For more resources, visit the Web site for

Crossroads and Cultures

A HISTORY OF THE WORLD'S PEOPLES

bedfordstmartins.com/smith

FREE **ONLINE STUDY GUIDE**

Get instant feedback on your progress with

- Chapter self-tests
- Key terms review
- Map quizzes
- Timeline activities
- Note-taking outlines

FREE **HISTORY RESEARCH AND WRITING HELP**

Refine your research skills and find plenty of good sources with

- A database of useful images, maps, documents, and more at *Make History*
- A guide to online sources for history
- Help with writing history papers
- A tool for building a bibliography
- Tips on avoiding plagiarism

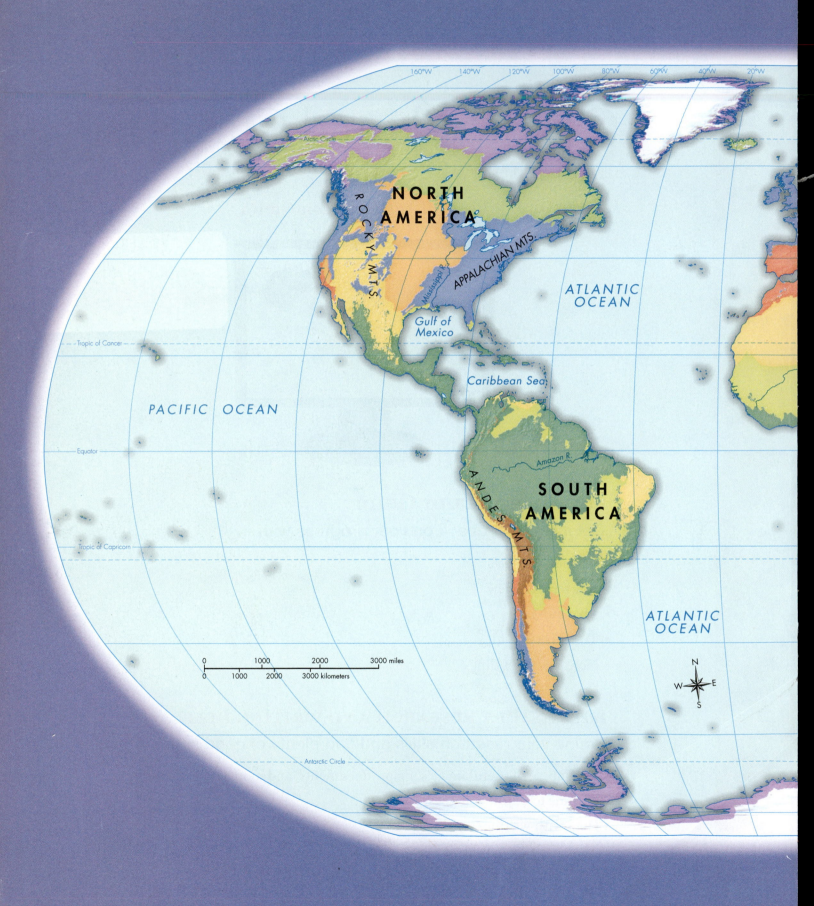

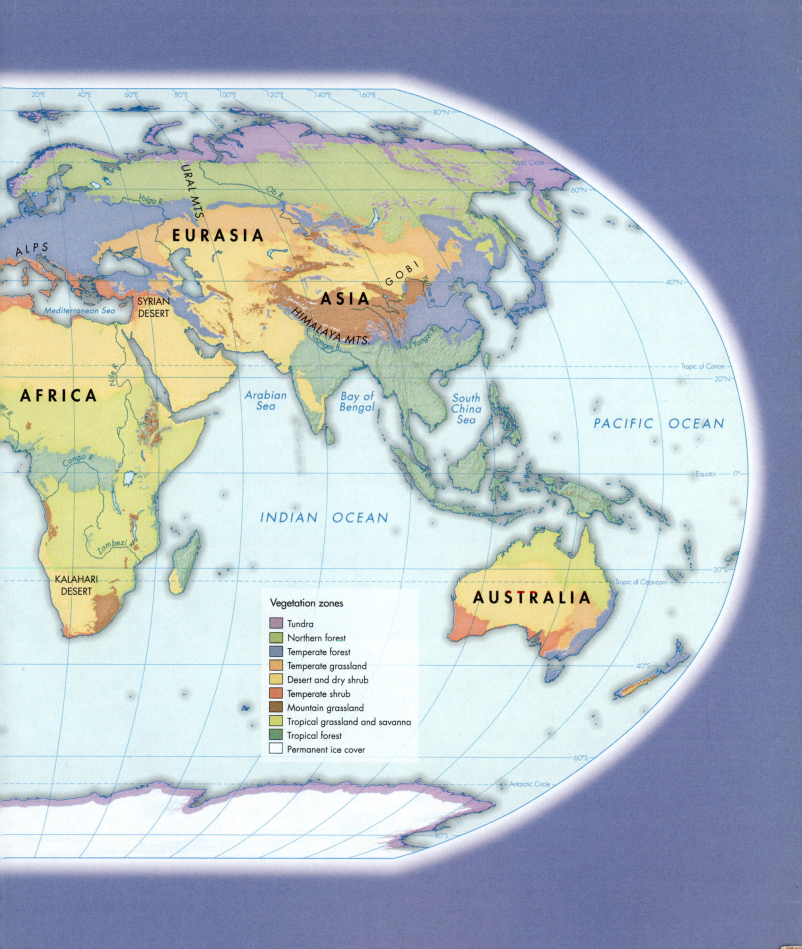

EURASIA

ASIA

AFRICA

AUSTRALIA

ALPS

URAL MTS.

Volga R.

Ob R.

GOBI

Yellow R.

HIMALAYA MTS.

Ganges R.

Yangzi

SYRIAN DESERT

Mediterranean Sea

Nile R.

Congo R.

Zambezi R.

KALAHARI DESERT

Arabian Sea

Bay of Bengal

South China Sea

PACIFIC OCEAN

INDIAN OCEAN

Arctic Circle

Tropic of Cancer

Equator

Tropic of Capricorn

Antarctic Circle

20°E 40°E 60°E 80°E 100°E 120°E 140°E 160°E

80°N

60°N

40°N

20°N

0°

20°S

40°S

60°S

80°S

Vegetation zones

- Tundra
- Northern forest
- Temperate forest
- Temperate grassland
- Desert and dry shrub
- Temperate shrub
- Mountain grassland
- Tropical grassland and savanna
- Tropical forest
- Permanent ice cover

VOLUME | TO 1450

Crossroads and Cultures

A History of the World's Peoples

Bonnie G. Smith
Rutgers University

Marc Van De Mieroop
Columbia University

Richard von Glahn
University of California, Los Angeles

Kris Lane
Tulane University

Bedford/St. Martin's
Boston ■ New York

FOR BEDFORD/ST. MARTIN'S

Publisher for History: Mary Dougherty
Executive Editor for History: Elizabeth M. Welch
Director of Development for History: Jane Knetzger
Senior Developmental Editor: Heidi Hood
Senior Production Editor: Anne Noonan
Senior Production Supervisor: Andrew Ensor
Executive Marketing Manager: Jenna Bookin Barry
Associate Editor: Jennifer Jovin
Assistant Production Editor: Laura Deily
Editorial Assistant: Emily DiPietro
Production Assistant: Elise Keller
Copy Editor: Dan Otis
Map Editor: Charlotte Miller
Indexer: Leoni Z. McVey
Cartography: Mapping Specialists, Ltd.
Photo Researcher: Rose Corbett Gordon
Permissions Manager: Kalina K. Ingham
Senior Art Director: Anna Palchik
Text Designer: Jerilyn Bockorick
Cover Designer: Billy Boardman
Cover Art: Pyramid of the Sun seen from Temple of Quetzalcoatl, Aztec, Teotihuacan, Mexico.
© The Art Archive/Gianni Dagli Orti/Art Resource
Composition: Cenveo Publisher Services
Printing and Binding: RR Donnelley and Sons

President: Joan E. Feinberg
Editorial Director: Denise B. Wydra
Director of Marketing: Karen R. Soeltz
Director of Production: Susan W. Brown
Associate Director, Editorial Production: Elise S. Kaiser
Managing Editor: Elizabeth M. Schaaf

Library of Congress Control Number: 2011943843

Manufactured in the United States of America.

7 6 5 4 3 2
f e d c b a

For information, write: Bedford/St. Martin's, 75 Arlington Street, Boston, MA 02116   (617-399-4000)

ISBN: 978-0-312-41017-9 (Combined edition)
ISBN: 978-0-312-57158-0 (Loose leaf)
ISBN: 978-0-312-44213-2 (Volume 1)
ISBN: 978-0-312-57159-7 (Loose leaf)
ISBN: 978-0-312-44214-9 (Volume 2)
ISBN: 978-0-312-57160-3 (Loose leaf)
ISBN: 978-0-312-57161-0 (Volume A)
ISBN: 978-0-312-57167-2 (Volume B)
ISBN: 978-0-312-57168-9 (Volume C)

A CONVERSATION WITH THE AUTHORS

The Story Behind *Crossroads and Cultures*

Bonnie G. Smith
Rutgers University

Marc Van De Mieroop
Columbia University

Richard von Glahn
University of California,
Los Angeles

Kris Lane
Tulane University

Bedford/St. Martin's is proud to publish *Crossroads and Cultures: A History of the World's Peoples,* which incorporates the best current cultural history into a fresh and original narrative that connects global patterns of development with life on the ground. This new synthesis highlights the places and times where people interacted and exchanged goods and ideas and in doing so joined their lives to the broad sweep of global history. Below the authors discuss their goals and approach.

Q. How does the title *Crossroads and Cultures: A History of the World's Peoples* tell the story of your book?

Crossroads

Bonnie: From the beginning we knew that we would be stressing interactions and engagements among the world's peoples. We looked for the places where they would meet—the **crossroads**— whether those were actual places or the intersections reflected in the practices of everyday life. We

want students to see how crossroads, interactions, and connections among the world's peoples have changed over time and continue to shape their own lives.

Richard: This focus is a result of our recognition that world history is not simply a matter of covering more areas of the world; it requires rethinking what matters in world history. World history must center on cross-cultural interactions and the ways in which peoples and cultures are influenced and are sometimes transformed by political engagement, cultural contact, economic exchange, and social encounters with other societies.

Cultures

Bonnie: The second half of our title reflects our heartfelt judgment that the past is shaped by **cultures**. Beliefs, ways of living, artistic forms, technology, and intellectual accomplishments are fundamental to historical development and are a part of the foundation of politics and economies. Cultures also produce structures such as caste, class, ethnicity, race, religion, gender, and sexuality—all of which are important themes in our book.

> **"We looked for the places where the world's peoples would meet —the crossroads—whether those were actual places or the intersections reflected in the practices of everyday life."**

A History of the World's Peoples

Marc: The book's subtitle, *A History of the World's Peoples*, is crucial. History often focuses on kings and states, but in the end the peoples of the past are the most interesting to study, however difficult that may be considering the nature of the sources for world history. People interact with their immediate and more distant neighbors, and these interactions are, indeed, often a cause of historical change.

Bonnie: *Crossroads and Cultures* focuses on people—individual and collective historical actors—who have lived the history of the world and produced global events. We want to capture their thoughts and deeds, their everyday experiences, their work lives, and their courageous actions—all of which have helped to create the crossroads we travel today.

Q. To follow up on the idea of "crossroads," what are some of the places and interactions that you emphasize in the book, and why?

Marc: In the ancient world, the period that I cover in the book (Part 1, from human origins to 500 C.E.), two regions figured prominently by virtue of their location—the Middle East and Central Asia. From earliest times, the Middle East formed a nexus of interactions among the African, European, and Asian continents, which I try to convey when I discuss the first human migrations out of Africa and when I show how the Roman and Persian empires met—and yes, battled! But I emphasize as well that vast open areas also served as crossroads in antiquity. Indeed, Central Asia, an enormous region, acted as a highway for contacts between the cultures at its fringes: China, South Asia, the Middle East, and Europe. Seas also can play this role, and I include the gigantic Pacific Ocean, which, although a formidable barrier, functioned as a road for migration for centuries.

Richard: Since I also deal with a period remote from the present (Part 2, 500–1450 C.E.), I try to balance my coverage between familiar and recognizable places that remain crossroads today—Rome and Jerusalem, Baghdad and Istanbul, Beijing and Delhi, the Nile Delta and the Valley of Mexico—and places that have faded from view, such as the trading cities of the West African savanna; Melaka, the greatest port of Asia in the fifteenth century; Samarkand, which had a long history as the linchpin of the Central Asian Silk Road; and the Champagne fairs in France, which operated as a "free trade" zone and became the incubator of new business practices that enabled Europeans to surpass the older economic centers of the Mediterranean world.

Kris: Since my section of the book (Part 3, 1450–1750) treats the early modern period, when the entire globe was interconnected for the first time in recorded history, I have almost too many crossroads to choose from. In this period, Seville and Lisbon emerged as hugely rich and important ports and sites of redistribution, but so also did Manila, Nagasaki, and Macao. Most of the obvious crossroads of this seafaring era were ports, but great mining centers like Potosí, deep in the highlands of present-day Bolivia, also became world-class cosmopolitan centers. In other books many of these sites have been treated simply as nodes in an expanding European world, but I try to show how local people and other non-European residents made Manila and Potosí quite different from what the king of Spain might have had in mind. Indeed, I emphasize crossroads as places of personal opportunity rather than imperial hegemony.

Bonnie: The crossroads that we describe are often the obvious ones of war, empire building, and old and new forms of trade, but we also enthusiastically feature the more ordinary paths that people traveled. For example, in my own section of the book (Part 4, 1750 to the present), I trace the route of the young Simon Bolivar, whose travels in Spain, France, and the new United States helped to inspire his own liberation struggles. I also follow the rough road from factory to factory along which a seven-year-old English orphan, Robert Blincoe, traveled. His life occurred at the crossroads of industrial development, where he suffered deliberate torture as the world began industrializing. For me, these personal journeys—filled with interactions—are at the heart of our endeavor to make history vivid and meaningful for students.

> "The crossroads that we describe are often the obvious ones of war, empire building, and old and new forms of trade, but we also enthusiastically feature the more ordinary paths that people traveled."

Q. Author teams of world history textbooks typically divide the work based on geographic specialty. Why did you decide to take responsibility for eras instead of regions?

Bonnie: Our goal is to show the interactions of the world's peoples over time and space. Had we divided history by region, our purpose would have been confounded from the start. Many books still take a "civilizational" approach, shifting from one region or nation to another and dividing each author's coverage according to national specialization. We aimed for a more interconnected result by each taking responsibility for narrating developments across the globe during a particular period of time.

Marc: When we look at any period globally, we can see certain parallels between the various parts of the world. There is a huge benefit to weighing what happened in different places at the same time.

Richard: Right. World history fundamentally is about making comparisons and connections. Defining our subject matter by time period rather than by geographic region enabled us to see the connections or parallel developments that make societies part of world history—as well as the distinctive features that make them unique. Our format has the virtue of bringing a coherent perspective to the many stories that each part of the book tells.

Kris: In my chapters, certain themes, such as slavery and the spread of silver money, took on new meaning as I traced them across cultures in ways that regional specialists had not considered. Writing the book this way entailed a huge amount of reading, writing, and reconsideration, but I feel it was a great decision. It allowed each of us to explore a bit before coming back together to hash out differences.

Q. The table of contents for *Crossroads and Cultures* blends both thematic and regional chapters. Why did you organize the book this way?

Bonnie: There is no orthodoxy in today's teaching of world history. Although textbooks often follow either a regional or a thematic structure, we felt that neither of these told the story that a blended approach could tell.

Richard: I particularly relished the opportunity to develop thematic chapters—for example, on cross-cultural trade and business practices, or on educational institutions and the transmission of knowledge—that illustrate both convergence and diversity in history. The thematic chapters were especially suitable for introducing individuals from diverse levels of society, to help students appreciate personal experiences as well as overarching historical trends.

Kris: In my period, the rapid integration of the world due to expanding maritime networks had to be balanced against the persistence of land-based cultures that both borrowed from new technologies and ideas and maintained a regional coherence. The Aztecs, the Incas, the Mughals, and the Ming were all land-based, tributary empires headed by divine kings, but whereas the first two collapsed as a result of European invasion, the latter two were reinforced by contact with Europeans, who introduced powerful new weapons. I felt it was necessary to treat these empires in macroregional terms before grappling with more sweeping themes. I found that in the classroom my students made better connections themselves after having time to get a firm handle on some of these broad regional developments.

> **"Defining our subject matter by time period rather than by geographic region enabled us to see the connections or parallel developments that make societies part of world history—as well as the distinctive features that make them unique."**

Q. Each chapter includes a Counterpoint section as substantial as the main sections of the narrative itself. What purposes do the Counterpoints serve?

Kris: The **Counterpoint** feature helps students and teachers remember that alternative histories—or paths—are not only possible but that they exist alongside "master narratives." In each chapter we have selected a people, a place, or a movement that functions as a Counterpoint to the major global development traced in that chapter. Some Counterpoints highlight different responses to similar circumstances—the successful resistance of the Mapuche of Chile against the European conquistadors, for example, in a chapter that tells the story of the collapse of the Aztec and Incan empires. Other Counterpoints show cultures adapting to a particular environment that either enables persistence or requires adaptation—such as the Aborigines of Australia, gatherer-hunters by choice, in a chapter that treats the rise of agriculture and spread of settled farming. Counterpoint is about human difference and ingenuity.

Richard: The Counterpoint feature is fundamental to our approach. It reminds us that there is much diversity in world history and helps us to think about the causes underlying divergence as well as convergence.

Marc: Right. It helps counter the idea that everyone goes through the same stages of evolution and makes the same choices. There is no uniform history of the world, as nineteenth-century scholars used to think.

Bonnie: One of my favorite Counterpoints centers on the importance of nonindustrialized African women farmers to the world economy during the Industrial Revolution. From a pedagogical standpoint, Counterpoints not only expose basic questions that historians grapple with but also offer material within a single chapter for compare-and-contrast exercises.

Q. Each chapter also offers a special feature devoted to the way that people made their living at different times and at different crossroads in the past. Would you explain how this Lives and Livelihoods feature works?

Richard: The **Lives and Livelihoods** feature helps us provide more in-depth study of one of our key themes, namely how people's lives intersect with larger cross-cultural interactions and global change.

Bonnie: We often spotlight new means of making a living that arose as the result of cross-cultural exchange or that contributed to major global developments. For example, the Lives and Livelihoods feature in Chapter 6 shows students how papermaking originated as a carefully guarded invention in classical China and became a worldwide technology that spawned numerous livelihoods. Similarly, the feature in Chapter 24 on workers on the trans-Siberian railroad exemplifies influence in both directions: the workers built a transportation network that advanced interconnections and fostered global change—change that they and their families experienced in turn.

> **"The Lives and Livelihoods feature supports one of our key themes: how people's lives intersect with larger cross-cultural interactions and global change."**

Q. *Crossroads and Cultures* **has a rich art and map program, and it also includes plentiful primary-source excerpts and clear reading aids. Can you talk about how you had students in mind as you developed these features of the book?**

Kris: Throughout the book we chose **images** to match as closely as we could the themes we wanted to stress. We did not conceive of the images as mere illustrations but rather as documents worthy of close historical analysis in their own right, products of the same places and times we try to evoke in the text.

Richard: And our carefully developed **map program** provides sure-footed guidance to where our historical journey is taking us—a crucial necessity, since we travel to so many places not on the usual Grand Tour! Our **Seeing the Past** and **Reading the Past** features, which provide excerpts from visual and written primary sources, give students direct exposure to the ideas and voices of the people we are studying. These features also help students build their analytical skills by modeling how historians interpret visual and written evidence.

Bonnie: Among the many reading aids, one of my favorites is the chapter-opening **Backstory**, which provides a concise overview of previously presented material to situate the current chapter for the student. It is at once a review and an immediate preparation for the chapter to come.

Richard: And we use every opportunity—at the start of chapters and sections, in the features, and at the end of each chapter—to pose **study questions** to help students think about what they are reading and make connections across time and space.

Kris: We wanted to hit as many bases as possible in order to make our book accessible for different kinds of learners. I imagine I'm like most teachers in that I never teach a course in exactly the same way each year. I like to use or emphasize different aspects of a textbook each time I assign it, sometimes hammering on chronology or working through study questions and sometimes paying closer attention to maps, works of art, or material culture. It all needs to be there; I like a complete toolbox.

Q. You have written many well-received and influential works. What response to *Crossroads and Cultures: A History of the World's Peoples* would please you most?

Bonnie: Our hope is that our approach to world history will engage students and help them master material that can otherwise seem so remote, wide-ranging, and seemingly disconnected from people's lives.

Richard: I would like from students who read this book what I want from my own students: a recognition and appreciation of the diversity of human experience that fosters understanding not only of the past and where we have come from but also of our fellow world citizens and the future that we are making together.

Kris: The practical side of me wants simply to hear, "At last, a world history textbook that works." The idealistic side wants to hear, "Wow, a world history textbook that makes both me and my students think differently about the world and about history."

Marc: And I hope that students start to realize not only that the pursuit of answers to such questions is absorbing and satisfying but also that the study of history is fun!

Crossroads and Cultures: A History of the World's Peoples makes its new synthesis accessible and memorable for students through a strong pedagogical design, abundant maps and images, and special features that heighten the narrative's attention to the lives and voices of the world's peoples. To learn more about how the book's features keep the essentials of world history in focus for students, see the "How to Use This Book" introduction on the following pages.

HOW TO USE THIS BOOK

Use the part opener's features to understand the place, time, and topic of the era.

PLACE
Ask yourself what regions are covered.

TIME
Ask yourself what era is under investigation.

TOPIC
Ask yourself what topics or themes are emphasized.

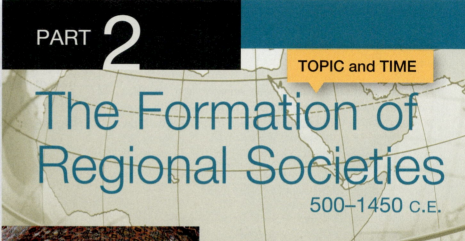

PART **2**

TOPIC and TIME

The Formation of Regional Societies
500–1450 C.E.

CH 9

ALTHOUGH NO SINGLE LABEL adequately reflects the history of the world in the period 500–1450, its most distinctive feature was the formation of regional societies based on common forms of livelihoods, cultural values, and social and political institutions. The new age in world history that began in around 500 C.E. marked a decisive break from the "classical" era of antiquity. The passing of classical civilizations in the Mediterranean, China, and India shared a number of causes, but the most notable were invasions by nomads from the Central Asian steppes. Beset by internal unrest and foreign pressures, the empires of Rome, Han China, and Gupta India crumbled. As these once-mighty empires fragmented into a multitude of competing states, cultural revolutions followed. Confidence in the values and institutions of the classical era was shattered, opening the way for fresh ideas. Christianity, Buddhism, Hinduism, and the new creed of Islam spread far beyond their original circles of believers. By 1450 these four religious traditions had supplanted or transformed local religions in virtually all of Eurasia and much of Africa.

The spread of foreign religions and the lifestyles and livelihoods they promoted produced distinctive regional societies. By 1000, Europe had taken shape as a coherent society and culture even as it came to be divided between the Roman and Byzantine Christian churches. The shared cultural values of modern East Asia—rooted in the literary and philosophical traditions of China but also assuming distinctive national forms—also emerged during the first millennium C.E. During this era, too, Indian civilization expanded into Southeast Asia and acquired a new unity expressed through the common language of Sanskrit. The rapid expansion of Islam across Asia, Africa, and

266

CH 10 →

TOPIC
Read the part overview to learn how the chapters that follow fit into the larger story.

xii

TOPIC, TIME, and PLACE

CH 11

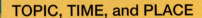

even parts of Europe demonstrated the power of a shared reli-

500–1450 C.E.

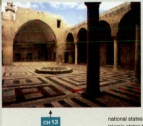

CH 13

faiths grew ever wider. The rise of steppe empires—above all, the explosive expansion of the Mongol empires—likewise transformed the political and cultural landscape of Asia. Historians today recognize the ways in which the Mongol conquests facilitated the movement of people, goods, and ideas across Eurasia. But contemporaries could see no farther than the ruin sowed by the Mongols wherever they went, toppling cities and laying waste to once-fertile farmlands.

After 1300 the momentum of world history changed. Economic growth slowed, strained by the pressure of rising populations on productive resources and the effects of a cooling climate, and then it stopped altogether. In the late 1340s the Black Death pandemic devastated the central Islamic lands and Europe. It would take centuries before the populations in these parts of the world returned to their pre-1340 levels.

By 1400, however, other signs of recovery were evident. Powerful national states emerged in Europe and China, restoring some measure of stability. Strong Islamic states held sway in Egypt, Anatolia (modern Turkey), Iran, and India. The European Renaissance—the intense outburst of intellectual and artistic creativity envisioned as a "rebirth" of the classical civilization of Greece and Rome—flickered to life, sparked by the economic vigor of the Italian city-states. Similarly, Neo-Confucianism—a "renaissance" of China's classical learning—whetted the intellectual and cultural aspirations of ed...

Eurasia's major land-based economies struggled to regain their earlier prosperity.

In 1453 Muslim Ottoman armies seized Constantinople and deposed the Byzantine Christian emperor, cutting the last thread of connection to the ancient world. The fall of Constantinople symbolized the end of the era discussed in Part 2. Denied direct access to the rich trade with Asia, European monarchs and merchants began to shift their attention to the Atlantic world. Yet just as Columbus's discovery of the "New World" (in fact, a very ancient one) came as a surprise, the idea of a new world order centered on Europe—the modern world order—was still unimaginable.

CH 15

TIME and PLACE
Scan the timeline to see how events and developments in different regions of the world fit together.

	500	750	1000	1250	1500
Americas	500 First permanent settlements in Chaco Canyon / 500–1000 Andean state of Tiwanaku / 550–650 Collapse of Teotihuacán / 700–900 Heyday of Andean state of Wari	800–900 Collapse of the Maya city-states / Rise of Chimu state 900	950–1150 Height of Toltec culture / 1050 Consolidation of Cahokia's dominance	1150 Abandonment of pueblos in Chaco Canyon / 1250–1300 Collapse of Cahokia / • 1200 Incas move into Cuzco region / • 1325 Aztecs found Tenochtitlán	Columbus reaches the Americas 1492 • / 1430–1532 Inca Empire
Europe	• 507 Clovis defeats Visigoths and converts to Christianity / 590–604 Papacy of Gregory I / Charles Martel halts Muslim advance into Europe 732 • / Charlemagne crowned emperor 800 •	• 793 Earliest record of Viking raids on Britain	988 Rus prince Vladimir converts to Christianity / • 1066 Norman conquest of England / Mongol conquest of Kiev 1240 •	• 1150 Founding of first university at Paris / 1150–1300 Heyday of the Champagne fairs / 1270–1300 Introduction of overseas navigational aids	1347–1350 Outbreak of Black Death / 1337–1453 Hundred Years' War / 1400–1550 Italian Renaissance / Reconquista completed 1492 •
Middle East	527–565 Reign of Byzantine emperor Justinian I / 570–632 Life of Muhammad	• 680 Permanent split between Shi'a and Sunni Islam / 750–850 Abbasid caliphate at its height / 661–743 Umayyad caliphate	First Crusade ends with Christian capture of Jerusalem 1099 • / Saladin recaptures Jerusalem 1187 •	• 1120 Founding of order of Knights of the Temple / • 1258 Mongols sack Baghdad	• 1291 Mamluks recapture Acre, last Christian stronghold in Palestine / 1347–1350 Outbreak of Black Death / • 1453 Fall of Constantinople to the Ottomans
Africa	500 Spread of camel use; emergence of trans-Saharan trade routes	• 750 Islam starts to spread via trans-Saharan trade routes	969 Fatimids capture Egypt / Fall of kingdom of Ghana 1076 •	Reign of Sunjata, founder of Mali Empire 1230–1255 • / 1100–1500 Extended dry period in West Africa prompts migrations	1250–1517 Mamluk dynasty / • 1250 Kingdom of Benin founded
Asia and Oceania	581–618 Sui Empire / 618–907 Tang Empire / 600–1000 Polynesian settlement of Pacific Islands	• 668 Unification of Korea under Silla rule / 755–763 An Lushan rebellion	850–1267 Chola kingdom / 939 Vietnam achieves independence from China / 960–1279 Song Empire	1100–1500 Easter Island's stone monuments / Formation of first Hawaiian chiefdoms 1200–1400 / 1206–1526 Delhi Sultanate / 1271–1368 Yuan Empire	1336–1573 Ashikaga Shogunate / 1368–1644 Ming Empire / 1392–1910 Korean Yi dynasty

STEP 2

Use the chapter's introductory features to understand the place, time, and topic of this chapter.

AT A CROSSROADS ▶

The fall of Constantinople to the Ottoman Turks in 1453 marked the end of the Byzantine Empire and heralded the coming age of gunpowder weapons. The Ottoman forces under Sultan Mehmed II breached the massive walls of Constantinople using massive cannons known as *bombards*. The Turkish cannons appear in the center of this book illustration of the siege of Constantinople, published in France in 1455. (The Art Archive/Bibliothèque Nationale Paris.)

PLACE and TOPIC
An important crossroads opens every chapter.

enough cannons to match the heavily armed Ottoman army and navy, which expelled the Venetians from the Black Sea in 1475. Although Venetian merchants still flocked to Constantinople, which Mehmed renamed Istanbul, to obtain spices, silks, and other Asian goods, the Ottomans held the upper hand and could dictate the terms of trade.

The fall of Constantinople to the Ottomans marks a turning point in world history. After perpetuating ancient Rome's heritage and glory for a thousand years, the Byzantine Empire came to an end. Islam continued to advance; in the fourteenth and fifteenth centuries, it expanded most dramatically in Africa and Asia. Italian merchants and bankers lost their dominance in the eastern Mediterranean and turned westward toward the Atlantic Ocean in search of new commercial opportunities. And this shift in commercial power and focus was not the only profound change that followed the Ottoman capture of Constantinople. The bombards cast by the Hungarian engineer for the Ottoman sultan heralded a military revolution that would decisively alter the balance of power among states and transform the nature of the state itself.

The new global patterns that emerged after Constantinople changed hands had their roots in calamities of the fourteenth century. The Ottoman triumph came just as Europe was beginning to recover from the previous century's catastrophic outbreak of plague known as the Black Death. The demographic and psychological shocks of epidemic disease had se-

PLACE and TOPIC
The Mapping the World feature gives a geographical overview of the chapter and highlights important routes and crossroads.

MAPPING THE WORLD
Afro-Eurasia in the Early Fifteenth Century

After the Mongol Empire disintegrated, trans-Eurasian trade shifted from the overland Silk Road to the maritime routes stretching from China to the Mediterranean. Muslim merchants crossed the Sahara Desert and the Indian Ocean in pursuit of African gold, Chinese porcelain, and Asian spices. Although Chinese fleets led by Admiral Zheng He journeyed as far as the coasts of Arabia and Africa, the Ming rulers prohibited private overseas trade.

ROUTES ▼
— Major trade route
— Silk Road
— Voyages of Zheng He

1315–1317 Great Famine in northern Europe
1325–1354 Travels of Ibn Battuta in Asia and Africa
1336–1573 Ashikaga shogunate in Japan
1337–1453 Hundred Years' War between England and France
• 1378 Ciompi uprising in Florence
• 1381 Peasant Revolt in England
1392–1910 Yi dynasty in Korea
• 1405 Death of Timur; breakup of his empire into regional states in Iran and Central Asia
• 1453 Ottoman conquest of Constantinople marks fall of the Byzantine Empire

1300   1325   1350   1375   1400   1425   1450

1347–1350 Outbreak of the Black Death in Europe and the Islamic Mediterranean
c. 1351–1782 Ayudhya kingdom in Thailand
1368–1644 Ming dynasty in China
1405–1433 Chinese admiral Zheng He's expeditions in Southeast Asia and the Indian Ocean
• 1421 Relocation of Ming capital from Nanjing to Beijing
1428–1788 Le dynasty in Vietnam

TIME and TOPIC
The timeline previews key events and developments discussed in the chapter.

Collapse and Revival in Afro-Eurasia

1300–1450

In 1453 the armies of the Ottoman sultan Mehmed II encircled Constantinople, the Byzantine emperor Constantine XI received a visit from a fellow Christian, a Hungarian engineer named Urban. Urban had applied metallurgical skills acquired at Hungary's rich iron and copper mines to the manufacture of large cannons known as *bombards*. He came to the Byzantine capital to offer his services to repel the Ottoman assault. But although Urban was a Christian, he was a businessman, too. When Constantine could not meet his price, Urban quickly left for the sultan's camp. Facing the famed triple walls of Constantinople, Mehmed promised to quadruple the salary Urban requested and to provide any materials and manpower the engineer needed.

Seven months later, in April 1453, Ottoman soldiers moved Urban's huge bronze bombards—with barrels twenty-six feet long, capable of throwing eight-hundred-pound shot—into place beneath the walls of Constantinople. Although these cumbersome cannons could fire only seven rounds a day, they battered the walls of Constantinople, which had long been considered impenetrable. After six weeks of siege the Turks breached the walls and swarmed into the city. The vastly outnumbered defenders, Emperor Constantine among them, fought to the death.

Urban's willingness to put business before religious loyalty helped tip the balance of power in the Mediterranean. During the siege, the Genoese merchant community at Constantinople—along with their archrivals, the Venetians—maintained strict neutrality. Although the Italian merchants, like Urban, were prepared to do business with Mehmed II, within a decade the Venetians and Ottomans were at war. Venice could not produce

BACKSTORY

In the fourteenth century, a number of developments threatened the connections among the societies of the Afro-Eurasian world. The collapse of the Mongol empires in China and Iran in the mid-1300s disrupted caravan traffic across Central Asia, diverting the flow of trade and travel to maritime routes across the Indian Ocean. Although the two centuries of religious wars known as the Crusades ended in 1291, they had hardened hostility between Christians and Muslims. As the power of the Christian Byzantine Empire contracted, Muslim Turkish sultanates—the Mamluk regime in Egypt and the rising Ottoman dynasty in Anatolia (modern Turkey)—gained control of the eastern Mediterranean region. Yet the Crusades and direct contact with the Mongols had also whetted European appetites for luxury and exotic goods from the Islamic world and Asia. Thus, despite challenges and obstacles, the Mediterranean remained a lively crossroads of commerce and cross-cultural exchange.

Fourteenth-Century Crisis and Renewal in Eurasia

FOCUS How did the Black Death affect society, the economy, and culture in Latin Christendom and the Islamic world?

Islam's New Frontiers

FOCUS Why did Islam expand dramatically in the fourteenth and fifteenth centuries, and how did new Islamic societies differ from established ones?

The Global Bazaar

FOCUS How did the pattern of international trade change during the fourteenth and fifteenth centuries, and how did these changes affect consumption and fashion tastes?

COUNTERPOINT Age of the Samurai in Japan, 1185–1450

FOCUS How and why did the historical development of Japan in the fourteenth and fifteenth centuries differ from that of mainland Eurasia?

bazaar, and this isolation contributed to the birth of Japan's distinctive national culture. For most Afro-Eurasian societies, however, the maritime world increasingly became the principal crossroads of economic and cultural exchange.

OVERVIEW QUESTIONS

The major global development in this chapter: Crisis and recovery in fourteenth- and fifteenth-century Afro-Eurasia.

As you read, consider:

1. In the century after the devastating outbreak of plague known as the Black Death, how and why did Europe's economic growth begin to surpass that of the Islamic world?

2. Did the economic revival across Eurasia after 1350 benefit the peasant populations of Europe, the Islamic world, and East Asia?

3. How did the process of conversion to Islam differ in Iran, the Ottoman Empire, West Africa, and Southeast Asia during this period?

4. What political and economic changes contributed to the rise of maritime commerce in Asia during the fourteenth and fifteenth centuries?

STEP 3

Use the chapter tools to understand what is important.

Focus questions, which also appear at the start and end of the chapter, tell you what you need to learn from each major section.

Topical headings in the margin focus on important topics and are useful for reviewing the chapter.

Marginal glossary definitions provide further explanation of key terms boldfaced in the narrative.

Sufism A tradition within Islam that emphasizes mystical knowledge and personal experience of the divine.

Islam's New Frontiers

FOCUS
Why did Islam expand dramatically in the fourteenth and fifteenth centuries, and how did new Islamic societies differ from established ones?

In the fourteenth and fifteenth centuries, Islam continued to spread to new areas, including central and maritime Asia, sub-Saharan Africa, and southeastern Europe. In the past, Muslim rule had often preceded the popular adoption of Islamic religion and culture. Yet the advance of Islam in Africa and Asia came about not through conquest, but through slow diffusion via merchants and missionaries. The universalism and egalitarianism of Islam appealed to rising merchant classes in both West Africa and maritime Asia.

During this period, Islam expanded by adapting to older ruling cultures rather than seeking to eradicate them. Timur, the last of the great nomad conquerors, and his descendants ruled not as Mongol khans but as Islamic sultans. The culture of the Central Asian states, however, remained an eclectic mix of Mongol, Turkish, and Persian traditions, in contrast to the strict adherence to Muslim law and doctrine practiced under the Arab regimes of the Middle East and North Africa. This pattern of cultural adaptation and assimilation was even more evident in West Africa and Southeast Asia.

Islamic Spiritual Ferment in Central Asia 1350–1500

The spread of Sufism in Central Asia between 1350 and 1500 played a significant role in the process of cultural assimilation. **Sufism**—a mystical tradition that stressed self-mastery, practical virtues, and spiritual growth through personal experience of the divine—had already emerged by 1200 as a major expression of Islamic values and social identity. Sufism appeared in many variations and readily assimilated local cultures to its beliefs and practices. Sufi mystics acquired institutional strength through the communal solidarity of their brotherhoods spread across the whole realm of Islam. In contrast to the orthodox scholars and teachers known as *ulama*, who made little effort to convert nonbelievers, Sufi preachers were inspired by missionary zeal and welcomed non-Muslims to their lodges and sermons. This made them ideal instruments for the spread of Islam to new territories.

Timur

One of Sufism's most important royal patrons was Timur (1336–1405), the last of the Mongol emperors. Born near the city of Samarkand (SAM-ar-kand) when the Mongol Ilkhanate in Iran was on the verge of collapse, Timur—himself a Turk—grew up among Mongols who practiced Islam. He rose to power in the 1370s by reuniting quarreling Mongol tribes in common pursuit of conquest. Although Timur lacked the dynastic pedigree enjoyed by Chinggis Khan's descendants, like Chinggis he held his empire together by the force of his personal charisma.

From the early 1380s, Timur's armies relentlessly pursued campaigns of conquest, sweeping westward across Iran into Mesopotamia and Russia and eastward into India. In 1400–1401 Timur seized and razed Aleppo and Damascus, the principal Mamluk cities in Syria. In 1402 he captured the Ottoman sultan in battle. Rather than trying to consolidate his rule in Syria and Anatolia (modern Turkey), however, Timur turned his attention eastward. He was preparing to march on China when he fell ill and died early in 1405. Although Timur's empire quickly fragmented, his triumphs would serve as an inspiration to later empire builders, such as the Mughals in India and the Manchus in China. Moreover, his support of Sufism would have a lasting impact, helping lay the foundation for a number of important Islamic religious movements in Central Asia.

The institutions of Timur's empire were largely modeled on the Ilkhan synthesis of Persian civil administration and Turkish-Mongol military organization. Like the Ilkhans and the Ottomans, Timur's policies favored settled farmers and urban populations over pastoral nomads, who were often displaced from their homelands. While Timur allowed local princes a degree of autonomy, he was determined to make Samarkand a grand imperial capital.

Cultural Innovations

Again, as with Islam in West Africa, the intellectual ferment of the Renaissance was nurtured in an urban environment. Humanist scholars shunned the warrior culture of the old nobility while celebrating the civic roles and duties of townsmen, merchants, and clerics. Despite their admiration of classical civilization, the humanists did not reject Christianity. Rather, they sought to reconcile Christian faith and doctrines with classical learning. By making knowledge of Latin and Greek, history, poetry, and philosophy the mark of an educated person, the humanists transformed education and established models of schooling that would endure down to modern times.

Nowhere was the revolutionary impact of the Renaissance felt more deeply than in visual arts such as painting, sculpture, and architecture. Artists of the Renaissance exuded supreme confidence in the ability of human ingenuity to equal or even surpass the works of nature. The new outlook was exemplified by the development of the techniques of perspective, which artists used to convey a realistic, three-dimensional quality to physical forms, most notably the human body. Human invention also was capable of improving on nature by creating order and harmony through architecture and urban planning. Alberti advocated replacing the winding narrow streets and haphazard construction of medieval towns with planned cities organized around straight boulevards, open squares, and monumental buildings whose balanced proportions corresponded to a geometrically unified design.

Above all, the Renaissance transformed the idea of the artist. No longer mere manual tradesmen, artists now were seen as possessing a special kind of genius that enabled them to express a higher understanding of beauty. In the eyes of contemporaries, no one exemplified this quality of genius more than Leonardo da Vinci (1452–1519), who won renown as a painter, architect, sculptor, engineer, mathematician, and inventor. Leonardo's father, a Florentine lawyer, apprenticed him to a local painter at age eighteen. Leonardo spent much of his career as a civil and military engineer in the employ of the Duke of Milan, and developed ideas for flying machines, tanks, robots, and solar power that far exceeded the engineering capabilities of his time. Leonardo sought to apply his knowledge of natural science to painting, which he regarded as the most sublime art (see Seeing the Past: Leonardo da Vinci's *Virgin of the Rocks*).

The flowering of artistic creativity in the Renaissance was rooted in the rich soil of Italy's com̄ [The final Counterpoint section offers an important exception to the Major Global Development discussed in the chapter.] from the Islamic world and Asia. Internā roduction across maritime Asia and gave nd consumption. In Japan, however, grow fostered the emergence of a national cultu ted the rest of East Asia.

The final Counterpoint section offers an important exception to the Major Global Development discussed in the chapter.

COUNTERPOINT

Age of the Samurai in Japan 1185–1450

FOCUS

How and why did the historical development of Japan in the fourteenth and fifteenth centuries differ from that of mainland Eurasia?

In Japan as in Europe, the term *Middle Ages* brings to mind an age of warriors, a stratified society governed by bonds of loyalty between lords and vassals. In Japan, however, the militarization of the ruling class intensified during the fourteenth and fifteenth centuries, a time when the warrior nobility of Europe was crumbling. Paradoxically, the rise of the **samurai** (sah-moo-rye) ("those who serve") warriors as masters of their own estates was accompanied by the increasing independence of peasant communities.

apter, Japan became more isolated from [Phonetic spellings follow many potentially unfamiliar terms.] ural exchanges with China reached a pea invasion of Japan in 1281, ties with contin panese see this era as the period in which Japan's unique national identity—expressed most distinctly in the ethic of *bushidō* (boo-shee-doe), the "Way of the Warrior"—took its definitive form. Samurai warriors became the

Phonetic spellings follow many potentially unfamiliar terms.

samurai Literally, "those who serve"; the hereditary warriors who dominated Japanese society and culture from the twelfth to the nineteenth centuries.

STEP 4
Do historical analysis.

LIVES AND LIVELIHOODS

> Lives and Livelihoods features underscore the connections between daily life and global developments.

Urban Weavers in India

Industry and commerce in India, especially in textiles, grew rapidly beginning in the fourteenth century. Specialized craftsmen in towns and regional groups of merchants formed guilds that became the nuclei of new occupational castes, *jati* (JAH-tee). Ultimately these new occupational castes would join with other forces in Indian society to challenge the social inequality rooted in orthodox Hindu religion.

It was growth in market demand and technological innovations such as block printing that drove the rapid expansion of India's textile industries. Luxury fabrics such as fine silks and velvet remained largely the province of royal workshops or private patronage. Mass production of textiles, on the other hand, was oriented toward the manufacture of cheaper cotton fabrics, especially colorful chintz garments. A weaver could make a woman's cotton *sari* in six or seven days, whereas a luxury garment took a month or more. Domestic demand for ordinary cloth grew steadily, and production for export accelerated even more briskly. At the beginning of the sixteenth century, the Portuguese traveler Tomé Pires, impressed by the craftsmanship of Indian muslins and calicoes (named after the port of Calicut), observed that "they make enough of these to furnish the world."[1]

Weaving became an urban industry. It was village women who cleaned most of the cotton and spun it into yarn; they could easily combine this simple if laborious work with other domestic chores. But peasants did not weave the yarn into cloth, except for their own use. Instead, weaving, bleaching, a[nd]
professional [...]
living in sep[...]

Like oth[er...]
pation that c[...]
Families of w[...]
guilds with b[...]
within their g[...]
not have exc[...]
could include [...]
could becom[e...]

Indian Block-Printed Textile, c. 1500
Block-printed textiles with elaborate designs were in great demand both in India and throughout Southeast Asia, Africa, and the Islamic world. Craftsmen carved intricate designs on wooden blocks (a separate block for each color), which were then dipped in dye and repeatedly stamped on bleached fabric until the entire cloth was covered. This cotton fabric with geese, lotus flower, and rosette designs was manufactured in Gujarat in western India. (Ashmolean Museum, University of Oxford)

[...] tions for social recognition. Amid the whirl and congestion of city life, it was far more difficult than in villages to enforce the laws governing caste purity and segregation. As a fourteenth-century poet wrote about the crowded streets of his hometown of Jaunpur in the Ganges Valley, in the city "one person's caste-mark gets stamped on another's forehead, and a brahman's holy thread will be found hanging around an untouchable's neck."[2] Brahmans objected to this erosion of caste boundaries, to little avail. Weaver guilds became influential patrons of temples and often served as trustees and accountants in charge of managing temple endowments and revenues.

In a few cases the growing economic independence of weavers and like-minded artisans prompted complete rejection of the caste hierarchy. Sufi preachers and *bhakti* (BAHK-tee)—devotional movements devoted to patron gods and goddesses—encouraged the disregard of caste distinctions in favor of a universal brotherhood of devout believers. The fifteenth-century *bhakti* preacher Kabir, who was strongly influenced by Sufi teachings, epitomized the new social radicalism coursing through the urban artisan classes. A weaver himself, Kabir joined the dignity of manual labor to the purity of spiritual devotion, spurning the social pretension and superficial piety of the brahmans ("pandits") and Muslim clerics ("mullahs"):

a trinity of labor, charity, and spiritual devotion. The Sikhs, who gained a following principally among traders and artisans in the northwestern Punjab region, drew an even more explicit connection between commerce and piety. In the words of a hymn included in a sixteenth-century anthology of Sikh sacred writings:

> The true Guru [teacher] is the merchant;
>
> The devotees are his peddlers.
>
> The capital stock is the Lord's Name, and
>
> To enshrine the truth is to keep His account.[4]

Sikh communities spurned the distinction between pure and impure occupations. In their eyes, holiness was to be found in honest toil and personal piety, not ascetic practices, book learning, or religious rituals.

1. Tomé Pires, *The Suma Oriental of Tomé Pires*, ed. and trans. Armando Cortes (London: Hakluyt Society, 1944), 1:53.
2. Vidyapati Thakur, *Kirtilata*, quoted in Eugenia Vanina, *Urban Crafts and Craftsmen in Medieval India (Thirteenth–Eighteenth Centuries)* (New Delhi: Munshiram Manoharlal, 2004), 443.
3. Quoted in Vanina, *Urban Crafts and Craftsmen*, 149.
4. *Sri Guru Granth Sahib*, trans. Gophal Singh (Delhi: Gur Das Kapur & Sons, 1960), 2:427.

[...at ease]
[...mullahs,]
[...come]
[...toil,]
[...asure.]
[...alesced]
[...red on]

[...th India. Delhi: Oxford University Press, 1985.]
[...India (Thirteenth–Eighteenth Centuries). New Delhi: Munshiram Manoharlal, 2004.]

SEEING THE PAST

> Reading the Past and Seeing the Past features provide direct exposure to important voices and ideas of the past through written and visual primary sources.

Leonardo da Vinci's *Virgin of the Rocks*

Virgin of the Rocks, c. 1483–1486
(Erich Lessing/Art Resource.)

Leonardo's Botanical Studies with Star-of-Bethlehem, Grasses, Crowfoot, Wood Anemone, and Another Genus, c. 1500–1506 (The Royal Collection © 2011 Her Majesty Queen Elizabeth II/Bridgeman Art Library.)

the menacing [...]
the cavern; de[...]
there was any[...]
thing within."[1]

Fantastic as the sce[ne...]
might seem, Leonardo's
meticulous rende[rings of]
rocks and p[...]
based on cl[...]
of nature. Th[...]
lehem flowe[r...]
left of the pa[...]
izing purity a[...]
also appear[...]
contempora[...]
cal drawing [...]
Geologists h[...]
Leonardo's l[...]
sandstone n[...]
and his prec[...]
of plants wh[...]
most likely t[...]

Master[...]
the *Virgin* o[...]
display Leonardo's careful study of human an[...]
landscapes, and botany. Although he admired [...]
tion of nature, Leonardo also celebrated the h[...]
rational and aesthetic capacities, declaring th[...]
arts may be called the grandsons of God."[2]

While living in Milan in the early 1480s, Leonardo accepted a commission to paint an altarpiece for the chapel of Milan's Confraternity of the Immaculate Conception, a branch of the Franciscan order. Leonardo's relationship with the friars proved to be stormy. His first version of the painting (now in the Louvre), reproduced here, apparently displeased his patrons and was sold to another party. Only after a fifteen-year-long dispute over the price did Leonardo finally deliver a modified version in 1508.

In portraying the legendary encounter between the child Jesus and the equally young John the Baptist during the flight to Egypt, Leonardo replaced the traditional desert setting with a landscape filled with rocks, plants, and water. Leonardo's dark grotto creates an aura of mystery and foreboding, from which the figures of Mary, Jesus, John, and the angel Uriel emerge as if in a vision. A few years before, Leonardo had written about "coming to the entrance of a great cavern, in front of which I stood for some time, stupefied and uncomprehending. . . . Suddenly two things arose in me, fear and desire: fear of

1. Arundel ms. (British Library), p. 115 recto, cited i[n...] *Leonardo da Vinci: The Marvelous Works of Nat[ure...]* (Oxford: Oxford University Press, 2006), 78.
2. John Paul Richter, ed., *The Notebooks of Leonar[do...]* of 1883 ed.; New York: Dover, 1970), Book IX, 32[...]

South[...]
and Rai[...]

READING THE PAST

A Spanish Ambassador's Description of Samarkand

Thus, China influenced patterns of international trade not only as a producer, as with

In September 1403, an embassy dispatched by King Henry III of Castile arrived at Samarkand in hopes of enlisting the support of Timur for a combined military campaign against the Ottomans. Seventy years old and in failing health, Timur lavishly entertained his visitors, but made no response to Henry's overtures. The leader of the Spanish delegation, Ruy Gonzalez de Clavijo, left Samarkand disappointed, but his report preserves our fullest account of Timur's capital in its heyday.

The city is rather larger than Seville, but lying outside Samarkand are great numbers of houses that form extensive suburbs. These lay spread on all hands, for indeed the township is surrounded by orchards and vineyards. . . . In between these orchards pass streets with open squares; these are all densely populated, and here all kinds of goods are on sale with breadstuffs and meat. . . .

Samarkand is rich not only in foodstuffs but also in manufactures, such as factories of silk. . . . Thus trade has always been fostered by Timur with the view of making his capital the noblest of cities; and during all his conquests . . . he carried off the best men to people Samarkand, bringing thither the master-craftsmen of all nations. Thus from Damascus he carried away with him all the weavers of that city, those who worked at the silk looms; further the bow-makers who produce those cross-bows which are so famous; likewise armorers; also the craftsmen in glass and porcelain, who are known to be the best in all the world. From Turkey he

had brought their gunsmiths who make the arquebus. . . . So great therefore was the population now of all nationalities gathered together in Samarkand that of men with their families the number they said must amount to 150,000 souls . . . [including] Turks, Arabs, and Moors of diverse sects, with Greek, Armenian, Roman, Jacobite [Syrian], and Nestorian Christians, besides those folk who baptize with fire in the forehead [i.e., Hindus]. . . .

The markets of Samarkand further are amply stored with merchandise imported from distant and foreign countries. . . . The goods that are imported to Samarkand from Cathay indeed are of the richest and most precious of all those brought thither from foreign parts, for the craftsmen of Cathay are reputed to be the most skilful by far beyond those of any other nation.

Source: Ruy Gonzalez de Clavijo, Embassy to Tamerlane, 1403–1406, trans. Guy Le Strange (London: Routledge, 1928), 285–289.

Review what you have learned.

Remember to visit the Online Study Guide for more review help.

REVIEW

Online Study Guide
bedfordstmartins.com/smith

The major global development in this chapter ▶ Crisis and recovery
in fourteenth- and fifteenth-century Afro-Eurasia.

Review the Major Global Development discussed in the chapter.

Review the Important Events from the chapter.

IMPORTANT EVENTS

1315–1317	Great Famine in northern Europe
1325–1354	Travels of Ibn Battuta in Asia and Africa
1336–1573	Ashikaga shogunate in Japan
1337–1453	Hundred Years' War between England and France
1347–1350	Outbreak of the Black Death in Europe and the Islamic Mediterranean
c. 1351–1782	Ayudhya kingdom in Thailand
1368–1644	Ming dynasty in China
1378	Ciompi uprising in Florence
1381	Peasant Revolt in England
1392–1910	Yi dynasty in Korea
1405	Death of Timur; breakup of his empire into regional states in Iran and Central Asia
1405–1433	Chinese admiral Zheng He's expeditions in Southeast Asia and the Indian Ocean
1421	Relocation of Ming capital from Nanjing to Beijing
1428–1788	Le dynasty in Vietnam
1453	Ottoman conquest of Constantinople marks fall of the Byzantine Empire

Review the Key Terms.

KEY TERMS

Black Death (p. 478)
humanism (p. 498)
janissary corps (p. 489)
Little Ice Age (p. 479)
Neo-Confucianism (p. 486)
oligarchy (p. 483)
pandemic (p. 478)
Renaissance (p. 498)
samurai (p. 501)
shogun (p. 503)
Sufism (p. 488)
theocracy (p. 489)
trade diaspora (p. 492)

CHAPTER OVERVIEW QUESTIONS

1. How and why did Europe's economic growth begin to surpass that of the Islamic world in the after the Black Death?

2. Did the economic revival across Eurasia a benefit the peasant populations of Europe Islamic world, and East Asia?

3. How did the process of conversion to Islam differ in Iran, the Ottoman Empire, West Africa, and Southeast Asia during this period?

4. What political and economic changes contributed to the rise of maritime commerce in Asia during the fourteenth and fifteenth centuries?

Answer these big-picture questions posed at the start of the chapter.

SECTION FOCUS QUESTIONS

1. How did the Black Death affect society, the omy, and culture in Latin Christendom and Islamic world?

2. Why did Islam expand dramatically in the fourteenth and fifteenth centuries, and how did new Islamic societies differ from established ones?

3. What were the principal sources of growth in international trade during the fourteenth and fifteenth centuries, and how did this trade affect patterns of consumption and fashion tastes?

4. How and why did the historical development of Japan in the fourteenth and fifteenth centuries differ from that of mainland Eurasia?

Explain the main point of each major section of the chapter.

MAKING CONNECTIONS

1. What social, economic, and technological c strengthened the power of European monar during the century after the Black Death?

2. How and why did the major routes and con ties of trans-Eurasian trade change after the collapse of the Mongol empires in Central Asia?

3. In what ways did the motives for conversion to Islam differ in Central Asia, sub-Saharan Africa, and the Indian Ocean during this era?

4. In this period, why did the power and status of the samurai warriors in Japan rise while those of the warrior nobility in Europe declined?

Connect ideas and practice your skills of comparison and analysis.

507

VERSIONS AND SUPPLEMENTS

Adopters of *Crossroads and Cultures: A History of the World's Peoples* and their students have access to abundant extra resources, including documents, presentation and testing materials, the acclaimed Bedford Series in History and Culture volumes, and much, much more. See below for more information, visit the book's catalog site at bedfordstmartins .com/smith/catalog, or contact your local Bedford/St. Martin's sales representative.

Get the Right Version for Your Class

To accommodate different course lengths and course budgets, *Crossroads and Cultures: A History of the World's Peoples* is available in several different formats, including three-hole punched loose-leaf Budget Books versions and e-books, which are available at a substantial discount.

- Combined edition (Chapters 1–31)—available in hardcover, loose-leaf, and e-book formats
- Volume 1: To 1450 (Chapters 1–16)—available in paperback, loose-leaf, and e-book formats
- Volume 2: Since 1300 (Chapters 15–31)—available in paperback, loose-leaf, and e-book formats
- Volume A: To 1300 (Chapters 1–14)—available in paperback
- Volume B: 500–1750 (Chapters 9–22)—available in paperback
- Volume C: Since 1750 (Chapters 23–31)—available in paperback

Your students can purchase *Crossroads and Cultures: A History of the World's Peoples* in popular e-book formats for computers, tablets, and e-readers by visiting bedfordstmartins .com/ebooks. The e-book is available at a discount.

Online Extras for Students

The book's companion site at bedfordstmartins.com/smith gives students a way to read, write, and study by providing plentiful quizzes and activities, study aids, and history research and writing help.

FREE Online Study Guide. Available at the companion site, this popular resource provides students with quizzes and activities for each chapter, including multiple-choice self-tests that focus on important concepts; flashcards that test students' knowledge of key terms; timeline activities that emphasize causal relationships; and map quizzes intended to strengthen students' geography skills. Instructors can monitor students' progress through an online Quiz Gradebook or receive e-mail updates.

FREE Research, Writing, and Anti-plagiarism Advice. Available at the companion site, Bedford's **History Research and Writing Help** includes **History Research and Reference Sources**, with links to history-related databases, indexes, and journals; **More Sources and How to Format a History Paper**, with clear advice on how to integrate primary and secondary sources into research papers and how to cite and format sources correctly; **Build a Bibliography**, a simple Web-based tool known as the Bedford Bibliographer that generates bibliographies in four commonly used documentation styles; and **Tips on Avoiding Plagiarism**, an online tutorial that reviews the consequences of plagiarism and features exercises to help students practice integrating sources and recognize acceptable summaries.

Resources for Instructors

Bedford/St. Martin's has developed a rich array of teaching resources for this book and for this course. They range from lecture and presentation materials and assessment tools to course management options. Most can be downloaded or ordered at bedfordstmartins.com/smith/catalog.

HistoryClass for Crossroads and Cultures. *HistoryClass*, a Bedford/St. Martin's Online Course Space, puts the online resources available with this textbook in one convenient and completely customizable course space. There you and your students can access an interactive e-book and primary source reader; maps, images, documents, and links; chapter review quizzes; interactive multimedia exercises; and research and writing help. In *HistoryClass* you can get all our premium content and tools and assign, rearrange, and mix them with your own resources. For more information, visit yourhistoryclass.com.

Bedford Coursepack for Blackboard, WebCT, Desire2Learn, Angel, Sakai, or Moodle. We have free content to help you integrate our rich materials into your course management system. Registered instructors can download coursepacks easily and with no strings attached. The coursepack for *Crossroads and Cultures: A History of the World's Peoples* includes book-specific content as well as our most popular free resources. Visit bedfordstmartins.com/ coursepacks to see a demo, find your version, or download your coursepack.

Instructor's Resource Manual. Written by Rick Warner, an experienced teacher of the world-history survey course, the instructor's manual offers both experienced and first-time instructors tools for preparing lectures and running discussions. It includes chapter review material, teaching strategies, and a guide to chapter-specific supplements available for the text.

Computerized Test Bank. The test bank includes a mix of fresh, carefully crafted multiple-choice, matching, short-answer, and essay questions for each chapter. It also contains the Overview, Focus, Making Connections, Lives and Livelihoods, Reading the Past, and Seeing the Past questions from the textbook and model answers for each. The questions appear in Microsoft Word format and in easy-to-use test bank software that allows instructors to easily add, edit, resequence, and print questions and answers. Instructors can also export questions into a variety of formats, including WebCT and Blackboard.

***The Bedford Lecture Kit:* Maps, Images, Lecture Outlines, and i>clicker Content.** Look good and save time with *The Bedford Lecture Kit*. These presentation materials are downloadable individually from the Instructor Resources tab at bedfordstmartins.com/smith/catalog and are available on *The Bedford Lecture Kit* Instructor's Resource CD-ROM. They provide ready-made and fully customizable PowerPoint multimedia presentations that include lecture outlines with embedded maps, figures, and selected images from the textbook and extra background for instructors. Also available are maps and selected images in JPEG and PowerPoint formats; content for i>clicker, a classroom response system, in Microsoft Word and PowerPoint formats; the Instructor's Resource Manual in Microsoft Word format; and outline maps in PDF format for quizzing or handing out. All files are suitable for copying onto transparency acetates.

***Make History*—Free Documents, Maps, Images, and Web Sites.** *Make History* combines the best Web resources with hundreds of maps and images, to make it simple to find the source material you need. Browse the collection of thousands of resources by course or by topic, date, and type. Each item has been carefully chosen and helpfully annotated to make it easy to find exactly what you need. Available at bedfordstmartins.com/makehistory.

Videos and Multimedia. A wide assortment of videos and multimedia CD-ROMs on various topics in world history is available to qualified adopters through your Bedford/St. Martin's sales representative.

Package and Save Your Students Money

For information on free packages and discounts up to 50%, visit bedfordstmartins.com/smith/catalog, or contact your local Bedford/St. Martin's sales representative.

Sources of Crossroads and Cultures. The authors of *Crossroads and Cultures* have carefully developed this two-volume primary source reader themselves to reflect the textbook's geographic and thematic breadth and the key social, cultural, and political developments discussed in each chapter. *Sources of Crossroads and Cultures* extends the textbook's emphasis on the human dimension of global history through the voices of both notable figures and everyday individuals. With a blend of major works and fresh perspectives, each chapter contains approximately six sources, an introduction, document headnotes, and questions for discussion. Available free when packaged with the print text.

***Sources of Crossroads and Cultures* e-Book.** The reader is also available as an e-book for purchase at a discount.

The Bedford Series in History and Culture. More than one hundred titles in this highly praised series combine first-rate scholarship, historical narrative, and important primary documents for undergraduate courses. Each book is brief, inexpensive, and focused on a specific topic or period. For a complete list of titles, visit bedfordstmartins.com/history/series. Package discounts are available.

Rand McNally Historical Atlas of the World. This collection of almost seventy full-color maps illustrates the eras and civilizations in world history from the emergence of human societies to the present. Available for $3.00 when packaged with the print text.

The Bedford Glossary for World History. This handy supplement for the survey course gives students historically contextualized definitions for hundreds of terms—from *abolitionism* to *Zoroastrianism*—that they will encounter in lectures, reading, and exams. Available free when packaged with the print text.

World History Matters: A Student Guide to World History Online. Based on the popular "World History Matters" Web site produced by the Center for History and New Media, this unique resource, edited by Kristin Lehner (The Johns Hopkins University), Kelly Schrum (George Mason University), and T. Mills Kelly (George Mason University), combines reviews of 150 of the most useful and reliable world history Web sites with an introduction that guides students in locating, evaluating, and correctly citing online sources. Available free when packaged with the print text.

Trade Books. Titles published by sister companies Hill and Wang; Farrar, Straus and Giroux; Henry Holt and Company; St. Martin's Press; Picador; and Palgrave Macmillan are available at a 50% discount when packaged with

Bedford/St. Martin's textbooks. For more information, visit bedfordstmartins.com/tradeup.

A Pocket Guide to Writing in History.   This portable and affordable reference tool by Mary Lynn Rampolla provides reading, writing, and research advice useful to students in all history courses. Concise yet comprehensive advice on approaching typical history assignments, developing critical reading skills, writing effective history papers, conducting research, using and documenting sources, and avoiding plagiarism—enhanced with practical tips and examples throughout—have made this slim reference a best-seller. Package discounts are available.

A Student's Guide to History.   This complete guide to success in any history course provides the practical help students need to be effective. In addition to introducing students to the nature of the discipline, author Jules Benjamin teaches a wide range of skills from preparing for exams to approaching common writing assignments, and he explains the research and documentation process with plentiful examples. Package discounts are available.

Worlds of History: A Comparative Reader.   Compiled by Kevin Reilly, a widely respected world historian and community college teacher, *Worlds of History* fosters historical thinking through thematic comparisons of primary and secondary sources from around the world. Each chapter takes up a major theme—such as patriarchy, love and marriage, or globalization—as experienced by two or more cultures. "Thinking Historically" exercises build students' capacity to analyze and interpret sources one skill at a time. This flexible framework accommodates a variety of approaches to teaching world history. Package discounts are available.

NOTE ON DATES AND USAGE

Where necessary for clarity, we qualify dates as B.C.E. ("Before the Common Era") or C.E. ("Common Era"). The abbreviation B.C.E. refers to the same era as B.C. ("Before Christ"), just as C.E is equivalent to A.D. (*anno Domini,* Latin for "in the year of the Lord"). In keeping with our aim to approach world history from a global, multicultural perspective, we chose these neutral abbreviations as appropriate to our enterprise. Because most readers will be more familiar with English than with metric measures, however, units of measure are given in the English system in the narrative, with metric and English measures provided on the maps.

We translate Chinese names and terms into English according to the *pinyin* system, while noting in parentheses proper names well established in English (e.g., Canton, Chiang Kai-shek). Transliteration of names and terms from the many other languages traced in our book follow the same contemporary scholarly conventions.

BRIEF CONTENTS

CONTENTS

PART 1   The Ancient World, from Human Origins to 500 C.E.

1

**Peopling the World,
To** 4000 B.C.E. 6

Major Global Development ▶ The adaptation of early humans to their environment and their eventual domestication of plants and animals.

2

**Temples and Palaces:
Birth of the City,**
5000–1200 B.C.E. 38

Major Global Development ▶ The rise of urban society and the creation of states in Southwest Asia.

7

The Unification of Western Eurasia,
500 B.C.E.–500 C.E. *202*

Major Global Development ▶ The unification of western Eurasia under the Roman Empire.

8

Reading the Unwritten Record: Peoples of Africa, the Americas, and the Pacific Islands,
3000 B.C.E.–500 C.E. *236*

Major Global Development ▶ The evolution of ancient cultures without writing and their fundamental role in world history.

11

Societies and Networks in the Americas and the Pacific, 300–1200 *338*

Major Global Development ▶ The formation of distinctive regional cultures in the Americas and the Pacific Islands between 300 and 1200.

12

The Rise of Commerce in Afro-Eurasia, 900–1300 *372*

Major Global Development ▶ The sustained economic expansion that spread across Afro-Eurasia from 900 to 1300.

13

Centers of Learning and the Transmission of Culture, 900–1300 *406*

Major Global Development ▶The expansion of learning and education across Eurasia in the period from 900 to 1300 and its relationship with the rise of regional and national identities.

14

Crusaders, Mongols, and Eurasian Integration, 1050–1350 *440*

Major Global Development ▶The Eurasian integration fostered by the clashes of culture known as the Crusades and the Mongol conquests.

15
Collapse and Revival in Afro-Eurasia, 1300–1450   *474*

Major Global Development ▶ Crisis and recovery in fourteenth- and fifteenth-century Afro-Eurasia.

16
Empires and Alternatives in the Americas, 1430–1530   *512*

Major Global Development ▶ The diversity of societies and states in the Americas prior to European invasion.

MAPS

SPECIAL FEATURES

ACKNOWLEDGMENTS

Writing *Crossroads and Cultures* has made real to us the theme of this book, which is connections among many far-flung people of diverse livelihoods and talents. From the first draft to the last, the authors have benefited from repeated critical readings by many talented scholars and teachers who represent an array of schools and historical interests. Our sincere thanks go to the following instructors, who helped us keep true to our vision of showing connections among the world's people and whose comments often challenged us to rethink or justify our interpretations. Crucial to the integrity of the book, they always provided a check on accuracy down to the smallest detail.

Alemseged Abbay, *Frostburg State University*

Heather J. Abdelnur, *Augusta State University*

Wayne Ackerson, *Salisbury University*

Kathleen Addison, *California State University, Northridge*

Jeffrey W. Alexander, *University of Wisconsin–Parkside*

Omar H. Ali, *The University of North Carolina at Greensboro*

Monty Armstrong, *Cerritos High School*

Pierre Asselin, *Hawai'i Pacific University*

Eva Baham, *Southern University at Baton Rouge*

William Bakken, *Rochester Community and Technical College*

Thomas William Barker, *The University of Kansas*

Thomas William Barton, *University of San Diego*

Robert Blackey, *California State University, San Bernardino*

Chuck Bolton, *The University of North Carolina at Greensboro*

Robert Bond, *San Diego Mesa College*

James W. Brodman, *University of Central Arkansas*

Gayle K. Brunelle, *California State University, Fullerton*

Samuel Brunk, *The University of Texas at El Paso*

Jurgen Buchenau, *The University of North Carolina at Charlotte*

Clea Bunch, *University of Arkansas at Little Rock*

Kathy Callahan, *Murray State University*

John M. Carroll, *The University of Hong Kong*

Giancarlo Casale, *University of Minnesota*

Mark Chavalas, *University of Wisconsin–La Crosse*

Yinghong Cheng, *Delaware State University*

Mark Choate, *Brigham Young University*

Sharon Cohen, *Springbrook High School*

Christine Colin, *Mercyhurst College*

Eleanor Congdon, *Youngstown State University*

Dale Crandall-Bear, *Solano Community College*

John Curry, *University of Nevada, Las Vegas*

Michelle Danberg-Marshman, *Green River Community College*

Francis Danquah, *Southern University at Baton Rouge*

Sherrie Dux-Ideus, *Central Community College*

Peter Dykema, *Arkansas Tech University*

Tom Ewing, *Virginia Polytechnic Institute and State University*

Angela Feres, *Grossmont College*

Michael Fischbach, *Randolph-Macon College*

Nancy Fitch, *California State University, Fullerton*

Terence Anthony Fleming, *Northern Kentucky University*

Richard Fogarty, *University at Albany, The State University of New York*

Nicola Foote, *Florida Gulf Coast University*

Deanna Forsman, *North Hennepin Community College*

John D. Garrigus, *The University of Texas at Arlington*

Trevor Getz, *San Francisco State University*

David Goldfrank, *Georgetown University*

Charles Didier Gondola, *Indiana University–Purdue University Indianapolis*

Sue Gronewold, *Kean University*

Christopher Guthrie, *Tarleton State University*

Anne Hardgrove, *The University of Texas at San Antonio*

Donald J. Harreld, *Brigham Young University*

Todd Hartch, *Eastern Kentucky University*

Janine Hartman, *University of Cincinnati*

Daniel Heimmermann, *The University of Texas at Brownsville*

Cecily M. Heisser, *University of San Diego*

Timothy Henderson, *Auburn University at Montgomery*

Ted Henken, *Baruch College, The State University of New York*

Marilynn J. Hitchens, *University of Colorado Denver*

Roy W. Hopper, *University of Memphis*

Timothy Howe, *St. Olaf College*

Delridge Hunter, *Medgar Evers College, The City University of New York*

Bruce Ingram, *Itawamba Community College*

Erik N. Jensen, *Miami University*

Steven Sandor John, *Hunter College, The City University of New York*

Deborah Johnston, *Lakeside School*

David M. Kalivas, *Middlesex Community College*

Carol Keller, *San Antonio College*

Ian Stuart Kelly, *Palomar College*

Linda Kerr, *University of Alberta*

Charles King, *University of Nebraska at Omaha*

Melinda Cole Klein, *Saddleback College*

Ane Lintvedt-Dulac, *McDonogh School*

Ann Livschiz, *Indiana University–Purdue University Fort Wayne*

George E. Longenecker, *Vermont Technical College*

Edward Lykens, *Middle Tennessee State University*

Susan Maneck, *Jackson State University*

Chandra Manning, *Georgetown University*

Michael Marino, *The College of New Jersey*

Thomas Massey, *Cape Fear Community College*
Mary Jane Maxwell, *Green Mountain College*
Christine McCann, *Norwich University*
Patrick McDevitt, *University at Buffalo, The State University of New York*
Ian F. McNeely, *University of Oregon*
M. E. Menninger, *Texas State University–San Marcos*
Kathryn E. Meyer, *Washington State University*
Elizabeth Mizrahi, *Santa Barbara City College*
Max Okenfuss, *Washington University in St. Louis*
Kenneth Orosz, *Buffalo State College, The State University of New York*
Annette Palmer, *Morgan State University*
David Perry, *Dominican University*
Jared Poley, *Georgia State University*
Elizabeth Ann Pollard, *San Diego State University*
Dana Rabin, *University of Illinois at Urbana-Champaign*
Norman G. Raiford, *Greenville Technical College*
Stephen Rapp, *Universität Bern*
Michele Reid, *Georgia State University*
Chad Ross, *East Carolina University*
Morris Rossabi, *Queens College, The City University of New York*
Steven C. Rubert, *Oregon State University*
Eli Rubin, *Western Michigan University*
Anthony Santoro, *Christopher Newport University*
Linda B. Scherr, *Mercer County Community College*
Hollie Schillig, *California State University, Long Beach*
Michael Seth, *James Madison University*
Jessica Sheetz-Nguyen, *University of Central Oklahoma*
Rose Mary Sheldon, *Virginia Military Institute*
David R. Smith, *California State Polytechnic University, Pomona*
Ramya Sreenivasan, *University at Buffalo, The State University of New York*
John Stavens, *Bristol Eastern High School*
Catherine Howey Stearn, *Eastern Kentucky University*
Richard Steigmann-Gall, *Kent State University*
Anthony J. Steinhoff, *The University of Tennessee at Chattanooga*
Stephen J. Stillwell, *The University of Arizona*
Heather Streets, *Washington State University*
Jean Stuntz, *West Texas A&M University*
Guy Thompson, *University of Alberta*
Hunt Tooley, *Austin College*
Wendy Turner, *Augusta State University*
Rick Warner, *Wabash College*
Michael Weber, *Gettysburg College*
Theodore Weeks, *Southern Illinois University*
Guy Wells, *Lorain County Community College*
Sherri West, *Brookdale Community College*
Kenneth Wilburn, *East Carolina University*
Pingchao Zhu, *University of Idaho*
Alexander Zukas, *National University*

Many colleagues, friends, and family members have helped us develop this work as well. Bonnie Smith wishes to thank in particular Michal Shapira and Molly Giblin for their research assistance and Patrick Smith, who gave helpful information on contemporary world religions. Her colleagues at Rutgers, many of them pioneers in world history, were especially helpful. Among these, expert historian Donald R. Kelley shaped certain features of the last section of the book and always cheered the author on. Marc Van De Mieroop thanks the friends and colleagues who often unknowingly provided insights and information used in this book, especially Irene Bloom, William Harris, Feng Li, Indira Peterson, Michael Sommer, and Romila Thapar. Richard von Glahn thanks his many colleagues at UCLA who have shaped his thinking about world history, especially Ghislaine Lydon, Jose Moya, Ron Mellor, Sanjay Subrahmanyam, and Bin Wong. He is also grateful for the exposure to pathbreaking scholarship on world history afforded by the University of California's Multi-Campus Research Unit in World History. Kris Lane thanks the many wonderful William & Mary students of History 192, "The World Since 1450," as well as colleagues Abdul-Karim Rafeq, Scott Nelson, Chitralekha Zutshi, Hiroshi Kitamura, Philip Daileader, Chandos Brown, and Ron Schechter. All offered valuable advice on framing the early modern period. He also owes a huge debt to the University of Minnesota for graduate training and teaching assistant experience in this field.

We also wish to acknowledge and thank the publishing team at Bedford/St. Martin's, who are among the most talented people in publishing that we as a group have ever worked with and who did so much to bring this book into being. Among them, our special thanks go to former publisher for history Patricia A. Rossi, who inspired the conceptual design of the book and helped bring us together. The current publisher for history, Mary Dougherty, then picked up the reins from Tisha and advanced the project, using her special combination of professional expertise and personal warmth. It is hard to convey sufficiently our heartfelt appreciation to president Joan E. Feinberg and editorial director Denise Wydra. They always kept us alert to Bedford's special legacy of high-quality textbooks, a legacy based on the benefits a book must have for students and teachers alike. We aimed to be part of that legacy while writing *Crossroads and Cultures*.

President emeritus and founder Charles Christensen was also present at the beginning of this project, and he always cheerfully lent his extraordinary knowledge of publishing to the making and actual production of this book. We know that it would have been less than it is without his wisdom. Alongside all these others, director of development for history Jane Knetzger patiently and skillfully guided the development process, during which each chapter (and sentence) was poked and prodded. We thank Jane for being such a quiet force behind the progress of *Crossroads and*

Cultures. Special thanks go to senior editor and expert facilitator Heidi Hood and the editorial assistants who joined Heidi in providing invaluable help on many essential tasks: Lynn Sternberger, Jennifer Jovin, and Emily DiPietro. All of them moved the project along in myriad ways that we hardly know. We also appreciate the countless schedules, tasks, and layouts juggled so efficiently and well by senior production editor Anne Noonan. On the editorial team were John Reisbord and Daniel Otis, who helped edit and polish our final draft. All along the way Rose Corbett Gordon and Charlotte Miller, our superb photo researcher and talented map editor, respectively, provided us with striking and thought-provoking images and up-to-date, richly informative, and gorgeous maps. No author team could ask for more than to have the book's content laid out in such a clear and attractive design as that provided by Jerilyn Bockorick, with assistance from senior art director Anna Palchik. Jerilyn's special attention to the overall look of our work makes us feel that we and our readers are especially lucky. Senior designer Billy Boardman created our six beautiful covers with help from senior art director Donna Dennison. We are grateful for their craft in building the book's appeal.

Crossroads and Cultures has a wealth of materials for students and teachers to help support the text. Editor Annette Fantasia has guided our creation of the sourcebook that accompanies the main book, and we could hardly have achieved this task without her help; she also edited the instructor's resource manual. The work of associate editor Jack Cashman, who supervised the development of the other elements in our impressive array of supplements, will be appreciated by all teachers and students who use these materials. Jenna Bookin Barry, senior executive marketing manager; Sally Constable, senior market development manager; and Katherine Bates, market development manager, have worked tirelessly at our side to ensure that the book is in the best shape to meet the needs of students and teachers. We are deeply grateful for all the work they have done in the past and all that they will do in so sincerely advocating for the success of *Crossroads and Cultures* in today's classrooms.

Among the authors' greatest *Crossroads* experiences has been our relationship with brilliant executive editor Elizabeth M. Welch and her support team of ace development editors Sylvia Mallory, Margaret Manos, and Jim Strandberg. Beth has guided many a successful book from inception to completion—all to the benefit of tens of thousands of students and their instructors. We thank her for bringing us her historical, conceptual, visual, and publishing talent, all of which she has offered with such generosity of spirit, good humor, and grace. It has been a privilege for all of us to work with Beth and to have spent these *Crossroads* years with the entire Bedford team.

Finally, our students' questions and concerns have shaped much of this work, and we welcome all our readers' suggestions, queries, and criticisms. We know that readers, like our own students, excel in spotting unintended glitches and also in providing much excellent food for thought. Please contact us with your comments at our respective institutions.

Bonnie G. Smith
Marc Van De Mieroop
Richard von Glahn
Kris Lane

Crossroads and Cultures

A History of the World's Peoples

The Ancient World

from Human Origins to 500 C.E.

CH 1

THE STORY WE TELL in this book begins around 4 million years ago, when the lines of human ancestors diverged from those of the great African apes, and our exploration of the ancient period of world history ends at about the year 500 C.E. If one wrote a four-hundred-page book that gave equal space to every century in all of world history, the period from 500 C.E. to today would take up only one-sixth of the final page. All previous pages would treat what we call the ancient world.

It would be hard for a historian to fill many of the four hundred pages of this book, however. The first 399 would describe foraging peoples who moved around during most of the year and consequently left little evidence for us to study. All the evidence is archaeological—that is, the material objects humans left behind. Only late in the period, some five thousand years ago, did people invent writing. That skill had a limited geographical spread, however, and even in societies that had developed writing, it was restricted by social class and to a small number of people. Archaeological remains provide much information, but they have limitations; they do not reveal what languages people spoke, their names, and many other things we know about those people to whom we have access through their writings.

This was the era of origins, the period in which human populations invented all the major elements we associate with culture. The modern human species itself originated over millions of years, and our ancestor species invented basic tools, some of which—such as the needle—we still use today. Humans migrated across the globe, sometimes helped by natural events; the last ice age, for instance, lowered sea level to create a land bridge that allowed people to move into the Americas. About ten thousand years ago, modern humans in various parts of the world invented agriculture, which remains an important livelihood for some of the world's peoples into the twenty-first century C.E. The development of agriculture allowed villages and, later, cities to arise, where people with special skills had an opportunity to invent and refine new technologies. As cities and states grew larger and people interacted more closely, they needed means of regulating their societies. This gave rise to such developments as laws, diplomacy, and tools for managing financial transactions, among many others.

CH 2

CH 3

All of the writing systems we use today had their roots in these early times. Some ancient scripts died out before 500 C.E., including Babylonian cuneiform, Egyptian hieroglyphs, and Greek Linear B. Others, such as Chinese script, have remained in use from the second millennium B.C.E. until today. The alphabet invented in western Asia in the second millennium B.C.E. had particularly widespread success, with Greeks, Romans, Indians, and many others adopting and then modifying it to serve their specific needs. In later history, it sometimes replaced long existing writing systems, such as those of the Americas.

Peoples of the ancient world also developed a wide variety of political structures. The overall trend was toward larger and more complex organizations, from small bands of up to forty gatherer-hunters to enormous empires incorporating millions of people. Eurasia's classical empires—so called because the revolutionary ideas that shaped these empires long outlived them and gave rise to the fundamental, or "classical," cultural traditions of Eurasia—flourished from about 500 B.C.E. to 500 C.E. Among them were the Qin Empire, which gave its name to the country of China, and the Old Persian Empire of Iran, whose Parthian and Sasanid successors inspired the people of the region until very recently. In western Eurasia, the Roman Empire gave us the term *empire* itself, which is derived from *imperium* (meaning "rule"), and its history inspired ideas of political domination up to modern times. We consider the classical period of antiquity to have ended at the time when many empires disappeared: the Roman in the Mediterranean, Sasanid in the Middle East, Gupta in India, and Han in China. Political organization was far from uniform

CH 5

CH 4

in this era, however, and states we give the same label—empire—took varied approaches to rule. Some states gave power to one individual, others to a group of bureaucrats. Still others professed ideals of popular participation in government, but even in these only a select group of people was involved in governing.

Although many people lived in relative isolation, ancient societies were often in contact over great distances. Trade routes ran across Eurasia, for example, and women in China made silk cloth that people in Rome would wear. Those contacts waxed and waned over time, but they ignored political boundaries, and often continued even between societies at war. Migrant peoples sometimes carried technologies over vast expanses; Bantu speakers, for instance, spread agriculture and ironworking over much of sub-Saharan Africa. Not all historical developments and innovations resulted from contact and migration, however. Often people living far apart separately created similar technologies and tools. Pottery, for example, was invented independently in Japan, the Middle East, Mesoamerica, and the Andes.

The ancient world produced the classical eras of the literate cultures of Eurasia. Many religions and philosophies begun in this period remain influential to this day, including Indian Buddhism and Hinduism, Chinese Confucianism, Daoism, and Legalism, and in the Mediterranean region Judaism, Christianity, and Greek philosophies. Major genres of literature stem from this period, and authors from a variety of cultures wrote works still read today, including Greek and Sanskrit epics and tragedies, the Five Classics of

	4000 B.C.E.	3000 B.C.E.	2000 B.C.E.
Americas	• 4000 Spread of agriculture	3000–1800 Norte Chico culture	
Europe	• 4000 Spread of agriculture and Indo-European languages	3000–1650 Minoan culture	
Middle East	• 4000 Spread of agriculture Uruk, the first city; Mesopotamian cuneiform script 3200 •	3000–2350 Competing city-states in Mesopotamia 2350–2200 Akkadian dynasty	
Africa	• 4000 Spread of agriculture	• 3000 Unification of Egypt; Egyptian hieroglyphic script; start of southward migration of the Bantu • 2550 Khufu's pyramid at Giza	
Asia and Oceania	• 4000 Spread of agriculture	2600–1900 Mature Indus Valley culture Oxus culture 2100–1700 3000–750 First wave of Austronesian migrations	

Chinese literature, and historical accounts, among many others. Some were short poems, others volumes of vast length.

World history was not a uniform process, however, as people everywhere chose the lifestyles and livelihoods best suited to their environments. Sometimes this led them to abandon techniques that most others saw as advances. People in Polynesia stopped making pottery, for example; people in Australia opted not to farm. In certain regions, structures that elsewhere provided the foundation for later developments suddenly ceased to exist. The urban cultures of the Oxus River Valley disappeared, for instance. Perhaps the primary characteristic of early world history is the sheer variety of the cultures that flourished in this period.

CH 8

NORTH AMERICA

EUROPE

ASIA

MIDDLE EAST

ATLANTIC OCEAN

AFRICA

PACIFIC OCEAN

SOUTH AMERICA

INDIAN OCEAN

AUSTRALIA

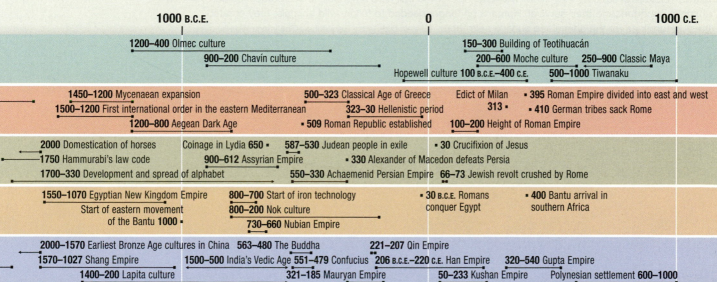

1000 B.C.E. 0 1000 C.E.

1200–400 Olmec culture
150–300 Building of Teotihuacán
900–200 Chavín culture
200–600 Moche culture   250–900 Classic Maya
Hopewell culture 100 B.C.E.–400 C.E.   500–1000 Tiwanaku

1450–1200 Mycenaean expansion
500–323 Classical Age of Greece
Edict of Milan
313
395 Roman Empire divided into east and west
1500–1200 First international order in the eastern Mediterranean
323–30 Hellenistic period
410 German tribes sack Rome
1200–800 Aegean Dark Age
509 Roman Republic established
100–200 Height of Roman Empire

2000 Domestication of horses
Coinage in Lydia 650
587–530 Judean people in exile
30 Crucifixion of Jesus
1750 Hammurabi's law code
900–612 Assyrian Empire
330 Alexander of Macedon defeats Persia
1700–330 Development and spread of alphabet
550–330 Achaemenid Persian Empire   66–73 Jewish revolt crushed by Rome

1550–1070 Egyptian New Kingdom Empire
800–700 Start of iron technology
30 B.C.E. Romans conquer Egypt
400 Bantu arrival in southern Africa
Start of eastern movement of the Bantu 1000
800–200 Nok culture
730–660 Nubian Empire

2000–1570 Earliest Bronze Age cultures in China   563–480 The Buddha
221–207 Qin Empire
1570–1027 Shang Empire
1500–500 India's Vedic Age 551–479 Confucius   206 B.C.E.–220 C.E. Han Empire   320–540 Gupta Empire
1400–200 Lapita culture
321–185 Mauryan Empire
50–233 Kushan Empire   Polynesian settlement 600–1000

AT A CROSSROADS ▲

In around 6000 B.C.E., the townspeople of Çatal Höyük in southern Turkey were on the cusp of one of the most important technological innovations in world history: the birth of agriculture. Wall paintings in their houses reveal how they lived. The large size of the bull here emphasizes this domesticated animal's importance to their survival. Humans no longer needed to follow wild animals; they created the surroundings for the animals to survive near them. (ullstein bild-Archiv Gerstenberg/The Image Works.)

Peopling the World
to 4000 B.C.E.

In August 1856 quarry workers opening up a cave in the Neander Valley of northwest Germany discovered a skull and bones. The skull was curious: it was long, with a bulge in the back, and the large brow ridges arched prominently over the eye sockets. Johann Fuhlrott, a local teacher and amateur student of natural history, identified them as the remains of an early species of human, thus challenging the ideas about creation that prevailed among the nineteenth-century Christians who lived in the area. Finds of other fossils and stone tools near lakes and riverbeds had convinced Fuhlrott and others, however, that modern humans had developed through a process of evolution rather than creation.

Three years later, in 1859, the British natural historian Charles Darwin published a detailed explanation of evolution in his famous book, *On the Origin of Species*. Darwin argued that the species of all living beings had evolved over millions of years through adaptation to their environment. He wrote in his *Autobiography* that, "Natural Selection . . . tends only to render each species as successful as possible in the battle for life with other species, in wonderfully complex and changing circumstances."[1] But many opposed the idea that earlier species of humans had existed and explained the strange fossil finds in the Neander Valley (*Neanderthal* in German) in other ways. One professor of anatomy claimed that the skeleton belonged to a man with severe vitamin deficiency and arthritis. Another said he was a Cossack horseman who had been wounded in battle and crawled into the

Human Origins

FOCUS What physical and behavioral adaptations and innovations characterized human evolution?

Paleolithic Food Gatherers, 2,000,000–9000 B.C.E.

FOCUS In the absence of written sources, what have scholars learned about the Paleolithic economy, adaptations to the natural world, and technological innovations?

The First Neolithic Farmers, 9000–4000 B.C.E.

FOCUS In what ways does the Neolithic agricultural economy reveal humans' increasing intent and ability to manipulate the natural world to their advantage?

COUNTERPOINT: Gatherer-Hunters by Choice: Aborigines of Australia

FOCUS Why did Australian Aborigines, in contrast to many of the world's other peoples, choose not to farm?

BACKSTORY

Some five billion years ago the earth came into being. For 99.9 percent of the time since then, the planet only gradually developed the conditions in which humans evolved. Humans with all the physical characteristics we have today have lived on the planet only for the last fifty thousand years, a short blip in the immense period that earth has existed. The era we can study through our ancestors' own written records is much shorter still. Less than five thousand years ago people in a few places invented writing, a skill that very gradually spread over the globe. Writing is the source that tells historians people's names and gives us access to their actions and thoughts.

We start this book by examining the period before people invented writing, however, at the moment when a separate species of uniquely human ancestors originated. With its appearance began world history—not the history of the world, but of humans in the world. Over time, people's interactions with one another and their environment caused fundamental changes not only in their physical features and behavior but in the natural world. We are one of the most recent species on earth, but we are also the one whose impact on the planet has been the greatest.

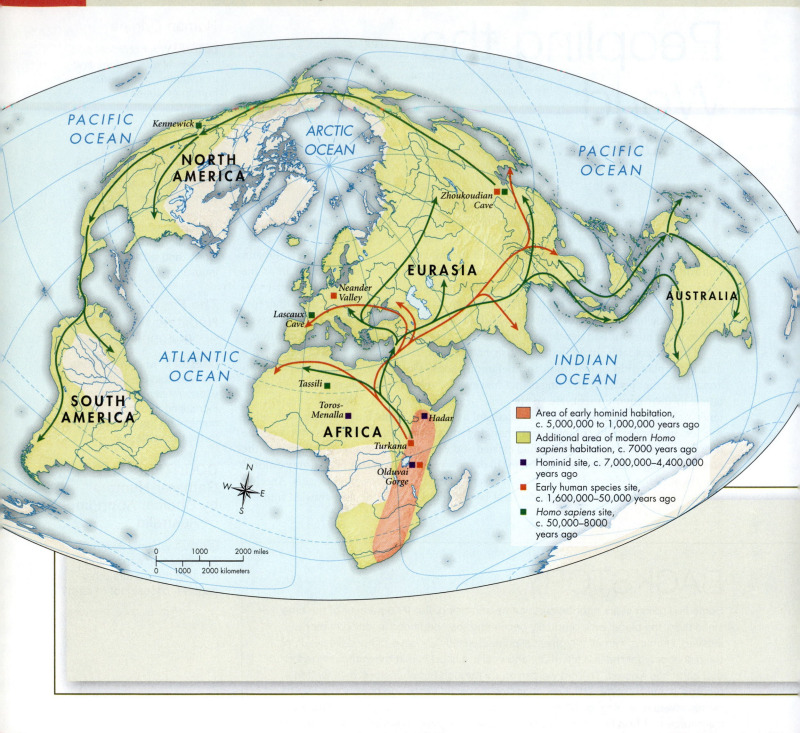

Area of early hominid habitation, c. 5,000,000 to 1,000,000 years ago

Additional area of modern *Homo sapiens* habitation, c. 7000 years ago

■ Hominid site, c. 7,000,000–4,400,000 years ago

■ Early human species site, c. 1,600,000–50,000 years ago

■ *Homo sapiens* site, c. 50,000–8000 years ago

▪ **c. 7 million years ago (mya)** Oldest hominid on record, *Sahelanthropus tchadensis*, lives in central Africa

▪ **c. 3.2 mya** *Australopithecus afarensis* (Lucy) lives in the region of modern Ethiopia

▪ **c. 1 mya** Ancestors of *Homo erectus* enter Asia

7 million years ago (mya)   **3 mya**   **1 mya**

▪ **c. 2 mya** First hominin and first stone tools

▪ **4.4 mya** *Ardipithecus ramidus* lives in the region of modern Ethiopia

cave; the agonizing pain he suffered had deformed his skull. Only in the early twentieth century, after numerous finds of similar fossils, were most scholars convinced that the Neanderthal represented an early human species, as Johann Fuhlrott had concluded.

Disagreements such as those over the Neanderthal skeleton characterize the study of early humans and their ancestors to the present day. Specialists often come to conflicting conclusions in their interpretation of such finds, and consequently they develop different narratives about the course of human evolution. This is understandable, given the challenges involved. Scholars have a limited number of archaeological remains, which come from all over the globe and cover a span of millions of years, and they must place them into a sequence that is logically consistent with the observable differences.

A major difficulty in interpretation is uncertainty in dating finds related to human evolution. Archaeologists assign widely differing dates to the skeleton remains they discover, which leads to divergent reconstructions of when certain human ancestors existed and how they relate to one another. Moreover, new finds often upset existing theories. In late 2009, for example, archaeologists announced the discovery in northern Ethiopia of remains that demonstrate the existence of an entirely new species of human ancestors, *Ardipithecus ramidus* (ahr-dih-PITH-eh-kihs rahm-IH-dihs), which lived 4.4 million years ago and had attributes scholars had thought developed more than a million years later. It will take years of further research to integrate these finds into the general reconstruction of human evolution.

Despite their varying viewpoints, scholars agree that humans developed over millions of years, and that a number of species preceded the modern human. The wide range of material evidence we explore in this chapter reveals that each species had distinctive characteristics that resulted from adaptations to different environments. Gradually our ancestors acquired the skills to manipulate the natural surroundings for their own purposes. After millions of years of gathering foodstuffs available in the wild, they began to control the growth of plants and animals through farming and herding. The implications of this development were numerous and profound. Farming made settled communities

MAPPING THE WORLD

Out of Africa

Several species of human ancestors migrated out of Africa at different times, ultimately settling in almost every part of the globe by 5000 B.C.E., about seven thousand years ago. Their ability to spread depended in part on ecological conditions such as the expansion of the Arctic ice cap and low sea levels, but it also involved such technological achievements as the construction of boats to reach islands. The first species to migrate were the ancestors of *Homo erectus* some one million years ago; the last was *Homo sapiens*, about one hundred thousand years ago.

ROUTES ▼

→ Migration of early *Homo* species, c. 1,000,000–500,000 years ago

→ Migration of *Homo sapiens*, c. 100,000–5000 years ago

- **c. 500,000 B.C.E.** Ancestors of Neanderthal enter western Eurasia
- **c. 400,000 B.C.E.** First evidence of *Homo sapiens* in Africa
- **c. 100,000 B.C.E.** Some *Homo sapiens* leave Africa
- **c. 30,000 B.C.E.** *Homo sapiens* becomes the only human species

500,000 B.C.E.	100,000 B.C.E.	50,000 B.C.E.	10,000 B.C.E.

c. 400,000–30,000 B.C.E. Neanderthal lives in western Eurasia

- **c. 15,000 B.C.E.** *Homo sapiens* enters the Americas

c. 35,000–10,000 B.C.E. Paleolithic cave paintings

c. 10,000–8,000 B.C.E. Development of agriculture in Southwest Asia

possible, which in turn led to the development of increasingly complex societies, cultures, and governments.

Not all humans decided to practice agriculture, however. In some parts of the world, such as Australia, they continued to forage even after they knew farming was possible. Examples like this show that natural conditions always influenced people's choices: they had to work with the resources available. To a great extent, the world's diverse geography explains the various forms of livelihood we observe in human history.

OVERVIEW QUESTIONS

The major global development in this chapter: The adaptation of early humans to their environment and their eventual domestication of plants and animals.

As you read, consider:

1. What caused humans to introduce technological and other innovations?

2. How did these innovations increase their ability to determine their own destinies?

3. How did the relationship between humans and nature change?

4. How have historians and other scholars reconstructed life in the earliest periods of human existence despite the lack of written records?

Human Origins

FOCUS

What physical and behavioral adaptations and innovations characterized human evolution?

Over the past two centuries archaeologists have uncovered fossils all over the world that show a startling range of human ancestors. The oldest finds come from Africa, which is also the source of the largest variety of fossils, especially the eastern part of the continent (see Map 1.1). Consequently, most scholars agree that Africa was the birthplace of the human species. Only after their origins in Africa did human ancestors start to spread out of the continent, which took place in several waves (see again Mapping the World, pages 8 and 9).

Students of human evolution have benefited immensely from recent advances in DNA analysis—in particular, the analysis of mitochondrial DNA, which passes on from the mother to her children. Similarities and differences in the mitochondrial DNA of populations across the world have enabled researchers to establish genetic connections among various population groups, as well as their ancestry. This information provides crucial support to the idea that Africa was the home of the modern human species.

Human evolution was not a process of constant, steady development. It unfolded unevenly, as bursts of change interrupted long periods of overall stability. Scholars understand human evolution in the context of changes in the natural environment, which often triggered and shaped physical and behavioral changes in human ancestors. Although today all humans belong to the same species, in the past different species of our ancestors coexisted. The sole surviving species, *Homo sapiens*, was the one best adapted to new conditions. Thus, from the very beginning, environmental adaptation and its consequences have been at the heart of the story of human history.

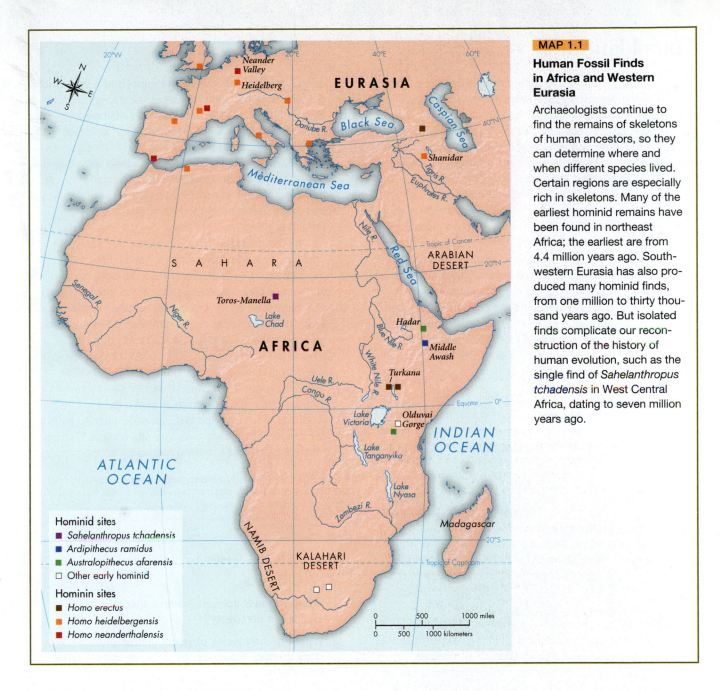

MAP 1.1

Human Fossil Finds in Africa and Western Eurasia

Archaeologists continue to find the remains of skeletons of human ancestors, so they can determine where and when different species lived. Certain regions are especially rich in skeletons. Many of the earliest hominid remains have been found in northeast Africa; the earliest are from 4.4 million years ago. Southwestern Eurasia has also produced many hominid finds, from one million to thirty thousand years ago. But isolated finds complicate our reconstruction of the history of human evolution, such as the single find of *Sahelanthropus tchadensis* in West Central Africa, dating to seven million years ago.

Hominid sites
- *Sahelanthropus tchadensis*
- *Ardipithecus ramidus*
- *Australopithecus afarensis*
- Other early hominid

Hominin sites
- *Homo erectus*
- *Homo heidelbergensis*
- *Homo neanderthalensis*

Evolution of the Human Species

The great African apes are the closest relatives of the human species. Indeed, we share 98 percent of our genetic makeup with them. Although recent finds suggest that human ancestors may have separated from those of the great apes beginning 7 million years ago (see Reading the Past: Fossil Hunting), secure evidence dates to only 5 to 4 million years ago. At that time, human ancestors, or **hominids**, moved out of dense forests into the more open woodlands and grasslands of eastern Africa; the ancestors of the great apes remained in the forest. A sustained drought that diminished the size of the African forest may have inspired the move. Adapting to the new environment led to several changes in the physical appearance and behavior of hominids. Three main physical traits came to distinguish humans from apes and other primates: upright walking, flexible hands, and the ability to communicate through speech.

hominid The biological family that includes modern humans and their human ancestors.

Fossil Hunting

New fossil finds occur regularly, and they often force scholars to reconsider existing theories of human evolution. Indeed, ideas about the evolutionary process have fundamentally changed in recent decades. Whereas scholars previously saw human evolution as linear, with each early species showing a single stage of evolution, today they see the various human species as coexisting during the same period, each having adapted to regional circumstances. Further, they now view evolutionary milestones as taking place not just in eastern Africa, where most early fossils were discovered, but in other parts of the world where they have found evidence of important developments. Moreover, scholars now think the divergence between the ancestors of humans and great African apes began earlier than they thought formerly. Until recently they thought this happened four or five million years ago. The discovery announced in 2002 of an almost complete skull that mixes ape and hominid features may force a reinterpretation. The find is surprising because of its very early date, 6–7 million years ago, and its location, Chad in central Africa.

The following is one of the earliest English-language reports on the remarkable find.

After more than a decade of digging, researchers working in Chad have made the fossil discovery of a lifetime: a nearly complete skull of the oldest and most primitive member of the human family yet known. Nicknamed Toumaï—or "hope of life" in the local Goran language—it belongs to an entirely new genus and species of hominid, *Sahelanthropus tchadensis*. And at almost 7 million years old, it has taken scientists several crucial steps closer to the point in time at which humans and chimpanzees diverged. Yet as is the case for most spectacular finds, this one raises as many questions, if not more, than it answers.

For one, until now almost all of the next earliest hominid fossils unearthed so far have come from East Africa, leading some scholars to posit that the origin of humans was essentially an "East Side story." Toumaï, however, comes from central Africa. And then there's his (the skull is thought to be that of a male) surprising

combination of primitive and advanced features. Characteristics of the face and teeth clearly align Toumaï with hominids, say team leader Michel Brunet of the University of Poitiers in France and his colleagues. But the braincase is comparable in size to that of a small ape. (Whether or not Toumaï and his kind were bipedal remains a matter of uncertainty. No skeletal elements have been found, but features on the base of the skull and the face resemble those of known bipedal hominids.)

As the oldest hominid on record, *S. tchadensis* could be the ancestor of all later hominids—including us—according to Brunet and his collaborators, who announced their discovery today in the journal *Nature*. But that will be difficult to prove, cautions Bernard Wood of George Washington University in an accompanying commentary. "My prediction is that *S. tchadensis* is just the tip of an iceberg of taxonomic diversity during hominid evolution 5–7 million years ago," he writes. Whatever the case, it seems certain that this find will have a tremendous impact on the study of human origins. "It's a lot of emotion to have in my hand the beginning of the human lineage," Brunet muses. "I have been looking for this for so long."

Source: Kate Wong, "Meet the Oldest Member of the Human Family," *Scientific American*, July 11, 2002, http://www.scientificamerican.com/article.cfm?id=meet-the-oldest-member-of.

EXAMINING THE EVIDENCE

1. What makes *S. tchadensis* an especially significant discovery?

2. What are the fossil's physical characteristics? Why does it upset the accepted theories about human evolution?

3. Why does a find such as this raise more questions than answers?

Upright Walking   Initially, the three developments that revealed an evolutionary split between humans and the great apes were all a matter of degree. Apes walk on two legs only in unusual circumstances, but people do so easily. This characteristic was the first of the three to develop, and the earliest signs of upright walking now seem to come from northern Ethiopia. The skeleton of the *Ardipithecus ramidus* from that region shows that the species could walk upright but did not yet have the arched foot that makes walking easy. The first evidence of smooth upright walking is fossilized footprints in what is today northern

Tanzania in a river canyon called Olduvai (ohl-DOO-vy) Gorge. These footprints show that 3.6 million years ago an adult and a child walked fully upright, using the same stride as modern humans.

Upright walking changed the skeleton and musculature and shifted the body's weight to a vertical axis. It reduced the space available for digestive organs, which led to a need for food that was easier to digest and more nutritious. Instead of hard plant materials, such as leaves, human ancestors now ate fruits and nuts. Moreover, the upright posture freed the hands for uses other than walking, such as carrying food, stones, and offspring—uses that offered potential survival advantages. Thus, upright walking created conditions favorable to the further evolution of human hands, because individuals with more flexible hands had improved chances of surviving and passing on their genetic inheritance.

Human hands and those of apes have thumbs that can face the four other fingers, but human hands have a much more powerful and precise grasp. Greater dexterity allowed humans to make tools to aid them in their daily tasks. The use of tools itself is not a distinguishing characteristic of humans—chimpanzees, for example, use peeled branches to catch ants. What is unique is the human capacity to use tools to create other tools. Many scholars agree that this skill may have developed late in human evolution, around 2 million years ago. The earliest preserved tools are made of stone, which because of their durability offer the archaeologist a rich set of evidence. With toolmaking, humans' ability to manipulate the environment to meet their needs took an enormous step forward.

Fossilized Footprints

In 1978, the archaeological team led by Mary Leakey discovered these revealing sets of footprints at Laetoli in northern Tanzania. Made by a child and an adult who walked through volcanic ash some 3.6 million years ago, they were preserved after the ash solidified. They are the earliest evidence of human ancestors walking upright using the same stride we use today. This change in walking resulted in important new skeletal and behavioral developments. (Tom Reader/PhotoResearchers, Inc.)

Flexible Hands

Humans took another step forward with speech, which gave them the capacity to work more effectively in groups and to pass on the benefits of experience to their offspring. Humans have a much greater ability to communicate than other primates. With their migration into the flat grasslands, human ancestors needed to live in larger groups for their safety. They were relatively small, weak, and slow—easy targets for predators—and cooperation offered their only defense. For example, they coordinated the throwing of rocks (a uniquely human and highly efficient skill), which gave them substantial protection. The heightened need for cooperation led to greater social interaction and organization, and over time, humans developed speech—the capacity to speak and to understand what others say.

Speech

The human attributes of walking upright, manual versatility, and speech both depended on and contributed to an increase in brain size. The brain became larger not only in absolute terms, but relative to the entire body. To accommodate the larger organ, the skull's shape had to change, and the new grasslands diet helped make that possible. The fruits and nuts human ancestors ate were easier to chew than the bark and leaves of the forest. Consequently, teeth and jawbones gradually grew smaller, which changed the shape of the skull. The very structure of the brain changed, too, as new areas developed, such as the one that controls speech and language. Thus, changes in human brains, like other key human characteristics, evolved out of a complex set of environmental pressures and corresponding adaptations. This pattern of adaptation to environmental pressures continued as humans evolved from the earliest human species to *Homo sapiens*, modern human beings.

The Changing Brain

As we have seen, recently published research on skeletal material from northern modern-day Ethiopia indicates that 4–5 million years ago a human ancestor lived who had

Human Ancestors

very apelike characteristics but also new abilities. This species, *Ardipithecus ramidus*, had a brain the size of a modern chimpanzee's and arms that permitted swift movement in trees, but it also had legs that enabled upright walking, albeit rather awkwardly. The species ate nuts and plants rather than the fruits that apes consume.

Around 4 million years ago, human ancestors of the *Australopithecus* (aw-strah-loh-PITH-uh-kihs) species developed. The term *Australopithecus* literally means "southern ape," and branches of the species inhabited eastern and southern Africa up to 1.5 million years ago. The most famous individual from this lengthy period is Lucy, a woman who lived 3.2 million years ago in what is now northern Ethiopia, near where the *Ardipithecus ramidus* remains were found. In 1974, archaeologists discovered her relatively well-preserved skeleton, and concluded from it that she was twenty-five to thirty years old, about 3.5 feet tall, and weighed no more than sixty pounds. She was much smaller and lighter than *Ardipithecus ramidus*, and she could walk much better because her foot had the archlike structure of the modern human. Her long arms indicated that Lucy still climbed trees, probably to escape from predators. Her teeth resembled those of hominids, and the wear on them suggested that she ate mostly fruits, berries, and roots. It is possible that all later hominids derived from Lucy's species, which we call *Australopithecus afarensis*.

Starting around 2 million years ago, the last members of the *Australopithecus* species started to coexist with the human ancestors we identify with the term **hominin**. They are distinguished from previous hominids by their much larger brains, which may have developed as a result of eating more nutritious foods, especially meat. Indeed, the eating habits of early hominins may have been their most important characteristic. They originated in a period when the climate fluctuated between wet and dry periods, forcing hominids to explore new sources of food. Among the foods most sought after, meat became preeminent.

One of the earliest representatives of hominins in the fossil record is Turkana boy, whose almost complete skeleton archaeologists found in the mid-1980s in the north of modern-day Kenya. He was no more than twelve years old when he died some 1.6 million years ago. Compared with Lucy, he stood more upright and his arms were shorter relative to the rest of his body. But his brain was larger and he was much taller. He already measured 5.3 feet at his young age, and biologists estimate he would have reached 6 feet when fully grown. Although his brain size was still very limited and he probably could not speak, Turkana boy resembled modern humans in many ways.

Around 1 million years ago, the first human ancestors moved from Africa into Asia,

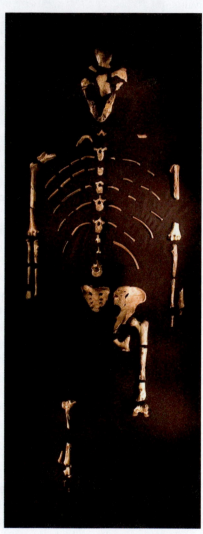

Comparing Skeletons

When paleontologists compare ancient skeletons to determine how human ancestors changed physically over time, they have to piece together evidence from many fragments. Compare the remains of an *Ardipithecus ramidus* more than 4 million years old (left) with those of the famous *Australopithecus afarensis*, Lucy, estimated to be 3.2 million years old (right). It is easy to see that the *Ardipithecus* had much longer arms and shorter legs, whereas Lucy's bones were lighter. Detailed analysis also shows that her skull had space for stronger teeth and a larger brain. (Tim White (left) and Dave Einsel/Getty Images (right).)

where they reached the areas of modern China and Indonesia. These groups developed into the species scholars call *Homo erectus* ("upright person"). Remains of their campsites show that they collaborated to kill large animals and they made fires. In fact, the use of fire made emigration out of Africa possible, because it allowed human ancestors to survive in the cold northern climates. Excavated hearths indicate that the fires, though small, allowed *Homo erectus* to shelter in caves. Fire also enabled them to cook, so they could soften otherwise inedible plants and more easily separate meat from bones. In this way, the invention of cooking meant that the frontal teeth could grow even smaller. *Homo erectus* existed in Asia until perhaps fifty thousand years ago, while in Africa and Europe new hominins developed.

At the same time that *Homo erectus* evolved in Asia, other human ancestors who remained in Africa developed substantially larger brains. One new African species, *Homo heidelbergensis*, was the first to migrate to Europe, establishing self-sustaining populations in Europe around five hundred thousand years ago. The hominids residing in Europe very slowly developed into a separate branch, *Homo neanderthalensis*, or **Neanderthals**, whose fossils led to the nineteenth-century debates over human origins discussed earlier. Flourishing in Europe and western Asia from four hundred thousand to thirty thousand years ago, Neanderthals had long, large faces that projected sharply forward, and they had larger front teeth than modern humans, which may have allowed them to consume the large amounts of meat they hunted. Their brains were slightly larger than those of modern humans, and their bones show that they were stockier. These physical characteristics may have helped them to survive in colder climates.

Simultaneous with the development of the Neanderthal in Europe, the earliest forms of the modern human species, **Homo sapiens** ("consciously thinking person"), arose in Africa around four hundred thousand years ago. This species continued to evolve slowly until it attained the physical characteristics humans have today, perhaps as recently as fifty thousand years ago. *Homo sapiens* is especially distinct from other hominids in the size and structure of the brain. Larger and more sophisticated brains allow them to improve skills such as tool-making and communication, giving the species a marked advantage over other hominids.

Homo sapiens may have used these abilities to monopolize available resources. For millions of years, various hominid species coexisted, but around thirty thousand years ago *Homo sapiens* became the sole human species on earth. It is possible that *Homo sapiens'* extraordinarily successful adaptation caused the extinction of all other human species. Then, as now, the development and adaptation of one human population had consequences for all human populations.

Homo Sapiens

Out of Africa

Various human ancestors migrated out of Africa at different times—the ancestors of *Homo erectus* some 1 million years ago, the ancestors of the Neanderthal some five hundred thousand years ago, and finally *Homo sapiens* about one hundred thousand years ago. Climate change, a desire to follow a particular type of prey, and social pressures probably triggered these movements. When the climate became wetter, for example, African animals grazing on grasslands spread into zones that were previously too dry to feed them, and the hominins who ate them probably followed. Moreover, when human groups became too large to survive on the natural resources of their territory, some members moved away and explored new areas.

The final migration—that of *Homo sapiens*—was a remarkable success. Scholars now think that the species survived times when its numbers dwindled to several thousand individuals, or even fewer. This did not prevent *Homo sapiens* from spreading to all corners of the earth, even into the most inhospitable environments, such as polar regions and desert fringes. The movement of early peoples from Africa into Eurasia was relatively easy, because these continents are connected by land. But to colonize the distant regions of the Americas, Australia, and other islands, humans had to take advantage of changes in the physical environment—as they did with the advent of the ice ages.

Hominin Migrations

hominin The biological subsection of the hominid family that includes species identified with the term *Homo*.

Neanderthal A hominid species that inhabited Europe and western Asia from four hundred thousand to thirty thousand years ago.

Homo sapiens The species of hominids to which modern humans belong; "*sapiens*" refers to the ability to think.

Ice Ages

In climatic terms, the earth's last seven hundred thousand years saw a series of dramatic fluctuations between warm and cold conditions. In cold periods, the so-called ice ages, the absorption of water into massive glaciers at the polar caps led to a drastic drop in the sea level, to more than 330 feet lower than today. As ocean waters receded into the ice sheets, islands grew larger and landmasses previously separated by water became connected.

The last ice age started 110,000 years ago and lasted almost 100,000 years. By 40,000 years ago, *Homo sapiens* had settled most of mainland Eurasia, and were migrating into Australia and its surrounding islands from southeast Asia. This required that they cross the sea by boat, often to places they could not see from the opposite shore.

Human Adaptation to the New Environment

There is much debate about when humans first entered the Americas, but no convincing evidence exists that any hominid species other than fully developed *Homo sapiens* made this journey. The earliest Americans had fire, stone tools, and the means to obtain clothing, food, and shelter. They most likely arrived fifteen thousand years ago when the last ice age lowered sea levels to produce a land bridge between northeast Asia and North America (see Map 1.2). Possibly others migrated by boat to the Americas from other parts of Asia. Kennewick Man, so-called from the site in the state of Washington where he was discovered in 1996, anatomically seems unlike other early humans of the continent, although he appears to have lived some eight thousand years ago. His physical characteristics resemble those of inhabitants of southeast Asia rather than of northeast Asia. Was he a descendant of another migration or not? The question remains unanswered.

The remarkable adaptability of *Homo sapiens* allowed the species to deal with differences in heat, sunlight, and other climatic and geographical conditions. Communities in various parts of the world developed diverse physical traits. One adaptation was a change in skin color. The pigment melanin, present in relatively high concentration in dark skin, protects against the ultraviolet in sunlight. This protection is essential in sun-drenched Africa or Australia, but not in the north, where it can even be counterproductive because it prevents absorption of vitamin D. Thus, through adaptation, inhabitants of most northern regions developed lighter skin to avoid vitamin deficiency.

Similarly, the size of human limbs varied from climate to climate. Long limbs allow for cooling of the body and short limbs retain heat. These and other distinctions are minor, however, when compared with the biological similarities that humans all over the globe share. The human genetic makeup is much more uniform than that of other species: two chimpanzees living in close proximity to one another have ten times as much variability in their DNA as two humans living on different continents.

A second vehicle for humans' adaptation to new environments is change in the languages they speak, change that can be substantial over short periods. The work of linguists—specialists in the study of language—suggests that on average, people who originally spoke the same language would preserve only 85 percent of the common features after living in separate communities for a thousand years. This relatively rapid change explains linguistic diversity. For example, many scholars assume that most inhabitants of the Americas before the arrival of the Italian explorer Christopher Columbus in

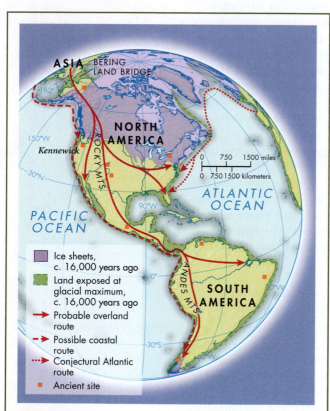

MAP 1.2

Settling the Americas

The last ice age created a land bridge across the Bering Sea, allowing humans to migrate from Eurasia into North America. The first humans probably entered fifteen thousand years ago, and their descendants continued expanding southward over land and by boat along the coasts. By seven thousand years ago, humans lived in the entire continent from the modern state of Alaska to the southern tip of South America, except for some regions in the dense Amazonian forest.

1492 C.E. descended from the people who had migrated there some fifteen thousand years earlier, and who had spoken a common language. Yet by Columbus's arrival, America had enormous linguistic variety, several thousand mutually unintelligible languages. This variety developed in part because populations lived in different environments and focused on different activities for their livelihoods. Some hunted, others fished, and later, farmers and herders developed vocabularies to suit their circumstances. Other processes also caused the languages of separate communities to diverge.

Any aspect of a language can change, including pronunciation, grammar, and vocabulary. Grammatical forms are abandoned or newly created; words change their meanings, disappear, or are invented. Word meanings can differ even among speakers of the same language. For example, *corn* in the United States refers to maize, whereas in England the word *corn* refers to wheat. Languages may drop the names of animals and plants if these species do not appear where the speakers live. They borrow terms from other languages to indicate new tools or foods. People all over the world today write "e-mails," using a newly invented English word in very different languages. The diversity of languages is one of the main features that distinguish human populations, and it shows how people adjust habits to their local situations. It also demonstrates that evolution is an ongoing process. Just as human language continues to develop in response to changing circumstances, humans themselves continue to evolve in response to new environmental conditions, whether those new conditions are the result of natural processes or of the impact of humans on their environment.

Paleolithic Food Gatherers   2,000,000–9000 B.C.E.

Having traced the biological evolution of *Homo sapiens*, we turn now to the development of human communities. To study the distant human past, scholars rely on archaeological remains, primarily tools made of hard stones such as flint and obsidian that leave a sharp edge when chipped. Items made of other materials, such as bone and wood, survive much less often. The record is thus biased toward stone tools, but they are undeniably important. Scholars commonly divide the period that used stone as the main material for tools into the **Paleolithic** ("Old Stone Age") and the **Neolithic** ("New Stone Age"). Based on the type of tools people used, these terms indicate critical differences in people's livelihoods as well: in the early period they hunted and gathered their food; in the later period they farmed. The transition from one livelihood to the other was not simultaneous worldwide. On the contrary, it took many millennia for agriculture to spread from the regions where it was first invented, and in some parts of the world people did not farm until the modern period.

The Paleolithic is by far the longest period of hominin existence. For close to 2 million years, our predecessors collected food from their environments using stone tools. Seasonal cycles determined what was available and when. Only in the recent past, starting eleven thousand years ago, did people in some parts of the world take a next step in manipulating the environment by controlling food supplies through farming.

The Gatherer-Hunter Economy

All living things need food to survive, and they use resources in their natural surroundings to secure it. Humans are the most versatile of all living primates in this respect. If necessary, they are willing to consume anything with nutritional value. This flexibility allowed humans to adapt to new environments as they migrated all over the globe.

A major breakthrough in the quest for food occurred around 2 million years ago with the use of stone tools, which gave human ancestors enormous advantages. They could

> **FOCUS**
>
> In the absence of written sources, what have scholars learned about the Paleolithic economy, adaptations to the natural world, and technological innovations?

Paleolithic Literally "Old Stone Age," the period when modern humans and their ancestors used stone tools and lived as foragers.

Neolithic Literally "New Stone Age," the period when humans developed a special set of stone tools to harvest cultivated plants.

quickly cut off parts of dead prey and run to a safe place. With tools they could pierce animal skins, cut meat from bones, and crush bones for marrow, increasing the availability of highly nutritious food. As we have seen, eating such foods allowed greater brain expansion, which in turn facilitated toolmaking abilities.

Paleolithic Toolmakers

At first, Paleolithic people did little to modify the stones they employed as tools. They chipped off flakes that had very sharp edges, allowing them to cut, and they used the cores as hammers to crush bones. Starting around 1.65 million years ago, however, they began to shape cores much more extensively, flaking off pieces symmetrically on both sides to create sharp hand axes that resembled large teardrops. This development reveals their ability to imagine in advance what the tool should look like. Hand axes were extremely popular and were an important part of the human tool arsenal until around 250,000 years ago. Human ancestors who migrated from Africa into Eurasia took the technology with them. Only when they reached distant regions such as China and southeast Asia did they stop making such hand axes, possibly because suitable stone was unavailable.

With the emergence of *Homo sapiens* toolmaking expanded dramatically. These physically modern humans created a wide variety of stone tools that were much sharper and easier to handle. They also fashioned tools from previously neglected materials, working antlers, bones, and ivory into various implements and inventing the needle, which made sewing possible. With these tools, they hunted, cut meat off bones, scraped skins, shaped wood, and turned dried tendons into strings. They used their increasingly ingenious creations to prepare food and to make clothing, shelter, and weapons. They turned shells into personal jewelry and began to fashion art. In short, increasingly sophisticated tools expanded their ability to manipulate the environment, which made possible the emergence of human society and culture.

Evolving Stone Tools

The development of tools, especially those of stone, which have survived much better than others, tells archaeologists about important changes in the technological abilities of human ancestors and early humans. The Oldowan tool shown here (left), used between 2.6 and 1.7 million years ago, was only slightly altered from the original rock in the effort to sharpen it. In contrast, the Acheulian ax (right), used between 1.65 million and 250,000 years ago, shows how its maker carefully flaked off pieces all over the original stone to turn it into a versatile hand tool. (National Museum of Tanzania, Dar es Salaam, ©1985 David L. Brill (left) and Werner Forman/Art Resource, NY (right).)

For the entire Paleolithic era, humans foraged for their food—that is, they gathered and hunted edible resources in their surroundings. The common idea that early humans were great hunters is a myth. Indeed, until *Homo sapiens*, they probably obtained meat only by competing with other scavengers for the flesh of dead animals. The earliest tools often occur near collections of bones from which meat was cut, indicating that Paleolithic peoples discarded tools after use. *Homo sapiens* dared to attack large animals only after they had developed a growing arsenal of tools—including sharp spears, bows, and arrows with stone tips—and could communicate through language.

Once early hominins had learned how to build and maintain fires some 1.5 million years ago, they cooked meat, making it much easier to chew. Much of their diet, however, consisted of other natural resources, including seeds, nuts, fruits, roots, small animals, fish, and seafood, depending on the area. They gathered food daily, but such work was not necessarily arduous, and Paleolithic gatherer-hunters probably had much more free time than many people today. The gatherer-hunters who still inhabit parts of Africa today collect all they need in a few hours, spending the rest of the day in leisure. Foraging was in many ways a very successful livelihood (see Counterpoint: Gatherer-Hunters by Choice: Aborigines of Australia). Observations of modern gatherer-hunters also show that women collect most foods, so world historians increasingly place woman, the gatherer, not man, the hunter, at the center of the Paleolithic economy.

Paleolithic Foragers

Life in Paleolithic Communities

Paleolithic gatherer-hunters typically lived in groups of fifteen to forty members, including several adult males, as well as females and children. Larger groups would have needed more resources than the surroundings could provide. Males probably supplemented gathered resources by providing food for the mothers of their children, strengthening emotional attachments and encouraging long-term relationships. Close connections developed not only between sexual mates but between parents and children. This may be due in part to the large size of the human head. To pass through the birth canal, humans need to be born earlier in their development than other primates. Because much maturation takes place outside the womb and humans must learn many skills, children need to be nurtured and protected for many years. Not until the ages twelve to fifteen do they become self-sufficient. The presence of children limits the mobility of human groups—babies need to be carried. These various aspects of Paleolithic life led to close-knit communities that stayed together for long periods. Thus, family relationships determined many characteristics of Paleolithic life. Such relationships would continue to shape the development of all subsequent human societies.

Small, Cohesive Groups

Paleolithic communities were egalitarian in character, largely because constant migration prevented individuals from accumulating much wealth. Because groups were small, conflicts were relatively easy to settle, and all adults, including women, could participate in most activities. When a group became too large for the region to support it, bands separated and found new places to live. Neighboring bands must have collaborated to a degree, determining borders, for example. These bands must have often exchanged reproductive partners to maintain social ties. As populations splintered, the new groups built and maintained connections with one another.

Societies of Equals

Early humans needed shelter, of course, especially when they moved into cold regions. At first they took advantage of natural features such as caves and overhanging rocks, often visiting them year after year for protection from the elements. Members of *Homo erectus* used the Zhoukoudian (choo-koot-jehn) cave west of Beijing in northern China, for example, from 460,000 to 230,000 years ago (see again Mapping the World, page 8). They left behind archaeological deposits 120 feet deep, which included some one hundred thousand artifacts. Ash layers in the cave, some of them eighteen feet deep, strongly suggest the cave dwellers' ability to light fires 460,000 years ago. Fire had many advantages: it made it possible to see in the dark, and it provided warmth and protection against animals. It also encouraged social interaction as people gathered around the fire.

Shelter and Fire

Mammoth Bone Dwelling
Human ingenuity in exploiting local resources is clear from circular huts built from the tusks, leg bones, and jaw bones of mammoths (extinct elephants) in eastern Europe between about 27,000 and 12,000 years ago. This example from Mezhirich in Ukraine included the remains of nearly one hundred animals and dates to about 15,000 years ago. Covered with hides, it allowed people to live outside caves in a cold climate. (C.M. Dixon, Ancient Art and Architecture Collection.)

Paleolithic peoples often improved natural shelters by building screens made of branches at the entrances of caves. They could also construct tent-like temporary shelters. Indeed, *Homo sapiens* showed great ingenuity in this respect. When wood was scarce, they built shelters by digging pits and constructing domes with mammoth bones or tusks, over which they draped animal skins. The earliest freestanding man-made shelters were round or oval with central hearths to keep inhabitants warm. Until agricultural communities arose, this remained the preferred design for huts and houses. Such shelters provided protection from the elements and promoted group interaction and cohesion.

Paleolithic Religious Beliefs

The emotional ties that held communities together also fostered a respect for the dead not found in other primates. Starting one hundred thousand years ago, Neanderthals began to bury their dead, at first in simple shallow pits in caves but with increasingly elaborate graves over time. The Neanderthal described at the start of this chapter may have been buried on purpose in the cave where he was found. Careful excavations at Shanidar cave in the mountains of modern Iraq uncovered a Neanderthal skeleton surrounded by large amounts of flower pollen. The archaeologists who found him believe that survivors covered the buried person with garlands of flowers. Other burials contain small objects such as pendants and beads. This archaeological evidence reveals that the living gave the dead material goods for the afterlife, suggesting that they believed in the survival of some aspect of the individual after death. The evolution of burial rites also suggests a growing sense among humans of the connections between generations. A community was more than its current members; it also included those who had come before, as well as the generations to come.

Paleolithic Art

Like burial rites, Paleolithic art gives us a glimpse of early human values and beliefs. Only humans create decorative objects. When did art first appear, and why? In 2001 C.E., archaeologists in southern Africa found a brown stone deliberately engraved with cross-hatchings on its surfaces and with long lines across the top, bottom, and center. They date the stone to at least sixty-five thousand years ago, which makes it the oldest purposefully decorated object ever found. What did the design mean? Was it merely ornamental, or did the people who carved it want to record something? These questions continue to excite debate.

It is clear, however, that, especially after forty thousand years ago, humans started to embellish objects and shape them to represent some of the living creatures that surrounded them. Typically, the first portable art objects were modified natural items such

Paleolithic Statuettes of Women

Paleolithic peoples of western Eurasia produced carved figurines of women for thousands of years, most abundantly,
in the archaeological record at least, between twenty-six
thousand to twenty-three thousand years ago. In regions
from Spain to central Russia, archaeologists have found
numerous individual statues and collections made from
materials such as mammoth ivory and soft stones. Among
them is what is called the Venus of Willendorf. Discovered
in the late nineteenth century C.E., it is 9-3/8 inches tall and
made from limestone. The representation focuses clearly on
the woman's hips, breasts, and vulva. Other parts of the
body, such as arms and legs, are very sketchily
fashioned, and the figure has no face at all.

Assessments of these figurines may say more about
the interpreter than about the ancient people who made
them. To call this statue a "Venus" after the Roman goddess
of love suggests a connection to sexuality and religion.
When they were first found, most scholars thought these
statuettes were magical objects connected to fertility and
childbirth. Recent interpretations are more varied and
involve other aspects of a woman's life. Some think the statues represent women in different stages of life, not just
when pregnant; others stress a role in social negotiations, or
think pregnant women carved these statuettes to communicate their experiences. Unfortunately, the archaeologists
who found the statuettes did not record what other objects
lay nearby and whether there were architectural remains.
Such information could have helped to explain the function
of these figurines.

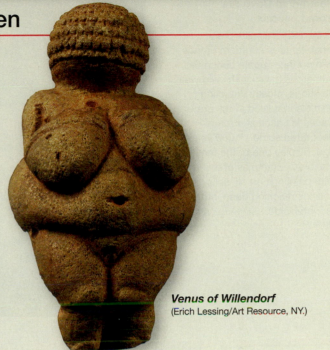

Venus of Willendorf
(Erich Lessing/Art Resource, NY.)

EXAMINING THE EVIDENCE

1. Why has this figurine caused scholars to dispute
the name, Venus of Willendorf?

2. How would better archaeological observation have
helped in understanding the purpose of such
female figurines?

as teeth and shells. People scratched geometric motifs on them and often pierced them
with a hole to hang them on a string to wear them as jewelry. Later they shaped stones
and bones to resemble living beings. Around twenty-five thousand years ago, people all
over western Eurasia sculpted small figurines of women with greatly exaggerated breasts
and hips. Although speculation is rife about the meaning of these figurines, their focus
on female sexuality has guided most interpretations. Many scholars believe the people
who owned them thought they would improve fertility (see Seeing the Past: Paleolithic
Statuettes of Women).

Between thirty-five thousand and eleven thousand years ago, people also painted elaborate scenes on walls and ceilings of caves. Archaeologists have found remains of portable
art objects all over the modern European continent, but for unknown reasons, cave paintings appear almost exclusively in southern France and northern Spain. Found in almost
250 caves, sometimes miles from the entrance, these paintings are the most dramatic example yet discovered of Paleolithic art. The artists worked by the light of lamps burning animal fat. Archaeological evidence in the Lascaux (la-SKOH) caves in France shows that they
even built scaffolding to reach the ceiling. The images in the caves range from small hand-
prints to life-size representations of animals hunted by their communities. Horses and

Paleolithic Cave Art from Lascaux

In the later Paleolithic era, inhabitants of southern France and northern Spain decorated numerous caves with vivid wall paintings, mostly depicting animals that lived in the area. Caves in Lascaux, France, decorated some 17,000 years ago, display one of the most elaborate examples of this art, with paintings on all walls and ceilings reaching deep into the mountainside. (Bridgeman Art Library.)

bison were the most popular subjects, but deer, ibexes, and mammoths were also abundant. Sometimes they even sculpted three-dimensional images of animals in clay against the walls. Whereas the painters represented animals with much realism, their rare depictions of humans are crude stick figures or blend animal and human features. The focus on animal images suggests the central importance of hunting to life in Paleolithic Europe.

Scholars have numerous interpretations of this magnificent artwork. Because the horse and the bison often appear in pairs, some specialists suggest that this pattern reflects male-female symbolism, which they also see in other motifs, including geometric designs. Others consider it very likely that the art expresses complex religious beliefs and theorize that the ideas behind the paintings changed over time because they were made over such a long period. Their subjects are clearly connected to life in the last ice age, because the paintings were no longer made after the climate warmed some eleven thousand years ago. The paintings' simplicity and power clearly reveal the remarkable intellectual abilities of early humans. They also reveal the emergence of a new dimension in human communication. Artwork and the meanings it embodies can survive long after its creator has perished, allowing the artist to connect with future generations. Thus art, like religion, contributed to the increasing sophistication and cohesion of human communities.

The First Neolithic Farmers 9000–4000 B.C.E.

FOCUS

In what ways does the Neolithic agricultural economy reveal humans' increasing intent and ability to manipulate the natural world to their advantage?

The invention of agriculture was one of the most important technological developments in human history. Daily life as we know it today depends on agriculture and the domestication of animals. Yet for most of their existence, human beings obtained their food by collecting what was naturally available. Even today a few populations have not turned to agriculture for their survival, and in many regions some people remained foragers while others farmed.

This novel interaction of humans with nature and agriculture, places them in control of the growth cycle and makes them responsible for the domestication of plants and animals. Those who plant must sow seeds at the right moment, protect plants during growth, harvest them on time, safely store the harvest, and save enough seed for the next season. Those who

TABLE 1.1

The Rise of Agriculture		
Region	**Main Plant Crops**	**Date**
Southwest Asia	wheat, barley	c. 10,000–9000 B.C.E.
China	rice, millet	c. 8000–6000 B.C.E.
New Guinea	taro, yams, banana	c. 7000–4000 B.C.E.
Sub-Saharan Africa	sorghum	c. 3000–2000 B.C.E.
Mesoamerica	maize, beans, squash	c. 3000–2000 B.C.E.
Andes	potato, manioc	c. 3000–2000 B.C.E.
Eastern North America	squash	c. 2000–1000 B.C.E.

raise animals must protect them against predators and provide fodder. These techniques developed independently in various areas of the world between 10,000 and 1000 B.C.E. and then spread from these core areas to almost all other parts of the globe (see Map 1.3).

The shift to a fully agricultural livelihood began the period scholars call the Neolithic. The shape of stone tools most clearly shows the transition to the Neolithic. Producers elaborately shaped stone flakes to turn them into sharp harvesting tools. Many other technological innovations occurred as well, and the equipment of Neolithic farmers was very different from that of earlier foragers. The processes behind the invention of agriculture are best understood by studying evidence from Southwest Asia, where farming probably originated first, between 10,000 and 9000 B.C.E.

The Origins of Agriculture

Out of thousands of plant species that humans potentially could have domesticated, humans selected very few to become the main staples of their diet. The skills to cultivate these plants developed separately in various parts of the world and at different times. It is difficult to determine where people invented agriculture independently, without influence from other groups, but today many scholars share the view that people developed farming in seven regions: Southwest Asia, China, New Guinea, sub-Saharan Africa, Mesoamerica, the Andes, and eastern North America (see Table 1.1). In each area, people learned to control the growth of local crops, and the technology they developed quickly spread to neighboring areas. The dates by which people in various regions developed farming are subject to much debate, and those provided here are just one of several possible reconstructions. In most places where people learned to control plant growth, they also began to domesticate selected local animals. This was not always the case, however. In New Guinea, for example, the earliest farmers did not keep animals. Most scholars of the rise of agriculture thus focus primarily on the interactions between humans and plants.

The advent of farming involved a long-term change in interactions between humans and naturally available resources, a change so gradual that people at the time probably barely noticed it. Throughout Southwest Asia runs a crescent-shaped belt richly supplied with wild plants and animals. Located at the foothills of mountain ranges, this zone, known as the **Fertile Crescent**, sweeps northward along the eastern Mediterranean coast into present-day southern Turkey and winds south again along the border between modern Iraq and Iran. In around 10,000 B.C.E. it was covered with fields of wild wheat and barley and inhabited by wild sheep, goats, pigs, and cattle. It is these resources that humans first learned to cultivate.

The Fertile Crescent

Fertile Crescent The region of Southwest Asia with rich natural resources arching along the Mediterranean coast and modern southern Turkey and eastern Iraq.

MAP 1.3

The Origins of Agriculture

In places across the globe early humans started to cultivate plants and herd animals, selecting from the locally available species. Most scholars agree that people invented agriculture independently in at least seven distinct regions at different moments in time between about 9000 and 1000 B.C.E. The crops listed here became the main staples of the local diets.

Eastern North America
Gourd
Squash
Sunflower

Mesoamerica
Avocado
Beans
Chili pepper
Gourd
Maize (Corn)
Pumpkin
Squash
Tomato
Cotton
Dog
Turkey

Andean region
Beans
Chili pepper
Gourd
Manioc
Potato
Quinoa
Alpaca
Guinea pig
Llama

☐ Area of independent development of agriculture
▨ Agricultural area and area in transition to agriculture, c. 2500 B.C.E.
▨ Gathering and hunting area
▨ Uninhabited area
→ Spread of agriculture

The Fertile Crescent, c. 7000–6000 B.C.E.

☐ Fertile Crescent
■ Neolithic settlement

Wild wheat and barley are difficult to gather and consume because of their natural characteristics, such as thick husks. Yet humans did collect their seeds, probably because other foods were insufficient. By doing so, they became familiar with the growth patterns of the plants—and they inadvertently changed the plants' characteristics to allow easier harvests. They favored species with tougher stalks (which could be more easily harvested and would remain upright when harvesters walked through the fields) and thinner husks (allowing easier preparation of food), and over many years these varieties became the only ones remaining in the area. Thus, even before deliberate farming began, humans exerted evolutionary pressure on the natural world, changing the environment and their own societies in the process.

At the same time, humans' relationships with certain animals changed. Whereas hunters continued to pursue deer and gazelles, early farmers nurtured and protected sheep, goats, pigs, and cattle (see Seeing the Past: Saharan Rock Art). Neolithic peoples probably recognized animals' breeding patterns and understood that they required fewer males than females. Farmers selectively slaughtered

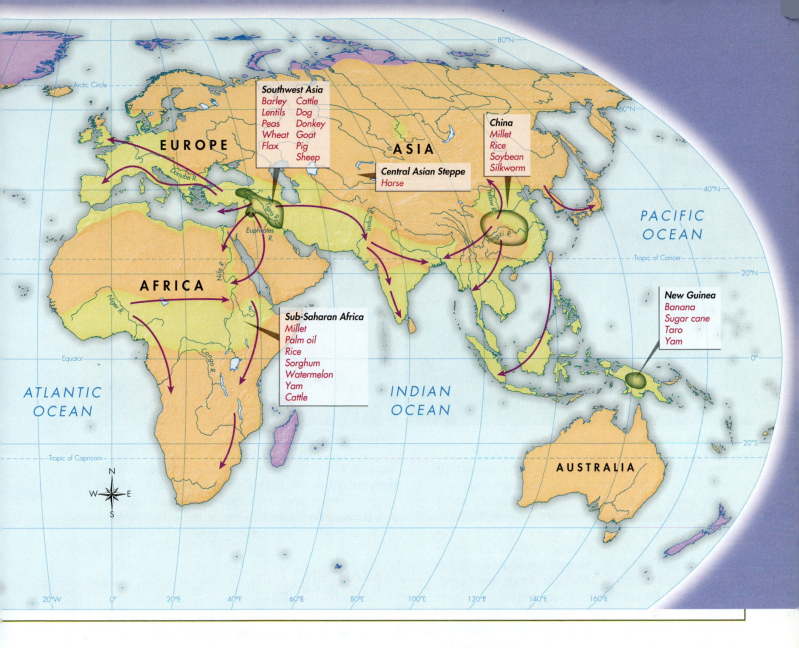

Southwest Asia
Barley   Cattle
Lentils   Dog
Peas   Donkey
Wheat   Goat
Flax   Pig
          Sheep

China
Millet
Rice
Soybean
Silkworm

Central Asian Steppe
Horse

Sub-Saharan Africa
Millet
Palm oil
Rice
Sorghum
Watermelon
Yam
Cattle

New Guinea
Banana
Sugar cane
Taro
Yam

EUROPE

ASIA

AFRICA

PACIFIC OCEAN

ATLANTIC OCEAN

INDIAN OCEAN

AUSTRALIA

young males for meat and kept females for reproduction and for milk. Like domesticated plants, domesticated animals changed in ways that better suited them to human needs. The protected animals generally became smaller and therefore easier to work with. In the case of goats, the animals' horns changed shape because they were no longer needed for defense, making them less dangerous to their human handlers.

Further, as Neolithic peoples increasingly took their domesticated animals into regions where they did not live in the wild, the animals had to adjust to the new environments; for example, they acclimated to the heat of the lowlands by losing some of their thick coats. Animals were also a convenient way to store calories; farmers could feed them extra plants that would otherwise be discarded, and in times of need slaughter them for their meat. They had many other practical uses, too. Sheep wool and goat hair made protective textiles, milk products were an excellent source of protein, and animal skins, bones, horns, hoofs, and sinews could be turned into a large array of utensils and other items. In a sense, humans learned to use animals as tools, discovering new uses over time and changing the animals themselves to improve their usefulness.

Although scholars have determined that these changes took place, they are less certain about why humans started to farm. Many suggest that the end of the last ice age around 10,000 B.C.E. brought warmer and drier conditions to Southwest Asia, drastically

Why Farm?

Saharan Rock Art

Wild Cattle (Image by Pierre Colombel/Corbis.)

Domesticated Cattle (Jean-Loïc Le Quellec.)

In the visual arts people often depict what they see in their surroundings, and when inhabitants of a region leave behind representations over long periods of time, scholars can infer changes in the environment from them. This is the case in the center of the Sahara Desert in the southern part of modern-day Algeria, where images of animals carved or painted on rocks show how people's interactions with them changed. Before 5000 B.C.E., the local climate was much wetter and more fertile than it is today, and the lush region supported a bounty of animal and human life. The earliest rock carvings in the Tassili region show humans hunting big game with spears and bows. One of the most commonly depicted hunted animals is the wild ancestor of cattle (left), which died out before 5000 B.C.E.

Rock paintings from about 4500 to 2500 B.C.E. show different animals. Instead of wild animals, the artists represented domesticated cattle, individually or in herds of up to one hundred head (right). People around the cattle seem to be herding them, showing us the earliest evidence of the domestication of cattle in Africa. After 2500 B.C.E. these images disappear because the climate became too dry and the herdsmen of the Sahara had to move elsewhere to feed their animals.

EXAMINING THE EVIDENCE

1. What do these examples of Saharan rock art tell us about changes in the environment?

2. How did people's interactions with animals change in this region in around 5000 B.C.E.?

3. Can you speculate why people of the Paleolithic era fashioned such representations?

reducing wild food supplies. According to this theory, humans tried to compensate for losses by moving plants to land where the plants did not reproduce naturally. Other scholars propose that human behavioral changes encouraged the shift to farming. The life of the gatherer-hunter lacked permanence, forcing small groups of people to move around even when women were pregnant or had small children. A desire to stay longer in one place may have pushed early peoples to more closely observe the growth cycles of the plants and animals around them. They may have learned the benefits of storing seeds and planting them for future harvests. Meanwhile, the permanence of their new way of life may have led to larger communities that could survive only if they grew food.

The archaeological record of Southwest Asia shows these processes at work in the period from 10,000 to 9000 B.C.E. The inhabitants increasingly left evidence of plant harvesting and processing in the form of flint and obsidian blades, pestles, mortars, and grinders. Although people still hunted and gathered extensively, by 9000 B.C.E. some lived in fully sedentary communities, where they relied on a combination of foraged and cultivated food.

Once Neolithic people developed agriculture, the technology spread rapidly into regions surrounding the Fertile Crescent, introducing crops and animals that had not existed in the wild. In the north and west, farming spread into the regions that are today Turkey and Europe. By 7000 B.C.E. people in northern Greece farmed, and by 4000 to 3000 B.C.E. the technology had reached Britain and Scandinavia. Wheat and barley cultivation arrived in the Indus Valley by 5000 B.C.E. and somewhat later in Egypt and North Africa. Farmers also moved into regions of Southwest Asia where rainfall was insufficient for farming. Their invention of irrigation agriculture made settlement possible even in the most arid zones (see Chapter 2).

As we saw earlier, not all populations of the world learned farming techniques from Southwest Asia. In China, people developed the skills independently several millennia after agriculture originated in Southwest Asia, focusing on locally available plants. In the middle part of the Yangzi (YANG-zuh) River Valley, where much water is available, wild rice started to grow when the climate became warmer after 8000 B.C.E. At first the local residents collected what was available naturally, but in the period from 8000 to 6000 B.C.E. they gradually used more cultivated rice, and at the end of that period they lived in villages, fully depending on their crops.

Although the crops and techniques used in farming varied from place to place, in every region agricultural life was more difficult than that of the gatherer-hunter. Early farmers had to work many more hours than gatherer-hunters, especially in certain seasons. Furthermore, farmers were more vulnerable to epidemic diseases because they lived together more closely. But farming had advantages. Cultivated crops produced much larger yields than wild plants, so farmers could live in larger communities than foragers. The increased permanence of agricultural communities led to expanded social interactions and a better survival rate for newborn babies. Whatever the reasons for the turn to agriculture, this livelihood became dominant over most of the world in the millennia after it developed. It was only well into the twentieth century C.E. that the majority of the earth's people stopped making a living as farmers.

Early Agriculture in China, c. 6000–5000 B.C.E.

Legend:
- Area of early millet cultivation
- Area of early rice cultivation
- Spread of rice cultivation
- Settlement site, 6000–5000 B.C.E.

Life in Neolithic Communities

As people began living year-round in the same location, the size and number of their material possessions expanded enormously. Their dwellings also changed. The earliest houses, imitating the temporary shelters of migratory foragers, were round or oval. Partly dug into the ground, they contained a central hearth, and floors were paved with stones. As agricultural communities spread over the world, however, the layout of houses evolved into a rectangular form, a layout that remains dominant in residential structures to the present day. This innovation allowed builders to create rooms with specialized functions, such as kitchens and bedrooms. The creation of separate spaces for men and women, for parents and children, and for certain activities reveals the relationships, beliefs, and priorities of the inhabitants. In this light, scholars see increasing complexity of design as a sign that the social organization of communities had become more complex.

New Household Technology

The house became the center of people's activities, the place where they kept the harvest and turned it into food. Because grain must be ground before it can be consumed, grinding stones are common in the archaeological record. Grinding was backbreaking. The first farmers used mortars and pestles, which permitted only small amounts to be ground at a time. Later, they crushed the grain between a flat or convex bottom stone and a smaller, handheld round stone. The millers were mostly women, who rubbed the stone back and forth until the flour was fine enough to use to prepare food. They sat bent over on their knees for such long periods that their wrists, toes, knees, and lower backs became deformed. Skeletons of Neolithic women excavated in the north of modern Syria show those physical injuries. Milling is but one example of a larger trend. As farming developed, the labor associated with farming was increasingly gendered, with some tasks seen as suitable for men and others for women.

Early farmers probably cooked gruel or mash from the flour, but by 3500 B.C.E. people consumed grain principally as bread and beer in Southwest Asia. They were probably invented accidentally. When roasted grains are mixed with water, they form a paste that can easily be baked on a hot stone, and adding other ingredients led to the invention and production of bread. Beer manufacture was very similar to that of bread, except that in brewing the grain mixture was soaked in water to ferment. Thus bread and beer together became essential nutrition to people in many parts of the world. Like milling, cooking and brewing became women's work in many regions.

Pottery and Metalworking

Clay, abundantly available in Southwest Asia, had long been used to form figurines. When early farmers realized the strength of baked clay, they started to create pots for storage and cooking. Pottery was a revolutionary innovation that allowed Neolithic farmers to build on the advantages of settled agriculture. Easily produced from local resources in all shapes and sizes, pottery provides both safe storage of grains against pests and moisture and a means to heat and cook food over a fire. First appearing in Japan around 12,000 B.C.E., pottery was independently invented in Southwest Asia around 6500 B.C.E. Because pottery is also easily decorated with carved incisions or painted designs, and because decorative styles changed rapidly, pottery finds have become the main evidence by which archaeologists date settlements.

The first farmers also liked to make small decorative objects out of metal; natural ore deposits, especially of copper, exist in many parts of Southwest Asia. Although copper ore could be hammered cold, by 5000 B.C.E. people had learned to heat ore to extract pure copper and pour it in liquid form into molds. They later expanded these techniques for use with other metals, and by 4000 B.C.E., people began to mix various metals to make stronger alloys. The most important was bronze, which they manufactured from copper and tin. The development of metallurgy was, in a sense, made possible by farming, because specialization of labor was an important feature of settled communities. Certain people in farming communities could devote themselves to a particular task, such as metalworking, while others went about the job of producing food.

Textile Production

Another vital innovation that agriculture made possible was textile weaving. Domestication made new fibers available, which people learned to twist into threads and wove into clothing, blankets, and many other fabrics. Some fibers derived from domesticated animals—sheep wool and goat hair—and others came from plants grown for the purpose, especially flax, used to make linen thread. The earliest pieces of cloth found so far are from the cave of Nahal Hemar (nak-hal HEY-mar) in modern Israel, dating to around 6500 B.C.E.

The earliest written documents available to us, written long after the invention of agriculture in Southwest Asia, show that women were mostly responsible for turning raw agricultural products into usable goods. They ground cereals and cooked food, and they wove textiles and made pots. They could perform these tasks while staying at home to take care of young children. Scholars assume that this was true in other early agricultural societies as well.

The division of labor along gender lines—with women primarily active around the house and men primarily outside—reflects the growing complexity of interactions in farming communities. Whereas bands of gatherer-hunters were probably egalitarian, in sedentary societies inequalities grew on the basis of wealth, status, and power. Some families accumulated more goods than others because, for example, they were able to harvest more. The greater wealth held by the heads of these families—all men, it seems—may have commanded community respect. Because the communities of the Neolithic period were larger and lived together for prolonged periods, they needed a means to settle conflicts peacefully, and wealthier men may have gained authority over the rest. The archaeological record shows differences in wealth of the inhabitants, albeit on a small scale, as early as 7000 B.C.E. Thus farming and the development of a hierarchical social structure seem to go hand in hand.

Çatal Höyük (cha-TAHL hoo-YOOK) in modern central Turkey is the largest Neolithic settlement yet excavated (see Lives and Livelihoods: The People of Çatal Höyük). Here, archaeologists found stone and clay figurines of women with enormous breasts and thighs, including one seated on a throne flanked by two catlike animals. As with Paleolithic figurines of women, scholars and others understand these statues in different ways, but the idea that they are fertility symbols is very popular. Some interpretations even suggest that they honor a "mother goddess" as the dominant primordial force of nature, but this theory is much disputed. It is possible that early peoples considered women to form the primary line of descent from one generation to the next and that family property passed along the female line—a system called **matrilineal**. But it is risky to conclude that women were in charge and had greater authority than men—a system called **matriarchy**. Nonetheless, a woman's ability to give birth was a force of nature that the people of early agricultural societies depended on for survival, and we can imagine that early farmers honored such forces of nature as being greater than themselves.

Among Paleolithic foragers the nomadic band was the primary social unit; in Neolithic farming communities the unit shifted to single families comprising several generations. The new rectangular form of the house made it possible for settled farmers to live together, close to other families yet separate from them. Neolithic people's burial practices reflect the more intimate family connections. Paleolithic people often buried their dead in caves that they periodically visited, but with the shift to farming people lived in the same house for long periods, and families buried at least some of the dead under the floors of their houses. How they did so varied, but it was common to detach the head from the rest of the body—probably after birds had picked the skeleton clean—and bury it separately. They often placed heads in groups and decorated some of them. Sometimes they filled the eyes with shells and modeled facial features with plaster.

Even more dramatic evidence of the practice of restoring the physical features of the dead comes from Ain Ghazal (ine gahz-AHL) in modern Jordan, a site occupied between 7200 and 5000 B.C.E. There, under floors of some houses, archaeologists found plaster human statues, some more than three feet high, with rudimentary bodies and large heads. The same site also yielded plaster masks modeled on human skulls. The exact interpretation of these practices is not certain, but it seems likely that they are the earliest evidence for a cult of ancestors, a way to preserve their presence in the house. They may even have received food offerings. People of many early cultures in world history maintained similar ties to the deceased.

In short, in religious practices, social structures, and technological and architectural innovations, we see evidence that the advent of settled agriculture produced a set of developments that led to increasingly complex human societies and cultures. This process was not inevitable, however, and not all ancient peoples considered it desirable. The gatherer-hunter lifestyle has certain advantages, and it is in no way obvious that settled agriculture represents a clearly superior alternative.

Growing Social Inequality

Women in the Neolithic Worldview

Neolithic Religious Beliefs

matrilineal A system of family descent that follows the female side of the family.

matriarchy The social order that recognizes women as heads of families and passes power and property from mother to daughter.

The People of Çatal Höyük

One of the most intriguing archaeological sites of the Neolithic era is Çatal Höyük, located in the south of modern Turkey. Occupied between 7200 and 6000 B.C.E., Çatal Höyük was an unusually large Neolithic settlement, some thirty-two acres in size, and it was home to perhaps as many as six thousand inhabitants. Some were farmers, who grew wheat and barley and herded sheep and goats. Numerous bones of wild animals discovered in the houses show that people also hunted the rich wildlife of the surroundings.

Çatal Höyük is remarkable for several reasons. Its mud-brick houses stood side by side without streets in between them and without doors or large windows. Those on the outside of the settlement formed a continuous wall for protection against intruders. The unusual layout forced residents to enter their homes by a ladder through a hole in the roof. The interiors of the houses were even more extraordinary for their time because of their extensive decoration. Many contained a room with paintings, engravings, or modeled reliefs, mostly representing wild animals of the surrounding countryside. Some of the scenes seem bizarre to us, including vultures attacking headless human corpses and women giving birth to bulls. These images must reflect the beliefs and perhaps the anxieties of Çatal Höyük's inhabitants, but their interpretation remains a problem.

We can explain the wealth and size of Çatal Höyük in terms of its location. A nearby volcano provided the hard rock obsidian, which craftsmen chipped and polished into tools and ornaments. Based on chemical analysis of such stone objects excavated all over Turkey, Syria, and Cyprus, archaeologists have determined that they originated at Çatal Höyük and that the town's inhabitants were in contact with people of these distant regions. They bartered the obsidian products for shells from the Mediterranean Sea and flint from Syria. Çatal Höyük's natural environment was so rich that some inhabitants could focus on obsidian work; others collected and grew food to support them. Given the vivid imagery of their work, the painters of the decorations inside the houses may also have been specialists.

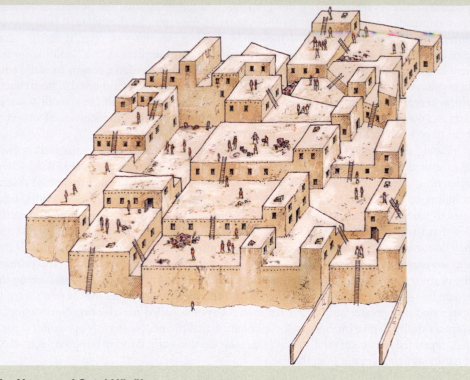

The Houses of Çatal Höyük

Although this reconstruction is hypothetical, it integrates the excavators' ideas about how the people of Çatal Höyük in southern Turkey lived. The remains of the houses suggest that residents entered them from the roofs, and it is clear that they decorated certain rooms with paintings of local animals. (© Dorling Kindersley.)

QUESTIONS TO CONSIDER

1. What factors explain the relatively large size of Çatal Höyük for a Neolithic settlement?

2. What material remains reveal information about the inhabitants' ideas?

3. Why did the inhabitants create, from our perspective, such an unusual layout and architecture?

For Further Information:
"Çatal Höyük: Excavations of a Neolithic Anatolian Höyük." http://www.catalhoyuk.com.
Hodder, Ian. *The Leopard's Tale: Revealing the Mysteries of Çatal Höyük*. New York: Thames & Hudson, 2006.
Mellaart, James. *Çatal Hüyük: A Neolithic Town in Anatolia*. New York: McGraw-Hill, 1967.

COUNTERPOINT
Gatherer-Hunters by Choice: Aborigines of Australia

Although agriculture spread rapidly across the globe, it was not universally practiced in ancient times. Until relatively recently, in fact, many people did not farm. Sometimes the local environment necessitated a forager lifestyle; it is impossible to farm in the Arctic Circle, for example. But in locales where *both* livelihoods are possible, people had a choice and they could select the one they preferred. Many of these people had contact with farmers and could have learned agricultural techniques if they had wanted to. In this Counterpoint we consider one such people who continue in a gatherer-hunter way of life to this day: Australian Aborigines.

> **FOCUS**
>
> Why did Australian Aborigines, in contrast to many of the world's other peoples, choose not to farm?

Understanding the History of Aborigines

The largest landmass in which people did not rely on agriculture (until it was forcibly introduced in the modern era) was Australia (see Map 1.4). Before European

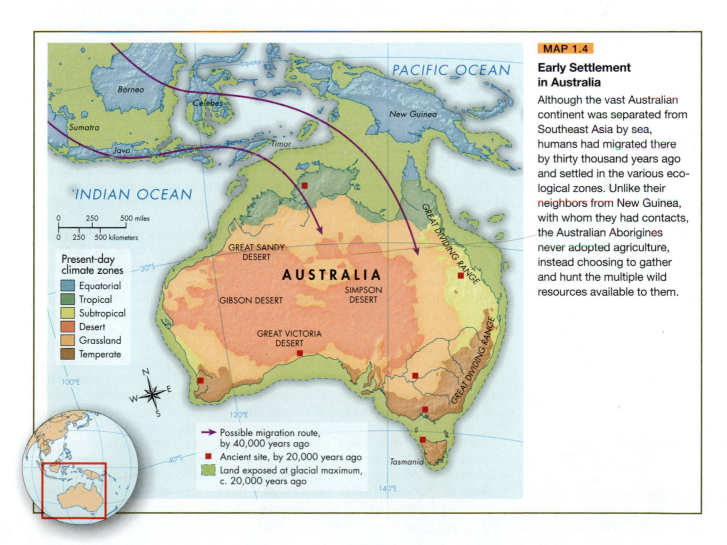

MAP 1.4

Early Settlement in Australia

Although the vast Australian continent was separated from Southeast Asia by sea, humans had migrated there by thirty thousand years ago and settled in the various ecological zones. Unlike their neighbors from New Guinea, with whom they had contacts, the Australian Aborigines never adopted agriculture, instead choosing to gather and hunt the multiple wild resources available to them.

Present-day climate zones
- Equatorial
- Tropical
- Subtropical
- Desert
- Grassland
- Temperate

→ Possible migration route, by 40,000 years ago
■ Ancient site, by 20,000 years ago
Land exposed at glacial maximum, c. 20,000 years ago

settlers first arrived in 1788 C.E., no one in this vast region farmed; the native inhabitants, or **Aborigines**, numbering perhaps 1 million at the time, lived as foragers. We have written descriptions and other sources of information about encounters between the Aborigines and modern Europeans. Reliable information of this sort is lacking for gatherer-hunters of the distant past, but European accounts of Aborigines are heavily biased. Their authors often saw Aborigines as primitive people who lacked the intelligence to farm. When historians took into account the Aborigines' rich archaeological remains and observations of gatherer-hunters who survive today, however, they concluded that Australian Aborigines consciously decided not to practice agriculture, because they knew that foraging was more suitable for their environment.

By thirty thousand years ago, gatherer-hunter immigrants from southeast Asia had settled the whole of the Australian continent. The water level was much lower due to the last ice age, and they had been able to cross the sea by boat—no small feat because even at the lowest sea level they had to sail at least forty miles. The ensuing ice melt, which started around twelve thousand years ago, widened the distance between Australia and adjacent islands and increased its population's isolation. The end of the ice age also caused the climate to dry considerably.

A Lifestyle in Harmony with the Natural World

Despite Australia's enormous variety of natural environments, ranging from tropical rain forests to desolate deserts, the foragers' lifestyles shared certain characteristics. Many scholars think these characteristics illustrate how gatherer-hunters of the distant past lived, and they use observations of modern gatherer-hunters to interpret archaeological evidence.

Although their existence was migratory, they were strongly attached to the regions they inhabited, and their migration patterns were fixed. In fertile regions near water, they maintained huts and shelters at seasonal campsites, where they could stay for several months. In arid regions they moved more often from one water hole to another, setting up temporary shelters. The whole community shared ownership of the land and its resources. In collecting food, they divided labor by gender. Women gathered plants and small animals such as lizards and turtles; men hunted large animals such as kangaroos and wallabies. The division of labor sometimes led men and women to be separated for prolonged periods.

Harvesting Nature's Bounty

So great is the ecological diversity of Australia that inhabitants could exploit a large variety of local resources, as foragers throughout world history have done. Yet the case of Australia shows especially vividly the enormous adaptability of humans and our willingness to take advantage of all potential food sources. In the Australian summer months, for example, moths migrate to the southeastern highlands to escape the heat, gathering in rock crevices in huge numbers. Local people scraped them off by the hundreds and grilled them on hot stones. After removing the moth's inedible parts, they had a high-protein, peanut-sized nugget that tasted like a roasted chestnut.

Another expedient use of local resources was the processing of macrozamia nuts for food. Poisonous when not treated, the kernels must be detoxified by soaking them in water, after which they were ground into flour used to bake a highly nutritious bread. Near the rivers of the southeast, people caught eels that migrate upstream in the spring and downstream in the fall. To trap the animals, they cleaned out channels and built retaining walls to guide them into nets and baskets made of bark and rushes. They then killed the eels—which could be up to three feet long and as thick as a man's arm—by biting them in the back of the head. Aborigines on the coasts used marine resources intensively but responsibly, taking care, for example, to harvest shellfish so that a species would not become extinct. Over time the discarded shells formed large heaps, in which archaeologists also have found

Aborigines Indigenous inhabitants of regions that Europeans colonized starting in the fifteenth century C.E.; the word is used especially in reference to Australia.

bones of birds eaten after they had washed up onto the beach. Coastal people fished in canoes, with men using spears and women using fish lines and hooks. These examples illustrate the resourcefulness of gatherer-hunters, and another important fact: far from being unsophisticated, gatherer-hunters develop highly effective specialized tools to harvest nature's resources.

Beyond collecting what nature provided, Aborigines manipulated the environment to increase the foodstuff available in the wild. In this effort, fire was an important tool. They burned areas with shrubs because they learned that the regenerative process produced a wide variety of edible plants. These plants were useful in their own right but also because they attracted animals that could be hunted. Selective burning also allowed certain desirable plants to grow better and to ripen simultaneously. For example, burning increased production of macrozamia nuts up to eight times. In addition, people replanted fruit seeds on fertile compost heaps near their camps, and when they collected wild yams and other tubers, they did not pull out the entire root but left the part that would regenerate. The Aborigines were thus well aware of the growth patterns of the plants and animals that surrounded them and adjusted natural circumstances so the desired species would thrive.

Increasing Nature's Bounty

The Conscious Choice to Gather and Hunt

Why Aborigines did not go one step further and independently develop agriculture or adopt it from abroad is an interesting question. Australia was not fully isolated before the Europeans' arrival in 1788 C.E.; peoples from neighboring regions such as Indonesia

Gathering Turtle Eggs
Gatherer-hunters ingeniously take advantage of everything nature provides and show great awareness of plants and animal behavior. These Australian Aboriginal women and children know that sea turtles come ashore to bury their eggs, and they collect the eggs before they hatch. (L. Kuipers.)

and New Guinea visited regularly. Inhabitants of these nearby areas farmed crops, including plants such as yams that can grow in Australia as well. Scholars thus believe that the absence of domestication was a conscious choice. They were content with the resources nature provided, which were adequate and easily available except in rare years of scarcity. Moreover, because much of Australia is dry—droughts can last for years—and has poor soil, farming is difficult in many parts of the continent and does not guarantee a stable food supply.

Moreover, farming is arduous and labor intensive compared with foraging. A woman harvesting and processing macrozamia nuts, for example, can feed herself for the whole day after only two hours of work. The relatively relaxed lifestyle of Aborigines made an impression on some of the earliest Europeans, who observed Australia before they started to settle there. In 1770 c.e., the English explorer James Cook wrote:

> [T]he Natives of New Holland [= Australia] . . . may appear to be the most wretched people upon Earth, but in reality they are far more happier than we Europeans. They live in a Tranquility which is not disturb'd by the Inequality of Condition: The Earth and sea of their own accord furnishes them with all things necessary for life, they covet not Magnificent Houses, Household-stuff &ca, they lie in a warm and fine Climate and enjoy a very wholesome Air, so that they have very little need of Clothing and this they seem to be fully sensible of, for many of who we gave Cloth &ca to, left it carelessly upon the Sea beach and in the woods as a thing they had no manner of use for. In short they seem'd to set no Value upon any thing we gave them, nor would they ever part with any thing of their own for any one article we could offer them; this in my opinion argues that they think themselves provided with all the necessarys of Life and that they have no superfluities.[2]

Religious Life and Social Organization

In contrast to the simplicity of their material culture, Aborigines had a complex religious life and social organization. Their worldview centered on the concept of "Dreaming" or "Dreamtime," which connected past, present, and future. In the distant past, according to Aboriginal belief, mythic beings created the land and its inhabitants and left rules on how humans should interact with one another and with nature. Then they withdrew into the spiritual world, but they continue to send messages through dreams and other altered states of consciousness. Humans needed to maintain contacts with these Dreaming beings through rituals and dances, for which Aborigines donned elaborate clothing, such as cloaks made of possum and wallaby skins. Ritual activity was primarily the domain of initiated men, who often temporarily withdrew from their communities for the purpose.

In Aboriginal society, a person gained respect through ritual knowledge, not wealth, because there was no accumulation of goods. Social interactions, including sexual intercourse and friendship, were allowed only between individuals with a specific family relationship. Marriages, an important way for families to establish ties, were often reciprocal—for example, men exchanged their sisters—and were arranged before those to be married were born. Likewise, gifts of tools, skins, ornaments, and the like were a crucial way to maintain good relations.

Despite these common characteristics, early Australia was culturally diverse, with practices varying from region to region. In the visual arts, for example, stone carvings and paintings on objects and rock surfaces show many regional styles, although treatments of subjects share basic similarities (for example, humans and animals are mostly represented as sticklike figures). The linguistic diversity of Aboriginal Australians was also enormous: in 1788 c.e. more than 250 languages were spoken on the continent.

The history of Australian Aborigines thus reveals that a nonagricultural life is possible, indeed preferable, under certain conditions. Native Australians' gatherer-hunter livelihood led to a distinctive historical development on the continent, with unique technologies and social, economic, and cultural practices.

Conclusion

Neanderthals, with whose discovery we began this chapter, differed greatly from modern humans. Not only did they not look like us, but they also led very different lives from ours. We should remember, however, that they too were a product of millions of years of evolution that had transformed human beings repeatedly.

Four million years ago, our ancestors depended entirely on the natural resources available in their immediate surroundings. They collected and ate plants and animals without tools or fire, relying only on their hands and teeth. But over long spans of time, they adapted to changes in their environments, acquired new skills, and started to modify what was available in their surroundings. Importantly, these developments allowed them to change physically, and they began to walk upright, hold things in their now-agile hands, speak, and think abstract thoughts. Tools and other inventions helped them in their quest for successful livelihoods. After millions of years, some began to domesticate plants and animals and to manage the forces of nature. Others, most notably Australian Aborigines, consciously decided to rely primarily on food available in the wild, for which they foraged.

By 4000 B.C.E., peoples in various parts of the world had learned to manipulate resources so that they could survive periods without naturally available food. They had developed the tools and skills needed to adapt elements of nature to their needs. As they lived in increasingly large communities, their social interactions, means of communication, and working conditions changed. The forces of nature were much more powerful than human abilities, but with a great deal of effort some people had developed the skills needed to spend their entire lives in one place. These early settlers went on to build up other aspects of human culture that are still with us today, such as cities and writing, the focus of our next chapter.

NOTES

1. Charles Darwin, *On the Origin of Species*, ed. Joseph Carroll (Peterborough, Ontario, Canada: Broadview, 2003), 432.
2. J. C. Beaglehole, ed., *The Voyage of the Endeavour 1768–1771: The Journals of Captain James Cook on His Voyages of Discovery* (Cambridge, U.K.: Cambridge University Press, 1955), 1:399.

RESOURCES FOR RESEARCH

Human Origins

The study of the human species draws on an assortment of disciplines, including anthropology, genetics, and linguistics. The literature is extensive, and ideas change rapidly. The selection of books and Web sites is vast; many are extensively illustrated. The book edited by Scarre gives a very up-to-date survey of all the issues discussed in this chapter.

Ardipithecus ramidus. Science, October 2, 2009. http://www.sciencemag.org/site/feature/misc/webfeat/ardipithecus/index.xhtml.

Fagan, Brian. *World Prehistory, A Brief Introduction*, 8th ed. 2010.

Johanson, Donald, and Blake Edgar. *From Lucy to Language*, 2d ed. 2006.

Klein, Richard G. *The Human Career: Human Biological and Cultural Origins*, 2d ed. 1999.

"The New Face of Human Evolution." http://archaeologyinfo.com/.

Scarre, Chris, ed. *The Human Past*. 2005.

"What Does It Mean to Be Human?" Smithsonian National Museum of Natural History. http://www.mnh.si.edu/anthro/humanorigins/.

Stringer, Chris, and Peter Andrews. *The Complete World of Human Evolution*. 2005.

Tattersall, Ian. *The World from Beginnings to 4000 B.C.E.* 2008.

Tattersall, Ian, and Jeffrey H. Schwartz. *Extinct Humans*. 2001.

Thomas, Herbert. *The First Humans: The Search for Our Origins*. 1996.

Paleolithic Food Gatherers, 2,000,000–9000 B.C.E.

Most of the books that treat human origins also discuss the Paleolithic. Additionally, these items more specifically address the art of that era.

Aujoulat, Norbert. "Lascaux: A Visit to the Cave." http://www.culture.gouv.fr/culture/arcnat/lascaux/en/.

Aujoulat, Norbert. *Lascaux: Movement, Space, and Time*. 2005.

Bahn, Paul G., and Jean Vertut. *Journey Through the Ice Age*. 1997.

The First Neolithic Farmers, 9000–4000 B.C.E.

The study of the origins of agriculture can be very technical, and scholars often introduce new ideas in publications of archaeological excavations that require processes or dates to be revised. Scholars often consider how the technology spread worldwide, which they regularly connect to the spread of languages. Several of the books mentioned in previous sections are useful for this period as well, especially Scarre's *The Human Past*. Nissen's somewhat older study provides an excellent survey of developments in Southwest Asia.

Bellwood, Peter. *First Farmers: The Origins of Agricultural Societies*. 2005.

Cauvin, Jacques. *The Birth of the Gods and the Origins of Agriculture*. Translated by Trevor Watkins. 2000.

Nissen, Hans J. *The Early History of the Ancient Near East, 9000–2000 B.C.* Translated by E. Lutzeier and K. Northcutt. 1988.

"Preserving Ancient Statues from Jordan." Arthur M. Sackler Gallery, Smithsonian Institution. July 28, 1996–April 6, 1997. http://www.asia.si.edu/jordan/html/jor_mm.htm.

Smith, Bruce D. *The Emergence of Agriculture*. 1995.

Wenke, Robert J., and Deborah I. Olszewski. *Patterns in Prehistory: Humankind's First Three Million Years*, 5th ed. 2006.

COUNTERPOINT: Gatherer-Hunters by Choice: Aborigines of Australia

The study of Australian aboriginal life involves a mixture of archaeological and ethnographic research, and many of the books discuss the people both before and after European settlement in 1788.

Chaloupka, George. *Journey in Time: The World's Longest Continuing Art Tradition*. 1993.

Flood, Josephine. *Archaeology of the Dreamtime: The Story of Prehistoric Australia and Its People*. 1989.

Kleinert, Sylvia, and Margot Neale, eds. *The Oxford Companion to Aboriginal Art and Culture*. 2000.

Mulvaney, D. J., and J. Peter White, eds. *Australians to 1788*. 1987.

▶ **For additional primary sources from this period**, see *Sources of Crossroads and Cultures*.

▶ **For Web sites, images, and documents related to topics in this chapter**, see Make History at bedfordstmartins.com/smith.

The major global development in this chapter ▶ The adaptation of early humans to their environment and their eventual domestication of plants and animals.

IMPORTANT EVENTS

c. 7 million years ago (mya)	Oldest hominid on record, *Sahelanthropus tchadensis*, lives in central Africa
c. 4.4 mya	*Ardipithecus ramidus* lives in the region of modern Ethiopia
c. 3.2 mya	*Australopithecus afarensis* (Lucy) lives in the region of modern Ethiopia
c. 2 mya	First hominin and first stone tools
c. 1 mya	Ancestors of *Homo erectus* enter Asia
c. 500,000 B.C.E.	Ancestors of Neanderthal enter western Eurasia
c. 400,000–30,000 B.C.E.	Neanderthal lives in western Eurasia
c. 400,000 B.C.E.	First evidence of *Homo sapiens* in Africa
c. 100,000 B.C.E.	Some *Homo sapiens* leave Africa
c. 35,000–10,000 B.C.E.	Paleolithic cave paintings
c. 30,000 B.C.E.	*Homo sapiens* becomes the only human species
c. 15,000 B.C.E.	*Homo sapiens* enters the Americas
c. 10,000–8000 B.C.E.	Development of agriculture in Southwest Asia

KEY TERMS

Aborigines (p. 32) matriarchy (p. 29)
Fertile Crescent (p. 23) matrilineal (p. 29)
hominid (p. 11) Neanderthal (p. 15)
hominin (p. 15) Neolithic (p. 17)
Homo sapiens (p. 15) Paleolithic (p. 17)

CHAPTER OVERVIEW QUESTIONS

1. What caused humans to introduce technological and other innovations?
2. How did these innovations increase their ability to determine their own destinies?
3. How did the relationship between humans and nature change?
4. How have historians and other scholars reconstructed life in the earliest periods of human existence despite the lack of written records?

SECTION FOCUS QUESTIONS

1. What physical and behavioral adaptations and innovations characterized human evolution?
2. In the absence of written sources, what have scholars learned about the Paleolithic economy, adaptations to the natural world, and technological innovations?
3. In what ways does the Neolithic agricultural economy reveal humans' increasing intent and ability to manipulate the natural world to their advantage?
4. Why did Australian Aborigines, in contrast to many of the world's other peoples, choose not to farm?

MAKING CONNECTIONS

1. What hominid species migrated across the globe, and for what reasons? How did natural conditions influence their migrations?
2. How did Neolithic peoples' livelihoods and daily lives compare with those of Paleolithic peoples?
3. What gender-specific roles can we discern in early human history, and how did they emerge?

2

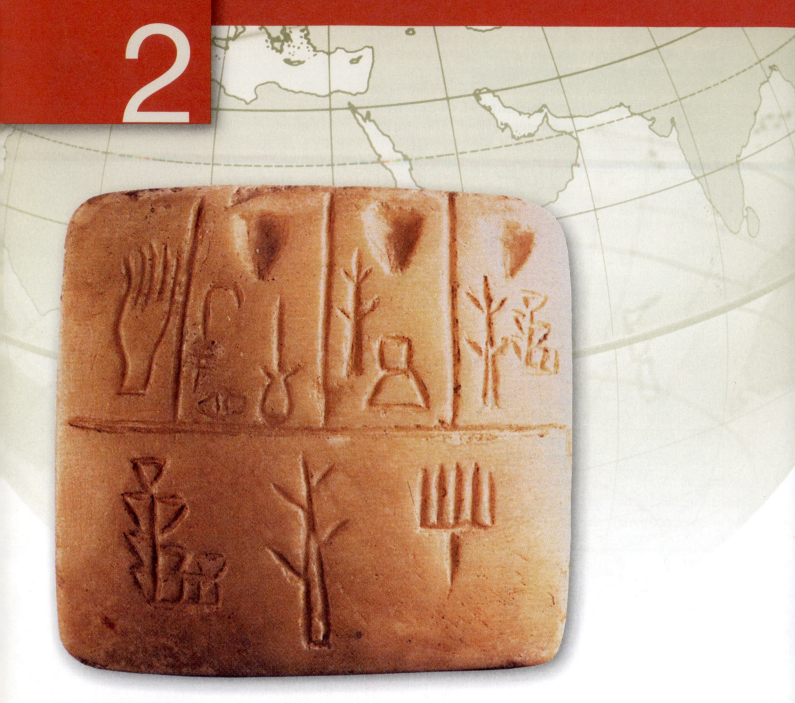

AT A CROSSROADS ▲

Unassuming clay objects such as this one show human beings' earliest ability to record information for the future. Dating to around 3200 B.C.E., this tablet from southern Mesopotamia is impressed with cuneiform signs that record the transfer of goods in the city of Uruk. Writing was one of many Uruk innovations that announced the birth of the first urban society in world history. (Science Source/PhotoResearchers.)

Temples and Palaces: Birth of the City

5000–1200 B.C.E.

In around 1800 B.C.E., scribes from Sumer, in the south of modern Iraq, wrote down the tale of Enmerkar and the Lord of Aratta. This Sumerian epic recounts the rivalry between Enmerkar, king of the Sumerian city of Uruk, and his unnamed counterpart in Aratta, a legendary city in what is today Iran. Both men wanted to be the favorite of the goddess Inanna, one of the many deities whom the people of this ancient world honored. The two kings communicated through a messenger, but at one point the message became too difficult for him to memorize, so the tale says:

> His speech was very great, its meaning very deep.
> The messenger's mouth was too heavy; he could not repeat it.
> Because the messenger's mouth was too heavy, and he could not repeat it,
> The lord of Uruk patted some clay and put the words on it as on a tablet.
> Before that day, there had been no putting words on clay;
> But now, when the sun rose on that day—so it was.
> The lord of Uruk had put words as on a tablet—so it was![1]

This passage describes in mythical terms the invention of the first writing system on earth, **cuneiform**, in which the writer used a reed to press wedge-shaped marks on a moist clay tablet. The invention of writing marked a major turning point in world history: it

BACKSTORY

As we saw in Chapter 1, people in Southwest Asia were the first in world history to invent agriculture, which allowed them to live in the same place for prolonged periods. The abundant natural resources of the Fertile Crescent, which runs from the eastern Mediterranean shore to the mountains between modern Iraq and Iran, allowed people to live in larger communities, in which social interactions became increasingly complex. In short, settled agriculture in Southwest Asia led to the birth of the city and the state.

In time, cities became major crossroads for peoples, goods, and ideas. It was in cities that the inhabitants of Southwest Asia developed a number of innovative concepts and technologies, including new forms of communication and political organization that remain important to this day. These changes did not happen in the Fertile Crescent itself, however, but in the adjacent river valleys, where natural challenges were much more severe. In this chapter we examine the origins and implications of urbanization, exploring the new patterns and connections that emerged as cities became central to Southwest Asian society and government.

Origins of Urban Society: Mesopotamia, 5000–3200 B.C.E.

FOCUS How do historians explain the rise of cities?

The First Cities, 3200–1600 B.C.E.

FOCUS How and why did the rise of the city lead to a more hierarchical society in early Mesopotamia?

City Life and Learning

FOCUS Why did ancient peoples develop writing systems, and what has been the enduring impact of this invention on intellectual expression?

The First International Order, 1600–1200 B.C.E.

FOCUS What were the main features of the first international order, and what developments explain its rise and fall?

COUNTERPOINT: Egypt's Distinct Path to Statehood

FOCUS In what ways did the early history of Egypt contrast with that of the ancient states of Southwest Asia?

cuneiform The dominant writing system of ancient Southwest Asia, which uses combinations of wedge-shaped symbols for words and syllables.

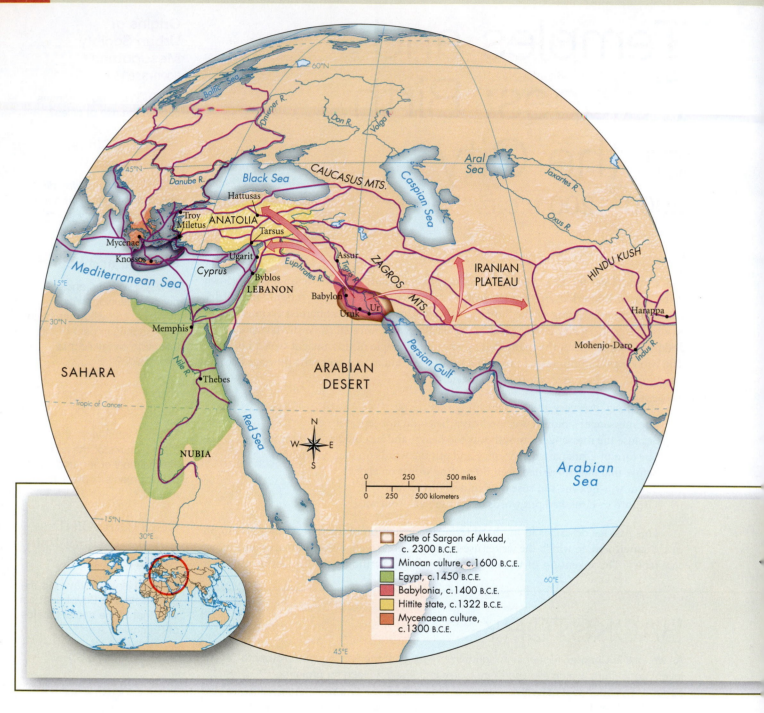

State of Sargon of Akkad, c. 2300 B.C.E.
Minoan culture, c. 1600 B.C.E.
Egypt, c. 1450 B.C.E.
Babylonia, c. 1400 B.C.E.
Hittite state, c. 1322 B.C.E.
Mycenaean culture, c. 1300 B.C.E.

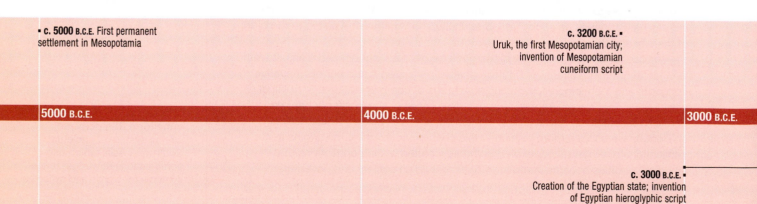

■ **c. 5000** B.C.E. First permanent settlement in Mesopotamia

c. 3200 B.C.E. ■
Uruk, the first Mesopotamian city; invention of Mesopotamian cuneiform script

5000 B.C.E.

4000 B.C.E.

3000 B.C.E.

c. 3000 B.C.E. ■
Creation of the Egyptian state; invention of Egyptian hieroglyphic script

reflected profound social and cultural developments and created a myriad of new connections, including connections between the present and the distant past. Hundreds of thousands of cuneiform tablets have survived, giving scholars the first written evidence and enormously expanding their access to the lives and thoughts of peoples from the past.

The written and archaeological evidence from ancient Sumer reveals the origins of the world's first urban culture and sheds light on its earliest characteristics. Before we begin exploring that evidence, however, we need to define what we mean by "city." Scholars characterize a **city** not just in terms of its size and large population, but by its role in the life of the region, which extends beyond its boundaries. Thus, the inhabitants of outlying areas relied on the cities of antiquity to meet important needs. People who lived many miles away may have venerated a god in the city temple, for instance, or they may have traveled there to obtain tools. At the same time, inhabitants of cities relied on nearby rural areas for basic needs, such as food, which they could not grow themselves. City dwellers tended to have specialized economic and social roles, such as metalworker, shopkeeper, or priest, and political elites usually controlled their interactions through rules and regulations. In ancient times, the growth of cities often led to a type of political organization we call the **city-state**: an independent urban center that dominates the surrounding countryside. Thus, as cities developed their own distinct economic, social, and political structures, they functioned as regional crossroads, connecting people with communities.

Throughout history, cities and city-states appeared in almost every part of the world as people decided to live together in denser concentrations. This arrangement often arose independently, centuries after cities first appeared in Southwest Asia, and the urban environments varied from place to place. Compared to Southwest Asian cities, for example, Chinese cities had similar numbers of residents but covered much larger areas. Some early cities in Mesoamerica were primarily ceremonial—their purpose

city A center of population, commerce, and culture that provides specialized services to people from surrounding areas.

city-state A form of political organization that incorporates a single city with its surrounding countryside and villages.

MAPPING THE WORLD

Southwest Asia and the Eastern Mediterranean, c. 5000–1200 B.C.E.

The earliest urban societies and states in world history arose in Southwest Asia. Southern Mesopotamia and Egypt were the leaders in urbanization and state creation, and with their extensive trade contacts they influenced adjacent regions and beyond. The use of cuneiform, the world's first writing, for example, spread from Mesopotamia to Iran, Anatolia, and Syria. By 1200 B.C.E., the area was home to a set of territorial states in constant contact—sometimes in peace and sometimes in military conflict.

ROUTES ▼

→ Spread of cuneiform writing, c. 3200 B.C.E.
— Major trade route

---

c. 2550 B.C.E. Khufu's pyramid at Giza

c. 1800–1700 B.C.E. Hammurabi's unification of southern Mesopotamia

• **c. 1800** B.C.E. Development of alphabetic script in Syria

2000 B.C.E.   **1000 B.C.E.**

c. 3000–2350 B.C.E. Competing city-states in Mesopotamia

c. 1600–1200 B.C.E. First international order in the eastern Mediterranean

• **c. 1650** B.C.E. End of the Minoan culture

c. 2350–2200 B.C.E. Dynasty of King Sargon of Akkad dominates Mesopotamia

• **c. 1450** B.C.E. Mycenaean expansion throughout the Aegean

FIRST APPEARANCE OF CITIES

c. 3200 B.C.E.	Southwest Asia
c. 3000 B.C.E.	Egypt
c. 2600 B.C.E.	Indus Valley
c. 2000 B.C.E.	Northern China
c. 1500 B.C.E.	Nubia
c. 1200 B.C.E.	Mesoamerica
c. 100 C.E.	Sub-Saharan West Africa
c. 1000 C.E.	Sub-Saharan East Africa

was apparently not to house people. But regardless of their size and purpose, all cities serve as important focal points for their society's activities.

Accordingly, it is not surprising that starting with the earliest city dwellers, many people have equated cities with civilization, seeing nonurban people as inherently backward and unsophisticated. Formerly, historians also equated urban societies with civilization, but we now realize we must be more flexible in applying terms. Although complex social and economic interactions and technological and cultural innovations often developed in cities, the many other forms of social and economic organization that have evolved over world history cannot be considered static or "uncivilized." As we examine developments in Southwest Asia, it is important to recognize that we are exploring the rise of cities, *not* the rise of civilization.

Moreover, although cities were the focus of cultural development in many regions, that was not universally true. In South Asia, for example, after a period of early urbanization people reverted to village life (see Chapter 3). In Egypt, bordering on Southwest Asia, a state with cities developed very early, but as the Counterpoint to this chapter will show, cities there had a limited role. The king was at the center of political, economic, and cultural life, and from the beginning of the Egyptian state, its inhabitants considered their status as royal subjects more important than their residence in a particular city. Thus, the central role of cities in Southwest Asia reflected a specific set of historical and environmental circumstances; it was not the product of a universal pattern followed by all complex societies.

The rise of cities in Southwest Asia was a long-term process marked by many social, economic, and technological advances that combined to fundamentally alter living conditions and livelihoods. The tale that begins this chapter reflects several elements of urban life that are still part of modern culture today: cities, communication by writing, political institutions, social hierarchies, and long-distance contacts. Once cities had developed, they became the sites of the characteristic culture of ancient Southwest Asia and provided the basis for further developments in every aspect of life.

OVERVIEW
QUESTIONS

The major global development in this chapter: The rise of urban society and the creation of states in Southwest Asia.

As you read, consider:

1. What types of political and social organization appeared in the early history of Southwest Asia?

2. What new technologies appeared, and how did they affect people's livelihoods?

3. How do urban societies differ from village societies?

4. How did the early states of Southwest Asia interact with one another?

Origins of Urban Society:
Mesopotamia 5000–3200 B.C.E.

Sumer, the land where the tale of Enmerkar and the Lord of Aratta took place, was located in southern Mesopotamia, an ancient region that occupied much the same territory as modern Iraq. It was in Mesopotamia that the first urban cultures arose. Abundant archaeological findings provide evidence of the earliest processes in city development, and many cuneiform tablets provide information on later stages. Together these sources allow scholars to reconstruct the development of an urban society, an evolution that occurred over several millennia.

FOCUS

How do historians explain the rise of cities?

The Environmental Challenge

Southern Mesopotamia is an extremely arid region where rain alone is insufficient to grow crops. It is also very hot—regularly more than 120 degrees Fahrenheit in the summer—and lacks certain basic natural resources, including trees, metal, and hard stone for building. So southern Mesopotamia may seem like an unlikely region to develop the world's first urban culture—but it did, mainly due to the inhabitants' ingenuity in facing the region's challenges. Two major rivers ran through the countryside, the Tigris and Euphrates, and people invented irrigation agriculture to use them to water fields (see Map 2.1).

Geography and Climate

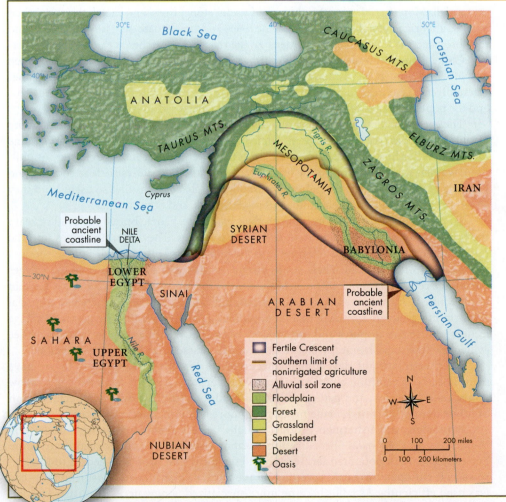

MAP 2.1

The Ecology of Southwest Asia

Southwest Asia, home to the earliest urban societies, includes many different ecological landscapes. In this map, the heavy line labeled "southern limit of nonirrigated agriculture" makes a critical distinction between zones that have enough rainfall for agriculture and zones where agriculture requires irrigation. In actuality, this boundary varies, depending on annual rainfall. It is clear, however, that the cultures of early Mesopotamia and Egypt developed where irrigation was always needed; ultimately, then, their rise depended on the Nile, Tigris, and Euphrates rivers.

By 8000 B.C.E., people in the Fertile Crescent zone of Southwest Asia had developed agriculture. The area had rich plant and animal life and rainfall sufficient to grow crops of wheat and barley. The early farmers kept domesticated animals such as cattle, sheep, goats, and pigs, which enabled them to reside year-round in villages with a few hundred inhabitants. Scholars speculate that some of them visited the arid areas nearby to graze herds and saw the opportunities this region provided—although rain was inadequate in Mesopotamia, the soil is extremely fertile. People discovered that when they guided water from the rivers into fields, barley grew abundantly. This simple innovation allowed farmers using irrigation to establish small villages throughout the southern Mesopotamian plain starting in around 5000 B.C.E.

Irrigation and Its Impact

Once they had invented the basic concept of irrigation, farmers dug canals to carry water over greater distances. But the construction and use of irrigation canals required planning and coordination. If farmers with fields near the head of the canal used too much water, those farther downstream could not irrigate their crops. Moreover, because flooding was a serious threat in the extremely flat Mesopotamian countryside, the canals and fields needed to be lined with strong dikes, which required maintenance. Such tasks demanded organization and cooperation in villages, as well as a system to resolve conflicts over water rights. From the very beginning, irrigation farming stimulated development of new forms of social organization and new connections among members of ancient communities.

Cooperation and Community Growth

Cooperation brought substantial benefits. In southern Mesopotamia, irrigation farmers could reap enormous yields and earn much more income than farmers elsewhere who relied on rainfall. Moreover, despite the absence of useful stone, trees, and metal, the region had several other rich natural resources. Near the rivers and canals, date orchards flourished, and they provided shade for vegetable gardens. In the rivers and marshes at the head of the Persian Gulf, inhabitants could catch loads of fish, as well as turtles, crabs, and water rats, which also provided protein. Herdsmen guided large flocks of sheep and goats to seasonal pastures. These diverse resources fueled the growth of larger communities and attracted outsiders, and the population of southern Mesopotamia rapidly increased after 5000 B.C.E.

Village Life and Social Development

The earliest settlers of Mesopotamia established villages like those of the surrounding Neolithic societies (see Chapter 1). All family members worked at agricultural tasks, some focusing on herding animals and others on growing crops. Because they cared for children, women were more tied to the house than men and had duties such as cooking and grinding grain. They made the pottery that modern archaeologists find so useful, and they wove sheep wool and goat's hair into clothing, blankets, and other textiles.

To maintain a close relationship with their ancestors, people buried the dead beneath the house floors and gave them food and drink offerings. They even dug pipes into the floors of houses to pour these offerings into the tombs. They also provided grave goods—items buried with the dead. These goods provide evidence of social change in the villages during the centuries from 5000 B.C.E. to the time of the origin of cities, 3200 B.C.E. Certain tombs came to include more and richer goods, indicating that their owners had a special status in life. Scholars speculate that communities gave these distinctive goods to village leaders who settled disputes and coordinated labor. Thus, even at this early stage, we see evidence of the social hierarchy that would come to characterize Mesopotamian cities.

Specialization of Labor

Another important development occurred during the same period. As we have seen, in early agricultural communities families performed all the tasks needed to grow crops, raise livestock, and gather additional food. Over time, however, **specialization of labor** developed, which made production more efficient. Specialist farmers, gardeners, herdsmen, and fishermen produced higher yields than families who undertook these tasks on their own. Specialization of labor also led to technological innovation. For example, Mesopotamian farmers invented a plow that dropped seeds into the furrows as it cut open the earth, speeding up the work of planting and ensuring that seed was used efficiently. As labor became more specialized, a new necessity arose: families

specialization of labor The organization of work such that individuals concentrate on specific tasks rather than engage in a variety of activities.

that were formerly self-sufficient had to trade to meet some of their basic needs. This crucial need for exchange was a major stimulus to the development of cities. People needed a central place to meet, a crossroads where they could connect with potential trading partners and exchange goods.

Many of the world's early urban cultures grew up in the valleys of mighty rivers, most notably in Mesopotamia along the Tigris and Euphrates, in Egypt along the Nile, in South Asia along the Indus, and in China along the Yellow (Huang He) and Yangzi rivers. With this in mind, many historians make a connection between irrigation agriculture and the centralized authority and social hierarchy typical of many ancient urban cultures. This line of argument suggests that irrigation depends on a strong central authority to coordinate its construction, use, and maintenance. Archaeological research does not, however, support this argument. Rather, the evidence shows that small communities initiated and maintained irrigation projects; centralized authority developed only long after such projects had begun. Nonetheless, it was the rich agricultural potential of the river valleys that led people in many parts of the world to establish densely populated urban centers.

River Valley Cultures

The First Cities 3200–1600 B.C.E

As we saw earlier, a crucial element in the definition of a city is that it serves communities in the surrounding countryside and that these communities provide goods to people in the city. The city is the center for many activities, including exchange of goods. Archaeological remains throughout Mesopotamia show that during the fourth millennium B.C.E. such central places grew increasingly large. This process culminated in around 3200 B.C.E. at Uruk—the home of Enmerkar in the Sumerian tale quoted at the start of the chapter (see again Mapping the World, pages 40 and 41). The population there became so large (perhaps thirty thousand individuals or more) and provided so many services to the surrounding region that we can consider it the first true city in world history.

> **FOCUS**
> How and why did the rise of the city lead to a more hierarchical society in early Mesopotamia?

Uruk exerted its influence in many ways. It was the economic hub for the exchange of goods and services. It was the religious center with temples for the gods. It was home to political and military powers who governed people, represented them in relations with others, and protected and controlled them.

Soon similar centers arose throughout southern Mesopotamia, organizing the inhabitants of cities and surrounding villages into the political structure historians call the city-state. In later centuries this form of political organization spread from Mesopotamia to the rest of Southwest Asia, characterizing the early history of the region from 3200 to 1600 B.C.E.

The Power of the Temple

What motivated the residents of Uruk and its surroundings to embrace the city as a hub of exchange? Dealing with the city could be inconvenient—for instance, the farmers, herders, fishermen, and others who delivered part of their products to the city sometimes had to wait several months for compensation. One reason they accepted the exchange arrangement was that it had the support of an ideology—that is, a set of ideas and values—to explain and justify it. That ideology was Mesopotamian religion.

In the center of Uruk was a gigantic temple complex, which must have required many community members to build and decorate. Not only did it house the city's gods and goddesses, but its staff also administered the economy. People contributed the products of their labor to the gods, whom they trusted to give something in return in the near or distant future. The head of the temple organization was the priest-king, the gods' representative on earth. A stone vase of the period, known as the Uruk vase, depicts the guiding

The Temple and Its Functions

The Uruk Vase

© Marc Van De Mieroop.

Uruk Vase (Bildarchiv Preussischer Kulturbesitz/Art Resource, NY.)

Archaeologists found this alabaster vase in the ruins of the Sumerian city of Uruk. It is over three feet high and dates to about 3200 B.C.E. Its surface is completely carved in an elaborate relief. Images in the bottom section represent the agriculture of the region; in the middle frame, a procession of naked men carry agricultural products in bowls, vessels, and baskets. The high point of the relief's story occurs in the top section, where a female figure faces the city's ruler. At some later date the ruler's depiction was cut out of the scene, but we can reconstruct his appearance from contemporaneous representations on other objects.

The female figure is the goddess Inanna, identified by the two symbols standing behind her, which were the basis for writing Inanna's name in later cuneiform script. Beyond those symbols are three animals amid storage jars for liquids and solid foods. Two small human figures, probably statues, stand on pedestals. The statue of the woman has the symbol of Inanna behind her. The statue of the man holding in his hands a stack of bowls and something like a box; bowls and box together form the shape of the cuneiform sign for "lord" in Sumerian. Scholars believe that sign, the most common in tablets from the period, indicates the highest temple official.

EXAMINING THE EVIDENCE

1. What does the relief on the vase tell us about the resources of the Uruk region?

2. What is the relationship among common people, secular ruler, and deity as expressed in this relief?

3. How can we interpret this relief as representing the ruling ideology of the time?

Ubaid and Uruk Pottery
Because archaeologists can see clear distinctions among pottery vessels from different periods, they rely on pottery to date the other remains they excavate. Production techniques can reveal other features of the potter's culture as well. Compare the two bowls here. The potter used great care to shape and decorate the one on the left, from the Ubaid period in the fifth millennium B.C.E. The bowl on the right, from the later Uruk period of the fourth millennium B.C.E., was made very quickly and left undecorated, demonstrating the ancient origin of mass production. (Réunion des Musées Nationaux/Art Resource, NY (right) and Image copyright © The Metropolitan Museum of Art/Art Resource, NY (left).)

ideology (see Seeing the Past: The Uruk Vase). Uruk's main goddess, Inanna, received the agricultural products of her people with the city-ruler as intermediary. In return, as the goddess of procreation, Inanna was expected to guarantee fertility and bountiful crops. Thus, city and country were connected by a divine cycle of exchange that benefited both.

Like almost all other ancient peoples, the Mesopotamians honored numerous deities, a system we call **polytheism**. Their gods and goddesses mostly represented aspects of the natural environment. There was a god of the sky, An; of the moon, Nanna; of grain, Ashnan; and many more. Some deities were the patrons of occupations, such as Dumuzi, the god of herding. Others were responsible for abstract concepts: the sun god, Utu, oversaw justice, and Inanna was the goddess of fertility, love, and war.

Every important deity was the patron of a specific city, which was the god or goddess's residence on earth. The Mesopotamians believed the gods controlled every aspect of their lives and were the source of all good and bad fortune. Literary compositions from later centuries sometimes expressed much pessimism about the gods' plans for humans. Their decisions were inscrutable, and life often seemed meaningless. Yet the Mesopotamians also believed they could encourage the gods to be kind through offerings and prayers, and one of their great preoccupations was to discover divine plans for the future (see Chapter 4).

The rise of the city had fundamental consequences for all the local people living in the vicinity; every aspect of life became more complex. In economic terms, specialization of labor soon extended beyond agriculture. The farming sector produced a surplus that could support people who were not farmers. Previously, for example, women had woven clothing for their families, but this task became the full-time occupation of teams of women who received food as compensation. Artisans in temple workshops worked faster and turned out standardized products. We see this in Uruk's pottery—archaeologists have excavated thousands of vessels produced by stamping clay into a mold and baking it. These simple bowls are very different from the wheel-made and painted vessels of the preceding centuries, which took much longer to make and varied in size and decoration. Thus, urbanization and the labor specialization changed the focus of Mesopotamian economic life. Instead of working to meet the needs of a self-sufficient family, people increasingly produced goods and services for a growing commercial marketplace.

Mesopotamian Gods and Goddesses

Expanded Specialization of Labor

polytheism A religious system that accepts the existence of many gods.

Crafts and Trade

Mesopotamian crafts and trade reflected this trend toward expanding economic connections. Artisans manufactured not only practical items but also luxury products using exotic materials from abroad. Merchants attached to the temple sometimes imported these materials from very distant regions. Mesopotamians prized the semiprecious blue stone lapis lazuli (LAP-is LAZ-uh-lee) for their jewelry. They could obtain it only through trade contacts with the mountain regions of modern Afghanistan, more than fifteen hundred miles away, yet substantial amounts appear in the archaeological record. They also imported copper from what is today the country of Oman in the Persian Gulf and tin from present-day Iran (see Map 2.2). Mixed together, copper and tin produce bronze, which is much more durable and versatile than the stone and copper earlier people had used to make tools. That this new metal was invented soon after the first cities arose is no surprise. Only cities had the collective resources to coordinate the import of ingredients from two separate distant sources. Cities became crossroads not only for their immediate surroundings, but for the people and products of different societies.

Uruk at Its Height

By 3200 B.C.E. Uruk was a fully developed city. It had many inhabitants, some of whom had great power over others and controlled much wealth. Its temple buildings were monumental in size, and its artisans had sophisticated skills that required much training. Uruk's residents greatly valued the building projects and the splendor of the city's art. In that sense they resembled many other people throughout history, who devoted much energy and wealth to show off their success. Other regions in Mesopotamia quickly developed cities as well. In their early history, the temple was the center of power, but this was soon to change.

MAP 2.2   **Sumer's Trade Contacts, c. 3200–1600** B.C.E.

Because Sumer's heartland in southern Iraq lacked metals, wood, and hard stone for building and tool-making, its inhabitants had to import them from as far away as Afghanistan and Egypt. The lapis lazuli, gold, silver, and other precious materials we find in the Royal Cemetery of Ur and elsewhere all came from distant sources. Even more important for the economy, however, were tin from Anatolia and copper from Oman, which the Sumerians combined to make bronze for tools and weapons.

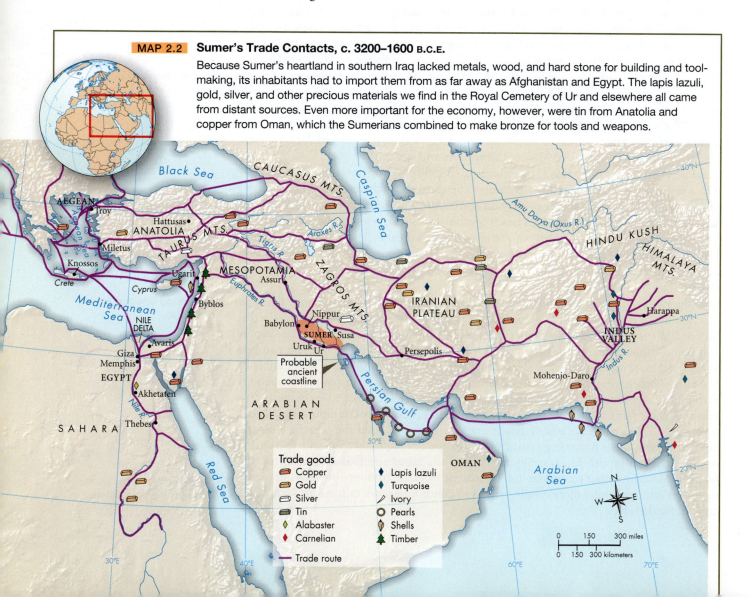

READING THE PAST

Royal Inscriptions from Early Mesopotamia

Inscriptions carved on stone or pressed into clay first appeared in southern Mesopotamia in around 2500 B.C.E. They honor the king's military feats and his patronage of public works, such as the construction of temples and irrigation canals. The inscriptions tie the king closely to the gods of the city, who are sometimes represented as his physical parents or as his caretakers in his youth. One such king was Eanatum of Lagash, who in around 2450 B.C.E. left several such inscriptions, among them the following example.

For the god Ningirsu—Eanatum, ruler of Lagash, whom the god Enlil named, whom the god Ningirsu gave strength, whom the god Nanshe selected, whom the goddess Ninhursag nourished with good milk, whom the goddess Inanna gave a good name, whom the god Enki gave wisdom, whom the god Dumuzi'abzu loves, whom the god Hendursag trusts, son of Akurgal, ruler of Lagash, restored the city Girsu for the god Ningirsu and built the wall of the city Uruku for him. For the god Nanshe he built the city Nina.

Eanatum . . . defeated the city Umma, and made twenty burial mounds for it. He gave back to the god Ningirsu the Gu'edena, his beloved field. He defeated the city Uruk, he defeated the city Ur, and he defeated the city Kiutu. He sacked the city Uruaz and killed its ruler. He sacked the city Mishime and he destroyed the city Arua. All the foreign lands trembled before Eanatum, named by the god Ningirsu. When the king of the city Akshak rebelled, Eanatum, named by the god Ningirsu, removed him from the Antasura-field of the god Ningirsu and destroyed the city Akshak.

After all that, Eanatum dug a new canal for the god Ningirsu.

Source: J. S. Cooper, trans., *Sumerian and Akkadian Royal Inscriptions* (New Haven: American Oriental Society, 1986), 1:42–43.

EXAMINING THE EVIDENCE

1. How does King Eanatum establish his relationship with various gods?
2. What are his achievements, according to this text?
3. What does the inscription reveal about the relationship among Mesopotamian city-states?

The Might of the Palace

Rise of Militarism

From its beginnings, the ideology of urban power had a military dimension, as evidenced by early art that shows the priest-king in battle or inspecting bound prisoners. But before 3000 B.C.E., artists emphasized nonmilitary functions. That imagery changed, however, as multiple urban centers emerged alongside Uruk, often as little as twenty miles apart. These cities housed fast-growing populations who needed ever-larger agricultural zones for food, and when both sides claimed an area their demands led to battles. In around 3000 B.C.E., the basis of power in cities began to shift from religion to the military. Neighboring city-states fought wars over territory and resources, and military leaders gained prominence, finally taking full control over political life; they absorbed some earlier religious functions as well. In archaeological sites, we see this change in the appearance of palaces next to temples and in massive walls built to protect cities. Increasingly, Mesopotamian cities were connected to one another primarily by conflict and war.

Royal Dynasties

Temples remained important institutions in Mesopotamian cities, and military leaders used them to legitimize their own rule. They created hereditary **dynasties**, that is, successions of rulers who belonged to different generations of the same family, claiming that the gods had chosen them to lead their city. In around 2450 B.C.E. Eanatum (AI-an-na-TOMB), king of Lagash, for example, declared that several gods had selected and nurtured him to lead his city in war, especially against the neighboring city of Umma. Both cities wanted control of an agricultural zone and repeatedly fought wars over it. Eanatum claimed his victory was a result of the gods' favor (see Reading the Past: Royal Inscriptions from Early Mesopotamia).

dynasty A succession of rulers from the same family.

49

Militarism thus became a fundamental element of political power and a driving force behind historical change in Mesopotamia. Many other ancient cultures repeated this pattern, including China and Rome. Each Mesopotamian city-state had an army commanded by its king, who consolidated his power at home and abroad through warfare. Some rulers grew so powerful that they could claim the lives of others for their own benefit. In around 2400 B.C.E., members of the royal house of Ur demanded that human attendants and soldiers accompany them to the afterlife. In a few tombs of the Royal Cemetery of Ur, occupants were surrounded by incredible luxuries, such as golden helmets, daggers, and inlaid musical instruments—and by the bodies of dozens of sacrificed men and women. Other rulers took their special connections to the divine world to a different extreme, professing to be gods themselves. Some kings had temples constructed in their own honor. These practices of human sacrifice and divine kingship were short-lived, however, and for most of Mesopotamian history kings were considered mortal representatives of the gods on earth. Nonetheless, these examples of extreme claims to power reflect a general trend toward the concentration of political authority in the hands of a single individual or family.

The political situation became more complex throughout Southwest Asia as a variety of peoples with different cultures and languages developed city-states. People who spoke Sumerian lived primarily in the far south of Mesopotamia. In the rest of the region they spoke mostly Akkadian, a Semitic language related to Hebrew and Arabic, and in Syria and western Iran people communicated in other Semitic and non-Semitic languages. For close to fifteen hundred years, from 3000 to 1600 B.C.E., the city-states of Southwest Asia were regularly in conflict. Some energetic rulers and dynasties gained great fame for conquering large territories. The dynasty of Akkad, the Akkadian-speaking ruler Sargon and his successors, dominated Mesopotamia from about 2350 to 2200 B.C.E. According to later traditions, the conquests of glorious Akkadian warriors reached the edges of the earth. The Sumerian dynasty of Ur was also famous; in the twenty-first century B.C.E. it imposed its rule over all of southern Mesopotamia.

Attempts at unification through conquest culminated in the eighteenth century B.C.E., when Hammurabi (r. 1792–1750 B.C.E.) created a large state around the city of Babylon. He molded southern Mesopotamia into a single political unit, which fundamentally shifted the base of power from the city-state to the territorial state. Although Hammurabi's kingdom soon disintegrated, the territorial state, not the city, would be the most important unit of political power in Southwest Asia during the second half of the second millennium B.C.E.

Sargon's Akkadian State, c. 2300 B.C.E.

The New Order of Society

Social Divisions and Political Centralization

Throughout history urban societies have differed radically from village communities in terms of social structure. Urban societies have a hierarchy of power based on professional specialization, with a small, but powerful elite. In the earliest Mesopotamian cities, as we have seen, priests monopolized political power. After 3000 B.C.E. military leaders, whom we call kings, replaced priests as city leaders. Palace households, including military commanders and administrators, supported the kings.

As in any ancient society, the great majority of people in Mesopotamia spent most of their energy producing food: they farmed, herded, hunted, and fished and often lived in outlying villages. But because they depended on the city's central institutions, its temples and palace, their lives differed from those of their ancestors who never experienced cities. As part of a large social structure, they had both responsibilities and benefits. They had to provide assistance to the state, usually through agricultural labor, but also through participating in building projects and military campaigns. In return, they counted on material support from the state.

A special characteristic of early Mesopotamian society is the ration system. Every man, woman, and child who depended on the central institutions received predetermined amounts of barley, oil, and wool. The amounts depended on one's status and gender. Leaders received larger payments than their supporters, and men received more than women. Despite its inequities, the system offered a safety net for individuals in economic trouble. It also helped widows and orphans who had no family support. Everyone but the old had to work, however, to qualify for these rations. This system of rations thus reflected both Mesopotamian social structure and Mesopotamian religious beliefs, with their emphasis on cycles of offerings and rewards. People worked for the city and, in exchange, the city rewarded them in proportion to their perceived contribution to the general well-being.

Kings came to play a key role in maintaining the health of this exchange society. If the powerful completely ignored the needs of those below them in society, the whole system would collapse. In early Mesopotamia, priests helped to prevent such imbalance by controlling the cycle of exchange, which centered on temples. With the growth of secular power (that is, worldly rather than religious authority), it became part of royal ideology that kings should protect the weak. The earliest written records of royal activities already express this idea. King Uruinimgina (ou-ROU-e-NIM-ge-na) of Lagash, for example, stated that he "promised the god Ningirsu [NEHN-gihr-su] that he would never subjugate the orphan and the widow to the powerful." He also gave examples of how he protected the rights of his subjects:

> When the house of a member of the elite borders on the house of a royal servant, and the member of the elite says to him: "I want to buy it from you," whether he answers: "When you buy it, pay me the price that I want" or "You cannot buy it," the member of the elite cannot hit the royal servant in anger.[2]

The idea that a good king guaranteed justice to his people remained part of Mesopotamian ideology for many centuries. Its most elaborate expression appeared in the laws of Hammurabi of Babylon. Carved on a seven-and-a-half-foot tall stone stele are some three hundred laws, all phrased in the same two-part form: an "if" action followed by consequences. The phrasing of the statements suggests general rules that judges needed to follow in court cases, but they are not abstract statements of principles. In cases of physical injury, for example, several laws describe distinct body parts:

> If a member of the elite blinds the eye of another member of the elite, they shall blind his eye. If he breaks the bone of another member of the elite, they shall break his bone (§§ 196-197).[3]

The concept underlying this system of justice is one of retribution: an eye for an eye, a tooth for a tooth. Hammurabi's law code was more complex than this, however, and penalties were related to the social structure. Only when a victim and a transgressor were of the same social level was the punishment equal. When the victim was of a lower class, a monetary fine was imposed:

Treasure from the Royal Cemetery of Ur

The treasures from the royal cemetery of Ur show the massive wealth of those buried in the tombs as well as the superior craftsmanship of Sumerian artisans. This eighteen-inch-tall ram is standing on its hind legs to eat the leaves of a tree. Its creator used gold leaf for the head and legs, copper for the ears, lapis lazuli for the horns and shoulder fleece, and shells for the body fleece. These precious materials were imported from distant regions. (© The Trustees of The British Museum/Art Resource, NY.)

Laws of Hammurabi

> If a member of the elite hits an elite woman, and causes her to miscarry her fetus, he shall pay 80 grams of silver for her fetus. Should that woman die, they will kill his daughter. If he causes a woman of the commoner class to miscarry her fetus, he shall pay 40 grams of silver. Should that woman die, he shall pay 240 grams of silver. If he hits a slave woman, and causes her to miscarry her fetus, he shall pay 16 grams of silver. Should that slave woman die, he shall pay 160 grams of silver. (§§ 209–214)[4]

If the victim was of a higher status than the transgressor, the punishment was more severe:

> If a member of the elite strikes the cheek of a member of the elite who is of a higher social status than him, he shall be flogged in public with sixty strikes of an ox whip. (§ 202)[5]

Hammurabi's laws and other contemporary sources indicate clearly that Mesopotamian society was a **patriarchy**: women were always subject to a man, at first their father, and then their husband. They moved from the father's house to the husband's upon marriage. A man could even sell his wife into servitude to pay off a debt. Women were somewhat protected, however. The wife's dowry was her own and could not be taken away upon divorce. A man could marry several women, but the woman's wealth went to her natural children alone. When a soldier went missing during a military campaign, his wife could remarry if she was unable to support herself. Some Babylonian women had considerable property that they could manage without the interference of their fathers or husbands. While their status was certainly below that of men, they had more rights and protection than women in many other ancient societies.

When Hammurabi set up his stele, he wanted to express how just his rule was. He stated its purpose as follows:

> In order that the mighty not wrong the weak, to provide just ways for the orphan and the widow, I have inscribed my precious pronouncements upon my stele and set it up before the statue of me, the king of justice, in the city of Babylon, the city which the gods Anu and Enlil have elevated, within the Esagila, the temple whose foundations are fixed as are heaven and earth, in order to render the judgments of the land, to give verdicts of the land, and to provide just ways for the wronged.[6]

Although protecting the weak was a central part of the ideology of power in Hammurabi's Babylon, that does not mean it was a society of equals. As we have seen, Babylonian law recognized and codified great inequalities rooted in gender and social status. When the number of people living together increased, social inequalities increased, and the new urban society that developed in Mesopotamia had a clear social hierarchy.

City Life and Learning

The rise of cities also fundamentally changed how humanity expressed itself intellectually. The invention of writing—the ability to express thoughts in a permanent form—was an enduring contribution of the first citizens of Mesopotamia. Because writing and reading required a group of well-trained specialists, it remained an urban phenomenon for all of Mesopotamian history. These specialists were relatively few in number, but they left us innumerable rich examples of the literature and scholarship of the time.

Hammurabi's Stele

This tall stone pillar is one of several that Hammurabi set up throughout his kingdom to proclaim his famous laws. The top of the monument shows the king receiving symbols of justice from the seated sun god. More striking is the lengthy, carefully carved inscription, which lists some three hundred laws and presents Hammurabi as a just ruler who protects the people of his land. (Réunion des Musées Nationaux/Art Resource, NY.)

FOCUS

Why did ancient peoples develop writing systems, and what has been the enduring impact of this invention on intellectual expression?

The Invention of Writing

Why Writing Arose

Probably the most famous writings from ancient Mesopotamia today are the Laws of Hammurabi we just discussed, or tales such as the *Epic of Gilgamesh* (see page 55), but script was not invented to write down those types of texts. The need for writing derived from the urban economy, which had become increasingly complex and required a system of record keeping. Administrators had to keep track of income and expenditures, and they needed a means of reviewing transactions that involved large quantities of goods. To address this need, an anonymous group (or perhaps even an individual) in Sumer developed a revolutionary invention: writing. Writing requires a connection between spoken language and the symbols written down. It enables someone who was not present to reconstruct events from the written account alone. The challenge to its inventors was to represent oral expression in graphic form.

Cuneiform Script

The Sumerian epic tale about the origins of writing at the beginning of this chapter does not address this challenge of translating spoken words into written symbols. It merely explains in mythic terms the physical characteristics of writing: the clay tablet into which cuneiform signs were pressed. Clay tablets did indeed appear with the emergence of the first city, Uruk, around 3200 B.C.E. They were pillow-shaped objects a person could hold in one hand. Scribes traced two types of signs with a reed stylus on them: numbers and word-signs.

The earliest scribes were mainly accountants, and it is no surprise that numbers were the most common characters on the first tablets. The tablets demonstrate that the Sumerians knew how to work with very large numbers and that they had a fully developed system of weights and measures. They counted, weighed, and indicated the values of a great variety of items, registering the names with a set of signs understood by everyone who handled the records. In the earliest stage of writing, each word was represented with one sign. It could be a graphic representation of the entire item, such as a drawing of a fish for the word *fish*, or of an emblematic part, such as the head of an ox for the word *ox*. The sign could also be purely abstract, such as a circle with a cross for *a sheep*. It was also crucial that written records express actions. For this purpose, the writers logically extended the meaning of items that they could draw. For example, the foot could communicate the verb *to go*. Sometimes they used similarities in sounds to make the drawing of an object represent an action. A word pronounced *ti* meant both *arrow* and *to receive* in Sumerian. Scribes thus could use the arrow sign to indicate the action of receiving.

The inventors of the script used these techniques to develop an inventory of signs that reproduced the Sumerian language they spoke. The earliest version of the script had some 950 signs and was difficult to use because each sign represented a separate word. In succeeding centuries, the script changed to make it easier to use and more adaptable to the spoken language. The signs developed from elaborate drawings to a handful of straight lines made by pushing a small piece of reed into the clay. The use of reeds created the impression of a wedge, a triangular head joined to a thin line, which inspired the modern name of the script, *cuneiform*, wedge-shaped (see Figure 2.1).

Soon the scribes invented signs that represented not only entire words but the sounds of syllables. This allowed them to reduce the number of signs in the script, because a limited number of syllable signs could be used to form many words; each word no longer required a distinct sign. A further benefit of the increased flexibility of script was that scribes could write down languages other than Sumerian. Throughout the long history of cuneiform, people used it to record many languages, not only in Mesopotamia but in neighboring regions. The cuneiform script was undoubtedly one of Sumer's most influential cultural exports, and it dominated written culture in Southwest Asia for some three thousand years.

After the Sumerians invented script in around 3200 B.C.E. other cultures independently came up with different writing systems: the Egyptians in around 3000 B.C.E., the Chinese after 2000 B.C.E., the Zapotecs (sah-po-TEHK) after 400 B.C.E., and many others

patriarchy A social system in which men hold all authority within the family and transfer their powers and possessions from father to son.

FIGURE 2.1

Cuneiform Writing

The earliest known form of writing originated in Sumer around 3200 B.C.E., when people began linking meaning and sound to signs such as these. Cuneiform was used for numerous ancient Middle Eastern languages and continued to be written for three thousand years.

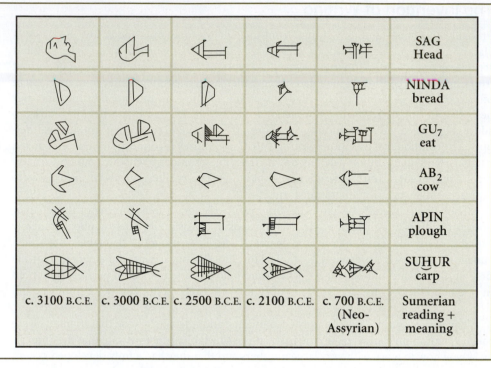

c. 3100 B.C.E.	c. 3000 B.C.E.	c. 2500 B.C.E.	c. 2100 B.C.E.	c. 700 B.C.E. (Neo-Assyrian)	Sumerian reading + meaning
					SAG Head
					NINDA bread
					GU$_7$ eat
					AB$_2$ cow
					APIN plough
					SUHUR carp

throughout history. Often they started out with very pictorial systems that became more schematic over time. Scholars in each case debate what motivated people to invent writing. Some say the Egyptians intended to honor their kings and the Chinese were primarily concerned with oracles, for example, but the economic needs that arose with the birth of urban societies seem to have been the main inspiration in most cases. Whatever the motivation for its invention, writing vastly increased the power of communication in the societies that possessed it. Written documents allowed ideas and information to be preserved and disseminated in ways that were previously impossible. Further, they created a community of readers who shared a familiarity with common texts, texts written by authors of both their generation and generations before. In this way, written documents created connections that were crucial to the expansion of knowledge.

INVENTION OF WRITING SYSTEMS

c. 3200 B.C.E.	Mesopotamian cuneiform
c. 3000 B.C.E.	Egyptian hieroglyphs
c. 2600 B.C.E.	Indus Valley script
c. 2000–1200 B.C.E.	Chinese writing
c. 1850 B.C.E.	Cretan Linear A
c. 1800 B.C.E.	Earliest alphabetic script, western Syria
c. 400 B.C.E.	Mesoamerican glyphs

The Expansion of Knowledge

First Literature

Although scribes originally wrote for the practical purpose of administering the complex economies of urban societies, they soon extended writing into all spheres of life. Kings commissioned inscriptions carved in stone to proudly proclaim their accomplishments as military leaders, builders, and caretakers of their people. Hammurabi's law code is a prime example. They also encouraged the creation of poetry, at first to sing praise to themselves and to the gods and heroes of the past. In the third millennium B.C.E. poetry was almost exclusively written in Sumerian, which people of the time regarded as the language of high culture. Most authors remain unknown because they did not sign their works, but there are a few remarkable exceptions. The earliest known author of world literature is Princess Enheduanna (ehn-hoo-DWAHN-ah), the daughter of King Sargon. In the twenty-fourth century B.C.E. she composed a long plea to the goddess Inanna to reinstate her as high priestess of the city Ur after her father's enemy had deposed her:

> He stood there in triumph and drove me out of the temple. He made me fly like a swallow from the window; I have exhausted my life-strength. He made me walk through the thorn bushes of the mountains. He stripped me of the rightful crown of the *en* priestess. He gave me a knife and a dagger, saying to me: "These are the appropriate ornaments for you."[7]

Inanna accepted her prayer and restored Enheduanna to her former status:

> The powerful lady, respected in the gathering of rulers, has accepted her offerings from her. Inanna's holy heart has been assuaged. The light was sweet for her, delight extended over her, she was full of fairest beauty. Like the light of the rising moon, she exuded delight.[8]

Students, mostly the sons of priests but also some girls, copied out these poems and many others. Archaeologists have found thousands of tablets containing their work, including some that described a typical schoolboy's day. A master and his assistant (who did not spare the cane) closely supervised the student, who copied out increasingly difficult and long texts: lists of cuneiform signs, words, short compositions, and excerpts and finally the full text of literary compositions.

We have a detailed view of the teaching profession from a set of cuneiform tablets dated from 1821 to 1789 B.C.E. that document the activities of Ku-Ningal, a schoolmaster who taught in his house near the main temple in the city Ur. He lived in a neighborhood densely populated with people attached to the temple as priests and administrators. Ku-Ningal's family were the temple archivists for at least three generations. In addition to working as an archivist, Ku-Ningal taught his neighbors' children to write. His house was small, with less than eleven hundred square feet of living space, so he probably offered instruction to only a few students at a time. He was relatively wealthy, however, and documents found in the house reveal that he acquired meadows outside the city and expanded his dwelling slightly by buying parts of his next-door neighbor's house. In his home he kept literary manuscripts, copies of royal inscriptions, mathematical texts, and lists of words students had to reproduce. Ku-Ningal may have had literary talents himself and probably composed a hymn in honor of the king, copies of which were found in his house. Thus, writing was the central activity of Ku-Ningal's profession, a skill he passed on to others, and a means of self-expression.

The early second millennium B.C.E. brought the beginnings of literature written in Akkadian, including compositions that would later become famous. Among them was an early form of the *Epic of Gilgamesh*, which describes the hero's search for immortality. Gilgamesh (GIHL-gah-mehsh) was a king of Uruk—the third successor of Enmerkar of the epic at the start of this chapter—who saw his friend Enkidu die and refused to accept that fate for himself. He traveled to the edge of the world to find the only humans to whom the gods had given immortality: Utnapishtim (UHT-nuh-PISH-teem) and his wife, who had

Mesopotamian Mathematical Tablet
Mesopotamian mathematical knowledge, famous in its day, was highly developed, as tablets used in teaching show. This one, from around 1800 B.C.E., asks the student to find the length and width of a rectangle, given the diagonal and area. Students who graduated became the accountants needed to keep track of Mesopotamia's extensive economic activity. (David Lees/CORBIS.)

survived a universal flood. A woman he met on his travels told Gilgamesh, "When the gods created humankind, they gave death to humans and kept life for themselves."

Gilgamesh's search was ultimately futile because physical immortality cannot be attained. But eternal fame is possible. If one's deeds are recorded, they will be remembered forever, something that writing can assure. In that way, Gilgamesh did succeed.

Mesopotamian Mathematics

Schoolboys also had to study mathematics, and they did so in the same way they learned language, by copying out increasingly complex texts. They started with standard lists of capacity, weight, area, length, division, and multiplication. Then they moved to mathematical problems formulated in words, such as how to determine the height of a pile of grain based on its circumference and shape. Early Mesopotamian mathematics was highly developed and had a lasting impact on world history. Its basis was a mix of the decimal (base-10) and sexagesimal (base-6) systems. The numbers 6, 60, 360, and so on, indicated new units of measure. This convention still influences us today; it is why, for example, 60 minutes make an hour and 360 degrees a full circle.

The First International Order 1600–1200 B.C.E.

FOCUS

What were the main features of the first international order, and what developments explain its rise and fall?

No state exists in isolation. Throughout world history we see many moments when contacts between neighboring states produced similarities in political and social structures. Such was the case from 1600 to 1200 B.C.E. in Southwest Asia and adjacent regions, where an international system of states developed. Although these states had similar social organization and culture and exerted increasing influence on one another, they remained distinct. Their close connections did not end their capacity to produce independent innovations.

From City-States to Territorial States in the Eastern Mediterranean

As we have seen, from the beginning of urbanism in 3200 to 1600 B.C.E., the city-state had been the dominant form of political organization throughout Southwest Asia. After 1600 B.C.E., however, a new political order emerged in the region, one characterized by **territorial states**. Territorial states controlled much larger landmasses and included several dependent cities. The king controlled his territory through a hierarchy of officials, governors, and others, who were personally beholden to him. The fact that kings could, and did, move their capitals from city to city within their realms underscores the political shift that had taken place. The primary focus of political loyalty was now the ruler, not the city.

In the centuries between 1600 and 1200 B.C.E, territorial states existed from western Iran to the Aegean Sea and from the Black Sea to south of Egypt (see Map 2.3). The elites who ruled these states knew they belonged to a collective system and maintained constant contact with one another. The development of their individual states became intertwined and an international system emerged that bound them in a shared history. Yet as we will see, the region was very diverse in every respect, including ecology, economy, political organization, and culture.

The Minoans and the Mycenaeans

On the western edge of this international system was the Bronze Age Aegean world, which historians know primarily from archaeological material. Since about 7000 B.C.E. agricultural societies had populated the Greek mainland and the Aegean islands. For millennia, people from the region had traded materials such as the volcanic stone obsidian, which could be made into cutting tools. Different regions had held on to their own cultural traditions, however, and in the second millennium B.C.E. these traditions coalesced into two main cultures: the Minoan, centered on the island of Crete, and the Mycenaean, which flourished in southern mainland Greece.

territorial state A centralized form of political organization that unites inhabitants of an often large geographical area.

Linear A The administrative writing system of the Minoans, which is still not deciphered.

Minoan Cretan society revolved around palaces, which served as the economic hubs of larger regions. Best known is the palace at Knossos (K-NOSS-oss), a sprawling building centered on a large open court and decorated with colorful wall paintings. Unlike

The Minoan Palace at Knossos

This is the throne room from the palace at Knossos, built in around 1450 B.C.E., and much restored after excavations by Sir Arthur Evans at the start of the twentieth century. It vividly illustrates aspects of Minoan culture. The colorful wall paintings show mystical creatures, griffins, beside an alabaster throne in front of a central fireplace. Scholars debate the function of this room, but all agree it must have been central to palace life at the time. (David Porges/Peter Arnold Images/Photolibrary.)

Mesopotamian palaces, the Knossos building and other Cretan palaces lacked defensive structures, which suggests that warfare played a small role in this society. The palaces did share important qualities with Mesopotamian cities, however. Like those cities, Cretan palaces served as crossroads, places where people collected and exchanged resources such as grain, wine, and oil. The Cretans kept track of the exchanges that took place in the palace with an as-yet-undeciphered writing system called **Linear A**. Although the signs in the Linear A system do not resemble those of Southwest Asia at all, they were traced onto clay tablets in imitation of the cuneiform records. Crete's central location in the northeastern Mediterranean gave it a prominent role in maritime trade, making it a regional crossroads. People of the island shipped goods as far away as Sicily and Egypt.

But its apparent prosperity did not protect Crete from disaster. Although it was spared the endemic warfare that characterized Mesopotamia, Crete fell victim to a natural catastrophe. Around 1650 B.C.E. a volcanic eruption on the island of Santorini (ancient Thera) created a tsunami that may have destroyed most of the palaces on Crete.

On the southern and eastern mainland of Greece a very different tradition developed. People here built fortresses, such as Mycenae (my-SEE-nee) and Tiryns (TIHR-ihnz), constructed with stones so large that later Greeks thought only giants could have built them. Nearby burials contained great riches, including weapons, golden masks, and jewelry. Around 1450 B.C.E., the people of this world, the Mycenaeans, expanded their influence throughout the Aegean Sea, including Crete, where all the palaces except Knossos had disappeared. The regional economic activity of the Mycenaeans was focused on fortresses, from which officials

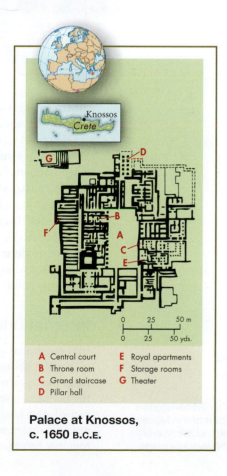

Palace at Knossos, c. 1650 B.C.E.

A Central court	**E** Royal apartments
B Throne room	**F** Storage rooms
C Grand staircase	**G** Theater
D Pillar hall	

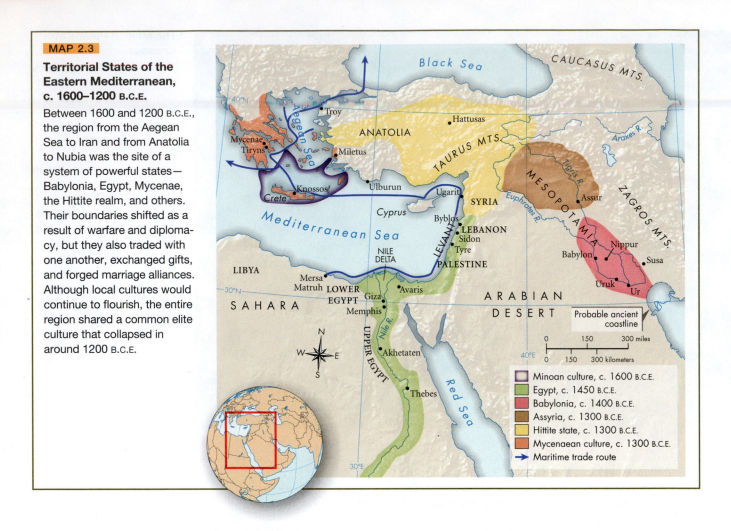

MAP 2.3

Territorial States of the Eastern Mediterranean, c. 1600–1200 B.C.E.

Between 1600 and 1200 B.C.E., the region from the Aegean Sea to Iran and from Anatolia to Nubia was the site of a system of powerful states— Babylonia, Egypt, Mycenae, the Hittite realm, and others. Their boundaries shifted as a result of warfare and diplomacy, but they also traded with one another, exchanged gifts, and forged marriage alliances. Although local cultures would continue to flourish, the entire region shared a common elite culture that collapsed in around 1200 B.C.E.

Map legend:
- Minoan culture, c. 1600 B.C.E.
- Egypt, c. 1450 B.C.E.
- Babylonia, c. 1400 B.C.E.
- Assyria, c. 1300 B.C.E.
- Hittite state, c. 1300 B.C.E.
- Mycenaean culture, c. 1300 B.C.E.
- Maritime trade route

controlled agriculture and craft production. Scribes recorded activities on clay tablets incised with a script that scholars call **Linear B**.

Linear B tablets do not reveal much about the social and political organization of this area, but they do mention a number of political and military titles, including one, *wanax*, that historians interpret as "ruler." The fortresses probably housed military leaders and their entourages, and Mycenae probably had several coexisting rulers. It seems likely, too, that rulers joined in alliances and accepted one man among them as overlord. The famous Greek poet Homer portrayed this world in the epics he wrote in the eighth century B.C.E. (see Chapter 5). His *Iliad* tells how Greeks joined forces to attack Troy, a city on the west coast of modern Turkey, under the leadership of Agamemnon. Although Homer certainly interpreted what were even in his time events from a distant past, his depiction may reflect the actual political situation in the Mycenaean world.

International Relations

In the regional system of the eastern Mediterranean, state relations ranged from peaceful to hostile. Because power in all of these states was based on military achievement, campaigning was a normal part of every king's career. Scholars could write the entire history of the period as a sequence of battles and conquests, because these are the focus of the ancient record. But kings, courtiers, and others had peaceful international contacts as well. The region's states were connected by competition and conflict, but they were also bound together by important diplomatic and economic ties.

Linear B The administrative writing system of the Mycenaeans, used to record an early form of the Greek language.

In around 1600 B.C.E., the introduction of the horse-drawn chariot fundamentally changed warfare in Southwest Asia. Previously, chariots had been heavy and slow, pulled by oxen and donkeys, but the use of fast, light vehicles allowed warriors to move rapidly over the battlefield. The equipment was expensive, however, and charioteers needed special training. The mass of the armies consisted largely of infantrymen, mostly farmers and others who performed military service for their states. Official inscriptions report on numerous battles and regularly boast about how many opponents were killed and captured. They glorify the king's success in war, but historians should remember that warfare caused misery for many. The official inscriptions and new nature of warfare both reflect the increasingly hierarchical nature of militarized Southwest Asia.

At the same time, however, diplomatic activity thrived. Kings exchanged letters, which scribes all over Southwest Asia wrote in Mesopotamian cuneiform on clay tablets. The letters show that the kings traded valuables to reinforce friendly relations based on mutual respect. The Egyptians mostly offered gold, on which they had a monopoly. In return, they received expensive items from other countries, such as copper from Cyprus or lapis lazuli that the Babylonians imported from Afghanistan. They also exchanged women, and many princesses married foreign kings. The Egyptians did not reciprocate in this respect, however. They loved to receive princesses from abroad but never gave one of their own in return. This angered other kings, who complained bitterly about it in writing.

Women of the courts, especially queens, were also in contact with one another during this era. We know of several letters that Egypt's Queen Nefertari (nehf-uhr-TAHR-ee) wrote Queen Puduhepa (Poo-doo-KHE-pa) in the thirteenth century B.C.E. Puduhepa was queen of the Hittite state that dominated modern-day central Turkey and northern Syria. Both writers were powerful women, and it is no surprise that they conducted their own diplomacy. They called each other "sister" to indicate their equal status, as if they were all part of the same large family.

> Thus speaks Nefertari, the great queen of Egypt, to Puduhepa, the great queen of the Hittites: My sister, I am well and my country is well. May you, my sister, be well and may your country be well. I have heard that you, my sister, have written to me to inquire about my well-being and that you write to me because of the peaceful relations and the good brotherhood that exists between the great king, king of Egypt, and the great king, king of the land of the Hittites, his brother.
>
> The sun god and the storm god will raise your head and the sun god will let goodness flourish and he will preserve the brotherhood between the great king, king of Egypt, and the great king, king of the Hittites, his brother. I am in peace and in brotherhood with you, my sister. Now I send you a present for well-wishing to my sister, and you, my sister, should know about the present I send to you with the royal messenger: 1 multicolored necklace of good gold made up of 12 strings and weighing 801 grams; 1 multicolored linen garment from the city Byssos; 1 multicolored linen tunic from the city Byssos; 5 multicolored linen garments with good thin weave, 5 multicolored linen tunics with good thin weave, a total of 12 linen textiles.[9]

This letter exemplifies how the elites of eastern Mediterranean societies saw themselves as equals with a shared culture and ideology. Both queens communicated in Akkadian, a language neither of them spoke, and appreciated luxuries that often could only be obtained in foreign countries.

Alongside court exchanges, a lively trade in luxury goods connected the societies of the eastern Mediterranean. From the Aegean, for example, people from Egypt and Syria imported wine and olive oil in typical Mycenaean jars. Seafaring merchants conducted much of this trade, and some shipwrecks reveal what they carried. A prime example is a ship found on the south coast of Anatolia (modern Turkey) at Uluburun, dating to around 1300 B.C.E (see again Map 2.3). The array of goods the ship carried was so diverse that it is impossible to identify its origin. The main load consisted of ten tons of copper and one ton of tin. The merchants probably picked up these metals in Cyprus and southern Anatolia, intending to exchange them for other goods in various harbors along the route. The ship contained tropical African ebony logs, obtained in Egypt, and cedar logs from Lebanon. The cargo's ivory tusks came from Egypt, and marine snail shells, prized for the dye they contained, were a special product of Syria. The ship also carried manufactured goods, such as Syrian jewelry, Cypriot pottery, and beads of gold, agate, and colored glass, each type from a different source. There was even a jeweler's hoard on board, with scraps of gold and silver and an amulet with the name of the Egyptian queen Nefertiti. The cargo was truly cosmopolitan in origin and reflected the desire for luxury items of elites throughout the region.

Influence of Mesopotamian Culture

The frequent contacts and shared interests extended to culture and art as well. Although each state had its own traditions, often many centuries old, the elites imported the literate culture of Mesopotamia. Earlier, cuneiform script had spread throughout Southwest Asia, inspiring writing in other languages. But now international correspondence was written in Akkadian, even if it involved two states where the language was not native, as we saw in the queens' correspondence. Palaces all over the region employed scribes who could read and write Akkadian. Their libraries contained works of Mesopotamian literature, sometimes adapted to local tastes. In the Hittite capital, for example, the *Epic of Gilgamesh* was read in both a Mesopotamian version and an abbreviated translation in the local Hittite language. Even in Egypt, which had an ancient and very distinct literate culture, some literature was written in Akkadian.

Alphabetic Script

The spread of Mesopotamian culture did not destroy local traditions; rather, a multiplicity of languages, scripts, and literatures flourished. In western Syria a new type of script had developed in around 1800 B.C.E., and its use expanded at this time. The writing was **alphabetic**. Instead of using signs to indicate entire words or syllables, a sign represented each consonant of the language. Vowels were not indicated. This type of writing required fewer than thirty characters. Various alphabetic scripts coexisted, but the system that survived into later periods had a set of characters whose pronunciation was based on a simple principle: each character was a drawing of an item, and the first sound of that item's name gave the character its pronunciation. For example, a drawing of a house represented the sound /b/, the first sound in the Semitic word for house, *baytu*. We know only a handful of such alphabetic inscriptions from the second millennium B.C.E., but this system of writing would spread enormously in the first millennium B.C.E. It is the basis of alphabetic scripts in use today all over the world.

Kings and Commoners: An Unequal System

The flourishing local traditions of the eastern Mediterranean were matched by strong interconnections throughout the region. The rulers knew that they were joined together in a system. The heads of the leading states were like members of a club whose membership was restricted to "Great Kings," the term they used to refer to one another. Always included in this elite group were the kings of Babylonia, the Hittite state, and Egypt. Other rulers joined when resources and fortune enabled them to do so. In around 1350 B.C.E., for example, the king of the Mediterranean island of Cyprus was included on the basis of his control of copper mines.

Growing Social Inequality

Throughout this world there was a similar social structure, one with greater inequality than in the past. The leading elites accumulated enormous wealth, whereas the general population lived in poverty. This social disparity was reflected in the contents of elite tombs. Treasures such as those of King Tutankhamun (tuht-uhnk-AH-muhn) in Egypt (r. 1333–1323 B.C.E.) show the amazing wealth reserved for a tiny ruling class. During their lifetimes, too, the elites basked in luxury, which they enjoyed in palaces in secluded walled sections of their cities. Kings often ordered their subjects to build entirely new, and often gigantic, cities for themselves and their entourages. Removed from the masses of the lower classes, they restricted their company to the palace household. Thus, just as kings emphasized

alphabetic A type of writing with a limited number of characters, each one representing a single sound.

King Tutankhamun's Mask

The contents of the tomb of the king Tutankhamun are a prime example of the vast wealth of Egyptian pharaohs. This mask is one of several found among thousands of objects of gold, silver, and other precious materials. It was made of gold and inlaid with lapis lazuli, quartzite, and colored glass. The combination of materials gives the king's face a vivid, colorful allure. (François Guenet/Art Resource, NY.)

their membership in an exclusive elite in their diplomatic relations with other kings, they built walls around themselves in their day-to-day lives to underscore the vast distance between the powerful and the powerless.

The rulers' lavish lifestyles were funded, in part, by the spoils of military conquest. Egyptians, for example, mined large amounts of gold in Nubia, which they conquered in the sixteenth century B.C.E. Yet it was local populations that bore the brunt of the unequal social system. Primarily farmers, the lower social classes throughout the eastern Mediterranean were compelled to produce surpluses for their urban ruling elites. Although they were not slaves, they were tied to the land and forced to hand over much of their produce. They were not free to leave their land to take up a new life elsewhere—many international agreements between kings stipulated that people fleeing a state should be returned. The kings of this era may have been engaged in almost constant warfare, but they recognized a common interest in maintaining strict control over their subjects, who were the true source of their wealth and power.

Western Syrian Cities at the End of the Bronze Age, c. 1200 B.C.E.

The inequality that characterized the international system may have been the primary cause of its collapse, in around 1200 B.C.E. The success of the system had relied on collaboration and sustained contacts among the various states, even if those interactions involved warfare. After 1200 B.C.E. individual states gradually failed to sustain their social and political systems, and they grew increasingly isolated from one another. Historians have difficulties determining what happened, but revolts from the lower classes seem to have initiated the process. Documentation from Egypt attests to the earliest workers' strikes on record in world history.

Increasing numbers of people seem to have left their villages, fleeing the control of urban elites. These uprisings prompted outsiders from the northern shores of the Mediterranean to immigrate to the unstable kingdoms. Their attacks on coastal cities made sea travel unsafe and unraveled the connections among the various states. Reports of these attacks speak of "Sea Peoples," migrants who forced their way into the rich areas of the eastern Mediterranean. The chaos that ensued changed life fundamentally all over this region. Archaeology shows that several cities disappeared forever. People of the Aegean abandoned their Mycenaean fortresses, and the Hittite state disintegrated. Many cities along the Syrian coast were destroyed, and states such as Egypt and Babylonia lost influence outside their borders and went into economic decline. The rapid and simultaneous decline of the region's states reflects the vital nature of their close connections. Just as these states rose together, creating a system of diplomatic, military, and economic connections that sustained them all, the disintegration of connections brought with it the collapse of the states themselves.

Not all was lost, however. Several places, such as the harbors of Lebanon, remained relatively unscathed, and they would carry second millennium traditions into the first millennium. But as we will see in Chapter 4, the Southwest Asian world after 1000 B.C.E. was very different from the one that gave rise to the first urban societies.

COUNTERPOINT
Egypt's Distinct Path to Statehood

FOCUS

In what ways did the early history of Egypt contrast with that of the ancient states of Southwest Asia?

In the evolution of societies documented in Southwest Asia, the city played a decisive role. It was the earliest unit of social and political organization, and cities dominated all aspects of life in the region for more than fifteen hundred years. The city-state was a stepping-stone to the formation of larger political units. This was the case in nearly all the regions Mesopotamia was in contact with, with one notable exception: Egypt. Egypt never had city-states. It was a highly centralized territorial state from the very beginning.

Egypt's Geography and Early History

The Nile River   Settled agriculture began in Egypt in around 5400 B.C.E. Egypt's farmers, like their counterparts in Mesopotamia, China, and elsewhere, had to rely on river water to grow their crops, because the region receives almost no rain. They were more fortunate than others, however. Every year the Nile rose at just the time when the crops needed water, turning large areas of land along its banks into rich and extremely fertile fields (see Map 2.4). Egypt was truly the gift of the Nile. By monitoring the height of the annual flood, the Egyptians could determine exactly how much land could be farmed each year. The predictability of Egyptian agriculture gave its people an enormous advantage, freeing them from the constant uncertainty about food supplies that plagued other peoples.

Egypt's territory along the Nile River, seven hundred miles long, comprises two regions, which the ancient Egyptians clearly distinguished. In the northern delta area the Nile separates into numerous branches in a flat countryside. Scholars call this region Lower Egypt because it lies where the river drains into the sea. To the south the river runs through a narrow valley in a clearly demarcated basin, the region called Upper Egypt. Prior to 3000 B.C.E., these visibly distinct geographical zones were not part of a single territorial state or dominated by powerful city-states. Instead, the long country stretching beside the Nile was dotted with villages, whose inhabitants farmed the fertile soil the annual floods created.

Then, quite suddenly in around 3000 B.C.E., a state arose that was very different from the city-states that emerged in Mesopotamia at about the same time. Instead of a small area centered on a city, the earliest state in Egypt incorporated a large territory from the Mediterranean Sea to the northernmost place where rapids interrupt the Nile River, preventing travel by boat. The Egyptians portrayed the emergence of the Egyptian state as the result of a campaign of military conquest. The earliest Egyptian historical document shows the victory of a king of Upper Egypt, Narmer, over his Lower Egyptian counterpart (see Seeing the Past: The Palette of Narmer). The document reflects an ideal that would survive throughout Egyptian history: the king held the two parts of the country together through his military might. Modern historians distinguish two types of periods in the three-thousand-year history of the country: when Upper and Lower Egypt were united, they speak of Kingdoms (Old, Middle, and New), and when political fragmentation existed, they speak of Intermediate Periods (First, Second, and Third).

Egyptian Ideology of Kingship

Cities did arise in Egypt, but unlike those in Mesopotamia, they did not become the center of political life and cultural development. Instead, the king played that role. He guaranteed the success and welfare of the country, and in return the entire population supported him and his entourage. This was true from the very beginning of the Egyptian state. The earliest monumental remains are massive tombs from around 3000 B.C.E. with offerings that show that the persons buried in them, the earliest kings, received grave goods that originated from all over the country. The wealth of these and later tombs show a tremendous concentration of Egypt's economic resources in the ruler's palace.

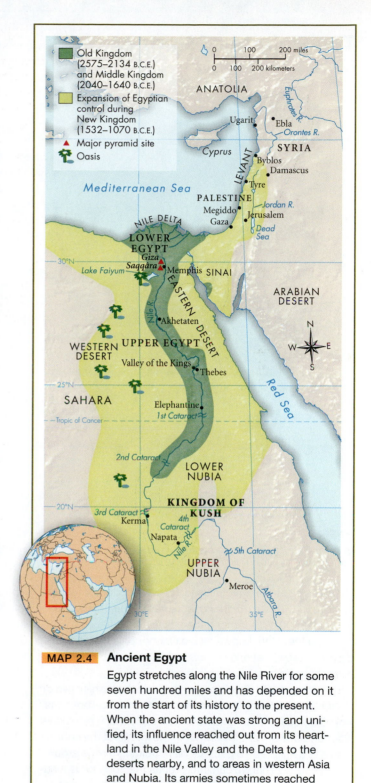

MAP 2.4 **Ancient Egypt**
Egypt stretches along the Nile River for some seven hundred miles and has depended on it from the start of its history to the present. When the ancient state was strong and unified, its influence reached out from its heartland in the Nile Valley and the Delta to the deserts nearby, and to areas in western Asia and Nubia. Its armies sometimes reached places thousands of miles from home.

The Palette of Narmer

Narmer Palette (front and back) (The Art Archive/Egyptian Museum Cairo/Dagli Orti (left) and The Art Archive/Egyptian Museum Cairo/Dagli Orti (right).)

In 1898 C.E., at the Egyptian site of Hierakonpolis, archaeologists excavated a number of sculpted stone objects dating to about 3000 B.C.E. Among them was a thin, flat slab a little over two feet high, known as the Narmer palette, bearing carved representations on both sides, as well as a few hieroglyphic signs.

The front (left) shows a king wearing the high crown of Upper Egypt beating another man with a mace. Above the king is a square that contains two hieroglyphs, which scholars read as "Nar" and "mer." Over the image of the subdued man sits a falcon on a papyrus plant holding a rope around a man's neck. This we can interpret as the god Horus (usually represented as a falcon) handing over the conquered Nile Delta to the king.

On the back of the palette (right), the same king wearing the square crown of Lower Egypt reviews troops holding standards. Beside them are two rows of decapitated bodies with heads at their feet. Two hieroglyphs record the name Narmer both in front of the king's face and on the top of the

palette. In other contemporary images, the same King Narmer appears with a double crown, a combination of the crowns of Upper and Lower Egypt, which in later Egyptian history characterizes the unified country.

EXAMINING THE EVIDENCE

1. How do the hieroglyphic signs and the visual elements of the palette combine to convey a message?

2. What message did Narmer hope to communicate with this palette?

3. How do the images on the palette of Narmer compare with the relief on the Uruk vase (see p. 46)?

Egyptian Women Weaving
Images such as this one from an Egyptian tomb represent an idealized view of daily life, yet they show that weaving was an important activity performed by women. The two weavers depicted here use a horizontal loom. Because the Egyptian artistic convention was to show all the important elements of an object, regardless of perspective, the painter depicted the loom from above, allowing us to see the weavers' tools and techniques. (Image copyright © The Metropolitan Museum of Art/Art Resource, NY.)

The difference between the role of cities in Egypt and in Mesopotamia is reflected in the palaces of the two societies. As in Egypt, the palaces of Mesopotamia were sites where great wealth was concentrated. However, their wealth and prominence came from their connection to the cities in which they were located. In contrast, the palaces of Egyptian rulers gained prominence through their connection to the king. This linkage of the palace with the king led the Egyptians to use the term for palace, *per-o*, for the title of king—hence our use today of the term **pharaoh** to refer to the ancient Egyptian king.

The Egyptians' ideology of kingship was closely tied to their religious ideas. Like the Mesopotamians, they honored a large number of gods, many of whom represented aspects of the universe. For example, Geb was the earth, Nut the sky, and Re the sun. The Mesopotamian gods had human forms, but the Egyptians visualized many gods as wholly or partly animal. The goddess Hathor was a cow or woman with a cow's head, the god Horus a falcon or falcon-headed man, and so on. Why this was the case we do not know, but many animals became objects of cults.

The king fit into this system, in that he was considered the earthly embodiment of the god Horus, who in mythology had inherited the throne from his father Osiris. To the Egyptians, history was the sequence of kings, each of whom was related to his predecessor just as Horus had been related to Osiris. The Egyptian king was not a god, nor was he a simple human; his status was somewhere in between. As such, he served as a connection between his people and the divine.

The majority of the Egyptian population seems to have accepted this system without much difficulty. Food and other resources were plentiful along the Nile, and they saw the king as a source of stability and peace who would help preserve their fortunate circumstances. In return for his safeguarding the country, they contributed their labor to the great monuments that today remain the greatest testimonies of Egypt's past. They built the

Gods and Kings

pharaoh The ancient Egyptians' title for their king.

The Pyramid Builders of the Pharaohs

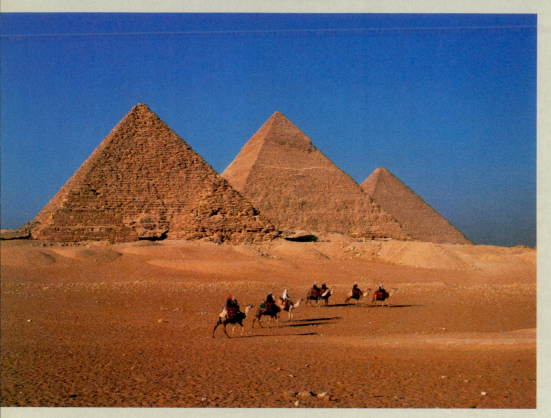

The Pyramids at Giza

To build the Giza pyramids the ancient Egyptians transported, carved, and set into place massive amounts of stone, using tools that were themselves made of stone or of the soft metal bronze. Archaeologists wonder how they managed to accomplish this work in less than a century. It is no surprise that the greatest of the three pyramids—the tomb of King Khufu—was considered one of the wonders of the ancient world. (Fuste Raga/Corbis.)

The three pyramids of Giza on the outskirts of modern Cairo are among the most awe-inspiring monuments of early world history. Archaeologists estimate that the largest of the three, the tomb of King Khufu, contained 2,300,000 blocks of stone with an average weight of $2\frac{3}{4}$ tons, some weighing up to 16 tons. Khufu ruled for twenty-three years, which meant that throughout his reign 100,000 blocks had to be quarried, transported, trimmed and finished, and put in place every year. That comes to about 285 blocks a day, or one for every two minutes of daylight.

The pyramids themselves are just one part of a much larger burial complex that included temples for offerings to the dead king, a ramp to transport the body to the pyramid, secondary burials for queens and others, and statuary. The latter could be as monumental as the Great Sphinx of Giza, the largest monolith (made from a single large block of stone) sculpture in the world.

pyramids and temples tourists see everywhere when they visit the country (see Lives and Livelihoods: The Pyramid Builders of the Pharaohs).

Most Egyptians lived in simple circumstances in villages. They farmed plots of land, which often belonged to the palace or a temple, and they paid part of their harvests as a rental fee. The Nile provided them with fish, and they hunted small animals and caught birds for food as well. Unlike in Southwest Asia, where people made their clothes from the wool of sheep they raised, Egyptians wore mostly linen textiles, which they made from the flax plant that grew throughout the country. Artistic representations show women weaving the cloth. As in Mesopotamia, weaving was an important domestic task in Egypt.

The New Culture of Statehood

Hieroglyphic Script   With the creation of the Egyptian state, new elements of culture appeared around the person of the king. These included monumental buildings, especially temples and tombs, as

Because the logistical requirements for these gigantic projects were daunting, the question of manpower is especially intriguing. Every district of Egypt had to supply laborers, which meant that some had to travel hundreds of miles. They were probably mostly men, but some women may have worked in auxiliary tasks. Scholars now estimate that about twenty-five thousand workers were active at a time, and they infer from later records of state enterprises that they worked three-month stints. The workers needed housing, food, and tools. They left their families behind and slept in crammed dormitories, each laborer being assigned a narrow space. They received rations of bread and beer, which were prepared on a massive scale in kitchens. Archaeologists have found some of the kilns used for baking, and also remains of workshops where tools were manufactured and repaired. Metal tools were mostly made of copper, which is soft, and they must have been sharpened very regularly.

Although no ancient Egyptian description exists of how the pyramids were built, the massive stones could only have been moved into place by dragging them on ramps constructed from wooden beams, stone rubble, and mud. The Giza plateau has little open space, so the architects must have laid out the ramps in circles around the pyramid base. They had to construct new ramps for every pyramid, and space must have become increasingly cramped as temples and secondary tombs surrounded earlier pyramids. We can imagine that workers suffered injuries and even died on the job, but no evidence of that has survived.

The labor must have been grueling, considering the weight of the stones and the height of the pyramids, let alone the heat and other conditions. The workers participated willingly, however, and were not slaves, foreign or Egyptian. We know that it would have been impossible to force them. They used axes, chisels, and other tools that were not much different from the weapons of the time. If workers had wanted to rebel, they could easily have overwhelmed whoever was in charge.

The willingness of Egyptians to participate in this massive enterprise tells us much about the king's position in society. The inhabitants of the entire country regarded him with so much respect that they willingly undertook these tasks. The projects required many years of work, and people had to forsake other responsibilities to work on them. After finishing their stint of pyramid building, these workers would resume their livelihoods as farmers, fishermen, or some other occupation, but with the memory of having contributed to the glory of their king.

QUESTIONS TO CONSIDER

1. How do scholars estimate the number of people involved in constructing Khufu's pyramid?

2. What were the logistical problems of the project?

3. Where did the workers come from, and how were they convinced to participate?

For Further Information:
For general information on Egyptian pyramids: Pyramids. http://www.pbs.org/wgbh/nova/pyramid/excavation.
Lehner, Mark. *The Complete Pyramids*. London: Thames & Hudson, 1997.

well as specialized craft products and writing. The Egyptians developed their own script, which we call **hieroglyphics**. The signs were distinct in form from those of Mesopotamian cuneiform, but they shared the same principles in how they rendered words. Hieroglyphic signs were pictorial and were painted on papyrus and pottery or carved in stone. Their meaning derived from accepted convention, and although scholars have identified over six thousand signs, in any period fewer than a thousand were in use. The script stayed in use from about 3000 B.C.E. to 400 C.E. and never lost its basic characteristics (see Figure 2.2). However, because hieroglyphs were very elaborate and cumbersome to write, over time the Egyptians developed derivative scripts.

As in Mesopotamia, the first writings Egyptians produced were limited to business transactions and short inscriptions celebrating the deeds of kings. Then people started to write down compositions, such as hymns and prayers to the gods. In around 2000 B.C.E. creativity flourished as authors composed the tales considered classics of Egyptian literature for centuries afterward. In their literature the Egyptians recorded their

hieroglyphics The writing system of ancient Egypt, which used detailed pictorial symbols to indicate words and syllables.

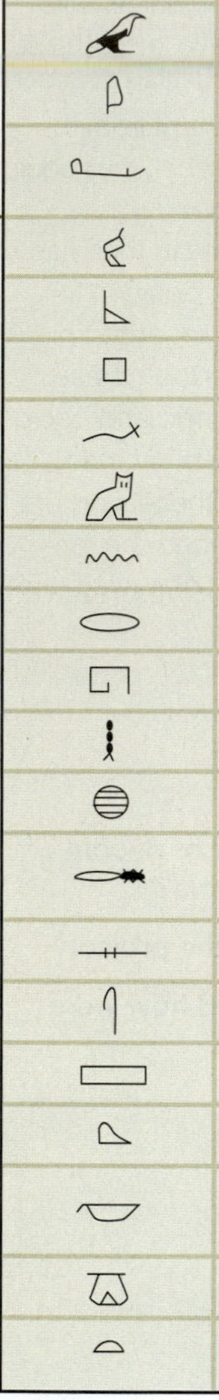

Hieroglyph	Meaning
	vulture
	flowering reed
	forearm and hand
	quail chick
	foot
	stool
	horned viper
	owl
	water
	mouth
	reed shelter
	twisted flax
	placenta (?)
	animal's belly
	door bolt
	folded cloth
	pool
	hill
	basket with handle
	jar stand
	loaf

FIGURE 2.2

Egyptian Hieroglyphs

Ancient Egyptians used pictures such as these to create their own system of writing around 3000 B.C.E. Because Egyptians used this formal script mainly for religious inscriptions, Greeks referred to it as *hieroglyphica* ("sacred carved letters"). Eventually Egyptians also developed the handwritten cursive script called demotic (Greek for "of the people"), a much simpler and quicker form of writing.

thoughts on the subjects most important to them, giving historians insight into their values, priorities, and beliefs. Among the most notable early Egyptian compositions are texts on death and burial.

The Egyptians viewed death not as an end, but as the beginning of a new existence that resembled life in many respects, one that required material goods such as food if the dead were to thrive. Thus, a tomb was more than a depository for the body—it also contained a chapel where surviving family members offered food to the dead. Unlike in Southwest Asia, where tombs were often placed beneath houses, in Egypt they were located apart from settlements in the desert. Egyptians expected to use their bodies after death, so they had to be preserved intact. To achieve this goal, the Egyptians developed mummification. They removed all perishable parts (lungs, intestines, etc.) and treated the other remains in such a way that they maintained their shape. Then they wrapped the bodies in linen and deposited them in coffins to protect them against possible damage. The dryness of the desert aided in preservation as well.

From the start of Egyptian history kings had enormous tombs, a practice that culminated in the great pyramids of Giza, built between 2550 and 2500 B.C.E. (see again Lives and Livelihoods: The Pyramid Builders of the Pharaohs). The masses of stone eloquently demonstrate how much energy the Egyptians would expend to guarantee the king a safe and impressive burial. Common people had the same hopes; they too wanted to be buried safely and to receive gifts into eternity. Royal cemeteries such as the one at Giza reflect the distinct nature of the early Egyptian state. The royal pyramids lie in the center, massive in size and bordered by temples for the cults of the dead kings. Numerous tombs of officials and others surround them. Just as the king was the center of power in life, it was desirable to be near him in death. Even many centuries later common people dug simple tombs near the old royal ones, hoping to benefit from the king's presence.

Although Egypt became part of the international system in the eastern Mediterranean after 1600 B.C.E., its earlier history contrasted notably with that of its neighbors. The king of Egypt was the center of power over the entire territorial state, which he personally held together. The strong unity of Egypt's territorial state led it to become the earliest empire in this part of the world, which we will discuss in Chapter 4.

Conclusion

After the rise of agriculture, the historical development of the world's peoples continued to unfold in Southwest Asia and North Africa, where the Eurasian and African continents meet. We have focused in this chapter on Mesopotamia and Egypt, which rapidly developed socially and economically complex cultures that left behind many remains for historians to study. Their invention of writing, which the mythical tale at the start of the chapter portrayed as a simple act to aid a messenger, had a fundamental impact on our understanding of people's lives in that era. These are the first cultures in history we can study at least in a limited way through the written expressions of the people themselves. We see a clear difference between these two regions: in Mesopotamia (and many other ancient cultures) the city was crucial to political life; in Egypt, it was the king.

After hundreds of years of separate developments, from about 3200 to 1600 B.C.E. the countries of Mesopotamia and Egypt united with others in the eastern Mediterranean region to form a much larger system of exchange in diplomacy, trade, and culture. From 1600 to 1200 B.C.E. states simultaneously competed and joined in a network of interdependence. Their fortunes were intertwined, and in around 1200 B.C.E. they all suffered decline. In the new world that would develop after 1000 B.C.E., the balance of power that undergirded the first international system no longer existed. The inhabitants of Southwest Asia and North Africa were the first in world history to develop the elements of culture we studied in this chapter, but soon afterward peoples elsewhere in Asia also did so. We will turn to these peoples living farther east in the next chapter.

NOTES

1. H. L. J. Vanstiphout, ed. *Epics of Sumerian Kings: The Matter of Aratta* (Atlanta, Ga.: Society of Biblical Literature, 2004), 85.
2. J. S. Cooper, *Sumerian and Akkadian Royal Inscriptions* I (New Haven: American Oriental Society, 1986), 72.
3. Martha T. Roth, *Law Collections from Mesopotamia and Asia Minor* (Atlanta, Ga.: Society of Biblical Literature, 1997), 121.
4. Ibid., 122–123.
5. Ibid., 121.
6. Ibid., 133–134.
7. J. A. Black, et al. *The Literature of Ancient Sumer* (Oxford: Oxford University Press, 2004), 319.
8. Ibid., 320.
9. Translated from Edel, E. *Die ägyptisch-hethitische Korrespondenz aus Boghazkoy.* 1994, 40–41.

RESOURCES FOR RESEARCH

Origins of Urban Society: Mesopotamia, 5000–3200 B.C.E.

Early developments in Mesopotamia interest historians, archaeologists, and anthropologists because Mesopotamia provides the first case in world history of the rise of a city-state. They are often studied using a long-term perspective. Pollock's book devotes special attention to issues of the economy and gender.

Nissen, Hans. *The Early History of the Ancient Near East 9000–2000 B.C.* Translated by E. Lutzeier and K. Northcutt. 1988.

Oates, David, and Joan Oates. *The Rise of Civilization.* 1976.

Pollock, Susan. *Ancient Mesopotamia: The Eden that Never Was.* 1999.

Roaf, Michael. *Cultural Atlas of Mesopotamia and the Ancient Near East.* 1990.

Wenke, Robert J., and Deborah I. Olszewski. *Patterns in Prehistory: Humankind's First Three Million Years,* 5th ed. 2006.

The First Cities, 3200–1600 B.C.E.

The origins of cities and the fundamental effects of urbanization on human society also attract the interest of scholars with varied approaches. Several of the books listed for the previous section are relevant as well to the early history of Southwest Asia.

Chadwick, Robert. *First Civilizations: Ancient Mesopotamia and Ancient Egypt,* 2d ed. 2005.

Liverani, Mario. *Uruk: The First City.* Translated by Z. Bahrani and M. Van De Mieroop. 2006.

Postgate, J. N. *Early Mesopotamia: Society and Economy at the Dawn of History.* 1992.

*Roth, Martha T. *Law Collections from Mesopotamia and Asia Minor,* 2d ed. 1997.

Van De Mieroop, Marc. *A History of the Ancient Near East ca. 3000–323 B.C.* Rev. ed. 2007.

City Life and Learning

The literature of early Mesopotamia, in both Sumerian and Akkadian, presents many challenges for the translator. A few famous works, especially the *Epic of Gilgamesh*, have been translated repeatedly in recent years, each version reflecting a somewhat different approach.

Black, Jeremy, and Anthony Green. *Gods, Demons and Symbols of Ancient Mesopotamia*. 1992.

*Cuneiform Digital Library Initiative. http://www.cdli.ucla.edu/.

*Dalley, Stephanie. *Myths of Mesopotamia: Creation, The Flood, Gilgamesh, and Others*. 1991.

The Electronic Text Corpus of Sumerian Literature. http://etcsl .orient.ox.ac.uk/.

*George, Andrew. *The Epic of Gilgamesh*. 2000.

Van De Mieroop, Marc. *The Ancient Mesopotamian City*. 1999.

*Vanstiphout, H. L. J. *Epics of Sumerian Kings: The Matter of Aratta*. 2004.

The First International Order, 1600–1200 B.C.E.

Many cultures of the international system in the eastern Mediterranean have received detailed attention, and their diplomatic and trade relations are a favorite topic of study. Studies of the demise of the system often focus on the Sea Peoples.

Aruz, Joan, ed. *Beyond Babylon: Art, Trade, and Diplomacy in the Second Millennium B.C.* 2008.

*Beckman, Gary. *Hittite Diplomatic Texts*, 2d ed. 1999.

Bryce, Trevor. *The Kingdom of the Hittites*, rev. ed. 2005.

Institute of Nautical Archaeology. http://ina.tamu.edu/vm.htm

*Moran, William L. *The Amarna Letters*. 1992.

Preziosi, Donald, and Louise A. Hitchcock. *Aegean Art and Architecture*. 1999.

Van De Mieroop, Marc. *The Eastern Mediterranean in the Age of Ramesses II*. 2007.

COUNTERPOINT: Egypt's Distinct Path to Statehood

There are innumerable books and Web sites on Egypt, and many cover the country's archaeological and artistic remains. The selection here focuses on the history and writings of the ancient Egyptians. Kemp's work is especially thought provoking.

Ancient Egyptian sites: http://egyptsites.wordpress.com/.

Baines, John, and Jaromír Málek. *Cultural Atlas of Ancient Egypt*, rev. ed. 2000.

Collier, Mark, and Bill Manley. *How to Read Egyptian Hieroglyphs*. 1998.

Digital Egypt for universities. http://www.digitalegypt.ucl.ac.uk.

Egyptian monuments. http://egyptsites.wordpress.com/

Kemp, Barry J. *Ancient Egypt: Anatomy of a Civilization*, rev. ed. 2006.

*Lichtheim, Miriam. *Ancient Egyptian Literature*, 3 vols. 2006.

Morkot, Robert G. *The Egyptians: An Introduction*. 2005.

Resources on Egypt. http://www.digitalegypt.ucl.ac.uk.

Robins, Gay. *Women in Ancient Egypt*. 1993.

Shaw, Ian. *Ancient Egypt: A Very Short Introduction*. 2004.

Van De Mieroop, Marc. *A History of Ancient Egypt*. 2011.

* Primary source.

▶ **For additional primary sources from this period**, see *Sources of Crossroads and Cultures.*

▶ **For Web sites, images, and documents related to this chapter**, see Make History at bedfordstmartins.com/smith.

REVIEW

The major global development in this chapter ▶ The rise of urban society and the creation of states in Southwest Asia.

IMPORTANT EVENTS

c. 5000 B.C.E.	First permanent settlement in Mesopotamia
c. 3200 B.C.E.	Uruk, the first Mesopotamian city; invention of Mesopotamian cuneiform script
c. 3000 B.C.E.	Creation of the Egyptian state; invention of Egyptian hieroglyphic script
c. 3000–2350 B.C.E.	Competing city-states in Mesopotamia
c. 2550 B.C.E.	Khufu's pyramid at Giza
c. 2350–2200 B.C.E.	Dynasty of King Sargon of Akkad dominates Mesopotamia
c. 1800 B.C.E.	Development of alphabetic script in Syria
c. 1800–1700 B.C.E.	Hammurabi's unification of southern Mesopotamia
c. 1650 B.C.E.	End of the Minoan culture
c. 1600–1200 B.C.E.	First international order in the eastern Mediterranean
c. 1450 B.C.E.	Mycenaean expansion throughout the Aegean

KEY TERMS

alphabetic (p. 60)
city (p. 41)
city-state (p. 41)
cuneiform (p. 39)
dynasty (p. 49)
hieroglyphics (p. 67)
Linear A (p. 56)
Linear B (p. 58)
patriarchy (p. 53)
pharaoh (p. 65)
polytheism (p. 47)
specialization of labor (p. 44)
territorial state (p. 56)

CHAPTER OVERVIEW QUESTIONS

1. What types of political and social organization appeared in the early history of Southwest Asia?
2. What new technologies appeared, and how did they affect people's livelihoods?
3. How do urban societies differ from village societies?
4. How did the early states of Southwest Asia interact with one another?

SECTION FOCUS QUESTIONS

1. How do historians explain the rise of cities?
2. How and why did the rise of the city lead to a more hierarchical society in early Mesopotamia?
3. Why did ancient peoples develop writing systems, and what has been the enduring impact of this invention on intellectual expression?
4. What were the main features of the first international order, and what developments explain its rise and fall?
5. In what ways did the early history of Egypt contrast with that of the ancient states of Southwest Asia?

MAKING CONNECTIONS

1. How did the development of agriculture in Southwest Asia lead to the first urban culture there?
2. What were the roles of cities in political developments in the regions discussed in this chapter?
3. What was the relationship between gods and humans in Mesopotamia and Egypt?
4. What are similarities and differences between Mesopotamian and Egyptian writing systems, and how do they differ from alphabetic writing?

AT A CROSSROADS ▲

The vast expanses of Central Asia opened up when people first domesticated horses around 2000 B.C.E. and could quickly cross large, arid areas. Central Asian horsemen connected the urban cultures at the fringes of Eurasia, and may have introduced technologies such as bronze manufacture into China. This decorated textile, dating to around 500 B.C.E., comes from Pazyryk, on the modern border between Russia and northern China. It depicts a man riding on horseback using a saddle and a bit, tools that revolutionized the use of horses and have not gone out of use since. (The State Hermitage Museum, St. Petersburg, Russia/Bridgeman Art Library.)

Settlers and Migrants: The Creation of States in Asia

5000–500 B.C.E.

A round the year 100 B.C.E., the Chinese historian and astrologer Sima Qian (sih-muh chee-en), in a massive work on the early history of his country, wrote these words about nomadic people living on the fringes of the Chinese state whose emperor he served:

> We hear of these people, known as Mountain Barbarians . . . wandering from place to place pasturing their animals. The animals they raise consist mainly of horses, cows, and sheep, but include such rare beasts as camels, asses, mules, and wild horses. . . . They move about in search of water and pasture and have no walled cities or fixed dwellings, nor do they engage in any kind of agriculture. . . . They have no writing and even promises and agreements are only verbal. . . . All the young men are able to use a bow and act as armed cavalry in times of war. It is their custom to herd their flocks in times of peace and make their living by hunting, but in periods of crisis they take up arms and go off on plundering and marauding expeditions. This seems to be their inborn nature.[1]

This is a stereotypically negative portrayal of nomadic people by an author living in an urban society. His perspective has parallels in writings worldwide and across millennia. Settled people provided almost all the written sources with which the historian works, and

BACKSTORY

In Chapter 1 we saw how humans developed, spread across the globe, and invented agriculture, which enabled them to establish permanent settlements. Societies in various parts of the world evolved differently, often in response to varying environmental challenges and opportunities. But wherever large numbers of people started to live together, they needed institutions and social arrangements to regulate their interactions. The peoples of Southwest Asia and Northeast Africa were the first to form large states, in around 3000 B.C.E. This ultimately led to a complex system of states throughout the region interconnected by diplomatic relations (discussed in Chapter 2). Sometime after the founding of Southwest Asian states, peoples in other parts of Asia also created large political and social entities, each in accordance with their particular circumstances. It is to these early states that we turn in this chapter.

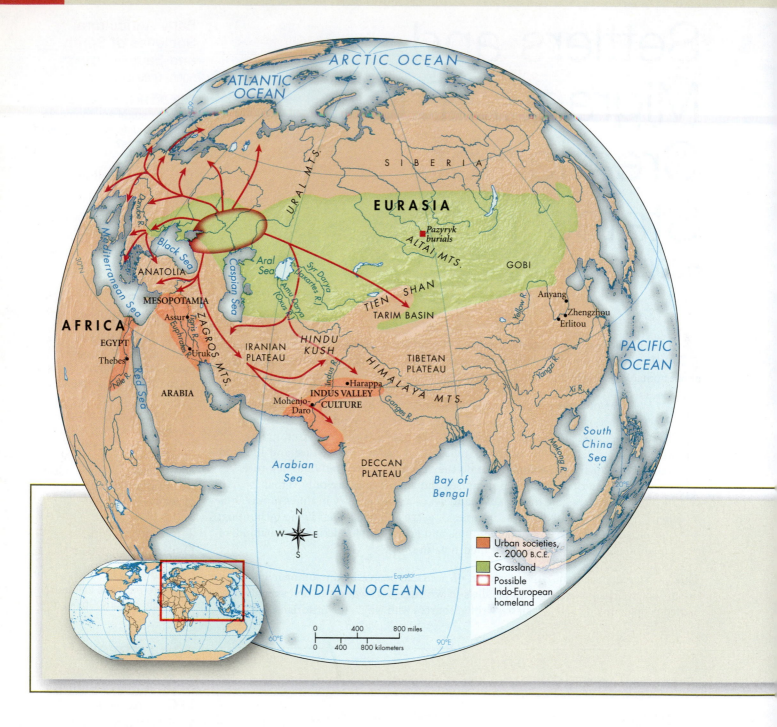

Urban societies, c. 2000 B.C.E.

Grassland

Possible Indo-European homeland

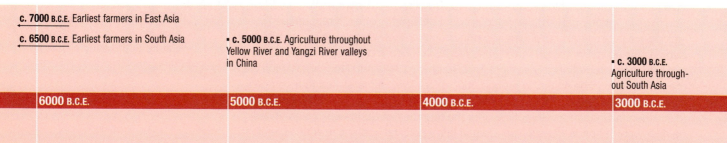

c. 7000 B.C.E. Earliest farmers in East Asia

c. 6500 B.C.E. Earliest farmers in South Asia

c. 5000 B.C.E. Agriculture throughout Yellow River and Yangzi River valleys in China

c. 3000 B.C.E. Agriculture through-out South Asia

6000 B.C.E.	5000 B.C.E.	4000 B.C.E.	3000 B.C.E.

typically they did not like, or even understand, those who did not live like themselves. The ancient history of Asia shows, however, that settled and nomadic peoples were connected in numerous and important ways. As alien as nomads may have seemed to urban peoples, the contacts, conflicts, and exchanges among nomadic and settled peoples profoundly influenced world history, shaping the lives of nomads and city dwellers alike.

Asia is a vast landmass with numerous natural environments, which support primarily two types of livelihood: farming and herding. Where sufficient rain fell or rivers allowed for irrigation, farmers worked the soil and lived in the same location year-round. The earliest urban cultures of Asian history arose especially in the river valleys, that is, in Southwest, South, and East Asia. In all these areas people developed large states with urban and literate cultures, but key differences distinguished them. The states of Southwest Asia show continuity from about 3000 B.C.E. to 600 C.E. In South Asia the urban Indus Valley culture, whose script we cannot read, arose around 2600 B.C.E. and ceased to exist after some 700 years. Several centuries later, the new Vedic culture provided the basis of all of the region's later history. In East Asia the Shang (shahng) state of 1570 to 1027 B.C.E. was the first in a long series of Chinese dynasties that continued into modern times. Elsewhere on the Asian continent, such as in the Oxus River Valley, some early urban cultures flourished only temporarily, however, and when people abandoned them, they left few traces for later history.

Whether particular urban cultures were to survive for a short or a long time, their emergence depended on suitable environmental conditions. Beyond Asia's river valleys, however, agriculture was often impossible, and people survived instead as **pastoralists**, nomadic animal herders who moved with their flocks in search of grazing land. The domestication of horses in around 2000 B.C.E. greatly increased the mobility of pastoralists, enabling some to migrate over great distances. These long-distance migrations created links among the urban states of Asia. Especially important were the migrations of speakers of Indo-European languages, whose nomadic lifestyle brought them to western

pastoralist Animal herder who moves around with a flock to find grazing land; the lifestyle of such people is called pastoralism.

MAPPING THE WORLD
The Nomads and Settlers of Early Eurasia

Throughout history, the native migrants crisscrossed the vast grasslands in the center of Eurasia, crucially influencing the urban cultures that arose on the fringes of the steppes. This map shows the situation in around 2000 B.C.E., when the urbanized regions of Egypt, the Middle East, and the Indus Valley, as well as the village culture of China, coexisted with Indo-European migrants, whose spread brought radical changes to Eurasian societies and cultures.

ROUTES ▼

→ Indo-European migration

- **c. 2000 B.C.E.** Spread of domesticated horses throughout Asia
- **c. 2600–1900 B.C.E.** Mature Indus Valley culture
- **1027 B.C.E.** Battle of Muye in China
- **c. 1500–500 B.C.E.** India's Vedic age

2000 B.C.E.	1000 B.C.E.	0 B.C.E.	1000 C.E.

- **c. 2100–1700 B.C.E.** Oxus River culture
- **1027–771 B.C.E.** Early Zhou dynasty in China
- **c. 2000–1570 B.C.E.** Earliest Bronze Age cultures in China
- **c. 1570–1027 B.C.E.** Shang dynasty in China
- **c. 2000 B.C.E.–100 C.E.** Indo-European migrations

China, western Europe, and the Indian subcontinent. Many other nomadic groups flourished as well, and the interactions between settled and pastoral peoples powerfully shaped the history of Asia from its beginning until recent times.

OVERVIEW QUESTIONS

The major global development in this chapter: The rise of large urban states in Asia and the interactions between nomadic and settled peoples that shaped them.

As you read, consider:

1. How did peoples living in far-flung regions of Asia develop societies that had many similarities?

2. What were the unique characteristics of the cultures studied here?

3. Which features of ancient Indian and Chinese society and culture shaped later developments most fundamentally?

4. What common trends in the interactions between settled and nomadic peoples can you discern?

Early Agricultural Societies of South and East Asia 5000–1000 B.C.E.

FOCUS

How did Asia's diverse natural environments shape the different lifestyles of its inhabitants?

By 8000 B.C.E., people in Southwest Asia had developed agriculture, which made it possible for them to live in the same place for their entire lives. In subsequent millennia, inhabitants of other regions of Asia started to farm as well, especially in river valleys, where the soil was fertile and people could use river water to irrigate crops when rainfall was insufficient. By 5000 B.C.E. farmers had settled throughout the valleys of the Yellow River (Huang He) and the Yangzi River in China, and by 3000 B.C.E. agriculture had spread into parts of the South Asian subcontinent, including the Indus Valley. Out of those communities the earliest urban cultures of East and South Asia would develop. Simultaneously, pastoralists survived by herding animals, grazing them on the continent's steppes, vast areas of semiarid and treeless grasslands. After some pastoralists domesticated the horse, they could cover long distances, which led to their migration over the entire Eurasian continent. These people became the nomads of Central Asia.

Settled Farmers of the River Valleys

The Asian continent has a great deal of natural variety, but most of the regions with agricultural potential lie along mighty rivers whose waters make the adjoining fields very fertile. Besides the Tigris and Euphrates valleys in Southwest Asia, the valleys of the Indus and Ganges in South Asia and those of the Yellow River and Yangzi to the east in China were home to early agricultural societies with intensive food production. The first farmers appeared by 7000 B.C.E. in East Asia and by 6500 B.C.E. in South Asia. Local conditions determined what crops these people could grow. In China they cultivated rice in the southern Yangzi Valley, because the large amounts of water the crop required were available there. In the northern Yellow River Valley, people grew millet, because that hardy grain could survive the region's chronic droughts. In the western Indian subcontinent people cultivated wheat and barley, plants that need a modest, yet annually recurring, amount of water. In each case, environmental conditions determined not only what kinds of crops people grew, but whether settled agriculture was possible at all.

Early Agriculture in China

The early farmers lived in villages and produced pottery in which to store produce and liquids and to cook. As we have seen, pottery provides an important key to archaeologists, for shapes and styles of decoration allow them to distinguish cultures and to study their geographical spread. These studies show that the early inhabitants of various regions of modern-day China had distinct customs and practices. On the coast of eastern China, for example, they made delicate vessels on potter's wheels in colored clay, whereas in the central Yellow River Valley they made large bulky vessels by placing bands of clay on top of one another and painting decorations on the upper half. Thus, although each agricultural region may have emerged in response to similar environmental opportunities, each developed distinct cultural characteristics.

Over time these diverse populations across China increased contacts and started to share cultural elements. Some of the interactions were violent rather than peaceful, so inhabitants of northern China began to protect their villages with walls. They employed a unique building technique that would remain characteristic for many centuries in the region. They filled a wooden frame with layers of earth, which they pounded until the wall became as solid as cement. When the builders removed the boards, straight and strong walls remained.

As in Mesopotamia and Egypt, the construction of such walls and other large projects in early China required organized communal labor and a hierarchical social structure. Again, as in the case of Mesopotamia and Egypt, burial sites provide evidence of this increasing social stratification. By 2000 B.C.E. social differences became evident in people's burials. While the vast majority of people were buried with only a few objects, a small number of elites took many gifts with them to their graves. The goods found in elite graves often had symbolic significance, revealing the owner's special status. That great power went with special status was made very clear by the human sacrifice of people of lower status to serve members of the elite in the afterlife. Archaeologists regularly find skeletons with their feet cut off placed near the principal occupants of rich Chinese graves. Both Mesopotamia and Egypt show evidence of human sacrifice in their early histories as well, but there the practice died out quickly, while in China it continued much longer.

Grave goods are not the only evidence we have of social stratification. As some members of Chinese society grew wealthy, they demanded new and more luxurious products. Highly skilled specialized laborers focused their attention on meeting such demands. One typically Chinese luxury product, silk cloth, provides an example of the specialization of labor that went along with social stratification. Starting in the third millennium B.C.E., Chinese women began weaving cloth from the cocoons of silkworms. They bred the worms and fed them masses of mulberry leaves to make them grow fast. The women unraveled the cocoons to obtain the delicate silk threads and wove them into valuable textiles. The silk trade became a key component of the Chinese economy, and silk production remained a Chinese monopoly until the sixth century C.E., when two Christian monks smuggled some silkworms out of China (see Chapter 10). Thus, silk production both reflected Chinese social structure and helped make China a global trading crossroads.

Similarly, villages appeared by 6500 B.C.E. in the northwestern part of the Indian subcontinent, where farmers grew barley and wheat using techniques probably imported from Southwest Asia. They gradually spread out into regions such as the Indus River Valley,

East Asian Settlers

South Asian Settlers

where the rich soil allowed increased agricultural production and, hence, population growth. Some larger villages may have served as centers of trade. Over time South Asian farmers extended the range of plants they grew and started to cultivate cotton, which they used to weave textiles. By 3500 B.C.E. village life was common in the fertile river valleys of South and East Asia.

Nomadic Herders of the Steppe

Agriculture involves not only farming but also the herding of animals. At the same time that they learned to domesticate plants, the early inhabitants of Asia became responsible for the survival of selected animals. They bred them, protected them against natural predators, milked and sheared them, and guided them to pastureland where they could feed. The search for pasture required herders to move around for at least part of the year, because most natural environments in Asia do not provide sufficient food for herds in the same place year-round. Nomadic herders did not wander at random but moved with their flocks along established routes. These settled patterns of movement reflected knowledge of the region's environment that had been passed down from generation to generation.

From about 3000 B.C.E. on, sheep, goats, and cattle were the most important domesticated animals throughout Asia. The settled farmers and nomadic herders exchanged the specialized goods they each produced. Farmers traded grains, pottery, and other craft goods for the herders' dairy products, wool, and skins. But tensions could arise between the two groups, especially in summer when herders drove their flocks from the dry steppe to the lush river valleys where their animals could graze. At just that time, the farmers' crops were nearly ready for harvest, so allowing flocks near them could prove disastrous. Many ancient accounts focus on these tensions and ignore the cooperation, but both were important. Each group provided the other with goods they could not otherwise acquire, and the need for exchange created a web of connections between nomadic and settled peoples that shaped both cultures. At the same time, the sometimes divergent demands of agriculture and herding led to serious and often violent conflict.

Domestication of the Horse

The pastoral lifestyle originally did not allow people to range over great distances as they moved on foot. A dramatic change happened around 2000 B.C.E., when they started to use horses. People of the Russian steppe may have domesticated the horse as early as 4000 B.C.E., but horses became truly important in world history only when they were hitched to chariots and wagons in around 2000 B.C.E. For both settled and pastoral populations, the two-wheeled horse-drawn chariot was an essential piece of equipment, used in warfare and for other purposes. By 1000 B.C.E., chariot technology had spread throughout Asia, and in pastoral societies charioteers became elites with great wealth and power. Their massive tombs were packed with rich grave goods, including their horses and chariot.

When people started to ride horses using saddles and bits, rather than bareback, their mobility increased even more, and the distances they could cover expanded drastically. By 500 B.C.E., animal herders on horseback roamed the Asian steppes. Their speed and agility made them feared in battle, but the armies of settled populations soon imitated their techniques. The use of the horse revolutionized warfare throughout Asia and beyond.

The mobility of mounted horsemen had a remarkable consequence: during the first millennium B.C.E., shared cultural elements appeared over a vast region, from eastern Russia to western China. From the Black Sea to Siberia, nomadic people used similar burial mounds. They placed the dead in a central chamber of wood or stone, over which they piled an earthen mound. As gifts, they included weapons and sacrificed animals—sheep, goats, cattle, and horses. These burial items reveal the people's preoccupations in life with warfare and animal husbandry.

The best examples of such tombs are found in the Altai Mountains on the modern border between Russia and northern China. At the site of Pazyryk (PA-zee-rick) in that region, Russian archaeologists excavated tomb remains that were extremely well preserved by permafrost, a permanently frozen layer of earth below the surface. The builders covered the tomb chambers with earthen mounds, on top of which they piled loose rocks. The tombs housed the bodies of horses, and of people whose skins had dried naturally, some of them completely tattooed. They also contained textiles (including carpets), leather, and felt, all decorated with images of humans, animals, and other special motifs, as well as weapons and precious goods, including imports from China, India, and Southwest Asia.

The people buried in them were leaders of nomadic groups, who received honors on their deaths. Among them was a young blond woman, covered with body tattoos, who died in around 500 B.C.E. Her tomb shows her special status in society. She was placed in a wooden coffin wearing a blouse imported from India and a three-foot-high felt headdress onto which gilded wooden birds had been sewn. Six horses accompanied her in death,

Burial Practices

Chariot from Pazyryk Burials in Central Asia

The people of Central Asia who relied on the horse for transport invented a new set of tools and equipment to use with the animal, including chariots. Chariots for the elite could be very elaborate. This chariot, found in one of the burials at Pazyryk, was reconstructed from pieces of wood and leather. The distance between the front and back wheels is only 2 inches, which suggests this was a ceremonial object. (The State Hermitage Museum, St. Petersburg. Photograph © The State Hermitage Museum /photo by Vladimir Terebenin, Leonard Kheifets, Yuri Molodkovets.)

which showed that she must have been very wealthy in life, and reflected the profound importance of the horse in the lives of Asian nomads.

Between 5000 and 1000 B.C.E., Asians had thus developed two basic means of survival. Across the wide steppes of Central Asia, they subsisted as nomadic herders who moved with their sheep, goats, cattle, and horses over long distances. In the fertile river valleys, they had become farmers, living in increasingly numerous villages that shared regionally characteristic social structure and agricultural practices. Interactions between the two groups would have an enormous impact on the subsequent history of Asia.

The Indus Valley Culture 2600–1900 B.C.E.

FOCUS

What were the main characteristics of South Asia's early urban culture?

In the third and second millennia B.C.E., the villages of South and East Asia had developed major urban societies in the valleys of the powerful Indus River and the Yellow River. The two regions were strikingly different, however. The Indus Valley had cities earlier than China, but they disappeared after 1900 B.C.E., whereas in China the building of the first cities started a long history of urban life. The Indus culture is also less accessible to us because its script has not yet been deciphered. Scholars thus do not know the names of peoples and places or the language they spoke, and they have no access to verbal expression of their ideas. Further, no later native Indian sources describe Indus elites and their activities. Archaeological remains fill some of the gaps, but uncertainties about their interpretation have led to competing theories about many features of the Indus Valley culture.

Urban Society in the Indus Valley

Archaeological evidence shows that the geographical spread of the Indus culture was enormous, stretching some 1100 miles from the northernmost reaches of the Indus River to the Arabian Sea and some 800 miles from east to west (see Map 3.1). The Indus culture existed in varied natural environments, including fertile agricultural zones with abundant rainfall near the mountains, a large alluvial plain that is naturally fertilized by annual flooding, and a marshy coastal area with islands and peninsulas.

Harappan Cities   Around 3200 B.C.E., villagers in the western part of South Asia started to build larger fortified settlements. This trend culminated suddenly in around 2600 B.C.E. with the creation of the mature Indus culture, which shows amazing shared cultural characteristics over a vast area of some 193,000 square miles. For unknown reasons numerous people moved into cities surrounded by villages. We know of five very large urban centers, whose inhabitants may have numbered thirty thousand (similar to the population of Uruk, discussed in Chapter 2), and more than thirty smaller cities. At the same time, the number of villages remained very high as well: archaeologists have identified more than fifteen thousand of them. Despite the great distances between them, the urban settlements were remarkably similar. Scholars often refer to them as *Harappan*, after the modern name of one of the large cities.

The uniformity is clear from the layout of the cities, although local variations appear. They were surrounded by thick mud-brick walls and contained various sectors. Each of the five large cities had a high sector, set on a mud-brick platform, with monumental buildings, and one or more lower sectors with residences and workshops. The interior layout of each sector was planned on a grid pattern oriented north to south and east to west. In some residential areas, streets up to thirty-three feet wide created city blocks, which were subdivided with narrower streets. Evidence that smaller settlements had the same layout indicates that people consciously planned cities and villages using an established pattern.

Mohenjo-Daro   Mohenjo-Daro (moe-hen-joe-DAHR-oh) in the east of modern Pakistan, the best-known and largest site of the culture, is often taken as the prime example of the layout of

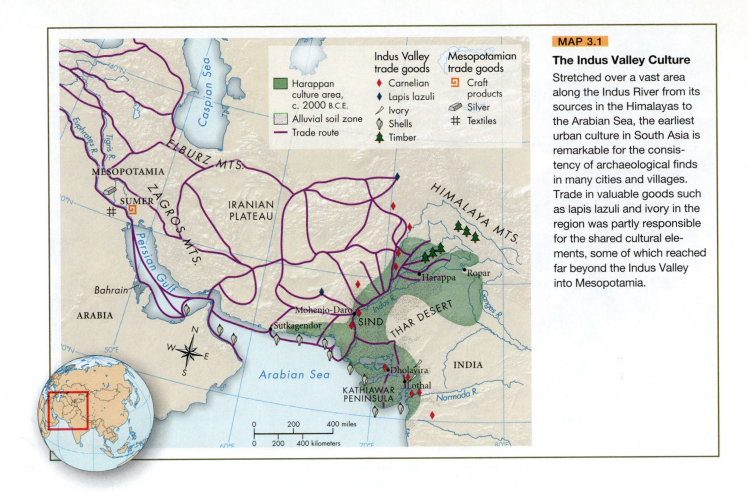

MAP 3.1

The Indus Valley Culture

Stretched over a vast area along the Indus River from its sources in the Himalayas to the Arabian Sea, the earliest urban culture in South Asia is remarkable for the consistency of archaeological finds in many cities and villages. Trade in valuable goods such as lapis lazuli and ivory in the region was partly responsible for the shared cultural elements, some of which reached far beyond the Indus Valley into Mesopotamia.

Indus Valley cities. Its monumental buildings on the high sector are relatively well preserved. They include the Great Bath, 23 feet wide by 39 feet long and 8 feet deep, made of baked bricks and lined with plaster. Around the outside of the bath was a three-inch layer of bitumen, a kind of asphalt used as waterproofing. People may have used the small rooms next to the bath to change clothing. Many scholars think the complex was used for ritual cleansing because it resembles later Indian purification pools. Next to the Great Bath was a vast storehouse for grain, 99 by 99 feet, and the platform also supported a large pillared hall. These structures indicate a communal effort to construct special edifices.

In the residential areas—which also housed the shops and craft workshops—people built their homes using uniformly sized bricks. Most houses had an entrance on a side street and consisted of a courtyard surrounded by rooms on two or three sides. The Harappan cities show a greater attention to sanitation than was seen anywhere else in the ancient world. Houses had private bathrooms and wells, and their sewage systems were connected to main channels underneath the streets. All cities had large artificial basins to collect water. Scholars believe that the Indus people planned these elaborate systems to protect themselves against the flooding of the rivers and heavy rains. They could have used some of the basins as harbors as well.

Although the archaeological remains of Harappan cities are abundant, they present many problems of interpretation. They suggest political and social structures that are very unlike those of other early urban cultures, but the differences may be more apparent than real. Urban societies usually have a hierarchy in which an elite holds power over the mass of the population, often by military means. The remains of the Indus society show no military activity, however. The people never depicted warfare, and none of their tombs con-

Social Structure

The Great Bath at Mohenjo-Daro
This building in the center of Mohenjo-Daro clearly had a use related to water: the bricks are neatly fitted together and sealed with plaster, and the outside is covered with bitumen, a waterproofing substance. Because of the stairs and the benchlike ledge, most archaeologists think it was used for ritual bathing. (Borromeo/Art Resource, NY.)

tained weapons. Further, houses or tombs show no grandiose displays of wealth such as we find in Mesopotamia, Egypt, China, and elsewhere. The archaeological material from the Indus Valley creates the impression (perhaps falsely) that the majority of people shared the existing wealth equally.

Some scholars argue that Harappan society was matriarchal. They think that property passed along the female line of the family rather than the male and that husbands moved into their wives' homes upon marriage. If true, this would make Indus Valley culture very different from other early urban cultures. But the evidence for an Indus matriarchy is far from conclusive.

The existence of massive public works, however, suggests that, as was the case in other urban societies, an elite group did have authority over the rest of the Harappan population. The basis of that authority remains a mystery, as there is no evidence of military control or, as far as we know, of temples that could indicate a religious basis of power. Because, as we will see, long-distance trade was crucial to the Indus Valley economy, many historians propose that a merchant class governed. Other scholars speculate that the Indus Valley culture featured certain people who gained authority by renouncing material goods and luxuries, as people in later Indian history did.

Indus Beliefs   We are as uncertain about Indus religion as we are about Indus society. Scholars have turned to visual and archaeological evidence for insight into Indus beliefs, and many specialists argue that several later Indian practices have their roots in Indus culture. They see the Great Bath at Mohenjo-Daro, for example, as a place for purification with sacred water. Images on the Indus seals regularly show human figures with legs spread in a position resembling later yoga postures. This may indicate that practices such as meditation already existed in the Indus culture. Scholars differ in their acceptance of such ideas, however. Those who see much continuity between the Indus Valley culture and later periods of South Asian history will interpret aspects of the early culture on the basis of later evidence. Those who see little continuity find different explanations.

How do we explain that the five major cities of the Indus Valley culture show an amazing cultural uniformity even though they are located two hundred to four hundred miles apart? The idea that a unified territorial state would have imposed the cultural norms seems improbable, as such a state would have been enormous in size. It seems more likely that each city controlled the territory surrounding it. The cultural similarity, however, indicates that the cities were in close contact with one another. Trade most likely played a key role in creating and reinforcing the contacts and connections that resulted in the uniformity of Indus culture.

Political Organization

Harappan Crafts and Long-Distance Trade

The archaeological evidence is more secure when we look at the role of crafts and trade in the Indus Valley culture. The people seem to have excelled in these activities and devoted much attention to both of them. They imported prized stones, such as carnelian and lapis lazuli, to carve valuable objects, including seals and beads. Wherever archaeologists find such objects, the objects are similar in shape and size, showing that craftsmen throughout the Indus Valley followed standard patterns. Traders also shipped craft items to other cities. All the settlements used a unified system of weights and measures, which greatly facilitated transactions among people of different towns. In every site, archaeologists found sets of stone weights that use the same measuring system. Trade must have been of great importance to the Indus people considering that they devoted so much effort to making it function smoothly and efficiently.

Writing is another indicator that trade was important in the Indus Valley. Although we cannot decipher the texts, all scribes over the vast region of the culture used the same signs and carved them on the same types of objects. Indus script appeared in two contexts that seem connected to trade. People inscribed vessels, probably to indicate who owned the contents; more dramatically, writing appears on stone seals (see Seeing the Past: Inscribed Seals from the Indus Valley). The appearance of these seals throughout the Indus Valley underscores the wide range of the exchanges.

Indus Valley Script

Traders also exported Indus Valley craft items to distant places, including Mesopotamia. Although an expanse of some one thousand miles separated Mesopotamia from the Indus River delta, sailors went back and forth by following the Pakistani and Iranian coasts. Archaeological finds in the Persian Gulf show that Indus Valley people traded on their way to Mesopotamia. Inhabitants of the island of Bahrain adopted the Indus system of weights and measures and produced seals in the Harappan style, sometimes inscribing them with signs of the Indus script. Thus Indus cities served as crossroads, connecting communities to one another and to the larger world.

Foreign Trade

The End of the Indus Valley Culture

How, when, and why did this remarkable urban culture disappear? Around 1900 B.C.E. people throughout the Indus Valley started to leave the great cities and many other settlements, and they abandoned the shared cultural practices, such as weights and measures. Most scholars argue that turmoil forced them to do so. Many of these historians theorize that the arrival of Indo-European-speaking migrants forced the Indus Valley inhabitants to change their lifestyles completely. But there is no clear evidence of conquest. The cities were not burned down or sacked, and there are no signs of violence.

The end of the Indus Valley cities was more likely due to a combination of factors. It is possible that the climate became drier in the early second millennium B.C.E. and that

Inscribed Seals from the Indus Valley

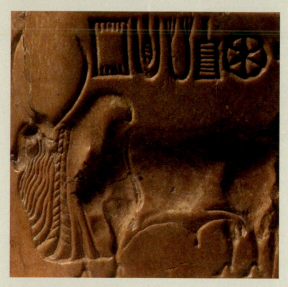

Seals from Mohenjo-Daro (Art Archive/National Museum Karachi/Dagli Orti (left) and Scala/Art Resource, NY (right).)

The people of the Indus Valley used a script that emerged in around 2600 B.C.E., remained in use until around 1900 B.C.E., and then disappeared forever. Some four thousand texts are known, mostly incised on stamp seals, pottery, or pieces of jewelry. People of the Indus Valley used the stone stamps to make an impression on a piece of soft clay, so they cut the inscriptions in mirror image. On these seals the signs often appear next to the image of a single standing animal. Archaeologists have found lumps of clay into which such seals were pressed, often on several sides.

The inscriptions were usually very short, on average containing about five signs. Thus they did not record long sentences or tales, but most likely administrative information, such as the amount of a commodity and the name of the person who supervised the transaction. There are about four hundred signs, which suggests that each sign expressed an entire word.

EXAMINING THE EVIDENCE

1. Although we cannot understand the writing on them, what do these seals tell us about record keeping in the Indus culture?

2. Comparing the two seals, what similarities do you observe? How would you describe the differences?

3. How do the Indus Valley seals differ from the first writings we discussed for other early cultures?

For Further Information:
Kenoyer, Jonathan M. *Ancient Cities of the Indus Valley*. New York: Oxford University Press, 1998.

urban residents could no longer grow enough food to live in large groups. According to this theory, people moved into villages, smaller communities that required smaller concentrations of food, or migrated eastward, where the climate was wetter. This movement disrupted the trade networks that had tied the vast region together, and by 1700 B.C.E. people used a variety of local traditions rather than those that had characterized the mature Indus Valley culture. Some aspects of that culture, such as the possible rejection of material wealth and the beliefs in certain gods, may have inspired later South Asian practices and, in that way, have exerted a deep impact on later history. But the great cities of the Indus Valley ceased to exist, and many centuries passed before urban culture returned to that area of the world.

Indo-European Migrations 3000–1000 B.C.E.

Above we considered the theory that the Indus Valley culture ended because of the immigration of people speaking an Indo-European language. Such migrants may have descended onto the Indian subcontinent and conquered local populations. The scholarly disagreement over exactly what happened illustrates how difficult it is to understand the process by which Indo-European languages came to be spoken over a vast area of Eurasia. However, the fact that by 100 B.C.E. people from western China to western Europe spoke related Indo-European languages certainly was the result of a crucial process in Eurasian history—a process likely connected to the interactions between farmers and pastoralists.

> **FOCUS**
>
> What does the concept "Indo-European" mean, and how important is it for the study of Eurasia?

Indo-European Languages

The term *Indo-European* does not refer to a race or an ethnic group but to a group of languages that are related in vocabulary and grammar. In the eighteenth century C.E., European scholars first observed that people from Britain to South Asia spoke languages that had many similarities. Their discovery of the links between Sanskrit, the sacred language of ancient India, and the European classical languages, Greek and Latin, also showed them that these similarities had existed for many centuries. Note, for example, how English, Sanskrit, Greek, and Latin use the same words to express mother, father, and house (domicile):

English	Sanskrit	Greek	Latin
mother	matar	meter	mater
father	pitar	pater	pater
domicile	dama	domos	domus

Linguists observed that many other European languages and several from South Asia—including Sanskrit and Persian along with their modern derivations, Hindi and Farsi—shared many words and grammatical structures. Hence they reasoned that the languages evolved from an original ancient language that spread when its speakers migrated. They grouped the languages derived from this ancient one under the name *Indo-European*. When Indo-European groups separated, they adjusted to new natural environments and interacted with populations who spoke non-Indo-European languages. Consequently, their languages developed differences, but still maintained clear common Indo-European roots. These roots now help us trace the course of their migrations.

Indo-European Migrations

Speakers of an Indo-European language who called themselves *Arya*, "noble," arrived in South Asia shortly after 2000 B.C.E. and started to displace the local people, who spoke non-Indo-European Dravidian languages. Dravidian languages persist in the southernmost Indian subcontinent today, which together with historical accounts shows that the spread of Indo-European speakers from north to south was gradual. Where the speakers of Indo-European speakers came from and what motivated them to migrate remain unresolved.

Theories of Indo-European Migrations

The two principal explanations for these migrations show how scholars can interpret the same set of evidence very differently. Some researchers suggest that Indo-European languages spread together with agriculture from the area of modern Turkey where farming originated. Farmers would have migrated east and west from this region starting after 7000 B.C.E. They would have altered not only the local populations' means of survival but also their languages, in a process parallel to that of the Bantu migrations in Africa (see Chapter 8).

Other scholars believe the speakers of Indo-European languages were pastoralists who moved into farming areas starting in around 2000 B.C.E. Most believe these migrants originated in the southern Russian steppes, but others argue for a homeland closer to India, and the answer remains elusive. Some suggest that the arrival of Indo-European speakers entailed the conquest and domination of local populations. The conquerors would have benefited greatly from their expertise in horsemanship and their invention of the horse-drawn chariot. It is equally possible, however, that pastoralists often integrated peacefully into existing farming communities.

Indo-European Speakers and Eurasian History

Spread of Indo-European Languages

Although we cannot precisely locate the Indo-European homeland, it is certain that speakers of Indo-European languages spread over Eurasia in the second and first millennia B.C.E., carrying their languages into regions where people spoke other vernaculars. Indo-European languages gradually came to dominate Eurasia. The earliest definitive evidence of an Indo-European language is from what is now Turkey, where, as we saw in Chapter 2, a people called the Hittites had established a powerful state by 1800 B.C.E. whose official court language was Indo-European Hittite. In Greece, evidence of Indo-European first appears in Linear B tablets from 1500 to 1200 B.C.E. that include Greek words. It is possible that Indo-European speakers lived in both Turkey and Greece for many centuries before they started to write.

The presence of Indo-European languages farther west and north in Europe is clear from the earliest written remains found there; that is, from about 500 B.C.E. onward. Although today Indo-European languages are dominant throughout Europe, a few regions remain in which non-Indo-European languages have survived over millennia, such as Finland and the Basque area of Spain.

INDO-EUROPEAN MIGRATIONS

c. 2000 B.C.E.	Aryas arrive in South Asia
c. 1800 B.C.E.	Creation of Hittite state in area of modern Turkey
c. 1500–1200 B.C.E.	Indo-European Greek words appear in Linear B texts
c. 1500–900 B.C.E.	Probable period of composition of the *Rig-Veda* in India
c. 1300 B.C.E.	*Gathas* composed in Iran
c. 1000 B.C.E.	Indo-European languages spoken throughout area of modern Europe

In Asia, Indo-European speakers did not become as dominant as they were in Europe. In the Middle East outside Turkey (where people today speak Turkish, the non-Indo-European language of later immigrants), people continued to use Semitic languages, such as Akkadian in antiquity and Arabic in more recent times. But migrants speaking Indo-European languages moved into southern Asia, arriving on the Iranian plateau in the second millennium B.C.E. The *Gathas*—songs of the Persian prophet Zoroaster (see Chapter 4)—were probably composed toward the end of that millennium, in around 1300 B.C.E., and their language is Indo-European with close similarities to the Sanskrit of India.

The most easterly evidence of Indo-European languages appears in the Central Asian provinces of modern China, where excavations have uncovered burials with naturally mummified human bodies in the Tarim Basin. Some of the burials date back to 2000 B.C.E., and they continued until 500 B.C.E. The dead people had European physical features, including fair skin and light hair, and some scholars believe that they were Indo-European speakers. They arrived in western China when the chariot first appeared in Shang China, and the two events seem to be related.

Vedas Early collections of Indian hymns, songs, and prayers that contain sacred knowledge; initially preserved in oral form, they were recorded in writing c. 600 B.C.E.

The spread of Indo-European languages was thus one of the most important events in the early history of the entire Eurasian continent. As a result, by the beginning of the Common Era, if not before, peoples from the Atlantic Ocean to the western regions of China spoke a variety of related languages that had a common source. The spread of Indo-European languages is but one example of the profound impact of nomadic peoples on the settled societies of Eurasia.

India's Vedic Age 1500–500 B.C.E.

By 1500 B.C.E. the Aryas had entered the Indian subcontinent from the Iranian plateau. They were probably pastoralists who migrated into the fertile river valleys in search of land, first in the northwest of India and later farther east. During their migrations, the Aryas encountered speakers of the non-Indo-European Dravidian languages. The mixture of peoples, traditions, and languages that resulted led to changes in customs and lifestyles that affected all, and this fusion became the foundation of classical Indian culture (see Map 3.2).

> **FOCUS**
>
> How did cultural developments in early Indian history shape the structure of society?

Vedic Origins

Ancient Indian literature contains many references to the new society that developed when Indo-European speakers migrated into the subcontinent. Unfortunately for historians, the accounts were written down long after the events they describe, raising questions about their accuracy. Historians who use such sources need to keep in mind that they likely tell us as much about the world of their authors as about early Vedic India.

The oldest compositions are the **Vedas**, collections of hymns, songs, prayers, and dialogues. The term *Veda* literally means "sacred knowledge," and the texts are written in a very early form of the Indo-European Sanskrit language. There are four Vedas, the oldest of which is the *Rig Veda*, a collection of 1028 hymns organized in ten books and addressed to various deities. Priests probably composed the *Rig Veda* between 1500 and 900 B.C.E., describing events of that period. The hymns were not written down until around 600 B.C.E., however, and the later authors likely modified their contents.

The authors of the Vedas portrayed a society torn by violent conflict. They depicted the Aryas as light-skinned nomadic warriors who conquered the local dark-skinned population, the *Dasa*, which means "enemy." The Aryas fought on horse-drawn chariots against the Dasa, who often lived in fortified settlements, and also against each other. According to the Vedas, the Aryas greatly valued cattle and needed access to grazing areas for their animals. Although the Vedas focus on military feats, many scholars now believe that they misrepresent actual events. They think it more likely that the Aryas spread throughout India through peaceful interaction and intermarriage with local populations. Thus, instead of the conflict between pastoralists and farmers described in the texts, the Aryas and the local population probably developed slowly and peacefully among people of different lifestyles.

Rise of a New Society: Families, Clans, and Castes

People in early Vedic society belonged to extended families organized along patriarchal lines, the leading men having full control over other members of the family. Women had

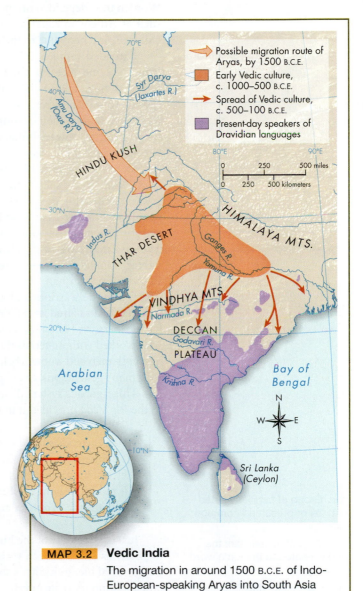

MAP 3.2 **Vedic India**

The migration in around 1500 B.C.E. of Indo-European-speaking Aryas into South Asia introduced radical changes in culture and society, which gradually spread from the northwest throughout much of the subcontinent. The Aryas' new ideas about social hierarchy, religion, and human nature would affect the region's culture for millennia.

Patriarchal Families

little authority and did not inherit family wealth unless there were no male heirs. The *Law-book of Manu*, although written down much later in the first century B.C.E., gives an idea of the low status of women in the Vedic age. The book states:

> I will now propound the eternal laws for a husband and his wife who keep to the path of duty, whether they be united or separated.
>
> Day and night women must be kept in dependence by the males of their families, and, if they attach themselves to sensual enjoyments, they must be kept under one's control. Her father protects her in childhood, her husband protects her in youth, and her sons protect her in old age; a woman is never fit for independence.[2]

Women thus depended on men throughout their lives. As in many other ancient societies, such as Athens in classical Greece (see Chapter 5), a woman's primary duty was to bear children, and her value to the community was measured in these terms.

Political Structure

Extended families joined together in **clans**, groups considered to have descended from the same ancestor. Clans were the basis of the early Vedic political structure. Family heads, all men, met in assemblies and accepted the leadership of a **raja**, a word that corresponds to the Latin *rex*, "king," although a translation of "chief" is more accurate. Clan members shared their resources and maintained strong social ties. Hundreds existed throughout northwest India, some settled in villages, others as pastoral groups. Clashes between clans were frequent, and the rajas had to be great military leaders to gain the respect of their people. This explains the atmosphere of conflict in the Vedas.

Varnas

In early Vedic society among both the indigenous Dasas and the Indo-European Aryas, it was membership in a clan believed to have a common ancestor that primarily determined people's identities. In around 1000 B.C.E., after the composition of the *Rig Veda*, different categorizations arose. One involved the concept of **varna**, which literally means "color." The idea may have originally derived from the division between dark-skinned Dasas and lighter-skinned Aryas, but later the word came to mean something like "class." Originally the varna system had four levels: Brahmans (BRAH-mihn), or priests; Kshatriyas (shuh-TREE-uh), the warriors and aristocrats; Vaishyas (VYSH-yuh), landowning peasants and merchants; and Shudras (SHOOD-ra), by far the largest group, composed of artisans, land-less farmers, and laborers. Later on came the addition of a fifth group, the Untouchables, who worked with materials that others refused to touch, such as animal skins. Entire families, both men and women, belonged to the same varna, and they stayed in the same category over many generations, as people were supposed to marry within their own varna.

This rigorous system of social hierarchy required justification, and a hymn added late to the *Rig Veda* provided it in these terms:

> When the gods spread the sacrifice with the Man as the offering . . .
> When they divided the Man, into how many parts did they apportion him? What do they call his mouth, his two arms and thighs and feet?
> His mouth became the Brahman; his arms were made into the Warrior (Kshatriya), his thighs the People (Vaishya), and from his feet the Servants (Shudra) were born.[3]

clan Group of families related to a real or presumed common ancestor.

raja Chief of Indian clan; the term is related to the Latin word for "king," *rex*.

varna Group identity in early Indian society, related to the concept of class; people belonged to one of four varna as a result of their birth.

jati Division of Indian society that identifies an individual's occupation and social standing.

Just as each part of the human body serves a specific purpose and has a fixed place in the body as a whole, each varna served a specific purpose in society and had a fixed place in the social hierarchy. This social order, like the body itself, had been created by the gods and could no more be questioned or changed than the human body.

Over time the structure of Vedic society became more complex, however. When increasing numbers of people lived together, labor became more specialized, and by 500 B.C.E. subdivisions of the varna system developed. These became known as **jati**. Although varnas continued to determine people's position in the social hierarchy, specific occupations grouped them into jatis. Every specialized occupation could create a new jati, each with its specific tasks and duties. Members of a jati lived together, married each other, and ate together. The designation thus passed on from parents to children, and in fact the term *jati* has the same root as the word for birth.

When Portuguese visitors to the Indian subcontinent in the sixteenth century C.E. observed these social groups, they gave them the name *casta*, which means "breed." That categorization led to the English designations of caste and the **caste system**. The caste system provided a social structure in which everyone had an allotted place. There were clear rules of behavior, which, if broken, would lead to expulsion from the caste—hence the term *outcast*. The upper castes had special rights and access to property, and the system protected their privileges. Social mobility was very difficult in Vedic society. Jatis could improve their lot as a group, but individuals rarely moved into a higher caste. The system had a particular advantage, however: it facilitated the integration of newcomers into Indian society, even those with different faiths. Many immigrants to the subcontinent could establish themselves as a defined jati. The caste system remained a central part of Indian society for thousands of years and still plays a role today.

Vedic Religion

The Vedas portray a rich religious system, one that shares ideas and gods described in other Indo-European writings, especially those from Iran and Greece. The atmosphere of conflict dominates in the divine world of the Vedas, and many of the gods represent forces of nature admired because of their strength.

As was true among humans, male gods dominated the Vedic divine world. Their leader was Indra, the war god, often violent and fond of drink. He wielded the thunderbolt and protected the universe against demons. The sky god, Varuna, maintained cosmic order and justice. He punished liars and evildoers, banishing their souls to the miserable netherworld, the House of Clay, whereas the souls of people who had behaved well dwelled in a heaven-like House of the Fathers. The god of fire, Agni, was the intermediary between humans and gods because, as fire, he made it possible for people to give sacrifices. All these gods were strong warriors, but some Vedic hymns emphasized their peaceful aspects as well. They honored the goddess of dawn, Usas, or the lady of the forest, in language that shows deep appreciation for the natural environment. Of dawn, they say, for example:

> She makes paths all easy, fair to travel, and, rich, has shown herself benign and friendly. We see that you are good: far shines your luster; your beams, your splendors have flown up to heaven.[4]

Humans could communicate with the gods through ritual sacrifice. Trained priests burned offerings to urge the gods to be kind. They slaughtered a variety of animals—horses, cattle, sheep, and goats—while reciting hymns. The priests also drank *soma*, extracted from unknown plants, that gave them divine inspiration. Sacrifice was so central in the Vedic culture that it became connected with creation itself. According to tradition, the gods had created the universe by sacrificing a Lord of Beings, the primeval man who had existed before the universe. Consequently, every time the priests performed a sacrifice, they repeated creation and thus became responsible for the order of the universe.

The most important sacrifices, especially those of horses, demanded the presence of the raja. Over time, the raja became the sole patron of sacrifices, and the priests gave him attributes of divinity. In this way a division of authority developed: the priests gained superiority in the ritual world, and the raja became the political, military, and administrative head of the clan. Women were fully excluded from this power structure. Thus Vedic religious practices and beliefs reinforced the social and political order.

The Brahmans' central role in sacrifices confirmed their uppermost status in the caste system and also had a unique effect on the spread of literacy in India. Only they knew the Vedic hymns that were essential during sacrifices. These songs were composed in the upper-class Sanskrit language, which contrasted with Prakrit, the dialect that most people

caste system Indian organization of society that identifies people's position and status on the basis of the group into which they were born.

The Upanishads

At the end of the Vedic period, anonymous mystics and others who rejected the existing social order started to formulate commentaries on the Vedas that reflect evolving religious ideas and speculations in a genre of Indian writing called the Upanishads. The Upanishads are often phrased as dialogues about religious questions between a teacher and a student "sitting in front" (the literal meaning of *Upanishad*). The oldest Upanishads were composed between 800 and 400 B.C.E., but they continued to appear in much later periods. Their main concern is to establish the unity of all things within the Brahman, the eternal entity that binds the universe together. Some Upanishads focus on the practice of meditation. The following passage recommends meditation on the syllable Om (ohm), which was pronounced at the start of every Vedic recitation. Its other designation is *udgitha*. The passage describes what the syllable could mean in the mind of a devotee.

> Let a man meditate on the syllable Om, called the udgitha; for the udgitha is sung, beginning with Om.
>
> The full account, however, of Om is this:
>
> The essence of all beings is the earth, the essence of the earth is water, the essence of water the plants, the essence of plants man, the essence of man speech, the essence of speech the Rig Veda, the essence of the Rig Veda the Sama Veda, the essence of the Sama Veda the udgitha (which is Om).
>
> That udgitha (Om) is the best of all essences, the highest, deserving the highest place, the eighth.
>
> . . .
>
> And that couple is joined together in the syllable Om. When two people come together, they fulfill each other's desire.
>
> Thus, he who knowing this, meditates on the syllable (Om), the udgitha, becomes indeed a fulfiller of desires.
>
> That syllable is the syllable of permission, for whenever we permit anything, we say Om, yes. Now permission is gratification. He who knowing this meditates on the syllable (Om), the udgitha, becomes indeed a gratifier of desires.
>
> By that syllable does the threefold knowledge proceed. When the Adhvaryu priest gives an order, he says Om. When the Hotri priest recites, he says Om. When the Udgatri priest sings, he says Om—all for the glory of that syllable. The threefold knowledge proceeds by the greatness of that syllable and by its essence.
>
> Now therefore it would seem to follow, that both he who knows this (the true meaning of the syllable Om), and he who does not, perform the same sacrifice. But this is not so, for knowledge and ignorance are different. The sacrifice which a man performs with knowledge, faith, and the upanishad is more powerful. This is the full account of the syllable Om.

Source: Nicol Macnicol, trans., *Hindu Scriptures* (London/New York: J. M. Dent & Sons, Ltd., E. P. Dutton & Co., Inc., 1938), 117–118.

EXAMINING THE EVIDENCE

1. How does this passage reflect Vedic ideas?

2. How does it aim to establish unity in the universe?

Brahmans spoke. Brahmans may have had such firm control over the literary tradition that they prevented the written recording of the Vedas and the use of writing in general. This monopoly on literacy strengthened the power of the Brahmans, but it slowed the spread of writing throughout Indian society. Only by 500 C.E. did writing become widespread in India, whereas in other equally complex societies—such as Mesopotamia, where, as we saw in Chapter 2, writing first served administrative functions—it caught on much earlier.

Developments in Vedic Ideas

The Upanishads Early Vedic society was primarily centered in the river valleys of northwest India, and the *Rig Veda* depicts the natural environment of that region. The dense forests farther east in the Ganges plain originally prevented extensive agriculture and herding there. It was only after 1000 B.C.E. when people began to use iron tools, that forests could be cleared. Aryas spread eastward, and during this period of expansion they encountered indigenous traditions that affected their own religious doctrines. Groups of people started to reject the structures of Vedic society and began to formulate new interpretations of the Vedas in a new type of text. Called *Upanishads* (oo-PAHN-ih-shhad), they combined indigenous and Vedic traditions (see Reading the Past: The Upanishads). The texts were only written down around 500 B.C.E., but they express older ideas. They shifted the strong focus on sacrifice that had dominated early Vedic religion toward an emphasis on living a righteous life. This shift was connected to changes in the beliefs about the afterlife and to the concept of **reincarnation**—rebirth in a new form.

The belief arose that every living creature had an immortal essence, something like a soul. Upon death this soul would leave the body and be reborn in another body. When people had behaved well, their souls reincarnated into higher bodies. But when they had misbehaved, they reincarnated into a lower life form, either a lower caste or an animal or plant. The outcome depended on a person's **karma**, his or her behavior in the former life. The idea of reincarnation supported the caste system—a person's position in the hierarchy was the result of earlier behavior and was one's own responsibility. At the same time, it opened up the possibility of upward social movement, even if such movement had to wait for the next life.

The belief in reincarnation tied all forms of life together into a single system, a universal and eternal entity called **Brahman**. Even the gods passed away, and other gods replaced them. The aim of the Upanishads was to make people conscious of their connection to the Brahman. In this view, each being has a Self, called the **atman**, understanding of which liberates people from the constant cycle of reincarnation. They would first attain a state of deep sleep without dreams, unaware of any physical reality. One teacher explained the state as follows:

> Now as a man, when embraced by a beloved wife, knows nothing that is without, nothing that is within, so does this person, when embraced by the intelligent Self (atman), knows nothing that is without, nothing that is within. This is indeed his true form, in which wishes are fulfilled, in which the Self only is his wish, in which no wish is left—free from sorrow.[5]

After achieving deep sleep, an individual could reach a level beyond this dreamless trance, in which he or she realizes that his or her Self is identified with the eternal entity (Brahman). One does not reach the higher stage through active life but by meditating, that is, reflecting on religious questions.

We see, then, that the expansion of the Aryas across India did not result in the simple dissemination of Vedic ideas. Rather, contact with indigenous traditions led to changes in Vedic ideas. A religion that emphasized individual transcendence replaced one that emphasized the role of social elites in divine sacrifice. It is within this later Vedic world that further developments in Indian religious thought would take place (which we will explore in Chapter 6).

Reincarnation

reincarnation Belief system that every living being's soul can be reborn in another life form after death in an eternal cycle of existence.

karma In Indian thought about reincarnation, the consequences of one's behavior in an earlier life that influence events in the present.

Brahman In Indian thought, a universal and eternal soul that binds all life forms together.

atman In Indian thought, the immortal essence of a living creature.

The Early Chinese Dynasties 2000–771 B.C.E.

In India of the second millennium B.C.E., we have seen how the arrival of new people caused sweeping social and religious changes. By contrast, in the region of East Asia that would develop into China, cultures in the early and later periods were linked by continuities. From the start of agricultural life in the vast landmass that constitutes modern China, multiple cultures coexisted, and through increased contacts and exchange they acquired common features. The middle Yellow River Valley was the seat of a succession of dynasties, and archaeological information from that region allows us to study how states governed by a powerful elite developed.

FOCUS

What factors account for the remarkable cultural continuity of early Chinese states?

Re-Creating Early China: Literary Traditions and the Archaeological Record

In around 100 B.C.E., Sima Qian, the court astrologer whom we met at the beginning of the chapter, wrote a history of his country up to his own day. He based his account on existing books that contained anecdotes, speeches, and chronicles of rulers from the beginning of time. His *Records of the Historian* contains historical tales, chronological tables, biographies, and treatises. Because Sima Qian lived in a time when a single dynasty, the Han, ruled China, he depicted the earlier history of his country as a sequence of similar dynasties. According to Sima Qian, after a period in which heroes and sages established the elements of culture, such as agriculture, music, and the arts, three dynasties governed in succession: the Xia (shah), Shang, and Zhou (joe).

For two millennia, Sima Qian and the literary sources he used provided the only evidence of China's early history. Then in the twentieth century C.E., archaeologists unearthed villages, cities, and cemeteries that tell a somewhat different story. The excavations provided evidence that from about 2000 to 771 B.C.E., a sequence of large urban centers flourished in China; they were probably the capital cities of states. In those cities lived elites who surrounded themselves with luxury goods in life and were buried in lavish tombs, similar to those we have seen in Southwest Asia and Egypt.

Oracle Bones   China's early history became clearer with the discovery of the first written material from the region. In the late nineteenth century C.E., farmers from Anyang (ahn-YAHNG) in the Yellow River Valley regularly dug up bones and turtle shells incised with what looked like characters of Chinese script. However, they could not read them. Believing that these "dragon bones" had the power to heal, they ground them into medicinal powders. When scholars saw the bones in 1898, they recognized that the inscriptions contained some of the royal names Sima Qian listed in his history of the Shang dynasty. Further excavations at Anyang revealed large deposits of bones and turtle shells, which scholars refer to as *oracle bones* because of their use in **divination**, that is, the prediction of the future. Some two hundred thousand oracle bones have been discovered, many of them fragmentary, containing mostly short inscriptions. They derive from the reigns of the last nine kings of the Shang dynasty, from about 1200 to 1027 B.C.E. (see Lives and Livelihoods: Chinese Diviners, page 96).

Chinese Writing   The oracle bones are the earliest preserved evidence of writing in China. Other types of records were probably written on perishable materials such as bamboo or silk. The script of the oracle bones uses a principle followed in the cuneiform and hieroglyphic writings we discussed in Chapter 2: a single sign represents an entire word. Some of the characters were pictures of the item they indicated (for example, a kneeling human for a woman), whereas conventional symbols conveyed abstract ideas (for example, a mouth for "to call"). Although many words in Chinese sound alike, each had its own representation in writing, and until the twentieth century C.E. Chinese script did not rely much on syllabic signs. In this respect, it departed from the early scripts of Southwest Asia and Egypt.

The Chinese script has a unique history. After the first emperor, Shi Huangdi (shee huang-dee, discussed in Chapter 6), ordered its standardization, its basic elements and characters did not change, although the shape of the signs evolved over time. The script had a deep effect on Chinese history in that it connected people from a wide geographical area to the same ancient past. As Chinese script spread, its use brought more and more people into a shared history.

The Growth of States 2000–1570 B.C.E.

Soon after 2000 B.C.E. the village cultures that had characterized China for millennia developed into a more uniform culture in which bronze played a major role. Copper had been used for tools since 5000 B.C.E., but around 2000 B.C.E., people started to mix it with tin to produce the much stronger bronze. Scholars disagree about how bronze working arrived in

divination The practice of seeking information about the future through sources regarded as magical.

China. Some argue for an indigenous invention, whereas others believe that Indo-European nomads brought the technology from western Asia to China.

Bronze production in ancient China was unparalleled in the ancient world. The elites valued the metal so much that they commissioned vast numbers of weapons and other items, especially vessels. Demand was so great that in around 1500 B.C.E. large-scale production started. Workers manufactured numerous objects. Many were of giant size—one tomb from around 1200 B.C.E. contained 3520 pounds of the metal, and the largest surviving bronze vessel from antiquity, which weighs 1925 pounds, is also from this era. All the bronze objects were cast in molds with intricate decorations, which were first impressed in clay and later refined by filing the bronze. Mining the metals, transporting them, and casting them required the handicraft of hundreds of workers, many with specialized skills. Thus, like the silk cloth production we discussed earlier in this chapter, the desires of elites stimulated bronze production and required the specialized labor that went along with social stratification.

The earliest large urban site in China is Erlitou (er-lee-toh), dating from around 1900 B.C.E. In its center on top of a pounded-earth platform archaeologists found the remains of a monumental building, measuring about 110 by 117 yards. In later periods of Chinese history, such imposing structures had an official character, and it is thus likely that this was a palace. The objects found at the site of Erlitou resemble those that later clearly showed political control and ritual activity, such as weapons and bronze vessels. Archaeologists also found many animal shoulder blades, and although they were not inscribed, they may have been oracle bones.

The archaeological remains from Erlitou belong to a culture that spread over the central Yellow River Valley and adjacent zones. Scholars used to believe that Erlitou was the capital of the dynasty that Sima Qian called Xia, but today most historians think that the Xia dynasty did not exist and that Sima Qian imposed an image of the state of his day onto an earlier period. Many of Erlitou's cultural elements survived into the succeeding period, which may characterize the start of what Sima Qian called the Shang dynasty. Historians feel that they are on firmer ground in the study of that dynasty, as oracle bones confirm its existence and contain information that archaeology on its own cannot provide.

The Shang Dynasty and the Consolidation of Power
1570–1027 B.C.E.

Several major cities in the Yellow River Valley seem to have been successive centers of political power in the second half of the second millennium B.C.E. (see Map 3.3). They differed from early cities in Southwest Asia and the Indus Valley; they covered a much larger area and had zones with clearly distinct functions that housed a hierarchy of social classes. The centers of the early Chinese cities contained large buildings on top of pounded-earth platforms reserved for the elites. Surrounding them were industrial areas with workshops that produced goods for these elites, such as bronze vessels. The common people lived in the outer rings of the cities in small houses partly dug into the ground. This helped inhabitants to keep warm in the winter and cool in the summer, but their living circumstances were generally very poor. On the outskirts of the cities were located the tombs for rulers and other elites, and nearby were sites for rituals related to the dead, such as the reading of oracle bones. Thus, Chinese cities were physical manifestations of Chinese social structure.

The city of Anyang shows the culmination of a process of increasing concentration of power and wealth in early China. Located one hundred miles to the north of the Yellow River and stretching over a huge area of some twenty square miles, it most likely was a capital of the Shang state. Anyang's cemetery shows the riches that elites accumulated. It had thirteen large tombs, dug into the ground up to forty-three feet deep and with wooden

Shang Dynasty Bronze Vessel
Shang period bronze work is famous for the skill and refinement the artists displayed in their creations. To produce a vessel like this one, they made a clay model of the desired object to create a mold, which they cut into pieces. They cast bronze segments in the clay molds and reassembled them before filling in the details. This process enabled them to produce large items with elaborate decoration. (akg-images/Werner Forman.)

Anyang

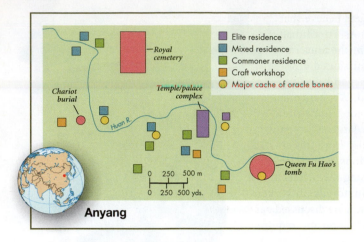

Anyang

Legend:
- Elite residence
- Mixed residence
- Commoner residence
- Craft workshop
- Major cache of oracle bones

Royal cemetery
Chariot burial
Temple/palace complex
Huan R.
Queen Fu Hao's tomb
0   250   500 m
0   250   500 yds.

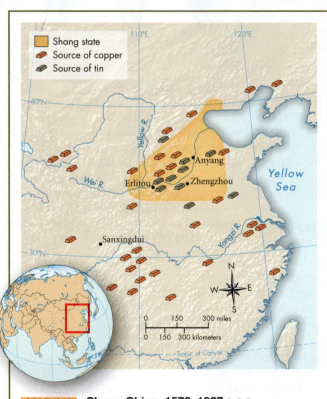

Legend:
- Shang state
- Source of copper
- Source of tin

MAP 3.3   Shang China, 1570–1027 B.C.E.
The Shang dynasty ruled the Yellow River Valley and its surroundings. They repeatedly moved the capital to sprawling new cities with massive earthwork constructions and impressive royal tombs. Famed for its bronzes, Shang China needed continued access to copper and tin, whose sources the state sought to control.

burial chambers at the bottom. These monumental tombs certainly belonged to Shang kings and queens, although the fact that all but one were looted prevents us from knowing exactly who was buried in them.

The only remaining intact tomb from Anyang contained dazzling wealth. In 1976 C.E., Chinese archaeologists discovered the tomb of Queen Fu Hao (foo HOW), wife of King Wu Ding, who lived in the thirteenth century B.C.E. Previously known oracle bones had already revealed that she was a highly unusual woman for her time, although she was only one of Wu Ding's many consorts. Some oracle bones state that Fu Hao prepared them, evidence that she took a leading role in divination, which was usually reserved for the king. The oracle bones also indicate that she actively participated in her husband's wars, raising troops and leading them into battle. The finds in the tomb confirmed her unusual status. They included over a hundred weapons—very uncommon for a woman's burial—and some were inscribed with her name. Several bronze vessels were also inscribed with Fu Hao's name or title. The splendor of her tomb goods was magnificent. They included more than 460 bronze objects, some 70 stone sculptures, nearly 705 jade objects, numerous bone hairpins, and some 7000 cowrie shells, which served as currency at the time. Alongside Fu Hao lay six sacrificed dogs and sixteen sacrificed humans. As in other ancient societies, the tombs of the Chinese elites displayed their wealth and power.

Surrounding the royal tombs of Anyang were more than twelve hundred pits containing the remains of people and animals. Human skeletons were the most numerous by far, but there were also twenty pits with horses, and fewer with other animals. Each of two pits held an elephant accompanied by its human attendants. The human sacrifices were usually young men, who were often beheaded or otherwise dismembered, with the heads buried apart from the bodies. Although some of these sacrifices were made at the time of a king's burial, most occurred later, as gifts to the dead. They were part of interactions between the king and his ancestors, which dominated the ritual life of the Shang state.

The cult of ancestors dominated Shang's ritual and religious ideas; the deceased were thought to have enormous powers over the living. A god called *Di* (dee) presided over hierarchically organized powers, which included natural phenomena such as rivers, mountains, and the sun and also people who had lived in the past. These included male and female Shang ancestors of the king, pre-Shang ancestors, and former regional lords. When an important person died, he or she became an ancestor and joined the group of powers. The honors awarded to these people while still alive continued after death and may even have expanded. Ancestors gained even more importance in the later Shang dynasty, at the expense of Di, who may ultimately have come to be considered the first royal ancestor.

The high respect for ancestors also explains the care the Shang gave to burials and the subsequent sacrifices. The living king had to keep ancestors satisfied so that they would not cause harm, and he constantly consulted them through oracle bones to divine the future. Oracle reading evidently took place continuously and required an infrastructure of specialists. These included people to slaughter the animals, which subject regions often provided as tribute; individuals to select and prepare the bones and shells; and scribes to record the questions, predictions, and other information on perishable materials before carving the text on the actual bones or shells (see Lives and Livelihoods: Chinese Diviners). Ancestor worship reinforced the power of kings by connecting them to a host of notable people stretching back through the generations to the beginning of time.

Ancestor Worship

The king enforced his rule through military means as well as rituals. Devotion to warfare was a Shang hallmark. The core of the army fought on chariots pulled by two horses and ridden by a warrior, an attendant, and a driver. The introduction of chariots after 1500 B.C.E. marked a major technological change in Chinese society. Because the earliest chariots in China were fully developed, many scholars think the innovation came from western Asia. Once again, nomads were key to this development. Indo-European-speaking nomads of Central Asia, such as those whose mummified bodies were found in the Tarim Basin, were probably the intermediaries between the two regions.

Warfare

Besides fighting, the Shang also loved to hunt. Excavations have revealed numerous bones of elephants, bears, rhinoceroses, tigers, leopards, deer, monkeys, foxes, and smaller game. Whereas northern China is now barren and treeless, in ancient times the region was blanketed with dense forests, home to many animals. The Shang hunted them in great numbers, partly for use in the sacrifices that were a major part of their ritual life, but also for sport.

All the monumental remains relate to the top level of Shang society, whose members had access to great wealth and power. A large majority of people, however, lived in poor conditions, working the fields, mining metals, building tombs and monumental residences, and providing other services to their masters. Many were slaves captured during military campaigns, and as we have seen, their lives could be sacrificed to benefit the Shang elites.

Social Order

Sima Qian's focus on the Shang dynasty, along with Anyang's status as the only city to provide written evidence of this period, creates the false impression that the Shang state was the only important one in late-second-millennium B.C.E. China. Recent archaeological work shows that other regions had their own cultures, which sometimes produced artwork as impressive as that of Anyang, but stylistically distinct. The people of some of these regions must have created states as well. It was one of these centers that ended the Shang dynasty: in the eleventh century B.C.E. the Zhou to the west of the Shang heartland defeated the last Shang ruler, Di Xin.

Shang's Neighbors

The Early Zhou Dynasty and the Extension of Power 1027–771 B.C.E.

During the Shang period many distinct groups controlled parts of northern China as either allies or opponents of Shang rulers. According to Sima Qian, the leader of one such group, the Zhou, defeated Di Xin at the Battle of Muye in 1027 B.C.E. King Wen, the Zhou ruler, justified the rebellion with a new ideology: he had received the **Mandate of Heaven** to replace an oppressive ruler. An ode in his honor from the *Book of Songs* states:

Mandate of Heaven Concept in Chinese thought that Heaven gave the right to rule to a king or emperor and could withdraw that right were the ruler to behave badly.

Statue of a Man from Sanxingdui

Outside the center of Shang rule Chinese artists produced refined bronze work that displays regional styles. One masterpiece is this 8-1/2-foot statue excavated at Sanxingdui to the west of Shang's heartland. Features such as the man's attenuated shape are very unlike the artistic style characteristic of Anyang at the time. (Sanxingui Museum/ChinaStock.)

Chinese Diviners

Just like other ancient peoples, such as the Mesopotamians, the Chinese were preoccupied with predicting the future. In the Shang period, this stimulated a massive enterprise based on oracle bones. Numerous people were involved, including the preparers of bones or shells, the scribes, and the diviners themselves, a post reserved for noblemen. The Shang king was the principal figure, however, as the questions and interpretations derived their authority from his person. The basic idea behind the divination practice was that ancestors could give guidance about the future and communicate their advice through oracle bones.

In typical practice, the king or his diviners first formulated a statement such as "we will receive millet harvest." The diviner then touched a previously prepared animal shoulder bone or turtle shell with a hot metal point until the bone or shell cracked. He numbered the cracks, and the king interpreted them as being auspicious—that is, indicating a good omen—or not. He then made a prediction such as "Auspicious: We will receive harvest." Next, a scribe carved the original question on the bone or shell, sometimes with the king's prediction and more rarely with a statement of what happened in reality.

The questions posed often involved the success of harvests or whether the queen would give birth to a boy or a girl. They ranged over a wide area of royal activities, however: Whom should the king appoint to a bureaucratic post? When should he make an offering? Will an act of his incur the displeasure of the powers? One group of early diviners often listed alternatives side by side. For example:

Divined: "On the next day, day 31, (we) should not make offering to Ancestor Yi."

Divined: "On the next day, day 31, (we) should make offering to Ancestor Yi."

Some statements contained an appeal for good luck or asked for guidance in the interpretation of an event or a dream. Others aimed to predict disasters, as in this example:

Crack-making on day 30, Que divined: "In the next ten days there will be no disasters." The king read the cracks, and said: "Not so. There will be trouble!" And so it was. On day 31, the king went to hunt buffaloes and the chariot of officer Zi hit the royal chariot. Prince Yang fell to the ground.

Crack-making on day 50, Que divined: "In the next ten days there will be no disasters." The king twice stated:

Oracle Bone

Bones inscribed with early Chinese characters present the first examples of Chinese writing dating to the late Shang period, 1200 to 1027 B.C.E. This oracle bone is from the hundreds of thousands that have been found near the Shang capital of Anyang. (Lowell Georgia/Corbis.)

"There will be trouble!" He predicted: "X will have trouble and an affliction." The fifth day came, day 54, X fell from the steps of the sacrificial room. The divination took place in the tenth month.

Oracle bone divination is closely tied to the Shang dynasty. It may have originated earlier in Chinese history, but archaeologists cannot determine from the uninscribed bones and shells they find whether they were consumed for food only or had uses in divination. The Shang dynasty elevated oracle bone divination to a major state enterprise, as the numerous remains show. With the Zhou, however, people turned to other means to find out what the future held in store.

Source: Redouan Djamouri, trans., "Écriture et divination sous les Shang," in *Divination et rationalité en Chine ancienne*, ed. Karine Chemla, Donald Harper, and Marc Kalinowski (Saint-Denis, France: Presses Universitaires de Vincennes, 1999), 19.

QUESTIONS TO CONSIDER

1. What areas of life did Shang divination cover?

2. How did oracle bone reading bolster the king's role in society?

For Further Information:
de Bary, William T., and Irene Bloom, eds., *Sources of Chinese Tradition*, 2d ed., Vol. 1. New York: Columbia University Press, 1999.
Ebrey, Patricia Buckley. *Chinese Civilization: A Source Book*, 2d ed. New York: Free Press, 1993.
Keightley, David N. *Sources of Shang History: The Oracle-Bone Inscriptions of Bronze Age China*. Berkeley: University of California Press, 1978.

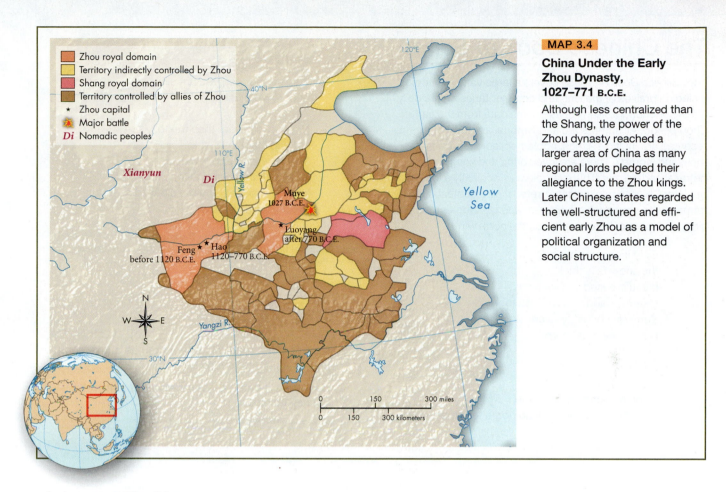

MAP 3.4

China Under the Early Zhou Dynasty, 1027–771 B.C.E.

Although less centralized than the Shang, the power of the Zhou dynasty reached a larger area of China as many regional lords pledged their allegiance to the Zhou kings. Later Chinese states regarded the well-structured and efficient early Zhou as a model of political organization and social structure.

Map legend:
- Zhou royal domain
- Territory indirectly controlled by Zhou
- Shang royal domain
- Territory controlled by allies of Zhou
- ★ Zhou capital
- Major battle
- *Di* Nomadic peoples

> August was King Wen,
> continuously bright and reverent.
> Great, indeed, was the Mandate of Heaven.
> There were Shang's grandsons and sons.
> Was their number not a hundred thousand?
> But the High God gave his Mandate,
> and they bowed down to Zhou.[6]

As a supreme divine force, Heaven, called Tian (ty-ehn) in Chinese, gave the right to rule to a just and honorable man. When that man maintained order and harmony on earth, the entire cosmos was harmonious. If he misbehaved, however, Heaven withdrew the mandate, natural disasters occurred, and the people were allowed to rebel. The idea of the Mandate of Heaven thus became a check on rulers and allowed the possibility of political change. All new Chinese dynasties adopted the ideology the Zhou created to justify their rebellion, and even the democracy-seeking protesters at Beijing's Tiananmen Square in May 1989 invoked the rejection of oppressive rulers.

The Zhou was the longest ruling dynasty in Chinese history (1027–221 B.C.E.), although, as we will see, its powers were only nominal after 771 B.C.E. The territory Zhou kings ruled was larger than that of the Shang, stretching beyond the Yellow River Valley, but their control was indirect. Zhou kings did not personally annex and govern all the regions included in the state but appointed family members to do so on their behalf. When it was impossible to subdue a territory fully, they established alliances with local lords who were willing to accept the kings' supremacy. Lords resided in fortified cities and often controlled only a small hinterland. By around 800 B.C.E. there existed some two hundred regional lords in the Zhou state. According to convention, they all belonged to one extended family, with the Zhou king being the oldest brother who deserved the most respect (see Map 3.4).

Political and Social Structure

READING THE PAST

The Chinese *Book of Songs*

The Chinese *Book of Songs* covers a large variety of topics, including praises of the king and commentaries on the daily life of commoners. Many of its poems date from the early Zhou period. All authors are anonymous, and the voices represented are multiple: kings, noblemen, soldiers, peasants, men, and women. There are love songs and songs about betrayal and sorrow. This example was originally a love song, but later Chinese thinkers interpreted it as a contest song by farmers who urge each other to escape government oppression, metaphorically referred to as the north wind.

> Cold is the north wind,
> the snow falls thick.
> If you are kind and love me,
> take my hand and we'll go together.
> You are modest, you are slow,
> but oh, we must hurry!
>
> Fierce is the north wind,
> the snow falls fast.
> If you are kind and love me,
> take my hand and we'll go home together.

> You are modest, you are slow,
> but oh, we must hurry!
>
> Nothing is redder than the fox,
> nothing blacker than the crow.
> If you are kind and love me,
> take my hand and we'll ride together.
> You are modest, you are slow,
> but oh, we must hurry!

Source: Burton Watson, trans., in Wm. Theodore de Bary and Irene Bloom, eds., *Sources of Chinese Tradition*, 2d ed., vol. 1 (New York: Columbia University Press, 1991), 40.

EXAMINING THE EVIDENCE

1. How can one read this poem both as a love song and as a contest song?

2. How does it use the natural environment to convey its message?

This structure provided a very strict hierarchy to Zhou society. Each local lord and state official had a well-defined rank and position assigned by birth. Sacrifices to ancestors continued. The king made offerings to the ancestors of the royal family, and local lords honored their own ancestors. By participating in these rituals, they reinforced their social ties.

Ritual Practices Under the Zhou, however, the ritual practices associated with ancestor cults changed. Instead of performing sacrifices, nobles contacted their ancestors by donating bronzes, which they inscribed with short texts listing the names of the donors and sometimes military events. In return, the ancestors were expected to provide favors to the living. The consultation of oracle bones also ended, and in its place kings determined the wishes of ancestors by reading messages in the lines sticks created when thrown down.

Some statements kings made in interpreting cast sticks became part of the major literary works of subsequent Chinese history. Later works, especially the *Book of Songs*, also include poems from the early Zhou period that reflect court life at the time (see Reading the Past: The Chinese *Book of Songs*). Later Chinese extensively edited this early material, however, so modern scholars have trouble determining what is original and what is not. It is clear, however, that many later generations in China saw the Zhou period as very special, with an ideal government and social structure. Just as ancestors provided models for the living to emulate, the Zhou provided a model for the current Chinese state. In this way the image of the Zhou state was fundamental to Chinese thought.

End of the Early Zhou The Zhou political organization fell apart in 771 B.C.E., when leaders of dependent states started to ignore the king's commands and to fight one another, ushering in a long period of internal warfare. Nonetheless, in the many preceding centuries, a large part of China had become organized culturally and politically along similar lines, and a distinctive Chinese identity had arisen. The cultural developments were the result of indigenous processes, but technological innovations from the nomadic outsiders had played a significant role. Although settled Chinese such as Sima Qian saw these intruders as "barbarians," they had been crucial in the evolution of Chinese culture.

COUNTERPOINT
The Oxus People: A Short-Lived Culture in Central Asia 2100–1700 B.C.E.

FOCUS

What are the unique characteristics of the Oxus culture in the early history of Asia?

The continuity that characterized the settled communities of China and India did not occur everywhere in Asia. In the Central Asian valleys of the rivers Amu Darya and Syr Darya rivers, in present-day Turkmenistan, northern Afghanistan, southern Uzbekistan, and western Tajikistan, a settled society emerged and disappeared over the course of four hundred years. Today's world politics have greatly influenced our knowledge of this region. Archaeological investigations of the area started in the 1970s C.E., when it was part of the former Soviet Union, and the excavators published their results in Russian articles and books that were little known outside the Soviet Union. Only after the end of the Soviet Union in 1991 were these works translated into other languages and these early cultures became known in other parts of the world.

One culture this archaeological research reveals was highly unusual. Scholars call it either the Oxus (OX-uhs) culture, after the Greek name *Oxus* for the Amu Darya River, or the Bactria-Margiana archaeological complex, derived from the names *Bactria* and *Margiana*, which the ancient Greeks gave to these regions of Central Asia. The rivers there have the special characteristic that they run dry in the desert and do not drain into a sea. These rivers enabled irrigation agriculture, as in other parts of Asia, but only in isolated oases and only when people built a complex system of canals.

It was in these fertile places, around 2100 B.C.E., that people of Central Asia unexpectedly established agricultural settlements in which they could live year-round while farming barley and wheat. They built walled fortresses with guard towers and reinforced gates; a single clan probably inhabited each fortress under a leader who resided in the center. These structures suggest that living conditions were unsafe and that inhabitants needed protection, most likely against neighbors who wanted access to the precious water. They may also have had to resist nomads who roamed the regions north of the Oxus River Valley and may have tried to settle in the oases. Unlike in the contemporary Indus Valley culture, warfare seems to have been a major preoccupation of these people.

One small seal with what may be signs of an unknown script was excavated among the remains of the Oxus culture, but no scholar can read its text. Thus we have no idea what language or languages the people of this culture spoke, but several historians have argued that they were Indo-European migrants who came from areas farther north. They may later have migrated south into Iran and southeast into the Indian subcontinent, where they could have caused the end of the Indus River culture. The creators of the Oxus culture would then have been crucial for the later history of South Asia. Other scholars argue that such theories are highly conjectural because archaeological remains don't tell us the origins and later destinations of this culture's people or what language they spoke.

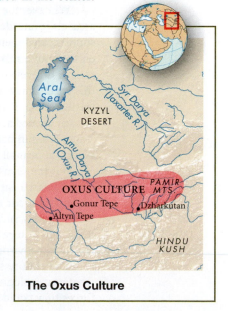

The Oxus Culture

Oxus Culture Fortress
The settlements of the Oxus culture were typically heavily fortified, surrounded by straight rectangular walls with guard towers. This is Gonur Tepe in modern Turkmenistan, which was fully excavated so that its entire plan is visible. The fortress measures 142 by 130 yards and may have contained a temple and a palace. (Kenneth Garrett.)

Whoever the people of the Oxus culture were, archaeological finds show that they created elaborate decorated axes, stamp seals, and vessels, all of which demonstrate very sophisticated metalworking skills. The region's artisans also produced sculptures of women made of a mixture of costly light and dark stones. These works are very distinctive in style and reveal that the society was rich enough to produce luxury goods. The source of this wealth may have been Oxus control of overland trade routes connecting eastern and western Asia. If true, this would show that forerunners of the Silk Road (see Chapter 6) already existed at this early date. In any event, it is clear that inhabitants of the Oxus River Valley were in contact with other regions of Asia by 2000 B.C.E., at which time their craft objects appear all over the Iranian plateau.

But the Oxus culture vanished around 1700 B.C.E., and permanent settlement in the region ceased for some five hundred years. Why? Scholars have come up with various explanations for the culture's demise, ranging from natural causes, such as droughts, to political ones, such as excessive conflict. The region's unusual ecological conditions, which made agriculture possible only in isolated oases, may explain why people saw it as a less-than-ideal environment and abandoned it so suddenly.

The culture shows, however, how people throughout world history sought to exploit whatever ecological niche was available and how their success in doing so depended on forces they could not always control. The circumstances of the Oxus River Valley around

2100 B.C.E. enabled people to live in these kinds of settlements and create a distinctive culture. The conditions that enabled settlement disappeared four hundred years later because of natural changes or for other reasons. People could no longer live in the oases, so they moved elsewhere or turned to a nomadic lifestyle. Whichever was the case, when the environment changed, the settled culture they had created ceased to exist.

Conclusion

The historian Sima Qian, whom we met at the start of this chapter, had a very low opinion of the nomadic people living on the edges of the Chinese state whose ruler he served. His disparaging remarks were misguided, however. Contacts between the settled and the nomadic people of Asia were constant, and throughout the entire history of the continent, the interactions between these two groups with distinct livelihoods were important to both. Their uses of the natural environment were complementary, and cultural exchanges went both ways. The boundaries between the two groups were also not absolute. Many nomadic groups became sedentary, as we saw with the Indo-European speakers in India, just as sedentary people could turn to nomadism, as was possibly the case at the end of the Oxus River culture. To understand the history of the region, we must take both groups into account.

The ancient histories of India and China show how long cultural traditions can last—their influences are still felt today. But historical differences between the two regions are clear. In India, an early urban culture of the Indus Valley ceased to exist before newly arrived Aryas, together with indigenous people, created the foundations of the region's culture. In China the earliest states—the Shang and Zhou—introduced elements such as a script and political ideology that survived into modern times.

Historians do not, however, find such continuity everywhere in Asia. Some ancient cultures, such as that of the Oxus River, disappeared completely. In the next chapter we will return to the western parts of Asia to see how its urban cultures developed new structures, political and otherwise. We will investigate how the first empires in world history evolved.

NOTES

1. Burton Watson, trans., *Records of the Grand Historian by Sima Qian: Han Dynasty II* (New York: Columbia University Press, 1993), 129.
2. *The Laws of Manu*, trans. Georg Bühler (New York: Dover Publications, 1969), 327–328.
3. Wendy Doniger O'Flaherty, *The Rig Veda: An Anthology* (New York: Penguin Books, 1981), 10.90, 30–31.
4. *Rig Veda*, trans. Ralph T. H. Griffith (Benares: E. J. Lazarus and Co., 1896), at sacred-texts.com, book VI, hymn 64.
5. *Hindu Scriptures*, trans. Nicol Macnicol (London/New York: J. M. Dent & Sons, Ltd./E. P. Dutton & Co., Inc., 1938), 93.
6. Burton Watson, trans., Book of Songs in Wm. Theodore de Bary and Irene Bloom, eds., *Sources of Chinese Tradition*, 2d ed., vol. 1 (New York: Columbia University Press, 1999), 38.

RESOURCES FOR RESEARCH

Early Agricultural Societies of South and East Asia, 5000–1000 B.C.E.

Most histories of early India and China include discussions of the periods before written sources appear. For a special focus on the pastoral aspects, see:

Golden, Peter B. "Nomads and Sedentary Societies in Eurasia." In *Agricultural and Pastoral Societies in Ancient and Classical History*, edited by M. Adas, 71–115. 2001.

The Indus Valley Culture, 2600–1900 B.C.E.

The archaeological literature on the Indus Valley culture is often very technical. Some recent overviews appeared in connection with museum exhibitions. Kenoyer's book is the most detailed general survey.

Allchin, Bridget, and Raymond Allchin. *The Birth of Indian Civilization.* 1968.

Aruz, Joan, ed. *Art of the First Cities: The Third Millennium B.C. from the Mediterranean to the Indus.* 2003.

(For the newest discoveries and much more): *The Indus Civilization.* http://www.harappa.com/har/har0.html

Kenoyer, Jonathan M. *Ancient Cities of the Indus Valley.* 1991.

Indo-European Migrations, 3000–1000 B.C.E.

This topic has created much controversy, with scholars disagreeing, especially on the homeland of the Indo-European speakers and on their ways of migrating. Mallory's book provides the broadest survey of the available information.

Encyclopædia Britannica Online, s.v. "Indo-European Languages," http://search.eb.com/eb/article-9109767 (accessed July 30, 2008).

Family Tree of Indo-European Languages. http://www.danshort.com/ie/

Mallory, J. P. *In Search of the Indo-Europeans.* 1991.

Renfrew, Colin. *Archaeology and Language: The Puzzle of Indo-European Origins.* 1990.

India's Vedic Age, 1500–500 B.C.E.

Many general surveys of Indian history include good chapters on the earliest periods. Basham's book, although older than the others cited, contains a particularly readable account.

Avari, Burjor. *India, the Ancient Past: A History of the Indian Sub-Continent from c. 7000 B.C. to A.D. 1200.* 2007.

Basham, A. L. *The Wonder That Was India: A Survey of the Culture of the Indian Sub-Continent Before the Coming of the Muslims.* 1981.

*Goodall, Dominic, ed. *Hindu Scriptures.* 1996.

(For ancient Indian sources): *Internet Indian History Sourcebook.* http://www.fordham.edu/halsall/india/indiasbook.html

The Rig-Veda. http://www.sacred-texts.com/hin/rigveda

Thapar, Romila. *Early India from the Origins to A.D. 1300.* 2002.

The Early Chinese Dynasties, 2000–771 B.C.E.

The literature on the history of China is vast. The works here provide especially accessible introductions.

Ebrey, Patricia Buckley. *The Cambridge Illustrated History of China.* 1996.

Gascoine, Bamber. *A Brief History of the Dynasties of China.* 2003.

Hansen, Valerie. *The Open Empire: A History of China to 1600.* 2000.

Internet East Asian History Sourcebook. http://www.fordham.edu/halsall/eastasia/eastasiasbook.html.

Loewe, Michael, and Edward L. Shaughnessy, eds. *The Cambridge History of Ancient China.* 1999.

Thorp, Robert L. *China in the Early Bronze Age: Shang Civilization.* 2006.

A Visual Sourcebook of Chinese Civilization. http://depts.washington.edu/chinaciv/index.html.

von Glahn, Richard. *The Sinister Way: The Divine and the Demonic in Chinese Religious Culture.* 2004.

COUNTERPOINT: The Oxus People: A Short-Lived Culture in Central Asia, 2100–1700 B.C.E.

Because the Oxus culture became known outside the former Soviet Union only recently, English-language publications on it are still few in number.

Aruz, Joan, ed. *Art of the First Cities: The Third Millennium B.C. from the Mediterranean to the Indus.* 2003.

Lamberg-Karlovsky, Carl C. *Beyond the Tigris and Euphrates: Bronze Age Civilizations.* 1996.

* Primary source.

▶ **For additional primary sources from this period**, see *Sources of Crossroads and Cultures*.

▶ **For Web sites, images, and documents related to topics in this chapter**, see Make History at bedfordstmartins.com/smith.

The major global development in this chapter ▶ The rise of large urban states in Asia and the interactions between nomadic and settled peoples that shaped them.

IMPORTANT EVENTS

c. 7000 B.C.E.	Earliest farmers in East Asia
c. 6500 B.C.E.	Earliest farmers in South Asia
c. 5000 B.C.E.	Agriculture throughout Yellow River and Yangzi River valleys in China
c. 3000 B.C.E.	Agriculture throughout South Asia
c. 2600–1900 B.C.E.	Mature Indus Valley culture
c. 2100–1700 B.C.E.	Oxus River culture
c. 2000 B.C.E.	Spread of domesticated horses throughout Asia
c. 2000–1570 B.C.E.	Earliest Bronze Age cultures in China
c. 2000 B.C.E.–100 C.E.	Indo-European migrations
c. 1570–1027 B.C.E.	Shang dynasty in China
c. 1500–500 B.C.E.	India's Vedic age
1027 B.C.E.	Battle of Muye in China
1027–771 B.C.E.	Early Zhou dynasty in China

KEY TERMS

atman (p. 91)
Brahman (p. 91)
caste system (p. 89)
clan (p. 88)
divination (p. 92)
jati (p. 88)
karma (p. 91)
Mandate of Heaven (p. 95)
pastoralist (p. 75)
raja (p. 88)
reincarnation (p. 91)
varna (p. 88)
Vedas (p. 87)

CHAPTER OVERVIEW QUESTIONS

1. How did peoples living in far-flung regions of Asia develop societies that had many similarities?
2. What were the unique characteristics of the cultures studied here?
3. Which features of ancient Indian and Chinese society and culture shaped later developments most fundamentally?
4. What common trends in the interactions between settled and nomadic peoples can you discern?

SECTION FOCUS QUESTIONS

1. How did Asia's diverse natural environments shape the different lifestyles of its inhabitants?
2. What were the main characteristics of South Asia's early urban culture?
3. What does the concept "Indo-European" mean, and how important is it for the study of Eurasia?
4. How did cultural developments in early Indian history shape the structure of society?
5. What factors account for the remarkable cultural continuity of early Chinese states?
6. What are the unique characteristics of the Oxus culture in the early history of Asia?

MAKING CONNECTIONS

1. How did the development of Indus Valley cities compare with the processes in Southwest Asia (see Chapter 2) and China?
2. How does the social structure of Vedic India compare with those of ancient Southwest Asia (see Chapter 2) and China?
3. In what ways do the interactions between settled and nomadic peoples explain the historical development of Asia?
4. What are the similarities in burial practices of the ancient cultures we have discussed so far, and what do they suggest about attitudes toward class and religion in these societies?

AT A CROSSROADS ▲

In around 500 B.C.E. the Persian emperor Darius started to build a new capital of astonishing magnificence at Persepolis in modern Iran, where he celebrated an annual ceremony of tribute delivery from all subject peoples. The reliefs that decorate the walls show the great diversity of the peoples in his empire, indicating the Persians' awareness of the novelty of this type of political organization. Depicted here are Babylonians on the top level, bringing cups, cloth, and a hump-backed bull, and Phoenicians on the lower level, bringing bracelets, metal vessels, and a horse-drawn chariot. The dress and headgear identify the tribute bearers' origins. (The Art Archive/Gianni Dagli Orti.)

Creation of Empire: North Africa and Southwest Asia

1550–330 B.C.E.

I n the late sixth century B.C.E., the Persian king Darius commissioned the carving of a long inscription on a cliff side. In the inscription he described his rise to power as emperor of Persia, the king of twenty-three countries from central Asia to Egypt. He had acquired these territories by defeating a succession of men who, in his words, had falsely claimed kingship over those states. Darius proudly proclaimed:

> Thus says Darius, the king: These are the countries that listen to me—it is under the protection of the god Ahuramazda that I am their king: Persia, Elam, Babylonia, Assyria, Arabia, Egypt, the Sealand, Sardis, Ionia, Media, Urartu, Cappadocia, Parthia, Drangiana, Aria, Choresmia, Bactria, Sogdiana, Gandhara, Scythia, Sattagydia, Arachosia, and Maka, in total twenty-three countries. . . .
>
> Thus says Darius, the king: this is what I have done in one year under the protection of the god Ahuramazda. After becoming king, I have fought nineteen battles in one year, and under the protection of Ahuramazda I won them. I captured nine kings: the Magian named Gaumata, who lied saying: "I am Bardiya, son of Cyrus, king of Persia," and who caused the lands of Persia and Media to rebel; an Elamite called Atrina, who lied saying: "I am the king of Elam," and who caused Elam to rebel; a Babylonian called Nidintu-Bel, who lied saying: "I am Nebuchadnezzar, son of Nabonidus, the king of Babylon," and who caused Babylonia to rebel.[1]

Imperial Egypt and Nubia, 1550 B.C.E.–350 C.E.

FOCUS How did Egyptians and Nubians interact in the two imperial periods that united them politically?

Rise and Fall of the Assyrian Empire, 900–612 B.C.E.

FOCUS What kind of power structure did the Assyrians impose on their subjects, and how did it lead to cultural assimilation in the empire?

The Persian Empire, 550–330 B.C.E.

FOCUS What imperial vision and style of government marked the rise of the vast Persian Empire and allowed it to endure for over two hundred years?

COUNTERPOINT: Assimilation and Resistance: The Peoples of Israel and Judah

FOCUS To what degree and in what ways did the peoples of Israel and Judah accept or reject the influences of the empires they confronted?

BACKSTORY

In Chapters 2 and 3 we saw how early states developed throughout the Asian continent and in North Africa. From its very beginnings, the state of Egypt incorporated a wide territory centered on the king; in Southwest Asia, India, and China, states first grew around cities and then expanded rapidly. Although a number of these states were quite large, their populations were relatively homogeneous, sharing a common culture and history.

Starting around 1550 B.C.E., however, the rulers of some of these early states began wide-ranging foreign conquests, bringing diverse peoples under their control and creating empires. Imperial rule created a new challenge, one that has confronted empires throughout history: the need to integrate diverse subjects into a single state. As we will see in this chapter, each empire developed its own solutions to this problem.

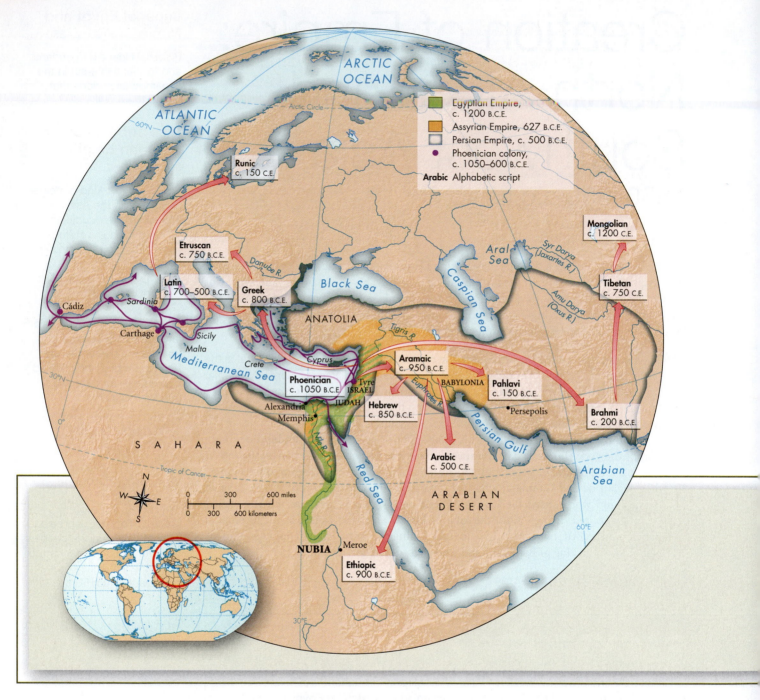

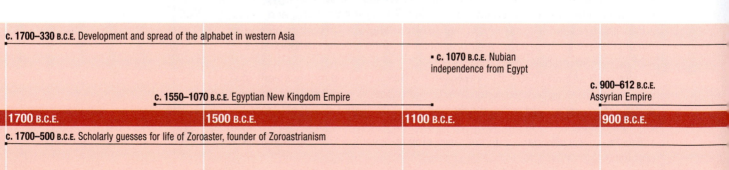

Darius was aware of the cultural and ethnic diversity of his vast empire, a fact he acknowledged by presenting his message in three different languages: his own, Old Persian; Babylonian, the language of Mesopotamia; and Elamite, the language of western Iran. He knew that the Persian Empire had brought together these and other regions in a single unit of unprecedented size. He also knew, however, that it was political and military power that held his empire together. His subjects did not see themselves as Persians, but as distinct peoples.

History has seen many empires, and their diversity makes it difficult to devise a definition of **empire** that encompasses all their variety. A common characteristic is clear, however: empires are very large political units whose leaders impose their rule over diverse countries, peoples, and cultures. Relations between empires and their subjects are complex and influence many spheres of life—political, economic, social, and cultural—so we can study empires from many perspectives. As we will discover in this chapter and others, each empire takes a different approach to the challenge of asserting imperial control. The extent to which the ruling authorities try to impose a single cultural identity on their subjects varies substantially. Moreover, even when a single culture becomes preeminent in an empire, it is not always the conquerors' customs that become dominant. Sometimes imperial powers impose their culture on the conquered territories, but sometimes they permit cultural freedom, and sometimes they embrace the cultures of the people they conquer.

empire A large political unit that imposes its rule over diverse regions, peoples, and cultures; empires can take many different forms.

MAPPING THE WORLD

Rise of the First Empires

The area at the junction of modern Africa, Asia, and Europe was the site of the first empires in world history. They appeared in a long sequence, and as empires rose and fell the sites of imperial centers moved from Egypt to Nubia, Assyria, Persia, and others that followed. Political unification aided the remarkable spread of a new system of writing invented in the heart of this area—the alphabet—but other factors also helped forms of the alphabet reach most of Eurasia and, later, the rest of the world.

ROUTES ▼

⟶ Spread of alphabetic writing
→ Phoenician trade route

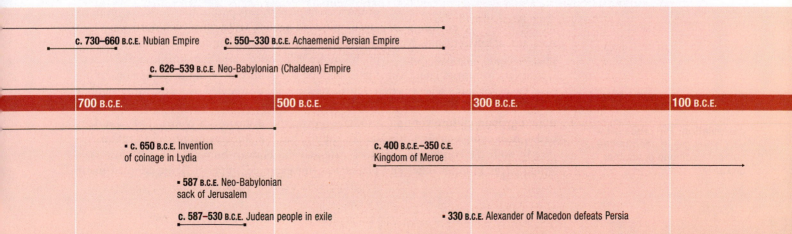

c. 730–660 B.C.E. Nubian Empire   c. 550–330 B.C.E. Achaemenid Persian Empire

c. 626–539 B.C.E. Neo-Babylonian (Chaldean) Empire

700 B.C.E.   500 B.C.E.   300 B.C.E.   100 B.C.E.

• c. 650 B.C.E. Invention
of coinage in Lydia

c. 400 B.C.E.–350 C.E.
Kingdom of Meroe

• 587 B.C.E. Neo-Babylonian
sack of Jerusalem

c. 587–530 B.C.E. Judean people in exile   • 330 B.C.E. Alexander of Macedon defeats Persia

Because the definition of what constitutes an empire is not simple, it is hard to say when the empires first appeared in world history. Historians agree, however, that a set of large states that incorporated many countries and peoples in much of North Africa and Southwest Asia from 1550 to 330 B.C.E. deserve the title. Thus, in this chapter we focus on the imperial efforts of the Egyptians, Nubians, Assyrians, and Persians. Although all these states constructed empires, their rulers' attitudes toward their subject populations varied. The pharaohs of Egypt showed little respect for the culture of Nubia, for example, whereas Nubian kings and elites eagerly absorbed their Egyptian subjects' cultural traditions and ways of life. Darius and other practical-minded Persian emperors took a middle path, tolerating local beliefs and adopting existing customs, but also demanding full obedience.

As the diverse subjects of empires went about their daily lives, they often started to share cultural habits and build a common cultural tradition. Yet some peoples of these early states, such as the people of Judah, consciously resisted adopting the ways of their conquerors. It is the diversity of interactions between the conquered and the conquerors that led to variation in empires throughout world history.

Imperial Egypt and Nubia   1550 B.C.E.–350 C.E.

In northeast Africa, where that continent borders Southwest Asia, the kingdoms of Egypt and Nubia dominated the Nile Valley from around 3000 B.C.E. From about 1550 to 660 B.C.E., first Egypt and then Nubia formed the core of the first empires in this part of the world. Egypt in its New Kingdom period expanded beyond its borders both northward into Asia and southward into Nubia, annexing huge territories. Under a sequence of strong pharaohs, the New Kingdom Egyptian Empire thrived for more than four hundred years.

Several centuries later, Nubia itself became the dominant power in the region, ruling over Egypt for some seventy years. Thus a region once dominated by a powerful neighbor itself developed into a force and overtook its master. Despite this reversal of political fortune, Egyptian culture continued to have a powerful influence in Nubia. The Egyptians had almost completely ignored Nubian culture, but the Nubians promoted Egyptian culture in both the conquered Egyptian state and the Nubian homeland. Similar reversals would occur in other times and places, too (for example, imperial Rome adopted many

assimilation The process by which one group absorbs the cultural traditions of another group.

aspects of Greek culture, as we discuss in Chapter 7). In the case of the Nubian Empire, this **assimilation**—absorption of the cultural traditions of others—produced a unique mix of local and foreign influences that characterized the region for many centuries after Nubia's empire had faded away.

The Imperial Might of New Kingdom Egypt 1550–1070 B.C.E.

Around 1550 B.C.E., the Egyptians started a sustained period of expansion. In the north, they first expelled the Hyksos—foreign rulers who had occupied the Nile Delta for some 150 years—and then marched into the area now occupied by Syria and Palestine. Large armies pushed deep into Asiatic territory, confronting states that belonged to the international system described in Chapter 2. King Thutmose III (r. 1479–1425 B.C.E.) stands out as an especially aggressive empire builder, driving his troops into Syria seventeen times to force local rulers into submission. The resistance remained strong, however, and two hundred years later King Ramesses (RAM-ih-seez) II (r. 1279–1213 B.C.E.) still had to fight massive battles against the Hittites to maintain control over part of the region. The most famous of these clashes was Ramesses's battle at Qadesh (KA-desh) in northern Syria (1275 B.C.E.), which in large relief carvings on several monuments he depicted as a great victory for the Egyptian army.

At the same time, Egypt expanded south into Nubia, occupying some seven hundred miles along the Nile River. There, the opposition was less organized, and once Egypt annexed the region after a century of campaigning, troops were more involved with peacekeeping than with further conquest (see Map 4.1).

Conquest brought tremendous riches to Egypt, allowing its pharaohs to build massive temples, palaces, and tombs stuffed with precious goods. Many pharaohs are famous today because of such monuments. An illustrious example is Queen Hatshepsut (hat-SHEP-soot), who seized power in 1473 B.C.E., when the legitimate heir Thutmose III was still a young boy, and ruled Egypt until 1458 B.C.E., the probable year of her death. To honor her after death, she ordered that a temple be constructed on the west Nile bank of the capital Thebes. Relief sculptures on the walls celebrate her accomplishments.

One depicts a naval expedition to Punt, a fabled land somewhere on the East African coast. The ships sailed down to obtain prized materials needed to construct the temple and worship the gods, such as incense and myrrh, jewels, ivory, and exotic animals and trees. The images show the sailors loading many boats with these goods. Several years after she died, the Egyptians turned against Hatshepsut and defaced the reliefs and statues that depicted her. We do not know why they took these actions, though some scholars think they reflect official opposition to a woman ruler. The Egyptians left her temple standing, however, and its remains today give a glimpse of the grandeur

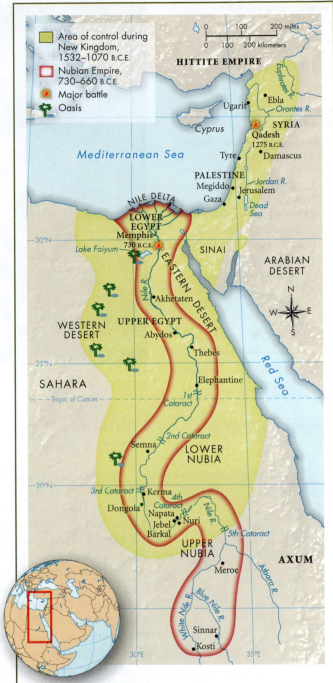

MAP 4.1   **New Kingdom of Egypt and Nubia, 1550–660 B.C.E.**

After ruling supreme in the northern Nile Valley and western Syria in the centuries from 1550 to 1070 B.C.E., Egypt itself was conquered by one of its earlier subjects, Nubia, whose kings extended their power up to the Mediterranean Sea from 730 to 660 B.C.E. Each empire controlled a massive area centered on the Nile, which facilitated constant movement of people and ideas along the river.

Queen Hatshepsut's Expedition to Punt

On the walls of her mortuary temple at Thebes, Hatshepsut had artists illustrate the highlights of her reign. These include an expedition she sent to the distant, fabled land of Punt to obtain exotic materials, including animal skins, incense plants, gold, and other precious materials. The detail here shows the Egyptian boat sailing down the Red Sea. Note the care with which the artist depicted the unusual sea creatures in the foreground; they may have been included to suggest the exceptional nature of the voyage. (Sandro Vannini/Corbis.)

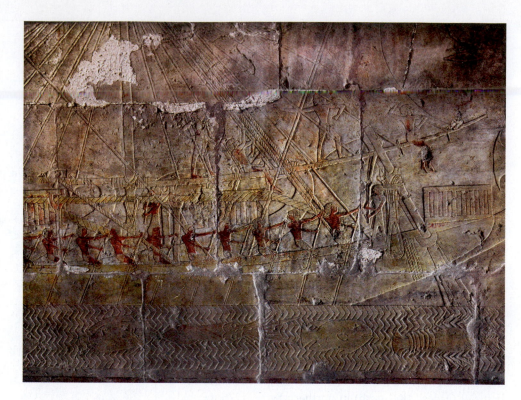

of New Kingdom Egypt. Although Hatshepsut was exceptional in that she became the acknowledged king, she was not the only woman in New Kingdom Egypt who acquired great power. In general, women in this period of Egypt's history seem to have possessed more influence and legal autonomy than anywhere else in the ancient world.

Akhenaten's Religious Reforms

The success of the New Kingdom empire and the wealth it brought the Egyptian elites may have inspired experiments with new ideas about the divine world and the pharaoh's place in it. The most remarkable episode in Egypt's religious history was the reign of King Amenhotep IV (r. 1352–1336 B.C.E.), who early in his rule adopted the name Akhenaten (ah-ken-AHT-en), meaning "servant of Aten." The king abandoned the cults of traditional deities, such as Amun, the highest god, and instead focused all his attention on the god of the sun disk, Aten. In hymns he portrayed Aten as the sole existing deity, and he built an entire city in his honor and made it his capital. Akhenaten depicted himself, his wife Nefertiti, and their daughters as the only humans who could communicate with Aten (see Reading the Past: Akhenaten Praises His God, Aten). Many scholars see in his ideas a form of **monotheism**, belief in the existence of one god only, but Akhenaten did not forbid his people to worship other deities.

Aten was Akhenaten's personal god and the ruler of the universe. This ideology gave the king a unique status, but it came at the expense of the priesthood, which in earlier Egyptian history had held enormous authority (see Chapter 2). Akhenaten's reforms did not last long, however, and soon after his death Amun and his priesthood regained their prominence in Egypt. Akhenaten's failed effort to alter Egypt's religious culture illustrates some of the complexities of cultural change brought about by empire. In this case, an emperor failed to impose long-term cultural change not because he lacked power while he lived, but because the changes he sought challenged the status of another powerful group in his state.

Class and Society in Imperial Egypt

Even during Akhenaten's unusual reign, New Kingdom Egypt was a very unequal society in terms of wealth and status. The empire's success affected people of all social levels, not just the elites. Historians estimate that New Kingdom Egypt had some 3 million inhabitants at its height, with a large proportion of the population serving the state, specifically its kings and its temples. As heads of the religious structure, pharaohs were in

Akhenaten Praises His God, Aten

King Akhenaten produced perhaps the most startling reforms in the long history of Egyptian religion. Whereas Egyptians usually honored a multitude of deities, the New Kingdom ruler focused on one god only: Aten, the sun disk. Akhenaten expressed his exclusive veneration especially through building and the visual arts. He only constructed in honor of Aten, leaving behind several temples and an entire city named Akhetaten after the god, and his artists carved numerous relief sculptures that depicted the king and his family praying to the sun disk. Such material remains leave much room for interpretation about the new ideology, but we have several copies of one long text that expresses Akhenaten's beliefs in words. It is a hymn to Aten praising the god for his beneficent powers. The end of the hymn reads:

Your rays nurse all fields,
When you shine, they live and grow for you.
You made the seasons to foster all that you made,
Winter, to cool them,
Summer, that they taste you.
You made the sky far to shine therein,
To see all that you make, while you are One,
Risen in your form of the living sundisk,
Shining and radiant,
Far and near.

You make millions of forms from yourself alone,
Towns, villages, fields,
Road and river.
All eyes behold you upon them,
When you are above the earth as the disk of daytime.

When you are gone there is no eye (whose eyesight you have created
in order not to look upon yourself as the sole one of your creatures),

But even then you are in my heart, there is no other who knows you,
Only your son, *Nefer-kheperu-Re Sole-one-of-Re* (Akhenaten),
Whom you have taught your ways and your might.

The earth comes into being by your hand as you made it,
When you dawn, they live,
When you set, they die;
You yourself are lifetime, one lives by you.

All eyes are on beauty until you set,
All labor ceases when you rest in the west;
But the rising one makes firm every arm for the king,
And every leg moves since you founded the earth.

You rouse them for your son who came from your body,
The king who lives by Ma'at, the lord of the two lands,
Nefer-kheperu-Re Sole-one-of-Re (Akhenaten),
The Son of Re who lives by Ma'at,
The lord of crowns, Akhenaten, great in his lifetime,
And the great Queen whom he loves,
The lady of the Two Lands, Nefertiti,
Who lives and rejuvenates,
For ever, eternally.

Source: Jan Assmann, *Moses the Egyptian* (Cambridge, MA: Harvard University Press, 1997), 175–177.

EXAMINING THE EVIDENCE

1. **What qualities does the hymn assign to Aten?**

2. **What is the relationship between the king and the god?**

charge of the temples, to which they assigned massive state resources. A document of the twelfth century B.C.E. indicates that about half a million people worked for temples across Egypt in activities such as farming fields the temples owned. They were not slaves, but people with personal freedom who received food in return for their labor. When the empire flourished, the supplies were guaranteed. Late in the New Kingdom, however, the empire declined, food supplies ran low, and people suffered hardship.

Determined to leave behind magnificent monuments, the pharaohs employed many specially trained craftsmen, including the men who dug and decorated tombs in the Valleys of the Kings and the Queens in the mountains facing the capital, Thebes. We are particularly well-informed about these craftsmen because archaeologists have excavated the village where they lived. The workmen's village, called Deir el Medina (dare uhl meh-DEE-nah) today, was

monotheism A religious system that tolerates the existence of one god only.

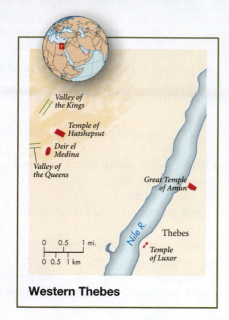

Valley of
the Kings

Temple of
Hatshepsut

Deir el
Medina

Valley of
the Queens

Great Temple
of Amun

Nile R.

Thebes

Temple
of Luxor

0   0.5   1 mi.

0 0.5 1 km

Western Thebes

in the desert between the Nile and the Valley of the Kings. Archaeologists have unearthed numerous writings detailing the lives of inhabitants.

One was a sculptor called Qen, who had two wives and at least ten children. Because the village was in the desert, the family could not grow its own food, which was delivered from the state's storehouses. They received grains, vegetables, fish, oil, and milk, as well as water and firewood. When Qen worked in the tombs, which were several hours by foot from Deir el Medina, he stayed overnight in a camp. Each day he and his colleagues worked two shifts of four hours each, with a lunch break in between. After men had dug and plastered long tunnels and a draftsman had traced the figures, Qen sculpted religious images and hieroglyphic texts to help the king on his way to the underworld, a journey central to the Egyptian religious beliefs discussed in Chapter 2. When Qen died, his children buried him in a tomb near the village. Over the years the pharaoh had rewarded him well for his work, so Qen had acquired precious objects himself, some of which accompanied him in his tomb for his use in the afterlife.

Qen and his coworkers were more privileged than most because of their much-desired skills. Historians cannot know for certain how the majority of people fared because we have no remains from them. We can imagine, however, that all Egyptians benefited to some extent from the empire's existence, at least insofar as it produced internal peace and economic stability. Like Qen, they were all part of an imperial system that connected Egypt to its territories, a system that allowed Egypt's rulers to draw resources from many distant lands to glorify themselves and to enrich their homeland.

Egypt's Attitude Toward Conquered Territories

The New Kingdom empire was so large and included such diverse peoples and countries that the Egyptians were obliged to adjust their attitude toward subjects in response to local conditions. In Southwest Asia, Egypt participated in the eastern Mediterranean system described in Chapter 2, using diplomacy to interact with rulers they considered equals. Vassal rulers, who paid taxes and allegiance to the Egyptian king, governed small kingdoms in the southern part of the Syria-Palestinian area. These vassals were politically dependent on Egypt, but the Egyptians treated them with respect, and sometimes adopted elements of their cultures. For example, New Kingdom Egyptians honored the storm god Baal (bahl) and the goddess of love Astarte (uh-STAHR-tee), both imported from Syria.

In contrast, the Egyptians showed no respect for the cultures and traditions of the Nubians, whom they considered inferior and uncivilized. Their primary interest in Nubia was its gold mines. Egyptian governors ignored the local culture and founded Egyptian-style settlements with administrative buildings and temples devoted to Egyptian gods. Some elite Nubians entered the Egyptian administration, adopting an Egyptian lifestyle to do so. One such man in the fourteenth century B.C.E. was Hekanefer, a prince of the Nubian region of Miam, just south of Egypt. His tomb near his hometown presents him in full Egyptian attire, and the accompanying hieroglyphics call him an admirer of the Egyptian god of the netherworld, Osiris. Interestingly, Hekanefer also features in paintings in a tomb in Thebes, where he appears with Nubian physical features and clothes, prostrating himself in front of an Egyptian official. Clearly, the Egyptians saw Hekanefer very differently than he saw himself. He seems proud to have adopted the dominant Egyptian culture, but for Egyptian elites his most important characteristic was his submission to their rule.

When the eastern Mediterranean system collapsed around 1200 B.C.E., the Egyptian Empire also disintegrated and gradually lost its foreign territories. By 1070 B.C.E. Nubia had become an independent kingdom. Four centuries of Egyptian imperial rule had fundamentally changed Nubia, however, and the kingdom retained the administrative centers the Egyptians had built. The Nubians used the practices they had observed among the

bureaucracy A system of government employing nonelected officials to administer a variety of specialized departments.

Nubian Prince Hekanefer Prostrates Before an Egyptian Official

The Egyptians as a rule depicted the people of Nubia as subjects who owed them allegiance and respect. This painting from the tomb of Tutankhamun's governor of Nubia in the fourteenth century B.C.E. shows local princes in submission, including one named Hekanefer in front of the group. In Hekanefer's own tomb in Nubia, he proudly represents himself in full Egyptian outfit, but here he is shown in Nubian attire, prostrate before the superior Egyptian official. (Francis Dzikowski/akg-images/The Image Works.)

Egyptians to develop a culture distinct from the rest of Africa, continuing such elements as writing and monumental building and maintaining a more centralized state organization than existed elsewhere on the continent.

Nubia's Rise and Rule of Egypt 1000–660 B.C.E.

The Nubians had their capital in Napata (nah-PAH-tuh), which had been the major Egyptian town in the region (see again Map 4.1). Napata was the site of a temple devoted to the leading Egyptian god Amun, whose cult had survived through the centuries. Nubia developed as a strong centralized state shortly after 1000 B.C.E., at a time when Egypt was divided among several competing dynasties and chiefdoms. In Egypt's south, from the area of the religious center Thebes to the Nubian border, the Theban high priest of Amun ruled as if he were a king. In the eighth century B.C.E., political control over Thebes shifted to a new system that centered on the women of the royal court. The highest religious office—which came with control over the vast properties controlled by temples and substantial political power—became that of the high priestess of Amun. She was always a princess of the most powerful political house in Egypt at the time of her selection. To maintain political control over her possessions, she could not marry and have children. Instead, she passed on her office by adopting her successor, again a princess from the strongest dynasty.

The growing power of Nubia in the region became clear when, in 736 B.C.E., its king, Piye (py), gave his sister the office of high priestess. In this way, a Nubian became in effect the ruler of southern Egypt. But northern Egyptian rulers did not accept Piye's authority and threatened to attack Thebes. In response, in around 730 B.C.E., Piye led his troops northward from Napata all the way to Memphis at the tip of the Nile Delta, forcing local rulers to submit. Egypt and Nubia reunited—but this time with Nubia in control. The succession of Nubian kings who ruled this new empire behaved in every respect like the earlier Egyptian pharaohs. They supported Egyptian cults, portrayed themselves as Egyptian rulers with the proper titles, and headed a **bureaucracy**, a group of officials who administered the country.

Although militarily superior to the Egyptians, the Nubians did not attempt to influence Egyptian culture. On the contrary, the Nubian elite absorbed Egyptian customs that they saw as expressions of power and prestige. Nubia's upper classes had imitated Egyptian

Nubia's Conquest of Egypt

Nubian Embrace of Egyptian Ways

culture in the past, but after the conquest they went further, pressing their claim to be the legitimate rulers of Egypt by presenting themselves as Egyptians rather than Nubians.

Nubian kings can be distinguished from native Egyptian rulers only by their retention of Nubian birth names. They used Egyptian titles and promoted Egyptian culture throughout their empire. In the Nubian capital, the cult of the Egyptian god Amun continued to flourish, and the Nubian rulers substantially enlarged and embellished Amun's temple in Napata to rival the one at Thebes, his main sanctuary. Nubian burial customs, inscriptions, and statues also showed a devotion to Egyptian traditions—after the conquest of Egypt, Nubian kings were buried in pyramids rather than the earlier round mounds of earth. Although the Nubian pyramids were smaller and had steeper sides than the older Egyptian structures, the Egyptian examples inspired their shape. Nubians also decorated the tomb chambers with scenes from the Egyptian books of the underworld. As in Egypt, they mummified corpses and set them in human-shaped coffins, placing hundreds of small statuettes in the tombs to assist the dead in the afterlife. The Nubians also used the Egyptian language and hieroglyphic script for their official inscriptions, and in statues of kings the poses matched those of the Egyptian pharaohs. Thus, in a myriad of ways, Nubian rulers demonstrated that their conquest of Egypt was not predicated on a sense of their own cultural superiority. Rather, they saw Egyptian culture as a key source of imperial power and unity, and they sought to use the cultural connections the Egyptians had created to reinforce the legitimacy of their own rule.

Survival of Nubian Traditions

Nonetheless, some local Nubian traditions survived—especially among the commoners of the Nubian state, but even among the elite. For example, in depictions of Nubian kings, artists accurately rendered their African physical features. A very un-Egyptian element in the Nubian burials was the interment of horses along with the king, something that Egyptians never did. The Nubians greatly admired horses, which had contributed to their military victories, and due to Nubian success in battle the horses they bred were in

Statues of Nubian Kings
These statues of Nubian rulers of the first millennium B.C.E., some up to ten feet high, were found in a pit, where they were preserved after a raiding Egyptian king had smashed them in 593 B.C.E. Reassembled, they show that in depicting kings, Nubian artists followed many Egyptian conventions, such as the erect posture, but they also reveal typically Nubian elements, such as indigenous physical features and the royal crown. (Kenneth Garrett.)

high demand in other countries. Thus the Nubians retained the things they valued most in their own culture, while adopting the aspects of Egyptian culture that seemed most useful.

The stability the Nubians brought to Egypt reflects their success in adopting Egyptian ways. The country flourished economically, and in many respects the Nubians oversaw a period of Egyptian prosperity. Although we have no evidence of popular resentment of Nubian rule among Egyptians, some elites, particularly in the north, seem to have wanted independence but lacked the military might needed to resist the Nubians. Then, around 660 B.C.E., the Assyrians of Southwest Asia invaded Egypt and drove the Nubians out of Egypt. When the Assyrians' grip on the country loosened a few years later, a family from the north of Egypt established itself as the new ruling dynasty.

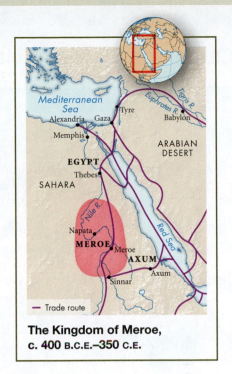

The Kingdom of Meroe, c. 400 B.C.E.–350 C.E.

The Nubian Kingdom of Meroe 400 B.C.E.–350 C.E.

Although driven from Egypt, the Nubians continued to rule their homeland. By 400 B.C.E. they moved their political capital to Meroe (MER-oh-ee), some seven hundred miles upstream from Napata. This shift took advantage of the greater fertility of the region surrounding Meroe and of the intersection of trade routes in the city. Those routes reached into regions of Africa farther south, east, and west and made Meroe a major trade crossroads for the continent.

Over time, the political situation in Egypt changed as first the Greeks (332–30 B.C.E.) and then the Romans (30 B.C.E.–395 C.E.) occupied it. The Meroites had mostly friendly contacts with the Greeks and Romans, who fancied African luxury goods such as gold, ivory, spices, animals, and slaves. During a long period of peace, the enormous Roman appetite for luxury items brought fantastic wealth and a flood of Mediterranean goods into Nubia. Trade with Rome not only made Nubia rich, but also brought Roman influences into Nubian life and culture.

Crossroads of Trade

After the first century C.E., however, Meroe's commercial advantage gradually declined. The kingdom of Axum, to Meroe's east on the Red Sea in what is today Ethiopia, became Rome's preferred center for access to African trade. As Axum's wealth grew, so did its military power, and in 350 C.E., the Axumites conquered Meroe.

After the political separation of Nubia from Egypt in the seventh century B.C.E., Egyptian influences in Nubia remained strong. Even after moving the capital to Meroe, the Nubians continued to honor Egyptian gods such as Amun, to bury kings in pyramids, and to depict themselves in an Egyptian style. Nonetheless, with fewer direct connections to Egypt, local Nubian culture grew more independent, and important changes occurred. In the second century B.C.E., for example, the Meroites started to write their own language, rather than Egyptian. They used two scripts: one based on Egyptian hieroglyphics but with only twenty-three symbols, and the other featuring entirely new sign forms that were much faster to write out. Scholars have not yet deciphered these inscriptions, whose language is unknown.

Culture and Society in Meroe

Women enjoyed a high status in the social structure of Meroe. In royal succession a king was followed by his sister's son, and from the second century B.C.E. on, several women became rulers themselves. Like their male counterparts, they were represented on monuments as defeating enemies and honoring gods. Classical Greek and Roman authors mistakenly concluded from these depictions that queens had always ruled in Nubian society (see Seeing the Past: The Queen of Meroe in Battle). As this example illustrates, the economic connections between Rome and Nubia facilitated cultural exchange and inquiry but did not eliminate misunderstandings and misinterpretations.

The Queen of Meroe in Battle

Naga Temple (front gate) (John Warburton Lee/ AWL Images.)

Queen Amanitare (From *Meroe: A Civilization of the Sudan* by P. L. Shinnie, Thames & Hudson Ltd., London.)

South of the capital Meroe, the Meroites of the late first century B.C.E. or early first century C.E. built a group of temples near a staging post for caravans traveling east. They dedicated one of the temples to the Meroite lion god Apedemak, and built it fully in accordance with an ancient Egyptian plan. Its decoration, however, shows a mixture of ancient Egyptian and local traditions.

The image on the front gate of the temple reveals this mixture. On the right side, the queen is battling enemies with the god's help; she is depicted as equal to her husband, who appears on the left. Both stand in the pose that Egyptian rulers of the distant past used to show their victories, wielding arms over opponents bunched together. Underneath them are rows of bound enemies representing defeated countries. Short Egyptian hieroglyphic inscriptions identify the figures as Queen Amanitare and King Netekamari. Above them, traditional Egyptian gods appear as birds.

These traditional Egyptian motifs are mixed with Meroitic details. The king and queen wield swords rather than the axes or maces that Egyptians would have used. Their dress and jewelry are local, and the lion god Apedemak (unknown in Egypt) assists them. Moreover, unlike Egyptian queens in images, Queen Amanitare is quite chubby, which may have been the local ideal of beauty.

EXAMINING THE EVIDENCE

1. Which decorative features of the front gate would most have startled Egyptians, and which would they have recognized as normal?

2. How does the temple illustrate contacts between Egypt and regions to its south?

For Further Information:
"Naga'a (Middle Sudan)," Poznan Archaeological Museum. http://www.muzarp.poznan.pl/muzeum/muz_eng/nagaa.htm.

The African kingdoms of Egypt and Nubia were thus at the core of the first empires in this part of the world. The Nubian rulers of Egypt showed a clear inclination to absorb the culture of the conquered territory, in sharp contrast with the Egyptians' behavior when they dominated Nubia. The Nubians' adoption of Egyptian culture led to a unique assimilation of local and foreign influences that characterized the region for many centuries after Nubia's imperial period.

Rise and Fall of the Assyrian Empire   900–612 B.C.E.

As we have seen, the Nubians were not driven from Egypt by the Egyptians but by the Assyrians. Waging unrelenting wars of conquest, the Assyrians built the first empire to encompass much of Southwest Asia. Assyria's martial character dominates our modern view of the empire, and the Assyrian state was indeed organized around the demands of warfare. But the Assyrian kings also commissioned engineering projects, built new cities, sponsored the arts, and powerfully influenced cultural developments in the empire. Despite their military successes, structural weaknesses in the empire would ultimately thwart the Assyrian kings' dreams of integrating the conquered territories into a coherent whole. Their conquests did, however, lay the groundwork for later empires in the region.

> **FOCUS**
>
> What kind of power structure did the Assyrians impose on their subjects, and how did it lead to cultural assimilation in the empire?

Assyria: A Society as War Machine

By 1000 B.C.E. Assyria was a state with a long history, but had little influence beyond its heartland in the north of modern-day Iraq. Then, starting around 860 B.C.E., Assyria began a series of wars that would lead to 250 years of dominance in Southwest Asia. The Assyrians defeated all their rivals, and by around 650 B.C.E. their control reached from western Iran to the Mediterranean Sea and from central Anatolia (modern Turkey) to Egypt (see Map 4.2).

Assyrian Militarism

The reasons for Assyria's expansion changed as the empire grew. At first, it was a defensive reaction against outside threats, especially those posed by nomads from Syria. But over time, as the Assyrians became used to the wealth that came with conquest, their expansion became more aggressive and more acquisitive. Instead of seeking to defend themselves, they were driven by a desire to seize the wealth and resources of their neighbors, including the Babylonians and the Egyptians.

The empire's militarism affected every level of Assyrian society. The state was organized as a military hierarchy with the king at the top. All state officers, whatever their responsibilities, had a military rank. The material demands of the Assyrian war machine were enormous. The army required massive amounts of weapons, clothing, and food and vast numbers of horses. But manpower was perhaps in the greatest demand: the central Assyrian state simply could not provide enough soldiers without drawing too many people away from other essential work, such as farming and building.

Deportation

The Assyrians filled their need for manpower through a policy of deporting conquered people. They were not the first empire—or the last—to employ this practice, but they were the most systematic in its use in early times. After the army defeated a region that had resisted Assyrian dominance, the troops forced large numbers of people to resettle elsewhere in the empire, typically hundreds of miles from their homes. These dislocated men, women, and children labored for the Assyrian state, working on farms and construction projects. Some of the men enlisted in the Assyrian army. Besides providing the state with workers, the policy of deportation effectively thwarted opposition to Assyrian expansion and rule. The Assyrians also used the threat of

MAP 4.2

The Empires of Assyria and Babylonia, 900–539 B.C.E.

From its small core in northern Mesopotamia, Assyria gradually extended its control over most of the Middle East and at times even Egypt, turning the entire region into a vast land-based empire by 650 B.C.E. By 610, however, the Babylonians had taken over most of Assyria's territory, expanding their empire into parts of the Arabian Desert. Both peoples used the enormous influx of resources to embellish their homelands, creating two of the most impressive cities of the ancient world, Nineveh and Babylon.

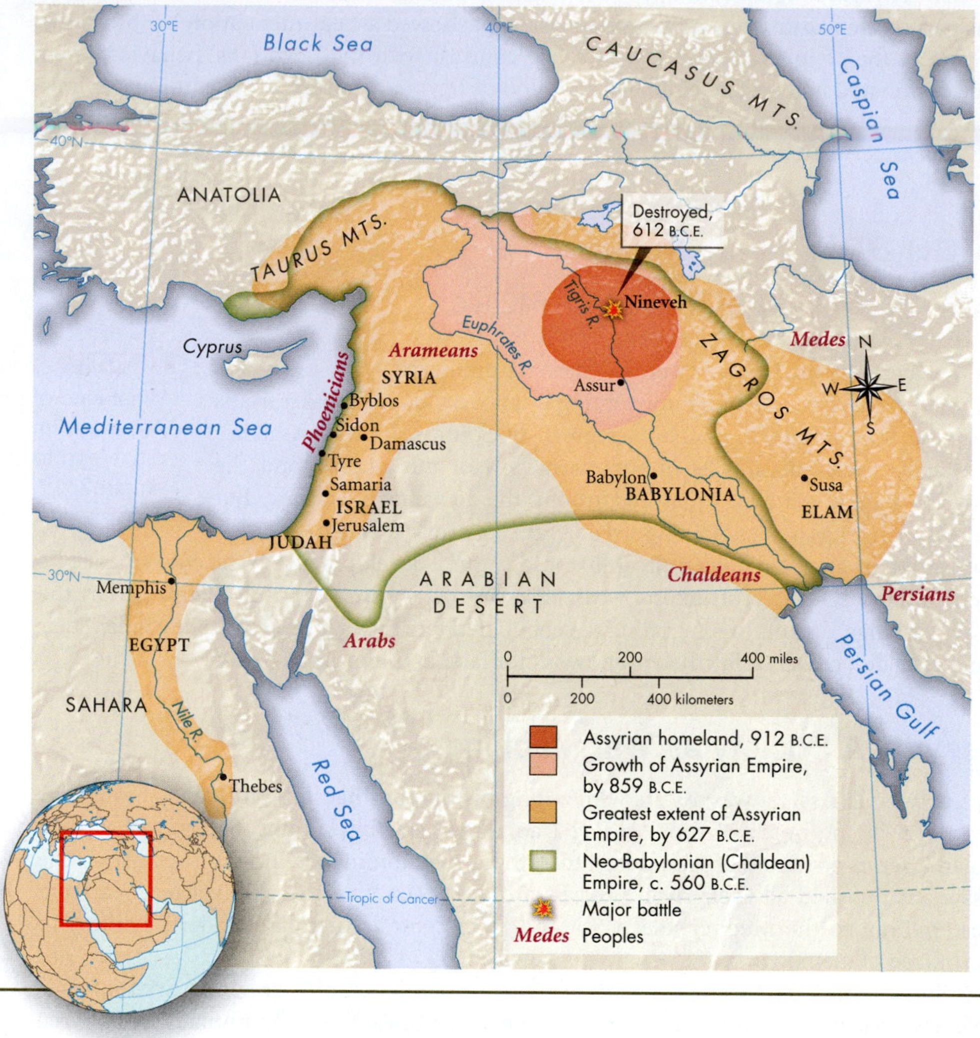

deportation as a scare tactic to cow opponents into submission. Moreover, deported people needed the protection of the empire in their new and strange environments. The policy thus aimed both to supply laborers and to reduce the chance of rebellion in the conquered territories.

King and Army

As head of the military hierarchy, the king was supreme commander of the army. The ultimate source of authority, he made all crucial political, military, and administrative decisions. His officials therefore had to be in constant communication with him, which slowed decision making. Couriers had to travel long distances to royal headquarters in the capital to obtain orders on how to proceed in the **provinces**, the territories fully administered by the Assyrians.

The incessant campaigning made the Assyrians seasoned warriors, and their military tactics were undeniably superior to those of their opponents. From about 745 B.C.E. on, the empire had a standing professional army rather than one made up of recruits called up seasonally after they had completed agricultural tasks. Despite the extensive written evidence we have from Assyria, we have little information about the composition and technical support of the army, and we do not know how long men served.

province In an empire, a region or country directly governed by an imperial official answering to the central administration.

Assyria's military culture was dominated by men, allowing most women a limited role in Assyrian society. The available evidence reveals little about ordinary women

Gold for the Assyrian Queen
We get an idea of the wealth of the Assyrian court from the recent find of tombs at the capital Nimrud. Buried with two queens of the ninth and eighth centuries B.C.E. were masses of finely worked gold jewelry, such as these solid gold bracelets decorated with lion heads. (Time & Life Pictures/Getty Images.)

and focuses instead on royal women—queens and princesses. As members of the court, these women led privileged lives and enjoyed fabulous wealth, as the intact tombs of two queens from the ninth and eighth centuries B.C.E. demonstrate. On the two women's bodies together were piled a total of seventy-seven pounds of gold and precious ornaments.

Royal Women

As wives and mothers, royal women could shape political affairs. We saw how Hatshepsut in Egypt rose to the top to become king; in Assyria no woman acquired such power, but certain queens exercised enormous influence. Queen Naqia (na-KEE-ah) married King Sennacherib (sehn-AK-er-ihb) (r. 704–681 B.C.E.) before he ascended the throne, and bore him a son called Esarhaddon (ee-sahr-HAD-in). He was not the first in line for succession, but after Sennacherib's eldest son was murdered, Naqia convinced Sennacherib to declare the young Esarhaddon his heir. Older sons by another wife rebelled, and one (or perhaps several) of them assassinated Sennacherib. This started a civil war, which Esarhaddon won after months of fighting. During Esarhaddon's subsequent rule from 680 to 669 B.C.E., the queen mother Naqia became his staunchest ally. She built a palace for the king, restored temples, and made grand offerings to the gods on his behalf. She corresponded with high officials of the empire, who paid her the same respect they gave the king. Even after Esarhaddon's death she remained prominent. Her last known act was to impose an oath on court officials to obey her grandson as king. As powerful as Naqia was, however, note that it ultimately derived from her status as the mother of a prince, not from her own independent political position. As in many other societies, elite Assyrian women could wield considerable influence, but it was almost always through their connections to powerful men.

Imperial Governance

All imperial powers face the challenge of administering territories after conquering them. We saw how the New Kingdom Egyptians used a system of dependent vassals in Southwest Asia, but at the same time they governed Nubian territories directly. The Assyrians were less eager to impose direct rule on defeated countries, however—it would have required large investments in infrastructure and administrators. Moreover, because the empire was centralized around a king who made all decisions, urgent issues in territories far from the king would have been difficult to deal with. Thus, when the military forced a population to submit, they left the local king on the throne but demanded obedience and

Indirect Rule

annual contributions. If the region rebelled—a common occurrence—troops returned to install a pro-Assyrian ruler in the local king's stead. If this arrangement also failed, Assyria annexed the region as a province. The Assyrians usually hesitated to take this drastic step, however. For example, only after repeated rebellions did the Assyrians turn Israel into a province in 722 b.c.e. But they never annexed the state of Judah, south of Israel (see Counterpoint: Assimilation and Resistance: The Peoples of Israel and Judah). As a vassal, Judah provided a useful buffer with Egypt, then part of the rival Nubian Empire.

Motives for Expansion

The Assyrians' preference for indirect rule was linked to their motives for expansion. They were not interested in ruling other peoples, but in acquiring the wealth and resources of other lands. With each conquest, the army captured huge amounts of booty, usually in the form of precious metals and luxury goods, which became palace property. In addition, the empire required yearly contributions, or **tribute**, from conquered territories. In an annual ceremony, ambassadors from Assyria's subject peoples renewed their states' loyalty oaths and brought tribute, often goods that were the region's special assets. Ambassadors from the mountain regions to the north and east of Assyria brought horses, for example, and those from western countries delivered manufactured craft products such as carved ivories and jewelry. In this way, Assyrian palaces became centers for collections of the empire's diverse resources and products.

City Building

Deported subjects gave Assyrian rulers the manpower to construct magnificent cities and to enlarge existing towns to serve as capitals. King Sennacherib, for example, refurbished and expanded the old city of Nineveh (NIN-uh-vuh). Its massive ruins still overlook the modern Iraqi city of Mosul. On these sites the kings erected monumental palaces and temples and decorated them with such materials as cedar wood, ivory, gold, and silver gathered from the entire empire. Although not the largest in the world at that time—Chinese cities were spread over vaster areas—the new Assyrian cities were too gigantic for the surrounding countryside to support. Because agriculture in the Assyrian core produced too little food to feed the city, products from elsewhere in the empire had to be imported. Assyria thus became an enormous drain on the resources of the conquered territories.

Independence Preserved: Phoenicians in the Assyrian Empire

As we have mentioned, the Assyrians shrewdly recognized that it was often preferable to grant independence to their subject peoples so that they could freely carry on activities that would benefit the empire economically. One such people was the Phoenicians, the inhabitants of Mediterranean port cities including Sidon (SIE-duhn), Byblos (BIB-loss), and Tyre (TY-er), which had been important hubs of trade for thousands of years. These cities occupied the thin ribbon of land between the sea and the high Lebanon Mountains. In addition to serving as a Mediterranean crossroads, Phoenician cities were famous for their craftwork, especially production of purple cloth dyed with extracts from the rare murex marine snails.

Phoenician Sea Trade

Benefiting from their extensive maritime trade, the Phoenicians had survived the devastation of the eastern Mediterranean system in the twelfth century b.c.e. In the tenth century b.c.e. they had begun to establish settlements overseas, first on the island of Cyprus and then along the Mediterranean coast in North Africa, in Spain, and on the islands of Malta, Sicily, and Sardinia, near Italy. From the territories surrounding these colonies, the Phoenicians collected metals and other valuable resources and shipped them to the East.

tribute Payment made from one state to another as a sign of submission.

colony A settlement or administrative district in a foreign country established and governed by people who intend to exploit the resources of that country.

The westernmost Phoenician **colony** was Cádiz on the Atlantic coast of Spain, beyond the Strait of Gibraltar (see again Mapping the World, page 106). There the Phoenicians established a fortified city that was completely Phoenician in character, with temples to Syrian gods such as Astarte and Baal. The settlers were interested in the nearby Spanish mines, which yielded gold, silver, copper, tin, and iron. Local populations extracted precious metal from ore and smelted it into bars that could be shipped east. This same pattern was repeated elsewhere in the Mediterranean. Everywhere they went, the Phoenicians established coastal outposts from which they sent local goods to their home cities.

The Phoenician system of trade was well established by 750 B.C.E., when Assyrian armies reached the Mediterranean coast. The encounter brought both sides mutual gain. For Phoenician traders, Assyria represented an enormous new market. For the Assyrians, Phoenicia provided access to goods they could not otherwise obtain. For example, the Phoenicians traded with Egypt, Assyria's rival at the time, to obtain papyrus, which scribes used for writing alphabetic scripts. So much papyrus entered the Mediterranean region through Phoenicia that the Greeks based the word for book, *biblion*, on the Phoenician city named Byblos, and this term has come down to us in the word *bible*.

Phoenician independence helped the Phoenicians preserve their cultural traditions from the second millennium B.C.E. into the first millennium. A fundamental element of that culture was the alphabet, a script with just twenty-two characters, used to indicate consonants only. The Phoenicians developed this script to record daily transactions on papyrus and parchment, now all decayed, and to chisel inscriptions on stone. Because the Phoenicians had extensive trade contacts, many foreign peoples adopted their alphabet to write their languages (see Figure 4.1). To the east of Phoenicia, these included speakers of the Semitic languages Aramaic and Hebrew, and to the west, the Indo-European-speaking Greeks also adopted it. Because both Aramaic and Greek adopters of the Phoenician alphabet later had broad cultural influence in the Mediterranean and Middle Eastern worlds, that script gained enormous reach. Today the Phoenician alphabet is the basis of all alphabetic scripts in the world.

The Phoenician Alphabet

SPREAD OF THE ALPHABET IN WESTERN EURASIA	
c. 1700 B.C.E.	Earliest alphabetic inscriptions in Palestine
c. 1400–1200 B.C.E.	Various alphabetic scripts in western Syria
c. 1050 B.C.E.	Early Phoenician alphabet
c. 950 B.C.E.	Earliest Aramaic alphabetic inscriptions
c. 850 B.C.E.	Earliest Hebrew alphabetic inscriptions
c. 800 B.C.E.	Earliest Greek alphabetic inscriptions
c. 750 B.C.E.	Earliest alphabetic writing in Italy
700–500 B.C.E.	Earliest Latin alphabetic inscriptions
c. 520–330 B.C.E.	Use of Old Persian cuneiform alphabet

Semitic name of letters	Phoenician	Hebrew	Greek name of letters	Greek	Roman
alef	✦	א	alpha	A	A
beth	⼂	ב	beta	B	B
gimel	⼂	ג	gamma	Γ	C, G
daleth	◁	ד	delta	Δ	D

FIGURE 4.1   **Comparative Alphabets**

In the Phoenician alphabet we can find the roots of our own. Our alphabet is based on that of the Romans, who borrowed their letter forms from the Greeks, who in turn adapted the Phoenician alphabet.

Culture and Identity in the Assyrian Empire

Through its far-reaching conquests, the Assyrian Empire brought people from a wide territory together under the same political structure. They spoke a variety of languages, followed different religious systems and customs, and must have been visually distinguishable to the people of the time. The Assyrians displayed different attitudes toward this cultural variety, depending on the region.

Cultural Assimilation

In the core of the empire, the Assyrians enforced assimilation. They relabeled existing cities with Assyrian names, built public buildings in the Assyrian style, and forced the people to support the cult of their leading god, Assur, the divine commander of the army, whose only temple was in the city of Assur on the Tigris River. But beyond this central zone, the Assyrians did not demand that people change their ways of life. Their only concern was that the subjects provide tribute and pay taxes.

Naturally, assimilation occurred because of the imperial deportation policy. When the Assyrians resettled an entire population in a foreign part of the empire, these immigrants maintained their identity for a while, but over generations they adopted local customs. Yet they also influenced the customs of their conquerors, leaving a cultural imprint on Assyria, especially in the realm of language. Many of the deportees came from the west and spoke Aramaic, which may have become the primary spoken language in the empire.

Babylonian and Syrian Influences

The Assyrians willingly accepted cultural influences from the conquered territories, especially when they felt those influences to be superior to their own traditions. This openness to foreign ways is most notable in literature and scholarship, but outsiders also influenced architecture, crafts, and religion. In the second millennium B.C.E., the country of Babylonia to the south of Assyria had been the center of literary and scholarly creativity in Southwest Asia. When the Assyrians conquered it in the late eighth century B.C.E., Babylonian scribes were still very actively composing and duplicating cuneiform texts. King Assurbanipal (ah-shur-BAH-nee-pahl) (r. 668–627 B.C.E.) used their output to build up the richest library of ancient Southwest Asia in his palace at Nineveh. He ordered his officials in Babylon to search for early, well-preserved manuscripts of texts of literary and scholarly character. He was especially interested in omen literature, the texts that guided scholars in interpreting the signs of the gods regarding the future, but all literary genres flourished in his reign. With its thousands of manuscripts, Assurbanipal's library gives us the most complete record of the Babylonian written tradition. Among its many treasures are multiple manuscripts of the *Epic of Gilgamesh* (see Chapter 2).

The literary Babylonian language influenced the Assyrian language used for official inscriptions. Kings commissioned increasingly lengthy records of their military campaigns. Although much of the phrasing in these accounts is repetitive (there are only so many ways to describe crushing an enemy), the authors regularly composed passages of high literary merit. For example, Sargon II (r. 721–705 B.C.E.) used these words to narrate his victory over an enemy army in the mountains:

> I massacred them in great numbers, the corpses of his warriors I spread out like grain, and I filled the mountain plains with them. Their blood I let rush like a river down the mountain gorges, and I dyed the fields, plains, and open country red.
> I slaughtered his fighters, the force of his army carrying bows and lances, like sheep and I chopped off their heads.[2]

In other forms of cultural expression, too, the Assyrians readily accepted outside influences. In architecture they imitated the palaces they saw in Syria. Assyrian craftwork showed a strong Syrian influence: the jewelry and ivory carvings found in Assyrian palaces were either produced in Syria or made locally using Syrian designs. These designs mixed motifs from the various cultures of the region, including Syria and

Egypt. The influx of expensive goods from foreign sources reflects not only that the Assyrian court was a rich market but that the Assyrians were very willing to accept foreign styles.

In religion, the Assyrians remained true to their old cults, but they attempted to harmonize them with Babylonian ideas. In Babylonian religion, the god Marduk was supreme, and common belief credited him with creating the universe. This event was the subject of a myth, the *Babylonian Creation Story*. It describes how Marduk defeated the forces of chaos and organized the universe, and how the other gods rewarded him by making him their king. The myth was an important element of the Babylonian New Year's festival, which intended to recreate the moment of creation. The Assyrians wanted to integrate their leading god Assur into this myth, and they either made him a forefather of Marduk or directly equated Assur with Marduk. They imported many other Babylonian gods and rites as well. Thus, in many ways, the Assyrian attitude toward foreign cultures mirrored their attitude toward foreign wealth and resources: they were interested in taking anything, and everything, that seemed valuable.

Failure of the Assyrian System

In 663 B.C.E., King Assurbanipal invaded Egypt and looted its rich cities, and in 647 he defeated the long-time rival state of Elam in western Iran. By this time, the Assyrian Empire encompassed an enormous territory, and huge amounts of wealth flowed from dependent peoples to the Assyrian homeland. Just forty years later, however, it would no longer exist. The collapse of the empire was precipitated by attacks launched by previously subjected peoples, but its causes lay in the structure of the system itself.

Structural Weakness and Military Defeat

The military events are clear: after the death of Assurbanipal in 627 B.C.E., Babylonia regained its independence under a local dynasty, which we call Neo-Babylonian or Chaldean (chal-DEE-uhn). Chaldean troops joined the Medes, an Iranian people from the eastern mountains, in an attack on the Assyrian heartland, and in 612 B.C.E. the combined armies destroyed the Assyrian capital, Nineveh. The Assyrians would resist a few years longer in northern Syria, but soon the Chaldeans had taken over almost their entire territory.

At the heart of Assyria's failure to rise to the military challenge from the Chaldeans and the Medes was a serious structural weakness. The centralized power structure required a strong king at the helm, and after Assurbanipal no such person stepped forward. Internal struggles for the throne produced instability and uncertainty. Moreover, the empire relied heavily on the conquered territories to sustain itself—it could not survive without their goods and manpower. Historians believe that when the pressures on the empire's core mounted, the subject states, which always had taken any opportunity to withhold tribute, probably cut off those supplies, and the empire fell apart. The exploitative economic policies on which Assyria depended could be sustained only when backed up by military might. When Assyria's military power faltered, the sources of Assyrian wealth dried up, further undermining the state and leading to collapse of the imperial system.

The Neo-Babylonian Empire

Assyria's successor, the Neo-Babylonian dynasty, soon restored order and extended the empire by annexing more territory (see again Map 4.2). The most famous Neo-Babylonian ruler was King Nebuchadnezzar II (NAB-oo-kuhd-nez-uhr) (r. 604–562 B.C.E.), who captured the kingdom of Judah in 587 B.C.E. Like his Assyrian predecessors, Nebuchadnezzar used the resources of conquered territories to embellish the cities of his homeland. Under Nebuchadnezzar's direction, Babylon became the most fabulous city in the western Eurasian world. We can still see remains from his time on the site or in museums around the world (see Lives and Livelihoods: Mesopotamian Astronomers). The Neo-Babylonian empire did not last long, however. Less than one hundred years after its creation, it was conquered by a far mightier force—the Persian Empire.

Mesopotamian Astronomers

Like the Chinese in the Shang period (see Chapter 3), the Mesopotamians were obsessed with predicting the future. But instead of asking specific questions and finding the answers in the cracks of oracle bones as the Chinese did, the Mesopotamians saw signs from the gods everywhere: in the birth of a malformed animal, the appearance of a large flock of birds, the occurrence of a lunar eclipse, and so on. The challenge to the people was to know how to read these omens.

From early in Mesopotamian history, scholars had compiled lists of guidelines for interpreting omens. The items were phrased in the same way as the Laws of Hammurabi (see pages. 51–52), as "if-then" statements. The "if" part could be any observable phenomenon or an effect produced through a special procedure. The second part indicated what the observation foretold. For example, "If a white cat is seen in a man's house, then hardship will seize the land." Often observations involved slaughtering a sheep to investigate the liver, an organ with many variations in color and shape, any of which could present a sign. For example, "If the left lobe of the liver is covered by a membrane and it is abnormal, the king will die from illness."

In the first millennium B.C.E., astronomical observations became very important to the Mesopotamians, and the longest lists of omens relate to events in the sky, such as planetary alignments, eclipses, and the appearance of stars. One series of omens, *Enuma Anu Enlil* (meaning, "When the gods Anu and Enlil"), was copied out on seventy clay tablets and included some seven thousand entries. It described omens dealing with the moon, including its visibility, eclipses, and conjunction with planets and fixed stars; with the sun, including aspects such as sunspots or a ring around

Assyrian Astronomy

The best evidence of the Assyrian reliance on the stars and other heavenly bodies to predict the future is written lists of astronomical omens, but their art reflects the same interest. This stele from Adad-nirari III in around 800 B.C.E. shows the king under the protection of the moon, Venus, and the Pleiades (seven stars). In front of him are other symbols of leading gods of the Assyrian pantheon. (Art Archive/Archaeological Museum Baghdad.)

The Persian Empire 550–330 B.C.E.

FOCUS

What imperial vision and style of government marked the rise of the vast Persian Empire and allowed it to endure for more than two hundred years?

In the sixth century B.C.E. the Persians, starting from what is today southern Iran, united all the existing empires and states from the Mediterranean coast to the Indus Valley. Remarkably, they were able to integrate an enormously diverse group of peoples and cultures into an imperial whole. Although they demanded obedience to their king, the Persians respected local cultures and identities, and this respect was key to their success. The Persians did encounter resistance from their subject peoples, but their empire—unprecedented in its scale—survived for more than two hundred years partly because of their tolerance. Although others replaced the Persians, the practices of government they initiated survived for many centuries after the empire's disintegration.

the sun; the weather—lightning, thunder, and clouds; and the planets, including their visibility, appearance, and stations. For example, one omen warned: "If the moon makes an eclipse in Month VII on the twenty-first day and sets eclipsed, they will take the crowned prince from his palace in fetters."

Although every Mesopotamian consulted omens, most of those recorded in writing deal with the king. They cover everything important to him personally and to his rule: the outcome of battles, deaths, births, illnesses, the success of the harvest, and many more concerns. Kings ordered scholars from all over the empire to examine anything that could be an omen and to report it to them. From their constant observation of phenomena in the sky, astronomers became aware of cyclical patterns. For example, they learned to calculate when events such as eclipses would occur and when a specific star would appear on the horizon. Ancient Mediterranean peoples thus regarded astronomy as a Mesopotamian science, and they considered the Babylonians its greatest experts.

The observation and interpretation of astronomical and other omens were not goals in themselves, however. Rather, Mesopotamians believed it was possible to change a predicted negative outcome. They aimed to produce this change mostly by appeasing the gods with prayers and offerings. But when an omen foretold the death of the king, the people would place a substitute on the throne and hide the real king in a safe place. They enacted a ritual in which the substitute was crowned, dressed in royal garb, and even provided with a queen. When they considered that the evil had passed, they removed the substitute (most often killing him to indicate that the prediction had been accurate) and restored the real king to the throne.

Omen readers, and especially astronomers, were thus very important, highly respected people in ancient Mesopotamia. They probably had to study for long periods to become familiar with the extensive writings that guided the interpretation of signs, and they had to thoroughly understand the intricacies of the cuneiform script and of Babylonian mathematics, which were at the basis of the analysis. The astronomers' accomplishments as observers of planetary behavior were remarkable, and their predictions of eclipses and the like were accurate. They were also meticulous record keepers, and to this day we identify many of the constellations they were the first to discern.

QUESTIONS TO CONSIDER

1. What was the purpose of omen reading in ancient Mesopotamia?

2. How did astronomers obtain their data?

3. What was the relationship between political rule and omen reading?

For Further Information:

Baigent, Michael. *From the Omens of Babylon: Astrology and Ancient Mesopotamia*. 1994.

Bottéro, Jean. *Mesopotamia: Writing, Reasoning, and the Gods*. Translated by Z. Bahrani and M. Van De Mieroop. Chicago: University of Chicago Press, 1992.

Rochberg, Francesca. *The Heavenly Writing: Divination, Horoscopy, and Astronomy in Mesopotamian Culture*. Cambridge, U.K.: University of Cambridge, 2004.

The Course of Empire

The Persian Empire was established by Cyrus the Achaemenid (a-KEY-muh-nid) (r. 559–530 B.C.E.), who in the sixth century rapidly annexed his neighbors' territories, including the large Neo-Babylonian Empire and the states of central Iran. His son and successor, Cambyses (kam-BIE-sees) (r. 530–522 B.C.E.), added Egypt to the empire, and for another fifty years the Persians campaigned in all directions to conquer new lands. By 480 B.C.E., the Achaemenid Empire incorporated the area from western India to the Mediterranean coast and from Egypt to the Black Sea and the fringes of Central Asia. Indeed, for more than a millennium, four ruling dynasties—the Achaemenids (559–330 B.C.E.), Seleucids (323–83 B.C.E.), Parthians (247 B.C.E.–224 C.E.), and Sasanids (224–651 C.E.)—maintained imperial rule over much of Southwest Asia (see Maps 4.3 and 4.4).

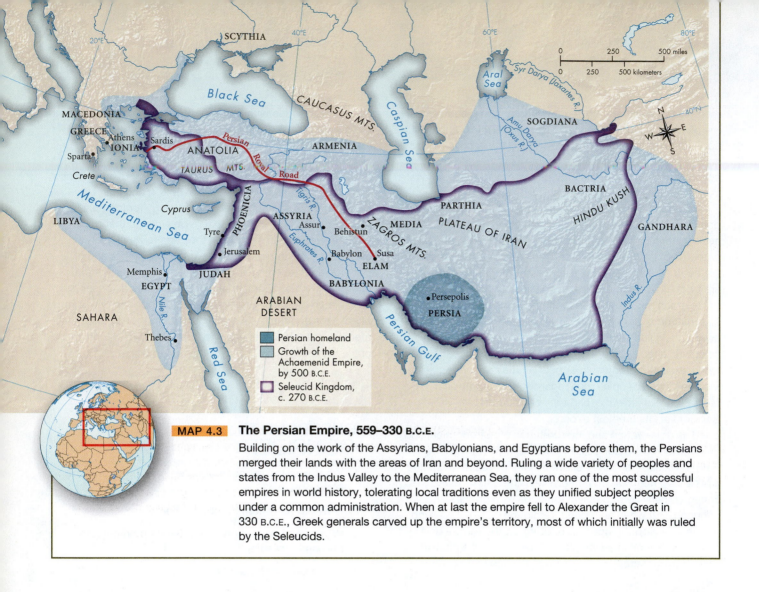

MAP 4.3 **The Persian Empire, 559–330 B.C.E.**

Building on the work of the Assyrians, Babylonians, and Egyptians before them, the Persians merged their lands with the areas of Iran and beyond. Ruling a wide variety of peoples and states from the Indus Valley to the Mediterranean Sea, they ran one of the most successful empires in world history, tolerating local traditions even as they unified subject peoples under a common administration. When at last the empire fell to Alexander the Great in 330 B.C.E., Greek generals carved up the empire's territory, most of which initially was ruled by the Seleucids.

Although they were foreign occupiers, the early Persian kings presented themselves as legitimate heirs to local thrones. Thus Cyrus became king of Babylon and continued local traditions of rule. When Cambyses became king of Egypt, he adopted an Egyptian throne name and was represented with traditional Egyptian royal garments and crowns. These men had to be strong individuals to assert their authority over various conquered peoples, who yearned for independence and the return of a native ruler. These feelings boiled over at the death of Cambyses in 522 B.C.E., and only after much campaigning—described in the passage at the beginning of this chapter—did the new Persian king, Darius (r. 521–486 B.C.E.), gain full control of the empire.

Imperial Structure

The difficulties Darius faced led him to undertake a program of reorganization and reform. In place of a collection of states held together by the person of the king, Darius created an imperial structure comprising twenty provinces, called **satrapies** (SAY-trap-eez), thereby extending a uniform system of government over an area of unprecedented size. Each satrapy had a Persian administrator (satrap) and was forced to provide tribute and troops to meet the empire's ever-increasing need for men and resources to control conquered territories. Imperial authorities exploited the skills of their subject peoples: Phoenicians manned the navy along with Cypriots and Ionians; in the army, Arabian camel drivers fought next to North African charioteers.

Greek Resistance

satrap A province in the Achaemenid Persian Empire, administered by a satrap.

Despite Persia's enormous power and military success, there were limits to its ability to expand. Most famous is the empire's failure to conquer Greece. Between 490 and 479 B.C.E., Darius and his son and successor Xerxes (r. 486–464 B.C.E.) invaded Greece twice, but the Greek city-states defeated the Persian army on land and at sea (as we will see in

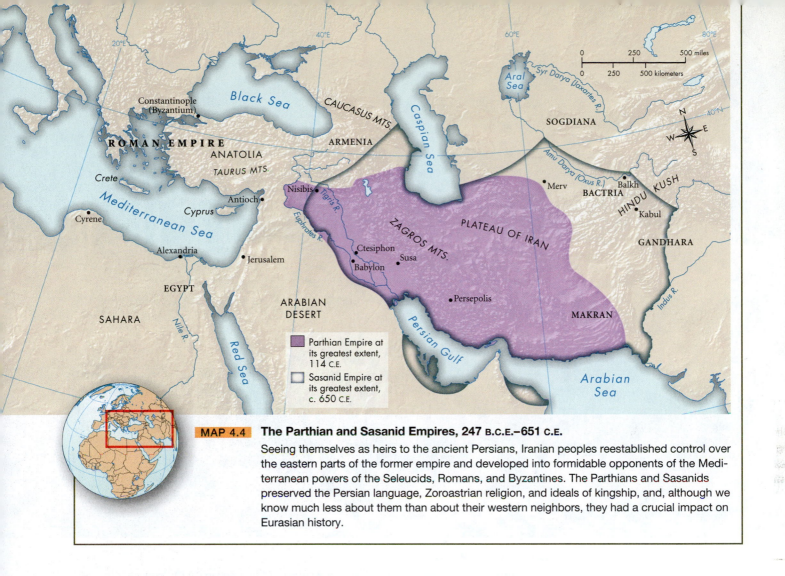

The Parthian and Sasanid Empires, 247 B.C.E.–651 C.E.

Seeing themselves as heirs to the ancient Persians, Iranian peoples reestablished control over the eastern parts of the former empire and developed into formidable opponents of the Mediterranean powers of the Seleucids, Romans, and Byzantines. The Parthians and Sasanids preserved the Persian language, Zoroastrian religion, and ideals of kingship, and, although we know much less about them than about their western neighbors, they had a crucial impact on Eurasian history.

Chapter 5). Resistance to Persia continued throughout the empire's history, and Egypt, for example, was able to gain independence from 404 to 343 B.C.E.

Yet these rebellions did not destroy the empire. That occurred only with the arrival of a young ruler, Alexander the Great, from Macedonia, the region just north of Greece. With his highly skilled troops, Alexander defeated the Persian King Darius III in three crucial battles, after which some of the king's noblemen killed him and delivered his body to Alexander. These events did not allow Alexander to inherit the entire empire at once, however. Victory came only after he led his troops on a long series of campaigns from Egypt to Iran and farther east, to claim control over these territories. In 324 B.C.E., Alexander set up his capital in Babylon, where, as we will see in Chapter 5, he died three years later.

Macedonian Conquest of Persia

Administering a Multicultural Empire

At Persepolis, in the heartland of Persia, Darius constructed a magnificent city where he annually celebrated the delivery of tribute. Persepolis's ruins still impress us by their grandeur and refinement. The emperor received an enormous tribute. Babylonia, for example, had to deliver 1000 talents (about 60,000 pounds) of silver. India paid 360 talents (about 21,600 pounds) of gold dust. The Persian treasuries were so rich that when later Macedonian conquerors put their contents into circulation, the value of gold and silver dropped steeply due to oversupply. The annual ceremony of tribute delivery had an ideological as well as economic value, for it showed the ruler as master of the subject regions, each dependent people offering him the specialties of their lands. Bactrians, for example, brought camels; Armenians, gold vessels; and Nubians, ivory tusks.

View of Persepolis

The imperial city of Persepolis (the Greek name meaning "the Persian City") dominated the countryside, to be seen from afar and stand as a symbol of the empire's power. Huge palaces with high stone pillars and walls decorated with relief sculptures provided a background for the annual ceremony in which representatives from all parts of the empire came to deliver their tribute as a sign of their submission (see "At a Crossroads," page 104). (akg-images/Suzanne Held.)

Communication with the Provinces

Because communication was of utmost importance in administering this colossal empire, the Persians developed an extensive road system to connect the capital to the provinces. Royal emissaries and trade caravans traveled along these routes to bring messages and goods over great distances. The king used messengers, known as "the eyes and ears of the king," to inspect his provincial officials and to make sure they obeyed his orders. The most famous road was the Royal Road from Susa in western Iran to Sardis in western Turkey, covering a distance of sixteen hundred miles, which a traveler could cover in ninety days. Rest houses along its route accommodated the king's representatives.

Given the empire's vast size and enormous bureaucracy, the efficiency-minded Persians readily adopted existing practices in the conquered territories, including writing and language. In Babylonia they continued to record on clay tablets; in Egypt they wrote on papyri. For affairs that crossed the borders of these earlier states, they used Aramaic language and script. Most people in Syria-Palestine already spoke that language, and the Aramaic alphabetic script was easier to use than the ancient scripts of Mesopotamia and Egypt. Unfortunately, Aramaic records were written on papyrus or parchment, which easily disintegrate, and therefore few such documents have survived.

The Persians' adoption of the Aramaic alphabet spread that system's use far to the east, and it inspired later alphabets as far east as India. Before their empire, the Persians did not have a script. They spoke an Indo-European language, Old Persian, in which they may have had a flourishing oral literature. When Darius became king, he instituted the use of a new script to write Old Persian, an alphabetic cuneiform intended for royal inscriptions. Like Darius's proclamation at the beginning of the chapter, these inscriptions appeared in three languages—Old Persian, Babylonian, and Elamite, the last being the official language of the Elamite state that had ruled western Iran for centuries until about 700 B.C.E. Sometimes scribes added translations into Egyptian as well. The intent was to show that the empire integrated several great literate cultures, and that the ruling Persians themselves also had a written tradition. At the same time, the use of multiple languages ensured that the desires of Persian rulers would be understood by all.

Coinage and Trade

An innovation that simplified trade and spread widely over the empire was the use of coins—small, portable disks of precious metal stamped by official mints to guarantee their value. In around 650 B.C.E., before the Persian Empire, people from the country of Lydia in western Anatolia had invented coinage. They made the earliest coins of electrum, a locally available mixture of silver and gold. Sometime later, others minted coins of pure gold and silver; each region or city could produce its own coins with distinctive stamps. Coins facilitated trade by providing an easily portable, guaranteed means of exchange. They were also used to pay soldiers and taxes.

Because the empire encompassed a vast area with no political boundaries, traders could travel safely and easily throughout Southwest Asia. Kings also encouraged trade through public projects, such as digging a canal from the Nile River to the Red Sea, and they may have sponsored exploration to expand trade contacts. The Persians controlled the Phoenician harbors, giving them access to the resources of the entire Mediterranean. Records show that ships from Anatolia docked in Egypt and that Babylonian merchants traveled in Iran. Taxes collected on trade became another major source of income. Thus, although the Persians extracted tribute as the Assyrians had before them, they took pains to ensure the overall economic health of the empire by promoting and protecting robust trade throughout their domain.

The First Coins

Because people who received payment in gold, silver, or other precious metals ran the risk of receiving inferior metal, in around 650 B.C.E. inhabitants of Lydia developed the idea of casting pieces with a mark stamped on them. Recipients would recognize the distinctive image from an authority that guaranteed the value. The earliest coins were of electrum, as are the examples shown here, but soon gold and silver were more common. The Persian Empire's need to pay soldiers promoted the use of coinage all over its vast territory and beyond. (Charles O'Rear/ Corbis.)

Tolerance of Local Traditions

As the empire's network of roads and trade routes eased the movement of people and resources, they helped disseminate Persian culture. Some local elites adopted Persian customs and artistic styles, but Persia's empire had a distinctive attitude toward local traditions and beliefs. Other imperial elites, such as the New Kingdom Egyptians and the Assyrians, were confident that their culture was superior, and their appearance and behavior always reflected that culture. By contrast, the Persians adopted the lifestyles and ideologies of the territories they annexed and integrated themselves into existing structures. As we have seen, the Persian king assumed the role of descendant of the native dynasties. He behaved as a local ruler, participating, for example, in traditional rituals to local gods. Further, the Persians restored local traditions that their imperial predecessors had recently disrupted. Most famous is Cyrus's decision to allow Judean deportees to return from Babylonia to Jerusalem and his promise of monetary support to rebuild the temple there (see Counterpoint: Assimilation and Resistance: The Peoples of Israel and Judah). The Hebrew Bible depicts Cyrus as the savior of the Judean people sent by their god Yahweh (YAH-way). Other literatures, too, presented the Persians as more devoted to the local gods than the rulers they replaced. Such observations may have been propagandistic, but they did contain a grain of truth. By respecting local identities and adopting local customs, the Persians reduced resistance to their rule and claimed political legitimacy in terms the local population understood. They saw themselves as heads of a multicultural empire and did not seek to impose a common Persian identity on their subject peoples.

Zoroastrianism in a Polytheistic World

The local religious practices the Persian kings promoted differed significantly from those of the Persians themselves. Persian religion followed the teachings of Zoroaster (the Greek rendering of the Iranian name Zarathushtra), and Zoroastrianism is still practiced today. He taught through **Gathas** (Songs), which are contained in the Avesta, a collection of writings recorded in around 500 C.E. The Gathas depict a world inhabited by pastoralists, probably located in eastern Iran, similar to the world described in the Indian Vedas (see Chapter 3). The languages of the Gathas and Vedas are closely related, and they both belong to the Indo-Iranian branch of Indo-European.

Zoroaster's Teachings

It is unclear when Zoroaster lived; scholars have suggested dates from 1700 to 500 B.C.E. Persian religion was **polytheistic**—they believed in the existence of many gods—but Zoroaster molded them into a structure that emphasized dualism. According to Zoroaster, the universe is divided into the two opposing forces, good and evil, which were represented by two spirits. A line in his teachings says: "Yes, there are two fundamental spirits, twins which are renowned to be in conflict. In thought and in word, in action, they are two: the good and the bad. And between these two, the beneficent have correctly chosen, not the maleficent."[3] Everything in the Zoroastrian world was characterized by this parallel dualism—good versus evil, truth versus untruth, light versus darkness—and all humans had to choose between them. Zoroastrians worshiped one god only, Ahuramazda (ah-HOOR-uh-MAZZ-duh) ("wise lord"), who was the father of both the beneficent and the hostile spirit and the force for keeping evil in check. The creator of heaven and earth, day and night, light and darkness, Ahuramazda provided ethical guidance to humans to seek truth, goodness, and light.

Because Zoroaster's teachings stressed that individuals had to seek purity in nature, the cult focused on the pure forces of fire and water. Unlike other peoples of Southwest Asia and neighboring regions, Zoroastrians did not build temples, and they burned sacrifices on altars standing in the open. As in Vedic India (see Chapter 3), priests, called Magi in Greek texts on Persia, played a key role in the sacrifices, and they drank a stimulant, haoma (HOW-muh), that was related to the Vedic drink soma.

It is unclear whether the Persian rulers were Zoroastrians, but historians know that they recognized Ahuramazda as the god who placed them on the throne and guided them

Gathas The songs that contain the prophet Zoroaster's teachings.

polytheism A religious system's belief in the existence of many gods.

Hebrew Bible The sacred books—in prose and poetry—that document the monotheistic religious ideas of the peoples of Israel and Judah.

in their search for truth. Representations of the king commonly show him next to a winged sun disk containing the upper body of a man, most likely the god Ahuramazda. The altars built near the royal tombs also suggest that kings adhered to Ahuramazda's cult.

Zoroastrianism's Lasting Influence

Zoroaster's teachings became the basis of the official religion of later Iranian dynasties (the Parthians and the Sasanids, as we will see in Chapter 7). But the ancient Persians did not force their subjects to honor Ahuramazda or adopt Persian cult practices, and Zoroaster's ideas probably had little impact on the general population of the empire. The focus on choosing between good and evil and on worshiping only the god Ahuramazda had a significant impact on Judaism, however, and through it on Christianity and Islam. With the spread of Islam (discussed in Chapter 9), Zoroastrianism became a minority religion in Iran, and its worshipers moved to India, where they are referred to today as Parsees.

COUNTERPOINT
Assimilation and Resistance: The Peoples of Israel and Judah

By their very nature, empires produce a degree of assimilation as diverse populations come together and absorb aspects of one another's cultures and lifestyles. The empires discussed in this chapter exposed people everywhere to foreign influences—voluntary or forced movement to new locations, new bureaucratic practices, and novel imperial dress and customs—and local people adopted some new practices. Even in empires that allowed local lifestyles and customs to persist, common practices arose, such as the use of Aramaic script in the Persian Empire. People subjected to mass deportations, such as those the Assyrians used systematically, had to adapt to their new environment, learn how to work the new land, and communicate with the local populations, and in so doing they lost part of their own identities.

> **FOCUS**
>
> To what degree and in what ways did the peoples of Israel and Judah accept or reject the influences of the empires they confronted?

In this Counterpoint we examine the effects of this process of assimilation —and resistance to it—in the two small states of Israel and Judah, strategically located in Syria-Palestine, where Asia and Africa meet. All the empires we discussed in this chapter sent armies to these territories in the effort to dominate Israel and Judah.

Reconstructing the Histories of Israel and Judah

Located in the south of the region between the Mediterranean coast and the Jordan River, Israel and Judah were surrounded by Philistine city-states on the southern coast, Phoenicia on the northern coast, the Aramaic kingdom of Damascus to the north, and the states of Ammon, Moab, and Edom to the east. All were small kingdoms centered on a capital city. For Israel that city was Samaria; for Judah, Jerusalem. The populations throughout the region spoke related languages. In Israel and Judah the language was Hebrew, which the people recorded in an alphabetic script derived from Phoenician.

Scholars reconstruct the histories of Israel and Judah on the basis of a monumental literary work of antiquity, the **Hebrew Bible**, which Christians call the Old Testament. The Bible provides a rich narrative

Ancient Israel and Judah

The Bible as a Historical Source

starting with the creation of the universe, but it is a very challenging historical source. A religious tract, the Hebrew Bible honors the god Yahweh and tells of his interactions with peoples of Israel and Judah. It contains, among much else, the Torah, a set of laws on how people should behave. Anonymous writers and adapters composed the Bible by combining existing myths and tales, historical narratives, king lists, poems, and laws, some of which tradition credits to figures, such as Moses. Judeans in exile in Babylonia probably wrote down the core of the Hebrew Bible in the fifth century B.C.E., but it was later reworked and expanded, and multiple versions circulated. The early Christians added New Testament books to the Old Testament, extending the narrative to include the teachings of Jesus (see Chapter 7). Today Jews and Christians consider the Bible their sacred text, but they diverge in what books they see as integral parts of the work.

Historians' Debate over the Bible

Historians hold a wide range of opinions about the historical value of the Bible. Some regard it as fundamentally factual with some inconsistencies arising from different traditions contained in it, but others question the accuracy of any statement not confirmed by sources other than the Bible. Archaeology has failed to provide much help. It can demonstrate the existence of the cities mentioned, but it cannot, for example, ascribe a building to a particular king. A remarkable aspect of the cultures of Israel and Judah is the rarity of monumental royal inscriptions of the type that existed in the neighboring states. Were such inscriptions destroyed on purpose in Israel and Judah? The reality of the individuals and events described in the Bible is mostly from external sources, especially Assyria.

Peoples Uprooted: Deportation and Exile

Israel and Assyria

The state of Israel arose at the turn of the second millennium B.C.E. when, archaeology shows, newcomers disrupted the existing political structures of Syria-Palestine. At this time, the Philistines settled on the southern coast, and Aramaic kingdoms appeared throughout Syria. Tension was rife. Possibly after a period of union in the tenth century under kings David and Solomon, Israel split into two kingdoms, Israel and Judah, which regularly clashed with each other and with other nearby states. Assyrian pressure, however, caused all of these states to join forces. When the Assyrians campaigned west of the Euphrates River in the ninth and eighth centuries B.C.E., they regularly engaged coalitions that included Israel and Judah. The only existing representation of an Israelite king is a relief of Jehu submitting to the Assyrian King Shalmaneser III (shal-muh-NEE-zer) (r. 858–824 B.C.E.). The Assyrians tried to control the Syrian-Palestinian states by installing pro-Assyrian locals on the throne, but rebellions and refusals to pay tribute were common. Thus, in 722 B.C.E., the Assyrian king Sargon II sacked Israel's capital Samaria, turned the region into a province, and deported most of the population of Israel to other parts of the empire. These deportees soon assimilated to their new surroundings and never emerged as a discernible entity again. Meanwhile Sargon settled people from the east of Assyria in the land of Israel.

Judah and Babylonia

The Assyrians allowed Judah to remain a separate state, although they raided much of its territory to enforce obedience. But the Neo-Babylonians, who replaced the Assyrians as the leading power in Southwest Asia in around 610 B.C.E., sealed Judah's fate. In 587 B.C.E., Nebuchadnezzar II sacked Jerusalem, deported a large proportion of the inhabitants, and imposed a governor on the region. When this governor was assassinated, Nebuchadnezzar returned to Judah in 582 B.C.E. and deported even more Judeans. This period became known as the Babylonian captivity, or the **Exile**.

Nebuchadnezzar settled the displaced people of Judah in the core of the empire near Babylon, where they experienced a very cosmopolitan culture. Babylon's inhabitants came from all over Southwest Asia and beyond, the city was a center of culture, and its ancient religious cults flourished under royal patronage. The Babylonian countryside where the Judeans lived prospered as the result of public works such as the digging of irrigation

Exile In the history of ancient Judah, the period when the Neo-Babylonians deported the Judeans to Babylonia, c. 587–530 B.C.E.

King Jehu of Israel

In contrast to the rulers of neighboring Egypt and Mesopotamia, those of Israel and Judah are not known to us from statuary and other representations. The exception is the ninth-century-B.C.E. King Jehu of Israel, who appears prostrate on a monument the Assyrian Shalmaneser III had carved showing Israel's submission. Why no other representations of the kings of Israel and Judah survive or were ever made remains a mystery. (Erich Lessing/Art Resource, NY.)

canals. The temptation to assimilate and to make the region a new home was great, and many of the deportees yielded to it.

Judean Resistance and Dispersal

Some Judeans reacted against this process by stressing a separate identity rooted in their relationship with their god, Yahweh. His only temple had been in Jerusalem, and the Babylonians had demolished it. Before the Exile, the cult of Yahweh had been central to the states of Israel and Judah, but not exclusive. Other cults flourished as well, especially those devoted to the Syrian gods Baal and Astarte. Debate over which god was supreme, Yahweh or Baal, seems to have taken place for centuries, but over time, most likely during the Exile, the veneration of Yahweh became a monotheistic creed. Yahweh was not only the supreme god, he was the only god. No other gods existed, and the people who revered other gods worshiped idols. Unlike the ideas of Akhenaten or Zoroaster, which allowed for the existence of divine beings alongside Aten or Ahuramazda, Judaism held that Yahweh was the one and only god.

When the Persian king Cyrus conquered Babylonia, his tolerance for local customs led him to issue an edict that allowed the Judeans to return home after some fifty years of exile. Some Judeans chose to remain in Babylon, but others felt that their duty to Yahweh demanded that they return home. They argued that a **covenant**—an agreement between Yahweh and the "people of Israel"—guaranteed Judeans success and a country in return for obedience to God (see Reading the Past: The God Yahweh and the People of Israel Form a Covenant). Yahweh could be worshiped only in the temple at Jerusalem, and it was the people's obligation to return home and rebuild that temple, a project for which Cyrus promised government funds.

Return to Judah

covenant In the Hebrew Bible, Yahweh's promise of success and a homeland in return for his people's obedience.

The God Yahweh and the People of Israel Form a Covenant

The monotheistic religion that developed among the Judeans was based on a covenant, an agreement between the people and their God. The terms of the covenant resembled those of treaties between a human emperor and his subjects. The Hebrew Bible stated this agreement several times; in this passage, Yahweh addresses the patriarch Abraham, who, according to the Book of Genesis, had first arrived in the region that would become the states of Israel and Judah.

When Abram was ninety-nine years old the Lord appeared to Abram, and said to him, "I am God Almighty; walk before me, and be blameless. And I will make my covenant between me and you, and will multiply you exceedingly." Then Abram fell on his face; and God said to him, "Behold my covenant is with you, and you shall be the father of a multitude of nations. No longer shall your name be Abram, but your name shall be Abraham; for I have made you the father of a multitude of nations. I will make you exceedingly fruitful; and I will

make nations of you, and kings shall come forth from you. And I will establish my covenant between me and you and your descendants after you throughout their generations for an everlasting covenant, to be God to you and your descendants after you. And I will give to you, and to your descendants after you, the land of your sojournings, all the land of Canaan, for an everlasting possession; and I will be their God."

Source: Genesis 17:1–8, Revised Standard Version.

EXAMINING THE EVIDENCE

1. What are the terms of the covenant between Yahweh and the people of Israel?
2. What relationship between God and Abraham does this passage indicate?

Judaism as an Identity

The Judeans who returned to Judah adopted firm rules that set them apart from other people in the region. Now known as Jews, they relied on teachers (rabbis) to guide them in their faith and lives and gathered in meeting places (synagogues) to pray as a community. The exclusive belief in one god was essential and strictly enforced. It was very important to observe the Sabbath (literally meaning "seven"), one day a week for rest from work, because God had rested after six days of creation. The Jews established dietary rules, prohibiting the consumption of foods such as pork and shellfish and the combination of dairy products with meat. Women were required to take baths after menstruation to renew ritual purity. These and other distinctive laws, such as a ban on marriage to non-Jews, produced a strong separate Jewish identity.

Jews Outside Judah

But not all Jews lived in Judah. Some remained in Babylonia, and others dispersed over the Persian Empire in a process known as the **Diaspora**. One such emigrant community lived on the Nile island of Elephantine on the southern border of Egypt. The residents left papyri, written in Aramaic, that detail their lives. Mercenaries (soldiers for hire) for the Persian king adhered to the faith in Yahweh and kept in constant contact with Jerusalem. They built their own temple, but the Jerusalem priesthood did not approve of it, and Egyptian opponents destroyed it. Because of the Diaspora, an identity based on a Jewish faith rather than a Judean people developed, with many adherents living abroad. The emigrants focused strictly on one god, but the world was predominantly polytheistic. Thus, regardless of where they lived, Jews maintained a sense of connection to a community, albeit a community of believers rather than of inhabitants of a particular city, state, or region.

Diaspora Dispersal of people from their homeland; the term originally referred to the Jews who left Palestine after the Babylonian and Roman sacks of Jerusalem, but it is now used for many other peoples as well.

Throughout the Hellenistic and Roman periods (see Chapters 5 and 7), the idea of monotheism would further develop. For a time, different interpretations of Judaism existed. These were consolidated, however, after the Jews were forced to leave Judah when the Romans destroyed the second temple of Jerusalem in 70 C.E. In the first century C.E. a Jewish sect following the teachings of Jesus of Nazareth would develop Christianity, which would have its immense impact on world history through its influence on the Roman Empire.

Conclusion

In North Africa and Southwest Asia, the earliest empires in world history arose beginning in the second millennium B.C.E. A sequence of political masters accumulated vast territories by defeating previously independent states and forcing their populations to contribute labor and goods to the empire. The emergence of empires prompted peoples with separate cultures and habits to interact, and they exchanged ideas and influenced one another in enduring ways.

The degree to which they assimilated and the sources of the most influential traditions varied enormously. Political domination could lead to cultural supremacy, as when Egypt conquered Nubia, but sometimes rulers eagerly adopted the practices and ideas of their subject people, as when Nubians ruled Egypt. Some imperial powers permitted their subjects to continue cultural practices and even promoted them; in the inscription quoted at the start of the chapter, the Persian King Darius depicted himself as a king of many countries. Others, such as Assyria, did not interfere with cultural matters and local customs as long as their subjects obeyed them. Some subject peoples consciously rejected assimilation, most notably the Judeans. Thus the cultural consequences of imperial rule took a wide variety of forms. This variation would continue throughout world history, and in the next chapter we will see how it emerged in the early empires of Eurasia.

NOTES

1. Translated from Florence Malbran-Labat, *La version akkadienne de l'inscription trilingue de Darius à Behistun* (Rome: GEI, 1994), 93–103.
2. Translated from F. Thureau-Dangin, *Une relation de la huitième campagne de Sargon* (Paris: Geuthner, 1912), lines 131–136.
3. Yasna 30:3. In S. Insler, *The Gathas of Zarathustra* (Leiden: Brill, 1975), 33.

RESOURCES FOR RESEARCH

Imperial Egypt and Nubia, 1550 B.C.E.–350 C.E.

In their general surveys of the culture, many of the books on ancient Egypt treat the New Kingdom's imperial period and the period when Nubians ruled Egypt. A number of works focus on Nubia, often looking at its entire ancient history.

Ancient Egypt Web site. http://www.ancient-egypt.co.uk.
Manley, Bill. *The Penguin Historical Atlas of Ancient Egypt.* 1996.
Morkot, Robert G. *The Black Pharaohs: Egypt's Nubian Rulers.* 2000.
Morkot, Robert G. *The Egyptians: An Introduction.* 2005.
O'Connor, David. *Ancient Nubia: Egypt's Rival in Africa.* 1993.
Romer, John. *Ancient Lives: The Story of the Pharaohs' Tombmakers.* 2003.
Taylor, John H. *Nubia and Egypt.* 1991.

Theban Mapping Project. http://www.thebanmappingproject.com.
Van De Mieroop, Marc. *A History of Ancient Egypt.* 2010.
Welsby, Derek A. *The Kingdom of Kush: The Napatan and Meroitic Empires.* 1996.

Rise and Fall of the Assyrian Empire, 900–612 B.C.E.

The Assyrians left extensive archaeological and written remains, which have been the subject of many specialized studies. General descriptions of the empire often appear in surveys of Mesopotamian history, as well as in more specialized books.

The British Museum. http://www.mesopotamia.co.uk.
Chadwick, Robert. *First Civilizations: Ancient Mesopotamia and Ancient Egypt,* 2d ed. 2005.

Curtis, J. E., and J. E. Reade. *Art and Empire: Treasures from Assyria in the British Museum*. 1995.

Joannès, Francis. *The Age of Empires: Mesopotamia in the First Millennium B.C.* Translated by A. Nevill. 2004.

Kuhrt, Amélie. *The Ancient Near East, c. 3000–330 B.C.* 1995.

Leick, Gwendolyn. *The Babylonians: An Introduction*. 2003.

Markoe, Glenn E. *Phoenicians*. 2000.

Oppenheim, A. Leo. *Ancient Mesopotamia*, 2d ed. 1977.

Saggs, H. W. F. *The Might That Was Assyria*. 1990.

Van De Mieroop, Marc. *A History of the Ancient Near East, ca. 3000–323 B.C.* 2d ed. 2007.

The Persian Empire, 550–330 B.C.E.

Much early work on the Persian Empire was based on Greek sources, which depicted the empire through the eyes of one of its greatest enemies. More recently, scholars have turned to sources from the empire itself, especially those from Mesopotamia and Egypt, to study how the empire functioned.

Allen, Lindsay. *The Persian Empire: A History*. 2005.

Briant, Pierre. *From Cyrus to Alexander: A History of the Persian Empire*. Translated by P. Daniels. 2002.

Brosius, Maria. *The Persians: An Introduction*. 2006.

Curtis, John. *Ancient Persia*, 2d ed. 2000.

*Kuhrt, Amélie. *The Persian Empire: A Corpus of Sources from the Achaemenid Period*. 2007.

Musée Achéménide. http://www.museum-achemenet.college-de-france.fr/.

Wiesehöfer, Josef. *Ancient Persia from 550 B.C. to 650 A.D.* Translated by A. Azodi. 1996.

COUNTERPOINT: Assimilation and Resistance: The Peoples of Israel and Judah

The literature on the ancient history of Israel and Judah is vast. In their use of the Hebrew Bible as a historical source, surveys vary from fully accepting the accuracy of the information to rejecting most of it as historically unreliable. The books below cover a spectrum of approaches, from heavy reliance on the biblical text (Bright; Miller and Hayes) to a critical attitude (Liverani, Soggin).

Bright, John. *A History of Israel*, 4th ed. 2000.

Kamm, Antony. *The Israelites: An Introduction*. 1999.

Liverani, Mario. *Israel's History and the History of Israel*. Translated by C. Peri and P. Davies. 2005.

Miller, J. Maxwell, and John H. Hayes. *A History of Ancient Israel and Judah*, 2d ed. 2006.

Moorey, P. R. S. *Biblical Lands*. 1975.

Soggin, J. Alberto. *An Introduction to the History of Israel and Judah*, 3d ed. Translated by J. Bowden. 1999.

* Primary source.

▶ **For additional primary sources from this period**, see *Sources of Crossroads and Cultures*.

▶ **For Web sites, images, and documents related to topics in this chapter**, see Make History at bedfordstmartins.com/smith.

The major global development in this chapter ▶ The rise of empires and the variety and consequences of imperial rule.

IMPORTANT EVENTS

c. 1700–500 B.C.E.	Scholarly guesses for life of Zoroaster, founder of Zoroastrianism
c. 1700–330 B.C.E.	Development and spread of the alphabet in western Asia
c. 1550–1070 B.C.E.	Egyptian New Kingdom Empire
c. 1070 B.C.E.	Nubian independence from Egypt
c. 900–612 B.C.E.	Assyrian Empire
c. 730–660 B.C.E.	Nubian Empire
c. 650 B.C.E.	Invention of coinage in Lydia
c. 626–539 B.C.E.	Neo-Babylonian (Chaldean) Empire
587 B.C.E.	Neo-Babylonian sack of Jerusalem
c. 587–530 B.C.E.	Judean people in exile
c. 550–330 B.C.E.	Achaemenid Persian Empire
c. 400 B.C.E.–350 C.E.	Kingdom of Meroe
330 B.C.E.	Alexander of Macedon defeats Persia

KEY TERMS

assimilation (p. 109)   **Gathas** (p. 130)
bureaucracy (p. 113)   **Hebrew Bible** (p. 131)
colony (p. 120)   **monotheism** (p. 110)
covenant (p. 133)   **polytheism** (p. 130)
Diaspora (p. 134)   **province** (p. 118)
empire (p. 107)   **satrapy** (p. 126)
Exile (p. 132)   **tribute** (p. 120)

CHAPTER OVERVIEW QUESTIONS

1. What were the main characteristics of the early empires?
2. How did the empires affect the peoples who created them and their subject populations?
3. How did imperial rulers adapt their control to local circumstances?
4. How did people resist empires?

SECTION FOCUS QUESTIONS

1. How did Egyptians and Nubians interact in the two imperial periods that united them politically?
2. What kind of power structure did the Assyrians impose on their subjects, and how did it lead to cultural assimilation in the empire?
3. What imperial vision and style of government marked the rise of the vast Persian Empire and allowed it to endure for more than two hundred years?
4. To what degree and in what ways did the peoples of Israel and Judah accept or reject the influences of the empires they confronted?

MAKING CONNECTIONS

1. How would you describe the different attitudes of the imperial elites discussed in this chapter toward the cultures of the conquered?
2. What languages and scripts were used in the different empires described in this chapter?
3. How did imperial policies and trade contacts influence the spread of writing systems?
4. What characteristics make these empires different from the earlier political structures we have studied?

5

AT A CROSSROADS ▲

The remains of the Acropolis ("top of the city") of Athens, towering over the modern city, include the majestic temple to Athena, divine protectress of the city, and the elaborate entrance gate on the left. Built under the world's first democratic government system, the Acropolis stands as a symbol of the Greeks' accomplishments in the first millennium B.C.E. (The Art Archive/Gianni Dagli Orti.)

The Greeks and the Wider World

1200–30 B.C.E.

Around 300 B.C.E., the Athenian Clearchus traveled to a city, now called Ai Khanoum, that Greeks had recently founded on the northern border of modern Afghanistan. On foot and horseback, he covered a distance equivalent to crossing the continental United States. At some point after he arrived, Clearchus inscribed on a rock sayings he had brought with him from the god Apollo's sanctuary at Delphi back home. He wrote:

> When a child, show yourself well behaved;
> When a young man, self-controlled;
> In middle age, just;
> As an old man, a good counselor;
> At the end of your life, free of sorrow.[1]

The inscription shows us that Clearchus actually visited Ai Khanoum and that he brought wisdom from his homeland with him, reflecting the spread of characteristic Greek values over a vast area. All we know about his life otherwise comes from quotes of his writings by later authors, and they show him as a typical Greek intellectual of his time. Born on the island of Cyprus, he had moved to Athens on the Greek mainland to study with the famous philosopher Aristotle. He wrote scholarly treatises on a wide variety of subjects, from water animals to human love. He was especially interested in Persia and India; recent conquests by Alexander the Great of Macedonia had connected Greece to the distant eastern places, which is why Clearchus could visit them. In his curiosity about

BACKSTORY

The historical developments we have studied so far took place primarily outside western Eurasia, the region of modern Europe. Nonetheless, through migration and cultural transmission, these developments did influence western Eurasia. *Homo sapiens*, for example, migrated from Africa to Southwest Asia and then to Europe about forty thousand years ago, and agriculture and Indo-European languages spread into the region after 7000 B.C.E. Central Asian horsemen reached this far west as well. By the second millennium B.C.E., part of Europe had joined the international order.

In the first millennium B.C.E., the first empires of Southwest Asia and North Africa still dominated the eastern Mediterranean. To the west, however, the inhabitants of Europe initiated changes—especially in politics and culture—that would have far-reaching effects on the rest of world history. We now turn our attention to these developments.

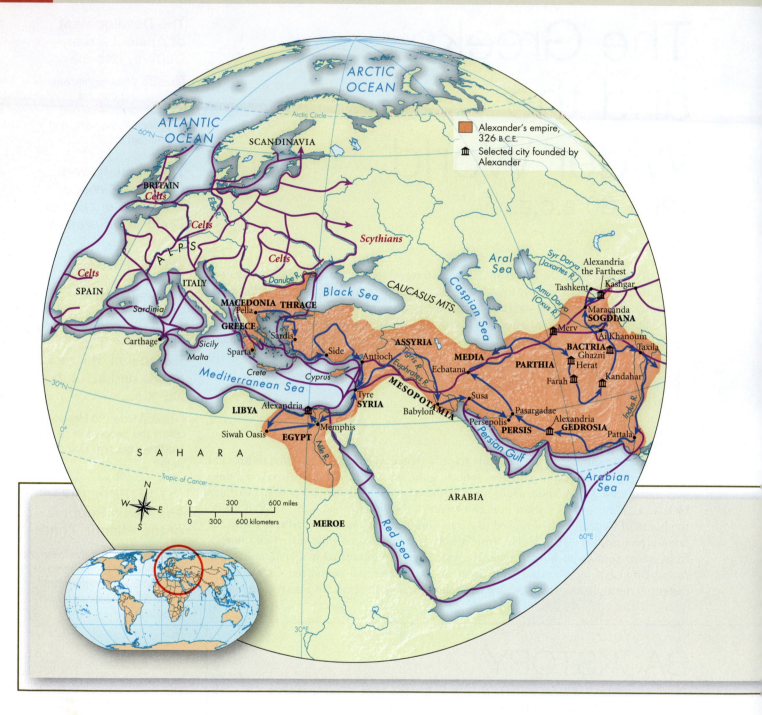

Alexander's empire, 326 B.C.E.

Selected city founded by Alexander

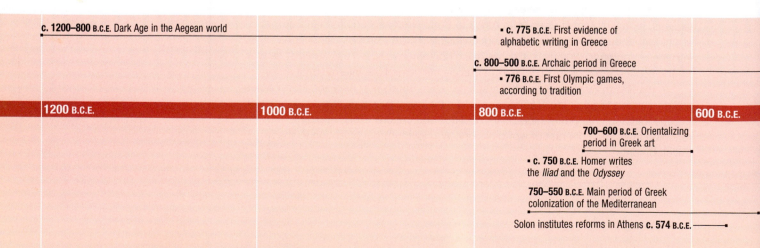

- **c. 775 B.C.E.** First evidence of alphabetic writing in Greece

c. 800–500 B.C.E. Archaic period in Greece

- **776 B.C.E.** First Olympic games, according to tradition

1200 B.C.E.	1000 B.C.E.	800 B.C.E.	600 B.C.E.

700–600 B.C.E. Orientalizing period in Greek art

- **c. 750 B.C.E.** Homer writes the *Iliad* and the *Odyssey*

750–550 B.C.E. Main period of Greek colonization of the Mediterranean

Solon institutes reforms in Athens **c. 574 B.C.E.**

the larger world, he was following an established Greek tradition. For centuries, Greeks had been exploring the Mediterranean region and beyond as merchants and travelers, observing foreign cultures and disseminating novel Greek ideas.

Although the large states and empires considered in previous chapters were forces for political unification and influenced broad territories, they tended to stress stability and generally avoided initiating fundamental political and cultural change. In this chapter we focus on a territory that was at first marginal in terms of political and military power but became a center of cultural and technological innovation: Greece in western Eurasia. In close contact with the nearby empires of Southwest Asia and North Africa, yet politically independent, the Greeks stimulated many political and cultural developments during the first millennium B.C.E. These groundbreaking innovations touched almost every aspect of life: government, human rationality, literature, visual art, and much more. Although Greek city-states were in almost perpetual military competition with one another, people throughout the region shared a common culture, and all experimented with new intellectual endeavors. After several centuries, the military successes of one state, Macedonia, which itself was originally secondary to the Greek world, propelled the spread of these innovations over a vast area, merging them with a host of local traditions.

The ancient Greeks are more accessible to historians than many of the peoples we studied earlier, for a remarkable number of their writings survived through the ages. Because later peoples studied them, at first mostly in the Middle East and Europe and more recently worldwide, these writings had an enormous impact. They give us insight into many later intellectual developments in human history.

Greece was not characteristic of all of western Eurasia, however. Other cultures, notably the Celtic peoples of the Atlantic zone, adhered to their own traditions despite contact with Greece. As we will see in the Counterpoint to this chapter, Celtic culture influenced parts of Europe for many centuries, and Celtic traditions are important to this day.

MAPPING THE WORLD

The Spread of Hellenism

In a rapid sequence of major battles, Alexander the Great conquered a vast empire that brought peoples from Greece to the Indus River Valley under his rule. Through the policy of establishing new cities of Greek immigrants alongside local peoples, he and his successors initiated the merging of cultural traditions known as Hellenism (from "Hellas," the native term for Greece). Hellenism shaped the histories of these regions for many centuries.

ROUTES ▼

— Trade route

➜ Campaign of Alexander, 334–324 B.C.E.

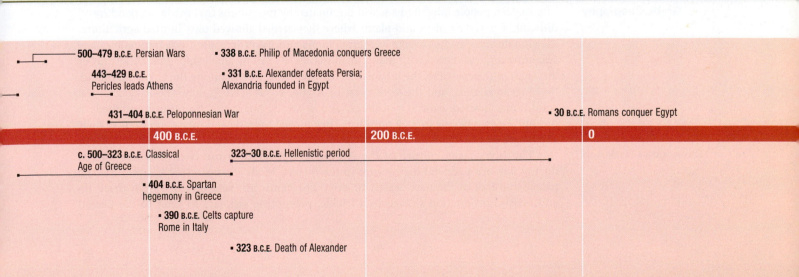

- **500–479** B.C.E. Persian Wars
- **443–429** B.C.E. Pericles leads Athens
- **431–404** B.C.E. Peloponnesian War
- **338** B.C.E. Philip of Macedonia conquers Greece
- **331** B.C.E. Alexander defeats Persia; Alexandria founded in Egypt
- **30** B.C.E. Romans conquer Egypt

400 B.C.E.   **200** B.C.E.   **0**

- **c. 500–323** B.C.E. Classical Age of Greece
- **323–30** B.C.E. Hellenistic period
- **404** B.C.E. Spartan hegemony in Greece
- **390** B.C.E. Celts capture Rome in Italy
- **323** B.C.E. Death of Alexander

OVERVIEW QUESTIONS

The major global development in this chapter: The cultural and political innovations of the ancient Greeks and the expansion of Greek ideals and institutions.

As you read, consider:

1. How did geography and contacts with other peoples shape Greek institutions and values?

2. What were the cultural and political innovations of the Greeks, and how have they proved enduring?

3. To what extent did these innovations affect the lives and livelihoods of ordinary Greeks?

4. How did the spread of Hellenism affect the Greeks and the other peoples of Eurasia and North Africa?

The Development of Ancient Greek Culture 1200–500 B.C.E.

FOCUS

What significant political and cultural developments emerged in Greece in the early first millennium B.C.E.?

Despite their unparalleled size, the empires of Southwest Asia and Egypt (see Chapter 4) had much in common with the states that preceded them. Like their predecessors, they were essentially kingdoms with centralized authority and clear distinctions between rulers and subjects. In contrast, the Aegean world took an entirely new trajectory in the first millennium B.C.E., launching bold experiments in politics, culture, and social organization. Energized by Eastern influences but operating in a different physical environment, the people of the Aegean created a unique culture that would have a great and lasting impact on world history.

A Dark Age in Aegean Life and Culture 1200–800 B.C.E.

Greek Geography

The Aegean people inhabited a world dominated by mountains that made overland travel difficult. The river valleys and plains where they settled allowed only limited agriculture; the climate was dry, but unlike in Mesopotamia and Egypt irrigation was impossible. The sea, however, was dotted with many small islands. By sailing small ships that almost never lost sight of the coastline, the inhabitants maintained contacts among the Greek mainland, the Aegean islands, and the west coast of Anatolia (modern Turkey). Poor agricultural conditions, limited natural resources, and a strong maritime tradition combined to prompt Aegean people to look outward. They turned to trade and migration to meet their challenges (see Map 5.1).

The Aegean Dark Age

The Mycenaean culture of the Aegean disappeared in the twelfth century B.C.E. during that era's general disruptions in the eastern Mediterranean (see Chapter 2). The palace cultures of the past ceased to exist. For centuries, written expression dried up and artistic production slowed to a trickle, prompting scholars to refer to the period from 1200 to 800 B.C.E. as the Aegean Dark Age. During the Dark Age, people deserted large settlements and seem to have survived in small, poor communities of farmers and migratory herders. They continued to produce pottery, however, and Mycenaean wares gradually gave way to what archaeologists call geometric pottery, vessels with intricate geometric patterns covering their entire surface. Inhabitants throughout the Aegean islands used this style of pottery. From this Aegean-wide tradition we can infer that although Dark Age conditions reduced settlement size and limited cultural activities, Aegean communities sustained their interconnections. Despite their hardships, the Aegean people continued to participate in a shared culture.

Greek Colonization of the Mediterranean 800–500 B.C.E.

The Aegean people abandoned rural life relatively suddenly around 800 B.C.E. Demographic growth, internal and external factors, and renewed contacts with the East produced radical social changes. Historians call this new era in Aegean history the Archaic period (c. 800–500 B.C.E.).

Archaeological evidence shows that the settled population of Greece dramatically increased in the eighth century B.C.E. More settlements appeared, and their populations rose substantially. The mushrooming of settled communities may reflect a change in attitudes—a desire to live in large settlements instead of moving around—rather than improvements in farming methods. Indeed, the dry, mountainous land could not support dense populations, and so many Greeks left their homeland, establishing colonies all around the Mediterranean and creating new communities modeled on those in Greece.

MAP 5.1

Greeks and Phoenicians in the Mediterranean

Throughout most of the first millennium B.C.E. Phoenician and Greek traders sailed the Mediterranean Sea, competing to bring natural resources from the west to urban centers in the east. Both peoples established trading posts on the coast as transit points for materials brought from farther inland. The Phoenicians focused especially on the south coast and the far west, while the Greeks settled mostly in the northern Mediterranean and explored the Black Sea coast.

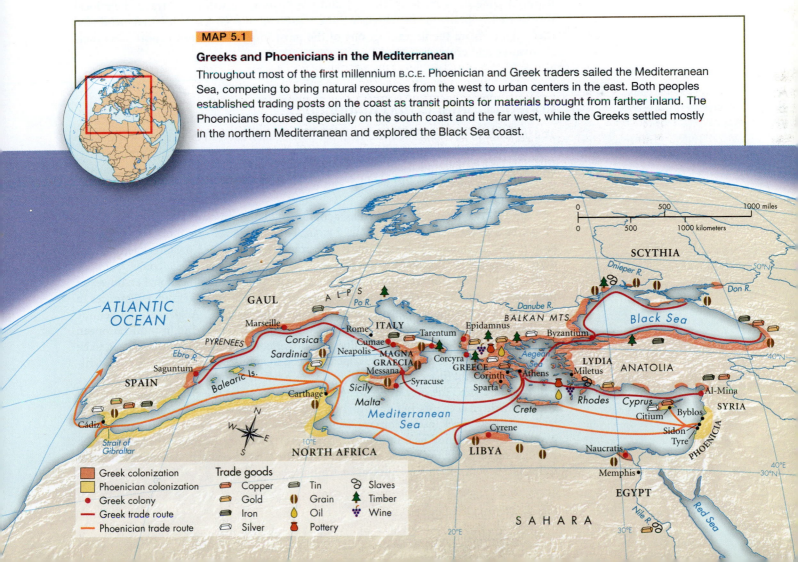

Colonization and Trade

The period of Greek colonization spanned more than two centuries, with most colonies originating between 750 and 550 B.C.E. Migrants fanned out in all directions from the Greek mainland: eastward to the modern Turkish coast and the Black Sea and westward to southern Italy, Sicily, southern France, and Spain. They also settled on the Libyan coast in North Africa.

In this widening circle of expansion, the Greeks competed with the Phoenicians, who had already colonized large parts of the western Mediterranean (see again Map 5.1). The Greeks settled eastern Sicily, for example; Phoenicians already controlled the western part of the island. The Greek colonies' economic bases varied, as did their importance to their home cities. Settlements in fertile agricultural zones shipped grain back home, while other outposts provided commodities such as timber and tin. Some special trading ports facilitated commerce with the great states of Assyria and Egypt; these typically were already established centers where Greeks simply set up business. Hence, in numerous ways, but most directly through trade, colonization strengthened the connections between Greeks and the larger world.

What did the Greeks have to offer areas that were richer in resources? The Greeks produced fine wines and olive oil, but the goods their artisans produced were especially in demand—in particular, pottery. Throughout ancient history Greek potters and painters manufactured exquisitely decorated ceramics, depicting with unprecedented liveliness scenes from epics and other literature. Because each city had its distinct style, modern scholars can easily determine where a vessel was made. Every city shipped large quantities of pottery abroad, either as empty vessels or as containers for wines and oil. People everywhere regarded them as the height of artistic accomplishment and proudly displayed them. Fancy banquets in Italy or France, for example, featured wine cups made in Greece, and the hosts were willing to trade their local resources to obtain them, increasing the wealth of the Greek cities that produced them. Thus, from the beginning, one of the most important Greek exports was their innovative and creative culture.

Foreign Contacts and Influences

The presence of Greeks abroad and visits by Phoenician traders in the Aegean world naturally led to a brisk exchange of ideas, practices, and people in the eighth century B.C.E. Because the East had much older and more developed traditions than the West, most of the inspiration went from east to west, and various Eastern cultural elements entered the Greek world.

Greek Alphabet

Most consequential was the Greeks' adoption of the Phoenician alphabet (see Chapter 4), perhaps as early as the ninth century B.C.E. The Phoenician origin of Greek letters is clear from the names, which are Semitic. For example, the name of the Greek letter *alpha* derives from the Semitic word *aleph*, meaning "ox-head"; the Greek *beta* comes from *bet*, "house"; and so on. The Greeks introduced a crucial innovation in the alphabet, however: they wrote down the vowels, which were not expressed in Semitic writing. Differences in the Greek and Semitic languages made this innovation essential. A speaker of a Semitic language knows what vowels to use from the grammatical context, but in Indo-European languages such as Greek, the context does not provide this clue and the vowels need to be explicitly expressed. Over time the scripts diverged in another way: whereas Semitic writing goes from right to left, Greek writing goes from left to right.

Why did the Greeks start to write again? Scholars assume that economic growth required written accounts, but none of the preserved earliest writing deals with business or trade. The first Greek inscriptions are names, short dedications, or curses. Often the writers state, "X wrote this," as if showing off a rare skill. Probably the majority of early Greek writings disappeared over time, and most likely the Greeks realized the multiple uses of script as a new means of communication from the beginning.

In the eighth to sixth centuries B.C.E., increasing prosperity from manufacturing and trade enabled the Greeks to buy art from foreign regions such as Phoenicia and Syria. Such art inspired Greek potters, painters, and other artists to include Eastern scenes and styles in their work. Sculptors carved human figures in imitation of Egyptian statues, and architects borrowed from Egypt techniques for constructing large buildings in stone. Given these Eastern influences, art historians refer to the seventh century B.C.E. in Greek art as the Orientalizing period, after the word *Orient*, meaning "East."

In the other direction, west to east, the Greeks provided manpower. Foreign empires greatly valued skilled Greek warriors. Greek mercenaries appeared in Egypt in the seventh century B.C.E. and soon afterward in Southwest Asia, where they remained a fixture for centuries. How and why had the Greeks developed such fighting skills? We find the answer in the emergence of powerful Greek city-states.

Growth of the City-State in Archaic Greece 800–500 B.C.E.

Population growth in the mid-eighth century B.C.E. led to fundamental changes in the political organization of the Aegean region. Village communities expanded or merged to form city-states, which became the characteristic political unit of Greek society. The Greeks referred to the city-state using the word **polis**, from which the modern term *politics* derives.

The polis was a self-governing community of citizens. It was administered by officials (who were themselves citizens) with defined responsibilities. There were numerous poleis, each controlling a relatively small territory comprising the city and its immediate surroundings. Although poleis were self-governing, they could be part of a larger political unit. In the fifth and fourth centuries B.C.E., for example, most Greek city-states fell under the hegemony of Sparta or Athens, and the poleis of western Turkey were subjects of the king of Persia for long periods. We have encountered city-states before—in Mesopotamia, for example (see Chapter 2)—but the Greeks added a further ideal to this concept. The citizens of the polis shared power rather than depended on a king. It must be emphasized, however, that most inhabitants of a polis were not citizens, a status reserved in most cases for native-born, male landowners. Women, the landless, slaves, and foreigners were all excluded from Greek government.

Like Mesopotamian city-states, neighboring Greek poleis often competed with one another over scarce resources. As a result, one of the most important duties of the citizen was to fight in the army. The eighth century B.C.E. saw radical changes in military tactics. Instead of a few heavily armed men riding to battle in chariots, from which they dismounted for individual combat, the soldiers formed **phalanxes**. Fighting on foot, these tightly organized groups relied on strict cooperation, every man holding a shield in his left arm to protect the right side of his neighbor. Each soldier, called a *hoplite*, was

Orientalizing Period

Woman's Statue in the Orientalizing Style

This statue, sculpted in Crete between 640 and 620 B.C.E., shows how much styles from Egypt and the Middle East influenced early Greek art. The woman's posture, dress, and hairstyle resemble those that Egyptian or Syrian sculptors of the same period would have shown (compare her to the Ptolemaic statues on page 162). The whole is distinctly Greek, however, and work like this lay at the basis of classical Greek sculpture. (Erich Lessing/Art Resource, NY.)

The Polis

polis The Greek city-state; in the ideal, a self-governing community of citizens.

phalanx A formation of soldiers who overlap their shields and swords to protect one another; developed in ancient Greece.

responsible for acquiring his own equipment: helmet, breastplate, leg armor, spear, and shield. Although much of the gear was made of iron, a cheaper metal than the previously used bronze, hoplites still faced considerable expense, and only landowners could serve. This common obligation, however, along with battle tactics relying on cooperation, created the strong sense of community that characterized the ideal of the polis. The way citizens fought on behalf of their communities mirrored the political connections that bound them to one another.

Shared Ideals

Despite frequent military conflicts among poleis, their inhabitants shared many cultural traits and ideals. They spoke dialects of the same Greek language, honored the same gods, and appreciated similar artistic styles. Sometimes they showed their competitive spirit in peaceful ways during festivals, including musical and literary contests. Most famous are the athletic competitions of the Olympic games. According to tradition, in 776 B.C.E. delegations of various city-states first met to compete in foot races, boxing, discus throwing, and other events in Olympia in southern Greece. The games continued in their original form for more than a thousand years, with cities from all over the Mediterranean sending athletes every four years. So strong were the cultural connections among the Greeks that even during the ruinous Peloponnesian War (discussed later in this chapter) cities of opposing factions participated in the games.

Political Diversity

Despite the shared characteristics of the city-states, their political organizations varied. The early city-states were dominated by aristocrats, a small group of people from wealthy families who inherited their status and made most of the important decisions for the community. When more people acquired wealth, the base of politically engaged men gradually expanded to include all citizens, with elected officials administering the state. These officials could reduce the power of the aristocratic families by issuing laws to regulate social and economic matters. Flouting the ideal of elected officials, from around 650 to 500 B.C.E. individuals seized power in many city-states. The Greeks called these men *tyrants*, which was at first a value-neutral term indicating "lord." People grew to resent this form of government, and rule by **tyranny** gave way to two new types of political organization. Many cities were controlled by an **oligarchy**, a small group of men who were usually wealthy, but not always from the old aristocratic families. Other cities embraced a more radical political system—the ideal of **democracy**, or rule by the people.

Athenian Democracy

Athens and Sparta, the two most prominent Greek city-states of the sixth and fifth centuries B.C.E., illustrate how geography shaped political developments in Greece. Athenians lived near the coast and relied on the sea for much of their livelihood. Starting in the seventh century B.C.E., many Athenians grew rich from maritime trade. They used this wealth to acquire land and built up large estates, dispossessing farmers in the countryside around Athens. As a result, small landowners often became indebted to wealthy city dwellers, and in the seventh century their discontent threatened the city's unity.

The tensions between classes weakened Athens, and various reformers—all aristocratic men themselves—introduced new policies intended to reduce conflict. The first measures were the work of Solon (c. 639–559 B.C.E.). Given full powers as lawgiver in 594 B.C.E., he cancelled all outstanding debts, freed all enslaved citizens, and made it illegal to force debtors into slavery. At the same time he resisted popular pressure to redistribute the lands of aristocrats and instead tried to increase wealth throughout Athenian society. Later reformers included Cleisthenes, who made all citizens equal before the law in 508 B.C.E., and—perhaps the most popular and influential of all—Pericles, who led Athens from 443 to 429 B.C.E. Pericles' many public works projects reduced unemployment, and his political initiatives brought more Athenians into the city's political structure. Collectively, these reforms turned Athens into the most developed democratic system of government in the ancient world (see Reading the Past: Pericles Praises the Democratic Ideal).

The basic principle of Athenian democracy was that all citizens—in the Greeks' limited sense of the term—could and should participate in government. All men over the age of eighteen decided on policy in an assembly that met four times every month. They debated laws, military strategy, diplomatic relations, and religious topics. They considered

tyranny A political system in which one person holds absolute power; originally value-neutral, the term has acquired the negative connotation of severe abuse of power.

oligarchy A political system in which a small group of people holds all powers.

democracy The political ideal of rule by the people.

Pericles Praises the Democratic Ideal

The ancient Greeks greatly admired the power of rhetoric, and certain speeches recorded from the time have become classics emulated to this day. Athens's leader Pericles delivered one such speech at the end of the first year of the Peloponnesian War, in 431 B.C.E. When he honored those who had fallen in battle, he extolled the virtues of the city of Athens and the institutions in whose defense they had died. This speech is the most eloquent description of the democratic ideal in world literature.

Let me say that our system of government does not copy the institutions of our neighbors. It is more the case of our being a model to others, than of our imitating anyone else. Our constitution is called a democracy because the power is in the hands not of a minority but of the whole people. When it is a question of settling private disputes, everyone is equal before the law; when it is a question of putting one person before another in positions of public responsibility, what counts is not membership of a particular class, but the actual ability which the man possesses. No one, so long as he has it in him to be of service to the state, is kept in political obscurity because of poverty. And, just as our political

life is free and open, so is our day-to-day life in our relations with each other. We do not get into a state with our next-door neighbor if he enjoys himself in his own way, nor do we give him the kind of black looks which, though they do no real harm, still do hurt people's feelings. We are free and tolerant in our private lives; but in public we keep to the law. This is because it commands our deep respect.

Source: From *Thucydides, History of the Peloponnesian War*, ed. M. I. Finley, trans. Rex Warner (London: Penguin Classics,1972), 145.

EXAMINING THE EVIDENCE

1. What characteristics of the Athenian political system does Pericles praise? Do you think his claims reflect the reality of life in ancient Athens?

2. Why was this speech pertinent in a period of war?

3. How do the ideals expressed here still echo in political discourse today?

the most important matters of state, listened to one another's arguments, and truly governed as a people. They even stood in judgment over one another—each citizen had the right to be judged by his peers.

Because the Athenian assembly was too large to manage daily business, they created a smaller body for this purpose. Each year five hundred men who were at least thirty years old were selected by lot to join a council, and they served in groups of fifty for a period of thirty-six days each. The council prepared laws for consideration by the assembly and executed the assembly's decisions. To prevent a small group of men from gaining a monopoly on executive power, no man was allowed to serve on the council for more than two years, and these years had to be nonconsecutive. Thus executive power was spread over the entire citizenry.

The ideal of the democratic system was clear: every citizen had the ability to make intelligent decisions and perform official duties. But not everyone thought this was true or that democracy was a good idea. Ancient philosophers such as Plato (see page 152) doubted that all men were equally capable of governing, and modern scholars often depict an Athenian assembly that was easily swayed by the false arguments of great orators. Yet despite the shortcomings Athenian democracy displayed in practice, its ideals have inspired political thinkers throughout world history, especially in modern times.

Sparta's geographical setting was very different from Athens's. In the eighth and seventh centuries B.C.E. the city conquered the fertile regions that surrounded it. The Spartans used this land, farmed by the forced labor of its inhabitants, to support its citizens. This enabled all Spartan citizens—again, the male inhabitants of the city—to sit in an assembly, unencumbered by agricultural work. The institution had much less power than the Athenian assembly, however, because it had to work in concert with an elected council

Spartan Oligarchy

of thirty men, all over sixty years old. A group of five officials, annually elected from among all citizens, held executive power. In practice wealthy families had more influence than poorer ones, because they could bribe officials. The highest Spartan officials were two kings, men from two wealthy families, who ruled simultaneously for life. Their primary role was to lead the army in war, but they had much influence at home as well. Real power in Sparta was thus in the hands of an oligarchy.

Spartan oligarchy and Athenian democracy thus shared several elements, but to us today their ideals seem very different. Athenians declared that citizens, however restricted that group was, could and should be involved in politics, whereas Spartans believed that only select men had the ability to govern. The Spartan economy depended on the control and exploitation of the nearby land and population. Athenians, in contrast, emphasized the sea and trade. The opposition of the two systems would grow over time and, as we shall see, lead to conflict.

A Cultural Reawakening

Homer and Sappho

During the Archaic period many Greek writers turned to poetry. Some of the earliest works had an enormous impact, influencing Western literature until the modern period. Of these early poets, Homer and Sappho stand out because of the beauty of their poetic language and their ability to depict human emotions.

Later Greeks regarded Homer as the greatest poet of their past and the authority on peoples, countries, gods, and events. He composed his two epics, the *Iliad* and the *Odyssey*, probably around 750 B.C.E. Models for all subsequent Western epic poetry, these lengthy poems (c. sixteen thousand and twelve thousand lines, respectively) use highly metaphoric language and a strict metric form. The *Iliad* depicts Greek and Trojan heroes engaged in a ten-year struggle; the *Odyssey* relates the adventures of one Greek warrior on his return home. Homer's intricate stories show acts of heroism, cunning, kindness, and cruelty. The Trojan War provides the background for a novel exploration of the sentiments, strengths, and weaknesses of the men and women involved: the anger of Achilles, the foolish pride of Agamemnon, the longing of Odysseus for his home and his wife, the steadfast love of Penelope. These characters lived a courtly life in which honor, hospitality, proper social behavior, and especially personal excellence were crucial

Sappho (c. 630–570 B.C.E.) was the first known woman poet of Greek literature. She led a community of young women on the island of Lesbos, near the modern Turkish coast. The strength of her poetry lay in her ability to describe human passions, especially love and friendship, often in the context of the religious festivals that occupied young women's lives before marriage. The literary quality of her writings earned her respect in her own lifetime, and her fame grew after her death. With her focus on women and their emotions, Sappho addresses a world that is different from Homer's, but they share an interest in human sentiments as well as the ability to write beautiful poetry.

Greek Temple in Agrigento, Sicily
Some of the best-preserved classical Greek temples are on the island of Sicily, where the Greeks had established colonies. This temple is one of seven built near the city of Agrigento in the sixth and fifth centuries B.C.E. and devoted to gods such as Zeus and his consort Hera. Its layout and the shape of its columns display one of the main styles of Greek architecture, the Doric order. (© DeA Picture Library/Art Resource, NY.)

Greek bards recited poems for entertainment, especially at religious festivals. Like the Mesopotamians, Egyptians, and others, the Greeks believed their gods to be immortal, but they saw them in far more human terms than did peoples elsewhere. The Greek gods loved, fought, lied, ate, drank, and behaved like humans in other ways, regularly interacting with mortals. Zeus, the ruler of heaven, had many affairs with women, divine and human, and sired numerous children.

Religious Ritual

Thus, in many ways the Greek gods simply reflected the Greeks themselves, but there was one crucial difference. The gods, of course, had the power to shape the universe and influence the fate of human beings. Accordingly, the Greeks were careful to appease them through established religious rites, rites in which women often played a major role. Citizens of Greek city-states had a civic duty to participate in public festivals, and the shared experience intensified their feeling of community. In their collective appeasement of the gods, Greek citizens shared the task of protecting and promoting their polis.

The most imposing monuments remaining from the Greeks are their temples, which display remarkable architectural and artistic skill. The temple of Athena, the goddess of wisdom, still defines the skyline of Athens. The basic structure was simple: a central room that held the cult statue (Athena's statue was made of ivory, silver, and gold and measured about forty-one feet high) and was surrounded by a wall and a row of columns. Mythological scenes carved in relief decorated the façades above the columns. In different parts of the Greek world various styles developed, but all Greeks on the mainland and in the colonies regarded the temple as an important sign of their city's wealth and grandeur.

Greek Temples

Although many elements of their culture received inspiration from the East, by 500 B.C.E. the Greeks had developed their own highly original literature, religion, art, and architecture, creating a distinct Greek cultural identity. Subsequent political events would sharpen the contrast between Greeks and other peoples even more.

The Persian Wars, Classical Greece, and the Concept of Cultural Difference 500–338 B.C.E.

For the Greeks, the fifth and fourth centuries B.C.E. were times of both endemic warfare and intellectual and cultural achievement. During this period, people all over the Greek world, but especially in Athens, produced revolutionary innovations in intellectual life. They developed new forms of scientific inquiry and artistic expression and experimented with political structures. Their accomplishments imbued the Greeks with pride and self-confidence, which they expressed in a worldview that made sharp distinctions between Greeks and outsiders. These developments took place against a backdrop of military conflict, both between Greeks and foreigners and among the Greeks themselves. Scholars refer to this period as Greece's Classical Age because it shows the culmination of earlier developments and because later Greeks and others in Western history saw its achievements as the height of human ingenuity in antiquity (see Map 5.2).

> **FOCUS**
>
> What cultural innovations appeared in Greece during its Classical Age?

Struggle Between Persia and Greece 500–479 B.C.E.

While the Greeks developed new political institutions in the city-states, the ideal of kingship, with inherited power held by one man, continued in Southwest Asia. As we saw in Chapter 4, increasingly large political units succeeded one another there, culminating in the late sixth century B.C.E. in the Persian Empire. By 500 B.C.E., Persian power extended from the Indus Valley to the Mediterranean Sea and from Central Asia to Egypt.

To the mighty Persian Empire, conquest of the small and divided city-states of Greece must have seemed like a minor challenge. Successive invasions, however, ended in disaster

Persian Wars

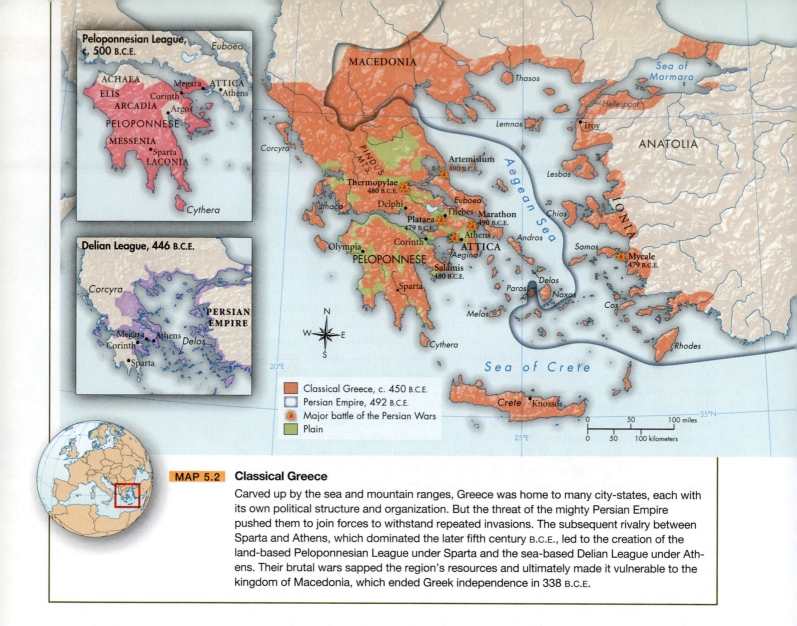

Peloponnesian League, c. 500 B.C.E.

ACHAEA
ELIS
ARCADIA
Corinth
Megara ATTICA
Athens
Argos
PELOPONNESE
MESSENIA
Sparta
LACONIA
Cythera
Euboea

Delian League, 446 B.C.E.

Corcyra
Megara Athens Delos
Corinth
Sparta
PERSIAN EMPIRE

MACEDONIA
Thasos
Sea of Marmara
Hellespont
Lemnos
Troy
ANATOLIA
Corcyra
PINDUS MTS.
Artemisium 480 B.C.E.
Lesbos
Thermopylae 480 B.C.E.
Ithaca
Delphi
Euboea
Chios
IONIA
Plataea 479 B.C.E.
Thebes Marathon 490 B.C.E.
Olympia
Corinth
Athens
Andros
Samos
Mycale 479 B.C.E.
PELOPONNESE
ATTICA
Aegina
Sparta
Salamis 480 B.C.E.
Paros
Delos
Naxos
Cos
Melos
Cythera
Rhodes
Sea of Crete
Crete Knossos
Aegean Sea

Classical Greece, c. 450 B.C.E.
Persian Empire, 492 B.C.E.
Major battle of the Persian Wars
Plain

0 50 100 miles
0 50 100 kilometers

MAP 5.2 Classical Greece

Carved up by the sea and mountain ranges, Greece was home to many city-states, each with its own political structure and organization. But the threat of the mighty Persian Empire pushed them to join forces to withstand repeated invasions. The subsequent rivalry between Sparta and Athens, which dominated the later fifth century B.C.E., led to the creation of the land-based Peloponnesian League under Sparta and the sea-based Delian League under Athens. Their brutal wars sapped the region's resources and ultimately made it vulnerable to the kingdom of Macedonia, which ended Greek independence in 338 B.C.E.

for Persia. In 490 B.C.E., the Athenians defeated the Persians soundly at the Battle of Marathon, relying on their heavy armor and tight battle formation. Ten years later, the Persian King Xerxes (r. 486–465 B.C.E.) invaded Greece on land and by sea with a gigantic army—the Greek historian Herodotus implausibly claims it included more than 2 million men. At a pass called Thermopylae, three hundred Spartans under King Leonidas stood firm to slow the Persian advance. Every Spartan died in several days of heavy fighting. Xerxes entered central Greece and burned down the temples and monumental buildings of Athens, which its citizens had evacuated without trying to resist a siege.

Despite the destruction of their city, the Athenians continued the fight at sea. They lured the massive Persian fleet into the narrow bay at Salamis, where, unable to maneuver, it fell prey to the smaller Greek ships. The playwright Aeschylus, who participated in the war and perhaps even fought in this battle, ascribes these words to the Persian messenger who reported the rout:

First the floods of Persians held the line,
But when the narrows choked them, and rescue hopeless,
Smitten by prows, their bronze jaws gaping,
Shattered entire was our fleet of oars.
The Grecian warships, calculating, dashed
Round, and encircled us; ships showed their belly:

> No longer could we see the water, charged
> With ships' wrecks and men's blood.
> Corpses glutted beaches and the rocks.
> . . . never in a single day
> So great a number died.[2]

The next year, in 479 B.C.E., the Greeks defeated the remainder of the Persian force and ended further threats of invasion.

The Persian Wars had tremendous consequences for the Greeks. Some thirty city-states had formed an unprecedented coalition, and for the rest of the fifth century B.C.E. Sparta and Athens, which had distinguished themselves militarily, used their fame to command the respect and gratitude of the other Greek city-states. The wars also raised the Greek self-image. A sense of superiority permeated political, social, and cultural life, and the Greeks came to believe that they were the only people capable of achieving the ideal of freedom.

The coalition of states built to resist the Persians did not outlast the war, and political fragmentation returned after 479 B.C.E. Nevertheless, Athens and Sparta used their special status to gain allies, by free will and by force. Each formed a league of allies (see again Map 5.2). Sparta, which had risen to power by exploiting land resources, allied itself primarily with states on the Greek mainland that had strong infantries and few ships. The Spartans dominated most of the city-states of the Peloponnese, that is, the southern Greek peninsula. Their coalition was called the Peloponnesian League. Athens, in contrast, looked outward to the sea, where its navy had crushed the Persians. The Athenians allied themselves with states on the Greek islands and the Ionian coast. They created the Delian League, so named because the coalition originally kept its treasury on the island of Delos. At first, members delivered contributions mainly in the form of ships and their crews, but over time this arrangement developed into silver payments to Athens, which used the money to build and crew ships of its own. Soon Athens had by far the region's largest navy, with which it imposed its will on the members of the Delian League, presenting itself as the protector of democracy against the oligarchic regimes of the Peloponnesian League.

Peloponnesian and Delian Leagues

Athens's Golden Age 500–400 B.C.E.

In the fifth century B.C.E., the substantial contributions that Delian League members made in lieu of ships and crews filled Athenian state coffers. Moreover, Athenian traders shipped pottery, wine, and oil from Greece to ports all along the eastern Mediterranean coast, turning the Athenian harbor, Piraeus, into the dominant commercial center of the region. Thus, political and economic connections dramatically increased Athenian power and wealth, which in turn made possible remarkable innovations in the city's political, scientific, and cultural life.

As we have seen, in the sixth century B.C.E. the Athenians took important steps toward democracy. In the fifth century B.C.E. Athenian democracy reached its zenith under the leadership of Pericles. Pericles sought to ensure that all Athenian citizens, rich or poor, were able to take an active role in government. Hence, he arranged for men who sat in council or on a jury to receive a daily stipend from the state so that poor citizens could take time off from work to fulfill their civic duties. As important as Pericles' policies were, we must remember that they aimed to increase the number of citizens who took part in civic life, not to increase the total number of citizens. Out of a mid-fifth-century population of between three and four hundred thousand, only about fifty thousand Athenians had any political rights.

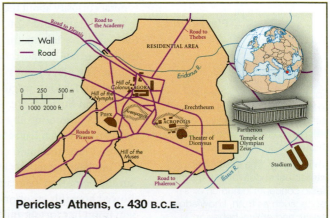

Pericles' Athens, c. 430 B.C.E.

Sophists

Those Athenians with political rights obviously wanted to present convincing arguments in the assembly. As a result, the art of rhetoric, or public speaking, gained importance unprecedented in world history. The need to speak persuasively created a niche for a new type of teacher, called a **sophist** ("wise man"), who offered instruction in rhetoric for a fee. Because of the sophists' focus on oratory technique and the payments, the term *sophist* has a negative connotation today, suggesting someone who makes an invalid argument with the appearance of truth. But in ancient Athens, these men were highly respected and considered much more than mere political "coaches" for hire. Many explored innovative ideas, subjecting Greek intellectual and religious traditions to a rigorous examination that pushed Greek thinking in new directions. Above all, the sophists believed in the power of human reason. Although many were religious and believed in the power of the gods, they saw human rationality as *the* crucial tool for explaining the workings of the universe. Many sophists came from outside Athens. Because of its wealth and vibrant cultural life, the city became an intellectual crossroads and the center of the new field of **philosophy**, a word literally translated as "love of wisdom."

Philosophers

The three most famous and influential Greek philosophers of antiquity were Socrates, Plato, and Aristotle. Although they distanced themselves from the sophists, their ideas and inquiries were made possible by the general atmosphere of intellectual curiosity that the sophists helped create in Athens. The three philosophers investigated all aspects of life and the physical environment using techniques that are still influential today. Although the three men were closely linked (Socrates taught Plato, who in turn taught Aristotle), each made distinctive contributions to Greek philosophy. Socrates developed a mode of questioning designed to help separate truth from assumption. Plato developed the notion of universal ideals. Aristotle analyzed everything from literature to the natural environment by classifying their elements. Together they laid the foundation of education and scientific investigation as practiced in the Middle East and Europe until the modern period (see Lives and Livelihoods: Philosophers of Athens's Golden Age).

Historians

Whereas philosophers investigated general principles, other Athenians explored the events that shaped Greek life, notably the wars that occupied much of fifth-century b.c.e. Greece. As we have seen, Herodotus (c. 485–425 b.c.e.) wrote on the Persian Wars, which ended when he was a young boy, and Thucydides (c. 460–400 b.c.e.) documented the Peloponnesian War between Athens and Sparta (discussed later in this chapter), in which he had fought. The elder of the two, Herodotus, became known in the West as the Father of History ("inquiry" in Greek) because he was the first who studied the past to find the causes of historical events.

Thucydides explained the war between Athens and Sparta as an unavoidable clash between two expansionist states, the former focusing on sea power, the latter on control of land. He used his work as a vehicle to express his support for democratic rule under a strong leader, connecting Athens's problems to deviations from this ideal. The works of Herodotus and Thucydides were revolutionary because they presented historical events as the consequences of human actions, rather than as the result of divine intervention. Moreover, they personified the general curiosity about the structure and causes of things that swept Athens in its Golden Age.

Playwrights

Herodotus and Thucydides had great literary skills and wrote engaging prose narratives. In these talents they were far from alone, for in the fifth century b.c.e. Athens was the hub of an extraordinary literary production including, most prominently, works of drama. The playwright's emphasis was not on action but on the beauty of poetic language. The most famous tragic authors—Aeschylus (525–456 b.c.e.), Sophocles (c. 496–406 b.c.e.), and Euripides (c. 485–406 b.c.e.)—examined human nature and society in all their aspects. A common subject was human *hubris*, the Greek term for excessive pride and self-confidence, which led to the hero's downfall. For example, in *Oedipus the King*, Sophocles explored how the main character's certainty that he could uncover the truth through his own intellect caused his utter ruin: he blinded himself and his mother committed suicide. Another emotion regularly depicted was the desire for vengeance. In *Medea*, Euripides showed how this emotion pushed a slighted wife, Medea, into killing her children to inflict pain upon her former husband. In the *Oresteia*, three plays that form a narrative sequence,

sophist Originally an ancient Greek teacher of rhetoric; today the term has the negative connotation of someone who convinces through false arguments.

philosophy The systematic intellectual endeavor of explaining basic concepts in human existence, such as truth, knowledge, reality, and ethical behavior.

Aeschylus demonstrated how vengeance becomes an endless cycle, as Clytaemnestra killed her husband Agamemnon because he had slaughtered their daughter. In retaliation, their son Orestes murdered her. The cycle ended only when a jury in Athens's law court decided guilt. The *Oresteia* explained how a new institution based on the judgment of humans superseded the older system of never-ending revenge. Indeed, the Golden Age dramatists probed into all aspects of society. In so doing they frequently criticized those characteristics of classical Greece that we now so often praise, such as rationality and self-confidence.

While the characters in the Greek tragedies were almost always figures from the ancient past, comedies featured living people and current events. Greek comedies used bawdy jokes and verbal puns to mock Athens's leaders and to make fun of their society's shortcomings. For example, actors often stood on stage wearing large leather phalluses, and sex and other bodily functions dominated the insults that the characters hurled at each other.

The best-known comic author was Aristophanes (c. 455–385 B.C.E.), whose barbed attacks spared no one. He depicted the philosopher Socrates as hanging in a basket staring at the sky, collecting fees from spoiled young men for teaching them how to win every argument. In the play *Lysistrata* Aristophanes has the women of Athens and Sparta withhold sex to force their husbands to recognize the senselessness of the Peloponnesian War. These plays were performed for a public that understood the allusions and were willing to see their political and intellectual leaders portrayed as buffoons.

Remarkably for a society that treated women as inferior, women were often the central characters of Greek tragedies. Sophocles' heroine Antigone, for example, stood against her uncle's decree that her brother should not be buried. She proudly obeyed divine laws and was willing to die for doing so:

> And so, for me to meet this fate, no grief.
> But if I left that corpse, my mother's son,
> dead and unburied I'd have cause to grieve
> as now I grieve not.
> And if you think my acts are foolishness
> the foolishness may be in a fool's eye.[3]

These female characters, fully developed by the genius of the playwrights, do not fight their inferior status but often uphold values that are more personal than those of the publicly oriented men.

The cultural and intellectual flourishing of Athens in the fifth century B.C.E. derived from the presence of great creative minds in a society that gave some of its people the freedom to explore everything. Out of this environment came a sense of Athenian superiority to the rest of the world. They scorned those who did not speak Greek as "barbarians," a term derived from "bar bar," after the sound of foreign languages to Greek ears. The Greeks depicted non-Greeks as lacking the sense to have proper political institutions, customs, and social behavior. Indeed, outsiders were presented as holding the opposite of Greek values: they tolerated despots, indulged in excess, and committed

Poking Fun at Greek Gods

The ancients took their gods very seriously, but they saw a comic side to them as well. This vase from about 350 B.C.E. shows Zeus (left), father of all the gods, as an old man carrying a ladder, assisted by Hermes (right), herald for the other gods. Zeus is attempting to visit the young Alcmene (in the window), who was thought to be the most beautiful mortal woman on earth. According to myth, Zeus and Alcmene's child was the Greek hero Heracles. (Scala/Art Resource, NY.)

Philosophers of Athens's Golden Age

Three Athenians of the fifth and fourth centuries B.C.E. stand out as giants in the history of Western philosophy: Socrates, Plato, and Aristotle. For some one hundred years their teaching and writing inspired intellectual life in the city and beyond, and ever since their ideas have engaged philosophers. Socrates (c. 470–399 B.C.E.) did not leave any written work; we know of his teachings primarily through his student Plato. Socrates' chief aim was to find justice, which he equated with truth. Questioning people who claimed to be wise in such a way that they realized the limitations of their knowledge, Socrates sought ways to discover true wisdom. Probably because he was, as he himself said, a gadfly constantly reproaching the Athenians, he was condemned to death in 399 B.C.E., ostensibly because he corrupted youth.

Aristotle in Medieval Islamic Tradition

The great classical Greek philosophers were remembered long after antiquity. In the Middle Ages they were especially treasured in the Islamic world, where scholars translated their works into Arabic and interpreted their ideas. This manuscript from the thirteenth century C.E. depicts the philosopher Aristotle teaching Alexander the Great. The manuscript contains a work by a physician of the Abbasid court called "The Usefulness of Animals," which draws from classical works such as Aristotle's. (British Library, London/British Library Board. All Rights Reserved/Bridgeman Art Library.)

incest. This contrast had a political value, for as we have seen, it enabled the Greeks to unite against the Persians. But it led to a skewed view in the historical record of the relationship between Greeks and foreigners. Stressing their own uniqueness, the Greeks downplayed the significant role that Southwest Asia and Egypt played in inspiring many of their cultural achievements.

He chose to commit suicide by drinking hemlock, rather than flee from prison as his friends had arranged for him.

It is hard to determine how much of Plato's (c. 428–348 B.C.E.) writing reflects Socrates' teaching and how much records his own philosophy. Plato used the dialogue form to communicate his ideas. He portrays Socrates as questioning persons in such a way that his ideas were arrived at as the only logical conclusion. The dialogues assume that all knowledge was innate in human beings and could be revealed by asking the right questions, through the so-called Socratic method. In one dialogue, Socrates takes a young slave of his friend Meno through a geometrical proof as if the boy knew the answer all along. In this view, the soul naturally possesses all knowledge; the philosopher needs only to find the key to unlock it. The Socratic method can be used to investigate all aspects of life, from mathematics to love.

Plato stressed the distinction between the physical, which he saw as imperfect, and the spiritual, which he viewed as perfect. Only the immortal human soul knows the spiritual, Plato believed. He also commented on political life in his dialogue, *Republic*, in which he questioned the democratic ideal on the grounds that not all men have the skills needed to make the right decisions. He proposed a hierarchy instead: on top would be "guardians," who are wise and well educated; in the middle, "auxiliaries" would provide protection; on the bottom, "producers" would provide food and manufactured goods. Laws would be the instruments to enable the guardians to carry out their decisions.

Plato founded a school, the Academy, that drew students from all over Greece, including his most famous pupil, Aristotle (384–322 B.C.E.). On Plato's death Aristotle tutored the young Alexander of Macedonia. He returned to Athens in 335 B.C.E. to found his own school, the Lyceum. Aristotle taught a vast array of subjects, from the natural sciences to literary criticism. He collected and analyzed biological samples and wrote about physics, chemistry, anatomy, and medicine, believing that one could classify every thing by analyzing its properties. He abandoned Plato's distrust of the physical, focusing instead on observing particulars, from which one could derive general conclusions through logical induction. Aristotle wrote many analytical treatises, including the famous work *Politics*, in which he described a state in which the virtues of people guided government. He disapproved of tyranny and rule by the masses and wanted a middle road with an assembly directed by able experts. Aristotle thought that slavery was a natural condition for some people and that these individuals should be captured for the benefit of the state. In the field of ethics, Aristotle warned against extremes and argued that people should strive for balance. He also wrote analyses of Greek literature in which he formulated the principles of poetry, using the great tragedies of the fifth century B.C.E. as models.

Because the three philosophers sought rational explanations and (especially Aristotle) formulated ideas very systematically, they became the models for scholarly investigation in the Hellenistic world. Philosophers in Alexandria and elsewhere turned to them for inspiration for centuries. When Christianity and Islam emerged, the thinkers who laid their intellectual foundations merged classical Greek philosophical ideas with biblical concepts. The works of Plato and Aristotle were translated into other languages, notably Arabic, which is how they survived, and for centuries they provided the foundation of scientific investigation in Europe and the Middle East. Even today no philosopher working in the Western tradition can ignore these thinkers.

QUESTIONS TO CONSIDER

1. How and why did approaches to philosophical inquiry differ among Socrates, Plato, and Aristotle?

2. Why did these three philosophers have such influence on later intellectual history?

For Further Information:
Ancient Greek philosophy: http://www.iep.utm.edu/greekphi/.
Annas, Julia. *Plato: A Very Short Introduction*. New York: Oxford University Press, 2003.
Barnes, Jonathan. *Aristotle: A Very Short Introduction*. New York: Oxford University Press, 2000.
Dean-Jones, Lesley. "Philosophy and Science." In *Cambridge Illustrated History of Ancient Greece*. Edited by Paul Cartledge, 288–319. Cambridge, U.K.: Cambridge University Press, 1998.
Taylor, Christopher. *Socrates: A Very Short Introduction.* Oxford, U.K.: Oxford University Press, 2000.

Greeks and Foreigners

Greek city-states were part of a larger Mediterranean economic system. The Greeks may have disliked foreigners, and contacts between Greeks and outsiders were often hostile, but trade never ceased. Their colonies throughout the Mediterranean and Black seas put the Greeks in contact with foreign people from Spain to Scythia. Greek merchants continued to trade with Egypt even when that country was under Persian rule. People everywhere wanted Greek decorated pottery and other luxury products. Moreover, foreign traders prized the silver that the Greeks paid for imported goods. Some Greeks observed foreign cultures firsthand and came to appreciate their unique characteristics, even if such encounters did not shake their confidence in Greek superiority. Herodotus, for example, was fascinated by Egypt, although he considered its culture to be almost the exact opposite of his own:

> For instance, women attend market and are employed in trade, while men stay at home and do the weaving. In weaving the normal way is to work the threads of the weft upwards, but the Egyptians work them downwards. Men in Egypt carry loads on their heads, women on their shoulders; women pass water standing up, men sitting down. To ease their bowels they go indoors, but eat outside in the streets, on the theory that what is unseemly but necessary should be done in private, and what is not unseemly should be done openly.[4]

The Peloponnesian War and the End of Athenian Supremacy 431–404 B.C.E.

Peloponnesian War

Athens's international trade and its control over the Delian League had funded the city's Golden Age. Over time, however, its ever-expanding power led to resentment among its rivals, especially Sparta, the leading city-state of the Peloponnese. The tensions between Athens and Sparta erupted in a generation-long conflict known as the Peloponnesian War (431–404 B.C.E.), which impoverished Greece and undermined its society. During the war years, the Athenians became increasingly authoritarian, extracting ever higher contributions from members of the Delian League, forcing other cities to choose sides, and punishing those who refused to join. They could be ruthless. When the inhabitants of the island of Melos asked to remain neutral, Athens massacred all the men and enslaved all the women and children. Despite such desperate acts, Athens failed to defeat its enemies, and in 404 B.C.E. Sparta prevailed. For the moment, Sparta was the dominant power in Greece.

Rise of Macedonia

Sparta's hegemony, however, did not last long, and the fourth century B.C.E. saw fierce struggles among Greek cities for preeminence. The power that ended this period of civil strife was Macedonia, a territory to the north of Greece that the Greeks had long regarded as backward. Macedonia was a kingdom, and in many respects its relationship to Greece was like that of Nubia to Egypt (see Chapter 4): it owed much of its culture to Greece, yet ultimately it came to dominate its neighbor. Inspired by Greek practices, the Macedonian King Philip II (r. 359–336 B.C.E.) greatly improved his army's strength and tactics by arming his phalanx of foot soldiers with 10-foot-long spears and coordinating their actions with those of the horse-mounted cavalry. With this military advantage, in 338 B.C.E. Philip defeated the city-states of southern Greece and forced them into an alliance under Macedonian leadership. The age of independent Greek poleis was over. Greek culture had reached its highest point after its city-states had united to oppose the might of Persia. When the connections among Greek city-states that had helped produce this vital unity deteriorated, the Greeks were left weak and divided, easy prey for a powerful and determined neighbor.

Macedonia, 359 B.C.E.
Territorial gains, by 336 B.C.E.
Macedonian dependencies and allies, 336 B.C.E.
Major battle

Macedonia Under Philip II, 359–336 B.C.E.

Daily Life in Classical Greece

Athens's acropolis, its famous hilltop covered with monumental marble buildings (see again At a Crossroads, page 138), was a physical expression of the city's wealth and power. Although many Athenians probably took pride in the acropolis, very few enjoyed the wealth and luxury suggested by the city's public spaces. As was the case elsewhere in the ancient world, social inequality was the norm in Greece. Most Greeks were poor and powerless, although conditions varied from place to place. A comparison of Athens and Sparta illustrates the range of social conditions that existed in classical Greece.

In Athens, most people were slaves, landless poor, or resident aliens (called *metics* in Greek), none of whom enjoyed political rights. The last group was especially large. Many metics came to Athens voluntarily, because it was the center of Greek economic and intellectual life. Because they could not own land, they often practiced crafts and trade, activities scorned by Athenian citizens. Slaves were always foreigners. The Athenian state used some of them in public works, such as mining, which was grueling and deadly work. Many slaves worked in private households. Slaves who managed to save money could buy their freedom, although they could not become citizens. Of an estimated total population of three to four hundred thousand people, fifth-century-B.C.E. Athens was home to perhaps one hundred thousand slaves.

Athenian Society

Women, even those of the elite class, had second-class status and little personal freedom. As in Vedic India (see Chapter 3), they were tied to households dominated by men. A father fully controlled a young girl's life and arranged her marriage in her teen years to a suitable man of around thirty years old. Once a wife entered her husband's house, she was responsible for its management but had little control over the property. Her father, husband, or brother acted in public on her behalf, and she could not go out without wearing a veil. When a man died, his sons inherited all he owned; if he left only a daughter, a male relative married her and took charge of the property she inherited (see Reading the Past: Semonides Catalogues the Evils of Women). Prevented from acquiring financial independence, women were defined entirely by their subordinate relationship to men as daughters and wives.

Meanwhile, Athenian men spent most of their time away from home for work or leisure. They often ate and drank with their friends until late at night while female musicians and dancers entertained them. Some women, mostly foreigners, attended those dinners to provide witty conversation, music, and sometimes sexual favors. Many prominent Athenians kept such women in luxurious circumstances as concubines. We should not, however, romanticize such women's lives. The story of Neaira (neh-EYE-ruh), a highly successful courtesan with many rich and influential clients, demonstrates the vulnerability of all Athenian women, regardless of their circumstances. We know her life in detail from the record of a trial involving her in mid-fourth-century-B.C.E. Athens. When Neaira was about ten she joined a brothel with an elite clientele in the city of Corinth. In 376 B.C.E. two men bought her and later offered her the chance to buy her own freedom. A third man gave her the funds and took her to Athens, where she was the victim of his abuse. When she fled to live with yet another man, her original benefactor forcibly reclaimed her, and the two men agreed to share her. Although Neaira was admired by many men, her freedom was always limited and her status depended on the whims of her lovers, who—as in many other ancient societies—could dispose of her as they saw fit.

Greek women from all walks of life shared Neaira's vulnerability. For the Greeks, the purpose of a marriage was to produce children, preferably boys. If a woman could not produce children, she had failed in her primary function and her husband often divorced her. Moreover, childbearing was dangerous in early societies, and scholars blame it for the high death rate of women in Athens. Studies of skeletons show that the life expectancy of women was thirty-six, whereas for men it was forty-five.

Seeing their wives as little more than the mothers of their children, Athenian men looked outside of the home for companionship and pleasure. Women like Neaira provided sexual favors to men, but male homosexual intercourse was also considered normal and acceptable in ancient Athens. Adolescents attached themselves to older men who became their guardians and taught them how to behave as adults.

The Spartan situation—although similarly unequal—was different from that in Athens. The Spartan state owned a large group of dependent laborers, who worked the land. These

Spartan Society

Semonides Catalogues the Evils of Women

Women's inferior status in Greek society is clear from actual practice, but many literary works also display misogynist attitudes. The Greeks accepted the superiority of men in every respect. Aeschylus's *Oresteia*, for example, presents women as mere incubators for the male semen, which they believed determined all of a child's characteristics. Murdering a mother was a lesser crime than killing a father. A number of literary passages lament the very existence of women, as does this poem, "On Women," by the sixth-century B.C.E. satirist Semonides of Amorgos.

For Zeus designed this as the greatest of all evils:

Women. Even if in some way they seem to be a help;

To their husbands especially they are a source of evil.

For there is no one who manages to spend a whole day

In contentment if he has a wife.

Nor will he find himself able to speedily thrust famine out of his house,

Who is a hateful, malicious god to have as a houseguest.

But whenever a man seems to be especially content at home,

Thanks either to good fortune from the gods or to his good relations with the rest

Of mankind, she'll find fault somewhere and stir up a dispute.

For whosoever wife she is, she won't receive graciously

Into the house a friend who comes to visit.

And you know, the very one who appears to be moderate and prudent

Actually turns out to be the most outrageous and shameful.

And when her husband is still in shock from finding out about her, the

Neighbors have a good laugh because even he made a mistake in his choice.

For each man likes to regale others with stories of praise about his own wife,

While at the same time finding fault with any other man's wife.

We don't realize that we all share the same fate.

For Zeus designed this as the greatest of all evils

And bound us to it in unbreakable fetters.

Source: M.L. West. *Greek Lyric Poetry* translated by M. L. West (1994), p. 19 'On Women' (21 lines of poetry). Used by permission of Oxford University Press.

EXAMINING THE EVIDENCE

1. What attributes does Semonides ascribe to women?

2. Why does he consider women to be the curse of all men?

3. What does this satirical poem suggest about the Greeks' attitude toward women?

slaves, called helots, were the descendants of the original population of the territory Sparta had conquered early in its history. Unlike slaves elsewhere in Greece, the helots were Greeks rather than foreigners, and at times they tried to rebel. The Spartans used terror tactics to try to keep them in their place. For example, they sent young men into the countryside at night to kill any helot they encountered for sport.

We use the word *Spartan* today to indicate an existence that is frugal, austere, and disciplined. That notion derives from ancient Sparta's education of its boys. The state took them from their mothers at age seven to train in military techniques and gymnastics. Between the ages of twenty and thirty, men lived in communal barracks, even if they were married, and in later life they had to dine with their peers rather than at home. Spartan citizens did not admire individualism; they wanted all men to share the same bravery and devotion to the state. They honed their military skills while helots provided their food.

Spartan women had greater freedom than those in Athens. Relieved of domestic duties by helots, they were responsible for household property, some of which they owned. Some women had large dowries, which husbands could not take away. According to Aristotle, women owned two-thirds of the land in Sparta. To learn how to protect the household, Spartan girls received physical training and exercised naked in public (as did boys). Although far from emancipated, they enjoyed more respect and greater independence than Athenian women.

In both societies, and throughout Greece, life for most people was difficult and dangerous. The wars of the fifth century B.C.E. brought ruin to the Greek countryside and sent many men to fight in distant conflicts. Thucydides describes brutality by all sides in the Peloponnesian War, including indiscriminate slaughter of men, women, and children, as we saw in the case of Melos. Civil wars erupted constantly between different political factions, and opponents received little mercy. The predominance of war in the fifth century B.C.E. explains why so many Greek men later hired themselves out as mercenaries to anyone willing to pay. When the wars ended, young Greek men were left with nothing but their hard-won military skills.

Hellenism: The Expansion of Greek Ideals and Institutions   323–30 B.C.E.

After establishing dominance over Greece, the new power of Macedonia conquered the vast Persian Empire and created in its stead a system of kingdoms ruled by Greeks. As the Greeks moved into Egypt, Southwest Asia, and beyond, contacts between Greeks and local populations led to a cultural fusion known as **Hellenism**, from *Hellas*, the native term for Greece. Although the precise mix of Greek and local culture varied from place to place, people throughout the Hellenistic world were connected through exposure to common language, literature, and intellectual and political ideas. Historians date the Hellenistic age from the death of Alexander in 323 B.C.E. to 30 B.C.E., when the Roman Empire (discussed in Chapter 7) conquered Egypt, the last major Hellenistic state. For most people, day-to-day life in the Hellenistic age was much the same as life in previous centuries. However, the blending of traditions that was the heart of Hellenism exposed men and women to a new and more varied set of beliefs and ideas. Those ideas would be at the center of many cultural developments in the later Mediterranean world.

> **FOCUS**
>
> How did Hellenism affect the peoples of Greece, North Africa, and Southwest Asia?

Creation of the Hellenistic Empires   323–275 B.C.E.

In 336 B.C.E., twenty-year-old Alexander succeeded his father Philip as king of Macedonia and leader of the league of Greek states. As we saw in Chapter 4, almost immediately he invaded the Persian Empire, which for two hundred years had dominated an enormous territory stretching from the Mediterranean coast to India. Defeating the Persians in a quick succession of battles, Alexander proclaimed himself the new master of the empire. The swift military successes earned him the title "the Great" in later tradition.

To thwart challenges to his rule, however, Alexander had to take his troops to every corner of his realm (see again Mapping the World, pages 140 and 141). When he finally reached the eastern border of the Persian Empire and the Indus Valley in 326 B.C.E., his troops rebelled and refused to go farther. Alexander settled in Babylon, where soon afterward, in 323 B.C.E., he died at the age of thirty-three. Did he succumb to the illnesses and wounds he had endured during his campaigns, or did his courtiers tire of the habits he acquired as emperor and assassinate him? Scholarly theories about the cause of his death abound, but it is certain that Alexander's role was paramount in bringing Greece into closer cultural contact with the wider world than ever before.

Because Alexander died without an heir, his generals fought over the giant territory he had conquered. They ultimately carved it into several states, each ruled by a former general

Hellenism The culture that derived from the merger of Greek, Southwest Asian, and Egyptian ideas through the creation of Alexander the Great's empire.

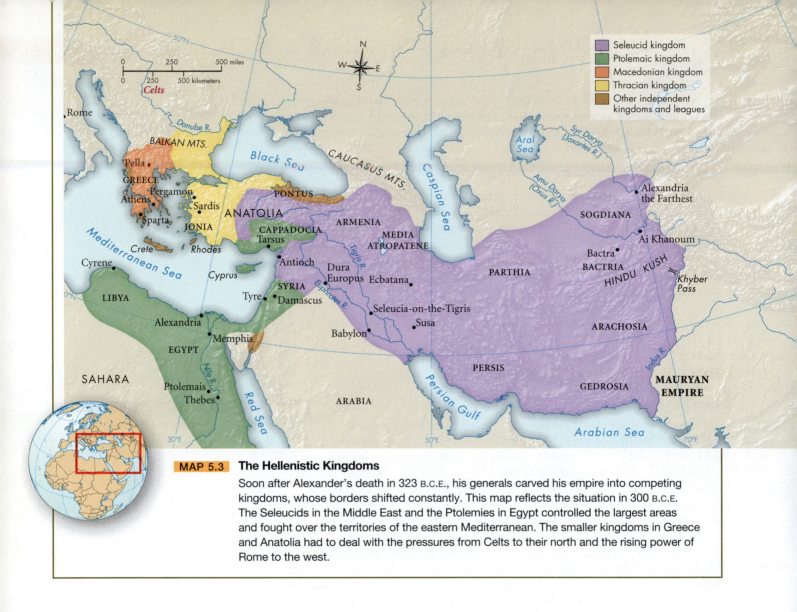

MAP 5.3 **The Hellenistic Kingdoms**

Soon after Alexander's death in 323 B.C.E., his generals carved his empire into competing kingdoms, whose borders shifted constantly. This map reflects the situation in 300 B.C.E. The Seleucids in the Middle East and the Ptolemies in Egypt controlled the largest areas and fought over the territories of the eastern Mediterranean. The smaller kingdoms in Greece and Anatolia had to deal with the pressures from Celts to their north and the rising power of Rome to the west.

Alexander's Successors

(see Map 5.3). The two largest kingdoms were the Seleucid Empire, which initially included lands from Syria to the Indus, and the Ptolemaic Empire, which controlled Egypt and the Libyan coast. To gain acceptance as legitimate rulers, the generals married local women and started dynasties of mixed descent, which governed the Seleucid and Ptolemaic empires for some three hundred years. Seeking legitimacy as kings within the local traditions, they celebrated local religious festivals, supported cults, and commissioned inscriptions in cuneiform (Seleucids) and hieroglyphics (Ptolemies). They also maintained the existing bureaucracies, although Greek gradually took over as the language of administration.

For common Egyptians and Babylonians, little changed. They worked the land and produced goods, interacting with their new authorities only through local government agents; the ruling elite remained mostly in the region's large cities. The Greeks, however, faced fundamental changes both at home and in the new empires. Before they had belonged to small political and social groups in which (ideally) everyone knew each other, but they now lived in immense empires and regularly mingled with people with whom they at first could barely communicate. They maintained the belief that Greek culture was superior, but over time they absorbed the ideas and traditions of the ancient cultures they encountered. The Greeks' political system also changed fundamentally: kingdoms in which absolute power passed from father to son (and also to daughters in the case of the Ptolemies) replaced city-states ruled by citizens. The ideal of the polis survived, however; many new city-states were founded all over the Hellenistic world. They were subject, however, to a king who dictated international affairs and imposed taxes and other obligations.

Statue of Philosopher from Ai Khanoum
Although located several thousand miles east of Greece, Ai Khanoum in modern Afghanistan felt the Hellenistic influence so strongly that this statue from the second century B.C.E. looks as though it could have been carved in Greece itself. The image of the pensive old man suggests that he was a philosopher, and evidence shows that the writings of Aristotle were known in Ai Khanoum. (Getty Images.)

The new political order facilitated intensified cultural exchange. Greek hegemony made travel safer, easier, and more common. Greeks settled throughout the Hellenistic world, looking for new opportunities in distant Hellenistic kingdoms. At the same time, many foreigners moved to Greece and actively participated in Greek intellectual and cultural life.

The Hellenistic City

In his march through the former Persian Empire, Alexander founded some seventy cities, which he used to help establish his local dominance. As his successors continued the policy, new cities took root across the Hellenistic world. Taking the form of city-states, they resembled Greek cities in layout, buildings, and government structures. The new city-states were often built in strategic locations. When they were established in previously urbanized areas, such as Mesopotamia and Egypt, they overtook the old centers in importance.

One such outpost was the city whose ruins are called Ai Khanoum (eye KHA-nuum) today. Built to defend the northeastern border at the Oxus River, until 100 B.C.E. the city successfully kept out tribal people encroaching from Central Asia. The city had a Greek-style palace, a gymnasium, administrative buildings, and a Greek theater, and it was adorned with a Greek-style statuary. It was here that Clearchus, whom we met at the beginning of this chapter, arrived around 300 B.C.E., bringing with him wise sayings from Delphi. Clearchus was not the only philosopher who visited. When archaeologists excavated the palace, they found imprinted on its floor the ink text from a decayed papyrus. It contained an extract from a philosophical dialogue that Aristotle may have written.

In the countries along the eastern Mediterranean coast, the cities were even grander than Ai Khanoum and drew more visitors. The most prominent was Alexandria, which Alexander had founded as the new capital of Egypt in 331 B.C.E. and whose population soon rose to half a million. Located on the Mediterranean Sea, Alexandria dazzled both in appearance and as a center of learning and culture. When Arab forces invaded the city in 642 C.E., they supposedly had to shield their eyes from the sunlight reflected off the city's marble buildings. Alexandria was laid out on a plan of straight streets that intersected at right angles. Palaces, temples, theaters, and an enormous library lined the streets; these were constructed in the Greek style, but the city was also clearly Egyptian. Kings and queens followed traditional styles as they filled the city with monumental statues of themselves as rulers. They also brought in statues from all over Egypt of earlier kings, such as the famous Ramesses II (see Chapter 4).

Alexandria and other cities were set up as Greek poleis, and

Alexandria in Egypt

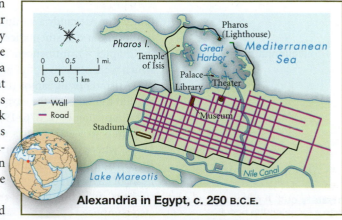

Alexandria in Egypt, c. 250 B.C.E.

Statues of Ptolemaic Royalty
Although the Ptolemies descended from Greek invaders of Egypt, spoke Greek, and promoted Greek culture in such institutions as the Library of Alexandria, they also were Egyptian rulers and had themselves represented in traditional Egyptian style. These statues from the third century B.C.E. show King Ptolemy II, his wife Arsinoe II, and an unknown princess. Nothing in the representations suggests that they are not typical Egyptian rulers. (Scala/Art Resource, NY.)

originally only Greeks and Macedonians qualified for citizenship and the political privileges that went with it. At first, accordingly, only Greeks could serve as administrators, but as natives learned the Greek language and adopted Greek cultural habits, they became eligible for offices and gradually gained civic rights as well. Documents from the period show that some local people took Greek names besides their own to conduct government business. For example, the Egyptian administrator Menches (Men-khez) also called himself Asklepiades (Ass-clay-pee-ja-dez). Over time, Greek and non-Greek populations mixed and intermarried. Alexandria became a melting pot that attracted people with diverse native languages, customs, and religions. Thus Alexandria, like cities throughout the Hellenistic world, became a crossroads, a place that attracted Greek migrants and served as a site of cultural exchange and transformation.

Hellenistic Learning and Livelihoods

Royal patronage drew scholars and artists from all over the Greek-speaking world and beyond to Alexandria. The city became a center of learning, which it actively promoted through the Library and Museum (literally, "House of the Muses"; the Muses were nine sister goddesses who presided over poetry, history, science, and the arts). The Museum housed poets and scientific researchers in all fields. The Library's aim was to collect copies of every known work of Greek literature. Because copyists had made errors over time, librarians also sought to establish an accurate original text for each work by comparing manuscripts. At one point, the Library borrowed from Athens the official copies of the works of the great authors of tragedies from the fifth century B.C.E. It paid an enormous deposit of silver as security, but when the texts arrived, the king willingly gave it up and kept the manuscripts. Alexandria's Library held 490,000 volumes, probably the largest collection of writings in the ancient world.

Hellenistic Scholarship   The promotion of learning epitomized by the Library at Alexandria stimulated intellectual innovation. Scientific inquiry relied on older traditions, and mathematics and astronomy, well-developed sciences in Babylonia (as seen in Chapter 4), influenced Greek science anew. Researchers made remarkable advances, which were often lost after antiquity and rediscovered only in more recent times. For example, Aristarchos of Samos (c. 310–230 B.C.E.) correctly recognized that the planets revolved around the sun, not the earth.

Eratosthenes (c. 276–194 B.C.E.) is a good example of the life of a scholar whose career took him to various parts of the Hellenistic world. He was born in Cyrene in northern Libya, where he received his basic training. After continuing his education in Athens, he accepted at the age of thirty-six the invitation of Egypt's king to become royal tutor and head of the Library in Alexandria. He was enormously erudite and wrote on numerous subjects, including literary criticism, philosophy, history, geography, and mathematics. He also composed epics and poems, which are known only from fragments today. In a treatise,

mystery cult A religious practice with a focus on the occult.

On the Measurement of the Earth, now lost but quoted by later authors, Eratosthenes calculated the earth's circumference with high accuracy. He compared the lengths of noon shadows cast at midsummer in places at the extreme ends of Egypt and so measured the curvature of the globe between them. He calculated that the distance between the two spots had to be multiplied fifty times to constitute a full circle. To determine this distance, the king gave him a group of men who walked with equal paces; they measured the length of Egypt to be about five hundred miles. Because of his versatility scholars often criticized Eratosthenes as only second best, although in every subject. Others likened him to Plato, however, recognizing his great knowledge.

Philosophy flourished in the Hellenistic world. When the polis disappeared as the center of political and social life, philosophers focused more on the individual, exploring ways to live a good and proper life. They presented a wide range of options. The Epicurians, for example, taught that one should enjoy every moment in the pursuit of simple pleasures and a quiet life. Cynics urged the rejection of social norms and conventional behavior, often living as beggars without any physical comfort. The Stoic school was the most influential throughout Greek and Roman antiquity. It granted women more consideration than earlier male-dominated philosophies, enabling some elite women to become involved in intellectual activities. Stoics encouraged intellectual inquiry to provide guidance in moral behavior, which would eliminate the anxieties of daily life and desire. "Freedom is secured not by the fulfilling of one's desires, but by the removal of desire," a Roman Stoic wrote. Such words resemble the somewhat earlier teachings of men like the Buddha and Laozi in India and China (discussed in Chapter 6). Although we cannot know if Hellenistic philosophers encountered these teachings directly, we can say that similar ideas developed in various parts of the ancient world.

Hellenistic Philosophy

While Hellenistic philosophies provided guidance to educated elites, many people, rich and poor, sought comfort and direction from religion. The Hellenistic world brought together an enormous variety of religious traditions and their gods. Although they maintained their cults, the Greeks lost faith in the old gods of the past and were drawn to the divine personification of Fortune—Tyche (TEE-chee) in Greek—in their efforts to deal with life's unpredictability. The ancient Egyptian goddess Isis became very popular outside Egypt in a different form: she was considered all-powerful, even surpassing Tyche. **Mystery cults** based on secret knowledge were very widespread. The Greek god of heaven, Zeus, was equated with leading deities elsewhere: Amun in Egypt, Marduk in Babylonia, Baal in Syria, and Yahweh in Judah. Exposure to Hellenistic culture in turn deeply influenced other religions. Many Jews who lived outside Judah absorbed the new ideas. They even forgot the Hebrew language for a time, and in the early third century B.C.E. the Ptolemaic ruler (Ptolemy II) commissioned a Greek translation of the Hebrew Bible.

Hellenistic Religion

Historians debate how much all this cultural mixing influenced the majority of the people. A Persian, Babylonian, Egyptian, or Greek farmer would still have been illiterate and would have adhered to old traditions and ideas. Even so, gods could and did achieve an unprecedented popularity outside their original place of worship, and people throughout the Hellenistic world were exposed to new ideas. Hellenism left no one totally unaffected.

COUNTERPOINT
The Celtic Peoples of the Atlantic Zone

Historians studying western Eurasia in the first millennium B.C.E. focus primarily on developments in Greece (and somewhat later in Roman Italy, discussed in Chapter 7) because sources are abundant and momentous developments occurred there. The Greeks expressed political ideals, ideas about self-governance, and concerns for aspects of the human condition in very explicit terms and in a rich textual record, inspiring a millennia-long tradition of

FOCUS

How did the lives and livelihoods of the peoples of Atlantic Europe differ from those of the Mediterranean peoples?

MAP 5.4

Celtic Peoples, c. 600–100 B.C.E.

Spread over much of the west and center of modern-day Europe, the Celtic peoples controlled natural resources of interest to Greece and Rome. Although at first Celtic warriors could threaten such places as Rome and Delphi and invade Galatia in Anatolia, in the first century B.C.E. Rome successfully annexed most Celtic territories.

intellectual development. These advances were restricted to a tiny part of the modern European continent, however. In the wide areas north and west of Greece, a different world existed. Although the inhabitants of these regions were in contact with the Greeks, they had different lifestyles and ideologies. They did not write much, except for short dedications scratched onto pots and metal strips using the Greek or Latin alphabets. Historians thus turn to archaeological remains to understand them. These peoples' oral literature depicted aspects of their world, and it survived for centuries in Ireland and elsewhere. Moreover, Greek and Roman Mediterranean authors provided useful information, although their writings were often biased. The Romans called them "Celts," a term many scholars and others still use today (see Map 5.4).

Who Were the Celts?

When in the first century B.C.E. and first century C.E. the Romans conquered much of the Atlantic region (see Chapter 7), their historians described the local peoples and their interactions with the new rulers. Like the Greeks, the Romans paid little attention to cultural distinctions among foreign peoples, and the term *Celts* covers a variety of groups and cultures. There was a unity among peoples of the Atlantic region in one sense, however: they all spoke languages that belong to the Celtic branch of Indo-European. Although they have changed greatly with time, some of the languages are still spoken in Ireland, Scotland, Wales, and Brittany (a region of northwestern France to which immigrants from the British

Isles introduced the language between 300 and 600 C.E.). The ideologies of these peoples also seem to have survived in the oral literary traditions of these regions.

Celtic Livelihoods

Throughout western Eurasia, from north of the Mediterranean to the Atlantic coast and the British Isles, the Celtic peoples of the first millennium B.C.E. were farmers living in small settlements and villages. The societies greatly valued warrior skills and were ruled by a military aristocracy. The elites inhabited fortresses on natural hills, which they encircled with moats and walls of earth, stone, and timber; they were buried in tombs with their swords, shields, and chariots. The Romans noted that these military leaders treated the general population as if they were slaves.

Warrior Aristocracy

The warlike culture is prominent in Celtic oral literature. The preserved tales recount how people raided, defended their honor in single combat, and bonded through feasts and hospitality. Unlike in Greece and most of the ancient societies discussed earlier, women actively participated in military life and could themselves become war leaders. Roman historians wrote in awe about Queen Boudicca (BOO-dee-kah), who led an army against them in the year 60 C.E. Goaded by the mistreatment her people suffered, including the rape of her own daughters, she rallied her own and neighboring groups in battle with these words:

> Look round, and view your numbers. Behold the proud display of warlike spirits, and consider the motives for which we draw the avenging sword. On this spot we must either conquer, or die with glory. There is no alternative. Though a woman, my resolution is fixed: the men, if they please, may survive with infamy, and live in bondage.[5]

Her troops lost the battle and she committed suicide, but in the nineteenth century C.E. British people revived Boudicca's memory as a symbol of resistance and woman's valor.

Like most ancient peoples, the Celts honored a multitude of gods who were closely connected to forces of nature. Roman authors provide some information on early religious practices and gods. They say, for instance, that the Celts called the goddess of wells and springs Coventina, and treated priests—whom the Romans called Druids—as the most honored group in Celtic society, equal to warriors. Religious ceremonies included human sacrifice. Throughout the Atlantic world archaeologists have discovered "bog people," men and women executed by strangulation or other means and buried in bogs as offerings to the gods. The Romans regarded Celtic religious practices as so uncivilized that they tried to ban them—without success.

Gaul Killing Himself and His Wife

Although ancient Greeks and Romans considered the Gauls to be barbarians, they also could credit them with a great sense of nobility and honor. The statue here is a marble Roman copy of a work originally created in Anatolian Pergamon around 220 B.C.E. It shows the defeated Gaul warrior choosing to kill his wife and himself rather than face capture. (Museo Nazionale Romano/Giraudon/Bridgeman Art Library.)

Contacts with the Mediterranean

The Celtic peoples did not live in isolation, however. Starting in the early first millennium B.C.E., contacts with the Mediterranean world were extensive, and they grew over time (see again Map 5.4). The Phoenician and Greek colonies in the western Mediterranean were places of exchange between the Atlantic and Mediterranean worlds. The Greeks obtained silver, tin, and copper from as far as Britain. Atlantic peoples transported amber, a fossilized resin popular in jewelry, all the way from the Baltic Sea to supply the Greeks. In return the Greeks and other Mediterranean peoples provided luxury goods such as drinking vessels. Wine was also an important export to the Celts, who were notorious for their heavy drinking of undiluted wine. A Greek author wrote that a trader could get a slave in return for one jar of wine.

These contacts gave some local Celtic elites access to Mediterranean luxury goods. For example, a woman buried in the late sixth century B.C.E. in a tomb at Vix in eastern France was honored with a massive bronze wine crater and other fancy Mediterranean goods (see Seeing the Past: The Vix Crater: A Greek Vessel in Northern France). Few Celtic people were able to acquire such luxuries, however, and most lived simple lives as farmers. As in the Greek world, social inequality was the rule.

The wealth of the Mediterranean may have inspired Celtic military forays and a desire among some Celts to establish settlements in the region. Several times Celtic groups raided deep into Italy and Greece. In 390 B.C.E., they captured most of Rome, and it took the Romans two centuries to fully drive them from Italy. In 279 B.C.E., one Celtic group tried to ransack the Greek sanctuary at Delphi. Also in the third century B.C.E., other Celts

SEEING THE PAST

The Vix Crater: A Greek Vessel in Northern France

Vix Crater
(Musée Archeologique, Chatillon Sur Seine, France/Giraudon/ Bridgeman Art Library.)

Around 530 B.C.E. a woman about thirty years old was buried in a tomb beneath an earthen mound 138 feet in diameter and 16 feet high. The tomb, near the modern town of Vix, east of Paris, is one of the richest in Atlantic Europe. It contained jewelry of gold (including a bracelet weighing 1.06 pounds) and of bronze, sometimes decorated with amber.

The most impressive goods were accessories for a drinking party: ceramic cups made in Athens, bronze basins and a jug for pouring made in Italy, and the largest metal vessel of Greek manufacture ever recovered, a crater to mix wine, shown here. This Vix crater, made of bronze, is nearly 5.5 feet tall and weighs 458 pounds. Its rim is decorated with a band of Greek hoplites on foot and on chariots. The handles contain images of the Greek female monster, the Gorgon. The creators of the crater were probably Greek colonists in southern Italy, and it took great effort to transport the heavy object to northern France. European elites could only afford such imported goods only because they controlled one of the metals people of the Mediterranean much desired: tin, which was indispensable in producing bronze.

EXAMINING THE EVIDENCE

1. How does the decoration of this vessel reveal contacts between the people of northern France and Greeks of the Mediterranean?

2. What does it and other burial goods tell us about the woman's social status?

3. Why would the scene on this crater have appealed to the Celts? Keep in mind the chapter discussion in considering this question.

migrated into central Turkey, where they were long known as Galatians, a name derived from one of the peoples of western Europe, the Gauls.

These raids and other clashes led authors from Greece and Rome to emphasize the physical strength and martial behavior of Celts. But they also saw them as noble savages. When in the late third century B.C.E. a Hellenistic king erected a monument in the city of Pergamon to celebrate his victory over the Galatians, he depicted them as honorable fighters who would rather commit suicide than be captured, mirroring the Roman portrayal of Boudicca.

Thus, at the edge of the Greek world lived a people with fundamentally different traditions. Their history has been overshadowed by that of their more powerful neighbor, whose culture has attracted the attention of scholars for more than two millennia. The Celts were connected to a larger world, however, and their influences on later periods, though less obvious than those of the Greeks, were no less real.

Military Encounters

Conclusion

Between 800 and 300 B.C.E., a very small part of the world's population, living in Greece, developed a new set of ideas about every aspect of their lives. Earlier traditions, both domestic and foreign, certainly inspired these ideas, but in questioning inherited practices and beliefs the Greeks created an environment that was unique in every respect: politically, socially, culturally, and intellectually. The benefits were restricted to the very few, but they expressed themselves in writings that were preserved and admired later on, and their thoughts dominate our understanding of this era.

When the Greeks conquered the Persian Empire to the east, their ideas spread over a wide area, enormously expanding their impact. This geographic diffusion explains how wise sayings from mainland Greece, such as those of Clearchus, came to be inscribed on stone as far away as northern Afghanistan. Greek intellectual influence was far reaching and long lasting. Not only did the Romans, whom we will discuss in Chapter 7, build purposely on Greek foundations, but the emperor of India, Ashoka, used the Greek language to spread Buddhist ideals, as we will see in the next chapter. And in many ways, still today, we hearken back to ideals that the Greeks first formulated in the distant past.

NOTES

1. Susan Sherwin-White and Amélie Kuhrt, *From Samarkhand to Sardis: A New Approach to the Seleucid Empire* (Berkeley: University of California Press, 1993), 179.
2. *Aeschylus II*, trans. Seth G. Bernadete (Chicago: University of Chicago Press, 2d ed., 1991), 62–63.
3. *Sophocles I*, trans. Elizabeth Wyckoff (Chicago: University of Chicago Press, 1954), 174.
4. *Herodotus: The Histories*, Book 2:35, ed. John M. Marincola, trans. Aubrey De Selincourt (London: Penguin Classics, 1996).
5. Tacitus, *Annals*, Book 14, Ch. 35. Quoted from http://www.athenapub.com/tacitus1.htm.

RESOURCES FOR RESEARCH

General Works

There are many books on ancient Greek history and culture, and new ones continue to be published. Ranging from broad surveys to detailed studies of specific topics, they take many different approaches to the subject, from chronological surveys to discussions of select topics. Here is a sample.

Cartledge, Paul, ed. *Cambridge Illustrated History of Ancient Greece*. 1998.

(For women in ancient Greece): Diotima: Materials for the Study of Women and Gender in the Ancient World. http://www .stoa.org/diotima/.

Grant, M., and R. Kitzinger, eds. *Civilization of the Ancient Mediterranean.* 1988.

(For translations of Greek literature and other writings): Internet Ancient History Sourcebooks: Full Texts. http://www .fordham.edu/halsall/ancient/asbookfull.html#Greece.

Morris, Ian, and Barry Powell, eds. *The Greeks: History, Culture, and Society.* 2006.

Osborne, Robin. *Greek History.* 2004.

(For translations and Greek text of literature and other writings): Perseus Digital Library. http://www.perseus.tufts.edu.

Pomeroy, Sarah. *Goddesses, Whores, Wives, and Slaves: Women in Classical Antiquity.* 1995.

Pomeroy, Sarah B., Stanley M. Burstein, Walter Donlan, and Jennifer Tolbert Roberts. *A Brief History of Ancient Greece: Politics, Society, and Culture.* 2004.

The Development of Ancient Greek Culture, 1200–500 B.C.E.

The period of the formation of Greek culture is the subject of many specialized studies, including these accessible works.

The British Museum: Ancient Greece. http://www.ancientgreece .co.uk/.

Coldstream, J. N. *Geometric Greece, 900–700 BC.* 2d ed. 2003.

Fischer, N., and H. van Wees, eds. *Archaic Greece: New Approaches and New Evidence.* 1998.

Hall, Jonathan M. *A History of the Archaic Greek World.* 2007.

Osborne, Robin. *Greece in the Making, 1200–479 BC.* 1996.

*Rhodes, P. J. *The Greek City States: A Source Book.* 1986.

The Persian Wars, Classical Greece, and the Concept of Cultural Difference, 500–338 B.C.E.

The Classical Age, the height of ancient Greek culture, is one of the best-studied eras in world history. Scholars have taken many approaches to a wide range of subjects. Hamel uses the life of Neaira as a gateway into many aspects of classical Greece.

The Ancient City of Athens. http://www.stoa.org/athens/.

Hall, Edith. *Inventing the Barbarian: Greek Self-Definition Through Tragedy.* 1989.

Hamel, Debra. *Trying Neaira: The True Story of a Courtesan's Scandalous Life in Ancient Greece.* 2003.

Hornblower, Simon. *The Greek World, 479–323 BC.* 1991.

Kagan, Donald. *The Peloponnesian War.* 2003.

Kinzl, Konrad H., ed. *A Companion to the Classical Greek World.* 2006.

Munn, Mark. *The School of History: Athens in the Age of Socrates.* 2000.

Osborne, Robin. *Classical Greece, 500–323 BC.* 2000.

Powell, Anton. *Athens and Sparta: Constructing Greek Political and Social History, 478 BC.* 1988.

Rhodes, P. J. *A History of the Classical Greek World.* 2006.

Hellenism: The Expansion of Greek Ideals and Institutions, 330–30 B.C.E.

Hellenism also has been studied in great detail, but until recently the work focused on Greek sources. The work of Sherwin-White and Kuhrt has started to rectify that situation by integrating information on the well-documented cultures to the east.

Cartledge, Paul. *Alexander the Great: The Hunt for a New Past.* 2004.

Errington, Malcolm. *A History of the Hellenistic World.* 2008.

Erskine, Andrew, ed. *A Companion to the Hellenistic World.* 2003.

Green, Peter. *Alexander to Actium: The Historical Evolution of the Hellenistic Age.* 1990.

Sherwin-White, Susan, and Amélie Kuhrt. *From Samarkhand to Sardis: A New Approach to the Seleucid Empire.* 1993.

COUNTERPOINT: The Celtic Peoples of the Atlantic Zone

Much more archaeological in nature are studies of the Atlantic peoples, who left no writings of their own.

Cunliffe, Barry. *The Ancient Celts.* 1997.

Cunliffe, Barry. *The Celts: A Very Short Introduction.* 2003.

Ellis, Peter Beresford. *The Ancient World of the Celts.* 1998.

James, Simon. *Exploring the World of the Celts.* 1993.

* Primary source.

▶ **For additional primary sources from this period**, see *Sources of Crossroads and Cultures*.

▶ **For Web sites, images, and documents related to topics in this chapter**, see Make History at bedfordstmartins.com/smith.

The major global development in this chapter: ▶ The cultural and political innovations of the ancient Greeks and the expansion of Greek ideals and institutions.

IMPORTANT EVENTS

c. 1200–800 B.C.E.	Dark Age in the Aegean world
c. 800–500 B.C.E.	Archaic period in Greece
776 B.C.E.	First Olympic games, according to tradition
c. 775 B.C.E.	First evidence of alphabetic writing in Greece
c. 750 B.C.E.	Homer writes the *Iliad* and the *Odyssey*
750–550 B.C.E.	Main period of Greek colonization of the Mediterranean
700–600 B.C.E.	Orientalizing period in Greek art
c. 574 B.C.E.	Solon institutes reforms in Athens
c. 500–323 B.C.E.	Classical Age of Greece
500–479 B.C.E.	Persian Wars
443–429 B.C.E.	Pericles leads Athens
431–404 B.C.E.	Peloponnesian War
404 B.C.E.	Spartan hegemony in Greece
390 B.C.E.	Celts capture Rome in Italy
338 B.C.E.	Philip of Macedonia conquers Greece
331 B.C.E.	Alexander defeats Persia; Alexandria founded in Egypt
323 B.C.E.	Death of Alexander
323–30 B.C.E.	Hellenistic period
30 B.C.E.	Romans conquer Egypt

KEY TERMS

democracy (p. 146)   philosophy (p. 152)
Hellenism (p. 159)   polis (p. 145)
mystery cult (p. 163)   sophist (p. 152)
oligarchy (p. 146)   tyranny (p. 146)
phalanx (p. 145)

CHAPTER OVERVIEW QUESTIONS

1. How did geography and contacts with other peoples shape Greek institutions and values?
2. What were the cultural and political innovations of the Greeks, and how have they proved enduring?
3. To what extent did these innovations affect the lives and livelihoods of ordinary Greeks?
4. How did the spread of Hellenism affect the Greeks and the other peoples of Eurasia and North Africa?

SECTION FOCUS QUESTIONS

1. What significant political and cultural developments emerged in Greece in the early first millennium B.C.E.?
2. What cultural innovations appeared in Greece during its Classical Age?
3. How did Hellenism affect the peoples of Greece, North Africa, and Southwest Asia?
4. How did the lives and livelihoods of the peoples of Atlantic Europe differ from those of the Mediterranean peoples?

MAKING CONNECTIONS

1. How do the political systems of the Greek city-states Athens and Sparta compare with those of contemporary empires in Asia and North Africa (see Chapter 4)?
2. How would you describe the cultural interactions between Southwest Asia and Greece from the Archaic to Hellenistic periods?
3. What ideals of classical Greece influenced later developments in world history?

6

AT A CROSSROADS ▶

The Kushan emperors promoted a cross-cultural art form that combined Hellenistic Greek styles with South Asian motifs. Known as "Gandharan" from the Kushan capital of Gandhara in modern northwest Pakistan, a typical example is this statue of the Buddha, dated sometime in the first to third centuries C.E. It shows an iconic South Asian figure, the Buddha, seated in a traditional pose of meditation. The realism and detail reflect Hellenistic art, especially in the carving of the folds of his dress. (Fitzwilliam Museum, University of Cambridge, UK/Bridgeman Art Library.)

Peoples and World Empires: Classical India, the Kushan Empire, and China

500 B.C.E.–500 C.E.

On the Indian peninsula sometime in the second century C.E., a man named Dashafota carved an inscription on a stone left by a well. The short text in the Sanskrit language reads:

> During the reign of the Maharaja, Rajatiraja, Devaputra, Kaisara Kanishka, the son of Vajheshka, the 41st year, on the 25th day of the month Jyaishtha, on this day a well was dug by Dashafota, the son of Poshapuri, in honor of his mother and father, in order to confer benefit on himself together with his wife and his son, for the welfare of all beings in the various births. And here I throw in 100,000 coins as a religious gift.[1]

Dashafota was a subject of Emperor Kanishka II, whose Kushan dynasty had conquered large parts of Central Asia and the Indian peninsula. The king's titles, taken from those of the great empires of Eurasia, show him to be an equal of the powerful rulers whose realms surrounded him. Those titles included the Indian *maharaja*, "Great King," and the Chinese *devaputra*, "son of God." *Rajatiraja*, "king of kings," is from the Parthian emperor, and *kaisara*, "Caesar," is from the Roman. Kanishka's empire was at the crossroads of large states that stretched from the China Sea to the Atlantic Ocean. His assumption of these titles

BACKSTORY

We left the discussion of Asia in Chapter 3 in 500 B.C.E. By this point, centuries of development in India and China had laid the foundations for the two regions' subsequent histories. In India, many had accepted the Vedic traditions and the caste system, whereas in China the ideal of political unification and dynastic rule had been firmly established. In other parts of Asia, such as the Oxus River Valley, early cultural developments had suddenly ended, and the people had abandoned the regions they formerly occupied. We return now to Asia to study how the peoples of China and India both built on and challenged their cultural inheritance.

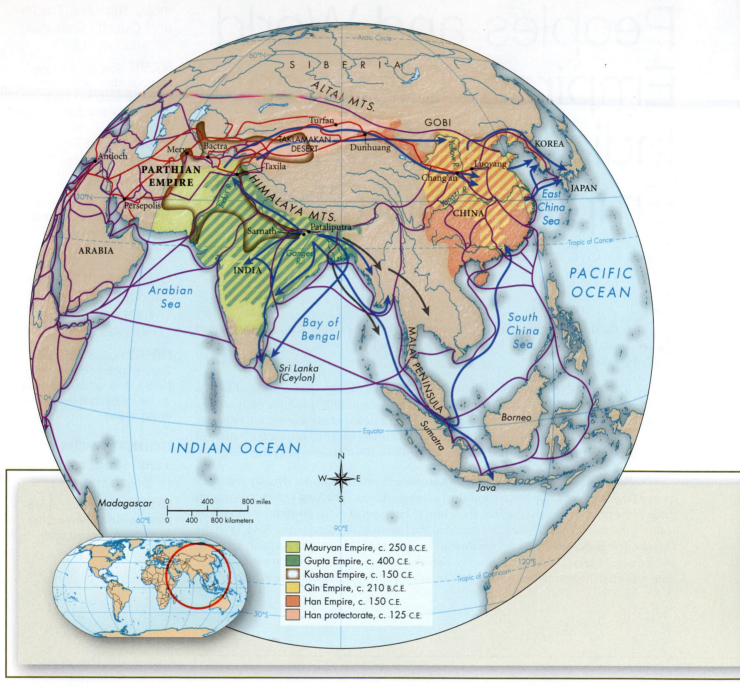

Mauryan Empire, c. 250 B.C.E.
Gupta Empire, c. 400 C.E.
Kushan Empire, c. 150 C.E.
Qin Empire, c. 210 B.C.E.
Han Empire, c. 150 C.E.
Han protectorate, c. 125 C.E.

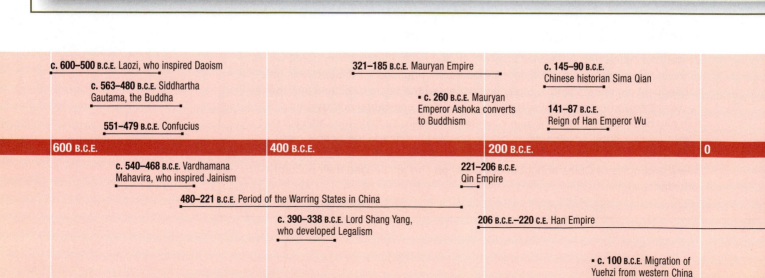

c. 600–500 B.C.E. Laozi, who inspired Daoism

c. 563–480 B.C.E. Siddhartha
Gautama, the Buddha

551–479 B.C.E. Confucius

321–185 B.C.E. Mauryan Empire

▪ c. 260 B.C.E. Mauryan
Emperor Ashoka converts
to Buddhism

c. 145–90 B.C.E.
Chinese historian Sima Qian

141–87 B.C.E.
Reign of Han Emperor Wu

600 B.C.E.   **400 B.C.E.**   **200 B.C.E.**   **0**

c. 540–468 B.C.E. Vardhamana
Mahavira, who inspired Jainism

480–221 B.C.E. Period of the Warring States in China

c. 390–338 B.C.E. Lord Shang Yang,
who developed Legalism

221–206 B.C.E.
Qin Empire

206 B.C.E.–220 C.E. Han Empire

▪ c. 100 B.C.E. Migration of
Yuehzi from western China

shows that he and his people knew of the other empires and their rulers, the result of frequent interactions through trade. Kanishka's empire was indeed equal to the others, and because of its central location in Asia, it acted as a conduit for their goods and ideas.

Dashafota's inscription acknowledges that the Eurasian world of the time was one of territorial empires. This was true for the entire period from 500 B.C.E. to 500 C.E., when centralized states incorporated varied regions and cultural traditions and established a degree of uniformity over them. In the east of this vast area, India, Central Asia, and China each saw a succession of such empires, including the Mauryan, Gupta, Kushan, Qin, and Han. As we will see, these imperial dynasties were interrupted by periods of political fragmentation, and some regions, such as the Tamil area in southern India, were never incorporated into an empire. The empires that did arise were in close contact with one another, bound together by trade that moved along the land and sea routes connecting the eastern and western borders of Asia.

These centuries saw a profuse cultural flowering that fed intellectual and artistic traditions for millennia. Like their Greek contemporaries, great thinkers in India and China developed new ideas about life and government that affected all levels of society. Their teachings launched religious and philosophical trends that were fundamental to the later histories of these countries and spread far beyond their borders. This creativity expressed the will and passion of untold individuals, often reacting against the political circumstances of their time. The intellectual currents these peoples engendered were spread through integration into imperial ideologies, but the ideas long outlived the empires that promoted them. Indeed, they shaped all subsequent thought in Asia. Thus we refer to the eras of their creation as the **classical** periods of both India and China.

classical The traditional authoritative form of a culture.

MAPPING THE WORLD

Empires and Exchange in Asia, 500 B.C.E.–500 C.E.

For a thousand years, the vast territories of Asia were connected through a vibrant trade in goods and ideas regardless of the political powers that dominated parts of the region. Qin and Han China in the east and the Mauryan, Kushan, and Gupta empires in South and Central Asia were hotbeds for the development of new ideas and technologies, many of which subsequently spread throughout Asia and beyond into the Parthian and Roman worlds.

ROUTES ▼

— Silk Road
— Other trade route
➤ Spread of Buddhism
➤ Spread of Hinduism

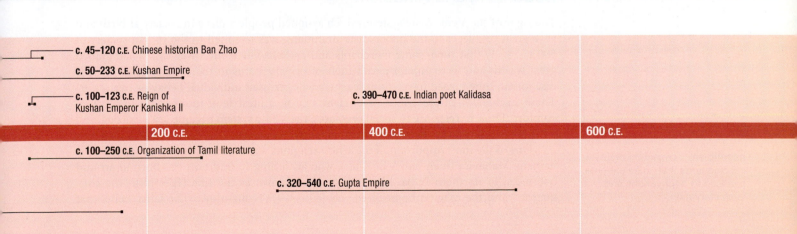

c. 45–120 C.E. Chinese historian Ban Zhao

c. 50–233 C.E. Kushan Empire

c. 100–123 C.E. Reign of Kushan Emperor Kanishka II

c. 390–470 C.E. Indian poet Kalidasa

200 C.E.   400 C.E.   600 C.E.

c. 100–250 C.E. Organization of Tamil literature

c. 320–540 C.E. Gupta Empire

India: Thinkers, Traders, and Courtly Cultures 500 B.C.E.–500 C.E.

FOCUS

How did the new religious ideas of the last centuries B.C.E. suit the social and political structures of India?

In around 500 B.C.E., Indian culture and society started to undergo fundamental changes that continued for almost a millennium. The teachings of several influential thinkers radically affected prevailing religious currents, changing the nature of the caste system (see Chapter 3) and stressing individual responsibility for all people. Politically the region saw the successive rise of the Mauryan and Gupta empires, which placed large parts of South Asia under centralized control. Culturally, Indian arts and scientific investigation blossomed. Exchanges of all kinds occurred between India and the larger world. People from China, Central Asia, and the Mediterranean came to India, often as traders, sometimes as conquerors, and people from India traveled far and wide as merchants and missionaries. India became a crossroads of connections that spread across the Asian continent, bringing outside influences to India and bringing Indian culture, ideas, and products to the rest of Asia.

Religious Ferment: The Rise of Jainism, Buddhism, and Hinduism

The rigor of the Vedic caste system, which assigned people a place in society at birth and gave great privileges to the upper-caste Brahmans, was ill suited to the Indian society of 500 B.C.E. By that time, some merchants and craftspeople from lower castes had gained great wealth and were unhappy with their secondary status in the caste system. In their discontent, they turned to religious teachers who stressed individual behavior over caste. These teachers often prescribed **asceticism**, that is, a lifestyle of indifference to physical comfort. Thus, in response to social pressures, the Vedic system became less rigorous, and a variety of new and profoundly influential religions emerged.

One of the most important of these new religions was based on the teachings of Vardhamana Mahavira (mah-hah-VEER-uh), who according to tradition was born in around 540 B.C.E. in northern India. Mahavira became known as the Jina (JYN-uh), "the conqueror," and the religion he inspired was Jainism (JYN-ihz-uhm). The Jains' belief that

asceticism A rejection of physical pleasures that, in its extreme, can lead to deprivations and even starvation.

everything—humans, animals, plants, and inanimate objects—had a soul led devotees to complete nonviolence. They believed that no creature whatsoever should be killed, even accidentally. Jains call the moral virtue that inspires such behavior **dharma**. In an extreme form of the religion, followers filtered their water to avoid swallowing small insects. They also tried to end the cycle of reincarnation (rebirth in a different form), which bolstered the caste system, and to free the soul from the body through ascetic behavior such as fasting. Because Mahavira himself had discarded clothing in his life, some of his followers insisted that devotees should be completely naked; others allowed only simple white robes.

Few could adhere fully to such a rigorous lifestyle, but Jainism was especially popular among urban merchants and artisans who were attracted to its rejection of castes. Its pacifism also had great appeal, inspiring men and women ever since its inception, including the twentieth-century Indian statesman Mahatma Gandhi, who grew up in a region where Jainism was widespread. Some political elites promoted Jainism, but the religion never spread beyond India.

In sharp contrast, another religion that originated in India, Buddhism, had a powerful impact on the entire Asian continent. Buddhism is based on the teachings of the Buddha, "the Awakened One"—that is, the one who awakened from a sleep of ignorance to find freedom from suffering. According to traditions written down centuries after his death, the Buddha was Prince Siddhartha Gautama from southern Nepal, who lived from about 563 to 480 B.C.E. Gautama's father shielded him from the evils of life, giving him access to all possible pleasures in his luxurious palaces. But when Gautama was twenty-nine years old, he insisted on going outside, and he was shocked to finally witness old age, illness, and death. When his father told him these conditions were inescapable, he moved into the forest to search for a state beyond birth and death. At first he joined other ascetics, but he realized self-mortification was not the answer. After weeks of meditation, resisting the temptations the god of desire showered upon him, he formulated the idea of "the middle way." A balanced way of life between the extremes of luxury and asceticism was the answer to human suffering. Having thus become the Buddha, he established the Four Noble Truths: (1) existence is suffering, (2) the cause of suffering is negative deeds of the body inspired by desire, (3) desire can be eliminated, and (4) the way to end desire lies in the eightfold path—right belief, resolve, speech, behavior, occupation, effort, contemplation, and meditation.

Buddhism's appeal relied on three elements, the "three jewels": (1) the charismatic teacher, the Buddha; (2) his teachings, the Buddhist interpretation of dharma; and (3) the community, **sangha**. For forty-five years after his awakening, the Buddha traveled throughout northeastern India to teach the religion. Most followers remained laypeople, but some devoted their lives to Buddhism, becoming monks and nuns and founding **monasteries**, communities reserved for followers. There they renounced material goods and led a life of moderation and meditation, supported by the donations of local populations. They strove to reach **nirvana**, a state without desire, hatred, and ignorance and, ultimately, without suffering and rebirth, in which the physical was completely removed from the spiritual.

After the Buddha died, followers cremated his remains and distributed them over large parts of India, where they were buried underneath earthen mounds called **stupas**. According to tradition, the emperor Ashoka built eighty-four thousand stupas after he converted to Buddhism in 260 B.C.E., giving the Buddha a physical presence throughout India. Pilgrims visited sites that had been important in the Buddha's life and spread the new religion, reaching a wide audience by using vernacular dialects rather than the obscure literary Sanskrit of the Brahmans. By promising an escape from the cycle of reincarnation and by rejecting the caste system, Buddhism appealed powerfully to the new wealthy mercantile class. Moreover, its "middle way" was an easier practice than the stricter Jainism.

As followers interpreted the Buddha's teaching, different schools of thought emerged. The most popular tradition, Mahayana Buddhism, became the "Greater Vehicle" to salvation; it was open to more people than the more restrictive Hinayana ("Lesser Vehicle") Buddhism, which more closely adhered to the Buddha's original dharma. Mahayana Buddhism portrayed

Jainism

The Buddha and His Teachings

dharma A term with slightly different meanings in various Indian religions, it refers in Jainism to moral virtue, in Buddhism to the teachings of the Buddha, and in Hinduism to duty.

sangha In Buddhism, the community of monks and nuns who see themselves as the successors of the people who traveled with the Buddha in his lifetime.

monastery A community of adherents to a particular religion, who often live in seclusion from general society.

nirvana In Buddhism, the goal of religious practice, a state of existence without desire, hatred, ignorance, suffering, and, ultimately, reincarnation.

stupa A Buddhist monument built to hold a part of the Buddha's remains or an object connected to him.

The Great Stupa of Sanchi, India

According to tradition, in 260 B.C.E. Emperor Ashoka built thousands of stupas across India to cover ashes of the cremated Buddha. This example from Sanchi is known to have a simple hemispherical brick core to hold the remains. In later centuries people turned the stupa into an elaborate construction with a large stone mound and entrance gates. The monument is still in use today. (Frédéric Soltan/Corbis.)

the Buddha as a divine being people could worship. Any man or woman who acquired freedom from suffering and postponed nirvana to teach it to others was a called a *bodhisattva*, an "enlightened being," who in turn became an object of veneration. The two schools coexisted, sometimes within the same monastery.

Spread of Buddhism

Royal support greatly facilitated the spread of Buddhism. Particularly important was the emperor Ashoka, a skillful military leader whose campaigns greatly expanded the Mauryan Empire (discussed later in this chapter). Sickened by the death and destruction of his conquest of Kalinga in 260 B.C.E., he converted to Buddhism, hoping to bring the various peoples in his empire together under the common ideal of humanity and virtue. Ashoka proclaimed his aspirations by inscribing them on rock surfaces and stone pillars in an assortment of languages and dialects. For example:

> This world and the other are hard to gain without great love of Righteousness [dharma], great self-examination, great obedience, great circumspection, great effort. Through my instruction respect and love of Righteousness daily increase and will increase. . . . For this is my rule—to govern by Righteousness, to administer by Righteousness, to please my subjects by Righteousness, and to protect them by Righteousness.[2]

bodhisattva In Buddhism, a person who found enlightenment and teaches others.

Thus, by promoting a universal religion, establishing precepts to govern all of his people, and translating his precepts into many languages so that all could understand them, Ashoka consciously sought to strengthen connections among the peoples and communities of his empire.

Ashoka's efforts to promote Buddhism were not confined to the Mauryan Empire. He sent missionaries to spread Buddhism beyond India, and later traditions regularly attribute the religion's arrival to his initiatives. In Sri Lanka, for example, they say that Ashoka's son Mahendra converted many people through acts of kindness and piety. Buddhism's spread also benefited from the support of merchants, who especially in early centuries C.E. traveled widely from India to other parts of Asia, as we will see. They carried Buddhist manuscripts to distant places, where scholars translated them into local languages and adapted them to local tastes. The spread of Buddhism beyond India proved crucial to the religion's survival. Hinduism eventually replaced Buddhism as India's dominant religion, but Buddhism continued to flourish abroad.

Buddhism and Jainism challenged the Vedic tradition and drew believers away from the older religion. But the Vedic tradition evolved rather than withered away. After 500 B.C.E. the Vedic tradition widened its appeal by abandoning its special treatment of the Brahmans and its rigorous adherence to the caste system. These developments coincided with the production of written Sanskrit versions of the Vedas, as well as of a large literature, both secular and religious. Although scholars call the new religion "Hinduism," that term did not appear until the eleventh century C.E., when India's Muslim conquerors used it to refer to the religious practices of the people of India in general. Influenced by Jainism and Buddhism, Hinduism found ways to emphasize the value of the individual within a caste framework. All people had an obligation to carry out the activities and duties of their caste, but proper behavior could free any individual from the cycle of reincarnation. Hence, Hinduism combined essential elements of the Vedic tradition with some of the beliefs and ideals of the tradition's critics, creating a stronger and more popular religion.

Hinduism honors many gods and goddesses, and their worship is an important duty. The major division in Hinduism is between devotees of the two most prominent male gods, Vishnu and Shiva. Both had been minor gods in Vedic times. Shiva was of Dravidian origin and remained more popular in the south of India, whereas Vishnu had an Indo-European background and was more popular in the north. Vishnu was a benevolent god who preserved and protected the universe. Shiva, however, had warlike characteristics and was present in places of disaster. Vishnu could appear in numerous incarnations, which linked him to the gods and heroes of other traditions. Thus, in one incarnation Vishnu could be Krishna, a warrior god and a shepherd; in another incarnation he was the Buddha. This flexibility was a key consequence of the Vedic tradition's evolution into Hinduism. One of Hinduism's strengths was its ability to incorporate elements from many religious traditions and to thrive in diverse communities across India.

The Hindu way of life encouraged a balanced pursuit of devotion and pleasure. People should seek righteousness, virtue, and duty, but they could also pursue material gain, love, and recreation. Correct balance among these pursuits would lead to liberation from worldly life. The poem known as the *Bhagavad Gita* ("Song of the Lord") explains how a person could attain the ideal balance in an active life. The poem is a dialogue between the hero

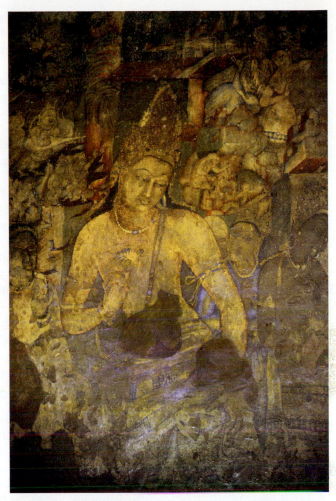

Image of a Bodhisattva

The bodhisattva—an individual who, through wisdom, moral behavior, and self-sacrifice, guided people to awakening— became a popular figure in Buddhist art and literature. This depiction of one comes from the Ajanta caves in western India, where Buddhist temples famous for their frescoes were excavated in the rock between the first century B.C. and the seventh century C.E. The bodhisattva is shown in a posture typical for meditation. (Frédéric Soltan/Corbis.)

Hinduism

Arjuna and his charioteer, Krishna, who is the incarnation of Vishnu. When Arjuna is reluctant to fight his family members and friends, Krishna convinces him that he will hurt only their bodies, which are renewable, and not their souls, which are immortal:

> Just as man, having cast off old garments, puts on other, new ones, even so does the embodied one, having cast off old bodies, take on other, new ones.
> Weapons do not cleave him, fire does not burn him; nor does water drench him, nor the wind dry him up.
> He is uncleavable, he is unburnable, he is undrenchable, as also undryable. He is eternal, all pervading, stable, immovable, existing from time immemorial.[3]

As a warrior, Arjuna has a specific role in society, just as everyone does, whatever their place in society. The idea of specific roles reinforced the caste system, in which the duty of the Brahman was to provide wisdom; of the warrior, valor; of the Vaishya, industry; and of the Shudra, service.

The centuries after 500 B.C.E. thus witnessed remarkable intellectual activity in India as thinkers reinterpreted the ancient Vedic ideals and sought to make them accessible to all people. Hinduism continued to stress the caste system, but people on every level could find spiritual liberation. In contrast, Buddhism and Jainism focused on the individual quest for salvation outside the caste system. All three religions proved to have widespread and long-lasting appeal, and they continue to inspire millions of people to this day.

Unity and Fragmentation: The Mauryan and Gupta Empires

With its vast size and varied ecology of forests, deserts, mountain ranges, and river valleys, it was not easy to bring the Indian subcontinent under central political control. Further, its population had varied cultural traditions, languages, and scripts. Nevertheless, between 500 B.C.E. and 500 C.E., a series of empires, including those of Persians, Macedonians, Mauryans, and Guptas, controlled large parts of India. Their leaders came from diverse backgrounds: some were from India itself, but others were outsiders who conquered parts of the subcontinent. All encouraged the merging of traditions throughout their realms, and some used the new religions to inspire a regional sense of community.

Rise of the Mauryan Empire

When the Aryas moved into the eastern Indian Ganges Valley sometime before 1500 B.C.E. (see Chapter 3), they established a number of kingdoms. In later centuries, these kingdoms were often at war with one another, but eventually these civil struggles ended, perhaps in part due to outside pressures. In 326 B.C.E. Alexander of Macedonia crossed the Indus River and confronted Indian armies. Greek sources say that a rebellious Indian prince, whose name they render in Greek as Sandracottos (san-droh-KOT-uhs), met Alexander and urged him to conquer the kingdom of Magadha in the Ganges Valley. Alexander's men refused to go farther east, however, and retreated. This, according to some, was Alexander's greatest mistake: "Sandracottos, when he was a stripling, saw Alexander himself, and we are told that he often said in later times that Alexander narrowly missed making himself master of the country, since its king was hated and despised on account of his baseness and low birth."[4]

Later Indian sources do not mention Alexander, but they do describe the Indian prince, using his Indian name, Chandragupta. He started out as a penniless servant but established himself as ruler of the kingdom of Magadha. Through conquest and clever diplomacy, he created the largest empire in Indian history—called Mauryan after the name of Chandragupta's dynasty—bringing the entire subcontinent except for the Tamil south under his control (see Counterpoint: Tamil Kingdoms of South India). By 321 B.C.E., Chandragupta had annexed the Indus Valley. He later acquired the Greek-controlled region of Bactria—northern Afghanistan today—from the Seleucid Empire in exchange for five hundred elephants (see Map 6.1).

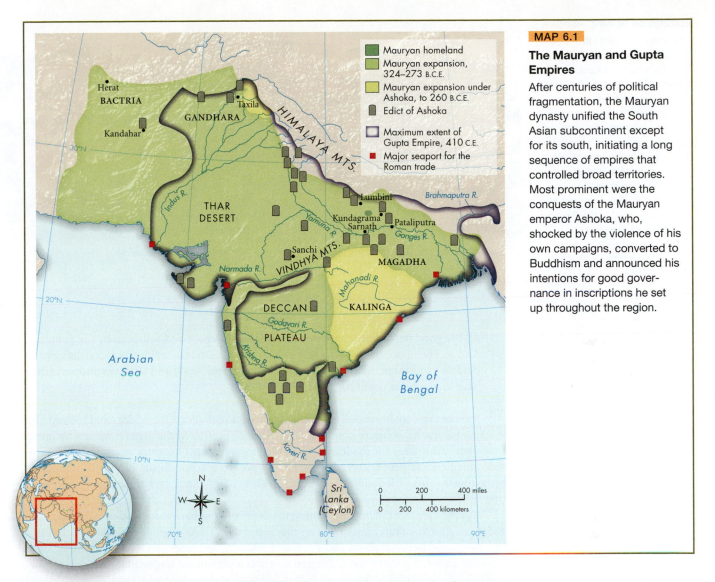

MAP 6.1

The Mauryan and Gupta Empires

After centuries of political fragmentation, the Mauryan dynasty unified the South Asian subcontinent except for its south, initiating a long sequence of empires that controlled broad territories. Most prominent were the conquests of the Mauryan emperor Ashoka, who, shocked by the violence of his own campaigns, converted to Buddhism and announced his intentions for good governance in inscriptions he set up throughout the region.

Chandragupta relied on his chief adviser, Kautilya, to create the empire's administration, which became famous for its efficiency. Kautilya left behind a handbook on government, the *Arthasastra*, or "Treatise on Material Gain," as a guideline for future officials. He presented the figure of the king as the center of the state and the source of people's wealth and happiness. The king was the sole guarantee against disorder and could use any means necessary to avoid it, including spies and political assassination. For much of his reign, Chandragupta followed Kautilya's advice, consolidating his own power and eliminating potential sources of opposition. It is possible, however, that he came to regret his ruthless policies, because in around 297 B.C.E. Chandragupta abdicated the throne, became a Jain monk, and starved himself to death in absolute asceticism.

King Ashoka

The religious climate of his day also deeply influenced Chandragupta's grandson and successor, Ashoka. As we have seen, the human cost of his wars of conquest prompted him to convert to Buddhism in around 260 B.C.E. Buddhist ideals inspired his government, and he announced his reforms publicly throughout the empire through the use of the carved inscriptions described earlier in this chapter. Ashoka's inscriptions are the oldest preserved writings from India, after the Indus Valley texts (see Chapter 3).

Ashoka ruled his empire in a way that was unique for his time. He urged nonviolence, humane treatment of servants, and generosity to all. He did not force his views on his people, instead leading through example. One of his statements was:

Inscription of King Ashoka

After his conversion to Buddhism in around 260 B.C.E., King Ashoka broadcast his message of tolerance and care for the people in his land in a series of inscriptions on pillars and rock façades. He used local languages and scripts to do so, and these inscriptions are the earliest evidence of writing in India after the Indus Valley script. This fragment of a pillar is inscribed in the Brahma script, the ancestor of all modern Indian scripts. (© The Trustees of The British Museum/Art Resource, NY.)

> All the good deeds that I have done have been accepted and followed by the people. And so obedience to mother and father, obedience to teachers, respect for the aged, kindness to Brahmans and ascetics, to the poor and weak, and to slaves and servants, have increased and will continue to increase.[5]

Ashoka dispatched specially appointed officers to broadcast these ideas and to keep him informed about his subjects' concerns. The emperor promoted the general welfare by lining roads with fruit trees for shade and food, digging wells, and building rest houses. He provided medicine to people and animals. He did not preach Buddhism, but instead hoped to bring together his varied subjects under an ideology of tolerance, seeking universal principles that all of his diverse subjects could accept.

Ashoka's empire did not long outlast the death of this charismatic leader in 232 B.C.E. By 185 B.C.E., the Mauryan Empire was no more, and the various regions of India had regained independence. Between about 200 B.C.E. and 300 C.E., foreigners such as the Central Asian Kushans annexed parts of India. Foreign invasion and political fragmentation did not, however, end India's cultural flowering. India's religious and intellectual vitality did not depend on political unity, and the arrival of outsiders created new conduits for the spread of Indian culture abroad.

Gupta Empire

The breakup of India was temporarily reversed when a dynasty from the Ganges Valley, the Guptas, unified the north and parts of the center between about 320 and 540 C.E. (see again Map 6.1). The dynasty's founder took the name Chandra Gupta to recall the Mauryan Empire of the past, but his state was smaller and much less centralized. The Guptas replaced the direct administration of the Mauryans with a system that relied on the cooperation of allies and vassals. Much of the conquest was the work of Chandra Gupta's son, Samudra Gupta (c. 330–380 C.E.). Later Indians saw him as the ideal king because he was a great warrior as well as a poet and musician.

Unlike Ashoka, who had sought to inspire the loyalty of his people through good works, Samudra Gupta used violence and the threat of violence to hold his empire together. This strategy proved effective, and he could control his subjects while expanding his empire. Inscriptions from his reign claim that he received tribute from places as distant as Central Asia in the north and Sri Lanka in the south. The Gupta Empire gradually came under increasing pressure from Central Asian nomads, who raided northwest India throughout the fifth century C.E. The expense and effort to keep these raiders out proved so great that by 540 C.E. the Gupta Empire had disappeared. Not until the Mughal dynasty in the sixteenth century C.E. would empire return to India.

A Crossroads of Trade

Like people all over the ancient world, most Indians devoted their lives to agricultural tasks. They lived in small villages, enjoying few if any luxuries. The work of this rural labor force was nonetheless crucial to India's cultural and material development. Food produced in the countryside made possible the growth of cities, which were at the heart of both internal and external trade. Indian urban artisans created products that appealed to elites all over India. Moreover, its location at the crossroads of land and sea trade routes across Asia and beyond placed India at the center of an enormous and dynamic international trading system. Despite the region's political turmoil from 500 B.C.E. to 500 C.E., long-distance trade continued to grow. India was in contact with far-flung lands, from China and Southeast Asia to East Africa and the Mediterranean world. As both importers and exporters of luxury goods, its merchants accumulated enormous wealth. Indian rulers, who also benefited financially from this trade, sent ambassadors to distant lands, promoting an exchange of ideas and styles as well as goods.

India's merchants looked both east and west to trade with Asia's great empires. Caravans to and from China took advantage of the age-old trade routes that crossed Asia to India's north, which later became known as the **Silk Road** or, sometimes, the "Silk Roads," as it was not a single route but instead incorporated various parallel branches. Leading four thousand miles through lush regions, deserts, and mountain ranges, it connected China to western Asia and the Mediterranean coast in ancient and medieval times (see again Mapping the World, page 172). The name derives from the Chinese monopoly on silk, which lasted until the fifth century C.E. People throughout Eurasia coveted the cloth so much that they shipped large amounts of gold, silver, and other products east to obtain it. Few traveled the entire Silk Road, instead passing goods on to others in trading stations in oases, near mountain passes, and in other strategic locations. Ideas as well as material goods moved along the road; it was the route by which Buddhism and Christianity spread into China.

Reliance on the Silk Road connected the fortunes of far-flung peoples. The empires of Rome and Byzantium in the Mediterranean area (discussed in Chapter 7) provided enormous markets for the products shipped along the Silk Road. While these empires thrived, so did the Asian trading cities along the western portion of the Silk Road, but when Rome and Byzantium declined, many of these cities were abandoned. In the thirteenth and fourteenth centuries C.E. the arrival of the Mongols in western Asia revived this region and enabled Marco Polo, a merchant from Venice, to reach the Chinese court and write one of the great works of travel literature. In time, trade with the East would enable Venice to build a maritime empire and become in its own right a crossroads for exchanges between Europe and Asia.

While traders from north India traveled the Silk Road, those from the south sailed the seas to gain access to goods and foreign markets. In Southeast Asia they obtained spices and semiprecious stones, luxury goods for which Indians found a large market among the Roman imperial elite. The Romans paid with gold coins, wine, copper, tin, and lead. An anonymous Greek traveler of the first century C.E. described ports and marketplaces from Egypt to the Indian Ocean, including various harbors on the Indian coast. Archaeologists have uncovered Roman objects in India that suggest the presence of Roman settlers. But more Indians sailed to the west than Romans to the east, as evidenced by the names that appear in Indian scripts on potsherds excavated in Red Sea ports. Situated between major empires, Indian traders could obtain goods in the empires of the east and sell them in the empires of the west. International trade brought many outside influences to India and helped disseminate Indian religions, ideas, and goods throughout Asia and beyond.

The rulers of many Indian states taxed international trade and so had a substantial stake in it. Hence it was in their interest to facilitate and encourage long-distance commerce through embassies. In about 25 B.C.E., one such Indian trade mission traveled to Rome. According to the Greek historian Nicholas of Damascus, they brought as gifts to the Roman emperor Augustus tigers, pheasants, snakes, giant tortoises, and an armless boy who could shoot arrows with his toes. Missions of this type presented exotic eastern products to an eager Roman clientele.

Silk Road

Trade with Rome

Silk Road The caravan route with various branches that connected China in the east to the Mediterranean Sea in the west, passing through regions such as South and Southwest Asia.

The economies of Asia were thus joined by an exchange of luxury products. For centuries, political changes in any region could affect the trade, but they did not fundamentally alter it. The decline of the Western Roman Empire in the fourth century C.E. and the end of the Gupta Empire soon thereafter, however, were a major blow to India's long-distance trade. Only in the ninth century C.E. did it revive.

Literary and Scientific Flowering

At around the time that Greece's culture reached new heights in its Classical Age, a period of great literary production began in India. It was to last from 500 B.C.E. to 500 C.E., India's own classical period. This flowering, which continued despite the region's shifting political circumstances, involved religious and secular poetry, drama, and prose. The Brahmans' control over literature through their teaching of the Vedas in memorized form weakened in the Mauryan period, when scribes started to write down the Vedas and their interpretations in the Upanishads. Ashoka's use of various languages and scripts in the third century B.C.E. encouraged the use of spoken dialects in writing and indicates that different literate traditions coexisted in his empire.

The language of the Vedas inspired the primary literary language of ancient India, Sanskrit. Although it was probably little spoken, it was used for much of Indian literature until the nineteenth century C.E. Sanskrit texts fall into a wide range of genres, but most prominent are the epics, or warrior songs. Previously passed down orally, epics began to be recorded in writing after 100 B.C.E. Although the epics represent the traditional values of Hinduism, their engaging stories fascinated people of varied religions all over India and Southeast Asia, and they became the basis for multiple interpretations in many languages and formats, including modern film.

Perhaps the longest single poem in world literature is the *Mahabharata*, the "Great Epic of the Bharata Dynasty," with one hundred thousand stanzas written in Sanskrit. It describes the contest between two branches of the same royal family, which culminated in an eighteen-day-long battle that involved all the kings of India and also Greeks, Bactrians, and Chinese. The epic showed how people of all ranks, including kings and warriors, should behave, following the rules of dharma, which in Hindu thought refers to "duty."

A shorter epic, the *Ramayana*, the "Story of Prince Rama," shows the adherence to dharma in practice. A plot against the prince forced Rama to flee to the forest with his wife Sita. Sita was kidnapped, taken to the island of Sri Lanka, and compelled to reside in the house of another man. After many adventures, Rama freed her with the help of monkeys, but because people doubted her chastity, he had to force her to live in the forest despite his great love for her. There she gave birth to

Delhi's Iron Pillar

Near Delhi in modern India stands an iron pillar whose characteristics demonstrate the great technical skills of Gupta craftsmen. Probably erected in around 400 C.E., the pillar is more than 13 feet tall and weighs about 6 tons. The iron is 98 percent pure, which is possible only when extremely high heat has been applied. The ability to work this enormous mass of metal was unparalleled in early world history and was not attained in Europe until the nineteenth century C.E. (Dinodia Photos.)

Rama's twin sons. In the end, the family was reunited, but Sita asked to be returned to her mother, the goddess Earth. The *Ramayana* and the *Mahabharata* enjoyed great popularity across India, providing common cultural touchstones for the continent's diverse peoples.

Indian poetry was not limited to sweeping epics. Most notable are the works of Kalidasa, who probably lived in the Gupta period between 390 and 470 C.E. In one short poem, the "Cloud Messenger," he describes how an exiled man asks a cloud to carry a message to his wife, whom he misses deeply. He declares:

Sanskrit Poetry and Plays

> In the vines I see your limbs, your look
> in the eye of a startled doe, the loveliness
> of your face in the moon, in the peacock's plumage your hair,
> the playful lift of your brows in the light ripples
> of rivers, but, O, sadly, nowhere, my passionate girl,
> is the whole of your likeness in any one of these.[6]

Kalidasa was also famous for his dramatic works, which were very popular as court entertainment. The stories featured gods, heroes, and courtiers who suffered a good deal of intrigue and hardship but always prevailed in the end.

Scholarship also flourished during India's classical period. In linguistics, Panini developed a grammar of the Sanskrit language in around the fifth century B.C.E., recording more than four thousand grammatical rules. His work impressed later generations so much that they used it as the absolute standard of the language, inhibiting change. Consequently, Sanskrit grew increasingly distant from the commonly spoken Prakrit.

Scholarship

Investigations in astronomy, medicine, physics, and chemistry brought technological wonders. Probably in about 400 C.E., ironsmiths set up a pillar 13 feet 8 inches tall near Delhi that was made of a single piece of iron so chemically pure that it has not rusted in sixteen hundred years. And Indian mathematicians would have a great impact on the world by inventing the concept of zero. The Indian number system, with its symbols from 0 to 9, spread east and west in the seventh century C.E., and western Europeans adopted it from the Middle East as "Arabic" numerals in around 1000 C.E.

The Kushan Peoples of Central Asia 100 B.C.E.–233 C.E.

As we saw in Chapter 3, in ancient times the vast treeless steppe of Central Asia was home to nomadic groups whose livelihood depended on animal husbandry. The settled inhabitants along the steppe's borders lived in fear of these horse-riding warriors. At various times, nomads entered the urbanized states, seized power, and created empires. The nomads ruled such empires through existing political and social structures, absorbing the customs and cultures of the sedentary peoples in the process.

> **FOCUS**
>
> How did the geographical location and trade relations of the Kushan Empire affect its cultural traditions?

An early example of this dynamic occurred from around 50 to 233 C.E., when tribes originally from the western borderlands of China built an empire that included large parts of south-central Asia and India. These people, the Kushans, ruled a thriving multicultural empire that lasted for nearly two centuries. As the inscription at the beginning of this chapter indicates, the Kushan ruler considered himself equal to the great emperors of his time who ruled large urbanized territories, both to his east (China) and to his west (Parthia and Rome). That was not an idle boast—the Kushan Empire rivaled the other great empires of Eurasia in political power, wealth, and cultural production. The Kushan peoples are an excellent example of how nomads of Central Asia shaped the history of Eurasia.

Foundations of Empire

The introduction of horses (discussed in Chapter 3) increased the mobility of nomadic herders, which brought them in contact with various urbanized regions at the edges of the Central Asian steppe. Because they did not leave any writings themselves, we must rely on descriptions from sedentary neighbors to reconstruct their histories. Chinese sources report on the early history of one of these peoples, who would become known as Kushans. They describe struggles between nomadic groups on the western border of the Han state in around 100 B.C.E. The previously dominant Yuehzi (YOU-EH-juh) came under attack by another group, the Xiongnu (SHE-OONG-noo), who killed their king. The Yuehzi subsequently migrated westward, where one faction, the Great Yuehzi, occupied the region north of the Oxus River Valley that had only recently been resettled. The Great Yuehzi remained organized as five nomadic tribes, although they controlled cities in the Oxus River Valley whose inhabitants practiced irrigation agriculture (see Reading the Past: A Family of Chinese Historians Trace Early Kushan History).

The social and political organization of the Yuehzi did not change for more than a century, until one tribe gained supremacy over the other four in about 50 C.E. The Chinese called these people Kuei-shuang, a Chinese rendering of the name *Kusana* from Indian sources; today we use the name *Kushan*. Soon after dominating the other tribes, the Kushans conquered the regions to their south: Parthia, Bactria, and Gandhara. At the height of its power, the empire incorporated modern-day Afghanistan, Pakistan, and

READING THE PAST

A Family of Chinese Historians Traces Early Kushan History

In around 80 to 100 C.E., Ban Biao, Ban Gu, and Ban Zhao wrote the *History of the Former Han Dynasty*, which includes an account of the early history of the Kushan Empire. Information about the distant country came from envoys of the Han court, who visited the region to establish alliances against the Xiongnu on the northern border.

The king of the country of the Great Yuehzi resides at the city of Chien-shih, at a distance of 11,600 *li* [about 3850 miles] from Changan. It is not controlled by the [Chinese] governor-general [in Central Asia]. It has a population of 100,000 households, with 400,000 people and 100,000 excellent soldiers. . . . Its soil, climate, products, prevailing popular customs and money are the same as those of the An-hsi [Parthia]. [This country] produces one-humped camels. The Great Yuehzi originally formed a nomadic state; they moved about following their cattle, and had the same customs as the Xiongnu. As their archers numbered more than a hundred thousand, they were strong and treated the Xiongnu with contempt. Originally they lived between Tunhuang and Ch'i-lien. But when Mao-tun [Xiongnu leader, c. 209–174 B.C.E.]

had attacked and defeated the Yuehzi, and when Lao-shang [Xiongnu leader, c. 174–161 B.C.E.] had killed the Yuehzi [king] and had made a drinking vessel from his skull, then the Yuehzi went far away. They passed through Ta-yüan [Ferghana] and to the west [of that country] they smote Ta-hsia and subdued it. They had their capital north of the Kuei [Oxus] River and [this] they made their royal court.

Source: E. Zürcher, trans., "The Yüeh-chih and Kaniska in the Chinese Sources," *Papers on the Date of Kaniska*, ed. A. L. Basham (Leiden, Netherlands: Brill, 1968), 364–365.

EXAMINING THE EVIDENCE

1. How do the authors explain the migration of the Yuehzi, the Kushans' ancestors?

2. What is the lifestyle of the Yuehzi and their opponents, the Xiongnu?

northwest India (see Map 6.2). These were very wealthy lands, densely urbanized and home to multiple flourishing cultural traditions that the Kushan rulers readily absorbed.

A Merging of Cultural Influences

The Kushan Empire brought together regions with manifold traditions, and its far-reaching contacts with peoples abroad helped make it a culture that embraced an enormous diversity of influences. Like the leaders of the Persian Empire (see Chapter 4), Kushan rulers did not seek to impose a uniform identity on their subjects, but instead embraced the diverse cultures of their domain.

Multicultural Religion

When the Yuehzi first arrived in the Oxus River region in the first century B.C.E., the people there worshiped a mixture of Iranian and Greek gods. The Iranian tradition was Zoroastrian, whereas the descendants of the Seleucid Empire worshiped Greek gods. The two traditions had already partly merged in that Iranian gods were equated with Greek deities. Indian influences were also present, representing both the Buddhist and Brahmanist traditions. When the Kushan Empire took over the region in around 50 C.E., its leaders sought to reinforce the legitimacy of their rule by using Greek, Iranian, and Bactrian imagery and ideas to explain and define their royal status.

The Kushans promoted Indian religious practices as well; later tradition honored the Kushan ruler Kanishka II as a great supporter of Buddhism. (The dates of the reign of

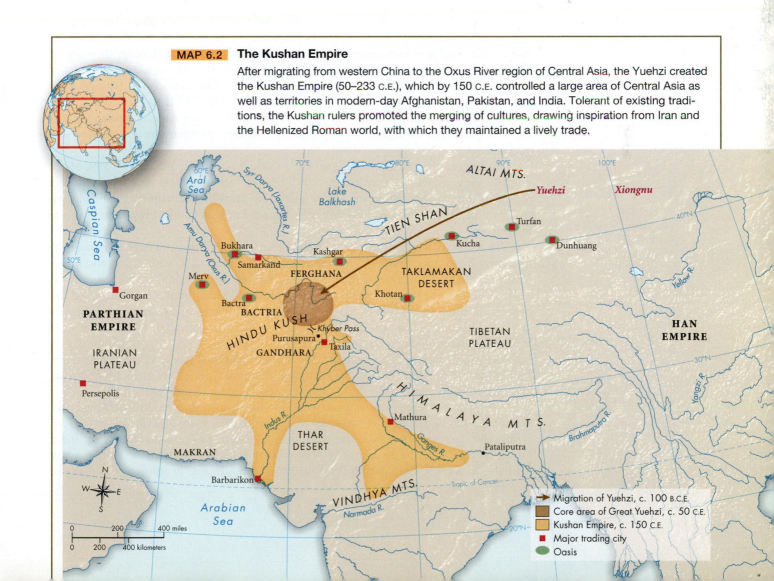

MAP 6.2   **The Kushan Empire**

After migrating from western China to the Oxus River region of Central Asia, the Yuehzi created the Kushan Empire (50–233 C.E.), which by 150 C.E. controlled a large area of Central Asia as well as territories in modern-day Afghanistan, Pakistan, and India. Tolerant of existing traditions, the Kushan rulers promoted the merging of cultures, drawing inspiration from Iran and the Hellenized Roman world, with which they maintained a lively trade.

Kanishka II are contested, but scholars agree that he ruled for twenty-three years starting sometime between 78 and 144 C.E.) One story relates that after he defeated the Indian state of Pataliputra, he chose the alms bowl of the Buddha rather than massive tribute as the price for his victory. Kanishka II built many Buddhist stupas and monasteries, and he sponsored the study of Buddhist texts. Because he encouraged contacts with China, Buddhism spread into that country; the earliest evidence for Chinese Buddhism dates to the second century C.E.

Gandharan Art and Writing

Art and literature also reflected the Kushan embrace of multiple cultural traditions. The Gandharan art style, which used Greek styles to portray traditional Indian figures such as the Buddha, flourished under the Kushans (see again At a Crossroads, page 170). Many Gandharan statues represent women with much sophistication and detail, and the art was a favorite of wealthy merchants. At the same time, imperial art represented the king in heavy robes and tall boots, based on Central Asian traditions. Local artistic practices in various regions of the Kushan Empire continued as well.

Likewise, many scripts and languages were in use. The Kushans used the Greek alphabet to write Greek and local languages. From India came two scripts called Brahmi and Kharosthi and the Prakrit and Sanskrit languages. The Kushans probably employed Indians as their administrators, and under them Buddhist monks spread Indian languages and scripts, which can be seen on coins and in official inscriptions. Sometimes they presented texts in several languages.

Farmers and Traders: The Kushan Economy

Farmers

The region north of the Oxus River receives too little rainfall for agriculture, but the river and its tributaries allow irrigation. People practiced irrigation before the Yuehzi arrived, and the Kushans greatly expanded and systematized the existing technology throughout their Central Asian provinces. They lengthened earlier canals and merged separate smaller systems into a network that covered mountain regions as well as lowlands. Farmers used plows with iron shears, which enabled more land to be cultivated than ever before. They grew highly varied crops, including cereals, fruits, and cotton. Animal husbandry was vitally important to the economy as well; the two-humped Bactrian camel was prized as a pack animal.

The large-scale agricultural infrastructure made it possible to build new cities. Many nomads were drawn to a sedentary life by urban economic possibilities, including the manufacture of household and luxury goods. The areas the Kushans commanded were rich in minerals and semiprecious stones, which were in high demand inside and outside the empire.

Traders

The Kushan Empire lay astride the transcontinental Silk Road and controlled many of its central Asian trading routes. The empire's territory linked India with China, and under Kushan protection traders from the Indian subcontinent spread out along the Silk Road to establish stations to the east. At its fullest extent, the Kushan Empire also controlled the harbors on the west Indian coast, leaving Kushan merchants at the center of exchanges among China, India, Iran, and the Mediterranean. The state gained an enormous income from taxes on this trade.

The production of coins greatly facilitated international trade. When the Kushans minted their first official coins, they imitated the Greek designs of their predecessors and inscribed the coins in Greek. To allow easy exchange with the Romans, they struck a gold coin with the same value as the one used in the Roman Empire. Kushan kings later abandoned Greek usages in coinage, however, introducing coins inscribed with various scripts and languages of the Kushan state and representing non-Greek gods from India and Iran. The Buddha occasionally appeared as well (see Seeing the Past: Kushan Coins). The Kushan Empire thus flourished economically, taking advantage of peaceful

SEEING THE PAST

Kushan Coins

Kushan Coin, c. 100 C.E. (Classical Numismatic Group, Inc.; http://www.cngcoins.com/.)

The Kushan emperors minted coins to facilitate trade with their neighbors. They provide a series of portraits of the various kings, who had themselves represented with inscriptions giving their names and titles and with religious figures whom they considered important. These coins vividly show how multiple cultures influenced the Kushans.

The gold coin shown here has the portrait of King Kanishka II on the front (left). He appears in clothing typical of horsemen of Central Asia—a heavy robe and thick boots—and he places an offering on a small altar to his right. His left hand holds a staff. The flames from his shoulders indicate his superhuman status. The inscription at the edge of the coin is in the Bactrian language using the Greek alphabet, to which a letter was added to render the sound /sh/. It reads "King of

Kings, Kanishka, the Kushan." On the back (right) appears an image of the Buddha, with his name written in Greek letters as "Boddo." Other coins of Kanishka depict Greek, Indian, and Iranian deities.

EXAMINING THE EVIDENCE

1. Judging from this example, in what ways do Kushan coins reflect the multiple religious influences on the empire?

2. What do these coins tell us about languages and scripts in the Kushan Empire?

conditions, the unification of diverse regions with different resources, and control over the trans-Asian trade routes.

The Kushans are one in a sequence of nomadic peoples from Central Asia whose interactions with surrounding urbanized areas profoundly influenced the histories of these regions. Through their wide-ranging contacts, the Kushans contributed to the development of all of Asia. Their acceptance of varied traditions led to a remarkable multiculturalism and the creation of dynamic new hybrid cultures. Although the nearly two-hundred-year Kushan supremacy ended with the rise of a new empire to the west, Sasanid Iran, remnants of a Kushan state survived into the ninth century C.E. In India, the disappearance of the Kushans gave the Guptas the freedom to create their own empire.

China's First Empires: The Qin and Han Dynasties 221 B.C.E.–220 C.E.

FOCUS

How did the early Chinese philosophers come to have a long-lasting influence on the intellectual development of the region?

In the east of Asia, the unified Shang and Zhou (joe) kingdoms of the second and early first millennia B.C.E. started to disintegrate in around 800 B.C.E. (see Chapter 3). Historians still see the period from 770 to 221 B.C.E. as part of the Zhou dynasty, but the political situation differed greatly from those of earlier centuries, when unity rather than fragmentation prevailed. The later Zhou dynasty is divided into the Spring and Autumn Period (770–481 B.C.E.) and the Period of the Warring States (480–221 B.C.E.). The name "Spring and Autumn Period" derives from a book called *The Spring and Autumn Annals*. It depicts a world of more than one hundred states routinely involved in wars, both among themselves and with inhabitants of the surrounding regions. Conflicts increased even more in the Period of the Warring States.

Perhaps inspired by the volatility of the time, revolutionary thinkers such as Confucius, Mencius (mehng-tsi-uz), Laozi (low-ZUH), and Lord Shang Yang founded intellectual movements that questioned human nature, the state, and political behavior. The implementation of their ideas led to a reconfiguration of political life that paved the way for the first Chinese empires, the Qin (chin), which was followed by the Han (hahn). These empires controlled a huge territory that at times stretched into Central Asia and southern China. Qin and Han rulers centralized and unified administrative practices. From about 500 B.C.E. to 200 C.E., culture flourished in China, especially scholarly writings. Scribes produced numerous copies of a wide variety of texts on law, medicine, divination, philosophy, and many other topics. In contrast to Indian thinkers, who generally focused on religious issues, Chinese scholars turned their attention to secular subjects and concerns. Therefore, we tend to label their teachings as philosophy—as we do for Greek thinkers of the time—rather than religion. Nonetheless, Indian, Chinese, and Greek thinkers were engaged in a common project. They all sought to understand and improve the societies in which they lived.

China's Warring States, 480–221 B.C.E.

Intellectual Churning: Confucians, Daoists, and Legalists

Confucius   Confucius (551–479 B.C.E.) dominates the intellectual history of this period, and his teachings have crucially influenced Chinese society and political life to this day. His own life, however, was rather uneventful. The son of an impoverished aristocrat from a small state of the later Zhou period, Confucius (from the Chinese name Kongfuzi, "Master Kong") was a good student and sought out teachers to learn new subjects. He obtained a minor government post in his native state, but in his thirties he turned to education, supporting himself by tutoring young aristocrats. Later in life he held higher government positions, but he fell out of favor with his local overlord because of his uncompromising support of the Zhou king. After traveling for twelve years to find employment in other states, he returned home to teach. During this time his fame grew as one who awakened the people from their ignorance. His followers grew in number, and the Han historian Sima Qian claims that, when Confucius died at the age of seventy-three, three thousand followers were studying with him.

It was these students who wrote down their conversations with him and thus preserved his teachings; Confucius himself did not write down his ideas. Probably compiled by 100 B.C.E. in the form known today, Confucius's *Analects* document the philosopher's ideas about human nature, behavior, and the state. He taught that proper conduct in all social interactions instilled in individuals a humaneness that emphasized benevolence and kindness. Like Indian thinkers of around the same time, Confucius urged that behavior adhere to a moral code: "For the gentleman integrity is the essence; the rules of decorum are the way he puts it into effect; humility is the way he brings it forth; sincerity is the way he develops it. Such indeed is what it means to be a gentleman."[7] As a former administrator, Confucius especially stressed respect for parents and superiors. He urged children to take care of their parents in old age and to mourn them after death for a three-year period, and he encouraged people to obey those above them in the social hierarchy.

Proper behavior, Confucius believed, should also be taught to highborn men who desired to become good rulers. He did not want to institute a new political system but to return to the centralized rule of the Zhou dynasty (see Chapter 3). He stressed that doing good would stop the forces of evil, including war. Confucius renounced coercion in government because it produced resentment among subjects rather than respect. Thus his teachings went beyond establishing moral guidelines for individuals. He believed that proper behavior by all men and women could help produce a more peaceful and prosperous society.

Confucian Interpretations

After Confucius's death, a number of different philosophers interpreted and further developed his teachings. Among the most influential was Mencius (c. 372–289 B.C.E.), who stressed the basic goodness of human nature. Mencius emphasized the importance of human compassion and believed all human beings shared the capacity to empathize with one another. The philosopher Xunzi (shoon-zuh) (c. 300–230 B.C.E.), by contrast, saw humans as basically greedy and selfish, and he urged leaders to adopt strict rules to prevent their subjects from doing evil.

Daoism

Confucius taught that proper behavior involved active participation in society. In contrast, those who came to be known as Daoists urged people to seek a simple and honest life. They should withdraw from society and meditate, forsaking the pursuit of wealth and prestige and seeking a peaceful inner life. If many people behaved well, the world would be in harmony and follow its natural course, which was far superior to a world that people tried to actively control. These teachings are ascribed to a sixth-century B.C.E. sage, Laozi, but they probably represent the work of more than one philosopher collected in the third century B.C.E. under Laozi's name. In the Later Han period after 25 C.E., Daoism became an official religion, closely associated with Buddhism, with which it shared many ideas, and Laozi was depicted as a god.

Legalism

Rather than stressing practical guidance to rulers and officials, Daoism focused on personal introspection. On the opposite end of the spectrum was a school of thought called Legalism, which focused on the ruler, the social hierarchy, and practical aspects of government. At the height of the political turbulence of the Warring States period, Lord Shang Yang (c. 390–338 B.C.E.) put legalistic ideas into practice in the then small state of Qin, paving the way for the later unification of China. He believed every man should have an occupation that benefited the state, so he introduced compulsory military service and forced others to become farmers, whose activities government administrators monitored closely. He introduced strict laws—hence the name *Legalism*—that harshly punished even the smallest crime. Leaving trash on the street, for example, could lead to the amputation of a hand or foot. He assumed that fear would prevent people from wrongdoing; the only reward they could expect for correct behavior was absence of punishment. Lord Shang also introduced the principle of collective responsibility. If a soldier disobeyed, his entire family was executed. When the Later Qin state forced Lord Shang's ideas onto the entire population of China, its ruler became so unpopular that the people rebelled and overthrew the government.

Unification and Centralization: The Worlds of Qin and Han

The great philosophers of ancient China lived in a period of political turmoil and fragmentation. Although the Zhou kings nominally ruled the entire region, after 771 B.C.E. China was actually carved into numerous small principalities. It was only after five hundred years of fragmentation that rulers, inspired by the teachings of Confucius, Lord Shang, and others, restored China's political unity (see Map 6.3).

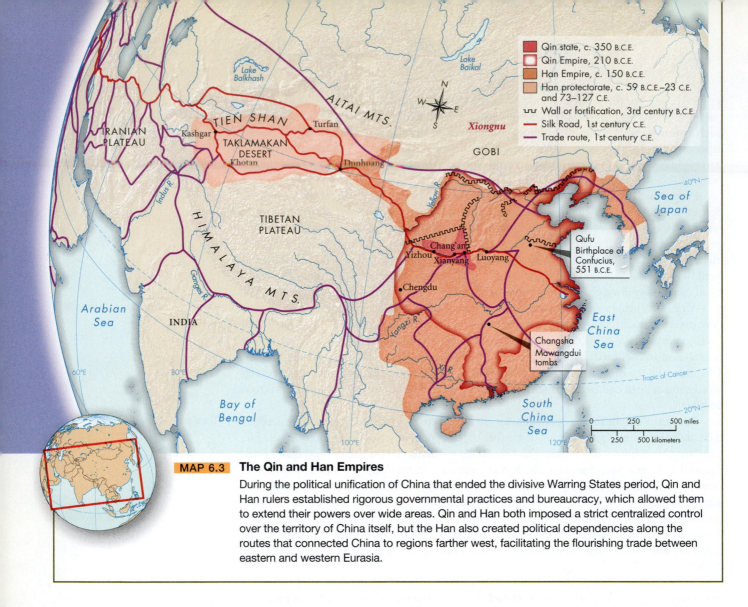

MAP 6.3 **The Qin and Han Empires**

During the political unification of China that ended the divisive Warring States period, Qin and Han rulers established rigorous governmental practices and bureaucracy, which allowed them to extend their powers over wide areas. Qin and Han both imposed a strict centralized control over the territory of China itself, but the Han also created political dependencies along the routes that connected China to regions farther west, facilitating the flourishing trade between eastern and western Eurasia.

Foundations for Qin Rule: Changes in Warfare and Administration

Two innovations dramatically changed the nature of warfare in the period of political fragmentation. First, chariotry had been the core of the Shang army, but it lost its effectiveness in mountainous or marshy terrain. In its place, infantry rose in importance, requiring local leaders to force thousands of farmers and other commoners to fight. The chariot-based aristocracy disappeared in favor of a more meritocratic army in which a soldier from any social background could rise up the military ranks, similar to what we saw in ancient Greece (discussed in Chapter 5). Second, after Central Asian nomads introduced iron technology into China, iron became the preferred metal for weapons. Not only were iron weapons much stronger than bronze, but iron ore was much more widely available than copper and tin. More and better weapons were thus produced more cheaply.

As the military aristocracy declined and family ties became less important in determining social status, bureaucracies arose to administer the states. Inspired by Legalism, lords instituted centralized systems of taxation and a military draft. Over time, some ten dominant states developed from the multitude of smaller ones, absorbing neighbors and adding new territories. Although they warred against one another regularly, they also traded goods, especially luxury items such as silk and craft products. A new educated elite arose among the administrators, trained in the ideas Confucius had introduced.

Shi Huangdi, First Emperor of China

The state that most successfully applied Legalism was Qin in western China, where Lord Shang had been minister of state. In 237 B.C.E., the Qin ruler started an all-out war, and after fifteen years he had unified an immense part of China (two-thirds of today's territory) under his rule. He succeeded because his state had a strong economic base and he could raise numerous troops and arm them with iron weapons. In 221 B.C.E., proclaiming himself Shi

Han Farmers at Work
Like that of all ancient states, imperial China's success depended to a great extent on agricultural development. The first emperor, Qin ruler Shi Huangdi, instituted reforms that expanded China's farming capabilities. Shown here is a stone relief from the Han dynasty of two men plowing with an ox-drawn plow. The relief was originally part of the decoration of a tomb built sometime between 200 B.C.E. and 200 C.E. (Werner Forman Archive/Topham/The Image Works.)

Huangdi (shee huang-dee), "First August Emperor," he began a series of reforms that would determine the political organization of China for more than four hundred years and inspire the norms of centralized rule in China up to the early twentieth century C.E. The modern name *China* derives from *Qin*.

Shi Huangdi (r. 221–210 B.C.E.) considered the expansion of China's agriculture the basis of progress, and, like the Babylonians, Kushans, and others we have discussed, he ordered large irrigation canals to be dug. He also sponsored the exploitation of new territories by giving land to farmers, whom the state closely supervised. Shi Huangdi first and foremost sought political centralization through three branches of government: taxation authorities, the military, and supervisors of officials. The Qin Empire was subdivided into provinces (at first thirty-six and later forty-two), and he and his successors governed it rigidly. They forced people to construct four thousand miles of roads to connect the provinces to one another and to the capital Xianyang (shan-yahng). Another large-scale public work, the result of backbreaking labor by three hundred thousand men, was the building of defensive walls at the northern border of the state, the forerunner to the Great Wall of China. Shi Huangdi also standardized the script his bureaucrats used. Instead of preserving the local variants that had developed out of Shang writing, he used a unified script to record the variety of languages spoken in the empire. He also imposed a single system of weights and measures and of coins.

The First August Emperor did not tolerate dissent. Indeed, according to late Han sources, Shi Huangdi assassinated 460 Confucian scholars who had criticized him, and in 213 B.C.E. he ordered that all books be burned except practical works on agriculture, medicine, and divination. The great classics of Chinese literature and philosophy would have disappeared had copies not been hidden or memorized by people who transmitted them orally. Thus Shi Huangdi sought to unify his people through very different policies than those of the Kushans or the Persians. They had seen diversity as a source of strength, but Shi Huangdi saw in it the potential for disorder, chaos, and rebellion. Suppressing difference and dissent, he sought to impose a unified culture on China, one in which all aspects of Chinese life served the interests of the centralized state.

One of the most massive building projects of Shi Huangdi's reign reflects the concentration of power in his hands. This is his tomb near his capital at Xianyang, which archaeologists have been excavating carefully since the 1970s. Only a small part has been uncovered so far, but what we already know is astounding. The emperor created an underground palace, surrounding himself with an army of seventy-three hundred life-size terra cotta statues. They depict footmen, archers, charioteers, and cavalry, and although the bodies were mass-produced, the faces show individual characteristics, as if real soldiers had posed for them.

Sima Qian described the central tomb (so far unexcavated) and claimed that it had a bronze foundation to protect against underground water, representations of seas and rivers composed of mercury made to flow by special mechanisms, and crossbow traps that the motion of an intruder would trigger. According to legend, seven hundred thousand men built the tomb and were imprisoned in it when they finished. Childless royal concubines also accompanied their master in death. Moreover, the tomb was filled with treasures from all over the land. Pearl-inlaid representations of the constellations of the sky covered the ceiling, and the floor displayed the extent of the empire. The entire complex seems to have been intended to continue the emperor's rule in the afterlife.

Rise of the Han Empire

The death of Shi Huangdi in 210 B.C.E. effectively meant the end of his dynasty, as subsequent palace intrigues weakened the central hold of the state and made peasant rebellions possible. Resentful of the Qin's harsh rule, mobs sacked the court and killed imperial officials. But China did not once again fall into pieces—a determined and popular rebel leader, Liu Bang (lee-OO bangh), managed to establish full dominance in 206 B.C.E. Liu Bang created a new nobility by giving two-thirds of the empire as kingdoms to relatives and supporters, keeping only one-third under direct state administration. His generosity generated support for himself and his dynasty, which he named Han after his home region (see again Map 6.3). The Han Empire governed China for four hundred years (206 B.C.E.–220 C.E.) with only a short interruption (9–24 C.E.). Historians refer to the first half of the Han period, in which the capital was at Chang'an in the west, as Former Han (206 B.C.E.–25 C.E.); they call the second half, in which the capital was at Luoyang farther east, Later Han (25–220 C.E.).

Although Liu Bang had moderated the Qin concentration of power by reestablishing the earlier system of inherited domains under aristocrats, the forces of centralization remained strong. The most prominent ruler of the Former Han, Emperor Wu, held the throne from 141 to 87 B.C.E.; he greatly expanded the government's powers and ruled with an iron fist. Wu needed a large bureaucracy administered by men with the proper skills to perform their tasks. Although local noble families recommended those who became officials, Wu introduced a **civil service examination** to determine where to place each appointee. He also centralized the education system. Whereas previously, private tutors (such as Confucius) had taught young men, Wu created a central school whose core was composed of five so-called Erudite Scholars, each a specialist in an aspect of Confucius's teaching. At first each scholar had fifty students apiece, but soon the student population swelled to three thousand, a number that grew larger over time. The graduates, who became the empire's officials, in turn formed a new class of educated men more loyal to the state than to the aristocratic families. Because Confucian ideas formed the basis of their education, the central role of these ideas in formal training was confirmed for two millennia. Emperor Wu's state thus combined the pragmatism of Legalism with an intellectual training based on Confucian traditions. In the process, he created a Chinese elite connected by their participation in a shared intellectual tradition.

Shi Huangdi's Terra Cotta Army
The tomb of the first emperor of China near his capital at Xianyang is one of the greatest archaeological sites of the ancient world, and it is still mostly unexcavated. A massive army of soldiers surrounds the tomb, each life-size figure made from baked clay and shaped to show the individual warrior's features. Created shortly before 200 B.C.E., the complex reveals a commitment to the dead emperor on a par with what we see in Egypt and other ancient cultures. (Alfred Ko/CORBIS.)

Highly centralized and well organized, the Former Han state relied on agricultural resources for its support. In addition, a state monopoly on iron and salt allowed the emperor to charge artificially high prices for these vital products. Trade of luxury goods, especially silk and lacquer ware, also brought substantial income to the empire. But the harsh system of government stirred the people's anger.

A combination of causes led to the collapse of the Han Empire. By the end of the first century B.C.E., a few local families had acquired huge estates and reduced the population to the status of slaves. A usurper seized the throne in 9 C.E., temporarily discontinued the Han dynasty, and freed the slaves. When the Han regained the throne by 25 C.E., the local landed gentry became even more powerful than before. In consequence, large numbers of peasants from several provinces rose in rebellion. Although the state crushed the uprisings, they weakened the central government, and by 220 C.E. the Han dynasty fell, leaving China politically fragmented once again.

Collapse of the Han Dynasty

The leaders of both the Qin and Han empires were driven by a desire to centralize power. In both dynasties, a government bureaucracy applied uniform practices throughout the empire. State-trained officials, chosen for their abilities rather than family connections, staffed the administration. Their allegiance to the state created a powerful unifying force. The pressures of decentralization remained strong, however—especially the resilience of aristocratic families, whose wealth allowed them to control local populations. The competing forces of centralization and decentralization led those in power to exploit the general population, who, pushed to the limit, grew to resent all authority and ultimately overthrew both empires.

Preserving and Spreading the Written Word

The Chinese political elite, interconnected by its education and intellectual training, placed special value on the written word. That written texts were important in Qin and Han China has been amply demonstrated in recent years through the excavation of elite tombs. Members of the bureaucracy buried themselves with their libraries, which consisted of manuscripts written on bamboo and silk. The physical objects themselves were very valuable. The use of bamboo forced the scribes to write the characters in long vertical columns, a layout that survived in Chinese writing until the twentieth century C.E., when writers began to use horizontal lines in letters and books (see Lives and Livelihoods: Papermakers).

Three tombs excavated in the 1970s at Mawangdui in the Hunan province of southern China reveal the high value that the Chinese elite accorded manuscripts. They belonged to a local lord who had supported the Han dynasty, his wife, and a man who died in his thirties, probably their son. Whereas the woman's burial stands out because of the perfect preservation of the tomb gifts, including clothing, lacquer ware, ceramics, and food, the son's burial is astonishing for its extensive library. On bamboo strips appear numerous medical treatises, including recipes to enhance sexual pleasure. The silk manuscripts uncovered in this tomb include several of the classic works of ancient Chinese philosophy, as well as books on astronomy, astrology, fortune-telling, calendar making, politics, military affairs, ideology, culture, science, and technology. Moreover, the earliest preserved maps from China come from this tomb: one shows the region around the tomb; another, the borderland with the south; and the third, the location of military garrisons. The fact that the dead man had his library buried with him suggests that he wanted to show off his ability to read and write, a rare skill that was the hallmark of the upper levels of Chinese society.

The Former Han period was crucial to the preservation of the Chinese literature of the earlier Zhou and Warring States periods—works that would determine the form of literary production for millennia. The great philosophers of early China were closely connected to this literary flowering. A tradition developed that Confucius, who left no writings of his own, had edited earlier literary works, such as the *Book of Songs* (see Chapter 3). When Emperor Wu made Confucius's teachings the basis of education, these works became mandatory reading for all Chinese bureaucrats. They memorized, for example, the 305 poems of the *Book of Songs*, whose rhyming format later Chinese poets imitated. Tradition credits the founder of Daoism, Laozi, as the author of the *Classic of Integrity and the Way*, a discussion in verse of a tranquil and harmonious life. The work uses a vivid and powerful poetic imagery that has inspired many later writers both in China and abroad. It has been translated more often than almost any other work in world literature, with some forty English translations published since 1900. *Classic of Integrity and the Way* is a rather short

Literary Flowering Under the Han

civil service examination First instituted in Han China, a centrally administered test for applicants to government jobs that measures their qualifications; the goal was to base appointments on merit rather than political or other connections.

Papermakers

Early Chinese Paper
The invention of paper made writing materials much cheaper in China. This early example of paper was used for administrative purposes. Meant to be read from right to left and from top to bottom, it gives accounts of grain with the prices at the end of each line. (© 2011 The British Library (Or. 8212/499, recto).)

History shows us countless instances of one region's invention spreading worldwide over the centuries and becoming so common that we now take it for granted. One such invention was paper, developed in China in around 100 C.E. According to Chinese tradition, a courtier named Ts'ai Lun (tsy loon) invented paper and presented it to the Han emperor in 105 C.E. Earlier Chinese had written on bamboo strips or on expensive materials such as silk. Ts'ai Lun produced his new writing material from vegetable fibers, as well as tree bark, hemp, rags, and fishing nets, all of which were relatively cheap.

The making of paper involved several steps. The raw materials were ripped into fibers that were washed, cooked, and mixed into a thick liquid. Workers then dipped rectangular wooden frames into the liquid to form thin sheets, which they left to dry on the moulds before removing the resulting sheets and bleaching and cutting them. We know little of the individual workers involved, but they clearly had very specialized skills. Chinese sources praise several of them for having refined the product over the centuries. One gave paper a shining appearance, for example, and another discovered that using a special tree bark made the paper ideal for calligraphy, the art of writing that Chinese much admired. Production by Chinese papermakers was enormous: in around 800 C.E. the finance ministry alone required half a million sheets annually.

At first, the Chinese carefully guarded the technique of papermaking, but they could not contain its spread. Traveling monks took it to Korea and Japan, where people started to produce the material in the early seventh century C.E. Later that century, people in India read paper books written in Sanskrit. Chinese prisoners captured in the 793 C.E. Battle of Talas River (discussed in Chapter 9) taught people of the Middle East how to manufacture paper, and one year

Sima Qian, Father of Chinese Dynastic History

text, only about some five thousand Chinese characters long, but its influence on later Chinese and world literature has been immense.

The writing of history in prose flourished under the Han dynasty. China's counterpart to Greece's Herodotus was Sima Qian (c. 145–90 B.C.E.), whose *Records of the Historian* has defined our modern understanding of early Chinese history. The work ends with an autobiographical section in which Sima Qian dramatically recounts how he fell from the emperor's favor for backing a disgraced general. He refused to commit suicide, which would have been considered honorable, accepting instead the punishment of castration so that he could continue his writing. So massive that no full translation in a European language exists, Sima Qian's history has 130 chapters containing more than half a million characters.

Whereas Herodotus had to rely heavily on secondary accounts from such sources as Egyptian priests, Sima Qian could base his work on earlier Chinese writings, including

later Baghdad opened its first paper mill. Because the Middle East lacked the plant materials used in China, papermakers found substitutes, mostly linen rags. Middle Eastern craftsmen produced increasing supplies of the paper, which was useful for writing but also for wrapping and as decoration. Europeans at first imported the material from Middle Eastern centers of production such as Damascus, but by the fourteenth century they had founded paper mills of their own. The earlier materials for writing—tree bark in India and parchment in the Middle East and Europe, for example—had long-lasting popularity, but the relative cheapness of paper and its ease of use finally made it the dominant medium for writing. When Europeans invented the printing press in around 1450, paper's success as a writing tool was guaranteed.

For centuries, paper manufacture was the domain of artisans who worked in small workshops and produced sheets individually. In around 1800 two inventions revolutionized production. The primary basic material became wood pulp, which is much more abundant than the rags and bark in use earlier, and in 1798, the Frenchman Nicholas-Louis Robert invented a machine that combined all production steps. Once a time-consuming and expensive process, papermaking became relatively quick and cheap.

Paper's effect on culture was far reaching. Its use allowed the written word to spread much more widely, and the increased access to writing encouraged literacy. The use of paper for pamphlets and newspapers in the modern period made it possible for political ideologies to reach large audiences. Even today, when we rely on our computers for so much of our communication, it is hard to imagine a world without paper.

PAPERMAKING

c. 100 C.E.	Paper invented in China
300–400 C.E.	Paper becomes the dominant writing material in China
600–610 C.E.	First paper in Korea and Japan
751 C.E.	First paper in Central Asia
793 C.E.	First paper in the Middle East
1300–1400 C.E.	First paper mills in Europe
c. 1450 C.E.	European invention of the printing press
1798 C.E.	Frenchman Nicholas-Louis Robert invents the papermaking machine

QUESTIONS TO CONSIDER

1. What writing materials existed before the invention of paper?

2. How long did it take for papermaking to spread all over Eurasia?

3. What explains the success of paper over other writing materials?

For Further Information:
Bunch, Bryan H. *The History of Science and Technology: A Browser's Guide to the Great Discoveries, Inventions, and the People Who Made Them, from the Dawn of Time to Today*, 2004.
Tsuen-Hsuin, Tsien. "Paper and Printing." In vol. 5, *Science and Civilisation in China*. Edited by Joseph Needham, 1985.
Twitchett, Denis. *Printing and Publishing in Medieval China*. New York: Frederick C. Beil, 1983.

records of speeches and events, lists of rulers, and similar documents. From these sources, he developed the idea that a sequence of dynasties had always ruled all of China, a tradition that has continued in Chinese historical writing until modern times. He started with a mythological distant past, when sages brought civilization to humanity. Afterward the Xia, Shang, and Zhou dynasties (discussed in Chapter 3) ruled the country as a whole. He even calculated the dates when kings ruled and gave details on battles and other events. By suggesting that unified centralization under a dynasty was normal for the region, Sima Qian wanted to show that Han efforts at empire building were in keeping with tradition.

Sima Qian's history stops at around 100 B.C.E., but a family of scholars from the first century C.E. carried on the tradition of dynastic history. The father, Ban Biao (bahn bi-ah-ow), started a work called *History of the Former Han Dynasty*, and his son, Ban Gu (bahn gu), continued it. Finally, the emperor ordered Gu's sister, Ban Zhao (bahn jow), to finish the work, giving her access to the state archives. Ban Zhao took the narrative up until the interruption of the Han dynasty in the first decade C.E. Others continued the genre of dynastic history, and in 1747 C.E. the combined work of this family and subsequent authors amounted to 219 volumes, an unparalleled continuous record of the history of a country.

Ban Zhao   Ban Zhao (c. 45–120 C.E.) was a remarkable woman in a period when most families saw their daughters as little more than economic burdens. Coming from a scholarly family, she was well educated before her marriage at the age of fourteen. Still young when her husband died, she joined her brother at court at age thirty, an unusual step when widows of the time were expected to stay with their husbands' families. At court she gained influence with the empress Dou, who in 92 C.E. was accused of treason; her supporters, including Zhao's brother Ban Gu, were exiled or executed. As a woman, Zhao escaped severe punishment, and she was given the task of finishing the official history of the Han dynasty. At the same time she taught young women, including a girl called Deng, who later went on to become empress. Zhao's political influence was enormous. She also wrote numerous literary and scholarly works, which her daughter-in-law collected after Zhao's death. At first, her fame derived primarily from her *History*, but from about 800 C.E. on, her *Lessons for Women* gained enormous popularity (see Reading the Past: Women in Han China). Men used it to justify the inferior role of women in society, but in

READING THE PAST

Women in Han China

Ban Zhao's *Lessons for Women* of the early second century C.E. made her the most famous female author in Chinese history. Although she wrote the work as personal advice to women, men later used the book to prescribe how women ought to behave in relation to men.

A woman ought to have four qualifications: 1. womanly virtue, 2. womanly words, 3. womanly bearing, and 4. womanly work. Now what is called womanly virtue need not be brilliant ability, exceptionally different from others. Womanly words need be neither clever in debate nor keen in conversation. Womanly appearance requires neither a pretty nor a perfect face and form. Womanly work need not be work done more skillfully than that of others.

To guard carefully her chastity, to control circumspectly her behavior, in every motion to exhibit modesty, and to model each act on the best usage—this is womanly virtue.

To choose her words with care, to avoid vulgar language, to speak at appropriate times, and not to weary others with much conversation may be called the characteristics of womanly words.

To wash and scrub filth away, to keep cloths and ornaments fresh and clean, to wash the head and bathe the body regularly, and to keep the person free from

disgrace and filth may be called the characteristics of womanly bearing.

With wholehearted devotion to sew and to weave, to love not gossip and silly laughter, in cleanliness and order to prepare the wine and food for serving guests may be called the characteristics of womanly work.

These four qualifications characterize the greatest virtue of a woman. No woman can afford to be without them. In fact they are very easy to possess if a woman only treasure them in her heart. The ancients had a saying: "Is Love far off? If I desire love, then love is at hand." So can it be said of these qualifications.

Source: Victor H. Mair, ed., "Pan Chao, *Lessons for Women*," *The Columbia Anthology of Traditional Chinese Literature* (New York: Columbia University Press, 1994), 537–538.

EXAMINING THE EVIDENCE

1. What are the basic tenets of Ban Zhao's advice to women?

2. Why can this passage from the independent and politically influential Zhao be interpreted as an argument for women's secondary role in society?

reality Zhao had written practical advice to her daughters on how to survive in their husbands' family homes. When Zhao died shortly before 120 C.E., Empress Deng officially mourned her, an unusual honor for a commoner.

From 500 B.C.E. to 200 C.E., then, the foundations of Chinese culture were established in arts and sciences as well as politics. The chaos and disorder of the Spring and Autumn Period and the Warring States period inspired many of these developments. Hoping to stabilize their society, scholars developed philosophies with long-lasting influence, and politicians gave these philosophies practical applications in statecraft. Politically, imperial administrations were highly centralized and harsh, but the forces of decentralization also remained strong. Both the central administration and the local elites demanded much from the general population, and in the end their excessive demands may have led to the collapse of the entire system.

COUNTERPOINT
Tamil Kingdoms of South India

The development of large, highly centralized empires characterized much of Eurasian history in the centuries from 500 B.C.E. to 500 C.E. But imperial states were not universal in Asia. On the fringes of the empires in this chapter were societies with very different social and political structures whose populations created their own classical traditions. One such nonimperial region is the south of the Indian peninsula, the Tamil regions, which preserved ancient cultural traditions from southern India that differed significantly from those of the Aryas in the north.

FOCUS

How did southern Indian developments differ from those in other parts of Asia?

Rise of the Tamil Kingdoms

In around 250 B.C.E., the Mauryan emperor Ashoka referred to people in the Tamil regions as Cholas, Cheras, and Pandyas. At that time they were still organized as chiefdoms—that is, social hierarchies whose leaders had authority over small clan groups. Despite their relatively simple social and political organization, the archaeological remains show that these societies had far-reaching trade contacts. Megalithic burials appear throughout southern India. These large stone monuments take a variety of forms, including dolmen (two or more vertical stones supporting a horizontal slab), single standing stones, stone circles, and rock-cut chambers. This variety suggests that the builders had different cultural traditions, but the burials all contained iron tools and the same type of pottery. The tombs contained the bodies of one or more persons, each with small amounts of valuables such as carnelian beads and gold objects. They date from the entire first millennium B.C.E.; the most recent ones contain Roman coins from the last century B.C.E. The coins show that Tamil areas benefited as much from long-distance trade as the regions under imperial control to the north. South India's main export was pepper, which people used as condiment, food preservative, and medication for digestive problems. The Romans imported so much pepper that in around the year 77 C.E. the writer Pliny claimed it drained the empire's cash resources. He grumbled, "Pepper has nothing to recommend it in either fruit or berry. To think that its only pleasing quality is pungency and that we go all the way to India to get this!"[8]

Probably because a more centralized political structure benefited trade, small kingdoms with a limited number of cities arose in southern India. No empires developed, but competition among these kingdoms was fierce and warfare was a regular aspect of people's lives.

Tamil Regions of Southern India

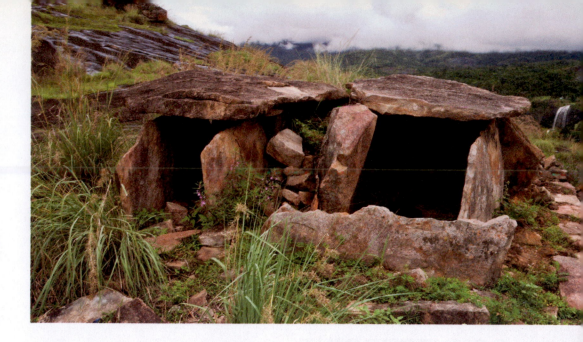

Dolmen in Southern India
The cultures of southern India were distinct from those in the north. Among the unique southern features is the use of megalithic constructions for burial, such as these dolmen from Marayoor in the state of Kerala, each made from four massive standing stone slabs with a fifth slab on top. Dolmen were used for burial for several centuries during the first millennium B.C.E., probably for the leaders of the communities who built and maintained them. (Dinodia Photos.)

Tamil Culture and Society

As in Archaic Greece, war inspired a literature that praised valor and glory in battle. Like Greek poets, Tamil poets composed works dealing with human emotions, such as love and friendship. Tamil poetry of the early centuries C.E. represents a rich South Asian tradition very distinct from the Sanskrit tradition of northern India, and it is still the pride of the region today. Tamil is a Dravidian language, fully distinct from the Indo-European languages of northern India. Although they had contacts with the north, until 250 C.E. Tamil writers resisted the influence of Sanskrit. The poets were mostly men, but thirty-two women have also been identified as authors. All belonged to the educated upper class, and some traveled from court to court to recite their work. One of the most renowned was the poet Auvaiyar. Fifty-nine of her poems are preserved, many of them in praise of King Atiyaman, at whose court she resided.

Contemporary Indians from the north saw the Tamils as unsophisticated barbarians, and modern scholars long ignored their literature. But today, scholars appreciate Tamil poetry's sophistication and its portrayals of the strength and nobility of human emotions under the hard conditions of incessant warfare. In this example, a wife mourns a dying warrior:

> I cannot cry out,
> I'm afraid of tigers,
> I cannot hold you,
> your chest is too wide
> for my lifting.
>
> Death
> has no codes
> and has dealt you wrong,
> may he
> shiver as I do!
>
> Hold my wrist
> of bangles,
> let's go to the shade
> of that hill.
> Just try and walk a little.[9]

The poems shed light on the position of women in Tamil society. They assign married women with children a positive role, representing them as a great asset to their husbands.

The poems portray widows, however, in a negative way. Widows were forced to lead an ascetic life to reduce the threat to others they were believed to pose. Poems suggest that they shaved their heads, slept on stone beds, and ate poor food.

The poems also clearly distinguish the various livelihoods practiced in southern India. Each depended on a specific natural environment—some groups gathered and hunted, others fished, others herded animals, and some farmed the fields. A fifth group made a living from trade. All the groups started out organized as clans, but as trade grew and cities developed, clans gave way to urban social hierarchies.

Political leaders in southern India seized control of the trade because of the wealth it produced. The poetry they sponsored in their courts celebrated their rule as kings, placing them at the center of society and honoring their military valor. Their power is reflected in the enormous size of their megalithic burial tombs, which required massive construction efforts. Although Tamil culture was exposed to influences from the north, it maintained its independence for centuries. In many ways, the grandeur of its culture equaled that of the great empires of Asia, but the kingdoms that produced Tamil culture were much less centralized and complex. Because great empires tend to dominate our view of the past, we sometimes get the false impression that only empires can develop enduring and influential cultural traditions. The Tamil kingdoms of ancient India prove this impression wrong.

Conclusion

When Dashafota carved the second-century-C.E. inscription translated at the start of this chapter, he knew that his king, Kanishka II, ruled one of a string of empires in Eurasia. In the east, the empires covered large parts of India, Central Asia, and China, and in each of these regions the teachings of great thinkers from the fifth to first centuries B.C.E. profoundly influenced later history. The Buddha and Confucius, among many others, had reacted to the tumultuous social and political conditions of their lifetimes, focusing on personal behavior and responsibility. The empires that arose after their deaths integrated their revolutionary religions and philosophies into ideas about the state, introducing a common ruling ideology to vast territories with multiple cultural traditions. Prescriptions for proper individual behavior and personal development could spread into regions with very different environments: nomads from the Central Asian steppe, for example, adopted teachings the Buddha had developed in the forested regions of northern India. Because every individual was part of a large state, new ideologies could define each person's role and responsibilities.

Although empires promoted the spread of new teachings, political centralization was not a precondition for cultural flowering. In south India too competing Tamil kingdoms developed enduring cultural traditions. Also, while the great empires of this period succumbed to the forces of decentralization, the traditions they had promoted survived and spread over all of Asia, a process aided by the continent's commercial connections. The multiplicity of ideas and traditions was never abandoned, and a myriad of religious teachings and philosophies coexisted in this world. When we turn next to the spread of the Roman Empire in western Eurasia, we will see similar cultural and religious innovations whose impact also persists today.

NOTES

1. Sten Konow, "The Ara Inscription of Kanishka II: The Year 41," *Epigraphica Indica* 14 (1917): 143 (with slight changes).
2. Ainslee T. Embree, ed., *Sources of Indian Tradition*, 2d ed. (New York: Columbia University Press, 1988), 1:144.
3. Ibid., 1:282.
4. Plutarch, "Life of Alexander," 62, 4.

5. *Sources of Indian Tradition*, 1:148.
6. Leonard Nathan, *The Transport of Love* (Berkeley: University of California Press, 1976), 83.
7. Confucius, *Analects* 15, 17, *Chinese Civilization: A Sourcebook*, 2d. ed., trans. Patricia Buckley Ebrey (New York: The Free Press, 1993), 18.
8. Pliny, *Natural History* 12.14, trans. H. Rackham (Cambridge, MA: Harvard University Press, 1968), 4:21.
9. Paul Davis et al., eds., *The Bedford Anthology of World Literature* (Boston: Bedford/St. Martin's, 2004), Book 2, 222–223.

RESOURCES FOR RESEARCH

India: Thinkers, Traders, and Courtly Cultures, 500 B.C.E.–500 C.E.

This period is discussed in numerous historical surveys of India. Because Buddhism and Hinduism had a long and continuing influence, many books treat the early developments of these religions within a long-term context.

Avari, Burjor. *India, the Ancient Past: A History of the Indian Sub-continent from c. 7000 B.C. to A.D. 1200.* 2007.
Basham, A. L., ed. *A Cultural History of India.* 1997.
Basham, A. L. *The Wonder That Was India: A Survey of the Culture of the Indian Sub-continent Before the Coming of the Muslims.* 1981.
*Embree, Ainslee T., ed. *Sources of Indian Tradition*, 2d ed., vol. 1. 1988.
* Internet Indian history sourcebook: http://www.fordham.edu/halsall/india/indiasbook.html.
Keown, Damien. *Buddhism: A Very Short Introduction.* 1996.
Knott, Kim. *Hinduism: A Very Short Introduction.* 1998.
Kulke, Hermann, and Dietmar Rothermund. *A History of India*, 3d ed. 1998.

The Kushan Peoples of Central Asia, 100 B.C.E.–233 C.E.

The Kushan Empire is often discussed within the wider context of the histories of India or Central Asia.

Frye, R. *The Heritage of Central Asia: From Antiquity to the Turkish Expansion.* 1996.
Harmatta, János, ed. *History of Civilizations of Central Asia.* Vol. 2, *The Development of Sedentary and Nomadic Civilizations: 700 B.C. to A.D. 250.* 1994.
Liu, Xinru. *Ancient India and Ancient China: Trade and Religious Exchanges A.D. 1–600.* 1988.
(A rough guide to Kushan history): http://www.kushan.org.
(For a selection of Kushan artworks): Heilbrunn timeline of art history. http://www.metmuseum.org/toah/hd/kush/hd_kush.htm.

China's First Empires: The Qin and Han Dynasties, 221 B.C.E.–220 C.E.

As is true for India, discussions of this period appear in various general histories of China. Because of the continuing impact of ancient Chinese philosophers, their ideas are often discussed in a long-term context.

Clements, Jonathan. *Confucius: A Biography.* 2004.
*de Bary, Wm. Theodore, ed. *Sources of Chinese Tradition.* 1999.
*Ebrey, Patricia Buckley, ed. *Chinese Civilization: A Sourcebook*, 2d ed. 1993.
Gascoine, Bamber. *A Brief History of the Dynasties of China.* 2003.
Hansen, Valerie. *The Open Empire: A History of China to 1600.* 2000.
(For a collection of ancient Chinese textual sources): Internet East Asian sourcebook. http://www.fordham.edu/halsall/eastasia/eastasiasbook.html.
*Mair, Victor H., ed. *The Columbia Anthology of Traditional Chinese Literature.* 1994.
Portal, Jane, ed. *The First Emperor: China's Terracotta Army.* 2007.
*Sima Qian. *The First Emperor: Selections from the *Historical Records. Edited by K. E. Brashier. Translated by Raymond Dawson. 2007.
Wei-ming, Tu. "Confucius and Confucianism," in the *New Encyclopaedia Britannica*, 15th ed., vol. 16. 1997.

COUNTERPOINT: Tamil Kingdoms of South India

Many books on India also discuss the Tamil area. The first two listed here translate numerous Tamil poems.

*Hart, George L., and Hank Heifetz, trans. and eds. *The Four Hundred Songs of War and Wisdom.* 1999.
*Ramanujan, A. K. *Poems of Love and War.* 1985.
Ray, H. P. *The Archaeology of Seafaring in Ancient South Asia.* 2003.
Thapar, Romila. *Early India from the Origins to A.D. 1300.* 2002.

* Primary source.

▶ **For additional primary sources from this period**, see *Sources of Crossroads and Cultures*.

▶ **For Web sites, images, and documents related to topics in this chapter**, see Make History at bedfordstmartins.com/smith.

The major global development in this chapter ▶ The revolutionary religious and cultural developments in India and China that took place between 500 B.C.E. and 500 C.E. and remained fundamental to the history of Asia.

IMPORTANT EVENTS

c. 600–500 B.C.E.	Laozi, who inspired Daoism
c. 563–480 B.C.E.	Siddhartha Gautama, the Buddha
551–479 B.C.E.	Confucius
c. 540–468 B.C.E.	Vardhamana Mahavira, who inspired Jainism
480–221 B.C.E.	Period of the Warring States in China
c. 390–338 B.C.E.	Lord Shang Yang, who developed Legalism
321–185 B.C.E.	Mauryan Empire
c. 260 B.C.E.	Mauryan Emperor Ashoka converts to Buddhism
221–206 B.C.E.	Qin Empire
206 B.C.E.–220 C.E.	Han Empire
c. 145–90 B.C.E.	Chinese historian Sima Qian
141–87 B.C.E.	Reign of Han emperor Wu
c. 100 B.C.E.	Migration of Yuehzi from western China
c. 45–120 C.E.	Chinese historian Ban Zhao
c. 50–233 C.E.	Kushan Empire
c. 100–123 C.E.	Reign of Kushan emperor Kanishka II
c. 100–250 C.E.	Organization of Tamil literature
c. 320–540 C.E.	Gupta Empire
c. 390–470 C.E.	Indian poet Kalidasa

CHAPTER OVERVIEW QUESTIONS

1. How did new social circumstances stimulate changes in religious beliefs and cultures?
2. What processes encouraged close connections among the various regions of Asia?
3. In what ways did the revolutionary thinkers discussed here have a lasting impact on the histories of the regions they inhabited and beyond?

SECTION FOCUS QUESTIONS

1. How did the new religious ideas of the last centuries B.C.E. suit the social and political structures of India?
2. How did the geographical location and trade relations of the Kushan Empire affect its cultural traditions?
3. How did the early Chinese philosophers come to have a long-lasting influence on the intellectual development of the region?
4. How did southern Indian developments differ from those in other parts of Asia?

MAKING CONNECTIONS

1. What ideas that emerged in classical India and China remained fundamental to the later histories of these countries?
2. How would you describe the cultural and intellectual interactions among the various Asian cultures discussed in this chapter?
3. How did the cultural innovations in India and China compare with those in Greece of the first millennium B.C.E. (see Chapter 5)?

KEY TERMS

asceticism (p. 174)
bodhisattva (p. 176)
civil service examination (p. 192)
classical (p. 173)
dharma (p. 175)
monastery (p. 175)
nirvana (p. 175)
sangha (p. 175)
Silk Road (p. 181)
stupa (p. 175)

AT A CROSSROADS ▲

Over the centuries from 500 B.C.E. to 500 C.E., Rome grew from a small village in the heart of the Italian peninsula into the crossroads of a vast empire dominating all of western Eurasia. Pictured here is the Roman Forum, the ancient square that was for centuries the center of Roman public life. Temples and government buildings surround the Forum, and looming in the background is the Colosseum, a massive amphitheater constructed for gladiatorial contests and other public spectacles. Completed in 80 C.E., the Colosseum is now one of imperial Rome's most iconic symbols. (Raimund Koch/Getty Images.)

The Unification of Western Eurasia

500 B.C.E.–500 C.E.

I n around 100 C.E., the Roman historian Tacitus (c. 56–117 C.E.) described how inhabitants of Britain, encouraged by the Roman governor Agricola, took on the habits of their Roman occupiers:

> To induce a people, hitherto scattered, uncivilized and therefore prone to fight, to grow pleasurably inured to peace and ease, Agricola gave private encouragement and official assistance to the building of temples, public squares, and private mansions. He praised the keen and scolded the slack, and competition to gain honor from him was as effective as compulsion. Furthermore, he trained the sons of the chiefs in the liberal arts and expressed a preference for British natural ability over the trained skill of the Gauls. The result was that in place of distaste for the Latin language came a passion to command it. In the same way, our national dress came into favor and the toga was everywhere to be seen.[1]

The Romans built their empire through military conquest, taking over new lands in order to dominate them. Roman expansion spread Roman culture, for, as this passage from Tacitus makes clear, conquered peoples were often as eager to adopt Roman practices as the Romans were to encourage their adoption. From North Africa to Britain and from the Atlantic coast to the Euphrates River, numerous peoples were "Romanized" to some degree, leaving behind aspects of their previous cultural identities to acquire the benefits of participating in the empire. This process worked both ways, because incorporating new cultures into the empire changed what it meant to be Roman.

The impact of the interactions between Romans and the peoples they conquered was all the more profound because the Romans sought to transform the territories they acquired. After each new conquest, they reorganized the subject region by introducing Roman administration, politics, social practices, and technology. Conquered territories were thus fully

BACKSTORY

As the Mauryan, Gupta, Kushan, Qin, and Han empires were bringing vast areas of Asia under one rule (see Chapter 6), a similar political unification occurred in western Eurasia, merging two regions with previously separate histories. In the Middle East and eastern North Africa, empires had existed since the second millennium B.C.E. New Kingdom Egypt, Nubia, Assyria, and Persia, for example, had all brought large and diverse populations under their rule (see Chapter 4). However, the peoples of the western Atlantic zone of modern-day Europe and the Mediterranean areas to its south had never known political union. The citizens of Rome would fundamentally change that situation, creating an empire that would profoundly influence the history of the world.

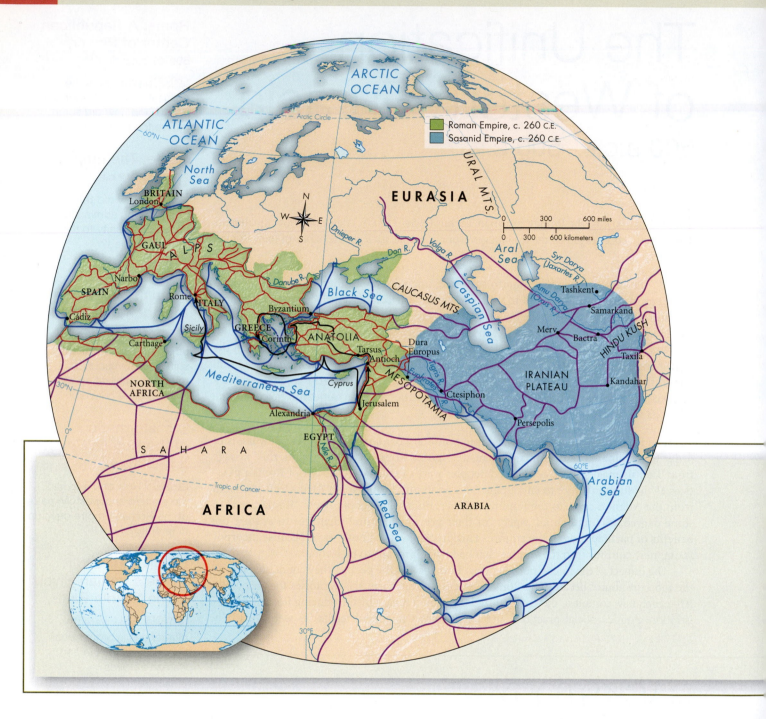

Roman Empire, c. 260 C.E.
Sasanid Empire, c. 260 C.E.

ARCTIC OCEAN

ATLANTIC OCEAN

Arctic Circle

60°N

North Sea

BRITAIN
London

GAUL

ALPS

Narbo

SPAIN

Cádiz

Rome
ITALY

Sicily

Carthage

NORTH AFRICA

30°N

Mediterranean Sea

SAHARA

AFRICA

0°

EGYPT

Nile R.

Danube R.

Dnieper R.

Black Sea

GREECE
Corinth

Byzantium

ANATOLIA

Cyprus

Alexandria

Jerusalem

EURASIA

URAL MTS.

Don R.

Volga R.

CAUCASUS MTS.

Aral Sea

Caspian Sea

Syr Darya (Jaxartes R.)

Amu Darya (Oxus R.)

Tashkent

Samarkand

Merv

Bactra

HINDU KUSH

Taxila

Dura Europus

Tarsus
Antioch

MESOPOTAMIA

Euphrates R.

Tigris R.

Ctesiphon

IRANIAN PLATEAU

Kandahar

Persepolis

60°E

Red Sea

Tropic of Cancer

ARABIA

Arabian Sea

30°E

300   600 miles

300   600 kilometers

N W E S

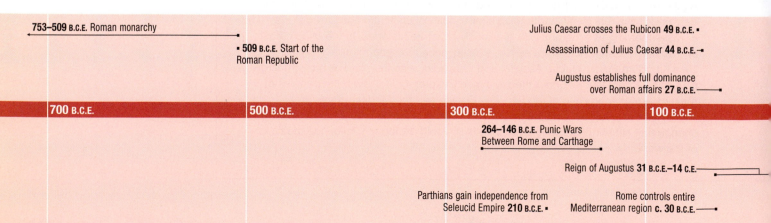

753–509 B.C.E. Roman monarchy

■ **509 B.C.E.** Start of the Roman Republic

Julius Caesar crosses the Rubicon **49 B.C.E.** ■

Assassination of Julius Caesar **44 B.C.E.** ■

Augustus establishes full dominance over Roman affairs **27 B.C.E.** —

700 B.C.E.	**500 B.C.E.**	**300 B.C.E.**	**100 B.C.E.**

264–146 B.C.E. Punic Wars Between Rome and Carthage

Reign of Augustus **31 B.C.E.–14 C.E.** —

Parthians gain independence from Seleucid Empire **210 B.C.E.** ■

Rome controls entire Mediterranean region **c. 30 B.C.E.** —

integrated into Roman political and administrative structures. In time, subject peoples gained the opportunity to become Roman citizens. Men from the provinces could even become emperors, which has no parallel in the earlier empires we have studied. Only eighty-four years after the death of the first emperor, Augustus, a man from Spain, Trajan (r. 98–117 C.E.), took the highest office in Rome, and many other provincials later attained the same position.

At the heart of the vast empire was the city of Rome. From its foundation—traditionally said to be in 753 B.C.E.—to its establishment as an imperial capital, Rome underwent a remarkable political evolution. After a period of rule by kings, the most common type of government in the ancient world, the Romans set up institutions, which were republics with the aim of preventing one man from holding all power. These included a Senate as a place of deliberation, rotating officials with executive powers, term limits, and other safeguards against tyranny. In spite of these carefully crafted institutions, the Roman Republic failed and descended into the chaos of civil wars until one man, Augustus, assumed full control in around 27 B.C.E.

Because the Romans were so successful and left behind so much evidence of their activities, Rome has become the foremost example of an ancient empire. Indeed, the term *empire* itself derives from the Romans' designation, *imperium*, which means "rule." Many Republican institutions are still held up today as ideals of representative government. Even though Roman history itself shows how these institutions can fail, the principles behind them continue to inspire admiration.

The standardization of imperial practices that Tacitus evokes in this chapter's opening lines also explains the success of a new religion, Christianity. Christianity originated in a small community in the Roman Middle East, finding its early adherents among the lower classes and the powerless. Spreading from the Middle East via the empire's network of roads

MAPPING THE WORLD

The Roman and Sasanid Empires, c. 260 C.E.

In around 260 C.E., nearly all of western Eurasia was in the hands of two large imperial powers, Rome and Sasanid Persia. The two empires had risen through very different processes: the citizens of Rome had annexed more territory over the centuries, whereas the Sasanids inherited the territories of the Parthians and earlier empire builders. Both controlled numerous peoples with varied cultures and histories, however, and both were home to intellectual and religious innovations that would radically affect the later histories of the regions. Despite their often hostile interactions, Rome and Sasanid Persia sustained a flourishing trade, one that included many luxury products from countries farther afield. Thus, although their rivalry was intense, they together forged a large exchange network for goods and ideas.

ROUTES ▼

— Major Roman road

— Caravan route

— Maritime trade route

→ Travels of Paul, c. 40–70 C.E.

- **100–200 C.E.** Pax Romana; height of the Roman Empire
- **313 C.E.** Constantine issues Edict of Milan, legalizing Christianity
- **410 C.E.** German tribes sack Rome

100 C.E.   **300 C.E.**   **500 C.E.**

- c. **4 B.C.E.–30 C.E.** Life of Jesus
- **224 C.E.** Sasanids overthrow Parthians
- **395 C.E.** Roman Empire divided into eastern and western parts
- **212 C.E.** Caracalla grants citizenship to nearly all free inhabitants of the empire
- **476 C.E.** German leader Odoacer forces last western Roman emperor to step down

and sea routes, it eventually became the official state religion, and its institutions merged with those of the state. Once this happened, the power of the state helped bring Christianity to all of the empire's peoples.

As powerful and important as the Roman Empire was, it was not without its peers, and ultimately it could not defeat its rivals to the east, the Parthians and Sasanids from Iran. Although in the history of Europe the Roman Empire was a watershed, in a global perspective it was one of a series of world empires that stretched across Eurasia from around 500 B.C.E. to 500 C.E. It is worth remembering that the Kushan emperor, Kanishka II (discussed in Chapter 6), placed the rulers of China, India, and Parthia on the same level as the emperor of Rome.

OVERVIEW
QUESTIONS

The major global development in this chapter: The unification of western Eurasia under the Roman Empire.

As you read, consider:

1. How are Roman political institutions still important to us today?

2. How did the Romans face the challenges of creating and maintaining an empire?

3. What impact did Rome have on the lives of the people it conquered?

4. How did Christianity's rise benefit from the Roman Empire?

5. What were the limits of Roman imperialism?

Rome: A Republican Center of Power 500–27 B.C.E.

FOCUS

What were the political ideals of Republican Rome, and how did some outlive the Republic itself?

In a sequence of increasingly far-ranging campaigns that started in the fifth century B.C.E. and continued into the second century C.E., Rome established military dominance over a large territory encircling the Mediterranean Sea and extending far inland into Atlantic Europe. Unlike Alexander of Macedonia, who had subdued the populations of an enormous landmass in one fell swoop (see Chapter 5), the Romans engaged in a long series of wars against neighbors ranging from tribal leagues to powerful unified states. The wars were ruthless, and more than once Rome seemed close to annihilation. But the perseverance and skill of Roman soldiers always won out in the end.

Rome's initial military success arose under a political system different from that of surrounding states. After an initial period of monarchy, traditionally said to have lasted from the founding of Rome in 753 to the expulsion of the last king in 509 B.C.E., Rome was officially a republic in which citizens shared power and elected their officials. In theory, all citizens represented Rome, so it was unimportant who held positions of power. In reality, however, social tensions created political division and conflict in Republican Rome. The acquisition of foreign territories and their wealth only exacerbated these problems, because social and economic inequality increased and military leaders played an ever greater role in domestic politics. These tensions underlay the entire Republican period and ultimately led to the collapse of Republican institutions and establishment of an imperial government.

From Village to World Empire

The origins of Rome are shrouded in mystery, but we know that in the eighth to fifth centuries B.C.E. various Latin-speaking people inhabited the center of Italy, a mountainous peninsula where a variety of groups shared power. In the north Celtic speakers dominated, just south of them the Etruscans had a powerful kingdom, and elsewhere tribal leagues held sway. Outsiders had also established colonies in Italy, especially in the south. Some were Greek, and others were settlements of the important North African city of Carthage, itself a colony of the Phoenicians.

In the late fifth century B.C.E., Rome—still a small settlement then—took advantage of Etruscan decline to start a sustained period of expansion fueled by the fighting skills of its landowning citizens. Progress was initially slow, but by 264 B.C.E. Rome was master of most of Italy (see Map 7.1). The successes altered the city's strategic position. Like the Spartans in Greece, the Romans originally concentrated on acquiring nearby territory. The conquest of Italy led the Romans to look across the sea to Sicily. There they faced a major foreign power, North African Carthage, which owned colonies on the island. Understanding that Carthage's power derived from its navy, the Romans built a fleet to confront their rival. They did so with great technological ingenuity, equipping battleships with platforms where foot soldiers could fight using the same techniques they used on land. Thus, they applied a Roman strength, their infantry, to an arena in which Carthage had the seeming advantage.

Punic Wars

Rome and Carthage fought three long wars between 264 and 146 B.C.E., called the Punic Wars after the Latin word *Poeni*, Phoenician. Rome won the First Punic War (264–241 B.C.E.), but imposed such harsh penalties that Carthage felt compelled to react. At the start of the Second Punic War (218–201 B.C.E.), its general, Hannibal, led an army to Italy through Spain, famously crossing the Alps with two dozen elephants, and ransacked the countryside, defeating Roman opposition repeatedly. He spent sixteen years in Italy but could not attack Rome itself because of the staunch resistance by the inhabitants of the surrounding area. The delay caused by this resistance allowed Rome's citizens to regroup, and after many bloody battles the Roman general Scipio Africanus crushed Hannibal on North African soil in 202 B.C.E. Following the Third Punic War (149–146 B.C.E.), Rome gained control over all of Carthage's territories on the Mediterranean islands, in North Africa, and in Spain. Thus Rome became the dominant military power in the western Mediterranean by 146 B.C.E.

Wars in the East

Meanwhile, in the eastern Mediterranean, the great empire of Alexander of Macedonia had split into rival kingdoms. Rome entered the region partly because some of the rival states sought the support of the Roman armies' superior fighting skills. Rome showed its ruthlessness in 146 B.C.E. by annihilating both Carthage and the Greek city of Corinth, slaughtering the men and enslaving the women and children. The whole Greek world was shocked by Rome's violence. By 100 B.C.E. much of Greece and Anatolia had become Roman territory.

Continued Expansion

Inspired by the wealth and glory that incessant campaigns could bring, ambitious Roman military leaders looked for new territories to conquer. One such leader, Julius Caesar (100–44 B.C.E.), marched his troops into Gaul, the region north of the Alps as far as Britain, turning the Atlantic zone into his personal power base. Soon afterward, in 31 B.C.E., the general and future first Roman emperor, Octavian (Augustus, 63 B.C.E.–14 C.E.), annexed Egypt and pushed Roman territory until it reached natural borders that his armies could more easily defend. In the south the Sahara Desert provided such an impassable barrier, and in the east the Euphrates River and Syrian Desert formed another natural border. In the north, Octavian conquered the passes through the Alps to

MAP 7.1

Roman Expansion Under the Republic, 500 B.C.E.–14 C.E.

From a village founded in around 500 B.C.E. in the center of Italy, over the next five hundred years Rome grew into a world power that encircled the Mediterranean and reached far into modern western Europe. At first, the expansion took place under the leadership of the Republic, with elected officials and generals. However, especially in the last century B.C.E., it gave ambitious men an opportunity to build power bases, which they used to force their will upon the people and institutions of Rome. This process ended when Octavian, who annexed the wealthy country of Egypt, acquired every powerful office and became Rome's first emperor, Augustus (r. 27 B.C.E.–14 C.E.).

the Danube so that the river could serve as a frontier. Along the Atlantic coast in the west, Rome's territory extended from Gibraltar to the Rhine (see again Map 7.1). Its control established, the Roman Empire would turn the regions within these borders into a coherent political whole, dominated by Roman culture, lifestyles, and livelihoods.

Society and Politics in the Republic

The essential unit of Roman society was the family, whose head was the oldest man, the ***pater familias***. Groups of families considered themselves to be descendants of a common ancestor, and each such group had its own religious and social practices. The family incorporated not only those related by blood but also slaves and what the Romans called **clients**. The latter

pater familias The head of a Roman household, with full power over other family members and clients.

client Within the early Roman social structure, a person who was economically dependent on an influential family head.

were persons of a lower social rank who were economically attached to the family and received assistance from the pater familias. In return he expected clients to support him, by voting for him in an election, for example, or even serving in his private militia. The pater familias had unrestricted powers over the other members of the family. Adult sons with children of their own did not have an independent legal status and could not own property. Thus, some men with very prominent official positions could be excluded from legal transactions while their fathers were still alive. Hence, the Roman family was like a miniature society, with the eldest male holding absolute authority over all of his dependents.

Women had a secondary role, although over time they gained financial power. At first, in the usual marriage a woman entered her husband's family and was under full control of its leader. But in the second century B.C.E. so-called free marriages became common: a married woman remained a member of her father's family and inherited a share of his property. Upon her father's death she became financially independent, and several affluent women acquired much influence in this way.

Wealthy family heads formed a hereditary aristocratic class, the **patricians**, who in Rome's early days held all political power. Most people did not belong to patrician families, however, especially the increasing number of people from conquered territories who had moved to Rome. These other folk, the **plebeians**, could not claim descent from the ancestors of the patrician families or participate in their religious rites. In the first two centuries of the Republic the plebeians' struggle to acquire political influence and their share of public assets dominated Rome's political and social life.

When the Romans ended the monarchy and created the Republic in 509 B.C.E., they sought a balance of power between the people and government officials, or **magistrates**. But the resulting system was less representative than that of classical Athens (see Chapter 5). Although all citizens sat in various assemblies and had the right to elect magistrates, real power was in the hands of the **Senate**, whose members were mostly patricians with lifelong terms. Senators voted on laws, represented Rome in foreign affairs, and appointed the governors of provinces. Because they nominated men for election by the assembly, they controlled access to the highest offices. Thus the Senate was a representative body only in the sense that it represented the interests of Rome's political and social elites.

The Romans were, however, more generous in granting citizenship than the Greeks, who limited citizenship to male landowners. Originally, only free inhabitants of Rome could become citizens, but in the early period of the Republic, people of conquered Italian territories, freed slaves, and others regularly became citizens. Only men were full citizens, because the status involved military service and political participation, and women could not participate in either of these spheres.

To limit the power of magistrates, the Romans restricted them to one-year terms and placed two men in each office. The two most prominent magistrates were the **consuls**. Patricians monopolized the office of consul until 367 B.C.E., when plebeians forced passage of a law requiring one consul to be from their ranks. As the state and the number of people governed expanded, other magistracies had to be created to carry out special tasks, but the concept of power sharing between two men remained a firm rule. The only exception occurred in times of crisis, when the Senate gave absolute power to a single magistrate, the dictator. The term *dictator* did not have the negative meaning then that it has today. He was someone who could make decisions on his own, and he returned to his former status after six months or when the emergency had passed, whichever came first.

In the struggle between plebeians and patricians, Rome's expansion tilted the balance of power in the plebeians' favor. Rome's wars of conquest and the need to control conquered territories continually increased reliance on the military. The growing army depended on plebeian recruits, and the plebeians used this to extract concessions from patricians. They forced the Senate to create the new government office of **tribune** to protect plebeians from arbitrary decisions by patrician magistrates. Tribunes could veto (a Latin term that means "I prohibit") acts by consuls and the Senate. At this time the plebeians also received their own temples, as well as their own assembly.

The Roman Family

Political Structure

patrician The Roman aristocratic class.

plebeian The Roman class of commoners.

magistrate A Roman government official.

Senate The Roman assembly of elderly men, usually patricians, whose main function was to deliberate important issues of state and give advice.

consul In the Roman Republic, one of the two highest magistrates.

tribune The Roman magistrate whose role was to protect the interests of the plebeians.

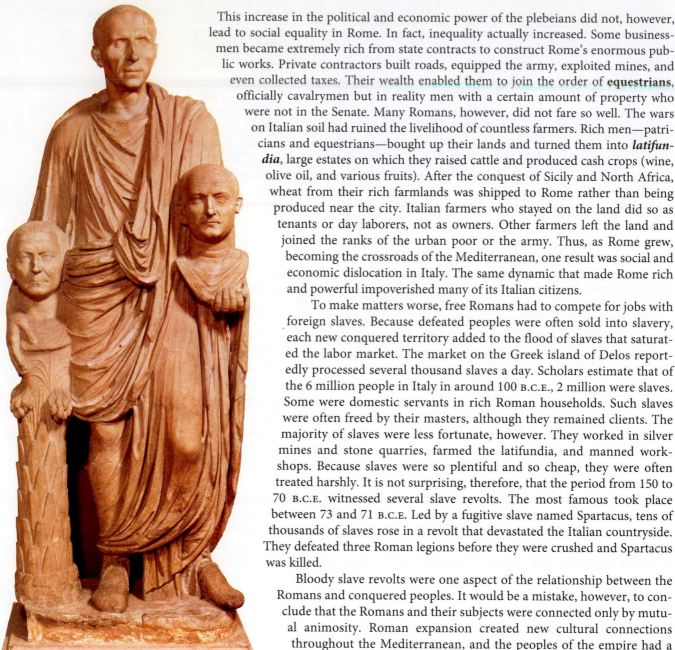

Statue of a Roman Patrician

In this typical example of Roman sculpture dating from around 25 B.C.E., the subject wears a toga that identifies him as a senator. Because family was so crucial for patrician leaders' social status, he holds the busts of his ancestors in his hands. (Scala/Art Resource, NY.)

Greek Cultural Influences

This increase in the political and economic power of the plebeians did not, however, lead to social equality in Rome. In fact, inequality actually increased. Some businessmen became extremely rich from state contracts to construct Rome's enormous public works. Private contractors built roads, equipped the army, exploited mines, and even collected taxes. Their wealth enabled them to join the order of **equestrians**, officially cavalrymen but in reality men with a certain amount of property who were not in the Senate. Many Romans, however, did not fare so well. The wars on Italian soil had ruined the livelihood of countless farmers. Rich men—patricians and equestrians—bought up their lands and turned them into *latifundia*, large estates on which they raised cattle and produced cash crops (wine, olive oil, and various fruits). After the conquest of Sicily and North Africa, wheat from their rich farmlands was shipped to Rome rather than being produced near the city. Italian farmers who stayed on the land did so as tenants or day laborers, not as owners. Other farmers left the land and joined the ranks of the urban poor or the army. Thus, as Rome grew, becoming the crossroads of the Mediterranean, one result was social and economic dislocation in Italy. The same dynamic that made Rome rich and powerful impoverished many of its Italian citizens.

To make matters worse, free Romans had to compete for jobs with foreign slaves. Because defeated peoples were often sold into slavery, each new conquered territory added to the flood of slaves that saturated the labor market. The market on the Greek island of Delos reportedly processed several thousand slaves a day. Scholars estimate that of the 6 million people in Italy in around 100 B.C.E., 2 million were slaves. Some were domestic servants in rich Roman households. Such slaves were often freed by their masters, although they remained clients. The majority of slaves were less fortunate, however. They worked in silver mines and stone quarries, farmed the latifundia, and manned workshops. Because slaves were so plentiful and so cheap, they were often treated harshly. It is not surprising, therefore, that the period from 150 to 70 B.C.E. witnessed several slave revolts. The most famous took place between 73 and 71 B.C.E. Led by a fugitive slave named Spartacus, tens of thousands of slaves rose in a revolt that devastated the Italian countryside. They defeated three Roman legions before they were crushed and Spartacus was killed.

Bloody slave revolts were one aspect of the relationship between the Romans and conquered peoples. It would be a mistake, however, to conclude that the Romans and their subjects were connected only by mutual animosity. Roman expansion created new cultural connections throughout the Mediterranean, and the peoples of the empire had a profound and multifaceted impact on Roman life. Among the slaves the Romans brought to Italy were educated Greeks who became physicians, secretaries, and tutors. The Romans were skilled warriors, but they had given little attention to intellectual pursuits such as philosophy and the arts. Thus, when they encountered Greek culture, first in Greek colonies in Italy and later in Greece itself and the Hellenistic world, they eagerly absorbed many elements of it. A Roman poet of the first century B.C.E. wrote: "Greece was captured but it captivated its wild conqueror."[2] The Romans imitated Greek styles in their buildings and artwork. They equated Roman gods with Greek ones: the Roman Jupiter with the Greek Zeus, the Roman goddess Minerva with the Greek Athena, and so on. They adopted Greek religious rites. Elite Roman children learned the Greek language, and Greek scholars came to Rome to form philosophical schools of the type that had existed earlier in the Hellenistic world. The Stoics especially had great success (see

Chapter 5). Not all Romans appreciated these influences, and some wrote that they inspired weakness and decadence. But the trend could not be stopped, and familiarity with Greek culture became a hallmark of Roman education. At the same time that the Romans transformed the political institutions and physical infrastructure of their provinces, contact with the Greek world forever altered Roman culture.

Thus expansion brought a host of changes in Roman life. Military success, however, did not bring economic equality or political stability. By 150 B.C.E., a small number of wealthy landowners, merchants, and entrepreneurs shared power, whereas the mass of the population was landless and had little political representation. A few politicians took up the cause of the poor, most famously Tiberius Gracchus (c. 163–133 B.C.E.). In 133 B.C.E. he became a tribune and tried to enforce an old law that no individual could cultivate more than about 300 acres (120 hectares) of land. The patrician owners of huge estates would not tolerate this, and a group of senators lynched Gracchus. This was the first in a long string of political assassinations, indications of the power struggles that would ultimately trigger the end of the Roman Republic.

Failure of the Republic

By 100 B.C.E. social tension and political intrigue pervaded Roman society. Individuals and families bought political influence with the wealth they looted from conquered regions. They broke the ancient rules on who could hold offices and for how long. Military men interfered in politics. Armies were often more loyal to their commanders than to the state, and commanders did not hesitate to use their armies to advance their personal political ambitions. Several civil wars broke out in the first century B.C.E., bringing enormous devastation and loss of life and draining the energy of the Roman people. By the end of the century, they were so war-weary that they granted one man, Octavian, supreme power.

Julius Caesar, who lived from 100 to 44 B.C.E., is a good example of the famous men—and some women—who struggled for power in the first century B.C.E. A member of an old, albeit not wealthy, Roman family, he started his political career by allying himself with powerful men to win a number of offices. He managed to gain the governorship of northern Italy, which he used as a springboard for the conquest of Gaul. His wars there from 58 to 50 B.C.E. were merciless—he exterminated entire tribes—and brought him unparalleled personal wealth.

Caesar used this wealth to broaden his political influence in Rome and to remain in elected offices despite legal restrictions. Others opposed him, however—at one point the Senate ordered him to lay down his army command. In response, on January 10, 49 B.C.E., Caesar led his troops across the Rubicon River, the northern border of Italy, which was an act of treason as no provincial army was allowed to pass that point. The ensuing civil war took Caesar and his army to distant Roman territories, and it was four years before he won the often brutal conflict. Back in Rome in 44 B.C.E., he tried to restore order, but he did not have time. On March 15—known in the Roman calendar as the Ides of March—opponents assassinated Caesar on his way to the Senate.

Not all people who lost their lives in these conflicts were leading politicians and military men. Another career steeped in intrigue was that of Marcus Tullius Cicero (106–43 B.C.E.). He was famous in his own day for the speeches he gave in prosecution or defense of public figures caught in political disputes. He devoted himself to philosophy, adopting Stoic values, and to poetry, and he wrote numerous letters (nine hundred of which are preserved). His speeches stand today as examples of great oratory, and already in antiquity people studied them to learn how to argue forcefully.

Roman Slave Tag
Roman slaves were clearly identified as someone's personal property and wore metal collars with tags attached such as the one shown here, dating to the fourth century C.E. The text written on it reads: "Stop me from running away and return me to my master, Viventius, who lives in Callistus's court." (©The Trustees of the British Museum/Art Resource, NY.)

Power Struggles and Civil Wars

equestrian The class of wealthy businessmen and landowners in ancient Rome, second only to the patricians in status and political influence.

latifundia Vast rural estates in ancient Rome whose owners employed a large number of tenant farmers and sometimes slaves.

Cicero's unhappy fate was the result of political misjudgment. After Caesar's death he attacked members of the powerful new coalition that grew around Octavian. They had him assassinated and displayed his head and hands on the speaker's platform in Rome.

Octavian (Augustus)

Caesar's assassination in 44 B.C.E. led to another thirteen-year-long civil war, fought in various battlefields throughout the Mediterranean. The population grew so tired of war and chaos that they did not object to one man taking control, as long as it would bring peace and stability. That man was Octavian, the creator of imperial rule in Rome. After crushing his opponents in 31 B.C.E., he developed a system in which he and his successors would exercise absolute control in practice, yet in theory would respect the old political institutions of the Roman Republic. Octavian obtained overall command of the army and of the provinces with the most important legions. He could propose and veto any legislation, overrule provincial governors, and sit with the highest magistrates, the consuls. In 27 B.C.E. the Romans awarded him the title *Augustus*, "noble one," suggesting he was closer to the gods than to humans.

Augustus's dominance of government was unprecedented in Roman history, but he cloaked his ambition by appearing to accumulate traditional Republican offices, which he held without the usual term limits. He called himself *princeps*, "the first citizen," not "king" or another title that would have indicated absolute rule. In that sense, Augustus was a master of diplomacy: he offered the war-weary people of Rome a new and efficient system of government without casting it as the monarchical system they had traditionally rejected.

Augustus's tactics won him the people's support and admiration, and in 2 B.C.E. they named him "father of the country," although he still claimed to be merely a consul. When he died in 14 C.E., he had ruled Rome as de facto emperor for forty-two years, and few Romans remembered life without him. Augustus's political acumen and the length of his reign contributed to the durability of the system of government he created. His successors would maintain it for the next two hundred years.

Rome: The Empire 27 B.C.E.–212 C.E.

FOCUS

How did the Roman Empire bring administrative and cultural unity to the vast territory it ruled?

Starting with Augustus, a succession of powerful Romans ruled an enormous territory that brought together numerous peoples with a variety of cultural backgrounds and traditions. A massive army enforced imperial control, but in a process known as Romanization, universal administrative and economic practices fused the regions of the Roman Empire into a cohesive whole. Retired Roman soldiers routinely moved to the provinces, as did others, and people from the provinces moved to Rome to work at running the empire. The system of government that dominated Roman life for several centuries became the archetype of an empire. Even though its structure contained weaknesses that would lead to its decline in the west, the Roman Empire was highly successful and fundamentally changed the histories of all the regions it controlled.

Emperors and Armies

With an emperor dominating a government that was still attached to its Republican roots, the Romans had to reorganize the other institutions of state. The Roman Senate lost its decision-making powers, but it retained important functions: senators filled the highest government and military offices, and the Senate acted as a court of law. The emperor decided who would receive magistracies, however, and the Senate always approved his choices.

The Emperor

The emperor exercised both military and civilian authority. As in the Republic, the military played a substantial role in Roman imperial politics. Thus the emperor's relationship to the army was pivotal, and most Roman emperors were active soldiers. The continuous campaigns sometimes extended the empire beyond its Augustan borders—in 43 C.E.,

MAP 7.2

Roman Expansion Under the Empire, 14–212 C.E.

Roman emperors attempted to enlarge the empire through repeated campaigns, but mostly they only succeeded in securing the borders along natural boundaries, such as the Sahara Desert and the Rhine and Danube rivers. Their activities consolidated Roman rule over the territory, however, and increased the integration of non-Italians into the imperial governmental structure. In certain periods, such as the second century C.E., Roman rule brought great stability and prosperity to a wide area.

for example, Claudius (r. 41—54 C.E.) annexed much of Britain—which could bring the emperor great wealth and glory (see Map 7.2). War could also lead to disaster, as when the Sasanid Persians captured the emperor Valerian (r. 253–260 C.E.) in 260 C.E. and tortured him to death (see Counterpoint: Rome's Iranian Rivals in the Middle East).

The emperor's civilian duties required his constant attention. He was flooded with requests for guidance and favors, and his answers, communicated by letter, had the force of law. The emperor controlled a massive treasury, which received income mostly from customs duties and taxes on sales, land, and agricultural products. The emperor also had enormous personal wealth, from his own estates, which he could extend by confiscating property, and from gifts by those who wished to obtain his favor. As the center of an imperial government that connected Rome to its provinces, the emperor had an unparalleled ability to shape the lives of Rome's citizens and subjects.

One way Roman emperors shaped Roman life was by commissioning extensive public works, many of which still stand today (see Lives and Livelihoods: Roman Engineers). They built majestic theaters and huge amphitheaters and erected triumphal arches to celebrate their military victories. They laid out forums—open places with temples, shops,

Public Works

Roman Engineers

Pont du Gard

The Romans are rightly famous for their engineering skills. A key concern was guaranteeing the water supply to cities throughout the empire, and several of their aqueducts still stand as major signs of their accomplishment. This is the Pont du Gard, part of an aqueduct in the south of modern France that was built in the first century C.E. The structure remained in use as a bridge into the eighteenth century. (akg-images/Bildarchiv Steffens.)

Throughout the territory of the former Roman Empire, we can still see the impressive remains of constructions put up some two thousand years ago. Numerous landmarks in the modern city of Rome date to ancient times. Visitors admire monuments such as the Colosseum, the giant amphitheater opened for gladiatorial games in 80 C.E. (see again At a Crossroads, page 202), and the Pantheon, whose present form dates to around 120 C.E. A temple for the veneration of all Roman gods, the Pantheon had the largest dome on earth until modern times, 142 feet wide. In the former provinces still stand Roman bridges, watermills, aqueducts, and other monuments equally old and sometimes still functional.

Roman engineers are famous not because of their originality—they mostly continued to use Greek inventions—but because they developed techniques to their fullest extent. They also left behind the most detailed writings on and public buildings in which citizens conducted government business. An elaborate road system extended from Scotland to the Sahara Desert. The roads ran straight for miles, extending over stone bridges when needed, and their surfaces were carefully paved to resist all weather. If two cities were more than a day's journey apart, they provided rest houses. At first the roads had military functions, but wheeled vehicles and messengers also used them. By building and improving the empire's transportation network, the emperors connected their provinces to Rome, making their capital the crossroads of the Mediterranean.

Imperial Succession   Because of the emperor's pivotal role in the political system, the empire's power centers viewed the choice of emperor with the utmost concern, and succession was highly contested. Rarely did a natural son succeed his father as emperor. This was true from the start of the empire: Augustus had no sons, so he groomed several relatives, including his daughter's sons, to succeed him. When they all died before him, he reluctantly chose Tiberius, his last wife's son from a previous marriage, as heir and adopted him as a stepson (see Seeing the Past: The Augustan Cameo Gem).

engineering in the ancient world. Most elaborate is the work of Vitruvius from the first century C.E. His *On Architecture* is ten volumes of information on materials, construction methods, water management, town planning, and many other subjects.

Engineers and skilled builders were organized in associations that grouped together specialists. The variety of these associations shows that skills were highly specialized: stonemasons, demolition experts, brickmakers, plasterers, painters, and many others had their own associations. Only people who belonged to the association could do the job. Access was restricted, however, and often only the sons of existing members could join. Young workers had to undergo a long apprenticeship before they could work independently. The associations also provided assistance to their members—for example, to pay for funerals or tombs. They worked under the supervision of architects, who were highly respected.

As groups of engineers traveled and worked in different regions, they contributed to the unity of the empire. They used the same techniques to create Roman buildings and monuments of similar appearance everywhere, from modern-day Britain to Syria. Among the most impressive Roman remains still standing are aqueducts—man-made channels that brought water from distant sources. Constructed in stone and concrete (lime, sand, and water poured into molds to obtain the desired shape), the aqueducts relied on gravity to move the water. Their builders sometimes used massive constructions to bypass natural obstacles. One amazing example is the Pont du Gard ("Bridge over the Gard") in the south of modern France. To allow passage over the Gard River valley, Roman engineers built three tiers of stone arches rising 180 feet above the riverbed. The water runs through a channel on top that is 4.5 feet wide and 5.5 feet deep, covered with stone slabs to protect against the sun and pollution. Many aqueducts supplied Rome with water, and some still feed fountains in the city today, including the landmark Trevi Fountain.

Military engineers were especially important in Rome's extensive wars. They devoted much effort to the development of artillery. One typical Roman piece of equipment was the ballista, a large crossbow, mounted on wheels, that could propel a projectile for one thousand feet or more with a high degree of accuracy.

Many of the techniques Roman engineers used were forgotten after the end of the empire, but once Europeans of the fifteenth and later centuries C.E. rediscovered the writings of Vitruvius and others and investigated the remains still standing, they used them as the basis for their constructions. Roman engineering is thus another connection between antiquity and modern times.

QUESTIONS TO CONSIDER

1. How did Roman engineers serve the needs of the empire?

2. How did they contribute to the spread of Roman culture?

3. How did their organization contribute to their success?

For Further Information:
Hodge, A. Trevor. *Roman Aqueducts and Water Supply*, 2d ed. London: Duckworth, 2002.
Landels, J. G. *Engineering in the Ancient World*, 2d ed. Berkeley: University of California Press, 2000.

From the early history of the empire, generals contested succession, relying on armies to enforce their claims. When Augustus's dynasty ended with the suicide of the childless Nero (r. 54–68 C.E.), four men in quick succession claimed the throne, each with the support of provincial troops. Finally Vespasian (vehs-PAYZ-ee-an) (r. 69–79 C.E.), backed by the troops in the east, seized full control.

The army sometimes sold the throne to the highest bidder. Because real power now derived from military support, the emperor's direct connection to the city of Rome and its aristocratic families vanished. Vespasian was not born in Rome, but in provincial Italy to humble parents. Ten years later a Spaniard, Trajan (r. 98–117 C.E.), became emperor. Soon afterward the rulers began to come from other regions of the empire—Gaul, North Africa, Syria, and the Balkans.

Nonetheless, because it was the capital of the empire, many emperors focused attention on the city of Rome, spending enormous amounts to construct fountains, theaters, stadiums, baths, and other monuments. The Roman historian Suetonius (c. 69–140 C.E.) quotes Augustus's boast that he found Rome a city of brick and left it a city of marble.

The City of Rome

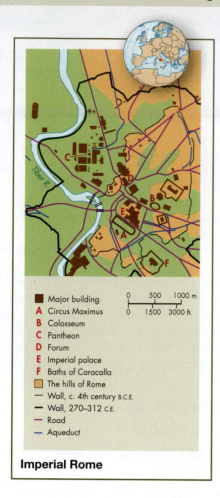

Imperial Rome

Workers and artisans from all over the empire flocked to the city to provide labor and craftsmanship. Its population grew to around a million. Most were poorly paid laborers and servants, but there were also numerous shopkeepers, bakers, fishmongers, and others who provided goods and services. Many inhabitants lived in terrible conditions, in city blocks packed with multiple-story wooden buildings. When in July 64 C.E. a fire erupted, it took almost a week to put it out; ten of the fourteen urban districts were damaged, and three were burned to the ground.

Because many Roman residents were poor and unemployed, emperors sought to ward off restlessness with "bread and circus games": food handouts, performances, races, and contests between gladiators, that is, enslaved men fighting to the death for public entertainment. (Spartacus had been a gladiator before leading his slave rebellion.) The Roman Colosseum, built in the first century C.E. for such games, could seat fifty thousand spectators. The games and food handouts diverted people's attention and made them feel as if the emperor cared about them.

In return for such benefits, the people awarded the emperor divine status. The Senate had declared Augustus a god after his death, and soon the idea took hold that the living emperor was a deity. The rulers themselves liked the idea; Emperor Domitian (r. 81–96 C.E.), for example, insisted that he should be addressed as "master and god." Other members of the imperial family were likewise deified to exalt their status. Visual imagery such as statues, relief sculptures, and coins that appeared throughout the empire broadcast the idea that the emperor was a god, and in the provinces temples existed for his cult.

The army was the central institution in Roman society, the backbone of the empire. It was enormous, although enlistments varied over time. Scholars estimate that more than 10 percent of the adult male population typically served in active duty at one time. In theory it was an army of landowning Romans: in the early Republic only men who could pay for their equipment were allowed to join, as had been the case with the Greek hoplites (see Chapter 5). Reforms enacted in 107 B.C.E. allowed landless poor men to enlist, and these recruits received farms when they returned to civilian life after many years of service.

The Roman Army

The core of Rome's army consisted of **legions**, infantry units of six thousand men each, divided into ten cohorts of six centuries—one hundred men—each. The legionaries of the empire were predominantly non-Italians, who received Roman citizenship when they enlisted. They trained hard to fight in unison and were well armed. Alongside the legionaries fought auxiliaries, non-Roman soldiers who often excelled in a special skill such as archery. They fought under a Roman officer in cohorts of five hundred or one thousand men each. Upon retirement they, too, as well as their sons, became Roman citizens, and their female family members acquired the rights of Roman women. Thus the army facilitated the fuller integration of provincials into Roman life.

Military service was long and arduous. A legionary served twenty years, an auxiliary twenty-five. Until the late second century C.E., soldiers were not allowed to marry, although they could have long-term relationships. The army's maintenance took up a major part of the state's finances. To keep soldiers loyal, their salaries were regularly increased, and they received a share of the booty, as well as special gifts (for example, to gain their allegiance when a new emperor took office) and a retirement bonus. Over time, the growing cost of maintaining the army, and through it control over the empire, would put a great strain on the imperial system.

Despite the frequent changes of emperors and their often erratic behavior and military adventures, the peoples of the empire enjoyed substantial periods of peace and prosperity.

legion A military unit in the Roman army consisting of six thousand infantry soldiers.

SEEING THE PAST

The Augustan Cameo Gem

(Erich Lessing/Art Resource, NY.)

Probably in around 50 C.E., an anonymous artist cut this stone (7½ inches high, 9 inches wide) in honor of Augustus, visually expressing the new idea of rule introduced by the first emperor of Rome. Although officially Augustus was only "a first citizen," in this piece the artist conveys the idea that he was a king linked to the gods. It may have been possible only after Augustus's death in 14 C.E. to express such an idea.

In the center of the top register we see the goddess Roma, along with Augustus as a heroic seminude; his image is based on that of statues representing Jupiter, head of the Roman pantheon. To the right are Gaia, the goddess of the earth, and Neptune, the sea god, to express the idea that Augustus's rule encompassed both land and sea. Oikumene (oy-ku-MEHN-ay), the personification of the civilized world, holds a crown over the emperor's head. On the left is Tiberius, Augustus's designated successor, descending from his chariot after he defeated the barbarian threat represented on the bottom register. Next to Tiberius stands a young man in military dress; he represents Germanicus, Tiberius's adopted son, who had died before Tiberius. The image thus represents the idea of a royal dynasty in which generations of the same family rule in succession.

EXAMINING THE EVIDENCE

1. What ideals of rule does the artist express in this piece?

2. How does this representation of Augustus diverge from his official status in society as *princeps*, "the first citizen"?

In particular, the second century C.E. was a time of ***Pax Romana***, or Roman peace: a sequence of competent rulers held power, the borders were secure, and internal tranquility generally prevailed. In this climate of peace and prosperity, Roman culture spread rapidly throughout the empire. This process of cultural exchange was accelerated by a shift in the role of the Roman army as the wars of conquest came to an end.

Pax Romana

The Provincial System and the Diffusion of Roman Culture

The Roman legions were stationed in the border areas, which initially functioned as sites to launch further expansion. From the late second century C.E. on, however, the legions took on a defensive role, protecting the borders against foreign invaders. The presence of legionaries and Roman bureaucrats fundamentally altered the local societies, especially in the west. The impact of this process is still visible today. Modern inhabitants of places that were once Roman provinces speak Romance languages—languages that developed from Latin—rather than Germanic and Slavic tongues. This is why the people of modern Romania still speak a language derived from Latin, whereas their neighbors, whose territories never became Roman provinces, use Slavic languages. Moreover, many ancient Roman settlements are important western European cities today, including

Pax Romana Literally, "Roman peace," the period in the second century C.E. when the empire was stable and secure.

London and Paris. In these and myriad other ways, Rome had a permanent impact on its territories.

Roman Settlements

The Romans influenced occupied territories most directly by creating various types of settlements. On the empire's borders, the Romans built military camps that became centers of trade and attracted the local populations. They turned existing settlements into Roman cities or founded new cities. These contained public baths, triumphal arches, temples, theaters, and amphitheaters, all patterned on those in Rome itself.

The new cities structured their governments on the Roman model. The local elite ran for election to high offices and sat on councils from which senators were often chosen. Like the emperor in Rome, these men were expected to lavish gifts upon the cities by constructing public monuments and buildings, organizing spectacles, and giving food hand-outs. At first they exercised a great deal of autonomy, and the Roman bureaucracy did not attempt to rule the empire directly. Over time, however, Roman emperors intervened more often in provincial affairs. Moreover, the great expense associated with holding office led to a shortage of local candidates. As a result, in the second century C.E. local autonomy gave way to direct rule by the emperor's representatives.

Romanization

Although Roman customs and lifestyles were not officially enforced, provincials who wanted to participate in the empire's business had to learn Latin in the west and Greek in the east and to dress and behave like Romans. Their material goods and houses reflected Roman styles. For example, floor mosaics such as those favored in Rome decorated houses built from North Africa to Britain, and provincial craftsmen produced items that imitated Italian products, such as clay lamps, for local consumption.

But **Romanization**, the process through which Roman culture spread into the provinces, was not wholesale adoption of Roman practices. Rather, local and imperial traditions merged as people retained the parts of their own culture they valued most while

A Roman Mosaic in England

With the military expansion of the Roman Empire throughout western Eurasia came the spread of Roman culture. The mosaic shown here, dating to around 350 C.E., is a typical example of Roman floor decoration. Not only is the style Roman, but so is the story illustrated, the tragedy of Dido and Aeneas, two lovers separated by the gods, as told in Virgil's *Aeneid*. The mosaic shows that the poem was known at the edges of the empire. (Somerset County Museum, Taunton Castle, UK/Bridgeman Art Library.)

Romanization The process by which Roman culture spread across the empire.

adopting aspects of Roman culture. Consequently, the east and the west of the empire were very different. Much of the western empire had been inhabited by nonliterate societies with few cities, and when the Romans annexed these regions, they introduced urban life, which naturally had a strong Roman character. In contrast, in the eastern territories, Hellenistic cultures had flourished before the Roman conquest, and many inhabitants were urban, literate, and educated (see Reading the Past: A Young Woman Laments Her Premature Death). Cities in the eastern empire remained Greek in character but prospered under Roman rule. Alexandria in Egypt was the second largest city of the empire after Rome, and its economy boomed because vast amounts of Egyptian grain were shipped through its harbor to Rome. Culturally it may have surpassed Rome itself, with its multitude of scholars and artists from all over the eastern world.

Spread of Citizenship

The diffusion of Roman culture coincided with the spread of citizenship. Only citizens could hold office, so non-Romans who wanted to participate in government had to become citizens. Over time the empire granted citizenship to more and more people, including other Italians, officials from the provinces, and former soldiers of foreign origin. Finally, in 212 C.E., Emperor Caracalla (cahr-ih-CAHL-ah) (r. 211–217 C.E.) gave nearly all free men in the empire Roman citizenship and all free women the same rights as Roman women. This created a new sense of unity, but at the same time it reduced the appeal of citizenship because it became less exclusive. Moreover, men from the provinces no longer needed to enlist in the army to become citizens, so to meet the constant demand for soldiers, the army increasingly turned to Germanic mercenaries.

The expansion of citizenship was part of a larger trend toward increased opportunities for provincials within the empire. Once the empire was established, ambitious men could move from one end to the other of a vast territory in pursuit of a career. Inscriptions honoring these men after their deaths report many such careers. In one example, Quintus Gargilius started out as a military officer in Britain. He then moved to North Africa, where he led Spanish troops and became responsible for governing two Roman cities in the north of what is today Algeria. After he died in an ambush, city leaders set up a monument to honor their fallen leader:

> To Quintus Gargilius, son of Quintus, member of the Quirina Martialis tribe, Roman equestrian, who was prefect of the first cohort of the Astyres in the province of Britannia, tribune of the Spanish cohort in the province of Mauritania Caesariensis [northern Algeria], after military service, set in charge of the cohort of Moorish aides and mounted detachments acting as protection in the territory of Auzia, decurio of the two colonies Auzia and Rusgunia and provincial patron, on account of his outstanding love for the citizens and his singular affection for the fatherland, and because, through his bravery and watchfulness against the rebel Faraxen, whom he captured with his associates and killed, the college of the colony of Auzia has made for him, at public expense [this monument] after he was deceived [and killed] by the ambush of the Bavares. It was dedicated on March 25 of the provincial year 221 [260 C.E.].[3]

Roman Law

Another means of unifying the empire was through law, which was evenly applied throughout the territories. From the Republican period on, legal experts had developed comprehensive procedures, mainly for private law, that is, interactions between individuals. Laws laid out rules for transactions in every aspect of life. They stipulated, for example, that a woman who married or divorced retained her property. They determined whether a neighbor could pick fruits from a tree overhanging his garden or collect water that ran off a roof. For transfers of property, they indicated what documentation was needed and whether or not witnesses had to be present.

Several emperors commissioned legal scholars to codify the laws and ensure their consistency. The laws had such an impact that people based their legal practices on them even after the empire's collapse. Roman law is the foundation of the continental European legal system to this day.

A Young Woman Laments Her Premature Death

To reconstruct Roman history we often rely on the extensive writings of ancient historians and official records. But many common people in the Roman Empire left documents as well, including business correspondence, letters, and the like, written on parchments and papyri that have survived only in Egypt, thanks to the region's dry climate. They also carved inscriptions on gravestones. This example of such an inscription comes from Egypt and was written in Greek. In it, a young woman asks passersby to mourn her premature death.

What profit is there to labor for children, or why honor them above all else, if we shall have for our judge not Zeus, but Hades [god of the underworld]?

My father took care of me for twice ten years, but I did not attain to the marriage bed of the wedding chamber,

Nor did my body pass under the bridal curtain, nor did the girls my age make the doors of cedar resound throughout the wedding night.

My virginal life has perished. Woe for that Fate, alas, who cast her bitter threads on me!

The breasts of my mother nourished me with their milk to no purpose at all, and to those breasts I cannot repay the favor of nourishment for their old age.

I wish I would have left my father a child when I died, so that he would not forever have an unforgettable grief through remembrance of me.

Weep for Lysandre, companions of my same age, the girl whom Philonike and Eudemos bore in vain.

You who approach my tomb, I implore you very much, weep for my youth, lost prematurely and without marriage.

Source: Jane Rowlandson, ed., *Women and Society in Greek and Roman Egypt* (Cambridge, U.K.: Cambridge University Press, 1998), 347.

EXAMINING THE EVIDENCE

1. What would have been expected from the deceased Lysandre had she lived longer?

2. What does this inscription tell us about the role of women in Roman society?

3. What does it tell us about the role of children in Roman society?

Christianity: From Jewish Sect to Imperial Religion

FOCUS

Why did imperial policy toward Christianity shift from persecution to institutionalization as Rome's state religion?

Roman culture profoundly influenced life throughout the empire, but as we have seen, cultural diffusion was a two-way process. We have already explored the Roman adoption of Greek culture in the second and first centuries B.C.E. In the first centuries C.E., the teachings of Jesus, a Jewish preacher in Palestine, fundamentally changed the religious outlook of many inhabitants of the Roman Empire, and by 325 C.E. his ideas would become the basis for a new state religion, Christianity. Christianity's absorption of classical Greek philosophical tradition and the merging of the church hierarchy with that of the imperial bureaucracy explain the new religion's remarkable success. These intellectual and bureaucratic foundations enabled the Christian church to survive the collapse of the Roman Empire in the west and to dominate the religious life of Europe for centuries.

Religions in the Roman Empire

The Roman Empire was home to numerous cultural and religious traditions. The Romans readily adopted foreign cults and religions, making no effort to monopolize the religious life of the empire. As a result, foreign gods found new adherents far from the regions where they originated. The Iranian god of light, Mithras, for example, was a favorite of soldiers throughout the empire because he was armed with a knife at birth.

Roman Depiction of the Iranian God Mithras
In the time of the empire, the Romans often adopted the religious cults of conquered peoples and incorporated foreign gods into their pantheon without difficulties. Especially popular was the Iranian god of light, Mithras, whose heroic deeds appealed to soldiers. In this marble relief of the second or third centuries C.E., he slays a bull to guarantee fertility. Overlooking him are images of the sun god and moon goddess, both also deities with eastern origins. (Louvre, Paris/Giraudon/Bridgeman Art Library.)

Mystery Religions

In the first century C.E., eastern mystery religions, or religions of salvation, gained much popularity throughout the empire. Under the new system of government, both ideas and populations could travel more easily over a vast area, which probably increased interest in foreign traditions and left people unsatisfied with their own. The cults of the Egyptian gods Osiris and Isis, which were seen as exotic and mysterious, were particularly popular. At the same time, a strong tendency arose to merge the gods of various cultures. Mithras, for example, came to be equated with the invincible Roman sun god, Sol Invictus. Moreover, that merged god was sometimes placed at the center of Roman religion as if he were the only deity. Thus the process of religious experimentation and exchange produced a Roman tendency toward monotheism, the belief in the existence of only one true deity.

Judaism in the Roman Empire

Although monotheism may have been a new concept to many Romans, in some parts of the empire it had a long history. In Palestine in the east of the empire, the monotheistic religion of Judaism had survived (see Chapter 4) and its temple hierarchy was integrated into the Roman administrative structure. In the capital city of Jerusalem, the aristocracy cooperated with the Romans, who kept them in power and allowed them to practice their faith. Several interpretations of Judaism coexisted, however, some focusing on adherence to established law, others more open to foreign cultural traditions. Certain Jewish groups wanted to overthrow Roman rule, among them the Zealots (originally a Greek term that indicates a zealous follower), some of whom were willing to assassinate Roman sympathizers. Thus in Palestine the process of Romanization was contested, with some Jewish groups choosing to adopt Roman ways and others seeing Roman rule and Roman culture as totally incompatible with the survival of an authentic Jewish identity.

Jesus

It was in this context of competing Jewish interpretations that the teachings of one preacher, Jesus of Nazareth, became popular. Focusing on personal faith, Jesus reached out to the disenfranchised of society, including women and the poor. We know of his teachings through accounts of his followers, whose story of his life situates him in the first decades of the first century C.E. Although the dates are uncertain, scholars estimate that he lived from about 4 B.C.E. to 30 C.E. Accounts of his life, which we call the New Testament gospels today, show that the traditional Jewish urban hierarchy rejected Jesus and that the Romans, who thought he advocated independence from the empire, executed him as a subversive and a rebel.

After his execution, a small community of Jesus's followers preserved his message and identified Jesus with the messiah, the "anointed one," whom earlier prophets had announced as the liberator of the Jews from imperial oppression. Jesus's disciples started to teach his message to other Jews. Initially their greatest appeal was to Jews who had partly assimilated into the Greek-speaking communities of Syria, and the gospels were written in Greek rather than Aramaic, the most common spoken language in the region. They used the Greek term *Christ* for messiah, which led to the word *Christians* for their followers. According to Christian tradition, Jesus's leading disciple, Peter, traveled to Rome to found a Christian community in the empire's capital.

Christianity's Spread Outside the Jewish Community

Travels of Paul

The earliest Christians saw themselves as Jews who could teach only those who obeyed the laws of circumcision and of the Jewish diet. A teacher from Anatolia called Paul especially advocated an end to that restriction, and in around 50 C.E. he began to spread Christianity among non-Jews. Addressing his message to people in Anatolia, Greece, Macedonia, and Rome, Paul established numerous Christian communities throughout the Eastern Roman Empire (see Map 7.3). The Roman communication and transportation network that connected the far-flung communities of the empire greatly facilitated Paul's missionary activities.

Jewish-Christian Split

Initially, Christian communities existed in harmony with the Jewish temple hierarchy in Jerusalem, but when the Christians failed to back a Jewish rebellion against the Romans in the years 66 to 74 C.E., many Jews considered Christians to be traitors. By 90 C.E., the two religions had split apart. At that time, a substantial number of Christian communities prospered in the regions of Syria-Palestine, Anatolia, and Greece. The two largest cities of the empire, Rome and Alexandria, also housed numerous Christians, and some Christian communities sprang up east of the Roman Empire in Parthian territory.

Early Christians

The early Christians were mostly urban merchants and members of the lower classes. They may have been drawn to the church because of its focus on human equality—slaves could hold leading offices—and support for the poor. That equality extended to women, who at first seem to have made up a large part of the congregations and to have held prominent roles. Rich women often made their homes available as gathering places and gave hospitality to traveling preachers. Paul often addressed his letters to women, advising them on how to teach the new religion. When the Christian church became more institutionalized, however, the role of women decreased, and the new church selected its leaders from among old men, the literal meaning of the Greek title given to them, *presbyteros*. By the early second century C.E., each Christian community elected one such elder as "overseer," *episkopos* in Greek, which became the title *bishop*. Various bishops vied for supremacy, which the bishop in Rome finally won by arguing that Peter had founded his church in Rome.

Toward a State Religion 50–324 C.E.

Persecution of Christians

Because they refused to honor other gods and formed close-knit communities, the early Christians grew apart from others in society—a development that made them an easy target for persecution by the authorities. As we have discussed, the Romans were generally tolerant of foreign religions, but not if such religions seemed to inspire rejection of the Roman community and state. At first, acts of persecution were tied to specific events, such as the burning of Rome in 64 C.E. Emperor Nero blamed the disaster on Christians and ordered the execution of those living in Rome. When the empire subsequently encountered military setbacks, the idea that the Christians' refusal to honor traditional gods had caused divine displeasure led to more general persecutions. In the mid-third century C.E., officials traveled across the empire and forced people to make offerings to Roman deities. If they refused, as Christians often did, they were killed. In addition, early Christians were sometimes attacked by non-Christian populations, who resented the isolation of Christian communities. Local governments tolerated such mob violence.

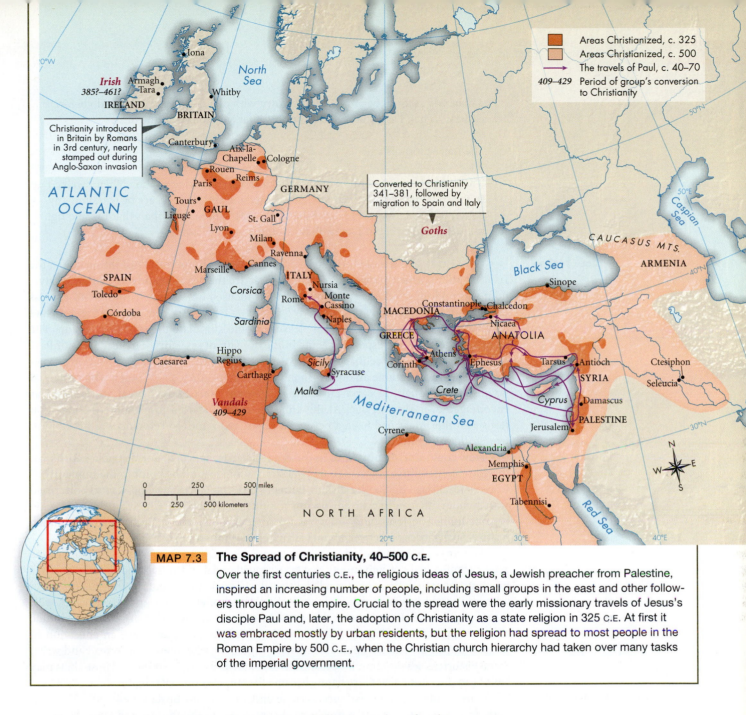

MAP 7.3 **The Spread of Christianity, 40–500 C.E.**

Over the first centuries C.E., the religious ideas of Jesus, a Jewish preacher from Palestine, inspired an increasing number of people, including small groups in the east and other followers throughout the empire. Crucial to the spread were the early missionary travels of Jesus's disciple Paul and, later, the adoption of Christianity as a state religion in 325 C.E. At first it was embraced mostly by urban residents, but the religion had spread to most people in the Roman Empire by 500 C.E., when the Christian church hierarchy had taken over many tasks of the imperial government.

Map labels: Iona; *Irish* 385?–461?; Armagh, Tara; Whitby; IRELAND; BRITAIN; North Sea; Christianity introduced in Britain by Romans in 3rd century, nearly stamped out during Anglo-Saxon invasion; Canterbury; Aix-la-Chapelle, Cologne; Rouen, Reims; Paris; ATLANTIC OCEAN; Tours; GAUL; Ligugé; Lyon; St. Gall; GERMANY; Milan; Converted to Christianity 341–381, followed by migration to Spain and Italy; *Goths*; CAUCASUS MTS.; Caspian Sea; Ravenna; ARMENIA; Marseille; Cannes; ITALY; Nursia; Black Sea; Sinope; SPAIN; *Corsica*; Rome; Monte Cassino; MACEDONIA; Constantinople; Chalcedon; Toledo; Naples; Nicaea; ANATOLIA; Córdoba; *Sardinia*; GREECE; Athens; Ephesus; Tarsus; Antioch; Ctesiphon; Hippo Regius; *Sicily*; Corinth; SYRIA; Seleucia; Caesarea; Carthage; Syracuse; Crete; *Cyprus*; Damascus; *Vandals* 409–429; *Malta*; Mediterranean Sea; Jerusalem; PALESTINE; Cyrene; Alexandria; Memphis; EGYPT; Tabennisi; Red Sea; NORTH AFRICA

Legend: Areas Christianized, c. 325 / Areas Christianized, c. 500 / The travels of Paul, c. 40–70 / *409–429* Period of group's conversion to Christianity

Scale: 0 250 500 miles / 0 250 500 kilometers

Persecution led to **martyrdom**, the execution of Christians who refused to renounce their faith. Such acts of defiance, even under the greatest tortures, became a sign of great devotion, to be admired and praised. Early Christian writings recount in detail the suffering of the faithful, including women, who through their trials acquired a status equal to men. One early record is the prison diary of Vibia Perpetua (WIHB-ee-ah pehr-PEHTCH-u-ah). The twenty-two-year-old woman described her imprisonment in the city of Carthage in the year 203 C.E. with her baby son, whom she was still nursing. When the child lost interest in breast milk, Perpetua saw this as a sign from God that she was free to go to her death. She and four other Christians were thrown to the animals: a wild cow trampled her, and a soldier killed her with his sword.

Perpetua described three visions she had in prison. In the final vision she saw herself in an arena facing a giant Egyptian. She wrote:

> Then came out an Egyptian against me, of vicious appearance, together with his seconds, to fight with me. There also came up to me some handsome young men to be my seconds and assistants. My clothes were stripped off, and suddenly I was

martyrdom The suffering of death for one's religious beliefs.

> a man. My seconds began to rub me down with oil (as they are wont to do before a contest). Then I saw the Egyptian on the other side rolling in the dust.
>
> She was victorious and
>
> The crowd began to shout and my assistants started to sing psalms. Then I walked up to the trainer and took the branch. He kissed me and said: "Peace be with you, my daughter!"... I awoke. I realized that it was not with wild animals that I would fight but with the Devil, but I knew that I would win the victory.[4]

Edict of Milan

In 313 C.E., about a century after Perpetua's death, Emperor Constantine issued the Edict of Milan, which allowed Christians to practice their faith openly. Now that martyrdom was no longer necessary, early Christians focused on an ascetic lifestyle to express devotion to the faith. They saw the body as merely a temporary container of the soul, and they believed that rejecting physical pleasure would stimulate the soul's perfection. The dislike of the body was especially acute in the domain of sexuality. The teachings of Paul already had celebrated celibacy as a virtue, but abstinence from sexual relations, especially for women, became an obsession in the second century C.E. Women who remained virgins were thought to carry an intact soul in an intact body. Sexual abstinence was encouraged even in marriage. At this time the church started to promote the idea that Jesus's mother Mary had been a perpetual virgin and removed references to his siblings from official literature.

How could Christianity, with its focus on austerity, appeal to a wide public? Although there are no definitive answers to this question, some historians point to the humanity of Christ's teachings: unlike the distant Roman gods, the Christian God was so concerned with humans that he sacrificed his son for their salvation. In Christian doctrine, God became human in Jesus, and Jesus was the force through which God influenced human history. Such closeness between humans and god was absent in other religions.

Moreover, Jesus preached love and compassion for one's peers, and his followers actively built a sense of community that transcended social and cultural boundaries and was much stronger than that of other religious groups. The new community served very well in a Roman world in which people moved around and often ended up in large cities with mixed populations. Furthermore, the early Christian church was well organized to provide services otherwise missing. It protected widows, fed the poor, and gave an education to some. Many of the empire's bureaucrats were Christians who knew how to read and write. Some historians see the church's organizational skills as its major strength. Those skills may have been the reason that Christianity became the empire's official religion.

Conversion of Constantine

Christianity's guarantee of success came under Emperor Constantine (r. 307–337 C.E.). Early in his reign Constantine fought rival contenders to the throne, and when he won a crucial battle in 312 C.E., he credited his victory to the Christian god and converted to Christianity. According to tradition, he did so because he saw a vision of Christ before the battle. Historians today debate whether Constantine was spiritually motivated or a pragmatist who recognized the growing influence of the religion in the empire and sought to win the support of its adherents.

In any case, Constantine's embrace of Christianity was of enormous historical significance. A year after his military victory, he promulgated the Edict of Milan, guaranteeing freedom of worship to Christians and all others. When Constantine became sole ruler of the Roman Empire in 324 C.E., he used the Christian church as an institution to unify the empire. He granted land to build churches, especially in places significant to the religion's history. In this cause, his mother, Helena, traveled through Palestine and financed the building of memorials in locations where, according to the gospels, crucial events in Jesus's life had taken place. A story developed that while supervising the construction of the Church of the Holy Sepulcher in Jerusalem she even found the cross on which he was crucified. Thus, in the early days of Christianity, Christians used the

The Church of the Holy Sepulcher in Jerusalem
After Constantine converted to Christianity in 312 C.E., his mother, Helena, commissioned the building of churches in or near places highlighted in stories about Jesus, including the church shown here, constructed over the spot where, according to tradition, he was crucified and buried. The Church of the Holy Sepulcher that exists today is very different from the original one built in the fourth century, but it continues to be a major pilgrimage site. (Erich Lessing/Art Resource, NY.)

roads and sea routes that connected the empire to spread their message and establish new outposts for their religion. By Constantine's day, Christianity had grown to such an extent that the empire turned to Christian institutions and networks to reinforce imperial unity.

Institutionalization of the Christian Church

After Constantine, the institutions of the empire and Christian church were increasingly intertwined, and the power of the church within the empire was irreversible. Changes in the imperial administration, which had become fully focused on the emperor's authority, confirmed the religion's grip. Whereas the empire's earlier administration had been decentralized, the concern of provincial governors and local wealthy citizens, by 300 C.E. the emperor's court had taken over most administrative tasks. Government offices were assigned with careful attention to rank and responsibilities. According to one estimate the imperial court controlled thirty to thirty-five thousand such offices by 400 C.E. The Christian church mirrored the centralized imperial bureaucracy when it stabilized its structure and hierarchy. The imperial and Christian administrative structures coincided, and soon religious leaders also adopted civilian roles.

As Christianity spread over the wide empire with its multiple cultural traditions, differences of opinion about aspects of the religion emerged. Especially controversial in Constantine's time was the question of the relationship between Jesus's divine and human natures. A doctrine called Arianism (AYR-ee-an-ihz-uhm), which originated with Arius, a priest of Alexandria, claimed that Jesus could not have been divine because he was born from the will of God and had died. Only God, the father, was eternal and divine. Constantine, to whom religious disagreement meant civil disorder, called a council of bishops at Nicaea in Anatolia in 325 C.E. to determine the official doctrine. The council rejected Arianism, but disagreements remained over such questions as exactly when in the year Jesus died and whether priests should remain celibate, among many others. Over the next centuries several councils followed, as we will see in Chapter 9. Opinion differed especially between eastern and western church leaders, who became more distant from each other as the eastern and western halves of the empire increasingly diverged.

At the same time, intellectuals refined the philosophical basis of the Christian creed. Particularly important in this context was the North African bishop Augustine

Doctrinal Debates

Augustine's Influence

RISE OF CHRISTIANITY

c. 20–30 C.E.	Jesus teaches in Palestine
c. 40–70 C.E.	Paul spreads Christianity in the Mediterranean
64 C.E.	Nero persecutes Christians in Rome
c. 90 C.E.	Split between Judaism and Christianity
312 C.E.	Constantine converts to Christianity
313 C.E.	Edict of Milan establishes freedom of worship for Christians
324 C.E.	Constantine makes Christianity the official state religion
325 C.E.	Council of Nicaea labels Arianism a heresy
c. 340–420 C.E.	Life of Jerome
354–430 C.E.	Life of Augustine
c. 400–500 C.E.	The Roman imperial and Christian church bureaucracies merge

(354–430 C.E.), who connected Christian thought to Plato's notions of universal ideals (see Chapter 5). Just as Plato believed that rigorous intellectual searching revealed the ideal form of the good, Augustine saw reading the Bible as a way to comprehend God's goodness. Thus the cultural exchanges that shaped the Roman Empire also shaped Christianity. Through the work of Augustine, the Greco-Roman intellectual tradition became embedded in Christian religious thought.

To explain the military difficulties Rome encountered in his lifetime, Augustine reinterpreted the history of the world in his *City of God* (written between 413 and 425 C.E.). He contrasted the "city of man," in which people pursue earthly pleasures, with the "city of God," in which they dedicate their lives to the promotion of Christian ideals. Roman gods and non-Christian philosophers had failed to provide true happiness to humanity; only the Christian God could do so. Even in this project, Augustine was influenced by Greek and Roman thought. Although Augustine attacked earlier philosophers, he was very familiar with their works and used their systems of reasoning. By helping to merge the Roman and Christian traditions, Augustine did much to help cement the place of Christianity in Roman life.

Jerome's Translation of the Bible

Others promoted the development of Christianity by making it more accessible. Jerome (c. 340–420 C.E.), who was born in the area of modern Slovenia but moved to Rome, translated the Bible from Hebrew and Greek into Latin. The Latin speakers of the western empire found his translation much easier to comprehend, which greatly facilitated conversion in that region.

The merger of Christian ideas with Roman imperial ideology and bureaucracy led to ultimate success for the religion, even while the empire collapsed in the west. Emperors credited military victories to Christianity and became the upholders of the faith, persecuting non-Christians and dissenting voices within the church. Civil and religious bureaucracies were combined—bishops were also judges, for example. Thus, to understand fully the success of Christianity, we must further explore political developments in the late Roman Empire.

Transformation of the Roman Empire 200–500 C.E.

FOCUS

How and why did the eastern and western parts of the Roman Empire develop differently?

The emperor Caracalla's edict of 212 C.E., which gave citizenship to nearly all free people in the Roman Empire, was the culmination of a long process that changed life for the masses. During the Pax Romana of the second century C.E. in particular, they had enjoyed a long period of stability and economic growth. In the third century C.E., however, severe social and economic crises gripped Rome. Divisions between the eastern and western parts became more acute, and after attempts to keep the empire together, a definitive partition took place in 395 C.E. In the following century, the pressures on the Western Roman Empire became too great, and it collapsed. To this day scholars debate the causes of Rome's collapse in the west. What is undeniable is that fundamental changes took place, and that western Eurasia in 500 C.E. was a very different place from that of 200 C.E.

Division Between East and West

The peace and stability of the Pax Romana was shattered when, in the third century C.E., generals using their legions in fights over the imperial throne devastated the land. Outsiders took advantage of the disarray to raid the empire, and in many places the economy collapsed. It was during this chaotic period that the eastern and western parts of the empire split—they had often served as distinct power bases for contenders to the throne. As we have seen, they had very different cultural histories, and in religious terms they grew further apart because their inhabitants interpreted Christianity differently.

In 324 C.E., Emperor Constantine turned the old city of Byzantium in the eastern part of the empire into a majestic new capital, which he called Constantinople ("city of Constantine"). He filled it with magnificent buildings and established a senate, calling his capital the "new Rome." Strategically located near the empire's borders and situated on major trade routes, Constantinople soon became the most important city of the east. Its rise exacerbated the growing division between the two parts of the empire, however, and by 395 C.E. a single ruler could no longer govern the Roman Empire. Rather, one emperor resided in Constantinople in the east; in the west another emperor ruled, at first from Rome and later from the Italian cities Milan and then Ravenna. The two halves had different histories thereafter: the western part declined and fell prey to Germanic invaders, but the eastern part remained an imperial power for centuries.

Division of the Roman Empire, c. 395 C.E.

Economic Strains and Social Tensions

Throughout its existence, the costs of running the Roman Empire had been enormous. In the third century C.E., the army, which had always been large, grew massive, and emperors gave soldiers increasingly high pay to gain their support. Already expected to

Growing Costs of Empire

Emperor Theodosius's Monument in Constantinople

Work to embellish Constantinople began soon after it became the capital of the Eastern Roman Empire. In 390 C.E. Emperor Theodosius I set up the oldest monument preserved today, an ancient obelisk taken from Egypt and placed on a platform decorated with reliefs carved in his time. This relief shows the emperor ready to hand the laurels of victory to the winner of a chariot race, an image befitting the location of the monument in the city's hippodrome, an arena for equestrian events. (The Art Archive/Gianni Dagli Orti.)

commission public works and monumental buildings, after the official conversion to Christianity, emperors were also obliged to build numerous churches and donate property to the church and its clergy. The imperial administration thus grew increasingly concerned over finances.

Social Impact   To guarantee state income and promote economic stability, the emperors took steps to limit economic and social mobility. Peasants were tied to the land, unable to leave to pursue other economic opportunities. Artisans were similarly tied to their workshops and had to pass on their occupations to their sons, and when soldiers retired their sons replaced them. The general population of the empire thus became tied to the land and fixed in a particular social class from which they could not advance. This new arrangement facilitated tax collection, because social class determined the level of taxation, but it severely limited people's freedom. In the country, peasants sought protection against the state from the landowners they worked for. In the cities, the poor turned to bishops, who had gained special prominence and who could act as people's patrons—in the fifth century c.e., bishops became the masters and protectors of entire cities, especially in the western empire. Thus, as the problems of the empire intensified, its inhabitants increasingly saw the imperial government as a threat rather than a protector, and they tried to establish a new set of social and political connections to guarantee their safety and security.

This transformation was accelerated by the decline of cities and towns in the west. They were victims of insufficient funds for public works, a disappearing imperial administration, and diminished trade. Economic power shifted to the landed estates, whose owners were masters over the people working for them and produced all they needed by themselves. This greatly reduced the western emperor's powers, and many regions became virtually autonomous. By contrast, in the east the cities were more resilient, and the peasants resisted forced settlement and retained their independence.

Collapse in the West and Revitalization in the East

After 200 c.e., outside pressures exacerbated the internal problems of the Roman Empire. In the east, the empire fought over border territories with the centralized states of Parthia and, after 224 c.e., Sasanid Persia. Because these wars involved two equal powers, they regularly ended in negotiated settlements. In the west, Rome confronted various Germanic tribal groups, which acted independently of one another. In time these groups breached the Rhine and Danube frontiers.

The Western Empire   The tribal threat had loomed since the beginning of the empire, and the Romans had strengthened the western border with a long line of walls and fortresses. Some tribes infiltrated imperial lands, however, and officials allowed them to settle there. Because German tribes themselves were under pressure from Central Asian nomadic Huns, they increased their efforts to enter the empire and broke down Rome's resistance. The Huns entered the fray themselves under their king, Attila, who acquired the epithet "scourge of God." He invaded Gaul in 450 and then assailed Italy, where the bishop of Rome had to pay him off. Although an emperor remained enthroned in the western empire, his influence was minor, and he watched feebly as various German leaders struggled for power. Thus nomadic peoples profoundly influenced the history of the sedentary peoples of the Roman Empire, duplicating a pattern we have seen in other societies around the world.

Despite the Germanic presence, there was much continuity in daily life in the western empire. The older inhabitants kept obeying Roman law, while the Germans followed their own legal traditions. Landed estates remained the focus of economic activities, the difference being that their lords now depended on German kings. Bureaucrats were still needed, and those of the empire continued to serve. Because many Germans converted to Christianity upon entering the empire, religious practices remained the same, and the church even increased its influence. Thus when in 476 c.e. Odoacer (OH-doo-way-sahr), the German king whose territory included Italy, forced the last Roman emperor, Romulus Augustulus, to abdicate, the event did not affect most people's lives. The western empire ceased to exist, and several Germanic kingdoms arose in its place, as we will see in Chapter 9.

The history of the eastern empire was very different from that of the west. Constantinople was a powerful major city and, notwithstanding outside pressures, its emperors governed large territories that remained urban and economically successful. The court saw itself as the protector of the Christian faith and of Roman civilization. A distinct eastern culture of the late world of antiquity developed; today historians call it Byzantine. The eastern empire and its culture would continue into the fifteenth century C.E., when the Turks captured Constantinople. Thus the urban culture of the eastern Mediterranean survived both integration into the Roman Empire in the second and first centuries B.C.E. and the western empire's disintegration some five hundred years later.

COUNTERPOINT
Rome's Iranian Rivals in the Middle East

To ancient Romans, their empire may easily have seemed the strongest power on earth, invincible and unlimited. In reality, however, Rome's dominion of western Eurasia was just one of a string of empires that stretched across Eurasia from the South China Sea in the east to the Atlantic Ocean in the west. We have discussed several of these empires before. The Han Empire in China (206 B.C.E.–220 C.E.) and the Kushan Empire in Central and South Asia (c. 50–233 C.E.) both controlled territories not much smaller than Rome's. Closer to Rome was a Southwest Asian power that never yielded to Roman armies. Centered in Iran and heirs to the ancient Persian Empire, two empires in succession withheld the forces of Roman expansion (see Map 7.4). From the moment Rome started to annex regions of the eastern Mediterranean in the first century B.C.E., it confronted the Parthians, who ruled Iran, Mesopotamia, parts of Syria, and eastern Anatolia. The Sasanids overthrew the Parthians in 224 C.E. and continued the competition with Roman Byzantium until their defeat by Muslim armies in the seventh century (discussed in Chapter 9).

> **FOCUS**
>
> What were the differences in organization between the Iranian and Roman empires?

These Iranian empires demonstrated not only that Rome's military dominance had limits but that the structure of a powerful empire did not have to resemble that of Rome. In contrast to the Roman style of control, which imposed a uniform system over subject territories, the Iranian empires were conglomerates of kingdoms and provinces whose kings and governors owed obedience to a "king of kings." These empires successfully ruled a vast area for more than nine centuries.

The Parthians 247 B.C.E.–224 C.E.

Soon after Alexander of Macedonia's death in 323 B.C.E., the territories he had conquered from the Mediterranean Sea to the Indus Valley had become the Seleucid Empire (see Chapter 5). Gradually, however, various regions of the Seleucid state gained independence. In the north, to the east of the Caspian Sea, was the province of Parthia, where in 247 B.C.E. a new people came to power under a leader called Arsaces (ar-SAY-sez). They may have originally been one of the many nomadic groups who seized control over the cities in the region and assumed rule. The Seleucids recognized Parthia's independence in around 210 B.C.E., and in succeeding decades Parthians annexed parts of Iran and Mesopotamia. When Rome conquered the remains of the Seleucid Empire in the eastern Mediterranean, it found itself faced with a formidable new opponent in the Parthians.

The Euphrates River formed a natural border between the two empires, but several Roman generals sought fame and fortune by leading their forces across the river. The results were often disastrous. In a battle in 53 B.C.E., for example, tens of thousands of Roman soldiers lost their lives. Likewise the Parthians regularly tried to annex Roman-

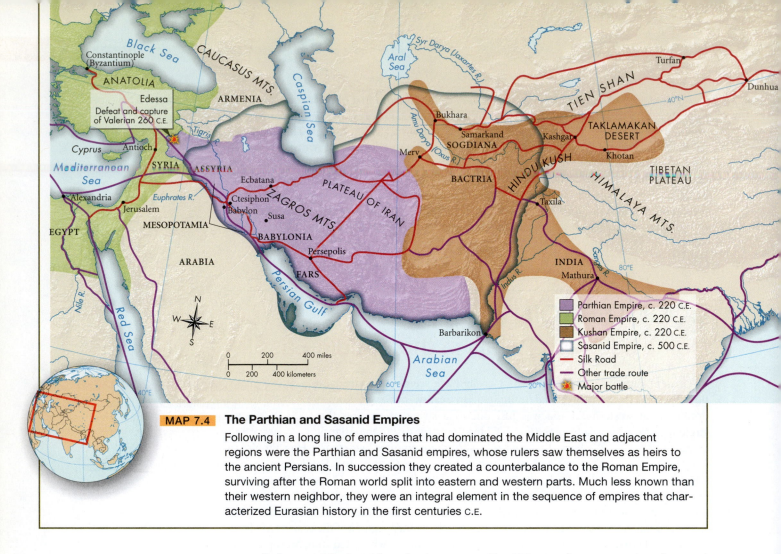

The Parthian and Sasanid Empires

Following in a long line of empires that had dominated the Middle East and adjacent regions were the Parthian and Sasanid empires, whose rulers saw themselves as heirs to the ancient Persians. In succession they created a counterbalance to the Roman Empire, surviving after the Roman world split into eastern and western parts. Much less known than their western neighbor, they were an integral element in the sequence of empires that characterized Eurasian history in the first centuries C.E.

controlled western Syria, without lasting success. For 250 years the wars continued: several Roman emperors of the second century C.E. made gains in northern Syria and Mesopotamia, but the territories were never truly integrated into the Roman Empire.

Imperial Organization

The Parthians could manage these territorial gains and losses because they saw their ruler as a "king of kings," a master of vassals from various states. This idea had already existed in the Persian Empire, and the Parthians claimed familial descent from these earlier rulers in their efforts to gain acceptance as kings. As in the past, the empire's cohesion depended greatly on the strength of the Parthian ruler; the local kings had a local power base and sufficient independence to switch allegiance at times. The cities, the hubs from which the Seleucids had governed the territory, also maintained the sovereignty they had before, and Greek speakers often preserved political organizations, such as the assembly. Nonetheless, the structure gave flexibility and resilience to the Parthian Empire: the loss of one territory would not have disastrous effects on the whole.

Trade

Despite the numerous wars between Parthians and Romans, the two rivals maintained important economic connections. Parthia controlled a large part of the Silk Road, which, as we saw in Chapter 6, brought luxuries from the East to Rome: Indian pepper, aromatics, perfumes, precious stones and pearls, and Chinese silk. In the first century C.E. the Romans tried to bypass the Parthians by establishing a direct link to India by sea, but the Roman elite's appetite for luxury goods was so great that they still needed overland trade. The Parthians contributed to this trade, exporting foods such as pomegranates and alfalfa to China, as well as Iranian horses, which the Chinese greatly admired.

The Sasanids 224–651 C.E.

In 224 C.E., Ardashir (AR-da-shear), the leader of a Parthian vassal kingdom, defeated the last Parthian king in battle and asserted supremacy over the entire empire. A native of the southwestern Iranian region of Fars, Ardashir claimed descent from a man named Sasan, and his dynasty is thus called the Sasanids. The structure of the Parthian Empire allowed for such a change of ruler; in essence, a new "king of kings" had arisen. The Sasanids developed the idea of "the empire of the Iranians," which the king was destined to rule because he was the descendant of mythical kings and of gods. His line of royal descent ran through the Persian emperors of the sixth to fourth centuries B.C.E. and gave rise to the idea of a history of the country of Iran with a long succession of rulers. The Sasanids thus inherited their concept of kingship from the Parthians, but added increased centralization of power to it.

Continued Wars with Rome

Diplomatically, the Sasanids carried on as the Parthians had, their trade with Rome being an enormous source of income. Simultaneously, wars with the Romans continued with some notable Sasanid successes: for example, in 260 C.E. King Shapur I defeated the Roman army of Valerian and captured the Roman emperor alive. This was the first time ever that a Roman emperor had been taken captive in battle. The wars did not end with the division of the Roman Empire, and Byzantine and Sasanid forces regularly fought each other, despite threats to both from the Huns of Central Asia. The end of the Sasanid dynasty came from the south, when Muslim armies from Arabia invaded Iran in the seventh century.

The Iranian Army

So for almost a thousand years the Parthians and Sasanids successfully ruled Iran and the surrounding regions, basing their authority on a system of supreme kingship over varied vassals. They enforced control through armies that were especially effective because of the cavalry. The core of the army consisted of mounted archers and heavily armored mounted spearmen, their horses covered with armor as well. The Romans were in awe of these opponents. One soldier wrote in 362 C.E.:

> The Persians opposed us with squadrons of mounted armored soldiers drawn up in such serried ranks that their movements in their close-fitting coats of flexible mail dazzled our eyes, while all their horses were protected by housings of leather.[5]

A Tapestry of Cultures and Religions

Like the other empires we have studied, those of the Parthians and Sasanids brought together people with diverse cultural backgrounds and religions, who spoke many languages and used different scripts. Like the Kushans of Central Asia, they tolerated these various

Shapur Celebrates the Capture of Valerian

In 260 C.E. the Sasanid ruler Shapur defeated the Roman army in northern Syria and captured its emperor Valerian alive, a feat unparalleled in Roman history. In this relief, carved on a rock near the tombs of the ancient Persian kings seven miles from Persepolis, the Persians celebrated by depicting the Roman emperor kneeling in submission. According to tradition, after the Roman emperor was killed in captivity, Shapur had him skinned and preserved. (The Art Archive/Gianni Dagli Orti.)

A Sasanid Account of the Wars with Rome

Near the ancient Persian city of Persepolis, the Sasanid king Shapur I (r. 239–270 C.E.) set up an inscription in three languages that described his wars with the Romans. The languages he used were Middle Persian, the language the court spoke at the time; Parthian, the language of the preceding rulers of Iran; and Greek, the language of the eastern Roman Empire. Although he glorifies his own actions in the account and perhaps ignores his military setbacks, his account is a useful balance to the Roman picture of wars in the east. Shapur boasts, for example:

> Just as we were ascended to the throne over the lands, the Caesar Gordian gathered in all of the Roman Empire an army of Goths and Germans and marched on Asurestan [Assyria], against Iranshahr and against us. On the border of Assyria, at Misike [where the Euphrates and Tigris rivers are close together], a great frontal battle took place. And Caesar Gordian was killed and we destroyed the Roman army. And the Romans proclaimed Philip Caesar. And Caesar Philip came to us to plead,

and paid us 500,000 denarii as ransom for his life and became tributary to us.

The inscription goes on to describe three wars against the Romans; the last one led to the capture of the Roman emperor Valerian in 260 C.E. Shapur I was so proud of that event that he ordered a large rock-relief carving in which the Roman is shown begging for his life (see page 231).

Source: Translation from Philip Huyse. *Die dreisprachige Inschrift Shabuhrs I. an der Ka'ba-i Zardusht (ShKZ)* (London: School of Oriental and African Studies, 1999), 26–27.

EXAMINING THE EVIDENCE

1. Why would Shapur I have commissioned an inscription in three languages?

2. Why are records of this type especially important for our knowledge of the Roman Empire?

---

traditions and even promoted them. The emperors spoke Aryan languages of Iran (Parthian and Middle Persian), which they used for official inscriptions often carved on rock surfaces and written in alphabetic scripts derived from Aramaic (see Reading the Past: A Sasanid Account of the Wars with Rome). They also used Greek as an official language, often on coins and also for translations of the rock inscriptions. The Semitic Aramaic language, written in its own script, was very important for administration. The use of a variety of Semitic (for example, Hebrew) and Indo-European (for example, Bactrian, Armenian) languages persisted throughout the entire period. Besides administrative and official records, a great variety of writings appeared, including literature translated from Greek and Indian originals.

Religious Toleration   Although the kings relied on Zoroastrianism (see Chapter 4) to support their rule, the variety of religions in the empire was equally great. A Zoroastrian priest wrote in the third century C.E. that the empire housed "Jews, Buddhists, Hindus, Nazarenes, Christians, Baptists, and Manicheans,"[6] that is, followers of the various religions from India and the Eastern Roman Empire, including various Christian sects.

Manichaeism   A new religion that originated in Iran perfectly illustrates a coalescence of various spiritual influences. Its founder, Mani (MAH-nee), was born in 216 C.E. in the Babylonian part of the then Parthian Empire. At age twenty-four, Mani started to preach a religion he hoped would appeal universally. He saw Buddha, Zoroaster, and Jesus as his precursors in a long line of prophets and borrowed from all their teachings. Like Zoroaster, Mani saw a strict opposition between soul and body, good and evil, and light and dark. To him life was painful, and the human soul had succumbed to evil. Only true knowledge would free the soul and return it to its original state of goodness, which it would share with God. Mani urged people to live an ascetic life, but realized that few people could do so at the desired level.

Mani traveled widely to spread his ideas, and he encouraged his followers to do the same. His teachings were so flexible that they could easily merge with existing religions, such as Buddhism, Daoism, Zoroastrianism, and Christianity. In the west they inspired many Christians of the Roman Empire, including Augustine, who followed Manichaean teachings for nine years, but the church hierarchy saw them as heresy. In Iran, too, the original toleration of Manichaeism gave way to persecutions. Mani himself died in prison sometime between 274 and 277 C.E., and his severed head was impaled on a pole for public display. His followers likened his death to Jesus's crucifixion. His religion survived, however, until persecutions in the Roman Empire in the fifth century and in the Middle East in the tenth century almost extinguished it.

Conclusion

When the Roman historian Tacitus wrote in around the year 100 C.E. that the empire he inhabited changed the way people lived as far away as Britain, he was not bragging groundlessly. Rome had created a world in which people from North Africa and Syria to Britain and France shared habits and tastes. A man born in one corner of the empire could make a career hundreds of miles away and end up in Rome as a politician. The cohesion of the Roman Empire explains why the ideas of a small Jewish sect could spread over an enormous area and why the Christian church it inspired could obtain an encompassing structure once it assimilated with the imperial bureaucracy. The Roman Empire was a crucial milestone in the history of western Eurasia, a structure that fundamentally shaped the region with effects still visible today. Its own development is a fascinating story of how strong Republican institutions with elected officials and term limits failed to prevent the consolidation of power in the hands of one man. In European tradition, the Roman Empire became the embodiment of the ancient world, a period of the past that produced great human achievements that needed to be recovered. The ancient Romans left behind so much material—written and nonwritten—that we can recreate their world in great detail and see it as the archetype of empire.

A subject of the empire may have imagined that Rome was unique and dominated the entire world. But students of world history today realize that it was merely part of a system of empires that stretched throughout Eurasia. Although we call them all empires, they had varied organizations and degrees of centralization. For each region, the empire constituted a finishing point of developments that had started thousands of years earlier, as politically united regions grew larger and cultural uniformity increased. These empires represent the culmination of ancient history throughout Eurasia.

NOTES

1. H. Mattingly, trans., *Tacitus on Britain and Germany* (Harmondsworth, Middlesex, U.K.: Penguin Books, 1978), 72.
2. Horace, *Epistles* 2.1, lines 156–157.
3. J. Parrès, http://rambert.francis.free.fr/aumale/aumalehisto/aumalerom3.htm.
4. Herbert Musurillo, ed. and trans., *The Acts of the Christian Martyrs* (Oxford: Clarendon Press, 1972), 119.
5. Ammianus Marcellinus, 24.6.7., qtd. in M. Brosius, *The Persians* (London: Routledge, 2006), 187.
6. Josef Wiesehöfer, *Ancient Persia from 550 B.C. to 650 A.D.* (London: Tauris, 1996), 199.

RESOURCES FOR RESEARCH

General Works

Ancient Rome is the subject of a vast amount of research and writing, and works continue to be published on every aspect of its history and culture. Most of the references listed here relate to this chapter as a whole.

Grant, Michael, and Rachel Kitzinger, eds. *Civilization of the Ancient Mediterranean*, 1988.
*(For quotes from ancient texts on numerous subjects): Internet Ancient History Sourcebook: Rome. http://www.fordham .edu/halsall/ancient/asbook09.html.

(For information on women): Materials for the Study of Women and Gender in the Ancient World. http://www.stoa.org/diotima.

McGeough, Kevin M. *The Romans: New Perspectives.* 2004.

*(For ancient texts in the original and in translation, and other online resources): Perseus Digital Texts. http://www.perseus.tufts.edu.

Woolf, Greg, ed. *Cambridge Illustrated History of the Roman World.* 2003.

Rome: A Republican Center of Power, 500–27 B.C.E.

To reconstruct the earliest history of Rome, modern historians rely on accounts that Romans such as Livy produced in the late Republic and early empire, and on archaeological remains. Some of the main political actors of later Republican times left their own writings—for example, Julius Caesar, whose war accounts are fascinating in their detail and information on the late Republic.

Cornell, T. J. *The Beginnings of Rome: Italy and Rome from the Bronze Age to the Punic Wars (c. 1000–264 B.C.).* 1995.

*Julius Caesar. *The Civil War.* Translated by John Carter. 1997.

*Lewis, Naphtali, and Meyer Reinhold, eds. *Roman Civilization: Selected Readings,* 3d ed. Vol. 1, *The Republic and the Augustan Age.* 1990.

*Livy. *The Early History of Rome.* Translated by Aubrey de Sélincourt. 1961.

Matyszak, Philip. *Chronicle of the Roman Republic: The Rulers of Ancient Rome from Romulus to Augustus.* 2003.

Rome: The Empire, 27 B.C.E.–212 C.E.

Ancient Roman historians such as Tacitus left us detailed biographies of emperors, which are engaging works with stories of court intrigues and other scandals. They have inspired modern fiction, which can represent Roman antiquity very realistically, as in Graves's novels. Because there is so much historical data, we have an enormous volume of publications on every aspect of the empire.

Bunson, Matthew. *Encyclopedia of the Roman Empire.* 1994.

Graves, Robert. *Claudius the God.* 1943.

Graves, Robert. *I, Claudius.* 1934.

*Lewis, Naphtali, and Meyer Reinhold. *Roman Civilization. Selected Reading.* Vol. 2, *The Empire,* 3d ed. 1990.

Online Encyclopedia of Roman Rulers and Their Families. http://www.roman-emperors.org.

Scarre, Christopher. *Chronicle of the Roman Emperors: The Reign-by-Reign Record of the Rulers of Imperial Rome.* 1995.

*Tacitus. *The Histories.* Translated by D. S. Levene. 1977.

Wells, Colin. *The Roman Empire,* 2d ed. 1992.

Christianity: From Jewish Sect to Imperial Religion

The birth and early development of Christianity continues to engage scholars and other writers. A vast literature approaches the subject from multiple angles.

Fox, Robin Lane. *Pagans and Christians.* 1986.

Hopkins, Keith. *A World Full of Gods: Pagans, Jews, and Christians in the Roman Empire.* 1999.

*MacMullen, Ramsay, and Eugene N. Lane, eds. *Paganism and Christianity, 100–425 C.E.: A Sourcebook.* 1992.

Markus, R. A. *Christianity in the Roman World.* 1974.

Stark, Rodney. *The Rise of Christianity: How the Obscure, Marginal Jesus Movement Became the Dominant Religious Force in the Western World in a Few Centuries.* 1997.

Transformation of the Roman Empire, 212–500 C.E.

The study of the later centuries of the Roman Empire is a relatively new academic pursuit that has become very popular because it allows scholars to deal with many traditions and cultures. Brown's book is often regarded as the work that gave rise to this new interest.

Bowersock, G. W., Peter Brown, and Oleg Grabar, eds. *Late Antiquity: A Guide to the Postclassical World.* 1999.

Brown, Peter. *The World of Late Antiquity.* 1971.

Cameron, Averil. *The Late Roman Empire, A.D. 284–430.* 1993.

Garnsey, Peter, and Caroline Humfress. *The Evolution of the Late Antique World.* 2001.

Mitchell, Stephen. *A History of the Later Roman Empire, A.D. 284–641: The Transformation of the Ancient World.* 2007.

COUNTERPOINT: Rome's Iranian Rivals in the Middle East

Until recently, study of the Parthians and Sasanids was a highly specialized academic field. Now, however, several scholars have written more accessible works that place these empires within the sequences of ancient Persian empires and that rely on indigenous as well as Roman sources. The Web site listed here contains an extensive collection of materials, including a massive bibliography.

Brosius, Maria. *The Persians: An Introduction.* 2006.

Garthwaite, Gene R. *The Persians.* 2005.

Harrison, Thomas, ed. *The Great Empires of the Ancient World.* 2009.

The Parthian Empire. http://parthia.com/.

Wiesehöfer, Josef. *Ancient Persia from 550 B.C. to 650 A.D.* 1996.

* Primary source.

▶ **For additional primary sources from this period**, see *Sources of Crossroads and Cultures.*

▶ **For Web sites, images, and documents related to topics in this chapter**, see Make History at bedfordstmartins.com/smith.

The major global development in this chapter ▸ The unification of western Eurasia under the Roman Empire.

IMPORTANT EVENTS

753–509 B.C.E.	Roman monarchy
509 B.C.E.	Start of the Roman Republic
264–146 B.C.E.	Punic Wars between Rome and Carthage
210 B.C.E.	Parthians gain independence from Seleucid Empire
49 B.C.E.	Julius Caesar crosses the Rubicon
44 B.C.E.	Assassination of Julius Caesar
31 B.C.E.–14 C.E.	Reign of Augustus
c. 30 B.C.E.	Rome controls entire Mediterranean region
27 B.C.E.	Augustus establishes full dominance over Roman affairs
c. 4 B.C.E.–30 C.E.	Life of Jesus
100–200 C.E.	Pax Romana; height of the Roman Empire
212 C.E.	Caracalla grants citizenship to nearly all free inhabitants of the empire
224 C.E.	Sasanids overthrow Parthians
313 C.E.	Constantine issues Edict of Milan, legalizing Christianity
395 C.E.	Roman Empire divided into eastern and western parts
410 C.E.	German tribes sack Rome
476 C.E.	German leader Odoacer forces last western Roman emperor to step down

KEY TERMS

client (p. 208)
consul (p. 209)
equestrian (p. 210)
latifundia (p. 210)
legion (p. 216)
magistrate (p. 209)
martyrdom (p. 223)

pater familias (p. 208)
patrician (p. 209)
Pax Romana (p. 217)
plebeian (p. 209)
Romanization (p. 218)
Senate (p. 209)
tribune (p. 209)

CHAPTER OVERVIEW QUESTIONS

1. How are the institutions of Republican Rome still important to us today?
2. How did the Romans face the challenges of creating and maintaining an empire?
3. What impact did Rome have on the lives of the people it conquered?
4. How did Christianity's rise benefit from the Roman Empire?
5. What were the limits of Roman imperialism?

SECTION FOCUS QUESTIONS

1. What were the political ideals of Republican Rome, and how did some outlive the Republic itself?
2. How did the Roman Empire bring administrative and cultural unity to the vast territory it ruled?
3. Why did imperial policy toward Christianity shift from persecution to institutionalization as Rome's state religion?
4. How and why did the eastern and western parts of the Roman Empire develop differently?
5. What were the differences in organization between the Iranian and Roman empires?

MAKING CONNECTIONS

1. How did the political and cultural achievements of Republican Rome compare with those of classical Greece (see Chapter 5)?
2. How did the world empires of the centuries from 500 B.C.E. to 500 C.E. facilitate the spread of new ideas and religions? Compare, for example, the Han (see Chapter 6) and Roman empires.
3. How does the level of cultural integration in the Roman Empire compare with that of the Eurasian empires we studied in earlier chapters?
4. In what sense did Christianity merge earlier traditions of the eastern Mediterranean world?

AT A CROSSROADS ▲

The ancient populations of South America developed textiles into an art form, experimenting with fiber materials and decorations. In the first millennium B.C.E., the people of Paracas in the southern Andes revolutionized textile production by introducing tapestry weaving and new techniques of dyeing. The fragment shown here, part of a mummy wrapping produced in the first century B.C.E., depicts a mythical monster we call the "Decapitator." (Private Collection/Boltin Picture Library/Bridgeman Art Library.)

Reading the Unwritten Record: Peoples of Africa, the Americas, and the Pacific Islands

3000 B.C.E.–500 C.E.

In 1769 C.E., Sir Joseph Banks visited the Polynesian islands in the South Pacific in his ship, the *Endeavour*. In describing the inhabitants in his journal, the English explorer remarked on their navigational skills:

> The people excell much in predicting the weather, a circumstance of great use to them in their short voyages from Island to Island. They have many various ways of doing this but one only that I know of which I never heard of being practisd by Europaeans, that is foretelling the quarter of the heavens from whence the wind shall blow by observing the Milky Way . . . in this as well as their other predictions we found them indeed not infallible but far more clever than Europaeans. In their longer voyages they steer in the day by the Sun and in the night by the Stars. Of these they know a very large part by their Names and the clever ones among them will tell in what part of the heavens they are to be seen in any month when they are above their horizon; they know also the time of their annual appearing and disapearing to a great nicety, far greater than would be easily believed by an Europaean astronomer.[1]

BACKSTORY

At the start of this book we looked at the evolution of the human species and our ancestors' migration throughout the globe. As the setting for the lives of the earliest humans, Africa played a major role in these events. Vast oceans separated Africa and its original human inhabitants from places such as the Americas and the islands of the Pacific Ocean. But over broad expanses of time, the significance of these gaps between the earth's far-distant realms diminished as African peoples responded to changes in their physical environment and migrated to other parts of the world. In this chapter, we shift our focus from the ancient cultures of Eurasia to Africa, the Americas, and the Pacific in the period 3000 B.C.E. to 500 C.E. In so doing, we explore a unique challenge these regions present to the historian: reconstructing the history of societies that did not leave a written record.

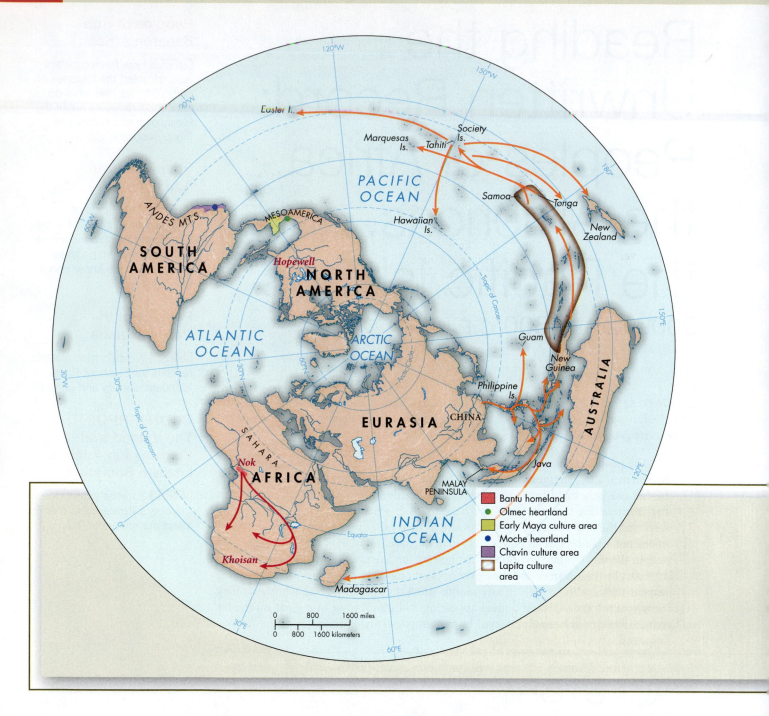

Legend:
- Bantu homeland
- Olmec heartland
- Early Maya culture area
- Moche heartland
- Chavín culture area
- Lapita culture area

Map labels: Easter I., Marquesas Is., Society Is., Tahiti, PACIFIC OCEAN, Samoa, Tonga, New Zealand, Hawaiian Is., ANDES MTS., MESOAMERICA, SOUTH AMERICA, Hopewell, NORTH AMERICA, ATLANTIC OCEAN, ARCTIC OCEAN, Guam, New Guinea, Philippine Is., AUSTRALIA, EURASIA, CHINA, SAHARA, Nok, AFRICA, Khoisan, Java, MALAY PENINSULA, INDIAN OCEAN, Madagascar

Scale: 0 800 1600 miles / 0 800 1600 kilometers

Timeline:

c. 3000–1800 B.C.E. Norte Chico culture in the Andes

c. 1400–200 B.C.E. Lapita culture in the Pacific Ocean

c. 900–200 B.C.E. Chavín culture in Mesoamerica

Start of iron technology in Africa c. 800–700 B.C.E.

3000 B.C.E.   **2000 B.C.E.**   **1000 B.C.E.**

c. 3000 B.C.E. Start of southward migration of the Bantu in Africa

c. 3000–750 B.C.E. First wave of Austronesian migrations

c. 1200–400 B.C.E. Olmec culture in Mesoamerica

c. 1000 B.C.E. Start of eastern movement of the Bantu in Africa

Savvy seafarers, the ancestors of these Polynesians had boldly spread over the myriad of islands in the Pacific Ocean, but they had maintained many of their original customs. Thus Banks stated:

> From the similarity of customs, the still greater of Traditions and the almost identical sameness of Language between these people and those of the Islands of the South Sea there remains little doubt that they came originally from the same source: but where that Source is future experience may teach us, at Present I can say no more than I firmly believe that it is to the Westward and by no means to the East.[2]

Banks was among the handful of early European explorers who drew the peoples of Polynesia into history by recording some of their customs, practices, and languages. Because these people did not write, our only records of their early histories are the accounts of literate visitors. Banks's efforts are all the more valuable because he carefully observed the Polynesians and willingly acknowledged their intelligence and skills. More often, however, European observers' comments were derogatory or patronizing, depicting the peoples of Africa, the Americas, and the Pacific Islands as savages without culture.

All peoples of the world have a history, but in ancient times very few people wrote. Historians today work primarily with written evidence that provides direct access to peoples of the past. Thus there are limits to what they can say about people who left no written documents, such as the early Polynesians whom Sir Joseph Banks described, or about cultures such as the Olmec of Mesoamerica, whose writings they do not comprehend. To explore the lives of such populations, researchers must rely on material remains, which can be anything from a massive city to a simple ax or knife used to build a boat or to harvest fruit. Scholars usually refer to this type of archaeological study as **prehistory**, a discipline that focuses on the remains of nonliterate peoples or peoples with early writing systems that are still not fully deciphered. Their artifacts can reveal developments as complex as those recorded by ancient literate cultures.

prehistory The scholarly discipline that studies peoples' histories before they left behind written evidence; also the time period during which cultures had no writing.

MAPPING THE WORLD

Peoples of Africa, the Americas, and the Pacific Islands, c. 3000 B.C.E.–500 C.E.

Throughout the ancient world, peoples without writing—and hence outside the traditional historical record—established vibrant cultures, which are known to us mostly from archaeological remains. In Africa and the Pacific Islands, migrants spread aspects of these cultures over wide areas and into different natural zones, whereas in the Americas, cultures developed distinctive elements in relative geographic isolation. Everywhere ancient peoples created traditions of lasting impact.

ROUTES ▼

→ Bantu migrations, c. 3000 B.C.E.–400 C.E.

→ Austronesian migrations, c. 3000 B.C.E.–1000 C.E.

c. 200–600 C.E. Moche culture in the Andes

▪ c. 400 C.E. Bantu arrival in southern Africa

0	1000 C.E.	2000 C.E.

c. 100 B.C.E.–400 C.E. Hopewell culture in eastern North America

c. 400 B.C.E.–250 C.E. Early Maya culture in Mesoamerica

c. 800 B.C.E.–200 C.E. Nok culture in West Africa

c. 400–1200 C.E. Second wave of Austronesian migrations

In this chapter we consider prehistoric cultures from various parts of the world as examples of historical developments in such societies. Literate observers often used to dismiss them as "peoples without history," but in the 1980s the anthropologist Eric Wolf laid the groundwork for a new attitude by showing how prehistoric cultures actively shaped world history. The examples in this chapter show that such societies could reach high levels of social and technological development and acquire many features of what we call civilization, including cities.

This is not to say that these societies closely resembled those of Eurasia in the same period. Some purposely rejected technologies that were almost universally used elsewhere in the ancient world, such as pottery. Members of these societies lived in smaller communities than their contemporaries in Eurasia, and they did not create the large states that emerged there. The prehistoric peoples we study here were more physically isolated from other cultures than those treated before, and local conditions had more impact than outside influences on their cultural development. Geographical features such as high mountain ranges and dense forests were harder to cross than in Eurasia, where transcontinental routes existed. Yet some of these small groups—especially among the Polynesians and Africa's Bantu speakers—migrated vast distances by water or land and in this way spread technologies and cultural traditions to a range of new environments.

As in Eurasian societies, in this period the inhabitants of Africa, the Americas, and the Pacific Islands laid the groundwork for later developments. In a sense, they are the voiceless peoples of early world history, for the absence of writing that we can comprehend makes them less approachable than other cultures we have studied. But it is important to remember that throughout the ancient world, very few people speak to us directly—as in every society we have discussed so far, the great majority of people were illiterate and remain equally voiceless.

OVERVIEW
QUESTIONS

The major global development in this chapter: The evolution of ancient cultures without writing and their fundamental role in world history.

As you read, consider:

1. How does the presence or absence of writing influence how we study ancient cultures?

2. Why did the ancient cultures of Africa, the Americas, and the Pacific often show similar developments in spite of their isolation from one another?

3. How is the spread of peoples, languages, and technologies interrelated, and in what ways can we study these processes?

Peoples of Sub-Saharan Africa

FOCUS

How have scholars reconstructed the histories of early Africans, and what do their sources reveal about the livelihoods and cultures of these peoples?

The human species originated in Africa, the continent with the longest history in the world. But except in northern Africa, the study of early African history must be based primarily on material remains, because there were no native writing systems, and accounts by foreign visitors are scarce until European reports from the seventeenth century C.E. Thus, we mainly reconstruct developments in sub-Saharan Africa in ancient times through archaeology, with some help from linguistics. These sources show a long-term process during which the livelihoods of most people changed from gathering and hunting to agriculture, as was the case in the Eurasian regions we studied before. In many parts of Africa, migrations by peoples speaking Bantu languages were responsible for the shift to settled farming. Geography and climate combined to keep these farming communities small, however, and large urban centers did not emerge in Africa in this period.

Early Hunters and Herders

The earliest inhabitants of Africa, as elsewhere, survived by gathering and hunting local resources. Animals and plants were abundant enough that small groups of people could comfortably survive throughout most of the continent. Africa has several ecological zones that provide a diversity of wild resources (see Map 8.1).

African Ecology

Around the equator lies a tropical rain forest. The area has few food sources and the climate promotes tropical diseases such as malaria, so in ancient times human occupation was very limited there. But **savannas**—tropical or subtropical grasslands with scattered trees and shrubs where plenty of animals reside and plant life is rich—cover large parts of Africa. These grassy expanses have drawn gatherers and hunters throughout history. Wild food supplies were especially plentiful near lakes, and ancient peoples who lived near them could spend most of the year in the same settlement without farming. Instead, they subsisted largely by fishing, hunting, and collecting plants and nuts.

Soon after 5000 B.C.E., some people in northern Africa moved from gathering and hunting to herding animals. This transition is vividly documented in cave paintings in the Tassili (TAH-sihl-ee) region, located in the midst of the Sahara Desert in southern modern-day Algeria (see again Chapter 1's Seeing the Past: Saharan Rock Art, page 21). Before 5000 B.C.E., the climate there was much wetter than it is today, and it supported a bounty of animal and human life. The earliest paintings, whose exact date we cannot establish, show humans hunting big game with spears and bows. But those painted from perhaps 4500 B.C.E. to 2500 B.C.E. depict people as herders of cattle, sheep, and goats. Wild cattle were native to the Sahara. Sheep and goats were not, however, so the Saharan people must have imported them from the Middle East, where these animals had been herded since 8000 B.C.E. Later art shows attempts to domesticate other native animals, such as giraffes and ostriches, a sign of the people's greater reliance on domesticated resources. Simultaneously, early Africans collected and cared for plants more intensively. Thus we can say that from 4500 B.C.E. to 2500 B.C.E., a widespread pastoral culture flourished in Africa north of the rain forest.

Bantu Migrations

Today some 85 million people in Africa speak a myriad of closely related languages that originate from one common source. Scholars call the linguistic group they belong to **Bantu**, after a native term for "persons" or "people." The expansion of Bantu languages all over the continent is related to the spread of agriculture and is fundamentally important to African history. The processes involved parallel those of the spread of Indo-European languages discussed in Chapter 3, and scholars study them in the same way. Linguistic analysis identifies similarities and differences among the various languages to determine how closely they are related and to estimate when their speakers became separated. As these examples from four central African languages show, the similarities are great, but there are clear differences.

savanna Tropical or subtropical grassland with scattered trees and shrubs.

Bantu The name for some five hundred closely related languages spoken in sub-Saharan Africa, and for the speakers of these languages.

English	Asu	Bemba	Koyo	Yao
husband	ume	lume	lomi	lume
house	umba	nganda	ndago	njuumba
cattle	ngombe	ngombe	(not used)	ngoombe

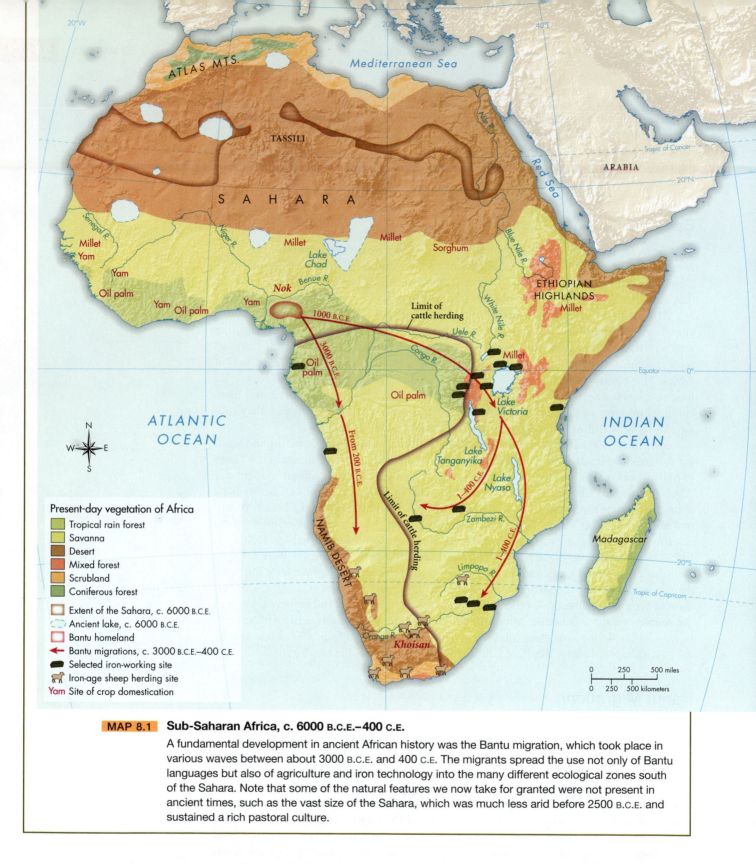

Present-day vegetation of Africa
- Tropical rain forest
- Savanna
- Desert
- Mixed forest
- Scrubland
- Coniferous forest
- Extent of the Sahara, c. 6000 B.C.E.
- Ancient lake, c. 6000 B.C.E.
- Bantu homeland
- Bantu migrations, c. 3000 B.C.E.–400 C.E.
- Selected iron-working site
- Iron-age sheep herding site
- Yam Site of crop domestication

MAP 8.1 **Sub-Saharan Africa, c. 6000 B.C.E.–400 C.E.**

A fundamental development in ancient African history was the Bantu migration, which took place in various waves between about 3000 B.C.E. and 400 C.E. The migrants spread the use not only of Bantu languages but also of agriculture and iron technology into the many different ecological zones south of the Sahara. Note that some of the natural features we now take for granted were not present in ancient times, such as the vast size of the Sahara, which was much less arid before 2500 B.C.E. and sustained a rich pastoral culture.

The roughly five hundred Bantu languages differ from one another to varying degrees. Most scholars accept that the first Bantu speakers had a single homeland in the southern region of modern-day Cameroon and eastern Nigeria. From this core, people migrated in successive waves south and east in a long-term process, until their descendants inhabited most of sub-Saharan Africa (see again Map 8.1). Scholars debate the dates of the migrations, but many agree that a first southward movement began in the west of Africa in about 3000 B.C.E. Another wave began in around 1000 B.C.E. and swept east to the region of the

Great Lakes in modern Kenya and Tanzania. This second wave moved into southern Africa and merged with the descendants of the first southward migration, a process that may have been completed by 400 C.E.

The speakers of Bantu languages had very diverse forms of social, political, and economic organization, but all based their economic lives on agriculture. The Sahara Desert had dried up after 5000 B.C.E., pushing people into the sub-Saharan savanna, and it was probably on the edges of the rain forest that they learned how to farm crops. The yam, the root of a tropical vine, proved especially important. The knowledge of how to cultivate yams probably arose accidentally as people observed that plants growing on rubbish heaps near settlements flourished more than fully wild plants. After the men cut down trees and other large plants, leaving some remains to screen the soil from heavy rains, the women made narrow furrows in the earth in which they planted yam cuttings. Similarly, the inhabitants of the savanna learned to farm sorghum and millet, local grasses that produce grains, and they promoted the growth of a palm tree whose nuts they could press for oil. The earliest farmers in sub-Saharan Africa also raised cattle.

In around 3000 B.C.E. these agriculturalists started to migrate. It was a slow process, and it did not begin for any one reason. Probably the most common cause was that a community grew too large for the local area to support, so part of the population had to leave. But other motivations existed—sometimes adventurous individuals set out on long journeys, or a community could expel people they considered undesirable. The migrants traveled on foot or by boat, searching for new areas suitable to their agriculture.

Wherever the Bantu migrants settled, their villages became the focal point for the smaller groups of gatherer-hunters in the area. These local groups were probably most attracted by the settlers' use of pottery, which made cooking easier (see Lives and Livelihoods: Potters of Antiquity). The gatherer-hunters exchanged their fish or meat with the settlers for farmed food, and Bantu languages were probably crucial to their interactions. Over time, the gatherer-hunters introduced the Bantu to the rain forest. This development may have harmed the local populations, because the forest clearance needed for the cultivation of yams drew malaria-bearing mosquitoes. In any event, the encounters between the original people and the newly arrived Bantu speakers led to cultural exchange and assimilation. Bantu speakers started to adopt non-Bantu words and expressions, and the original populations adopted agriculture and other Bantu practices.

Bantu speakers moved everyplace in eastern and southern Africa where farming was possible, but they did not enter zones too dry to cultivate their crops. Into these areas they pushed people who maintained a gathering and hunting lifestyle until modern times. Prominent among them were the Khoisan (KOI-sahn), gatherer-hunters and pastoralists from southern Africa who spoke languages in which a clicking sound is used for consonants. Although the Bantu displaced the Khoisan in many parts of southern Africa, Khoisan gatherer-hunters survived in desert areas into the modern period.

Farming became more efficient with the arrival of iron technology, which deeply influenced Bantu society and agriculture. Iron has several advantages over other metals: iron ore is found in numerous locations, and the metal is stronger than the bronze that many cultures used before iron. The first evidence for working iron ore in world history comes from about 2000 B.C.E. in the Middle East, but people in the region started to use the metal extensively to arm soldiers and make tools only in about 800 B.C.E. Soon afterward, iron technology appeared in sub-Saharan Africa. Most scholars think it arrived from the Middle East, because to work iron one must know how to regulate air flow in furnaces; people in sub-Saharan Africa did not melt any metals before, and without experimenting with softer metals it seems unlikely that they would have developed the skills to work iron. It remains unclear how the technology reached sub-Saharan Africa, however, and other scholars argue that people developed it locally. In any case, the replacement of stone tools with iron tools had a great impact on agriculture. It became much easier to clear trees in the previously impenetrable rain forest, rendering new areas fit for farming.

Those who could work iron could make much better weapons than the stone arms others used. This military advantage may have encouraged them to drive out gatherer-

Farmers and Migrants

Bantu Relations with Gatherer-Hunters

Iron Technology

Potters of Antiquity

With very few exceptions, people in agricultural societies produce pottery, that is, containers made of clay that have been baked to keep their shape. In antiquity all pottery was fired at a relatively low temperature, between 1652° and 2192° F, and needed to be glazed (coated with a special layer) to become waterproof. Archaeologists find broken and whole pots in large quantities in almost every excavation. These remains are crucially important to our understanding of ancient societies because of their enormous variety in shape and decoration.

Pottery manufacture began in Japan in around 12,000 B.C.E. From the start, people shaped pots in different ways and decorated them according to local tastes. They molded them into countless forms, painted them with various pigments, and incised them or added such elements as knobs. Shapes and decorations changed rapidly, giving the archaeologist an effective means for dating. Variations in the quality and care of pottery decoration inform historians about class differences, and the presence of foreign pottery in certain places reveals trade contacts. Beyond their importance to the modern scholar, potters were crucial contributors in ancient societies, creating valuable utensils as well as expressing ideologies and aesthetic values.

Pottery revolutionized cooking, allowing people to heat liquids and other food products such as fats and store them for prolonged periods. This feature of pottery had the greatest effect on women's lives. It is likely that pottery was mainly the work of women who shaped, decorated, and baked basic pots as part of their domestic chores. Because basic pots are easy to make, the earliest potters worked at home or in simple communal installations. From the beginning, these women showed imagination and the desire to make something beautiful. The creative possibilities of working with clay are almost limitless because it is flexible and easy to decorate, and so for peoples all over the world, pots are often the most prominent and plentiful art forms.

Many of the cultures discussed in this chapter had especially skilled potters. The Moche potters of the Andes, for example, fashioned vessels in the shape of human heads, creating what may have been portraits of their patrons. At the same time, people living in southern Peru used the patterns of Paracas textiles to adorn their pots in colorful ways. Although the meanings of these decorations are mysterious to us, they may have had great symbolic importance to the pots' owners. Unfortunately, we do not know the identities of the individual potters. In ancient literate societies where pottery remained valuable, we do

Moche Vessel
Once baked, clay survives extremely well in most climates, and the potters of antiquity left much remarkable artwork for us to study. Particularly famed for the skills of their potters are the Moche from the South American Andes, whose state lasted from about 200 to 600 C.E. Many vessels represent human heads, probably those of the men who commissioned them. They show the men as warriors, strengthening the view that the Moche were a militaristic society. (Private Collection/Paul Maeyaert/AISA/Bridgeman Art Library.)

sometimes know the maker. A Greek vase from around 530 B.C.E. contains the remark, "Exekias made and painted me," but such signatures are rare. Roman potters regularly impressed a stamp that identified their workshop.

Artistic experimentation with pottery inspired other forms of creativity. The earliest preserved sculptures of sub-Saharan Africa are the terra cotta heads of the Nok culture in Nigeria (see page 246). Potters' work with clay must have been instrumental in teaching the sculptors of these striking figures what shapes they could obtain.

Thus, the potters of antiquity were not mere artisans who provided for basic needs. They were also artists who imaginatively expressed their societies' ideas and tastes, which we can study today through their enduring creations.

QUESTIONS TO CONSIDER

1. In what ways is pottery useful to the scholar?

2. How can pottery reveal the social conditions of an ancient society?

For Further Information:
Barnett, William K., and John W. Hooper, eds. *The Emergence of Pottery: Technology and Innovation in Ancient Societies*. Washington, D.C.: Smithsonian Institution Press, 1995.
Orton, Clive, Paul Tyers, and Alan Vince. *Pottery in Archaeology*. Cambridge, U.K.: Cambridge University Press, 1993.

hunters by force. Iron weapons were also better for hunting large animals. Further, iron had a powerful social impact, because people used the metal as a measure of value for exchange. Objects of high-quality iron brought prestige to those who possessed them.

Bantu Society

Matrilineal descent was the cornerstone of Bantu social organization. Status, goods, and political office were inherited from mothers, and a man usually moved to his wife's village upon marriage. Adolescent boys were initiated into adult life in circumcision rituals, secret ceremonies that could last for several weeks. Circumcision rituals inducted young men into community-wide fraternities that shouldered many of the collective tasks of the village, both in peace and in war.

In these societies, marriage was a less significant rite of passage into adult society than it was in the Eurasian societies we have studied. Childbearing, not marriage, signified a woman's entry into full adulthood. Although men cleared forests for cultivation, women did virtually all the farming. This division of labor encouraged polygamy. Women's labor made valuable contributions to household wealth, and a man with several wives could farm more land, produce more food, and raise more children. Despite the prevalence of matrilineal descent and the central place of women in production as well as reproduction, decision-making authority within families was usually a male privilege.

With the migrations, Bantu social and political institutions changed significantly, especially in East Africa. The dislocations of migration and the intermarriage with indigenous peoples caused a steady shift away from the Bantu tradition of matrilineal descent and inheritance to patrilineal descent and strict gender roles in food production. This change also resulted from the growing importance of herding, especially cattle raising. Cattle became the crucial form of wealth in East African societies, and this wealth went to the men who tended the cattle. Agriculture remained a woman's task with little prestige. As cattle herds increased in size, ownership of cattle conferred status as well as wealth. Men who owned large herds of cattle could attract many followers and dependents and assume positions of leadership in their communities. Moreover, the authority of chiefs derived increasingly from wealth; previously, it had depended heavily on ties to the spirits of their ancestors residing at the ancestral burial grounds. Thus, the cultural exchanges that accompanied Bantu migrations changed the societies of both the Bantu migrants and the peoples they encountered. Encounters with Bantu speakers introduced new languages, technologies, and forms of subsistence to local populations, and the connections between Bantu speakers and their new neighbors led to a significant reorganization of Bantu society.

Bantu Religion

Because sub-Saharan Africans did not write until their encounters with Europeans in the modern period, we have no texts on Bantu religious beliefs. Accordingly, to reconstruct early Bantu ideas, historians of religion use tales and customs that exist today or that earlier visitors recorded. Just as scholars use similarities in language to trace Bantu migrations, they use similarities in myths and beliefs among distant African peoples to identify the original, common set of religious ideas. For example, many modern Bantu speakers think that proper human conduct was part of the natural order established at the time of creation, but that the creator has remained distant ever since. They believe that natural disasters and evil arise from human transgressions that disturb the cosmic order. To restore the essential positive nature of things, mortals must perform rituals to clear away anger and calm the spirits. Although these views are widespread and probably originated with the earliest Bantu, scholars accept that ideas and rituals change over time, so they cannot firmly establish what the Bantu speakers of antiquity believed and how they expressed those beliefs.

Bantu Art

The archaeological remains of ancient Africa—mostly tools, pottery, and dwellings—are largely devoted to basic human needs such as food and housing. But the early sub-Saharan Africans also produced nonutilitarian goods. From around 800 B.C.E. to around 200 C.E., for example, people of the Nok culture in modern northern Nigeria created remarkable artwork in terra cotta. Their baked clay human heads, often life-size, show unique skills of representation. Throughout their history, the Khoisan people of southern Africa produced many cave paintings, representing their lives as hunters of local animals such as giraffes and elands. People from sub-Saharan Africa undoubtedly fashioned many other objects of art as well, but they were often made of materials that have now decomposed.

A Nok Figurine

In the centuries between 800 B.C.E. and 200 C.E., the Nok culture of western Africa produced impressive statues of terra cotta (baked clay), the oldest known figurative sculpture south of the Sahara. Made, like the culture's pottery, from coils of clay, these statues are hollow. Most of the remains are heads or other body parts from large statues, which were close to life-size when complete but often broke over time. For reasons scholars continue to debate, Nok artists tended to emphasize certain elements of the person's appearance—in this example, the woman's eyes and jewelry. (Museum of Fine Arts, Houston/Funds from the Brown Foundation Accessions Endowment Fund/ Bridgeman Art Library.)

Thus, ancient Africa produced diverse and dynamic communities, connected by a common thread of Bantu culture, society, and technology. The cultural richness of sub-Saharan Africa in ancient times had parallels in other parts of the world where prehistoric cultures flourished. Those of the Americas will draw our attention next.

Peoples of the Americas

FOCUS

What kinds of evidence have scholars used to recreate the experience of ancient American peoples, and what do we know about these cultures?

As we saw in Chapter 1, the most widely accepted theory about the peopling of the world holds that migrants crossed into North America from northeastern Asia during the last Ice Age about fifteen thousand years ago and then spread throughout the Americas. When the glaciers gradually melted, rising sea levels cut off the Americas from the rest of the world. Although sailors from Europe and perhaps from Africa could still reach American shores, these visits did not introduce lasting changes until the sixteenth century C.E. Thus, all technological and social developments after people arrived in the ancient Americas were due to internal processes until European contact.

In Central and South America, societies developed first into states and later into empires. Mountain ranges created separate areas with distinct natural conditions. Despite the difficulties of overland contacts and the region's enormous ecological diversity, cultural similarities developed over wide areas, and a number of populations seem to have shared ideologies and religious beliefs. In Central America, or Mesoamerica, and the Andes Mountains of South America, archaeological evidence reveals a variety of advanced cultures. By contrast, the peoples of North America remained mostly isolated from their southern neighbors and pursued a gatherer-hunter lifestyle for much longer. As we explore the cultures of ancient America, we will look at societies in both regions to illustrate key historical developments in this part of the world.

The Olmecs 1200–400 B.C.E.

Volcanoes in the narrow strip of land that connects North and South America created high mountain barriers between numerous valleys and coastal zones. Because these natural barriers created relatively isolated areas with distinct natural environments, it is no surprise that several centers of cultural development arose (see Map 8.2). One such area occupies the modern Mexican states of Tabasco and Veracruz, south of the Gulf of Mexico. Between 1200 and 400 B.C.E., this region had a flourishing common culture that influenced others for hundreds of miles beyond its heartland. Scholars today call the culture in Tabasco and Veracruz *Olmec*, after the name Spanish conquerors in the sixteenth century C.E. gave the region's people.

The Olmecs, or their ancestors, were one of the few peoples on earth who invented agriculture independently, sometime between 3000 and 2000 B.C.E. Their crops differed from those of Eurasia and North Africa, however, because their indigenous plants were different. The cereal they cultivated was maize (corn), and beans and squash were also very important. Moreover, unlike Eurasia and Africa, the Americas had no large native mammals that could be domesticated for food. So before the arrival of the Spanish in the sixteenth century C.E., the main sources of protein for all Mesoamerican people were hunted animals (rabbits, deer, and iguanas), domesticated turkeys and dogs, and fish, which supplemented the crops they grew.

Olmec Livelihoods

Although agriculture was not as productive in Mesoamerica as in the river valley cultures of South Asia and northern Africa, the Olmecs could concentrate enough resources to construct elaborate ceremonial centers. The earliest such center, San Lorenzo, was inhabited beginning in 1500 B.C.E. In around 1200 B.C.E., the people leveled the mountain top where the settlement was situated and created a platform some 2500 by 3300 feet in size and 165 feet higher than the surrounding countryside. On top of this platform they built podiums and pyramids of clay and erected numerous sculptures, including ten massive stone heads. These sculptures were made of the volcanic rock basalt, which the Olmecs could have obtained only in mountains some fifty miles away; they probably placed the rocks on rafts to float downriver to the ceremonial center. The stone heads represented men who must have been important to the people of San Lorenzo, but scholars do not

Olmec Ceremonial Centers

MAP 8.2

Mesoamerica, c. 1200 B.C.E.–250 C.E.

Mesoamerica forms a land bridge between North and South America, yet is itself fragmented by mountain ranges and valleys. It was home to a variety of highly developed cultures between 1200 B.C.E. and 250 C.E., Olmec and Maya prominent among them. Both cultures left behind impressive buildings and monumental artwork, which shed light on elaborate ceremonial activity, including blood sacrifices and ballgames. These traditions would survive in the region after ancient times.

An Olmec Colossal Head

The Olmec had a centuries-long tradition of setting up colossal heads of men with helmetlike headgear, which may indicate that they were warriors or participants in ceremonial ballgames. The example shown here is 10 feet high and 7 feet wide and made of basalt, a volcanic rock imported from distant mountains. This head is one of the earliest from San Lorenzo, the largest city in Mesoamerica and the leading Olmec site from about 1200 to 900 B.C.E. (Art Archive/Xalapa Museum Veracruz Mexico/Gianni Dagli Orti.)

know their identity. They could have been kings, chiefs, or participants in the ballgames characteristic of later Mesoamerican culture.

In around 900 B.C.E., the Olmecs shifted the focus of their building activity fifty-five miles to the northeast to the site that is now called La Venta. Between 800 and 400 B.C.E., they developed the locale into their most elaborate ceremonial center. At its core stood a clay pyramid (badly destroyed today) with a base measuring 420 by 240 feet and a height of over 108 feet. Bordering the pyramid to the north and south were plazas that contained magnificent stone monuments: colossal heads, massive thrones, stelae decorated with carved relief sculptures, and statues. Also carved from imported stone, the heads in some cases are 11 feet high and weigh 20 tons. The complex at La Venta contained a jaguar mask of green serpentine stone and what seems to be a tomb chamber filled with jade.

The remains at La Venta tell an intriguing and puzzling story. The stone sculptures were regularly damaged on purpose: faces were erased, arms and heads cut off, and pieces removed. The Olmecs then buried the sculptures and displayed new ones, which indicates that they were responsible for the mutilations. It is possible that the monuments' destruction was part of a ceremony performed at the death of the person portrayed. Speculation about the reasons for these acts continues, however. The size, complexity, and artistry of Olmec ceremonial centers speaks to the sophistication of Olmec culture, but like so much else about prehistory, we have more questions than answers about the Olmecs and their practices.

Just as we cannot offer verified explanations of Olmec practices, the absence of written evidence makes it difficult to explain the overarching purpose of the complexes at San Lorenzo and La Venta. Although they share certain elements with the cities of Eurasia, such as monumental buildings, they seem not to have been large population centers, as those cities were. They appear instead to have been primarily ceremonial in character, and ideas about what ceremonies took place there often depend on theories about the relationship between the Olmecs and later Mesoamerican cultures, especially the better-known Maya. Ceremonial centers with pyramids and intricate sculptures remained a part of Mesoamerican culture until the Spanish conquest in the sixteenth century C.E., and later practices are easier to understand because we have early European accounts and some written Maya evidence. For example, in the classical Maya period of 250–900 C.E. (discussed in Chapter 11), the ballgame ritual was very important; it ended in a blood sacrifice to renew the life-giving powers of the gods. It appears very likely that the Olmecs played the ballgame, as a dozen rubber balls were found as ritual deposits in a spring to the east of San Lorenzo, together with Olmec wooden sculptures. Because the game may have been important to the Olmecs, some scholars interpret the culture's colossal sculpted heads as representations of ball players.

Olmec Society and Ideology   It is clear that Olmec society was hierarchical, with an elite who had the power to demand labor from the general population. Based on Maya parallels, many archaeologists believe that the elites could even claim the lives of commoners and that they regularly practiced human sacrifice. The source of the elite's authority is debated. Many Olmec representations show men involved in rituals, which, along with their interpretations of Maya culture leads some scholars to suggest that Olmec leaders derived power from their role as **shamans**, individuals who have the ability to communicate with nonhuman powers and who safeguard the community's prosperity. The shaman's consumption of hallucinogenic drugs, such as extracts from toads, facilitated the dialogue with supernatural forces. Shamans appear in many parts of the world, and throughout history various societies have seen certain persons, often with unusual physical characteristics, as crucial to communication with greater powers, and the Olmecs may indeed have been among the peoples with this view. The leaders' powers probably had more secular aspects as well. The ceremonial centers gave prominence to stones imported from distant places, and it is likely that only elites could obtain them. This privilege must have confirmed their special status.

The validity of these scholarly interpretations of Olmec culture and ideology depends strongly on the Olmecs' connection to later Mesoamerican societies. Because their monuments are similar, many scholars see Olmec as the "mother culture" and inspiration of all subsequent Mesoamerican cultures. In this interpretation, the Olmecs would have spread their ideas and practices through trade to regions as distant as the Mexican west coast and El Salvador to the south, where later Mesoamerican cultures flourished. The appearance of Olmec objects and artistic motifs in these regions supports this view. Others disagree, however, and consider the various cultures of Mesoamerica to be of local origin, the result of internal developments.

The Early Maya 400 B.C.E.–250 C.E.

Olmec culture had disappeared by 400 B.C.E., for reasons that are unclear to us, and several major Mesoamerican cultures developed to the east and west of the Olmec heartland. In some of these cultures, people such as the Zapotecs (sah-po-TEHK) started to write, typically carving a few **glyphs**—symbolic characters used to record a word or a syllable in writing—beside the image of a person. Scripts survive in a variety of languages, but scholars can read none of them. The highly pictorial glyphs suggest that the content of the inscriptions resembles that of later Maya texts and deals with sacrifice, war, and the capture of enemies. The texts also use the calendar of the classic Maya, which allows scholars to date the inscriptions very accurately. Most of the inscriptions derive from western Mexico, with a few from the east coast (see Reading the Past: The La Mojarra Stele). Our inability to read Zapotec writing leaves us guessing about much of their early history; we know more about another Mesoamerican society, the Maya.

One of the best-documented Mesoamerican cultures in the archaeological record was that of the Maya, centered in the Yucatan Peninsula in the southeast corner of the Gulf of Mexico (see again Map 8.2). Although the culture achieved its height after 250 C.E., it originated earlier, in a time when various early Maya kingdoms existed side by side. Beginning in around 800 B.C.E., in an area of dense forest, the early Maya developed a number of complexes that included massive stone buildings, pyramids, and platforms. Throughout the first millennium B.C.E. and early first millennium C.E., they established several ceremonial centers. The largest was at El Mirador in the remote jungle of Guatemala, where between 150 B.C.E. and 50 C.E. the inhabitants built numerous tall pyramids, plazas, platforms, causeways, and elite houses in stone, decorating them with stone reliefs. How such a complex came to be constructed in such surroundings remains a mystery, because the area has insufficient agricultural land to support a large labor force.

El Mirador was not the only large Maya religious complex. In around 50 B.C.E., the site of Cerros (SEHR-roh), in a more hospitable environment near the sea, suddenly grew from a small village into a major center. The inhabitants leveled existing houses and shattered their contents—pottery, ornaments, and other objects. On top of the rubble they

Maya Ceremonial Centers

shaman A tribal member who acts as an intermediary between the physical and spiritual worlds.

glyph A figurative symbol, usually carved in stone, that imparts information.

The La Mojarra Stele

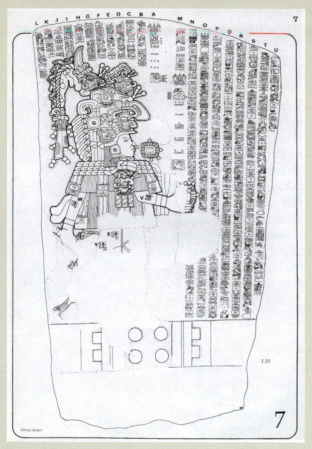

The La Mojarra Inscription, c. 160 C.E.
(Courtesy of George Stuart.)

Although the first Mesoamerican writing dates to about 400 B.C.E., historians cannot read the earliest inscriptions with certainty, because they often do not know what language the texts record. Yet scholars do find continuity between the earliest scripts and the later, better-known classic Maya script (discussed in Chapter 11). For example, many topics addressed in classic Maya inscriptions, such as warfare and the glorification of the leader, also appear much earlier. Moreover, the calendar used was the same, which allows scholars to date inscriptions with confidence.

In 1986 archaeologists discovered one early inscription on this stele, or stone tablet, at La Mojarra (la moh-HAH-rah), in the province of Veracruz in eastern Mexico, a region the Olmecs had occupied before the inscription was carved (see again Map 8.2). It contains two dates, 143 and 156 C.E., and seems to have been carved soon afterward. The language of the inscription is a matter of debate among scholars, as is the exact content, but all agree that the man with the elaborate cloak and headdress must be some kind of leader. They speculate that the stele deals with issues of sacrifice and war in parallel with later Maya inscriptions, which often deal with these concerns. The man's elaborate headdress resembles that of Maya war leaders. The La Mojarra inscription raises various puzzling questions, however. Why is this the only lengthy inscription from early Mesoamerica so far discovered? Is its language related to that of the Olmecs? And what is the relationship between this script and the later Maya?

EXAMINING THE EVIDENCE

1. In the absence of knowledge of the language, how have scholars sought to interpret the La Mojarra inscription?

2. What enables scholars to relate the inscription to the Olmecs?

erected a temple, surrounding it with plazas, pyramids, causeways, and other monuments characteristic of Maya settlements. The transformation occurred so abruptly that it must have resulted from the arrival of some powerful authority, who ordered the construction of a new settlement.

Maya Script   Early Maya sites contain a few glyphs that scholars can connect to a later stage of the Maya script. Much of the interpretation of the early inscriptions remains uncertain, but they clearly focus on the deeds of kings, especially in war. By understanding the calendar, scholars can assign precise dates to some early Maya monuments. For example, one stele was carved in the year 197 C.E. It shows a leader, whose name in the accompanying text is expressed by the combination of a bone and a rabbit skull, which scholars read as Bak T'ul. He is dressed as the rain god and surrounded by scenes of human sacrifice, fertility, and renewal. Beneath his hand are the severed bodies of three victims going down into the underworld.

As in Eurasia, all of the evidence indicates that a political and social elite in Mesoamerica held power over the mass of the population whose labor they commanded. The leaders of these societies commissioned representations showing them participating in rituals that often involved bloodletting and human sacrifice. Those rituals probably gave them a special connection to the gods: they were not methods of punishment but rather events that gave prestige to their participants. Men and women pierced themselves with stingray spines, thorns, or lancets, especially through the tongue, ears, and genitals. They usually collected the blood on clothlike paper, which they burned so that the gods could consume the blood in the form of smoke (see Seeing the Past: Early Maya Frescoes).

The early Maya cultures arose in a range of natural environments, as Map 8.2 reveals, and people's choice of a particular location for settlement was probably connected to their ideas about the universe and the king's role in connecting the human and supernatural worlds. We can scarcely imagine the massive amounts of labor and coordination involved in early Maya building projects; they were undertaken either without bureaucratic accounting records or with documents that have been lost over time, if indeed they ever existed. Such accomplishments as these led to the network of Maya city-states in the classical age, which we will study in Chapter 11.

Maya Society and Ideology

Andean Peoples 900 B.C.E.–600 C.E.

Along the west coast of South America runs a narrow finger of land that contains an amazing variety of ecological zones (see Map 8.3). Here the Pacific Ocean and the tops of the Andes Mountains, which can reach heights of over four miles, are only sixty miles apart.

Andean Ecology

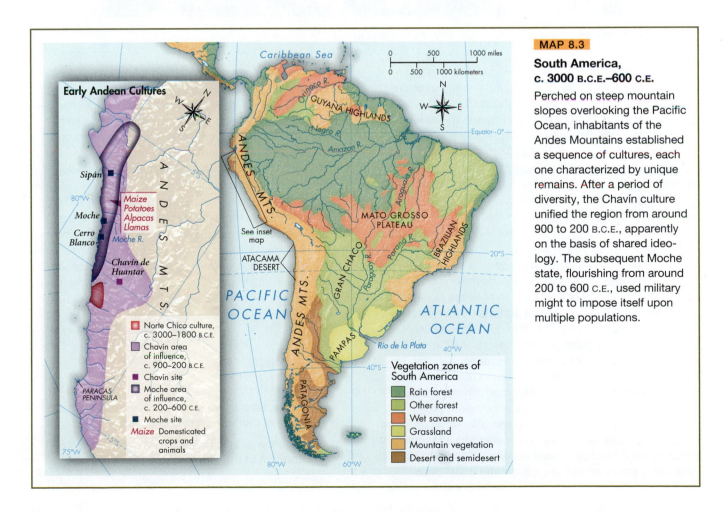

MAP 8.3

South America, c. 3000 B.C.E.–600 C.E.
Perched on steep mountain slopes overlooking the Pacific Ocean, inhabitants of the Andes Mountains established a sequence of cultures, each one characterized by unique remains. After a period of diversity, the Chavín culture unified the region from around 900 to 200 B.C.E., apparently on the basis of shared ideology. The subsequent Moche state, flourishing from around 200 to 600 C.E., used military might to impose itself upon multiple populations.

Early Maya Frescoes

Fresco from San Bartolo, c. 100 B.C.E. (Kenneth Garrett.)

In archaeology, chance discoveries can provide unexpected insights into past cultures. A stunning example is a find in 2001 by an archaeologist studying Meso-american culture. When making a day trip to the site of San Bartolo in the Guatemalan jungle (see again Map 8.2), he rested in a tunnel dug by looters. His flashlight revealed a chamber with traces of early Maya frescoes. Subsequent excavations of the entire room uncovered remarkable paintings on all the walls. The Maya artists who created them in around 100 B.C.E. displayed skills that scholars previously thought were not achieved until some four hundred years later.

The murals tell the story of the original creation of order in the world. They show four gods making offerings next to four trees that connect the earth to the sky in the Maya view of the universe. Each god's offering relates to an aspect of the universe. The third god, depicted here, offers an elaborate creature with aspects of a bird and a snake (in the lower right corner) representing the sky. At the same time, the gods provide a blood offering by piercing their penises with a lance. Blood offerings were very important in Maya religion, because they guaranteed renewal. The ideas about creation and offerings expressed here are the same as those in much later Maya material, including the *Popul Vuh*, written between 1554 and 1558 C.E. to tell local traditions about creation, the gods' deeds,

and the history of the people and kings of the region of modern Guatemala.

Another scene in the room depicts the original crowning of the maize god alongside the crowning of a Maya king, who thereby obtained legitimacy for his rule from the god. Before this image was found, there was no firm evidence that the early Maya people had a fully developed ideology of kingship under divine protection.

Originally located next to a pyramid from about 100 B.C.E., the painted room was soon thereafter buried below a larger pyramid. The complex was part of a settlement with some one hundred buildings, including a palace, a ball court, and another small pyramid, underneath which archaeologists excavated the earliest known Maya royal tomb. Overall, people seem to have developed the site in around 600 B.C.E. and stayed there at least until 100 C.E.

EXAMINING THE EVIDENCE

1. How does later Maya evidence help clarify the meaning of the San Bartolo frescoes?

2. What do the murals reveal about Maya ideas on the creation of the universe?

Between them is a diverse array of environments, including a coastal area that is arid except where rivers run through it. Marine resources are abundant, however, because the current that brings cold water from the South Pole carries vital nutrients that feed a wide variety of fish, shellfish, and sea mammals. Thanks to this sea life, early Andean coastal residents did not need to practice agriculture.

At irregular intervals this cold-water current is reversed by a global climatic event called *El Niño* (ehl NEEN-yoh) (Spanish for "the Christ Child," as the name derives from its occurrence around Christmas). When El Niño appears, warm water from the north chases away the marine life, while rainstorms sweep across and devastate the countryside. The unpredictable disruptions of El Niño take years to repair, and these times of crisis may have led to social and political upheaval among Andean peoples throughout history.

Perhaps to offset the uncertainties of marine supplies, the peoples of the Andes started to farm plants on the mountain slopes, potatoes possibly as early as 4400 B.C.E. and maize after 1500 B.C.E. Farther up the mountains they herded the alpaca and the llama, the only domesticated beasts of burden in South America. The tops of the Andes Mountains are so high that only people who have physically adjusted to the scarcity of oxygen can be active there. Thus in the Andean peoples we see a clear example of the profound impact of ecology on social development. As the peoples of the Andes adapted to local conditions and environmental change, unique communities evolved that reflected the challenges and opportunities the region's ecology presented.

As they adapted to their region's ecological diversity, early Andean peoples developed complex societies with a large array of intricate cultural expressions. One such local culture emerged in valleys of the Norte Chico region on the coast some one hundred miles north of Peru's modern capital, Lima, where between 3000 and 1800 B.C.E. people constructed large ceremonial centers, apparently for religious purposes. In some twenty centers, they built platforms on artificial mounds with circle-shaped plazas partially sunken into the ground. Buildings surrounded these platforms. The people of this culture did not yet make pottery, but they used gourds as containers, sometimes decorated with the image of a god holding a staff. They lived off the resources from the sea and practiced agriculture inland, including cotton, which they grew with irrigation.

Norte Chico Culture

In around 900 B.C.E., the cultural diversity of the Andes gave way to relative uniformity when a new culture, called Chavín (cha-BEAN), came to dominate a wide area of north and central Peru. In the Chavín culture, people used the same style of pottery decoration, similar artifacts, and the same architecture for about seven hundred years. The ceramics of Chavín show remarkable skill; the artisans shaped the vessels in many different forms, including elaborately decorated human and animal figures. They often depicted hybrid creatures, combining human and animal attributes, as well as snakes, birds, crocodiles, and fish. These animals came from different ecological zones within the region, including the Amazon forest on the east side of the Andes, which indicates that the Chavín people traveled widely. They also refined metalworking techniques, using pure gold or alloys of gold with silver or copper. Chavín artisans knew how to solder pieces together and how to shape them into three dimensions. At the site that gave the culture its name, Chavín de Huantar, 170 miles north of Lima, stood a stone temple complex with galleries, stairs, and ramps looking out over a plaza that was partly sunken into the ground. Fantastical stone carvings decorated the complex, including sculpted heads of humans, birds, and canines, as well as reliefs of felines, serpents, and supernatural beings made up of the body parts of various creatures. Once again, as we saw in Africa and other American societies, isolation and the challenges presented by geographical boundaries by no means inhibited creativity and innovation.

Chavín Culture

The Chavín culture inspired peoples over a wide stretch of the Andean region, including those of the south-central Peruvian peninsula of Paracas (pah-RAH-kas), 150 miles south of Lima. This area is especially famous for its long history of textile production. Even before the introduction of agriculture, people in this region wove fibers from cacti, grasses, and other

El Niño A periodic change in the sea current in the Pacific Ocean west of South America, which brings about severe climatic change in regions in and near the Pacific.

Weavers of Paracas

plants into textiles. When they domesticated cotton in around 3500 B.C.E., it became the main vegetable fiber for weaving, but people also used alpaca and llama hair.

In the late first millennium B.C.E., the introduction of tapestry weaving and new techniques of dyeing revolutionized textile production. The weavers produced intricate patterns and figures using multicolored threads and further decorated the cloth with feathers, metal strips, and other embellishments. The textiles had great importance in people's lives, especially at crucial events such as birth, marriage, and death, when individuals received special cloth. The most remarkable textiles produced by the inhabitants of Paracas are those used in the burials of wealthy people. The dead sat in a fetal position, wrapped in thick layers of multicolored cotton garments. These included embroidered mantles, tunics, and headbands that depicted mythical creatures and humans in ornate dress. Some of the dead were wrapped in more than one hundred such garments. The resulting mummy bundles were covered with white cotton sheets and placed in an underground vault, with up to forty individuals in one vault.

The Militaristic Moche State

The shared artistic motifs in the Chavín area and beyond suggest the region shared a common belief system that accorded great significance to animals and the forces of nature. Because there is no evidence of military conquest, it was evidently ideology rather than conquest that produced this cultural unity. In around 200 B.C.E., however, this unity ended, and the appearance of massive defensive structures around settlements suggests that wars may have torn the different peoples apart. After a period of disintegration, a new set of states arose, but the basis for control differed dramatically from that of the Chavín culture. One such state, in northern Peru, is called Moche (MOH-che) today, after the river in its center (see again Map 8.3). Flourishing from around 200 to 600 C.E., the Moche state was highly militaristic and hierarchical, as evidenced by its art, which teems with brutal images of warfare, torture, and other forms of violence.

The Moche economy was based on an elaborate system of irrigation agriculture. The people laid out a large network of mud canals on the mountain slopes, guiding the water for miles into the valleys. The farmers cultivated a mixed crop of maize, beans, squash, and chili peppers and fertilized the fields with guano (bird dung). With increased resources gained through agricultural development and military muscle, more people could live in cities, where they constructed huge ceremonial complexes.

At the Moche capital in Cerro Blanco, a few miles south of the modern city of Trujillo in northwestern Peru, the people built two enormous mud-brick temples in pyramid shapes. One of the largest solid structures in the Americas, the Pyramid of the Sun stood at least 130 feet high, measured 1115 feet by 525 feet at its base, and contained some 143 million bricks. Nearby rose the slightly smaller Pyramid of the Moon, made up of three separate platforms. The leaders of Moche society lived on top of these giant pyramids. But the structures also formed a ceremonial complex in which human sacrifice was central, as was the case in Maya culture. Excavations of nearby plazas have revealed the remains of seventy individuals who were killed and dismembered, their body parts having been thrown off the platforms. Human sacrifice is also prominent in the representational arts of the Moche. Humans in bird costumes slit the throats of prisoners, drank their blood, and cut off their heads, feet, and hands. The goal of the many wars the Moche

A Mummy from Paracas

Mummies are found not only in Egypt but also in many parts of the ancient world. Examples like this one from Paracas in the southern Andes show how much attention the people there paid to burial, dressing the dead with finely woven textiles and adorning them with jewelry made from bones. These mummies were usually placed in a seated position and wrapped with multiple layers of decorated textiles, such as those shown here and in At a Crossroads on page 236. (Museo del Oro, Lima, Peru/ Bridgeman Art Library.)

appear to have waged was probably not to kill enemies on the battlefield but to capture them and bring them home for these sacrifices.

Other Moche archaeological sites had similar ceremonial complexes. At Sipán (SHEE-pan) in northern Peru, archaeologists in 1987 C.E. discovered tombs that were also connected with human sacrifice. So far, these excavations have uncovered twelve tombs, three of them beneath large pyramids. The occupants of the pyramid tombs were buried with enormous amounts of grave goods—including pottery, jewelry, and textiles—as well as other humans (see again Lives and Livelihoods: Potters of Antiquity). In the richest tomb, said to be of "the lord of Sipán," eight individuals accompanied the dead, including three adult men, one adult woman, three young women, and one child. On top of the burial chamber lay the body of a young man whose feet had been amputated, seemingly to prevent his escape. The garments of the tomb occupants suggest that they were the central figures in the sacrificial ceremonies, as represented in Moche art.

The Moche state went into decline in the sixth century C.E., probably due to natural disasters, including a long drought. By 800 C.E. other states would arise to replace it. In around 1400 the entire Andean zone would be incorporated into the Inca Empire, which would continue some of the practices the Moche people had begun.

Ritual and Human Sacrifice

Gatherer-Hunters of North America 800 B.C.E.–400 C.E.

The vast North American continent contains many varied natural environments, and for millennia after humans arrived the relatively few inhabitants survived by hunting and collecting wild resources (see Map 11.3, page 357). Hunters in the Great Plains, for example, killed large bison herds after driving them into closed-off canyons. At times the meat was so abundant that they butchered only the best parts. These folk also gathered plants and hunted small game, however; the bison were caught mostly in the fall to provide meat for the winter months.

Great Plains Hunters

Eastern North America, between the Great Plains and the Atlantic Ocean, was a vast wooded region with a network of rivers centered on the Mississippi Valley, an area the size of India. Although this region had great agricultural potential because of its rich alluvial soils, until 400 C.E. most inhabitants survived by hunting and gathering the rich wild resources. They made simple pottery and crafted artwork, often using materials that had to be imported from distant regions. These materials were items of exchange among the small communities that lived throughout the region. The men who arranged for the exchange became community leaders and settled disputes in the mostly egalitarian societies. They or others may also have been shamans.

Eastern Woodlanders

The people of these communities joined forces to construct large earthworks, mostly low mounds that covered tombs, but also fortifications and platforms for buildings. The areas inside these fortifications were used for ceremonial rather than residential purposes. The largest known site of the period, at Newark in modern Ohio, belonged to what archaeologists call the Hopewell culture, which lasted from about 100 B.C.E. to 400 C.E. This site includes a large rectangular enclosure,

The Hopewell Shaman

This small stone figure was discovered near a burial mound of the Hopewell culture, which flourished from 100 B.C.E. to 400 C.E. along rivers in northeastern and midwestern North America. The figure wears a bearskin and appears to be holding a decapitated head in its lap. It probably represents a shaman, a man or woman who acted as an intermediary between humans and the forces of nature and the gods. (Ohio Historical Society.)

The Hopewell Culture, c. 100 B.C.E.–400 C.E.

one hundred acres in size, that surrounded forty mounds. Those mounds contained many crafted objects, often in hoards. The materials came from distant sources: shell from the Gulf of Mexico, copper from the Great Lakes, mica from the Carolinas, and obsidian (a glass-like volcanic rock) from the Rocky Mountains. The mound-building culture continued in the eastern woodlands after 400 C.E., when the introduction of agriculture fundamentally changed its social and economic structures (see Chapter 11). Even in this early period, however, we see evidence of sophisticated social organization and long-distance economic connections.

Thus, in ancient times various regions in the Americas developed cultures of different levels of complexity. All this took place without an extensive written tradition—in Mesoamerica the few examples of writing are brief official statements regarding wars and kingship, and in the Andes and North America no documents are preserved for this period. Although the absence of writing denies us access to many aspects of these cultures, archaeology provides us with abundant evidence of the energy and diversity of ancient American societies.

Peoples of the Pacific Islands

FOCUS

What do their material remains tell us about the Pacific Islanders' society and culture?

The Pacific Ocean, stretching 12,500 miles along the equator, covers much of the globe's tropical zone. This expanse is dotted with a myriad of small islands, mostly of volcanic origin or taking the form of **atolls**, rings of coral that grew up around sunken islands (see Map 8.4). Although their natural resources are limited to a few native plants, humans inhabit some fifteen hundred of the twenty-five thousand islands, the result of a colonization process that spanned millennia. These people did not create scripts, so their written histories begin with European descriptions from the eighteenth century C.E., such as the account by Sir Joseph Banks quoted at the start of this chapter.

Archaeology has helped to fill gaps in the study of these peoples' ancient past. Because archaeological exploration of the islands started only in the 1950s, it is still in its early phases, and many conclusions about the islands' early history are tentative. They do demonstrate, however, that people in this part of the world had the initiative and courage to sail across enormous distances to discover new lands—and that they brought their agricultural lifestyle with them.

Agricultural Livelihoods

Fishers, Farmers, and Herders

The early inhabitants of the Pacific Islands derived much of their food from the sea. Archaeological finds of food remains and simple agricultural tools show that they also cultivated plants and herded animals that their ancestors brought with them during migrations. Only a few native plants and fruits of the Pacific Islands became important foods; the islanders' main crops—coconut, taro, yam, banana, and breadfruit—were not native, and farmers had imported them from elsewhere. The peoples of the Pacific Islands promoted their growth using simple yet efficient techniques. For example, taro, a plant with an edible root, requires a very wet soil, so in some places the islanders created irrigation systems. By contrast, the yam, another root plant, needs a much drier soil, and the people drained marshes to grow it. Their domesticated animals were few—chickens, pigs, and dogs—but they were found on all inhabited islands. We see, then, that human needs profoundly shaped the ecology of the Pacific Islands. Islanders introduced new plant and

atoll A small ringlike island made of coral.

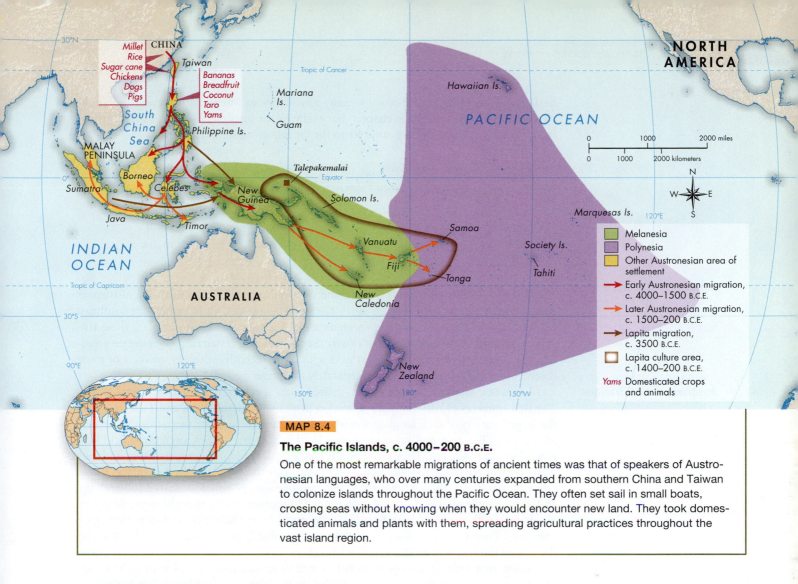

MAP 8.4

The Pacific Islands, c. 4000–200 B.C.E.

One of the most remarkable migrations of ancient times was that of speakers of Austronesian languages, who over many centuries expanded from southern China and Taiwan to colonize islands throughout the Pacific Ocean. They often set sail in small boats, crossing seas without knowing when they would encounter new land. They took domesticated animals and plants with them, spreading agricultural practices throughout the vast island region.

animal species and altered the land itself to create environments capable of sustaining their communities.

Scholars believe that much of the colonization of new islands was deliberate, displacing the earlier theory that drifters settled the islands by accident. As with Bantu migrants in Africa, Polynesian peoples set out with the plants and animals they intended to grow and breed, and they established permanent dwellings soon after arriving in the new land. In Africa the Bantu speakers moved on land or traveled along rivers in boats; in the Pacific, migration required sailing, sometimes across great distances. Because the supply of food was steady, Polynesians did not decide to move because the natural resources of their original islands were insufficient. More likely, younger sons initiated the adventures to find places where they could head their own families, a status that was denied them in hierarchical systems that gave precedence to the eldest son.

Peopling the Islands

Analysis of the migrations that populated the Pacific Islands uses the same methodologies as studies of Bantu and Indo-European migrations, and it faces the same uncertainties. All reconstructions of migrations rely on a mixture of linguistic and archaeological evidence to determine what modern populations share common ancestors and when they became separated from one another. The dating of events is especially problematic, because it relies on scant archaeological evidence.

The peoples of the Pacific Islands speak languages that belong to the Austronesian family, which also includes modern Malayan and Indonesian. Some one thousand Austro-

Colonization of Islands

nesian languages exist, and they show many similarities, as Joseph Banks recognized in the passage at the beginning of the chapter. For example, the inhabitants of three island groups in Polynesia use almost all the same terms for the following English words:

English	Society Islands (includes Tahiti)	Tonga	New Zealand
two	rooa	looa	rooa
five	reema	neema	reema
eye	matta	matta	matta
to drink	ainoo	ainoo	ainoo

The indigenous peoples of Taiwan and of some areas in southern China also speak Austronesian languages, as do the inhabitants of Madagascar, an island off the southeast coast of Africa. By comparing the vocabularies and grammatical features of all these languages, linguists can determine how closely they are related. If two languages are very similar, the peoples speaking them must have split quite recently, whereas speakers of more divergent languages must have lived separately for longer periods.

Austronesian Migrations

Linguistic analysis indicates that Austronesian speakers migrated in several waves. The first speakers of Austronesian languages lived in southern China and Taiwan, where the largest variety of such languages exists today. These early Austronesians were farmers who grew millet, rice, and sugar cane; they lived in wooden houses, used boats, and kept pigs, dogs, and chickens. They knew how to make pottery but did not use metals, and they had a typical Neolithic lifestyle that they shared with the people of farther inland China (see Chapter 3). In around 3000 B.C.E. this homogenous population started to break up, and some people migrated south by sea to the Philippines, where they discovered tropical plants for cultivation, such as breadfruit, coconut, bananas, yams, and taro (see again Map 8.4). They improved the canoes they used, probably by adding sails and outriggers (beams on the side that greatly increased stability).

These new technologies enabled the people to spread rapidly and widely. In subsequent centuries Austronesian speakers settled on the islands of Southeast Asia to the west and of Melanesia and western Polynesia to the east, a process that seems to have ended around 750 B.C.E. Then there was a pause of about a thousand years before further expansion occurred in around 400 C.E., as we will see in Chapter 11. Many of the islands at which the Austronesians arrived had only small gatherer-hunter communities that were easily displaced, and members of these communities gradually learned how to farm. On the large island of New Guinea, however, indigenous people had developed agriculture in the highlands long before the arrival of the Austronesians, and with their larger numbers they restricted Austronesian settlement to areas on the shores.

Lapita Culture

The migrating Austronesians took with them a mixture of technologies and styles that gives us another means of using the archaeological record to trace their movements. From 1400 to 200 B.C.E., those living in Melanesia surrounded themselves with material goods that archaeologists identify as belonging to the Lapita (lah-PEE-tah) culture. Most distinctive is the pottery—although the pots were poorly made and not well fired, they were extensively decorated by incising lines or impressing comb-like toothed instruments, which left a series of dots. The lines formed geometric motifs and occasionally human features such as faces, and they were probably filled with lime and other white substances. The designs resembled the body tattoos popular among Austronesian speakers.

The pottery, fishhooks, and other implements of the Lapita culture spread eastward from Melanesia into western Polynesia by 1000 B.C.E. The migration was amazingly

The Lapita Culture, c. 1400–200 B.C.E.

fast: scholars estimate that they explored 2800 miles of the ocean over as few as fifteen to twenty-five human generations. In the end, Lapita culture appeared across 4050 miles, from northeastern New Guinea to Samoa. Although some pots were traded among islands, local artisans produced most pottery using the same techniques as their forebears. After 750 B.C.E. the quality of their pottery declined even further, however, and by the beginning of the common era some Polynesians stopped producing pottery altogether.

The Polynesians' decision to abandon the use of pottery is unique in world history. Everywhere else, people considered the technology superior because pots could be used to store and cook foods (see again Lives and Livelihoods: Potters of Antiquity). The absence of pottery in Polynesia is easily understandable, however, because atolls lack the clay needed to make it. On other islands, however, people consciously decided to stop using pots even when clay was present. Instead of boiling foods, they baked them in underground ovens, and for storage, drinking cups, and the like, the islanders used coconut shells, which were readily available. In short, they had no need to continue using advanced pottery technology.

The people of the Lapita culture inhabited small villages, living in houses they sometimes built on stilts. They grew taro, yams, and other tropical plants and kept dogs, pigs, and chickens. They were mostly self-sufficient, with trade in obsidian for stone tools the only essential link among the islands. Because of their self-sufficiency, and the influence of the indigenous populations on the settlers, Lapita communities developed many local characteristics, making Melanesia a highly diverse world.

Lapita Lifestyles

When the descendants of the Austronesian migrants came into contact with Europeans in the eighteenth century C.E., the islanders may still have adhered to practices that dated back many centuries. But we must take care not to imagine these societies as static and unchanging. Rather, we should acknowledge that throughout history the peoples of this region were experts at adapting their lifestyles to the local circumstances of numerous islands. As members of small communities, they did not need writing, instead passing on their knowledge, skills, and beliefs orally, from person to person, over many centuries.

COUNTERPOINT
The Voiced and Voiceless in Ancient Literate Societies

When we study peoples of the ancient past, we find a wealth of visible, physical artifacts, which can be astonishingly rich and appealing. In this chapter we have seen Nok sculptures, Olmec colossal heads, Andean textiles, and many other examples of human ingenuity that tell us much about their creators. But historians are especially attracted to written documentation, because it can reveal elements of ancient cultures about which there is no other evidence, such as the languages people spoke, the names they gave themselves and the things that surrounded them, their literary creativity, and much more. The advent of writing in the various cultures of the world is thus an important turning point, because it opens new pathways for us to approach the peoples of the past.

> **FOCUS**
>
> To what extent does a society's literacy or nonliteracy affect our study of it?

The first humans to invent writing lived some 5300 years ago in the Middle East, as we saw in Chapter 2. Others developed new writing systems independently, such as the people in Shang China, discussed in Chapter 3, or the Zapotecs in Mesoamerica, considered in this chapter. More often, however, cultures eagerly adopted writing technology from neighboring societies, adjusting it to suit their languages. Almost everywhere, writing emerged as a tool when societies reached a level of complexity that made the memorization of important information impossible.

We should not, however, overestimate the impact of writing on ancient societies. In all the cultures we have studied so far, only a very small segment of the population used writing, and these people were mostly wealthy, male, and urban. Before modern times, literacy remained a rare skill. The inequality of access to literacy can distort the historian's picture of the past, because the voices of those who wrote are so much clearer and so much louder than the voices of those who did not.

Uses of the Written Record

The earliest known written records vary considerably in their nature and purpose. In Babylonia, where script appeared around 3200 B.C.E., its primary purpose was to record the exchange of goods. The Egyptians soon afterward also noted down economic information, but they used script mainly to commemorate the deeds of kings. In China, the earliest preserved written sources were the oracle-bone inscriptions that kings started to commission in around 1200 B.C.E. as a way to determine future events. In Mesoamerica, where writing appeared in the last centuries B.C.E., the Zapotec and early Maya inscriptions on stone—still not fully deciphered—dealt with the heroic acts of kings. These are the purposes of writing that we can ascertain from the preserved records. But it is likely that much of the earliest writing in these and other cultures appeared on materials that have since disintegrated and are thus lost from the historical record. The earliest manuscripts from Central Asia, for example, were made of tree bark, and that material survives only in very unusual circumstances.

Despite these differences in focus of the earliest preserved writings, many scholars believe that economic needs everywhere inspired the desire to keep records. Those needs began when people started to live together in large communities and were involved in so many transactions that it was impossible to keep track of them without written records. After the technology to record the spoken language in written form had been invented for administrative purposes, people could write down anything, including tales, accounts of military accomplishments, consultations with their gods, and much more. In most cultures the purposes of writing multiplied quickly after script came into use.

The Voiceless Many

As we have discussed, however, literacy was never very widespread in ancient cultures. To learn how to read and write required training from which most people were excluded. Moreover, there are degrees of literacy that require different periods of training. In a culture such as that of classical Greece, for example, many citizens of Athens may have been able to read basic words such as signs and the names of people. But they may not have managed to comprehend a treatise of Aristotle, and they would not have known how to compose a long letter. And consider this: the citizenry of Athens was a highly select group of landowning men. Among those excluded from citizenship, literacy was even more restricted.

Whether a person was included in or excluded from literate life depended mostly on economic factors. Only those who were involved with activities beyond a subsistence level would have needed to record anything in writing. Such people would usually have been city residents with substantial economic assets: landowners who received accounts from their estates, financiers who had to keep track of the loans they issued, merchants with goods in transit to foreign destinations, and so on. These people would join large-scale organizations such as palaces, temples, and monasteries that kept accounts of their holdings. Furthermore, some of those propertied individuals, or people supported by them, could engage in activities that did not produce economic benefit, such as composing plays and epics. The large majority of these people were men because, for the most part, males alone received an education.

For a woman in an ancient society to become literate, a good deal of luck and probably a very strong will were essential. In all early literate societies some women did write, however, and their writings constitute a small portion of the material that historians use as sources. In ancient Mesopotamia, women scribes recorded economic transactions, usually for institutions that provided services to women. For example, some Babylonian cities had **cloisters**, places devoted to religious observation in which rich families housed daughters they did not want to marry off. Were they to marry, these girls would take a share of the family property with them, and the family's total assets would correspondingly shrink. Although these girls were kept in seclusion, they engaged in financial activities and used the services of women scribes.

A small number of the earliest figures in world literature are women. The first known author in history is Enheduanna, a Babylonian princess. Living in around 2400 B.C.E., she was a priestess of the moon god in the city of Ur, and we know that she composed several poems in the Sumerian language (see Chapter 2). Likewise, in China of the first century C.E., the historian Ban Biao gave his daughter a literary education. As we saw in Chapter 6, Ban Zhao finished her father's *History of the Han Dynasty* and wrote other works of literature.

One of the most renowned poets of Greek antiquity was Sappho (c. 630–570 B.C.E.), whom we met in Chapter 5. The daughter of an aristocratic family, Sappho wrote poetry about religious festivals, military celebrations, and life at court. In her moving poems she focused on her emotions, which often involved the young women who were her friends and companions. Due to a military coup, her family was forced to leave their home on the Aegean island of Lesbos for a period of exile in Sicily, which she described with anger. But she was already so famous that the inhabitants of Sicily welcomed her with great ceremony.

Much of Sappho's poetry has been lost through the ages, but the pieces that remain show a remarkable sensitivity and ability to describe human feelings. Fortunately, scholars continue to discover some of her poems on fragmentary manuscripts preserved in the dry sands of Egypt. One such discovery on a papyrus from the third century B.C.E., made in 2004, contains a description of old age. Because the beginning of the papyrus is damaged, the words in parentheses are the translator's conjecture:

> (You for) the fragrant-bosomed (Muses') lovely gifts
> (be zealous,) girls, (and the) clear melodious lyre:
> (but my once tender) body old age now
> (has seized;) my hair's turned (white) instead of dark;
> my heart's grown heavy, my knees will not support me,
> that once on a time were fleet for the dance as fawns.
> This state I oft bemoan; but what's to do?
> Not to grow old, being human, there's no way.
> Tithonus once, the tale was, rose-armed Dawn,
> love-smitten, carried off to the world's end,
> handsome and young then, yet in time grey age
> o'ertook him, husband of immortal wife.[4]

Women such as Enheduanna, Ban Zhao, and Sappho were exceptional, however. In general, most known and unknown writers of ancient societies were men.

Outside the urban centers, in the villages and temporary settlements where most ancient peoples lived, very few were literate, if any. Thus their lives are often not revealed to us, or we view their experience only through the eyes of urban dwellers with very different concerns and lifestyles. One notable nonliterate group was the pastoral nomads who cared for herds of animals, which they led to various pastures at different times of the year—often the mountains in the summer when the snow melted and the valleys in the winter. Only in the winter would they interact with people living in cities, exchanging goods with them. Some of these interactions are reported in the writings of urban residents who did not look upon the pastoralists positively; they typically found the herders

cloister A place, usually a monastery or convent, in which people live in seclusion to concentrate on religious observation.

A Fragment of Sappho's Poetry

The dry climate of Egypt allowed numerous papyri to be preserved, including many that contain literature from Greek antiquity. The fragmentary papyrus shown here, dating from the third century B.C.E., contains the text of a poem that Sappho wrote in around 600 B.C.E. It was only in 2004 that a scholar recognized that the fragment recorded a previously unknown work from the famed Greek poet. (Papyrus Collection, The Institute for Ancient Studies, University of Cologne.)

uncivilized and dangerous. Sima Qian's quote at the beginning of Chapter 3 is just one of the many statements of this nature.

These exclusions from the technology of writing limit modern historians' view of the peoples of the past. Scholars can rarely close this gap through the archaeological record: archaeologists seldom excavate the remains of villages, and the temporary camps of nomads left virtually no traces. In investigations of urban remains, historians can focus on aspects traditionally associated with women, such as kitchens in the houses. But they must be careful not to impose a presumed gender division of labor upon all peoples of the past. Within ancient literate societies there are always large numbers of people whose voices we cannot hear.

Conclusion

Were we to imagine a woman making a tour around the world in the year 1 C.E. (an improbable adventure), we could reconstruct who her hosts would have been and how she would have been received for many stages of the voyage. She would have stayed in a city only very rarely, but when she did we can picture her as the guest of a courtier of the Roman, Parthian, Kushan, and Han emperors as she made her way across Eurasia, and we could even think of a name for that courtier. In Mesoamerica she might have seen the ceremonial centers of the early Maya, people whose names we do not know. Most days, however, she would have visited people in small villages or in temporary settlements whose names we cannot even guess. Many of her hosts in Eurasia, Africa, the Pacific Islands, and the Americas would have been farmers, but others would have foraged or raised herds of animals to feed themselves.

At a distance of more than two thousand years, the details of the histories of most of the world's inhabitants in the year 1 C.E. are vague to us, but there is much that we do know. A crucial distinction in our ability to study the peoples of that past is whether or not they wrote down information that tells us their names, their activities, and the languages they spoke. Few literate cultures existed. The archaeological remains of cultures without writing show us, however, how much they could accomplish, even in areas where in other cultures writing was crucial. The Polynesian sailors Joseph Banks described at the start of this chapter could navigate without the written records or maps that were indispensable to that eighteenth-century European explorer.

All over the world, the foundations of later histories developed in the long period from the evolution of the human species to 500 C.E. They settled most parts of the globe; they invented most of the tools we consider part of civilization, such as agriculture, writing, cities, and metalwork; and they developed elements of culture that were not utilitarian, such as literature, philosophy, and the visual arts. In many parts of the world, these innovations were fundamental to later historical developments. For their cultural and intellectual lives, people in Europe, the Middle East, and South and East Asia still rely on the creations of their ancestors. So, too, do people whose ancestors did not write. In ancient times, people all over the globe contributed to the world that we live in today.

NOTES

1. *The Endeavour Journal of Joseph Banks, 1768–1771*, ed. J. C. Beaglehole (Sydney, Australia: Halstead Press, 1962), 1:368, 2:37. Spellings from the original source.
2. Ibid.
3. Eric R. Wolf, *Europe and the People Without History* (Berkeley: University of California Press, 1982).
4. Martin West, trans., "A New Sappho Poem," *The Times Literary Supplement*, June 24, 2005.

RESOURCES FOR RESEARCH

General Works

In the absence of written sources, historians draw deeply on works from the archaeological perspective. Milleker's book gives an interesting idea of what high art a traveler would encounter on a trip around the world in the year 1 C.E.

Milleker, Elizabeth J., ed. *The Year One: Art of the Ancient World East and West*. 2000.

Scarre, Chris, ed. *The Human Past: World Prehistory and the Development of Human Societies*. 2005.

Wenke, Robert J., and Deborah I. Olszewski. *Patterns in Prehistory: Humankind's First Three Million Years*, 5th ed. 2006.

Peoples of Sub-Saharan Africa

Works that treat the history of the continent until European colonization in the eighteenth century often include studies of Africa's early history. Vansina's book excels in its use of linguistic data for historical reconstructions.

(For archaeological sites in Africa): African Archaeology, http://www.african-archaeology.net/, and Society of Africanist Archaeologists, http://safa.rice.edu/links.cfm.

Ehret, Christopher. *The Civilizations of Africa: A History to 1800*. 2002.

(For sources of African history): H-Africa. http://www.h-net.org/~africa/.

Stahl, Ann, ed. *African Archaeology: A Critical Introduction*. 2005.

Vansina, Jan. *Paths in the Rainforests: Toward a History of Political Tradition in Equatorial Africa*. 1990.

Peoples of the Americas

Many works focus on just one of the many cultures of the early Americas. They usually concentrate on either archaeological research or the fine arts of these cultures.

Burger, Richard L. *Chavín and the Origins of Andean Civilization*. 1995.

Fagan, Brian. *Ancient North America*, 4th ed. 2005.

(Hopewell culture): Ohio History Central. http://www.ohiohistorycentral.org/entry.php?rec=1283.

(Moche culture): http://www.huacas.com/.

(Norte Chico culture): http://www.fieldmuseum.org/research_Collections/anthropology/anthro_sites/PANC/default.htm.

Pillsbury, Joanne, ed. *Moche Art and Archaeology in Ancient Peru*. 2001.

(San Bartolo frescoes): http://www.sanbartolo.org/research.htm.

Peoples of the Pacific Islands

Because the archaeological exploration of this vast region is still in its infancy, relatively few books providing general overviews have been published.

Bellwood, Peter. *Man's Conquest of the Pacific*. 1979.

Kirch, Patrick V. *The Lapita Peoples*. 1997.

Kirch, Patrick V. *On the Road of the Winds: An Archaeological History of the Pacific Islands Before European Contact*. 2000.

(Lapita culture): Report of the 1997 Lapita Project. http://www.sfu.ca/archaeology/museum/tonga/toc.html.

Spriggs, Mathew. *The Island Melanesians*. 1997.

COUNTERPOINT: The Voiced and Voiceless in Ancient Literate Societies

Issues of ancient literacy are usually addressed in studies that focus on a specific culture.

Harris, William V. *Ancient Literacy*. 1989.

Houston, Stephen D., ed. *The First Writing: Script Invention as History and Process*. 2004.

▶ **For additional primary sources from this period**, see *Sources of Crossroads and Cultures*.

▶ **For Web sites, images, and documents related to topics in this chapter**, see Make History at bedfordstmartins.com/smith.

REVIEW

The major global development in this chapter ▶ The evolution of ancient cultures without writing and their fundamental role in world history.

IMPORTANT EVENTS

c. 3000 B.C.E.	Start of southward migration of the Bantu in Africa
c. 3000–1800 B.C.E.	Norte Chico culture in the Andes
c. 3000–750 B.C.E.	First wave of Austronesian migrations
c. 1400–200 B.C.E.	Lapita culture in the Pacific Ocean
c. 1200–400 B.C.E.	Olmec culture in Mesoamerica
c. 1000 B.C.E.	Start of eastern movement of the Bantu in Africa
c. 900–200 B.C.E.	Chavín culture in Mesoamerica
c. 800–700 B.C.E.	Start of iron technology in Africa
c. 800 B.C.E.–200 C.E.	Nok culture in West Africa
c. 400 B.C.E.–250 C.E.	Early Maya culture in Mesoamerica
c. 100 B.C.E.–400 C.E.	Hopewell culture in eastern North America
c. 200–600 C.E.	Moche culture in the Andes
c. 400 C.E.	Bantu arrival in southern Africa
c. 400–1200 C.E.	Second wave of Austronesian migrations

KEY TERMS

atoll (p. 256)　　**glyph** (p. 249)
Bantu (p. 241)　　**prehistory** (p. 239)
cloister (p. 261)　　**savanna** (p. 241)
El Niño (p. 253)　　**shaman** (p. 249)

CHAPTER OVERVIEW QUESTIONS

1. How does the presence or absence of writing influence how we study ancient cultures?

2. Why did the ancient cultures of Africa, the Americas, and the Pacific often show similar developments in spite of their isolation from one another?

3. How is the spread of peoples, languages, and technologies interrelated, and in what ways can we study these processes?

SECTION FOCUS QUESTIONS

1. How have scholars reconstructed the histories of early Africans, and what do their sources reveal about the livelihoods and cultures of these peoples?

2. What kinds of evidence have scholars used to recreate the experience of ancient American peoples, and what do we know about these cultures?

3. What do their material remains tell us about Pacific Islanders' society and culture?

4. To what extent does a society's literacy or nonliteracy affect our study of it?

MAKING CONNECTIONS

1. Consider the agricultural techniques and resources of the inhabitants of Africa, the Americas, and the Pacific. What do the similarities and differences reveal about the development of their cultures?

2. Why did Eurasian societies develop the features we associate with civilization before their counterparts elsewhere in the world?

3. What are the similarities and differences between the major cities of Eurasia and the ceremonial centers of the Americas?

PART 2

The Formation of Regional Societies

500–1450 C.E.

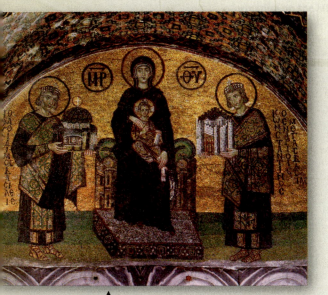

CH 9

ALTHOUGH NO SINGLE LABEL adequately reflects the history of the world in the period 500–1450, its most distinctive feature was the formation of regional societies based on common forms of livelihoods, cultural values, and social and political institutions. The new age in world history that began in around 500 C.E. marked a decisive break from the "classical" era of antiquity. The passing of classical civilizations in the Mediterranean, China, and India shared a number of causes, but the most notable were invasions by nomads from the Central Asian steppes. Beset by internal unrest and foreign pressures, the empires of Rome, Han China, and Gupta India crumbled. As these once-mighty empires fragmented into a multitude of competing states, cultural revolutions followed. Confidence in the values and institutions of the classical era was shattered, opening the way for fresh ideas. Christianity, Buddhism, Hinduism, and the new creed of Islam spread far beyond their original circles of believers. By 1450 these four religious traditions had supplanted or transformed local religions in virtually all of Eurasia and much of Africa.

The spread of foreign religions and the lifestyles and livelihoods they promoted produced distinctive regional societies. By 1000, Europe had taken shape as a coherent society and culture even as it came to be divided between the Roman and Byzantine Christian churches. The shared cultural values of modern East Asia—rooted in the literary and philosophical traditions of China but also assuming distinctive national forms—also emerged during the first millennium C.E. During this era, too, Indian civilization expanded into Southeast Asia and acquired a new unity expressed through the common language of Sanskrit. The rapid expansion of Islam across Asia, Africa, and

CH 10 →

CH 11

even parts of Europe demonstrated the power of a shared religious identity to transcend political and cultural boundaries. But the pan-Islamic empire, which reached its height in the eighth century, proved unsustainable. After the authority of the Abbasid caliphs ebbed in the ninth century, the Islamic world split into distinctive regional societies in the Middle East, North Africa, Central and South Asia, and Southeast Asia.

We also see the formation of regional societies in other parts of the world. Migrations, the development of states, and commercial exchanges with the Islamic world transformed African societies and brought them into more consistent contact with one another. The concentration of political power in the hands of the ruling elites in Mesoamerica and the Andean region led to the founding of mighty city-states. Even in North America and the Pacific Ocean—worlds without states—migration and economic exchange fostered common social practices and livelihoods.

Nomad invasions and political disintegration disrupted economic life in the old imperial heartlands, but long-distance trade flourished as never before. The consolidation of nomad empires and merchant networks stretching across Central Asia culminated in the heyday of the overland "Silk Road" linking China to the Mediterranean world. The Indian Ocean, too, emerged as a crossroads of trade and cultural diffusion. After 1000, most of Eurasia and Africa enjoyed several centuries of steady economic improvement. Rising agricultural productivity fed population expansion, and cities and urban culture thrived with the growth of trade and industry.

Economic prosperity and urban vitality also stimulated intellectual change. Much of the new wealth was channeled into the building of religious monuments and institutions. New institutions of learning and scholarship—such as Christian Europe's universities, the madrasas of the Islamic world, and civil service examinations and government schooling in China—spawned both conformity and dissent.

Cross-cultural interaction also brought conflict, war, and schism. Tensions between Christians and Muslims erupted into the violent clashes known as the Crusades beginning in the late eleventh century. The boundaries between Christendom and the House of Islam shifted over time, but the rift between the two

CH 12

faiths grew ever wider. The rise of steppe empires—above all, the explosive expansion of the Mongol empires—likewise transformed the political and cultural landscape of Asia. Historians today recognize the ways in which the Mongol conquests facilitated the movement of people, goods, and ideas across Eurasia. But contemporaries could see no farther than the ruin sowed by the Mongols wherever they went, toppling cities and laying waste to once-fertile farmlands.

After 1300 the momentum of world history changed. Economic growth slowed, strained by the pressure of rising populations on productive resources and the effects of a cooling climate, and then it stopped altogether. In the late 1340s the Black Death pandemic devastated the central Islamic lands and Europe. It would take centuries before the populations in these parts of the world returned to their pre-1340 levels.

By 1400, however, other signs of recovery were evident. Powerful national states emerged in Europe and China, restoring some measure of stability. Strong Islamic states held sway in Egypt, Anatolia (modern Turkey), Iran, and India. The European Renaissance—the intense outburst of intellectual and artistic creativity envisioned as a "rebirth" of the classical civilization of Greece and Rome—flickered to life, sparked by the economic vigor of the Italian city-states. Similarly, Neo-Confucianism—a "renaissance" of China's classical learning—whetted the intellectual and cultural aspirations of educated elites throughout East Asia. Maritime Asia, spared the ravages of the Black Death, continued to flourish while

CH 13

CH 14 →

	500		750	
Americas	• 500 First permanent settlements in Chaco Canyon 500–1000 Andean state of Tiwanaku 550–650 Collapse of Teotihuacán		800–900 Collapse of the Maya city-states Rise of Chimu state 900 700–900 Heyday of Andean state of Wari	
Europe	• 507 Clovis defeats Visigoths and converts to Christianity 590–604 Papacy of Gregory I	Charles Martel halts Muslim advance into Europe 732 • Charlemagne crowned emperor 800 •	• 793 Earliest record of Viking raids on Britain	
Middle East	527–565 Reign of Byzantine emperor Justinian I 570–632 Life of Muhammad	• 680 Permanent split between Shi'a and Sunni Islam 661–743 Umayyad caliphate 750–850 Abbasid caliphate at its height		
Africa	• 500 Spread of camel use; emergence of trans-Saharan trade routes	• 750 Islam starts to spread via trans-Saharan trade routes		
Asia and Oceania	581–618 Sui Empire 618–907 Tang Empire 600–1000 Polynesian settlement of Pacific Islands	• 668 Unification of Korea under Silla rule 755–763 An Lushan rebellion		

Eurasia's major land-based economies struggled to regain their earlier prosperity.

In 1453 Muslim Ottoman armies seized Constantinople and deposed the Byzantine Christian emperor, cutting the last thread of connection to the ancient world. The fall of Constantinople symbolized the end of the era discussed in Part 2. Denied direct access to the rich trade with Asia, European monarchs and merchants began to shift their attention to the Atlantic world. Yet just as Columbus's discovery of the "New World" (in fact, a very ancient one) came as a surprise, the idea of a new world order centered on Europe—the modern world order—was still unimaginable.

CH 15

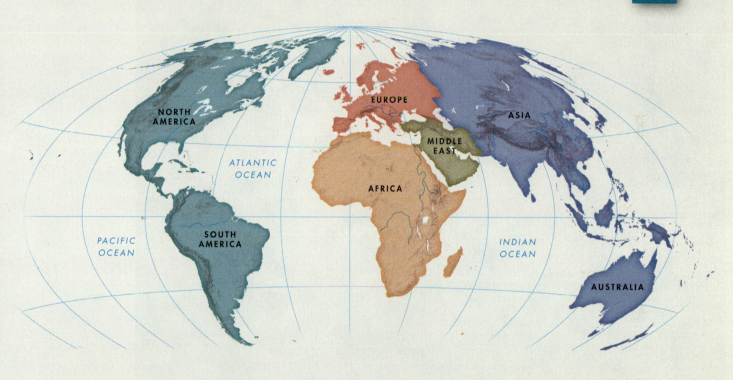

1000	1250	1500

950–1150 Height of Toltec culture · 1200 Incas move into Cuzco region Columbus reaches the Americas 1492 ·
· 1050 Consolidation of Cahokia's dominance · 1150 Abandonment of pueblos in Chaco Canyon · 1325 Aztecs found Tenochtitlán 1430–1532 Inca Empire
1250–1300 Collapse of Cahokia

· 988 Rus prince Vladimir converts to Christianity · 1066 Norman conquest of England · 1150 Founding of first university at Paris 1347–1350 Outbreak of Black Death 1400–1550 Italian Renaissance
1150–1300 Heyday of the Champagne fairs 1337–1453 Hundred Years' War Reconquista completed 1492 ·
Mongol conquest of Kiev 1240 · 1270–1300 Introduction of overseas navigational aids

First Crusade ends with Christian capture of Jerusalem 1099 · · 1120 Founding of order of Knights of the Temple · 1291 Mamluks recapture Acre, last Christian stronghold in Palestine
·1258 Mongols sack Baghdad 1347–1350 Outbreak of Black Death · 1453 Fall of Constantinople to the Ottomans
Saladin recaptures Jerusalem 1187 ·

· 969 Fatimids capture Egypt Reign of Sunjata, founder of 1250–1517 Mamluk dynasty
Fall of kingdom of Ghana 1076 · Mali Empire 1230–1255 · 1250 Kingdom of Benin founded
1100–1500 Extended dry period in West Africa prompts migrations

850–1267 Chola kingdom 1100–1500 Easter Island's stone monuments 1336–1573 Ashikaga Shogunate
939 Vietnam achieves independence from China Formation of first Hawaiian chiefdoms 1200–1400 1206–1526 Delhi Sultanate 1368–1644 Ming Empire
960–1279 Song Empire 1271–1368 Yuan Empire 1392–1910 Korean Yi dynasty

AT A CROSSROADS ▲

The emperors of Constantinople had grand ambitions to rebuild the Roman Empire on new foundations of Christian faith. They displayed special devotion to the Virgin Mary, the patron saint of their capital. This mosaic in the Hagia Sophia, Constantinople's greatest Christian church, shows Emperor Constantine (right) offering a model of the city to Mary and the infant Jesus. Emperor Justinian I (left) presents a model of the Hagia Sophia, which he rebuilt in 562. (Erich Lessing/Art Resource, NY.)

The Worlds of Christianity and Islam

400–1000

In 550, Médard, the bishop of Noyon, northeast of Paris, faced a dilemma. Radegund, the pious wife of the Germanic king Clothar, had come to him seeking to become a nun. But Médard was reluctant to offend Clothar, his patron and benefactor, and the king's men had threatened to drag him from his church should he attempt to place a nun's veil on their queen. According to her biographers, Radegund, sizing up the situation, entered the sacristy, put on a monastic garb, and proceeded straight to the altar, saying, 'If you shrink from consecrating me, and fear man more than God, pastor, He will require His sheep's [Radegund's] soul from your hand.'" Chastened, Médard laid his hands upon Radegund and ordained her as a deaconess.

Radegund (520–587) was the daughter of a rival German king who was a bitter enemy of Clothar's tribe, the Franks. When Radegund was eleven, the Franks slaughtered her family and took her prisoner. Later she was forced to marry Clothar and became, in her words, "a captive maid given to a hostile lord." Raised a Christian, Radegund took refuge in religion. Even before renouncing secular life, "she was more Christ's partner than her husband's companion."[1] Her biographers describe in great detail the physical torments she inflicted on herself, her ministrations to the poor and the sick, the miracles she performed, and the rich gifts she bestowed on the church and the needy. After Clothar's death, Radegund founded a convent at Poitiers and took up a life of full seclusion. But she continued to play the role of Christian queen, maintaining a vigorous correspondence with the leading clergy of the day and trying to act as peacemaker between feuding Frankish kings.

BACKSTORY

As we saw in Chapter 7, the Roman Empire enjoyed a period of renewal in the early fourth century under Constantine, who reinvigorated imperial rule and adopted Christianity as an official religion. But the western part of the empire, wracked by internal conflicts and Germanic invasions, crumbled in the fifth century. By contrast, the emperors at Constantinople, buoyed by the diverse and resilient economy of the eastern Mediterranean, continued to preside over a strong state, which historians call the Byzantine Empire. The resurgent Persian Empire of the Sasanid dynasty struggled with the Romans for control of Syria, Mesopotamia, and Armenia. The rise of Islam in the seventh century would transform political, religious, and economic life from the Mediterranean to Persia.

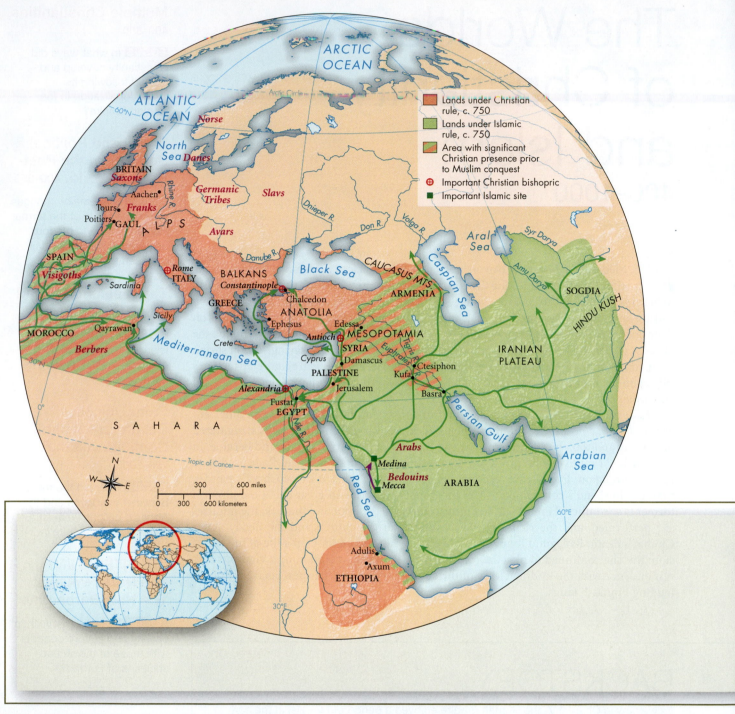

Legend:
- Lands under Christian rule, c. 750
- Lands under Islamic rule, c. 750
- Area with significant Christian presence prior to Muslim conquest
- ⊕ Important Christian bishopric
- ■ Important Islamic site

ARCTIC OCEAN

ATLANTIC OCEAN

North Sea

Norse

Danes

BRITAIN
Saxons

Aachen

Tours
Poitiers
GAUL

Franks

Germanic Tribes

Slavs

Avars

Rhine R.

Danube R.

Dnieper R.

Don R.

Volga R.

Aral Sea

Syr Darya

Amu Darya

SOGDIA

HINDU KUSH

Caspian Sea

CAUCASUS MTS

ARMENIA

Black Sea

⊕ Rome
ITALY

BALKANS

Constantinople

GREECE

Chalcedon

ANATOLIA

Ephesus

Edessa

Antioch ⊕

MESOPOTAMIA

SYRIA

Damascus

Cyprus

PALESTINE

Jerusalem

Kufa

Ctesiphon

Basra

Euphrates R.

Tigris R.

IRANIAN PLATEAU

SPAIN

Visigoths

Sardinia

Sicily

Crete

Mediterranean Sea

MOROCCO

Qayrawan

Berbers

ALPS

Alexandria ⊕

Fustat
EGYPT

SAHARA

Nile R.

Tropic of Cancer

Arabs

Medina ■

Bedouins
Mecca

ARABIA

Persian Gulf

Arabian Sea

Red Sea

Adulis

Axum

ETHIOPIA

N W S E

0   300   600 miles
0   300   600 kilometers

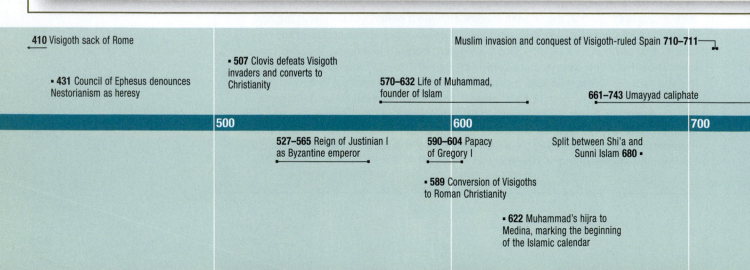

410 Visigoth sack of Rome

Muslim invasion and conquest of Visigoth-ruled Spain **710–711**

507 Clovis defeats Visigoth invaders and converts to Christianity

431 Council of Ephesus denounces Nestorianism as heresy

570–632 Life of Muhammad, founder of Islam

661–743 Umayyad caliphate

500

527–565 Reign of Justinian I as Byzantine emperor

600

590–604 Papacy of Gregory I

Split between Shi'a and Sunni Islam **680**

700

589 Conversion of Visigoths to Roman Christianity

622 Muhammad's hijra to Medina, marking the beginning of the Islamic calendar

By Radegund's day, Christianity had become deeply entrenched in all of the Roman Empire's former territories and had spread beyond to Iran, Armenia, and Ethiopia. Pagan societies on the fringes of the old empire, such as the roving Germanic tribes and the Slavic peoples of Eastern Europe, gradually adopted the Christian religion as well. Even the Norse Vikings, at first reviled as the mortal enemies of Christianity, remade themselves into models of Christian piety.

Unity proved elusive in Christendom (the realm of Christianity), however. Radegund's contemporary Justinian I (r. 527–565), the emperor at Constantinople, tried to reunify the old Roman Empire through military conquest. But Justinian's triumphs barely outlasted his death in 565. New adversaries in the east—above all, the rising religion of Islam—drew the emperors' attention away from the western provinces of the old empire. The rulers of Constantinople began to identify themselves exclusively with their capital's Greek heritage, spurning Roman traditions and replacing Latin with Greek as the official language of the empire. By 600 the religious and cultural gulf between the Latin west and the Greek east had so widened that historians speak of the latter as the Byzantine Empire (from *Byzantium*, the Greek name for Constantinople).

At the same time that the Latin west and the Greek east took increasingly divergent paths, a new and powerful culture arose that would challenge both. The emergence and spread of Islam in the 600s occurred with astonishing speed and success. The Muslim conquests sowed the seeds of Islamic faith and Arab social institutions in diverse societies in Africa, Europe, and Asia. The pace of conversion to Islam varied greatly, however. Islam quickly made deep inroads among urban merchants and among pastoral nomads such as the Berbers of North Africa. In agrarian societies such as Syria, Mesopotamia, and Spain, the Arabs long remained a tiny elite ruling over Christian majorities, who only gradually accepted Islam. In regions hemmed in by the expansion of Islam, such as Armenia and Ethiopia, the Christian faith became the hallmark of political independence. Thus Islamic expansion did not impose a uniform culture over a vast empire. Local conditions in each

MAPPING THE WORLD

Christian and Islamic Lands, c. 750

By 750, the old Roman Empire had been partitioned between two faiths, Christianity and Islam. Christendom itself was increasingly becoming a house divided between two rival churches centered at Constantinople and Rome. The Abbasid caliphate had deposed the Umayyad dynasty of caliphs, based at Damascus, in 747. The new Abbasid capital at Baghdad soon eclipsed Damascus and the holy cities of Mecca and Medina as the political and religious center of the Islamic world.

ROUTES ▼

➤ Major campaign of Islamic forces, 625–732

➤ Muhammad's hijra, 622

868–883 Zanj revolt against the Abbasid regime

793 Earliest record of Viking raids on Britain

988 Vladimir, the Rus prince of Kiev, converts to Christianity

870–930 Vikings colonize Iceland

| 800 | 900 | 1000 |

747–1258 Abbasid caliphate

800 Coronation of Charlemagne as emperor by Pope Leo III

909 Fatimid dynasty founded

732 Charles Martel halts Muslim advance into Europe

Muslim territory shaped the terms and consequences of cultural exchange among Muslim conquerors, subject peoples, and neighboring states.

However, like Christianity, Islam claimed to be a universal religion. Both religions offered a vision of common brotherhood that brought a new religious sensibility to daily life and integrated disparate peoples into a community of faith. Although Christianity and Islam spread along different paths, both were beset by an abiding tension between sacred and secular authority. The Christian church preserved its autonomy amid political disorder in the Latin west, whereas the Byzantine emperors yoked imperial power and clerical leadership tightly together. The vision of a universal Islamic empire combining spiritual faith with political and military strength was crucial to the initial expansion of Islam. In the ninth and tenth centuries, however, the Islamic empire fragmented into numerous regional states divided by doctrine, culture, and way of life. Nonetheless, the economic vibrancy and religious ferment of the far-flung Islamic world created a vast territory through which Muslim merchants, missionaries, and pilgrims moved freely, drawing together the separate worlds of Asia, Africa, and Europe. Islamic cities and ports became global crossroads, centers for the exchange of goods and ideas that helped create new cultural connections stretching from the Iberian peninsula to China.

OVERVIEW
QUESTIONS

The major global development in this chapter: The spread of Christianity and Islam and the profound impact of these world religions on the societies of western Eurasia and North Africa.

As you read, consider:

1. How and why did the development of the Christian church differ in the Byzantine Empire and Latin Christendom?

2. In what ways did the rise of Christianity and Islam challenge the power of the state?

3. Conversely, in what ways did the spread of these faiths reinforce state power?

4. Why did Christianity and Islam achieve their initial success in towns and cities rather than in the rural countryside?

Multiple Christianities 400–850

FOCUS

In what ways did Christianity develop and spread following its institutionalization in the Roman Empire?

In the century following the Roman emperor Constantine's momentous conversion to Christianity in 312, Christian leaders were confident that their faith would displace the classical Mediterranean religions (see Chapter 7). Yet the rapid spread of the Christian religion throughout Roman territories also splintered the Christian movement. Their fierce independence honed by hostility and persecution, Christian communities did not readily yield to any universal authority in matters of doctrine and faith. Efforts by the Byzantine emperors to impose their will on the Christian leadership met strong resistance. The progress of conversion throughout the territories of the old Roman Empire came at the cost of increasing divisions within the church itself.

The Christian Church in Byzantium

In the eastern Mediterranean, where imperial rule remained strong, the state treated the Christian church and clergy as a branch of imperial administration. Although the Christian communities of the eastern Mediterranean welcomed imperial support, they also sought to preserve their independence from the emperors' direct control. For example, bishops elected by their local followers exercised sovereign rule over religious affairs within their jurisdictions. In the late fourth century a council of bishops acknowledged the special status of the bishop of Constantinople by designating him as patriarch, the supreme leader of the church. But the bishops of Alexandria in Egypt and Antioch in Anatolia (modern Turkey) retained authority and influence nearly equal to that of Constantinople's patriarch (see Map 9.1). Thus, although Byzantine emperors sought to use the Christian church as a vehicle to expand and reinforce their power, church leaders contested this agenda throughout the empire.

Tensions between secular and religious officials were not the only source of division in eastern Christianity. The urban elite of imperial officials and wealthy merchants adopted the new religion, but alongside such new Christian practices as prayer, repentance, and almsgiving they often continued to uphold the old forms of Greek religion. Their vision of Christianity reflected the strong influence Greek culture continued to exert on Byzantine city life. These were urban people, and their religious beliefs and practices grew out of a cosmopolitan urban context.

The Ascetic Movement

In Syria and Egypt, however, rural inhabitants embraced a more austere form of Christian piety. Some of the most impassioned Christians, deploring the persistence of profane Greco-Roman culture in the cities, sought spiritual refuge in the sparsely inhabited deserts, where they devoted themselves to an ascetic life of rigorous physical discipline and contemplation of the divine. Perhaps the most famous of these ascetics was Symeon the Stylite, who for many years lived and preached atop a sixty-foot pillar. After his death in 459, thousands of pilgrims flocked each year to Symeon's shrine in northern Syria.

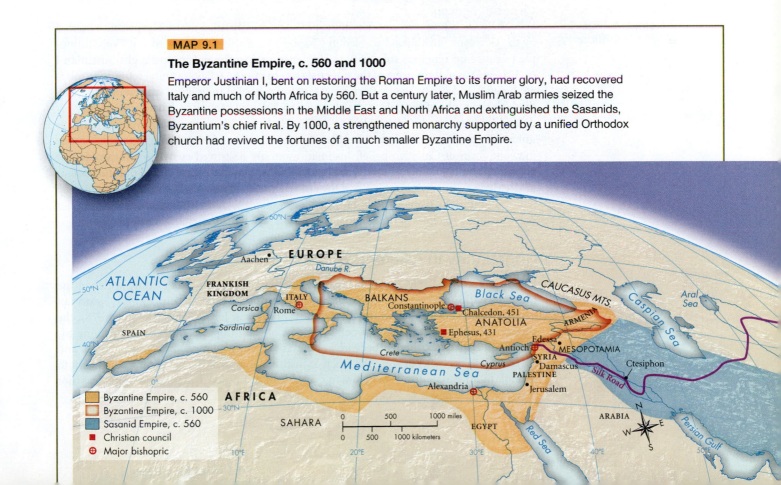

MAP 9.1

The Byzantine Empire, c. 560 and 1000

Emperor Justinian I, bent on restoring the Roman Empire to its former glory, had recovered Italy and much of North Africa by 560. But a century later, Muslim Arab armies seized the Byzantine possessions in the Middle East and North Africa and extinguished the Sasanids, Byzantium's chief rival. By 1000, a strengthened monarchy supported by a unified Orthodox church had revived the fortunes of a much smaller Byzantine Empire.

Byzantine Empire, c. 560
Byzantine Empire, c. 1000
Sasanid Empire, c. 560
■ Christian council
⊕ Major bishopric

Rise of Christian Monasteries

While also serving as spiritual guides for the Christian population at large, other ascetics founded monasteries that attracted like-minded followers. The monastic movement began sporadically in Egypt and Syria in the late third century and surged in the fourth and fifth centuries. The austerity of monastic life endowed monks with an aura of holiness and sacred power that outshone the pomp and finery of church leaders in the cities. Whether hidden away in the monasteries or preaching their convictions among the people, these holy men became alternative sources of sacred authority independent of the official church hierarchy.

Disputes over Doctrine

The divisions within eastern Christianity went beyond differences in style and presentation to disagreements over basic Christian beliefs. Straying from orthodoxy—established church doctrines—became common among recluses, itinerant preachers, and even those in the church's highest ranks. Already in the time of Constantine, the bishops had been locked in debate over the divinity of Jesus (see Chapter 7). Nestorius (neh-STORE-ee-us), elected patriarch of Constantinople in 428, renewed this controversy by proclaiming that Jesus had two natures, one human and one divine. Nestorius especially objected to the idea that a human woman, Mary, could give birth to the son of God. But Nestorius's views outraged Cyril, the bishop of Alexandria, who insisted that Jesus had a single, fully divine nature, a principle that became known as the Monophysite ("single nature") doctrine. Councils of bishops held at Ephesus (431) and Chalcedon (KAL-suh-dahn) (451) denounced Nestorius's views as heresy (see again Map 9.1). To counter the claims of Nestorius, the Ephesus council formally declared Mary "mother of God" (see Seeing the Past: Mary as Mother of God). The Chalcedon council, in an effort to heal the split among the clergy, adopted a compromise position, that Jesus was both "fully divine and fully human." But the bishops of Alexandria remained committed to their Monophysite views, whereas the Nestorian doctrine gained a considerable following among local clergy in Syria and Mesopotamia. This debate may seem esoteric to modern observers, but it is important to remember that, from the point of view of the participants, the stakes could not have been higher. At issue was the very nature of Jesus and, thus, the essential nature of Christianity. It is, therefore, not surprising that this debate led to long-lasting divisions within the Christian community.

Justinian's Imperial Orthodoxy

There were, however, countervailing pressures for Christian unity. The pressure exerted by the Germanic invasions discussed in Chapter 7 compelled the emperors at Constantinople to shore up religious solidarity as a defense against the pagan onslaught. Justinian I (r. 527–565) used the powers of the imperial state to impose religious unity, refusing to tolerate heretics and nonbelievers. Born a peasant but schooled in political intrigue while rising through the ranks of the palace guard, Justinian believed himself to have been divinely ordained to restore order to the Roman world. He began his campaign to impose religious uniformity on his empire soon after his coronation. "His ambition being to force everyone into one form of Christian belief, Justinian wantonly destroyed everyone who would not conform," wrote Procopius, the great historian of Justinian's reign.[2] He also put the content of Christianity in service of his drive toward religious orthodoxy as a means of promoting political unity. The theology elaborated at Constantinople during the next several centuries reiterated the principles of order and hierarchy on which the imperial state was built.

Christianity in Asia and Africa

Far from restoring unity, though, Justinian's often strong-arm tactics only widened the fractures within the church. Alexandria resisted imperial domination, and the Nestorian heresy became entrenched in the easternmost provinces. Jacob Baradaeus (died 578), the Monophysite bishop of Edessa, openly defied Constantinople's authority by forming his own separatist church (what became known as the Jacobite movement) in Anatolia and Syria. Christians living beyond the reach of Justinian's control were even more reluctant to submit to imperial dictates. Justinian's vision of a unified Christian empire was not matched by the power to impose his will.

Mary as Mother of God

***The Virgin of Vladimir* (artist unknown):** This icon, sent to the Rus prince of Kiev from Constantinople in 1131, became renowned for its miracle-working powers. (Scala/Art Resource, NY.)

There is little scriptural authority for the central place that Mary, mother of Jesus, eventually came to occupy in Christian beliefs and rituals. The few references to Mary in the Gospels make no mention, for example, of her lifelong virginity or her ascent to heaven. Nonetheless, early Christian writings singled Mary out as a role model for women, stressing her obedience and virginity in contrast to the biblical Eve. The virginity of Mary also provided inspiration for the ascetic and monastic movements that began to flourish in the third and fourth centuries. Ultimately, the theological controversy over the question of Jesus's divinity that reached a climax at the 431 Council of Ephesus elevated Mary to a position in Christian devotion second only to Jesus himself.

Devotion to Mary intensified through a proliferation of festival days, liturgies, miracle stories, and visual images. When Constantinople's patriarch renovated the city's principal Christian church, Hagia Sophia, after the defeat of the iconoclasm movement in the mid-ninth century (see page 281), the mosaic shown at the start of this chapter of an enthroned Mary and the child Jesus flanked by two haloed Byzantine emperors was placed prominently over an entrance to the church's nave.

Icons intended for personal, private devotion depicted the Virgin and Child in a very different manner. The example reproduced here, known as the Virgin of Vladimir (the Kievan prince who commissioned it), portrays the Virgin and Child locked together in a tender maternal embrace, faces touching. The tiny head and hands of Jesus accentuate his infantlike helplessness. In contrast to her public portrayal as the enthroned Mary, in this personal icon Mary's gaze is fixed on the viewer, with her left hand upraised in a gesture of prayer that likewise beckons toward the viewer. Many icons of this type also were brought to Italy and had a strong influence on the religious art of the early Renaissance, a European cultural movement that we will discuss in Chapter 15.

Source: Maria Vassilaki, ed., *Mother of God: Representations of the Virgin in Byzantine Art* (Milan: Skira editore, 2000), plates 61, 24.

EXAMINING THE EVIDENCE

1. How does the "At a Crossroads" mosaic from Hagia Sophia (see page 270) and the icon shown here differ in their depiction of Mary as a maternal figure? What do these contrasts tell us about the differences between public and private devotion to Mary?

2. How does the Byzantine conception of imperial authority expressed in the mosaic from Hagia Sophia compare with the Roman conception as evidenced in the image of Augustus on page 217?

Armenia, at the frontier between the Roman Empire and the Persian Sasanid Empire, nurtured its own distinctive Christian tradition. Christianity had advanced slowly in Armenia following the conversion of its king in the early fourth century. But after Armenia was partitioned and occupied by Roman and Sasanid armies in 387, resistance to foreign rule hardened around this kernel of Christian faith. With the invention

Christianity in Armenia

Byzantine Emperorship

This mosaic from the San Vitale church in Ravenna, Italy, depicts Justinian surrounded by his civil, military, and ecclesiastic officials—a clear effort to project the emperor's identity as head of both state and church. The mosaic was commissioned in around 550 not by Justinian, however, but by Maximian, archbishop of Ravenna in Italy, the only figure labeled by the artist. (Giraudon/Bridgeman Art Library.)

of the Armenian alphabet in around 400 came a distinctive Armenian literary heritage of Christian teachings. Christianity had become the hallmark of Armenian independence, and the Armenian clergy also repelled Justinian's attempts to impose religious orthodoxy.

Sasanid Toleration of Christianity

Except in Armenia, where Christians suffered political persecution, the Sasanids generally tolerated Christianity, which along with Judaism was well entrenched in Mesopotamia. The Nestorian church enjoyed a privileged position at the Sasanid capital of Ctesiphon (TEH-suh-fahn), south of modern Baghdad, and a number of Nestorian clergy attained high office at court. Nestorian Christians celebrated the Sasanid seizure of Jerusalem from Constantinople in 618 as a triumph over heresy. Nestorian missionaries traveled eastward and established churches along the trade routes leading from Persia to Central Asia. Merchants from the caravan settlements of Sogdia carried their adopted Nestorian faith eastward along the Silk Road as far as China, as we will see in Chapter 10. In this way, Sasanid political policies and economic connections facilitated the growth and spread of a distinctive form of Christianity.

Christianity also gained a foothold in Ethiopia, at the northern end of the Rift Valleys in eastern Africa, and once again trade played a key role. Long a bridge between sub-Saharan Africa and the Mediterranean, Ethiopia also became the main channel of trade and cultural contact between the Roman world and the Indian Ocean. Both Jewish and Christian merchants settled in the Ethiopian towns that served this trade, chief of which was Axum (AHK-soom).

Rise and Fall of Axum

By the first century C.E., Axum was a thriving metropolis connected to the Mediterranean trade network through the Red Sea port of Adulis (ah-DOOL-iss). Axum was the chief marketplace for exotic African goods such as ivory, gold, precious stones, and animal horns and skins. Although the majority of the population consisted of herders and farmers, townsmen made pottery, worked leather and metal, and carved ivory. The use at the Axum court of Greek and Syriac, along with Ge'ez (geeze), the native written language of Ethiopia, reflected the multinational character of the merchant and official classes.

Commercial wealth led to the creation of a powerful monarchy. During the early fourth century the rulers of Axum officially recognized Christianity as their state religion. Intolerance of other creeds hardened as the pace of conversion to Christianity accelerated.

Axum's Jews emigrated farther inland, where they formed the nucleus of their own independent state, which would later be known as Falasha.

But the Islamic conquests in the seventh century disrupted the lucrative trade on which Axum's vitality depended. Trade routes shifted away from the Red Sea to Syria, and Damascus became the new commercial capital of the eastern Mediterranean. When the Axum monarchy declined, a class of warrior lords allied with Christian monasteries gained both economic and legal control of the agrarian population. As in Europe, most of the population was reduced to servile status, and much of the produce of the land supported Christian monasteries, which remained the repositories of learning and literate culture. In this way, trade brought Christianity to Axum and created the wealth that built its Christian monarchy. When regional trade patterns changed, Christianity in Axum changed as well.

In the twelfth and thirteenth centuries, new royal dynasties arose in the highlands of Ethiopia that became great patrons of Christianity. These dynasties claimed direct descent from the ancient kings of Israel, but they also drew legitimacy from African traditions of sacred kingship. Ethiopia endured as a Christian stronghold down to modern times, although hemmed in by the hostile pastoral nomads of the coastal lowlands, who converted to Islam. Not surprisingly, isolated as it was from the larger Christian world, the Ethiopian church developed its own distinctive Christian traditions.

Ethiopia, Christian Stronghold

Christian Communities in Western Europe

While the Christian movements in Asia and Africa strove to maintain their independence from Constantinople, the collapse of the imperial order in the west posed different challenges for the Christian faithful. In the absence of the patronage (and interference) of the Byzantine emperors, a variety of distinctive Christian cultures emerged throughout the former western provinces. With imperial Rome in ruins, local communities and their leaders were free to rebuild their societies on the pillars of Christian beliefs and practices. When the Frankish king Charlemagne achieved military supremacy in western Europe at the end of the eighth century, his contemporaries heralded their new emperor as having been chosen by God "to rule and protect the Christian people."[3]

When imperial Rome fell, Christianity in the west was largely an urban religion. Amid ongoing warfare and violence, the beleaguered Christian towns in Gaul and Spain turned for leadership to provincial notables—great landowners and men of the old senatorial class. The bishops of Rome proclaimed their supreme authority in doctrinal matters as popes (from *papa*, or "grand old man"), the successors of St. Peter, who represented the universal ("Catholic") church. But Christian communities in the provinces of western Europe entrusted their protection to local men of wealth and family distinction, whom they elected as bishops. Bred to govern in the Roman style, these aristocrats took firm control of both secular and religious affairs. Although many of these men had been born to luxury and comfort, they embraced the austerity of monastic life, which further enhanced their aura of holiness. In time, with the assistance of zealous Christian missionaries, they negotiated settlements with their new Germanic overlords—the Franks in Gaul, the Visigoths in Spain, and the Saxons in Britain—that fully welcomed the Christian religion.

Bishops of the West

In an increasingly uncertain and violent world, the bishops of the west rallied their followers around collective religious ceremonies and the cults of saints. From at least the second century, Christians had commemorated beloved and inspiring martyrs and bishops as saints. Later, hermits, monks, and outstanding laypeople, both men and women, were also honored as saints. Christians viewed saints as their patrons, persons of power and influence who protected the local community and interceded on its behalf for divine blessings. They regarded the bodily remains of saints as sacred relics endowed with miraculous potency. Thus, worship of saints at the sites of their tombs became a focal point of Christian life. Just as Christian communities turned to provincial elites for protection, Christians looked to the saints to keep them safe in a hostile world.

Pope Gregory I

Pope Gregory I exercised firm personal leadership over the Latin Christian church through his voluminous correspondence with bishops, missionaries, and noble laypeople. At least twenty thousand letters were dispatched from Rome under his name during the fourteen years of his papacy. This ivory carving shows the pope at his writing desk, with scribes below copying his writings. (Erich Lessing/Art Resource, NY.)

In the 460s, the bishop of Tours built a huge and ornate basilica at the site of the grave of the martyr St. Martin (335–397). Its reputation swelled by a flood of reports of miracles, it became a fortress of Christian faith and attracted pilgrims from throughout Gaul and beyond. When the Frankish king Clovis challenged the Visigoth ruler Alaric for control of southern Gaul in 507, he sought (and reportedly received) divine blessing at St. Martin's shrine. After defeating the Visigoths, Clovis returned to Tours laden with booty that he donated to the shrine. Similar cults and networks of pilgrimage and patronage sprung up around the relics of other saints.

Pope Gregory I (540–604) typified the distinctive style of leadership in the western Christian church. Born into a prominent Roman aristocratic family, Gregory entered the imperial service in 573 as the governor of Rome. Pulled by a strong religious calling, however, he soon retired to become a monk. After achieving fame for his devotion to learning and ascetic lifestyle, Gregory yielded to repeated summons to return to public service. He spent a decade as the papal envoy to the Byzantine court before returning to Rome upon his election as pope in 590. Keenly aware of the divisions within the Christian world, Gregory strove to make the papacy the centerpiece of a church administration that stretched from Britain to North Africa. Mindful, too, of the limited penetration of Christian religion in the countryside, he worked tirelessly to instill a sense of mission among the Christian clergy. "The art to end all arts is the governing of souls," wrote Gregory, insisting that the contemplative life of the monastery must be joined to the pastoral duty of saving sinners.[4]

Slowly but surely, Gregory's vision of the Christian clergy as the spiritual rulers of the humble peasantry gained converts. By the eighth century, social life in the western European countryside revolved around the village church and its liturgies. Christian sacraments marked the major stages of the individual's life from birth (baptism) to death (last rites), and the religious calendar, with high points at the celebrations of Christ's birth (Christmas) and resurrection (Easter), introduced a new rhythm to the cycle of the seasons.

Still, Latin Christendom was far from united. Distinctive regional Christian churches and cultures had emerged in Italy, Gaul, Britain, and Spain; indeed, we can think of these as a cluster of micro-Christendoms clinging to the fragments of the former Roman Empire. During the eighth century, however, the rise of the Carolingian dynasty and its imperial aspirations would bring these regional Christendoms into a single European form.

Social and Political Renewal in the Post-Roman World 400–850

FOCUS

What major changes swept the lands of the former Roman Empire in the four centuries following the fall of imperial Rome?

The Byzantine emperors in the east and the Germanic chieftains who ruled the empire's former western European provinces shared a common heritage rooted in the Roman imperial past and Christian religion. The Byzantine Empire faced a profound crisis in the sixth and seventh centuries. Protracted wars with the Sasanids, the Slavs, and the Avars were followed by the loss of two-thirds of Byzantium's realm to the rapid advance of Muslim Arab armies. Yet the Byzantine Empire survived, thanks to the revitalization of the imperial state and a resilient economy. Byzantine political institutions and especially its distinctive version of Christianity also exerted a powerful influence on the Slavic peoples and led to the formation of the first Rus state. Although Byzantium regained its political and cultural vigor in the ninth century, their fellow Christians, the Frankish empire of the Carolingian dynasty, proved to be more a rival than an ally.

Crisis and Survival of the Byzantine Empire

Justinian I's conquests in Italy and North Africa had once again joined Constantinople and Rome under a single sovereign, but this union was short-lived. Lengthy wars and the enormous costs of Justinian's building programs sapped the fiscal strength of the empire. Although the Byzantine forces repulsed a Sasanid-led attack on Constantinople in 626, this victory was eclipsed within fifteen years by the loss of Syria, Palestine, and Egypt to Muslim armies, as we shall see. By 700 the Byzantine Empire was a shrunken vestige of Justinian's realm, consisting essentially of Constantinople and its immediate environs, a few territories in Greece, and Anatolia. Once-flourishing commercial cities lost much of their population and were rebuilt as smaller, fortified towns to defend the local bishop and his church.

Constantinople alone stood out as a thriving crossroads of trade, learning, and aristocratic culture. Home to a dense mosaic of languages and nationalities united by the Christian faith, Constantinople numbered five hundred thousand inhabitants at its peak in Justinian's age. Social frictions frequently ignited outbursts of violence, such as the Nika (Greek for "conquer") Revolt of 532, a weeklong protest against Justinian's high-handed officials that left nearly half of the city burned or destroyed. To soothe these tensions, the emperors staged an elaborate cycle of public rituals—military triumphs, imperial birthdays, and Christian festivals—that showcased their essential role in fostering unity and common purpose among Constantinople's populace.

Accompanying Byzantium's declining power and prestige were worsening relations with Rome. Emperor Justinian II (r. 685–695) convened a council of bishops at Constantinople in 692 that granted the emperor greater control over the church and its clergy. The council rejected Latin customs such as priestly celibacy and affirmed the independence of the patriarch of Constantinople from the Roman pope in matters of religious doctrine. This rupture between the emperor and the pope was partially mended in the later years of Justinian II's reign, but over the course of the eighth century the religious **schism** widened. The Frankish king Charlemagne's coronation as emperor by Pope Leo III in 800 in effect declared Charlemagne to be the protector of the church, usurping the Byzantine emperor's role. Although Charlemagne negotiated a compromise in 813 that recognized the Byzantine monarch as "emperor of the Romans" and pledged friendship between the two rulers, Latin Christendom had clearly emerged as a separate church.

Schism Between Constantinople and Rome

Within Byzantium, debate raged over the proper conduct of life and religion in a Christian society, especially concerning the veneration of icons—painted images of Jesus, Mary, and the saints. The powerful new faith of Islam denounced any representation of the divine in human form as idolatry. This radical **iconoclasm** (Greek for "image-breaking") struck a responsive chord among the many Byzantines who saw the empire's political reversals as evidence of moral decline. Throughout the eighth century a bitter struggle divided Byzantium. On one side were the iconoclasts, who sought to match Muslim religious fervor by restoring a pristine faith rooted in Old Testament values. On the other side were the defenders of orthodoxy, who maintained that the use of explicitly Christian images of Jesus and Mary was an essential component of the imperially ordained liturgy on which social unity depended. In the mid-ninth century the proponents of orthodoxy prevailed over the iconoclasts. Henceforth Byzantine Christianity became known as the Orthodox Church, in which religious authority became tightly interwoven with imperial power.

The Iconoclastic Controversy

In the second half of the ninth century the Muslim threat abated, and the Byzantine Empire enjoyed a rebirth. Resurgent economic strength at home fueled military success against the Muslims and the Slavs. The church and the army supported efforts to enhance the power and authority of the emperor and the central state. Yet as the leading classes of Byzantine society rallied around a revitalized imperial institution, the estrangement between the churches of Constantinople and Rome intensified. The split between the two churches was about more than conflicts over theology and church hierarchy. The peoples of the Latin west and the Greek east, who had once shared a common history and culture as subjects of the Roman Empire, were moving in different directions.

schism A split in any organized group (especially a church or religious community) resulting in a formal declaration of differences in doctrine or beliefs.

iconoclasm Literally, "destruction of images"; the word originates with the movement against the veneration of images in the Byzantine Empire in the eighth and ninth centuries.

Christ Pantokrator

Following the final defeat of iconoclasm, images of Christ Pantokrator (Greek for "ruler of all") became a standard feature of Byzantine church decoration. Typically placed on vaulted domes, these images emphasized Jesus's transcendent divinity. This version of the Pantokrator, which portrays Jesus as a teacher, was created in 1148 by Byzantine mosaic artists hired by Roger II, king of Sicily, to decorate his newly built Cefalu Cathedral. (Corbis.)

The Germanic Successor States in Western Europe

At the peak of the Roman Empire, its northern frontier stretched three thousand miles, from the British Isles to the Black Sea. From the vantage point of Rome, this frontier marked a sharp boundary between civilized and barbarian peoples. But as we saw in Chapter 7, provincial Romans had frequent social and economic interactions with their Celtic and Germanic neighbors. Many Germanic chieftains who became overlords of the empire's western provinces in the fifth and sixth centuries had previously served as mercenaries defending the territories they now ruled. In a sense, they were at least partially Romanized before they conquered Rome (see Map 9.2).

Livelihoods of the Germanic Peoples

Similar patterns of livelihood prevailed among the Germanic peoples—and indeed among all the peoples of northern and eastern Europe. In most of the region, small, patriarchal farming communities predominated, in which men had full authority over members of their families or clans. The most important crop was barley, which was consumed as porridge, bread, and beer. Cattle-raising also was important, both to feed the community and as an index of positions in the social hierarchy. The number of cattle a household possessed determined its wealth and prestige, and acquiring cattle was a chief objective of both trade and warfare.

Valor and success in warfare also conferred prestige. Village communities organized themselves into warrior bands for warfare and raiding, and at times these bands joined together to form broad confederations for mutual defense and campaigns of plunder. These groups were primarily political alliances, and thus they constantly dissolved and reformed as the needs and interests of their constituent tribes shifted. Kinfolk found solidarity in their common genealogical descent, but marriage ties, gift giving, and sharing food and drink at feasts helped nurture bonds of fellowship and loyalty. Contact with the Roman world, through both trade and war, magnified the roles of charismatic military leaders, men skilled at holding together their fragile coalitions of followers and negotiating with the Roman state. As we saw in Chapter 7, Rome's eagerness to obtain the military services of these confederations further encouraged the militarization of Germanic society.

The Goths

One such confederation, the Goths, arrived in Italy and Gaul as refugees, driven westward by the invasions of the Hun nomads from Central Asia in the fifth century (see Chapter 7).

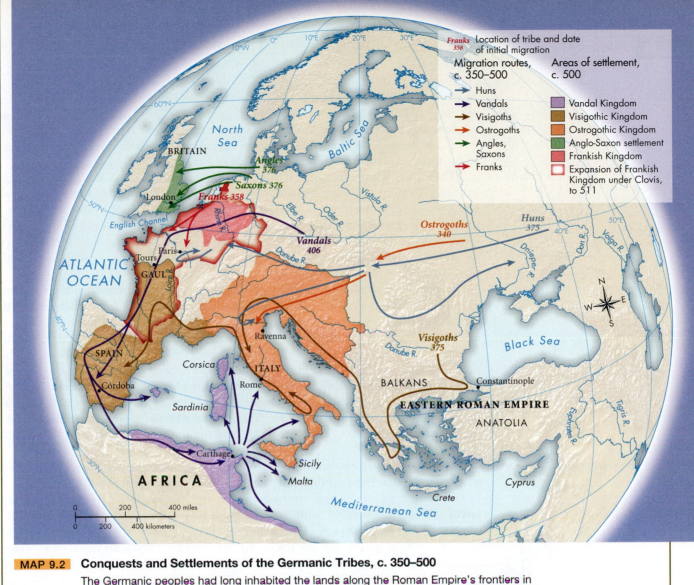

Franks 358 Location of tribe and date of initial migration

Migration routes, c. 350–500
- → Huns
- → Vandals
- → Visigoths
- → Ostrogoths
- → Angles, Saxons
- → Franks

Areas of settlement, c. 500
- Vandal Kingdom
- Visigothic Kingdom
- Ostrogothic Kingdom
- Anglo-Saxon settlement
- Frankish Kingdom
- Expansion of Frankish Kingdom under Clovis, to 511

MAP 9.2 **Conquests and Settlements of the Germanic Tribes, c. 350–500**

The Germanic peoples had long inhabited the lands along the Roman Empire's frontiers in northern and eastern Europe. In the fourth and fifth centuries, as Rome's authority disintegrated, Germanic chieftains led their followers to invade and occupy Roman territories. The new Germanic rulers such as the Franks and the Goths cultivated alliances with local leaders and the Christian church and restored a measure of stability.

Expelled from their homeland in the lower Danube region, the Visigoths (Western Goths) followed their king Alaric into the Balkans and Italy. Driven more by desperation and hunger than by greed, Alaric's army captured and plundered Rome in 410. In 418 the Visigoths negotiated an alliance with the Byzantine emperor that allowed them to occupy southern Gaul—the first Germanic people to complete the transition from confederation to kingdom.

The Ostrogoths (Eastern Goths) emerged as an independent force in the late fifth century, following the death of the Hun leader Attila, whom the Ostrogoths loyally served. After Attila's empire disintegrated, the Ostrogoths shifted their allegiance to Constantinople. In 488 the Byzantine emperor dispatched the Ostrogoth leader Theodoric to subdue Odoacer, the German king who had seized Rome and deposed its last emperor in 476. Theodoric conquered the Italian peninsula in 493 but refused to relinquish control to Constantinople. The Ostrogoths ruled Italy until they were overwhelmed by Justinian's armies in 553.

Only a small number of the Goths entered Gaul and Italy as members of the warrior ruling elite, entitled to the privileges of "Gothic freedom." Most were farmers whose livelihood scarcely differed from that of their Roman neighbors. Sensational images of "barbarian invasions" obscure the fact that many Germans wanted to assimilate into the Roman world. The Romans likewise welcomed the peace and security brought by the German kings. Acceptance of "barbarian" rule accelerated most rapidly where the German rulers converted to Roman Christianity. We should not think of the fall of the western empire as the destruction of one culture and its replacement by another. What took place, instead, was a complex process of cultural exchange shaped by changes in the political and economic fortunes of the empire and by the needs and ambitions of nomadic peoples.

The Franks

The Franks, a league of German tribes in the lower Rhine River Valley, had long lived in close proximity to the Roman world. So thoroughly had the Franks been assimilated into Roman life that their own legends about their ancestry had faded by 600, the approximate date of the earliest Latin accounts of their history and origins. The "long-haired kings"—as the Romans called them—of the Franks gained power through loyal military service to the empire. When the Roman state collapsed, the Frankish kings allied with Christian bishops in the interest of preserving local order.

Under the leadership of Clovis (r. 482–511), the Franks consolidated their control over the Rhineland and Gaul. Although the circumstances of Clovis's conversion to Roman Christianity are murky, we have seen that he credited to St. Martin his decisive victory in 507 over the Visigoths in southern Gaul. Clovis also issued a law code, Roman in form but German in substance, of rules governing crime and property, including the principle, later widely adopted in Europe, that "no portion of the inheritance [of land] shall come to a woman."[5] When Clovis died in 511, his kingdom was divided among his four sons, including Clothar, future husband of Radegund (whom we met at the beginning of this chapter). But the fundamental unity of the Frankish kingdom endured, held together by Frankish law, Christian faith, and the unwavering allegiance of the old Roman aristocrats.

The Carolingian Dynasty

The Franks added new conquests during the sixth and seventh centuries, but the pattern of decentralized rule continued. The lightning conquest of Spain by Muslim armies in 710–711 triggered a crisis that reversed this erosion of royal power. When the Muslim forces subsequently invaded southern Gaul, local nobles turned to a Frankish warlord, Charles Martel, for protection. Martel's decisive victory over the Muslims at Tours in 732 made him the undisputed leader of the Franks; his descendants would rule as the Carolingian (from *Carolus*, Latin for "Charles") dynasty of kings.

Frankish political power reached its height under Martel's grandson Charlemagne (r. 768–814). Drawing on the Roman Empire as a model, Charlemagne's conquests added substantial territories to the Frankish empire, extending from the Baltic Sea to the Adriatic Sea. Charlemagne incorporated these new dominions into his empire by sharing power with local rulers and allowing their peoples to be governed in accordance with their own laws and customs. This policy also allowed colonists who migrated to newly conquered regions of the empire to preserve their distinct legal status and autonomy. Thus the Carolingian Empire created new ethnic identities among its diverse subjects.

Charlemagne sought to elevate himself and his empire to the imperial dignity enjoyed by Byzantium. He made protection of the pope and Roman orthodoxy an essential component of his mandate. The culmination of his efforts took place on Christmas Day, 800, when Pope Leo III placed a crown on Charlemagne's head and proclaimed him Augustus, the title of the first Roman emperor. Although recognition of Charlemagne and his successors as "emperors" only partially reversed the political fragmentation of post-Roman Europe, it forged a lasting bond between the papacy and the secular rulers of Latin Christendom. Compared with Byzantium, church and state remained more independent of each other in western Europe. Nonetheless, Charlemagne established a new ideology of Christian kingship.

Frankish Kingdom, 768
Areas conquered by Charlemagne, to 814
Tributary peoples
Byzantine Empire

Empire of Charlemagne, 814

Economic Contraction and Renewal in Christendom

Although the Franks preserved the rural aristocracy's control over the land and patronized the Christian church and monasteries, the urban culture of the Roman world withered. The nobility retreated to the security of their rural estates, and the great monasteries in the countryside, enriched by royal land grants, began to overshadow the urban bishops. The Carolingian monarchs, too, abandoned the old Roman towns, preferring to hold court at rural villas such as Charlemagne's capital at Aachen, along the modern border between Germany and Belgium. Both secular lords and monastic abbeys built up vast estates; for labor, they subjected the rural population to increasingly servile status. Throughout the Carolingian realm this new institution, the **manor**, was widely adopted. The tenants became **serfs**, tied to the land and subject to the legal authority of the lord. The obligations of serfs could vary significantly, but in general they owed labor services to the lord, as well as rents and fees for the right to graze animals and collect firewood. Women provided labor as well, either in the manor's workshops or by making cloth in their own homes.

Whereas the expansion of the Carolingian Empire stimulated commercial exchange with Saxon lands in Britain and Denmark, elsewhere industry and trade diminished. Towns and commerce in Europe declined in part from the rise of the new rural manors, but more fundamental was the contraction of the international trading system centered on Constantinople. A terrible plague that swept across the Mediterranean from Egypt to Europe in 541–542 dealt a devastating blow to the urban network of the Roman world, which had survived the decline of the empire itself. Byzantine officials reported that 230,000 died in Constantinople alone, and Mediterranean cities from Antioch to Alexandria also suffered huge losses. Slav and Avar raids decimated the once-thriving cities of the Balkans, and the Sasanid and Muslim conquests of the seventh century deprived the empire of its richest domains. These cumulative demographic and territorial losses greatly reduced economic productivity. Egypt no longer delivered the ample grain tribute upon which the Byzantine state depended to feed its cities and armies, and in much of Anatolia farmland reverted to sheep pasture for lack of labor to grow cereal crops.

Political setbacks, the decline of towns, and the shrinking population led to a downturn in the Byzantine economy. The circulation of money slowed and in many parts of the empire disappeared altogether between the mid-seventh and early ninth centuries. Yet the Byzantine state still appropriated a significant share of agricultural surpluses, which it distributed as salaries to its officials and soldiers. Hit hardest by the waning economic fortunes of the empire was the provincial landowning aristocracy. Peasants who owned their own land increased in numbers and importance, and the state benefited from the taxes they paid.

Yet even as it hit bottom, the Byzantine economy displayed far more vigor than that of the Germanic kingdoms. During the sixth and seventh centuries, the Italian cities under Byzantine rule were the major exception to the pervasive decline of urban population and economic activity throughout Europe. Throughout the empire, political stability rekindled population growth in both town and countryside, especially in the long-settled coastal regions. By 800 unmistakable signs of economic prosperity had reappeared: the demand for coinage increased, new lands were put under the plow, and reports of famine became less frequent and less desperate. The Mediterranean trade network centered on Constantinople began to recover as tensions with Islamic rulers eased. A Muslim scholar writing in around 850 listed among Baghdad's imports from the Byzantine Empire "gold and silver wares, coins of pure gold, medicinal plants, gold-woven textiles, silk brocade, spirited horses, female slaves, rare copperware, unpickable locks, lyres, hydraulic engineers, agrarian experts, marble workers, and eunuchs."[6]

The quickening prosperity of the Byzantine economy promoted commerce across the Mediterranean. Silks produced in Constantinople's workshops ranked among the most prized luxury goods in the Carolingian world (see Lives and Livelihoods: Constantinople's

The Manorial Order

Decline of Towns and Commerce

Economic Recovery in Byzantium

manor A great estate, consisting of farmlands, vineyards, and other productive assets, owned by a lord (which could be an institution, such as a monastery) and cultivated by serfs.

serf A semifree peasant tied to the land and subject to the judicial authority of a lord.

Constantinople's Silk Producers

During the heyday of the Roman Empire, when silk was said to be worth its weight in gold, Romans depended entirely on imports of silk from China. According to the historian Procopius, sericulture—the raising of silk-worms to make silk—first appeared in the Byzantine Empire in his own time, during the reign of Emperor Justinian I (r. 527–565). Several Indian monks arrived at Constantinople offering to reveal the secrets of sericulture:

> When the Emperor questioned them very closely and asked how they could guarantee success in the business, the monks told him that the agents in the production of silk were certain caterpillars, working under nature's teaching, which continually urged them to their task. To bring live caterpillars from that country would be impracticable indeed, but . . . it was possible to hatch their eggs long after they had been laid by covering them with dung, which produced sufficient heat for the purpose.[1]

The monks delivered the eggs as promised, and silk manufacture subsequently became a pillar of the Byzantine economy.

Since Roman times, silk clothing had become a conspicuous mark of wealth and social distinction. The Byzantine government issued numerous decrees restricting the wearing of certain kinds of silk to the nobility. Purple-dyed silks—the "royal purple," a pigment derived from a tropical sea snail—were reserved for the emperor alone. Silk also served as a valuable tool of diplomacy. The Byzantine emperors regularly sent gifts of silk fabrics to the Frankish kings and the Islamic caliphs. In the Carolingian Empire, Byzantine silks were coveted luxury goods, flaunted by male aristocrats and well-born nuns no less than by royal princesses. The prominence of silk garments, furnishings, and liturgical vestments in wills, dowry and marriage contracts, and church inventories attests to both their economic value and their social prestige.

Emperor Justinian I restricted silk manufacture to imperial workshops, but the Islamic conquests deprived the Byzantine state of its monopoly on silk production. Muslim

Byzantine Silk Shroud
Byzantine silk fabrics were highly prized in Latin Christendom. Tradition has it that this piece was placed in the tomb of the Frankish ruler Charlemagne after his death in 814. The design features a charioteer—probably an emperor—driving a four-horse chariot. Attendants in the background hold out crowns and whips; those at the bottom pour coins onto an altar. (Erich Lessing/Art Resource, NY.)

entrepreneurs took over the flourishing silk industry in Syria and introduced sericulture to Sicily and Spain. Then, as the demand for luxury silk goods surged, in the ninth century the Byzantine court allowed private merchants to manufacture and trade silk. At the same time the imperial government imposed tight controls on the private silk trade. These laws have been preserved in the *Book of the Prefect*, a set of commercial regulations issued by the chief magistrate of Constantinople in around 912.

Silk manufacture involves a complex series of operations, ranging from low-skilled tasks such as raising silk-worms and reeling yarn to those requiring high technical proficiency, such as weaving, dyeing, and embroidery. In late Roman times, imperial textile workers, both men and

Silk Producers). Significant economic growth, however, would not return to the European heartland until the late tenth century, well after the expansion of the Byzantine economy was under way.

Origins of the Slavs and the Founding of Rus

During its crisis of the sixth and seventh centuries, the Byzantine empire confronted a new people on its borders, the Slavs. Today nearly 300 million people in Eastern Europe

women, had been reduced to hereditary occupational castes. By Justinian's day, the standing of skilled silk artisans had risen appreciably, and government employment was considered a privilege, not a burden. In the tenth century shortages of skilled labor grew so acute that the government prohibited private merchants from offering artisans wage advances or contracts of more than one month's duration. The intent behind this rule was to ensure that all firms had competitive access to the best craftsmen. Further, the government required these private craftsmen to belong to one of five separate guilds.

This kind of intervention in the marketplace exemplified the Byzantine state's economic philosophy. By splitting the private silk industry into separate guilds, the state enforced a strict division of labor that prevented a few large firms from consolidating control over silk manufacture and trade. Thus, the reeling workshops had to purchase raw silk from middlemen dealers rather than from the producers themselves; after the raw silk was reeled into yarn, it had to be sold back to the middlemen, who in turn marketed the yarn to the silk clothiers. The clothiers produced finished cloth but could sell it only to wholesale merchants, not directly to retail customers.

Yarn production was largely a family business. The silk clothiers, in contrast, combined weaving, dyeing, and tailoring workshops under one management, relying mostly on hired labor but employing household slaves as well. Slaves also operated workshops as agents for their masters. Government workshops employed skilled craftsmen divided into guilds of clothiers, purple dyers, and gold embroiderers, who made richly decorated fabrics for the emperor and his officials. Menial tasks were relegated to servile labor, including foreign slaves.

Although keen to profit from the high prices its silks commanded in foreign markets, the Byzantine government also sought to protect the domestic industry from international competition. The Byzantine rulers kept foreign silk importers, chiefly Muslims and Jews, under close surveillance. After depositing their goods in a government warehouse, foreign merchants were sequestered in special lodgings, where they were permitted to remain for a maximum of three months. Domestic silk importers could not deal directly with foreign merchants. Instead, they negotiated collectively for the purchase of imported wares. This practice, too, ensured that all firms, small and large, had some access to imported products.

The Byzantines also feared the loss of trade secrets to foreign competitors. Foreign merchants were prohibited from taking certain silk goods and unsewn fabrics out of Constantinople, and their cargoes were carefully inspected before they could leave the city. The city magistrate decreed that "every dyer who sells a slave, a workman, or a foreman craftsman to persons alien to the city or the Empire shall have his hand cut off."[2] But these efforts to monopolize technological know-how proved futile. By 1000, technical mastery of silk manufacture had become widely disseminated. Surviving silk specimens show that Byzantine and Muslim artisans freely borrowed weaving techniques, artistic motifs, and color patterns from each other, to the point where it is nearly impossible to distinguish their handiwork.

1. Procopius, *The History of the Wars*, 4:17.
2. *Book of the Eparch*, Chapter 8, in E. H. Freshfield, *Roman Law in the Later Roman Empire: Byzantine Guilds, Professional, Commercial; Ordinances of Leo VI, c. 895, from The Book of the Eparch* (Cambridge, U.K.: Cambridge University Press, 1938), 26.

QUESTIONS TO CONSIDER

1. Did the Byzantine government's measures to regulate the silk industry stimulate or discourage competition among producers?

2. Did guild organizations in the Byzantine silk industry exist primarily to promote the interests of artisans, merchants, or the government?

For Further Information:

Laiou, Angeliki E., and Cécile Morrisson. *The Byzantine Economy*. Cambridge, U.K.: Cambridge University Press, 2007.

Laiou, Angeliki E., ed. *The Economic History of Byzantium from the Seventh Through the Fifteenth Century*. 3 vols. Washington, DC: Dumbarton Oaks Research Library and Collections, 2002.

and Russia speak a Slavic language. They trace their ancestry back to peoples known as *Sclavenoi* in Greek, who first appear in sixth-century Byzantine chronicles. As the Goths migrated westward into the former Roman territories, they abandoned their homelands to the Slavs, small, independent communities who rejected the imperial order of Byzantium. As contact with the Roman world declined, the material culture beyond the eastern frontiers of the old empire became more impoverished. Early Byzantine accounts classified the Slavs, together with the Avars and the Goths, as pagan savages and mortal enemies of Christendom. Between the fifth and tenth centuries, however, Byzantine interaction with

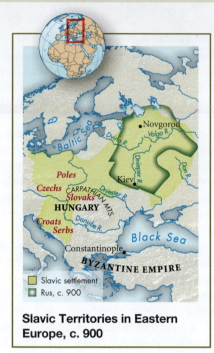

Slavic Territories in Eastern Europe, c. 900

Legend:
- Slavic settlement
- Rus, c. 900

both settled and nomadic Slavic populations led to the crystallization of an identifiable Slavic culture with its own written languages and to the assimilation of the Slavs into a larger Christian civilization.

Like the Germanic peoples, most Slavs lived in small farming settlements consisting of several extended related families: "each living with his own clan on his own lands," in the words of a Russian chronicler.[7] The Slavs practiced shifting cultivation, regularly moving into wilderness areas and cutting down virgin forest to plant barley and millet, using the nitrogen-rich ash of burnt trees as fertilizer. Procopius portrayed the Slavs as leading "a primitive and rough way of life. . . . They are neither dishonorable nor spiteful, but simple in their ways, like the Huns."[8] Another Byzantine writer complimented Slavic women as "chaste beyond all measure," willing to kill themselves upon the death of their husbands because they "regard widowhood as no life at all."[9]

Social stratification increased by the eighth century; chiefs and their retinues crowned the social order, and hilltop strongholds with timber fortifications proliferated. Distinctive Slavic forms of pottery and silver jewelry appeared, but the material culture of the forest-dwelling Slavs was dominated by wood products and has mostly vanished. Trading posts for bartering furs and slaves sprang up near major crossroads, and craftsmen such as blacksmiths and silversmiths wandered from place to place offering their services.

Slavic Conversion to Christianity

In the ninth and tenth centuries the Slavic peoples were strongly influenced by Byzantine and Frankish models of government, law, and religion. The uniform Slavic culture divided into separate societies and political allegiances, leading to the emergence of Serb, Croat, Polish, and other Slavic national identities. The most far-reaching change was the conversion of most Slavic peoples to Christianity. Slav rulers, pressured by hostile Christian adversaries, were the first to convert. The Slavic adoption of Christianity only heightened frictions between Rome and Constantinople, however, because the southern and eastern Slavs adhered to Byzantine rites and beliefs, whereas Latin teachings prevailed among western Slavs.

Emergence of Rus

According to later (and not wholly reliable) Russian chronicles, the first state of Rus was formed in 862 when Scandinavian communities in the Novgorod region elected a Viking chieftain as their ruler. But a Rus confederation of Viking settlements engaging in slave raiding and fur trading had already emerged some decades before. Lured by the riches of the Mediterranean world, the Rus pushed southward toward the Black Sea along the Dnieper and the Volga rivers. A major assault by the Rus on Constantinople in 911 forced the Byzantine emperor to sue for peace by conceding generous trading privileges. At some point, probably in the 930s, the Rus princes shifted their capital to Kiev in the lower Dnieper valley.

By the late tenth century Kievan Rus had emerged as the dominant power in the Black Sea region. Prince Vladimir (r. 980–1015) consolidated Rus into a more unified state and adopted the Christian religion of Byzantium. Conversion to Christianity and deepening commercial and diplomatic ties with Byzantium marked a decisive reorientation of Rus away from its Scandinavian origins. Drawn south by Byzantine wealth, Rus invaders did not destroy the culture they encountered but instead became part of it, adding their own cultural heritage to that of the eastern Christian world.

Thus the middle centuries of the first millennium C.E. saw both the growth and the splintering of Christianity, as competing visions of Christianity emerged. This competition would soon become more complex with the arrival of a new religion. Although the Latin and Orthodox churches continued to win new converts in eastern and northern Europe, the sudden emergence of Islam in the seventh century transformed the religious landscape of the Mediterranean world. Even though large Christian communities persevered under Muslim rule in regions such as Syria, Iran, and Spain, the Mediterranean Sea took on new significance as a boundary between religious faiths.

The Rise and Spread of Islam 610–750

In the early seventh century, the Arab prophet Muhammad (c. 570–632) founded what became a new religion, Islam, rooted in the Judaic and Christian traditions but transformed by the divine revelations he proclaimed. Muhammad was more than a religious teacher, however. He envisioned the community of believers as a tight-knit movement dedicated to propagating the true faith, and his successors fashioned Islam into a mighty social and political force. Within a century of Muhammad's death in 632 an Islamic empire had expanded beyond Arabia as far as Iran to the east and Spain to the west. As in Christendom, tensions arose between political rulers and religious authorities. During the tenth century the united Islamic empire fractured into a commonwealth of independent states. Yet the powerful inspiration of Muhammad's teachings and Islam's radical egalitarian ideals sustained a sense of community that transcended political and ethnic boundaries.

FOCUS

In what ways did Islam instill a sense of common identity among its believers?

The Prophet Muhammad and the Faith of Islam

The Arabian Background

Muhammad's call for a renewal of religious faith dedicated to the one true God must be seen in the context of social and religious life in the Arabian peninsula. The harsh desert environment of Arabia could sustain little more than a nomadic pastoral livelihood. Domestication of the camel since about 1000 B.C.E. allowed small, clan-based groups known as Bedouins to raise livestock. During the summer the Bedouins gathered at oases to exchange animal products for grain, dates, utensils, weapons, and cloth. Some of these oases eventually supported thriving commercial towns, of which the most prosperous was Mecca.

The Bedouin (BED-uh-wuhn) tribes regularly came to Mecca to pay homage at the Ka'aba (KAH-buh) shrine, which housed the icons of numerous gods worshiped throughout the region. Mecca thus served as a sanctuary where different tribes could gather to worship their gods in peace. The religious harmony that prevailed at Mecca also offered opportunities to settle disputes and conduct trade. The Meccan fairs gave birth to a common culture, language, and social identity among the leading clans of Arabia.

Building on its status as an Arabian crossroads, Mecca developed economic connections with the larger world. During the sixth century, it blossomed into a major emporium of international trade between the Mediterranean and the Indian Ocean. Yet urban growth was accompanied by social tensions. Clan solidarity remained paramount, and the gap between rich and poor widened. No single ruler presided over Mecca, and economic inequality sowed dissension. It was here that Muhammad, the founder of Islam, was born in around the year 570.

Muhammad's Life and Message

Muhammad belonged to a once-prominent clan whose fortunes were in decline. As a young man he worked as a caravaner for a woman named Khadija, a rich widow older than Muhammad, whom he married when he was twenty-five. Although Muhammad seemed to have gained a secure livelihood, moral doubts and growing contempt for what he regarded as the arrogance and greed of his fellow Meccans deeply troubled him. Beginning in around 610 he experienced visions of a single, true God ("Allah") who did not cater to the worldly wishes of worshipers as the pagan gods of his countrymen did but instead imposed an uncompromising moral law upon all peoples. Muhammad's revelations were suffused with a deep sense of sin inspired by Christianity. From Judaism Muhammad incorporated devotion to the one true God, a sense of personal mission as a prophet sent to warn the world against impiety, and a regimen of ritual prayer intended to instill rightful thought and conduct. Thus Muhammad's message was shaped by both the social and economic conflicts of his day and the long religious history of the region.

Hijra of Muhammad, 622

Initially, Muhammad communicated his visions only to a small group of confidants. In 613, however, a revelation instructed him to "rise and warn," and he began to preach publicly. Muhammad's egalitarian vision, in which all believers were equal before God, directly challenged tribal loyalties and clan leaders. Like Jesus, his teachings won favor among the lower classes, the poor and propertyless, while making him a pariah among the affluent and powerful clans. Persecution forced Muhammad and his followers to seek sanctuary in Medina, a nearby oasis town, in 622. Muhammad's move to Medina, known as the *hijra* (HIJ-ruh) ("migration"), subsequently marked the beginning of the Muslim calendar.

In Medina, Muhammad's reputation for holiness and fairness and his vision of a united community bound by a single faith elevated him to a position of leadership. The primary obstacle to the consolidation of his power in Medina was the town's large Jewish population, which rejected Muhammad's claims of prophethood and allied with his Meccan enemies. Muhammad began to issue new revelations accusing the Jews of breaking the covenant with God and declaring that he himself was the direct successor of the first and greatest prophet, Abraham. Muhammad vowed that his own creed of Islam ("submission") would supersede both Judaism and Christianity. Backed by Medina's clan leaders, Muhammad executed or exiled the town's leading Jewish citizens, thereby securing unchallenged authority in political as well as spiritual matters.

Subsequently Muhammad and his followers warred against Mecca—the first instance of a *jihad* ("struggle") of the sword, a holy war fought against those who persecute believers. In 630, the Meccans surrendered their city to Muhammad, who destroyed the idols of pagan gods in the Ka'aba and instead established it as the holiest shrine of Islam. Most Bedouin tribes soon capitulated to Muhammad as well. Preparing in 632 for an invasion of Syria, Muhammad was struck down by an illness and died in Medina. By the time of his death, he had created the basis for a new political order founded on a universal religion and a faith in the oneness of God that transcended clan, ethnic, and civic identities.

The revelations of Muhammad were written down in Arabic in the **Qur'an**, which Muslims regard as the completion of earlier revelations from God set down in the Jewish Torah and the Christian Gospels. The Qur'an elaborates the "five pillars of faith": (1) bearing witness to the unity of God and the prophethood of Muhammad; (2) daily prayers while facing the direction of Mecca; (3) fasting during Ramadan, the ninth month of the Islamic calendar; (4) giving alms to the poor; and (5) for those physically able and with the financial means, the obligation to make a pilgrimage (*hajj*) to Mecca. Performance of the "five pillars" gave public expression to membership in the **umma**, the community of the faithful. The daily regimen of prayer, the annual observation of Ramadan, and the duty to complete the hajj at least once during one's lifetime transformed the rhythms and purpose of life for herders and townfolk alike. All of these practices were joyous public ceremonies that served as visible symbols of submission to divine will. In the absence of a formal priesthood, the **ulama**—scholars and teachers steeped in study of the Qur'an—acted as the custodians and interpreters of divine teachings.

Several principles set Islam apart from the earlier monotheistic traditions of Judaism and Christianity: the stress on complete subjugation to God's commands—the fundamental tenet of Islam; the subordination of all other identities and loyalties to the community of believers; and dedication to defending the community and spreading the true religion. Although the Qur'an modified some of the prevailing norms of Bedouin society—for example, by recognizing women and children as individuals with their own needs and some limited rights—on the whole it reinforced the patriarchal traditions of clan society (see Reading the Past: Women and Property in Islam). At the same time, the charismatic leadership of clan elders yielded to the higher authority of divine will. Aspects of Islam were rooted in Bedouin culture, but the

The Five Pillars of Islam

hijra Muhammad's move from Mecca to Medina in 622, which marks year 1 of the Islamic calendar.

jihad Literally, "struggle"; a key concept in the Qur'an, which can refer to the individual's spiritual effort to follow "the path of God" (jihad of the soul) or to a holy war (jihad of the sword) against those who persecute Islam.

Qur'an The book recording the revelations of the Prophet Muhammad; regarded as the most sacred scripture in Islam.

umma The worldwide community of believers in Islam.

ulama Scholars learned in Islamic scripture and law codes who act as arbiters of Islamic teachings.

Women and Property in Islam

Under laws that prevailed in Latin Christendom until the nineteenth century, women had no right to inherit property, even from their deceased husbands. The Jewish legal tradition allowed only limited inheritance rights to women, generally for unmarried daughters or to perpetuate the family line when a man had no male heirs. Islamic law, by contrast, explicitly granted women certain property rights and control over their own earnings. In practice, however, the property rights of Islamic women and their access to gainful employment have been shaped and in some cases curtailed by social practices and scriptural interpretation.

Islam establishes men as the guardians of women, responsible for both their material welfare and their moral conduct, obligations that entail the right to punish women for their moral failings. At the same time, in keeping with the commandment against coveting the wealth and property of others, women are entitled to whatever earnings they receive from their work, trade, or property.

> Men are the ones who support women since God has given some persons advantages over others, and because they should spend their wealth on them. Honorable women are steadfast, guarding the Unseen just as God has it guarded. Admonish them, foresake them in beds apart, and beat them if necessary. If they obey you, do not seek any way to proceed against them.
> Qur'an, 4.34

> In no way covet those things in which God has bestowed his gifts more freely on some of you than on others: to men is allotted what they earn, and to women what they earn.
> Qur'an, 4.128

In both the Jewish and Islamic traditions, at the time of marriage the husband must provide the wife with a dowry that becomes her irrevocable personal property. Whereas the husband has free use of this property during the marriage under Jewish law, Islamic law places the dowry entirely at the disposal of the wife. The Qur'an also guarantees women an inheritance from their parents and close kin, though their share is usually less than the portion received by male heirs.

> [Upon marriage], give women their dowry as a free gift. If they of their own good wish remit any part of it to you, take it and enjoy it with good cheer.
> Qur'an, 4.4

> From what is left by parents and near relatives there is a share for men and a share for women, whether the property be small or large.
> Qur'an, 4.7

> God instructs you concerning your children's inheritance: a son should have a share equivalent to that of two daughters: if you have only daughters, two or more, their combined share is two-thirds of the inheritance; if only one, her share is a half.
> Qur'an, 4.11

Under Jewish law, both men and women could initiate a divorce, but one of the radical reforms of Christianity was to abolish divorce. Islamic law granted the right of divorce to men but not to women. The Qur'an allows the husband to divorce a wife without her consent, but it also requires that he provide financial support for a divorced wife, as well as a widow. Following a period of mourning, widows are free to leave their husband's household together with their property and remarry if they wish.

> A divorce may be pronounced twice [to give the parties a chance to reconcile]: after that, the parties should either hold together on equitable terms, or separate with kindness.
> Qur'an 2.229

> Those of you who die and leave widows should bequeath for their widows a year's maintenance and residence.
> Qur'an, 2.240

> For divorced women, maintenance should be provided on a reasonable scale.
> Qur'an, 2.241

EXAMINING THE EVIDENCE

1. Did Islamic law strengthen or weaken women's economic dependence on men?

2. Did Islamic laws on divorce and women's property correspond more closely to Jewish or to Christian precedents?

Divorce Hearing

Although permitted under Islamic law, divorce was regarded as a last resort. In this illustration from *The Assemblies* of al-Hariti, dated 1237, a man accompanied by his several wives pleads his case before the judge, who sits on a raised platform in front of a curtain of authority. Both the husband and the accused wife are portrayed as stubborn; the judge dismisses the case by giving each a gold coin. (Bibliothèque nationale de France.)

Factions Within Islam

caliph The designated successor to Muhammad as leader of the Muslim faithful in civil affairs.

imam The supreme leader of the Islamic community (especially in the Shi'a tradition), the legitimate successor to Muhammad; or any Islamic religious leader.

Shi'a A branch of Islam that maintains that only descendants of Muhammad through his cousin and son-in-law Ali have a legitimate right to serve as caliph.

Sunni The main branch of Islam, which accepts the historical succession of caliphs as legitimate leaders of the Muslim community.

religion pointed toward a new understanding of community in which membership was defined not by kinship or geography but by assent to a common set of religious principles.

The Islamic Empire of the Umayyad Caliphs 661–743

Muhammad's stature as the Prophet made him unique in the Islamic community. After his death the community faced the thorny problem of choosing his successor. Although Kadijah is said to have borne Muhammad four daughters and two sons, only two of his daughters outlived him. Eventually a compromise was reached that recognized Muhammad's father-in-law, Abu Bakr (AH-boo BOCK-ear), as **caliph** (KAY-luhf) ("deputy"). The caliph would inherit Muhammad's position as leader of the Islamic community, but not his role as prophet. As caliph, Abu Bakr led the community in wars of conquest and submission. The Byzantine and Sasanid empires, weakened by three decades of wars against each other, were no match for the Arabs. The Arabs decisively defeated the Byzantine army in Palestine in 634 and proceeded to capture Syria, Mesopotamia, and Egypt by 641. The Byzantine Empire lost most of its territories in the east but survived. The Sasanid Empire, however, utterly collapsed after Arab armies seized its capital of Ctesiphon in 637.

Abu Bakr and his immediate successors as caliphs ruled by virtue of their close personal relationships to the Prophet Muhammad, but disputes over succession persisted. The third caliph, Uthman (r. 644–656), a Meccan aristocrat of the Umayya (oo-MY-uh) clan, sought to resolve the succession problem by creating a family dynasty. Uthman's grab for power provoked civil war, however, and he was assassinated in 656. Ali, Muhammad's cousin and husband of his daughter Fatima, was elected to replace Uthman, but he failed to unite the warring Arab tribes. In 661 Ali, too, was assassinated. Mu'awiya (moo-AH-we-yuh) (r. 661–680), a cousin of Uthman and governor of Syria, emerged as the most powerful Muslim leader and succeeded in establishing a hereditary dynasty of Umayyad caliphs. Hence politics shaped Islam during Muhammad's lifetime and continued to affect its development long after his death. Just as the expansion of Christianity brought with it divisions and conflicts, Islam's success undermined its unity as factions formed within the Islamic world.

Although Mu'awiya cemented dynastic control over the caliphate and built up an imperial government in his new capital of Damascus, the wounds opened by the succession dispute failed to heal. When Mu'awiya died in 680, Ali's son Husayn (hoo-SANE) launched an insurrection in an attempt to reclaim the caliphacy. The Umayyads defeated the rebels, and Husayn was captured and killed. Nonetheless, a faction of Muslims remained who contended that the only rightful successors to the caliphate were Ali and his descendants, known as the *imam* ("leaders"). This group, which became known as the **Shi'a**, regarded Husayn as a great martyr. Another group, the Khariji, had turned against Ali because of his vacillating leadership and perceived moral failings. The Khariji rejected hereditary succession to the office of caliph in favor of election, insisting that religious devotion and moral purity were the only proper criteria for choosing the caliph. Both the Shi'a and the Khariji emphasized the role of the caliph as an infallible authority in matters of religious doctrine. Supporters of the Umayyad caliphs, known as the **Sunni**, instead regarded the caliph primarily as a secular ruler. Although the Sunni believed that the chief duty of the caliph was to protect and propagate Islam, they turned to the ulama rather than the caliph for interpretation of Islamic doctrine and law. Thus the divisions in Islam that grew out of disputes over the succession evolved into divergent understandings of the nature of the Islamic community and Islamic institutions.

When Abd al-Malik (r. 685–705), following a bloody struggle, assumed the office of Umayyad caliph in 685, the Muslim world was in disarray after a half century of astonishingly rapid expansion. Abd al-Malik succeeded in quelling uprisings by Shi'a and Khariji dissidents and restoring the caliph's authority over Arabia and Iran. He retained much of the administrative system of the Byzantine and Sasanid states, while substituting Arabic for Greek and Persian as the language of government. He also enacted currency reform, replacing images of human rulers with quotations from scripture, thereby providing another powerful symbol of Islamic unity. Abd al-Malik upheld the supremacy of Arabs in

Umayyad Reform and Expansion

government as well as faith, but bureaucratic office and mastery of the written word displaced martial valor as marks of leadership. He thus succeeded in creating a powerful monarchy supported by a centralized civilian bureaucracy.

Abd al-Malik and his successors continued to pursue vigorous expansion of *dar-al-Islam* ("the House of Belief") through military conquest, extending the Umayyad realm across North Africa and into Central Asia. In 710–711 a coalition of Arab and Berber forces from Morocco invaded the Iberian peninsula and quickly overran the Visigoth kingdom, stunning Latin Christendom. This invasion marked the beginning of a conflict between Christians and Muslims in the Iberian peninsula that would continue for centuries.

At first, to preserve the social unity of the conquerors, the Arabs ruled from garrison cities deliberately set apart from older urban centers. The Arabs thus became an elite military class based in garrison cities such as Basra and Kufa (both in Iraq), Fustat (modern Cairo), and Qayrawan (KYE-rwan) (in Tunisia), living off taxes extracted from farmers and merchants. Regarding Islam as a mark of Arab superiority, they made little effort to convert their non-Arab subjects. "Peoples of the Book"—Jews, Christians, and Zoroastrians, collectively referred to as *dhimmi* (DEE-me)—were permitted to practice their own religions, which the Arabs regarded as related but inferior versions of Islam, but under certain restrictions (see Reading the Past: The Pact of Umar). The dhimmi also had to pay a special tax (*jizya*) in return for the state's protection.

The segregation of Arabs from the conquered peoples could not be sustained indefinitely, however. Settlement in garrison towns transformed the lifestyle of the nomadic Arabs, and interactions with native populations led to assimilation, especially in Iran, far from the Arabian homeland. After a century of trying to maintain a distinct Arab-Muslim identity separate from local societies, the Umayyad caliphs reversed course and instead began to promote Islam as a unifying force. Caliph Umar II (r. 717–720) encouraged conversion of local rulers, merchants, and scholars. Although most people remained faithful to their ancestral religions, many members of the local elites were eager to ally with their Arab rulers. They converted to Islam, adopted the Arabic language, and sought places in the military and government service as equals to Arabs on the basis of their shared religion.

dar-al-Islam Literally, "the House of Belief"; the name given to the countries and peoples who profess belief in Islam; in contrast to *dar-al-harb* ("the House of War"), where Islam does not prevail and Muslims cannot freely practice their religion.

dhimmi The Arabic term for "peoples of the book" (i.e., the Bible), namely Jews and Christians, who are seen as sharing the same religious tradition as Muslims.

From Unified Caliphate to Islamic Commonwealth 750–1000

Umar II's efforts to erase the distinctions between Arabs and non-Arabs and create a universal empire based on the fundamental equality of all Muslims stirred up strong opposition from his fellow Arabs. Although the creation of a unified Islamic state fostered the emergence of a

FOCUS

How did the tensions between the ulama and the Abbasid caliphs weaken a unified Islamic empire?

The Pact of Umar

The Pact of Umar purports to be a letter from a Christian community in Syria seeking a truce with their Muslim overlords after the caliph Umar I conquered Syria in 637. Most scholars doubt that this document actually was written by Christians of that era. Rather, it was probably composed in the ninth century by Islamic jurists who wished to prescribe the conditions under which Muslims would tolerate the dhimmi communities, Jews as well as Christians, under their rule. But at least some of these regulations were enacted by the Abbasid caliphs. It has also been suggested that the restrictions on religious activities derived from Sasanid policies toward religious minorities within their empire. Regardless of its true origins, Muslim rulers frequently invoked the Pact of Umar as a model for regulating the conduct of Christians and Jews.

This is a letter to the servant of God Umar, Commander of the Faithful, from the Christians of [specific city]. When you came against us, we asked you for safe-conduct for ourselves, our descendants, our property, and the people of our community, and we undertook the following obligations toward you:

We shall not build, in our cities or in their neighborhood, new monasteries, churches, convents, or monks' cells, nor shall we repair, by day or by night, such of them as fall in ruins or are situated in the quarters of the Muslims.

We shall keep our gates wide open for passersby and travelers.

We shall give board and lodging to all Muslims who pass our way for three days.

We shall not give shelter in our churches or in our dwellings to any spy, nor hide him from the Muslims.

We shall not teach the Qur'an to our children.

We shall not manifest our religion publicly nor convert anyone to it. We shall not prevent any of our kin from entering Islam if they wish it.

We shall show respect toward the Muslims, and we shall rise from our seats when they wish to sit. We shall not seek to resemble the Muslims by imitating any of their garments, the qalansuwa [a fez-like cap], the turban, footwear, or the parting of the hair.

We shall not speak as they do, nor shall we adopt their kunyas [honorific names].

We shall not mount on saddles, nor shall we gird swords nor bear any kind of arms nor carry them on our persons.

We shall not engrave Arabic inscriptions on our seals. We shall not sell fermented drinks. . . . We shall not display our crosses or our books in the roads or markets of the Muslims.

We shall use only clappers [percussion instruments to accompany singing] in our churches very softly.

We shall not raise our voices when following our dead.

We shall not show lights on any of the roads of the Muslims or in their markets. We shall not bury our dead near the Muslims.

We shall not take slaves who have been allotted to Muslims.

We shall not build houses overtopping the houses of the Muslims.

(When I brought the letter to Umar, may God be pleased with him, he added, "We shall not strike a Muslim.")

We accept these conditions for ourselves and for the people of our community, and in return we receive safe-conduct. If we in any way violate these undertakings for which we ourselves stand surety, we forfeit our covenant, and we become liable to the penalties for contumacy [falsehood] and sedition [treason].

Source: A. S. Tritton, *The Caliphs and Their Non-Muslim Subjects*, by A. S. Tritton (1930): "The Pact of Umar." By permission of Oxford University Press.

EXAMINING THE EVIDENCE

1. In what ways were Christians expected to show deference to the superiority of Islam? Why were these visible expressions of subjugation considered important?

2. What Christian religious activities and symbols were deemed offensive to Muslims? Why?

cosmopolitan society and culture, rebellions by Bedouin tribes and Shi'a and Khariji communities caused the collapse of the Umayyad regime in 743. A new lineage of caliphs, the Abbasids, soon reestablished a centralized empire. But by 850, Abbasid power was in decline, and regional rulers and religious leaders began to challenge the caliphs' authority (see Map 9.3).

Rise of the Abbasid Caliphs

In 747, the Abbasids (ah-BASS-id), a branch of Muhammad's clan that had settled in Khurasan in northern Iran, seized the caliphate in their own name. They based their legitimacy on their vow to restore the caliphacy to the imams descended from Muhammad, a vow that won them the crucial support of Shi'a Muslims. Once securely in power, however, the Abbasids revived Umar II's vision of a pan-Islamic empire. Proclaiming the universal equality of all Muslims, the Abbasids stripped the Arabs of their military and economic privileges while recruiting non-Arab officers and administrators loyal to the new dynasty.

The Abbasid dynasty perpetuated the image of the caliph as a universal sovereign and supreme defender of Islam. When the Abbasid caliph al-Mansur (r. 754–775) began building his new capital of Baghdad on the banks of the Tigris River, near the former Sasanid capital of Ctesiphon, in 762, he claimed to be fulfilling a prophecy that a city would be built at this spot, at "the crossroads of the whole world."[10] Baghdad soon mushroomed into a giant complex of palaces, government offices, military camps, and commercial and industrial quarters.

The New Capital of Baghdad

At the heart of Baghdad, al-Mansur built the so-called Round City, more than a mile in diameter, which housed the caliph's family and the offices of government. At the center of the Round City, the green-domed palace of the caliph and the city's Grand Mosque stood together in the middle of a large open plaza, accentuating the unique majesty of the caliph's authority

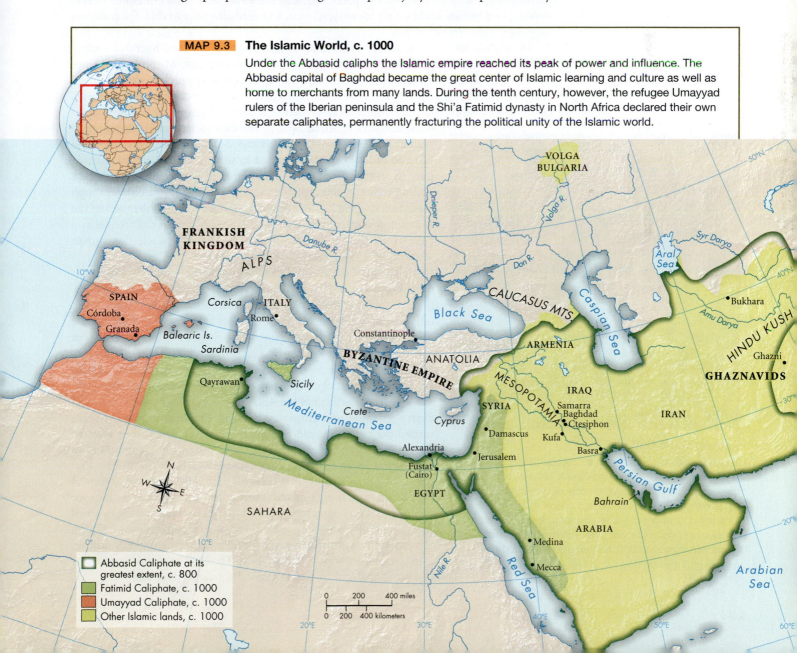

MAP 9.3   The Islamic World, c. 1000

Under the Abbasid caliphs the Islamic empire reached its peak of power and influence. The Abbasid capital of Baghdad became the great center of Islamic learning and culture as well as home to merchants from many lands. During the tenth century, however, the refugee Umayyad rulers of the Iberian peninsula and the Shi'a Fatimid dynasty in North Africa declared their own separate caliphates, permanently fracturing the political unity of the Islamic world.

☐ Abbasid Caliphate at its greatest extent, c. 800
☐ Fatimid Caliphate, c. 1000
☐ Umayyad Caliphate, c. 1000
☐ Other Islamic lands, c. 1000

0   200   400 miles
0   200   400 kilometers

over both civil and religious affairs. In Baghdad, as in other Islamic cities, the mosques, bazaars, and public baths became the centers of community life. Baghdad was divided into numerous residential neighborhoods, which acquired some measure of informal autonomy. The caliphs entrusted many tasks of municipal government to quasi-autonomous judicial, police, and fiscal officials, while the ulama dispersed across the city's neighborhoods performed informal but vital roles as community leaders. Well-regarded professionals, such as jewelers, perfumers, and booksellers, opened shops adjacent to the mosques, whereas those in dirty industries, such as tanners and butchers, were banished to the city's outskirts. House architecture and the winding, narrow city streets were designed to render women invisible to the public eye. Open public spaces such as squares and parks were notably absent. But Islamic rulers seldom imposed residential segregation based on ethnicity or religion.

Baghdad's Cosmopolitan Culture

The merchant communities of Baghdad and other cities included a mix of Jews, Christians, Persians, and Central Asians, as well as Muslims. Abbasid policies favoring conversion to Islam isolated Christians and Jews, turning them into ethnic minorities. Nonetheless, Jews and Nestorian Christians enjoyed better opportunities to earn a living and practice their religions in the Muslim world than they had under Byzantine rule.

The Abbasid rulers cultivated a cosmopolitan court life that blended Persian culture and Islamic faith. The court and wealthy officials and merchants in Baghdad became great patrons of scholars, physicians, and poets. Baghdad's scholars translated numerous Greek, Persian, and Indian works on philosophy, science, and medicine into Arabic, the common language of the Islamic world.

Alongside its officials, scholars, merchants, soldiers, and artisans, Baghdad society included a significant number of slaves. According to Islamic law, Muslims could not enslave their fellow Muslims. Thus, slaves were mostly obtained by purchase from Central Asia, the Slavic lands, and Africa. Elite households employed slaves as domestic servants, concubines, guards, and entertainers. Despite their legal status as slaves, they could acquire some measure of social rank in Muslim society, as the example of Arib al-Ma'muniya (797–890) shows. Sold as a young girl to a high Abbasid official, Arib was trained in singing and music, talents that were in great demand in the elite homes of Baghdad. Arib became a leading figure in the capital's musical and literary salons. Through these contacts and her love affairs with high-ranking members of the Abbasid government and army, she acquired powerful friends and patrons. By the end of her life Arib had become a wealthy woman who owned and trained her own slave singers.

The rise of the Abbasid caliphate drew the Islamic world farther from its roots in Arabia. The Umayyad caliphs had been tied to the culture and society of the Arabian deserts. After the founding of the Abbasid caliphate, however, Arabia was no longer at the center of the Islamic world. Mecca and Medina remained the holy cities, where pilgrims from every corner of the Muslim world gathered and intermingled. But religious leadership, like political and economic power, shifted to Baghdad and other commercial centers such as Damascus, Basra, and Cairo.

Iraq, the heartland of the Abbasid caliphate, experienced extraordinary economic and urban development. Building on improvements carried out by the Sasanid Empire, the Abbasid government invested heavily in the irrigation works needed to sustain agriculture. Muslim landowners in southern Iraq imported slaves from the nearby East African region of Zanj to work on sugar cane plantations and to convert the salt marshes into farmland. Foreign trade introduced both exotic goods and new manufacturing technologies. Papermaking, learned from China, displaced the practice of writing on papyrus leaves. Cotton textile manufacture and sugar refining emerged as major industries using techniques imported from India. The Muslim world became part of a vast global trading network, with Baghdad at its center.

Abbasid Court Culture

The Abbasid caliphs favored a cosmopolitan cultural style drawn from Persian and Greek, as well as Islamic, traditions. Frescoes from the ruins of the Abbasid palace at Samarra in Iraq—such as this scene of two dancing girls pouring wine—celebrate hunting, feasting, and the pleasures of court life. But after the caliphs' power began to decline in around 900, human figures disappeared almost entirely from Islamic art for centuries. (bpk/Art Resource, NY.)

Rise of the Religious Scholars

Whereas the power of the caliphs rested on their wealth, their legitimacy ultimately derived from their role as defenders of Islamic orthodoxy. Yet the caliphs did not inherit Muhammad's stature as prophet, and the Qur'an remained the indisputable testament of religious wisdom. Through their commentaries on scripture, the ulama taught how to apply the Qur'an to the conduct of social life. Religious teachers also compiled records of the deeds and words of Muhammad, known as *hadith*, as guides to the proper fulfillment of divine commandments. The caliphs thus occupied an ambiguous space in Islamic religious life. It was their job to defend Islamic orthodoxy, but they lacked the power to define that orthodoxy.

Their position was made even more difficult by the proliferation of scriptural commentaries and hadith, which widened the scope for individual interpretation of Islamic doctrine. In response, the caliphs sought to ensure orthodoxy by creating formal legal codes (*shari'a*) and law courts that combined religious and civil authority. Schools of law sprang up in major seats of Islamic learning such as Baghdad, Basra, Fustat, and Medina (see Chapter 13). However, because no consistent body of law could be applied uniformly throughout the caliphate, this initiative only added to the profusion of scriptural commentary and legal opinion that threatened to splinter the unity of Islamic teachings.

Faced with the potential fracturing of Islam, the ulama largely reconciled themselves to the caliphs' authority to maintain unity and order. Yet beneath this acceptance of Abbasid rule simmered profound discontent. "The best ruler is he who keeps company with scholars," proclaimed a leading religious teacher, "but the worst scholar is he who seeks the company of kings."[11] For the ulama, the special privileges and riches of the caliph and his courtiers betrayed Islam's most basic principles. The fundamental conflict remained. The caliphs sought to merge political and religious authority in a centralized state. The ulama, in contrast, worked to redefine the role of the caliph to establish clear limits to the caliph's power. In their view, the role of the caliph was not to determine Islamic law but rather to ensure the just administration of the shari'a for the benefit of all.

Relations between the caliphate and the ulama sank to their lowest point during the reign of al-Mamum (r. 813–833). Confronted with fierce opposition among the leading ulama and civil officials, al-Mamum launched a harsh campaign to force the ulama to acknowledge the caliph's higher authority in theological matters. His heavy-handed tactics failed, however. The spiritual leadership of the ulama rested securely on the unswerving allegiance of ordinary citizens, which the caliph was powerless to usurp.

Collapse of the Unified Caliphate

Unable to command the loyalty of its subjects and with its very legitimacy in question, the Abbasid regime grew weaker and ultimately collapsed. Al-Mamum's brother and successor as caliph, al-Mutasim (r. 833–842), faced growing dissent among both his officials and the ulama. He withdrew from Baghdad and took up residence at a new capital he built at Samarra, seventy miles to the northwest. Al-Mutasim also made the fateful decision to recruit Turkish slaves from Central Asia to form a new military force loyal to the caliphate. The slave soldiers soon ousted civil officials from the central government and provincial posts. In 861 a regiment of Turkish troops revolted and murdered the caliph, plunging the caliphate into anarchy. In 868 a renegade imam roused the Zanj slaves and other disaffected people in southern Iraq to revolt, promising "to give them slaves, money, and homes to possess for themselves."[12] The Zanj rebellion lasted fifteen years, claiming many thousands of lives and draining the fiscal and military resources of the Abbasid regime. Some measure of stability was restored in 945, when a Persian military strongman took control of Baghdad, reducing the Abbasid caliph to a mere figurehead. But by then rulers in Spain and North Africa had claimed the mantle of caliph for themselves.

In the early years of the Abbasid caliphate, the sole survivor of the Umayyad clan, Abd al-Rahman (ahbd al-rah-MAHN) (r. 756–788), had assembled a coalition of Berber and Syrian forces and seized power in Muslim Spain. Too far removed from the Muslim heartland

Islamic Teachings and Law Schools

Tensions Between the Caliphs and the Ulama

Rival Caliphates

to pose a threat to the Abbasids, the Umayyad regime in Spain coexisted uneasily with the Baghdad caliphate. In 931, as Abbasid authority ebbed, the Umayyad ruler Abd al-Rahman III (r. 912–961) declared himself the rightful caliph in the name of his forebears.

Another claim to the caliphacy arose in North Africa, a stronghold of a messianic Shi'a movement known as the Ismaili. The Ismaili believed that soon the final prophet, the true successor to Muhammad and Ali, would appear in the world to usher in the final judgment and the resurrection of the faithful. Hounded from Baghdad, Ismaili evangelists had instigated secessionist movements in North Africa, Bahrain, and the Caspian region. In 909, an Ismaili leader in Algeria proclaimed himself caliph, founding what came to be called (in homage to Muhammad's daughter Fatima) the Fatimid dynasty. In 969 the Fatimids captured Egypt and made Cairo the capital of their caliphate.

Flowering of Islamic Culture   By the middle of the tenth century, then, the unified caliphate had disintegrated into a series of regional dynasties. The collapse of political unity, however, did not lead to decline of Islamic social and cultural institutions. On the contrary, the tenth century was an age of remarkable cultural flowering in the Islamic world. The sharpening doctrinal disputes of the age produced an outpouring of theological scholarship and debate, and conversion of non-Arabs to Islam accelerated. Sufism, a mystical form of Islam based on commitment to a life of spirituality and self-denial, acquired a large following (see Chapter 13). Despite its political fragmentation, the Islamic world retained a collective identity as a commonwealth of states united by faith. The networks of travel and communications formed during the heyday of the Umayyad and Abbasid caliphates continued to help the circulation of people, goods, ideas, and technology throughout the Islamic lands.

COUNTERPOINT
The Norse Vikings: The New Barbarians

FOCUS

How did the Vikings' society and culture contrast with those of the settled societies of Europe?

The Norse Vikings ("sea raiders") who terrified Latin Christendom for more than two centuries can be seen as the maritime equivalent of the steppe nomads of Central Asia. The Vikings operated as independent bands of pirates and rarely acknowledged any authority other than the captains of their ships. Their Nordic homelands did not shift to formal centralized authority until the mid-eleventh century. Ultimately, however, the Vikings, like the nomadic peoples of the Central Asian steppes, were transformed by their interactions with the settled peoples whose goods they coveted.

The Viking Raids 790–1020

The earliest record of the Vikings relates that in the year 793 strange omens appeared in the skies over northeastern England, followed by a dire famine; then, "on June 8th of the same year, merciless heathens laid waste the Church of God in Lindisfarne [in northeast England], with plundering and killing."[13] By 799 the Vikings were launching raids along the coast of France. They would return to plunder the peoples to their south virtually every spring thereafter until the early eleventh century. The leaders of Christendom were aghast at what they interpreted as a brutal assault on the church and true religion. The Vikings were not, however, motivated by hatred of Christianity. They wanted money, goods, and slaves, and they were just as likely to prey on their fellow pagans as on Christians.

The Viking marauders originated from the Nordic, or Scandinavian, lands ringing the Baltic and North seas, whose thick forests, thin soils, and long winters discouraged agriculture (see Map 9.4). Like the Germans, the Norse prized cattle. Pasture was scarce, though, and in many places overgrazing had forced the inhabitants to replace cattle with less demanding sheep. Given this harsh and unpromising environment, it is not surprising that many Vikings turned to military raids to acquire what they could not produce themselves.

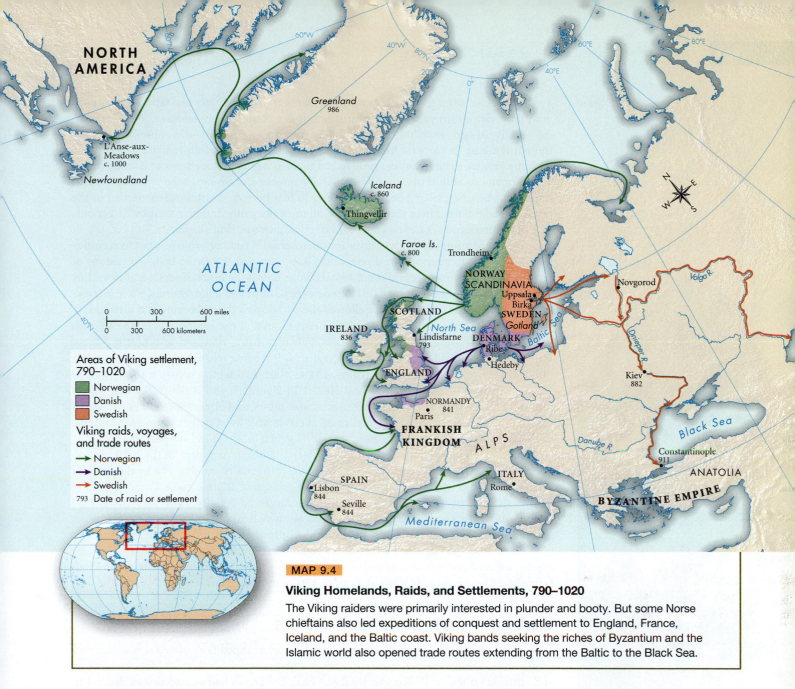

MAP 9.4

Viking Homelands, Raids, and Settlements, 790–1020

The Viking raiders were primarily interested in plunder and booty. But some Norse chieftains also led expeditions of conquest and settlement to England, France, Iceland, and the Baltic coast. Viking bands seeking the riches of Byzantium and the Islamic world also opened trade routes extending from the Baltic to the Black Sea.

Viking Warriors

Warfare had a long history in this region, but Nordic settlements rarely were fortified. The object of war was booty rather than seizing land, and the evolution of Viking military technology reflected this goal. Instead of developing the castles and stone fortifications that proliferated in northern Europe, the Vikings concentrated on improving their ability to launch seaborne raids. Between the fifth and eighth centuries, Norse shipbuilders developed larger and more seaworthy longboats, equipped with keels and powered by sails and by crews of thirty to sixty oarsmen. Using these vessels, roving Viking bands crossed the North Sea to pillage the unsuspecting coastal communities of Britain and France.

During the eighth century local chieftains all around the Nordic coasts constructed great halls, the "mead halls" celebrated in *Beowulf*, a tenth-century epic recounting the feats of a heroic Norse warrior. (Mead is a potent alcoholic beverage made from fermented honey and water.) Yet the great halls typically housed no more than thirty warriors and their families, and outfitting a single longboat required recruiting additional men beyond the chieftain's immediate retinue. For raiding expeditions, convoys of longboats were assembled under the leadership of a king, or paramount chief. Although these alliances were often renewed from season to season, the captains of these expeditions exercised little control over the subordinate chieftains, except in war and plunder. Such alliances did not reflect permanent connections among Viking groups or the beginnings of durable political institutions. Rather, they were arrangements of convenience, kept in place only as long as all involved profited from them.

Viking Kings

As a result, amid the conflict and rivalries of this warrior class few families could uphold their claim to royal authority for more than a couple of generations. The Christian missionary Ansgar, traveling in southern Sweden in around 865–875, observed that although the king at Uppsala led armies overseas and conducted diplomatic negotiations with the Franks, in civil matters he deferred to an assembly of chieftains and landowners. The anonymous author of *Beowulf* boasted of a mighty Danish king who "shook the halls, took mead-benches, taught encroaching foes to fear him . . . until the clans settled in the seacoasts neighboring over the whale-road all must obey him and give tribute."[14] Yet outside of the epics and sagas, few kings commanded such awe and allegiance.

The Norse kings did not levy taxes in coin or grain. The king's role was not to accumulate wealth, but to distribute it. Extravagant banqueting in the mead halls—occasions of majesty in lands of meager and monotonous diets—lay at the heart of social and ritual life. Feasting enabled kings and chieftains to renew friendships and allay rivalries, while bestowing gifts of gold and other treasures allowed them to display their liberality and lordship.

In contrast to the settled peoples of Christendom and the Islamic world, the Vikings were indifferent town builders and traders. Few merchants ventured into hostile Viking waters. Those who did briefly disembarked at seaside trading posts during the summer but did not settle permanently in the region. In the ninth and tenth centuries a few of these seasonal markets—including Ribe and Hedley in Denmark and Birka in Sweden—grew into towns, with their own Christian bishops and mints, and attracted colonies of foreign merchants. But these towns remained small enclaves of at most two thousand inhabitants. Only after 1000 did Nordic iron, furs, and slaves gain a foothold in European markets.

Islamic silver coins imported from the Black Sea began to appear in the Baltic region at the close of the eighth century. Silver was made into jewelry, used to pay legal fines, and offered as gifts to win allies and favors. The abundance of Islamic coins found in Viking hoards should not be taken as a measure of commercial activity, however. The richest hoards of Islamic coins have been discovered on the island of Gotland, midway between Latvia and Sweden. Yet Gotland lacked good harbors and towns. Most likely the islanders obtained their troves of silver from piracy rather than trade. Despite their treasure, they rigidly adhered to their traditional ways of life, to judge by the evidence of their small farms and the conservative dress and ornaments of their women.

Norse Emigration and Colonization

In the ninth century the Norse chieftains began to conduct expeditions aimed at conquest and colonization. Danish marauders seized lands in eastern England and imposed their own laws and customs on the Anglo-Saxons. By about 1000, the Danes had extended their control to parts of Norway, Sweden, and, under King Cnut (Keh-NEWT) (r. 1017–1035), all of England. Vikings also occupied parts of Ireland and coastal lands on the European continent from Normandy to Denmark.

Legends relate that the island of Iceland was first colonized during 870–930 by hundreds of families fleeing the tyranny of the Norwegian king Harald Fair-haired. More likely the immigrants were driven by hunger for land. Iceland, with its relatively mild winters, ample pasture for cattle, and abundant game, must have seemed a windfall. But human settlement soon upset the island's fragile ecology. Forests and fields were ruined by timber cutting, erosion, and overgrazing, while the game was hunted to extinction. By 1000 the settlers were desperately short of fuel and timber, and fishing had become the staple of their livelihood.

In around 980 Icelanders in search of virgin territories made landfall on Greenland, only to discover that this new world was even less well endowed with forests, pasture, and arable land. Subsequent foraging expeditions took them to Newfoundland, but there, too, the prospects for farming and stock raising were dim, and settlements were short-lived.

The maritime conquests of the Vikings proved to be more fleeting than the far-flung empires of the Central Asian nomads. Prolonged contact with Latin Christendom eventually eroded the Viking way of life. From about 1000 on, towns and merchants proliferated, local chieftains yielded to the rule of royal dynasties, and kings submitted to baptism and the Christian church's authority. As these new forms of economic, religious, and political

Viking Memorial Stone

Viking picture stones such as this eighth-century one from the island of Gotland off the coast of Sweden are believed to have been memorials dedicated to dead warriors and chiefs. Scholars disagree about the precise meaning of the scenes shown on this stone. One interpretation suggests that the stone depicts the death of a warrior in battle and his final journey to the underworld on the Viking longboat at bottom. (Courtesy of The Bunge Museum, an open air museum in Gotland, Sweden, displaying 8th century picture stones, and allowing visits to 17th, 18th and 19th century homes, mills, gardens, and workshops. www.bungemuseet.se.)

life permeated the Nordic world, the Vikings' plundering ceased. Yet even as the Norse peoples were pulled into the orbit of Latin Christendom, their songs and legends continued to celebrate the deeds of their pagan ancestors.

Conclusion

By the year 1000 the classical civilizations of western Eurasia had been reshaped by their new dominant religious cultures, Christianity and Islam. Christianity had spread throughout the European provinces of the old Roman Empire, whereas Islam prevailed in the heartlands of the ancient Persian and Egyptian empires and among the pastoral desert tribes of Arabia and North Africa. Christianity and Islam both flourished most vigorously in the cities. By 1000 the Christian church had made a concerted effort to extend its reach into village society through its legions of parish priests, and monastic orders ranked among the greatest landowners of Europe. The penetration of Islam into the countryside in long-settled areas such as Syria, Iraq, and Iran came more slowly.

The Christian communities allied with their secular rulers, whether they were Roman aristocrats, German chieftains, or the Byzantine emperor. From its inception, Islam became a political force as well as a religious movement, and the Umayyad caliphs created a vast Islamic empire. Despite efforts by the Byzantine emperors and the Muslim caliphs to impose religious orthodoxy, however, both Christendom and the Islamic empire fractured into competing religious traditions and a multitude of states.

At the same time, these religious faiths advanced into new frontiers. German kings and warriors followed in the footsteps of our chapter-opening heroine Radegund in embracing Christianity. Cultural, economic, and political interaction with the Byzantine Empire brought most Slavic peoples into the Christian fold. The arrival of Christianity in the Norse lands of northern Europe brought an end to the Viking menace. Although the prospects for a unified Muslim empire receded, Islamic religion and culture had become deeply implanted in a vast territory stretching from Iran to Spain. Starting in around 1000, Islam again underwent rapid expansion, notably in Africa and Asia, where, as we shall see in the next chapter, the Indian religions of Buddhism and Hinduism had shaped many diverse societies.

NOTES

1. Jo Ann McNamara and John E. Halborg, eds. and trans., *Sainted Women of the Dark Ages* (Durham, NC: Duke University Press, 1992), 65, 72, 75.
2. Procopius, *The Secret History*, trans. G. A. Williamson (London: Penguin, 1966), 106.
3. Alcuin, "Letter 8" (to Charlemagne), in Stephen Allott, *Alcuin of York, c. A.D. 732 to 804: His Life and Letters* (York, U.K.: Sessions, 1974), 11.
4. Gregory, *Pastoral Care*, 1.1, trans. Henry Davis, in *Ancient Christian Writers* (New York: Newman Press, 1950), 11:21.
5. Roy Cave and Herbert Coulson, eds., *A Source Book for Medieval Economic History* (New York: Biblo and Tannen, 1965), 336.
6. Al Djahiz, *A Clear Look at Trade*, quoted in Michael McCormick, *Origins of the European Economy: Communications and Commerce, A.D. 300–900* (Cambridge, U.K.: Cambridge University Press, 2001), 591.
7. S. H. Cross and O. P. Sherbovitz-Wetzor, *The Russian Primary Chronicle, Laurentian Text* (Cambridge, MA: Mediaeval Academy of America, 1953), 53, referring to the Poliane people inhabiting modern-day Ukraine.
8. Procopius, *History of the Wars*, trans. H. B. Dewing (Cambridge, MA: Harvard University Press, 1924), 7:14, 22–30.
9. Pseudo-Maurice, *Strategikon*, 11.4, quoted in P. M. Barford, *The Early Slavs: Culture and Society in Early Medieval Eastern Europe* (London: British Museum Press, 2001), 68.
10. Quoted in Gaston Wiet, *Baghdad: Metropolis of the Abbasid Caliphate* (Norman: University of Oklahoma Press, 1971), 11.
11. Sufyan al-Thawri, quoted in Francis Robinson, ed., *The Cambridge Illustrated History of the Islamic World* (Cambridge, U.K.: Cambridge University Press, 1996), 22.
12. *The History of al-Tabari* (Albany: State University of New York Press, 1992), vols. 36, 38.
13. Charles Plummer, ed., *Two of the Saxon Chronicles* (Oxford: Clarendon Press, 1892), 57.
14. *Beowulf*, lines 4–11, from *Beowulf: A Verse Translation*, trans. Michael Alexander (London: Penguin, 1973), 3.

RESOURCES FOR RESEARCH

Multiple Christianities, 400–850

Spearheaded by the pathbreaking work of Peter Brown, scholars now emphasize the continuation of the culture and institutions of the Roman Empire in the worlds of both Latin and Byzantine Christianity, as well as the multitude of distinct forms that Christianity took in different societies. MacMullen and the essays in Kreuger's volume focus on the religious experiences of ordinary people.

Brown, Peter. *The Rise of Western Christendom*, 2d ed. 2003.

Burstein, Stanley, ed. *Ancient African Civilizations: Kush and Axum*, rev. ed. 2009.

Kreuger, Derek, ed. *Byzantine Christianity*. 2006.

MacMullen, Ramsay. *Christianity and Paganism in the Fourth to the Eighth Centuries*. 1997.

McNamara, Jo Ann, and John E. Halborg, eds. and trans. *Sainted Women of the Dark Ages*. 1992.

Social and Political Renewal in the Post-Roman World, 400–850

In contrast to the conventional images of the Germans and Slavs as alien barbarians, recent studies—such as Geary's work—emphasize the fluidity of social and cultural identity and the dynamic interactions among peoples in post-Roman Europe. Angold provides a brief but compelling portrait of the early Byzantine Empire in relation to both Latin Christendom and the Islamic world.

Angold, Michael. *Byzantium: The Bridge from Antiquity to the Middle Ages*. 2001.

(Byzantium): Byzantine Studies on the Internet. http://www.fordham.edu/halsall/byzantium/index.html.

Franklin, Simon, and Jonathan Shepard. *The Emergence of Rus, 750–1200*. 1996.

Geary, Patrick J. *Before France and Germany: The Creation and Transformation of the Merovingian World*. 1988.

McKitterick, Rosamond, ed. *The Early Middle Ages: Europe, 400–1000*. 2001.

Treadgold, Warren. *A History of the Byzantine State and Society*. 1997.

Worlds of Late Antiquity. http://www9.georgetown.edu/faculty/jod/wola.html.

The Rise and Spread of Islam, 610–750

Gordon's highly accessible text is a useful introduction to the origins and early history of the Islamic movement. Berkey's book combines narrative and thematic approaches to the development of Islam in the Middle East before modern times. Muhammad remains an elusive biographical subject; Rodinson's study, though dated (originally published in 1961), is still regarded as reliable.

Berkey, Jonathan. *The Formation of Islam: Religion and Society in the Near East, 600 to 1800*. 2003.

Bulliet, Richard. *Islam: The View from the Edge*. 1994.

Crone, Patricia. *Meccan Trade and the Rise of Islam*. 1987.

Gordon, Matthew S. *The Rise of Islam*. 2005.

Rodinson, Maxime. *Muhammad*, 2d ed. 1996.

From Unified Caliphate to Islamic Commonwealth, 750–1000

Lapidus's encyclopedic survey is especially valuable for its detailed regional-focused reviews of the varieties of Islamic society and culture. Hodgson remains a classic work in terms of both its erudition and its emphasis on the world-historical context of the rise and development of Islam. Daftary provides an authoritative introduction to the history, doctrines, and practice of one of the most important branches of Shi'a Islam.

(Byzantium): Byzantine Studies on the Internet. http://www.fordham.edu/halsall/islam/islamsbook.html.

Daftary, Farhad. *A Short History of the Ismailis: Traditions of a Muslim Community*. 1998.

Hodgson, Marshall. *The Venture of Islam: Conscience and History in a World Civilization*. Vol. 1, *The Classical Age of Islam*. 1974.

Kennedy, Hugh. *The Court of the Caliphs: The Rise and Fall of Islam's Greatest Dynasty*. 2004.

Lapidus, Ira M. *A History of Islamic Societies*, 2d ed. 2002.

Lewis, Bernard, ed. *Islam: From the Prophet Muhammad to the Capture of Constantinople*. 2 vols. 1974.

COUNTERPOINT: The Norse Vikings: The New Barbarians

Recent archaeological research—as exemplified by Christiansen's meticulous study—challenges many of the prevailing assumptions about the Vikings' society and livelihood. The Sawyers chronicle the transformation of Norse life and culture after the conversion to Christianity. Jochens, drawing primarily on Icelandic sources, argues that conversion brought few changes to the lives of Norse women.

Christiansen, Eric. *The Norsemen in the Viking Age*. 2002.

Jochens, Jenny. *Women in Old Norse Society*. 1995.

Logan, F. Donald. *The Vikings in History*, 3d ed. 2005.

Page, R. I. *Chronicles of the Vikings: Records, Memorials, and Myths*. 1995.

Sawyer, Birgit, and Peter Sawyer. *Medieval Scandinavia: From Conversion to Reformation, circa 800–1500*. 1993.

▶ **For additional primary sources from this period**, see *Sources of Crossroads and Cultures*.

▶ **For Web sites, images, and documents related to topics in this chapter**, see Make History at bedfordstmartins.com/smith.

The major global development in this chapter ▶ The spread of Christianity and Islam and the profound impact of these world religions on the societies of western Eurasia and North Africa.

IMPORTANT EVENTS

410	Visigoth sack of Rome
431	Council of Ephesus denounces Nestorianism as heresy
507	Clovis defeats Visigoth invaders and converts to Christianity
527–565	Reign of Justinian I as Byzantine emperor
570–632	Life of Muhammad, founder of Islam
589	Conversion of Visigoths to Roman Christianity
590–604	Papacy of Gregory I
622	Muhammad's hijra to Medina, marking the beginning of the Islamic calendar
661–743	Umayyad caliphate
680	Split between Shi'a and Sunni Islam
710–711	Muslim invasion and conquest of Visigoth-ruled Spain
732	Charles Martel halts Muslim advance into Europe
747–1258	Abbasid caliphate
793	Earliest record of Viking raids on Britain
800	Coronation of Charlemagne as emperor by Pope Leo III
868–883	Zanj revolt against the Abbasid regime
870–930	Vikings colonize Iceland
909	Fatimid dynasty founded
988	Vladimir, the Rus prince of Kiev, converts to Christianity

KEY TERMS

caliph (p. 292)
dar-al-Islam (p. 293)
dhimmi (p. 293)
hijra (p. 290)
iconoclasm (p. 281)
imam (p. 292)
jihad (p. 290)
manor (p. 285)

Qur'an (p. 290)
schism (p. 281)
serf (p. 285)
Shi'a (p. 292)
Sunni (p. 292)
ulama (p. 290)
umma (p. 290)

CHAPTER OVERVIEW QUESTIONS

1. How and why did the development of the Christian church differ in the Byzantine Empire and Latin Christendom?

2. In what ways did the rise of Christianity and Islam challenge the power of the state?

3. Conversely, in what ways did the spread of these faiths reinforce state power?

4. Why did Christianity and Islam achieve their initial success in towns and cities rather than in the rural countryside?

SECTION FOCUS QUESTIONS

1. In what ways did Christianity develop and spread following its institutionalization in the Roman Empire?

2. What major changes swept the lands of the former Roman Empire in the four centuries following the fall of imperial Rome?

3. In what ways did Islam instill a sense of common identity among its believers?

4. How did the tensions between the ulama and the Abbasid caliphs weaken a unified Islamic empire?

5. How did the Vikings' society and culture contrast with those of the settled societies of Europe?

MAKING CONNECTIONS

1. How did the political institutions and ideology of the Islamic empire of the Umayyad and Abbasid caliphates differ from those of the Roman Empire (see Chapter 7)?

2. In what ways did the spiritual authority of the Islamic ulama differ from that exercised by the Christian popes and bishops?

3. How does the Islamic conception of the community of the faithful compare with Jewish and Christian ideas of community?

4. What were the causes and effects of the Viking raids and invasions in Europe in the eighth through tenth centuries, and how did these compare with the early invasions of the Roman Empire by the Germanic peoples (see Chapter 7)?

AT A CROSSROADS ▲

The Chinese monk Xuanzang's epic journey to India epitomized the cross-cultural exchanges that took place across Asia during the heyday of the Silk Road. In this Japanese painting commemorating Xuanzang's life, the pilgrim monk parades in triumph through the Chinese capital of Chang'an, preceded by horses bearing the precious Buddhist scriptures he brought back from India. The painting was commissioned in around 1300 by the Kofukuji Monastery in Nara, the headquarters of a Buddhist school dedicated to Xuanzang's teachings. (From the Collection of the Fujita Museum, Osaka, Japan. First section, tenth chapter of the painted scroll, *Genjo sanzo e* (Japanese National Treasure).)

Religion and Cross-Cultural Exchange in Asia

400–1000

In 642, a Chinese Buddhist pilgrim named Xuanzang (shoo-wen-zhang) (c. 602–664) was enjoying a leisurely stay at the court of the king of Assam, in the Himalayan foothills of northern India. Thirteen years before, Xuanzang had left China, where he had studied Buddhist scriptures and Indian languages at Chang'an, capital of the recently founded Tang dynasty (618–907). As his studies progressed, however, Xuanzang concluded that he could obtain authentic scriptures that preserved the Buddha's original teachings only by traveling to India, homeland of the Buddha, "the Awakened One." Defying an imperial decree that forbade travel abroad, Xuanzang embarked across the deserts and mountain ranges of Central Asia and spent years retracing the footsteps of the Buddha. It was these travels that had brought him to the court of Assam.

Xuanzang's visit, however, was interrupted by an urgent summons from King Harsha (r. 606–647), the most powerful Indian monarch at the time. During his time in India, Xuanzang had acquired a reputation as a great philosopher and skilled orator, and he had come to the attention of King Harsha, a pious man and an earnest patron of both Hindu Brahman priests and Buddhist monks. "He divided the day into three parts," commented Xuanzang, "the first devoted to affairs of state, and the other two to worship and charitable works, to which he applied himself tirelessly, as there were not enough hours in the day to complete his ministrations."[1] Harsha now wished to host a grand philosophical debate featuring his Chinese guest.

On the appointed day King Harsha led a vast procession of princes, nobles, soldiers, and priests to a parade ground on the banks of the Ganges River. Xuanzang wrote, "In the

BACKSTORY

In China as in the Roman world, invasions and migrations by "barbarian" peoples followed the collapse of the empire. After the Han Empire fell in the third century C.E. (see Chapter 6), endemic fighting among regional warlords weakened China and made it possible for steppe nomads to conquer the north China heartland in the early fourth century. Pressure from central Eurasian nomads also contributed to the demise of the Gupta Empire in northern India at the end of the fifth century (see Chapter 6). Yet political turmoil and the fragmentation of India and China into smaller rival kingdoms did not breed isolation. On the contrary, the Silk Road flourished as a channel of trade and cultural exchange during these centuries. Traversing both overland and overseas trade routes, missionaries and merchants carried Indian religions to China and Southeast Asia, where they profoundly influenced not only religious beliefs and practices but political and social institutions as well.

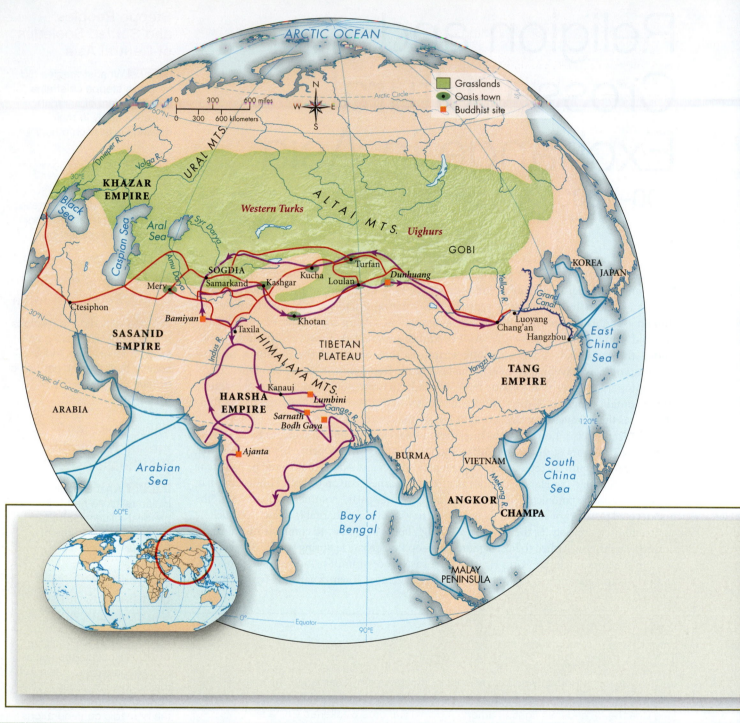

386–534 Northern Wei dynasty in north China and Mongolia

581–618 Sui dynasty in China

c. 670 ▪
The Khazars conquer and
supplant the Bulgar khanate

552–603 First Turkish empire

618–907 Tang dynasty in China

400   500   600   70

Prince Shōtoku reorganizes the
Yamato kingdom in Japan **604 ▪**

690 ──
Empress Wu declares the founding
of her Zhou dynasty in China

606–647 Reign of King Harsha as
paramount ruler of north India

629–645 Journey of the Chinese
Buddhist monk Xuanzang to India

Unification of the Korean peninsula under the rule of the Silla kingdom **668 ▪**

center strode a huge, elaborately caparisoned elephant bearing a golden statue of the Buddha more than three feet high. On the left went King Harsha, dressed as [the Hindu god] Indra and holding aloft a jeweled parasol, while on the right was the King of Assam, wearing the regalia of [the Hindu god] Brahma and grasping a white fly-whisk."[2] The theological tournament lasted five days, during which the rhetorical clashes grew increasingly fierce. When Harsha declared Xuanzang the victor, his Brahman opponents allegedly set fire to the shrine housing the Buddha's image, and one of them tried to assassinate the king. Harsha, keen to avert religious strife among his subjects, punished the ringleader but pardoned the rest of the disgruntled Brahmans.

Four months later, Xuanzang departed for home. Although he had left China illegally, he returned in triumph. The Tang emperor anointed him "the jewel of the empire" and built a magnificent monastery to house the precious Buddhist icons, relics, and books that he had brought back from India. A legend in his own lifetime, Xuanzang devoted the last twenty years of his life to translating Buddhist texts and to seeking refuge from his admirers.

Xuanzang's remarkable experiences were part of the larger pattern of cross-cultural encounters and exchanges that shaped Asia in the second half of the first millennium C.E. Since the inception of the Silk Road route in the first century C.E. (see Chapter 6), Buddhist missionaries had accompanied the caravans setting out from the frontiers of India to seek the fabled silks of China. As we will explore in this chapter, in later centuries others traveled between India and China bearing goods and ideas that fertilized cross-cultural exchange, including nomad warriors from Central Asia, long-distance traders such as the Sogdians, and missionaries and pilgrims. A similar interweaving of commerce and evangelism also drew Southeast Asia into sustained contact with India, and to a lesser extent with China.

The resulting spread of Buddhism and Hinduism from India provided the foundations for distinctive regional cultures across Asia. Political and social crises in China and India prompted serious questioning in those countries of traditional beliefs and values, creating a climate more receptive to new ideas. At the same time, the leaders of newly emerging states

MAPPING THE WORLD

Cross-Cultural Exchange in Asia

Both goods and ideas flowed across the Silk Road, the name given by a nineteenth-century German geographer to the network of caravan routes crossing Central Asia from China to Iran. During the peak of the Silk Road from the fourth to the eighth century C.E., Sogdian merchants dominated East-West trade. Buddhist missionaries journeyed from India to China by following the overland Silk Road, as did the Chinese monk Xuanzang on his pilgrimage to India in the early seventh century.

ROUTES ▼

— Silk Road, c. 600

— Maritime trade route, c. 600

→ Travels of Xuanzang, 629–645

755–763 A Lushan rebellion in north China severely weakens the Tang dynasty

▪ **802** Consolidation of the Angkor kingdom in Cambodia by Jayavarman II

▪ **939** Vietnam achieves independence from China

800

900

1000

▪ **c. 760** Sailendra kings in Java begin construction of the Borobudur monument

▪ **965** Rus invaders destroy the Khazar khanate

▪ **861** Conversion of the Khazars to Judaism

▪ **792** Kyoto established as Japan's new capital

in East and Southeast Asia looked toward China and India for models of political institutions and cultural values. A common civilization inspired by Chinese political, philosophical, and literary traditions and permeated by Buddhist beliefs and practices emerged in East Asia. In Southeast Asia, a more eclectic variety of societies and cultures developed, one that blended Indian influences with native traditions. In time, the emergence of new societies throughout Asia would give rise to new trade patterns. By the tenth century the maritime realm stretching from Korea and Japan to Java and Malaysia had supplanted the overland Silk Road as the major channel of economic and cultural interaction within Asia.

OVERVIEW QUESTIONS

The major global development in this chapter: The cultural and commercial exchanges during the heyday of the Silk Road that transformed Asian peoples, cultures, and states.

As you read, consider:

1. In what ways did Asian societies respond to cross-cultural interaction during the period 400–1000?

2. What strategies did pastoral nomads adopt in their relations with settled societies, and why?

3. What patterns of political and cultural borrowing characterized the emerging states in East and Southeast Asia?

4. Why did India and China experience different outcomes following the collapse of strong and unified empires?

Steppe Peoples and Settled Societies of Central Asia

FOCUS

What strategies did nomadic steppe chieftains and the rulers of agrarian societies apply in their dealings with each other?

Neither the fall of the Han dynasty in China in the early third century nor the collapse of the Roman Empire in the West in the fifth century resulted directly from invasions by pastoral nomads from the steppes of Central Asia. In both cases, imperial decline was the cause rather than the consequence of nomadic invasions. Political instability following the demise of the Han encouraged raids by nomadic groups on China's northern frontiers. During the fifth century, one of these groups, the Tuoba confederation, gradually occupied nearly all of northern China, as well as Manchuria and Mongolia.

Despite the political instability on the Eurasian steppe in this era, trade and cultural exchange flourished as never before. The heyday of the Silk Road between the fifth and the eighth centuries witnessed major changes in the societies and cultures of Asia. No group was more deeply affected by these changes than the pastoral nomads of the Central Asian steppe. The empires of the Tuoba, the Turks, and the Khazars marked a new stage in state formation among the nomadic tribes. The military ingenuity and political skills these nomad confederations developed would later make possible the greatest nomad conquerors of all, the Mongols.

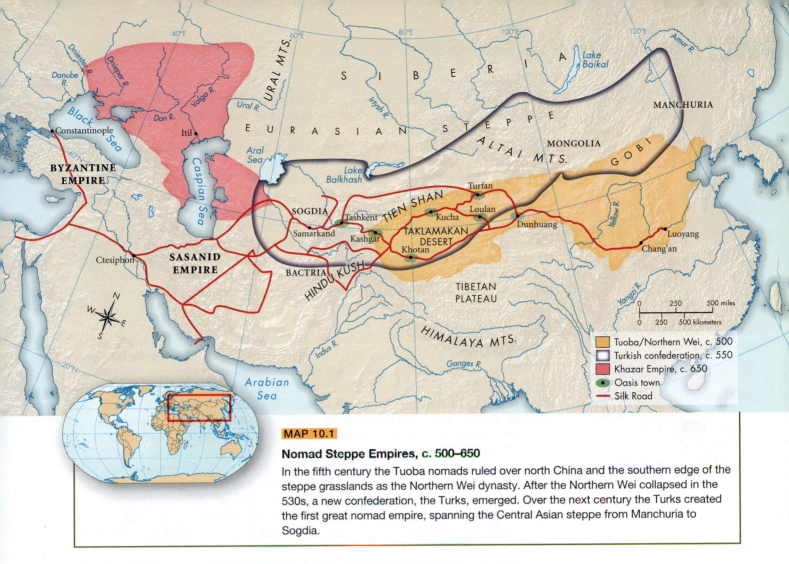

MAP 10.1

Nomad Steppe Empires, c. 500–650

In the fifth century the Tuoba nomads ruled over north China and the southern edge of the steppe grasslands as the Northern Wei dynasty. After the Northern Wei collapsed in the 530s, a new confederation, the Turks, emerged. Over the next century the Turks created the first great nomad empire, spanning the Central Asian steppe from Manchuria to Sogdia.

Nomad Conquerors of China: The Northern Wei 386–534

China had a frontier stretching thousands of miles along the border of the steppe grasslands. Throughout the more than four hundred years of the Han dynasty (202 B.C.E.–220 C.E.), steppe nomads had shifted between a "hard" strategy of invading China and extorting tribute during times of strength and a "soft" strategy of allying with Chinese rulers and symbolically acknowledging their overlordship during times of weakness. The nomads were primarily interested in obtaining scarce resources they could not produce themselves, such as grain. They also sought precious goods, notably gold, metal wares, and silk cloth, which they needed to cement the alliances that held their confederations together. Nomad chieftains had no desire to conquer the agrarian states and adopt their lifestyle. They preferred to acquire the goods they desired through tribute and trade rather than direct rule.

Nomad Conquest of North China

The demise of the Han dynasty in 220 ushered in a century of civil wars that sapped the empire's defenses and left China vulnerable to foreign invasion. In 311, steppe invaders sacked Luoyang (LWAUGH-yahng), the capital of the reigning Jin dynasty. The Jin emperor fled with his court to the Yangzi River delta, leaving the Chinese heartland in the north at the mercy of marauding armies. For the next three centuries, a series of foreign rulers controlled north China; some were wise, and many were rapacious. Then, in the late fourth century, a measure of stability was restored to north China by the rulers of a new confederation of steppe peoples, the Tuoba (TWAUGH-bah).

Northern Wei State

The rise of the Tuoba marked the first attempt by steppe nomads to build enduring institutions for governing agrarian China, rather than merely seeking to extract booty from it. In 386 the Tuoba declared their imperial ambitions by adopting a Chinese-style dynastic name, Northern Wei (way). From 430, when the Tuoba captured the former Han capital of Chang'an, down to the 530s, the Northern Wei reigned virtually unchallenged across a wide swath of Asia from Manchuria to Bactria (see Map 10.1).

To reinforce their legitimacy and further their imperial ambitions, the Northern Wei promoted cross-cultural exchange between themselves and their Chinese subjects. The Northern Wei rulers avidly embraced the Buddhist faith that, as we will see, had spread throughout Central Asia. Emperor Xiaowen (SHIAW-when) (r. 471–499) encouraged intermarriage between the Tuoba nobility and the leading Chinese aristocratic clans, as well as adoption of Chinese language, dress, and customs. Xiaowen sought to create a hybrid ruling class that combined the martial traditions of the steppe with the cultural prestige and administrative acumen of imperial China. Ultimately, however, his policies divided the "sinified" Tuoba—those who adopted Chinese ways—within China from the Tuoba nobles based in the steppe grasslands, who staunchly resisted Chinese habits and values. This split widened when purist Tuoba chiefs from the steppes revolted in 524. The Northern Wei state crumbled ten years later. A cultural policy meant to unify the Tuoba and the Chinese and thereby cement Northern Wei rule ended up creating fatal divisions among the Tuoba themselves.

Rise of the Turks

The return of tribal strife to the eastern steppe gave charismatic leaders among the pastoral nomads a chance to forge new coalitions. In Mongolia, a chieftain named Bumin (BOO-min) (d. 552) emerged as the **khan** ("lord") of a new confederation called the Heavenly Turks. Bumin initially allied with the purist Tuoba chiefs, but he soon became their overlord. Bumin's successors extended the Turkic conquests eastward to Manchuria, but they were content to exact tribute from, rather than conquer, the Tuoba-Chinese states that had succeeded the Northern Wei in north China.

Turkic Warriors   Technology played a role in the Turks' rise to prominence. Recent innovations in warfare, such as the use of stirrups, had become widespread in the eastern steppe in the fifth century. The stirrup gave horse-riding archers a steadier posture from which to shoot. Turkic warriors cloaked themselves in mailed armor and wielded large bows and curved sabers. Thus equipped, the Turkic cavalry transformed themselves into a far more deadly force than the mounted warriors of the past.

The Turks' most dramatic advance occurred in the western steppe. They swallowed up the oasis towns and principalities of the Silk Road, reaching as far west as the Black Sea, and negotiated a marriage alliance with the Sasanid king. Like earlier steppe confedera-

Central Asian Horse Riders
The invention of the metal stirrup marked an important advance in warfare, enabling riders to wield bows and swords more effectively. By 200 C.E. Chinese craftsmen were making iron and bronze stirrups like the ones shown in this mural from the tomb of a Chinese general. Widely adopted by the steppe nomads of eastern Asia by 400, the stirrup spread westward and reached Europe in the eighth century. (Shaanxi Museum/ChinaStock.)

khan The Turkish word for "lord," used especially for rulers of the nomad empires of the central Eurasian steppes.

tions, the Turks preferred tribute and trade as means of obtaining booty. The merchants of Sogdia, in modern Uzbekistan, became key advisers and agents of the Turkic leaders. Control of the entire length of the Silk Road by a single power was a boon to trade, and the Sogdian capital of Samarkand (SAM-mar-kand) flourished as a great crossroads for merchant caravans (see Counterpoint: Sogdian Traders in Central Asia and China). This robust commercial activity also stimulated trade along the lower reaches of the Volga River and opened a route that the Vikings would later exploit.

In diplomatic negotiations with the autocratic empires of Iran and China, the Turkic khans presented themselves as supreme monarchs. Nevertheless, the Turkic confederation remained a loose band of tribes whose chieftains retained considerable autonomy. When, as we will see, a strong empire reemerged in China under the Sui dynasty in the late sixth century, the Turks lacked effective leadership to counter a resurgent China. By 603 the Sui captured the eastern portion of the Silk Road corridor, splitting the Turks into separate eastern and western groups.

Breakup of the Turkic Confederation

A Turkic Khanate in the West: The Khazars

Khazar Expansion

Following the division of the Turkic Empire in 603, local tribal identities once again came to the fore in the western part of the former empire, where few people were of Turkic ancestry. The Khazars (hus-ahr), based in the Caucasus region between the Black and Caspian seas, emerged as an independent khanate allied with the Byzantines against the Sasanids. In around 650 the Khazars conquered the rival Bulgar khanate that had been established northeast of the Black Sea (see again Map 10.1). Later, in the tenth century, the Khazars drove the Magyar chieftains westward into the Danube River basin, where they established a durable state, Hungary, and converted to Christianity.

Following their triumph over the Bulgars, the Khazars moved their capital to Itil in the Volga River delta. In the mid-eighth century the Khazars developed close diplomatic and commercial relations with the Abbasid caliphs. Although Itil consisted of little more than a massed array of felt tents, the Khazar capital attracted merchants from distant regions. Many Muslims resided there, along with a sizable community of Jewish merchants who had fled Constantinople because of the anti-Jewish policies of the Byzantine government. Commercial exchange with the Muslim world was fed by the rich mines of the Caucasus region, the tribute of furs collected from Slavs in the Dnieper River Valley, and the steady flow of slaves seized as war captives. Despite the Khazars' nomadic lifestyle, their capital became a crossroads for trade and cultural exchange.

Conversion to Judaism

This openness was dramatically demonstrated when, in around 861, the reigning Khazar khan abruptly converted to Judaism, reportedly after listening to debates among a Muslim mullah, a Christian priest, and a Jewish rabbi. The khan adopted the Jewish Torah as the legal code of the Khazars, although Christians and Muslims continued to be judged according to their own laws. Hebrew became the primary written language of government and religion. Subsequently the head of the Jewish community gained effective power over political affairs, relegating the khan to the role of a symbolic figurehead. The Khazar khanate did not long survive this dramatic shift. In 965 Rus armies overran Itil and other Khazar towns, bringing the khanate to an end and opening the region to settlement by Christian Slavs.

The Shaping of East Asia

The culture and technology of the Chinese Empire—and of course its political and military muscle—could not fail to have a powerful impact on its neighbors. Chinese agriculture and metalworking were adopted in the Korean peninsula from the eighth century B.C.E. and in the Japanese archipelago after the fourth century B.C.E. Rapid advances in agricultural production and the rise of local and regional chiefdoms followed.

FOCUS

How did the spread of Buddhism transform the politics and societies of East Asia?

Buddhist Family Shrine

Although the Buddha had presented the pursuit of enlightenment as an individual quest, Mahayana Buddhists in China promoted devotional acts intended to earn karmic merit for the entire family. This stone stele, dated 562, features carvings of numerous Buddhas and bodhisattvas. The name of the donor is inscribed alongside each image. Nearly all the donors were surnamed Chen, suggesting that the monument was a collective family project. (Collected in Shanxi Museum.)

The imposition of direct Chinese rule on part of the Korean peninsula and on Vietnam during the Han dynasty left a deep imprint on these regions. Independent Korean states arose after the Han Empire collapsed in the early third century C.E., but Vietnam remained under Chinese rule until the tenth century. In the Japanese islands, contact and exchange with the continent stimulated the progress of state formation beginning in the third century.

Although both Korea and Japan preserved their independence from the resurgent Sui (581–618) and Tang (618–907) empires in China, the societies of both the peninsula and the archipelago were shaped by Chinese political and cultural models and traditions. The farthest-reaching cultural transformation of this era was the adoption of a foreign tradition, Buddhism, as the dominant religion within China, and subsequently in the rest of East Asia. With the waning of Tang imperial might after the mid-eighth century, however, Japan and Korea shifted away from Chinese models and developed their own distinctive political and social identities. After Vietnam gained independence in the early tenth century, the multistate system of modern East Asia assumed definitive form.

The Chinese Transformation of Buddhism

From the first century C.E., Buddhist missionaries from India had crossed the steppe grasslands of Central Asia and reached China. The rise of the kingdom of the Kushans, great patrons of Buddhism, at the intersection of the trade routes linking China with India and Iran had stimulated the spread of Buddhism along these thoroughfares (see Chapter 6). Although the Kushan kingdom disintegrated in the second century, the rulers and inhabitants of the oasis towns of central Eurasia had converted to Buddhism, creating a neat path of stepping-stones for the passage of Buddhist monks and doctrines from India to China.

The collapse of the Han Empire and subsequent foreign invasions prompted many Chinese to question their values and beliefs and to become receptive to alternative ideas and ways of life. Buddhism was well known in Chinese philosophical circles by the third century, but it was not until the fifth century that this nonnative religion began to penetrate deeply into Chinese society.

In its original form, Buddhism could not be readily assimilated into the Chinese worldview. Its rejection of the mundane world and its stress on a monastic vocation conflicted with the humanist goals and family-centered ethics of Confucianism. As we saw in Chapter 6, however, the **Mahayana** school of Buddhism maintained that laypeople in any walk of life had equal potential for achieving enlightenment and salvation. The figure of the **bodhisattva** (boh-dihs-SAHT-vah), an enlightened being who delays entry into nirvana to aid the faithful in their own religious quests, exemplified the Mahayana ideal of selfless compassion and provided a model for pious laypeople and clergy alike. The Mahayana vision of a multitude of Buddhas (of whom the historical Buddha was only one) and bodhisattvas as divine saviors also encouraged the prospect of gaining salvation within a person's present lifetime, rather than after many lives of suffering. It was the Mahayana school of Buddhism, therefore, that made broad inroads in China.

Mahayana Buddhism's compatibility with existing Chinese cultural and intellectual traditions was crucial to its acceptance. The Buddhist doctrine of *karma*—the belief that the individual's good and evil actions determine one's destiny in the next reincarnation—was revised to allow people to earn merit not just for themselves but also for their parents and children. The pursuit of merit and eradication of sin became a collective family endeavor rather than a solitary, self-centered enterprise.

This understanding of karma fit well with the Chinese practice of ancestor worship and the emphasis on the family as the fundamental moral unit. Moreover, the Buddhist regimen of mastery of scripture, lavish donations to support the clergy, and ritual observances governing all aspects of daily life fit readily into the lifestyles of the educated, wealthy, and ritual-bound upper classes in China. Indeed, the lay religious practices of Buddhism served to confirm the Chinese aristocracy's own sense of social superiority. Not surprisingly, Buddhist missionaries in China initially directed their conversion efforts at the rulers and aristocrats, whose faith in Confucianism had been badly shaken by the collapse of the Han.

During the fifth century, devotion to Buddhism spread swiftly among the ruling classes in both north and south China. The Tuoba rulers of the Northern Wei dynasty had long been familiar with Buddhism. Several Northern Wei emperors converted to Buddhism and became avid patrons of Buddhist institutions. Buddhism also served useful political purposes. In a world fractured by warfare and political instability, the universalist spirit of Buddhism offered an inclusive creed that might ease social and ethnic frictions among the Chinese and the diverse foreign peoples who had settled within China. The Northern Wei rulers were especially attracted to the Buddhist ideal of the *chakravartin* (chuhk-ruh-VAHR-tin), the "wheel-turning king" (controller of human destiny) who wages righteous wars to bring the true religion to the unenlightened peoples of the world. The chakravartin ideal was founded on the historical precedent of Ashoka (see Chapter 6), the great Mauryan king of the third century B.C.E., whose imperial dominion was closely tied to his support and patronage of Buddhism.

Chinese rulers in the south also became patrons of Buddhism. The desire to earn religious merit through acts of faith and charity spurred Chinese aristocrats to donate land, money, and goods to support the Buddhist clergy. The profusion of domestic shrines and devotional objects illustrates the saturation of upper-class life in China by Buddhist beliefs and practices.

In the sixth century, two interrelated developments profoundly altered the evolution of Buddhism in East Asia. First, Chinese monastic communities and lay congregations created their own forms of Buddhist theology and religious discipline, forms that were more closely attuned to the concerns of their Chinese audience. Second, these new movements reached well beyond the elite and led to the emergence of Buddhism as a religion of the masses. As a reaction against the exclusivity of earlier forms of Buddhism, two new forms of Buddhism developed—Pure Land Buddhism and Chan (Zen) Buddhism.

Pure Land Buddhism first emerged as a coherent religious movement in China during the sixth century. Born amid the incessant war and deepening poverty that afflicted the Chinese world after the collapse of the Northern Wei state in 534, Pure Land expressed deep pessimism about mortal existence. The formidable burden of sins accumulated over countless lifetimes made the possibility of attaining salvation through one's own merit-earning actions appear hopelessly remote. Yet people of sincere faith could obtain rebirth in the Pure Land, a celestial paradise, through the aid of savior figures such as Amitabha (Ah-MEE-tah-bah), the presiding Buddha of the Pure Land, or Guanyin (GWAHN-yin), the bodhisattva of compassion.

Like the later Protestant Reformation of Christianity, Pure Land Buddhism emphasized salvation through faith alone rather than good works. One did not achieve nirvana by making large donations to Buddhist monasteries, but by fully committing oneself to a spiritual life. Thus, it offered the hope that through sincere piety all persons, no matter how humble, might attain salvation within their present lifetimes. Originating among lay congregations alienated by the luxury and splendor that increasingly enveloped the monastic establishments, Pure Land teachings found favor among poor and illiterate people. Its devotions focused on simple rituals, such as chanting the names of Amitabha and Guanyin, that did not require wealth, learning, or leisure. Because of the universal appeal of its message, the Pure Land movement transformed Chinese Buddhism into a mass religion focused on the worship of compassionate savior figures.

From an Elite to a Mass Religion

Mahayana A major branch of Buddhism that emphasizes the potential for laypeople to achieve enlightenment through the aid of the Buddha and bodhisattvas.

bodhisattva In Mahayana Buddhism, an enlightened being who delays entry into nirvana and chooses to remain in the world of suffering to assist others in their quest for salvation.

chakravartin In Indian political thought, the "wheel-turning king," a universal monarch who enjoys the favor of the gods and acts as a defender of religious orthodoxy.

Pure Land A school of Mahayana Buddhism, originating in China, that emphasizes the sinfulness of the human condition and the necessity of faith in savior figures (the Buddha and bodhisattvas) to gain rebirth in paradise.

Eleven-Headed Guanyin

Guanyin, the bodhisattva of compassion, became the most popular figure in East Asian Buddhism. This tenth-century banner depicts Guanyin with eleven heads and six arms, symbolizing Guanyin's role as a savior. Guanyin is surrounded by scenes from the *Lotus Sutra* in which the bodhisattva rescues devout followers from perils such as fire and bandits. The donor, dressed as a Chinese official, appears at bottom right. (Arthur M. Sackler Museum, Harvard University Art Museums/Bequest of Grenville L. Winthrop/Bridgeman Art Library.)

China's Grand Canal

Like Pure Land, **Chan Buddhism**—better known by its Japanese name, Zen—reacted against the unseemly wealth and privileges enjoyed by the clergy. Also like Pure Land, Chan Buddhists rejected a religious life centered on what they perceived to be rote recitation of scripture and performance of complex rituals. Chan instead embraced strict discipline and mystical understanding of truth as the genuine path of enlightenment. But in contrast to Pure Land, Chan Buddhism continued to honor the monastic vocation, and as the ultimate goal of its religious quest it emphasized sublime spiritual mastery of Buddhist teachings rather than rebirth in a paradise of material comfort. The Chan movement gained a widespread following among the clergy beginning in the eighth century and subsequently became the preeminent monastic tradition throughout East Asia.

Reunification of the Chinese Empire: The Sui Dynasty 581–618

The collapse of the Northern Wei in 534 once again plunged northern China into anarchic warfare. In 581, Yang Jian (d. 604), a member of the mixed-blood Tuoba-Chinese aristocracy, staged a bloody coup in which he deposed and killed his own grandson and installed himself as emperor. As iron-fisted ruler of the Sui dynasty (581–618), Yang Jian quickly reasserted military supremacy. In 589 he conquered southern China and restored a unified empire.

Yang Jian was determined to resurrect the grandeur of the Han by rebuilding a centralized bureaucratic state. He immediately abolished the entitlements to political office enjoyed by aristocratic families during the centuries of disunion. Although the inner circle of his government would still be drawn from the hybrid aristocracy fostered by the Northern Wei, high office was a privilege the emperor could bestow or take away as he saw fit.

Yang also retained the system of state landownership that the Northern Wei had put in place. The Northern Wei rulers, descended from nomad chiefs, had introduced policies designed to simplify the task of administering the unfamiliar agrarian world of China. Under the **equal-field system**, the Northern Wei government allocated landholdings to individual households according to formulas based on the number of able-bodied adults the household had to work the land and how many mouths it had to feed. Each household was expected to have roughly equal productive capabilities, so that the state could collect uniform taxes in grain, cloth, and labor or military service from all households. Although aristocratic families largely preserved their extensive landholdings, this system of state landownership provided the Northern Wei with dependable sources of tax revenues and soldiers.

Yang Jian's son and successor, Yang Guang (r. 604–618), further centralized control over resources by building the Grand Canal. This artificial waterway connected the Sui capital at Chang'an in northwestern China with the rice-growing regions of the Yangzi River delta. With the Grand Canal, the central government could tap the burgeoning agricultural wealth of southern China to feed the capital and the military garrisons surrounding it. As we have seen in previous chapters, ancient cities originally depended on their immediate surrounding rural areas for food and other products. The construction of the Grand Canal was important, because it allowed Chang'an to draw resources from further away in the countryside with greater ease, thereby increasing its size and power.

The Sui rulers differed sharply from their Han predecessors in their commitment to Buddhism rather than Confucianism. Unlike the uniform culture of the Han rooted in Confucian traditions, the Sui realm encompassed a heterogeneous collection of peoples divided by ancestry, language, and customs. A devout believer in Buddhism since childhood, Yang Jian recognized Buddhism's potential to aid him in rebuilding a universal empire. Buddhism was equally entrenched in all of China and could provide a set of common values that would unite his subjects. Yang Jian cultivated his self-image as a chakravartin king and imitated the example of Ashoka by building hundreds of Buddhist shrines and monasteries throughout the empire.

Yet the Sui dynasty ended as abruptly as it began. Foreign affairs, rather than domestic problems, proved the dynasty's undoing. From the outset the Sui had tempestuous relations with their Korean neighbors. In 612 Yang Guang launched an invasion of the Korean peninsula that ended in disastrous defeat. When the emperor insisted on preparing a new offensive, his generals revolted against him, and he was assassinated in 618. One of his former generals, Li Yuan (565–635), declared himself emperor of a new dynasty, the Tang.

The Power of Tang China 618–907

The coup that brought the Tang dynasty to power was only the latest in a series of coups led by the Tuoba-Chinese aristocratic clans dating back to the fall of the Northern Wei. Yet unlike its predecessors, the Tang fashioned an enduring empire, the wealthiest and most powerful state in Asia (see Map 10.2). Given their roots in both the Chinese and Tuoba nobilities, the Tang rulers laid equal claim to the worlds of the steppe nomads and settled peoples. They extended Chinese supremacy over the oasis city-states of the eastern steppe, which further fragmented the Turkic confederation. Within China, they revived Confucian traditions while building on the institutional foundations of the Northern Wei and Sui to reestablish a strong bureaucratic state.

At the pinnacle of its political supremacy in the late seventh century, the Tang dynasty was beset by a jarring crisis. During the reign of the sickly emperor Gaozong (r. 650–683), the empress Wu Zhao (625–705) took an increasingly assertive role in governing the empire. Fierce opposition from the aristocrats who dominated the Tang court provoked Empress Wu to unleash a campaign of terror against her enemies. At the same time she carefully nurtured support among lesser aristocrats, expanding the use of civil service examinations to broaden access to bureaucratic office.

In 690 Wu Zhao set aside the Tang dynasty and declared her own Zhou dynasty, becoming the only woman ever to rule as emperor of China. Although Confucian historians depicted her in the harshest possible light, there is little evidence that the empire's prosperity diminished during her reign. Shortly before her death in 705, however, Empress Wu was forced to abdicate, and the Tang dynasty was restored.

The Tang capital of Chang'an had been built by the Sui founder, Yang Jian, near the site of the ancient Han capital. The Chinese conceived of their capital not only as the seat of government but also as the axis of cosmological order. The capital's design—laid out as a nearly perfect square, with its main gate facing south—expressed the principles of order and balance that imperial rule was expected to embody. Imperial palaces, government offices, marketplaces, and residential areas were symmetrically arranged along a central north-south avenue in checkerboard fashion. Two great marketplaces, enclosed by walls and gates, were laid out in the city's eastern and western halves. The bustling Western Market, terminus of the Silk Road, teemed with foreign as well as Chinese merchants. The more sedate Eastern

Chan Buddhism A Buddhist devotional tradition, originating in China, that emphasizes salvation through personal conduct, meditation, and mystical enlightenment; also known as Zen Buddhism.

equal-field system A system of state-controlled landownership created by the Northern Wei dynasty in China that attempted to allocate equitable portions of land to all households.

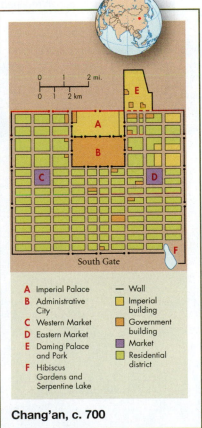

A	Imperial Palace	— Wall
B	Administrative City	▢ Imperial building
C	Western Market	▢ Government building
D	Eastern Market	
E	Daming Palace and Park	▢ Market
F	Hibiscus Gardens and Serpentine Lake	▢ Residential district

Chang'an, c. 700

The Imperial Capital of Chang'an

Market catered to an elite clientele of officials and aristocrats. The cosmopolitan styles of life and culture radiating from Chang'an reverberated throughout East Asia, shaping tastes in fashion, furnishings, and pastimes, as well as music, dance, and art (see Lives and Livelihoods: Tea Drinkers in Tang China). Chang'an was an economic and cultural crossroads of immense importance not just to China, but to all of Asia.

Demise of Tang Power

Yet the gilded glory of Tang civilization masked deepening political and economic divisions. In some ways, the Tang were victims of their own success. Aristocratic factions jockeyed for control of the court and the riches and privileges at its disposal. Economic prosperity and commercial growth unleashed market forces that eroded the foundations of the equal-field landownership system and jeopardized the state's financial stability. The gravest challenge to Tang rule came in 755, when An Lushan (ahn loo-shahn), a Sogdian general who commanded the Tang armies along the northeastern frontier, revolted. Convinced that he was about to fall victim to court intrigues, An rallied other generals to his side and marched on Chang'an. The emperor was forced to abandon the capital and seek sanctuary in the remote southwest. The dynasty survived, but probably only because An Lushan was assassinated—by his son—in 757. The rebellion finally was suppressed in 763, thanks to the crucial aid of Turkic Uighur mercenaries from Central Asia.

Although the Tang dynasty endured for another 150 years, it never recovered from the catastrophe of the An Lushan rebellion. The court ceded much military and civil authority to

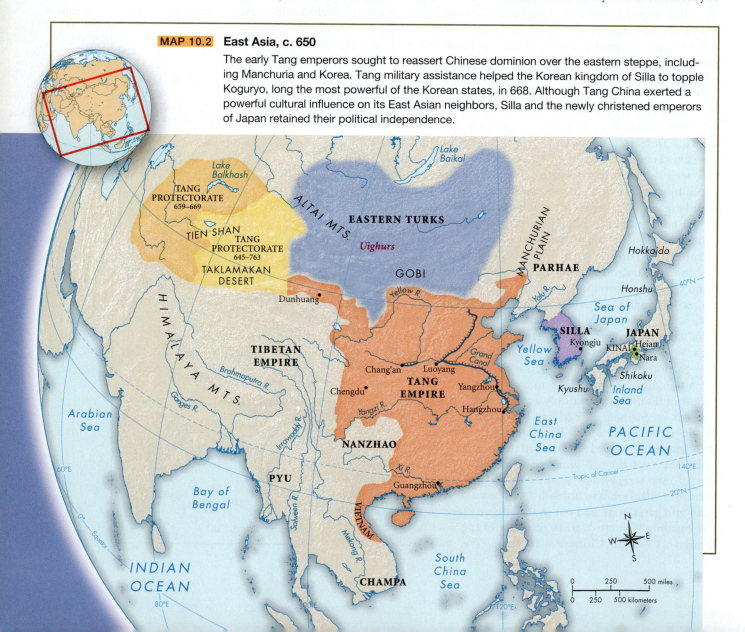

MAP 10.2 **East Asia, c. 650**

The early Tang emperors sought to reassert Chinese dominion over the eastern steppe, including Manchuria and Korea. Tang military assistance helped the Korean kingdom of Silla to topple Koguryo, long the most powerful of the Korean states, in 668. Although Tang China exerted a powerful cultural influence on its East Asian neighbors, Silla and the newly christened emperors of Japan retained their political independence.

provincial warlords. The rebellion wrecked the empire's finances by forcing the government to abandon the equal-field system and relinquish its control over landholdings. Many of the millions of peasants displaced by marauding armies took refuge in the south, which escaped much of the devastation suffered by the north China heartland. The aristocratic families who had dominated government and society since the Han dynasty were perhaps the major casualties of the rebellion. Tethered to the weakened Tang court, their estates lying in ruin, the old aristocracy clung to its prestige but never regained its power.

China and Its Neighbors

At the height of its power in the late second century B.C.E., the Han Empire had annexed portions of the Korean peninsula and Vietnam and established colonial rule over the native peoples of these regions. The introduction of the Chinese written language, as well as China's political institutions and cultural heritage, exerted a lasting influence on Korea and Vietnam, and later on Japan as well. The rise and fall of the Sui and Tang empires gave birth to East Asia as a common civilization divided into separate national states. Although each state had a unique identity and aggressively asserted its independence, Chinese policies and influences profoundly shaped how each of them developed. Elites in Korea, Vietnam, and Japan all looked to China for political and cultural models, adapting Chinese practices to suit local conditions.

Vietnam

Local rulers continued to resist foreign domination after the Han Empire conquered northern Vietnam in 111 B.C.E. In 40 C.E. a Viet queen, Trung Trac, and her sister led a revolt against the tribute demands of the Han officials. A Han general ruthlessly crushed the rebellion, executed the Trung sisters, and imposed more direct Chinese control over local society. He also erected a pair of bronze pillars along Vietnam's central coast to mark the boundary of Chinese rule—and by extension to symbolize the limits of civilization itself. Vietnam remained under Chinese dominion after the fall of the Han dynasty, but actual authority passed to a landlord class of mixed Chinese and Vietnamese ancestry linked by cultural and literary traditions to the Chinese world.

Korea

Chinese rule in Korea continued until the nomad invasions that overran north China in the early fourth century C.E. In 313 the Chinese-ruled territories in Korea were seized by Koguryo (koh-goo-ryuh), a recently formed confederation based in southern Manchuria. Pressure from nomad invaders soon forced Koguryo out of Manchuria. Koguryo moved its capital to the site of modern Pyongyang, but it became embroiled in conflict with the states of Paekche (pock-CHAY) and Silla (SHEE-lah), which had sprung up in the southern peninsula.

Japan

The earliest reference to the Japanese islands in Chinese records refers to an embassy dispatched to the Chinese court in 238 by Himiko (hee-mee-KOH), queen of the Japanese Wa people. Himiko was described as a spinster sorceress whom the Wa had elected as ruler to instill unity and curb the violent disorder that had wracked the archipelago for generations. Himiko's stature as supreme ruler reflected a pattern of dual-gender rulership that was a distinctive feature of early states in Japan.

At the time that Himiko's envoys arrived in China, influences from the mainland had only recently set in motion what would become a profound transformation in the economy and society of the Japanese islands. Settled agriculture based on rice cultivation had developed in Japan only since the fourth century B.C.E. Bronze and iron wares—chiefly weapons and prestige goods such as bronze mirrors—appeared together in the archipelago, probably in the first century C.E. During the first four centuries C.E., the population of the Japanese islands grew rapidly, in part because of immigration from the continent.

During the fourth century the Yamato kingdom in Kinai, the region around the modern city of Osaka, gained dominance in the Japanese islands. The Yamato "great kings" may or may not have descended from the Wa lineage of Himiko, but their power clearly derived from their success as warrior chiefs. Although the Yamato won the Chinese court's

Tea Drinkers in Tang China

Tea Drinking and Buddhist Hospitality

During the Tang dynasty tea drinking became an indispensable part of Chinese social life. This painting is a sixteenth-century copy of one attributed to the Tang artist Yan Liben (d. 673). It illustrates the story of a scholar who visits an elderly monk, intending to steal a famous work of calligraphy for the Tang emperor. After the monk and the scholar devote several days to lofty talk of art, the monk finally shows the treasured heirloom to his guest, who snatches it away. Here the scholar and the monk converse while two servants prepare tea for them. (National Palace Museum, Taiwan, Republic of China.)

The wild tea plant is native to the mountainous borderlands between China and India. References to drinking an infusion of fresh tea leaves in hot water date back to the first century B.C.E., but the vogue for drinking tea made from roasted leaves became widespread during the Tang dynasty. In the mid-eighth century a Tang scholar-official named Lu Yu wrote *The Classic of Tea*, which became so widely celebrated as a handbook of connoisseurship that tea merchants made porcelain statues of Lu Yu and worshiped him as their patron deity.

In Lu Yu's estimation, the finest teas were produced in Sichuan in western China and in the hilly region south of the Yangzi River, along China's eastern coast. Tea plants flourished best in a humid climate and in stony, well-drained soils on mountain slopes. After the outbreak of the An Lushan rebellion in 755, many peasants fled war-torn northern China and settled in the upland valleys of the south, where the rugged terrain was far better suited to tea cultivation than to rice agriculture. Over the next four centuries, as the popularity of tea drinking rose, tea cultivation

recognition as rulers of Japan, they only gradually extended their authority over the heterogeneous local chiefdoms scattered across the archipelago.

Warrior Rule in Korea and Japan

Meanwhile, in the Korean peninsula, the practice of mounted warfare developed by steppe nomads such as the Tuoba upset the balance of power. Koguryo had quickly imitated the Tuoba style of mounted warfare, in which both warriors and horses were clad in full body armor. At the start of the fifth century, Koguryo decisively defeated the combined armies of Paekche and their Yamato allies. The Paekche king abandoned his capital near modern Seoul and resettled in the southwestern corner of the peninsula. The militarization of the Yamato state in the fourth and fifth centuries was accompanied by a sharp increase in the incidence of warfare in the Japanese islands, fueled by imports of iron weapons from Korea. As in Korea, a warrior aristocracy now dominated in Japan.

spearheaded settlement of the interior provinces of southern China.

Tea was harvested in the spring. Although large tea plantations hired both men and women, in peasant households the task of tea picking fell almost exclusively to women, of all ages. "Tea comes in chopped, loose, powdered, and brick varieties, but in all cases the tea leaves are simply picked, steamed, roasted, pounded, and sealed in a ceramic container,"[1] Lu wrote, but he scrupulously differentiated many types of tea and methods of preparation. In Lu Yu's day, roasted tea leaves usually were pressed into bricks for ease of storage and transport. Fragments of these bricks were crushed or ground into a fine powder before brewing.

Originally, drinking tea was a leisurely pastime of the elite, but over the course of the Tang dynasty, tea became a common staple in all social classes. Lu Yu greatly esteemed tea for its medicinal value:

> Because tea is of "cold" nature it is most suitable as a beverage. A person who ordinarily is moderate in disposition and temperament but feeling hot and dry, melancholic, or suffering from headaches, soreness of the eyes, aching in the four limbs, or pains in the hundred joints should take four or five sips of tea. Its flavor can compare favorably with the most buttery of liquors, or the sweetest dew of Heaven.[2]

Feng Yan, a contemporary of Lu Yu, attributed the rising popularity of tea to Chan Buddhist monks, who drank tea to remain wakeful and alert during their rigorous meditation exercises. Monastic regulations prohibited monks from eating an evening meal but allowed them to drink tea while fasting. The diary of the Japanese Buddhist monk Ennin, who traveled throughout China on a pilgrimage between 838 and 847, contains many references to tea as a courtesy provided to guests, as a gift, and as an offering placed on the altars of Buddhist divinities and saints.

The habit of tea drinking also spread beyond the borders of China. Feng Yan reported that "Uighur Turks who came to the capital bringing herds of fine horses for sale would hasten to the marketplace and buy tea before returning home."[3] The stock-raising nomads of Central Asia and Tibet flavored their tea with butter or fermented milk.

Lu Yu's commentary bristles with sharply worded judgments about the aesthetics of preparing and drinking tea. For example, he observed that it was common to "stew tea together with finely chopped onion, fresh ginger, orange peel, or peppermint, which is boiled until a glossy film forms, or the brew turns foamy."[4] But in Lu's view such vile concoctions were "like water tossed into a ditch."[5] In choosing tea bowls Lu favored the celadon (sea green) hue of the Yue porcelains of eastern China as a fitting complement to the greenish color of tea. Later generations of tea connoisseurs in China and Japan developed complex tea ceremonies that became fixtures of refined social life.

1. Translated from Lu Yu, *The Classic of Tea*, Chapter 6.
2. Ibid., Chapter 1.
3. Translated from Feng Yan, *Master Feng's Record of Things Seen and Heard*, Chapter 6.
4. Lu, *The Classic of Tea*, Chapter 6.
5. Ibid.

QUESTIONS TO CONSIDER

1. How did Buddhist religious practices promote tea drinking?

2. Why did the cultivation of tea in China increase dramatically during the Tang dynasty?

For Further Information:
Evans, John C. *Tea in China: The History of China's National Drink*. New York: Greenwood Press, 1992.
Sen Shōshitsu XV. *The Japanese Way of Tea: From Its Origins in China to Sen Rikyū*. Honolulu: University of Hawaii Press, 1998.

Spread of Buddhism to Korea and Japan

Buddhism first arrived in Korea in the mid-fourth century. The Koguryo kings lavishly supported Buddhist monasteries and encouraged the propagation of Buddhism among the people. Paekche and Silla adopted Buddhism as their official religion in the early sixth century. In 552 a Paekche king sent a letter to the Yamato ruler in Japan urging him to adopt Buddhism, which "surpasses all other doctrines," adding that in Korea "there are none who do not reverently receive its teachings."[3] Koguryo and Silla also dispatched Buddhist monks to Japan, and it was a Koguryo monk, Hyeja (tee ay-JUH), who after his arrival in Japan in 595 became tutor to the regent Prince Shōtoku (SHOW-toe-koo) (573–621). Shōtoku subsequently sent missions to China, and their reports inspired him to imitate both the Sui system of imperial government and its fervent devotion to Buddhism. In both Korea and Japan, Buddhist monasteries became far more

Korea, c. 600

powerful institutions than in China, but they still looked to China for innovations in religious doctrines and practices.

The fall of the Sui dynasty did not resolve the tense confrontation between the Chinese empire and Koguryo. The Tang rulers formed an alliance with Silla, the rising power in the southern part of the Korean peninsula. With Chinese support, Silla first defeated Paekche and then in 668 conquered Koguryo, unifying Korea under a single ruler for the first time. Although the Tang court naively assumed that Silla would remain a client state under Tang imperial dominion, the Silla kings quickly established their independence.

The growing power of the Tang was witnessed with great trepidation at the Yamato court. In 645, after a violent succession dispute, sweeping political reforms recast the Yamato monarchy in the image of Tang imperial institutions. Efforts to strengthen the hand of the Yamato king and his government intensified after the Tang-Silla alliance heightened fears of invasion from the mainland. The court issued a law code, based on that of the Tang, that sought to adapt Chinese institutions such as the equal-field landownership system to Japanese circumstances. At the same time, the Japanese court remade its national identity by replacing the dynastic title Yamato with a Chinese-inspired name, Nihon (nee-HOHN) ("Land of the Rising Sun"). Although their concepts of rulership were partly borrowed from Chinese models, the Japanese emperors (as they now called themselves) also asserted their independence from and equality with the Tang Empire.

Tang Influence on East Asian Neighbors

In the early eighth century, Tang China reached the height of its influence on its East Asian neighbors. In Korea, Japan, and Vietnam alike, the Chinese written language served as the *lingua franca*, or common language, of government, education, and religion. Adoption of Chinese forms of Buddhism reinforced Tang China's cultural preeminence. In northern Vietnam, Chinese ways of life became deeply implanted in the fertile plains of the Red River delta around modern Hanoi. Although the Vietnamese inhabitants of the plains chafed under Tang rule, their adoption of rice farming and settled livelihoods in-

Horyuji Monastery

After gaining the patronage of rulers and aristocrats in China in the fourth century C.E., Buddhism soon spread to Korea and Japan. The Horyuji monastery, founded by Japan's Prince Shōtoku in the seventh century, was built in a Chinese architectural style adjacent to the prince's palace. The five-story pagoda, believed to be the world's oldest wooden building, houses a statue of the bodhisattva Guanyin (known in Japan as Kannon). (Vanni/Art Resource, NY.)

creasingly alienated them from the forest-dwelling highland peoples, the ancestors of the modern Hmong (mahng). Thus Chinese culture created connections between all of the states of East Asia. Elites in China, Korea, Vietnam, and Japan were bound together by a common language, similar political ideas and institutions, and shared religious beliefs. East Asian elites outside of China had something else in common, however: they were united in resisting Chinese rule.

By the early tenth century, the political boundaries of East Asia had assumed contours that would remain largely intact down to the present. Silla (supplanted by the new Koryo dynasty in 935) ruled over a unified Korea. Most of the Japanese archipelago acknowledged the sovereignty of the emperor at Kyoto, the new capital modeled on the design of Chang'an and founded in 792. In 939, after the Tang dynasty was finally deposed, local chieftains in Vietnam ousted their Chinese overlords and eventually formed their own Dai Viet kingdom. Although Korea, Japan, and Vietnam achieved lasting political independence, they remained within the gravitational pull of a common East Asian cultural sphere centered on China. At the same time, the decline of the Silk Road caravan trade and the waning popularity of Buddhism in the land of its origin loosened the ties between China and India. Henceforth, the cultural worlds of East Asia and South Asia increasingly diverged.

East Asian Political Boundaries and Common Culture

The Consolidation of Hindu Society in India

The period of the Gupta Empire (c. 320–540) often is regarded as India's classical age. Indian historians portray the Guptas as the last great native rulers of India—a dynasty under which a revived Vedic religion surpassed the appeal of the dissident religions of Buddhism and Jainism. Yet the power of the Gupta monarchs was less extensive than that of the Mauryan emperors they claimed as their forebears. Gupta rule was largely confined to the Ganges River Valley heartland, and by the 480s the Hun invasions had already dealt the dynasty a mortal blow (see Chapter 6).

> **FOCUS**
>
> Why did the religious practices of Hinduism gain a broader following in Indian society than the ancient Vedic religion and its chief rival, Buddhism?

The demise of the Gupta Empire, like that of the Roman Empire in Europe, resulted in the fragmentation of political power and the formation of a system of regional states. Unlike in China, however, political disunity remained the norm in India for centuries to come. Not until the rise of the Mughal Empire in the sixteenth century would India be unified again. The absence of a unified state did not deflect the emerging cultural and social trends of the Gupta era, however. On the contrary, in post-Gupta India, as in post-Roman Europe, common values, social practices, and political institutions penetrated more deeply into all corners of the subcontinent.

Land and Wealth

The Chinese pilgrim Xuanzang, whom we met at the start of this chapter, arrived in India during the heyday of King Harsha (r. 606–647), perhaps the most powerful of the post-Gupta monarchs (see Map 10.3). Yet Harsha's kingdom depended on his own charismatic leadership, and it perished soon after his death. Other dynasties survived longer, but their authority was confined to the ruling families' regional power base. Nonetheless, a strikingly uniform political culture spread throughout India. In addition, regional states expanded their reach into hinterland territories, bringing neighboring hill and forest tribes under their sway and assimilating them to the norms of caste society. Thus, although political ties among Indian peoples were weak, the cultural connections were increasingly strong.

The Gupta monarchs, recognizing that their control over local societies was limited, had started awarding royal lands to their officials and Brahman priests. The Gupta expected the recipients to take charge of settling and cultivating these lands. In post-Gupta

Land Grants and Village Society

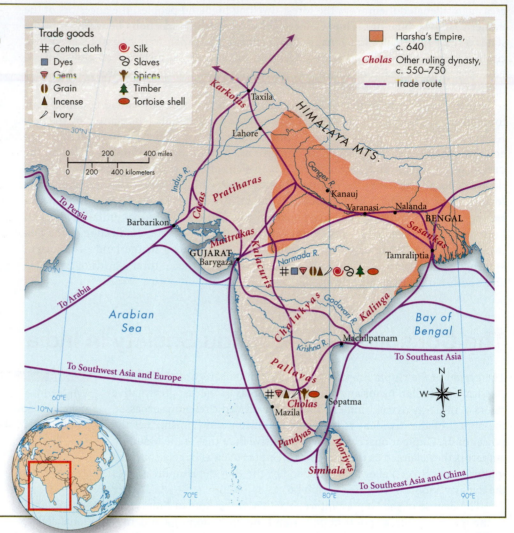

MAP 10.3

The Indian Subcontinent in the Age of Harsha, c. 640

A century after the demise of the Gupta Empire, King Harsha succeeded in restoring unified rule over most of the Gupta territories in northern India. Although tolerant of all religious faiths, Harsha became a devoted follower of Buddhism and patron to the Chinese pilgrim Xuanzang. After Harsha's death in 647, his empire disintegrated into numerous small states.

times, such land grants were often bestowed on corporate bodies such as temples, monasteries, and Brahman communities. Xuanzang observed that "the royal lands are divided into four parts: one portion provides for the needs of the court and sacrificial offerings; the second portion is given as compensation to officers and ministers for their service; the third is awarded to men of intelligence, learning, and talent; and the fourth establishes charitable endowments for religious institutions."[4] In some cases the grants included whole villages and their populations, and the peasants fell under the administrative and legal jurisdiction of the grant recipients (see Reading the Past: A Copper-Plate Land Grant Inscription).

This system of royal land grants stabilized the agricultural base of society and the economy while fostering a landlord class of Brahmans who combined religious authority, caste prestige, and landed wealth. Yet nothing like the large manors or serfdom characteristic of Latin Christendom at this time appeared in India. The peasant household remained the basic unit of work and livelihood. Rural society, especially in the south, typically was governed by village assemblies that enjoyed some measure of independence from their lords.

The practice of royal land grants transferred most wealth to temples and Brahman landlords. These landowners dominated the local economy, garnering tribute from the lands and peasants attached to them and controlling enterprises such as mills, oil presses, and moneylending. Beginning in the tenth century, temples dedicated to gods such as Shiva and Vishnu were built on an unprecedented monumental scale, symbolizing the

A Copper-Plate Land Grant Inscription

This inscription from 753 records a land grant made by the king of the Pallava dynasty in southern India to the king's religious teacher, a local Brahman. The grant was recorded on eleven copper plates that were strung together on a copper wire and stamped with the Pallava royal seal—a bull and the phallic symbol associated with the god Shiva.

The inscription begins with a eulogy written in Sanskrit lauding the king. Details of the land grant, written in the local language, Tamil, follow. This passage from the Tamil portion defines the relationship between the land grant recipient and the local village community.

> Having seen the order . . . we, the inhabitants, went to the boundaries which the headman of the district pointed out, walked around the village from right to left, and planted milk-bushes and placed stones around it. . . . The recipient shall enjoy the wet land and the dry land included within these four boundaries, wherever the iguana runs and the tortoise crawls, and shall be permitted to dig river channels and irrigation channels. . . . Those who take and use the water in these channels by pouring out baskets, by cutting branch channels, or by employing small levers shall pay a fine to be collected by the king. The recipient and his descendants shall enjoy the houses, house gardens, and so forth, and shall have the right to build houses and halls of burnt tiles. The land included

within these boundaries we have endowed with all exemptions. The recipient shall enjoy the exemptions obtaining in this village without paying for the oil-mill and looms, the hire of the well-diggers, the share of the Brahmans of the king, the share of shengodi [a plant], the share of figs, the share of lamp black, the share of corn-ears, the share of the headman, the share of the potter, the sifting of [rice] paddy, the price of ghee [clarified butter], the price of cloth, the share of cloth, the hunters, messengers, dancing-girls, the grass, the best cow and the best bull, the share of the district, cotton-threads, servants, palmyra molasses, the fines to the accountant and the minister.

Source: Kasakkudi Plates of Nandivarman, *South Indian Inscriptions,* Archaeological Survey of India, vol. 2, part 3 (Madras: Government Press, 1896), 360–362.

EXAMINING THE EVIDENCE

1. What services—supported by the taxes and fees explicitly exempted from this land grant—did the village community provide to its members?

2. Why did rights to water figure so prominently in this grant?

---

dominance of the temple over community life. In this way, royal land grants established a connection between local elites and institutions and the king, even as they increased the wealth and power of land grant recipients.

Devotional Worship in Hinduism

Beginning in Gupta times, Brahmanical religion regained its primacy, while competing religious movements such as Buddhism and Jainism retreated to the margins of Indian society. The resurgence of Brahmanical religion during this period—in the form now called **Hinduism**—stemmed both from changes in religious practice and from the wealth and power Brahman groups obtained through royal patronage.

The farthest-reaching change in Hindu practice was displacement of the sacrificial rituals only Brahmans could perform by forms of worship all ranks of society could participate in. Personal devotion to gods such as Shiva and Vishnu—whose cults took many distinct forms, depending on regional traditions and even individual imagination—replaced Brahmanical rituals as the core of religious life.

Devotional worship, or *bhakti*, was celebrated as the highest form of religious practice in religious texts known as the **Puranas**. The Puranas instructed believers in the proper forms for worshiping a specific god. Hinduism, like Buddhism and Jainism, centered on the salvation of the individual, regardless of one's caste. At the same time, Hinduism fostered collective worship of the gods enshrined at local village temples. Bhakti worship also encouraged more active participation by women, who previously had been excluded from religious life.

Hinduism The name given (first by Muslims) to the body of religious teachings, derived from the Brahmanical religion of the Vedic era, that developed in response to the challenge of Buddhism.

Puranas Religious writings, derived from oral tradition and written down during the first millennium C.E., that recount the legends of the gods and serve as the canonical texts of popular Hinduism.

Proliferation of Hindu Temples and Deities

Hindu temples joined religious piety to political power. The Puranas constructed genealogical ties between ancient heroes and gods and present-day rulers. Royal inscriptions also celebrated the close relationship between kings and the gods, in some cases asserting that the king was an incarnation of a god such as Shiva or Vishnu.

The focus on worshiping images of the gods that accompanied the spread of Hinduism accelerated the trend of founding temples through royal land grants. Temples grew in size and splendor. Major temples employed large retinues of Brahman priests, students, and caretakers. Many temples also maintained troupes of female attendants—known as *devadasis*—who were "married" to the local god. The devadasis performed rituals that combined music and dance and served as temple wardens. Devadasis at major temples often were highly educated and accomplished artists, respected in local society and accorded a freedom from social convention denied to married women. At poorly endowed temples, however, devadasis sometimes had no choice but to sell their sexual services to support themselves.

The rapid growth of local temples and bhakti devotion spurred intense adoration of a multitude of new or transformed deities. The proliferation of deities resulted from the absorption of local cults into Hindu religion. People worshiped the principal Hindu gods, Shiva and Vishnu, in many different incarnations. Krishna, an incarnation of Vishnu, appeared both as the wise philosopher-warrior of the celebrated philosophical poem *Baghavad Gita* ("Song of the Lord") and as a rustic herdsman, the patron of cowherds and devoted lover of the milkmaid Radha. Kings and warriors particularly venerated Shiva, an icon of sovereign authority and wielder of terrible powers of destruction. The elephant-headed god Ganesh was recast as the offspring of Shiva and his elegant consort (or spouse) Parvati.

Worship of goddesses who originated in local fertility cults marked a significant departure in Hinduism from the older Vedic tradition. Consort goddesses were seen as necessary complements to male gods such as Shiva, whose power and energy could be activated only through union with a female. Yet goddesses such as Lakshmi, the consort of Vishnu, and Shiva's many wives also attracted their own personal followings. Brahman priests condoned these goddess cults, which became a distinctive feature of Hinduism.

As he traveled about India, Xuanzang was appalled by the decayed state of Buddhism in its homeland. Monuments lay in ruin; once-grand monasteries stood desolate. Arriving at Varanasi (the modern city of Benares in northern India), which Buddhists revered as the site of the Buddha's first sermon, the Chinese pilgrim found "a densely crowded city teeming with rich and prosperous inhabitants, their houses filled with great wealth and rare goods." But "few of them revered Buddhist teachings. . . . Of Deva [Hindu] temples there were more than a hundred, and more than ten thousand adherents of the non-Buddhist sects, the great majority professing devotion to Shiva."[5] Popular devotion to Buddhism was fading, and by the thirteenth century it would vanish altogether.

The Many Faces of Shiva

Hindus worship the god Shiva in many forms, as both a creator and a destroyer. The faces on this sculpture—which include a bust of Shiva's consort Parvati, the embodiment of feminine composure and wifely devotion—portray Shiva as both a fierce exterminator and a serene ascetic. The four faces encircle a *linga*, an erect phallus symbolizing Shiva's powers of fertility and procreation. (Erich Lessing/Art Resource, NY.)

New Economic and Social Trends

The land grant system and the temple-centered economy it spawned stimulated the expansion of agriculture and village settlement into frontier areas. New irrigation and fertilization techniques also promoted the growth of the agricultural economy. The encroaching agrarian states with their caste-based social order incorporated many tribal groups in the forests and hills. An inscription dated 861 celebrated the conquest of a frontier area in western India by a king of the Pratihara dynasty, boasting that he had made the land "fragrant with the leaves of blue lotuses and pleasant with groves of mango and *madhuka*-fruit trees, and covered it with leaves of excellent sugarcane."[6]

The prominence of the temple-centered economy in these centuries also reflected the decline of towns and trade. Xuanzang sadly observed that people had abandoned many of the great cities in which Buddhism had thrived in the past. Archaeological research confirms the decline of urban centers in the Ganges Valley between the seventh and tenth centuries. Circulation of coins ceased in many areas. The proliferation of land grants attests to the growing importance of wealth in the form of landed property and goods rather than money.

As local agricultural economies became more important, international trade declined. Arab seafarers frequented the western coast of the peninsula to obtain spices, pepper, gems, and teak in exchange for horses, but India was largely severed from the lucrative Central Asian caravan trade now in the hands of hostile Turkic and Muslim neighbors. Itinerant traders and local merchants remained active, however, supplying agricultural produce, ghee (clarified butter), betel leaves (a popular stimulant), and cotton cloth to ordinary villagers and procuring ritual necessities and luxury goods for temples and royal courts.

As Brahman religion and social norms became more deeply entrenched in village society and the frontier tribal regions, the structure of caste society underwent profound changes. Many of the upstart regional dynasties came from obscure origins. Although these ruling families strove to invent a noble ancestry in the *Kshatriya* (warrior) caste, status in court society depended more on personal relations and royal favor than caste standing.

The rigid formal hierarchy of the four major caste groups—Brahmans (priests), Kshatriyas (warriors), Vaishyas (merchants and farmers), and Shudras (servile peoples)—could not contain the growing complexity of Indian society, especially with the inclusion of pastoral nomads and forest-dwelling tribes. Social status based on occupation—known as *jati*—often superseded ancestral birth, at least on the lower rungs of the caste hierarchy. Jatis developed their own cultural identities, which were expressed in customs, marriage rules, food taboos, and religious practices. Merchant and artisan jati groups acquired an institutional identity as professional guilds. Leaders of wealthy jatis sometimes became temple wardens and persons of distinction in local society.

Yet the status of merchants and artisans often varied from place to place. In some localities, certain craftsmen jati—for example, butchers, shoemakers, and cloth fullers—were required to live outside the town walls, like Untouchables and other social groups deemed ritually unclean. Blacksmiths and carpenters formed special organizations in an effort to raise their social standing. The court also granted special privileges to groups of artisans who worked for it, such as copperplate engravers, weavers in the employ of the royal family, and masons building royal temples and palaces.

The rights and privileges of women, like those of men, differed according to caste and local custom. As in most cultures, writers and artists often idealized women, but they did so in terms that distinguished feminine from masculine qualities. Whereas the ideal man was described in strongly positive language—emphasizing, for example, ambition, energy, mastery of knowledge and spiritual paths, and skill in poetry and conversation—female virtues were often conveyed through negative constructions, such as absence of jealousy, greed, arrogance, frivolity, and anger. These characterizations reflect prevailing notions of women's weaknesses.

Women were encouraged to marry young and remain devoted to their husbands throughout their lives. The earliest reference to the practice of *sati*, in which a widow commits suicide following the death of her husband, dates from the sixth century. Yet only women of the Kshatriya caste were expected to perform sati, primarily when the husband had died heroically in battle. But the fate of a widow in this patriarchal society was often grim. Unable to inherit her husband's property or to remarry, a widow depended on her husband's family for support. However, women who chose not to marry, such as nuns and devadasis, were accepted as normal members of society.

Court Society and Culture

The gradual unraveling of the Gupta Empire left a multitude of local kings. Each claimed exalted ancestry and strove to shore up his social base by awarding land grants. In this political world—referred to as the "circle of kings" in the *Arthashastra* ("The Science of Material Gain"), a renowned treatise on statecraft—each ruler pursued his advantage through complex maneuvers over war and diplomacy involving numerous enemies and

jati In India, a caste status based primarily on occupation.

The Lure of Court Life

The sumptuous splendor of Indian court life drew sharp criticism from Buddhist and Jain ascetics. At the left of this mural, created in around 500 to represent a Buddhist legend, King Mahajanaka, wearing a crown and garlanded with pearls, sits in a stately palace. His wife and palace ladies fail to persuade him to continue his life of ease and luxury, however— at the right the king rides away from the palace, having renounced worldly pleasures. (Frédéric Soltan/Corbis.)

allies. Kings achieved political dominance by gaining fealty and tribute, not by annexing territory, as was usual in China, for example. The consequence was that connections between rulers were of paramount importance.

Given the treachery and uncertainty of the "circle of kings," rulers eagerly sought divine blessings through lavish patronage of temples and their gods. They portrayed themselves as devoted servants of the supreme gods Shiva and Vishnu, and they demanded similar reverence and subservience from their courtiers and subjects. The rituals of the royal court gave monarchs an opportunity to display their majesty and affirm their authority over lesser lords. As we also see in Europe and the Islamic world at this time, royal courts became the main arenas of political intercourse, social advancement, and cultural accomplishment.

Attendance at court and participation in its elaborate ceremonial and cultural life was crucial to establishing membership in the ruling class. Marrying a daughter to a powerful king was the surest means of securing a family's social and political eminence. Important kings had numerous wives, each with her own residence and retinue. Relations within royal households were governed by the same strategies of alliance, rivalry, and intrigue that characterized the political realm of the "circle of kings." In both cases, personal connections played a central role in the distribution and exercise of power.

Kama Sutra

The lifestyle of the courtly elite was exemplified in the *Kama Sutra* ("The Art of Pleasure"), composed during the Gupta period. Most famous for its frank celebration of sexual love, the *Kama Sutra* was intended as a guidebook to educate affluent men in the rules of upper-class social life. It is addressed to a "man about town" who has received an education, obtained a steady source of wealth (whether from land, trade, or inheritance), established a family, and settled in a city populated by other men of good birth and breeding. The book enumerates sixty-four "fine arts" that a cultivated man should master, from dancing and swordsmanship to skill in conversation and poetry. The *Kama Sutra* also dwells on the protocols of courtship and erotic love, although only one of its seven books is devoted to sexual techniques. Above all, the *Kama Sutra* exalts mastery of the self: only through discipline of the mind and senses can a man properly enjoy wealth and pleasure while avoiding the pitfalls of excess and indulgence.

The *Kama Sutra* describes an urbane lifestyle that imitated the worldly sophistication and conspicuous consumption of the king and his court. It dismisses rural society, in contrast, as boorish and stultifying. Village life dulls one's sensibilities and coarsens manners and speech. Village youths, complained a contemporary poet, "cannot grasp facial expressions, nor do they have the intelligence to understand subtle meanings of puns and innuendos."[7] Despite such assertions that a vast cultural gulf separated the court from the countryside, courtly culture and its values permeated the entire ruling class, including local lords and Brahman landowners.

The post-Gupta era witnessed steady cultural integration throughout the Indian subcontinent, even in the absence of political unity. Non-Brahman religions and social values were increasingly marginalized, and by the tenth century Hindu religious culture, as well as the norms of caste society, prevailed in almost all regions.

Cultural Integration

The Diffusion of Indian Traditions to Southeast Asia

Indian culture and religions spread to Southeast Asia before the emergence of indigenous states or literary and philosophical traditions, in a process resembling how China influenced its East Asian neighbors. Thus Indian traditions had a powerful effect on the development of Southeast Asian ideas about kingship and social order and provided a new vocabulary to express cultural and ethical values.

FOCUS

What aspects of Indian religions had the greatest influence on the societies and cultures of Southeast Asia?

Southeast Asian religious beliefs and practices integrated aspects of two Indian religions, Hinduism and Buddhism. As in East Asia, Mahayana Buddhist teachings were readily adapted to local cultures. Hinduism, with its roots in Indian social institutions, especially the caste system, proved less adaptable. Yet some elements of Hinduism, such as bhakti devotional cults and the worship of Shiva, also flourished in Southeast Asia. Given the Brahman priesthood's prominent role in Southeast Asia—despite the absence there of caste societies—it would be more appropriate to refer to this tradition as **Brahmanism** than as Hinduism. Across the mainland and islands of Southeast Asia, aspects of both Buddhism and Brahmanism would intermingle in novel ways, fusing with ancient local traditions to produce distinctive religious cultures (see Map 10.4).

Commerce and Religious Change in Southeast Asia

The spread of Indian religions and cultural traditions to Southeast Asia occurred gradually beginning in the early centuries C.E. Indian influence did not result from conquest or large-scale migration and colonization. Rather, it was carried by Indian merchants and missionaries following the maritime routes from the Bay of Bengal to the South China Sea. Buddhist missionaries were crossing the Southeast Asian seas to China by the second and third centuries C.E. Brahmans, in contrast, lacked the evangelical zeal of Buddhist monks, and Indian law prohibited Brahmans from traveling abroad for fear of jeopardizing their purity of body and spirit. Brahmanism was disseminated to Southeast Asia, therefore, largely via Indian merchant colonies, and also by Southeast Asian natives who traveled to India for study and training and returned as converts.

Historians find evidence for the diffusion of Brahmanism to Southeast Asia in Funan, the first identifiable state in the region, and in Java during the early centuries C.E. The Funan state, based in the lower Mekong River Valley (in present-day Vietnam and Cambodia), flourished during the first to fourth centuries C.E. as the principal trading center between India and China. Contemporary Chinese observers noted that Indian beliefs and practices were prevalent in Funan, as was the use of Indic script in writing. Local lore even attributed the ancestry of the Funan rulers to the marriage of a local princess with an Indian Brahman.

Brahmanism in Funan and Java

Brahmanism also flourished in central Java, as attested by the presence of Brahman monastic communities and the adoption of many Indian gods into local religion. The

Brahmanism The distinctive Hindu religious tradition of Southeast Asia, in which the Brahman priesthood remained dominant despite the absence of a caste system.

MAP 10.4 **States in Southeast Asia, c. 800**
Many Southeast Asian states, such as Angkor in the lower Mekong River Valley and the Sailendra dynasty in Java, were based in fertile agricultural regions. But the Champa and Srivijaya confederations ruled the seas and derived their power from the profits of trade. During its heyday from the seventh to the twelfth centuries, Srivijaya dominated the maritime trade routes linking China with India and the Islamic world.

earliest inscriptions in Old Javanese, dating from the late fourth to early fifth centuries, refer to gifts of cattle and gold to Brahman priests and to royal ceremonies apparently derived from Indian precedents.

As in India, local rulers in Southeast Asia appropriated Hindu religious ideas and motifs that meshed with their own worldviews and grafted them onto ancient local traditions. In Champa (along Vietnam's central coast), the cult of Shiva, centered on the worship of stone phalli, resembled older fertility rituals in which people presented offerings to rough stone icons of local gods. In Java, the high gods of Hinduism came to be identified with the island's fearsome volcanoes, which the inhabitants regarded as the homes of the gods. Mountain symbolism is also striking in the architecture of the Buddhist monument of Borobudur (booh-roe-boe-DOOR) in central Java, and in the temple complexes of Angkor in Cambodia (see Seeing the Past: Borobudur: The World's Largest Buddhist Monument, page 331).

Religion and the Constitution of State Power

From the beginning, Southeast Asia's borrowing of religious ideas from India was closely linked to the ambitions of Southeast Asian rulers. Indian traditions that related kingship to all-powerful gods had obvious appeal to local chieftains seeking to augment their authority and power. Both Buddhism and Brahmanism provided models for divine blessing of royal authority. In the Buddhist tradition, the universal monarch, the chakravartin, achieved supremacy through lavish acts of piety and devotion. In the Brahmanical tradition, by contrast, the king partook of divine power by identifying with the high gods, above all Shiva, and received worship from his subjects much as the gods did. This association of the king with the gods sanctified the king's role as ruler and protector of his people. Although the gods might lend aid to the king, ultimately it was the king's personal charisma that endowed him with sovereign power.

The earliest appearance of the worship of Shiva in Southeast Asia is found in Champa, where a loose confederation of local rulers shared power under a weak royal overlord (see again Map 10.4). One Champa king instituted a Shiva cult at the royal shrine at Mi-son, the ritual center of the Champa confederation, in the fourth century. Yet the Champa chiefdoms never coalesced into a centralized state, perhaps because the small coastal plains yielded only meager agricultural

Brahmanism in Champa   surpluses. The Champa chieftains instead relied on piracy and plunder to obtain wealth. Thus Indian political and religious ideas alone were not enough to create a powerful king. Without the resources to pay soldiers and officials and reward allies, kings could never be powerful enough to dominate their wealthiest subjects.

Brahmanism and Buddhism in Angkor   However, where ample resources were combined with a compelling political ideology, powerful kings did emerge. For example, worship of Shiva aided consolidation of state power in the broad plains around the Tonle Sap Lake in the lower Mekong River Valley. The founder of the Angkor kingdom, Jayavarman (JUH-yuh-vahr-mon) II, was pro-

Angkor's Oldest Temple
The earliest kings in Southeast Asia often claimed to be avatars, or incarnations, of the Hindu god Shiva. Upon moving his capital to the new site of Angkor, the Khmer king Yasovarman I (r. 889–910) built Phnom Bahkeng, a temple dedicated to Shiva, on a hill overlooking the city. In the shape of a six-tiered pyramid, the temple symbolizes Mount Meru, the home of the Hindu gods. (Hervé Champollion/ akg-images.)

claimed universal monarch by his Brahman advisers in 802; he consolidated his dominion over the region's local lords by combining devotion to Shiva with homage to himself as deva-raja (divine lord).

During the early phase of the Angkor state, kings delegated control over the land and its inhabitants to officials assigned to temples established throughout the realm by royal charter. The Brahman priesthood managed the administrative affairs as well as the ritual ceremonies of these temples. Not until a century later did one of Jayavarman's successors, Yasovarman (YAH-suh-vahr-mon) I (r. 889–c. 910), consolidate royal authority by establishing his capital at Angkor and building the first of its numerous temple complexes. The many temples he founded at Angkor and elsewhere were dedicated primarily to Shiva, Vishnu, and Buddha. Depending on individual inclinations, later Angkor kings sometimes favored worship of Vishnu—the chief deity at Angkor's most famous temple complex, Angkor Wat—or patronage of Mahayana Buddhism, and their temple-building projects reflected these personal religious allegiances.

Apart from Brahmanism, Mahayana Buddhism was the other Indian religious tradition that initially attracted devotion and patronage in Southeast Asia. Chinese pilgrims in the seventh century described the Pyu and Mon city-states of lower Burma, which had ready access by sea to the great Mahayana monasteries in Bengal, as "Buddhist kingdoms." Burmese ambassadors to the Tang court in the ninth century reported that all children were required to spend some time as novices in Buddhist monasteries. Mahayana Buddhism was also enthusiastically welcomed by Malay chiefs in Sumatra, who had begun to capitalize on a major reorientation of maritime trade routes that occurred between the fourth and sixth centuries.

Previously, merchants had avoided the monsoon winds that dictated the rhythms of seafaring in the Southeast Asian seas. Instead of sailing around the Malay peninsula,

Mahayana Buddhism in Burma and Sumatra

Maritime Trade

ships would land at the Kra Isthmus, the narrowest point along the peninsula. From there, they would carry their goods overland to the Gulf of Siam before setting sail again for the Indochina peninsula. Funan used its strategic location on the more protected eastern shore of the Gulf of Siam to become the major crossroads where merchants from the Indian Ocean could meet those from China. Beginning in the fourth century, however, Malay navigators pioneered an all-sea route through the Straits of Melaka, bypassing the Gulf of Siam altogether. Funan's prosperity abruptly ended, and the ports of southeastern Sumatra replaced Funan as the linchpin of maritime trade (see again Map 10.4).

Trade routes shifted in part because of the growing importance of Southeast Asian products in international trade. Earlier, trade between India and China consisted largely of exchanging Chinese silk for products from western Asia (frankincense, myrrh, and other substances used to make perfume and incense). Gradually, cheaper local substitutes, such as Sumatran camphor and sandalwood from Timor, began to enter this trade, and by the seventh century both Arab and Chinese merchants had become avid buyers of Sumatran pepper and the fine spices (cloves, nutmeg, and mace) from the Molucca Islands far to the east. The Sumatran ports were ideally situated to capture this trade.

The Buddhist Kingdoms of Srivijaya and Sailendra

In the late seventh century, the ruler of the Sumatran port of Palembang founded the first of a series of kingdoms known collectively as Srivijaya (sree-vih-JUH-yuh). Our first image of a ruler of Srivijaya comes from an inscription of 683, which tells how the king celebrated his conquest of a rival city-state and gravely admonished his vanquished foe to accept Buddhism. The rulers of Srivijaya became great patrons of Mahayana Buddhism. The large international community of monks that gathered at Palembang included novices from China seeking instruction from Indian monks.

The rise of Srivijaya was soon followed by the emergence of a lineage of kings in the Kedu Plain of central Java. Known as the Sailendra (SIGH-len-drah) dynasty, these monarchs were equally dedicated to Mahayana Buddhism. Although boasting a rich rice agriculture, the Kedu Plain was isolated from the coast by a ring of mountains, and thus did not have direct access to the maritime commercial world. Nonetheless, in the mid-eighth century the Sailendra kings achieved dominance over the Kedu Plain by borrowing heavily from Indian religious and political traditions, probably through the cordial relations they cultivated with Srivijaya.

The Sailendra kings used Sanskrit sacred texts and administrative language to construct a network of religious and political allegiances under their leadership. They also founded many Buddhist shrines, which attracted monks from as far away as Bengal and Gujarat. The massive monument of Borobudur in central Java testifies to the Sailendra kings' deep faith in Mahayana Buddhism (see Seeing the Past: Borobudur: The World's Largest Buddhist Monument).

Allied to Srivijaya by their common faith and intermarriage between the royal families, the Sailendra dynasty flourished from 750 to 850. In around 850, however, the Sailendra were suddenly expelled from Java by an upstart rival devoted to Shiva. The royal house fled to Sumatra, where they joined their Srivijaya kin. Bereft of Sailendra patronage, the Buddhist monasteries in Java plunged into irreversible decline. Henceforth, Brahmanism predominated in Java until a wave of conversions to Islam began in the fifteenth century.

Indian Religions in Southeast Asia: A Summing-up

Indian religions were assimilated in Southeast Asia as the existing cultural and social frameworks adapted foreign ideas. The potent ideologies of the Sanskrit literary heritage and the organizational skills of Buddhist and Brahman holy men stimulated the formation of states based on divinely sanctioned royal authority. Both the Brahmanical and Buddhist traditions contributed to the rise of monarchies in the maritime realm, in the rice-growing plains of the great river valleys, and in central Java. The Angkor kingdom

SEEING THE PAST

Borobudur: The World's Largest Buddhist Monument

The Monument at Borobudur (Luca Tettoni/Corbis.)

The Sailendra kings never built palaces or cities for themselves. Instead they devoted their wealth and resources to building vast monuments displaying their devotion to the Buddhist faith. The massive stone edifice they erected at Borobudur in central Java rises from a fertile plain ringed by imposing volcanoes. Construction of Borobudur began in around 760 and took seventy years to complete.

The exact purpose of the Borobudur monument, which was neither a temple nor a monastery, continues to provoke scholarly debate. Borobudur consists of ten concentric terraces of decreasing size crowned by a bell-shaped stupa, a Buddhist shrine used as a repository for relics or other sacred objects. The terraces are adorned with carved reliefs depicting many episodes from the basic scriptures of Mahayana Buddhism and with more than five hundred statues of Buddhas. The carved reliefs provide a virtual

encyclopedia of Mahayana teachings. But they also include many scenes from court life, which spoke more directly of the royal majesty of the Sailendras. Some scholars have suggested that the mountainlike edifice celebrated the Sailendras' exalted stature as "Lords of the Mountains" and marked the dynasty's original home.

By visiting Borobudur, the Buddhist faithful could pass physically and spiritually through the ten stages of devotion necessary to attain enlightenment. Entering from the eastern staircase, they would proceed slowly around each terrace, studying and absorbing the lessons told by the carved reliefs before passing to the next level. To see all the reliefs one must walk around the monument ten times, a distance of three miles. Reliefs at the lower levels retell well-known stories from the life of the Buddha and other holy figures. The higher levels are devoted to the pilgrim Sudhana, who visited 110 teachers in his quest for enlightenment. On the upper levels the narrow galleries of the lower levels give way to three round open terraces surmounted by numerous latticelike stupas enclosing life-size statues of Buddhas. The devotee's ascent of the monument symbolized a spiritual progress from the world of illusion to the realm of enlightenment.

Source: John Miksic, *Borobudur: Golden Tales of the Buddhas* (Hong Kong: Periplus, 1990).

EXAMINING THE EVIDENCE

1. How can we see the architectural design of Borobudur as a physical representation of the world, which in Buddhist cosmology is depicted as a series of circular oceans and continents surrounding a sacred mountain at the center?

2. In what ways does the monument reflect Buddhism's renunciation of worldly life?

represents the most striking case of simultaneous patronage of both Brahmanism and Mahayana Buddhism, but to a lesser degree this eclectic adoption of Indian religions occurred throughout Southeast Asia.

Royal temples and monuments became focal points for amassing wealth in service to the gods, while also serving as testaments to the kings' piety. Local temples likewise accumulated landholdings and stores of treasure, serving as both the economic and the ceremonial hubs of community life. In contrast to Islam, which exercised a powerful centralizing pull and created a common brotherhood of faith across national, ethnic, and cultural boundaries, Indian religions in Southeast Asia—as in India itself—spawned a diverse array of regional religious cultures.

COUNTERPOINT
Sogdian Traders in Central Asia and China

FOCUS

How did the social and economic institutions of the Sogdian merchant network differ from those of the nomadic confederations and the agrarian empires?

The heyday of the overland caravan routes of Central Asia—the Silk Road—was between the fifth and the eighth centuries. Chinese and Persian emperors, nomad chieftains, and kings of oasis city-states all struggled to capture a share of the lucrative Silk Road trade. Yet the great length of the trade routes and the harsh deserts and mountains through which they passed made it impossible for any single political power to dominate the Silk Road. Instead, rulers great and small had to cultivate close ties with those who, in the words of a Moroccan spice merchant turned Christian monk, "to procure silk for the miserable gains of commerce, hesitate not to travel to the uttermost ends of the earth."[8] The Sogdian merchants who linked the steppe lands of the nomads with Asia's great agrarian empires did so through economic enterprise rather than military might or political power.

A Robust Commercial Economy

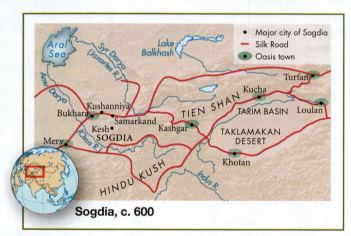

Sogdia, c. 600

Sogdia (SUGG-dee-yah) (now divided between Uzbekistan and Tajikistan) was a fertile agricultural region surrounded by the grassland habitat of the central Eurasian nomads. Persian in language and religion, Sogdian culture was also enriched by contact with the Indian and Greek worlds. Alexander the Great conquered the region in the fourth century B.C.E.

Sogdia's commercial economy began to develop slowly beginning in the first century C.E. Sogdian merchants achieved success by leaving their homeland and traveling to distant regions, especially eastward to China. The dispersion of Sogdian merchants took the form of a **trade diaspora** (*diaspora* was the Greek word for scattering grain), a network of merchant settlements spread throughout foreign lands. These communities remained united by their common origins, religion, and language, as well as by family ties and business partnerships (see Reading the Past: Letters from a Sogdian Castaway).

Nomad incursions in the fifth and sixth centuries ruined many cities in Central Asia, as the Chinese pilgrim Xuanzang observed. Sogdia's city-states were largely spared this devastation and began to enjoy unprecedented prosperity. Agriculture and trade supported ambitious building projects, including an extensive system of irrigation canals and long walls to fend off both nomad attacks and encroaching desert sands.

Sogdian-Turkic Alliance

The creation of the Turkic nomad empire in the mid-sixth century catapulted Sogdian merchants to dominance over the Silk Road trade. Sogdian merchants forged an alliance with the Turks and entered the administration, army, and diplomatic service of the Turkic khan. When the Sasanid king rebuffed the Turkic khan's offer of trade, a Byzantine historian tells us, it was "Maniakh, the leader of the Sogdians" who advised the khan "that it would be better for the Turks to cultivate the friendship of the Romans [i.e., the Byzantines] and send their raw silk for sale to them, because they made more use of it than other people."[9]

trade diaspora A network of merchants from the same city or country who live permanently in foreign lands and cooperate with one another to pursue trading opportunities.

Prominent Sogdians intermarried with the Turks, and the Turks adopted the written language of the Sogdians. Under the umbrella of Turkic military power, Sogdian merchant colonies sprouted in Mongolia and on the frontiers of China, and they spread westward as far as the Black Sea. Sales contracts found at Turfan, the principal hub of the Silk Road,

Letters from a Sogdian Castaway

In 1907, while surveying the ruins of a guardhouse near Dunhuang, the westernmost outpost of the Tang Empire, the British explorer Aurel Stein found a post bag that had been lost in transit. The letters, written in Sogdian and dating from the early fourth century, perhaps had been confiscated by Chinese border officials. Among the contents were two letters written by Miwnay, a Sogdian woman living in Dunhuang—one to her husband, a traveling merchant, and the other to her mother in Loulan, a desert town hundreds of miles farther west.

In the letter to her husband, Nanai-dhat, Miwnay complains that it had been three years since he abandoned her and her daughter in Dunhuang. She implores him to return. Miwnay had appealed to Artivan, a relative of her husband, and Farnkhund, apparently one of his business associates, as well as the leaders of the Sogdian community at Dunhuang, but they refused her requests for help. Here Miwnay describes her plight to her mother:

> I am very anxious to see you, but have no luck. I petitioned the councilor Sagharak, but the councilor says, "Here there is no other relative closer to [my husband] than Artivan." And I petitioned Artivan, but he says: "Farnkhund is . . . [missing text], and I refuse to hurry, . . ." And Farnkhund says, "If [Artivan] does not consent that you should go back to your mother, how should I take you? Wait until . . . comes; perhaps Nanai-dhat will come." I live wretchedly, without clothing, without money. I ask for a loan, but no one consents to give me one, so I depend on charity from the priest. He

said to me, "If you go, I will give you a camel, and a man should go with you, and on the way I will look after you well." May he do so for me until you send me a letter!

In a postscript to the letter to the husband, Miwnay's daughter adds that Farnkhund had run away and the Chinese authorities were holding her mother and herself liable for Farnkhund's debts. Miwnay's closing words convey her bitterness toward her husband:

> I obeyed your command and came to Dunhuang. I did not observe my mother's bidding, nor that of my brothers. Surely the gods were angry with me on the day when I did your bidding! I would rather be wife to a dog or pig than to you!

Source: Nicholas Sims-Williams, "Towards a New Edition of the Sogdian Ancient Letters: Ancient Letter 1," in Étienne de la Vaissière and Eric Trombert, eds., *Les Sogdiens en Chine* (Paris: École française d'Extrême Orient, 2005), 185–187.

EXAMINING THE EVIDENCE

1. What does Miwnay's predicament tell us about the status of women in Sogdian society?

2. What do these letters reveal about the role of the family in the organization of the Sogdian merchant network?

---

show Sogdian merchants buying and selling silk, silver, gold, perfume, saffron, brass, medicines, and cane sugar. Horses ranked first among the goods they brought to China, while slaves, Siberian furs, and gems and spices from India filled the markets of Samarkand and other Sogdian cities.

The dominance of Sogdians over Silk Road commerce fed stereotypes about their immense wealth and shallow morals. Xuanzang, who passed through Samarkand in 630, pronounced the Sogdians "greedy and deceitful," snidely observing that "fathers and sons scheme for profit, because everyone, noble and commoner alike, regards wealth as the measure of distinction."[10] At the same time, Sogdian merchants living in Chinese cities occupied a prominent place in the cosmopolitan cultural world of Tang China. The popularity of Persian fashions, music, dance, and sports such as polo at the Tang court can be attributed to the influence of Sogdians who settled in Chang'an. Sogdian merchants' homes, as well as temples dedicated to Persian religions, clustered around the Tang capital's Western Market, the gateway to the Silk Road.

The Sogdian émigré communities in Central Asia and China drew strength from their strong communal bonds, but as the generations passed, many Sogdians in China began to assimilate to the cosmopolitan Chinese culture. The Sogdian silk merchant He Tuo, who settled in China in the mid-sixth century, joined the entourage of a Chinese prince and

Sogdian Communities in Central Asia and China

amassed a great fortune. His eldest son and nephew became experts at cutting gemstones, and the Sui emperor Yang Jian placed the nephew in charge of the imperial jewelry workshop. The He family is credited with introducing the techniques of glassmaking to China. Another of He Tuo's sons had a brilliant career as a Confucian scholar in service to the Sui court. The Tang emperors also frequently employed Sogdians in important civil and military offices, most notoriously the general An Lushan, whose rebellion nearly brought down the Tang dynasty.

Breakdown of the Trade Network

Muslim Takeover of Sogdia

The Muslim conquest of Sogdia in the early eighth century marked the beginning of the end of Sogdian prosperity. When Samarkand surrendered to an Islamic army in 712, the city's population was forced to pay an indemnity of two million silver coins and three thousand slaves and agreed to submit annual tribute of two hundred thousand silver coins. Unlike many of their neighbors, however, the Sogdians stubbornly resisted both their new Arab overlords and Islamic religion. As a result Sogdia remained isolated from the commercial and cultural worlds of the Islamic empire.

Impact of An Lushan Rebellion

The An Lushan rebellion of 755–763 dealt another major blow to the Sogdian trade network. It severely damaged the Chinese economy, and after the rebels were defeated many Sogdians in China disguised their ancestry and abandoned their culture out of fear of persecution.

Rise of Asian Maritime Trade

Finally, with the rise of maritime trade routes connecting the Islamic world and China, overland traffic across the Silk Road dropped off steeply. By the late tenth century, the Sogdian language and culture were on the verge of extinction in Sogdia itself, and the scattered Sogdian communities had blended into the foreign societies they inhabited. Samarkand, however, would enjoy a brilliant revival in the fourteenth century under the Turkic emperor Timur, when the city was reborn as an Islamic metropolis (see Chapter 15).

Conclusion

Commercial and cultural exchanges across the Silk Road during the first millennium C.E. linked the distant agrarian empires of China, India, and Iran. The interactions that resulted transformed the peoples and cultures along the Central Asian trade routes. Nomad chieftains, for example, developed the political acumen to knit together tribal confederations and pursue profits through trade, plunder, and conquest. The Tuoba, the Turks, and the Khazars all transcended their original predatory purposes by creating empires that spanned both the pastoral nomadic and the settled agrarian worlds. In each case, however, these empires failed to create political institutions that might have perpetuated their dominion over settled societies. The Sogdian merchant communities forged very different commercial and cultural linkages across Asia, but these networks, too, proved vulnerable to shifts in political fortunes and trade patterns.

The movement across the Silk Road of goods and of people such as the Buddhist pilgrim Xuanzang fostered unprecedented cosmopolitan cultural intercourse throughout Asia. The complex intermingling of peoples, cultures, and religious faiths peaked with the rise of the Sui and Tang empires in China. The spread of Buddhism to China and from there to Korea, Japan, and Vietnam provided the foundation for a common East Asian culture. The political dominance of the Chinese empires also spread China's written language, literary heritage, and social values among its neighbors. Correspondingly, the demise of Tang power after the An Lushan rebellion in the mid-eighth century undermined China's cultural dominance. Subsequently a new order of independent states emerged in East Asia that has persisted down to the present.

In India, too, a cosmopolitan culture and a more homogeneous ruling class formed during the first millennium C.E., despite the absence of political unity. This elite culture was based on Gupta political institutions and Hindu religious beliefs and social values expressed through the new lingua franca, or common language, of Sanskrit. Some scholars have dubbed it "the Sanskrit cosmopolis." The royal lineages and noble classes that founded the first states in Southeast Asia during this period participated fully in creating this cosmopolitan culture. Yet by the tenth century, as in East Asia, the common elite culture encompassing South and Southeast Asia had begun to fragment into more distinctive regional and national traditions.

Between the fifth and tenth centuries, regional cultures in East and South Asia were formed by the movement of people and goods across trade routes, the mixture of religious and political ideas, and the spread of common forms of livelihood. The same forces were also at work in the formation of regional societies in the very different worlds of the Americas and the Pacific Ocean, as we will see in the next chapter.

NOTES

1. Translated from Xuanzang, *Record of the Western Regions.*
2. Ibid., Book 5.
3. Translated from *The Chronicles of Japan*, Chapter 19.
4. Translated from Xuanzang, *Western Regions*, Book 2.
5. Ibid., Book 7.
6. Translated in Munshi Debiprasad, "Ghatayala Inscription of the Pratihara Kakkuka of [Vikrama-]Samvat 918," *Journal of the Royal Asiatic Society* (1895): 519–520.
7. Quoted in Daud Ali, *Courtly Culture and Political Life in Early Medieval India* (Cambridge, U.K.: Cambridge University Press, 2004), 197.
8. Cosmas Indicopleustes, *Christian Topography* (c. 547–550) (London: Hakluyt Society, 1897), Book II, 47.
9. R. C. Blockley, *The History of Menander the Guardsman* (Liverpool, U.K.: Cairns, 1985), 115.
10. Translated from Xuanzang, *Western Regions*, Book 1.

RESOURCES FOR RESEARCH

Steppe Peoples and Settled Societies of Central Asia

The centrality of Central Asia to world history has been analyzed from a variety of perspectives. Bentley focuses on the spread of world religions, Beckwith on political interactions and the formation of empires, and Christian on the movements of peoples and social transformations. Liu offers a lively discussion of cultural life across the Silk Road.

Barfield, Thomas. *The Perilous Frontier: The Nomadic Empires and China.* 1989.

Beckwith, Christopher I. *Empires of the Silk Road: A History of Central Eurasia from the Bronze Age to the Present.* 2009.

Bentley, Jerry H. *Old World Encounters: Cross-Cultural Contacts and Exchanges in Pre-Modern Times.* 1993.

Christian, David. *A History of Russia, Central Asia, and Mongolia.* Vol. 1, *Inner Eurasia from Prehistory to the Mongol Empire.* 1998.

Liu, Xinru, *The Silk Road in World History.* 2010.

The Shaping of East Asia

Although he overstates the degree of Chinese influence, Holcombe provides a succinct digest of the formation of a shared East Asian civilization. Adshead likewise exaggerates China's cultural dominance, but his detailed comparison of Chinese, Islamic, Indian, and both Latin and Byzantine Christian civilizations contains many important insights. Farris and Pai offer sure-handed guidance through the thorny debates over foreign influence and cultural identity that have dominated the study of the emergence of the Japanese and Korean states, respectively.

Adshead, S. A. M. *T'ang China: The Rise of the East in World History.* 2004.

Benn, Charles. *Daily Life in Traditional China: The Tang Dynasty.* 2002.

Farris, William Wayne. *Sacred Texts and Buried Treasures: Issues in the Historical Archaeology of Ancient Japan.* 1998.

Holcombe, Charles. *The Genesis of East Asia, 221 B.C.–A.D. 907.* 2001.

Pai, Hyung-Il. *Constructing "Korean" Origins: A Critical Review of Archaeology, Historiography, and Racial Myth in Korean State-Formation Theories.* 2000.

A Visual Sourcebook of Chinese Civilization. http://depts .washington.edu/chinaciv/.

The Consolidation of Hindu Society in India

In contrast to earlier studies that defined post-Gupta India in terms of political and economic regression, recent work argues that the Indian economy and society continued to be vital despite political fragmentation. Thapar's encyclopedic yet accessible survey caps a distinguished career as the most important interpreter of India's early history. Ali's illuminating investigation of court society reconceptualizes the nature of kingship in Indian culture.

Ali, Daud. *Courtly Culture and Political Life in Early Medieval India.* 2004.

Basham, A. L. *The Origins and Development of Classical Hinduism.* 1989.

Champakalakshmi, R. *Trade, Ideology, and Urbanization: South India, 300 B.C. to A.D. 1300.* 1996.

Chattopadhyaya, Bradjadulal. *The Making of Early Medieval India.* 1994.

Thapar, Romila. *Early India: From the Origins to A.D. 1300.* 2002.

The Diffusion of Indian Traditions to Southeast Asia

Hall provides a comprehensive introduction to the impact of maritime trade on the political, economic, and religious transformations of the region during this formative era. Wolters's collection of essays examines conceptual approaches for the study of this highly diverse region. Higham, an archaeologist, admirably synthesizes current scholarship on Angkor.

Hall, Kenneth R. *A History of Early Southeast Asia: Maritime Trade and Societal Development, 100–1500.* 2011.

Higham, Charles. *The Civilization of Angkor.* 2002.

Shaffer, Lynda. *Maritime Southeast Asia to 1500.* 1996.

Tarling, Nicholas, ed. *Cambridge History of Southeast Asia.* Vol. 1, Part 1. 1992.

Wolters, O. W. *History, Culture, and Region in Southeast Asian Perspectives.* 1999.

COUNTERPOINT: Sogdian Traders in Central Asia and China

Little scholarship on Sogdia and its merchants is available in English, but the translation of de la Vaissière's landmark study helps to remedy this omission. Schafer catalogues the impact of the rich material culture of Central Asia on Tang culture and literature.

Schafer, Edward. *The Golden Peaches of Samarkand: A Study in T'ang Exotics.* 1963.

de la Vaissière, Étienne. *Sogdian Traders: A History.* 2005.

▶ **For additional primary sources from this period**, see *Sources of Crossroads and Cultures*.

▶ **For Web sites, images, and documents related to topics in this chapter**, see Make History at bedfordstmartins.com/smith.

The major global development in this chapter ▶ The cultural and commercial exchanges during the heyday of the Silk Road that transformed Asian peoples, cultures, and states.

IMPORTANT EVENTS

386–534	Northern Wei dynasty in north China and Mongolia
552–603	First Turkish empire
581–618	Sui dynasty in China
604	Prince Shōtoku reorganizes the Yamato kingdom in Japan
606–647	Reign of King Harsha as paramount ruler of north India
618–907	Tang dynasty in China
629–645	Journey of the Chinese Buddhist monk Xuanzang to India
668	Unification of the Korean peninsula under the rule of the Silla kingdom
c. 670	The Khazars conquer and supplant the Bulgar khanate
690	Empress Wu declares the founding of her Zhou dynasty in China
755–763	An Lushan rebellion in north China severely weakens the Tang dynasty
c. 760	Sailendra kings in Java begin construction of the Borobudur monument
792	Kyoto established as Japan's new capital
802	Consolidation of the Angkor kingdom in Cambodia by Jayavarman II
861	Conversion of the Khazars to Judaism
939	Vietnam wins independence from China
965	Rus invaders destroy the Khazar khanate

KEY TERMS

bodhisattva (p. 312)
Brahmanism (p. 327)
chakravartin (p. 313)
Chan Buddhism (p. 314)
equal-field system (p. 314)
Hinduism (p. 323)

jati (p. 325)
khan (p. 310)
Mahayana (p. 312)
Puranas (p. 323)
Pure Land (p. 313)
trade diaspora (p. 332)

CHAPTER OVERVIEW QUESTIONS

1. In what ways did Asian societies respond to cross-cultural interactions during the period 400–1000?

2. What strategies did pastoral nomads adopt in their relations with settled societies, and why?

3. What patterns of political and cultural borrowing characterized the emerging states in East and Southeast Asia?

4. Why did India and China experience different outcomes following the collapse of strong and unified empires?

SECTION FOCUS QUESTIONS

1. What strategies did nomadic steppe chieftains and the rulers of agrarian societies apply in their dealings with each other?

2. How did the spread of Buddhism transform the politics and societies of East Asia?

3. Why did the religious practices of Hinduism gain a broader following in Indian society than the ancient Vedic religion and its chief rival, Buddhism?

4. What aspects of Indian religions had the greatest influence on the societies of Southeast Asia?

5. How did the social and economic institutions of the Sogdian merchant network differ from those of the nomadic confederations and the agrarian empires?

MAKING CONNECTIONS

1. How and why did the spread of Buddhism from India to China and Southeast Asia differ from the expansion of Islam examined in Chapter 9?

2. Do you think that the invasions of Germanic peoples into the Roman Empire had more lasting consequences (see Chapter 9) than the invasions in China by steppe nomad peoples? Why or why not?

3. Compare the main values of Hinduism in the post-Gupta period with those of the ancient Vedic religion (see Chapter 3). How had the goals of religious practice changed, and what effect did these changes have on Indian society?

AT A CROSSROADS ▶

The Mesoamerican ball-game, which spread as far as northeastern North America, was charged with powerful ritual and religious meaning. Maya myths associate the ballgame with the Hero Twins' triumph over the gods of the underworld and with the gift of agriculture. This stone disk, which dates from about 590 and once marked the site of a ball court in the modern Mexican province of Chiapas, displays a ballplayer striking the ball with his hip. The headdress and inscriptions suggest that the ballplayer is a royal figure reenacting the feats of the Hero Twins. (Giraudon/ Bridgeman Art Library.)

Societies and Networks in the Americas and the Pacific

300–1200

W hen Holy Lord Eighteen Rabbit (r. 695–738) became king of the Maya city-state of Copán (co-PAHN) in today's western Honduras, his society was at the peak of its wealth and strength. Eighteen Rabbit's building projects reflected Copán's power. He commissioned an impressive series of stone monuments, adding major new temples in the heart of the city and laying out a Great Plaza to the north. He rebuilt Copán's magnificent ball court, where the warriors reenacted the Maya myth of creation as a gladiatorial contest culminating in the blood sacrifice of captured nobles. At the entrance to the Great Plaza, Eighteen Rabbit erected a stone pillar commemorating his accession as king, and the plaza itself was studded with carved stelae depicting Eighteen Rabbit as a multifaceted deity. One stele shows him as a mighty warrior holding up the sky; others portray him dressed as the Maize God and the spirit of the planet Venus.

After ruling Copán for forty-three years, Eighteen Rabbit was betrayed by one of his followers. In 725 he had installed a man named Cauac (kah-WOK) Sky as ruler of the nearby city of Quiriga (kee-REE-gah). In 738 Cauac Sky captured Eighteen Rabbit and carried the Copán king back to Quiriga, where he was killed as a sacrificial victim. Copán preserved its independence after Eighteen Rabbit's execution; Cauac Sky made no attempt

BACKSTORY

As we saw in Chapter 8, during the first millennium B.C.E. signs of growing social complexity and a hierarchy of villages and towns emerged in both the Olmec culture on Mexico's Atlantic coast and the Chavín culture along Peru's Pacific coast. By 200 B.C.E., however, the Olmec and Chavín societies had been eclipsed by the rising city-states of the Maya and Moche, respectively. These city-states concentrated political and military power by mobilizing massive amounts of labor to build monumental cities and irrigation systems for agriculture. Meanwhile, in North America, agriculture and settled societies did not appear until the first millennium C.E., when native peoples began to adopt Mesoamerican food crops and farming techniques. In the Pacific Ocean, once the Lapita migrations ceased in around 200 B.C.E., many islands remained undisturbed by human occupation. Colonization of the Pacific Islands would not resume until after 500 C.E.

The Classical Age of Mesoamerica and Its Aftermath

FOCUS What common beliefs and social and political patterns did the various local societies of Mesoamerica's classical age share?

City and State Building in the Andean Region

FOCUS How did environmental settings and natural resources shape livelihoods, social organization, and state building in the Andean region?

Agrarian Societies in North America

FOCUS How did the introduction of Mesoamerican crops transform North American peoples?

Habitat and Adaptation in the Pacific Islands

FOCUS In what ways did the habitats and resources of the Pacific Islands promote both cultural unity and cultural diversity?

COUNTERPOINT: Social Complexity in Bougainville

FOCUS Why did the historical development of the Melanesian island of Bougainville depart so sharply from that of contemporaneous societies in the Americas and the Pacific?

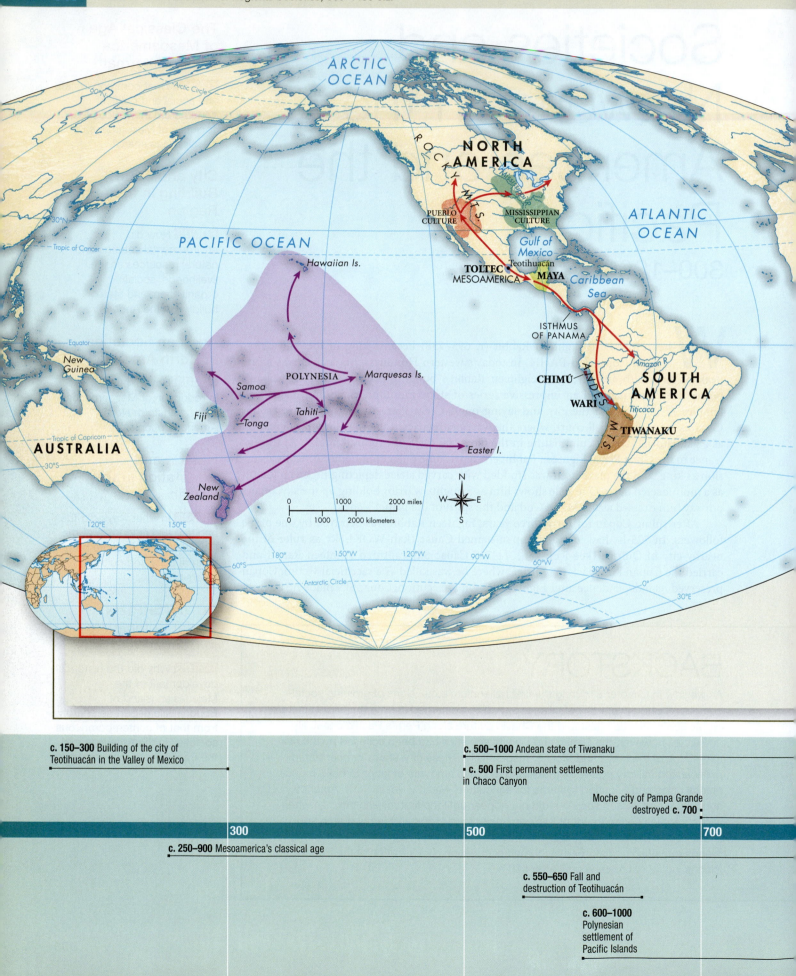

c. 150–300 Building of the city of Teotihuacán in the Valley of Mexico

c. 500–1000 Andean state of Tiwanaku

c. 500 First permanent settlements in Chaco Canyon

Moche city of Pampa Grande destroyed **c. 700**

300

500

700

c. 250–900 Mesoamerica's classical age

c. 550–650 Fall and destruction of Teotihuacán

c. 600–1000 Polynesian settlement of Pacific Islands

to occupy Copán or destroy its monuments. In fact, Eighteen Rabbit's successor as Copán's ruler completed one of his predecessor's most ambitious projects, a pyramid staircase that set down in stone the history of his dynasty. The inscription carved into the staircase steps reaffirmed the power of Copán by celebrating the accomplishments of its ancient warrior kings. The seated sculptures of earlier rulers placed at ascending intervals include an image of Eighteen Rabbit. His death—"his breath expiring in war"—was duly noted, but only as an unfortunate episode in an otherwise heroic history. He received full honors as a noble martyr and sacred ancestor.

The life and death of Eighteen Rabbit recorded in his city's monuments exemplify the obsession with dynastic continuity that was so central to the Maya kings' identity. The rulers of the Maya city-states devoted enormous resources to asserting their godlike power to command their subjects' labor and wealth. Their monuments wove together history and myth to tell the story of conquests, captives, slain enemies, and military alliances. Yet this wealth of historical documentation speaks in a single uniform voice. It is the speech of kings and nobles and sheds little light on the lives of the commoners who toiled under their rule.

As we saw in Chapter 8, the scarcity of written records, especially in comparison to Eurasia, complicates scholars' efforts to recover the histories of peoples of the Americas, the Pacific Islands, and most of sub-Saharan Africa. Only in Mesoamerica, stretching from central Mexico to Honduras, do we find substantial indigenous writings, which are as yet only partly deciphered. But the absence of documentary evidence does not indicate social or cultural isolation. Throughout the period from 300 to 1200, movements of peoples, goods, and ideas had far-reaching influences on these regions of the world. As in Eurasia, cross-cultural interaction played a significant role in shaping peoples and cultures.

The intensity of interaction and degree of cultural convergence varied with time and place. In Mesoamerica, cross-cultural interactions created a set of institutions and ideologies that knitted together local societies and cultures from the highland plateaus of central Mexico to the tropical rain forests of the Maya world. In the Andean region of South

MAPPING THE WORLD

Formation of Regional Societies in the Americas and the Pacific

In the Americas and the Pacific—as in Eurasia and Africa during this era—migration and trade promoted cultural exchange and the formation of regional societies. Complex states based on intensive agriculture arose in Mexico, the Maya region, and the Andes, but the southwestern deserts and eastern woodlands of North America fostered sharply distinct societies. The Polynesian migrations spawned a remarkable cultural unity across the central and eastern Pacific Ocean.

ROUTES ▼

→ Spread of maize cultivation, c. 1000 B.C.E.–700 C.E.

→ Polynesian migration, c. 300–1000 C.E.

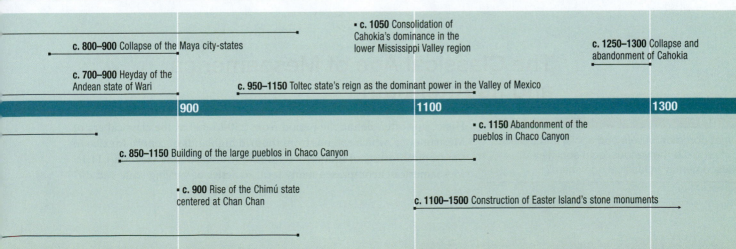

- **c. 1050** Consolidation of Cahokia's dominance in the lower Mississippi Valley region

c. 800–900 Collapse of the Maya city-states

c. 1250–1300 Collapse and abandonment of Cahokia

c. 700–900 Heyday of the Andean state of Wari

c. 950–1150 Toltec state's reign as the dominant power in the Valley of Mexico

900 **1100** **1300**

- **c. 1150** Abandonment of the pueblos in Chaco Canyon

c. 850–1150 Building of the large pueblos in Chaco Canyon

- **c. 900** Rise of the Chimú state centered at Chan Chan

c. 1100–1500 Construction of Easter Island's stone monuments

America, too, inhabitants of the coastal plains and the highlands developed common political and cultural institutions. In contrast, cross-cultural influences touched virtually all of the local societies of North America without producing a shared cultural and political identity. In the Pacific Islands, migration, trade, and social interchange produced both the high degree of cultural uniformity of Polynesia and the remarkable cultural diversity found on the single island of Bougainville.

Equipped only with stone tools, these peoples faced formidable obstacles in their efforts to create stable agricultural economies. Landscapes as diverse as the alpine plateaus of the Andes, the barren deserts of southwestern North America, and the volcanic islands of the Pacific posed daily challenges to farming folk. Their success produced larger surpluses, greater social stratification, and more hierarchical political systems than before. In North America and the Pacific Islands, political and religious authority was dispersed among numerous hereditary chiefs. But in Mesoamerica and the Andean region, where irrigated agriculture supported denser populations, large states emerged. A distinct ruling class governed these states; their authority rested on an ideology that defined the cosmic order and explained the rights and obligations of all members of society, as well as the special status of the ruling class. The rulers of these states, such as Eighteen Rabbit, expressed their ideologies not only in words but in the design of their settlements and cities, in monumental architecture and sacred objects, and in rituals performed on behalf of both their deceased ancestors and their living subjects.

OVERVIEW
QUESTIONS

The major global development in this chapter: The formation of distinctive regional cultures in the Americas and the Pacific Islands between 300 and 1200.

As you read, consider:

1. How did these societies, equipped with only Stone Age technologies, develop the social and political institutions and the patterns of exchange to tame often hostile environments and build complex civilizations?

2. How did differences in environment and habitat foster or discourage economic and technological exchanges among adjacent regions?

3. What were the sources of political power in the societies discussed in this chapter, and how were they similar or dissimilar?

4. How did differences in urban design reflect distinctive forms of political and social organization?

The Classical Age of Mesoamerica and Its Aftermath

FOCUS

What common beliefs and social and political patterns did the various local societies of Mesoamerica's classical age share?

Historians often define the period from 250 to 900 as the classical era of Mesoamerica, which extends from the arid highlands of central Mexico to the tropical forests of modern Honduras and Nicaragua (see Map 11.1). Mesoamerica encompassed many local societies of varying scale and dif-

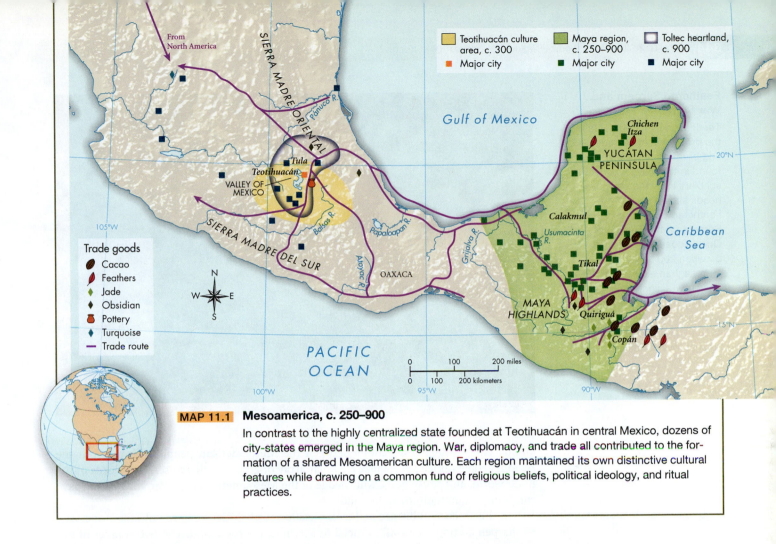

MAP 11.1 **Mesoamerica, c. 250–900**
In contrast to the highly centralized state founded at Teotihuacán in central Mexico, dozens of city-states emerged in the Maya region. War, diplomacy, and trade all contributed to the formation of a shared Mesoamerican culture. Each region maintained its own distinctive cultural features while drawing on a common fund of religious beliefs, political ideology, and ritual practices.

ferent degrees of integration and complexity. What united it as a regional society was a set of shared ideas about the operation of the cosmos. This common ideology produced similar patterns of elite status, political power, and economic control.

Between the first and ninth centuries, Mesoamerica underwent a remarkable cycle of political consolidation and disintegration. At the beginning of this period, Mesoamerica was home to numerous **chiefdoms**, in which a hereditary chief exercised political and religious authority and military leadership over a group of tribes or villages. By the third century, more complex and more steeply stratified political orders—**city-states**—dominated both the highlands and the lowlands by extracting labor and tribute from their subjects.

Bronze and iron metallurgy were unknown in Mesoamerica during this period. Yet despite the limitations of Stone Age technology, the people built great cities, and their skilled craft industries flourished. Highly productive agriculture based on maize, beans, squash, and chili peppers supported some of the world's densest populations.

The monumental metropolis of Teotihuacán (teh-o-tee-WAH-kahn) in central Mexico and the dozens of Maya city-states testify to the strong control the rulers wielded over their subjects' lives. As was true of the classical ages of Eurasia and Africa, the classical era of Mesoamerica was a time of strife and crisis as well as expanding economic and cultural interchange.

Political Power and Ideology in Mesoamerica

Scholars have traced the origins of Mesoamerican cultural and political traditions to the ancient Olmec civilization (see Chapter 8). Powerful Mesoamerican city-states emerged during the first centuries C.E., and cross-cultural exchange intensified as trade and warfare

chiefdom A form of political organization in which a hereditary leader, or chief, holds both political and religious authority and the rank of members is determined by their degree of kinship to the chief.

city-state A small independent state consisting of an urban center and the surrounding agricultural territory.

Feathered Serpent and War Serpent

Teotihuacán's monuments lack the prolific historical records and portraits of royal figures found in the Maya world. But scholars think the sculpted heads shown here of the Feathered Serpent and the War Serpent on the Temple of Queztalcoatl, constructed between 200 and 250, may represent an expression of power by a single ruler or dynasty. Many of these images were defaced in the fourth century, perhaps as a warning against royal ambitions. (Photolibrary.)

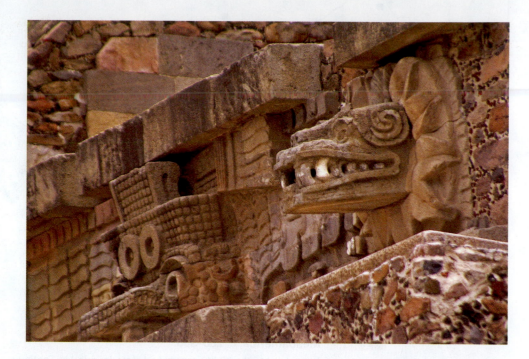

among cities forged connections between the Mesoamerican peoples. Throughout the region, people came to recognize a similar array of gods—feathered serpents, lords of the underworld, and storm gods. Knowledge of the Mesoamerican calendar and writing gave rulers important tools for state-building.

In the absence of bronze and iron metallurgy, **obsidian**—a hard volcanic stone used to sharpen cutting tools—was crucial to agricultural production. The two sources of obsidian in the region, the northern part of the Valley of Mexico and highland Guatemala, emerged as early centers of economic exchange and state formation. Poor transportation limited the reach of political control, however; in the absence of draft animals (domesticated beasts of burden) and wheeled vehicles, people could transport only what they could carry on their backs. Long-distance exchange was therefore difficult, and it was restricted to the most highly desired goods. Political power was based more on controlling labor than on accumulating property. Yet the possession of rare and exotic **prestige goods** gave rulers awesome authority, and so items such as jade, gold, jaguar skins, feathers, and cacao seeds (for making chocolate) acquired great value. Rulers of the Mesoamerican city-states constantly warred against each other, vying for control of labor resources and prestige goods and exacting tribute from their defeated enemies.

Mesoamerican political power was explained and legitimated by a political ideology that many scholars argue was rooted in memories of the great rulers and cities of antiquity. The people collectively associated these memories with a mythical city known as **Tollan** ("the place of reeds"), which they saw as a paradise of fertility and abundance, the place where human and animal life began. They believed Tollan was the earthly abode of the god Feathered Serpent (whom the Aztecs would later name Quetzalcoatl [kate-zahl-CO-ah-tal]), the creator and patron of humanity. Mesoamerican myths associated the Feathered Serpent with elemental forces such as wind and fire, and also with the planet Venus, the "morning star" that heralds the arrival of the life-giving sun. Mythological lore credited the Feathered Serpent with creating the sun and moon, inventing the calendar and thus the cycles of time, and bestowing basic necessities such as maize, their staple food.

But Mesoamerican concepts of cosmic order, in which cycles of time are punctuated by violence and death, required that the Feathered Serpent sacrifice his own life to

Sources of Political Power and Ideology

obsidian A hard volcanic stone used to sharpen cutting tools and thus one of the most valuable natural resources for Stone Age peoples.

prestige good A rare or exotic item to which a society ascribes high value and status.

Tollan In Mesoamerican myths, the name of the place where the gods created human beings, and thus the place of origin for all of humanity.

renew the creative powers of the universe. Human rulers in turn could acquire and maintain political power only through offering frequent blood sacrifices to the gods. These blood sacrifices involved both the execution of war captives and bloodletting rituals by rulers and priests, who used needles of obsidian, bone, or stingray spines to pierce their tongues and ears and extract blood. Human rulers embodied the divine powers of the Feathered Serpent and reenacted his heroic exploits through ritual performance.

Mesoamericans believed that all humans originally spoke a common language and lived under the benign rule of the Feathered Serpent. Gradually, though, groups of people developed their own languages, customs, and beliefs and went their separate ways. By building temples and cities, rulers sought to renew the common community of the original Tollan. Claiming the heritage of Tollan gave legitimacy to new rulers and dynasties and provided a rationale for accepting foreign conquerors. Thus political power in Mesoamerica was rooted in a shared cultural heritage and a vision of cultural unity.

The City-State of Teotihuacán

The rise of Teotihuacán, about thirty miles northeast of present-day Mexico City, as the dominant center in the Valley of Mexico was due largely to its location near the region's major obsidian mines and irrigated farmland. Only a few fragments of Teotihuacán writing have survived, so we have far less direct evidence of Teotihuacán's history than we do for the Maya city-states. We do know that in the first two centuries C.E., Teotihuacán's founders constructed a magnificent city with wide avenues, numerous walled residential complexes, and a massive open plaza anchored by giant pyramids and temples.

Most of the population of the valley, farmers and craftsmen alike, lived in this vast city. To house all these people, apartment-like stone buildings—the first apartment compounds in world history—were constructed. These compounds housed an average of fifty to one hundred persons in a series of apartments built around a central patio, which in some cases had its own ritual mound. The apartments usually housed members of a single kinship group, but some were for craftsmen working in the same trade. This residential pattern suggests that the city's people were divided into groups (probably based on kinship) that shared everyday life, collective rituals, and in some cases specialized trade and craft occupations.

Social and Economic Organization

These groups may also have been the basic units of the city's economy. Although the scale of Teotihuacán's buildings and monuments shows that the state could command vast amounts of labor, there is little evidence that its rulers exercised direct control over the inhabitants' ordinary working lives. Even the obsidian tool–making industry, the mainstay of the city's economic dominance, was dispersed among hundreds of small domestic workshops, not centralized in large state-run industrial enterprises.

Priestly Rule and Ritual

Despite the extensive centralization of the Teotihuacán state, scholars have not found evidence of a hereditary dynasty of kings. Most believe that in its formative stages, Teotihuacán—like the city-states of Mesopotamia discussed in Chapter 2—was ruled by a cadre of priests rather than a military elite. Ritual action, including blood offerings, dominates the art and imagery of Teotihuacán, but warriors and scenes of warfare rarely appear until the fourth century C.E. Human sacrifice was a notable aspect of Teotihuacán's public culture. Nearly two hundred sacrificial victims, bound and dressed in war regalia, were

Teotihuacán

0   250   500 m
0   750   1500 ft.

A Temple of the Feathered Serpent
B Pyramid of the Sun
C Plaza of the Moon
D Pyramid of the Moon
E Great Compound (possibly marketplace?)

■ Major temple platform
■ Residential compound
■ Avenue of the Dead

San Juan R.

buried beneath the Temple of the Feathered Serpent, the hub of government, when it was constructed in the early third century.

Teotihuacán's precise gridlike layout reflects a paramount desire to impose human order on an unpredictable natural world. The city's planners aligned its pyramids and plazas with crucial astronomical phenomena to provide a consecrated space to perform sacred rituals at the proper times. The Temple of the Feathered Serpent was flanked by twelve platforms, which served as stages for elaborate seasonal rites to ensure abundant harvests, cosmic balance, and social stability. The technologies of architecture, astronomy, and calendrical calculation were essential to maintain the orderly structure of the cosmos. Above all, the city's builders intended Teotihuacán to be seen as the Tollan of its day, a ceremonial complex dedicated to perpetuating the power and authority of its ruling class through awesome public rituals. It was for this reason that centuries later, the Aztecs named the city's massive ruins Teotihuacán, "the place where men become gods." In every way, the city was designed to function as a place of connection between the human and the divine.

Teotihuacán's Power and Influence

By 500 C.E. Teotihuacán's population had swelled to as many as two hundred thousand inhabitants, surpassed probably only by Constantinople among contemporary cities worldwide. The rise of Teotihuacán signaled the ascendancy of the central Mexican highlands as the dominant economic, political, and cultural region in Mesoamerica. Yet Teotihuacán's rulers pursued imperial expansion only fitfully, if at all. The area under their direct control seems to have been fairly limited, perhaps just the Valley of Mexico. Nevertheless, the city's influence radiated to the entire region through the prestige of its artifacts and culture, both of which were widely imitated throughout Mesoamerica. Visiting merchants and diplomatic missions from the Oaxaca (wah-HAH-kah) highlands, the Gulf Coast, and the Maya region inhabited their own special quarters in Teotihuacán. These foreigners' barrios (neighborhoods) were crossroads of cultural and economic exchange that helped disseminate sacred knowledge, ritual culture, political intelligence, and prestige goods throughout Mesoamerica.

By the fifth century, the Teotihuacán state exerted a far-reaching influence over the Mesoamerican world through its splendid monuments, its grand public ceremonies, and the abundant output of its craft workshops. At the same time, Teotihuacán's leaders took a more aggressive stance toward rival chiefs and foreign states. This shift would have crucial consequences for the Maya city-states.

The Maya City-State Network

The Maya city-states developed before the rise of Teotihuacán in central Mexico. Like other Mesoamerican cultures, the Maya inherited many features of the ancient Olmec civilization of the Gulf coast, including its monumental architecture, social institutions, calendar, and ritual art. In contrast to the Mexican highlands, however, where the massive scale of Teotihuacán dwarfed all other cities and polities, the Maya region never had a single dominant power.

In both the highlands near the Pacific coast and the lowland rain forests to the north, the early phase of Maya political and economic expansion was suddenly interrupted in the second and third centuries C.E. Major cities were abandoned, especially in the Pacific highlands, and new building and settlement came to a halt. The causes of this disruption are unknown, but its pervasive effects have led scholars to speculate that it resulted from some ecological catastrophe, perhaps a volcanic eruption. This catastrophe did not bring an end to Maya society, but it did alter the political landscape. By the time economic and demographic growth recovered at the beginning of the fourth century, political power had shifted decisively from the highlands to the city-states of the lowlands, such as Copán and Tikal (tee-KAHL).

Contraction and Recovery

The period from 250 to 900, the classical age of Maya civilization, witnessed the founding of nearly forty city-states. During these centuries the **Holy Lords**, as the Maya rulers called themselves, engaged in prodigious building of cities and monuments. But this era was also marked by succession struggles, dynastic changes, and perpetual political insecurity. The Holy Lords of powerful city-states frequently resorted to war to subdue neighbors and rivals. Victors rarely established direct rule over vanquished enemies, however. Unlike the Eurasian rulers we studied in earlier chapters, Maya elites did not dream of creating vast empires.

Warring City-States of the Classical Age

Instead, they were more likely to seek booty and tribute, and above all to seize war captives. Conquerors often brought back skilled craftsmen and laborers to their home city, reserving captives of high rank, such as the unfortunate Eighteen Rabbit, for blood sacrifices. Maya ceramic art often depicts tribute bearers offering cloth, foodstuffs, feathers, and cacao to enthroned rulers. Thus the Maya nobility may have conceived of war as a sacred ritual, but one that also furthered their ambitions for wealth and power. At the same time, armed conflict resulted in the exchange of people and goods among Maya city-states, contributing to the Maya region's cultural uniformity.

Maya myths about the origins of the gods and humanity have been preserved in the *Popol Vuh*, or "Book of Council." The descendants of a former Maya royal family wrote down these legends in the Latin alphabet after the Spanish conquest of Mesoamerica in the sixteenth century (see Reading the Past: The Maya Hero Twins Vanquish the Lords of the Underworld). The *Popul Vuh* portrays humans as the servants of the all-powerful gods who created them. In return for the gods' gifts of maize and timely rains, humans were obliged to build monuments to glorify the gods, to offer them sacrifices (especially human blood), and to regulate their own lives according to a sacred calendar. The Maya believed that all human beings possess a sacred essence, *ch'ulel* (choo-LEL), which is found in blood. The exalted status of kings and nobles endowed them with more potent ch'ulel, and so they were especially prized as blood sacrifices. Although the Maya kings depicted themselves as

Myths of Origins in the *Popol Vuh*

Holy Lord The title given by the Maya to the rulers of their city-states.

ch'ulel In Maya belief, the sacred essence contained in human blood that made it a potent offering to the gods.

The Maya Hero Twins Vanquish the Lords of the Underworld

The *Popol Vuh* records the myths about the world's creation and the origins of human society as handed down by the Quiché, a late Maya people. Central to the mythology of the Popol Vuh is the struggle between the gods and the Xibalba (shee-BAHL-ba), the lords of the underworld. The narrative focuses mostly on the exploits of the Hero Twins, whose father had been defeated by the Xibalba in a ball-game contest and decapitated. The Hero Twins travel to the underworld, outwit the Xibalba, and avenge their father's death.

In the following passages from the *Popol Vuh*, the Hero Twins inform the defeated Xibalba that as punishment for their heinous deed they will no longer receive blood sacrifices—and thus they will lose their power over mortals. Then the Hero Twins resurrect their father and assure him that in the future he will receive worship from the as-yet-unborn humans. Their triumph complete, the twins become transformed into the sun and moon (or, in other versions, the planet Venus), whose daily progressions through the heavens remind humanity of the triumph of the gods over the lords of death.

Passage 1:

"Here then is our word that we declare to you. Hearken, all you of Xibalba; for never again will you or your posterity be great. Your offerings also will never again be great. They will be reduced to croton [a shrub] sap. No longer will clean blood be yours. Unto you will be given only worn-out griddles and pots, only flimsy and brittle things."

"You shall surely eat only the creatures of the grass and the creatures of the wastelands. No longer will you be given the children of the light, those begotten in the light. Only things of no importance will fall before you." . . . Thus began their devastation, the ruin of their being called upon in worship. . . .

Here now is the adornment of their father by them. . . . His sons then said to him: "Here you will be called upon. It shall be so." Thus his heart was comforted.

"The child who is born to the light, and the son who is begotten in the light shall go out to you first. Your name shall not be forgotten. Thus be it so," they said to the father when they comforted his heart.

"We are merely the avengers of your death and your loss, for the affliction and misfortune that were done to

you." Thus was their counsel when they had defeated all Xibalba.

Then [the Hero Twins] arose as the central lights. They arose straight into the sky. One of them arose as the sun, and the other as the moon.

Passage 2:

Now when they came from Tulan Zuyva [Tollan], they did not eat. They fasted continuously. Yet they fixed their eyes of the dawn, looking steadfastly for the coming forth of the sun. They occupied themselves in looking for the Great Star, called Icoquih [Venus], which appears first before the birth of the sun. The face of this Green Morning Star always appears at the coming forth of the sun.

When they were there at the place called Tulan Zuyva, their gods came to them. But it was surely not then that they received their ultimate glory or their lordship. Rather it was where the great nations and the small nations were conquered and humiliated when they were sacrificed before the face of Tohil. They gave their blood, which flowed from the shoulders and armpits of all the people.

Straightaway at Tulan came the glory and the great knowledge that was theirs. It was in the darkness, in the night as well, that they accomplished it. . . .

[Tohil spoke to them]: "You shall first give thanks. You shall carry out your responsibilities first by piercing your ears. You shall prick your elbows. This shall be your petition, your way of giving thanks before the face of god."

"Very well," they said. Then they pierced their ears. They wept as they sang of their coming from Tulan.

Source: Allen J. Christenson. Popol Vuh, The Sacred Book of the Maya, *translated by Allen Christenson. Copyright © 2003 by O Books. University of Oklahoma Press, 2007. Used by permission of the publisher.*

EXAMINING THE EVIDENCE

1. Why did the Maya believe that human beings must offer blood sacrifices to the gods?

2. Why might the Maya have been so deeply interested in the movements of the sun, moon, and planets?

gods, they attained immortality only after death, and the natural death of a king was considered a necessary sacrifice to ensure the renewal of divine blessings. Women of high birth also participated in the political and ceremonial life of the Maya ruling class, and Maya inscriptions record that several women ruled as Holy Lords. Maya elites thus occupied a unique position at the intersection of the human and the divine, ensuring the world's continuity both by demanding labor and sacrifices from the Maya population and by becoming sacrifices themselves.

The Mesoamerican ballgame, which dates back at least to Olmec times, was no mere spectator sport. On important ritual occasions, the ballgame became a solemn restaging of the mythical contest in which the Hero Twins triumphed over the lords of the underworld. When Eighteen Rabbit renovated Copán's ball court, he made it the city's ceremonial centerpiece, surrounding it with the greatest temples and monuments. The object of the ballgame, played by two teams of up to four players each, was to keep a rubber ball up in the air without using hands or feet. The slope-sided arenas represented the crack in the earth leading to the underworld. Allowing the ball to strike the ground risked incurring the wrath of the underworld gods. After the outcome was decided, the ball court became a sacrificial altar where the losers' heads were impaled on a skull rack alongside the court. These blood sacrifices not only commemorated the victory of the Hero Twins but also renewed the life-giving power of the gods.

The intricate Maya calendar determined the timing of war, sacrifice, agricultural work, and markets and fairs. The Maya believed that time and human history moved in elaborate cycles determined by the movements of the sun, moon, and planets—especially Venus, which in Maya belief governed sacrifice and war. To ensure a favorable outcome, the Maya people sought to align major actions in the present, such as attacks on enemies, with heroic events and accomplishments in the past. Thus the Maya took great care to observe and record astronomical phenomena. Maya astronomers calculated eclipses and the movements of planets with astonishing precision: their charts of the movements of Venus, which survive in bark-paper books, are accurate to within one day in five hundred years.

Bloodletting by a Maya Queen
Blood sacrifices offered to the gods occupied a central place in Mesoamerican political life. This stone monument shows the king of Yaxchilan holding a torch over the head of his queen, who is performing a ritual bloodletting by passing a spiked cord through her tongue. The ritual celebrated the birth of the king's son in 709. (Erich Lessing/Art Resource.)

Maya Social Order

Maya society revolved around the activities of the king and the royal clan. Beneath this ruling elite existed a multitiered social order based on class, residence, and kinship. As in many early Eurasian cultures, astrologers, diviners, and especially scribes occupied privileged positions in Maya society. These groups possessed the knowledge crucial to maintaining the royal mystique and to carrying out the tasks of government. The cities also housed large groups of specialized craftworkers in trades such as pottery manufacture, stone and wood carving, weaving, toolmaking, and construction. Urban artisans who made luxury goods for the nobility lived in larger dwellings near the cities' ceremonial centers, which indicates that they had higher socioeconomic status. At Tikal one artisans' compound was reserved for dentists who specialized in inlaying the teeth of the nobility with jade and other precious stones.

In the countryside, three to four families, probably kinfolk, lived in a common compound, each family in its own one-room building. The residential compound included a common kitchen and storage facilities, which they all shared. Clusters of residential compounds formed hamlets of several hundred persons. The considerable differences in the richness of burial goods suggest that the size, wealth, and prestige of the kin groups of commoners varied widely.

Larger outlying settlements, where powerful noble families resided, had paved plazas, pyramids, and temples but lacked the altars and ball courts of royal cities. These local nobles governed the surrounding population and organized the delivery of tribute and labor demanded by the supreme Holy Lords. The burden of labor service—to construct cities and to serve in the military—weighed heavily on the subject population. Like other ancient city-states we have studied, Maya city-states turned to the surrounding area for resources and labor and thereby became local crossroads for people, goods, and ideas.

Maya Family Life

Written records from the Maya classical age say little about family life. Although descriptions of Maya society compiled by the Spanish conquerors in the sixteenth century suffer from biases and misrepresentations, they reveal aspects of Maya culture that cannot be gleaned from archaeological evidence. According to these accounts, children were considered members of their fathers' lineage and took their surnames, but they also acquired "house names" from their mothers. Property and status passed from parents to children: sons inherited from fathers, and daughters inherited from mothers. Upon marriage, the husband usually moved in with his wife's family for a period of service lasting six or more years. Thereafter the couple might live with the husband's family or set up their own separate household.

Maize, usually made into steamed cakes known as *tamales*, was the staple of the Maya diet. The lowland Maya practiced both dry-land and intensive wet-land agriculture, growing maize, cotton, beans, squash, chili peppers, root crops, and many other vegetables. Hunting also provided food, but the only domestic animals the Maya possessed were dogs and turkeys. Maya rulers also received fish and shellfish as tribute from coastal areas.

Population Growth and Long-Distance Exchange

During the prosperous classical era the Maya population grew rapidly. In a pattern we have seen repeated around the world, population growth stimulated regular contact and communication throughout the region, and also the specialized production of agricultural and craft goods. The urban ruling elites, while continuing to war against one another, exchanged prestige goods over long distances. The unusual uniformity in spoken languages and pottery manufacture suggests that ordinary people also interacted frequently.

Influence of Teotihuacán

It was during the classical age, too, that Teotihuacán's influence left a clear imprint on the Maya world. Obsidian tools, ceramics, stone pyramid architecture, and other artifacts imported into Maya city-states show that cultural interaction and trade with Teotihuacán were well established (see again Map 11.1). Long-distance trade between the central Mexican highlands and the Maya lowlands was complemented by reciprocal gift giving and the dispatch of emissaries among rulers. The circulation of exotic goods charged with sacred power—feathers, pelts, and precious stones—reinforced elite status and helped spread religious practices.

In the fourth century Teotihuacán also became a major political force in the Maya region. Teotihuacán trade and diplomatic missions made forays into Maya lands and cultivated local clients, who reaped political and economic benefits from allying with Teotihuacán. The sudden appearance of Teotihuacán building styles, pottery, and tomb goods suggests that some cities, particularly in the coastal plains and highlands of Pacific Guatemala, fell under the rule of governors dispatched from Teotihuacán. At the very least, some Maya elites, especially upstart contenders for power seeking to unseat established royal dynasties, emulated certain features of Teotihuacán's political ideology. At Tikal and Copán, mysterious figures identified as "Lords of the West" overthrew previous rulers and founded new royal dynasties. These foreign regimes quickly assimilated into the native ruling elites of their cities. Economic ties to Teotihuacán, and perhaps adoption of Teotihuacán's more centralized system of administration and tribute collection, enriched Tikal and Copán. Both cities developed their own networks of client cities and exercised at least informal dominance over their local regions.

The Passing of Mesoamerica's Classical Age

Destruction of Teotihuacán

Between 550 and 650 Teotihuacán was destroyed. Sacred monuments were cast down, civic buildings were burned, and at least some portion of the population was slaughtered, leaving little doubt that the destruction was politically motivated. Historians do not know whether the razing of Teotihuacán resulted from foreign invasion or domestic political strife. Clearly, the perpetrators aimed not merely to overthrow the current regime but to obliterate the city's sacred aura. Most of Teotihuacán's population scattered, and the city never regained its preeminence. No successor emerged as the dominant power. For the next three or more centuries, the Valley of Mexico was divided among a half-dozen smaller states that warred constantly against one another.

In 562 an alliance of rival states vanquished Tikal, the most powerful Maya city-state, and sacrificed its king. As was Maya practice, however, the allies did not attempt to establish direct rule over Tikal, and by 700 it had recovered and its kings once again became the paramount lords of an extensive network of allies and trading partners. Interestingly, Maya royal monuments of the eighth century at Tikal (and at Copán during the reign of Eighteen Rabbit and his successors) feature a great revival of Teotihuacán imagery, even though the Mexican city had long been reduced to ruin. The reverence shown to Teotihuacán as a royal capital illustrates the lasting appeal of its ideas and institutions throughout Mesoamerica.

From Ruin to Recovery in Tikal

The brilliant prosperity that Tikal and other Maya city-states enjoyed in the eighth century did not last. Over the course of the ninth century, monument building ceased in one Maya city after another. Although there is evidence of internal struggles for power and of interstate warfare, scholars believe that population pressure or an ecological disturbance triggered a more profound economic or demographic crisis. The collapse of the Maya city-state network not only ended individual ruling dynasties but also dismantled the basic economy of the region. Cities and cultivated fields were abandoned and eventually disappeared into the encroaching jungle. The region's population fell by at least 80 percent. New—but much more modest—cities arose along the Gulf coast of the Yucatan peninsula in the following centuries, but the cities of the Maya classical age never recovered.

Collapse of the Maya City-States

The crumbling of the entire region's political and economic foundations reveals the tight web of interdependence within the Maya city-state network. The Maya peoples were more culturally uniform than peoples in other parts of Mesoamerica, sharing common languages, material culture, ritual practices, aesthetic values, and political institutions. Their diversified regional economy promoted specialized production and reliance on exchange to meet subsistence needs. Yet the competition among many roughly equal city-states also produced an unstable political system rife with conflict. Sharp reversals in political fortunes, booms in monument building followed by busts of destruction and abandonment, and frequent changes of ruling dynasties (which court historians took great pains to conceal) shaped the Maya world. Ultimately the political instability of the Maya city-state network eroded its infrastructure of production, labor, transport, and exchange.

By 900, with the passing of both Teotihuacán and the Maya city-states, Mesoamerica's classical age had ended. Yet the region's cosmopolitan heritage endured in the Toltec state that dominated the central Mexican highlands from around 950 to 1150 (see again Map 11.1). Although descended from nomadic foragers from Mexico's northern deserts, the Toltecs resurrected the urban civilization, craft industries, and political culture of Teotihuacán. The Toltec capital of Tula became the new Tollan. According to Toltec annals written shortly after the Spanish conquest, the founder of Tula bore the name Quetzalcoatl (Feathered Serpent). Images of the Feathered Serpent frequently recur among Tula's ruins. Once again, in a pattern we have seen in other parts of the world, a nomadic people had inherited the culture of an urban society.

Post-Classical Mesoamerica: The Toltecs and Chichen Itza

This era also produced a remarkable synthesis of Mexican and Maya traditions. Chichen Itza (chuh-chen uht-SAH), in the heart of the Yucatan peninsula, dominated the northern Maya region in the tenth century. The art and architecture of Chichen Itza so closely resembles that of Tula that some scholars believe Chichen Itza was a colony of the Toltec state. But Chichen Itza's major monuments are older than those of Tula. Relief carvings on the temples surrounding Chichen Itza's ball court depict the lords of Itza (the name means "sorcerer of water") summoning the Feathered Serpent, who grants them the right to rule this land. Although it is unlikely that the Toltecs ruled over Chichen Itza, there is little doubt that both cities were conceived as reincarnations of ancient Tollan and shared a political ideology centered on the Feathered Serpent. The striking similarities between Tula and Chichen Itza offer compelling evidence of the growing cultural integration of Mesoamerica.

City and State Building in the Andean Region

FOCUS

How did environmental settings and natural resources shape livelihoods, social organization, and state building in the Andean region?

At the height of Mesoamerica's classical age, a series of rich and powerful states, centered on spectacular adobe and stone cities, sprouted in both the northwestern coastal lowlands and the Andean highlands of South America (see Map 11.2). But the narrow land bridge of the Isthmus of Panama, covered by thick tropical forests, hampered communication between North and South America. Despite similarities in art, architecture, ritual, and political ideology, there is scant evidence of sustained contact between Mesoamerican and Andean societies during this era. Indeed, their differences are striking. Metalworking, already highly refined in the Andean region in the first millennium B.C.E., was unknown in Mesoamerica until the seventh century C.E. The massive irrigation systems of the Andean region had no parallel in Mesoamerica, and urbanization and trade networks were far more extensive in Mesoamerica than in the Andes. And although the Andean region was characterized by strong states and powerful rulers, they did not develop the traditions of writing and record keeping that became vital to political life in the Maya city-states.

All along the Pacific coast of South America, the abrupt ascent of the Andean mountain chain creates a landscape of distinctive ecological zones. Low coastal deserts give way to steep valleys and high mountain ranges interspersed with canyons and plateaus. Marked differences in climate and resources within relatively short distances led local populations to practice a variety of subsistence strategies, while also encouraging cooperation and exchange. Still, the formidable geographical barriers and uneven distribution of resources favored social and cultural diversity and inhibited imperial control by highly centralized states.

Nonetheless, Andean rulers strove to forge regional connections, promoting economic integration by bringing together diverse groups, resources, and technologies. These efforts met with some success. Careful use of the region's material wealth produced impressive achievements, most spectacularly in the monumental cities built in both the highlands and lowlands. Yet the challenges of the Andean environment and the resulting fragility of its agriculture continually threatened the social and political institutions that produced these achievements.

States and Societies in the Coastal Lowlands

Demise of the Moche and Rise of the Chimu

As we saw in Chapter 8, the earliest Andean states, Chavín and Moche, were founded in the arid coastal valleys of northern Peru. Moche, which had supplanted the earlier Chavín cultures by the first century C.E., was dominated by a powerful warrior elite who mobilized large numbers of forced laborers to build monumental pyramids and irrigation systems. But Moche was beset by climatic and political upheavals. In the early seventh century the grand ceremonial complex at Cerro Blanco was abandoned. Evidence from tree rings indicates that in the late sixth century the region suffered a drought lasting more than thirty years, followed by decades of unusually heavy rains and severe flooding, which partly destroyed Cerro Blanco's great pyramids in around 635. Scholars speculate that the El Niño currents might have caused these climatic upheavals. The largest late Moche city,

Pampa Grande, was burned to the ground in around 700. Whether the city's destruction resulted from domestic unrest or foreign invasion is unclear.

In the late ninth century a new state, Chimú (chee-MOO), arose in the Moche valley. Chimú's rulers, like the Moche leaders, depicted themselves as godlike figures and dramatized their authority through rituals of human sacrifice. But Chimú achieved far more political control over the coastal region than Moche had. It would thrive for over five centuries before succumbing to the Incas.

At its peak, the Chimú capital of Chan Chan comprised a vast maze of adobe-walled enclosures covering eight square miles. The city included at least nine palace compounds, residences for members of the royal clan who shared paramount rulership. There were also some thirty smaller residences of minor nobility and state officials, and densely packed barrios where the city's artisans, laborers, and traders lived in cramped dwellings made of mud-covered cane. Caravansaries (inns with large courtyards and stables) at the city's center welcomed llama caravans bringing trade goods from the highlands, especially alpaca wool, gold, silver, and copper.

Chan Chan was built on a barren plain near the Peruvian coast. Its inhabitants, and the power of its rulers, were nourished by irrigated agriculture and the construction of a much more extensive network of canals than that of Moche. In the thirteenth and fourteenth centuries the Chimú state expanded into neighboring valleys to tap additional land and water supplies. Military conquest was undoubtedly important in this expansion, but the stability of the Chimú state owed much more to trade and economic integration. Local rulers enjoyed substantial autonomy, and they had access to an enormous range of fine prestige goods produced in Chan Chan's workshops. Centuries later, Inca conquerors relocated large numbers of Chan Chan artisans to their capital at Cuzco after annexing Chimú in the 1460s.

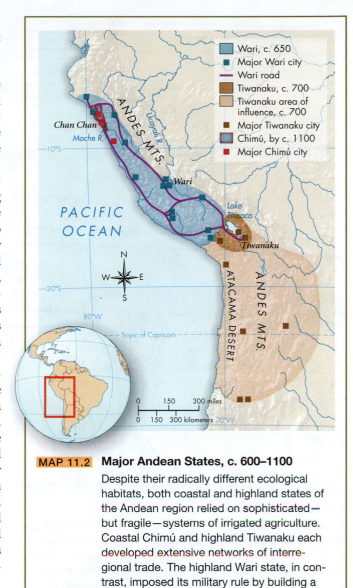

MAP 11.2 **Major Andean States, c. 600–1100**
Despite their radically different ecological habitats, both coastal and highland states of the Andean region relied on sophisticated—but fragile—systems of irrigated agriculture. Coastal Chimú and highland Tiwanaku each developed extensive networks of interregional trade. The highland Wari state, in contrast, imposed its military rule by building a series of fortified towns to control local populations.

States and Societies in the Andean Highlands

Inhabitants of the Andean highlands developed sophisticated agricultural systems to overcome the high altitude, erratic rainfall, and short growing season of the region. Indigenous crops, chiefly potatoes and quinoa (a native cereal), were the staples of the highland diet. Cultivation of raised fields constructed on cobblestone bases and fed by runoff of rain from the surrounding mountains began as early as 800 B.C.E.

Raised-field agriculture relied on an intricate system of irrigation but did not require complex technology, intensive labor, or large-scale organization. Local groups of farmers, known to the Inca as *ayllu* (aye-YOO), constructed the fields well before the appearance of complex political systems. The ayllu were essentially based on cooperative labor, though in some cases they relied on real or invented kinship ties to reinforce group solidarity. Ayllu typically owned lands in different locations and ecological zones (valley floors, hillsides, pasture) to minimize risk of crop failures. Groups of ayllu periodically pooled their labor to construct and maintain extensive networks of fields, canals, and causeways.

Raised-Field Farming

ayllu Groups of farmers (or other specialized occupations) in the Andean highlands who shared claims to common lands and a common ancestry.

Andean Agriculture

Farmers in the arid Andean highlands irrigated their fields with water stored in stone-lined reservoirs. The public benefits of irrigation encouraged the formation of cooperative labor groups known as ayllu. This depiction of Andean raised-field farming was included in a chronicle written by a native Peruvian in around 1615. (Photo: akg-images.)

In contrast to Mesoamerican peoples, who lacked economically useful domesticated animals, Andean peoples used the llama as a beast of burden and the alpaca as a source of meat and wool; the latter was especially important in this bitterly cold environment. Llama caravans traveled up and down the spine of the Andes ranges, trading in local specialties such as woolen cloth, pottery, and bone tools and utensils. Small towns near Lake Titicaca became trading posts that fed this growing interregional exchange. In the fifth century C.E. the city of Tiwanaku (tee-wah-NAH-coo), at the southern end of Lake Titicaca, became the dominant economic and political center of the region, serving as a crossroads connecting the environmentally diverse Andean communities (see again Map 11.2).

Tiwanaku included ceremonial centers with grand temples and public plazas, a large square stone-walled administrative center, and extensive residential barrios. At its peak between 500 and 800 the city may have housed as many as sixty thousand inhabitants, so it was roughly the same size as Chan Chan but less than one-third of Teotihuacán's maximum population. Some scholars believe that by this time Tiwanaku had developed from a major metropolis into a highly centralized state led by a small group of priestly clans or perhaps a royal dynasty. The power of the ruling elite rested on a highly ordered cosmology expressed through the precise spatial layout of the city and its lavish culture of rituals and feasting. The religious symbols and images of gods found at Tiwanaku were clearly ancestral to those of the Incas. As in Mesoamerica, public ceremony was central to religious and political life. The many drinking vessels and snuff tubes, spoons, and trays found among the ruins of Tiwanaku confirm that consumption of alcohol and hallucinogenic plants was important during these ceremonies. The prodigious drinking and eating at these events also provided occasions for rulers to demonstrate their generosity and to strengthen social and political bonds with their subjects (see Seeing the Past: Images of Power in Tiwanaku Art).

Tiwanaku's Broad Influence   The uniformity of Tiwanaku ceramic art and architecture, which came to be widely dispersed throughout the region, suggests that Tiwanaku's political ideology and craft traditions exercised a strong influence over local communities. Some scholars interpret Tiwanaku's pattern of development—intensification of agriculture, specialization of craft manufactures, road building, and resettlement of the population on farmland reclaimed from the lake bed—as evidence of strong state control. Others question the portrayal of Tiwanaku as a centralized empire whose rule rested on colonial domination and extraction of tribute. Although there is ample archaeological evidence of human sacrifice and display of decapitated enemies as trophies, Tiwanaku had no fortifications. Weapons and images of warfare are rare in Tiwanaku art, suggesting that the city's power derived more from its economic strength and religious ideology than from military aggression.

Wari's Militarized State   Tiwanaku was not the only significant political force in the Andean highlands. During the seventh and eighth centuries the city-state of Wari (WAH-ree), four hundred miles to the north, established a far-flung network of walled settlements in the highland valleys to its north and south, extending almost the entire length of modern Peru. In contrast to

Images of Power in Tiwanaku Art

Wool Tunic from Tiwanaku, c. 200–400 (Private Collection.)

The lack of written records leaves us with many mysteries about the composition, character, and even the names of the ruling elites who lived in the sumptuous palaces of the city of Tiwanaku. But artistic and architectural evidence gives important clues about the self-image of Tiwanaku's rulers. Decorated wool garments and tapestries provide us with rich visual materials of a sort rarely found for other ancient civilizations. The extreme dryness of the Andean highland environment preserved organic materials such as textiles that would have quickly disintegrated in humid climates.

Scholars interpret the dense patterns on the wool tunic shown here as a representation of Tiwanaku and its ruling powers. The face of a god, shown as a many-rayed sun, dominates the center. Below the god's face is a stepped structure that resembles the principal shrine at Tiwanaku. On the lowest tiers of this structure stand two winged figures with feline faces (their heads turned back over their

shoulders) and gold ankle bracelets. These figures are probably priests wearing ritual costumes.

Flanking the central images on each side are rows of human figures in elaborate dress holding staffs, arrows, or plants. All of the figures, like the central deity, have vertically divided eyes, which are thought to be a mark of ancestral or divine status. Three upturned animal heads are attached to each headdress, and each figure wears three gold ornaments on its chest. Yet the great variety of headdress styles, facial markings, and garment patterns indicates that each figure represents a specific identity, most likely the heads of the ruling lineages of Tiwanaku or the leaders of subordinate towns and social groups. The array of images suggests a religious festival or procession in which the leaders of human society pay homage to the gods and ancestors.

The Incas who later ruled the Andean region believed that festivals were occasions when the living could connect with their ancestors and invoke divine power to bring life-giving rain to their fields and pastures. The dominant images in Tiwanaku art suggest that the Tiwanaku shared such beliefs.

Source: From Margaret Young-Sánchez, ed., *Tiwanaku: Ancestors of the Inca* (Lincoln: University of Nebraska Press, 2004), 47, Figure 2.26a.

EXAMINING THE EVIDENCE

1. The figures in the wool tunic hold staffs that take the form of hybrid creatures with serpent bodies and feline (perhaps jaguar) heads. Why do you think Tiwanaku's leaders chose these animals to represent their power?

2. What does the emphasis on symmetry and repetition in Tiwanaku art, architecture, and urban design suggest about their rulers' ideas of social and cosmic order?

Tiwanaku, the Wari state set up military outposts to control and extract tribute from local populations.

Wari was located on a plateau at a lower altitude than Tiwanaku, but the region was drier and more dependent on irrigation for agriculture. Wari farmers grew maize along with highland crops such as the mainstays, potato and quinoa, in terraced fields constructed on hillsides and watered by canals. Tiwanaku and Wari shared a common religious heritage but had markedly different forms of religious practice. Wari architecture suggests a more exclusive ceremonial culture restricted to private settings and a small elite, in contrast to the grand temples and public plazas of Tiwanaku.

Decline of the Highland States

Archaeological evidence reveals that by the ninth century Wari's colonial empire had collapsed and new building in the city had come to a halt. In around 1000 the same fate befell Tiwanaku. Prolonged drought had upset the fragile ecological balance of raised-field agriculture, and food production declined drastically. The city of Tiwanaku was abandoned, and political power came to be widely dispersed among local chieftains solidly entrenched in hilltop forts. Highland peoples continued some irrigated agriculture, but they relied heavily on animal herds for subsistence. Incessant warfare merely produced a political standoff among local chiefdoms, with no escalation into conquest and expansion until the rise of the Inca Empire in the fifteenth century.

Agrarian Societies in North America

FOCUS

How did the introduction of Mesoamerican crops transform North American peoples?

North America, like the Andean region, long remained isolated from developments in Mesoamerica. The deserts of northern Mexico impeded movement of peoples and technologies from the centers of Mesoamerican civilization to the vast landmass to the north. Although North American peoples cultivated some native plants as food sources as early as 2000 B.C.E., agriculture did not emerge as a way of life in North America until maize was introduced from Mesoamerica in around 1000 B.C.E. (see again Mapping the World, page 340).

Maize first appeared in North America's southwestern deserts, but the transition to agriculture in this arid region was gradual and uneven. The eastern woodlands had a greater variety of subsistence resources and a longer tradition of settled life, yet here, too, Mesoamerican crops eventually stimulated the emergence of complex societies and expanding networks of communication and exchange (see Map 11.3).

Pueblo Societies in the Southwestern Deserts

Shift to Settled Life

Mesoamerican agriculture penetrated the deserts of northern Mexico and the southwestern United States slowly. Farmers gradually adapted Mesoamerican crops to this hot, arid environment by carefully selecting seeds, soils, and naturally irrigated lands for cultivation. But it was only after 200 C.E. that yields from growing crops encouraged the southwestern desert peoples to abandon gathering and hunting in favor of settled agriculture. Clay pots used for food storage and cooking also first appeared in the Southwest at this time. Another important cause of the shift to farming was, ironically, the bow and arrow, introduced by bison hunters of North America's Great Plains, also in around 200 C.E. By providing more protein from game, use of the bow and arrow made it easier to adopt maize, which supplies ample calories but is very low in protein, as a staple food.

Early agricultural settlements in the southwestern deserts tended to be small, loose clusters of oval pit dwellings. But even these small villages contained special buildings used for ritual purposes. These buildings were the forerunners of the *kivas*, or large ceremonial rooms, of the later pueblo societies in which people lived in large complexes of adjoining adobe buildings.

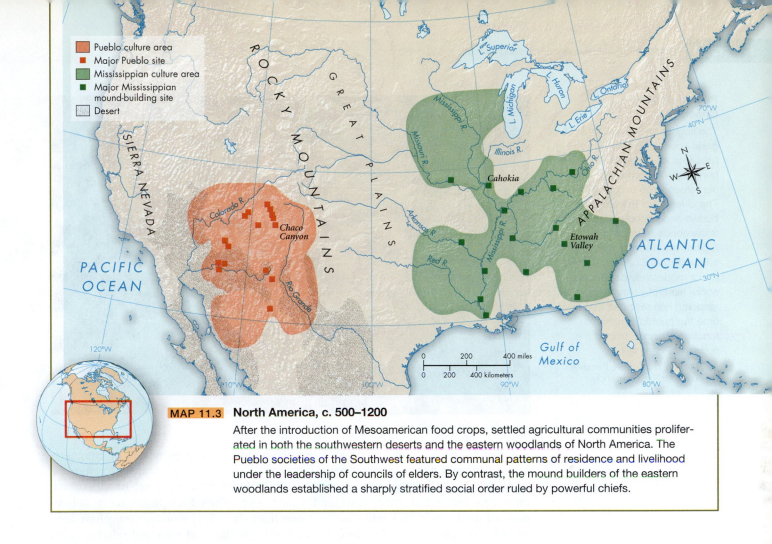

MAP 11.3 **North America, c. 500–1200**

After the introduction of Mesoamerican food crops, settled agricultural communities proliferated in both the southwestern deserts and the eastern woodlands of North America. The
Pueblo societies of the Southwest featured communal patterns of residence and livelihood
under the leadership of councils of elders. By contrast, the mound builders of the eastern
woodlands established a sharply stratified social order ruled by powerful chiefs.

Legend
- Pueblo culture area
- Major Pueblo site
- Mississippian culture area
- Major Mississippian mound-building site
- Desert

Pueblo Villages

The limited productivity of the land made self-sufficiency difficult. Farmers often
traded to obtain food as well as salt, stone for toolmaking, and prestige goods, including
hides and precious stones such as turquoise. After 700 C.E., population growth and
increasing dependence on agriculture led to replacement of the pithouse villages with
pueblos, in which hundreds or even thousands of people lived in contiguous buildings
constructed of adobe clay or stone. By 900, pueblo villages had spread throughout much of
the northern tier of the southwestern deserts, especially on the Colorado River plateau.

Chaco Canyon

Chaco Canyon, in northwestern New Mexico, dramatically illustrates the transformation of social life in the southwestern deserts as its agricultural livelihood matured. The first
villages, along with maize and squash agriculture, appeared in the canyon in around 500
C.E. The largest of these early villages consisted of no more than twenty pithouses. Between
700 and 900, large pueblos replaced the pithouse villages. The dwelling spaces in the pueblos were arranged in semicircular arcs so that each multiroom family unit was equidistant
from a central chamber, the **kiva** that served as the community's ceremonial nucleus.

During the tenth century, Chaco Canyon's population exploded. Much larger pueblos
with more than two hundred rooms appeared. By the twelfth century the canyon had thirteen of these large pueblos housing a population of approximately six thousand people.

Both large and small settlements in Chaco Canyon contained turquoise workshops
that manufactured a wide range of ritual ornaments. Because the nearest sources of turquoise were in the modern Santa Fe area, about one hundred miles to the east, craftsmen
had to obtain their raw material through trade or possibly tribute. Exchange networks
linked Chaco Canyon with at least seventy communities dispersed across more than ten
thousand square miles throughout the Colorado River plateau. These outlying settlements
also featured pueblo construction and were connected to Chaco Canyon by a network of

pueblo A communal village
built by the peoples of southwestern North America, consisting of adjoining flat-roofed
stone or adobe buildings
arranged in terraces.

kiva A large ceremonial chamber located at the center of the
pueblo.

Pueblo Bonito, Chaco Canyon

The largest of Chaco Canyon's great houses, Pueblo Bonito rose four stories and contained hundreds of rooms and numerous large circular kivas. The diversity of Pueblo Bonito's burials and artifacts—including trade goods from coastal regions and Mesoamerica—suggests that Chacoan society had a moderately developed social hierarchy. Archaeological research has revealed that over time the pueblo's primary function changed from residential complex to ceremonial center. (R. Perron/Art Resource, Art Resource, NY.)

rudimentary roads. Most likely the outlying communities were populated by emigrants forced to leave Chaco Canyon as population growth overburdened local food resources. Although Chaco Canyon may have served as a ritual hub for the entire web of settlements, centralized rule was absent even within the canyon's confines. Each pueblo seems to have pursued similar industrial, trade, and ceremonial activities. Historians generally have concluded that councils of elders coordinated these activities and managed relations with neighboring communities but that no privileged groups of families attained exclusive rights to political office. Hence in Chaco Canyon we see another example of the diversity of historical development. Agriculture led to population growth and large settlements, but, unlike in much of Eurasia, it did not lead to the emergence of kingship or empire building.

Abandonment of Chaco Canyon

In the early twelfth century prolonged drought weakened the canyon's fragile agricultural base. Many inhabitants migrated elsewhere, and others probably returned to foraging. Pueblo societies continued to flourish in other parts of the southwestern deserts where local conditions remained favorable to farming or trade. Although long-distance exchange continued, none of the other pueblo societies developed an integrated network of settlements like that of Chaco Canyon.

Some scholars believe that regional exchange and the founding of pueblo towns were stimulated by long-distance trade with merchants from the central Mexican highlands. Others contend that trade emerged in the southwestern deserts as a practical response to the unreliability of agriculture in this harsh environment. Environmental changes—especially soil exhaustion and increasingly irregular rainfall—may also have led to the abandonment of concentrated pueblo settlements and the return to more dispersed settlement beginning in the twelfth century. However, a similar trend toward concentration of political power and wider networks of exchange during the period 1000 to 1200, followed by a reversion to smaller and more isolated communities in the centuries before European contact, also occurred in the temperate woodlands of the Mississippi Valley, where livelihoods were less vulnerable to climatic change.

Mound-Building Societies in the Eastern Woodlands

Spread of Mesoamerican Agriculture

Beginning in around 700 C.E., the introduction of new technologies radically altered the evolution of eastern woodland societies in North America. The most important innovation was the cultivation of Mesoamerican food crops. The widespread cultivation of maize, perhaps prompted by greater control over labor and resources by a rising class of chiefs, revolutionized agriculture and transformed the woodlanders' economic livelihood. At the same time, the flint hoes that accompanied the spread of maize farming made it possible to construct mounds on a much larger scale, and the introduction of the bow and arrow from the Great Plains led to new hunting tactics.

The spread of Mesoamerican agriculture encouraged migration, regional exchange, and the formation of chiefdoms. Unlike the southwestern deserts, where the founding of settled communities followed the transition to agriculture, the eastern woodlands already had permanent villages. Still, population growth triggered by the capacity to produce more food led to greater occupational specialization and social complexity. Favorably located mound settlements conducted a lively trade in stone tools made from chert (a flintlike rock) and obsidian, marine shells from the Gulf of Mexico, and copper from the upper Great Lakes region, as well as salt, pottery, and jewelry. Population growth also caused friction among neighboring groups competing for land, and farmers displaced foragers from the river valleys best suited to agriculture.

As a result of these developments, the middle and lower reaches of the Mississippi River Valley experienced rapid economic and political changes. Scholars have given the name **Mississippian emergence** to the spread of common technologies, cultural practices, and forms of social and political organization among Mississippi Valley farming societies from the eighth century onward (see Lives and Livelihoods: The North American Mound Builders).

Although most Mississippian societies remained small, in some cases regional trading centers blossomed into powerful chiefdoms. The most famous is Cahokia (kuh-HOH-kee-uh), at the junction of the Illinois and Mississippi rivers just east of modern St. Louis. At its fullest extent, the settlement at Cahokia covered an area of eight square miles. Surrounded by four sets of wooden fortifications, it contained at least ten thousand people, and perhaps as many as thirty thousand. Cahokia's physical size and population thus were comparable to those of the city-states of ancient Mesopotamia, as well as Mesoamerica, in their formative stages of development.

Mound building at Cahokia began in around 900. From 1050 the pace of construction quickly accelerated, and by 1200 Cahokia's inhabitants had erected more than one hundred mounds surrounding a four-tiered pyramid set in the middle of four large plazas oriented north, south, east, and west. Five woodhenges (circles marked by enormous upright cedar posts) enclosed additional ceremonial sites.

Some of Cahokia's mounds were used for elite burials, but most served as platforms for buildings. The height of a mound was an index of prestige. The central pyramid, covering fourteen acres and rising over one hundred feet, was crowned by an enormous pole-and-thatch building covering five thousand square feet, which scholars believe was the residence of Cahokia's paramount chief. As was the case with the monuments of Mesoamerican cities, the placement of Cahokia's mounds was apparently determined by observations of crucial celestial events.

Also as in Mesoamerican cities, Cahokia's impressive mounds, plazas, and woodhenges displayed the power of its rulers to command labor and resources. The Grand Plaza of Cahokia served as a stage from which the chiefs presided over celebratory feasts, fiercely competitive games played with small stone disks known as chunkeys, and solemn death rites in which troops of young women, probably obtained as tribute from outlying areas, were sacrificed. Nonetheless, despite the similarity of Cahokia's plaza-and-pyramid

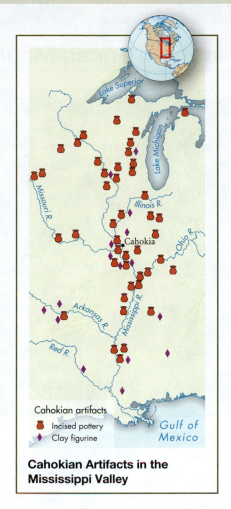

Cahokian Artifacts in the Mississippi Valley

Cahokian artifacts
- Incised pottery
- Clay figurine

Cahokia

Mississippian emergence The name scholars give to the spread of common technologies, cultural practices, and forms of social and political organization among a wide range of farming societies in the Mississippi Valley of North America, beginning in around 700 and peaking between 1000 and 1500.

The North American Mound Builders

Artist's Reconstruction of Cahokia

Compared to Chaco Canyon (see pages 357–358), Cahokia exhibited a more steeply graded social order. Moreover, in contrast to other mound-building societies—which gradually increased the size of their mounds—construction at Cahokia began with the massive pyramid and great plaza at its core. From the outset Cahokia's rulers displayed an ability to mobilize community labor on a scale unparalleled anywhere else in North America. (Richard Schlecht, National Geographic Image Collection.)

Scholars generally believe that the mounds built by North American woodlands societies symbolized the fertility of the earth and its inhabitants. The idea was that the act of building mounds renewed the fertility of the earth and the welfare of the community. Mound construction strengthened social solidarity by bringing people together in activities intended to ensure the prosperity of all. Moreover, mound building was accompanied by feasting that celebrated communal solidarity. Yet as the woodlands societies grew more complex and stratified, mound-building began to serve other purposes. Paramount chiefs and elite families often appropriated the mounds' symbolic power by reserving them as burial grounds for their exclusive use or by erecting temples on their summits to glorify their ancestors.

The Etowah (EE-toe-wah) River Valley in northwestern Georgia provides evidence of this process of social and political change. Here, as in many parts of the eastern

architecture to Mesoamerican prototypes, there is no evidence of direct Mesoamerican influence at Cahokia or other Mississippian mound-building sites. Indeed, archaeologists have not found imported Mesoamerican manufactured goods anywhere in the eastern woodlands. Although Mesoamerican beliefs and rituals may have had some influence on them, Cahokia's elite generated its own distinctive cosmology and ideology (see Seeing the Past: Symbols of Fertility in Cahokian Sculpture).

Cahokia's Influence

Following the abrupt and dramatic consolidation of power at Cahokia in around 1050, its influence radiated outward throughout the Mississippi Valley. A number of other regional centers, perhaps rivals of Cahokia, emerged from the area of modern Oklahoma to the Atlan-

woodlands, the adoption of maize agriculture led to greater social and political complexity. Etowah, which eventually boasted six mounds, became the region's major political center. It first achieved local prominence in the eleventh century, but over the next five centuries its history showed a cyclical pattern of development and abandonment.

In the eleventh century Etowah was a small settlement with residences, community buildings, and perhaps a small mound and plaza. Ritual life was confined to feasting, and there was a notable absence of prestige goods that would signify a strong social hierarchy. The earliest confirmed evidence of mound building dates from the twelfth century, when several other mound settlements appear in the Etowah Valley. Although these settlements were probably the capitals of independent chiefdoms, archaeological evidence of social ranking at this time is slim. Apparently these settlements were still organized around principles of community solidarity rather than hierarchy and stratification.

In the first half of the thirteenth century, the entire Etowah Valley was abandoned, for unknown reasons. When settlement resumed after 1250, a social transformation occurred. Over the next century mound building expanded dramatically, and a sharply stratified chiefdom emerged that exercised overlordship over at least four neighboring mound settlements. Monuments were built at the site, including a large ceremonial hall and a raised central plaza. In a burial mound reserved exclusively for Etowah's ruling elite, archaeologists have found prestige goods such as engraved shell ornaments, flint swords, embossed copper plates, and copper headdress ornaments. The wide dispersal of these items across the southeastern woodlands in the thirteenth and fourteenth centuries indicates that there were strong networks of regional exchange.

In Etowah and elsewhere in the region, wooden fortifications and ceremonial art featuring motifs of violence and combat testify to increasing political conflict and warfare. Copper plates depicting winged warriors found in Etowah burial mounds were almost certainly imported from the Mississippian heartland, if not from Cahokia itself.

The concentration of power that was evident in the Etowah chiefdom during the thirteenth and fourteenth centuries proved to be unstable. After 1375 Etowah and other large chiefdoms in the southeastern woodlands collapsed. The inhabitants again abandoned the site of Etowah. Regional trade networks became constricted, and the flow of prestige goods diminished. Whether chiefly authority was weakened by enemy attack or internal strife is uncertain. By the time the Spanish explorers arrived in 1540, another trend toward concentration of political power and expansion of territorial control was well under way. At this point, however, the capacity to organize mound building and the possession of prestige goods were no longer sufficient to claim political authority. Warfare had supplanted religious symbolism as the source of a chief's power.

QUESTIONS TO CONSIDER

1. In what ways did the purposes of the North American mound builders resemble those of the builders of monumental cities in Mesoamerica and the Andean region? In what ways did they differ?

2. How did changes in the structure and purpose of mound building at Etowah and Cahokia reflect new developments in social organization and the basis of political power in North American societies?

For Further Information:

King, Adam. *Etowah: The Political History of a Chiefdom Capital*. Tuscaloosa: University of Alabama Press, 2003.

Reilly, F. Kent, III, and James F. Garber, eds. *Ancient Objects and Sacred Realms: Interpretations of Mississippian Iconography*. Austin: University of Texas Press, 2007.

tic coast. Local chiefs imitated the mound building and sacred ceremonies of the Mississippian culture. Control of prestige goods acquired through trade enhanced the charismatic authority of these chiefs. Still, the power of the paramount chiefs at Cahokia and elsewhere rested on their alliances with lesser chiefs, who were the heads of their own distinct communities, rather than on direct control of the settled population. Political power thus remained fragile—vulnerable to shifts in trade patterns, economic fortunes, and political loyalties.

Cahokia declined after 1250 as competition from rival chiefs grew and as its farming base shrank due to prolonged droughts and deforestation. After 1300, Cahokia's inhabitants abandoned its grand ceremonial center and dispersed. Other smaller Mississippian

Cahokia's Collapse

Symbols of Fertility in Cahokian Sculpture

Birger Figurine (Courtesy of the Illinois State Archaeological Survey, University of Illinois.)

Mississippian peoples rarely incorporated images of humans and their activities into their art. Scholars have therefore closely scrutinized a small number of flint clay sculptures in the form of human beings for clues to Mississippian ideas about themselves and their world. These figurines mostly depict men engaged in battle, beheading enemies, and making offerings to ancestors and gods. Only in a few rare cases, such as the so-called Birger figurine shown here, do they include images of women.

Unearthed at Cahokia, the Birger figurine dates to the early twelfth century, the peak of Cahokia's dominance. It depicts a woman kneeling on a coiled snake, her left hand resting on the serpent's feline head (perhaps a puma) and her right hand holding a hoe. On her back she wears a square pack. Vines entwine the woman's body and stretch up her spine, putting forth fruit resembling squash or gourds. The figurine, discovered at a mortuary temple reserved for priests and nobles, was apparently deliberately broken during a ritual dedicated to the dead.

The association with serpents and agricultural tools and crops is typical among the small number of female Mississippian flint clay figures. Scholars generally agree that these symbols link the fertility of women as childbearers to the fertility of the earth. The snake symbolizes the earth itself, which the woman cultivates with her hoe. The plants and fruit wrapped around the woman's body signify both the fertility of women and their prominent role in farming. Images of the land and farming appear only in connection with female figures in Mississippian art.

Some scholars go further to argue that the Birger figurine and similar objects express a mythology in which women are associated with an underworld (symbolized by the serpent) that is the source of water, fertility, and the power of water-dwelling monsters. Male chiefs and warriors, by contrast, appear together with signs of the heavens, such as the sun and birds. The imagery of the Birger figurine also suggests a connection to the Earth Mother or Corn Mother myths that recur frequently in the ceremonial traditions of later eastern woodland peoples. The Earth Mother symbolized the life-giving power of plants and women, as well as the cycles of regeneration in which crops sprung from seeds and the souls of the dead were reborn in children. The Earth Mother thus was a goddess of both life and death.

Mississippian art and mythology exhibit a profound dualism: the underworld associated with women and water is strictly divided from the upper world of men and its motifs of sun, fire, and birds. This rigid gender segregation undoubtedly reflects a society that sharply separated the spheres, activities, and powers of men and women.

Source: Birger Figurine: From Rinita A. Dalan et al., *Envisioning Cahokia: A Landscape Perspective* (DeKalb: Northern Illinois University Press, 2003), 202, Figure 47. (Courtesy of Illinois Transportation Archaeological Research Program, University of Illinois.)

EXAMINING THE EVIDENCE

1. In what ways do Mississippian ideas about female qualities and powers, as revealed in the Birger figurine, differ from the Mesoamerican conception of masculine power expressed by the "At a Crossroads" ballplayer illustration on page 338?

2. Why would the priests break objects such as this figurine during the rituals performed in honor of the dead?

chiefdoms persisted down to the first contacts with Europeans in the sixteenth century and beyond. But in the wake of Cahokia's collapse, long-distance economic and cultural exchanges waned, and the incidence of violence grew. The prevalence of warrior imagery, the concentration of the population in fortified towns, and the ample evidence of traumatic death from excavated cemeteries all point to the emergence of warfare as a way of life.

The scale and complexity of the settlements and ritual complexes at Cahokia were unique in North America. Yet its influence as a panregional cultural force is reminiscent of other urban centers in the Americas. As in Tiwanaku, feasting, sacrifice, and resettlement of rural inhabitants in the urban core forged a distinctive cultural identity at Cahokia. Also like Tiwanaku, Cahokia apparently served as a ritual center for a group of independent chiefdoms that for a time merged into a single political entity. At the peak of its power, Cahokia's culinary habits, pottery styles, and agricultural techniques spread over a vast area. In this sense, as an economic and political crossroads, Cahokia was central to the emergence of a distinctive Mississippian society.

Habitat and Adaptation in the Pacific Islands

The Lapita colonization (see Chapter 8) transformed the landscapes and seascapes of the western Pacific, or Near Oceania. After approximately 200 B.C.E., though, what historians call the "long pause" in transoceanic migrations set in. Subsequently the cultural unity spawned by the Lapita migrations fragmented as local groups adapted to their diverse island habitats. Trade networks collapsed, and pottery making declined everywhere.

> **FOCUS**
>
> In what ways did the habitats and resources of the Pacific Islands promote both cultural unity and cultural diversity?

The "long pause" may reflect not people's lack of effort, but rather their lack of success in making landfall on the smaller and far more widely dispersed islands of the central and eastern Pacific, or Remote Oceania. But in around 300 C.E. (some scholars would say even several centuries earlier), a new wave of migration began with a leap eastward of more than twelve hundred miles from Samoa to the Marquesas and Society Island archipelagoes. This second wave of exploration brought human colonists to virtually every habitable island in the Pacific Ocean by the year 1000 (see Map 11.4).

In Near Oceania, the interaction of the Lapita peoples with the native Papuan societies had generated extraordinary cultural diversity. In contrast, this second wave of migrations into the farthest reaches of Remote Oceania fostered a culturally unified set of islands known as Polynesia. Still, Polynesian settlers did modify their livelihoods and social and political institutions to suit the resources of their island habitats. **Human ecology**—the ways in which people adapt to their natural environment—was as flexible in the Pacific Islands as in the world's great continental landmasses.

Polynesian Expansion

The Pacific Islands are commonly divided into three parts: Melanesia ("Middle Islands"), Micronesia ("Small Islands"), and Polynesia ("Many Islands"). Yet Melanesia makes sense only as a geographic label, not as a social or cultural unit. In fact, the peoples of Melanesia (if we include New Guinea) make up the most diverse and complex assembly of peoples and cultures on earth. Similarly, Micronesia had at least two major language groups and was populated over the course of four separate periods of immigration.

Polynesian societies, in contrast, share a strong social and cultural identity. Polynesian culture emerged from the Lapita settlements of Tonga and Samoa in the first millennium B.C.E. Following the leap to the Marquesas and Society archipelagoes, Polynesians spread through a chain of migrations westward into Micronesia, northward to the Hawaiian Islands, and eastward as far as Easter Island.

human ecology Adaptation of people to the natural environment they inhabit.

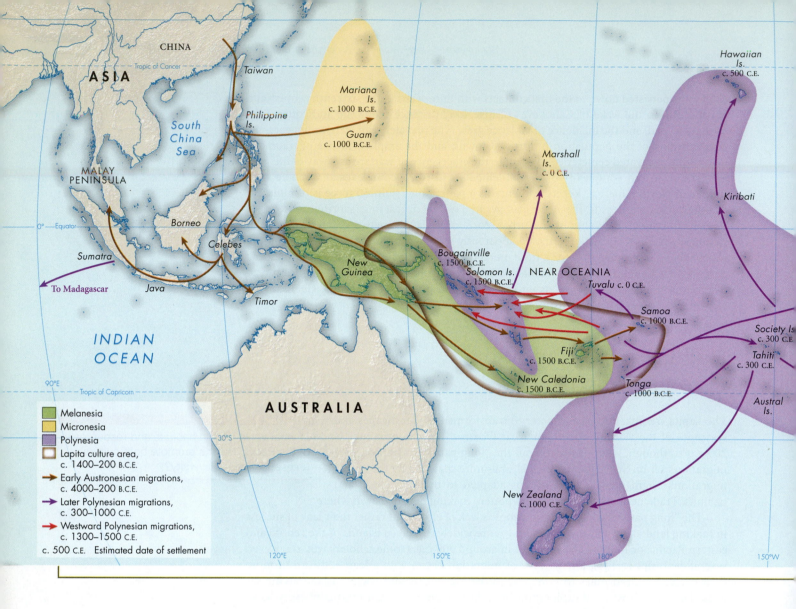

Melanesia
Micronesia
Polynesia
Lapita culture area,
c. 1400–200 B.C.E.
Early Austronesian migrations,
c. 4000–200 B.C.E.
Later Polynesian migrations,
c. 300–1000 C.E.
Westward Polynesian migrations,
c. 1300–1500 C.E.
c. 500 C.E.   Estimated date of settlement

Polynesia's Cultural Unity

Like the Lapita colonization, the Polynesian expansion included a cycle of vigorous interisland interactions during the initial phase of colonization, followed by progressive isolation and interruption of communication and exchange. The most remote parts of Polynesia, such as Easter Island and the Hawaiian archipelago, became solitary worlds.

The distinctive character of Polynesian societies owes much to their isolation. Fiji was virtually unique in maintaining exchanges of goods, people, and cultural influences with Melanesian societies; Tonga and the rest of Polynesia lost all contact with Melanesia. But however isolated the Polynesian societies of the central Pacific became, their recent common ancestry gave them similar languages, social practices, and forms of livelihood. One striking feature of the Polynesian expansion was the widespread abandonment of pottery manufacture. In contrast to the Lapita peoples, who regarded elaborately decorated pottery as a sign of high social rank, pottery—for reasons still unknown—lost its status as a prestige good among the Polynesians. Pottery was also replaced by coconut shells and wooden bowls for utilitarian purposes such as storing and cooking food.

Although Polynesian settlers had reached all of the habitable Pacific Islands by 1000, migration among settled islands continued. In around the year 1300 Polynesian voyagers would begin to travel westward into Micronesia and the southern parts of Melanesia. On some small islands, such as Tikopia (TEE-co-pi-ah) in Melanesia, Polynesians would wholly replace the native population, but more commonly the migrants mixed with the native peoples to produce hybrid cultures. Micronesian peoples, living in unstable envi-

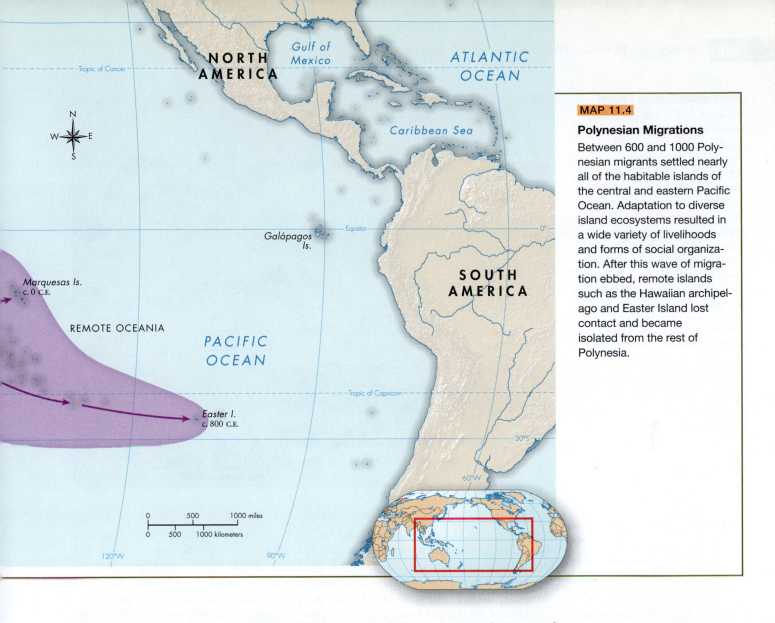

MAP 11.4

Polynesian Migrations
Between 600 and 1000 Polynesian migrants settled nearly all of the habitable islands of the central and eastern Pacific Ocean. Adaptation to diverse island ecosystems resulted in a wide variety of livelihoods and forms of social organization. After this wave of migration ebbed, remote islands such as the Hawaiian archipelago and Easter Island lost contact and became isolated from the rest of Polynesia.

ronments with limited resources, displayed enormous flexibility in changing their ways of life and welcoming strangers into their communities.

Distinctive ecosystems nurtured a wide range of livelihoods and political systems across the Polynesian Pacific. Larger islands with richer and more varied resources, among them Tahiti, Tonga, and Hawaii, gave rise to highly stratified societies and complex chiefdoms with tens of thousands of subjects. The rigid hierarchical structure of the Polynesian chiefdoms was based on command of economic resources. The vast majority in their populations were landless commoners. Local chiefs held title to cultivated lands but owed **fealty** (allegiance to a higher authority) and tribute to paramount chiefs, who wielded sacred power over entire islands (as we will see in Chapter 12's Counterpoint on the Hawaiian Islands, page 398).

Ecosystems and Social Stratification

Subsistence and Survival in the Pacific Islands

Counter to the romantic fantasies of nineteenth-century European travelers and twentieth-century anthropologists, the Pacific Islands were not pristine natural worlds undisturbed by their "primitive" human inhabitants. On the contrary, human hands had radically transformed the island ecosystems. For example, the islands of Remote Oceania originally lacked plant and animal species suitable for human food consumption. Polynesian settlers changed all that by bringing with them pigs, dogs, chickens, yams, taro, sugar cane,

fealty An expression of allegiance to a higher political authority, often verified by swearing an oath of loyalty, giving tribute, and other gestures of submission.

Polynesian Sailing Vessel
Although the age of great long-distance voyaging had ceased by the time Europeans reached the Pacific, Polynesians continued to make open-ocean journeys of hundreds of miles. In 1616 a Dutch mariner drew this illustration of a Polynesian double-hulled canoe sailing between Tonga and Samoa. The largest Polynesian canoes were roughly the same length as the sailing vessels of the European explorers. (*A Chronological History of the Voyages & Discoveries in the South Sea or Pacific Ocean*, London: Lake Hansard & Sons.)

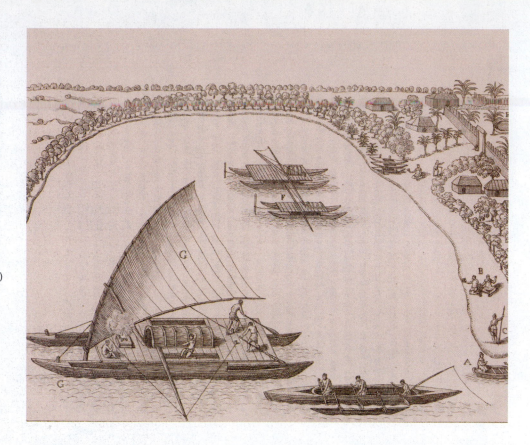

bananas, coconuts, breadfruit, and various medicinal and fiber plants. The intrusion of these alien species and human manipulation of fragile island landscapes had large and long-lasting consequences for both the environment and its human inhabitants. In many places native bird, turtle, and sea mammal species were hunted to extinction, and **deforestation**, the cutting down of forests, sharply reduced the islands' natural resources.

Environmental Transformation and Population Growth

Most of the tropical food plants transported by colonizers readily thrived in the Pacific Islands. Settlers practiced horticulture (the cultivation of fruits and vegetables), planting orchards of coconuts and bananas around their villages while cutting down rain forests to make room for root and tuber crops that required little care. As in Iceland's early history (see Chapter 9), explosive population growth typically followed initial settlement on uninhabited islands. Settlers had a compelling reason—fear of extinction—to have enough children to attain populations large enough to maintain their societies. Population densities on many islands reached 250 persons per square mile. Ecological constraints, however, ultimately curbed unrestricted population growth.

Micronesia's low-lying atolls—rings of coral surrounding a central lagoon—presented the most challenging environments. Exposed to destruction by typhoons and tsunamis, lacking fresh water other than rainfall, with just sand and crushed coral for soil, atolls offered only slender footholds for human colonists. Because cultivating taro and breadfruit was impossible on many coral atolls, coconut trees were essential to human survival. In addition to depending on coconuts for food, atoll dwellers used coconut leaves for textile fiber and for construction material. Lacking ceramics and metals, the atoll peoples fashioned utensils and tools from coconuts, seashells, and fish bones.

deforestation The cutting down of forests, usually to clear land for farming and human settlement.

On many islands, population pressure began to strain resources after 1100. Where possible, islanders applied more laborious agricultural methods, building irrigation canals and terraced or walled garden plots. In the Marquesas, swelling population growth increased competition and warfare. More fortified villages were built, and the authority of warrior chiefs rose. Settlement became concentrated in the island interiors, which afforded not only protection from sea raiders but lands more suitable for intensive cultivation. A similar pattern of intensified agriculture and warfare in response to population pressure appeared in Fiji. The growing diversity of local ceramic styles in Fiji also suggests a greater demarcation of ethnic groups and political boundaries. Here, too, constant warfare shifted the basis of chiefship from priestly duties to military leadership.

The most striking example of the fragility of island ecosystems and the risk of demographic catastrophe is Easter Island. When Polynesian voyagers originally settled Easter Island sometime after 600 C.E., the island was well endowed with fertile soils and abundant forests. These rich resources supported a population that at its peak numbered ten thousand people. Easter Island's famous stone monuments—thirty-ton sculptures believed to be images of ancestors who were transformed into gods—were carved and installed on more than two hundred temple platforms across the island between 1100 and 1500. But the clearing of forests for agriculture depleted fuel and construction resources, and erosion and exposure to wind and surf ruined soil fertility. After 1500, the island was plunged into incessant raiding and warfare, accompanied by ritual cannibalism. Construction of stone monuments halted. As the once plentiful flora and fauna of Easter Island were decimated, its human population dwindled to a mere several hundred persons subsisting mainly on fishing, the Pacific Ocean's most reliable resource.

Increased Competition and Warfare

Easter Island

COUNTERPOINT
Social Complexity in Bougainville

Bougainville (bow-gahn-VEEL), one of the chain of islands stretching in a long arc southeastward from New Guinea, typifies the phenomenon of **ethnogenesis**, the formation of separate ethnic groups from common ancestors. In contrast to the underlying social and cultural unity of many of the societies studied in this chapter, the long-settled islands of Melanesia display extraordinary social and cultural diversity. The complexity of the Melanesian world presents an important challenge for any theory of the evolution of human societies. Here the progress of history fostered not closer interaction and cross-cultural borrowing but rather more acute social differences and strong ethnic boundaries.

> **FOCUS**
>
> Why did the historical development of the Melanesian island of Bougainville depart so sharply from that of contemporaneous societies in the Americas and the Pacific?

Bougainville's Diverse Peoples

Situated slightly below the equator, Bougainville has a tropical climate with virtually no seasonal variation, enabling the island's farmers to cultivate food crops, mainly taro, year-round. Yet with four active volcanoes, Bougainville is one of the most geologically unstable places on earth. Volcanic eruptions have periodically covered major portions of the island with ash and forced the inhabitants to relocate, at least temporarily. The island, roughly the size of Puerto Rico, is sparsely populated even today. The mountainous interior remains virtually uninhabited. Settlements are concentrated along streams on the relatively flat terrain of the northern coast and in the southern interior.

Twenty different languages are spoken on Bougainville today. Scholars classify twelve of these languages as Austronesian (AW-stroh-NEE-zhuhn), the language group of the seafarers who settled in the islands of Southeast Asia and the Pacific during the Lapita colonization. Linguists broadly define the rest as Papuan (PAH-poo-en), the languages spoken by the ancient inhabitants of New Guinea, although their relationship to the other Papuan languages is uncertain. Four of Bougainville's languages are so idiosyncratic that the associations among them confound linguists.

Linguistic and Cultural Diversity

ethnogenesis The formation of separate ethnic groups from common ancestors.

Bougainville

Beyond the striking language differences, Bougainville's inhabitants also vary so much in stature, body type, and biological chemistry that Bougainville islanders rank among the most genetically diverse populations on the planet. Cultural variation is similarly striking. Although pottery manufacture on Bougainville dates back to the pre-Lapita era, some groups apparently have never made pottery and rarely sought ceramic wares from those who did.

What accounts for such remarkable diversity within the confines of this one island? One popular theory is that the kind of tropical agriculture practiced in Bougainville is relatively rich and reliable, and so the islanders have not had to build trading networks or other kinds of connections between communities to meet their needs. Traditions of matrilineal descent and local **endogamy**— marriage within the group—reinforced this pattern of isolated village life. The social isolation of individual villages also tended to raise language barriers over time. With two exceptions, the geographical range of the languages spoken on Bougainville does not exceed fifteen miles in diameter. Further, as modern biological research shows, small populations are more likely to experience large genetic fluctuations from one generation to the next, which fosters more, not less, genetic diversity. Not surprisingly, genetic variation among Bougainville's modern populations correlates strongly with language groups.

The Historical Roots of Social Difference

Yet the diversity of Bougainville's languages did not result from a long period of isolation. The island probably experienced a number of separate immigrations both before and after the Lapita era. The island's Austronesian speakers did not simply all arrive together at the time of the Lapita migrations. There is clear evidence that some coastal regions were resettled by Austronesian speakers after volcanic eruptions displaced the previous inhabitants.

The Siwai and the Buin: A Case Study

Further, it is not possible to make neat distinctions between the cultures of "native" Papuan speakers and "immigrant" Austronesian speakers. The Siwai (sih-why), a Papuan-speaking community in southern Bougainville, is noted in anthropological theory as a model **big man society**. According to the American anthropologist Marshall Sahlins, so-called big man societies are characterized by an egalitarian social structure and strong communal identity based on sharing and reciprocal exchange. The role of the big man is to redistribute wealth among members of the community to ensure the well-being of all, but the big man does not hold a position above the rest of society. Sahlins has contrasted Melanesian big man societies with the sharply stratified social hierarchy of Polynesian chiefdoms, in which a hereditary elite of chiefs monopolized political power and the control of economic resources. Near the Siwai in southern Bougainville, however, is another Papuan-speaking group, the Buin (boo-een), whose society developed the high degree of stratification and inherited rank and privilege typical of Polynesian chiefdoms.

Environmental adaptation does not explain the different social structures of the Siwai and the Buin: the two groups occupy virtually identical habitats, practice similar forms of irrigated taro agriculture, and speak closely related languages. Despite their similar livelihoods, the Siwai and Buin embraced different notions of prestige and status. For example, the Buin regarded pottery making as women's work, whereas the Siwai, uniquely among Melanesian societies, reserve pottery making exclusively for men. Scholars have explained this peculiar feature of Siwai culture as a consequence of the unusually cloistered life of Siwai women. According to this theory, knowledge of pottery making was acquired by men, who, unlike women, could travel outside the village, and it became a mark of their superior status.

This contrast underscores one important difference between the Buin and their Siwai neighbors. The Buin had access to the coast and, unlike the Siwai, interacted with peoples in neighboring islands. They learned their techniques of pottery making from Austronesian-speaking inhabitants of the nearby Shetland Islands in around 1000. Indeed, immigrants

endogamy Marriage within a defined group, such as a village or a kinship network.

big man society In modern anthropological theory, an egalitarian society in which a chosen leader, the "big man," supervises the distribution of the community's collective wealth and resources.

from the Shetlands probably arrived in southern Bougainville at that time and may have been absorbed into Buin society.

Yet differences in contact with the outside world cannot fully explain the variations in social practices among Bougainville societies. Some scholars have suggested that in the past, a more pronounced social hierarchy was common in Melanesian societies. In their view, the egalitarian big man societies for which Melanesia became the model were not ancient or primitive forms of social organization; rather, they resulted from the profound changes set in motion by contact with Europeans, including population losses from disease. At the very least, we can no longer attribute the complex human ecology of Melanesia in general, and of Bougainville in particular, to the former historical interpretation of unchanging island cultures cut off from the march of history by the encircling ocean.

Conclusion

During the period 300 to 1200, distinctive regional cultures coalesced in many parts of the Americas and the Pacific Islands. As in Latin Christendom and East Asia, the spread and intensification of agriculture, expanding networks of trade and cultural exchange, and the founding of cities and states led to the formation of common civilizations.

This period marked the classical age in Mesoamerica and the Andean region. There, the development of urban societies and states generated lasting traditions concerning knowledge, livelihoods, and social organization. Rulers such as the Maya Holy Lord Eighteen Rabbit built monumental cities and conducted elaborate public rituals to display their supreme power and bind their subjects to their will.

Permanent towns and long-distance networks of exchange also developed in North America. The spread of prestige goods and ritual art in the eastern woodlands and the southwestern deserts also indicates active cross-cultural borrowing in these regions, at least among elites.

The rapid peopling of the islands of Remote Oceania between 600 and 1000 gave this vast region a common cultural identity as Polynesia. Similar political and social structures and forms of livelihood took root across Polynesia, even though many island populations, such as those of the Hawaiian archipelago and Easter Island, lost contact with the outside world.

Striking, too, are patterns of regional diversity. Different types of social order evolved as new crops and technologies diffused and were adopted, people adjusted social and political institutions and forms of livelihood to new or transformed habitats, and notions of prestige, status, and authority changed. In all of these regions—even among the small village societies of Bougainville, which mostly shunned contact and interaction with their neighbors—social identities and community boundaries changed constantly. Ethnogenesis was a dynamic, continuous, and open-ended process.

By the year 1200, many of these societies were suffering from economic decline and political fragmentation. Scholars have attributed the collapse of the Maya city-state network in the ninth century, the disintegration of the Tiwanaku state in around 1000, and the abandonment of Chaco Canyon and Cahokia in the twelfth and thirteenth centuries primarily to ecological causes: either some climatic catastrophe, or the inability of the existing agricultural technologies and political systems to provide for their growing populations. The collapse of these societies reminds us of the fragility of their agricultural systems, still limited to Stone Age technologies, and their vulnerability to long-term ecological and climatic changes. As we shall see in the next chapter, advances in agricultural and industrial technology and the development of new economic institutions in Eurasia during the eleventh to thirteenth centuries laid the foundations for more sustained economic and demographic growth.

RESOURCES FOR RESEARCH

General Works

Our knowledge of the history of all the societies in this chapter except the Maya depends on research in fields such as archaeology and linguistics rather than written sources. The essays in Quilter and Miller use broad comparative and interdisciplinary analysis to survey the Americas as a whole in the era before the arrival of Europeans. Diamond's provocative analysis of human responses to ecological crises and the collapse of social systems includes case studies of Easter Island, the southwestern deserts of North America, and the Maya.

Diamond, Jared. *Collapse: How Societies Choose to Fail or Succeed.* 2004.

Quilter, Jeffrey, and Mary Miller, eds. *A Pre-Columbian World.* 2006.

Renfrew, Colin, and Steven Shennan, eds. *Peer Polity Interaction and Socio-Political Change.* 1986.

The Classical Age of Mesoamerica and Its Aftermath

The scholarship on the Maya is especially rich. Drew provides an excellent overview of both Maya civilization and the development of scholarship on the Maya. Carrasco's study of the Feathered Serpent is a pioneering investigation of the common cultural heritage of Mesoamerica as a whole.

Carrasco, David. *Quetzalcoatl and the Irony of Empire: Myth and Prophecies in the Aztec Tradition*, rev. ed. 2000.

Drew, David. *The Lost Chronicles of the Maya Kings.* 1999.

Pasztory, Esther. *Teotihuacan: An Experiment in Living.* 1997.

Schele, Linda, and Peter Mathews. *The Code of Kings: The Language of Seven Sacred Maya Temples and Tombs.* 1998.

Sharer, Robert J. *Daily Life in Maya Civilization*, 2d ed. 2009.

City and State Building in the Andean Region

Recent studies have sought to trace the social and political evolution of precolonial Andean societies through comparative studies of archaeological remains. Kolata's study remains the most thorough examination of Tiwanaku's archaeological record. Janusek proposes new models for understanding the formation of social identity and political power in the Andean region in a very accessible fashion.

Janusek, John Wayne. *Ancient Tiwanaku.* 2008.

Janusek, John Wayne. *Identity and Power in the Ancient Andes: Tiwanaku Cities Through Time.* 2004.

Kolata, Alan. *The Tiwanaku: Portrait of an Andean Civilization.* 1993.

Stanish, Charles. *Ancient Titicaca: The Evolution of Complex Society in Southern Peru and Northern Bolivia.* 2003.

von Hagen, Adriana, and Craig Morris. *The Cities of the Ancient Andes.* 1998.

Agrarian Societies in North America

Reconstruction of the history of North American societies during this period relies especially heavily on the fruits of archaeological research. Fagan's skill at weaving up-to-date coverage of new archaeological evidence into a compelling narrative is displayed in both his textbook survey of North American societies and his Chaco Canyon volume.

Emerson, Thomas E. *Cahokia and the Archaeology of Power.* 1997.

Fagan, Brian. *Ancient North America: The Archaeology of a Continent*, rev. ed. 2005.

Fagan, Brian. *Chaco Canyon: Archaeologists Explore the Lives of an Ancient Society.* 2005.

Milner, George R. *The Moundbuilders: Ancient Peoples of Eastern North America.* 2005.

Pauketat, Timothy R. *Ancient Cahokia and the Mississippians.* 2004.

Habitat and Adaptation in the Pacific Islands

Kirch's 2000 book provides the most comprehensive survey of settlement and social development in the Pacific Islands, and the essays in Howe focus on voyaging and exploration. Challenging the idea of universal stages of social evolution, Earle marshals evidence from case studies of Denmark, Hawaii, and the Andes to distinguish the sources of power in chiefdom societies.

Earle, Timothy. *How Chiefs Come to Power: The Political Economy in Prehistory.* 1997.

Howe, K. R., ed. *Vaka Moana, Voyages of the Ancestors: The Discovery and Settlement of the Pacific.* 2007.

Kirch, Patrick V. *The Evolution of the Polynesian Chiefdoms.* 1984.

Kirch, Patrick V. *On the Road of the Winds: An Archaeological History of the Pacific Islands Before European Contact.* 2000.

Terrell, John. *Prehistory in the Pacific Islands: A Study of Variation in Language, Customs, and Human Biology.* 1986.

COUNTERPOINT: Social Complexity in Bougainville

Since the 1930s anthropologists have considered Melanesia, and Bougainville in particular, as a laboratory for the study of social evolution. The classic works by Sahlins and Service drew on extensive cross-cultural comparisons to develop highly influential models of the emergence of complex social organization and political hierarchy in human societies.

Sahlins, Marshall. *Social Stratification in Polynesia.* 1958.

Service, Robert. *Origins of the State and Civilization: The Process of Cultural Evolution.* 1975.

Spriggs, Matthew. *The Island Melanesians.* 1997.

▶ **For additional primary sources from this period**, see *Sources of Crossroads and Cultures*.

▶ **For Web sites, images, and documents related to topics in this chapter**, see Make History at bedfordstmartins.com/smith.

The major global development in this chapter ▶ The formation of distinctive regional cultures in the Americas and the Pacific Islands between 300 and 1200.

IMPORTANT EVENTS

c. 150–300	Building of the city of Teotihuacán in the Valley of Mexico
c. 250–900	Mesoamerica's classical age
c. 500	First permanent settlements in Chaco Canyon
c. 500–1000	Andean state of Tiwanaku
c. 550–650	Fall and destruction of Teotihuacán
c. 600–1000	Polynesian settlement of Pacific Islands
c. 700	Moche city of Pampa Grande destroyed
c. 700–900	Heyday of the Andean state of Wari
c. 800–900	Collapse of the Maya city-states
c. 850–1150	Building of the large pueblos in Chaco Canyon
c. 900	Rise of the Chimú state centered at Chan Chan
c. 950–1150	Toltec state's reign as the dominant power in the Valley of Mexico
c. 1050	Consolidation of Cahokia's dominance in the lower Mississippi Valley region
c. 1100–1500	Construction of Easter Island's stone monuments
c. 1150	Abandonment of the pueblos in Chaco Canyon
c. 1250–1300	Collapse and abandonment of Cahokia

KEY TERMS

ayllu (p. 353)
big man society (p. 368)
chiefdom (p. 343)
ch'ulel (p. 347)
city-state (p. 343)
deforestation (p. 366)
endogamy (p. 368)
ethnogenesis (p. 367)
fealty (p. 365)

Holy Lord (p. 347)
human ecology (p. 363)
kiva (p. 357)
Mississippian emergence (p. 359)
obsidian (p. 344)
prestige good (p. 344)
pueblo (p. 357)
Tollan (p. 344)

CHAPTER OVERVIEW QUESTIONS

1. How did these societies, equipped with only Stone Age technology, develop the institutions and patterns of exchange to tame often hostile environments and build complex civilizations?

2. How did differences in environment foster or discourage exchanges among adjacent regions?

3. What were the sources of political power in the societies discussed in this chapter, and how were they similar or dissimilar?

4. How did differences in urban design reflect distinctive forms of political and social organization?

SECTION FOCUS QUESTIONS

1. What common beliefs and social and political patterns did the various local societies of Mesoamerica's classical age share?

2. How did environmental settings and natural resources shape livelihoods, social organization, and state building in the Andean region?

3. How did the introduction of Mesoamerican crops transform North American peoples?

4. In what ways did the habitats and resources of the Pacific Islands promote both cultural unity and cultural diversity?

5. Why did the historical development of Bougainville depart so sharply from that of contemporaneous societies in the Americas and the Pacific?

MAKING CONNECTIONS

1. Why were the human populations of the regions covered in this chapter more vulnerable to ecological changes than the settled societies of Eurasia?

2. How did the political and social organization of North American chiefdoms compare with those of the Maya city-states?

3. Although North America's eastern woodlands farmers began to cultivate the same food crops as Mesoamerican peoples during the Mississippian emergence, their societies developed in different ways. What might explain these variations?

371

12

القــرآن ثمّ وأبعد اساطير لأها ورخارف جلّها وقال ازكبوا فيها بسم اللّه مجراها
ومسـاهاته ثمّ نفس نفس المغرمين أوعباد اللّه للكرمين وقال لها انا

AT A CROSSROADS ▶

Arabs and Persians dominated the Indian Ocean trade routes, but by the eleventh century Indian and Malay mariners also plied Asian seas from Africa to China. This thirteenth-century illustration depicts a dhow, the most common type of Indian Ocean sailing vessel, on a voyage from East Africa to Basra, the great port linking Mesopotamia to the Persian Gulf. Indian Ocean trade vastly expanded cultural as well as economic exchange: although the passengers are Arabs, the crew appears to be Indian. (Bibliothèque Nationale, Paris, France/Bildarchiv Preussischer Kulturbesitz/Art Resource, NY.)

The Rise of Commerce in Afro-Eurasia

900–1300

Early in the twelfth century, the Jewish merchant Allan bin Hassun wrote home from Aden, in Yemen on the coast of the Arabian Sea, upon his return from India. Allan had been sent to Yemen by his father-in-law, a prominent Cairo cloth merchant, to sell the purple-dyed cloth that was the father-in-law's specialty. But the cloth had proved unprofitable, so Allan persuaded his reluctant father-in-law to supply him with coral and perfume for a trading venture to India. The journey to India and back had been long and dangerous, and Allan's return had been delayed repeatedly by local uprisings, storms, and accidents.

Upon finally reaching Aden, Allan reported, "I sold the iron for a good price, 20 gold dinars a *bahar* [one bahar equaled 300 pounds]. I had with me 72 bahars and 50 separate pieces, 30 *mann* [one mann equaled 2 pounds] of spices, and 40 mann of cloves. After customs I had obtained 1500 dinars and a lot in other currencies." Allan had intended to return to Cairo, but the high prices that pepper fetched in Aden instead spurred him to immediately set out for India again.

Only fragments of Allan's correspondence survive today, and we do not know how he fared during his return voyage to India. But however successful he was as a businessman, Allan's long sojourns took their toll on his family. In a letter his wife sent to Allan in North

BACKSTORY

The collapse of the Han Empire in China and the Western Roman Empire ended a prolonged era of growth in agriculture and trade in the agrarian heartlands of Eurasia (see Chapters 6 and 7). The steppe nomad invasions devastated many cities in China, India, and the Roman Empire's former territories. Political disunity hindered efforts to revive agriculture and commerce. Yet the rise of steppe empires such as that of the Turks also fostered trade and cultural exchange across the caravan routes of Central Asia.

In the seventh century, the formation of a vast Islamic empire and the reestablishment of a unified empire in China by the Sui and Tang dynasties created stable political and social foundations for economic recovery (see Chapters 9 and 10). Latin Christendom remained divided into many kingdoms and city-states, and here the reinvigoration of trade and industry came later. The expanding Islamic world also began to reach across the seas and deserts to bring parts of sub-Saharan Africa into its orbit.

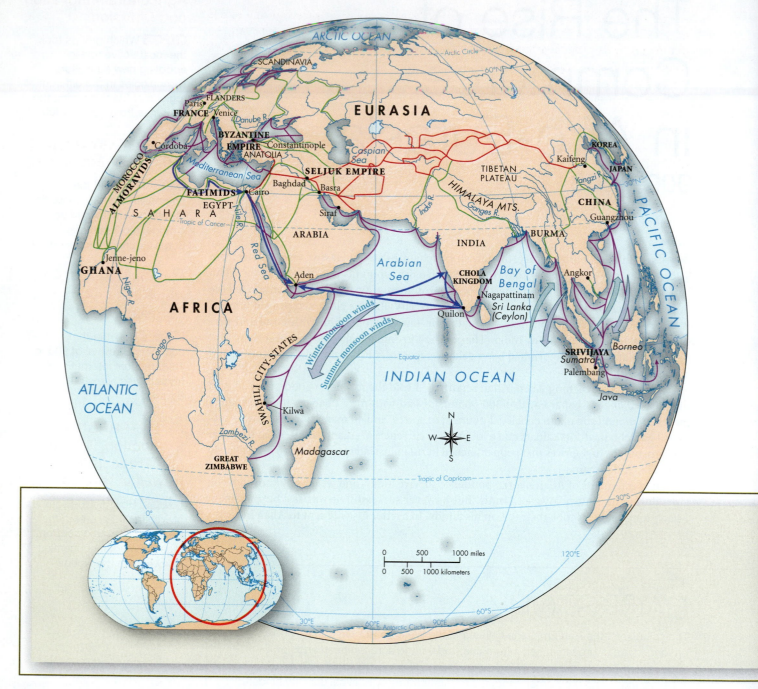

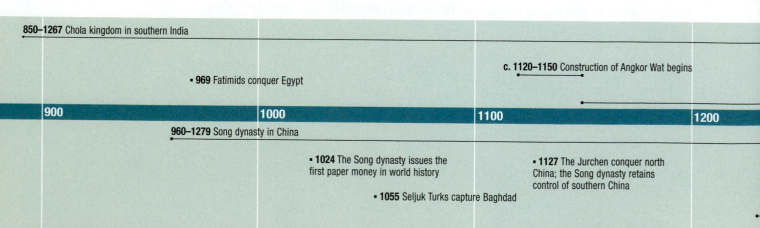

Africa, she bitterly chided him for his absence: "We are in great distress, owing to bad health and loneliness." Caring for their sick infant had forced her to sell furniture and rent out the upper story of their house to pay for doctors and medicines. Lamenting that her father was abroad on business at the same time, the wife urged her husband, "By God, do not tarry any longer . . . we remain like orphans without a man."

Allan's last surviving letter, written when he was an old man about to embark on another expedition to India, warned his adult sons not to abandon their families as he had done. He advised his sons, merchants themselves, to form a partnership that would spread the burdens of travel among them, and admonished them to take good care of their families and one another. His letter conveyed heartfelt regrets about the personal costs of his life as a merchant: "Had I known how much I would be longing after you, I would not have undertaken this voyage altogether."[1]

Merchants such as Allan bin Hassun faced formidable challenges: slow and frail modes of transportation, unfamiliar and sometimes dishonest clients and competitors, and the constant threat of bandits, pirates, and greedy rulers. To overcome these obstacles they devised new business organizations and practices. Allan, an Arabic-speaking Jew from Cairo who roamed westward to Spain and eastward to India, epitomized this cosmopolitan merchant class.

In Allan bin Hassun's day, a sustained economic expansion was spreading across Eurasia and Africa. Favorable climatic conditions, improved agricultural efficiency and output, increases in population and growth of cities, and new patterns of consumption led to rapid expansion of the money economy, culminating in a veritable commercial revolution. Long-distance merchants such as Allan opened new trade routes that connected Europe and the Mediterranean with the Islamic lands and the Indian Ocean. Vigorous commercial growth in China stimulated an unprecedented flowering of maritime trade between East Asia and the Indian Ocean world. The thirst for gold brought parts of sub-Saharan Africa into these trade networks as well. In all of these places, commercial wealth reshaped social and political power.

MAPPING THE WORLD

Commercial Crossroads in Afro-Eurasia, c. 900–1300

After 900, the maritime routes across the Mediterranean Sea and the Indian Ocean eclipsed the overland Silk Road as the great avenues of Eurasian trade. The shift in trade patterns led to the rise of new centers of international trade: Venice became the gateway to Europe, Cairo replaced Baghdad as the commercial capital of the Islamic world, and Nagapattinam, the chief port of the Chola kingdom, flourished as the main crossroads of the Indian Ocean.

ROUTES ▼

— Old Silk Road
— Other land trade route
— Maritime trade route
➜ Voyages of Allan bin Hassun, c. 1115

1250–1517 Mamluk dynasty in Egypt

c. 1150–1300 Heyday of the Champagne fairs

1300   **1400**   **1500**

1323–1325 Pilgrimage to Mecca of Musa Mansa, ruler of Mali

1258 The Italian city-states of Florence and Genoa mint the first gold coins issued in Latin Christendom

c. 1400–1450 Great Zimbabwe in southern Africa reaches peak of prosperity

1230–1255 Reign of Sunjata, founder of the Mali Empire in West Africa

c. 1200–1400 Formation of first chiefdoms in the Hawaiian Islands

Although the pace and dynamics of economic change varied from region to region, the underlying trends were remarkably consistent. Similarly, in the fourteenth century this surge in economic prosperity suddenly ended across all of Eurasia, from Spain to China. This cycle of economic growth and decline was powered by the progressive integration of local economies into regional and cross-cultural networks of exchange. Parts of the world, however, were still cut off from this web of economic connections. In relatively isolated places such as the Hawaiian Islands, more intensive exploitation of economic resources also had important social and political consequences, but with strikingly different results.

OVERVIEW
QUESTIONS

The major global development in this chapter: The sustained economic expansion that spread across Afro-Eurasia from 900 to 1300.

As you read, consider:

1. How did agricultural changes contribute to commercial and industrial growth?

2. What technological breakthroughs increased productivity most significantly?

3. What social institutions and economic innovations did merchants devise to overcome the risks and dangers of long-distance trade?

4. In what ways did the profits of commerce translate into social and economic power?

5. Above all, who benefited most from these economic changes?

Agricultural Innovation and Diffusion

FOCUS

Which groups took the most active role in adopting new agricultural technologies in the different regions of Eurasia during the centuries from 900 to 1300?

Commercial growth, the most robust feature of economic change during these centuries, was rooted in an increasingly productive agrarian base. The invention, adaptation, and diffusion of new farming techniques raised yields and encouraged investment in agriculture and specialization of production. Rulers, landowners, and peasants all contributed innovations and more intense agricultural production. As urban demand for foodstuffs and industrial raw materials increased, it became more rewarding to produce goods for sale than for household consumption. Increased agricultural production transformed patterns of rural life and community, and changed the relationship between peasants working the land and the lords and states that commanded their loyalty and labor.

Retrenchment and Renewal in Europe and Byzantium

serf A peasant who was legally bound to the land and who owed goods, labor, and service to the lord who owned the land.

The third-century collapse of the unified Roman Empire disrupted economic life in the cities, but it had little direct impact on work and livelihoods in the countryside. In subsequent centuries great lords and peasant smallholders alike concentrated on growing food for their own consumption. Even in the tenth and eleventh centuries, when political stability had restored some measure of economic prosperity in the Byzantine Empire and Latin Europe, self-sufficiency was the goal. Kekaumenos, an eleventh-century Byzantine official, instructed his sons that proper household management meant minimizing expenses, diversifying assets, and avoiding dependence on the market. His first priority was to ensure that the family had "an abundance of wheat, wine, and everything else, seed and livestock, edible and movable." In addition, Kekaumenos advised, "Make for yourself things that are 'self-working'—mills, workshops, gardens, and other things as will give you an annual return whether it be in rent or crop."[2] Vineyards, olives, and fruit trees would yield steady income year after year with the least amount of effort or expenditure. The greatest danger was debt, and the worst evil was to lose one's property to moneylenders.

Great landowners were the main agents of agricultural development and innovation in Europe. Although the population of Europe rose in the tenth and eleventh centuries, labor remained scarce. After the death of Charlemagne in 814, the imperial authority of the Frankish kings declined, and power was largely privatized. The warrior nobility and monastic establishments founded manorial estates that reduced the rural population to the condition of **serfs**, who were bound to the soil they tilled as well as to their masters' will. The spurt of castle-building that swept across western Europe beginning in the late tenth century remade the landscape. Lords gathered their serfs into compact villages and subjected them to their laws as well as the rules of parish priests. Although free smallholder farmers were probably still the majority, they too sought the protection of local lords.

As lordship came to be defined in terms of control over specific territories and populations, the nobility took greater interest in increasing their revenue. Landowners began to invest in enterprises such as watermills, vineyards, and orchards that required large initial outlays of capital but would yield steady long-term returns. In addition to owing their lords numerous dues and services, serfs were obliged to grind their grain at their master's mill, bake their bread in their master's ovens, and borrow money from their master.

Manorial lords also introduced other new technologies, such as the wheeled moldboard plow. Pulled by horses rather than oxen, this device was better than the light Mediterranean-style plow at breaking up northern Europe's heavy, clayey soils. Monasteries and manorial lords also promoted grape cultivation and wine making. Still, some fundamental aspects of European agriculture continued unchanged in both the Latin west and the Byzantine east. Wheat and barley remained the dominant crops. Farmers combined livestock-raising with cereal cultivation, providing more protein in European diets. The large amount of land needed to pasture animals kept population densities relatively low, however.

Agricultural innovation had less impact in the Byzantine Empire than in western Europe. For example, waterwheels were conspicuously absent, perhaps because Byzantine peasants, unlike European serfs, were not compelled to use the mills of the great landowners, who thus had less incentive to invest in expensive machinery. The recovery of Byzantium's political fortunes in the tenth and eleventh centuries led to renewed economic growth. Cultivation of olives, grapes, and figs expanded throughout the Mediterranean

Manorial Lords and Serfs

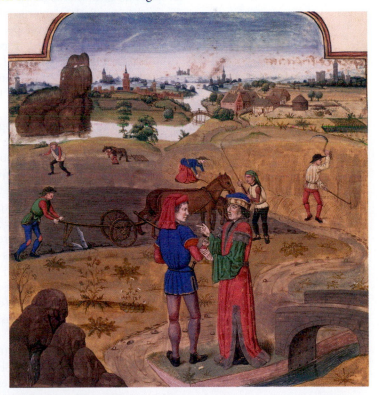

A Managerial Landlord

In this illustration from a fifteenth-century French handbook on farming, a landowner personally supervises the agricultural work on his estate. The laborers are engaged in various tasks, including plowing, sowing, and harvesting. The team of horses is pulling a wheeled moldboard plow, which allowed farmers to till the heavy soils of northern Europe more efficiently. (HIP/Art Resource, NY.)

lands. In Anatolia (modern Turkey), however, the scarcity of labor prompted landowners to replace agriculture with stock-raising—a trend that accelerated when the Seljuk (SEL-juk) Turks, nomadic Muslim warriors from Central Asia, conquered most of Anatolia in the late eleventh century.

Agricultural Transformation in the Islamic World

Emergence of Landed Estates

The Arab conquerors of Syria, Iraq, and Iran initially were confined to towns, and thus had little immediate impact on the already well-developed agricultural systems in these regions. Undeveloped areas were another matter, however. The new rulers awarded wilderness lands to Arab governors to reduce the fiscal burdens of the caliphate's far-flung empire. The governors were expected to convert the wastelands to agriculture and use the revenues to defray the costs of public administration. In the ninth and tenth centuries, as the caliphate began to lose its grip over the provinces, local governors turned to slave armies to maintain control. They allocated landed estates, *iqta* (ihk-ta), to military commanders for the upkeep of these slave forces. Under the rule of the Seljuk Turks, first in Iran and subsequently in the central Muslim lands, most of the land was held as iqta estates to support the slave armies.

New Crops and Farming Practices

Islamic agriculture was transformed by new crops and farming practices. The burgeoning trade with Asia (discussed later in this chapter) introduced into Islamic domains a host of new crops—including rice, cotton, sugar cane, sorghum, and citrus fruits—from the lands surrounding the Indian Ocean. Cultivating these tropical imports as summer crops in the arid Middle East and North Africa required more elaborate irrigation systems. Thus, the spread of Asian crops in Syria, Egypt, and Spain was accompanied by irrigation technologies originally developed in India and Iran.

By 1200, Asian tropical crops had been domesticated throughout the Islamic world, from Iran to Spain (see Map 12.1, page 380). In addition to providing a more diverse diet and better nutrition, the new imports spurred industrial production and trade. New processing industries such as cotton textile manufacture and sugar refining emerged, primarily in Egypt and Syria.

Surprisingly, Europeans adopted few of the new crops and farming practices that were spreading throughout the Islamic world. One exception was hard wheat (durum), a variety developed in North Africa in about 500 to 600. Muslims introduced hard wheat, used to make pasta and couscous (and now pizza crust), to Spain and Italy. The earliest mention of pasta making in Italy dates from the thirteenth century, but it is unclear whether this was an Italian novelty or a Muslim export.

In northern Europe, climate prevented cultivation of most warm-weather crops. Yet prevailing habits and food preferences also figured significantly in Europeans' lack of interest in Muslim innovations, as the experience of Spain shows. Rice, citrus fruits, and sugar cane were widely grown in Muslim-ruled Spain, whose rulers also invested heavily in irrigation projects. But in the wake of the Christian reconquest of Spain in the thirteenth and fourteenth centuries (discussed in Chapter 14), the new landowners converted the wheat and cotton fields to pasture for sheep and allowed the irrigated rice fields to revert to swamps.

Retreat to Pastoral Livelihoods

The Seljuk conquests disrupted the agrarian basis of the Islamic world's economic prosperity. As nomadic warriors, the Seljuks were ill suited to maintaining the fragile ecology of intensive irrigated farming in these arid regions. Moreover, unlike in the manorial order of Western Europe, possession of an iqta estate gave the owner no political or legal powers over the peasants who worked it. Further, the estates could not be sold, leased, or passed on to one's heirs. Lacking ownership of the land and control over the peasants' labor, estate holders had little incentive to try to improve the efficiency of agriculture. Economic regression was most severe in Iraq and Anatolia. Neglect of irrigation systems and heavy taxation prompted massive peasant flight, leading to depopulation and a retreat from farming to pastoralism.

iqta In the Islamic world, grants of land made to governors and military officers, the revenues of which were used to pay for administrative expenses and soldiers' salaries.

Rice Economies in Monsoon Asia

Between 700 and 1200, an agricultural revolution also transformed economic life and livelihoods throughout monsoon Asia. Earlier Asian farmers had mainly grown dry land cereals such as wheat and millet. Beginning in the eighth century, however, Asian agriculture shifted to irrigated rice as the main staple food. The high efficiency and yields of irrigated rice agriculture, which can feed six times as many people per acre as wheat, generated substantial surpluses and fostered rapid population growth.

Nowhere was the scale of this agricultural transformation greater than in China. The An Lushan rebellion in the mid-eighth century had devastated the north China plain, the traditional Chinese heartland (see Chapter 10). Refugees fleeing the war-torn north resettled in the south, especially in the well-watered plains of the Yangzi River Valley. Massive investment of labor and capital in dikes, canals, and irrigation channels made it possible to control the annual Yangzi floods and reclaim land in the Yangzi Delta. Man-made canals, along with the abundant natural waterways of southern China, also encouraged mobility and trade. Southern products such as tea, sugar, porcelain, and later cotton led to new industries and new patterns of consumption. The unprecedented growth of cities and towns widened the circulation of goods and made it possible to acquire great fortunes through landowning and commerce. Yet the imperial state, which gained renewed strength under the Song dynasty (960–1279), strictly limited the social and legal powers exercised by the landed elite. In contrast to other parts of Eurasia during this era, in China small property owners drove agricultural expansion and economic growth.

Water conservation, irrigation technologies such as pedal-powered water pumps, and the construction of terraced fields along hillsides dramatically increased the amount of land under rice cultivation. The introduction of faster-ripening, drought-resistant rice varieties from Southeast Asia allowed Chinese farmers to develop a double-cropping rotation. Fields were planted with rice during the summer, and then reused to cultivate winter crops such as wheat, barley, and soybeans. Yangzi Delta farmers also planted mulberry trees, whose leaves provided fodder for silkworms, on the embankments dividing the rice paddies.

Growing exchanges between town and countryside also altered dietary and consumption habits. The brisk market activity in the Yangzi Delta countryside deeply impressed one thirteenth-century visitor from another province. He observed that peasants coming to town to sell rice returned home "arms laden with incense, candles, paper money offerings for the ancestors, cooking oil, salt, soy sauce, vinegar, flour, noodles, pepper, ginger, and medicines."[3] The introduction of irrigated rice cultivation thus had consequences well beyond the production of more food for rural families. The surplus food made possible by rice cultivation helped create new connections between rural and urban peoples, changing both city and country life in the process.

In mainland Southeast Asia, wet rice cultivation became common probably in the first centuries C.E., and it had spread to Java by the eighth century. Fish and coconuts (a source of fruit, sugar, oil, and wine) also were important staple foods in tropical agriculture. Dried or fermented fish could be stored for lengthy periods, and coconut trees typically yielded fruit four times a year. Tuber crops such as taro and yams provided alternative sources of subsistence.

Women Making Pasta

The Chinese made noodles from millet flour as early as 3000 B.C.E., but pasta was introduced to Europe from the Islamic world much later. A twelfth-century Muslim geography mentions that *itriya*—long, thin noodles like those being made by the women in this fourteenth-century Italian illustration—was manufactured in Sicily and exported throughout Muslim and Christian lands around the Mediterranean. (Alinari/Art Resource, NY.)

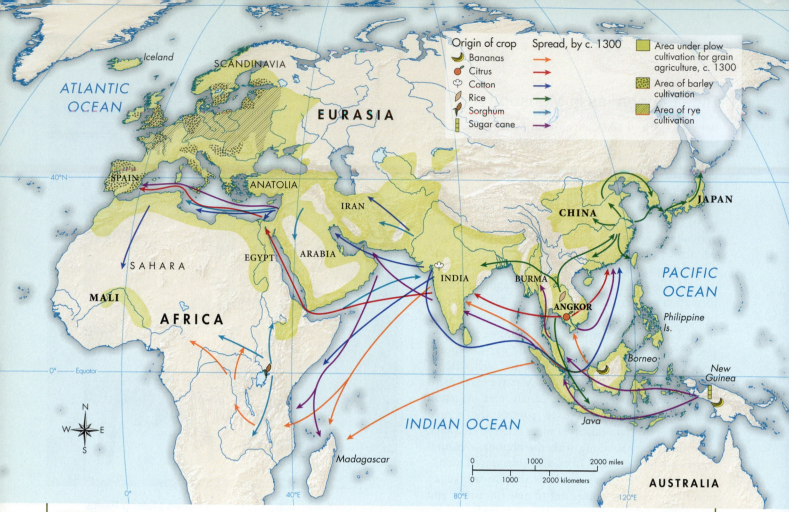

MAP 12.1

Principal Crops of Afro-Eurasia, c. 1300

The commercial prosperity of this era rested on the population growth made possible by the rising productivity of agriculture. New staple crops expanded the frontiers of agriculture: irrigated rice in Southeast Asia, rye and barley in northern Europe, and bananas in tropical Africa. Techniques of sugar and cotton production developed in India spread west to the Middle East and east to China.

Rise of Powerful Monarchies in Southeast Asia

The development of irrigated rice agriculture from the eighth century onward laid the economic foundations for the rise of powerful monarchies, most notably Angkor in Cambodia. In contrast to Chinese traditions, the Khmer kings of Angkor never created a centralized bureaucratic state. Instead, they extended their overlordship by recruiting local landowning elites as allies. The Angkor kings established networks of royal temples supported by ample land endowments. In addition to revenue from landholdings, royal and aristocratic patrons gave temples donations of rice, cattle, goats, coconut palms, fruit trees, betel nuts, and clothing. The temples became storehouses of goods shared with the whole community. Java and Burma had similar patterns of intensive rice cultivation, organized by allocating land and labor rights to temple networks. Hence, in Angkor, Java, and Burma, temples acted as local crossroads, functioning as hubs for the collection and distribution of resources and as points of connection between rural communities and the king.

In keeping with Indian political traditions, the Angkor monarchs portrayed themselves as servants of the gods and custodians of their temples. The kings ceded neither sacred authority nor temple administration to an independent priesthood, however. Even without a centralized bureaucracy, the Angkor kings retained control over temples and the land and wealth attached to them. The revenues that flowed to Angkor from the temple network financed massive construction projects, including irrigation works and new temple complexes. The power and wealth of Angkor reached its peak during the twelfth cen-

Annual Cycle of Rice Cultivation
Highly productive rice agriculture fueled Song China's dramatic economic growth. Irrigated rice fields could feed six times as many people per acre as dry-land crops such as wheat or maize. This twelfth-century painting depicts the annual cycle of rice farming in the Yangzi Delta (clockwise from top): sowing, irrigation with pedal-powered water pumps, harvesting, threshing, husking, and storing the husked grain in a granary. (The Palace Museum, Beijing/ChinaStock.)

tury, when Angkor Wat was built. The world's largest religious monument, it was originally covered in gold leaf. Designed to represent the world in miniature, it served both as a shrine dedicated to the Hindu god Vishnu and as a royal mausoleum.

In Japan, too, land reclamation efforts organized by aristocratic and religious estates fostered the spread of rice cultivation. Because most large landowners lived in the capital at Kyoto, actual cultivation of the land was divided among tenant farmers and serflike laborers working under the direction of a village headman. The estate economy remained highly localized and self-sufficient until the early fourteenth century, when double-cropping (combining, as in China, a winter harvest of wheat or soybeans with the summer rice crop) and other technical improvements raised rural incomes. Peasants began to sell their surplus produce at rural markets. Although traders still conducted most exchange through barter, imported Chinese coins began to appear in local markets as well.

Favorable climatic trends also contributed to agricultural expansion across Eurasia. After 900 warmer temperatures set in, lengthening growing seasons and boosting yields. With rising agricultural productivity, farmers could feed more people, leading to population expansion and the growth of cities. Increasing commercial ties between the countryside and the towns brought more people into the market economy: rural inhabitants obtained more of their daily necessities from markets and fairs, while urban merchants and artisans developed new products to satisfy the mounting consumer demand.

Estate-Based Economy in Japan

Industrial Growth and the Money Economy

Economic growth during these centuries was driven by rising agricultural productivity, population increases, and the expansion of markets, rather than revolutionary changes in industrial organization and technology. A world in which labor was cheap and often unfree offered little incentive for investing in labor saving technology. Although no "industrial revolution" occurred, important strides in technological progress stimulated expansion of manufacturing and transport. In both technical innovation and scale of output, textiles,

FOCUS
How did the composition and organization of the industrial workforce change in different parts of Eurasia during this period?

metallurgy, and shipbuilding were the leading industries. As the volume of transactions increased, so did the demand for money and credit. Money became the lifeblood of urban society and an increasingly important measure of social status.

Technological Change and Industrial Enterprise

Human and animal power continued to serve as the main sources of energy in both agriculture and industry. However, water and windmills, first used in Europe in Roman times, proliferated rapidly from the tenth to the thirteenth centuries. People used mills primarily to grind grain, but they also adapted milling techniques to industrial purposes such as crushing ore, manufacturing woolen cloth, and pressing oil seeds.

Increased Iron Production

The production of iron expanded in Europe during these centuries, though no significant technological breakthrough occurred until blast furnace technology using water-driven bellows emerged in Germany sometime after 1300. In China, innovations such as piston-driven blast furnaces and the use of coke (refined coal) as fuel made vigorous growth in iron and steel output possible. In the eleventh century China produced perhaps as much as 125,000 tons of iron per year, more than twice the entire output of Europe. The loss of China's chief iron mines after the Jurchen conquest of the north in 1127 severely slowed iron production, however, and even led to regression to more primitive iron-making techniques.

Advances in Shipbuilding and Navigation

Probably the farthest-reaching technological advances during this era came in shipbuilding and navigation. Arab seafarers had conquered the monsoon winds of the Indian Ocean by rigging their ships (known as *dhows*) with lateen sails, which allowed them to sail against the wind. By the thirteenth century, Arabian ships were equipped with stern-post rudders that greatly enhanced their maneuverability. Because of the dhow's relatively flimsy hull, though, its range was limited to the placid waters of the Indian Ocean (see At a Crossroads, page 372).

The Chinese were slow to develop seagoing vessels, for reasons we will consider in Chapter 15. But by the twelfth century, Chinese merchants were sailing to Korea, Japan, and Southeast Asia in "Fuzhou ships," which featured deep keels, stern-post rudders, nailed planking, and waterproofed bulkheads. The magnetic compass had been known in China since ancient times, but the earliest mention of its use as a navigational aid at sea refers to Arab and Persian vessels in the Indian Ocean in the eleventh century.

Important innovations in seafaring and navigation came somewhat later in Europe. The traditional Mediterranean galley, powered by oars, was designed for war rather than commerce, and had little space for cargo. Beginning in the late thirteenth century, the Venetians developed more capacious galleys specifically designed as cargo vessels. In addition, a new kind of sailing ship known as the "cog" was introduced from northern Europe in the early fourteenth century. Equipped with square-sail rigging and stern-post rudders, the cogs could be built on a much larger scale, yet they required only one-fifth the crew needed to man a galley.

Equally important to the expansion of European maritime trade were innovations in navigation. The nautical compass came into use in the Mediterranean in around 1270. At around the same time, European navigators began to compile sea charts known as "portolans" that enabled them to plot courses between any two points. The combination of compass, portolans, and the astrolabe—introduced to Europe via Muslim Spain—vastly broadened the horizons of European seafarers. Mediterranean mariners began to venture beyond the Straits of Gibraltar into the Atlantic Ocean. A Genoese ship made the first voyage from Italy to Flanders in 1277, the initial step in the reorientation of European trade away from the Mediterranean and toward the Atlantic.

Expansion of Textile Manufacture

In addition to metallurgy and shipbuilding, textile manufacture—the most important industrial enterprise in every premodern society—was also transformed by technological innovation. Egypt, renowned for its linen and cotton fabrics, continued to produce high-quality cloth that was sold across the Islamic world and in Europe as well. Egyptian cloth-making techniques were copied in many other Muslim societies. Knowledge of silk manufacture, brought to Iran from China by the seventh century, was later passed on to Syria and Byzantium. Woolen cloth manufacture was the largest industry in Europe. The expansion of textile weaving sparked the rise of industrial towns in Flanders (modern Belgium), while Italian cities such as Milan and Florence specialized in dyeing and finishing cloth.

Innovations such as spinning wheels, treadle-operated looms, and water mills sharply increased productivity at virtually every step in textile manufacturing. The new technologies also encouraged a more distinct division of labor. As textile manufacture shifted from a household or manorial activity to an urban, market-oriented industry, skilled tasks such as weaving and dyeing became the exclusive preserve of male artisans. Women were relegated to the low-skilled and laborious task of spinning yarn.

In the twelfth century the Chinese silk industry underwent momentous changes. Previously, silk production had been almost exclusively a northern industry, carried out in state-run workshops or by rural women working at home. However, in 1127 the Jurchen Jin kingdom in Manchuria seized north China, forcing the Song court to take refuge at a new capital at Hangzhou (hahng-jo) in the Yangzi Delta. Subsequently China's silk industry shifted permanently to the Yangzi Delta, where the humid climate was more conducive to raising silkworms (see Map 12.2, page 394). New machinery such as the silk spinning reel and the treadle-operated loom greatly increased the output of silk yarn and cloth.

Like woolen manufacture in Europe, silk production in China steadily ceased to be a cottage industry and moved into urban industrial workshops. Instead of weaving cloth themselves, peasant households increasingly specialized in producing raw silk and yarn for sale to weaving shops. Although state-run silk factories continued to employ some women, private workshops hired exclusively male weavers and artisans.

Indeed, as the role of the market in the household economy grew, men began to monopolize the more skilled and better-paid occupations throughout Eurasia. In European cities especially, women found their entry barred to occupations that had formerly been open to them. Moreover, for urban women throughout Eurasia, public participation in social and economic activities became a mark of lower-class status.

Cultural preconceptions about the physical, emotional, and moral weaknesses of women aroused anxieties about their vulnerability in the public realm. The Muslim philosopher and

Exclusion of Women from the Workforce

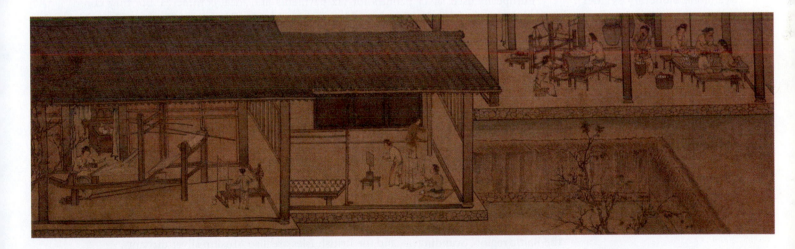

Chinese Silk Weaving

Growing demand for luxury silks with fancy weaves stimulated technological innovations in the Chinese silk industry. This thirteenth-century scroll painting shows various stages of silk production, including sorting cocoons, extracting the silk filaments (right background), and winding yarn on a silk reeling machine (center foreground). At left a female weaver operates a treadle-powered loom. Peasant women could not afford such expensive equipment, however; most stopped weaving and concentrated on raising silkworms and producing raw silk.
(Attributed to Liang Kai (Chinese). Sericulture (The Process of Making Silk), early 13th Century. Handscroll, ink and color on silk. 27.3x93.5 cm. The Cleveland Museum of Art. John L. Severance Collection 1977.5.)

jurist Ibn Hazm (994–1064) warned that men preyed on women working outside the home: "Women plying a trade or profession, which gives them ready access to people, are popular with lovers [men looking for sexual partners]—the lady broker, the coiffeuses, the professional mourner, the singer, the soothsayer, the school mistress, the errand girl, the spinner, the weaver, and the like."[4] At the same time, the segregation of women in Muslim societies conferred high status on women doctors and midwives, which were considered necessary and honorable professions. Muslim women's control over their dowries enabled them to invest in moneylending, real estate, and other commercial activities.

Hazm's list of occupations that exposed women to public scrutiny provides a glimpse of women's jobs in his home city, Córdoba in Muslim Spain. Household surveys conducted in Paris in around 1300 show that female taxpayers were represented in more than a hundred trades at all levels of income. Many worked as independent artisans, although nearly three-quarters were employed as servants, in preparing and selling food, and in the textile and clothing industries. But the urban economy of Paris was relatively open. Elsewhere, merchant and artisan guilds (see page 388) almost always excluded women. By the fifteenth century, independent wage-earning women had virtually disappeared from European cities, even in Paris. The majority of women who earned wages were domestic servants. Married women typically worked at family businesses—as innkeepers, butchers, bakers, and clothiers—serving as helpers to their husbands.

Expanding Circulation of Money

Before 1000, most parts of Eurasia suffered from acute shortages of money. The use of money in Latin Christendom sharply contracted after the demise of the Roman Empire. Local rulers began to issue their own coins, but their circulation was limited. With gold scarce, the Frankish kings minted silver coins known as pennies. Kings and princes across Europe also frequently granted coinage privileges to various nobles and clerical authorities, and a great profusion of currencies resulted. Silver pennies were still relatively high in value, though, and their use was largely restricted to the nobility and merchants. The great majority of European peasants paid their lords in goods and services rather than money.

Byzantine Monetary System   Europeans used silver pennies for tax payments and local commerce, but they conducted international trade using the gold coins issued by the Byzantine emperors. The gold *nomisma* (nom-IHS-mah) coin, the cornerstone of Byzantine monetary and fiscal systems, ruled supreme throughout the Mediterranean world from Justinian's time until the end of the eleventh century. The Byzantine state collected taxes in gold coins, which it spent on official salaries, public works, foreign subsidies, the ecclesiastic establishment, and above all its standing army. Payment of soldiers' salaries in gold coin ensured their wide dispersal throughout the empire. Byzantium's prominence as the main trading partner of Italy's mercantile cities established the nomisma as the monetary standard in Italy as well.

Islamic Monetary System   The Umayyad caliph Abd al-Malik's currency reforms in the 690s had established the silver *dirham* (DEER-im) as the monetary standard for the Islamic world (see Seeing the Past: Imitation and Innovation in Islamic Coinage). The ease with which merchants circulated throughout the Islamic world is demonstrated by a hoard of nine hundred dirhams buried in Oman in around 840, which included coins issued by fifty-nine different mints from Morocco to Central Asia. Most of the coins found in Viking hoards scattered across the Baltic region, Scandinavia, and the British Isles are also Muslim silver dirhams.

The Islamic world suffered from shortages of gold until, as we will see, the rise of trans-Saharan trade in the ninth century. North African rulers reaped enormous profits from minting this gold into coins known as *dinars*. The Arab geographer Ibn Hawqal reported that the king of Sijilmasa (sih-jil-MAS-suh), in southern Morocco, obtained annual revenues of 400,000 gold dinars, equivalent to 1.9 tons of gold, from commercial tolls and his mint.

European Monetary System   The revival of gold coinage in Italy in the mid-thirteenth century, first by Florence and Genoa in 1258 and later by Venice, confirms Italian merchants' growing supremacy over Mediterranean trade. The dominance of Venice and Genoa in trade with Byzantium enabled the Italian city-states to supply their mints with gold imported from Constantinople. Italian merchants also obtained an increasing portion of the African gold crossing the Sahara. The Venetian gold ducat, introduced in 1284, soon established itself as the new monetary standard of Mediterranean commerce. Although gold coins filled the purses of nobles and great merchants throughout Europe, artisans continued to receive their wages in silver coin, and so-called black money (silver debased with lead and other cheap metals that gave it a black color) was widely used for everyday purchases and almsgiving.

Chinese Monetary System

The Chinese Empire developed an entirely different monetary system based on low-value bronze coins rather than precious metals. Shortages of bronze coins had forced the Tang government to collect taxes in grain, bolts of cloth, and labor services, with only a few commercial duties paid in coin. In the early eleventh century the Song dynasty launched an ambitious policy of monetary expansion. By the 1020s, the output of Song mints already far surpassed that of earlier dynasties, and it soared to nearly 6 billion coins per year (requiring ninety-six hundred tons of copper) in the 1070s. Yet even this level of coinage failed to satisfy the combined needs of the state and the private market. Beginning in the early eleventh century, the Song government introduced paper money to expand the money supply and facilitate the movement of money across long distances.

Credit and the Invention of Paper Money

Despite the influx of African gold, shortages of gold and silver coin persisted in the Mediterranean world. These shortages, coupled with the high risk and inconvenience of shipping coin over long distances, encouraged the development of credit and the use of substitutes for metallic currency, including bank money, deposit certificates, and bills of exchange. The growing sophistication of business skills and commercial practices during this period was the product of pragmatic solutions to the problems of long-distance trade.

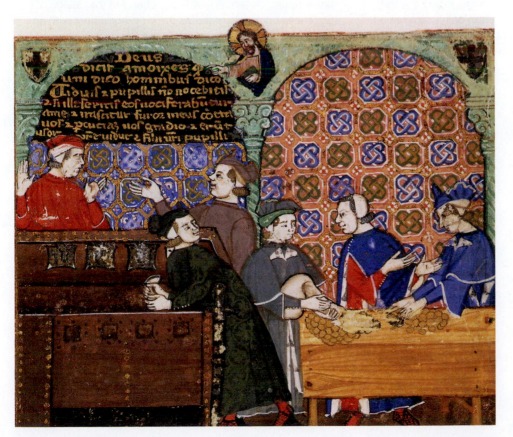

Genoese Bankers

The Christian church's ban on usury clashed with the financial needs of Europe's rising merchant class. In his *Treatise on the Seven Vices* (c. 1320), an Italian nobleman chose to portray the sin of greed with an illustration of the counting house of a Genoese banker. Genoa's bankers were pioneers in the development of bills of exchange and interest-bearing deposit accounts. (© 2011 The British Library Add. 27695, f.8.)

Imitation and Innovation in Islamic Coinage

Since their invention in the sixth century B.C.E., metallic coins have served a variety of purposes. The first goal of Eurasian rulers who issued the coins was to facilitate trade, but coins were also used to pay taxes, and in many cultures coins played an important role in religious ritual and offerings to the gods. Coins also possessed symbolic significance. The stamp or design on a coin became synonymous with the authority of the ruler or state that minted it. Coins thus became vehicles for expressing sovereign power and political and religious beliefs.

During its rapid expansion in the seventh and eighth centuries C.E., the Islamic realm spread over two distinct monetary zones: the Mediterranean region, where Byzantine gold coins prevailed as the international monetary standard, and the former Sasanid Empire in Iran and Mesopotamia, where Sasanid silver coins known as *drachm* dominated. At first Muslim rulers imitated the design, weight, and metallic content of Byzantine and Sasanid coins. Thus the first Muslim coins minted in Iran (known as *dirham*, an Arabic rendering of *drachm*) continued to display a bust of the Sasanid king on one side and a fire altar, the centerpiece of the Zoroastrian religion, on the reverse; the words "In the name of God" in Arabic were added along the edge. In 661 the first Umayyad caliph, Mu'awiya, issued a new coin that retained the imagery of the Sasanid king's bust and the fire altar, but a Persian inscription identified the ruler as Mu'awiya.

Similarly, the first Umayyad gold coins (dinars) portrayed the caliphs in the style of Byzantine emperors (A), but they removed the cross that Byzantine coins prominently displayed atop the tiered platform (B). Moreover, the legend encircling the image of the caliph defiantly proclaims that "Muhammad is the Prophet of God whom He sent with guidance and the religion of truth that he may make it victorious over every other religion" (Qur'an IX: 33).

A   B

(© The Trustees of the British Museum/Art Resource, NY.)

Provoked by this religious broadside, in 692 the Byzantine emperor Justinian II radically changed the design of Byzantine coins. He replaced the emperor's bust with an image of Jesus Christ and made the Christian cross even more obvious.

Overcoming Bans Against Usury

In Muslim and Christian societies, merchants had to overcome strong religious objections to profiting from commercial enterprise, especially the prohibitions against **usury**, the practice of charging interest on debts. The Qur'an, which took shape within the commercial world of Mecca, devotes much attention to codifying ethical principles for merchants. The Qur'an firmly forbids usury, but later Islamic jurists devised means of permitting buying and selling on credit as well as investments aimed at earning a profit. Christian merchants evaded similar prohibitions against usury by drawing up contracts that disguised interest payments as fees or fines. In cases such as loans for overseas trading expeditions, where the borrower was obligated to repay the loan only if the ship and its cargo returned safely, clerical authorities allowed lenders to collect interest as compensation for the high risk.

The global connections created by long-distance trade required institutional support, mechanisms to facilitate the exchanges of goods and wealth between peoples from distant parts of the world. Thus, every major trading city had moneychangers to handle the diverse assortment of coins in use. Rudimentary banks that acted primarily as safe deposits but also transferred funds to distant cities were operating in China and the Islamic world by the ninth century and appeared in Genoa and Venice by the early twelfth century.

Long-distance merchants also benefited from new forms of credit such as the **bill of exchange**. The bill of exchange was a written promise to pay or repay a specified sum of money at a future time, which enabled a merchant to deposit money with a bank in one place and collect payment from the bank's agent in another place. Bills of exchange were

usury The practice of charging interest on loans, forbidden under Christian and Muslim legal codes.

bill of exchange A paper note that allowed the bearer to receive money in one place and repay the debt in another currency at another place at a later date.

In response, the caliph Abd al-Malik introduced a change in 696, one that would establish the style for Islamic coins for centuries to come. Abd al-Malik removed all images, including the depiction of the ruler, and replaced them with quotations from the Qur'an (C, D).

C **D**

(© The Trustees of the British Museum/Art Resource, NY.)

The main face of the coin shown here (C) bears the Islamic declaration of faith (*shahada*): "There is no god but God; there is no partner with him." In addition to other quotations from the Qur'an, such coins often state the name of the caliph or provincial governor who issued them. This change reflected Muslim clerics' growing concern that the images of rulers on coins violated the Muslim prohibition against idolatry.

Later Muslim rulers modified this basic model to reflect their political or doctrinal independence. The Fatimid rulers in Egypt, for example, issued coins with legends testifying to their Shi'a affiliation. Thanks to their control over the trans-Saharan gold trade, the Fatimids and the Almoravid dynasty in Morocco began to issue gold dinars in such

great quantities that they displaced the Byzantine coin as the international monetary standard of the Mediterranean. Some Christian rulers in Iberia and Italy issued their own copies of Islamic dinars. The gold coin struck by King Alfonso VIII (r. 1158–1214) of Castile imitated the style of the Almoravid dinar, but replaced the shahada with professions of Christian faith (still written in Arabic) and the image of a cross (E, F).

E **F**

(Courtesy of the American Numismatic Society.)

EXAMINING THE EVIDENCE

1. Why did Muslim rulers at first retain the images of Byzantine and Sasanid rulers on their own coins?

2. How did Muslim and Christian rulers differ in expressing their religious commitments and values through the images on their coins?

---

used in the Islamic world by the tenth century, when we hear of a Moroccan merchant using one to remit a payment of 42,000 gold dinars to a client in a Saharan oasis town. In Europe, traders at the Champagne fairs, which, as we will see, began in the twelfth century, conducted most of their business on the basis of credit. But not until the fourteenth century, about three hundred years later than financiers in Baghdad and Cairo, did European bankers begin to issue bills of exchange that were payable on demand.

Development of Credit

The flood of African gold into the Fatimid capital of Cairo in the tenth and eleventh centuries made that city the first great international financial center. The Arab geographer Al-Muqaddasi, writing in about 985, boasted that Cairo "has superseded Baghdad and is the glory of Islam, and is the marketplace for all mankind."[5] Muslim, Jewish, and Christian merchants in Cairo did business with each other and frequently cooperated in business deals, money transfers, and information sharing. The Cairo Exchange acted as a clearinghouse for moneychanging and the settlement of debts for merchants from Morocco to Persia. The guiding principle of trade was to keep one's capital constantly at work. "Do not let idle with you one dirham of our partnership, but buy whatever God puts into your mind and send it on with the very first ship sailing," wrote a Spanish merchant in Lebanon to his partner in Cairo.[6]

Cairo, a Commercial Crossroads

In China, too, merchants used letters of credit to transfer funds to distant regions. In the late tenth century, private merchants in western China began to issue their own bills of exchange. In 1024 the Song government replaced these private bills with its own official

Invention of Paper Money in China

387

ones, creating the world's first paper money. By the thirteenth century paper money had become the basic currency of China's fiscal administration, and it was widely used in private trade as well. At the same time merchants carried great quantities of Chinese bronze coin overseas to Japan, where by 1300 nearly all Japanese paid their rent and taxes and conducted business using imported Chinese coin.

The flow of money across borders and oceans testified to the widening circulation of goods. Few villagers would ever see a gold coin. Yet the demand for gold, luxury goods, and industrial raw materials drew many peasants—however unwittingly—into networks of long-distance trade.

Merchants and Trade Networks in Afro-Eurasia

FOCUS

How did the commercial revival of 900 to 1300 reorient international trade routes across Afro-Eurasia?

During the period 900 to 1300, major trading centers across Eurasia and Africa came to be linked in a series of regional and international networks of exchange and production. To be sure, the great majority of rural inhabitants remained largely disengaged from the commercial life of the cities and toiled strictly to feed their families and fulfill their obligations to their lords. Yet if the channels of commerce remained narrow, they were far more extensive than ever before, reaching from China to Europe and from southern Africa to the Mediterranean.

Much of this trade consisted of luxury goods such as spices, silk, and gold intended for a select few—rulers, nobles, and urban elites. Yet bulk products such as grain, timber, and metal ores also became important commodities in maritime trade, and processed goods such as textiles, wine, vegetable oils, sugar, and paper became staple articles of consumption among the urban middle classes. Although the movement of goods would seem sluggish and sporadic to modern eyes, the volume of trade and its size relative to other forms of wealth grew enormously. Genoa's maritime trade in 1293 was three times greater than the entire revenue of the kingdom of France.

Merchant Partnerships and Long-Distance Trade

Long-distance merchants venturing far from their homelands had to overcome the hazards of travel across dangerous seas and alien lands; cultural barriers created by different languages, religions, and laws; and the practical problems of negotiating with strangers. The expansion of trade required new forms of association and partnership and reliable techniques for communication, payment, credit, and accounting. Notable advances in all of these spheres of trade and finance were made during the "commercial revolution" of the twelfth and thirteenth centuries.

Guild System

Not all innovations in commercial institutions promoted open access to trade. The **guild** system that took root in European towns during this period reflected the corporate character of urban government and merchant society. Guilds were granted extensive authority to regulate crafts and commerce, restrict entry to a trade, and dictate a wide array of regulations ranging from product specifications to the number of apprentices a master might employ. In the name of guaranteeing a "just" price and goods of uniform quality, the guild system also stifled competition and technical innovation. In China and the Islamic world, by contrast, guilds were formed chiefly to supply goods and services to the government, and they had no authority to regulate and control trade. Muslim rulers appointed market inspectors to supervise commerce and craftsmen. These officials upheld Islamic law, adjudicated disputes, and collected taxes and fees.

Merchants who engaged in international trade usually operated as individuals, carrying with them their entire stock of goods and capital, although they often traveled in cara-

guild An association of merchants or artisans organized according to the kind of work they performed.

vans and convoys for protection against bandits and pirates. As in the case of the Jewish trader Allan bin Hassun, whose story opened this chapter, a family firm might dispatch its members to foreign markets, sometimes permanently, to serve as agents. But as the volume of trade grew, more sophisticated forms of merchant organization emerged.

Commercial Partnerships

Islamic legal treatises devoted much attention to commercial partnerships. Muslim law permitted limited investment partnerships in which one partner supplied most of the capital, the other traveled to distant markets and conducted their business, and the two shared the profits equally. Apparently caravan traders of the Arabian deserts first developed such cooperative agreements in pre-Islamic times. Italian merchants later imitated this type of partnership in what became known as the *commenda* (coh-MEHN-dah) (see Reading the Past: The Commenda Partnership Among Venetian Merchants). Artisans such as bakers, tailors, silversmiths, and pharmacists as well as entrepreneurs in industrial enterprises such as weaving, metalworking, wine making, and sugar refining also formed investment partnerships. Chinese merchants likewise created joint trading ventures in the form of limited partnerships for both domestic and international trade.

READING THE PAST

The Commenda Partnership Among Venetian Merchants

New institutions and business practices to raise capital for conducting long-distance trade facilitated the expansion of Mediterranean trade in the eleventh century. One new practice was the *commenda*, a form of partnership in which one partner provides investment capital and the other partner acts as business agent. Byzantine and Jewish merchants in the Mediterranean developed similar partnerships, but the precise model for the commenda was the Muslim *qirad* contract, which appeared in Islamic law codes by the eighth century. The following commenda contract drawn up in Venice is the earliest known example from Latin Christendom.

> In the year . . . 1073, in the month of August . . . I, Giovanni Lissado of Luprio, together with my heirs, have received in partnership from you, Sevasto Orefice, son of Ser Trudimondo, and from your heirs, the amount of £200 [Venetian]. And I myself have invested £100 in it. And with this capital we have acquired two shares in the ship of which Gosmiro da Molino is captain. And I am under obligation to bring all of this with me on a commercial voyage to Thebes [in Greece] in the ship in which the aforesaid Molino sails as captain. Indeed, by this agreement and understanding of ours I promise to put to work this entire sum and to strive the best way I can. Then, if the capital is preserved, we are to divide whatever profit the Lord may grant us from it by exact halves, without fraud and evil device. And whatever I can gain with those goods from any source,

I am under obligation to invest all of it in the partnership. And if all these goods are lost because of the sea or of people [pirates], and this is proved—may this be averted—neither party ought to ask any of them from the other. If, however, some of them remain, in proportion as we invested so shall we share. Let this partnership exist between us so long as our wills are fully agreed.

But if I do not observe everything just as is stated above, I together with my heirs then promise to give and to return to you and your heirs everything in the double, both capital and profit, out of my land and my house or out of anything that I am known to have in this world. [signed by Lissado, two witnesses, the ship captain, and the clergyman who acted as notary]

Source: Robert S. Lopez and Irving W. Raymond, eds., *Medieval Trade in the Mediterranean World: Illustrative Documents* (Cambridge, U.K.: Cambridge University Press, 1955), 176–177.

EXAMINING THE EVIDENCE

1. What did these Italian merchants regard as the greatest risks in investing in maritime trade?

2. In what ways was the commenda partnership different from modern business organizations such as corporations?

Joint Stock Companies

The commenda partnerships were the forerunners of permanent **joint stock companies**, which were first founded in Italian cities in the thirteenth century. These companies, in which investors pooled their capital for trading ventures, engaged in finance as well as trade and often maintained their own fleets and branch offices in foreign cities. The merchant banks of Florence and other cities of northern Italy gradually became involved in fund transfers, bills of exchange, and moneychanging. Bardi, the largest Florentine bank, had over three hundred agents stationed throughout Europe and the Mediterranean in 1340, and its capital resources were more than four times as large as the annual income of the English crown, one of its main customers. Apart from trade and banking, such firms provided insurance for maritime trading expeditions; insuring such expeditions became a common practice after 1350.

Karimi Merchant Associations

In the late twelfth century, merchants based in Egypt created a commercial association known as the *karimi* (KUH-ree-mee) to organize convoys for trading expeditions in the Indian Ocean. Cairo's karimi merchants became a powerful **cartel**—a commercial association whose members join forces to fix prices or limit competition—that squeezed small entrepreneurs out of the lucrative spice trade. The karimi merchants cooperated closely with the sultans of Egypt, especially under the Mamluk dynasty (1250–1517), generating substantial tax revenue for the state in exchange for their trade privileges. By 1300 Cairo's two-hundred-plus karimi merchants had become the chief middlemen in trade between Asia and Europe.

Merchants and Rulers

The sumptuous wealth and rising social stature of merchant groups such as the Italian bankers and Cairo's karimi inevitably altered relationships between government and commerce. Rulers who had formerly depended almost exclusively on revenue from the land increasingly sought to capture the scarcely imaginable profits of the money economy. In places as far removed as England and Japan, landowners and governments began to demand payments in money rather than agricultural products or labor services. In Europe the expanding availability of credit was an irresistible temptation to monarchs whose ambitions outgrew their resources. Italian bankers became the chief lenders to the papacy and to the kings and princes of Latin Christendom.

Merchant-Ruler Relations in Europe

The Italians took the lead in putting private capital to work in service to the state. Merchant communities became closely allied with political leaders in the Italian city-states, most notably in Venice. In the late twelfth century the Venetian government imposed a system of compulsory loans that required contributions from every citizen. In 1262, the city's magistrates consolidated all of these debts into a single account. Public debt proved to be more efficient than taxation for raising revenue quickly to cope with war and other emergencies. Investment in state debt provided the men, fleets, and arms that enabled Venice to become the great maritime power of the Mediterranean.

As mercantile interests came to dominate the Venetian state, the government took charge of the republic's overseas trade. The state directed commercial expeditions, dictated which merchants could participate, built the vessels at its publicly funded shipyard, and regulated the prices of exports as well as crucial imports such as grain and salt. Venice was fortunate in its ability to maintain civic solidarity even as its mercantile oligarchy tightened its grip on the state and its resources.

Economic regulation was a powerful unifying force elsewhere in Europe as well. For example, the merchant communities of the trading cities along the Baltic seacoast formed an alliance known as the Hanseatic League. The League acted as a cartel to preserve its members' monopoly on the export of furs, grain, metals, and timber from the Baltic region to western Europe.

Efforts to merge commercial and political power did not, however, always result in increased prosperity and political strength. In Genoa,

• Principal Hanseatic League member
▲ Hanseatic trading partner

The Hanseatic League

antagonisms between the landed aristocracy and the city's rising merchant and financier families provoked frequent and sometimes bloody feuds that paralyzed the city's leadership. In the industrial cities of Flanders, fiscal policies and economic regulation that favored merchants over workers ultimately incited revolts that undermined Flanders' preeminence in the textile industry.

Merchant-Ruler Relations in the Islamic World

In most of the Islamic world, merchants—regardless of their religious commitments—enjoyed high status and close ties to the political authorities. The Fatimid government in Egypt largely entrusted its fiscal affairs to Coptic Christian officials, and Jewish merchant houses achieved prominence as personal bankers to Muslim rulers in Baghdad and Cairo. Private trade and banking were largely free of government interference during the Fatimid dynasty. But state intervention in commerce intensified under the Mamluk sultans, who came to power in Egypt after a palace coup in 1250.

The Mamluks' political and military strength rested on their slave armies, which were supported by revenues from iqta estates and commercial taxes. The karimi-controlled spice trade was an especially important source of income for the Mamluk state. Karimi merchants—most of whom were Jewish—also managed the fiscal administration of the Mamluk regime, helping to collect provincial revenues, pay military stipends, and administer state-run workshops and trade bureaus. Like European monarchs, the Mamluk sultans became heavily dependent on loans from private bankers to finance wars. And, again like their European counterparts, Mamluk sultans were always on the lookout for new sources of revenue. In the fifteenth century the Mamluk government took over many commercial enterprises, most notably the spice and slave trades and sugar refining, and operated them as state monopolies.

Merchant-Ruler Relations in China

In China, the fiscal administration of the imperial state penetrated deeply into the commercial world. The revenues of the Song Empire far exceeded those of any other contemporary government. The state generated more than half of its cash revenue by imposing monopolies on the production of rice wine and key mineral resources such as salt, copper, and alum. Yet in the most dynamic commercial sectors—iron mining and metallurgy, silk textiles, and the emerging industries of south China such as tea, porcelain, paper, and sugar—private enterprise was the rule. The Song government mainly intervened in private commerce to prevent private cartels from interfering with the free flow of goods.

The Song thus effectively stifled the formation of strong merchant organizations such as the European guilds. The state also assumed major responsibility for famine relief, stockpiling grain in anticipation of periodic harvest failures. Foreign trade was strictly regulated, and the export of strategic goods such as iron, bronze coin, and books was prohibited. Still, Chinese officials recognized the value of international trade as a source of revenue and of vital supplies such as warhorses, and they actively promoted both official trade with foreign governments and private overseas trading ventures.

Merchants in China did not enjoy the social prestige accorded to their Italian or Muslim counterparts. Confucianism viewed the pursuit of profit with contempt and relegated merchants to the margins of respectable society. Yet Confucian moralists expressed even greater hostility toward government interference in the economy than to private profit-seeking. Moreover, Confucian values applauded the prudent management of the household economy and the accumulation of wealth to provide for the welfare of one's descendants. As a minor twelfth-century official named Yuan Cai (you-ahn tsai) wrote in his *Family Instructions*, "Even if the profession of scholar is beyond your reach, you still can support your family through recourse to the arts and skills of medicine, Buddhist or Daoist ministry, husbandry, or commerce without bringing shame upon your ancestors."[7] Like his Byzantine counterpart Kekaumenos, Yuan Cai counseled his peers to be frugal in spending, to invest wisely in land, moneylending, and business ventures, to diversify their assets, and to never become dependent on the goodwill and honesty of those with whom one does business (see Reading the Past: A Chinese Official's Reflections on Managing Family Property).

joint stock company A business whose capital is held in transferable shares of stocks by its joint owners.

cartel A commercial association whose members join forces to fix prices or limit competition.

Despite their wealth, merchants led a precarious existence. Long-distance trade offered opportunities to make great profits, but the risks of failure were equally great. To lessen these risks, merchants built communities, negotiated alliances with ruling authori-

A Chinese Official's Reflections on Managing Family Property

In *Precepts for Social Life* (1179), Yuan Cai departed from the focus on personal ethics found in earlier Chinese writings on the family. A Chinese official living in a time of rapid economic change, Yuan concentrated on the practical problems of acquiring wealth and transmitting it to future generations. Yuan also adopted a more pragmatic attitude toward individual behavior in addressing the inevitable conflicts that arise within families. In the following selections, Yuan confronts the problem of disparities of wealth among relatives who live together as a joint family.

Wealth and liberality will not be uniform among brothers, sons, and nephews. The rich ones, only pursuing what's good for them, easily become proud. The poor ones, failing to strive for self-improvement, easily become envious. Discord then arises. If the richer ones from time to time would make gifts of their surplus without worrying about gratitude, and if the poorer ones would recognize that their position is a matter of fate and not expect charity, then there would be nothing for them to quarrel about. . . .

Some people actually start from poverty and are able to establish themselves and set up prosperous businesses without making use of any inherited family resources. Others, although there was a common family estate, did not make use of it, separately acquiring their individual wealth through their own efforts. In either case their patrilineal kinsmen will certainly try to get shares of what they have acquired. Lawsuits taken to the county and prefectural courts may drag on for decades until terminated by the bankruptcy of all parties concerned. . . .

When brothers, sons, and nephews live together, it sometimes happens that one of them has his own personal fortune. Worried about problems arising when the family divides the common property, he may convert his fortune to gold and silver and conceal it. This is perfectly foolish. For instance if he has one million cash [bronze coins] worth of gold and silver and used this money to buy productive property, in a year he would gain 100,000 cash; after ten years or so, he would have regained the one million cash and what would be divided among the family would be interest. Moreover, the one million cash could continue to earn interest. If it were invested in a pawnbroking business, in three years the interest would equal the capital. . . . What reason is there to store it in boxes rather than use it to earn interest for the profit of the whole family?

Source: Patricia Buckley Ebrey, *Family and Property in Sung China: Yuan Ts'ai's* Precepts for Social Life (Princeton, NJ: Princeton University Press, 1984), 197–200.

EXAMINING THE EVIDENCE

1. What did Yuan identify as the greatest threats to the preservation of the family's wealth and property?

2. What values did Yuan regard as crucial for gaining and maintaining wealth?

---

ties, and developed reliable methods of communication. Although some rulers coveted the profits of trade for themselves, and others treated merchants as pariahs, traders and rulers usually reached an accommodation that benefited both. The spread of new techniques and institutions for conducting trade strengthened the foundations of international commerce.

Maritime Traders in the Indian Ocean

The seventh century, when the Tang dynasty in China was at its height (see Chapter 10), marked the heyday of trade and travel along the Silk Road across Central Asia. As we have seen, however, overland commerce between India and China collapsed after the outbreak of the An Lushan rebellion in 755. By the time the Song dynasty was founded in 960, China's principal trade routes had shifted away from Central Asia to the maritime world (see Map 12.2).

Dominance of Muslim Merchants

Muslim merchants, both Arab and Persian, dominated Indian Ocean trade in the ninth century thanks to their superior shipbuilding and organizational skills. Travel across the Indian Ocean was governed by monsoon winds, which blew steadily from east to west in winter and from west to east in summer, making it impossible to complete a round trip between China and India in a single year. Initially, Muslim seafarers from Persian Gulf ports sailed all the way to China, taking two or three years to complete a round-trip voyage. A ninth-century Arab chronicler claimed that more than half of the two hundred thousand residents of Guangzhou (gwahng-joe) (Canton), southern China's principal port, were Arab, Persian, Christian, and Jewish traders, a testimony to the dense web of trading connections that had developed by this time.

By the tenth century, merchants more commonly divided the journey to China into shorter segments. By stopping at ports along the Strait of Melaka (Malacca), between Sumatra and the Malay peninsula, Muslim merchants could return to their home ports within a single year. The Srivijaya (sree-vih-JUH-yuh) merchant princes of Sumatra grew wealthy from their share of profits in this upsurge in trade between India and China.

Chola's Quest for Maritime Supremacy

In the eleventh century, however, new maritime powers arose to contest the dominance of Srivijaya and the Muslim merchants in Asian international commerce. The most assertive new entrant into the Indian Ocean trade was the Chola (chohz-ah) kingdom (907–1279), at the southeastern tip of the Indian peninsula. At first Chola nurtured cordial diplomatic and commercial relations with Srivijaya. The Chola port of Nagapattinam (Nah-gah-POT-tih-nahm) flourished as an international trading emporium under the patronage of both the Chola and Srivijaya rulers, who funded the construction of mosques, temples, and shrines for the city's expatriate merchant communities of Muslims, Jews, Christians, Parsis (Zoroastrian immigrants from Iran), and Chinese. Yet in 1025 Chola suddenly turned against Srivijaya, and its repeated attacks on Sumatran ports over the next fifty years fatally weakened the Srivijaya princes. But Chola's aggressiveness made many enemies, including the Sinhala kings of Sri Lanka, who stymied its attempt to succeed Srivijaya as the region's supreme maritime power.

Tamil Merchants and the China Trade

Chola's foreign trade was controlled by powerful Tamil merchant guilds that mobilized convoys and founded trading settlements overseas. Tamil merchants carried cargoes of Indian pepper and cotton cloth and Sumatran ivory, camphor, and sandalwood to the southern Chinese ports of Guangzhou and Quanzhou (chwehn-joe). Numerous architectural and sculptural fragments from Hindu temples found in Quanzhou attest to the city's once-thriving Tamil merchant colony.

Silk textiles had long been China's principal export commodity. After the tenth century, however, the growth of domestic silk industries in India and Iran dampened demand for Chinese imports. Although Chinese luxury fabrics such as brocades and satins still were highly prized, porcelain displaced silk as China's leading export. Maritime trade also transferred knowledge of sugar refining and cotton manufacture from India to China, leading to major new industries there.

During the twelfth century Chinese merchants began to mount their own overseas expeditions. Chinese commercial interests increasingly turned toward the Indonesian archipelago in search of fine spices such as clove and nutmeg (which grew only in the remote Moluccas, the so-called Spice Islands), and other exotic tropical products. Chinese merchants also imported substantial quantities of gold, timber, and sulfur (used in gunpowder and medicines) from Japan in exchange for silk, porcelain, and contraband bronze coin.

Swahili Merchants and East African Trading Cities

The advent of Muslim traders in Indian Ocean trade had stimulated commerce along the east coast of Africa as well. The Swahili peoples of the coasts of Tanzania and Kenya were descended from Bantu settlers who arrived in the region in around 500 C.E. The Swahili lived in coastal villages or on offshore islands, where they combined farming and fishing with small-scale trade. Beginning in the ninth century, Swahili merchants transformed the island towns of Shanga and Manda into major trading ports that functioned as regional crossroads, exporting ivory, hides, and quartz and other gems to the Islamic heartland in return for cotton, pottery, glass, and jewelry. When Swahili merchants ventured southward in search of ivory, they discovered an abundance of gold as well.

South African Gold Trade

The reorientation of East African trade networks toward the export of gold had far-reaching political and economic repercussions. In the twelfth century, Mapungubwe

International Commerce in Afro-Eurasia, c. 1150

New developments on opposite ends of Afro-Eurasia spurred the expansion of international trade. Song China became the world's most dynamic economy thanks to the dramatic growth of its silk, porcelain, iron, and shipbuilding industries. Muslim merchants pioneered trade routes across the Sahara Desert and along the eastern coast of Africa in pursuit of gold, ivory, copper, and other precious goods.

Rise and Fall of Great Zimbabwe

(Ma-POON-goo-bway), the first identifiable state in southern Africa, arose in the middle Limpopo River Valley, at the junction of the trade routes bringing ivory and copper from the south and gold from the north. The monsoon winds allowed Arab merchants to sail as far south as Kilwa, which eclipsed the older towns of Shanga and Manda as the preeminent trading center along the East African coast (see again Map 12.2). Control of the gold trade greatly enriched the Muslim sultans, possibly of Arabian origin, who ruled Kilwa. By the early fourteenth century the city boasted stone palaces, city walls, a Muslim law school, and a domed mosque constructed in the Indian style. South of Kilwa trade goods were relayed by local merchants from the interior and the Swahili colonies along the coast.

The mid-thirteenth century brought the rise of another powerful state, Great Zimbabwe, that would exert direct control over the main goldfields and copper mines in the interior. The capital of Great Zimbabwe consisted of a large complex of stone towers and enclosures housing a warrior elite and perhaps as many as eighteen thousand inhabitants. Similar but smaller stone enclosures (known as *zimbabwe*), built to shelter livestock as

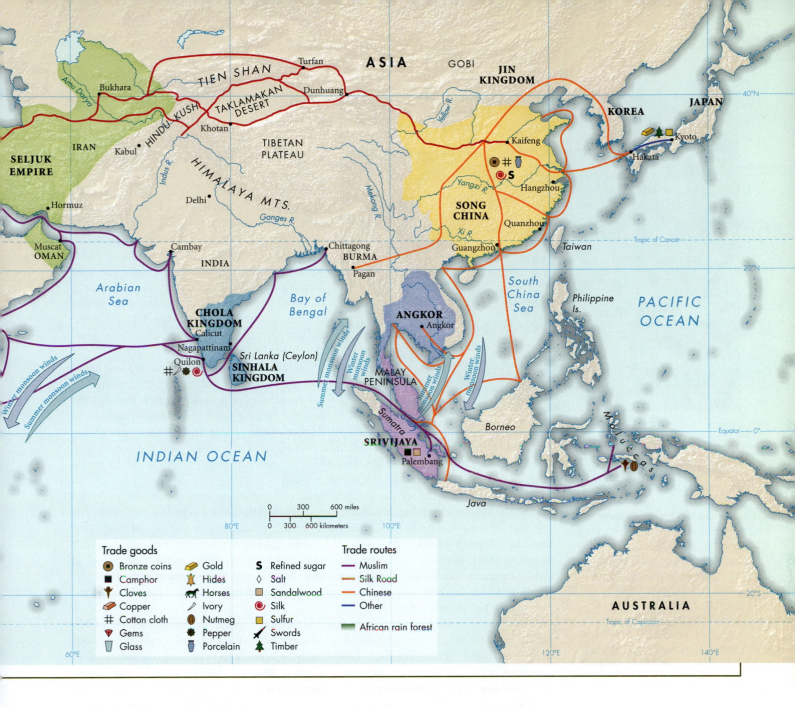

Trade goods

- ⊙ Bronze coins
- ■ Camphor
- ⚱ Cloves
- ▱ Copper
- # Cotton cloth
- ▽ Gems
- ▯ Glass
- ▮ Gold
- ⚱ Hides
- 🐎 Horses
- ✎ Ivory
- ◉ Nutmeg
- ✿ Pepper
- ▮ Porcelain
- **S** Refined sugar
- ◇ Salt
- ▢ Sandalwood
- ◉ Silk
- ▢ Sulfur
- ✕ Swords
- 🌲 Timber

Trade routes

- —— Muslim
- —— Silk Road
- —— Chinese
- —— Other
- ▬ African rain forest

well as protect their inhabitants, sprang up throughout the region. The abandonment of Mapungubwe at around the same time can probably be attributed to the diversion of commercial wealth to Great Zimbabwe. Traders prized gold for its value as an export commodity and conducted local exchange using cross-shaped copper currency. The rich array of copper goods in royal and elite burials across southern Africa confirms the importance of copper as the chief sign of wealth and status. Textiles made of raffia palm fronds, bark cloth, and cotton were also important trade items in the continent's interior.

Great Zimbabwe's dominance over the export trade could not be sustained indefinitely. In the fourteenth century the copper and ivory trade routes shifted to the Zambezi River Valley to the north. The empire fashioned by the rulers of Great Zimbabwe disintegrated in the early fifteenth century, and the capital city was abandoned by the 1450s. Although no single dominant state emerged, trade continued to flourish. The great volume of Chinese coins and porcelain shards that archaeologists have found at Great Zimbabwe and sites along the coast documents East Africa's extensive trade across the Indian Ocean.

Kilwa

Located on an island off the coast of Tanzania, Kilwa grew rich and powerful thanks to its dominance over the trade in African gold and ivory. The large quantities of Chinese pearls, porcelains, and coins unearthed at Kilwa attest to its prominence in Indian Ocean trade as well. In this German engraving from 1572, the city's domed mosques stand out among a dense cluster of multistory buildings made from stone and coral. (The National Library of Israel, Shapell Family Digitization Project and The Hebrew University of Jerusalem, Department of Geography — Historic Cities Research Project.)

Trans-Saharan Traders

The vast Sahara Desert separated most of the African continent from the Mediterranean world, but the thirst for gold breached this seemingly impenetrable barrier in the wake of the Muslim conquest of North Africa. The conversion of the Berbers to Islam and their incorporation into the far-flung Muslim trading world during the seventh century provided the catalyst for the rapid escalation of trans-Saharan trade. Reports of the fabulous gold treasure of *al-Sudan* ("country of the blacks"), the Sahel belt of grasslands spanning the southern rim of the Sahara from the Atlantic to the Indian Ocean, lured Berber and Arab merchants across the desert.

Trade across the western Sahara was negligible before the second century C.E., when Berber camel caravans began to trek through the desert, bringing food and animal products to remote salt and copper mines. Salt, essential for sustaining life in arid climates, was a valuable commodity, so precious that Saharan peoples used salt rather than gold as money. Gold from the mines at the headwaters of the Senegal and Niger rivers began to trickle northward across the Sahara by the fourth century.

Well before the rise of the trans-Saharan trade, growing interaction and exchange among the Sahel societies had begun to generate social differentiation and stratification. The majority of the population, the farmers and herders, remained free people not assigned a caste. In villages, however, communities began to specialize in manufacturing activities such as ironworking, pottery, leather making, and cotton weaving. Many in these occupational groups began to marry only among themselves. Occupational specialization, residential segregation, and endogamy—marriage within a closed group of families—fostered the formation of castes of skilled tradesmen.

By 400 C.E., clusters of specialized manufacturing villages in the inland delta of the Niger River coalesced into towns trading in iron wares, pottery, copper, salt, and leather goods as well as foodstuffs and livestock. Towns such as Jenne-jeno preserved the independent character of its various artisan communities. But in other Sahelian societies, powerful warrior elites dominated. Originating as clan leaders, these warrior chiefs appropriated ideas of caste status to define themselves as an exclusive and hereditary nobility. They also drew on traditions of sacred kingship originating in the eastern Sudan, which exalted the king as a divine figure and required him to live a cloistered private life, rarely visible to his subjects.

Gold Trade and Ghana

The earliest Muslim accounts of West Africa, dating from around 800, report that a great king—whose title, Ghana, came to be applied to both the ruler's capital and his state—monopolized the gold trade. Ghana's exact location remains uncertain, but its ruler, according to Muslim merchants, was "the wealthiest king on the face of the earth because of his treasures and stocks of gold."[8] The Muslim geographer al-Bakri described the capital of Ghana as consisting of two sizable towns, one in which the king and his court resided and a separate Muslim town that contained many clerics and scholars as well as merchants. Although the king was a pagan, al-Bakri deemed him to have led a "praiseworthy life on account of his love of justice and friendship for Muslims."[9]

Advance of Islam

At first the impact of Islam on the indigenous peoples was muted. Berber caravans halted at the desert's edge, because camels had little tolerance for the humidity and diseases of the savanna belt. Confined to segregated enclaves within the towns, Muslim merchants depended on the favor of local chiefs or the monarchs of Ghana. Yet local rulers found the lucrative profits of trade in gold and slaves irresistible, and the wealth and literacy of Muslim merchants made them valuable allies and advisers. Trade also yielded access to coveted goods such as salt, glass, horses, and swords (see again Map 12.2). The kings of Ghana and other trading cities converted to Islam by the early twelfth century, and to varying degrees required their subjects to embrace the new religion as well. At the same time Muslim commercial towns displaced many of the older trading centers such as Jenne-jeno, which were abandoned. Thus, the desire to engage in trade was a major stimulus for cultural exchange and adaptation in West Africa.

Rise of Mali

During the twelfth century Ghana's monopoly on the gold trade eroded, and its political power crumbled as well. In the thirteenth century a chieftain by the name of Sunjata (r. 1230–1255) forged alliances among his fellow Malinke to create a new empire known as Mali. Whereas Ghana probably exercised a loose sovereignty within the savanna region, Mali enforced its dominion over a much larger territory by assembling a large cavalry army equipped with horses and iron weapons purchased from Muslim traders. Unlike Ghana, Mali exercised direct control over the gold mines.

The kings of Mali combined African traditions of divine kingship with patronage of the Islamic faith. The Mali monarch Mansa Musa (MAHN-suh MOO-suh) (r. 1312–1337) caused a great sensation when he visited Cairo on his pilgrimage to Mecca in 1325. According to a contemporary observer, "Musa flooded Cairo with his benefactions, leaving no court emir nor holder of a royal office without a gift of a load of gold. . . . They exchanged gold until they depressed its value in Egypt and caused its price to fall."[10] The visit provided evidence of both the power and wealth of Mali and the increasing cultural connections between West Africa and the rest of the Muslim world.

Trade and industry flourished under Mali's umbrella of security. Muslim merchants formed family firms with networks of agents widely distributed among the oasis towns and trading posts of the Sahara. Known as *Juula* (meaning "trader" in Malinke), these Muslim merchants also extended their operations into the non-Muslim states of the rainforest belt and brought a variety of new goods, such as kola nuts, textiles, and brass and copper wares, into the Saharan trading world. Like other town-dwelling craftsmen and specialists, such as the blacksmiths and leatherworkers, the Juula became a distinct occupational caste and ethnic group whose members lived in separate residential quarters and married among themselves (see Lives and Livelihoods: The Mande Blacksmiths).

Mediterranean and European Traders

Revival of Towns

The contraction of commerce that followed the fall of the western Roman Empire persisted longer in Europe than did the economic downturn in Asia and the Islamic world. By the twelfth century, however, the rising productivity of agriculture and population growth in western Europe had greatly widened the horizons for trade. Lords encouraged the founding of towns by granting **burghers**—free citizens of towns—certain legal liberties as well as economic privileges such as tax exemptions, fixed rents, and trading rights. In England and Flanders a thriving woolen industry developed—the towns of Flanders, notably Bruges, Ghent, and Ypres, became highly specialized in weaving cloth using raw wool imported from Britain. Merchant guilds in both England and Flanders grew so powerful that they chose their own city councils and exercised considerable political autonomy. In northern Europe, repeating a dynamic we have seen before in other parts of the world, commercial expansion altered the political landscape (see Map 12.3, page 399).

Growing Power of the Italian City-States

The prosperity of the woolen industry made Flanders the wealthiest and most densely urbanized region in twelfth-century northern Europe, yet the Flemish towns were dwarfed by the great cities of Italy. Although social tensions often flared between the landed aristocracy and wealthy town-dwellers, the political fortunes of the Italian city-states remained firmly wedded to their mercantile interests. The city-states of Pisa, Genoa, and Venice aggressively pursued trade opportunities in the Mediterranean, often resorting to force to seize trade routes and ports from Muslim, Greek, and Jewish competitors. By the twelfth century Italian navies and merchant fleets dominated the Mediterranean, with Genoa paramount in the west and Venice the major power in the east.

burgher In Latin Christendom, a free citizen residing in a town who enjoyed certain legal privileges, including the right to participate in town governance.

Champagne Trade Fairs

Economic revival in northern and western Europe breathed new life into the long-defunct Roman commercial network. In the county of Champagne, southeast of Paris, a number of towns located at the intersections of Roman roads had continued to serve as local markets and sites of periodic fairs. In the twelfth century the counts of Champagne offered their protection and relief from tolls to the growing number of merchants who traveled between the textile manufacturing towns of Flanders and Italy's commercial centers. They established an annual cycle of six two-month fairs that rotated among the towns. Champagne's location midway between Flanders and Italy enhanced its stature as the major crossroads of international commerce and finance in western Europe. Merchants adopted the coins and weights used at the fairs as international standards.

Champagne's heyday as a medieval version of a free-trade zone came to an end in the early fourteenth century. Political tensions between Champagne's counts and the French monarchy frequently interrupted the smooth flow of trade. The Champagne fairs were also victims of their own success: the innovations in business practices spawned by the Champagne fairs, such as transfers of goods and money via agents and bills of exchange, made actual attendance at the fairs unnecessary. Champagne would regain fame after the seventeenth century, when its famous sparkling wine was invented, but trade and finance shifted to the rising commercial cities of northern Europe such as Antwerp and London.

COUNTERPOINT
Production, Tribute, and Trade in the Hawaiian Islands

FOCUS

How did the sources of wealth and power in the Hawaiian Islands differ from those of market economies elsewhere in the world?

During the period of this chapter, rulers everywhere sought to regulate the exchange of goods to both preserve the existing social structure and enhance their own authority. In the temple- and estate-based economies of India, Southeast Asia, Japan, and western Europe, payments in goods and services prevailed over market exchange. These payments took the form of **tribute**, obligations social inferiors owed to their superiors; thus, by its very nature tribute reinforced the hierarchical structure of society. Yet in all of these societies markets played some role in meeting people's subsistence needs. Expansion of the market economy provided access to a wider range of goods and allowed entrepreneurs to acquire independent wealth. Both the circulation of goods and the new concentrations of commercial wealth threatened to subvert the existing social hierarchy.

In societies that lacked market exchange, such as the Hawaiian Islands, rulers maintained firmer control over wealth and social order. During the thirteenth and fourteenth centuries, when hierarchical chiefdoms first formed in Hawaii, investment in agricultural production remained modest. Intensive agricultural development took off after 1400, however, as chiefs consolidated their control over land and labor. The construction of irrigation systems further strengthened the chiefs' authority, allowing them to command more resources, mobilize more warriors, and expand their domains through conquest. Complex systems of tribute payment—from commoners to local chiefs and ultimately to island-wide monarchs—facilitated the formation of powerful states.

tribute Submission of wealth, labor, and sometimes items of symbolic value to a ruling authority.

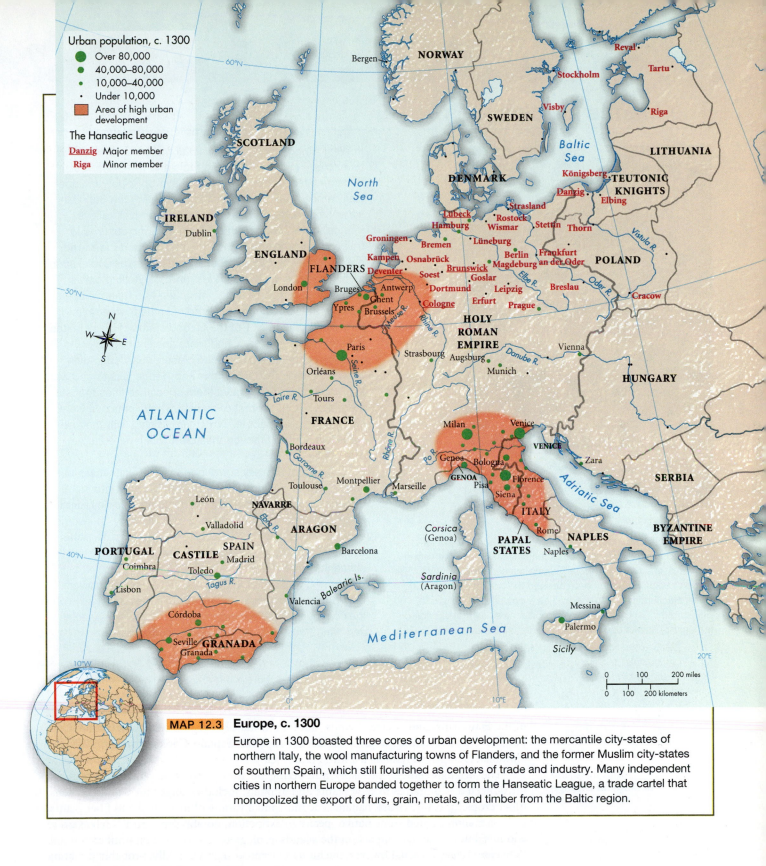

Urban population, c. 1300
- ● Over 80,000
- ● 40,000–80,000
- ● 10,000–40,000
- · Under 10,000
- ▨ Area of high urban development

The Hanseatic League
- Danzig Major member
- Riga Minor member

MAP 12.3 Europe, c. 1300

Europe in 1300 boasted three cores of urban development: the mercantile city-states of northern Italy, the wool manufacturing towns of Flanders, and the former Muslim city-states of southern Spain, which still flourished as centers of trade and industry. Many independent cities in northern Europe banded together to form the Hanseatic League, a trade cartel that monopolized the export of furs, grain, metals, and timber from the Baltic region.

Settlement and Agriculture

Humans first arrived in the Hawaiian Islands during the great wave of Polynesian voyaging of the first millennium C.E. (see Chapter 11). The dating of the initial settlement of Hawaii is disputed, with scholarly opinion ranging from as early as 300 C.E. to as late as 800. The early colonists maintained contact with distant societies in the Marquesas (the most likely origin

The Mande Blacksmiths

Komo Mask

Among the Mande peoples of West Africa, komo associations governed many aspects of community life, such as the secret rites of passage that inducted young males into adulthood. The komo associations may date back to the period 700 to 1100, when blacksmiths first emerged as a powerful social caste. Blacksmiths, who worked with wood as well as metal, carved the animal masks used in komo religious rituals. (Barakat Gallery.)

In West Africa, ironworking was far more than a useful technology for manufacturing tools and weapons. It also became a fearsome instrument of symbolic power, especially among the Mande peoples inhabiting the Sahelian savanna between the Senegal and Niger river valleys. Mande society was divided into three principal groups: free persons (including both commoners and the warrior nobility); specialized professional castes (*nyamakala*) such as blacksmiths, leatherworkers, and storytelling bards; and slaves. This three-tiered structure had taken shape at least by the time of the Mali Empire in the thirteenth and fourteenth centuries. But the unique status of blacksmiths in Mande society clearly had more ancient origins.

The nyamakala possessed closely guarded knowledge of technical arts, and this knowledge was tinged with supernatural power. It gave them special abilities that set them apart from the rest of society. The nyamakala were considered alien peoples who married only with their own kind. The right to practice their craft was a hereditary monopoly.

An aura of mystery surrounded the blacksmiths in particular, whose work involved transforming rock into metal through the sublime power of fire. Ordinary people regarded them with a mixture of dread and awe. Similarly, the women of blacksmith clans had the exclusive right to make pottery. Like iron metallurgy, pottery making required mastery of the elemental force of fire.

Armed with secret knowledge and "magical" powers, blacksmiths occupied a central place in the religious life of the community. The right to perform circumcision, a solemn and dangerous ritual of passage to adulthood, was

of the Hawaiians) and Society Islands. But long-distance voyaging ceased in around 1300. For the next five centuries, until the British explorer Captain Cook arrived in 1788, the Hawaiian archipelago remained a world unto itself.

Agriculture and Ecological Change

The original settlers, probably numbering no more than a few hundred persons, introduced a wide range of new plants and animals, including pigs, dogs, and chickens, tuber crops (taro and yams), banana, coconut, and a variety of medicinal and fiber plants. Colonists soon hunted some native species to extinction, notably large birds such as geese and ibis, but the human impact on the islands' ecology remained modest until after 1100. Between 1100 and 1650, however, the human population grew rapidly, probably doubling every century. Agricultural exploitation intensified, radically transforming the natural environment. In the geologically older western islands, the inhabitants constructed irrigated taro fields fed by stone-lined canals on the valley floors and lower hillsides. But irrigation was not practicable on the large eastern islands of Hawaii and Maui because they were largely covered by lava flows. As a result agriculture in the eastern islands lagged behind that of the western islands.

entrusted to blacksmiths. Blacksmiths also manufactured ritual objects, such as the headdresses used in religious ceremonies. They were believed to have healing powers, too. Together with leatherworkers, they made amulets (charms) for protection against demonic attack.

The social distance that separated blacksmiths from the rest of Mande society enhanced their reputation for fairness. Blacksmiths commonly acted as mediators in disputes and marriage transactions. Mande peoples often swore oaths upon a blacksmith's anvil. Most important, only blacksmiths could hold leadership positions in *komo* associations, initiation societies composed mostly of young men and charged with protecting the community against human and supernatural enemies. The ritual masks used by komo associations in their religious ceremonies were carved by blacksmiths, whose occult powers imbued the masks with magical potency.

The caste status of blacksmith clans affirmed their extraordinary powers, but it simultaneously relegated them to the margins of society. In Mande origin myths, blacksmiths appear as a powerful force to be tamed and domesticated. The Mande epics trace the founding of the Mali Empire to an intrepid warrior hero, the hunter Sunjata (see page 397), who is said to have overthrown the "blacksmith king" Sumanguru (soo-mahn-guh-roo) in the mid-thirteenth century. Sumanguru is depicted as a brutal tyrant. Sunjata's triumph over Sumanguru enabled him to gain mastery of spiritual forces without being polluted and corrupted by them. In the new social order of the Mali Empire, the dangerous powers of the blacksmiths were contained by marginalizing them as an occupational caste that was excluded from warfare and rulership and forbidden to marry outside their group. Despite their crucial importance to economic and religious life, the caste identity of the blacksmiths branded them as inferior to freeborn persons in Mande society.

QUESTIONS TO CONSIDER

1. Why did Mande society regard blacksmiths as exceptional?

2. In what ways was the caste system of West African peoples such as the Mande different from the caste system in India discussed in Chapter 6?

3. Why did the rulers of Mali perceive the Mande blacksmiths as a threat?

For Further Information:

McIntosh, Roderick. *The Peoples of the Middle Niger: The Island of Gold.* Oxford, U.K.: Blackwell, 1998.
McNaughton, Patrick R. *The Mande Blacksmiths: Knowledge, Power, and Art in West Africa.* Bloomington, IN: Indiana University Press, 1988.

Population growth and the building of irrigation systems reached their peak in the fifteenth and sixteenth centuries. This was also the period when the *ahupua'a* (ah-HOO-poo-ah-hah) system of land management developed. The ahupua'a consisted of tracts of land running down from the central mountains to the sea, creating wedge-shaped segments that cut across different ecological zones. Each ahupua'a combined a wide range of resources, including forests, fields, fishponds, and marine vegetation and wildlife.

In other Polynesian societies, kinship groups possessed joint landownership rights, but in Hawaii the land belonged to powerful kings. These rulers claimed descent from the gods and sharply distinguished themselves from the rest of society. The kings distributed the ahupua'a under their control to subordinate chiefs in return for tribute

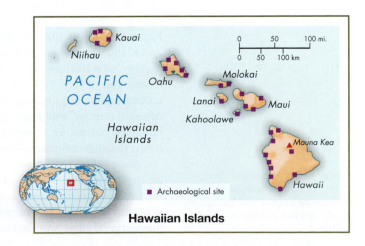

Hawaiian Islands

Hawaiian Landscape
The first European visitors to Hawaii were impressed by the intensive agriculture practiced by the Hawaiian islanders. This sketch of a Hawaiian village was drawn by a member of the expedition led by the British explorer George Vancouver, who landed at Hawaii in 1792. Cultivated fields lined with stone irrigation channels can be seen in the background. (Bishop Museum Library & Archives.)

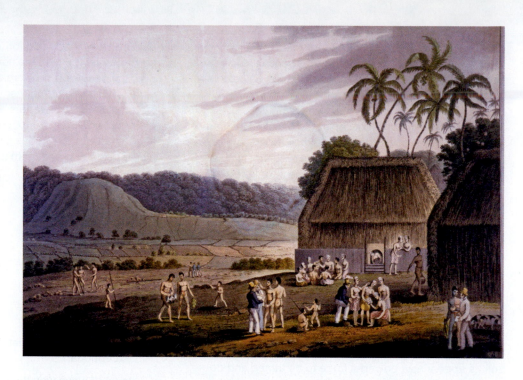

and fealty, especially in times of war. Local chiefs in turn allocated rights to land, water, and fishing grounds to commoners, who were obliged to work on the personal lands of the chief and to pay tribute in produce. These rights were etched into the landscape by the construction of stone walls that lined fields, ponds, and canals.

Exchange and Social Hierarchy

Social Stratification   Strict rules of descent and inheritance determined social rank in Hawaiian society, and an elaborate system of **taboos** reinforced social stratification. Taboos also regulated gender differences and boundaries. Women were forbidden to eat many foods, including pork, bananas, and certain kinds of fish, and had to cook their food in separate ovens and eat apart from men. Chiefs proclaimed their exalted status through temple construction, ritual performances, and personal dress. Specialized craftsmen directly under the control of the chief class fashioned the elaborate feather cloaks, capes, and helmets worn by rulers that signified their divine status.

Omnipotent Kings   In the genealogical lore of Hawaii, the oldest royal lineages were in the densely populated islands of Kauai (kah-WAH-ee) and Oahu. The ruling elites of these islands drew their power and wealth from irrigated agriculture and focused their religious worship on Kane (KAH-nay), the god of flowing waters and fertility. On the larger islands of Hawaii and Maui, where chiefs and kings derived their power from military might rather than the meager harvests from dry-land farming, their devotion centered instead on Ku, the bloodthirsty god of war. From 1400 onward the local rulers in Hawaii and Maui incessantly warred against neighboring rivals. Temple-building on Maui escalated dramatically in the fifteenth century, when two regional chiefdoms formed on opposite ends of the island and struggled bitterly for supremacy. By 1650, single, island-wide kingdoms would be established through conquest on both Maui and Hawaii.

Long before contact with Europeans, then, Hawaiian rulers forged powerful states based on highly stratified systems of social ranking. Private property did not exist. All land and resources belonged to chiefs and kings, who were regarded as gods. In the absence of the kind of market networks that emerged in Eurasia and Africa, rulers could effectively monopolize the prestige goods that gave them exalted status. Through their monopoly of not only productive

taboo In Polynesia, the designation of certain actions or objects as sacred and forbidden to anyone not of royal or chiefly status.

resources but the exchange and use of goods, Hawaiian rulers gained full command over the wealth of their realm and the labor of their subjects. Taboos served above all to regulate consumption and to enforce the sharp social divide between rulers and commoners.

Conclusion

Beginning in the tenth century, agricultural growth and commercial integration generated a sustained economic expansion across much of Eurasia and Africa. A warmer global climate and the introduction of new crops increased agricultural productivity in both the ancient centers of civilization of the Mediterranean, India, and China and the newly developing areas of settlement such as northern and eastern Europe and mainland Southeast Asia. Larger and more stable food supplies nourished population growth in cities and the countryside alike.

The farthest-reaching transformations in economic life and livelihood were the expansion of trade networks and the growing sophistication of commercial practices. Cairo, Venice, Quanzhou, and other leading commercial cities served as the crossroads for enterprising merchants such as Allan bin Hassun; their trade ventures linked the Mediterranean and the Middle East to sub-Saharan Africa, the Indian Ocean, and China. The cosmopolitan merchant communities of these cities were the forefathers of this "commercial revolution" and the new forms of business organization and banking that it spawned. In contrast to places such as Hawaii, where wealth remained yoked to political power, the dynamic market economy threatened to subvert the existing social order. Commercial cities harbored new centers of education and intellectual inquiry, too, and these also posed challenges to established political and cultural authority, as we will see in the next chapter.

Dramatic as the changes in economic life were during these centuries, we should remember their limitations. Population growth eventually outpaced increases in productivity. The profits generated by commerce accrued mainly to merchants and their fellow investors—including religious establishments and landowning aristocrats—rather than producers. Hunger was a constant threat, and the poor had to survive on the last dregs of grain and chaff in the final months before the new harvest.

By 1300, the capacities of existing agricultural and commercial systems were reaching their limits. Under the intensifying strain of population growth, natural disasters, and political pressures, the commercial networks spanning Eurasia and Africa began to break down, ushering in an age of crisis and economic contraction that we will consider in Chapter 15.

NOTES

1. Quotations from S. D. Goitein, "Portrait of a Medieval India Trader: Three Letters from the Cairo Geniza," *Bulletin of the School of Oriental and African Studies,* 50, no. 3 (1987): 461; S. D. Goitein, *A Mediterranean Society: The Jewish Communities of the World as Portrayed in the Documents of the Cairo Geniza* (Berkeley: University of California Press, 1978–88), 3:194; 5:221.
2. Kekaumenos, *Strategikon,* quoted in Angeliki E. Laiou, "Economic Thought and Ideology," in Angeliki E. Laiou, ed., *The Economic History of Byzantium from the Seventh Through the Fifteenth Century* (Washington, DC: Dumbarton Oaks Research Library and Collection, 2002), 3:1127.
3. Quotation from Fang Hui (1227–1307), cited in Richard von Glahn, "Towns and Temples: Urban Growth and Decline in the Yangzi Delta, 1100–1400," in Paul Jakov Smith and Richard von Glahn, eds., *The Song Yuan-Ming Transition in Chinese History* (Cambridge, MA: Harvard University Council on East Asian Studies, 2004), 182.
4. Ibn Hazm, *The Ring of the Dove: A Treatise on the Art and Practice of Arab Love* (London: Luzac, 1953), 74.
5. Al-Muqaddasi, *The Best Divisions for Knowledge of the Regions,* trans. Basil Anthony Collins (Reading, U.K.: Garnet Publishing, 1994), 181.
6. Quoted in Goitein, *A Mediterranean Society,* 1:200.
7. Translation adapted from Yuan Ts'ai, *Family Instructions for the Yuan Clan,* quoted in Patricia Buckley Ebrey, *Family and Property in Sung China* (Princeton, NJ: Princeton University Press, 1984), 267.

8. Ibn Hawqal, *The Picture of the Earth*, translated in N. Levtzion and J. F. P. Hopkins, eds., *Corpus of Early Arabic Sources for West African History* (Cambridge, U.K.: Cambridge University Press, 1981), 49.

9. Al-Bakri, *Kitab al masalik wa-'l-mamalik*, translated in Levtzion and Hopkins, eds., *Corpus of Early Arabic Sources*, 79.

10. Al-Umari, "The Kingdom of Mali and What Appertains to It" (1338), cited in Levtzion and Hopkins, eds., *Corpus of Early Arabic Sources*, 270–271.

RESOURCES FOR RESEARCH

Agricultural Innovation and Diffusion

The diffusion of crops and the invention of new technologies gave impetus to major advances in agricultural productivity across Eurasia between 900 and 1300. Duby's classic work on the early medieval European economy remains unsurpassed, but Verhulst, who reviews the large historiography on this topic and the growing body of archaeological evidence, provides a valuable supplement for the early part of this period.

Bray, Francesca. *The Rice Economies: Technology and Development in Asian Societies.* 1986.

Chaudhuri, K. N. *Asia Before Europe: Economy and Civilization of the Indian Ocean from the Rise of Islam to 1750.* 1990.

Duby, Georges. *The Early Growth of the European Economy: Warriors and Peasants from the Seventh to the Twelfth Century.* 1974.

Verhulst, Adriaan. *The Carolingian Economy.* 2002.

Watson, A. M. *Agricultural Innovation in the Early Islamic World: The Diffusion of Crops and Farming Techniques, 700–1100.* 1983.

Industrial Growth and the Money Economy

Technological innovation was also a key stimulus to industrial growth, especially in China. Lopez was the pioneer in establishing the now widely accepted idea of a "commercial revolution" in medieval Europe. Herlihy and Bray are landmarks in the study of women, work, and the domestic economy.

Bray, Francesca. *Technology and Gender: Fabrics of Power in Late Imperial China.* 1997.

Epstein, Steven A. *An Economic and Social History of Later Medieval Europe, 1000–1500.* 2009.

Herlihy, David. *Opera Muliebria: Women and Work in Medieval Europe.* 1990.

Laiou, Angeliki E., and Cécile Morrison. *The Byzantine Economy.* 2007.

Lombard, Maurice. *The Golden Age of Islam* (rpt.). 2004.

Lopez, Robert S. *The Commercial Revolution of the Middle Ages, 950–1350.* 1976.

Merchants and Trade Networks in Afro-Eurasia

We have much more abundant documentary evidence of the increasingly far-flung activities of merchants than we have for those of farmers and industrialists. Abu-Lughod provides the most comprehensive synthesis of the development of cross-cultural exchange and commercial practices in this era. Favier and Constable both marshal impressive bodies of evidence on the merchant world of western Europe.

Abu-Lughod, Janet. *Before European Hegemony: The World System, A.D. 1250–1350.* 1989.

Constable, Olivia Remie. *Trade and Traders in Muslim Spain: The Commercial Realignment of the Iberian Peninsula, 900–1500.* 1994.

Coquery-Vidrovitch, Catherine. *The History of African Cities South of the Sahara: From the Origins to Colonization.* 2005.

Favier, Jean. *Gold and Spices: The Rise of Commerce in the Middle Ages.* 1998.

Sen, Tansen. *Buddhism, Diplomacy, and Trade: The Realignment of Sino-Indian Relations, 600–1400.* 2003.

COUNTERPOINT: Production, Tribute, and Trade in the Hawaiian Islands

Through painstaking archaeological research, the major developments in land use and economic life in the Pacific Islands before European contact are gradually becoming clear. Kirch is the foremost authority on the archaeology of the Hawaiian Islands and Polynesia generally. Earle's study of the different types of chiefdom societies emphasizes the crucial importance of economic power in the formation of Hawaiian chiefdoms.

Earle, Timothy. *How Chiefs Come to Power: The Political Economy in Prehistory.* 1997.

Kirch, Patrick V. *Feathered Gods and Fishhooks: An Introduction to Hawaiian Archaeology and Prehistory.* 1985.

Kirch, Patrick V., and Jean-Louis Rallu, eds. *The Growth and Collapse of Pacific Island Societies: Archaeological and Demographic Perspectives.* 2007.

▶ **For additional primary sources from this period**, see *Sources of Crossroads and Cultures.*

▶ **For Web sites, images, and documents related to topics in this chapter**, see Make History at bedfordstmartins.com/smith.

The major global development in this chapter ▶ The sustained economic expansion that spread across Afro-Eurasia from 900 to 1300.

IMPORTANT EVENTS

850–1267	Chola kingdom in southern India
960–1279	Song dynasty in China
969	Fatimids conquer Egypt
1024	The Song dynasty issues the first paper money in world history
1055	Seljuk Turks capture Baghdad
c. 1120–1150	Construction of Angkor Wat begins
1127	The Jurchen conquer north China; the Song dynasty retains control of southern China
c. 1150–1300	Heyday of the Champagne fairs
c. 1200–1400	Formation of first chiefdoms in the Hawaiian Islands
1230–1255	Reign of Sunjata, founder of the Mali Empire in West Africa
1250–1517	Mamluk dynasty in Egypt
1258	The Italian city-states of Florence and Genoa mint the first gold coins issued in Latin Christendom
1323–1325	Pilgrimage to Mecca of Musa Mansa, ruler of Mali
c. 1400–1450	Great Zimbabwe in southern Africa reaches peak of prosperity

KEY TERMS

bill of exchange (p. 386)   serf (p. 376)
burgher (p. 397)   taboo (p. 402)
cartel (p. 390)   tribute (p. 398)
guild (p. 388)   usury (p. 386)
iqta (p. 378)
joint stock company
   (p. 391)

CHAPTER OVERVIEW QUESTIONS

1. How did agricultural changes contribute to commercial and industrial growth?

2. What technological breakthroughs increased productivity most significantly?

3. What social institutions and economic innovations did merchants devise to overcome the risks and dangers of long-distance trade?

4. In what ways did the profits of commerce translate into social and economic power?

5. Above all, who benefited most from these economic changes?

SECTION FOCUS QUESTIONS

1. Which groups took the most active role in adopting new agricultural technologies in the different regions of Eurasia during the centuries from 900 to 1300?

2. How did the composition and organization of the industrial workforce change in different parts of Eurasia during this period?

3. How did the commercial revival of 900 to 1300 reorient trade routes across Afro-Eurasia?

4. How did the sources of wealth and power in the Hawaiian Islands differ from those of market economies elsewhere in the world?

MAKING CONNECTIONS

1. In what ways did the spread of new crops and farming technologies during this period have a different impact in the Islamic world and in Asia?

2. How had the principal east-west trade routes between Asia and the Mediterranean world changed since the time of the Han and Roman empires (see Chapters 6 and 7)?

3. To what extent did the Christian, Jewish, and Muslim merchant communities of the Mediterranean adopt similar forms of commercial organization and business practices during the "commercial revolution" of 900 to 1300? How can we explain the differences and similarities among these groups?

13

AT A CROSSROADS ▲

Schools in Latin Christendom organized the learning of ancient Greece and Rome into the seven liberal arts. The trivium (Latin for "three roads") of logic, rhetoric, and grammar endowed the student with eloquence; the quadrivium ("four roads") of arithmetic, geometry, astronomy, and music led to knowledge. This detail from a mural composed between 1365 and 1367 for a Franciscan chapel in Florence depicts the trivium (at right in first row) and the quadrivium (at left) in the persons of the ancient scholars credited with their invention; behind each scholar sits his muse, represented in female form. (Scala/Art Resource, NY.)

Centers of Learning and the Transmission of Culture

900–1300

In her masterful novel of court life in Heian Japan, *The Tale of Genji*, Murasaki Shikibu (c. 973–1025) sought to defend the art of fiction and women as readers of fiction. Murasaki's hero, Genji, finds his adopted daughter copying a courtly romance novel and mocks women's passionate enthusiasm for such frivolous writings. Genji protests that "there is hardly a word of truth in all of these books, as you know perfectly well, but here you are utterly fascinated by such fables, taking them quite seriously and avidly copying every word." At the end of his speech, though, Genji reverses his original judgment. Romance novels, he concludes, may be fabricated, but they have the virtue of describing "this world exactly as it is."[1]

Many of Murasaki's contemporaries shared Genji's initial low opinion of the content of courtly romances, but they also rejected such works at least in part because they were written in vernacular Japanese—the language of everyday speech. In Lady Murasaki's day, classical Chinese was the language of politics and religion at the Heian court. Writing in the Japanese vernacular was considered at best a trifling skill, acceptable for letters and diaries but ill-suited to the creation of literature or art.

Lady Murasaki had been born into an aristocratic family of middling rank. She was a quick study as a child and, she tells us, far more proficient at Chinese than her brother.

BACKSTORY

As we saw in Chapters 9 and 10, from 400 to 1000 religious traditions consolidated in the main centers of civilization across Eurasia. Christianity prevailed in many parts of the former Roman Empire, but divisions deepened between the Greek church, which was closely allied with the Byzantine Empire, and the Latin church of Rome. Islam was fully established as the official religion across a vast territory extending from Spain to Persia. In India, the classical Brahmanic religion, recast in the form of Hinduism, steadily displaced Buddhism from the center of religious and intellectual life. In contrast, the Mahayana tradition of Buddhism enjoyed great popularity at all levels of society in East Asia. In China, however, Buddhist beliefs clashed with the long-cherished secular ideals of Confucian philosophy. In all of these regions, the study of scripture—and the written language of sacred texts—dominated schooling and learning.

Church and Universities in Latin Christendom

FOCUS What political, social, and religious forces led to the founding of the first European universities?

Students and Scholars in Islamic Societies

FOCUS To what extent did Sunni and Sufi schools foster a common cultural and religious identity among Muslims?

The Cosmopolitan and Vernacular Realms in India and Southeast Asia

FOCUS What political and religious forces contributed to the development of a common culture across India and Southeast Asia and its subsequent fragmentation into regional cultures?

Learning, Schools, and Print Culture in East Asia

FOCUS To what extent did intellectual and educational trends in Song China influence its East Asian neighbors?

COUNTERPOINT: Writing and Political Power in Mesoamerica

FOCUS How did the relationship between political power and knowledge of writing in Mesoamerica differ from that in the other civilizations studied in this chapter?

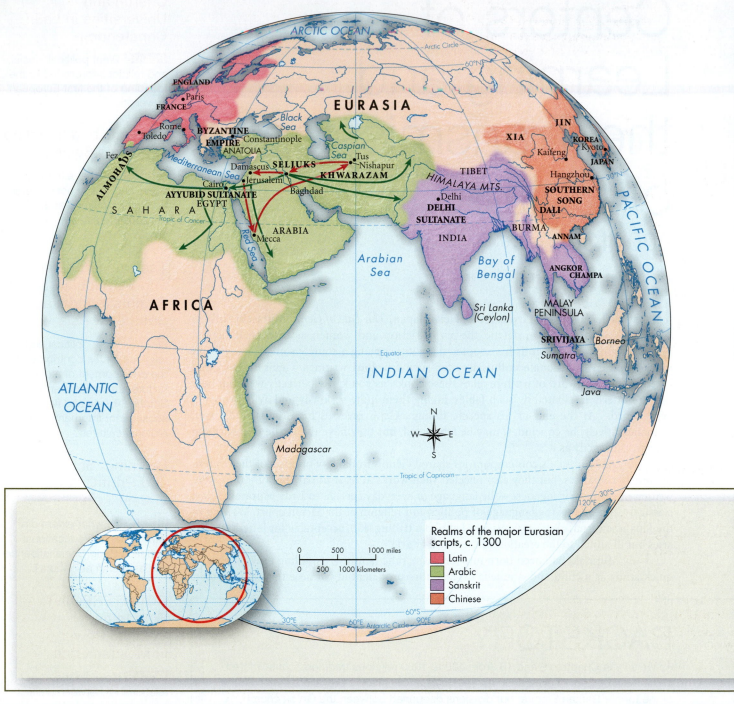

Realms of the major Eurasian
scripts, c. 1300

- Latin
- Arabic
- Sanskrit
- Chinese

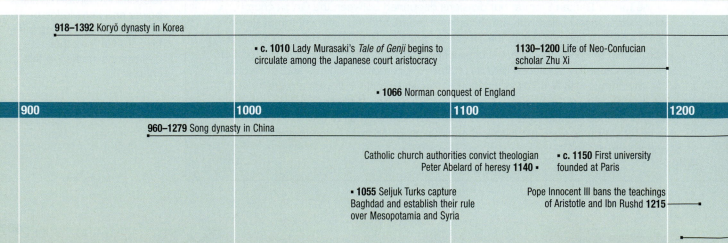

918–1392 Koryŏ dynasty in Korea

- c. 1010 Lady Murasaki's *Tale of Genji* begins to
circulate among the Japanese court aristocracy

1130–1200 Life of Neo-Confucian
scholar Zhu Xi

- 1066 Norman conquest of England

900   **1000**   **1100**   **1200**

960–1279 Song dynasty in China

Catholic church authorities convict theologian
Peter Abelard of heresy 1140 ▪

- c. 1150 First university
founded at Paris

- 1055 Seljuk Turks capture
Baghdad and establish their rule
over Mesopotamia and Syria

Pope Innocent III bans the teachings
of Aristotle and Ibn Rushd 1215

Knowledge of Chinese was considered unbecoming in a woman, however. Calligraphy (brush writing), poetry, and music were deemed appropriate subjects for female education. Like many women of her class, Murasaki was also fond of romance tales, which typically revolved around the lives, loves, and marriages of court women. Widowed in her twenties, Murasaki had already acquired some fame as a writer when she was summoned in around 1006 to serve as lady-in-waiting to the empress. During her years at the court Murasaki completed her *Tale of Genji*. Manuscript copies circulated widely among court women in Murasaki's lifetime and captivated a sizable male readership as well. From Murasaki's time forward, fiction and poetry written in the Japanese vernacular gained distinction as serious works of literature.

Yet Chinese remained the language of officials, scholars, and priests. The role of Chinese as the language of public discourse and political and religious authority throughout East Asia paralleled that of Latin in western Europe, of Arabic in the Islamic world, and of Sanskrit in South and Southeast Asia. Between the tenth and the fourteenth centuries these cosmopolitan languages—languages that transcended national boundaries—became deeply embedded in new educational institutions, and as a result their intellectual and aesthetic prestige grew. Although writing in vernacular languages gained new prominence as well, the goal was not to address a wider, nonelite audience. Rather, the emergence of vernacular literature was often closely tied to courtly culture, as in Murasaki's Japan. Authors writing in the vernacular still wrote for elite, learned readers.

Choosing to write in the vernacular was both a political and an artistic statement. The turn toward the vernacular was undoubtedly related to the ebbing authority of vast multinational empires and the rise of national and regional states. But the emergence of vernacular literary languages did not simply reflect existing national social and political identities; they were instrumental in inventing regional and national identities. Thus, both cosmopolitan and vernacular languages helped create new cultural connections, the former by facilitating the development of international cultural communities, and the latter by broadcasting the idea that nations were defined, in part, by the shared culture of their inhabitants.

MAPPING THE WORLD

The Major Written Languages of Eurasia, c. 1300

The use of a common written language fostered cultural unity within each of the four major regional societies of Eurasia. The spread of the four "classical" languages—Latin, Arabic, Sanskrit, and Chinese—resulted from their prominent role as the written word of religious scriptures. After 1000, a shift toward vernacular, or everyday, written languages occurred in all of these regions, but the classical languages retained their cultural authority, especially in religion and higher education.

ROUTES ▼

→ Spread of Sufi orders, 1150–1300

→ Travels of Abu Hamid al-Ghazali, 1091–1111

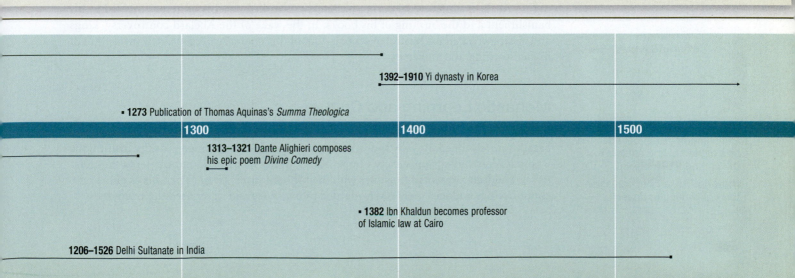

1392–1910 Yi dynasty in Korea

▪ 1273 Publication of Thomas Aquinas's *Summa Theologica*

1300 **1400** **1500**

1313–1321 Dante Alighieri composes his epic poem *Divine Comedy*

▪ 1382 Ibn Khaldun becomes professor of Islamic law at Cairo

1206–1526 Delhi Sultanate in India

OVERVIEW
QUESTIONS

The major global development in this chapter: The expansion of learning and education across Eurasia from 900 to 1300 and its relationship to the rise of regional and national identities.

As you read, consider:

1. Did the spread of higher learning reinforce or undermine established political and religious authority?

2. How did educational institutions reshape social hierarchy and elite culture?

3. What were the different uses of cosmopolitan languages (which transcended national boundaries) and vernacular (everyday) languages, and to what degree did they broaden access to written knowledge?

4. How did the different technologies of writing affect the impact of the written word?

Church and Universities in Latin Christendom

FOCUS

What political, social, and religious forces led to the founding of the first European universities?

Between the tenth and the fourteenth centuries, Latin Christendom witnessed the emergence of a unified learned culture. The values and self-images of clergy and knights increasingly converged. For knights, chivalric virtue and dedication to defense of the Christian faith replaced the wanton lifestyle of the Germanic warriors. At the same time, the clergy became more militant in their promotion of orthodoxy, as reform-minded religious orders devoted themselves to spreading the faith and stamping out heresy.

Schooling created a common elite culture and a single educated class. The career of Peter Abelard (1079–1142) captures this transformation. Abelard's father, a French knight, engaged a tutor to educate young Peter in his future duties as a warrior and lord. Abelard later recalled that "I was so carried away by my love of learning that I renounced the glory of a soldier's life, made over my inheritance and rights of the elder son to my brothers, and withdrew from the court of Mars [war] in order to kneel at the feet of Minerva [learning]."[2] Abelard's intellectual daring ultimately provoked charges of heresy that led to his banishment and the burning of his books. In the wake of the Abelard controversy, kings and clerics wrestled for control of schools. Out of this contest emerged a new institution of higher learning, the university.

Monastic Learning and Culture

cathedral school In Latin Christendom, a school attached to a cathedral and subject to the authority of a bishop.

rhetoric The art of persuasion through writing or speech.

From the time of Charlemagne (r. 768–814), royal courts and Christian monasteries became closely allied. Royally sponsored monasteries grew into huge, wealthy institutions whose leaders came from society's upper ranks. Many monks and nuns entered the cloisters as children, presented (together with their inheritances) by their parents as gifts to the church. Kings and local nobles safeguarded monasteries and supervised their activities.

Devoted to the propagation of right religion and seeking educated men to staff their governments, Charlemagne and his successors promoted a revival of classical learning consistent with the established doctrines of Latin Christianity. Charlemagne summoned famous scholars to his court and gave them the tasks of reforming ecclesiastic practices and establishing an authoritative text of the Bible. Although he never realized his hope that schooling would be widely available, local bishops began to found **cathedral schools**— schools attached to a cathedral and subject to a bishop's authority—as a complement to monastic education.

Elementary schools trained students to speak and read Latin. Advanced education in both monasteries and cathedral schools centered on the "liberal arts," particularly the Roman *trivium* (TREE-vee-um) (Latin for "three roads") of grammar, rhetoric, and logic. Roman educators had championed **rhetoric**—the art of persuasion through writing or speech—and especially oratorical skill as crucial to a career in government service. Monastic teachers likewise stressed the importance of rhetoric and oratory for monks and priests. Unlike the Romans, however, the clergy deemphasized logic; they sought to establish the primacy of revelation over philosophical reasoning. Similarly, the clergy separated the exact sciences of the Greeks—the *quadrivium* (kwo-DRIV-ee-uhm) ("four roads") of arithmetic, geometry, music, and astronomy—from the core curriculum of the trivium and treated these fields as specialized subjects for advanced study.

Bishops appointed "master scholars" to take charge of teaching at the cathedral schools. The masters in effect had a monopoly on teaching within their cities. Individuals who ventured to teach without official recognition as a master faced excommunication. The privileged status of these masters and their greater receptivity to logic and the quadrivium caused friction between cathedral schools and monasteries.

The revival of learning encouraged by Charlemagne and the Germanic kings led to a dramatic increase in book production, including theological works, biblical commentaries, encyclopedias, and saints' lives. The kings distributed manuscripts to monasteries, where scribes and artists made copies. By the eleventh century many religious texts were created as lavish works of art featuring copious illustration and expensive materials such

Cathedral Schools

Emphasis on Liberal Arts

Boom in Book Production

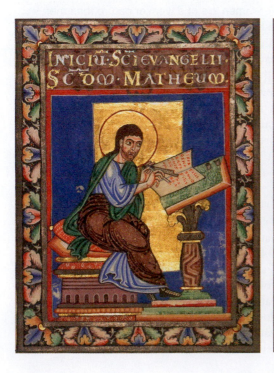

Deluxe Illustrated Manuscript
Monastic communities in Latin Christendom created many beautifully illustrated copies of the Gospels, the accounts of the life of Christ. The first page of this *Gospel of Matthew*, produced at a German monastery in around 1120 to 1140, shows Saint Matthew writing with a quill pen and sharpening knife. On the next page the first line of the Gospel begins with a large letter *L* (the beginning of the word *liber*, "book"), nested among golden vines against a background resembling the luxurious Byzantine silks highly prized in Europe. (The J. Paul Getty Museum, Los Angeles, Ms. Ludwig II 3, fol.10, Decorated Incipit Page, ca.1120-1140, Temera colors, gold and silver on parchment, Leaf: 9 × 6 ½ in.)

Medical Professionals of Latin Christendom

Economic revival and urban growth in Europe after 1000 spurred major changes in the practice and study of medicine. The rising urban commercial and professional classes increasingly demanded academically trained physicians. The cathedral schools, and later the universities, added medicine as an advanced subject of study. The institutionalization of medicine as an academic discipline transformed learned doctors into a professional class that tightly regulated its membership, practices, and standards.

In around 1173, the Jewish traveler Benjamin of Tudela described Salerno, in southern Italy, as the home of "the principal medical university of Christendom." By *university* Benjamin meant an organized group of scholars, not a formal educational institution. By the tenth century Salerno had already achieved renown for its skilled doctors. Many hailed from the city's large Jewish and Greek communities and were familiar with Arabic and Byzantine medical traditions. Beginning in the eleventh century, Salerno's learned doctors produced many medical writings that profoundly influenced medical knowledge and training across Latin Christendom.

Among the notable scholars at Salerno was Constantine the African, a Muslim who arrived from North Africa, possibly as a drug merchant, in around 1070. Constantine converted to Christianity and entered the famed Montecassino monastery north of Salerno. His translations of Muslim, Jewish, and Greek works on medicine became the basis of medical instruction in European universities for centuries afterward.

Salerno's doctors also contributed important writings on gynecology and obstetrics. A local female healer named Trota became a famed authority on gynecology ("women's medicine"). A Salerno manuscript falsely attributed to Trota justified singling out women's illnesses as a separate branch of medicine:

Trota Expounds on the Nature of Women

The *Trotula*, a set of three treatises on gynecology and women's health, was probably composed in Salerno in the twelfth century. All three works were attributed to Trota, a healer acclaimed as an authority on female physiology, although only one is likely to have come from her hand. In this illustration from a fourteenth-century French encyclopedia on natural science, Trota sits before a large open book and instructs a clerk in "the secrets of nature." (Bibliothèque de Rennes Métropole, MS593, folio 532.)

Because women are of a weaker nature than men, so more than men they are afflicted, especially in childbirth. It is for this reason also that more frequently diseases abound in them than in men, especially around the organs assigned to the work of nature. And because only with shame and embarrassment do they confess the fragility of the condition of their diseases that occur around their secret parts, they do not dare reveal their distress to male physicians. Therefore,

as gold leaf. A strikingly different style of creating manuscripts, however, was developed by the Cistercians, a new religious order that spread like wildfire across Europe within fifty years of its founding in 1098 (see Chapter 14). The Cistercians rebelled against the opulent lifestyle of wealthy monastic communities and dedicated themselves to lives of simplicity and poverty. In keeping with its principles of frugality, the Cistercian order produced great numbers of religious texts without elaborate decoration. Cistercian clergy also abhorred the growing importance of reasoning and logic in the cathedral schools, instead emphasizing religious education based on memorization, contemplation, and spiritual faith. Thus, the expansion of learning created both new connections and new divisions in Europe's intellectual and cultural elite.

their misfortune, which ought to be pitied, and especially the sake of a certain woman, moved me to provide some remedy for their above-mentioned diseases.[1]

The author attributed women's infirmity to their physical constitution and the trauma of childbirth, but also noted that women were less likely to seek treatment from male doctors. Local authorities, however, typically prohibited women other than midwives from treating patients.

Despite its outpouring of medical treatises, Salerno had no formal institution for medical training until the thirteenth century. By that time the universities of Bologna and Paris had surpassed Salerno as centers of medical learning. Bologna, for example, revived the study of anatomy and surgery and introduced human dissection as part of the curriculum. At the universities, students studied medicine only after completing rigorous training in the liberal arts.

The growing professionalization of medicine nurtured a new self-image of the doctor. Guy de Chauliac, a surgeon trained at Paris in the fourteenth century, wrote:

> I say that the doctor should be well mannered, bold in many ways, fearful of dangers, that he should abhor the false cures or practices. He should be affable to the sick, kindhearted to his colleagues, wise in his prognostications. He should be chaste, sober, compassionate, and merciful: he should not be covetous, grasping in money matters, and then he will receive a salary commensurate with his labors, the financial ability of his patients, the success of the treatment, and his own dignity.[2]

The emphasis on high ethical standards was crucial to the effort to elevate medicine's stature as an honorable occupation given the popular image of doctors and pharmacists as charlatans who, in the English poet Chaucer's mocking words, "each made money from the other's guile."[3]

This professional class of doctors steeped in rigorous study and guided by Christian compassion largely served the upper classes, however. Care of the poor and the rural populace was left to uneducated barber-surgeons, bonesetters, and faith healers.

---

1. Monica H. Green, ed. and trans., *The Trotula: An English Translation of the Medieval Compendium of Women's Medicine* (Philadelphia: University of Pennsylvania Press, 2002), 65.
2. Guy de Chauliac, "Inventarium sive chirurgia magna," quoted in Vern L. Bullough, *The Development of Medicine as a Profession: The Contribution of the Medieval University to Modern Medicine* (New York: Hafner Publishing, 1966), 93–94.
3. Geoffrey Chaucer, "Prologue," *The Canterbury Tales* (Harmondsworth, U.K.: Penguin), 30.

QUESTIONS TO CONSIDER

1. What kind of education and personal characteristics were considered necessary to become a professional physician?

2. Why did the public hold doctors in low regard? How did university education aim to improve that image?

For Further Information:
Bullough, Vern L. *The Development of Medicine as a Profession: The Contribution of the Medieval University to Modern Medicine*. New York: Hafner Publishing, 1966.
Siraisi, Nancy. *Medieval and Early Renaissance Medicine: An Introduction to Knowledge and Practice*. Chicago: University of Chicago Press, 1990.

The Rise of Universities

During the eleventh and twelfth centuries, demand for advanced education rose steadily. Eager young students traveled to distant cities to study with renowned masters. Unable to accommodate all of these students by themselves, masters began to hire staffs of specialized teachers who taught medicine, law, and theology in addition to the liberal arts. Certain schools acquired international reputations for excellence in particular specialties: Montpellier and Salerno in medicine, Bologna in law, Paris and Oxford in theology. These schools also applied higher learning to secular purposes. Montpellier and Salerno incorporated Greek and Arabic works into the study of medicine (see Lives and Livelihoods: Medical Professionals of Latin Christendom). At Bologna separate schools were established for civil and church law.

Increased Demand for Advanced Education

Influence of Greek and Muslim Learning

Christian conquests of Muslim territories in Spain and Sicily in the eleventh century reintroduced Greek learning to Latin Christendom via translations from Arabic. In 1085, King Alfonso VI (r. 1072–1109) of Castile captured Toledo, a city renowned as a center of learning where Muslims, Jews, and Christians freely intermingled. He made it his capital, and he and his successors preserved its multicultural heritage and spirit of religious toleration. In the twelfth century Toledo's Arabic-speaking Jewish and Christian scholars translated into Latin the works of Aristotle and other ancient Greek writers as well as philosophical, scientific, and medical writings by Muslim authors. Access to this vast body of knowledge had a profound impact on European intellectual circles. The commentaries on Aristotle by the Muslim philosopher Ibn Rushd (IB-uhn RUSHED) (1126–1198), known in Latin as Averröes (uh-VERR-oh-eez), sought to reconcile the paradoxes between faith and reason. They attracted keen interest from Christian theologians grappling with similar questions.

Ibn Rushd's insistence that faith is incomplete without rational understanding, for which he was persecuted and exiled, added new fuel to the intellectual controversies that flared up in Paris in the 1120s. Peter Abelard, who based his study of theology on the principle that "nothing can be believed unless it is first understood," attracted thousands of students to his lectures. Abelard's commitment to demonstrating the central tenets of Christian doctrine by applying reason and logical proof aroused heated controversy. Church authorities in 1140 found Abelard guilty of heresy and exiled him from Paris. He died a broken man two years later.

The First European Universities

The dispute over the primacy of reason or faith continued after Abelard's death. Paris's numerous masters organized themselves into guilds to defend their independence from the local bishop and from hostile religious orders such as the Cistercians, who had led the campaign against Abelard. The popes at Rome, eager to extend the reach of their own authority, placed Paris's schools of theology under their own supervision. In 1215 Pope Innocent III (1198–1216) formally recognized Paris's schools of higher learning as a **university**—a single corporation including masters and students from all the city's schools—under the direction of the pope's representative. Universities at Oxford and Bologna soon gained similar legal status.

In the end, though, chartering universities as independent corporations insulated them from clerical control. European monarchs, eager to enlist educated men in government service, became ardent patrons of established schools and provided endowments to create new ones. Consequently, during the thirteenth century more than thirty universities sprang up in western Europe (see Map 13.1). Royal patrons gave the universities leverage against local bishops and municipal councils. In some places, such as Oxford in England, the university became the dominant institution in local society, thanks to its substantial property holdings and control over both ecclesiastic and civil courts.

Among all the university towns, Paris emerged as the intellectual capital of Latin Christendom in the thirteenth century. Despite a papal ban on teaching Aristotle's works on natural science, the city swarmed with prominent teachers espousing Aristotle's ideas and methods. Even conservative scholars came to recognize the need to reconcile Christian doctrine with Greek philosophy. Thomas Aquinas (c. 1225–1274), a theologian at the University of Paris, incorporated Abelard's methods of logical argument into his great synthesis of Christian teachings, *Summa Theologica*. It stirred turbulent controversy, and much of it was banned until shortly before Aquinas's canonization as a saint in 1323. Academic freedom in the universities, to the extent that it existed, rested on an insecure balance among the competing interests of kings, bishops, and the papacy for control over the hearts and minds of their students.

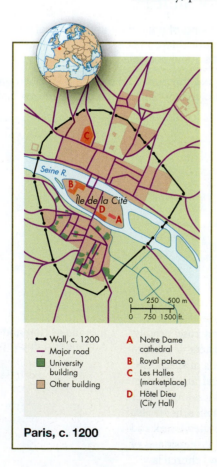

Wall, c. 1200
— Major road
■ University building
■ Other building

A Notre Dame cathedral
B Royal palace
C Les Halles (marketplace)
D Hôtel Dieu (City Hall)

Paris, c. 1200

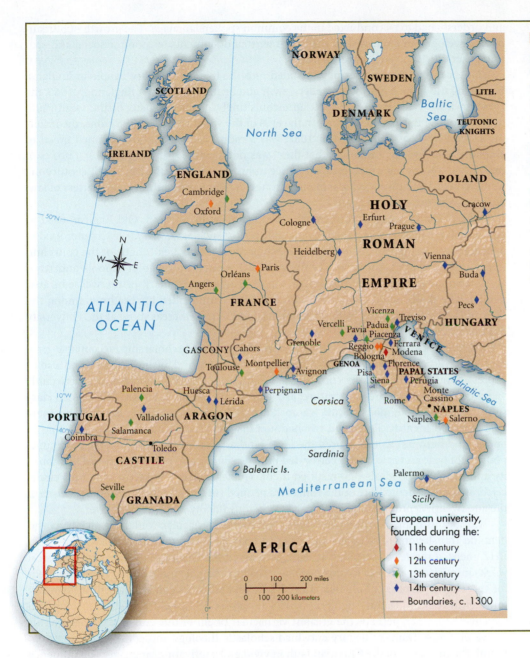

MAP 13.1

Founding of Universities in Latin Christendom, c. 1150–1400

By the twelfth century, universities eclipsed monasteries and cathedral schools as the most prestigious centers of learning in Latin Christendom. Universities were created by royal or municipal charters that affirmed their independence from clerical control. They attracted students from many lands and thus helped to forge a common elite culture across most of Europe.

European university, founded during the:
- 11th century
- 12th century
- 13th century
- 14th century
- Boundaries, c. 1300

Vernacular Language and Literature

The growing need for literacy was a driving force behind the expansion of schooling and the founding of universities in Latin Europe. The mental agility and practical knowledge obtained by mastering the liberal arts curriculum had wide applications in bureaucratic and ecclesiastic office, professional careers, and private business. Schooling based on literacy in Latin fostered a unified elite culture across western Europe, well beyond national boundaries. At the same time, however, the practical needs of government and business and changes in the self-image of the rising administrative and commercial classes encouraged writing in a **vernacular language**—the language of everyday speech.

Despite the dominance of Latin in formal education, commercial growth and political expansion demanded more practical forms of literacy. The everyday business of government—recording disputes and judicial settlements, collecting vital statistics, transmitting warrants

university In Latin Christendom, a single corporate body that included teachers and students from a range of different academic disciplines.

vernacular language The language of everyday speech, in contrast to a language that is mainly literary.

Practical Uses of Vernacular Writing

and orders—had to be conducted in the common spoken language. The growth of bureaucracy developed in tandem with the use of written documents to monitor social and economic activities and control resources.

Government most powerfully intruded into the lives of ordinary people in England. Following the French Norman invaders' swift and brutal conquest of England in 1066, the Norman king William I undertook an astonishingly detailed census of the wealth and property of the English population. In the eyes of the vanquished Anglo-Saxons, the resulting *Domesday Book*, completed in 1087, was a monument to the unrestrained greed of William, who "was not ashamed that there was not a single [parcel of land] . . . not even one ox, or cow, or pig which escaped notice in his survey."[3] By the thirteenth century the written record had displaced oral memory as the indispensable authority in matters of law, business, and government.

The Norman conquest also transformed language in England. Old English, used to compose the Anglo-Saxon law codes and epic poetry such as *Beowulf* (see Chapter 9), disappeared as a written language, while French became the spoken tongue of the court and upper-class society. Latin served as the standard written language of schools and royal government. Mastery of the three main languages became a mark of the well-educated person. The mathematician Roger Bacon (d. 1294) commended his brethren among the Oxford faculty for teaching in English, French, and Latin, whereas those at the University of Paris exclusively used Latin.

Vernacular Literary Traditions

Although Latin prevailed as the language of liturgy and scholarship, acceptance grew for the use of vernacular languages to manage government and business affairs, and also to express emotion. Enriched by commercial wealth and land revenues, court society cultivated new fashions in dress, literature, art, and music. Yet the Bible and the Roman classics offered few role models with whom kings and princes, let alone knights and merchants, could identify. Poets and troubadours instead used vernacular speech to sing of heroes and heroines who mirrored the ideals and aspirations of their audiences. An outpouring of lyric and epic poetry celebrated both the public and private virtues of the nobility and the chivalric ideals that inspired them. The legends of King Arthur and his circle, celebrated most memorably in the romances penned (in French) by Chrétien de Troyes in the late twelfth century, mingled themes of religious fidelity and romantic love.

Royal and noble patrons who eagerly devoured vernacular romances also began to demand translations of religious and classical texts. Scholars such as Nicole Oresme (or-EHZ-meh), a master of theology at Paris, welcomed the challenge of translating classical works into French as a way to improve the vernacular language and enable people to use it for the higher purposes of philosophical debate and religious contemplation. In the early fourteenth century, Dante Alighieri (DAHN-tay ah-lee-JIHR-ee) (1265–1321), composed his *Divine Comedy*, perhaps the greatest vernacular poem of this era, in the dialect of his native Florence. Dante's allegory entwined scholastic theology and courtly love poetry to plumb the mysteries of the Christian faith in vivid and captivating language. The influence of Dante was so great that modern Italian is essentially descended from the language of the *Divine Comedy*. Thus, even as the rise of universities promoted a common intellectual culture across Latin Christendom, the growth of vernacular languages led to the creation of distinctive national literary traditions.

Students and Scholars in Islamic Societies

FOCUS

To what extent did Sunni and Sufi schools foster a common cultural and religious identity among Muslims?

In contrast to Latin Christendom, in the Islamic world neither the caliphs nor dissenting movements such as Shi'ism sought to establish a clergy with sacred powers and formal religious authority. Instead, the task of teaching the faithful about matters of religion fell to the **ulama** (oo-leh-MAH), learned persons whose wisdom and holiness earned them the respect of their peers. But the ulama did not claim any special relationship to God.

The ulama remained immersed in the secular world because Islam disdained the celibacy and monastic withdrawal from society that were so central to Latin Christianity. Ulama could be found in all walks of life, from wealthy landowners and government officials to ascetic teachers and humble artisans and shopkeepers. Some ulama earned their living from official duties as judges, tax collectors, and caretakers of mosques. But many were merchants and shopkeepers; the profession of religious teacher was by no means incompatible with pursuit of personal gain.

During the heyday of Abbasid power in the eighth and ninth centuries (discussed in Chapter 9), educated professional men such as bureaucrats, physicians, and scribes—often trained in Persian or Greek traditions of learning—competed with theologians for intellectual leadership in the Islamic world. Following the decline of caliphal authority in the tenth century, religious scholars regained their privileged status. The ulama codified what became the Sunni orthodoxy by setting down formal interpretations of scriptural and legal doctrine, founding colleges, and monopolizing the judgeships that regulated both public and private conduct.

The Rise of Madrasas

During the Umayyad and Abbasid caliphates, scriptural commentators sought to apply Muhammad's teachings to social life as well as religious conduct. Scholars compiled anthologies of the sayings and deeds of Muhammad, known as **hadith** (hah-DEETH), as guidelines for leading a proper Muslim life. The need to reconcile Islamic ethical principles with existing social customs and institutions resulted in the formation of a comprehensive body of Islamic law, known as **shari'a** (sha-REE-ah). Yet the formal pronouncements of hadith and shari'a did not resolve all matters of behavior and belief.

Hadith and Shari'a

During the eighth and ninth centuries four major schools of legal interpretation emerged in different parts of the Islamic world to provide authoritative judgments on civil and religious affairs. These schools of law essentially agreed on important issues. Yet as in Latin Christendom, the tension between reason and revelation—between those who emphasized rational understanding of the divine and the free will of the individual and those who insisted on the incomprehensible nature of God and utter surrender to divine will—continued to stir heated debate. The more orthodox schools of law—Hanafi, Maliki, and Shafi'i—were receptive to the rationalist orientation, but the Hanbali tradition firmly rejected any authority other than the revealed truths of the Qur'an and the hadith.

Varying Interpretations of Islamic Law

These schools of law became institutionalized through the founding of **madrasas** (MAH-dras-uh), formal colleges for legal and theological studies. Commonly located in mosques, madrasas received financial support from leading public figures or the surrounding community. In addition, charitable foundations often subsidized teachers' salaries, student stipends, and living quarters and libraries. In the twelfth and thirteenth centuries, donations to construct madrasas became a favorite form of philanthropy.

Founding of Madrasas

Higher education was not confined to the madrasas. The world's oldest university, in the sense of an institution of higher education combining individual faculties for different subjects, is Al-Qarawiyyin, founded at Fez in Morocco in 859 by the daughter of a wealthy merchant. In 975, the Fatimid dynasty established Al-Azhar University, attached to the main mosque in their new capital at Cairo, as a Shi'a theological seminary. Al-Azhar grew into a large institution with faculties in theology, law, grammar, astronomy, philosophy, and logic. In the twelfth century, Saladin, after ousting the Fatimids (see Chapter 14), reorganized Al-Azhar as a center of Sunni learning, which it remains today.

Islamic education revolved around the master-disciple relationship. A madrasa was organized as a study circle consisting of a single master and his disciples. Most madrasas were affiliated with one of the four main schools of law, but students were mainly attracted by the master's reputation rather than school affiliation. "One does not acquire learning nor profit from it unless one holds in esteem knowledge and those who possess it," declared a thirteenth-century manual on education.[4] Several assistants might instruct students in subjects such as Qur'an recitation and Arabic grammar, but Islamic schools had

ulama Deeply learned teachers of Islamic scripture and law.

hadith Records of the sayings and deeds of the Prophet Muhammad.

shari'a The whole body of Islamic law—drawn from the Qur'an, the hadith, and traditions of legal interpretation—that governs social as well as religious life.

madrasa A school for education in Islamic religion and traditions of legal interpretation.

Firdaws Madrasa

The proliferation of madrasas beginning in the eleventh century strengthened the dominance of Sunni teachings in Islamic intellectual circles. Far from being cloistered enclaves of students and scholars, however, madrasas served as the centers of religious life for the whole community. Aleppo in Syria reportedly had forty-seven madrasas, the grandest of which was the Firdaws madrasa, built in 1235. (Photograph by K.A.C. Creswell, © The Creswell Photographic Archive, Ashmolean Museum of Art and Archaeology, University of Oxford.)

no fixed curriculum like the trivium and quadrivium of Latin Europe. Knowledge of hadith and shari'a law and insight into their application to social life were the foundations of higher education. Because learning the hadith was a pious act expected of all Muslims, schools and study circles were open to all believers, whether or not they were formally recognized as students. Although madrasas rarely admitted women as formal students, women often attended lectures and study groups. In twelfth-century Damascus, women took an especially active role as patrons of madrasas and as scholars and teachers as well.

Under the Seljuk sultans (1055–1258), who strictly enforced Sunni orthodoxy and persecuted Shi'a dissidents, the madrasas also became tools of political propaganda. The Seljuks lavishly patronized madrasas in Baghdad and other major cities (see Map 13.2). The Hanafi school became closely allied with the sultanate and largely dominated the judiciary. The Hanbalis, in contrast, rejected Seljuk patronage and refused to accept government positions. The Hanbalis' estrangement from the Seljuk government made them popular among the inhabitants of Baghdad who chafed under Seljuk rule. Charismatic Hanbali preachers frequently mustered common people's support for their partisan causes and led vigilante attacks on Shi'a "heretics" and immoral activities such as drinking alcohol and prostitution.

Role of the Ulama   Turkish military regimes such as the Seljuks in Mesopotamia and Syria, and later the Mamluks in Egypt, came to depend on the cooperation of the ulama and the schools of law to carry out many government tasks and to maintain social order. Yet the authority of the ulama was validated by their reputation for holiness and their personal standing in the community, not by bureaucratic or clerical office. Urban residents were considered adherents of the school of law that presided over the local mosque or madrasa and were subject to its authority. The common people often turned to the neighborhood ulama for counsel, protection, and settlement of disputes, rather than seeking recourse in the official law courts. Ulama were closely tied to their local communities, yet at the same time the ulama's membership in a school of law enrolled them in fraternities of scholars and students spanning the whole Muslim world.

The proliferation of madrasas between the tenth and thirteenth centuries promoted the unification of Sunni theology and law and blurred the boundaries between church and state. The Islamic madrasas, like the universities of Latin Christendom, helped to forge a common religious identity. But to a much greater degree than the Christian universities, the madrasas merged with the surrounding urban society and drew ordinary believers, including women, into their religious and educational activities.

Sufi Mysticism and Sunni Orthodoxy

In addition to the orthodox schools of law and the tradition of revelation expressed in hadith, an alternative tradition was **Sufism** (SOO-fiz-uhm)—a mystical form of Islam that emphasizes personal experience of the divine over obedience to scriptures and Islamic law. Sufis cultivated spiritual and psychological awareness through meditation, recitation, asceticism, and personal piety. Over the course of the ninth century Sufi masters elaborated comprehensive programs of spiritual progress that began with intensely emotional expressions of love of God and proceeded toward a final extinction of the self and mystical union with the divine. Some Sufis spurned the conventions of ordinary life, including the authority of the Qur'an and hadith, instead claiming to directly apprehend divine truth. This version of Sufism, deeply unsettling to political authorities, thrived in the distant regions of

Sufism A mystical form of Islam that emphasizes personal experience of the divine over obedience to the dictates of scripture and Islamic law.

MAP 13.2

Postimperial Successor States in the Islamic World

By 1000 the Islamic world had fragmented into many regional states, and upstart regimes such as the Shi'a Fatimids in North Africa vied with the Sunni Abbasid caliphs based in Baghdad for supremacy. Nomadic Turkish warriors such as the Seljuks became fierce champions of Islam in Central Asia. After the Seljuk conquest of Baghdad in 1055, the Abbasids ceded political authority to the Seljuk sultans, who strictly upheld Sunni teachings.

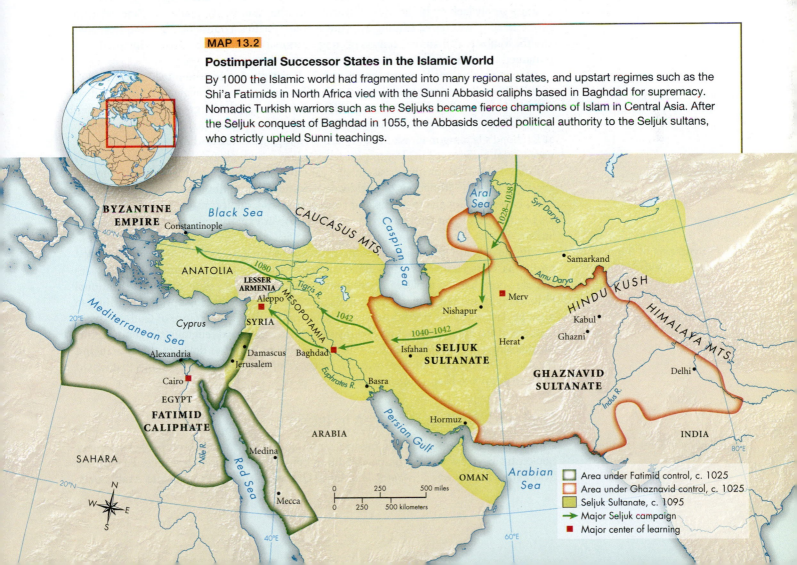

Iran and Central Asia. A more sober-minded form of Sufism, endorsing practical virtue and conformity to Islamic law, flourished in Baghdad and the central Islamic lands.

Sufism's Broad Appeal

Originating as a quest for personal enlightenment, Sufism evolved into a broad social movement. Sufis, like the madrasas, reached out to the common faithful. In their public preaching and missionary work, Sufis addressed everyday ethical questions and advocated a life of practical morality and simplicity. The Sufi ethic of personal responsibility, tolerance and sympathy toward human failings, and moderation in enjoyment of worldly pleasures, had broad appeal among all social classes.

Revered as holy persons with a special relationship to God, Sufi masters acquired an aura of sainthood. Tombs of renowned Sufi masters became important pilgrimage sites that drew throngs of believers from near and far, helping forge a sense of community among like-minded devotees. Women played a more prominent role in Sufism than in other Islamic traditions. One of the earliest Sufi teachers, Rabi'a al-'Adawiyya (717–801), attracted many disciples, chiefly men, with her fierce asceticism and her insistence that God should be loved for God's own sake, not out of fear of punishment or desire for reward. In the words of her biographer, Rabi'a was "on fire with love and longing, enamored of the desire to approach her Lord," and men accepted her "as a second spotless Mary."[5]

By the eleventh century the Sufi masters' residences, known as *khanaqa* (CON-kah) had developed into lodges where religious teachers lived, taught their disciples, and provided accommodations for traveling Sufis. Relationships between master and disciple became more formalized, and Sufis expected each student to submit wholeheartedly to the master's instruction and guidance. In the early thirteenth century Sufis began to form brotherhoods that integrated groups of followers into far-flung religious orders. Bonds of Sufi brotherhood cut across national borders and parochial loyalties, restoring a measure of unity sorely lacking in the Islamic world since the Abbasid caliphate's decline. Muslim rulers warmly welcomed leading Sufi masters as spiritual counselors. Yet the khanaqas and the tombs of Sufi saints—centers of congregational devotion and religious instruction—remained the heart of the Sufi movement.

Ongoing tensions between reason and faith sharply divided the intellectual world of Islam. This dilemma was epitomized by the personal spiritual struggle of Abu Hamid al-Ghazali (AH-boo hah-MEED al-gahz-AHL-ee) (1058–1111), the greatest intellectual figure in Islam after Muhammad himself. Al-Ghazali was appointed to a senior professorship at Baghdad's leading madrasa in 1091, at the young age of thirty-three. Although he garnered great acclaim for his lectures on Islamic law and theology, al-Ghazali was beset by self-doubt and deep spiritual crisis. In 1095, al-Ghazali found himself "continuously tossed about between the attractions of worldly desires and the impulses toward eternal life" until "God caused my tongue to dry up and I was prevented from lecturing."[6] He then resigned his position and spent ten years as a wandering scholar exploring the mystical approach of Sufism.

Synthesis of Sunni and Sufi Teachings

In the end, al-Ghazali's immersion in Sufism restored his faith in Muslim beliefs and traditions. In the last years of his life, al-Ghazali returned to the academy and wrote a series of major philosophical treatises that reaffirmed the primacy of revelation over rational philosophy in matters of faith and morals. According to al-Ghazali, a proper Muslim life must be devoted to the purification of the soul and the direct experience of God that lay at the core of the Sufi quest. But he also insisted that the personal religious awakening of individuals must not violate the established principles of Islam set down in the Qur'an and the hadith. Al-Ghazali's ideas provided a synthesis of Sunni and Sufi teachings that would come to dominate Islamic intellectual circles.

Oral and Written Cultures in Islam

Primacy of Oral Traditions

As the teaching methods of the madrasas reveal, oral instruction took precedence over book learning in Islamic education. Tradition holds that the Qur'an was revealed orally to Muhammad, who was illiterate. The name *Qur'an* itself comes from the Arabic verb "to recite," and recitation of the Qur'an became as fundamental to elementary education as it was to religious devotion. Moreover, the authority of any instruction rested on the reputation of the teacher, which in turn was validated by chains of transmission down through generations of scholars. Sufism reinforced this emphasis on direct person-to-person oral instruction. The persistence of ambivalent attitudes toward written documents is also evident in the priority Islamic law gives to the oral testimony of trustworthy witnesses over documents that could be easily forged or altered. Nonetheless, by the eleventh century books were regarded as indispensable aids to memorization and study, though learning solely from books was dismissed as an inferior method of education (see Reading the Past: Ibn Khaldun on Study and Learning). This preference for oral communication would ensure that the connections between individuals formed by Islamic schooling would be direct and deeply personal.

As the sacred language of scripture, Arabic occupied an exalted place in Islamic literary culture. To fulfill one's religious duty one had to master the Qur'an in Arabic. Arabic

Primacy of Arabic Language

READING THE PAST

Ibn Khaldun on Study and Learning

Ibn Khaldun (ee-bin hal-DOON) (1332–1406), born in Tunis in North Africa, was one of the greatest Islamic historians and philosophers. Khaldun served various Muslim rulers in North Africa before devoting himself to study and teaching. He spent the last twenty-four years of his life in Cairo, where he completed his monumental *Universal History*.

In the prologue of his *Universal History* Khaldun discusses the proper methods of study and learning. Like other Muslim scholars, he valued oral instruction over mere book learning. A good scholar was expected to be well traveled, seeking insight from a variety of teachers. Citing Muhammad bin Abdallah (1077–1148), Khaldun urges that education begin with the study of Arabic and poetry.

Human beings obtain their knowledge and character qualities and all their opinions and virtues either through study, instruction, and lectures, or through imitation of a teacher and personal contact with him. The only difference here is that habits acquired through personal contact with a teacher are more strongly and firmly rooted. Thus, the greater the number of authoritative teachers, the more deeply rooted is the habit one acquires.

When a student has to rely on the study of books and written material and must understand scientific problems from the forms of written letters in books, he is confronted by the veil that separates handwriting and the form of the letter found in writing from the spoken words found in the imagination.

Judge Abdallah places instruction in Arabic and poetry ahead of all other sciences: "Poetry is the archive of the Arabs. . . . From there, the student should go on to arithmetic and study it assiduously, until he knows its basic norms. He should then go to the study of the Qur'an, because with his previous preparation it will be easy for him." He continues, "How thoughtless are our compatriots in teaching children the Qur'an when they are first starting out. They read things they do not understand. . . . He also forbids teaching two disciplines at the same time, save to the student with a good mind and sufficient energy."

Source: Ibn Khaldun, *The Muqaddimah: An Introduction to History*, trans. Franz Rosenthal (Princeton, NJ: Princeton University Press, 1967), 426, 431, 424.

EXAMINING THE EVIDENCE

1. Why did Ibn Khaldun value oral instruction over reading books?

2. To what extent was the curriculum proposed by Ibn Khaldun parallel to the study of the liberal arts found in the cathedral schools and universities of Latin Christendom?

Basra Library

Although Islamic scholars esteemed oral instruction by an outstanding teacher over book learning, libraries served as important places for intellectual exchange as well as repositories of knowledge. In this illustration to a story set in the Iraq seaport of Basra—a city renowned as a seat of scholarship—a group of well-dressed men listen to a lecture on Arabic poetry delivered by the figure at right. In the background, leather-bound books are stacked on their sides in separate cupboards. (Bibliothèque Nationale, Paris, France; Scala/White Images/Art Resource, NY.)

became the language of government from Iran to Spain. The Sunni orthodoxy endorsed by the Abbasid caliphs and the Seljuk sultans was also based on codification in Arabic of religious teachings and laws. Thus, the Arabic language came to occupy an important place in the developing Islamic identity.

Book collecting and the founding of libraries helped expand book learning in Islamic society. The size of Muslim libraries dwarfed the relatively small libraries of Latin Christendom. The most eminent Christian monasteries in France and Italy had libraries of about four hundred to seven hundred volumes, and an inventory of the University of Paris collections from 1338 lists about two thousand books. By contrast, the House of Knowledge, founded by an Abbasid official at Baghdad in 991, contained over ten thousand books. The Islamic prohibition against the worship of images discouraged the use of illustrations in books, but Arabic calligraphy became an extraordinarily expressive form of art (see Seeing the Past: A Revolution in Islamic Calligraphy).

The breakup of the Abbasid caliphate and the rise of regional states fractured the cultural and linguistic unity of the Islamic world. In the ninth century, Iranian authors began to write Persian in the Arabic script, inspiring new styles of poetry, romance, and historical writing. The poet Firdausi (fur-dow-SEE) (d. c. 1025), for example, drew from Sasanid chronicles and popular legends and ballads in composing his *Book of Kings*. This sprawling history of ancient monarchs and heroes has become the national epic of Iran. The Persian political heritage, in which monarchs wielded absolute authority over a steeply hierarchical society, had always clashed with the radical egalitarianism of Islam and the Arabs. But the reinvigorated Persian poetry of Firdausi and others found favor among the upstart Seljuk sultans.

Court poets and artists drew from the rich

Revival of Persian Literature

trove of Persian literature—ranging from the fables of the sailor Sinbad to the celebrated love story of Warqa and Gulshah—to fashion new literary, artistic, and architectural styles that blended sacred and secular themes. The Seljuks absorbed many of these Persian literary motifs into a reinvented Turkish language and literature, which they carried with them into Mesopotamia and Anatolia. Persian and Turkish gradually joined Arabic as the classical languages of the Islamic world. Following the founding of the Muslim-ruled Delhi Sultanate in the early thirteenth century (discussed later in this chapter), Persian and Turkish literary cultures expanded into India.

In the absence of a formal church, the Islamic schools of law, madrasas, and Sufi khanaqa lodges transmitted religious knowledge among all social classes, broadening the reach of education to a wider spectrum of society than the schools and universities of Latin Christendom. The schools of law and madrasas helped to unify theology and law and to forge a distinct Sunni identity.

Nevertheless, regional and national identities were not completely subsumed by the overarching Islamic culture. Moreover, although most religious teachers harbored a deep

A Revolution in Islamic Calligraphy

Early Kufic Script on Parchment (©The Trustees of the Chester Beatty Library, Dublin.)

Calligraphy of Ibn al-Bawwab (©The Trustees of the Chester Beatty Library, Dublin.)

During the early centuries of Islam, the sacredness of the Qur'an was reflected in the physical books themselves. Early manuscripts of the Qur'an, like this example, are invariably written in an Arabic script known as Kufic on parchment. The introduction of paper into the Islamic world from China in the late eighth century led to an explosion in the output of Qur'an manuscripts. Legal and administrative texts, poetry, and works on history, philosophy, geography, mathematics, medicine, and astronomy also began to appear in great numbers in the tenth century. At the same time professional copyists developed new cursive styles of script, easier to write as well as to read, that revolutionized the design and artistry of the Qur'an and other sacred texts.

A leading figure in this revolution in Islamic calligraphy, Ibn al-Bawwab (ih-bihn al-bu-wahb) (d. 1022), had worked as a house decorator before his elegant writing launched him into a career as a manuscript illustrator, calligrapher, and librarian. Only six specimens of Ibn al-Bawwab's calligraphy have survived, the most famous being a complete Qur'an in 286 folio sheets, one of which is shown here. The writing—a graceful and flowing script, with no trace of the ruling needed for parchment—is more compact than the Kufic script, but also more legible. Unlike Kufic, Ibn al-Bawwab's writing is composed in strokes of uniform thickness, with each letter equally proportioned. On this page, which contains the opening verses of the Qur'an, the first two chapter headings appear in large gold letters superimposed on decorative bands with dotted frames. By contrast,

the parchment Qur'an simply marks the end of chapters by inserting small decorative bands without text. Ibn al-Bawwab also indicated the beginning of each of the Qur'an's 114 chapters with large, colored roundels in the margin. The roundels are generally floral designs, such as the lotus in the bottom roundel shown here, but no two are exactly alike. Smaller roundels in the margins mark every tenth verse and passages after which prostrations should be performed.

This copy lacks a dedication, and scholars believe that it was made for sale rather than on commission from a mosque or other patron. Ibn al-Bawwab reportedly made sixty-four copies of the Qur'an in his lifetime.

EXAMINING THE EVIDENCE

1. How does the design of Ibn al-Bawwab's Qur'an make it easier to use for prayer than the parchment manuscript?

2. How does the style of decoration of Ibn al-Bawwab's Qur'an differ from that of the Latin Christian Gospel pages shown on page 411? What religious and aesthetic values might account for these differences?

suspicion of the "rational sciences" of the ancient Greeks, in the Islamic world—as in Latin Christendom—the tension between reason and revelation remained unresolved. The Sunni ulama were also troubled by the claims of Sufi masters to intuitive knowledge of the divine, and by the tendency of Sufis to blur the distinction between Islam and other religions. Nowhere was the Sufi deviation from orthodox Sunni traditions more pronounced than in India, where Sufism formed a bridge between the Islamic and Hindu religious cultures.

The Cosmopolitan and Vernacular Realms in India and Southeast Asia

FOCUS

What political and religious forces contributed to the development of a common culture across India and Southeast Asia and its subsequent fragmentation into regional cultures?

Between the fifth and the fifteenth centuries, India and Southeast Asia underwent two profound cultural transformations. In the first phase, from roughly 400 to 900, a new cultural and political synthesis emerged simultaneously across the entire region. Local rulers cultivated a common culture reflecting a new ideology of divine kingship. Sanskrit became a cosmopolitan language for expressing rulers' universal claims to secular as well as sacred authority. In the second phase, from 900 to 1400, rulers instead asserted sovereign authority based on the unique historical and cultural identity of their lands and peoples. The spread of diverse vernacular cultures fragmented the cosmopolitan unity of Sanskrit literary and political discourse. The growing differentiation of India and Southeast Asia into regional vernacular cultures after 900 received added impetus from the Turkish conquests and from the founding of the Delhi Sultanate in 1206.

The Cosmopolitan Realm of Sanskrit

Beginning in about the third century C.E., Sanskrit, the sacred language of the Vedic religious tradition, became for the first time a medium for literary and political expression as well. The emergence of Sanskrit in secular writings occurred virtually simultaneously in South and Southeast Asia. By the sixth century a common cosmopolitan culture expressed through Sanskrit texts had become fully entrenched in royal courts from Afghanistan to Java. The spread of Sanskrit was not a product of political unity or imperial colonization, however. Rather, it came to dominate literary and political discourse in the centuries after the demise of the Gupta Empire discussed in Chapter 6, when the Indian subcontinent was divided into numerous regional kingdoms (see Map 13.3).

Sanskrit and Political Ideology

Sanskrit's movement into the political arena did not originate with the Brahman priesthood. Instead, the impetus came from the Central Asian nomads, notably the Kushan, who, as we saw in Chapter 6, ruled over parts of Afghanistan, Pakistan, and northwestern India from the first century B.C.E. to the fourth century C.E. The Kushan kings patronized Buddhist theologians and poets who adopted Sanskrit both to record Buddhist scriptures and to commemorate their royal patrons' deeds in inscriptions and eulogies. Later, the Gupta monarchs used Sanskrit to voice their grand imperial ambitions. The Gupta state collapsed in the mid-fifth century, but subsequent rulers embraced its ideology of kingship centered on the ideal of the *chakravartin*, or universal monarch.

This conception of kingship connected political authority to the higher lordship of the gods, above all Shiva and Vishnu. Temples became not only centers of community life but also places for individual worship. Modest acts of devotion—offerings of food presented to a deity's image, vows and fasting, and pilgrimages to temples—complemented Brahmanic rituals. Thus the egalitarian ethic and more personal relationship to the divine espoused by Buddhism left a lasting legacy in the devotional cults dedicated to the Hindu gods.

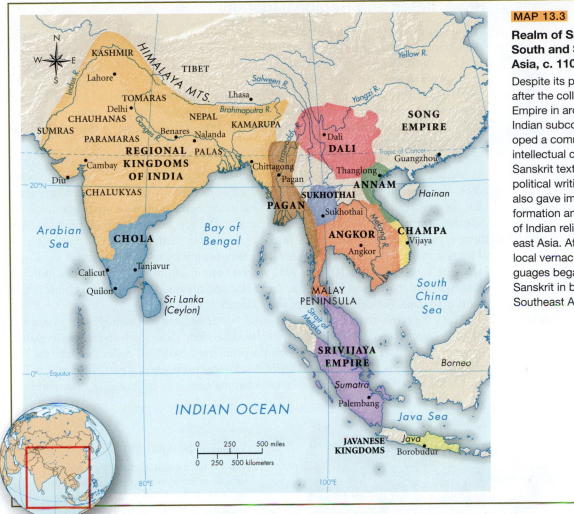

MAP 13.3

Realm of Sanskrit in South and Southeast Asia, c. 1100

Despite its political disunity after the collapse of the Gupta Empire in around 540, the Indian subcontinent developed a common literary and intellectual culture based on Sanskrit texts. Religious and political writings in Sanskrit also gave impetus to state formation and the expansion of Indian religions into Southeast Asia. After 900, however, local vernacular written languages began to displace Sanskrit in both India and Southeast Asia.

Brahmanic colleges attached to temples and Buddhist and Jain monasteries provided formal schooling. These colleges were open to anyone from the "twice-born" (that is, ritually pure) castes of Brahmans, warriors, and *Vaishya* (herders, farmers, and merchants). Beginning in the eighth century, hostels known as *mathas*, often devoted to the worship of a particular deity, became important as meeting places where students, scholars, and pilgrims gathered for religious discussion. Above all, royal courts served as the centers of intellectual life and literary production. The cultural realm of Sanskrit lacked a single paramount center such as the capitals of the Roman or Chinese empires, but through borrowing and imitation, political ideology and royal government assumed remarkably similar forms in many lands.

The predominance of Sanskrit was equally strong in the Angkor state in Cambodia and in the Javanese kingdoms. Public display of royal power and virtue through monumental architecture and Sanskrit inscriptions took forms in Angkor identical to those found in the Indian subcontinent. Although Khmer (kih-MAY) served as the language of everyday life, used to record matters such as land grants, tax obligations, and contracts, Sanskrit prevailed as the language of politics, poetry, and religion in Cambodia down to the seventeenth century.

Sanskrit's rise as a cosmopolitan language thus allowed local rulers and intellectual elites to draw on a universal system of values and ideas to establish their claims to authority. Royal mystique was expressed symbolically through courtly epics, royal genealogies, and inscriptions that depicted the ruler as a divinely ordained monarch.

Centers of Sanskrit Learning

Sanskrit Culture in Southeast Asia

Rival States and Regional Identity

By the tenth century, a long period of economic expansion produced a series of powerful states across the Sanskrit realm. Most prominent were Angkor in Cambodia and Chola in southern India (see again Map 13.3), but there were also a number of smaller regional kingdoms. The rulers of these states deemed themselves "great kings" (*maharajas*), the earthly representatives of the gods, particularly Shiva and Vishnu. Actual political power rested on the growing interdependence between the kings and the Brahman priesthood. At the same time, the kings sought to affirm and extend their authority through ostentatious patronage of gods and their temples.

Temple architecture most strikingly reveals the maharajas' (mah-huh-RAH-juh) ruling ideology. A wave of temple-building, most of it funded by royal donations, swept across the Sanskrit realm between 1000 and 1250. In contrast to the Buddhist cave temples, the new temples were freestanding stone monuments built on a vastly greater scale. Affirming the parallels between gods and kings, the builders of these temples conceived of them as palaces of the gods, but the rituals performed in them imitated the daily routines of human monarchs. Dedicated to Shiva, the temple built by royal command at the Chola capital of Tanjavur (tan-JOOR) in 1002 received tribute from more than three hundred villages, including some as far away as Sri Lanka, and maintained a staff of six hundred, in addition to many hundreds of priests and students.

Rising Regional Identity   From the tenth century onward, as royal power became increasingly tied to distinct territories, appeals to regional identity replaced Sanskrit claims to universal sovereignty. Regional identity was expressed through the proliferation of legal codes that, like the law codes of post-Roman Europe, were considered unique products of a particular culture and people. Kings asserted their rule over local temple networks by stressing their common

Tanjavur Temple

The Chola era was marked by a wave of temple-building on a grand scale across southern India. Many of these building projects, such as the Rajarajeshvara temple at the Chola capital of Tanjavur seen here, benefited from royal donations intended to underscore the connections between divine authority and kingship. But Hindu temples also attracted patronage from merchant and artisan guilds and obtained revenues from their landholdings, commercial activities, and contributions by village assemblies. (Bob Krist/CORBIS.)

identity with a distinct territory, people, and culture. Consequently the cosmopolitan cultural community based on Sanskrit writings no longer suited their political goals.

The displacement of Sanskrit by vernacular languages accompanied this political transformation. Between the tenth and fourteenth centuries, political boundaries increasingly aligned with linguistic borders. By the tenth century royal inscriptions began to use local vernacular languages rather than Sanskrit. The Chola kings, for example, promoted a Tamil cultural identity defined as "the region of the Tamil language" to further their expansionist political ambitions. Royal courts, the major centers of literary production, also championed a rewriting of the Sanskrit literary heritage in vernacular languages. The first vernacular versions of the *Mahabharata* epic (discussed in Chapter 6) appeared in the Kannada (kah-nah-DAH) language of southwestern India in the tenth century and in the Telugu (tehl-oo-JOO) and Old Javanese languages in the eleventh century. The poet Kamban composed his celebrated Tamil version of the *Ramayana* at the Chola court at the same time. These vernacular versions of the epics were not merely translations, but a rewriting of the classic works as part of local history rather than universal culture. Although Sanskrit remained the language of Brahmanic religion (and many sacred scriptures were never translated into vernacular languages), after 1400 Sanskrit all but disappeared from royal inscriptions, administrative documents, and courtly literature. The turn toward vernacular literary languages did not broaden the social horizons of literary culture, however. Vernacular literatures relied heavily on Sanskrit vocabulary and rhetoric and were intended for learned audiences, not the common people.

Displacement of Sanskrit by Vernacular Languages

Sufism and Society in the Delhi Sultanate

In the late twelfth century Muhammad Ghuri, the Muslim ruler of Afghanistan, invaded India and conquered the Ganges Valley. After Ghuri's death in 1206, a Turkish slave-general declared himself sultan at Delhi. Over the next three centuries a series of five dynasties ruled over the Delhi Sultanate (1206–1526) and imposed Muslim rule over much of India. By about 1330 the Delhi Sultanate reached its greatest territorial extent, encompassing most of the Indian peninsula.

The Delhi sultans cast themselves in the mold of Turko-Persian ideals of kingship, which affirmed the supremacy of the king over religious authorities. Nonetheless, like their Turkish predecessors, the Delhi sultans cultivated close relations with Sufi masters. Sufism affirmed the special role of the saint or holy man as an earthly representative of God, insisting that it was the blessing of a Sufi saint that conferred sovereign authority on monarchs. A leading Iranian Sufi proclaimed that God "made the Saints the governors of the universe . . . and through their spiritual influence [Muslims] gain victories over the unbelievers."[7] Implicitly recognizing the practical limits of their authority, the Delhi sultans sought to strengthen their control over their Indian territories by striking an alliance between the Turkish warrior aristocracy and the revered Sufi masters.

Initially the Delhi sultans staffed their government with Muslims, recruiting ulama and Sufis, mostly from Iran and Central Asia. The sultans also founded mosques and madrasas to propagate Islamic teachings, but the ulama and their schools had little impact on the native Hindu population. Instead, it was the missionary zeal of the Sufi orders that paved the way for Islam's spread in South Asia.

In the wake of Muslim conquests, the Sufi orders established khanaqa lodges in the countryside as well as in the cities, reaching more deeply into local society. United by total devotion and obedience to their master, the Sufi brotherhoods formed tightly knit networks whose authority paralleled that of the sultans, and in some respects surpassed it.

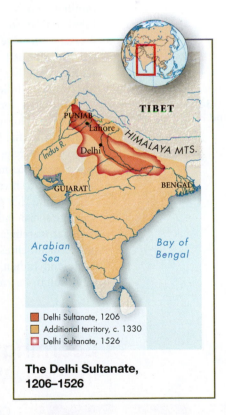

Delhi Sultanate, 1206
Additional territory, c. 1330
Delhi Sultanate, 1526

The Delhi Sultanate, 1206–1526

Sufi Influence in the Sultanate

Sufi masters presided over the khanaqas much like princes over their courts. For example, they welcomed local people seeking justice, dispute mediation, and miraculous cures. Learned dignitaries, both Muslim and Hindu, sought out Sufi masters for spiritual counsel and instruction. The monumental tombs of renowned saints became cultural and religious crossroads as they attracted steady streams of both Hindu and Muslim worshipers and pilgrims.

Sufis used vernacular language to address local audiences. In the Delhi region they adopted Hindi as a spoken language, and it was Sufis who developed Urdu, a literary version of Hindi, as the common written language among Muslims in South Asia. In the fifteenth century, as the political fortunes of the Delhi Sultanate waned, provincial Muslim regimes promoted the integration of Hindu and Muslim cultures and the use of vernacular literary languages. For example, the independent sultans of Bengal sponsored translations of the epics and other Sanskrit classics into Bengali, and they also patronized Bengali writers. A Chinese visitor to Bengal in the early fifteenth century reported that although some Muslims at the court understood Persian, Bengali was the language in universal use.

Sufi-Hindu Accommodation

Leading Sufis often sought spiritual accommodation between Islamic and Hindu beliefs and practices. In their quest for a more direct path to union with the divine, many Sufis were attracted to the ascetic practices, yoga techniques, and mystical knowledge of Hindu yogis. Similarly, Hindus assimilated the Sufi veneration of saints into their own religious lives without relinquishing their Hindu identity. Most important, the Sufi ethic of practical piety in daily life struck a responsive chord among Hindus. Sufis, like Brahmans, valued detachment from the world but not rejection of it. They married, raised families, and engaged in secular occupations. Nizam al-Din Awliya (1236–1325), an eminent Sufi master, ministered to the spiritual needs of Hindus as well as Muslims. His message—forgive your enemies, enjoy worldly pleasures in moderation, and fulfill your responsibilities to family and society—was closely aligned with the basic principles of Hindu social life. Thus, Sufism served as a bridge between the two dominant religious traditions of India.

Relations Between Muslim Leaders and Hindu Subjects

Although some sultans launched campaigns of persecution aimed at temples and icons of the Hindu gods, most tolerated the Hindu religion. Particularly in the fourteenth century, after the Delhi Sultanate extinguished its major Hindu rivals, the sultans adopted more lenient religious and social policies. They also made greater efforts to recruit Brahmans for government office. Sultans and regional governors even bestowed patronage on major Hindu shrines as gestures of magnanimity toward their non-Muslim subjects.

Despite this growing political accommodation, Muslim and Hindu elites preserved separate social and cultural identities. Both groups, for example, strictly forbade intermarriage across religious lines. Nonetheless, the flowering of regional cultures and inclusion of non-Muslim elites into government and courtly culture foreshadowed the synthesis of Islamic and Indian cultures later patronized by the Mughal Empire, which replaced the Delhi sultans as rulers of India in 1526 (see Chapter 19).

Learning, Schools, and Print Culture in East Asia

FOCUS

To what extent did intellectual and educational trends in Song China influence its East Asian neighbors?

Compared to the worlds of Christendom and Islam, in East Asia learning and scholarship were much more tightly yoked to the state and its institutions. Beginning with the Song dynasty (960–1279), the civil service examination system dominated Chinese political life and literary culture. At the same time the political and social rewards of examination success led to a proliferation of schools and broader access to education (see Map 13.4).

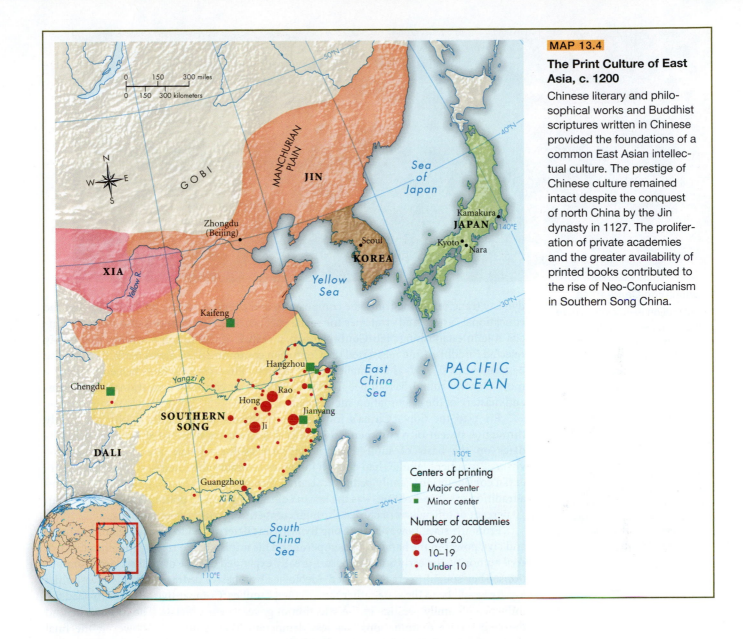

MAP 13.4

The Print Culture of East Asia, c. 1200
Chinese literary and philosophical works and Buddhist scriptures written in Chinese provided the foundations of a common East Asian intellectual culture. The prestige of Chinese culture remained intact despite the conquest of north China by the Jin dynasty in 1127. The proliferation of private academies and the greater availability of printed books contributed to the rise of Neo-Confucianism in Southern Song China.

The invention and spread of printing transformed written communication and intellectual life in China. Neither the state nor the Confucian-educated elite played a significant role in the invention and early development of printing. Yet throughout the Song dynasty, the period when Confucian education and examination success became the marks of elite status in China, the emerging culture of the educated classes dominated printing and publishing. Elsewhere in East Asia, however, the spread of printing and vernacular writing had a much more limited impact on government and social hierarchy. In Japan and Korea, literacy and education remained the preserve of the aristocratic elites and the Buddhist clergy.

Civil Service Examinations and Schooling in Song China

Chinese civil service examinations were a complex series of tests based on the Confucian classics, history, poetry, and other subjects. They served as the primary method for recruiting government officials from the eleventh century onward. Their use starting in the Song

Institution of Civil Service Exams

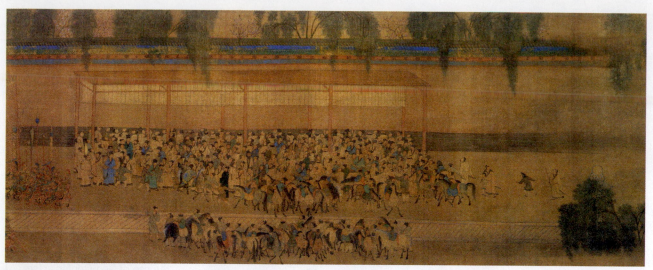

Examination Candidates

No institution exercised a more powerful influence on the culture and lifestyle of China's ruling class than the civil service examinations. Success in the examinations not only opened the path to a political career but also conferred prestige and privileges on the whole family. In this sixteenth-century painting, a crowd of men dressed in scholars' robes anxiously scan the lists of successful candidates posted outside the examination hall. (National Palace Museum, Taiwan, Republic of China.)

dynasty transformed not only the composition and character of the political elite, but the educational system and strategies for social success. The examinations also played a crucial role in establishing **Neo-Confucianism**, a revival of Confucian teachings that firmly rejected Buddhism and reasserted the Confucian commitment to moral perfection and the betterment of society, as an intellectual orthodoxy. Finally, the system helped produce a more uniform ruling class of people connected by their common educational experiences and mastery of the examination subject matter.

Prior to the Song, China's imperial governments recruited their officials mostly through a system of recommendations. Local magistrates nominated promising candidates on the basis of subjective criteria such as literary talent and reputation for virtue. Prominent families had enough influence to ensure that their sons received preferential consideration. Family pedigree, secured through wealth, marriage connections, and a tradition of office-holding, was the key to continued access to political office. Fewer than 10 percent of officials were chosen through competitive written examinations.

From the start, however, the Song dynasty was determined to centralize both military and civil power in the hands of the emperor and his ministers. To restore the supremacy of civil authority, the early Song emperors greatly expanded the use of civil service examinations. They sought to create a skilled, ideologically cohesive cadre of officials whose chief loyalty would be to the state rather than to their families. Competitive tests diminished the influence of family prestige in the selection of government officials. The impulse behind the civil service examinations was less democratic than autocratic, however: the final choice of successful candidates rested with the emperor.

State Schools

By the mid-thirteenth century four hundred thousand men had taken the civil service examinations. Of this number, only eight hundred were selected for appointment to office. The enormous number of examination candidates reflected the crucial importance of government office to achieving social and political success. It also testified to the powerful influence of schooling in shaping the lives and outlook of the ruling class. The Song government set up hundreds of state-supported local schools, but budget shortfalls left many of them underfunded. For the most part, primary education was limited to those who could afford private tutors.

At every level of schooling, the curriculum mirrored the priorities of the civil service examinations. Although the central government constantly tinkered with the content of the examinations, in general the examinations emphasized mastery of the Confucian classics, various genres of poetry, and matters of public policy and statecraft. Over time the prominence of poetry diminished, and the application of classical knowledge to public policy and administrative problems grew in importance.

Neo-Confucianism The revival of Confucian teachings beginning in the Song dynasty that firmly rejected Buddhist religion and reasserted the Confucian commitment to moral perfection and the betterment of society.

Critics of the civil service examinations complained that the impartiality of the evaluation procedures did not allow for proper assessment of the candidates' moral character. They advocated replacing the examinations with a system of appointment based on promotion through the state school system, in which student merit would be judged on the basis of personal qualities as well as formal knowledge. Other critics condemned the examination system and government schools for stifling intellectual inquiry. In their view, the narrow focus of the curriculum and the emphasis on rote knowledge over creative thinking produced petty-minded pedants rather than dynamic leaders.

Private Academies

These various criticisms spurred the founding of private academies. Moreover, many leading scholars rejected political careers altogether. This trend received a major boost from Zhu Xi (jew she) (1130–1200), the most influential Neo-Confucian scholar, who reordered the classical canon to revive humanistic learning and infuse education with moral purpose. Zhu mocked the sterile teaching of government schools, instead engaging his students (and critics) in wide-ranging philosophical discussions, often held under the auspices of private academies. Zhu Xi championed the private academy as the ideal environment for the pursuit of genuine moral knowledge. His teachings inspired the founding of at least 140 private academies during the twelfth and thirteenth centuries. Nevertheless, many students enrolled at private academies out of the self-serving conviction that studying with a renowned scholar would enhance their prospects for success in the examinations.

Influence of Zhu Xi's Neo-Confucianism

Ironically, later dynasties would adopt Zhu Xi's philosophical views and interpretations of the classics as the official orthodoxy of the civil service examinations. Consequently, his Neo-Confucian doctrines were more influential even than Thomas Aquinas's synthesis of Greek philosophy and Christian revelation, or al-Ghazali's contributions to Islamic theology.

For educated men, the power of the examination system was inescapable. Only a few rare individuals would ever pass through, as contemporaries put it, "the thorny gate of learning." Yet examination learning defined the intellectual and cultural values not only of officials, but of the educated public at large. In a poem, a Song emperor exhorted young men to apply themselves to study:

> To enrich your family, no need to buy good land;
> Books hold a thousand measures of grain.
> For an easy life, no need to build a mansion;
> In books are found houses of gold.
> When traveling, be not vexed at the absence of followers;
> In books, carriages and horses form a crowd.
> When marrying, be not vexed by lack of a good matchmaker;
> In books there are girls with faces of jade.
> A boy who wants to become somebody
> Devotes himself to the classics, faces the window, and reads.[9]

The average age of men who passed the highest level of the civil service examinations was thirty-one. Thus China's political leaders commonly underwent a long apprenticeship as students that lasted well into their adult life.

The Culture of Print in Song China

Invention of Printing

Just as papermaking originated in China (see Chapter 6), the Chinese invented the technology of printing, probably in the early eighth century. The Chinese had long used carved stone, bronze, and wood seals to make inked impressions on silk, and the process of using carved wooden blocks to print on paper probably derived from this practice.

The earliest known example of woodblock printing is a miniature Buddhist charm dating from the first half of the eighth century. Chinese inventors devised movable type by the mid-eleventh century, but this technology was not widely used. Chinese is a **logographic** language that uses symbols to represent whole words, not sounds. Given the large number of Chinese logographs in common use, printers found that carving entire pages of

logographic A system of writing that uses symbols to represent whole words, not sounds (as in the case of alphabetic writing systems).

Chinese Woodblock Printing

The religious merit earned for spreading Buddhist teachings appears to have been the motivating force behind the invention of printing in China. Nearly all early printed Chinese books are Buddhist scriptures and other religious works. This copy of the *Diamond Sutra*, a popular digest of Mahayana Buddhist teachings, bears the date 868, making it the oldest known dated example of block printing. (©2011 The British Library Or.8210.)

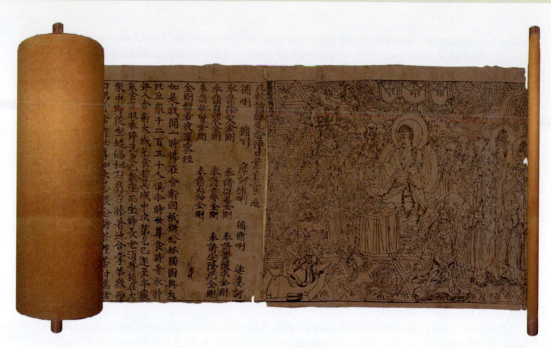

a book was less laborious than producing fonts that would require tens of thousands of individual pieces of type.

Mass Production of Books

By the ninth century printing had developed into a substantial industry in China. Printers produced a wide range of written materials, ranging from single-sheet almanacs to poetry anthologies and commentaries on the Confucian classics. But the most important use of print was to reproduce Buddhist scriptures and other religious texts. Buddhists regarded the dissemination of scriptures as an important act of piety that earned karmic merit for the sponsor. Mass production of religious texts and icons was very probably the original motivation behind the invention of printing.

Song Sponsorship

The founding of the Song dynasty marked the ascendancy of government-sponsored printing. Just as the Song took the lead in education to reinforce their rule, the Song government used printing to help disseminate official ideas and values. In the 970s the Song emperor ordered government workshops to print encyclopedias, dictionaries, literary anthologies, and official histories of all earlier dynasties, in addition to the Confucian classics. One of the government's largest printing projects was an official edition of the Buddhist canon, consisting of 1076 titles, published in 983. This project required the carving of 130,000 woodblocks and took twelve years to complete.

Before the twelfth century, the Song government dominated the world of publishing. The state printed collections of statutes, laws, and government procedures and works on medicine, astronomy, and natural history, as well as standard editions of classics, histories, and literary anthologies. Many of these works were sold through private booksellers or donated to government schools. In the twelfth century, however, private publishers, including schools as well as commercial firms, surpassed the Song government as the main source of printed books. Schools and academies had the intellectual and financial resources to publish fine-quality, scrupulously edited editions (see again Map 13.4).

Commercial firms usually issued cheaply printed texts that catered to market tastes, especially demand for a wide variety of aids to prepare students for the civil service exams. These works included classical commentaries by famous scholars, dictionaries, school primers, writing manuals, phrase books, collections of examination essays by the highest-ranked candidates, and—most notorious of all—so-called kerchief albums, crib sheets that candidates could fold like a kerchief and smuggle into the examination hall. Books largely for personal enjoyment, such as poetry and prose anthologies by famous authors and works of drama and fiction, also became staples of commercial publishing, along with medical and divination texts purveying practical knowledge.

Despite the advantages of printing as a means of mass reproduction, the technology of printing spread slowly. Elsewhere in East Asia, state and religious institutions monopolized printing. Although Muslims were aware of printing by the eleventh century, they felt deep reverence for the handwritten word and fiercely opposed mechanical reproduction of the sacred words of the Qur'an and other religious texts. No printing presses were established in the Islamic world before the eighteenth century. The printing press invented by the goldsmith Johannes Gutenberg in the German city of Mainz in the 1440s appears to have been a separate invention unrelated to Chinese printing technology.

Classical and Vernacular Traditions in East Asia

Just as Latin endured as the common literary language of Latin Christendom, the classical Chinese language unified East Asian intellectual life. Since the logographic forms of written Chinese could not be adapted to represent sounds in other languages, Korean and Japanese writers at first composed their works in classical Chinese. Even in China the written language had long been divorced from vernacular speech.

The earliest writings that use vernacular Chinese are all Buddhist works, especially translations of Indian texts but also sermons, hymns, and parables, written by monks in China to make the foreign religion more familiar and comprehensible to ordinary Chinese. Although works of popular entertainment such as drama and fiction begin to include colloquial speech during the Song period, classical Chinese prevailed as the dominant literary language of East Asia down to modern times.

In Korea, mastery of Chinese literary forms, especially poetry, became an essential mark of accomplishment among aristocrats. The advent of the Koryŏ (KAW-ree-oh) dynasty (918–1392), which brought the Korean peninsula under unified rule in 935, signaled the dominance of Confucianism in Korean political culture. The Koryŏ state preserved aristocratic rule, but it also instituted civil service examinations. Schooling and the examination system were highly centralized in the capital of Kaesong, and they were largely restricted to aristocratic families. From the mid-eleventh century, eminent officials and scholars encouraged the study of Confucian ideas at private academies. Although Buddhism continued to enjoy public and private patronage, study at a private academy became a badge of honor for sons of the aristocracy.

Confucian culture became even more deeply entrenched in the ruling class during the succeeding Yi dynasty (1392–1910). The Yi monarch Sejong (SAY-johng) (r. 1418–1450) took the initiative in creating a native writing system, known as *han'gul* (HAHN-goor), to enable his people to express themselves in their everyday tongue. But the Korean aristocracy, determined to preserve its monopoly over learning and social prestige, resisted the new writing system. As in Japan, it was women of aristocratic families who popularized the native script by using it extensively in their correspondence and poetry.

In Japan, too, Chinese was the learned, formal, written language of public life. Aristocratic men studied the Chinese classics, history, and law and composed Chinese poetry. By 850 the Japanese had developed a phonetic system for writing Japanese, but they rarely used it in public life. The Japanese kana script instead was relegated to the private world of letters and diaries; it became so closely associated with women writers that it was called "woman's hand." Women of the Heian aristocracy were expected to be well versed in poetry and composition, and this era witnessed a remarkable outpouring of great literature by women writing vernacular Japanese. In fact, women composed much of the memorable writing of this era. Men confined themselves to writing in Chinese, whereas gifted women of the Japanese aristocracy used the full resources of their native language to express themselves in the frank and evocative styles found in outstanding works such as the *Pillow Book* of Sei Shōnagon (SAY SHON-nah-gohn) and Lady Murasaki's *Tale of Genji*. Although the world immortalized by Murasaki was narrowly self-centered, she and her fellow women writers gave birth to Japanese as a written language, and in so doing gave Japanese literature its distinctive genius (see Reading the Past: Lady Murasaki on Her Peers Among Women Writers).

Printing Outside China

China

Korea

Japan

The heyday of women's literature in Japan had no parallel elsewhere in the premodern world, but it was short-lived. By 1200 the Japanese court had been reduced to political impotence, and a rising class of warrior lords seized political power (as we will see in Chapter 15). New cultural forms replaced both Chinese literary fashions and the courtly romances of the Heian era. Prose narratives chronicled not the love affairs of courtiers but the wars and political rivalries among warrior brotherhoods. Women often strode onto the political stage in the era of the shoguns, but they were no longer at the center of its literary culture.

To different degrees, the spread of vernacular writing broadened access to written knowledge throughout East Asia. In China, the classical language retained its preeminence as a literary language, but the early development of printing and public schools fostered a relatively high level of literacy. In Mesoamerica, by contrast, writing remained a jealously guarded prerogative of the ruling class.

READING THE PAST

Lady Murasaki on Her Peers Among Women Writers

In addition to her great novel *Tale of Genji*, Lady Murasaki composed a memoir, covering a brief period from 1008 to 1010, that reflects on events and personalities at the Heian court. Among its more personal elements are Murasaki's observations about other women writers of her day, such as Izumi Shikibu (EE-zoo-mee SHEE-kee-boo), who earned the scorn of many for the frankly amorous tone of her poems and her flamboyant love affairs, and Sei Shōnagon, the renowned author of the *Pillow Book*, a collection of writings on taste and culture. Murasaki's tart judgments reveal the intense rivalry for literary fame among women in the court's status-conscious circles.

Now someone who did carry on a fascinating correspondence was Izumi Shikibu. She does have a rather unsavory side to her character but she has a talent for tossing off letters with ease and seems to make the most banal statement sound special. Her poems are most interesting. Although her knowledge of the canon and her judgments of other people's poetry leave something to be desired, she can produce poems at will and always manages to include some clever phrase that catches the attention. Yet when it comes to criticizing or judging the works of others, well, she never really comes up to scratch—the sort of person who relies on a talent for extemporization, one feels. I cannot think of her as a poet of the highest rank.

Sei Shōnagon, for instance, was dreadfully conceited. She thought herself so clever and littered her writings with Chinese words; but if you examined them closely, they left a great deal to be desired. Those who think of themselves as being superior to everyone else in this way will inevitably suffer and come to a bad end.[1]

Yet Murasaki is no less harsh in her self-appraisal:

Thus do I criticize others from various angles—but here is one who has survived this far without having achieved anything of note. . . . Pretty yet shy, shrinking from sight, unsociable, fond of old tales, conceited, so wrapped up in poetry that other people hardly exist, spitefully looking down on the whole world—such is the unpleasant opinion that people have of me.[2]

1. Ivan Morris, *The World of the Shining Prince: Court Life in Ancient Japan* (New York: Knopf, 1964), 251.
2. *The Diary of Lady Murasaki*, trans. Richard Bowring (London: Penguin, 1996), 53–54.

EXAMINING THE EVIDENCE

1. Although women writers such as Murasaki did not compose their major works in Chinese, they still held literary skill in Chinese in high regard. Why?

2. Why might Lady Murasaki have believed that a woman writer's talent was best expressed by poetry? (Consider the chapter narrative as well as this excerpt in formulating your response.)

COUNTERPOINT
Writing and Political Power in Mesoamerica

The Greeks coined the word *hieroglyph* (priestly or sacred script) for the Egyptian language, whose signs differed radically from their own alphabetic writing. In ancient societies such as Egypt, writing and reading were skills reserved for rulers, priests, and administrators. Writing was both a product and an instrument of political control. Because of their sacred character or strategic importance, written records were closely guarded secrets. Rulers denied ordinary people access to books and other forms of written knowledge.

This monopoly over the written word vanished in the major civilizations of Eurasia and Africa during the first millennium B.C.E. Subsequently the evangelical zeal of Buddhists, Christians, and Muslims encouraged the spread of literacy and written knowledge. The desire to propagate Buddhist scriptures appears to have been the catalyst for one of the most significant technological milestones of human history, the invention of printing. But in more isolated parts of the world, such as Mesoamerica, writing, like ritual, served to perpetuate the profound social gulf that separated the rulers from the common people.

FOCUS

How did the relationship between political power and knowledge of writing in Mesoamerica differ from that in the other civilizations studied in this chapter?

Mesoamerican Languages: Time, History, and Rulership

In Mesoamerica, written languages took the form of symbols with pictorial elements, much like the hieroglyphs of ancient Egypt. Mesoamerican texts also display many parallels with Egyptian writings. Writing was a product of the violent competition for leadership and political control. Most surviving texts are inscriptions on monuments that commemorate the great feats and divine majesty of rulers. Knowledge of astronomical time-keeping, divination and prophecy, and rituals intended to align human events with grand cycles of cosmic time were indispensable to political power.

The earliest writing in Mesoamerica was the Zapotec (sah-po-TEHK) script of the Monte Alban state in southern Mexico, which was in use at least as early as 400 B.C.E. The Zapotec language achieved its mature form in 300–700 C.E., the Monte Alban state's heyday. Unfortunately, the Zapotec language remains undecipherable: the ancient written language does not correspond to modern spoken

Mesoamerican Scripts (Based on Andrew Robinson, *Lost Languages: The Enigma of the World's Undeciphered Scripts.* Copyright © 2002 McGraw-Hill Companies, Inc. Used by permission of the publisher.)

Zapotec Script

Classic Maya Script

Zapotec. Nonetheless, Zapotec inscriptions display many of the same themes found in later Mesoamerican literary traditions. For example, the earliest Zapotec monuments with writing depict slain enemies and captives, a common motif in Maya monuments. Like Maya texts, too, Zapotec inscriptions apparently focus on diplomacy and war.

Maya rulers wielded the written word to consolidate their power, using it to display both divine approval of their reign and the fixed course of human history. Maya scribes used calendrical calculation to create genealogical histories organized around the crucial events and persons—birth, marriage, ancestors, offspring—in the lives of royal and noble persons. Maya inscriptions also commemorated the rulers' accomplishments by portraying them as reenacting the triumphs of ancient heroes (see Reading the Past: The Maya Hero Twins Vanquish the Lords of the Underworld, page 348). Creating new monuments gave rulers opportunities to rewrite history, but only within the framework of a set interpretation of the past that affirmed the social order of the present. The regular destruction of monuments

Maya Scribe

In the Maya classical age, the power of the pen often was mightier than that of the sword. Court scribes combined writing ability, artistic skill, and esoteric knowledge of such fields as calendrical science to create the monuments and artifacts that perpetuated the authority of Maya royalty. Scribes were also associated with divine figures, as in this painted vase from the period 600 to 900 c.e., which depicts a scribe in the guise of the maize god. (Photograph K1185 ©Justin Kerr.)

testifies to the power of the visible word in Mesoamerican societies. The Zapotecs at Monte Alban plastered over or reused old monuments in new construction. The Maya frequently defaced, sawed, buried, or relocated monuments of defeated enemies or disgraced persons.

In addition to stone inscriptions on monuments, temples, and dwellings, a handful of Maya bark-paper books have survived. Whereas stone monuments served as public propaganda, the bark-paper books contained the technical knowledge of astronomy, calendrical science, divination, and prophecy that governed the lives of the Maya elite.

The tradition of monument-building lapsed almost entirely after the demise of the classic Maya city-states in the ninth and tenth centuries. Yet the nobility preserved knowledge of the Maya script down to the Spanish conquests in the sixteenth century. Early Spanish accounts observed that although only noble Maya could read, they instructed the commoners in history through storytelling and song. Spanish missionaries deliberately destroyed nearly all of the bark-paper books, which they condemned as works of the devil. In their place the Spanish taught the Maya to write their language using the Roman alphabet. The *Popul Vuh*, the "Book of Council" that has served as a rich mine of information about Maya mythology and religion, was composed in Roman script in the mid-sixteenth century (see Chapter 11). After an alphabet was adopted, however, knowledge of the Maya hieroglyphic script died out.

The Legacy of Mesoamerican Languages

Although the classical Maya language became extinct, scholars today can decipher as much as 80 percent of surviving Maya texts. Linguists have found that the political institutions and cultural values embedded in the Maya literary legacy also appear, in altered form, in the later written records of the Mixtecs and Aztecs of central Mexico. All of these languages, as well as Zapotec, were part of a broader Mesoamerican tradition that used writing and calendrical science to create histories designed to enhance rulers' prestige and power. Although command of writing was restricted to a tiny elite, Mesoamerican rulers addressed the mass of the populace through public monuments, which were intended to convey a sense of the immobility of history and the permanence of the present-day social order. Here, as in many cultures, the sacred and imperishable character of writing, in contrast to the fleeting nature of ordinary speech, endowed the ruler's words with a powerful aura of truth.

Yet it was precisely because of such tight control that written languages like classic Maya became extinct once the social and political systems that created them disappeared. In the cosmopolitan civilizations of Eurasia, by contrast, rulers and religious authorities failed to maintain a monopoly over the power of the written word, especially when vernacular tongues displaced classical languages as the chief media of written communication.

Conclusion

The tenth to the fourteenth centuries witnessed a remarkable expansion of learning and schooling across Eurasia. This expansion of knowledge and education was fostered by the growing penetration of religious institutions and values in local society and by the creation of formal institutions of higher learning. The languages of sacred texts and religious instruction—Latin, Arabic, Sanskrit, and Chinese—achieved new prominence in higher education and intellectual discourse. The growing prestige of these cosmopolitan languages led them to be adopted in government and literary expression as well.

The deepening infusion of religious faith into traditions of learning thus produced more distinct and coherent cultural identities in each of the major civilizations of Eurasia. At the same time the friction between sacred and secular learning—between faith and reason—intensified. In Latin Christendom, struggles erupted among the Roman church, monarchs and city councils, and guilds of masters, each seeking to dictate the structure and content of university education. In the Islamic world, in the absence of a centralized religious authority or even an ordained clergy, individual ulama and madrasas aligned themselves with one of several separate traditions of Islamic law and theological study. Sufis proposed a radically different understanding of Islam. In China, a resurgent, secular Neo-Confucianism dominated public discourse through the state-run civil service examinations and schools, pushing Buddhism to the margins of intellectual life. In the Maya world, by contrast, the rulers' monopoly of the written word ensured their domination over all aspects of political, social, and religious life.

The unity of learned culture was increasingly undercut by the emergence of vernacular literary languages. Writing in the vernacular was stimulated by political fragmentation and rivalry, governments' desire to intrude more deeply into the everyday lives of their subjects, and the flowering of local and regional literary and artistic expression in an era of vigorous economic prosperity. By the tenth century the cosmopolitan Sanskrit culture had fragmented into a chain of regional literary cultures across South and Southeast Asia. In the eleventh century Japanese authors, notably elite women such as Lady Murasaki, fashioned a new national literary culture written in the Japanese vernacular. In much of the Islamic world, Arabic persevered as the dominant written and spoken language, but Persian and Turkish achieved new stature in religion, government, and literature. Despite this proliferation of vernacular literatures, however, the cultural and social gulf between the literate and the illiterate remained as wide as ever.

The intense struggles over the definition of religious truth and social values in the major regions of Eurasia during these centuries aggravated conflicts between different civilizations and ways of life. As we will see in the next chapter, the launch of the Crusades and the Mongol conquests inflamed the already smoldering tensions between Christians and Muslims and between nomadic and settled peoples.

NOTES

1. Lady Murasaki, *The Tale of Genji*, quoted in Ivan Morris, *The World of the Shining Prince: Court Life in Ancient Japan* (New York: Knopf, 1964), 308–309.
2. *The Letters of Abelard and Heloise*, trans. Betty Radice (Harmondsworth, U.K.: Penguin, 1974), 58.
3. *The Anglo-Saxon Chronicle*, trans. G. N. Garmonsway (London: J. M. Dent, 1954), 216.
4. Burhan ad-Din Az-Zarnuji, *Ta'lim al-Muta'allim-Tariq at-Ta'allum, Instruction of the Student: The Method of Learning*, trans. G. E. von Grunebaum and Theodora M. Abel (New York: King's Crown Press, 1947), 32.
5. Farid al-Din Attar, *Tadhkirat al-Awliya*, quoted in Margaret Smith, *Rabi'a the Mystic and Her Fellow Saints in Islam* (Cambridge, U.K.: Cambridge University Press, 1928), 3–4.

6. W. Montgomery Watt, *The Faith and Practice of al-Ghazali* (London: George Allen & Unwin, 1967), 57.

7. Ali Hujwiri, *The Kashf al-Mahjūb: The Oldest Persian Treatise on Sufism*, trans. Reynold A. Nicholson (rpt. ed.; London: Luzac & Co., 1976), 213.

8. *The Itinerary of Rabbi Benjamin of Tudela*, trans. A. Asher (New York: Hakesheth Publishing, n.d.), 43.

9. Quoted in Ichisada Miyazaki, *China's Examination Hell: The Civil Service Examinations of Imperial China* (New Haven, CT: Yale University Press, 1981), 17.

RESOURCES FOR RESEARCH

Church and Universities in Latin Christendom

Scholars regard the rediscovery of Greek philosophy and science via translations from Arabic and the rise of the universities as the catalysts for a "twelfth-century renaissance" in European intellectual life. Moore's examination of the emergence of a distinctive European ruling culture provides historical background for assessing the political and social influence of higher learning. Cobban's classic study highlights the distinctive characters of the major European universities.

Clanchy, M. T. *Abelard: A Medieval Life*. 1997.

Cobban, A. B. *The Medieval Universities: Their Development and Organization*. 1975.

Ferruolo, Steven. *The Origins of the University: The Schools of Paris and Their Critics, 1100–1215*. 1985.

Moore, R. I. *The First European Revolution, c. 970–1215*. 2000.

Pedersen, Olaf. *The First Universities: Studium Generale and the Origins of University Education in Europe*. 1997.

Students and Scholars in Islamic Societies

Much scholarship has been devoted to the educational and legal institutions that shaped Islamic intellectual and cultural life. In recent years, scholars such as Chamberlain and Ephrat have examined the role of knowledge and teaching in the social life of the ulama and urban society in general. Trimingham remains the basic work on the social history of Sufism.

Berkey, Jonathan. *The Transmission of Knowledge in Medieval Cairo: A Social History of Islamic Education*. 1992.

Chamberlain, Michael. *Knowledge and Social Practice in Medieval Damascus, 1190–1350*. 1994.

Ephrat, Daphna. *A Learned Society in a Period of Transition: The Sunni Ulama of Eleventh-Century Baghdad*. 1995.

Makdisi, George. *The Rise of Colleges: Institutions of Learning in Islam and the West*. 1981.

Trimingham, J. S. *The Sufi Orders in Islam*. 1971.

The Cosmopolitan and Vernacular Realms in India and Southeast Asia

After the demise of the Gupta Empire, India's intellectual and political culture initially remained unified, but the Muslim conquests fostered strong regional diversity in vernacular languages and literary cultures. Pollock's seminal work on "the Sanskrit cosmopolis" has dramatically enhanced our understanding of the relationship between language and political and cultural authority.

Asher, Catherine B., and Cynthia Talbot. *India Before Europe*. 2006.

Eaton, Richard M., ed. *India's Islamic Traditions, 711–1750*. 2003.

Pollock, Sheldon. *The Language of the Gods in the World of Men: Sanskrit, Culture, and Power in Premodern India*. 2006.

Talbot, Cynthia. *Precolonial India in Practice: Society, Religion, and Identity in Medieval Andhra*. 2001.

Wink, André. *Al-Hind: The Making of the Indo-Islamic World*, 2d ed. 1997.

Learning, Schools, and Print Culture in East Asia

Civil government by officials selected through competitive examinations shaped the distinctive political, social, and cultural traditions not only of China but of East Asia as a whole. Chaffee provides a succinct institutional history of the Song civil service examinations that focuses on the question of social mobility, while Miyazaki offers a lively social history spanning the late imperial era. Morris remains the most engaging introduction to the literary culture of Heian Japan.

Bol, Peter K. *Neo-Confucianism in History*. 2008.

Chafee, John. *Thorny Gates of Learning in Song China: A Social History of Examinations*, 2d ed. 1995.

Chia, Lucille. *Printing for Profit: The Commercial Publishers of Jianyang, Fujian (11th–17th Centuries)*. 2002.

Miyazaki, Ichisada. *China's Examination Hell: The Civil Service Examinations of Imperial China*. 1981.

Morris, Ivan. *The World of the Shining Prince: Court Life in Ancient Japan*. 1964.

COUNTERPOINT: Writing and Political Power in Mesoamerica

Scholars' painstaking efforts to decode the Maya language have now yielded impressive results. Schele and Mathews combine archaeology, art history, and linguistic analysis to retrieve the history and meaning of key Maya monuments. Tedlock's study provides translations of a wide range of Maya literary texts down to modern times.

Coe, Michael D. *Breaking the Maya Code*, rev. ed. 1999.

Marcus, Joyce. *Mesoamerican Writing Systems: Propaganda, Myth, and History in Four Ancient Civilizations*. 1992.

Schele, Linda, and Peter Mathews. *The Code of Kings: The Language of Seven Sacred Maya Temples and Tombs*. 1998.

Tedlock, Dennis. *2000 Years of Mayan Literature*. 2010.

▶ **For additional primary sources from this period**, see *Sources of Crossroads and Cultures.*

▶ **For Web sites, images, and documents related to topics in this chapter**, see Make History at bedfordstmartins.com/smith.

REVIEW

The major global development in this chapter ▶ The expansion of learning and education across Eurasia from 900 to 1300 and its relationship to the rise of regional and national identities.

IMPORTANT EVENTS

918–1392	Koryŏ dynasty in Korea
960–1279	Song dynasty in China
c. 1010	Lady Murasaki's *Tale of Genji* begins to circulate among the Japanese court aristocracy
1055	Seljuk Turks capture Baghdad and establish their rule over Mesopotamia and Syria
1066	Norman conquest of England
1130–1200	Life of Neo-Confucian scholar Zhu Xi
1140	Catholic church authorities convict theologian Peter Abelard of heresy
c. 1150	First university founded at Paris
1206–1526	Delhi Sultanate in India
1215	Pope Innocent III bans the teachings of Aristotle and Ibn Rushd
1273	Publication of Thomas Aquinas's *Summa Theologica*
c. 1313–1321	Dante Alighieri composes his epic poem *Divine Comedy*
1382	Ibn Khaldun becomes professor of Islamic law at Cairo
1392–1910	Yi dynasty in Korea

KEY TERMS

cathedral school (p. 410)
hadith (p. 417)
logographic (p. 431)
madrasa (p. 417)
Neo-Confucianism (p. 430)
rhetoric (p. 410)

shari'a (p. 417)
Sufism (p. 419)
ulama (p. 417)
university (p. 415)
vernacular language (p. 415)

CHAPTER OVERVIEW QUESTIONS

1. Did the spread of higher learning reinforce or undermine established political and religious authority?

2. How did educational institutions reshape social hierarchy and elite culture?

3. What were the different uses of cosmopolitan languages and vernacular languages, and to what degree did they broaden access to written knowledge?

4. How did the different technologies of writing affect the impact of the written word?

SECTION FOCUS QUESTIONS

1. What political, social, and religious forces led to the founding of the first European universities?

2. To what extent did Sunni and Sufi schools foster a common cultural and religious identity among Muslims?

3. What political and religious forces contributed to the development of a common culture across India and Southeast Asia and its subsequent fragmentation into regional cultures?

4. To what extent did intellectual and educational trends in Song China influence its East Asian neighbors?

5. How did the relationship between political power and knowledge of writing in Mesoamerica differ from that in the other cultures in this chapter?

MAKING CONNECTIONS

1. In what ways did the cathedral schools and universities of Latin Christendom modify the classical traditions of learning of ancient Greece and Rome?

2. How did the madrasas of the Islamic world differ from European universities in their curricula, their teachers, and their relationships with political and religious authorities?

3. How can we explain the failure of printing technology to spread from China to neighboring societies such as Japan, India, or the Islamic world until centuries later?

14

AT A CROSSROADS ▶

Qubilai, grandson of the great conqueror Chinggis, cemented his claim as Great Khan of all the Mongols only after winning a bloody struggle against one of his brothers. In his single-minded quest to make himself the first foreign emperor of China, Qubilai turned his back on the Mongols' steppe homeland. His success in conquering China came at the cost of undermining the unity of the Mongol Empire, which fragmented into four separate khanates. (The Art Archive.)

Crusaders, Mongols, and Eurasian Integration
1050–1350

"The empire can be won on horseback, but it cannot be ruled from horseback." Reciting this old Chinese proverb, Yelu Chucai, a Chinese-educated adviser, delivered a tart rebuke to the Mongol Great Khan Ogodei (ERG-uh-day). A council of Mongol princes had just chosen Ogodei (r. 1229–1241) to succeed his father, Chinggis (CHEEN-gihs). The Mongol armies had overrun much of the territory of the Jin kingdom that then ruled north China. Now the princes urged Ogodei to massacre the defeated population and turn their farmlands into pasture for the Mongol herds. But Yelu Chucai persuaded Ogodei that preserving China's agricultural way of life would generate far greater rewards.

Yelu Chucai had served as a Jin official until the Mongols captured him in 1215. Three years later Yelu accompanied Chinggis (Genghis was the Persian version of his name) on his campaigns in western Asia, serving the Mongol khan as scribe, astrologer, and confidential adviser. Upon gaining the confidence of Ogodei, Yelu in effect became chief minister of the Mongol Empire and began to construct a strong central government based on Chinese models. But Yelu made many enemies among the Mongol princes, who distrusted his promotion of Chinese ways. After initially approving Yelu's plans, Ogodei withdrew his support.

BACKSTORY

By the twelfth century, economic revival and commercial integration had begun to stimulate unprecedented cultural contact and exchange across Eurasia (see Chapters 12 and 13). But economic prosperity did not necessarily translate into political strength. The weakened Abbasid caliphs, already challenged by rival caliphates in Egypt and Spain, had become pawns of the Seljuk Turks, invaders from Central Asia. In China, the Song dynasty was also vulnerable to invasion by its northern neighbors. In 1127 Jurchen Jin invaders from Manchuria seized the northern half of the empire, forcing the Song court to flee to the south. Within Christendom, the division between the Latin West and the Byzantine East widened into outright hostility, and the Roman and Byzantine churches competed against each other to convert the pagan peoples of eastern Europe and Russia to Christianity.

441

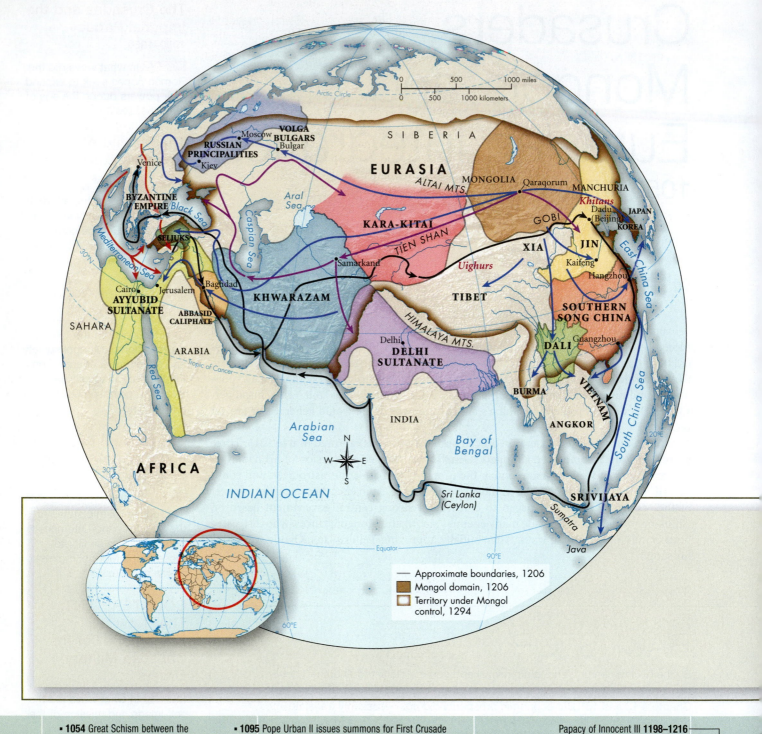

Approximate boundaries, 1206

Mongol domain, 1206

Territory under Mongol control, 1294

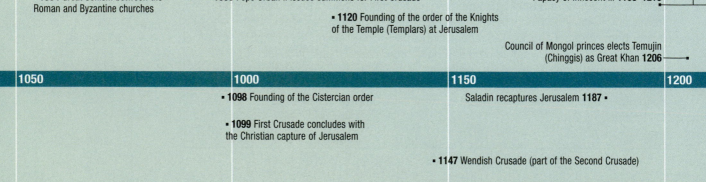

- 1054 Great Schism between the Roman and Byzantine churches

- 1095 Pope Urban II issues summons for First Crusade

Papacy of Innocent III 1198–1216

- 1120 Founding of the order of the Knights of the Temple (Templars) at Jerusalem

Council of Mongol princes elects Temujin (Chinggis) as Great Khan 1206

1050	1000	1150	1200

- 1098 Founding of the Cistercian order

Saladin recaptures Jerusalem 1187 -

- 1099 First Crusade concludes with the Christian capture of Jerusalem

- 1147 Wendish Crusade (part of the Second Crusade)

Following Ogodei's death in 1241 and Yelu Chucai's death two years later, Mongol leaders dismantled Yelu's efforts to remake the Mongol Empire in the likeness of China. Wracked by conflict among the sons and grandsons of Chinggis, the empire fragmented into a series of independent regional khanates. Two decades later, many features of Yelu's vision of bureaucratic government were adopted by Qubilai (KOO-bih-lie) Khan, who made himself emperor of China. But by then the unified Mongol Empire had ceased to exist.

The Mongol conquests dominate the history of Eurasia in the thirteenth century. From humble origins among the nomadic herders of Central Asia, the Mongols became world conquerors. They terrified settled peoples from Korea to Hungary, laid waste to dozens of cities, and toppled many rulers. Yet they also unified Eurasia in unprecedented ways. Merchants and missionaries, groups who received special favor from the Mongols, moved with ease from the Mediterranean to China. The Mongol Empire exerted a powerful influence on the histories of China, Russia, and the Islamic world.

A century before the Mongol armies swept across Eurasia, another clash of civilizations, the Crusades, had erupted—this one in the Mediterranean world. In this conflict, the tense hostility that had divided Christians and Muslims exploded into a succession of religious wars. Although the Crusaders ultimately failed to turn the Holy Land into a Christian stronghold, the Crusades marked a crucial moment in the definition of Europe as the realm of Latin Christendom. At the same time, centralization of administrative control and theological orthodoxy within the Latin church brought about a final rupture between Rome and the Christian churches of Byzantium and Asia. But the papacy's drive to create a united Latin Christendom under clerical leadership collapsed, and national monarchies enhanced their power throughout Europe.

For all of the destruction they caused, both the Mongol conquests and the Crusades expanded the horizons of cross-cultural contact and influence. Exotic goods whetted new appetites—elites in Europe and China alike craved the pepper grown in India. The Mongols introduced knowledge of gunpowder and cannon to the Islamic world, from whence it spread to Europe. Christian missionaries journeyed to the courts of the Mongol khans,

MAPPING THE WORLD

Eurasian Integration, c. 1050–1350

Although the Mongol conquests caused much devastation and loss of life, they also stimulated an unprecedented surge of people and goods across Eurasia. The Venetian Marco Polo, who after traveling overland to the court of Qubilai Khan returned to Italy via maritime routes through Southeast Asia and the Indian Ocean, exemplified this new mobility. The Crusades intensified religious and political tensions between Christians and Muslims, but also led to greater economic interaction between Europe and the Middle East.

ROUTES ▼

→ Mongol campaigns under Chinggis, 1206–1227

→ Later Mongol campaigns, 1229–1295

→ General routes of the Crusades, 1096–1291

→ Travels of Marco Polo, 1271–1295

▪ **1240** Mongol conquest of Kiev

1271–1368 Rule of Mongols over China as the Yuan dynasty

1274–1295 Journey of Marco Polo to China

1250–1517 Mamluk Sultanate in Egypt and Syria

| 1250 | 1300 | 1350 |

▪ **1248** Christian armies capture the Almohad stronghold of Seville

▪ **1291** Mamluks recapture Acre, last Christian stronghold in Palestine

▪ **1258** Mongols sack Baghdad

1295–1304 Rule of Ghazan as Ilkhan; conversion of Ilkhan Mongols to Islam

seeking converts and allies in their holy war against Islam. The Mongols, rulers of the largest contiguous land empire in human history, built bridges that connected diverse civilizations rather than walls that divided them. But ultimately the contradictions between the political and cultural traditions of the nomadic Mongols and the settled lives of the peoples they conquered proved too great, and the Mongol empires collapsed. By 1400 Europe and Asia had once again grown distant from each other.

OVERVIEW
QUESTIONS

The major global development in this chapter: The Eurasian integration fostered by the clashes of culture known as the Crusades and the Mongol conquests.

As you read, consider:

1. In what ways did the growing economic and cultural unity of Latin Christendom promote the rise of powerful European national monarchies?

2. To what degree did the expansion of Latin Christendom remake eastern Europe in the image of western Europe?

3. In what ways did the Mongol conquests foster cultural and economic exchange across Eurasia?

4. How and why did the Mongol rulers of China, Iran, and Russia differ in their relationships with the settled societies they ruled?

The Crusades and the Imperial Papacy 1050–1350

FOCUS

In what ways did the Roman popes seek to expand their powers during the age of the Crusades?

The **Crusades** are generally understood as an effort to reclaim control of the sacred sites of the Christian religion from Muslim rule. More broadly, the Crusades developed into an evangelical movement to Christianize the world. The summons to rescue Jerusalem from the "heathen" Muslims, announced at a church council in 1095, escalated to include campaigns to recover Islamic Spain; to impose orthodox Christianity on the pagan Celtic, Slavic, and Baltic peoples of Europe; and to eradicate heresy—doctrines contrary to the church's official teachings—from within Latin Christendom. The era of the Crusades also witnessed the temporary rise of an "imperial" papacy as administrative reforms within the church broadened the Roman popes' authority over secular affairs as well as the spiritual life of the Christian faithful. Both "Christendom" and "Europe" acquired more precise meaning: the lands of the Christian peoples subject to the spiritual commands of the Roman pope.

The Papal Monarchy

Crusades The series of military campaigns instigated by the Roman papacy with the goal of returning Jerusalem and other holy places in Palestine to Christian rule.

The transformation of Latin Christendom that led to the crusading movement began with initiatives to reform the church from within. In the eyes of both lay and clerical critics, abuses such as violations of celibacy and the sale of church offices had compromised the clergy's moral authority. The reformers also sought to renew the church's commitment to spread the teachings of Christ to all peoples of the world. Pope Gregory VII (r. 1073–1085) was the staunchest advocate of the primacy of the pope as the leader of all Christian peoples. Within the church, Gregory campaigned to improve the moral and educational caliber of the clergy by holding the priesthood to high standards of competence, and also—especially in matters of sexual behavior—to stringent standards of conduct. Gregory also demanded strict conformity to the standard religious services authorized by the church hierarchy and the use of Latin as the universal language of Christianity. Thus, under Gregory VII, the movements for clerical reform and centralization of authority within the church merged. As a result, clerical reform became a force for the religious and cultural unification of Europe.

Long before Gregory VII's papacy, the rivalry between the Roman and Byzantine churches had resulted in bitter division in the Christian world. The Roman pope's claim to supreme authority over all Christians rankled both the Byzantine emperor and the patriarch at Constantinople. Half-hearted efforts at reconciliation came to an end in 1054, when the Roman pope and the patriarch at Constantinople expelled each other from the church. This mutual excommunication initiated a formal break between the Latin and Orthodox churches that came to be known as the **Great Schism**. As the split between the Christian leadership widened, Rome and Constantinople openly competed for the allegiance of new converts in eastern Europe and Russia.

The leaders of the Orthodox church were not the only powerful figures who challenged the supremacy of the Roman popes. In their efforts to assert and consolidate their authority, the popes faced competition from within Europe as well as from without. Secular leaders in many parts of Europe had the right to make appointments to key church positions in their domains. In effect, this gave them control over church lands and officials. Pope Gregory demanded an end to such secular control, seeing it as a threat to the papacy's dominion over Latin Christendom. In a deliberately public disagreement with the Holy Roman Emperor Henry IV (r. 1056–1106) known as the **investiture controversy** (*investiture* refers to the appointment of church officials), Gregory challenged the emperor's authority to appoint bishops within his domains. The struggle for control of the church pitted the most powerful secular and sacred rulers of Christendom against each other. Gregory invalidated Henry's right to rule over his territories, provoking the emperor's enemies among the German princes to rise against him. Henry was forced to prostrate himself before the pope and beg forgiveness. Ultimately, a compromise gave kings and princes some say in appointments to major church offices in their territories but ceded leadership of the church to the papacy.

Deprived of control over the church, the Holy Roman emperors lost their primary base of support. The German princes consolidated their power over their own domains, reducing the emperorship to a largely ceremonial office. The Roman papacy, in contrast, increasingly resembled a royal government, with its own law courts, fiscal officers, and clerical bureaucracy.

Although the assertion of papal authority was originally linked to the movement for clerical reform, ironically, papal success and the church's growing immersion in worldly affairs gave rise to a new round of calls for change within the church. The Cistercian order, founded in France in 1098, epitomized the renewed dedication to poverty, chastity, and evangelism among the Latin clergy. Within half a century the Cistercians had more than three hundred affiliated monasteries stretching from Spain to Sweden—even while refusing to admit female convents into their order. Although the Cistercians preserved the tradition that monks must confine themselves to their monastery for life, the order developed elaborate networks of communication to coordinate their activities. Passionate defenders of Roman orthodoxy, the Cistercians worked tirelessly to uproot what they perceived as the heresies of their fellow Christians. It was the Cistercians who secured the papal condemnation that ended the career of the Parisian theologian Peter Abelard in 1140 (discussed in Chapter 13).

Great Schism of the Christian Churches

Investiture Controversy

Cistercian Religious Order

Great Schism The separation of the Latin Catholic and Greek Orthodox churches following the mutual excommunication by the Roman pope and the Byzantine patriarch in 1054.

investiture controversy Conflict between the pope and the Holy Roman emperor over who had the authority to appoint bishops and other church officials.

Crusaders Voyaging to Holy Land

Pope Urban's summons for a crusade to recapture Jerusalem was directed at knights and other men experienced in war. Nonetheless, people of all walks of life—including women and the urban poor—rallied to the Crusader cause. This Spanish illustration from 1283 shows the Crusaders embarking for the Holy Land aboard galleys powered chiefly by oars, the typical type of warship used in the Mediterranean Sea. (Biblioteca Monasterio del Escorial, Madrid/ Giraudon/Bridgeman Art Library.)

The Crusades 1095–1291

The First Crusade

Upon receiving an appeal from the Byzantine emperor for aid against the advancing armies of the Seljuk Turks in 1095, Pope Urban II (r. 1088–1099) called upon "the race of Franks [Latin Christians] . . . beloved and chosen by God" to "enter upon the road to the Holy Sepulcher; wrest that land from the wicked race, and subject it to yourselves."[1] Urban II's summons for a crusade to liberate Jerusalem drew inspiration from the reform movements within the church, and from a desire to transform the warrior rulers of Latin Christendom, constantly fighting among each other, into a united army of God. A papal dispensation granted to the Crusaders by Urban II transformed participation in the crusade into a form of penance, for which the Crusader would receive a full absolution of sins. This helped create enthusiasm for crusading among the knightly class, which saw the crusade as a means of erasing the heavy burden of sin that inevitably saddled men of war and violence.

The Crusader forces, more a collection of ragtag militias under the command of various minor nobles than a united army, suffered setbacks, yet achieved surprising success in capturing Jerusalem in 1099 (see Map 14.1). To some extent this success reflected the disunity prevailing in the Islamic world. The Seljuk sultans of Baghdad had ceded control of Palestine and Syria to the emirs of individual towns, who had failed to join forces for common defense. Yet the victors also lacked strong leadership and failed to follow up their initial success by establishing unified political and military institutions. Spurning the Byzantine emperor's claims to sovereignty, the Crusaders divided the conquered territories among themselves and installed a French duke as king of Jerusalem and defender of the Holy Land. Perhaps the greatest beneficiaries of the crusading movement were Venice and Genoa, whose merchants rushed to secure trading privileges in the Crusader kingdoms along the eastern shores of the Mediterranean. The capture of the Holy Land also prompted the founding of **military orders** that pledged themselves to the defense of the Holy Land (see Counterpoint: The "New Knighthood" of the Christian Military Orders). But in the long run, lack of coordination and unity of purpose among the leaders of

military order One of the new monastic orders, beginning with the Knights of the Temple founded in 1120, that combined the religious vocation of the priesthood with the military training of the warrior nobility.

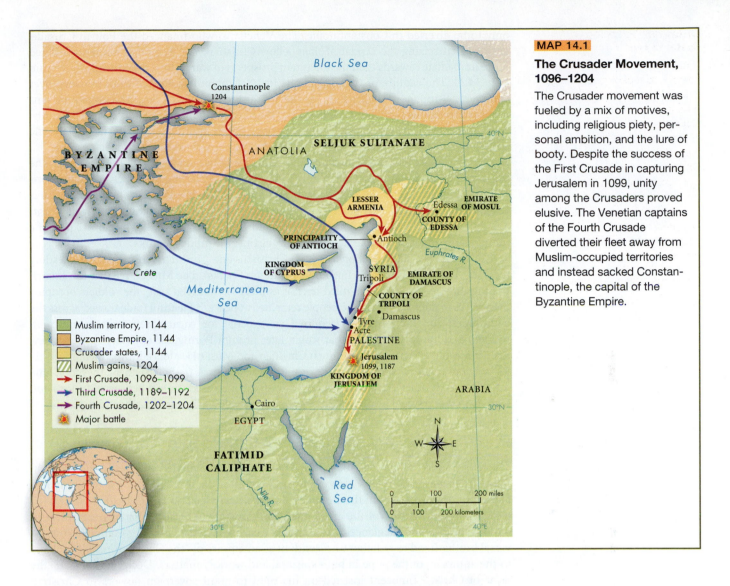

MAP 14.1

The Crusader Movement, 1096–1204

The Crusader movement was fueled by a mix of motives, including religious piety, personal ambition, and the lure of booty. Despite the success of the First Crusade in capturing Jerusalem in 1099, unity among the Crusaders proved elusive. The Venetian captains of the Fourth Crusade diverted their fleet away from Muslim-occupied territories and instead sacked Constantinople, the capital of the Byzantine Empire.

Crusader kingdoms, merchants, and military orders would doom Christian aspirations for permanent domination of the Holy Land.

At first Muslims did not understand the religious aspirations of the Crusaders and failed to rally against the Christian invaders. Nearly a century elapsed before a serious challenge arose to Christian rule over Jerusalem. In 1169 the Seljuk emir of Damascus dispatched one of his lieutenants, Saladin (c. 1137–1193), to Egypt to shore up defenses against a possible Christian attack. Saladin soon seized power from the much-weakened Fatimid caliphate and declared himself an independent sultan. He sought to muster support by declaring a holy war against the Christian occupiers of Jerusalem. In 1187 Saladin conquered Jerusalem and most of the Crusader principalities.

Saladin's Recapture of Jerusalem

This unexpected reversal prompted Christendom's leading monarchs—the kings of England and France and the Holy Roman emperor—to join together in what became known as the Third Crusade (1189–1192). Dissension among the Christian kings hobbled the military campaign, however, and the crusade ended with a truce under which the Christian armies withdrew in exchange for a Muslim pledge to allow Christian pilgrims access to holy sites.

Over the next century new crusades were repeatedly launched, with little success. Moreover, the original religious motivations of the Crusaders came to be overshadowed by political and economic objectives. The riches of Egypt beckoned but proved to be an elusive prize. The army mustered under the banner of the Fourth Crusade initially set sail for Egypt,

Failure of the Later Crusades

only to be diverted to Constantinople. The Venetians, who financed the Fourth Crusade, decided that seizing the capital of their fellow Christian, the Byzantine emperor, offered more immediate rewards than the uncertain prospects of war against the Muslims (see again Map 14.1). The capture of Constantinople in 1204 catapulted Venice to dominance over commerce throughout the eastern Mediterranean and the Black Sea. The Byzantine emperor recovered his capital in 1260 thanks to the naval support of Genoa, Venice's perennial rival. After the Venetian seizure—with the pope's tacit approval—of Constantinople, the schism between the Roman Catholic and Greek Orthodox churches became irreparable.

The Crusades also intensified the cultural divide between Christians and Muslims. The militant rhetoric and propaganda of holy war rendered any lasting peace between Christians and Muslims inconceivable. Chronicles from both sides are filled with grotesque caricatures and misconceptions of each other's beliefs and customs. The proliferation of new *madrasas* and Sufi lodges following the Muslims' humiliating defeat in the First Crusade was part of a moral rearmament of the Islamic community against the infidel "Franks."

In reality, not all interactions between Christians and Muslims were hostile (see Reading the Past: A Muslim Courtier's Encounters with the Franks). The Muslim pilgrim Ibn Jubayr, passing through the Crusader-ruled territories in 1184, observed that "the soldiers occupied themselves in their war, while the people remained at peace."[2] Plentiful trade flowed across the battle lines, and the Crusaders acquired an appetite for sugar (previously unknown in Europe) and the spices of Asia that would later prompt Portuguese seafarers to seek a new maritime route to Asia. However much Christian and Muslim leaders admired their adversaries' religious zeal and courage in battle or valued each other as trading partners, they took little interest in each other's cultures or ideas. Indeed, the increased contact between Muslims and Christians that resulted from the Crusades only intensified religious and ethnic differences.

Papal Supremacy and the Christian People

Expansion of Papal Authority

The reorientation of the Crusades toward political aims originated within the papacy itself. Pope Innocent III (r. 1198–1216) tried to capitalize on the crusading spirit to strengthen papal authority both within the church and over secular society. The Crusaders had rallied together under the sign of the cross, the common symbol of all Christians regardless of national origins and allegiances. Innocent likewise invoked the Crusaders' language of universal brotherhood to redefine Christendom as an empire of "the Christian people" subject to the authority of the pope in both spiritual and worldly matters. Declaring himself "the vicar of Christ," Innocent insisted on his right to grant sovereign powers to Christian kings and princes. Legislation enacted at Innocent's instigation created a more centralized Christian church and deprived bishops of much of their independence. Civil matters such as marriage now fell under church jurisdiction. Innocent also established a judicial body, the **Inquisition**, to investigate and punish anyone who challenged the pope's supreme authority. The Inquisition expanded, with the eager support of lay monarchs, into a broad-based campaign directed against heretics and nonbelievers alike. Thus, it became, in many ways, an internal Crusade. In the view of European elites, just as military expeditions to the Holy Land would strengthen Christendom by bringing sacred sites outside of Europe under Christian control, the Inquisition would strengthen Christendom by eliminating religious diversity within Europe.

Persecution of Jews

Jewish communities in Christian Europe were early targets of Innocent's Inquisition. Many Christians regarded Jews as an alien race whose presence corrupted Christian society. Jews had suffered various kinds of legal discrimination since Roman times, but their persecution intensified from the eleventh century onward. Christian rulers prohibited Jews from owning land, forcing them to take up occupations as urban craftsmen and merchants. Jews were often vilified because of their prominence in trades such as moneylending, which tainted them with the stigma of usury. In many places Jews lacked legal protections and were subject to the arbitrary whims of kings and princes. Innocent's new orders, which compelled Jews to wear distinctive forms of dress such as special badges or hats, were intended to reinforce existing laws forbidding marriage between Christians and Jews.

Inquisition A system of courts and investigators set up by the Roman papacy in the early thirteenth century to identify and punish heretics.

A Muslim Courtier's Encounters with the Franks

Usamah ibn Mundiqh (1095–1188) was a Muslim courtier in the entourage of Mu'in ad-Din Unur, a general in command of Damascus. Usamah fought in numerous battles against the Crusaders, but he also frequently visited Christian-ruled Jerusalem on diplomatic business and had cordial relations with some Christians. He wrote his *Learning by Example*, a book of moral advice and instruction, as a gift to Saladin, who conquered Jerusalem four years later.

Among the Franks—God damn them!—no quality is more highly esteemed in a man than military prowess. The knights have a monopoly of the positions of honor and importance among them, and no one else has any prestige in their eyes. . . .

The Franks are without any vestige of a sense of honor and jealousy. If one of them goes along the street with his wife and meets a friend, this man will take the woman's hand and lead her aside to talk, while the husband stands by waiting until she has finished the conversation. . . .

I was present myself when one of them came up to the emir Mu'in ad-Din—God have mercy on him—in the Dome of the Rock and said to him: "Would you like to see God as a baby?" The emir said he would, and the fellow proceeded to show us a picture of Mary with the infant Messiah on her lap. "This," he said, "is God as a baby." Almighty God is greater than the infidels' concept of him! . . .

[Upon entering a Christian church I found] about ten old men, their bare heads as white as combed cotton. They were facing the east, and wore on their breasts staves ending in crossbars turned up like the rear of a saddle. They took their oath of this sign, and gave hospitality to those who needed it. The sight of their piety touched my heart, but at the same time it displeased and saddened me, for I had never seen such zeal and devotion among the Muslims. . . . One day, as Mu'in ad-Din and I were passing the Peacock House, he said to me, "I want to dismount and visit the Old Men.". . . [Inside] I saw about a hundred prayer-mats, and on each a Sufi, his face expressing peaceful serenity, and his body humble devotion. This was a reassuring sight, and I gave thanks to Almighty God that there were among the Muslims men of even more zealous devotion than those Christian priests. Before this I had never seen Sufis in their monastery, and was ignorant of the way they lived.

Source: Usamah ibn Mundiqh, *The Book of Learning by Example*, quoted in Francesco Gabrieli, ed., *Arab Historians of the Crusades* (Berkeley: University of California Press, 1969), 73, 77, 80, 84.

EXAMINING THE EVIDENCE

1. What virtues did Usamah admire in the Christians, and why?

2. Why did Usamah find the picture of Mary and the child Jesus offensive?

Franciscan and Dominican Religious Orders

Efforts to impose religious conformity on Latin Christendom received further impetus from the formation of new religious orders, most notably the Franciscans and the Dominicans. Like the Cistercians, these new orders dedicated themselves to the principles of poverty and evangelism. Unlike the Cistercians, who remained confined to their monasteries, Franciscan and Dominican friars traveled widely, preaching to the populace and depending on almsgiving for their livelihood. The new preaching orders sought to carry out the church's mission to regulate and reform the behavior of lay believers. The Dominicans assumed a conspicuous role in leading the Inquisition. The Franciscan and Dominican orders were also in the forefront of campaigns to convert the non-Christian peoples of eastern Europe.

End of the Crusades

During the thirteenth century the precarious position of the Christian outposts along the coast of Palestine and Syria became dire. The rise of a powerful Islamic state under the Mamluk dynasty in Egypt (discussed later in this chapter) after 1250 sealed the fate of the crusading movement. In 1291 the Mamluks captured Acre, the last Christian stronghold in Palestine. Dissension among the leaders of Christendom, especially between the pope and the French king, made it impossible to revive an international alliance to recapture the Holy Land.

The Making of Christian Europe   1100–1350

FOCUS

How did the efforts to establish Christianity in Spain and eastern Europe compare with the Crusaders' quest to recover Jerusalem?

Despite their ultimate failure, the Crusades had profound consequences for the course of European history. Among the most important was their role in consolidating the social and cultural identity of Latin Christendom. Even as the movement to retake the Holy Land from the Muslim occupiers foundered and sank, the crusading spirit provided the crucial momentum for Christendom to expand into northern and eastern Europe.

The crusading ideal also encouraged assimilation of the warrior class into the monastic culture of the Christian church. This merger produced the culture of **chivalry**—the knightly class's code of behavior, which stressed honor, piety, and devotion to one's ideals. The code of chivalry confirmed the moral as well as social superiority of the warrior nobility. Knights played at least as great a role as clerical evangelists in spreading Christian culture.

We can see the connection between the Crusades and the expansion of Latin Christendom in the use of the term "Franks," the term both Christian and Islamic chroniclers used to refer to the Crusaders. Along the frontiers of Latin Christendom, the term assumed a special meaning. "Frankish" knights were aggressive colonizers who combined ambitions for conquest with the missionary zeal of the Roman church. In the thirteenth and fourteenth centuries such kings and knights conquered and colonized territories from Spain in the west to the Baltic Sea in the east. Europe took form out of the processes of military conquest, migration, and cultural colonization that would later also characterize European expansion into the Americas.

The Reconquest of Spain   1085–1248

Under its Umayyad dynasty (756–1030), Muslim-ruled Spain had enjoyed relative religious peace. Although religious toleration was often compromised by sharp differences in social standing among Muslims, Jews, and Christians, the Umayyad rulers fostered a tradition of mutual accommodation. Yet the subjection of Christian peoples to Muslim rulers in Spain, as in Palestine and Syria, became increasingly intolerable to Christian rulers and church leaders alike. At the same time that he issued his summons for the First Crusade, Pope Urban II urged Christian rulers in northern Spain to take up arms against their Muslim neighbors. The *Reconquista* ("reconquest" of Spain) thus became joined to the crusading movement.

Muslim Rule in Spain

In its heyday the Umayyad caliphate in Spain was the most urbanized and commercially developed part of Europe. In the early eleventh century, however, the Umayyad caliphate disintegrated, and Muslim-ruled Spain splintered into dozens of feuding city-states. The conquest of Toledo, Spain's second-largest city, by King Alfonso of Castile in 1085 lifted Castile into a preeminent position among Spain's Christian kingdoms. The Muslim emirs turned to the Almoravid (al-moe-RAH-vid) rulers of North Africa for protection. The Almoravids, fervently devoted to the cause of holy war, halted the Christian advance but imposed their own authoritarian rule over the Muslim territories in Spain.

The Almohad (AHL-moh-had) dynasty, which supplanted the Almoravids in North Africa and Spain in 1148, was even more fiercely opposed to the Umayyad heritage of tolerance toward non-Muslims. Almohad policies, which included the expulsion of all Jews who refused to convert to Islam, were highly unpopular. Despite a major victory over Castile in 1195, the Almohads were unable to withstand intensified Christian efforts to "reconquer" Spain. Between 1236 and 1248 the major Muslim cities of Spain—Córdoba, Valencia, and finally Seville—fell to Castile and its allies, leaving Granada as the sole remaining Muslim state in Spain.

After capturing Toledo in 1085, the kings of Castile made the city their capital. Toledo was renowned as a cultural and intellectual crossroads and, despite the rhetoric of holy war, the Castilian kings preserved Toledo's multicultural character. Toledo's large

chivalry The code of behavior, stressing honor, piety, and devotion to one's ideals, of the knightly class of medieval Europe.

Arabic-speaking Christian and Jewish communities epitomized this spirit of religious pluralism. During the twelfth century, Toledo prospered as Europe's brightest intellectual center, a city in which Arabic and Jewish culture and learning flourished under Christian rule.

But Toledo's intellectual and religious tolerance steadily eroded as the Reconquista advanced. Christian monarchs expelled most of the Muslims from the cities and awarded Muslim lands and dwellings to Christian princes, bishops, and military orders. The religious toleration that the kings of Castile had extended to Muslim and Jewish minorities gradually dissipated. At first, the Christian kings allowed their Muslim subjects, known as Mudejars (mu-DAY-hahr), to own property, worship in mosques, and be judged by Islamic law before *qadi* jurists. After 1300, however, judicial autonomy eroded, and Mudejars accused of crimes against Christians were tried in Christian courts under Christian law. Christian rulers also converted the great mosques of Córdoba, Seville, and Toledo into Christian cathedrals.

The place of Jews also deteriorated in a European world that had come to define itself as the realm of "the Christian people." Attacks on Jews escalated dramatically with the onset of the Crusades. In the 1230s, when the Inquisition began a deliberate persecution of Jews, many fled from France, England, and Germany to seek sanctuary in Spain. Yet in Spain, too, Jews occupied an insecure position. In the fourteenth century, as in other parts of Latin Christendom, violence against Jews swept Spain. Anti-Jewish riots in Toledo in 1370, encouraged by the Castilian king, wiped out the city's Jewish population almost overnight. In 1391 wholesale massacres of Jews in Spain's major cities dealt a catastrophic blow to Jewish communities from which they never recovered. Rigid intolerance had replaced the vibrant multiculturalism of Umayyad Spain.

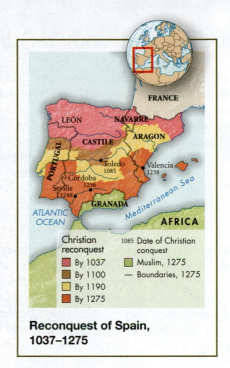

Reconquest of Spain, 1037–1275

Christianizing Eastern Europe 1150–1350

In issuing a summons in 1145 for the Second Crusade to recover territories retaken by the Muslims, Pope Eugene III also invited the knights of Christendom to launch a crusade against the non-Christian populations of northern and eastern Europe—collectively referred to as the Wends. The pope acted at the instigation of his teacher Bernard of Clairvaux (d. 1153), the Cistercian abbot who had put Peter Abelard on trial for heresy. Bernard had urged Christian knights to take up arms against pagan peoples everywhere "until such a time as, by God's help, they shall be either converted or wiped out" (see Reading the Past: Bernard of Clairvaux's Summons to the Wendish Crusade).[3] In the three centuries following the Wendish Crusade of 1147, Latin Christendom steadily encroached upon the Baltic and Slavic lands. Latin Christendom incorporated northern and eastern Europe through a combination of conquest and colonization that transformed political, cultural, and economic life.

Wendish Crusade

The fissure that split the Latin and Greek Christian churches also ran through eastern Europe. In the tenth and eleventh centuries, the rulers of Poland and Hungary had chosen to join the Roman church, but Christian converts in the Balkans such as the Serbs and Bulgars as well as the Rus princes had adopted the Greek Orthodoxy of Constantinople. In subsequent centuries, Latin and Greek clerics waged war against each other for the allegiance of the eastern European peoples along a frontier stretching from the Adriatic Sea to the Baltic Sea (see Map 14.2).

Freebooting nobles enthusiastically joined the Wendish Crusade and were the first to profit from its military successes. The lightly armed Wendish foot soldiers and cavalry were no match for the mounted Frankish knights, clad in heavy armor, and their superior siege weapons. Small groups of knights subjugated the Wendish peoples in piecemeal fashion, built stoutly fortified castles to control them, and recruited settlers from France

Bernard of Clairvaux's Summons to the Wendish Crusade

In March 1147, the Cistercian abbot Bernard of Clairvaux came to Frankfurt to promote what would become the Second Crusade. Few German knights expressed enthusiasm for a new crusade in the east, but they clamored to attack their pagan Slav and Balt neighbors in eastern Europe. Eager to capitalize on this fervor, Bernard secured the pope's permission to launch the part of the Second Crusade known as the Wendish Crusade. In this letter—addressed "to all Christians"—Bernard seeks to drum up recruits for the Wendish Crusade.

[Satan] has raised up evil seed, wicked pagan sons, whom, if I may say so, the might of Christendom has endured too long, shutting its eyes to those who with evil intent lie in wait, without crushing their poisoned heads under its heel. . . . Because the Lord has committed to our insignificance the preaching of this crusade, we make known to you that at a council of the king, bishops, and princes who had come together at Frankfurt, the might of Christians was armed against them, and that for the complete wiping out or, at any rate, the conversion of these peoples, they have put on the Cross, the sign of our salvation. And we by virtue of our authority promised them the same spiritual privileges as those enjoy who set out toward Jerusalem. Many took the Cross on the spot, the rest we encouraged to do so, so that all Christians who have not yet taken the Cross for Jerusalem may know that they will obtain the same spiritual privileges by undertaking this expedition, if they do so according to the advice of the bishops and princes. We utterly forbid that for any reason whatsoever a truce should be made with these peoples, either for the sake of money or for the sake of tribute, until such a time as, by God's help, they shall be either converted or erased. . . . The uniform of this army, in clothes, in arms, and in all else, will be the same as the uniform of the other, for it is fortified with the same privileges.

Source: Bernard of Clairvaux, *Letters,* trans. Bruno Scott James (London: Burns, Oates, 1953), 466–468.

EXAMINING THE EVIDENCE

1. In Bernard's view, who is the real enemy of the Christian faithful?

2. How and why does Bernard link the Wendish Crusade to the original crusading goal of capturing Jerusalem?

---

and the Low Countries to clear the forests for cultivation. The colonists were accompanied by missionaries, led by the Cistercians, seeking to "civilize" the Slavs by converting them to Latin Christianity. Thus, from the start the goal of the Frankish conquerors was to remake the east in the image of Latin Christendom.

Colonization and Conversion in Eastern Europe

Many Slavic princes opted to embrace Latin Christianity and to open their lands to settlement by immigrants from the west. Conversion not only preserved the political independence of native rulers but offered material rewards: willing settlers knowledgeable about advanced farming techniques, more reliable revenues from the land, and a retinue of Christian clerics determined to impose discipline on their subjects using the long arm of church law. For their part, Christian missionaries believed that the salvation of the pagan peoples required changing their work habits as well as ministering to their souls. A poem penned by a Cistercian monk in the early fourteenth century depicted Poland at the time his predecessors first arrived there as backward and poverty-stricken:

> The land lacked cultivators and lay under wood
> And the Polish people were poor and idle,
> Using wooden ploughs without iron to furrow the sandy soil,
> Knowing only how to use two cows or oxen to plough.
> There was no city or town in the whole land,
> Only rural markets, fallow fields, and a chapel near the castle.

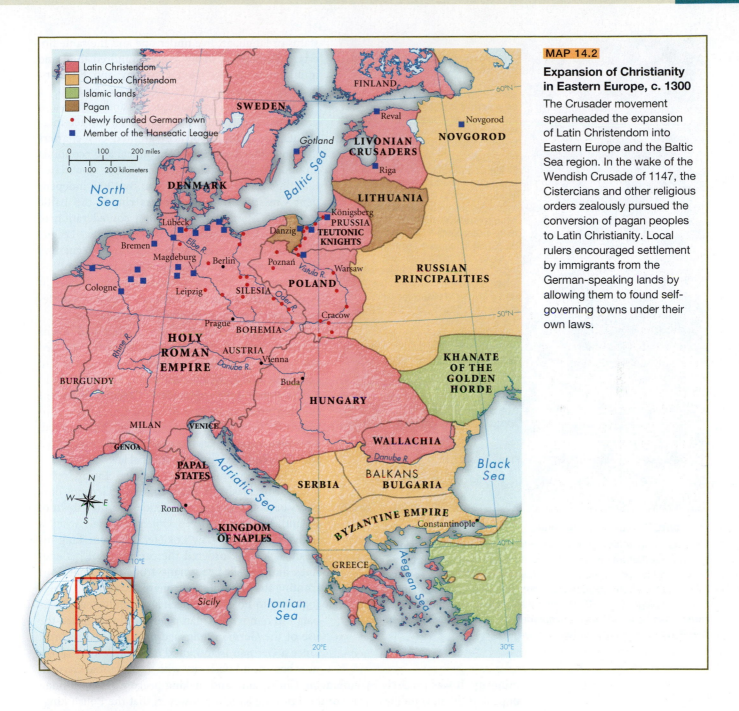

MAP 14.2

Expansion of Christianity in Eastern Europe, c. 1300

The Crusader movement spearheaded the expansion of Latin Christendom into Eastern Europe and the Baltic Sea region. In the wake of the Wendish Crusade of 1147, the Cistercians and other religious orders zealously pursued the conversion of pagan peoples to Latin Christianity. Local rulers encouraged settlement by immigrants from the German-speaking lands by allowing them to found self-governing towns under their own laws.

Neither salt, nor iron, nor coinage, nor metal,
Nor good clothes, nor even shoes
Did that people have; they just grazed their flocks.
    These were the delights that the first monks found.[4]

Hence, remaking the east would require more than the religious conversion of its people. It would require the reordering of the region's society and economy. With this belief in mind, princes, bishops, and monks often took the lead in recruiting farmers and craftsmen from the west to settle newly opened territories in the east. To attract settlers, local lords usually exempted homesteaders from feudal obligations and the legal condition of serfdom. For example, a charter issued by the king of Hungary in 1247 to new settlers in a sparsely populated corner of his realm declared, "Let the men gathered there, of whatever

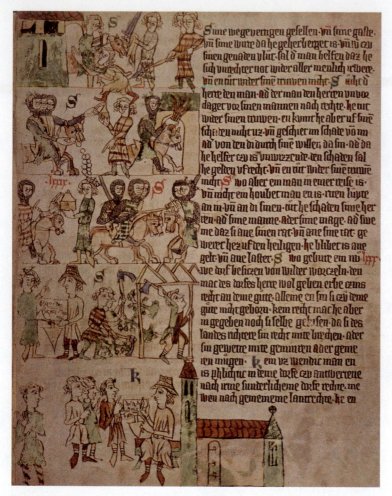

Peasants Receiving Land Title

New peasant settlers brought fresh labor and superior farming technology that transformed the landscape of eastern Europe. The legal and economic privileges granted to immigrants created conditions favorable for economic development. This illustration from the *Sachsenspiegel* (c. 1220), the first major law code written in German rather than Latin, shows homesteaders receiving titles of ownership to the lands they cleared for farming. (akg-images.)

status or language, live under one and the same liberty."[5] Perhaps as many as two hundred thousand immigrants, mostly from Germany and Flanders, had already settled east of the Elbe River by 1200.

Local princes, both conquerors and natives, also promoted the founding of cities. To attract merchants and artisans, princes granted city charters that guaranteed considerable political and economic autonomy. Lübeck, founded in 1159, dominated maritime trade in the Baltic Sea. By 1300, independent Christian trading colonies ringed the Baltic (see again Map 14.2). In 1358, a confederation of commercial cities formed the Hanseatic League discussed in Chapter 12. In addition to regulating trade among its more than one hundred members, the Hanseatic League provided a counterweight against rulers seeking to extort heavy customs duties from traders passing through their lands.

Throughout eastern Europe, cities and towns became oases of foreign colonists who differed sharply from the rural inhabitants in language and culture as well as wealth and status. For example, in 1257 a Polish duke reestablished Cracow, an ancient Polish fortress, as a center of international trade populated by German immigrants whom he recruited. The duke forbade Poles to reside in the town, which was governed by German municipal law.

This Germanization of eastern Europe provoked a backlash. In 1312, Cracow's German burghers backed a German contender for the crown of Poland, but they suffered violent reprisals when a native Pole, Wladyslaw Lokieteck, became king instead. Lokieteck ordered the execution of his enemies and expelled Germans from their mansions fronting the city's market square, turning the buildings over to Poles. Lokieteck also conducted a campaign to remove German priests and prohibited the use of the German language in municipal records. Once a German island amid a sea of Poles, Cracow now became a Polish city with a substantial German minority. It was precisely by embracing Christianity and making peace with the Roman pope and the new military order of the Teutonic Knights, however, that the Polish kings could establish themselves as independent monarchs within the expanding realm of Christendom.

Rise of National Monarchies

By 1350, Latin Christianity was firmly implanted in all parts of Europe except the Balkan peninsula. But the rise of strong national monarchies had thwarted the Roman popes' ambitions to create a unified Christendom under papal rule. The vigorous commercial expansion during this era discussed in Chapter 12 had swelled royal treasuries. Kings and princes increased their demands for tax revenue, extended the jurisdiction of royal courts, and convened assemblies (known as "parliaments") of leading nobles, clergy, and townsmen to rally support for their policies. Europe's patchwork of feudal domains and independent cities began to merge into unified national states, especially in England and France. The French philosopher Nicole Oresme (c. 1323–1382) expressed the spirit of his age when he rejected a "universal monarchy" as "neither just nor expedient."[6] Instead,

Oresme argued, practical necessity dictated that separate kingdoms, each with its own laws and customs, should exercise sovereign power over their own people.

Neither did the Muslims' success in repelling the Crusaders restore unity to the Islamic world. After enduring for sixty years, the Ayyubid dynasty founded by Saladin was overthrown in 1250 by Turkish slave soldiers. At that same time, the Islamic world faced a new challenge, the Mongol invasions, that would have a far more lasting impact on the development of Islamic societies than did the Crusades.

The Mongol World-Empire 1100–1368

The era of Mongol domination marked a watershed in world history. Although the Mongols drew on long-standing traditions of tribal confederation, warfare, and tribute extraction, the Mongol Empire was unprecedented in its scope and influence. Historians give much of the credit for the Mongols' swift military triumphs and political cohesion to the charismatic authority of the empire-builder Chinggis Khan. Later generations of Mongol rulers built upon Chinggis's legacy, seeking to adapt steppe traditions of rulership to the complex demands of governing agrarian societies.

FOCUS

How did the organization of Mongol society and government change from the time of Chinggis Khan to that of his grandson Qubilai, the ruler of China?

Despite the brutality and violence of the Mongol conquests, the Mongol Empire fostered far-reaching economic and cultural exchanges. The Mongols encouraged the free movement of merchants throughout their domains and embraced religious and intellectual diversity. Wherever they went the Mongols sought to impose their own political, social, and military institutions, but the Mongol conquerors of Iran and central Asia adopted the Islamic religion of their subjects. The Mongol courts also became flourishing centers of artistic, literary, and religious patronage. The Mongols transformed the world—and were themselves transformed by the peoples they subjugated.

Rise of the Mongols

In the several centuries before the rise of the Mongols, the dynamics of state formation in the Eurasian steppe underwent dramatic transformation. The Turkish and Uighur confederations had depended on control of the lucrative Silk Road trade routes and extraction of tribute from the settled empires of China and Iran (see Chapter 10). In the aftermath of the Tang dynasty in 907, the Khitans (kee-THANS) of eastern Mongolia annexed Chinese territories around modern Beijing and established a Chinese-style dynasty, Liao (lee-OW) (937–1125). The new dynasty was a hybrid state that incorporated elements of Chinese bureaucratic governance, including the taxation of settled farmers, while retaining the militarized tribal social structure and nomadic lifestyle of the steppe.

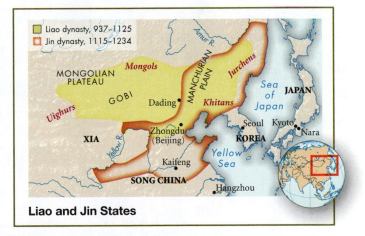

Liao and Jin States

In the 1120s the Jurchens, a seminomadic group from northern Manchuria, overran the Liao and the rest of northern China and founded their own state of Jin (1115–1234). The Jin state largely retained the dual administrative structure of the Liao. But in contrast to the Liao, the Jin conquerors were dwarfed by the enormous Chinese population under their rule. The Jin rulers struggled to preserve their cultural identity in the face of overwhelming pressures to assimilate to Chinese ways.

Temujin (teh-MU-jihn) (c. 1167–1227), the future Chinggis Khan, was born into one of the numerous tribes living in eastern Mongolia, on the margins of the Jin realm. Tribal affiliations were unstable, however, and at that time the "Mongol people" was not a clearly

Steppe Society

Mongol Women in the Household Economy and Public Life

The prominent roles of women in the social and economic life of the pastoral nomads of the Eurasian steppe contrasted starkly with women's reclusive place in most settled agrarian and urban societies. Under Chinggis Khan's permanently militarized society, nearly all adult men had to embark on lengthy campaigns of conquest far from home. The women left behind were compelled to shoulder even the most arduous tasks. Kinship and gender relations among the pastoral nomads also differed in many ways from the practices of settled societies. Mongol women remained subservient to their husbands, but royal and noble women participated vigorously in public life and political affairs.

European travelers to the Mongol domains expressed surprise at women's key roles in the pastoral economy. John of Plano Carpini, a papal envoy dispatched to the Mongol court in 1245, claimed that productive labor fell entirely to the Mongol women:

> The men do not make anything at all, with the exception of arrows, and they sometimes tend the flocks, but they hunt and practice archery. . . . Their women make everything, including leather garments, tunics, shoes, and everything made of leather. They also drive the carts and repair them. They load the camels, and in all tasks they are very swift and energetic. All the women wear breeches, and some of them shoot like the men.[1]

Marco Polo agreed that Mongol women "do all the work that is needed for their lords and family and themselves" while the men "trouble themselves with nothing at all but with hunting and with feats of battle and of war and with hawking [falconry]."[2]

Despite women's vital contributions to the family's economic welfare, however, Mongol society was based on a patrilineal system of inheritance in which men controlled property and wealth. Mongol women had no property of their own. Women who lacked the protection of a husband often found themselves abandoned and destitute. Such was

Mongol Empress Chabi

Mongol leaders often had multiple wives, each of whom took charge of her own household. Chabi, the second of Qubilai's four wives, became one of the most powerful figures at the Mongol court after Qubilai's election as Great Khan. Her ambition to become empress of China rather than merely the wife of a tribal chieftain was a driving force behind Qubilai's conquest of the Southern Song. (National Palace Museum, Taiwan, Republic of China.)

defined group. Family and clan were the basic units of Central Asian nomadic societies. Tribal allegiances grew out of political expediency, providing the means for mobilizing isolated groups for common purposes ranging from herding and migration to trade and war.

The pastoral livelihood of the steppe nomads was vulnerable to catastrophic disruptions, such as prolonged drought, severe winters, and animal diseases. Scarcity of resources often provoked violent conflict among neighboring tribes. Raiding to steal livestock, women, slaves, and grazing lands was common. The constant violence of the steppe produced permanently militarized societies. For most of the male population, warfare became a regular profession, and women took charge of tending herds and other activities usually reserved for men in the premodern world (see Lives and Livelihoods: Mongol Women in the Household Economy and Public Life).

the fate that befell Chinggis's mother, Hoelun, whose husband was murdered when Chinggis was nine years old. Deserted by her husband's kinfolk, Hoelun doggedly raised her sons on her own, at times forced to forage for roots and berries to survive.

Nonetheless, royal Mongol women were outspoken figures whose voices carried much weight in court deliberations. When Ogodei died in 1241, his widow ruled over the Mongol confederation for five years before ceding power to one of her sons. Qubilai's mother, Sorqaqtani-Beki, likewise played a decisive role in the history of the Mongol Empire. The pastoral nomads of the Eurasian steppe commonly protected widows by remarrying them to younger male relatives of their deceased husbands, and when Sorqaqtani-Beki's husband, Tolui, died in 1232, Ogodei offered to marry her to one of his sons. She firmly declined Ogodei's proposal and instead demanded a fiefdom to provide for her upkeep. Ogodei reluctantly granted her a fief of eighty thousand households in northern China, which Sorqaqtani-Beki insisted on governing herself. In keeping with the policies of Ogodei's minister Yelu Chucai, Sorqaqtani-Beki instituted a Chinese-style civil administration and engaged Chinese scholars to tutor her sons. Qubilai's upbringing thus turned his attention, and the direction of the Mongol Empire, away from the Mongols' steppe homeland and toward China.

Sorqaqtani-Beki proved to be a shrewd politician who earned wide admiration among Mongols and foreigners alike. She had converted to Nestorian Christianity, but promoted toleration of all of the major faiths of the subject peoples. The Ilkhan historian Rashid al-Din, a Muslim, wrote that "in the care and supervision of her sons and in the management of their affairs and those of the army and the people, Sorqaqtani-Beki laid a foundation that would have been beyond the capability of any crowned head."[3]

In 1251, her popularity and political agility paid off when she succeeded in elevating her son Mongke to the position of Great Khan, displacing the lineage of Ogodei. Sorqaqtani-Beki died the following year, but the supreme authority of the Great Khans remained with her sons, including Qubilai, the future emperor of China.

1. Christopher Dawson, ed., Mission to Asia: Narratives and Letters of the Franciscan Missionaries of Mongolia and China in the Thirteenth and Fourteenth Centuries (New York: Harper & Row, 1966), 18.
2. Marco Polo: The Description of the World, eds. A. C. Moule and Paul Pelliot (London: George Rutledge & Sons, 1938), 1:169.
3. Rashiduddin Fazullah's Jami'u't-tawarikh (Compendium of Chronicles): A History of the Mongols, trans. W. M. Thackston (Cambridge, MA: Harvard University, Department of Near Eastern Languages and Civilizations, 1999), Part II, 400–401.

QUESTIONS TO CONSIDER

1. How did the division of household work in pastoral societies such as the Mongols differ from that found among settled farming peoples?

2. How might the role of women in the Mongol household economy explain the power they wielded in tribal affairs?

For Further Information:
Lane, George. Daily Life in the Mongol Empire. Westwood, CT: Greenwood Press, 2006.
Rossabi, Morris. Khubilai Khan: His Life and Times. Berkeley: University of California Press, 1988.

The instability of steppe life worked against social stability, but it also created opportunities for new leadership. Personal charisma, political skills, and prowess in war counted far more than hereditary rights in determining chieftainship. We see this fluidity of Mongol society reflected in Temujin's rise to power. Orphaned at age nine and abandoned by his father's tribe, Temujin gained a following through his valor and success as a warrior. Building on this reputation, he proved extraordinarily adept at constructing alliances among chiefs and transforming tribal coalitions into disciplined military units. By 1206 Temujin had forged a confederation that unified most of the tribes of Mongolia, which recognized him as Chinggis (meaning "oceanic"), the **Great Khan**, the universal ruler of the steppe peoples.

Chinggis Khan

Great Khan "Lord of the steppe"; the Great Khan of the Mongols was chosen by a council of Mongol chiefs.

Creation and Division of the Mongol Empire 1206–1259

Maintaining unity among the fractious coalition of tribal leaders required a steady stream of booty in the form of gold, silk, slaves, and horses. Thus, once installed as Great Khan, Chinggis led his army in campaigns of plunder and conquest. Initially he set his eye on the riches of China and aimed at conquering the Jin kingdom. But in 1218, Chinggis's attention turned toward the west after the Turkish shah of Khwarazam (in Transoxiana) massacred a caravan of Muslim merchants traveling under the Mongol khan's protection. Enraged, Chinggis laid waste to Samarkand, the shah's capital, and other cities in Transoxiana and eastern Iran in what was perhaps the most violent of the Mongol campaigns. After deposing the Khwarazam shah, Chinggis returned to the east and renewed his campaign to conquer China.

By the time of Chinggis's death in 1227, Mongol conquests stretched from eastern Iran to Manchuria. Up to this point, the impact of the Mongol invasions had been almost wholly catastrophic. Solely interested in plunder, Chinggis had shown little taste for the daunting task of ruling the peoples he vanquished (see Map 14.3).

Chinggis's Successors   Throughout Central Asian history the death of a khan almost always provoked a violent succession crisis. But Chinggis's charisma sufficed to ensure an orderly transition of power. Before he died, Chinggis parceled out the Mongol territories among his four sons or their descendants, and he designated his third son Ogodei to succeed him as Great Khan.

The Mongol state under Chinggis Khan was a throwback to the Turkish-Uighur practice of allowing conquered peoples to maintain their own autonomy in exchange for tribute. Ogodei, in contrast, began to adopt features of the Liao-Jin system of dual administration under the direction of the Khitan statesman Yelu Chucai, whom we met at the start of this chapter. Creating an enduring imperial system required displacing tribal chiefs with more centralized political and military control. Thus Ogodei also established a permanent capital for the Mongol Empire at Qaraqorum.

Formation of Independent Mongol Khanates   Under Ogodei's leadership the Mongols steadily expanded their dominions westward into Russia, and they completed the conquest of the Jin. Mongol armies had invaded Hungary and Poland and were threatening to press deeper into Europe when Ogodei's death in 1241 halted their advance. After Ogodei's nephew Mongke was elected Great Khan in 1252, he radically altered Chinggis's original allocation of Mongol territories, assigning the richest lands, China and Iran, to his brothers Qubilai and Hulegu. Mongke's dispensation outraged the other descendants of Chinggis. By the end of his reign, the Mongol realm had broken into four independent and often hostile khanates (see again Map 14.3).

Qubilai Khan and the Yuan Empire in China 1260–1368

Conquest of China   The death of Mongke in 1259 sparked another succession crisis. After four years of bitter struggle Mongke's brother Qubilai secured his claim as Great Khan. Qubilai devoted his energies to completing the conquest of China. In 1271 he adopted the Chinese-style dynastic name Yuan and moved the Great Khan's capital from Mongolia to China, where he built a massive city, Dadu, at the former capital of Zhongdu (modern Beijing). Five years later, Mongol armies captured the Southern Song capital of Hangzhou, and by 1279 Chinese resistance to Mongol rule had ceased. The Yuan Empire (1271–1368) would last only about one hundred years, but for the first time all of China had fallen under foreign rule.

Qubilai was not content with the conquest of China. In 1281, he mustered a great armada, carrying forty-five thousand Mongol soldiers and their horses, for an invasion of Japan. Most of the Mongol fleet was destroyed by a typhoon, which the Japanese gratefully saluted as the *kamikaze*, the "divine wind" that defended them from the Mongol onslaught. The would-be invaders abandoned their effort to take over Japan. Qubilai's army captured the central plains of Burma in 1277, but attempts to conquer Vietnam and naval invasions of Java and Sumatra failed. After 1285, when one of his favorite sons died fighting in Vietnam, Qubilai halted his campaigns of conquest.

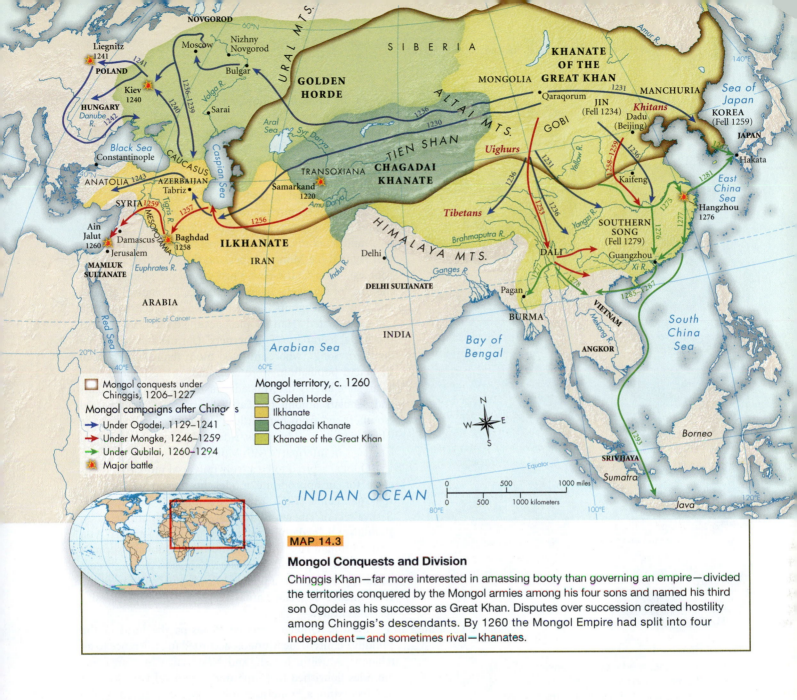

MAP 14.3

Mongol Conquests and Division

Chinggis Khan—far more interested in amassing booty than governing an empire—divided the territories conquered by the Mongol armies among his four sons and named his third son Ogodei as his successor as Great Khan. Disputes over succession created hostility among Chinggis's descendants. By 1260 the Mongol Empire had split into four independent—and sometimes rival—khanates.

Qubilai envisioned himself not merely as first among the Mongol princes but also as an exalted "Son of Heaven" in the style of the Chinese emperors. He surrounded himself with foreign advisers, including Muslims, Uighurs, and Chinese, and laid the foundations for permanent Mongol rule over China. Building on the precedents of the Liao and Jin states, Qubilai created a highly centralized administration designed to extract the maximum revenue from China's land, people, and commerce. The Venetian merchant Marco Polo (1254–1324), astonished at the splendor of the Great Khan's capital, proclaimed that Qubilai was "the most powerful man in people and in lands and in treasure that ever was in the world or that now is from the time of Adam our first father till this moment."[7]

Although Qubilai was a conscientious and diligent ruler, his successors gave little attention to the tasks of maintaining the infrastructure of the agrarian economy or protecting people's welfare. Instead, they relied on a system of **tax farming** that delegated tax collection privileges to private intermediaries, mostly Muslim merchants. Many of these tax farmers abused their authority and demanded exorbitant payments from an increasingly disgruntled agrarian population.

Qubilai as Chinese Emperor

tax farming The assignment of tax collection powers to private individuals or groups in exchange for fixed payments to the state.

Religious Tolerance

Mongol Passport

The Mongols established a comprehensive network of post stations to maintain communications with their far-flung armies. Only those with proper authorization, in the form of metal or wooden paiza tablets, were allowed use of the lodgings, supplies, and horses provided at these post stations. The Mongolian inscription on this silver paiza reads, "By the power of the Eternal Heaven, may the name of Mongke Khan be sacred. He who does not honor it shall perish and die." (© The State Hermitage Museum/photo by Vladimir Terebenin, Leonard Kheifets, Yuri Molodkovets.)

At the same time, however, the Mongols strongly encouraged commerce, and international trade flourished. The Mongols created a vast network of post stations and issued passports to merchants to ensure safe passage throughout the Mongol realm. The chief beneficiaries of expanding trans-Eurasian trade were the Uighur and Muslim merchants who acted as commercial agents for their Mongol patrons.

The Yuan Empire maintained the Central Asian tradition of a social structure based on tribal loyalties. Political, legal, and economic privileges rested on an ethnic hierarchy that favored the Mongol tribes and the so-called "affiliated peoples"—non-Chinese who had served the Mongols since the time of Chinggis, including Turks, Tibetans, Persians, and above all Uighurs. Former Chinese subjects of the Jin state, designated "Han people," occupied the third rung of this social hierarchy. "Southerners" (former subjects of the Southern Song), who composed more than 80 percent of the Yuan population, were relegated to the bottom. The Yuan state largely drew its administrators from merchants and scholars among the "affiliated peoples" and barred "southerners" from high office. The Mongols also forbade Chinese to possess firearms, ride horses, learn the Mongol language, or intermarry with Mongols.

Qubilai aspired to be a truly universal monarch. In his quest for an appropriate model, he turned to Phags-pa (pak-pa) Lama (1235–1280), the spiritual leader of the Saskya sect of Tibetan Buddhism. As a transnational faith, Buddhism helped unite the diverse peoples of eastern Asia under Mongol rule. At the same time, Qubilai's support enabled Phags-pa and the Saskya Lamas to gain supreme authority over Tibet, a position they would hold until the rival lineage of Dalai Lamas displaced them in the sixteenth century.

Even as Qubilai declared Phags-pa the head of the Buddhist church, the Mongols accorded full tolerance to all religions. Muslim, Jewish, and Nestorian Christian communities flourished in China under Mongol rule. John of Montecorvino, a Franciscan missionary dispatched by the pope, arrived at the Yuan capital in 1294. John erected a church near the khan's palace, translated the New Testament into Chinese and Uighur, and by his own estimate attracted six thousand converts—mostly non-Chinese—to Christianity. Pleased with John's reports of the progress of his missionary work, in 1308 the pope consecrated him as the first Latin bishop of Beijing.

Under Qubilai's leadership the Mongol Empire in China departed from the practices of the early steppe empires, which relied on plunder and extraction of tribute from settled societies. Instead the Yuan state, like its Liao and Jin predecessors, developed institutions for imposing direct rule on its Chinese subjects, even if it did not penetrate local society to the extent that native Chinese empires had. At the same time, the Mongols in China turned their backs on their steppe homeland. By 1300 the Yuan emperors were raised exclusively within the confines of the capital at Dadu and had largely severed their connections with the independent Mongol khanates in central and western Asia.

The Mongol Khanates and the Islamic World 1240–1350

FOCUS

In what respects did the Turkish Islamic states of the Mamluks and Ottomans pursue policies similar to those of the Mongol regimes in Iran and Russia?

In 1253 the Great Khan Mongke assigned his brother Hulegu (HE-luh-gee) responsibility for completing the Mongol conquest of Iran and Mesopotamia. In 1258 Baghdad fell to Hulegu's army, and the last Abbasid caliph was reportedly wrapped in a carpet and trampled to death, to avoid spilling royal blood on the ground. In their hunger for booty, the Mongol victors utterly destroyed the city of Baghdad, the official capital of Islam. By Hulegu's own estimate, two hundred thousand people perished. Survivors of the Mongol conquest fled to Cairo, where the Mamluk (MAM-luke) sultanate, a regime of military slave origins, had overthrown the dynasty of Saladin and was consolidating its power over Egypt and Syria. The Mamluks became the new political leaders of the Islamic world, rallying their fellow Muslims to the cause of holy war against the Mongol onslaught.

The conquest of Baghdad was the last great campaign conducted jointly by the Mongol princes. As we have seen, by the time of Qubilai's succession in 1263 as Great Khan, rivalry among Chinggis's heirs had fractured the Mongol Empire into four independent khanates: the Golden Horde along the frontiers of Russia; the Chagadai (shah-gah-TY) khanate in Central Asia; the Ilkhanate based in Iran; and the khanate of the Great Khan in China (see again Map 14.3).

Mongol Rule in Iran and Mesopotamia

After conquering Iran and Mesopotamia, Hulegu's army suffered a decisive defeat at the hands of the Mamluks in Palestine in 1260 and withdrew. At around this time Hulegu adopted the Turkish title of *Ilkhan* ("subordinate khan"), implying submission to his brother Qubilai, the Great Khan. Hulegu and his successors as Ilkhan (il-con) also made diplomatic overtures to the Christian monarchs of Europe with the goal of forming an alliance against their common enemy, the Mamluks. In 1287 the Ilkhanate sent Rabban Sauma, a Nestorian Christian monk from China, as an envoy to the courts of England, France, and the Roman pope to enlist their aid against the Mamluks, to no avail.

The Ilkhans ruled over their domains from a series of seasonal capitals in Azerbaijan, a region in the northwestern corner of Iran where good pastureland was plentiful. Unlike Qubilai in China, the Ilkhans did not build a fixed, monumental capital in the style of their subjects. Instead they followed the nomadic practice of moving their camps in rhythm with the seasonal migrations of their herds. The Mongol conquests of Iran and Mesopotamia had caused immense environmental and economic harm. Abandonment of farmlands and the deterioration of irrigation systems

Mongol Siege of Baghdad

The Mongol conquest of Baghdad in 1258 ended the caliphate, the main political institution of the Islamic world since the death of Muhammad. In this illustration of the siege of Baghdad, a group of Mongols at lower right beat a flat drum; the archers and soldiers are all in Persian dress. At upper left the last Abbasid caliph makes a futile attempt to escape by boat. (Bildarchiv Preussischer Kulturbesitz/ Art Resource.)

sharply curtailed agricultural production. Much land was turned over to pasture or reverted to desert.

As in China, Mongols composed a tiny minority of the Ilkhanate's population. Even in the Ilkhan armies, Turks far outnumbered Mongols. Like the Yuan state, the Ilkhanate initially recruited its administrative personnel from foreigners and members of minority groups. Christian communities, notably the Nestorians and Armenians, had been quick to side with the Mongol invaders against their Muslim overlords. Christians hoped that their connections to the Ilkhan court—Hulegu's queen was a Christian, and a number of Christians rose to high positions in the Ilkhanate government—might win official endorsement of their religion. Instead, the Mongols in Iran increasingly turned toward the faith of the Muslim majority. The proselytizing efforts of Sufi sheikhs attracted many converts, especially among the Mongol and Turkish horsemen who were the backbone of the Ilkhanate's military strength. Muslim advisers became influential in the ruling circles of the Ilkhanate as well.

By the late thirteenth century, escalating religious tensions and the familiar pattern of violent succession disputes among the Mongol leaders threatened to tear apart the Ilkhan state. The ascension of Ghazan (haz-ZAHN) (r. 1295–1304) as Ilkhan revived the Ilkhanate and marked a decisive turning point in Mongol rule in Iran.

Ghazan's Reforms

A convert to Islam, Ghazan took pains to show his devotion to the faith of the great majority of his subjects. Ghazan reduced Christians and Jews to subordinate status and banished Buddhist monks from the Ilkhan realm. He also placed the Ilkhanate government on sounder footing by reforming the fiscal system, investing greater resources in agriculture, instituting a new currency system, and reducing taxes. Ghazan broke with the practice of seasonal migration and constructed a permanent capital at Tabriz appointed with palaces, mosques, Sufi lodges, a grand mausoleum for himself, and baths and caravanserais to accommodate traveling merchants. Tabriz quickly developed into a major center of international trade and artistic production.

Rashid al-Din (ra-SHEED al-DEEN) (1247–1318), a Jewish doctor who converted to Islam, served as chief minister and architect of Ghazan's program of reform. Rashid al-Din also carefully embellished Ghazan's image as ruler, forging a new ideology of sovereignty that portrayed Ghazan as a devout Muslim, a Persian philosopher-king, and a second Alexander the Great. Ghazan ceased to refer to himself as Ilkhan, a title that implied subordination to the rulers of Yuan China, and adopted the Turkish and Persian royal titles sultan and *shah*. Under Rashid al-Din's direction, court scholars compiled the *Compendium of Chronicles*, a history of the world that glorified the Mongol rulers as rightful heirs to the legacies of the Persian kings and the Abbasid caliphate.

Patronage of Arts and Letters

The Ilkhans became great patrons of arts and letters. Rashid al-Din boasted that "in these days when, thank God, all corners of the earth are under our rule and that of Chinggis Khan's illustrious family, philosophers, astronomers, scholars, and historians of all religions and nations—Cathay and Machin (North and South China), India and Kashmir, Tibetans, Uighurs, and other nations of Turks, Arabs, and Franks—are gathered in droves at our glorious court."[8] Manuscript painting, luxury silks, architectural decoration, metalworking, and ceramics all reflected the impact of new aesthetic ideas and motifs, with Chinese influences especially prominent. Prolific production of luxury editions of the Qur'an and lavish decoration of mosques, shrines, and tombs also attest to the vitality of the religious art promoted by the Muslim Ilkhans.

Under Rashid al-Din's stewardship, the ideological basis of the Ilkhanate shifted away from descent from Chinggis Khan and toward the role of royal protector of the Islamic faith. Nonetheless, diplomatic ties and cultural and economic exchanges with China became even closer. In the early fourteenth century, a renewal of cordial relations among the leaders of the four Mongol khanates eased the passage of caravans and travelers across the Silk Road. Conversion to Islam did not alienate their fellow Mongols, but neither did it repair the breach with the Mamluk regime.

Sultan, Poet, and Courtiers
The Mongol elite of the Ilkhanate quickly became ardent patrons of Islam after Ghazan's conversion in 1295. In addition to building religious monuments and establishing charitable foundations, Mongol leaders commissioned numerous lavishly illustrated manuscripts attesting to their Muslim faith. In this illustration from a poetry anthology copied in 1315, a poet holding a scroll recites poetry before a seated Mongol ruler surrounded by his courtiers. (©2011 The British Library I.O. Islamic 132.)

End of the Ilkhanate

Ghazan's reforms failed to ensure the long-term stability of the Ilkhanate regime, however. Ghazan's attempt to recast the Ilkhanate as a monarchy in the tradition of the Islamic caliphate ran into strong opposition among Mongol leaders accustomed to tribal independence and shared sovereignty. The reign of Ghazan's nephew Abu Said (r. 1316–1335) was wracked by factional conflicts that sapped the Ilkhan leadership and cost Rashid al-Din his life. After Abu Said died without an heir in 1335, the Ilkhanate's authority steadily disintegrated. In 1353 members of a messianic Shi'a sect murdered the last Ilkhan.

The Golden Horde and the Rise of Muscovy

Founding of the Golden Horde

The Golden Horde in Central Asia and Russia proved more durable than the Ilkhanate. In 1237 a Mongol army led by Chinggis's grandson Batu conquered the Volga River Valley and sacked the main cities of the Bulgars and the Rus princes, including the fortified outpost of Moscow. In 1240 Kiev succumbed to a Mongol siege, and the Mongol armies quickly pushed westward into Poland and Hungary, prompting the Roman pope to declare a crusade against this new menace. But feuding among the Mongol princes after the death of Ogodei in 1241 halted the Mongol advance into Europe. Instead, Batu created an independent Mongol realm known as the **Golden Horde**, with its capital at Sarai in the lower Volga River Valley (see again Map 14.3).

Batu's successor, Berke (r. 1257–1267), was the first of the Mongol khans to convert to Islam. A fierce rivalry erupted between Berke and the Ilkhan Hulegu for control over the Caucasus region. Berke allied with the Mamluks against the Ilkhanate and opposed the election of Hulegu's brother Qubilai as Great Khan. Political and commercial competition with the Ilkhanate also prompted the khans of the Golden Horde to seek close ties with Genoese merchant colonies around the shores of the Black Sea and with the Byzantine emperors.

Indirect Rule in Russia

In the Rus lands, as in Iran, the Mongols instituted a form of indirect governance that relied on local rulers as intermediaries. The Mongols required that the Rus princes conduct censuses, raise taxes to support the Mongol army, maintain post stations, and personally appear at the khan's court at Sarai to offer tribute. The Golden Horde and the Ilkhanate both adopted the Persian-Turkish institution of *iqta*, land grants awarded to

Rus's Commercial Growth and Religious Independence

military officers to feed and supply the soldiers under their command. The administrative structure of the Golden Horde and its system of military estates were subsequently adopted by the expanding Muscovy state in the fifteenth century.

As elsewhere in the Mongol realms, the khans of the Golden Horde strongly encouraged commerce, and their favorable policies toward merchants increased the volume of trade passing through Rus lands. The Rus princes and the Christian church benefited enormously from the profits of commerce. Moscow flourished as the capital of the fur trade. As a result of this commercial prosperity, the first Grand Prince of Muscovy, Ivan I (r. 1328–1340), nicknamed "Moneybags" by his subjects, was able to build the stone churches that became the heart of the Kremlin, the seat of future Russian governments. New commercial towns were founded, most importantly Nizhny Novgorod (1358), populated by German and Scandinavian merchants from the Baltic region. The wealth accumulated by the Orthodox Christian clerics and the protection they enjoyed under the traditional Mongol respect for religious institutions strengthened the church's position in Rus society and fostered greater independence from the Byzantine patriarch.

The Golden Horde and the Mongol Heritage

Despite its commercial expansion, Rus was marginal to the khanate, which focused its attention instead on controlling the steppe pasturelands and trade routes. In contrast to the Yuan dynasty and the Ilkhanate, the Golden Horde retained its connections to the steppe and the culture of pastoral nomadism. Nor did conversion to Islam bring about substantial changes in the Golden Horde culture comparable to those that occurred in the Ilkhanate. Berke's conversion to Islam arose from personal conviction and was not accompanied by a mandate to adopt the new faith. Not until the 1310s did the Golden Horde adopt Islam as its official religion. Although conversion to Islam pulled the Mongols of the Golden Horde more firmly into the cultural world of their Turkish subjects (and away from that of Christian Rus), it did not lead them to abandon their pastoral way of life.

Retrenchment in the Islamic World: The Mamluk and Ottoman States

The fall and destruction of Baghdad in 1258 delivered a devastating blow to the Islamic world—even greater than the shock that reverberated across Latin Christendom when Jerusalem fell to Saladin in 1187. The sack of Baghdad and the execution of the Abbasid caliph left the Islamic confederacy leaderless and disorganized. Out of this political crisis emerged two new dynastic regimes, the Mamluks in Egypt and the Ottomans in Anatolia (modern Turkey). Together, these two dynasties restored order to the Islamic lands of the eastern Mediterranean and halted further Mongol advances (see Map 14.4). Both the Mamluks and the Ottomans were warrior states, but they owed their political longevity to their ability to adapt to the requirements of governing large settled populations. The Mamluk Sultanate ruled from 1250 to 1517, nearly three times as long as the Yuan dynasty. The Ottoman Empire would prove to be one of the most enduring in world history, stretching from its origins in the late thirteenth century to final eclipse in 1923, following World War I.

Rise of the Mamluk Sultanate

In 1250 the Mamluks, a regiment of Turkish slave soldiers, overthrew the Ayyubid dynasty in Egypt and chose one of their officers as sultan. The Mamluk regime gained enormous stature among Muslims when it repelled the Mongol incursions into Syria in 1260. Its prestige was further burnished after it expelled the last of the Crusader states from Palestine in 1291.

The Mamluk elite consisted solely of foreigners, predominantly Turks, who had been purchased as slaves and raised in Egypt for service in the Mamluk army or administrative corps. Sons of Mamluk soldiers were excluded from government and military service, which therefore had to be replenished in each generation by fresh slave imports from the steppe. The Mamluk soldiers and administrators were bound to the state by personal allegiance to their officers and the sultan. Except from 1299 to 1382, when a form of hereditary succession prevailed, the sultans were chosen by the officer corps.

The Mamluk regime devoted itself to promoting the Islamic faith and strengthening state wealth and power. Although barred from the overland caravan trade by the Ilkhans, Mamluk Egypt sat astride the maritime routes connecting the Mediterranean to the Indian Ocean. Revenues from the burgeoning commerce with Asia, driven especially by Europeans' growing appetite for spices such as pepper and ginger, swelled the coffers of the Mamluk treasury. To offset the Ilkhanate's partnership with Byzantium and the Genoese merchants, the Mamluk regime cultivated close commercial and political ties with Venice—evidence that the Mamluks, like the Ilkhans, were willing to set aside intense religious differences with their Christian allies to further their own political and commercial interests.

Stability Under Mamluk Rule

Relations with the Ilkhanate thawed, however, after Ghazan's conversion to Islam. In 1322 the Mamluks concluded a commercial treaty with the Ilkhans that ensured free movement of slave caravans from the Black Sea through Ilkhan territories to Egypt. Although the Ilkhan regime would unravel during the next several decades, the Mamluk state now enjoyed peace and prosperity.

Despite the stability of the Mamluk regime, membership in the ruling class was insecure. Not only were sons of the slave-soldiers excluded from military and government service, but family fortunes were often vulnerable to confiscation amid the factional conflicts that beset the Mamluk court. Sultans and other affluent notables sought to

MAP 14.4

Islamic Empires, c. 1350

The Mongol leader Hulegu captured Baghdad in 1258, but his attempt to conquer Syria and Palestine was repelled by the Mamluk sultanate based in Egypt. Later rulers of the Ilkhanate founded by Hulegu converted to Islam, as did the Mongol chiefs of the Golden Horde in Russia. The disruptions caused by the Mongol invasions eventually led to the rise of another Turkish warrior sultanate, the Ottomans, in the early fourteenth century.

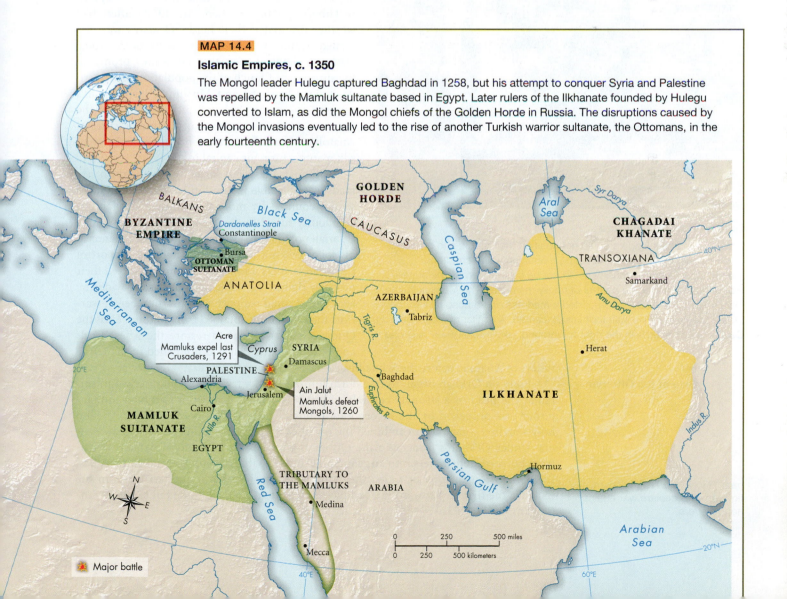

Qala'un Complex in Cairo

Since the Mamluk leaders could not pass on their status and privileges to their sons, they turned to creating monuments and charitable foundations—whose property could not be confiscated by the state—that remained under the control of family members. The Mamluk sultan Qala'un (r. 1280–1290) incorporated a madrasa and a hospital into the ornate mausoleum he built for himself (center). A similar complex built by Qala'un's son stands in the right foreground. (akg-images/Gerard Degeorge.)

preserve control of their wealth by establishing charitable trusts that were exempt from such seizures. The founding patrons often used the resources of these trusts to build large ceremonial complexes that housed a variety of religious and charitable institutions, including mosques, madrasas, elementary schools, hospitals, and Sufi hospices, as well as their own tombs.

Another Islamic warrior state, one that would ultimately contest the Mamluks' leadership within the Islamic world, emerged in Anatolia. The Ottomans traced their origins to Osman (d. 1324), who arose as the leader of an expanding confederation of nomadic warriors in the late thirteenth century. In Osman's day, Anatolia was the frontier between the Byzantine Empire and the Ilkhanate (see again Map 14.4). There, tribes of Muslim herders competed with Christian farmers and pagan nomads for lands and followers. Like other nomadic confederations, the Ottoman alliance was based on political expediency rather than permanent ethnic allegiances, and Osman's first invasions targeted neighboring Turks. Then, in 1302, after bad weather decimated their herds, Osman's warriors turned against the Byzantine towns of Anatolia. Osman's victories over the Byzantines prompted the surrender of much of the population of western Anatolia, Christians and Muslims alike. Osman's son and successor Orkhan (r. 1324–1362) led the Ottoman army in conquests of the major cities of Anatolia and made Bursa, a prosperous center of silk manufacture, his capital in 1331.

Although the tribal society of the Turkish nomads was a flexible institution in which loyalty and service counted far more than lineage and faith, it was poorly suited to the needs of governing a large agrarian population. Osman granted pasturelands to his followers, but he also cultivated the support of Christian farmers and town folk and protected their property rights. The stable revenue base provided by agriculture could support a greater number of warriors than the booty obtained from raiding. Thus the Ottoman rulers sought to restore the wheat fields and olive orchards that had flourished in the fertile valleys of Anatolia before the Seljuk invasions in the eleventh century.

Rise of the Ottomans

Early on Orkhan began to transform himself from a tribal chief into a Muslim sultan at the head of a strongly centralized state. The rapid growth of Ottoman military power was propelled by the incorporation into the army's ranks of bands of Muslim holy warriors—**gazi**, who combined the qualities of frontier bandits and religious zealots. Under Orkhan's leadership the Ottoman army also underwent a metamorphosis from horse-riding archers into large infantry units capable of sophisticated siege tactics. In 1354, Ottoman forces crossed the Dardanelles to seize Byzantine territories in the Balkans, the first step toward the conquest of Constantinople and the fall of the Byzantine Empire in 1453.

gazi "Holy warriors"; in Islam, fighters who declare war against nonbelievers.

COUNTERPOINT
The "New Knighthood" of the Christian Military Orders

Following the success of the First Crusade, a new church institution was formed: the military orders, religious orders that combined the vocations of monk and warrior. Inspired by new international monastic orders dedicated to the spread of the Christian faith, such as the Cistercians, these armed monks redefined both the monastic calling and the ideals of knighthood.

FOCUS

In what ways did the self-image and mission of the Christian military orders resemble or differ from those of the papal and royal leaders of the Crusades?

Their movement began with the Knights of the Temple, an order founded in 1120 to protect Christian pilgrims and merchants; it was named after their headquarters near the site of the ancient Temple of Solomon in Jerusalem. Subsequently, the Templars (as they were commonly known) and other military orders spearheaded the militant Christian expansionism that resulted in the "reconquest" of Spain and the conversion of much of eastern Europe to Latin Christianity. Yet in the end Christian monarchs and the papacy turned against the military orders, annihilating the Templars and sharply restricting other military orders' activities. The ideal of an international brotherhood united in faith and in arms—the Crusader ideal—was swept away by the rising tide of national monarchies.

The Templar Model and the Crusading Movement

The Templar knights were expected to maintain equal fidelity to both the code of chivalry and monastic rules. Like the Cistercians, the Templars took vows of poverty, chastity, and obedience. The Cistercian abbot Bernard of Clairvaux praised what he called the "new knighthood" of the Templars for its steadfast commitment to combating both the evil within—the temptations of the devil—and the external enemy, the Muslims.

The Templars and Their Followers

Critics of the military orders voiced misgivings about their unseemly combination of religious devotion with armed violence. Nonetheless, donations to the orders, strongly encouraged by the church, led to rapid expansion of their ranks. Within thirty years the Templars had taken proprietorship of scores of estates and castles throughout western Europe and in the Crusader states. The outpouring of patronage for the Templar order encouraged imitation. Two new military orders based on the Templar model, the Hospitallers and the Teutonic Knights, were formed to tend to the poor and infirm among the pilgrims to the Holy Land. In the late twelfth century a number of military orders also sprang up in Spain to aid the cause of the "reconquest."

Members of the military orders committed themselves to lifelong service. Strict rules imbued the military orders with the discipline and solidarity that other Crusaders lacked. The knights' brave defense of the Christian enclaves against the Muslim counterattack led by Saladin earned them high regard from the enemy as well as from their fellow Christians. After vanquishing Christian armies, Saladin ordered the immediate beheading of captured Templars and Hospitallers, whom he regarded as the backbone of the Christian defenders.

Despite Jerusalem's fall to Saladin in 1187, the military orders continued to attract new recruits and donations. Pope Innocent III staunchly supported the military orders, which he regarded as crucial allies in his campaign to create an imperial papacy. But the Mamluks' final expulsion of Latin Christians from Acre in 1291 deprived the military orders of their reason for existence. Moreover, the Templars had powerful enemies, especially the French king Philip IV (r. 1285–1314), who resented their autonomy and coveted

Destruction of the Templars

Domains of the Teutonic Knights, 1309–1410

their wealth. With the cowardly consent of a weak pope, Philip launched a campaign of persecution against the order. The officers of the Inquisition found the Templars guilty of heresy. Hundreds of knights were burned at the stake, and in 1312 the pope disbanded the Templar order.

The Teutonic Knights and Christian Expansion in Eastern Europe

In contrast to the Templars, the Teutonic military order gained renewed life after the failure of the Crusades. In the late 1220s a Polish duke recruited members of the Teutonic order (so called because nearly all its members were German) to carry out a crusade against his rivals among the pagan lords of Prussia. Anticipating sharing in the spoils of victory, German princes and knights rushed to join the new crusading enterprise in their own backyard. The popes claimed sovereign authority over Prussia and delegated the Teutonic order to rule the region on their behalf. In 1309 the Teutonic Knights relocated to Prussia and focused exclusively on building up their own territorial state in the Baltic region.

After 1370, when the Teutonic Knights defeated the pagan princes of Lithuania, new commercial towns affiliated with the Hanseatic League arose and the Baltic region was rapidly colonized. Town charters gave urban burghers considerable independence but reserved sovereign rights to the order, which possessed large rural estates and received annual tribute from town dwellers.

Marienburg Castle

After withdrawing from the Mediterranean, the Teutonic Knights found a new mission: spearheading the Christian advance among the pagan peoples of eastern Europe. From 1309 the order's leaders took up residence at a grand new headquarters at Marienburg on the Vistula River (now Malbork, Poland). The state created by the Teutonic order in the Baltic Sea region was considered a model of bureaucratic efficiency. (Photolibrary.)

Unschooled in Latin, the Teutonic order promoted Christianity through books, libraries, and schools in the German vernacular. The law codes adopted by the German overlords reminded the natives of their subordinate status by imposing various forms of legal discrimination. For example, the fine for killing a German was twice that for killing a native Prussian. Ethnic tensions were also evident in the rule that when drinking together, the Germans required the Prussians to drink first, for fear of poisoning.

When economic conditions worsened in the waning years of the fourteenth century, local landowners began to challenge the order's autocratic rule. The marriage of the Lithuanian king and the Polish queen in 1386 prompted Lithuanians to convert to Christianity, removing the last justification for the Teutonic order's holy war against paganism. During the fifteenth century the Prussian towns and rural lords gained independence from the order's rule. By the early sixteenth century the order had ceased to function as a sovereign state.

End of the Teutonic State

The Teutonic order was thus a victim of its own success. Once the order completed its mission of implanting Christianity through conquest, colonization, and conversion of pagans, the Knights no longer had a cause to serve. The military orders had represented the ideal of a universal Christian brotherhood championed by the Roman popes. Yet the dramatic expansion of Christendom to all corners of Europe between the twelfth and the fifteenth centuries had fostered national rivalry rather than political unity. With the failure of the Crusades and the demise of the military orders, the papacy's ambitions to rule over a united Christian people likewise perished.

Demise of the Crusader Ideal

Conclusion

The initial waves of the Mongol invasions spread fear and destruction across Eurasia, and the political and cultural repercussions of the Mongol conquests would resound for centuries. Adapting their own traditions to vastly different local settings, the Mongols reshaped the societies and cultures of Iran, Russia, and China as well as Central Asia. The Mongol legacy of steppe empires spanning the pastoral and settled worlds would inspire later empire-builders from Timur to the Mughals and the Manchus.

The Mongol incursions most profoundly affected the Islamic states and societies of Iran and Mesopotamia and the Rus lands. Many areas never recovered from the disruption of irrigated agriculture and reverted to pasture for stock raising, and in some cases even to barren desert. The Mongol invasions also erased the last of the Seljuk emirates, clearing the ground for the rise of new Turkish sultanates, the Mamluks and the Ottomans.

Like the Ilkhans in Iran, the Mongols of the Golden Horde converted to Islam, although their Rus subjects remained Christians. The rising Muscovy state would retain Mongol military and political institutions in building its own Russian empire. In China, by contrast, the Mongol legacy proved fleeting. Ignoring Yelu Chucai's warning that "the empire cannot be ruled on horseback," the Mongols failed to adapt their style of rule to the requirements of a large agrarian empire. The Yuan regime in China had badly deteriorated by the 1330s and collapsed into civil war and rebellion in the 1350s. As we will see in the next chapter, the founder of the Ming Empire (1368–1644) in China would seek to eliminate all traces of Mongol influence.

The Mongols brought the worlds of pastoral nomads and settled urban and agrarian peoples into collision, but a different kind of clash of civilizations had been triggered by the Crusades. Although the Crusaders failed to achieve their goal of restoring Christian rule over Jerusalem, the crusading movement expanded the borders of Latin Christendom by advancing the "reconquest" in Spain and by converting the Wendish peoples of eastern Europe.

The crusading movement and institutions such as the Christian military orders played a crucial role in the formation of Europe as the realm of "the Christian people" obedient to the Roman papacy. But the growing power of national monarchies frustrated the popes' efforts to establish supreme rule over secular as well as spiritual affairs. The unity imposed by the Mongol conquests also was short-lived. Although the creation of the Mongol Empire made possible an unprecedented movement of people, goods, and ideas throughout Eurasia, such cross-cultural exchanges vanished almost completely after the collapse of the Ilkhan and Yuan states in the mid-fourteenth century. By then, as the next chapter will reveal, both Europe and the Islamic lands had plunged into a new era of crisis following the devastating catastrophe of the Black Death.

NOTES

1. *The Deeds of the Franks and the Other Pilgrims to Jerusalem*, cited in James Harvey Robinson, ed., *Readings in European History* (Boston: Ginn & Co., 1904), 1:312.
2. Ibn Jubayr, "Relation de voyages," *Voyageurs arabes: Ibn Fadlan, Ibn Jubayr, Ibn Battuta et un auteur anonyme*, trans. Paul Charles-Dominique (Paris: Éditions Gallimard, 1995), 310.
3. Bernard of Clairvaux, *Letters*, trans. Bruno Scott James (London: Burns, Oates, 1953), 467.
4. Cited in Robert Bartlett, *The Making of Europe: Conquest, Colonization and Cultural Change, 950–1350* (Princeton, NJ: Princeton University Press, 1993), 154.
5. Cited in Bartlett, *The Making of Europe*, 132.
6. Nicole Oresme, "Le Livre de Politiques d'Aristotle," *Transactions of the American Philosophical Society*, new series, vol. 60, part 6 (1970), 292.
7. *Marco Polo: The Description of the World*, eds. A. C. Moule and Paul Pelliot (London: George Routledge & Sons, 1938), 1:192.
8. *Rashiduddin Fazullah's* Jami'u't-tawarikh (Compendium of Chronicles): *A History of the Mongols*, trans. W. M. Thackston (Cambridge, MA: Harvard University, Department of Near Eastern Languages and Civilizations, 1998), Part I, 6.

RESOURCES FOR RESEARCH

The Crusades and the Imperial Papacy, 1050–1350

The story of the Crusades has almost always been told from European and Christian perspectives. Hillenbrand's survey of Muslim attitudes helps to correct this bias. In his short, provocative study Tyerman challenges the conventional historiography and questions whether the Crusades constituted a coherent movement.

(Crusades: Introduction): http://www.theorb.net/encyclop/religion/crusades/crusade_intro.html.

France, John. *The Crusades and the Expansion of Catholic Christendom, 1000–1714*. 2005.
*Gabrieli, Francesco, ed. *Arab Historians of the Crusades*. 1969.
Hillenbrand, Carole. *The Crusades: Islamic Perspectives*. 2000.
Madden, Thomas F. *A Concise History of the Crusades*. 1999.
Tyerman, Christopher. *The Invention of the Crusades*. 1998.

The Making of Christian Europe, 1100–1350

Recent scholarship considers this the formative period for the emergence of a distinct European political and cultural identity. In Bartlett's view, this European identity was closely interwined with Latin Christendom's expansion and colonization of eastern and northern Europe and Spain. Nirenberg's pathbreaking work analyzes the culture of violence that led to persecution of Jews and other minorities.

Bartlett, Robert. *The Making of Europe: Conquest, Colonization, and Cultural Change, 950–1350*. 1993.
Christiansen, Eric. *The Northern Crusades: The Baltic and the Catholic Frontier, 1100–1525*, 2d ed. 1997.
Nirenberg, David. *Communities of Violence: Persecution of Minorities in the Middle Ages*. 1996.
Reilly, Bernard F. *The Medieval Spains*. 1993.
Reynolds, Susan. *Kingdoms and Communities in Western Europe, 900–1300*. 1984.

The Mongol World-Empire, 1100–1368

Despite the wealth of books on the Mongols, there is no comprehensive study of the Mongol Empire in its entirety. Lane and Morgan, both Islamic specialists, concentrate primarily on the Mongol domains in the west. Most treatments of the Mongols focus on the lives and deeds of the great khans, but Lane details many features of Mongol social life and customs.

Biran, Michal. *Chinggis Khan*. 2007.
Lane, George. *Daily Life in the Mongol Empire*. 2006.

Larner, John. *Marco Polo and the Discovery of the World*. 1999.
Morgan, David. *The Mongols*. 2d ed. 2007.
*Polo, Marco. *The Travels of Marco Polo*. 1958.

The Mongol Khanates and the Islamic World, 1240–1350

Revisionist scholars, while acknowledging the destructive effects of the Mongol conquests in Russia and Iran, have emphasized the transformative influences of Mongol rule as well. Lane rejects depictions of Ilkhan rule in Iran as a "dark age" and instead sees this period as one of cultural renaissance.

Allsen, Thomas. *Culture and Conquest in Mongol Eurasia*. 2001.
Kafadar, Cemal. *Between Two Worlds: The Construction of the Ottoman State*. 1995.
Lane, George. *Early Mongol Rule in Thirteenth-Century Iran: A Persian Renaissance*. 2003.
Morgan, David. *Medieval Persia, 1040–1797*. 1988.
Ostrowski, Donald. *Muscovy and the Mongols: Cross-Cultural Influences on the Steppe Frontier, 1304–1589*. 1998.

COUNTERPOINT: The "New Knighthood" of the Christian Military Orders

The history of the military orders is full of drama and controversy, and modern scholars have struggled to separate fact from fiction. Barber has written the definitive scholarly study of the Templar order, and the same can be said of Riley-Smith's work on the Hospitallers.

Barber, Malcolm. *The New Knighthood: A History of the Order of the Temple*. 1994.
(Military Orders: A Guide to On-line Resources): http://www.theorb.net/encyclop/religion/monastic/milindex.html .
Nicholson, Helen. *Templars, Hospitallers and Teutonic Knights: Images of the Military Orders, 1128–1291*. 1993.
Riley-Smith, Jonathan. *Hospitallers: The History of the Order of St. John*. 1987.

* Primary source.

> ▶ **For additional primary sources from this period**, see *Sources of Crossroads and Cultures*.

> ▶ **For Web sites, images, and documents related to topics in this chapter**, see Make History at bedfordstmartins.com/smith.

REVIEW

Online Study Guide
bedfordstmartins.com/smith

The major global development in this chapter ▶ The Eurasian integration fostered by the clashes of culture known as the Crusades and the Mongol conquests.

IMPORTANT EVENTS

1054	Great Schism between the Roman and Byzantine churches
1095	Pope Urban II issues summons for First Crusade
1098	Founding of the Cistercian order
1099	First Crusade concludes with the Christian capture of Jerusalem
1120	Founding of the order of the Knights of the Temple (Templars) at Jerusalem
1147	Wendish Crusade (part of the Second Crusade)
1187	Saladin recaptures Jerusalem
1198–1216	Papacy of Innocent III
1206	Council of Mongol princes elects Temujin (Chinggis) as Great Khan
1240	Mongol conquest of Kiev
1248	Christian armies capture the Almohad stronghold of Seville
1250–1517	Mamluk Sultanate in Egypt and Syria
1258	Mongols sack Baghdad
1271–1368	Rule of Mongols over China as the Yuan dynasty
1274–1295	Journey of Marco Polo to China
1291	Mamluks recapture Acre, last Christian stronghold in Palestine
1295–1304	Rule of Ghazan as Ilkhan; conversion of Ilkhan Mongols to Islam

KEY TERMS

chivalry (p. 450)
Crusades (p. 444)
gazi (p. 466)
Great Khan (p. 457)
Great Schism (p. 445)

Inquisition (p. 448)
investiture controversy (p. 445)
military order (p. 446)
tax farming (p. 459)

CHAPTER OVERVIEW QUESTIONS

1. In what ways did the growing economic and cultural unity of Latin Christendom promote the rise of powerful European national monarchies?

2. To what degree did the expansion of Latin Christendom remake eastern Europe in the image of western Europe?

3. In what ways did the Mongol conquests foster cultural and economic exchange across Eurasia?

4. How and why did the Mongol rulers of China, Iran, and Russia differ in their relationships with the settled societies they ruled?

SECTION FOCUS QUESTIONS

1. In what ways did the Roman popes seek to expand their powers during the age of the Crusades?

2. How did the efforts to establish Christianity in Spain and eastern Europe compare with the Crusaders' quest to recover Jerusalem?

3. How did the organization of Mongol society and government change from the time of Chinggis Khan to that of his grandson Qubilai, the ruler of China?

4. In what respects did the Turkish Islamic states of the Mamluks and Ottomans pursue policies similar to those of the Mongol regimes in Iran and Russia?

5. In what ways did the self-image and mission of the Christian military orders resemble or differ from those of the papal and royal leaders of the Crusades?

MAKING CONNECTIONS

1. How did the relationship between the Roman popes and the Christian monarchs of western Europe change from the reign of Charlemagne (see Chapter 9) to the papacy of Innocent III?

2. In what ways did the Crusades contribute to the definition of Europe as the realm of Latin Christendom?

3. To what extent were the policies of the Mongols similar to those of earlier Central Asian nomad empires such as the Khazars and the Turks (see Chapter 10)?

15

AT A CROSSROADS ▶

The fall of Constantinople to the Ottoman Turks in 1453 marked the end of the Byzantine Empire and heralded the coming age of gunpowder weapons. The Ottoman forces under Sultan Mehmed II breached the massive walls of Constantinople using massive cannons known as *bombards*. The Turkish cannons appear in the center of this book illustration of the siege of Constantinople, published in France in 1455. (The Art Archive/Bibliothèque Nationale Paris.)

Collapse and Revival in Afro-Eurasia

1300–1450

In August 1452, as the armies of the Ottoman sultan Mehmed II encircled Constantinople, the Byzantine emperor Constantine XI received a visit from a fellow Christian, a Hungarian engineer named Urban. Urban had applied metallurgical skills acquired at Hungary's rich iron and copper mines to the manufacture of large cannons known as *bombards*. He came to the Byzantine capital to offer his services to repel the Ottoman assault. But although Urban was a Christian, he was a businessman, too. When Constantine could not meet his price, Urban quickly left for the sultan's camp. Facing the famed triple walls of Constantinople, Mehmed promised to quadruple the salary Urban requested and to provide any materials and manpower the engineer needed.

Seven months later, in April 1453, Ottoman soldiers moved Urban's huge bronze bombards—with barrels twenty-six feet long, capable of throwing eight-hundred-pound shot—into place beneath the walls of Constantinople. Although these cumbersome cannons could fire only seven rounds a day, they battered the walls of Constantinople, which had long been considered impenetrable. After six weeks of siege the Turks breached the walls and swarmed into the city. The vastly outnumbered defenders, Emperor Constantine among them, fought to the death.

Urban's willingness to put business before religious loyalty helped tip the balance of power in the Mediterranean. During the siege, the Genoese merchant community at Constantinople—along with their archrivals, the Venetians—maintained strict neutrality. Although the Italian merchants, like Urban, were prepared to do business with Mehmed II, within a decade the Venetians and Ottomans were at war. Venice could not produce

Fourteenth-Century Crisis and Renewal in Eurasia

FOCUS How did the Black Death affect society, the economy, and culture in Latin Christendom and the Islamic world?

Islam's New Frontiers

FOCUS Why did Islam expand dramatically in the fourteenth and fifteenth centuries, and how did new Islamic societies differ from established ones?

The Global Bazaar

FOCUS How did the pattern of international trade change during the fourteenth and fifteenth centuries, and how did these changes affect consumption and fashion tastes?

COUNTERPOINT Age of the Samurai in Japan, 1185–1450

FOCUS How and why did the historical development of Japan in the fourteenth and fifteenth centuries differ from that of mainland Eurasia?

BACKSTORY

In the fourteenth century, a number of developments threatened the connections among the societies of the Afro-Eurasian world. The collapse of the Mongol empires in China and Iran in the mid-1300s disrupted caravan traffic across Central Asia, diverting the flow of trade and travel to maritime routes across the Indian Ocean. Although the two centuries of religious wars known as the Crusades ended in 1291, they had hardened hostility between Christians and Muslims. As the power of the Christian Byzantine Empire contracted, Muslim Turkish sultanates—the Mamluk regime in Egypt and the rising Ottoman dynasty in Anatolia (modern Turkey)—gained control of the eastern Mediterranean region. Yet the Crusades and direct contact with the Mongols had also whetted European appetites for luxury and exotic goods from the Islamic world and Asia. Thus, despite challenges and obstacles, the Mediterranean remained a lively crossroads of commerce and cross-cultural exchange.

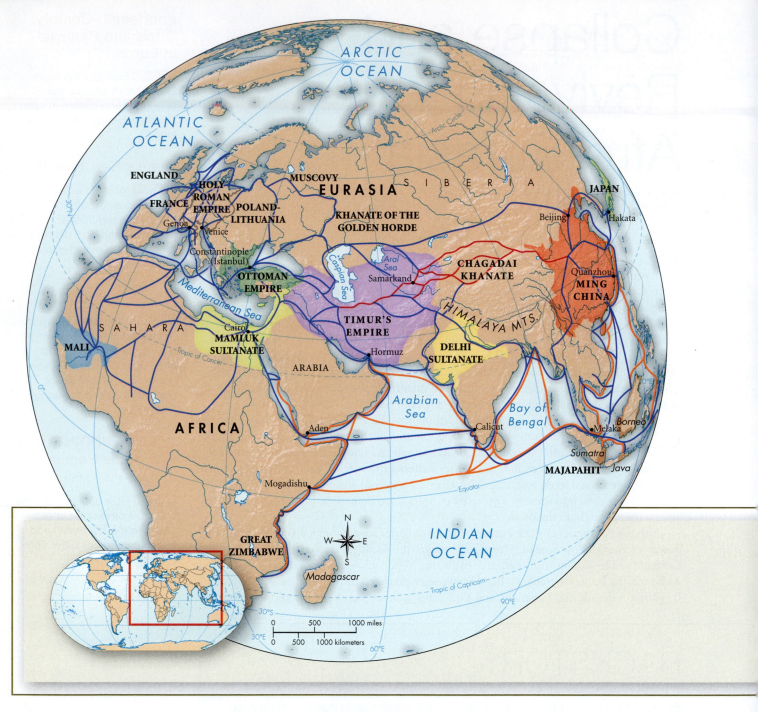

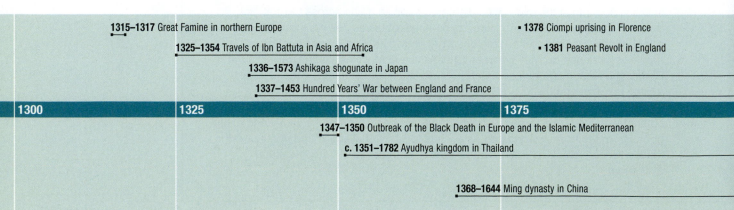

1315–1317 Great Famine in northern Europe

▪ 1378 Ciompi uprising in Florence

1325–1354 Travels of Ibn Battuta in Asia and Africa

▪ 1381 Peasant Revolt in England

1336–1573 Ashikaga shogunate in Japan

1337–1453 Hundred Years' War between England and France

1300	1325	1350	1375

1347–1350 Outbreak of the Black Death in Europe and the Islamic Mediterranean

c. 1351–1782 Ayudhya kingdom in Thailand

1368–1644 Ming dynasty in China

enough cannons to match the heavily armed Ottoman army and navy, which expelled the Venetians from the Black Sea in 1475. Although Venetian merchants still flocked to Constantinople, which Mehmed renamed Istanbul, to obtain spices, silks, and other Asian goods, the Ottomans held the upper hand and could dictate the terms of trade.

The fall of Constantinople to the Ottomans marks a turning point in world history. After perpetuating ancient Rome's heritage and glory for a thousand years, the Byzantine Empire came to an end. Islam continued to advance; in the fourteenth and fifteenth centuries, it expanded most dramatically in Africa and Asia. Italian merchants and bankers lost their dominance in the eastern Mediterranean and turned westward toward the Atlantic Ocean in search of new commercial opportunities. And this shift in commercial power and focus was not the only profound change that followed the Ottoman capture of Constantinople. The bombards cast by the Hungarian engineer for the Ottoman sultan heralded a military revolution that would decisively alter the balance of power among states and transform the nature of the state itself.

The new global patterns that emerged after Constantinople changed hands had their roots in calamities of the fourteenth century. The Ottoman triumph came just as Europe was beginning to recover from the previous century's catastrophic outbreak of plague known as the Black Death. The demographic and psychological shocks of epidemic disease had severely tested Europe's political and economic institutions—indeed, even its Christian faith.

The Black Death also devastated the Islamic world. Economic depression struck hard in Egypt, Syria, and Mesopotamia, the heartland of Islam. However, Europe's economy recovered more quickly. One consequence of the plague was the slow demise of serfdom, which contributed to the growing political and economic power of European monarchs and the urban merchant classes. By 1500 European merchants, bankers, and artisans had surpassed their Muslim counterparts in innovation and efficiency.

In Asia, the fourteenth century witnessed the rise and fall of the last Mongol empire, that of Timur (also known as Tamerlane). The end of the Mongol era marked the passing of nomadic rule, the resurgence of agrarian bureaucratic states such as Ming China and

MAPPING THE WORLD
Afro-Eurasia in the Early Fifteenth Century

After the Mongol Empire disintegrated, trans-Eurasian trade shifted from the overland Silk Road to the maritime routes stretching from China to the Mediterranean. Muslim merchants crossed the Sahara Desert and the Indian Ocean in pursuit of African gold, Chinese porcelain, and Asian spices. Although Chinese fleets led by Admiral Zheng He journeyed as far as the coasts of Arabia and Africa, the Ming rulers prohibited private overseas trade.

ROUTES ▼

— Major trade route
— Silk Road
— Voyages of Zheng He

1392–1910 Yi dynasty in Korea

▪ **1405** Death of Timur; breakup of his empire into regional states in Iran and Central Asia

▪ **1453** Ottoman conquest of Constantinople marks fall of the Byzantine Empire

| 1400 | 1425 | 1450 |

1405–1433 Chinese admiral Zheng He's expeditions in Southeast Asia and the Indian Ocean

▪ **1421** Relocation of Ming capital from Nanjing to Beijing

1428–1788 Le dynasty in Vietnam

the Ottoman Empire, and the shift of trade from the overland Silk Road to maritime routes across the Indian Ocean. Commerce attained unprecedented importance in many Asian societies. The flow of goods across Eurasia and Africa created new concentrations of wealth, fostered new patterns of consumption, and reshaped culture. The European Renaissance, for example, although primarily understood as a rebirth of the classical culture of Greece and Rome, also drew inspiration from the wealth of goods that poured into Italy from the Islamic world and Asia. By contrast, Japan remained isolated from this global bazaar, and this isolation contributed to the birth of Japan's distinctive national culture. For most Afro-Eurasian societies, however, the maritime world increasingly became the principal crossroads of economic and cultural exchange.

OVERVIEW
QUESTIONS

The major global development in this chapter: Crisis and recovery in fourteenth- and fifteenth-century Afro-Eurasia.

As you read, consider:

1. In the century after the devastating outbreak of plague known as the Black Death, how and why did Europe's economic growth begin to surpass that of the Islamic world?

2. Did the economic revival across Eurasia after 1350 benefit the peasant populations of Europe, the Islamic world, and East Asia?

3. How did the process of conversion to Islam differ in Iran, the Ottoman Empire, West Africa, and Southeast Asia during this period?

4. What political and economic changes contributed to the rise of maritime commerce in Asia during the fourteenth and fifteenth centuries?

Fourteenth-Century Crisis and Renewal in Eurasia

FOCUS

How did the Black Death affect society, the economy, and culture in Latin Christendom and the Islamic world?

Black Death The catastrophic outbreak of plague that spread from the Black Sea to Europe, the Middle East, and North Africa in 1347–1350, killing a third or more of the population in afflicted areas.

pandemic An outbreak of epidemic disease that spreads across an entire region.

No event in the fourteenth century had such profound consequences as the **Black Death** of 1347–1350. The unprecedented loss of life that resulted from this **pandemic** abruptly halted the economic expansion that had spread throughout Europe and the Islamic heartland in the preceding three centuries. Although the population losses were as great in the Islamic world as in Latin Christendom, the effects on society, the economy, and ideas diverged in important ways.

Largely spared the ravages of the Black Death, following the collapse of the Mongol empires in the fourteenth century Asian societies and economies faced different challenges. Expanding maritime trade and the spread of gunpowder weapons gave settled empires a decisive edge over nomadic societies, an edge that they never again relinquished. The founder of the Ming dynasty (1368–1644) in China rejected the Mongol model of "universal empire" and strove to restore a purely Chinese culture and social order. The prestige, stability, and ruling ideology of the Ming state powerfully influenced neighbors such as Korea and Vietnam—but had far less effect on Japan.

The "Great Mortality": The Black Death of 1347–1350

On the eve of the Black Death, Europe's agrarian economy already was struggling under the strain of climatic change. Around 1300 the earth experienced a shift in climate. The warm temperatures that had prevailed over most of the globe for the previous thousand years gave way to a **Little Ice Age** of colder temperatures and shorter growing seasons; it would last for much of the fourteenth century. The expansion of agriculture that had occurred in the Northern Hemisphere during the preceding three centuries came to a halt. The Great Famine of 1315–1317, when severe winters and overly wet summers brought on successive years of crop failure, killed 10 percent of the population in northern Europe and the British Isles. Unlike famine, though, the Black Death pandemic struck the ruling classes as hard as the poor. Scholars estimate that the Black Death and subsequent recurrences of the pandemic killed approximately one-third of the population of Europe.

Although the catastrophic mortality (death rates) of the Black Death is beyond dispute, the causes of the pandemic remain mysterious. The Florentine poet Giovanni Boccaccio (1313–1375), an eyewitness to the "great mortality," described the appearance of apple-sized swellings, first in the groin and armpits, after which these "death-bearing plague boils" spread to "every part of the body, wherefrom the fashion of the contagion began to change into black or livid blotches . . . in some places large and sparse, and in others small and thick-sown." The spread of these swellings, Boccaccio warned, was "a very certain token of coming death."[1]

The prominence of these glandular swellings, or buboes, in eyewitness accounts has led modern scholars to attribute the Black Death to bubonic plague, which is transmitted by fleas to rats and by rats to humans. Yet the scale of mortality during the Black Death far exceeds levels expected in plague outbreaks. Moreover, in Egypt the Black Death struck in winter, when bubonic plague is usually dormant, and the chief symptom was spitting blood rather than developing buboes, suggesting an airborne form of the plague. The pandemic killed as many livestock, especially cattle, as it did humans. Although it is difficult to identify the Black Death with any single modern disease, there is no doubt that the populations of western Eurasia had no previous experience of the disease, and hence no immunity to it. Outbreaks of plague continued to recur every decade or two for the next century, and intermittently thereafter.

Boccaccio and other eyewitnesses claimed that the Black Death had originated in Central Asia and traveled along overland trade routes to the Black Sea. The first outbreak among Europeans occurred in 1347 at the Genoese port of Caffa, on the Crimean peninsula. At that time Caffa was under siege by Mongols of the Golden Horde. Legend relates that the Mongols used catapults to lob corpses of plague victims over the city walls. Whether or not the Mongols really used this innovative type of germ warfare, the Genoese fled, only to spread the plague to the seaports they visited throughout the Mediterranean. By the summer of 1350 the Black Death had devastated nearly all of Europe (see Map 15.1).

The historian William McNeill has suggested that the Black Death was a byproduct of the Mongol conquests. He hypothesized that Mongol horsemen carried the plague bacillus from the remote highland forests of Southeast Asia into Central Asia, and then west to the Black Sea and east to China. The impact of the plague on China remains uncertain, however. The Mongol dynasty of Kubilai (Qubilai) (KOO-bih-lie) Khan already was losing its hold on China in the 1330s, and by the late 1340s China was afflicted by widespread famine, banditry, and civil war. By the time the Ming dynasty took control in 1368, China's population had fallen substantially. Yet Chinese sources make no mention of the specific symptoms of the Black Death, and there is no evidence of pandemic in the densely populated areas of South and Southeast Asia.

The demographic collapse resulting from the Black Death was concentrated in Europe and the Islamic lands ringing the Mediterranean. In these regions population growth halted for over a century. England's population did not return to pre-plague levels for four hundred years.

Causes and Spread of the Black Death

Demographic Consequences

Little Ice Age Name applied by environmental historians to periods of prolonged cool weather in the temperate zones of the earth.

MAP 15.1 **Spread of the Black Death, 1347–1451**

From Caffa on the shores of the Black Sea, Genoese merchant ships unwittingly carried the plague to Constantinople and other Mediterranean ports in the summer of 1347. Over the next four years the Black Death advanced across the Mediterranean Sea and throughout central and northern Europe. Hundreds of Jewish communities were attacked or destroyed by Christians who blamed the pandemic on the Jews.

Population losses from the Black Death were equally devastating in the Islamic parts of the Mediterranean. Italian ships brought the plague to Alexandria in the autumn of 1347. The Egyptian historian al-Maqrizi (al-mak-REE-zee) recorded that twenty thousand people died each day in Cairo, then the most populous city in the world. Although this estimate surely is exaggerated, the plague probably did cause more than one hundred thousand deaths in Cairo alone. In the Islamic world, as in Europe, the loss of human lives and livestock seriously disrupted agriculture. While rural inhabitants flocked to the towns in search of food and work, urban residents sought refuge in the countryside from the contagion that festered in crowded cities.

Decline of the Mamluk Sultanate

The devastation of the plague dealt a serious blow to the agricultural economy of the Mamluk (MAM-luke) Sultanate, which ruled over Egypt and Syria. The scarcity of labor following the pandemic prompted a return to pastoral nomadism in many rural areas, and the urban working classes who survived benefited from rising wages. "The wages of skilled artisans, wage workers, porters, servants, stablemen, weavers, masons, construction workers, and the like have increased manyfold," wrote al-Maqrizi, who served as Cairo's market inspector from 1399 to 1405. But, he added, "of this class only a few remain, since most have died."[2]

The Mamluk Sultanate depended on agricultural wealth for its support, so population losses and declining agricultural production following the Black Death undermined the Mamluk government. A struggle for power broke out among rival factions. Bureaucratic mismanagement compounded the economic distress. Faced with decreasing revenues, the sultanate tried to squeeze more taxes from urban commerce and industry. But the creation of state monopolies in the spice trade and the sugar industry throttled private enterprise and undermined the commercial vitality of Cairo and Damascus. The impoverishment of the urban artisan and merchant classes further weakened the Mamluk regime, leading to its ultimate downfall at the hands of Ottoman conquerors in 1517. In the fall of the Mamluk Sultanate, we can see how the plague produced a chain of interconnected consequences. Population decline led to agricultural decline, which in turn produced economic problems, undermined political authority, and created the conditions for significant social, political, and military upheaval.

Although the horrific mortality caused by the Black Death afflicted Latin Christendom and the Islamic world in equal measure, their responses to the epidemic diverged in significant ways. Christians interpreted the plague as divine punishment for humanity's sins (see Reading the Past: A French Theologian's View of the Black Death). Acts of piety and atonement proliferated, most strikingly in the form of processions of flagellants (from *flagella*, a whip used by worshipers as a form of penance), whose self-mutilation was meant to imitate the sufferings of Christ. In many places Christians blamed vulnerable minorities—such as beggars, lepers, and especially Jews—for corrupting Christian society. Although the Roman Church, kings, and local leaders condemned attacks against Jews, their appeals often went unheeded. For example, the citizens of Strasbourg threw the municipal council out of office for trying to protect the city's Jewish population and then burned nine hundred Jews on the grounds of the Jewish cemetery. The macabre images of death and the corruption of the flesh in European painting and sculpture in the late fourteenth and fifteenth centuries vividly convey the anguish caused by the Black Death.

Christian Responses to the Black Death

Dance of Death

The scourge of the Black Death pandemic dramatically influenced attitudes toward death in Latin Christendom. Literary and artistic works such as this woodcut of skeletons dancing on an open grave vividly portrayed the fragility of life and the dangers of untimely death. For those unprepared to face divine judgment, the ravages of disease and death were only a prelude to the everlasting torments of hell. (akg-images/Imagno.)

A French Theologian's View of the Black Death

This account of the Black Death comes from Jean de Venette (d. c. 1368), a monk and master of theology at the University of Paris who compiled, probably in the late 1350s, a chronicle of his own lifetime.

Some said that this pestilence was caused by infection of the air and waters. . . . As a result of this theory. . . . the Jews were suddenly and violently charged with infecting wells and water and corrupting the air. . . . In Germany and other parts of the world where Jews lived, they were massacred and slaughtered by Christians, and many thousands were burned everywhere, indiscriminately. . . . But in truth, such poisonings, granted that they actually were perpetrated, could not have caused so great a plague nor have infected so many people. There were other causes; for example, the will of God and the corrupt humors and evil inherent in air and earth. . . .

After the cessation of the epidemic, or plague, the men and women who survived married each other. There was . . . fertility beyond the ordinary. Pregnant women were seen on every side. . . . But woe is me! The world was not changed for the better but for the worse by this renewal of the population. For men were more avaricious and grasping than before, even though they had far greater possessions. They were more covetous and disturbed each other more frequently with suits, brawls, disputes, and pleas. Nor by the mortality resulting from this terrible plague inflicted by God was peace between kings and lords established. On the contrary, the enemies of the king of France and of the Church were stronger and wickeder than before and stirred up wars on sea and on land. Greater evils than before pullulated everywhere in the world. And this factor was very remarkable. Although there was an abundance of all goods, yet everything was twice as dear, whether it were utensils, victuals, or merchandise, hired helpers or peasants and serfs, except for some hereditary domains which remained abundantly stocked with everything. Charity began to cool, and iniquity with ignorance and sin to abound, for few could be found in the good towns and castles who knew how or were willing to instruct children in the rudiments of grammar.

Source: Richard A. Newhall, ed., *The Chronicle of Jean de Venette* (New York: Columbia University Press, 1953), 50–51.

EXAMINING THE EVIDENCE

1. How did Venette's interpretation of the causes of the epidemic differ from those of his European contemporaries?

2. In Venette's view, what were the social and moral consequences of the Black Death?

Muslim Responses to the Black Death   Muslims did not share the Christian belief in "original sin," which deemed human beings inherently sinful, and so they did not see the plague as a divine punishment. Instead, they accepted it as an expression of God's will, and even a blessing for the faithful. The Muslim cleric Ibn al-Wardi (IB-unh al-wahr-dee), who succumbed to the disease in 1349, wrote that "this plague is for Muslims a martyrdom and a reward, and for the disbelievers a punishment and rebuke."[3] Most Muslim scholars and physicians rejected the theory that the pandemic was spread through contagion, counseling against abandoning stricken family members. The flagellants' focus on atonement for sin and the scapegoating of Jews seen in Christian Europe were wholly absent in the Islamic world.

Rebuilding Societies in Western Europe 1350–1492

Just as existing religious beliefs and practices shaped Muslim and Christian responses to the plague, underlying conditions influenced political and economic recovery in the two regions. Latin Christendom recovered more quickly than Islamic lands. In Europe, the death toll caused an acute labor shortage. Desperate to find tenants to cultivate their lands, the nobility had to offer generous concessions, such as release from labor services, that liberated the peasantry from the conditions of serfdom. The incomes of the nobility and the Church declined by half or more, and many castles and monasteries fell into ruin. The shortage of labor enabled both urban artisans and rural laborers to bargain for wage increases. Rising wages improved living standards for ordinary people, who began to consume more meat, cheese, and beer. At the same time, a smaller population reduced the demand for grain and manufactured goods such as woolen cloth. Many nobles, unable to find tenants, converted their agricultural land into pasture. Hundreds of villages were abandoned. In much of central Europe, cultivated land reverted back to forest. Thus, the plague redrew the economic map of Europe, shifting the economic balance of power.

Economic change brought with it economic conflict, and tensions between rich and poor triggered insurrections by rural peasants and the urban lower classes throughout western Europe. In the Italian city-states, the working classes of Florence, led by unemployed wool workers, revolted against the patricians (the wealthy families who controlled the city's government) in 1378. Their demand for a greater share of wealth and political rights alarmed the city's artisan guilds, which allied with the patricians to suppress what became known as the Ciompi revolt ("uprising by the little people"). While the revolt failed, it clearly demonstrated the awareness of Florence's working classes that the plague had undermined the status quo, creating an opportunity for economic and political change.

The efforts of elites to respond to the new economic environment could also lead to conflict. In England, King Richard II's attempt to shift the basis of taxation from landed wealth to a head tax on each subject incited the Peasant Revolt of 1381. Led by a radical preacher named John Ball, the rebels presented a petition to the king that went beyond repeal of the head tax to demand freedom from the tyranny of noble lords and the Christian Church:

> Henceforward, that no lord should have lordship but that there should be proportion between all people, saving only the lordship of the king; that the goods of the holy church ought not to be in the hands of men of religion, or parsons or vicars, or others of holy church, but these should have their sustenance easily and the rest of the goods be divided between the parishioners, . . . and that there should be no villeins [peasants subject to a lord's justice] in England or any serfdom or villeinage, but all are to be free and of one condition.[4]

In the end the English nobles mustered militias to suppress the uprising. This success could not, however, reverse the developments that had produced the uprising in the first place. High wages, falling rents, and the flight of tenants brought many estates to the brink of bankruptcy. Declining aristocratic families intermarried with successful entrepreneurs, who coveted the privileges of the titled nobility and sought to emulate their lifestyle. A new social order began to form, one based on private property and entrepreneurship rather than nobility and serfdom, but equally extreme in its imbalance of wealth and poverty.

Perhaps nowhere in Europe was this new social order more apparent than in Italy. In the Italian city-states, the widening gap between rich and poor was reflected in their governments, which increasingly benefited the wealthy. Over the course of the fifteenth century, the ideals and institutions of republican (representative) government on which the Italian city-states were founded steadily lost ground. A military despot wrested control of Milan in 1450. Venice's **oligarchy**—rule by an exclusive elite—strengthened its grip over the city's government and commerce. In Florence, beset by constant civil strife after the Ciompi uprising, the Medici family of bankers dominated the city's political affairs. Everywhere, financial power was increasingly aligned with political power.

In the wake of the Black Death, kings and princes suffered a drop in revenues as agricultural production fell. Yet in the long run, royal power grew at the expense of the nobility and the Church. In England and France, royal governments gained new sources of income and established bureaucracies of tax collectors and administrators to manage them. The rulers of these states transformed their growing financial power into military and political strength by raising standing armies of professional soldiers and investing in new military technology. The French monarchy, for instance, capitalized on rapid innovations in gunpowder weapons

Social Unrest and Rebellion

Rise of National States

oligarchy Rule by a small group of individuals or families.

to create a formidable army and to establish itself as the supreme power in continental Europe. Originally developed by the Mongols, these weapons had been introduced to Europe via the Islamic world by the middle of the fourteenth century.

Hundred Years' War

The progress of the Hundred Years' War (1337–1453) between England and France reflected the changing political landscape. On the eve of the Black Death pandemic, the war broke out over claims to territories in southwestern France and a dispute over succession to the French throne. In the early years of the conflict, the English side prevailed, thanks to the skill of its bowmen against mounted French knights. As the war dragged on, the English kings increasingly relied on mercenary armies, paid in plunder from the towns and castles they seized. By 1400, combat between knights conducted according to elaborate rules of chivalry had yielded to new forms of warfare. Cannons, siege weapons, and, later, firearms undermined both the nobility's preeminence in war and its sense of identity and purpose. An arms race between France and its rivals led to rapid improvements in weaponry, especially the development of lighter and more mobile cannons. Ultimately the French defeated the English, but the war transformed both sides. The length of the conflict, the propaganda from both sides, and the unified effort needed to prosecute the increasingly costly war all contributed to the evolution of royal governments and the emergence of a sense of national identity.

Consolidating State Power

To strengthen their control, the monarchs of states such as France, England, and Spain relied on new forms of direct taxation, as well as financing from bankers. The French monarchy levied new taxes on salt, land, and commercial transactions, wresting income from local lords and town governments. The kings of England and France promoted domestic industries such as textiles and metallurgy to enhance their national power. The marriage of Isabella of Castile and Ferdinand of Aragon in 1469 created a unified monarchy in Spain. This expansion of royal power in Spain depended heavily on loans from Genoese bankers, who also financed the maritime ventures of the Portuguese and Spanish monarchs into the Atlantic Ocean. Thus, in all three of these states, new economic conditions contributed to the growth of monarchical power (see Map 15.2).

Ultimately, consolidation of monarchical power in western Europe would create new global connections. In their efforts to consolidate power, Ferdinand and Isabella, like so many rulers in world history, demanded religious conformity. In 1492 they conquered Granada, the last Muslim foothold in Spain, and ordered all Jews and Muslims to convert to Christianity or face banishment. With the *Reconquista* (Spanish for "reconquest") of Spain complete, Ferdinand and Isabella turned their crusading energies toward exploration. That same year, they sponsored the first of Christopher Columbus's momentous transatlantic voyages in pursuit of the fabled riches of China.

Wheeled Cannon

The Hundred Years' War between England and France touched off an arms race that spurred major advances in the technology of warfare. Initially, gunsmiths concentrated on making massive siege cannons capable of firing shot weighing hundreds of pounds. By 1500, however, military commanders favored more mobile weapons, such as this wheeled cannon manufactured for the Holy Roman Emperor Maximilian I. (Erich Lessing/Art Resource.)

MAP 15.2

Europe and the Greater Mediterranean, 1453

The century following the Black Death witnessed the growth of royal power and territorial consolidation across Europe, most notably in England and France. But central Europe and Italy remained politically fragmented. The Ottoman conquest of Constantinople in 1453 extinguished the Byzantine Empire and sharpened the conflict between Christendom and the Islamic world in southeastern Europe.

Ming China and the New Order in East Asia 1368–1500

State building in East Asia, too, fostered the development of national states. The Yuan dynasty established in China by the Mongol khan Kubilai had foundered after his death in 1294. Kubilai's successors wrung as much tribute as they could from the Chinese population, but they neglected the infrastructure of roads, canals, and irrigation and flood-control dikes that the Chinese economy depended on. By the time the Mongol court at Dadu (modern Beijing) began to enlist the services of the Confucian-educated elite in the late 1330s, economic distress and social unrest already had taken a heavy toll. When peasant insurrections and civil wars broke out in the 1350s, the Mongol leaders abandoned China and retreated to their steppe homeland. After a protracted period of war and devastation, a Chinese general of peasant origin restored native rule, founding the Ming dynasty in 1368 (see Map 15.3).

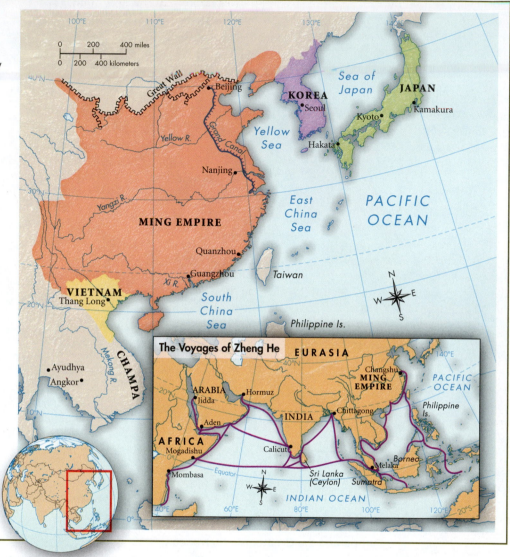

MAP 15.3

The Ming Empire, 1449

After expelling the Mongols, the rulers of the Ming dynasty rebuilt the Great Wall to defend China from nomad invasions. Emperor Yongle moved the Ming capital from Nanjing to Beijing and launched expeditions commanded by his trusted aide Zheng He that voyaged throughout Southeast Asia and the Indian Ocean.

Ming Autocracy

Neo-Confucianism The reformulation of Confucian doctrines to reassert a commitment to moral perfection and the betterment of society; dominated Chinese intellectual life and social thought from the twelfth to the twentieth centuries.

The Ming founder, Zhu Yuanzhang (JOO yuwen-JAHNG) (r. 1368–1398)—better known by his imperial title, Hongwu (hoong-woo)—resurrected the basic Chinese institutions of civil government. But throughout his life Hongwu viewed the scholar-official class with suspicion. Born a peasant, Hongwu saw himself as a populist crusading against the snobbery and luxurious lifestyle of the rich and powerful. Once in command, he repeatedly purged high officials and exercised despotic control over his government. Hongwu reinstituted the civil service examinations system to select government officials, but he used the examinations and the state-run school system as tools of political indoctrination, establishing the teachings of twelfth-century Neo-Confucian philosopher Zhu Xi (JOO shee) as the standard for the civil service exams. Zhu shared the Neo-Confucian antipathy toward Buddhism as a foreign religion and sought to reassert the Confucian commitment to moral perfection and the betterment of society. **Neo-Confucianism** advocated a strict moral code and a patriarchal social hierarchy, and the Ming government supported it with the full force of imperial law. Thus, Hongwu drew on tradition and a belief in China's cultural superiority as he created a new state.

This strong sense of Chinese superiority can be seen in many of Hongwu's policies. Determined to eradicate any taint of Mongol customs, Hongwu rejected the Mongol model of a multiethnic empire and turned his back on the world of the steppe nomads. He located his capital at Nanjing, on the south bank of the Yangzi River, far from the Mongol frontier. Foreign embassies were welcome at the Ming court, which offered trading privileges in return for tribute and allegiance to the Chinese emperor. But Hongwu distrusted merchants as much as he did intellectuals. In 1371 he forbade Chinese merchants from engaging in overseas commerce and placed foreign traders under close government scrutiny.

Hongwu's son, the Emperor Yongle (r. 1402–1424), reversed his father's efforts to sever China from the outside world. Instead, Yongle embraced the Mongol vision of world empire and rebuilt the former Mongol capital of Dadu, creating the modern city of Beijing. Throughout his reign Yongle campaigned to subdue the Mongol tribes along the northern frontier, but with little success. He also wanted to expand southward. In 1405 he launched a series of naval expeditions under Admiral Zheng He (JUNG-huh) that, as we will see, projected Chinese power deep into the Indian Ocean, and in 1407 he invaded and conquered Vietnam (see again Map 15.3). Nonetheless, Yongle's reign did not represent a complete break with that of Hongwu. Like his father, Yongle was an autocrat who promoted Neo-Confucian policies, even as he sought to reestablish some of the global connections Hongwu had tried to sever.

The impact of Hongwu's policies went far beyond the realms of court politics and international diplomacy. He envisioned his empire as a universe of self-sufficient and self-governing villages, where men worked in the fields and women remained at home. The Neo-Confucian ideology of Hongwu emphasized the patriarchal authority of the lineage, and his policies deprived women of many rights, including a share in inheritance. It outlawed the remarriage of widows. By the fourteenth century, many elite families practiced foot binding, which probably originated among courtesans and entertainers. From around age six the feet of young girls were tightly bound with bandages, deforming the bones and crippling them. The feet of adult women ideally were no more than three to four inches long; they were considered a mark of feminine beauty and a symbol of freedom from labor. Foot binding accompanied seclusion in the home as a sign of respectable womanhood.

Despite the strictures of patriarchal society, in the households of nonelite groups, women played an essential economic role. Women worked alongside men in rice cultivation and performed most tasks involved in textile manufacture. As national and international markets for Chinese silk expanded beginning in the twelfth century, male artisans in urban workshops took over skilled occupations such as silk weaving. But the spread of cotton, introduced from India in the thirteenth century, gave peasant women new economic opportunities. Most cotton was grown, ginned (removing the seeds), spun into yarn, and woven into cloth within a single household, principally by women. Confucian moralists esteemed spinning, weaving, and embroidery as "womanly work" that would promote industriousness and thrift; they became dismayed, however, when women displayed entrepreneurial skill in marketing their wares. Nevertheless, women did engage in commercial activities, suggesting that there were limits to the moralists' control of women's lives.

The Ming dynasty abandoned its designs for conquest and expansion after the death of Yongle in 1424. Yet the prestige, power, and philosophy of the Ming state continued to influence its neighbors, with the significant exception of Japan (see Counterpoint: Age of the Samurai in Japan, 1185–1450). Vietnam regained its independence from China in 1427, but under the long-lived Le dynasty (1428–1788), Vietnam retained Chinese-style bureaucratic government. The Le rulers oversaw the growth of an official class schooled in Neo-Confucianism and committed to forcing its cultural norms, kinship practices, and hostility to Buddhism on Vietnamese society as a whole. In Korea, the rulers of the new Yi dynasty (1392–1910) also embraced Neo-Confucian ideals of government. Under Yi rule the Confucian-educated elite acquired hereditary status with exclusive rights to political office. In both Vietnam and Korea, aristocratic rule and Buddhism's dominance over daily life yielded to a "Neo-Confucian revolution" modeled after Chinese political institutions and values.

Ming Patriarchal Society

Neo-Confucianism in Vietnam and Korea

Islam's New Frontiers

FOCUS

Why did Islam expand dramatically in the fourteenth and fifteenth centuries, and how did new Islamic societies differ from established ones?

In the fourteenth and fifteenth centuries, Islam continued to spread to new areas, including central and maritime Asia, sub-Saharan Africa, and southeastern Europe. In the past, Muslim rule had often preceded the popular adoption of Islamic religion and culture. Yet the advance of Islam in Africa and Asia came about not through conquest, but through slow diffusion via merchants and missionaries. The universalism and egalitarianism of Islam appealed to rising merchant classes in both West Africa and maritime Asia.

During this period, Islam expanded by adapting to older ruling cultures rather than seeking to eradicate them. Timur, the last of the great nomad conquerors, and his descendants ruled not as Mongol khans but as Islamic sultans. The culture of the Central Asian states, however, remained an eclectic mix of Mongol, Turkish, and Persian traditions, in contrast to the strict adherence to Muslim law and doctrine practiced under the Arab regimes of the Middle East and North Africa. This pattern of cultural adaptation and assimilation was even more evident in West Africa and Southeast Asia.

Islamic Spiritual Ferment in Central Asia 1350–1500

The spread of Sufism in Central Asia between 1350 and 1500 played a significant role in the process of cultural assimilation. **Sufism**—a mystical tradition that stressed self-mastery, practical virtues, and spiritual growth through personal experience of the divine—had already emerged by 1200 as a major expression of Islamic values and social identity. Sufism appeared in many variations and readily assimilated local cultures to its beliefs and practices. Sufi mystics acquired institutional strength through the communal solidarity of their brotherhoods spread across the whole realm of Islam. In contrast to the orthodox scholars and teachers known as *ulama*, who made little effort to convert nonbelievers, Sufi preachers were inspired by missionary zeal and welcomed non-Muslims to their lodges and sermons. This made them ideal instruments for the spread of Islam to new territories.

Timur

One of Sufism's most important royal patrons was Timur (1336–1405), the last of the Mongol emperors. Born near the city of Samarkand (SAM-ar-kand) when the Mongol Ilkhanate in Iran was on the verge of collapse, Timur—himself a Turk—grew up among Mongols who practiced Islam. He rose to power in the 1370s by reuniting quarreling Mongol tribes in common pursuit of conquest. Although Timur lacked the dynastic pedigree enjoyed by Chinggis Khan's descendants, like Chinggis he held his empire together by the force of his personal charisma.

From the early 1380s, Timur's armies relentlessly pursued campaigns of conquest, sweeping westward across Iran into Mesopotamia and Russia and eastward into India. In 1400–1401 Timur seized and razed Aleppo and Damascus, the principal Mamluk cities in Syria. In 1402 he captured the Ottoman sultan in battle. Rather than trying to consolidate his rule in Syria and Anatolia (modern Turkey), however, Timur turned his attention eastward. He was preparing to march on China when he fell ill and died early in 1405. Although Timur's empire quickly fragmented, his triumphs would serve as an inspiration to later empire builders, such as the Mughals in India and the Manchus in China. Moreover, his support of Sufism would have a lasting impact, helping lay the foundation for a number of important Islamic religious movements in Central Asia.

The institutions of Timur's empire were largely modeled on the Ilkhan synthesis of Persian civil administration and Turkish-Mongol military organization. Like the Ilkhans and the Ottomans, Timur's policies favored settled farmers and urban populations over pastoral nomads, who were often displaced from their homelands. While Timur allowed local princes a degree of autonomy, he was determined to make Samarkand a grand imperial capital.

Sufism A tradition within Islam that emphasizes mystical knowledge and personal experience of the divine.

He forcibly relocated artists, craftsmen, scholars, and clerics from many regions and put them into service in Samarkand (see Reading the Past: A Spanish Ambassador's Description of Samarkand). The citadel and enormous bazaar built by Timur have long since perished, but surviving mosques, shrines, and tombs illuminate Timur's vision of Islamic kingship: all-powerful, urbane and cosmopolitan, and ostentatious in its display of public piety.

After Timur's death in 1405, his sons carved the empire into independent regional kingdoms. Like Timur, his successors sought to control religious life in royal capitals such as Herat and Samarkand by appointing elders (*shayks*) and judges (*qadis*) to administer justice, supervise schools and mosques, and police public morality. Yet Sufi brotherhoods and the veneration of Sufi saints exerted an especially strong influence over social life and religious practice in Central Asia. Timur had lavished special favor on Sufi teachers and had strategically placed the shrines of his family members next to the tombs of important Sufi leaders. The relics of Timur in Samarkand, along with the tombs of Sufi saints, attracted pilgrims from near and far.

Elsewhere in the Islamic world, a number of religious movements combined the veneration of Sufi saints and belief in miracles with unorthodox ideas derived from Shi'ism, the branch of Islam that maintains that only descendants of Muhammad's son-in-law Ali have a legitimate right to serve as caliph. Outside the major cities, Islamic leadership passed to Sufis and popular preachers. One of the most militant and influential of these radical Islamic sects was the Safavid (SAH-fah-vid) movement founded by a Sufi preacher, Safi al-Din (SAH-fee al-dean) (1252–1334). Like other visionary teachers, Safi preached the need for a purified Islam cleansed of worldly wealth, urban luxury, and moral laxity. His missionary movement struck a responsive chord among the pastoral Turk and Mongol tribes of Anatolia and Iran. The Safavids roused their followers to attack Christians in the Caucasus region, but they also challenged Muslim rulers such as the Ottomans and Timur's successors. At the end of the fifteenth century, a charismatic leader, Shah Isma'il (shah IS-mah-eel), combined Safavid religious fervor with Shi'a doctrines to found a **theocracy**—a state subject to religious authority. It would rule Iran for more than two centuries and shape modern Iran's distinctive Shi'a religious culture.

Timur Enthroned

We can glean some sense of Timur's self-image from the *Book of Victories*, a chronicle of Timur's campaigns commissioned by one of his descendants in the 1480s. This scene portrays the moment in 1370 when Timur declared himself successor to the Chagadai khans. (Rare Books and Manuscripts Department, The Sheridan Libraries, The Johns Hopkins University.)

Ottoman Expansion and the Fall of Constantinople 1354–1453

The spread of Islam in Central Asia would have profound consequences for the region. In the eyes of Europeans, however, the most significant—and alarming—advance was the Ottoman expansion into the Balkan territories of southeastern Europe. The Byzantine state was severely shaken by the Black Death, and in 1354 the Ottomans took advantage of this weakness to invade the Balkans. After a decisive victory in 1389, the Ottoman Empire annexed most of the Balkans except the region around Constantinople itself, reducing it to an isolated enclave.

The growing might of the Ottoman Empire stemmed from two military innovations: (1) the formation of the **janissary corps**, elite army units composed of slave soldiers, and (2) the use of massed musket fire and cannons, such as the bombards of Urban, the Hungarian engineer whom we met at the start of this chapter. In the late fourteenth century the Ottomans adopted the Mamluk practice of organizing slave armies that would be more reliably loyal to the sultan than the unruly *ghazi* ("holy warrior") bands that Osman

theocracy A state ruled by religious authorities.

janissary corps Slave soldiers who served as the principal armed forces of the Ottoman Empire beginning in the fifteenth century; also staffed much of the Ottoman state bureaucracy.

A Spanish Ambassador's Description of Samarkand

In September 1403, an embassy dispatched by King Henry III of Castile arrived at Samarkand in hopes of enlisting the support of Timur for a combined military campaign against the Ottomans. Seventy years old and in failing health, Timur lavishly entertained his visitors, but made no response to Henry's overtures. The leader of the Spanish delegation, Ruy Gonzalez de Clavijo, left Samarkand disappointed, but his report preserves our fullest account of Timur's capital in its heyday.

The city is rather larger than Seville, but lying outside Samarkand are great numbers of houses that form extensive suburbs. These lay spread on all hands, for indeed the township is surrounded by orchards and vineyards. . . . In between these orchards pass streets with open squares; these are all densely populated, and here all kinds of goods are on sale with breadstuffs and meat. . . .

Samarkand is rich not only in foodstuffs but also in manufactures, such as factories of silk. . . . Thus trade has always been fostered by Timur with the view of making his capital the noblest of cities; and during all his conquests . . . he carried off the best men to people Samarkand, bringing thither the master-craftsmen of all nations. Thus from Damascus he carried away with him all the weavers of that city, those who worked at the silk looms; further the bow-makers who produce those cross-bows which are so famous; likewise armorers; also the craftsmen in glass and porcelain, who are known to be the best in all the world. From Turkey he had brought their gunsmiths who make the arquebus. . . . So great therefore was the population now of all nationalities gathered together in Samarkand that of men with their families the number they said must amount to 150,000 souls . . . [including] Turks, Arabs, and Moors of diverse sects, with Greek, Armenian, Roman, Jacobite [Syrian], and Nestorian Christians, besides those folk who baptize with fire in the forehead [i.e., Hindus]. . . .

The markets of Samarkand further are amply stored with merchandise imported from distant and foreign countries. . . . The goods that are imported to Samarkand from Cathay indeed are of the richest and most precious of all those brought thither from foreign parts, for the craftsmen of Cathay are reputed to be the most skillful by far beyond those of any other nation.

Source: Ruy Gonzalez de Clavijo, *Embassy to Tamerlane, 1403–1406,* trans. Guy Le Strange (London: Routledge, 1928), 285–289.

EXAMINING THE EVIDENCE

1. What features of Timur's capital most impressed Gonzalez de Clavijo?

2. How does this account of Samarkand at its height compare with the chapter's description of Renaissance Florence?

(r. 1280–1324), the founder of the Ottoman state, had gathered as the core of his army. At first, prisoners and volunteers made up the janissary corps. Starting in 1395, however, the Ottomans imposed a form of conscription known as *devshirme* (dev-SHEER-may) on the Christian peoples of the Balkans to supplement Turkish recruits. Adolescent boys conscripted through the devshirme were taken from their families, raised as Muslims, and educated at palace schools for service in the sultan's civil administration as well as the army. The Mamluks purchased slaves from Central Asia, but the Ottomans obtained a cheaper and more abundant supply from within their empire. At the same time, they created a government and military wholly beholden to the sultan. Janissaries were forbidden to marry and forfeited their property to the sultan upon their death.

Practical concerns dictated Ottoman policies toward Christian communities. Where Christians were the majority of the population, the Ottomans could be quite tolerant. Apart from the notorious devshirme slave

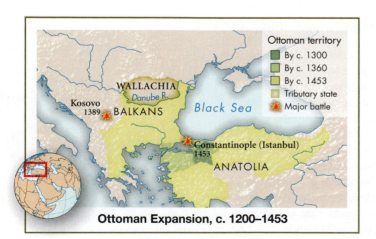

Ottoman Expansion, c. 1200–1453

levy, the Ottoman impositions were less burdensome than the dues the Balkan peoples had owed the Byzantine emperor. The Ottomans allowed Balkan Christians freedom to practice their religion, and they protected the Greek Orthodox Church, which they considered indispensable to maintaining social order. In Anatolia and other places where Christians were a minority, however, the Ottomans took a much harder line, seeing such minorities as a potential threat to the Ottoman order. Muslim governors stripped Christian bishops of their authority, seized church properties and revenues, and curbed public worship. By 1500 Christian society in Anatolia had nearly vanished; most Christians had converted to Islam.

Like the Ming emperors of China, Ottoman rulers favored the creation of a stable peasant society that would serve as a reliable source of revenue. A married peasant with a plot of land that could be worked by two oxen became the basic unit of Ottoman society. The state controlled nearly all cultivated land, but peasant families enjoyed permanent rights to farm the land they occupied. The government sold the rights to collect land taxes (a practice known as tax farming) to merchants and other wealthy individuals, including non-Muslims such as Greeks and Jews. The practice of tax farming guaranteed revenues for the state, but it distanced Ottoman officials from their subjects.

Despite their own nomadic origins, the Ottomans regarded nomadic tribes, like religious minorities, as a threat to stability. Many nomads were forcibly deported and settled in the Balkans and western Anatolia, where they combined farming with stock raising. Due to heavy taxes imposed on animal herds, nomads had to earn additional income through transport, lumbering, and felt and carpet manufacture. The push toward such activities created by harsh Ottoman policies was matched by the pull of global trade connections. Strong demand from European customers and the imperial capital of Istanbul (the name Mehmed II gave to Constantinople) stimulated carpet weaving by both peasants and herders.

The patriarchal family, in which the wife is subject to her husband's control, was a pillar of Ottoman law, just as it was in Ming China. Although the Ottoman state barred women from owning cultivated land, it did not infringe on women's rights to a share of family inheritance, as prescribed in the Qur'an. Thus, although men usually controlled property in the form of land and houses, women acquired wealth in the form of money, furnishings, clothes, and jewelry. Women invested in commercial ventures, tax farming, and moneylending. Because women were secluded in the home and veiled in public— long-established requirements to maintain family honor and status in the central Islamic lands—women used servants and trusted clients to help them conduct their business activities.

The final defeat of the Byzantine Empire by Ottoman armies in 1453 shocked the Christian world. Mehmed II's capture of Constantinople also completed a radical transformation of the Ottoman enterprise. The Ottoman sultans no longer saw themselves as roving ghazi warriors, but as monarchs with absolute authority over a multinational empire at the crossroads of Europe and Asia: "ruler of the two seas and the two continents," as the inscription over Mehmed's palace gate proclaimed. A proudly Islamic regime, the Ottoman sultanate aspired to become the centerpiece of a broad cosmopolitan civilization spanning Europe, Asia, and Africa.

Commerce and Culture in Islamic West Africa

West African trading empires and the merchants they supported had long served as the vanguard of Islam in sub-Saharan Africa. The Mali Empire's adoption of Islam as its official religion in the late thirteenth century encouraged conversion to Islam throughout the West African savanna. Under Mali's protection, Muslim merchant clans expanded their activities throughout the towns of the savanna and the oasis trading posts of the Sahara. Islam continued to prosper despite the collapse of Mali's political dominion in the mid-fourteenth century.

Timbuktu Manuscript
Timbuktu became the hub of Islamic culture and intellectual life in the western Sahara. Scholars and students at Timbuktu assembled impressive libraries of Arabic texts, such as this twelfth-century Qur'an. Written mostly on paper imported from Europe, Timbuktu's manuscripts were preserved in family collections after the city's leading scholars were deported to North Africa by Moroccan invaders in 1591. (Candace Feit.)

Muslim Merchants and Scholars

The towns of Jenne and Timbuktu, founded along the Niger River by Muslim merchants in the thirteenth century, emerged as the new crossroads of trans-Saharan trade. Jenne benefited from its access to the gold mines and rain forest products of coastal West Africa. Timbuktu's commercial prosperity rose as trade grew between West Africa and Mamluk Egypt. Islamic intellectual culture thrived among the merchant families of Timbuktu, Jenne, and other towns.

As elsewhere in the Islamic world, West African trader families readily combined religious scholarship with mercantile pursuits. Thus, in West Africa, trade and Islamic culture went hand in hand. In fact, West Africa saw the development of a profitable trade *in* Islamic culture. Since the eleventh century, disciples of renowned scholars had migrated across the Sahara and founded schools and libraries. The Moroccan Muslim scholar and traveler Ibn Battuta (IB-uhn ba-TOO-tuh), who visited Mali in 1352–1353, voiced approval of the people's "eagerness to memorize the great Qur'an: they place fetters on their children if they fail to memorize it and they are not released until they do so."[5] Books on Islamic law, theology, Sufi mysticism, medicine, and Arabic grammar and literature were staple commodities of trans-Saharan trade. The Muslim diplomat Hasan al-Wazzan (hah-SAHN al-wah-zan), whose *Description of Africa* (published in Italian in 1550) became a best-seller in Europe, wrote that in Timbuktu "the learned are greatly revered. Also, many book manuscripts coming from the Berber [North African] lands are sold. More profits are realized from sales of books than any other merchandise."[6]

Muslim Clerics and Native Religious Leaders

Muslim clerics wielded considerable influence in the towns. Clerics presided over worship and festival life and governed social behavior by applying Muslim law and cultural traditions. Yet away from the towns the majority of the population remained attached to ancestral beliefs in nature spirits, especially the spirits of rivers and thunder. Healer priests, clan chiefs, and other ritual experts shared responsibility for making offerings to the spirits, providing protection from evil demons and sorcerers, and honoring the dead. Much to the chagrin of purists such as Ibn Battuta, West African rulers maintained their authority in rural areas by combining Muslim practices with indigenous rituals and traditions. Islam in West Africa was largely urban, and West African rulers knew that their control of the countryside depended on religious accommodation.

trade diaspora A network of merchants from the same city or country who live permanently in foreign lands and cooperate with one another to pursue trading opportunities.

Advance of Islam in Maritime Southeast Asia

Muslim Arab merchants had dominated maritime commerce in the Indian Ocean and Southeast Asia since the seventh century. Not until the thirteenth century, however, did Islam begin to gain converts in Malaysia and the Indonesian archipelago. By 1400 Arab and Gujarati traders and Sufi teachers had spread Islam throughout maritime Asia. The dispersion of Muslim merchants took the form of a **trade diaspora**, a network of merchant settlements dispersed across foreign lands but united by common origins, religion, and language, as well as by business dealings.

Political and economic motives strongly influenced official adoption of Islam. In the first half of the fourteenth century, the Majapahit (mah-jah-PAH-hit) kingdom (1292–1528), a bastion of Hindu religion, conquered most of Java and the neighboring islands of Bali and Madura and forced many local rulers in the Indonesian archipelago to submit tribute. In response, many of these rulers adopted Islam as an act of resistance to dominance by the Majapahit kings. By 1428 the Muslim city-states of Java's north coast, buoyed by the profits of trade with China, secured their independence from Majapahit. Majapahit's dominion over the agricultural hinterland of Java lasted until 1528, when a coalition of Muslim princes forced the royal family to flee to Bali, which remains today the sole preserve of Hinduism in Southeast Asia.

Politics of Conversion

Cosmopolitan port cities, with their diverse merchant communities, were natural sites for religious innovation. The spread of Islam beyond Southeast Asia's port cities, however, was slow and uneven. Javanese tradition attributes the Islamization of the island to a series of preachers, beginning with Malik Ibrahim (mah-leek EE-bra-heem) (d. 1419), a Gujarati spice trader of Persian ancestry. Because merchants and Sufi teachers played a far greater role than orthodox ulama in the spread of Islam in Southeast Asia, relatively open forms of Islam flourished. The Arab shipmaster Ibn Majid (IB-uhn maj-jid), writing in 1462, bemoaned the corruption of Islamic marriage and dietary laws among the Muslims of Melaka (mah-LAK-eh): "They have no culture at all. The infidel marries Muslim women while the Muslim takes pagans to wife. . . . The Muslim eats dogs for meat, for there are no food laws. They drink wine in the markets and do not treat divorce as a religious act.[7] Enforcement of Islamic law often was suspended where it conflicted with local custom. Southeast Asia never adopted some features of Middle Eastern culture often associated with Islam, such as the veiling of women.

Religious Diversity

Local pre-Islamic religious traditions persisted in Sumatra and Java long after the people accepted Islam. The most visible signs of conversion to Islam were giving up the worship of idols and the consumption of pork and adopting the practice of male circumcision. In addition, the elaborate feasting and grave goods, slave sacrifice, and widow sacrifice (*sati*) that normally accompanied the burials of chiefs and kings largely disappeared. Yet Southeast Asian Muslims continued to honor the dead with prayers and offerings adapted to the forms of Islamic rituals. Malays and Javanese readily adopted veneration of Sufi saints and habitually prayed for assistance from the spirits of deceased holy men. Muslim restrictions on women's secular and religious activities met with spirited resistance from Southeast Asian women, who were accustomed to active participation in public life. Even more than in West Africa, Islam in Southeast Asia prospered not by destroying existing traditions, but by assimilating them.

In regions such as West Africa and Southeast Asia, then, Islam diffused through the activities of merchants, teachers, and settlers rather than through conquest. The spread of Islam in Africa and Asia also followed the rhythms of international trade. While Europe recovered slowly from the Black Death, thriving commerce across the Indian Ocean forged new economic links among Asia, Africa, and the Mediterranean world.

The Global Bazaar

Dynastic changes, war, and the Black Death roiled the international economy in the fourteenth century. Yet even before the end of the century, trade and economic growth were reviving in many areas. The maritime world of the Indian Ocean, largely spared both pandemic and war, displayed unprecedented commercial dynamism. Pepper and cotton textiles from India, porcelain and silk from China, spices and

> **FOCUS**
>
> How did the pattern of international trade change during the fourteenth and fifteenth centuries, and how did these changes affect consumption and fashion tastes?

other exotic goods from Southeast Asia, and gold, ivory, and copper from southern Africa circulated through a network of trading ports that spanned the Indian Ocean, Southeast Asia, and China. These trading centers attracted merchants and artisans from many lands, and the colorful variety of languages, dress, foods, and music that filled their streets gave them the air of a global bazaar.

The crises of the fourteenth century severely disrupted the European economy, but by 1450 Italy regained its place as the center within Latin Christendom of finance, industry, and trade. Previously, European craftsmen had produced only crude imitations of Islamic luxury wares. By the early fifteenth century, however, mimicry had blossomed into innovation, and Italian production of luxury goods surpassed Islamic competitors' in both quantity and quality. Wealth poured into Italy, where it found new outlets in a culture of conspicuous consumption. In contrast, the Islamic heartlands of the Middle East never recaptured their former momentum. In sum, the crises of the fourteenth century did not destroy the shared economy and commerce of the Afro-Eurasian world, but they did reshape them in profound and long-lasting ways (see Map 15.4).

Economic Prosperity and Maritime Trade in Asia 1350–1450

In Kubilai Khan's day, hostility among the Mongol khanates disrupted Central Asian caravan trade. Thus when the Venetian traveler Marco Polo returned home in 1292, he traveled by ship rather than retracing the overland route, known as the Silk Road, that had brought him to China two decades before. Polo's experience was a sign of things to come. After 1300 maritime commerce largely replaced inland trade over the ancient Silk Road. Asian merchants from India to China would seize the opportunities presented by the new emphasis on maritime commerce.

India: Cotton and Pepper

In India, improvements in spinning wheels and looms, and above all the invention of block printing of fabrics in the fourteenth century, led to a revolution in cotton textile manufacture. Using block printing (carved wooden blocks covered with dye), Indian weavers produced colorful and intricately designed fabrics—later known in Europe as chintz, from the Hindi *chint* ("many-colored")—that were far cheaper than luxury textiles such as silk or velvet. Gujarat in the northwest and the Tamil lands in southeastern India became centers of cotton manufacture and trade. Although cotton cultivation and weaving spread to Burma, Thailand, and China, Indian fabrics dominated Eurasian markets (see Lives and Livelihoods: Urban Weavers in India).

Along with textiles, India was famous for its pepper, for which Europeans had acquired a taste during the age of the Crusades. Muslim merchants from Gujarat controlled both cotton and pepper exports from the cities of Calicut and Quilon (KEE-lon). By 1500 Gujarati merchants had created a far-flung trade network across the Indian Ocean from Zanzibar to Java. Gujarati *sharafs* (from the Persian word for "moneylender") and Tamil *chettis* ("traders") acted as bankers for merchants and rulers alike in nearly every Indian Ocean port.

China: Silk and Porcelain

China's ocean-going commerce also flourished in the fourteenth century. The thriving trade between India and China deeply impressed Ibn Battuta, who found thirteen large Chinese vessels, or *junks*, anchored at Calicut when he arrived there in 1341. These junks, Battuta tells us, carried a complement of a thousand men and contained "four decks with rooms, cabins, and saloons for merchants; a cabin has chambers and a lavatory, and can be locked by its occupant, who takes along with him slave girls and wives."[8]

Silk had long dominated China's export trade, but by the eleventh century domestic silk-weaving was flourishing in Iran, the Byzantine Empire, and India. Because Iranian and Byzantine silk manufacturers were better positioned to respond to changing fashions in the Islamic world and Europe, China primarily exported raw silk rather than finished fabrics. At the same time, China retained its preeminent place in world trade by exporting porcelain, which became known as "chinaware."

Much admired for their whiteness and translucency, Chinese ceramics already had become an important item of Asian maritime trade in the tenth century. Bulky and fragile,

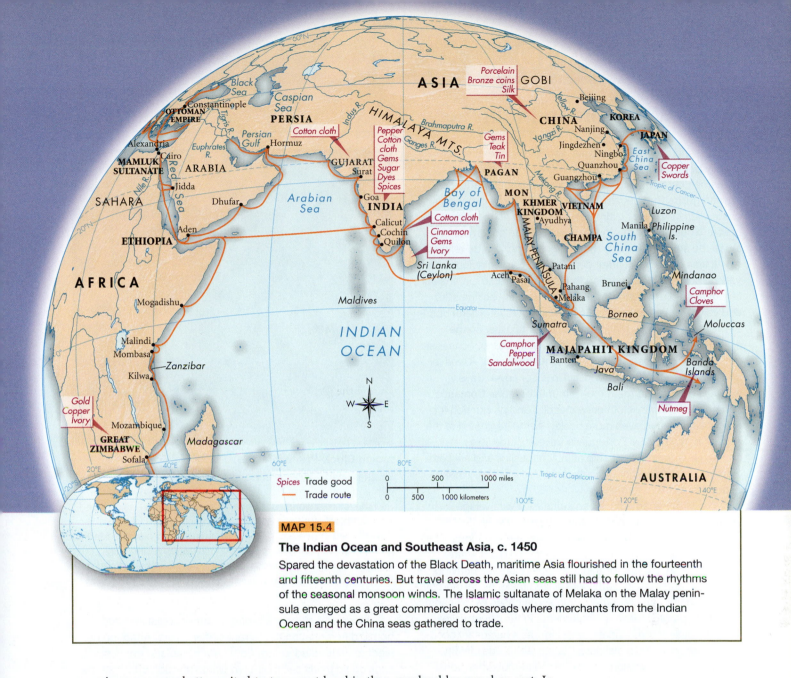

MAP 15.4

The Indian Ocean and Southeast Asia, c. 1450

Spared the devastation of the Black Death, maritime Asia flourished in the fourteenth and fifteenth centuries. But travel across the Asian seas still had to follow the rhythms of the seasonal monsoon winds. The Islamic sultanate of Melaka on the Malay peninsula emerged as a great commercial crossroads where merchants from the Indian Ocean and the China seas gathered to trade.

ceramic wares were better suited to transport by ship than overland by camel or cart. In the thirteenth century, artisans at Jingdezhen (JING-deh-JUHN) in southern China perfected the techniques for making true porcelains, which transform into glass the glaze and pigments, as well as the body of the piece. Porcelain wares, which were harder and whiter than previous types of ceramics, could be made into thin yet strong vessels. Although the Chinese preferred monochromatic (single-colored) porcelains that imitated the colors and texture of jade, consumers in the Islamic world prized intricate designs executed with the metallic pigments used by glassmakers. Muslim merchants introduced the cobalt blue pigment (which Chinese potters called "Mohammedan blue") used to create blue-and-white decorated porcelains. By 1400, Jingdezhen had become the largest manufacturing city in the world, housing more than one thousand kilns with some seventy thousand craftsmen engaged in several dozen specialized tasks. Thus, technological innovation and the demands of the international marketplace shaped both the production and decoration of Chinese ceramics.

The most avid consumers of Chinese porcelains were in the Islamic world, reflecting the global nature of the Chinese ceramics industry. Muslims used Chinese porcelains both as eating and drinking vessels and to decorate mosques, tombs, and other holy places. Imports of Chinese porcelain devastated local ceramic manufacturing in many parts of maritime Asia,

Urban Weavers in India

Industry and commerce in India, especially in textiles, grew rapidly beginning in the fourteenth century. Specialized craftsmen in towns and regional groups of merchants formed guilds that became the nuclei of new occupational castes, *jati* (JAH-tee). Ultimately these new occupational castes would join with other forces in Indian society to challenge the social inequality rooted in orthodox Hindu religion.

It was growth in market demand and technological innovations such as block printing that drove the rapid expansion of India's textile industries. Luxury fabrics such as fine silks and velvet remained largely the province of royal workshops or private patronage. Mass production of textiles, on the other hand, was oriented toward the manufacture of cheaper cotton fabrics, especially colorful chintz garments. A weaver could make a woman's cotton *sari* in six or seven days, whereas a luxury garment took a month or more. Domestic demand for ordinary cloth grew steadily, and production for export accelerated even more briskly. At the beginning of the sixteenth century, the Portuguese traveler Tomé Pires, impressed by the craftsmanship of Indian muslins and calicoes (named after the port of Calicut), observed that "they make enough of these to furnish the world."[1]

Weaving became an urban industry. It was village women who cleaned most of the cotton and spun it into yarn; they could easily combine this simple if laborious work with other domestic chores. But peasants did not weave the yarn into cloth, except for their own use. Instead, weaving, bleaching, and dyeing cloth were skilled tasks performed by professional urban craftsmen, or in some cases by artisans living in separate weavers' settlements in the countryside.

Like other trades in India, weaving was a hereditary occupation that conferred a distinct *jati* caste status and identity. Families of weavers belonged to one of a number of regional guilds with branches in different towns, and members married within their guilds. Unlike European guilds, Indian guilds did not have exclusive monopolies over their trades. A single town could include a number of different weaving guilds, which could become fierce economic and social rivals.

Indian Block-Printed Textile, c. 1500

Block-printed textiles with elaborate designs were in great demand both in India and throughout Southeast Asia, Africa, and the Islamic world. Craftsmen carved intricate designs on wooden blocks (a separate block for each color), which were then dipped in dye and repeatedly stamped on bleached fabric until the entire cloth was covered. This cotton fabric with geese, lotus flower, and rosette designs was manufactured in Gujarat in western India. (Ashmolean Museum, University of Oxford/ Bridgeman Art Library.)

Increased affluence brought further social and economic differentiation to the ranks of weavers. Although guild leaders negotiated orders from merchants and princes, artisans could freely sell their own wares through urban shops and country fairs. The most successful weavers became merchants and brokers, buying more looms and hiring others to work under their supervision. By the fourteenth century some weavers had begun to add the honorific title *chetti* (merchant) to their names.

Southeast Asia: Spices and Rain Forest Products

from the Philippines to East Africa. Chinese porcelains became potent prestige goods among the tribal societies of the Philippines and Indonesia, who attributed magical powers to them.

In mainland Southeast Asia, the shift in political power from the inland rice-growing regions toward coastal port cities reflected the new prominence of maritime trade in the region's economic life. Burma exported cotton to China as early as 1400 and became an important source of metals, gems, and teak for shipbuilding. The profits of maritime commerce fueled the emergence of Ayudhya (a-YOOD-he-ya) in Thailand as the dominant power in mainland Southeast Asia in the late fourteenth century. By 1400 Ayudhya was challenging Majapahit for control of the Southeast Asian trade routes between India and China.

The rising prosperity of weavers whetted their aspirations for social recognition. Amid the whirl and congestion of city life, it was far more difficult than in villages to enforce the laws governing caste purity and segregation. As a fourteenth-century poet wrote about the crowded streets of his hometown of Jaunpur in the Ganges Valley, in the city "one person's caste-mark gets stamped on another's forehead, and a brahman's holy thread will be found hanging around an untouchable's neck."[2] Brahmans objected to this erosion of caste boundaries, to little avail. Weaver guilds became influential patrons of temples and often served as trustees and accountants in charge of managing temple endowments and revenues.

In a few cases the growing economic independence of weavers and like-minded artisans prompted complete rejection of the caste hierarchy. Sufi preachers and *bhakti* (BAHK-tee)—devotional movements devoted to patron gods and goddesses—encouraged the disregard of caste distinctions in favor of a universal brotherhood of devout believers. The fifteenth-century bhakti preacher Kabir, who was strongly influenced by Sufi teachings, epitomized the new social radicalism coursing through the urban artisan classes. A weaver himself, Kabir joined the dignity of manual labor to the purity of spiritual devotion, spurning the social pretension and superficial piety of the brahmans ("pandits") and Muslim clerics ("mullahs"):

> I abandoned kin and caste, I weave my threads at ease
>
> I quarrel with no one, I abandoned the pandits and mullahs,
>
> I wear what I have woven; forgetful of myself, I come close to God.[3]

In Kabir's mind, genuine piety was rooted in honest toil, devotion to family, and abstinence from sensual pleasure.

By the seventeenth century, such ideas had coalesced into a separatist religious movement, Sikhism, centered on a trinity of labor, charity, and spiritual devotion. The Sikhs, who gained a following principally among traders and artisans in the northwestern Punjab region, drew an even more explicit connection between commerce and piety. In the words of a hymn included in a sixteenth-century anthology of Sikh sacred writings:

> The true Guru [teacher] is the merchant;
>
> The devotees are his peddlers.
>
> The capital stock is the Lord's Name, and
>
> To enshrine the truth is to keep His account.[4]

Sikh communities spurned the distinction between pure and impure occupations. In their eyes, holiness was to be found in honest toil and personal piety, not ascetic practices, book learning, or religious rituals.

---

1. Tomé Pires, *The Suma Oriental of Tomé Pires*, ed. and trans. Armando Cortes (London: Hakluyt Society, 1944), 1:53.
2. Vidyapati Thakur, *Kirtilata*, quoted in Eugenia Vanina, *Urban Crafts and Craftsmen in Medieval India (Thirteenth–Eighteenth Centuries)* (New Delhi: Munshiram Manoharlal, 2004), 443.
3. Quoted in Vanina, *Urban Crafts and Craftsmen*, 149.
4. *Sri Guru Granth Sahib*, trans. Gophal Singh (Delhi: Gur Das Kapur & Sons, 1960), 2:427.

QUESTIONS TO CONSIDER

1. In what ways did the organization of textile production reinforce or challenge the prevailing social norms of Hindu society?

2. In what ways did religious ideas and movements reflect the new sense of dignity among prosperous Indian merchants and craftsmen?

For Further Information:

Ramaswamy, Vijaya. *Textiles and Weavers in Medieval South India*. Delhi: Oxford University Press, 1985.

Vanina, Eugenia. *Urban Crafts and Craftsmen in Medieval India (Thirteenth–Eighteenth Centuries)*. New Delhi: Munshiram Manoharlal, 2004.

Thus, China influenced patterns of international trade not only as a producer, as with ceramics, but as a market for exported goods large enough to shape production elsewhere in the world. China was the principal market for the international trade in pepper, and it was Chinese demand that drove the rapid expansion of pepper cultivation in Southeast Asia, in particular Sumatra, during the fifteenth century. In return for exports of pepper, sandalwood, tin and other metals, fine spices, and exotic products of the tropical rain forests, Southeast Asia imported cotton cloth from India and silks, porcelain, and bronze coins from China. In the wake of this trade boom, Indian and Chinese merchant communities sprouted across maritime Southeast Asia. The trade diasporas of Gujarati Muslims and Chinese from Guangzhou

Wedding Present of Chinese Porcelains

Avid demand in the Muslim world stimulated development of China's renowned blue-and-white porcelains. This Persian miniature from around 1480 illustrates the story of a Chinese princess who in a gesture of diplomacy is sent to marry a Turkish nomad chieftain. The dowry that accompanies the reluctant bride includes blue-and-white porcelains and brass wares of Turkestan design. (The Art Archive/Topkapi Museum Istanbul/Gianni Dagli Orti.)

(Canton) and Quanzhou (CHYWAN-joe) created networks of cultural as well as economic influence, ultimately altering the balance of political power as well (see again Map 15.4).

China's Overseas Overture: The Voyages of Zheng He 1405–1433

The growth of South Asian maritime trade attracted the attention of the Chinese government, and in the early fifteenth century, the Ming dynasty in China took a more active role in maritime Southeast Asia, becoming a rival for political and economic supremacy. From the 1390s Malay princes in Sumatra appealed to the Ming court for protection against the demands of the Majapahit kings. In 1405 the Ming emperor Yongle decided to intervene by sending a naval expedition to halt the expansionist aggression of Majapahit and Ayudhya and to assert Chinese authority over the maritime realm.

Zheng He's Mission

Yongle entrusted the fleet to the command of a young military officer named Zheng He (1371–1433). Zheng was born into a Muslim family who had served the Mongol rulers of the Yuan dynasty. In 1383, Zheng He, then age twelve, was conscripted into the eunuch corps (castrated males employed as guardians of the imperial household) and placed in the retinue of the prince who would become Emperor Yongle. Zheng assisted the prince in the overthrow of his nephew that brought Yongle to the throne in 1402, and became his most trusted confidant.

For his mission to Southeast Asia, Yongle equipped Zheng He with a vast armada, a fleet of sixty-three ships manned by nearly twenty-eight thousand sailors, soldiers, and officials. Zheng's seven-masted flagship, more than four hundred feet long, was a marvel of Chinese nautical engineering. His fleet later became known as the "treasure ships" because of the cargoes of exotic goods and tribute they brought back from Southeast Asia, India, Arabia, and Africa. But Zheng's primary mission was political, not economic. Yongle, as we have seen, had a vision of world empire, in part borrowed from the Mongols, in which a multitude of princes would pay homage to Ming sovereignty. The constant flow of foreign embassies, the display of exotic tribute, and the emperor's pivotal role as arbitrator of disputes among lesser rulers were crucial to his sense of imperial dignity.

Departing in November of 1405, Zheng's fleet sailed first to Java in a show of force designed to intimidate Majapahit. He then traveled to Sumatra and Melaka and across the Indian Ocean to Ceylon and Calicut. No sooner had Zheng He returned to China in the

Renaissance A period of intense intellectual and artistic creativity in Europe, beginning in Italy in the fourteenth century as a revival of the classical civilization of ancient Greece and Rome.

humanism The study of the humanities (rhetoric, poetry, history, and moral philosophy), based on the works of ancient Greek and Roman writers, that provided the intellectual foundations for the Renaissance.

autumn of 1407 than Yongle dispatched him on another voyage. Yongle had recently launched his invasion of Vietnam, and the purpose of the second voyage was to curtail Ayudhya's aggression and establish a Chinese presence at strategic ports such as Melaka along the Straits of Sumatra. Altogether Yongle commissioned six expeditions under Zheng He's command. During the fourth and subsequent voyages, Zheng He sailed beyond India to Arabia and down the east coast of Africa.

The projection of Chinese power over the sea-lanes of maritime Asia led to far-reaching economic and political changes. The close relations Zheng He forged with rulers of port cities strengthened their political independence and promoted their commercial growth. Under the umbrella of Chinese protection, Melaka flourished as the great crossroads of Asian maritime trade.

The high cost of building and equipping the treasure ships depleted the Ming treasury, however, and after Yongle's death in 1424, Confucian ministers at the Ming court prevailed on his young successor to halt the naval expeditions. In 1430, Yongle's successor nonetheless overcame bureaucratic opposition and dispatched Zheng He on yet another voyage, his seventh. After traveling once again to Africa, Zheng died during his return home. With the passing of the renowned admiral, enthusiasm for the expeditions evaporated. Moreover, the Ming court faced a new threat: a resurgent Mongol confederation in the north. In 1449 a foolish young Ming emperor led a military campaign against the Mongols, only to be taken captive. The Ming court obtained the emperor's release by paying a huge ransom, but its strategic priorities had been completely transformed. Turning its back on the sea, the Ming state devoted its energies and revenues to rebuilding the Great Wall, much of which had crumbled to dust, as a defense against further Mongol attacks. The Great Wall that survives today was largely constructed by the Ming dynasty.

The Last of the Treasure Fleets

The shift in Chinese policy did not mean the end of Chinese involvement in maritime trade. Chinese merchants continued to pursue trading opportunities in defiance of the imperial ban on private overseas commerce. Even though Muslim merchants dominated Asian maritime commerce, Chinese merchant colonies dotted the coasts of Southeast Asia. Melaka's rulers converted to Islam but welcomed merchants from every corner of Asia. The population probably reached one hundred thousand before Melaka was sacked by the Portuguese in 1511. The Portuguese, like the Chinese before them, were drawn to Southeast Asian waters by the tremendous wealth created by maritime trade. Spurred by the growing European appetite for Asian spices, the violent intrusion of the Portuguese would transform the dynamics of maritime trade throughout Asia.

Commerce and Culture in the Renaissance

European expansion in the late fourteenth and early fifteenth centuries was preceded and influenced by a period of dramatic cultural change. The century after the outbreak of the Black Death marked the beginning of a sweeping transformation in European culture known as the **Renaissance**. In its narrow sense *Renaissance* (French for "rebirth") refers to the revival of ancient Greek and Roman philosophy, art, and literature that originated in fourteenth-century Italy. Scholars rediscovered classical learning and began to emulate the language and ideas of Greek and Roman philosophers and poets; these individuals became known as humanists, students of the liberal arts or humanities. The new intellectual movement of **humanism** combined classical learning with Christian piety and dedication to civic responsibilities.

At the same time the Renaissance inaugurated dramatic changes in the self-image and lifestyle of the wealthy. The new habits of luxurious living and magnificent display diverged sharply from the Christian ethic of frugality. Innovations in material culture and aesthetic values reflected crucial changes in the Italian economy and its relationship to the international trading world of the Mediterranean and beyond. These transformations in turn led to a reorientation of Europe away from Asia and toward the Atlantic world.

The Black Death had hit the Italian city-states especially hard. Some contemporary observers claimed that the pandemic had radically reshaped the social order. Although

Italy's Economic Transformation

artisan guilds became a powerful force in urban government for a time in Florence, Siena, and other cities, over the long term the patrician elite of wealthy merchants and landowners reasserted their oligarchic control. The rich became richer, and status and power were increasingly measured in visible signs of wealth.

Still, the economies of the Italian city-states underwent fundamental transformation. Diminishing profits from trade with the Islamic world prompted many Italian merchants to abandon commerce in favor of banking. Squeezed out of the eastern Mediterranean by the Turks and Venetians, Genoa turned its attention westward. Genoese bankers became financiers to the kings of Spain and Portugal and supplied the funds for their initial forays into the Atlantic in search of new routes to African gold and Asian spices. European monarchs' growing reliance on professional armies, naval fleets, and gunpowder weapons also stimulated demand for banking services, forcing them to borrow money to meet the rising costs of war.

Italy became the primary producer of luxury goods for Europe, displacing the Islamic world and Asia. Before 1400, Islamic craftsmanship had far surpassed that of Latin Christendom. The upper classes of Europe paid handsome sums to obtain silk and linen fabrics, ceramics, rugs, glass, metalwork, and jewelry imported from the Mamluk Empire. "The most beautiful things in the world are found in Damascus," wrote Simone Sigoli, a Florentine who visited the city in 1386. "Such rich and noble and delicate works of every kind that if you had money in the bone of your leg, without fail you would break it to buy these things. . . . Really, all Christendom could be supplied for a year with the merchandise of Damascus."[9] But the Black Death, Timur's invasions, and Mamluk mismanagement devastated industry and commerce in Egypt and Syria. According to a census of workshops in Alexandria recorded in 1434, the number of looms operating in the city had fallen to eight hundred, compared with fourteen thousand in 1395.

Seizing the opportunity these developments created, Italian entrepreneurs first imitated and then improved on Islamic techniques and designs for making silk, tin-glazed ceramics known as *maiolica* (my-OH-lee-kah), glass, and brassware. By 1450 these Italian products had become competitive with or eclipsed imports from Egypt and Syria. Italian firms captured the major share of the international market for luxury textiles and other finished goods, and the Islamic lands were reduced to being suppliers of raw materials such as silk, cotton, and dyestuffs.

A Culture of Consumption

Along with Italy's ascent in finance and manufacturing came a decisive shift in attitudes toward money and its use. The older Christian ethics of frugality and disdain for worldly gain gave way to prodigal spending and consumption. This new inclination for acquisition and display cannot be attributed simply to the spread of secular humanism. Indeed, much of this torrent of spending was lavished on religious art and artifacts, and the Roman papacy stood out as perhaps the most spendthrift of all. Displaying personal wealth and possessions affirmed social status and power. Civic pride and political rivalry fueled public spending to build and decorate churches and cathedrals. Rich townsmen transformed private homes into palaces, and artisans fashioned ordinary articles of everyday life—from rugs and furniture to dishes, books, and candlesticks—into works of art. Public piety blurred together with personal vanity. Spending money on religious monuments, wrote the fifteenth-century Florentine merchant Giovanni Rucellai (ROO-chel-lie) in his diary, gave him "the greatest satisfaction and the greatest pleasure, because it serves the glory of God, the honor of Florence, and my own memory."[10]

"Magnificence" became the watchword of the Renaissance. Wealthy merchants and members of the clergy portrayed themselves as patrons of culture and learning. Their private townhouses became new settings for refined social intercourse and conspicuous display. Magnificence implied the liberal spending and accumulation of possessions that advertised a person's virtue, taste, and place in society. "The magnificence of a building," the architect Leon Battista Alberti (1404–1472) declared, "should be adapted to the dignity of its owner."[11] Worldly goods gave tangible expression to spiritual refinement. The paintings of Madonnas and saints that graced Renaissance mansions were much more than objects of devotion: they were statements of cultural and social values. Thus, as with Islam in West Africa, changes in commerce and culture were closely linked. New commercial wealth created an expanded market for art, which was in turn shaped by the values associated with commerce.

Cultural Innovations

Again, as with Islam in West Africa, the intellectual ferment of the Renaissance was nurtured in an urban environment. Humanist scholars shunned the warrior culture of the old nobility while celebrating the civic roles and duties of townsmen, merchants, and clerics. Despite their admiration of classical civilization, the humanists did not reject Christianity. Rather, they sought to reconcile Christian faith and doctrines with classical learning. By making knowledge of Latin and Greek, history, poetry, and philosophy the mark of an educated person, the humanists transformed education and established models of schooling that would endure down to modern times.

Nowhere was the revolutionary impact of the Renaissance felt more deeply than in visual arts such as painting, sculpture, and architecture. Artists of the Renaissance exuded supreme confidence in the ability of human ingenuity to equal or even surpass the works of nature. The new outlook was exemplified by the development of the techniques of perspective, which artists used to convey a realistic, three-dimensional quality to physical forms, most notably the human body. Human invention also was capable of improving on nature by creating order and harmony through architecture and urban planning. Alberti advocated replacing the winding narrow streets and haphazard construction of medieval towns with planned cities organized around straight boulevards, open squares, and monumental buildings whose balanced proportions corresponded to a geometrically unified design.

Above all, the Renaissance transformed the idea of the artist. No longer mere manual tradesmen, artists now were seen as possessing a special kind of genius that enabled them to express a higher understanding of beauty. In the eyes of contemporaries, no one exemplified this quality of genius more than Leonardo da Vinci (1452–1519), who won renown as a painter, architect, sculptor, engineer, mathematician, and inventor. Leonardo's father, a Florentine lawyer, apprenticed him to a local painter at age eighteen. Leonardo spent much of his career as a civil and military engineer in the employ of the Duke of Milan, and developed ideas for flying machines, tanks, robots, and solar power that far exceeded the engineering capabilities of his time. Leonardo sought to apply his knowledge of natural science to painting, which he regarded as the most sublime art (see Seeing the Past: Leonardo da Vinci's *Virgin of the Rocks*).

The flowering of artistic creativity in the Renaissance was rooted in the rich soil of Italy's commercial wealth and nourished by the flow of goods from the Islamic world and Asia. International trade also invigorated industrial and craft production across maritime Asia and gave birth there to new patterns of material culture and consumption. In Japan, however, growing isolation from these cross-cultural interactions fostered the emergence of a national culture distinct from the Chinese traditions that dominated the rest of East Asia.

COUNTERPOINT
Age of the Samurai in Japan 1185–1450

In Japan as in Europe, the term *Middle Ages* brings to mind an age of warriors, a stratified society governed by bonds of loyalty between lords and vassals. In Japan, however, the militarization of the ruling class intensified during the fourteenth and fifteenth centuries, a time when the warrior nobility of Europe was crumbling. Paradoxically, the rise of the **samurai** (sah-moo-rye) ("those who serve") warriors as masters of their own estates was accompanied by the increasing independence of peasant communities.

In contrast to the regions explored earlier in this chapter, Japan became more isolated from the wider world during this era. Commercial and cultural exchanges with China reached a peak in the thirteenth century, but after the failed Mongol invasion of Japan in 1281, ties with continental Asia became increasingly frayed. Thus, many Japanese see this era as the period in which Japan's unique national identity—expressed most distinctly in the ethic of *bushidō* (boo-shee-doe), the "Way of the Warrior"—took its definitive form. Samurai warriors became the

FOCUS

How and why did the historical development of Japan in the fourteenth and fifteenth centuries differ from that of mainland Eurasia?

samurai Literally, "those who serve"; the hereditary warriors who dominated Japanese society and culture from the twelfth to the nineteenth centuries.

Leonardo da Vinci's *Virgin of the Rocks*

Virgin of the Rocks, c. 1483–1486
(Erich Lessing/Art Resource.)

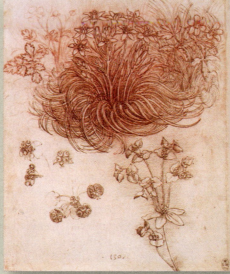

Leonardo's Botanical Studies with Star-of-Bethlehem, Grasses, Crowfoot, Wood Anemone, and Another Genus,
c. 1500–1506 (The Royal Collection © 2011 Her Majesty Queen Elizabeth II/Bridgeman Art Library.)

the menacing darkness of the cavern; desire to see if there was any marvelous thing within."[1]

Fantastic as the scene might seem, Leonardo's meticulous renderings of rocks and plants were based on close observation of nature. The Star of Bethlehem flowers at the lower left of the painting, symbolizing purity and atonement, also appear in the nearly contemporaneous botanical drawing shown here. Geologists have praised Leonardo's highly realistic sandstone rock formations and his precise placement of plants where they would most likely take root.

Masterpieces such as the *Virgin of the Rocks* display Leonardo's careful study of human anatomy, natural landscapes, and botany. Although he admired the perfection of nature, Leonardo also celebrated the human mind's rational and aesthetic capacities, declaring that "we by our arts may be called the grandsons of God."[2]

While living in Milan in the early 1480s, Leonardo accepted a commission to paint an altarpiece for the chapel of Milan's Confraternity of the Immaculate Conception, a branch of the Franciscan order. Leonardo's relationship with the friars proved to be stormy. His first version of the painting (now in the Louvre), reproduced here, apparently displeased his patrons and was sold to another party. Only after a fifteen-year-long dispute over the price did Leonardo finally deliver a modified version in 1508.

In portraying the legendary encounter between the child Jesus and the equally young John the Baptist during the flight to Egypt, Leonardo replaced the traditional desert setting with a landscape filled with rocks, plants, and water. Leonardo's dark grotto creates an aura of mystery and foreboding, from which the figures of Mary, Jesus, John, and the angel Uriel emerge as if in a vision. A few years before, Leonardo had written about "coming to the entrance of a great cavern, in front of which I stood for some time, stupefied and uncomprehending. . . . Suddenly two things arose in me, fear and desire: fear of

1. Arundel ms. (British Library), p. 115 recto, cited in Martin Kemp, *Leonardo da Vinci: The Marvelous Works of Nature and Man* (Oxford: Oxford University Press, 2006), 78.
2. John Paul Richter, ed., *The Notebooks of Leonardo da Vinci* (rpt. of 1883 ed.; New York: Dover, 1970), Book IX, 328 (para. 654).

EXAMINING THE EVIDENCE

1. How does Leonardo express the connection between John (at left) and Jesus through position, gesture, and their relationships with the figures of Mary and the angel Uriel?

2. The friars who commissioned the painting sought to celebrate the sanctity and purity of their patron, the Virgin Mary. Does this painting achieve that effect?

patrons of new forms of cultural expression whose character differed markedly from the Chinese traditions cherished by the old Japanese nobility. A culture based on warriors, rather than Confucian scholars, created a different path for the development of Japanese society.

"The Low Overturning the High"

During the Kamakura period (1185–1333), the power of the **shogun**, or military ruler, of eastern Japan was roughly in balance with that of the imperial court and nobility at Kyoto in the west. Warriors dominated both the shogun's capital at Kamakura (near modern Tokyo) and provincial governorships, but most of the land remained in the possession of the imperial family, the nobility, and religious institutions based in Kyoto. The shoguns appointed low-ranking samurai among their retainers to serve as military stewards on local estates, with responsibility for keeping the peace.

After the collapse of the Kamakura government in 1333, Japan was wracked by civil wars. In 1336 a new dynasty of shoguns, the Ashikaga (ah-shee-KAH-gah), came to power in Kyoto. Unlike the Kamakura shoguns, the Ashikaga aspired to become national rulers. Yet not until 1392 did the Ashikaga shogunate gain uncontested political supremacy, and even then it exercised only limited control over the provinces and local samurai.

In the Kamakura period, the samurai had been vassals subordinated to warrior clans to whom they owed allegiance and service. But wartime disorder and Ashikaga rule eroded the privileges and power of the noble and monastic landowners. Most of their estates fell into the hands of local samurai families, who formed alliances known as *ikki* ("single resolve") to preserve order. The *ikki* brotherhoods signed pacts pledging common arbitration of disputes, joint management of local shrines and festivals, and mutual aid against outside aggressors.

Rise of the Samurai

Just as samurai were turning themselves into landowners, peasants banded together in village associations to resist demands for rents and labor service from their new samurai overlords. These village associations began to assert a right to self-government, claiming legal powers formerly held by the noble estate owners.

Like the *ikki* leagues, villages and districts created their own autonomous governments. Their charters expressed resistance to outside control while requiring strict conformity to the collective will of the community. As one village council declared, "Treachery, malicious gossip, or criminal acts against the village association will be punished by excommunication from the estate."[12] Outraged lords bewailed this reversal of the social hierarchy, "the low overturning the high," but found themselves powerless to check the growing independence of peasant communities.

The political strength of the peasants reflected their rising economic fortunes. Japan's agrarian economy improved substantially with the expansion of irrigated rice farming. The village displaced the manorial estate as the basic institution of rural society. Rural traders, mostly drawn from the affluent peasantry, formed merchant guilds and obtained commercial privileges from local authorities. Japan in the fifteenth century had little involvement in foreign trade, and there were few cities apart from the metropolis of Kyoto, which had swelled to 150,000 inhabitants by mid-century. Yet the prosperity of the agrarian economy generated considerable growth in artisan crafts and trade in local goods.

Japan, 1185–1392

The New Warrior Order

After the founding of the Ashikaga shogunate, provincial samurai swarmed the streets of Kyoto seeking the new rulers' patronage. Their reckless conduct prompted the shoguns to issue regulations forbidding samurai to possess silver swords, wear fine silk clothing, gamble, stage tea-drinking competitions, and consort with loose women—to little effect. In this world of "the low overturning the high," warriors enjoyed newfound wealth while much of the old nobility was reduced to abject poverty.

shogun The military commander who effectively exercised supreme political and military authority over Japan during the Kamakura (1185–1333), Ashikaga (1338–1573), and Tokugawa (1603–1868) shogunates.

Night Attack on the Sanjo Palace
The Heiji Revolt of 1159 marked a key turning point in the shift from aristocratic to warrior rule in Japan. This scene from a thirteenth-century scroll painting depicts the samurai rebels storming the imperial palace and taking the emperor hostage. Although the leaders of the insurrection were captured and executed, the revolt plunged Japan into civil wars that ended only when the Kamakura shogun seized power in 1185. (Werner Forman/Art Resource.)

**Cultural and Social Life
of the Samurai**

While derided by courtiers as uneducated and boorish, the shoguns and samurai became patrons of artists and cultural life. The breakdown of the traditional social hierarchy allowed greater intermingling among people from diverse backgrounds. By the early fifteenth century the outlandish antics of the capital's samurai had been tempered by a new sense of elegance and refinement. The social and cultural worlds of the warriors and courtiers merged, producing new forms of social behavior and artistic expression.

In the early years of the Ashikaga shogunate, the capital remained infatuated with Chinese culture. As the fourteenth century wore on, however, this fascination with China was eclipsed by new fashions drawn from both the court nobility and Kyoto's lively world of popular entertainments. Accomplishment in poetry and graceful language and manners, hallmarks of the courtier class, became part of samurai self-identity as well. A new mood of simplicity and restraint took hold, infused with the ascetic ethics of Zen Buddhism, which stressed introspective meditation as the path to enlightenment.

The sensibility of the Ashikaga age was visible in new kinds of artistic display and performance, including poetry recitation, flower arrangement, and the complex rituals of the tea ceremony. A new style of theater known as *nō* reflected this fusion of courtly refinement, Zen religious sentiments, and samurai cultural tastes. The lyrical language and stylized dances of *nō* performances portrayed samurai as men of feeling rather than ferocious warriors. Thus, the rise of warrior culture in Japan did not mean an end to sophistication and refinement. It did, however, involve a strong focus on cultural elements that were seen as distinctly Japanese.

In at least one area, developments in Japan mirrored those in other parts of the world. The warriors' dominance over Ashikaga society and culture led to a decisive shift toward patriarchal authority. Women lost rights of inheritance as warrior houses consolidated landholdings in the hands of one son who would continue the family line. Marriage and sexual conduct were subject to stricter regulation. The libertine sexual mores of the Japanese aristocracy depicted in Lady Murasaki's *Tale of Genji* (c. 1010) gave way to a new emphasis on female chastity as an index of social order. The profuse output of novels, memoirs, and diaries written by court women also came to an end by 1350. Aristocratic women continued to hold positions of responsibility at court, but their literary talents were devoted to keeping official records rather than expressing their personal thoughts.

By 1400, then, the samurai had achieved political mastery in both the capital and the countryside and had eclipsed the old nobility as arbiters of cultural values. This warrior culture, which combined martial prowess with austere aesthetic tastes, stood in sharp contrast to the veneration of Confucian learning by the Chinese literati and the classical ideals and ostentatious consumption prized by the urban elite of Renaissance Italy.

Conclusion

The fourteenth century was an age of crisis across Eurasia and Africa. The population losses resulting from the Black Death devastated Christian and Muslim societies and economies. In the long run Latin Christendom fared well: the institution of serfdom largely disappeared from western Europe; new entrepreneurial energies were released; and the Italian city-states recovered their commercial vigor and stimulated economic revival in northern Europe. However, the once-great Byzantine Empire succumbed to the expanding Ottoman Empire and, under fire by Urban's cannon, came to an end in 1453. Although the Ottoman conquest of the Balkan peninsula threatened Latin Christendom, the central Islamic lands, from Egypt to Mesopotamia, never regained their former economic vitality. Still, the Muslim faith continued to spread, winning new converts in Africa, Central Asia, and Southeast Asia.

The fourteenth century also witnessed the collapse of the Mongol empires in China and Iran, followed by the rise and fall of the last of the Mongol empires, that of Timur. In China, the Ming dynasty spurned the Mongol vision of a multinational empire, instead returning to an imperial order based on an agrarian economy, bureaucratic rule, and Neo-Confucian values. New dynastic leaders in Korea and Vietnam imitated the Ming model, but in Japan the rising samurai warrior class forged a radically different set of social institutions and cultural values.

The Black Death redirected the course of European state-making. Monarchs strengthened their authority, aided by advances in military technology, mercenary armies, and fresh sources of revenue. The intensifying competition among national states would become one of the main motives for overseas exploration and expansion in the Atlantic world. At the same time, the great transformation in culture, lifestyles, and values known as the Renaissance sprang from the ruin of the Black Death. But the Renaissance was not purely an intellectual and artistic phenomenon. Its cultural innovations were linked to crucial changes in the Italian economy and the international trading world of the Mediterranean and beyond.

Asia was largely spared the ravages of the Black Death pandemic. Maritime Asia, from China to the east coast of Africa, enjoyed a robust boom in trade during the fifteenth century, in contrast to the sluggish economic recovery in much of Europe and the Islamic world. The intrusion of the Portuguese into the Indian Ocean in 1498 would upset the balance of political and economic power throughout Asian waters and dramatically alter Asia's place in what became the first truly global economy. But the arrival of the Europeans would have far more catastrophic effects on the societies of the Americas, which were unprepared for the political and economic challenges—and especially the onslaught of epidemic disease—that followed Columbus's landing in the Caribbean islands in 1492.

NOTES

1. Giovanni Boccaccio, *The Decameron* (New York: Modern Library, 1931), 8–9.
2. Quoted in Adel Allouche, *Mamluk Economics: A Study and Translation of Al-Maqrizi's* Ighathah (Salt Lake City: University of Utah Press, 1994), 75–76 (translation slightly modified).
3. Quoted in Michael W. Dols, "Ibn al-Wardi's *Risalah al-naba' 'an al'waba'*: A Translation of a Major Source for the History of the Black Death in the Middle East," in *Near Eastern Numismatics, Iconography, Epigraphy and History: Studies in Honor of George C. Miles*, ed. Dickran K. Kouymjian (Beirut, Lebanon: American University of Beirut, 1974), 454.
4. *Anonimalle Chronicle*, in *The Peasants' Revolt of 1381*, ed. R. B. Dobson (London: Macmillan, 1970), 164–165.
5. Ibn Battuta, "The Sultan of Mali," in *Corpus of Early Arabic Sources for West African History*, trans. J. F. P. Hopkins, ed. N. Levtzion and J. F. P. Hopkins (Cambridge, U.K.: Cambridge University Press, 1981), 296.
6. Leo Africanus, *History and Description of Africa*, trans. John Poy (London: Hakluyt Society, 1896), 3:825.
7. Shihab al-Din Ahmad ibn Majid, "Al'Mal'aqiya," in *A Study of the Arabic Texts Containing Material of South-East Asia*, ed. and trans. G. R. Tibbetts (Leiden, Netherlands: Brill, 1979), 206.

8. Ibn Battuta, *Travels in Asia and Africa, 1325–1354*, trans. H. A. R. Gibb (London: Routledge & Kegan Paul, 1929), 235.

9. Simone Sigoli, "Pilgrimage of Simone Sigoli to the Holy Land," in *Visit to the Holy Places of Egypt, Sinai, Palestine and Syria in 1384 by Frescobaldi, Gucci, and Sigoli*, trans. Theophilus Bellorini and Eugene Hoade (Jerusalem: Franciscan Press, 1948), 182.

10. Quoted in Lisa Jardine, *Worldly Goods: A New History of the Renaissance* (New York: Doubleday, 1996), 126.

11. Quoted in Richard A. Goldthwaite, *Wealth and the Demand for Art in Italy, 1300–1600* (Baltimore: Johns Hopkins University Press, 1993), 220.

12. Declaration of Oshima and Okitsushima shrine association, dated 1298, quoted in Pierre François Souyri, *The World Turned Upside Down: Medieval Japanese Society* (New York: Columbia University Press, 2001), 136.

RESOURCES FOR RESEARCH

Fourteenth-Century Crisis and Renewal in Eurasia

William McNeill's landmark work drew attention to the profound impact of epidemic diseases on world history. The exact cause of the Black Death remains a subject of debate, as the works of Cantor and Herlihy show, but few dispute that the pandemic had lasting consequences for European history. The influence of the Black Death in the Islamic world is less well studied, but Borsch's recent study seeks to explain why the economic depression it caused lasted longer in Egypt than in Europe.

Borsch, Stuart J. *The Black Death in Egypt and England: A Comparative Study*. 2005.

British History in Depth: The Black Death. http://www.bbc.co.uk/history/british/middle_ages/black_01.shtml

Brook, Timothy. *The Confusions of Pleasure: Commerce and Culture in Ming China*. 1998.

Cantor, Norman. *In the Wake of the Plague: The Black Death and the World It Made*. 2001.

Herlihy, David. *The Black Death and the Transformation of the West*. 1997.

McNeill, William H. *Plagues and Peoples*. 1976.

Islam's New Frontiers

The study of Islam in Africa has advanced rapidly in recent years. Robinson serves as a good overview; the essays in Levtzion and Pouwells provide comprehensive regional coverage. Imber provides the best introduction to the early history of the Ottoman Empire.

Dunn, Ross E. *The Adventures of Ibn Battuta: A Muslim Traveler of the 14th Century*. 1989.

Imber, Colin. *The Ottoman Empire, 1300–1650: The Structure of Power*, 2d ed. 2009.

Levtzion, Nehemia, and Randall L. Pouwells, eds. *The History of Islam in Africa*. 2000.

Manz, Beatrice Forbes. *The Rise and Rule of Tamerlane*. 1989.

Robinson, David. *Muslim Societies in African History*. 2004.

The Global Bazaar

New scholarship has erased the older image of this period as "the Dark Ages." The original understanding of the Renaissance as an intellectual and artistic movement centered in Italy has been broadened to include transformative changes in trade, industry, material culture, and lifestyles. Similarly, accounts of voyages of Zheng He—lucidly described by Levathes—have opened a window on the vigorous cultural and economic interchange across Asia; Reid examines this topic in greater detail.

Burke, Peter. *The European Renaissance: Centres and Peripheries*. 1998.

Finlay, Robert. *The Pilgrim Art: Cultures of Porcelain in World History*. 2010.

Goldthwaite, Richard A. *Wealth and the Demand for Art in Italy, 1300–1600*. 1993.

Jardine, Lisa. *Worldly Goods: A New History of the Renaissance*. 1996.

Levathes, Louise. *When China Ruled the Seas: The Treasure Fleet of the Dragon Throne, 1405–1433*. 1994.

Reid, Anthony. *Southeast Asia in the Age of Commerce, 1350–1750*. Vol. 1, *The Land Below the Winds*; Vol. 2, *Expansion and Crisis*. 1989, 1993.

COUNTERPOINT: Age of the Samurai in Japan, 1185–1450

Recent years have seen a wave of revisionist scholarship on medieval Japan. Souyri's work stands out for its finely detailed depiction of social diversity. *Tale of the Heike*, an account of the struggle between warlords that led to the founding of the Kamakura shogunate, provides a sharp contrast to earlier courtly literature such as Lady Murasaki's *Tale of Genji*.

Adolphson, Mikael S. *The Gates of Power: Monks, Courtiers, and Warriors in Premodern Japan*. 2000.

Mass, Jeffrey P., ed. *The Origins of Japan's Medieval World: Courtiers, Clerics, Warriors, and Peasants in the Fourteenth Century*. 1997.

McCullough, Helen Craig, trans. *Tale of the Heike*. 1988.

Souyri, Pierre-François. *The World Turned Upside Down: Medieval Japanese Society*. 2001.

Wakita, Haruko. *Women in Medieval Japan: Motherhood, Household Economy, and Sexuality*. 2006.

▶ **For additional primary sources from this period**, see *Sources of Crossroads and Cultures*.

▶ **For Web sites, images, and documents related to topics in this chapter**, see Make History at bedfordstmartins.com/smith.

The major global development in this chapter ▶ Crisis and recovery in fourteenth- and fifteenth-century Afro-Eurasia.

IMPORTANT EVENTS

1315–1317	Great Famine in northern Europe
1325–1354	Travels of Ibn Battuta in Asia and Africa
1336–1573	Ashikaga shogunate in Japan
1337–1453	Hundred Years' War between England and France
1347–1350	Outbreak of the Black Death in Europe and the Islamic Mediterranean
c. 1351–1782	Ayudhya kingdom in Thailand
1368–1644	Ming dynasty in China
1378	Ciompi uprising in Florence
1381	Peasant Revolt in England
1392–1910	Yi dynasty in Korea
1405	Death of Timur; breakup of his empire into regional states in Iran and Central Asia
1405–1433	Chinese admiral Zheng He's expeditions in Southeast Asia and the Indian Ocean
1421	Relocation of Ming capital from Nanjing to Beijing
1428–1788	Le dynasty in Vietnam
1453	Ottoman conquest of Constantinople marks fall of the Byzantine Empire

KEY TERMS

Black Death (p. 478) pandemic (p. 478)
humanism (p. 498) Renaissance (p. 498)
janissary corps (p. 489) samurai (p. 501)
Little Ice Age (p. 479) shogun (p. 503)
Neo-Confucianism Sufism (p. 488)
  (p. 486) theocracy (p. 489)
oligarchy (p. 483) trade diaspora (p. 492)

CHAPTER OVERVIEW QUESTIONS

1. How and why did Europe's economic growth begin to surpass that of the Islamic world in the century after the Black Death?

2. Did the economic revival across Eurasia after 1350 benefit the peasant populations of Europe, the Islamic world, and East Asia?

3. How did the process of conversion to Islam differ in Iran, the Ottoman Empire, West Africa, and Southeast Asia during this period?

4. What political and economic changes contributed to the rise of maritime commerce in Asia during the fourteenth and fifteenth centuries?

SECTION FOCUS QUESTIONS

1. How did the Black Death affect society, the economy, and culture in Latin Christendom and the Islamic world?

2. Why did Islam expand dramatically in the fourteenth and fifteenth centuries, and how did new Islamic societies differ from established ones?

3. What were the principal sources of growth in international trade during the fourteenth and fifteenth centuries, and how did this trade affect patterns of consumption and fashion tastes?

4. How and why did the historical development of Japan in the fourteenth and fifteenth centuries differ from that of mainland Eurasia?

MAKING CONNECTIONS

1. What social, economic, and technological changes strengthened the power of European monarchs during the century after the Black Death?

2. How and why did the major routes and commodities of trans-Eurasian trade change after the collapse of the Mongol empires in Central Asia?

3. In what ways did the motives for conversion to Islam differ in Central Asia, sub-Saharan Africa, and the Indian Ocean during this era?

4. In this period, why did the power and status of the samurai warriors in Japan rise while those of the warrior nobility in Europe declined?

PART 3

The Early Modern World

1450–1750

CH 16

CH 17

MAJOR GLOBAL CHANGES occurred between 1450 and 1750, as regional societies gave way to multiethnic empires, and horse-borne raiders gave way to cannon and long-distance sailing craft. Historians call this era "early modern" because it was marked by a general shift toward centralized, bureaucratic, monetized, and technologically sophisticated states. Yet nearly all of these "modern" states also clung to divine kingship and other remnants of the previous age, and most sought to revive and propagate older religious or philosophical traditions. Some states embraced mutual tolerance, but many others fought bitterly over matters of faith.

One of the most striking breaks with the past was the creation of new linkages between distant regions, most notably the Americas and the rest of the world. Early globalization accelerated changes in everything from demography to commerce to technology, allowing populations to grow and many individuals to get rich. Yet globalization also enabled the spread of disease, and some technical innovations increased the scale and deadliness of warfare; early modernity did not promise longer and better lives for everyone. The shift to modernity was not a uniquely Western phenomenon either, although western Europeans were key players in its spread, usually as traders, missionaries, or conquerors.

Beginning in around 1450, Iberians—the people of Spain and Portugal—used new ships and guns to venture into the Atlantic, where they competed in overseas colonization, trade, and conquest. They set out to claim new territories for their monarchs and to spread their Roman Catholic faith. They did both at the expense of many millions of native peoples, first in Africa and the East Atlantic and then throughout the Americas and beyond. Wherever they went, Iberians moved quickly from plunder to the creation of settled colonies, creating a new trading sphere that historians call the "Atlantic world." Other Europeans soon followed in the Iberians' wake, but the silver of Spanish America became the world's money.

Modernity affected Africa most deeply via the slave trade. The older flow of captive workers to the Muslim Middle East and Indian Ocean basin continued well into early modern times, but it was soon overshadowed by a more urgent European demand in the Atlantic. This desire for slaves to staff distant plantations and mines fueled

CH 18

existing antagonisms within Africa even as it spawned new ones, each generating captives and refugees to be traded abroad for select commodities, including firearms, textiles, and metal ware. Europeans did not penetrate, much less conquer, sub-Saharan Africa at this time, however, in part due to their general lack of resistance to tropical disease.

In the vast Indian Ocean basin a freer model of interaction and integration developed. Islamic merchants had come to dominate these seas by 1450, not through imperial means but rather by establishing trading networks from East Africa to Southeast Asia. Luxury products from the African interior were traded abroad for spices, cloth, porcelain, and other compact valuables. Ships also carried bulk commodities and religious pilgrims. After 1500, European interlopers discovered that in such a thriving, diverse, and politically decentralized region, they would have to compete fiercely for space. This they did, first by establishing coastal trading forts, then by moving inland.

On the Eurasian mainland, with the aid of modern firearms, powerful Ottoman, Russian, Safavid, and Mughal leaders turned from regional consolidation to massive imperial expansion by the sixteenth century. Each combined religious fervor with considerable political ambitions, but several of these states, notably the Ottomans and Mughals, embraced religious diversity. Collecting tributes in cash and establishing the appropriate bureaucracies to collect them were shared objectives. Unlike the Safavids and Mughals, the Ottomans sought to extend their empire overseas, taking on Venice and the Habsburgs in the Mediterranean and the Portuguese in the Indian Ocean. Russia would venture abroad under Peter the Great.

Europe remained mostly embroiled in religious and political conflict. The religious schism known as the Protestant Reformation touched off over a century of bloody war after 1500, and doctrinal disputes would carry on well into modern times. Warfare itself was transformed from knightly contests and town sieges to mass infantry mobilization and bombardment of strategic fortresses. These models would be exported, along with armed sailing ships. Europe's political fractures enabled the rise of market economies as well, with more states sponsoring overseas colonizing ventures

CH 19

over time to augment their share of business. New forms of government emerged, and also a marked tendency to question ancient authorities. From this came a revolution in science, emphasizing physical observation and secular reasoning, and at the end of the early modern period, a new intellectual movement known as the Enlightenment.

In East Asia, by contrast, introversion rather than foreign engagement was the rule in early modern times. Although both China and Japan had strong seafaring traditions by 1450, state policies from the fifteenth to sixteenth centuries gradually discouraged external affairs. Despite official isolation, both regions proved to be extraordinarily dynamic. Political consolidation and population growth were matched with a general shift from tributary to money economies. In the Chinese Ming and Qing empires this led to a massive rise in demand for silver, stimulating global circulation of this mostly American-produced metal. Porcelain and silk, much of it produced by poor women working in the household, were sent abroad in exchange. With the patronage of newly wealthy merchants and bureaucrats, the arts flourished on a scale not seen before.

By 1700, the American colonies were not the neo-Europes their first colonizers had envisioned. Centuries of ethnic and cultural mixture, forced labor regimes, frontier expansion, and export-oriented economies all led to the formation of distinct societies. Native populations were recovering in some areas, and African and African-descended populations had grown to dominate whole regions. Europeans continued to migrate to the colonies in search of new livelihoods, but most soon adopted the nativist attitudes of earlier colonizers. In much of the Americas, the different outlooks of European colonizers and colonists would prove irreconcilable by the end of the early modern era.

CH 21

	1400		1500	
Americas	1325–1521 Aztec Empire	1430–1532 Inca Empire ▪ Columbus reaches the Americas 1492 ▪ Portuguese reach Brazil 1500 ▪	Spanish conquest of Aztecs 1519–1521 ▪ Spanish conquest of Inca 1532–1536	Discovery of silver at Potosí 1545 ▪
Europe		1462–1505 Ivan III unites Russia Christian reconquest of Spain completed 1492 ▪ 1473–1543 Copernicus	▪ 1517 Luther confronts Catholic Church, sparking the Protestant Reformation	
Middle East		▪ 1453 Ottoman conquest of Constantinople	Ottoman conquest of Egypt 1517 ▪ 1520–1566 Reign of Suleiman the Magnificent	Battle of Lepanto 1571
Africa	First sub-Saharan Africans captured and taken to Portugal 1441 ▪	▪ 1450 Height of kingdom of Benin 1464–1492 Reign of Songhai emperor Sunni Ali	1506–1543 Reign of Afonso I of Kongo	
Asia and Oceania	1405–1433 Voyages of Ming admiral Zheng He ▪ 1421 Relocation of Ming capital to Beijing 1428–1788 Vietnamese Le dynasty		▪ 1498 Vasco da Gama reaches India Portuguese establish fort in Ceylon 1517 ▪	

Despite these profound transformations, many people remained largely unaffected by the currents of early modernity. Though not densely populated, most of North and South America, Polynesia, Oceania, central and southern Africa, and highland Asia remained beyond the zone of sustained contact with foreigners. New commodities and biological transfers were only beginning to be felt in many of these places at the end of the early modern period. As a result of their long isolation, inhabitants of these regions would be among the most drastically affected by modernity's next wave.

CH 22

1600	1700	1800

- **1625** Dutch settle New Amsterdam; English establish colony on Barbados
- **1607** English establish colony at Jamestown, Virginia
- **1608** French establish colony at Quebec City
- **1695–1800** Brazil's "gold rush"
- **1763** Rio de Janeiro becomes capital of Brazil

1588 English defeat Spanish Armada
1618–1648 Thirty Years' War
1643–1715 Reign of Louis XIV
1600 English East India Company founded
1642–1727 Newton
1688 England's Glorious Revolution
1712–1714 War of the Spanish Succession
1712 Peter the Great founds St. Petersburg
1700–1800 The Enlightenment

1600–1629 Peak of Safavid Empire
Last Ottoman siege at Vienna defeated **1683**
1722 Fall of Safavid Empire
1736–1747 Nadir Shah reunites Iran

1591 Moroccan raiders conquer Songhai Empire
1624–1663 Reign of Queen Nzinga in Ndongo
1638–1641 Dutch seize São Jorge da Mina and Luanda
1680s Rise of kingdom of Asante
1720s Rise of kingdom of Dahomey
1750–1800 Height of Atlantic slave trade

1602–1867 Tokugawa Shogunate
1644 Manchu invasion of Beijing; Ming Empire replaced by Qing
1500–1763 Mughal Empire
1736–1799 Reign of Qing emperor Qianlong
1751 Qing annexation of Tibet

16

AT A CROSSROADS ▲

Perched on a granite ridge high above Peru's Urubamba River, the Inca site of Machu Picchu continues to draw thousands of visitors each year. First thought to be the lost city of Vilcabamba, then a convent for Inca nuns, Machu Picchu is now believed to have been a mid-fifteenth-century palace built for the Inca emperor and his mummy cult. It was probably more a religious site than a place of rest and recreation. (The Art Archive/Gianni Dagli Orti.)

Empires and Alternatives in the Americas

1430–1530

In 1995, American archaeologist Johan Reinhard and his assistants discovered a tomb atop Mount Ampato, a peak overlooking the Peruvian city of Arequipa. Inside were the naturally mummified remains of a fourteen-year-old girl placed there some five hundred years earlier. Material and written evidence suggests she was an *aclla* (AHK-yah), or "chosen woman," selected by Inca priests from among hundreds of regional headmen's daughters. Most aclla girls became priestesses in temples and palaces dedicated to the Inca emperor or the imperial sun cult. Others became the emperor's concubines or wives. Only the most select, like the girl discovered on Mount Ampato, were chosen for the "debt-payment" sacrifice, or *capacocha* (kah-pah-KOH-chah), said to be the greatest honor of all.

According to testimonies collected soon after the Spanish conquest of the Incas in 1532 (discussed in the next chapter), the capacocha sacrifice was a rare and deeply significant event preceded by numerous rituals. First, the victim, chosen for her (and rarely, his) physical perfection, trekked to Cuzco, the Inca capital, to be feasted and blessed. The child's father brought gifts and sacred objects from his province and in turn received fine textiles from the emperor. Following an ancient Andean tradition, reciprocal ties between ruler and ruled were reinforced through such acts of ritualized gift exchange, feasting, and finally, sacrifice. The girl, too, received fine alpaca and cotton skirts and shawls, along with tiny gold and silver votive objects, a necklace of shell beads, and tufts of tropical bird feathers. These items adorned her in her tomb, reached after a long journey on foot from Cuzco.

As suggested by later discoveries in Chile and Argentina, at tomb-side the aclla girl was probably given a beaker filled with beer brewed from maize. In a pouch she carried coca leaves. The sacred coca, chewed throughout the Andes, helped fend off the headaches

BACKSTORY

By the fifteenth century, the Americas had witnessed the rise and fall of numerous empires and kingdoms, including the classic Maya of Mesoamerica, the wealthy Sicán kingdom of Peru's desert coast, and the Cahokia mound builders of the Mississippi Basin. Just as these cultures faded, there emerged two new imperial states that borrowed heavily from their predecessors. The empires treated in this chapter, the Aztec and Inca, were the largest states ever to develop in the Americas, yet they were not all-powerful. About half of all native Americans, among them the diverse peoples of North America's eastern woodlands, lived outside their realms.

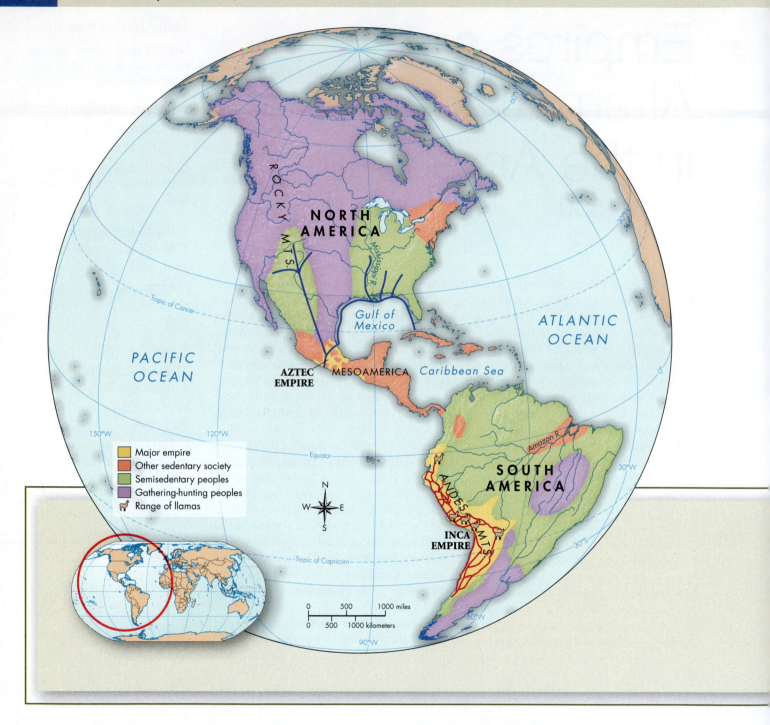

Major empire
Other sedentary society
Semisedentary peoples
Gathering-hunting peoples
Range of llamas

c. 900–1600 Late Woodland period of dispersed farming and hunting

c. 1100 Aztecs leave Aztlán

c. 1200 Incas move into Cuzco region

| 900 | 1000 | 1100 | 1200 |

and nausea brought on by oxygen starvation at high altitude, whereas the maize beer induced sleepiness. Barely conscious of her surroundings, the girl was lowered into her grass-lined grave, and, according to the forensic anthropologists who examined her skull, struck dead with a club. Other Inca sacrificial victims appear to have been buried alive and left to freeze to death, as described in postconquest accounts.

Why did the Incas sacrifice children, and why in these ways? By combining material, written, and oral evidence, scholars are beginning to solve the riddle of the Inca mountain mummies. From what is now known, it appears that death, fertility, reciprocity, and imperial links to sacred landscapes were all features of the capacocha sacrifice. Although macabre practices such as this may challenge our ability to empathize with the leaders, if not the common folk, of this distant culture, with each new fact we learn about the child mummies, the closer we get to understanding the Inca Empire and its ruling cosmology.

The Incas and their subjects shared the belief that death occurred as a process rather than in an instant, and that proper death led to an elevated state of consciousness. In this altered state a person could communicate with deities directly, and in a sense join them. If the remains of such a person were carefully preserved and honored, they could act as an oracle, a conduit to the sacred realms above and below the earth. Mountains, as sources of springs and rivers, and sometimes fertilizing volcanic ash, held particular spiritual significance.

In part, it was this complex of beliefs about landscape, death, and the afterlife that led the Incas to mummify and otherwise preserve respected ancestors, including their emperors, and to bury chosen young people atop mountains that marked the edges, or heights, of empire. Physically perfect noble children such as the girl found on Mount Ampato were thus selected for the role of communicants with the spirit world. Their sacrifice unified the dead, the living, and the sacred mountains, and also bound together a far-flung empire that was in many ways as fragile as life itself.[1]

MAPPING THE WORLD

The Western Hemisphere, c. 1500

Native Americans inhabited the entire Western Hemisphere from the Arctic Circle to the tip of South America. Their societies varied tremendously in density and political sophistication, largely as a result of adaptation to different natural environments. Empires were found only in the tropical highlands of Mesoamerica and the Andes, but large chiefdoms based on farming could be found in eastern Canada, the bigger Caribbean islands, and the lower Amazon Basin. Gatherer-hunters were the most widespread of all native American cultures, and despite their relatively small numbers they proved most resistant to conquest by settled neighbors.

ROUTES ▼

— Inca road
— Other trade route

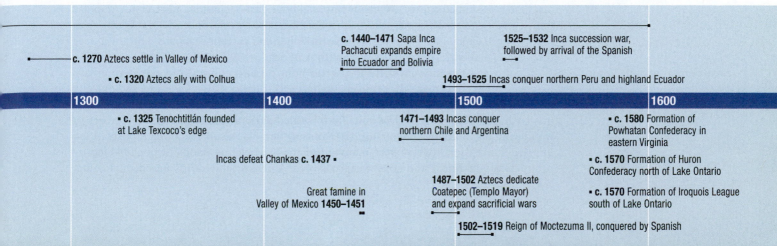

c. 1270 Aztecs settle in Valley of Mexico

▪ c. 1320 Aztecs ally with Colhua

c. 1440–1471 Sapa Inca Pachacuti expands empire into Ecuador and Bolivia

1525–1532 Inca succession war, followed by arrival of the Spanish

1493–1525 Incas conquer northern Peru and highland Ecuador

1300	1400	1500	1600

▪ c. 1325 Tenochtitlán founded at Lake Texcoco's edge

1471–1493 Incas conquer northern Chile and Argentina

▪ c. 1580 Formation of Powhatan Confederacy in eastern Virginia

Incas defeat Chankas c. 1437 ▪

▪ c. 1570 Formation of Huron Confederacy north of Lake Ontario

Great famine in Valley of Mexico 1450–1451

1487–1502 Aztecs dedicate Coatepec (Templo Mayor) and expand sacrificial wars

▪ c. 1570 Formation of Iroquois League south of Lake Ontario

1502–1519 Reign of Moctezuma II, conquered by Spanish

But this fragility was not evident to the people gathered at the capacocha sacrifice. By about 1480, more than half of all native Americans were subjects of two great empires, the Aztec in Mexico and Central America and the Inca in South America. In part by drawing on ancient religious and political traditions, both empires excelled at subduing neighboring chiefdoms through a mix of violence, forced relocation, religious indoctrination, and marriage alliances. Both empires demanded allegiance in the form of tribute. Both the Aztecs and Incas were greatly feared by their many millions of subjects. Perhaps surprisingly, these last great native American states would prove far more vulnerable to European invaders than their nonimperial neighbors, most of whom were gatherer-hunters and semisedentary villagers. Those who relied least on farming had the best chance of getting away.

OVERVIEW QUESTIONS

The major global development in this chapter: The diversity of societies and states in the Americas prior to European invasion.

As you read, consider:

1. In what ways was cultural diversity in the Americas related to environmental diversity?

2. Why was it in Mesoamerica and the Andes that large empires emerged in around 1450?

3. What key ideas or practices extended beyond the limits of the great empires?

Many Native Americas

FOCUS

What factors account for the diversity of native American cultures?

Population Density

Scholars once claimed that the Western Hemisphere was sparsely settled prior to the arrival of Europeans in 1492, but we now know that by the end of the fifteenth century the overall population of the Americas had reached some 60 million or more. Vast open spaces remained, but in places the landscape was more intensively cultivated and thickly populated than western Europe (see Map 16.1). Fewer records for nonimperial groups survive than for empire builders such as the Incas and Aztecs, but by combining archaeological, artistic, anthropological, linguistic, and historical approaches, scholars have shed much new light on these less-studied cultures. Outside imperial boundaries, coastal and riverside populations were densest. This was true in the Caribbean, the Amazon and Mississippi river basins, the Pacific Northwest, parts of North America's eastern seaboard, and the upper Río de la Plata district of southeastern South America.

Environmental and Cultural Diversity

Ecological diversity gave rise in part to political and cultural diversity. America's native peoples, or Amerindians, lived scattered throughout two vast and ecologically diverse continents. They also inhabited a variety of tropical, temperate, and icy environments that proved more or less suitable to settled agriculture. Some were members of wandering, egalitarian gatherer-hunter bands; others were subjects of rigidly stratified imperial states. In between were many alternatives: traveling bands of pilgrims led by prophets, as in Brazil and southeastern North America; chiefdoms based on fishing,

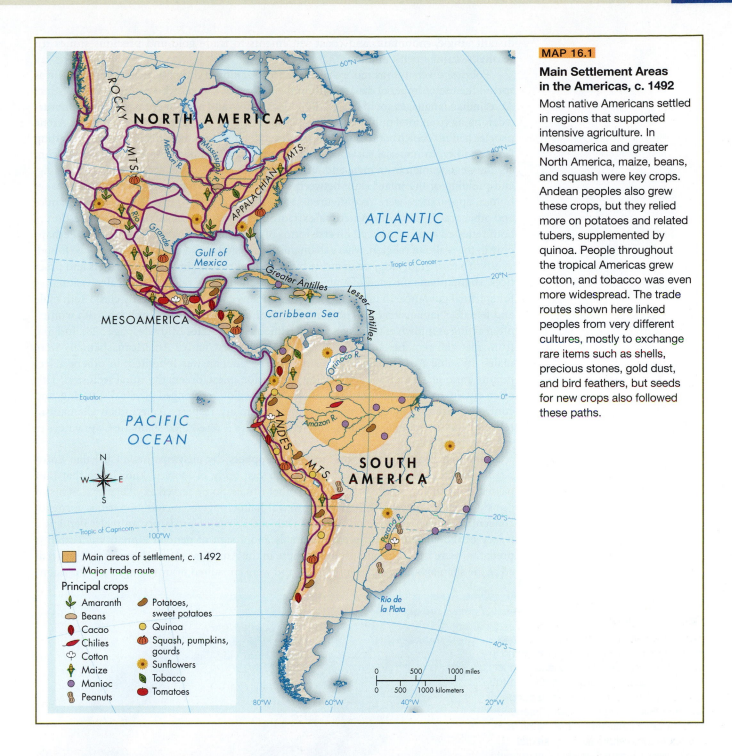

MAP 16.1

Main Settlement Areas in the Americas, c. 1492

Most native Americans settled in regions that supported intensive agriculture. In Mesoamerica and greater North America, maize, beans, and squash were key crops. Andean peoples also grew these crops, but they relied more on potatoes and related tubers, supplemented by quinoa. People throughout the tropical Americas grew cotton, and tobacco was even more widespread. The trade routes shown here linked peoples from very different cultures, mostly to exchange rare items such as shells, precious stones, gold dust, and bird feathers, but seeds for new crops also followed these paths.

whaling, or farming, as in the Pacific Northwest and Greater Antilles; large confederacies of chiefdoms as in highland Colombia and northeastern North America; commercially vibrant and independent city-states as in the Maya heartland of Central America. Others, such as the peoples of coastal Ecuador and the Lesser Antilles, had mastered the sea, routinely ferrying goods and ideas from one continent to the other, and throughout the Caribbean islands. Gold working and maize farming were among the many technologies that traversed American waters. Long-distance overland traders were equally important, carrying copper and tropical feathers from Central America to North America's desert Southwest in exchange for turquoise or, in South America, trekking between distant jungle, mountain, and coast settlements to trade gold and precious stones for seashells, animal pelts, and salt.

Political diversity was more than matched by cultural diversity. The Aztecs and Incas spread the use of imperial dialects within their empires, but elsewhere hundreds of distinct Amerindian languages could be heard. Modes of dress and adornment were even more varied, ranging from total nudity and a few tattoos to highly elaborate ceremonial dress. Arctic peoples had no choice but to bundle up, yet even their style choices distinguished one group from another. In imperial societies strict rules of dress and decorum separated elites from commoners, women from men, and juniors from seniors. Lip and ear piercing, tooth filing, and molding of the infant skull between slats of wood were but a few of the many ways human appearances were reconfigured. Architecture was just as varied, as were ceramics and other arts. In short, the Americas' extraordinary range of climates and natural resources both reflected and encouraged diverse forms of material and linguistic expression. Perhaps only in the realm of religion, where shamanism persisted, was a unifying thread to be found.

Shamanism

Not a formal ideology or doctrine but rather a broadly similar set of beliefs and practices, **shamanism** consisted of a given tribe's or chiefdom's reliance on healer-visionaries for spiritual guidance. In imperial societies shamans constituted a priestly class. Both male and female, shamans had functions ranging from fortuneteller to physician, with women often acting as midwives (see Lives and Livelihoods: The Aztec Midwife, page 528). Judging from material remains and eyewitness accounts, most native American shamans were males. In some Amerindian cultures the role of shaman was inherited; in others, select juniors announced their vocation following a vision quest, or lengthy ritual seclusion. This often entailed a solo journey to a forest or desert region, prolonged physical suffering, and controlled use of hallucinogenic substances. In many respects Amerindian shamanism reflected its Central Asian origins, and in other ways it resembled shamanistic practices in sub-Saharan Africa.

Often labeled "witch-doctors" or "false prophets" by unsympathetic Christian Europeans, shamans maintained and developed a vast body of esoteric knowledge that they passed along to juniors in initiations and other rituals. Some served as village or clan historians and myth-keepers. Most used powerful hallucinogens, including various forms of concentrated tobacco, to communicate with the spirits of predatory animals. Perhaps a legacy of the ancient era of great mammals and a sign of general human vulnerability, predators were venerated almost everywhere in the Americas. Animal spirits were regarded as the shaman's alter ego or protector, and were consulted prior to important occasions

Canadian War Club

This stone war club with a fish motif was excavated from a native American tomb in coastal British Columbia, Canada, and is thought to date from around 1200 to 1400 C.E. Such items at first suggest a people at war, but this club was probably intended only for ceremonial use. Other clubs from the same tomb share its overt sexual symbolism. Modern Tsimshian inhabitants of the region, who still rely on salmon, describe the exchange of stone clubs in their foundation myths. (National Museum of the American Indian, Smithsonian Institution. Catalog number: 5/5059. Photo by Katherine Fogden.)

shamanism Widespread system of religious belief and healing originating in Central Asia.

such as royal marriages, births, and declarations of war. Shamans also mastered herbal remedies for virtually all forms of illness, including emotional disorders. These rubs, washes, and infusions were sometimes highly effective, as shown by modern pharmacological studies. Shamans nearly always administered them along with complex chants and rituals aimed at expelling evil spirits. Shamans, therefore, combined the roles of physician and religious leader, using their knowledge and power to heal both body and spirit.

Range of Livelihoods

The many varieties of social organization and cultural practice found in the early modern Americas reflect both creative interactions with specific environments and the visions of individual political and religious leaders. Some Amerindian gatherer-hunters lived in swamplands and desert areas where subsistence agriculture was impossible using available technologies. Often such gathering-hunting peoples traded with—or plundered—their farming neighbors. Yet even farming peoples, as their ceramic and textile decorations attest, did not forget their past as hunters. As in other parts of the world, big-game hunting in the early modern Americas was an esteemed, even sacred activity among urban elites, marked by elaborate taboos and rituals.

Just as hunting remained important to farmers, agriculture could be found among some of the Americas' least politically complex societies, again characterized by elaborate rituals and taboos. According to many early modern observers, women controlled most agricultural tasks and spaces, periodically making offerings and singing to spirits associated with human fertility. Staple foods included maize, potatoes, and manioc, a lowland tropical tuber that could be ground into flour and preserved. Agricultural rituals were central in most cultures, and at the heart of every imperial state. With the ebb and flow of empires, many groups shifted from one mode of subsistence to another, from planting to gathering-hunting and back again. Some, such as the Kwakiutl (KWAH-kyu-til) of the Pacific Northwest, were surrounded by such abundant marine and forest resources that they never turned to farming. Natural abundance combined with sophisticated fishing and storage systems allowed the Kwakiutl to build a settled culture of the type normally associated with agricultural peoples. Thus, the ecological diversity of the Americas helped give rise to an equally diverse array of native American cultures, many of which blurred the line between settled and nomadic lifestyles.

Kwakiutl Culture Area, c. 1500

Tributes of Blood:
The Aztec Empire 1325–1521

Mesoamerica, comprised of modern southern Mexico, Guatemala, Belize, El Salvador, and western Honduras, was a land of city-states after about 800 C.E. Following the decline of ancient cultural forebears such as Teotihuacán (tay-oh-tee-wah-KAHN) in the Mexican highlands and the classic Maya in the greater Guatemalan lowlands, few urban powers, with the possible exception of the Toltecs, managed to dominate more than a few neighbors at a time.

FOCUS

What core features characterized Aztec life and rule?

This would change with the arrival in the Valley of Mexico of a band of former gatherer-hunters from a mysterious northwestern desert region they called Aztlán (ost-LAWN), or "place of cranes." As newcomers these "Aztecs," who later called themselves Mexica (meh-SHE-cah, hence "Mexico"), would suffer a number of humiliations at the hands of powerful city-dwellers centered on Lake Texcoco, now overlain by Mexico City. The Aztecs were at first regarded as coarse barbarians, but as with many conquering outsiders, in time they would have their revenge (see Map 16.2).

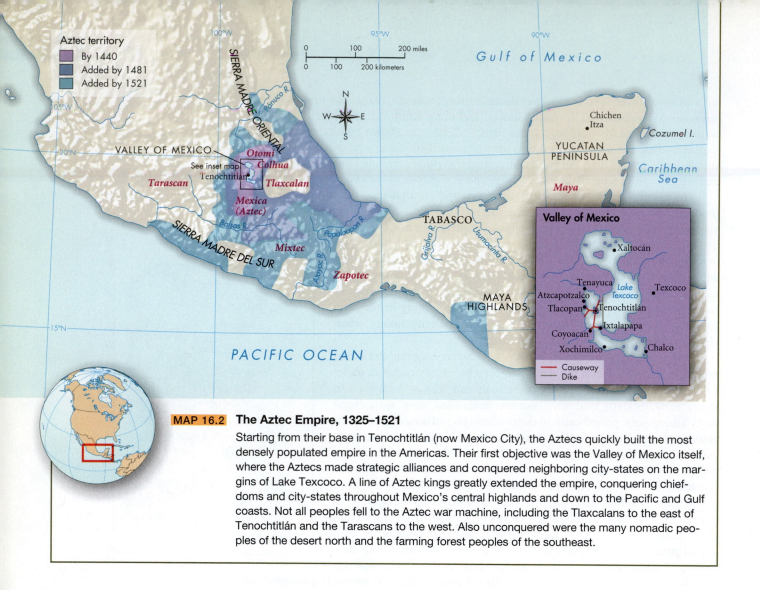

Aztec territory
- By 1440
- Added by 1481
- Added by 1521

Valley of Mexico
- Causeway
- Dike

MAP 16.2 The Aztec Empire, 1325–1521

Starting from their base in Tenochtitlán (now Mexico City), the Aztecs quickly built the most densely populated empire in the Americas. Their first objective was the Valley of Mexico itself, where the Aztecs made strategic alliances and conquered neighboring city-states on the margins of Lake Texcoco. A line of Aztec kings greatly extended the empire, conquering chiefdoms and city-states throughout Mexico's central highlands and down to the Pacific and Gulf coasts. Not all peoples fell to the Aztec war machine, including the Tlaxcalans to the east of Tenochtitlán and the Tarascans to the west. Also unconquered were the many nomadic peoples of the desert north and the farming forest peoples of the southeast.

Humble Origins, Imperial Ambitions

Unlike the classic Maya of preceding centuries, the Aztecs did not develop a phonetic writing system. They did, however, preserve key aspects of their history in a mix of oral and symbolic, usually painted or carved, forms. Aztec elders developed and maintained a series of chronicles of the kind historians call master narratives, or state-sponsored versions of the past meant to glorify certain individuals or policies. These narratives related foundation myths, genealogies, tales of conquest, and other important remembrances. Though biased, fragmentary, and otherwise imperfect, many Aztec oral narratives were preserved by dozens of young native scribes writing in Nahuatl (NAH-watt), the Aztec language, soon after the Spanish Conquest of 1519–1521 (discussed in the next chapter).

Historical Documentation

Why is it that the Spanish victors promoted rather than suppressed these narratives of Aztec glory? In one of history's many ironic twists, Spanish priests arriving in Mexico in the 1520s taught a number of noble Aztec and other Mesoamerican youths to adapt the Latin alphabet and Spanish phonetics to various local languages, most importantly Nahuatl. The Spanish hoped that stories of Aztec rule and religion, once collected and examined, would be swiftly discredited and replaced with Western, Christian versions. Not only did this quick conversion not happen as planned, but an unintended consequence of the information-gathering campaign was to create a vast and diverse body of Mesoamerican literature written in native languages.

Despite the agony of the immediate postconquest years, the Aztecs were a quick study in the production of written historical documents. Indeed, most of what we know of Aztec history relies heavily on these hybrid and often enigmatic sixteenth-century sources (see Seeing the Past: An Aztec Map of Tenochtitlán). Aside from interviews with the elders,

An Aztec Map of Tenochtitlán

Tenochtitlán, from the *Codex Mendoza* (The Granger Collection, New York.)

contains an illustrated history of Aztec conquests, crimes and punishments, and even a map of Tenochtitlán, the Aztec capital. This symbol-filled map is reproduced here.

According to legend, the Aztec capital came into existence when an eagle landed on a cactus in the middle of Lake Texcoco. This image, now part of the Mexican national flag, is at the center of the map. Beneath the cactus is a picture of a stone carving of a cactus fruit, a common Aztec symbol for the human heart, emblem of sacrifice. Beneath this is a third symbol labeled afterwards by a Spanish scribe "Tenochtitlán."

The city, or rather its symbol, marks the meeting of four horizontal, spatial quarters as well as a vertical axis linking the sky, earth, and watery underworld. In each quarter are various Aztec nobles, only one of whom, Tenochtli (labeled "Tenuch" on the map), is seated on a reed mat, the Aztec symbol of supreme authority. He was the Aztecs' first emperor; the name "Tenochtli" means "stone cactus fruit."

The lower panel depicts the Aztec conquests of their neighbors in Colhuacan and Tenayuca. Framing the entire map are symbols for dates, part of an ancient Mesoamerican system of time keeping and prophesying retained by the Aztecs. Finally, barely legible in the upper left-hand corner is the somewhat jarring signature of André Thevet, a French priest and royal cosmographer who briefly possessed the *Codex Mendoza* in the late sixteenth century.

Named for Mexico's first Spanish viceroy, the *Codex Mendoza* was painted by Aztec artists about a dozen years after the Spanish Conquest of 1519–1521. It was commissioned by the viceroy as a gift for the Holy Roman emperor and king of Spain, Charles V. After circulating among the courts of Europe, the *Codex Mendoza* landed in the Bodleian Library in Oxford, England, where it remains. Much of the document consists of tribute lists, but it also

EXAMINING THE EVIDENCE

1. What does this map reveal about the Aztec worldview?

2. How might this document have been read by a common Aztec subject?

521

several painted books, or codices, marked with precise dates, names, and other symbols, survive, along with much archaeological and artistic evidence. In combining these sources with Spanish eyewitness accounts of the conquest era, historians have assembled a substantial record of Aztec life and rule.

Aztec Origins   According to most accounts, the Aztecs arrived in the Valley of Mexico sometime in the thirteenth century, but it was not until the early fourteenth that they established a permanent home. The most fertile sites in the valley were already occupied by farmers who had no interest in making room for newcomers, but the Aztecs were not dissuaded; they had a reputation for being tough and resourceful. Heeding an omen in the form of an eagle perched on a cactus growing on a tiny island near the southwest edge of Lake Texcoco, the refugees settled there in 1325. Reclaiming land from the shallow lakebed, they founded a city called Tenochtitlán (teh-noach-teet-LAWN), or "cactus fruit place." Linked to shore by three large causeways, the city soon boasted imposing stone palaces and temple-pyramids.

The Aztecs quickly transformed Tenochtitlán into a formidable capital. By 1500 it was home to some two hundred thousand people, ranking alongside Nanjing and Paris among the world's five or six most populous cities at the time. At first the Aztecs developed their city by trading military services and lake products such as reeds and fish for building materials, including stone, lime, and timber from the surrounding hillsides. They then formed marriage alliances with regional ethnic groups such as the Colhua, and by 1430 initiated the process of imperial expansion.

Intermarriage with the Colhua, who traced their ancestry to the mighty Toltec warriors, lent the lowly Aztecs a new, elite cachet. At some point the Aztecs tied their religious cult, focused on the war god Huitzilopochtli (weetsy-low-POACH-tlee), or "hummingbird-on-the-left" to cults dedicated to more widely known deities, such as Tlaloc, a powerful water god. Also known to the distant Maya, the fearsome Tlaloc resembled a goggle-wearing crocodile, and was usually surrounded by shells and other marine symbols. A huge, multilayered pyramid faced with carved stone and filled with rubble, now referred to by archaeologists as the Templo Mayor, or "Great Temple," but called by the Aztecs Coatepec, or "Serpent Mountain," became the centerpiece of Tenochtitlán. At its top, some twenty stories above the valley floor, sat twin temple enclosures, one dedicated to Huitzilopochtli, the other to Tlaloc. Like many imperial structures, Coatepec was built to awe and intimidate. In the words of one native poet:

—— Causeway	**A** Great Temple
—— Major road	**B** Ritual center
—— Major canal	**C** Palace
—— Aqueduct	**D** Assembly hall

Lake Texcoco and Tenochtitlán, c. 1500

Proud of itself
Is the City of Mexico-Tenochtitlán
Here no one fears to die in war
This is our glory

This is Your Command
Oh Giver of Life
Have this in mind, oh princes
Who could conquer Tenochtitlán?
Who could shake the foundation of heaven?[2] *

As these words suggest, the Aztecs saw themselves as both stagehands and actors in a grand-scale cosmic drama centered on their great capital city.

* Miguel Leon-Portilla. *Pre-Columbian Literatures of Mexico*, by and Leon-Portilla, translated from the Spanish by Grace Lobanov. Copyright © 1969 by The University of Oklahoma Press. Used by permission of the publisher.

Enlarging and Supplying the Capital

With Tenochtitlán surrounded by water, subsistence and living space became serious concerns amid imperial expansion. Fortunately for the Aztecs, Lake Texcoco was shallow enough to allow an ingenious form of land reclamation called *chinampa* (chee-NAHM-pah). Still visible in a few Mexico City neighborhoods today, **chinampas** were long, narrow terraces built by hand from dredged mud, reeds, and rocks, bordered by interwoven sticks and live trees. Chinampa construction also created rows of deep canals, which served as waterways, or suburban "canoe roads." Because the Aztecs lacked iron or bronze metallurgy, wheeled vehicles, and draft animals, construction of large-scale agricultural works such as chinampas and massive temple-pyramids such as Coatepec absorbed the labors of many thousands of workers. Their construction, therefore, is a testimony to the Aztecs' ability to command and organize large amounts of labor.

Over time, Tenochtitlán's canals accumulated algae, water lilies, and silt. Workers periodically dredged and composted this organic material to fertilize maize, bean, and tomato plantings on the newly formed island-terraces. Established chinampa lands encompassing several square miles were eventually used for building residences, in part to help ease urban crowding. Always hoping not to anger Tlaloc, the fickle water god, by the mid-fifteenth century the Aztecs countered problems such as chronic flooding and high salt content at their end of the lake with dikes and other complex, labor-intensive public works.

Earlier, in the fourteenth century, an adjacent "twin" city called Tlatelolco (tlah-teh-LOLE-coe) had emerged alongside Tenochtitlán. Tlatelolco served as the Aztec marketplace. Foods, textiles, and goods from throughout Mesoamerica and beyond were exchanged here. Highly prized cocoa beans from the hot lowlands served as currency in some exchanges, and more exotic products, such as turquoise and the iridescent tail feathers of the quetzal bird, arrived from as far away as northern New Mexico and southern Guatemala, respectively. Though linked by trade, these distant regions fell well outside the Aztec domain. No matter how far they traveled, all products were transported along well-trod footpaths on the backs of human carriers. Only when they arrived on the shores of Lake Texcoco could trade goods be shuttled from place to place in canoes. Tlatelolco served as crossroads for all regional trade, with long-distance merchants, or *pochteca* (poach-TEH-cah), occupying an entire precinct. For the Aztecs, Tenochtitlán was the center of the political and spiritual universe. Tlatelolco was the center of Aztec commerce, connecting the peoples of the Valley of Mexico to diverse societies scattered across the Americas.

Genuine Aztec imperial expansion began only in around 1430, less than a century before the arrival of Europeans. An auspicious alliance between Tenochtitlán and the neighboring city-states of Texcoco and Tlacopan led to victory against a third, Atzcapotzalco (otts-cah-poat-SAUL-coh). Tensions with Atzcapotzalco extended back over a century to the Aztecs' first arrival in the region, and these early slights were not forgotten. Whether motivated by revenge or something else, the Aztecs used the momentum of this victory to overtake their allies and lay the foundations of a regional, tributary empire. Within a generation they controlled the entire Valley of Mexico, exacting tribute from several million people representing many distinct cultures. The Nahuatl language helped link state to subjects, although many newly conquered and allied groups continued to speak local languages. These persistent forms of ethnic identification, coupled with staggering tribute demands, would eventually help bring about the end of Aztec rule.

Holy Terror: Aztec Rule, Religion, and Warfare

A series of six male rulers, or *tlatoque* (tlah-TOE-kay, singular *tlatoani*), presided over Aztec expansion. When a ruler died, his successor was chosen by a secret council of elders from among a handful of eligible candidates. Aztec kingship was sacred in that each tlatoani traced his lineage back to the legendary Toltec warrior-sages. For this, the incorporation of the Colhua lineage had been essential. In keeping with this Toltec legacy, the Aztec

chinampa A terrace for farming and house building constructed in the shallows of Mexico's Lake Texcoco by the Aztecs and their neighbors.

The Coyolxauhqui Stone

Coyolxauhqui Stone (The Art Archive/Museo del Templo Mayor Mexico/Gianni Dagli Orti.)

Like many imperial peoples, the Aztecs sought to memorialize their deities in stone. The Aztec war god Huitzilopochtli was central, but as in other traditions, so were his mother and other female relatives. Huitzilopochtli's mother was Coatlicue (kwat-lih-KWAY), "Serpent Skirt," a fearsome and not obviously maternal figure. Huitzilopochtli's birth was said to be miraculous; Coatlicue had been inseminated by downy feathers while sweeping a temple, a ruse of the trickster-creator god Tezcatlipoca (tess-caught-lee-POH-cah), "Smoking Mirror."

A daughter, Coyolxauhqui (coe-yole-SHAU-key), "She Who is Adorned with Copper Bells," was so outraged at her mother's suspicious pregnancy that she incited her four hundred siblings to attempt matricide. Coatlicue was frightened at the prospect, but her unborn child, Huitzilopochtli, spoke from the womb to calm her. Upon the arrival of the angry children, dressed for war and led by Coyolxauhqui, Huitzilopochtli burst out of his mother's womb fully grown. He quickly prepared for battle and confronted his sister, whom he dismembered with a fire serpent. Huitzilopochtli went on to rout his other siblings, running them down like a proper Aztec warrior, stripping and sacrificing each without mercy.

The circular stone shown here, discovered by electrical workers near Mexico City's cathedral in 1979, depicts Coyolxauhqui dismembered on the ground. Some ten feet across, this stone apparently sat at the base of the Aztec Templo Mayor. Sacrificed warriors from all over the Aztec Empire probably got a good look at it before climbing the temple stairs to their deaths. Although shown in defeat, Coyolxauhqui is the ideal woman warrior, her serpent belt buckled with a human skull. Earth Monster knee- and elbow-pads, as well as heel-cups, add to her fearsome appearance, as do serpent ties on her severed arms and legs. An elaborate headdress and huge, Toltec-style ear-spools top off the battlefield ensemble.

EXAMINING THE EVIDENCE

1. How does the Coyolxauhqui stone reflect women's roles in Aztec society?

2. What does the stone suggest about death in Aztec thought?

Empire was characterized by three core features: human sacrifice, warfare, and tribute. All were linked to Aztec and broader Mesoamerican notions of cosmic order, specifically the fundamental human duty to feed the gods.

Sacrifice   Like most Mesoamerican peoples, the Aztecs traced not only their own but all human origins to sacrifices made by a wide range of deities. In most origin stories male and female gods threw themselves into fires, drew their own blood, and killed and dismembered one another, all for the good of humankind. These forms of sacrifice were considered essential to the process of releasing and renewing the generative powers that drove the cosmos (see Seeing the Past: The Coyolxauhqui Stone).

According to Aztec belief, humans were expected to show gratitude by following the example of their creators in an almost daily ritual cycle. Much of the sacred calendar had been inherited from older Mesoamerican cultures, but the Aztecs added many new holidays to celebrate their own special role in cosmic history. The Aztecs' focus on sacrifice also appears to have derived from their acute sense that secular and spiritual forces were

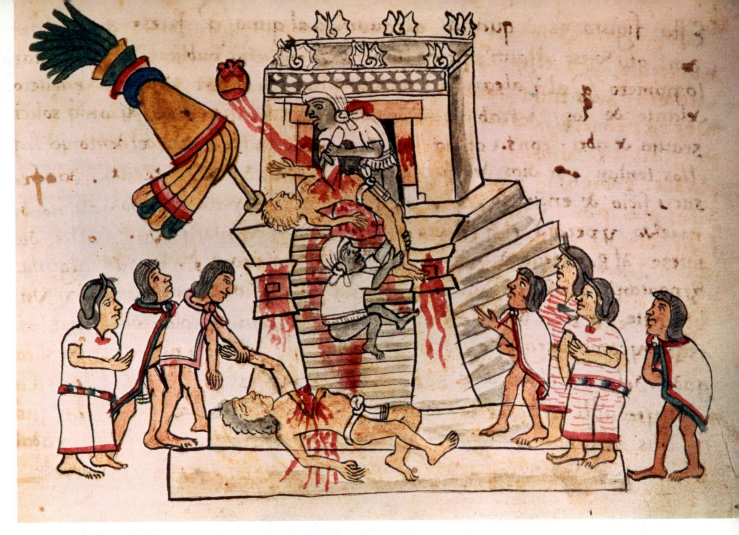

Aztec Human Sacrifice

This image dates from just after the Spanish Conquest of Mexico, but it was part of a codex about Aztec religious practices and symbols. Here a priest is removing the beating heart of a captive with a flint knife as an assistant holds his feet. The captive's bloody heart, in the form of a cactus fruit, ascends, presumably to the gods (see the same icon in Seeing the Past: An Aztec Map of Tenochtitlán, page 521). At the base of the sacrificial pyramid lies an earlier victim, apparently being taken away by noble Aztec men and women responsible for the handling of the corpse. (Scala/Art Resource, NY.)

inseparable and interdependent. Affairs of state were affairs of heaven, and vice versa. Tenochtitlán was thought to be the foundation of heaven, its enormous temple-pyramids the center of human-divine affairs. Aztec priests and astrologers believed that the universe, already in its fifth incarnation after only three thousand years, was inherently unstable, always on the verge of chaos and collapse. Only human intervention in the form of sustained sacrificial ritual could stave off apocalypse.

As an antidote, or at least a brake against impending doom, the gods had given humans the "gift" of warfare. Human captives, preferably able-bodied, energetic young men, were to be hunted and killed so that the release of their blood and spirits might satisfy the gods. Warrior sacrifice was so important to the Aztecs that they believed it kept the sun in motion. Thus the act of human sacrifice, which involved removing the hearts of live victims using a flint knife, was in part a reenactment of several creator gods' own acts of self-sacrifice.

Devout Aztec subjects, rather like the classic Maya before them, also took part in nonlethal cosmic regeneration rituals in the form of personal bloodletting, or **autosacrifice**. According to a number of eyewitness sources, extremities and genitals were bled using thorns and stone blades, with public exhibition of suffering as important as blood loss. Blood offerings were absorbed by thin sheets of reed paper, which were burnt before an

autosacrifice The Mesoamerican practice of personal bloodletting as a means of paying debts to the gods.

altar. These bloodlettings, like captive sacrifices, emphasized the frailty of the individual, the pain of life, and most of all indebtedness to the gods. Autosacrifice was, in short, a physical expression of the empathy and subordination humans were to feel before their creators. Human blood fueled not only the Aztec realm, but the cosmos.

Warfare

Given these sacrificial obligations, Aztec warfare was aimed not at the annihilation, but rather at live capture of enemies. This is not to say that "stone age" weapons technology was an impediment to determined killers: two-handed broadswords with razor-sharp obsidian blades could slice feather-clad warriors to ribbons, and ceramic projectiles could be hurled from slings with deadly accuracy. Spears, lances, clubs, and other weapons were equally menacing. Still, according to most sources, Aztec combat was ideally a stylized and theatrical affair similar to royal jousts in contemporary Eurasia, with specific individuals paired for contest.

In the field, Aztec warriors were noted for their fury, a trait borrowed from their patron deity, Huitzilopochtli. Chronic enemies such as the Tlaxcalans of east-central Mexico, and the Tarascans to the west, apparently learned to match the ferocious Aztec style. Despite their proximity to Tenochtitlán, they remained unconquered when Europeans arrived. Some enemies, such as the nearby Otomí, were eventually overwhelmed, then incorporated into Aztec warrior ranks.

All Mesoamerican warriors considered death on the battlefield the highest honor. But live capture was the Aztecs' main goal, and most victims were marched naked and bound to the capital to be sacrificed. Although charged with religious meaning, Aztec warrior sacrifices were also intended to horrify enemies; visiting diplomats were made to watch them, according to sources. Aztec imperial expansion depended in part on religious terror, or the ability to appear chosen by the gods for victory.

Tribute

In addition to sacrificial victims, the Aztecs demanded **tribute** of conquered peoples, a common imperial practice worldwide. In addition to periodic labor drafts for temple building and other public works, tribute lists included useful things such as food, textiles, and craft goods, crucial subsidies for the empire's large priestly and warrior classes. Redistribution of certain tribute items to favored subjects of lower status, a tactic also practiced by the Incas, further helped cement loyalties. Other tribute items were purely symbolic. Some new subjects were made to collect filth and inedible insects, for example, just to prove their unworthiness before the Aztec sovereign. As an empire that favored humiliation over co-optation and promotion of new subjects, the Aztecs faced an ever-deepening reservoir of resentment.

Daily Life Under the Aztecs

Class Hierarchy

Aztec society was highly stratified, and class divisions firm. As in most imperial societies, Mexica nobles regarded commoners, particularly farming folk, as uncouth and generally beneath contempt. In between were imperial bureaucrats, priests, district chiefs, scribes, merchants, and artisans. Although elites at several levels showed off the fruits of their subordinates' labors in lavish displays, most Aztec art seems to have been destined not for wealthy people's homes but rather for temples, tombs, and religious shrines. Despite heavy emphasis on religious ceremonies, the Aztecs also maintained a multitiered civil justice system. In many instances, and quite unlike most of the world's imperial cultures, including the Incas, Aztec nobles received harsher punishments than commoners for similar misdeeds.

Class hierarchy was further reinforced by a host of detailed dress and speech codes, along with many other social rules and rituals. The tlatoani, for example, could not be touched or even looked in the face by any but his closest relatives, consorts, and servants. Even ranking nobles were supposed to lie face down on the ground and put dirt in their mouths before him. Nobles guarded their own rank with vigilance, going so far as to develop a restricted form of speech. Chances for social advancement were severely limited, but some men, all of whom were expected to serve in the military for a period, gained status on the battlefield.

At the base of the social pyramid were peasants and slaves. Some peasants were ethnic Aztecs, but the vast majority belonged to city-states and clans that had been conquered after 1430. In either case, peasants' lives mostly revolved around producing food for subsistence

tribute Taxes paid to a state or empire, usually in the form of farm produce or artisan manufactures but sometimes also human labor or even human bodies.

and providing overlords with tribute goods and occasional labor. Slavery usually took the form of crisis-driven self-indenture; it was not an inherited social status. Chattel slavery existed, in which slaves were treated as property and traded in the marketplace, but slavery remained unimportant to the overall Aztec economy.

Merchants, particularly the mobile pochteca, responsible for long-distance trade, occupied an unusual position. Although the pochteca sometimes accumulated great wealth, they remained resident aliens much like other ethnic merchant communities operating in the contemporary Mediterranean and Indian Ocean basins. They had no homeland, but made a good living supplying elites with exotic goods, including slaves. Yet even among merchants there seems to have been little interest in capital accumulation in the form of money, land, or saleable goods. There is no evidence of complex credit instruments, industrial-style production, or real estate exchange of the sort associated with early merchant capitalism in other parts of the world at this time. The Aztec state remained at root tributary, the movement of goods mostly a reflection of power relations underpinned by force. Merchants, far from influencing politics, remained ethnic outsiders. Thus, both the Aztec economy and social structure reinforced the insularity of Aztec elites. The inflexible Aztec society could not incorporate outsiders, and economic exchange, even long-distance trade, did little to add new ideas and beliefs to Aztec culture.

The life of an Aztec woman was difficult even by early modern standards. Along with water transport and other heavy household chores, maize grinding and tortilla making became the core responsibilities of most women in the Valley of Mexico, and indeed throughout Mesoamerica. Without animal- or water-driven grain mills, food preparation was an arduous, time-consuming task, particularly for the poor. Only noblewomen enjoyed broad exemption from this and other forms of manual work.

Women's Roles

Sources suggest that some women achieved shaman status, performing minor priestly roles and working as surgeons and herbalists. Midwifery was also a fairly high-status, female occupation (see Lives and Livelihoods: The Aztec Midwife). These were exceptions; women's lives were mostly hard under Aztec rule. Scholars disagree, however, as to whether male political and religious leaders viewed women's substantial duties and contributions as complementary or subordinate. Surviving texts do emphasize feminine mastery of the domestic sphere and its social value. However, this emphasis may simply reflect male desire to limit the sphere of women's actions, since female reproductive capacity was also highly valued as an aid to the empire's perpetual war effort.

Indeed, Aztec society was so militarized that giving birth was referred to as "taking a captive." This comparison reflects the generalized Aztec preoccupation with pleasing their gods: women were as much soldiers as men in the ongoing war to sustain human life. Women's roles in society were mostly domestic rather than public, but the home was a deeply sacred space. Caring for it was equivalent to caring for a temple. Sweeping was a genuine ritual, for example, albeit one with hygienic benefits. Hearth tending, maize grinding, spinning, and weaving were also highly ritualized tasks, each accompanied by chants and offerings. Insufficient attention to any of these daily rituals put families and entire lineages at risk.

Children's Lives

Aztec children, too, lived a scripted existence, their futures predicted at birth by astrologers. Names were derived from birthdates, and in a way amounted to a public badge of fate. According to a variety of testimonies taken just after the Spanish Conquest, Aztec society at all levels emphasized duty and good comportment rather than rights and individual freedom. Parents were admonished to police their children's behavior and to help mold all youths into useful citizens. Girls and boys at every social level were assigned tasks considered appropriate for their sex well before adolescence. By age fourteen, children of both sexes were fully engaged in adult work. One break from the constant chores was instruction between ages twelve and fifteen in singing and playing instruments, such as drums and flutes, for cyclical religious festivals. Girls married at about age fifteen, and boys nearer twenty, a pattern roughly in accordance with most parts of the world at the time. Elder Aztec women usually served as matchmakers, and wedding ceremonies tended to be elaborate, multiday affairs. Some noblemen expanded their prestige by retaining numerous wives and siring dozens of children.

The Aztec Midwife

Aztec Midwife

Women were expected to be tough in Aztec culture, which described giving birth as "taking a captive." But as in war, medical attention was often required, so a trained class of professional midwives stood by to administer aid. This image accompanies a description in Nahuatl, the Aztec language, of the midwife's duties written soon after the Spanish Conquest. (Firenze, Biblioteca Medicea Laurenziana, Ms. Med. Palat. 219, c. 132v.)

In Aztec culture, childbirth was a sacred and ritualized affair. Always life-threatening for mother and child, giving birth and being born were both explicitly compared to the battlefield experience. Aside from potential medical complications, the Aztecs considered the timing of a child's birth critical in determining his or her future. This tricky blend of physical and spiritual concerns gave rise to the respected and highly skilled livelihood of midwife. It is not entirely clear how midwives were chosen, but their work and sayings are well described in early postconquest records, particularly the illustrated books of Aztec lore and history collectively known as the *Florentine Codex*. The following passage, translated directly from sixteenth-century Nahuatl, is one such description. Note how the midwife blends physical tasks, such as supplying herbs and swaddling clothes, with shamanistic cries and speeches.

And the midwife inquired about the fate of the baby who was born.

When the pregnant one already became aware of [pains in] her womb, when it was said that her time of death had arrived, when she wanted to give birth already, they quickly bathed her, washed her hair with soap, washed her, adorned her well. And then they arranged, they swept the house where the little woman was to suffer, where she was to perform her duty, to do her work, to give birth.

If she were a noblewoman or wealthy, she had two or three midwives. They remained by her side, awaiting her word. And when the woman became really disturbed internally, they quickly put her in a sweat bath [a kind of sauna]. And to hasten the birth of the baby, they gave the pregnant woman cooked *ciuapatli* [literally, "woman medicine"] herb to drink.

And if she suffered much, they gave her ground opossum tail to drink, and then the baby was quickly born. [The midwife] already had all that was needed for the baby, the little rags with which the baby was received.

And when the baby had arrived on earth, the midwife shouted; she gave war cries, which meant the woman had fought a good battle, had become a brave warrior, had taken a captive, had captured a baby.

Then the midwife spoke to it. If it was a boy, she said to it: "You have come out on earth, my youngest one, my boy, my young man." If it was a girl, she said to it: "My young woman, my youngest one, noblewoman, you have suffered, you are exhausted.". . . [and to either:] "You have come to arrive on earth, where your relatives, your kin suffer fatigue and exhaustion; where it is hot, where it is cold, and where the wind blows; where there is thirst, hunger, sadness, despair, exhaustion, fatigue, pain. . . ."

And then the midwife cut the umbilical cord. . . .

Source: Selection from the *Florentine Codex* in Matthew Restall, Lisa Sousa, and Kevin Terraciano, eds., *Mesoamerican Voices: Native-Language Writings from Colonial Mexico, Oaxaca, Yucatan, and Guatemala* (New York: Cambridge University Press, 2005), 216–217.

QUESTIONS TO CONSIDER

1. Why was midwifery so crucial to the Aztecs?
2. How were boys and girls addressed by the midwife, and why?

For Further Information:
Carrasco, Davíd, and Scott Sessions. *Daily Life of the Aztecs, People of the Sun and Earth*, 2d ed. Indianapolis, IN: Hackett Publishing, 2008.
Clendinnen, Inga. *Aztecs: An Interpretation*. New York: Cambridge University Press, 1994.

At around harvest time in September, Aztec subjects of all classes ate maize, beans, and squash lightly seasoned with salt and ground chili peppers. During other times of the year, and outside the chinampa zone, food could be scarce, forcing the poor to consume roasted insects, grubs, and lake scum. Certain items, such as frothed cocoa, were reserved for elites. Stored maize was used to make tortillas year-round, but two poor harvests in a row, a frequent occurrence in densely populated highland Mexico, could reduce rations considerably.

Food and Scarcity

In addition to periodic droughts, Aztec subjects coped with frosts, plagues of locusts, volcanic eruptions, earthquakes, and floods. Given such ecological uncertainty, warfare was reserved for the agricultural off-season, when hands were not needed for planting, weeding, or harvesting. In the absence of large domesticated animals and advanced metallurgy, agricultural tasks throughout Mesoamerica demanded virtual armies of field laborers equipped only with fire-hardened digging sticks and obsidian or flint knives.

Animal protein was scarce in highland Mexico, especially in urban areas where hunting opportunities were limited and few domestic animals were kept. Still, the people of Tenochtitlán raised significant numbers of turkeys and plump, hairless dogs (the prized Xolo breed of today). Even humble beans, when combined with maize, could constitute a complete protein, and indigenous grains such as amaranth were also highly nutritious. Famines still occurred, however, and one in the early 1450s led to mass migration out of the Valley of Mexico. Thousands sold themselves into slavery to avoid starvation.

The Limits of Holy Terror

As the Aztec Empire expanded in the later fifteenth century, sacrificial debts grew to be a consuming passion among pious elites. Calendars filled with sacrificial rites, and warfare was ever more geared toward satisfying what must have seemed a ballooning cosmic budget.

By 1500 the Aztec state had reached its height, and some scholars have argued that it had even begun to decline. Incessant captive wars and related tribute demands had reached their limits, and old enemies such as the Tlaxcalans and Tarascans remained belligerent. New conquests were blocked by difficult terrain, declining tributes, and resistant locals. With available technologies, there was no place else for this inherently expansive empire to grow, and even with complex water works in place, agricultural productivity barely kept the people fed. Under the harsh leadership of Moctezuma II ("Angry Lord the Younger") (r. 1502–1520), the future did not look promising. Although there is no evidence to suggest the Aztec Empire was on the verge of collapse when several hundred bearded, sunburnt strangers of Spanish descent appeared on Mexico's Gulf Coast shores in 1519, points of vulnerability abounded.

Underlying Weaknesses

Tributes of Sweat: The Inca Empire 1430–1532

At about the same time as the Aztec expansion in southernmost North America, another great empire emerged in the central Andean highlands of South America. There appears to have been no significant contact between them. Like the Aztecs, the Incas burst out of their highland homeland in the 1430s to conquer numerous neighboring cultures and huge swaths of territory. They demanded tribute in goods and labor, along with allegiance to an imperial religion. Also like the Aztecs, the Incas based their expansion on a centuries-long inheritance of technological, religious, and political traditions.

> **FOCUS**
>
> What core features characterized Inca life and rule?

Despite enormous geographical, technological, and cultural barriers, by 1500 the Incas ruled one of the world's most extensive, ecologically varied, and rugged land empires, stretching nearly three thousand miles along both sides of the towering Andean mountain range from just north of the equator to central Chile. Like most empires ancient and modern, extensive holdings proved to be a mixed blessing (see Map 16.3, page 531).

From Potato Farmers to Empire Builders

Inca Origins

Thanks to abundant archaeological evidence and early postconquest interviews and narratives, much is known about the rise and fall of the Inca state. Still, like the early Ottoman, Russian, and other contemporary empires, numerous mysteries remain. As in those cases, legends and sagas of the formative period in particular require careful and skeptical analysis. The Inca case is somewhat complicated by the fact that their complex knotted-string records, or *khipus* (also *quipus*, KEY-poohs), have yet to be deciphered.

Scholars agree that the Incas emerged from among a dozen or so regional ethnic groups or allied clans living in the highlands of south-central Peru between 1000 and 1400 C.E. Living as scattered and more-or-less egalitarian potato and maize farmers, the Incas started out as one of many similar groups of Andean mountaineers. Throughout the Andes, clan groupings settled in and around fertile valleys and alongside lakes between eighty-five hundred and thirteen thousand feet above sea level. Though often graced with clear mountain springs and fertile soils, these highland areas were subject to periodic frosts and droughts, despite their location within the tropics. Even more than in the Aztec realm, altitude (elevation above sea level), not latitude (distance north or south of the equator), was key.

Environment and Exchange

Anthropologist John Murra once described Inca land use as a "**vertical archipelago,**" a stair-step system of interdependent environmental "islands." Kin groups occupying the altitudes best suited to potato and maize farming established outlying settlements in cold uplands, where thousands of llamas and alpacas—the Americas' only large domestic animals—were herded, and also in hot lowlands, where cotton, peanuts, chilis, and the stimulant coca were grown. People, animals, and goods traveled constantly between highland and lowland ecological zones using well-maintained and often stone-paved trails and hanging bridges, yet the incredibly rugged nature of the terrain (plus the stubborn nature of llamas) made use of wheeled vehicles impractical.

vertical archipelago Andean system of planting crops and grazing animals at different altitudes.

Clans with highland ties and even some states of considerable size inhabited Peru's long desert coast. Here, urban civilization was nearly as old as that of ancient Egypt. Andean coast dwellers engaged in large-scale irrigated agriculture, deep-sea fishing, and long-distance trade. Trading families outfitted large balsawood rafts with cotton sails and plied the Pacific as far as Guatemala. Inland trade links stretched over the Andes and deep into the Amazon rain forest. Stopping at pilgrimage sites along the way, coast-dwelling traders exchanged salt, seashells, beads, and copper hatchets for exotic feathers, gold dust, and pelts. The Incas would move rapidly to exploit all of these diverse Andean regions and their interconnections, replacing old exchange systems and religious shrines with their own. Around 1200 C.E. they established a base near Cuzco (KOOS-coh), deep in the highlands of Peru not far from the headwaters of the Amazon, and soon after 1400 they began their remarkable drive toward empire.

The Great Apparatus: Inca Expansion and Religion

Cuzco, located in a narrow valley at a breathtaking altitude of over two miles above sea level, served as the Incas' political base and religious center. Like the Aztecs, the Incas saw their capital as the hub of the universe, calling it the "navel of the world." An array of dirt paths and stone-paved roads radiated out in all directions and tied hundreds of subsidiary shrines to the cosmically-ordained center. Much like the Aztecs' Tenochtitlán, Cuzco served as both the preeminent religious pilgrimage site and the empire's administrative capital. Compared with the Aztec capital, however, the city was modest in size, perhaps home to at most fifty thousand. Still, Cuzco had the advantage of being stoutly built

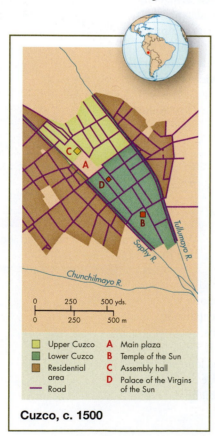

▢ Upper Cuzco	**A**	Main plaza
▢ Lower Cuzco	**B**	Temple of the Sun
▢ Residential area	**C**	Assembly hall
— Road	**D**	Palace of the Virgins of the Sun

Cuzco, c. 1500

0   250   500 yds.

0   250   500 m

of hewn stone. Whereas most of Tenochtitlán's temples and palaces were dismantled in the centuries following the Spanish Conquest, Cuzco's colossal stone foundations still stand.

For obscure reasons, the Incas in the early fifteenth century began conquering their neighbors. In time each emperor, or Sapa ("Unique") Inca, would seek to add more territory to the realm, called Tawantinsuyu (tuh-wahn-tin-SUE-you), or, "The Four Quarters Together." The Sapa Inca was thought to be descended from the sun and was thus regarded as the natural lord and sustainer of all humanity. To worship the sun was to worship the Inca, and vice versa. Devotion to lesser mountain and ancestor deities persisted, however, absorbed over time by the Incas in a way reminiscent of the Roman Empire's assimilation of regional deities and shrines. This religious inclusiveness helped the empire spread quickly even as the royal cult of the sun was inserted into everyday life. In a similar way, *runasimi*, later mislabeled "Quechua" (KETCH-wah) by the Spanish, became the Incas' official language even as local languages continued to be spoken.

Inca expansion was so rapid that the empire reached its greatest extent within a mere four generations of its founding. In semilegendary times, Wiracocha Inca (r. 1400–1438) was said to have led an army of followers to defeat an invading ethnic group called the Chankas near Cuzco. According to several royal sagas, this victory spurred Wiracocha to improve the defensive position of his people further by annexing the fertile territories of other neighbors. Defense turned to offense, and thus was primed the engine of Inca expansion.

Wiracocha's successor, Pachacuti Inca Yupanki (r. 1438–1471), was far more ambitious, so much so that he is widely regarded as the true founder of the Inca Empire. Substantial archaeological evidence backs this claim. Pachacuti (literally "Cataclysm") took over much of what is today Peru, including many coastal oases and the powerful Chimú kingdom. Along the way, Pachacuti perfected the core strategy of Inca warfare: amassing and mobilizing such overwhelming numbers of troops and backup forces that actual fighting was usually unnecessary.

Thousands of peasants were conscripted to bear arms, build roads, and carry grain. Others herded llamas, strung bridges, and cut building stone. With each new advance, huge masonry forts and temples were constructed in the imperial style, leaving an indelible Inca stamp on the landscape still visible today from Ecuador to Argentina. Even opponents such as the desert-dwelling Chimú, who had their aqueducts cut off to boot, simply capitulated in the face of the Inca juggernaut. Just after the Spanish Conquest, Pachacuti was remembered by female descendants:

> As [Pachacuti] Inca Yupanki remained in his city and town of Cuzco, seeing that he was lord and that he had subjugated the towns and provinces, he was very pleased. He had subjugated more and obtained much more importance than any of his ancestors. He saw the great apparatus that he had so that whenever he wanted to he could subjugate and put under his control anything else he wanted.[3]

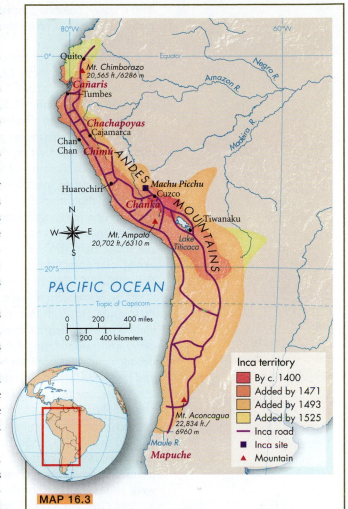

MAP 16.3

The Inca Empire, 1325–1521

Starting from their base in Cuzco, high in the Andes, the Incas built the most extensive empire in the Americas, and the second most populous after that of the Aztecs. They linked it by a road system that rivaled that of the ancient Romans. Inca expansion was extremely rapid as each ruler competed with his predecessor to extend tributary control. Some groups, such as the Cañaris and Chachapoyas, resisted Inca domination for many years, and the Mapuche of Chile were never conquered.

Imperial Expansion

These early colonial remembrances underscore the Sapa Inca's tremendous power. Pachacuti could at any time deploy the "great apparatus" of empire as his personal conquest machine.

Pachacuti's successors continued in the same vein, extending conquests southward deep into what are today Chile and Argentina, and also eastward down the slope of the Andes and into the upper Amazon Basin. It is from this last region, the quarter the Incas called Antisuyu (auntie-SUE-you), that we derive the word *Andes*. On the northern frontier, the Incas fought a series of bitter wars with Ecuadorian ethnic groups to extend Inca rule into the southernmost part of present-day Colombia (see again Map 16.3). Here the imperial Inca conquest machine met its match: instead of capitulating, awestruck by the Inca, many Ecuadorian and Colombian highlanders fought to the death.

According to most sources, Inca advances into new territory were couched in the rhetoric of diplomacy. Local headmen were told they had two options: (1) to retain power by accepting Inca sovereignty and all the tributary obligations that went with it, or (2) to defy the Inca and face annihilation. Most headmen went along, particularly once word of the Incas' battlefield prowess spread. Those who did not were either killed in battle or exiled, along with their subject populations, to remote corners of the empire. Several of these exile colonies are still identifiable today in southern Ecuador and northern Bolivia.

The Incas seem to have been most interested in dominating productive peoples and their lands, although they also succeeded to some extent in spreading their imperial solar cult. Whatever their motives, like the Aztecs they defined political domination in simple, easily understood terms: tribute payment. Conquered subjects showed submission by rendering significant portions of their surplus production—and also labor—to the emperor and his subordinates. Tribute payment was a grudgingly accepted humiliation throughout the Andes, one that many hoped to shake off at the first opportunity.

Inca Religion

Scholars argue that to understand Inca religion one must set aside familiar distinctions between sacred and secular and between life and death. As the chapter-opening description of child sacrifice suggests, a continuum of life was assumed throughout the Andes, despite permanent loss of consciousness, and spirit and body were deemed inseparable. Likewise, features in the landscape, ranging from mountain springs and peaks to ordinary boulders, were almost always thought to house or emit spiritual energy (see Reading the Past: An Andean Creation Story). Even practical human-made landforms, such as irrigation canals, walls, and terraces, were commonly described as "alive." These sacred places, **wakas** (or *huacas*), received sacrifices of food, drink, and textiles from their human caretakers in exchange for good harvests, herd growth, and other bounties. In addition, most Andeans venerated images and amulets carved from wood, shell, stone, metal, and bone.

Andeans also venerated the human corpse. As long as something tangible remained of one's deceased relatives or ancestors, they were not regarded as entirely dead. It was generally thought wise to keep them around. Of course it helped that the central Andes' dry highland and coastal climates were ideal for mummification: preservation often required little more than removal of internal organs. In wetter areas, the dead were sometimes smoked over a slow fire, a process that led some outsiders to suspect cannibalism. In fact, it would have been fairly common in Inca times to encounter a neighbor's "freeze-dried" or smoked grandparents hanging from the rafters, still regarded as very much involved in household affairs. Andeans sometimes carried ancestor mummies to feasts and pilgrimages as well. Thus, Inca society included both past and present generations.

The Incas harnessed these and other core features of Andean society at its most ancient, yet like the Aztecs they put a unique stamp on the vast and diverse region they came to dominate. Though warlike, the Incas rarely sacrificed captive warriors, a ritual archaeologists now know was practiced among ancient coastal Peruvians. As for cannibalism, it was something the Incas associated with barbaric forest dwellers. Inca stone architecture, though clearly borrowing from older forms such as those of Tiwanaku, a temple complex in modern Bolivia, is still identifiable thanks to the frequent use of trapezoidal (flared) doors, windows, and niches (see the illustration of Machu Picchu in At a

waka A sacred place or thing in Andean culture.

An Andean Creation Story

The small Peruvian town of Huarochirí (wahr-oh-chee-REE), located in the high Andes east of Lima, was the target of a Spanish anti-idolatry campaign at the end of the sixteenth century. The Spanish conquest of the Incas, which began in 1532 (see Chapter 17), had little effect on the everyday life of Andean peasants, and many clung tenaciously to their religious beliefs. In Huarochirí, Spanish attempts to root out these beliefs and replace them with Western, Christian ones produced written testimonies from village elders in phonetically rendered Quechua, the most commonly spoken language in the Inca Empire. Like the Aztec codices, the resulting documents—aimed at eradicating the beliefs they describe—have unwittingly provided modern researchers with a rare window on a lost mental world. The passage here, translated directly from Quechua to English, relates an Andean myth that newly arrived or converted Christians considered a variation on the biblical story of Noah and the Great Flood. In the Christian story, God, angered by the wickedness of man, resolves to send a flood to destroy the earth. He spares only Noah, whom he instructs to build an ark in which Noah, his family, and a pair of every animal were saved from the Great Flood.

In ancient times, this world wanted to come to an end. A llama buck, aware that the ocean was about to overflow, was behaving like somebody who's deep in sadness. Even though its owner let it rest in a patch of excellent pasture, it cried and said, "In, in," and wouldn't eat. The llama's owner got really angry, and he threw a cob from some maize he had just eaten at the llama. "Eat, dog! This is some fine grass I'm letting you rest in!" he said. Then that llama began speaking like a human being. "You simpleton, whatever could you be thinking about? Soon, in five days, the ocean will overflow. It's a certainty. And the whole world will come to an end," it said. The man got good and scared. "What's going to happen to us? Where can we go to save

ourselves?" he said. The llama replied, "Let's go to Villca Coto mountain. There we'll be saved. Take along five days' food for yourself." So the man went out from there in a great hurry, and himself carried both the llama buck and its load. When they arrived at Villca Coto mountain, all sorts of animals had already filled it up: pumas, foxes, guanacos [wild relatives of the llama], condors, all kinds of animals in great numbers. And as soon as that man had arrived there, the ocean overflowed. They stayed there huddling tightly together. The waters covered all those mountains and it was only Villca Coto mountain, or rather its very peak, that was not covered by the water. Water soaked the fox's tail. That's how it turned black. Five days later, the waters descended and began to dry up. The drying waters caused the ocean to retreat all the way down again and exterminate all the people. Afterward, that man began to multiply once more. That's the reason there are people until today.

[The scribe who recorded this tale, an Andean converted by Spanish missionaries, then adds this comment:] "Regarding this story, we Christians believe it refers to the time of the Flood. But they [i.e., non-Christian Andeans] believe it was Villca Coto mountain that saved them."

Source: Excerpt from *The Huarochirí Manuscript: A Testament of Ancient and Colonial Andean Religion*, trans. and ed. Frank Salomon and George L. Urioste (Austin: University of Texas Press, 1991), 51–52.

EXAMINING THE EVIDENCE

1. What do the similarities and differences between the Andean and Judeo-Christian flood stories suggest?

2. What do the differences between them reveal?

For Further Information:
Spalding, Karen. *Huarochirí: An Andean Society Under Inca and Spanish Rule*. Stanford: Stanford University Press, 1988.
Urton, Gary. *Inca Myths*. Austin: University of Texas Press, 1999.

Crossroads, page 512). It is worth noting, however, that the cult of the sun, which the Incas transformed and elevated to something new and imperial, proved far less durable than local religious traditions once the empire fell. Despite the Incas' rhetoric of diplomacy, most Andeans appear to have associated their rule with tyranny. Like the Aztecs, they failed to inspire loyalty in their subjects, who saw Inca government as a set of institutions designed to exploit, rather than protect, the peoples of the empire.

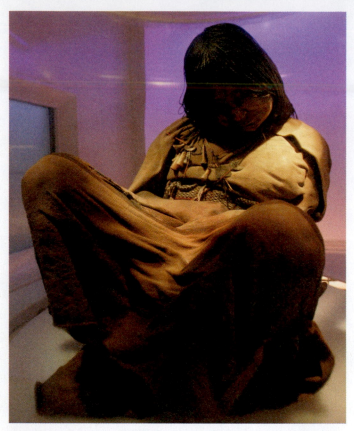

Inca Mummy

The Incas did not sacrifice humans as often as the Aztecs did, but headmen in newly conquered regions were sometimes required to give up young sons or daughters for live burial on high mountains. The victims, including this adolescent girl found in a shallow tomb atop 20,000-foot Mount Lullaillaco in the Argentine Andes, died of exposure after the long climb, but the Incas believed them to remain semiconscious and in communication with the spirit world. The girl seen here wears fine camelid-fiber garments bound by a *chumbi* (traditional Andean belt) and silver *topos* (shawl pins). She is also adorned with a shell necklace and other amulets, and her hair is pleated as described in early postconquest accounts. Such sacrifices were known as *capacocha*, or "debt payment." (AP Photo/Natacha Pisarenko.)

Daily Life Under the Incas

Inca society, like Aztec society, was highly stratified, with few means of upward mobility. Along with class gradations tied to occupation, the Incas maintained a variety of divisions and ranks according to sex, age, and ethnic or regional origin. Everyday life thus varied tremendously among the Inca's millions of subjects, although the vast peasant majority probably had much in common with farming folk the world over. Seasonal work stints for the empire were a burden for men, whereas women labored constantly to maintain households, raise children, and care for elderly kin. Unlike that of the Aztec, the Inca legal system, in common with most such systems in early modern times, appears to have been more harshly punitive against commoners than nobles. Exemplary elite behavior was expected, but not so rigidly enforced.

At the pinnacle of society was the Sapa Inca himself, the "son of the Sun." As in most imperial cultures, the emperor's alleged divinity extended to matters of war; he was believed to be the greatest warrior in the world. As a sign of unworthiness, everyone who came before him was obliged to bear a symbolic burden, such as a load of cloth or large water vessel. Only the Inca's female companions had intimate, daily contact with him. Although the ideal royal couple according to Inca mythology was a sibling pair, it was in fact dozens of wives and concubines who assured that there would be numerous potential heirs. Unlike monarchs in Europe and parts of Africa, the imperial household did not practice primogeniture, or the automatic inheritance of an estate or title by the eldest son. Neither did they leave succession to a group of elders, the method preferred by the Aztecs. Violent succession struggles predictably ensued. Though barred from the role of Inca themselves, ambitious noblewomen came to exercise considerable behind-the-scenes power over imperial succession.

Just beneath the Inca imperial line was an assortment of Cuzco-based nobles, readily identifiable by their huge ear-spools and finely woven tunics. Rather like their Aztec counterparts, they spoke a dialect of the royal language forbidden among commoners. Among this elite class were

Class Hierarchy decorated generals and hereditary lords of prominent and ancient clans. Often drawn from these and slightly lower noble ranks was a substantial class of priests and astrologers, charged with maintaining a vast array of temples and shrines.

Many noble women and girls deemed physically perfect, like the sacrificial victim described at the start of this chapter, were also selected for religious seclusion, somewhat like nuns in contemporary Western societies. Seclusion was not always permanent, because some of these women were groomed for marriage to the Inca. Still more noblewomen, mostly wives and widows, were charged with maintaining the urban households and country estates of the Incas, dead and alive.

Next came a class of bureaucrats, regional military leaders, and provincial headmen. Bureaucrats kept track of tribute obligations, communal work schedules, and land appropriations. Following conquest, up to two-thirds of productive land was set aside in the name of the ruling Inca and the cult of the sun. Bureaucrats negotiated with headmen as to which lands these would be, and how and when their subjects would be put to work on behalf of their new rulers. If negotiations failed, the military was called in for a show of force. Lower-ranking Inca military men, like bureaucrats, often faced service at the most hostile fringes of empire. They had little beyond the weak hold of local power to look forward to. As a result, in sharp distinction with the Aztecs, death in battle was not regarded as a glorious sacrifice among the Incas, but rather as yet another humiliation. Furthermore, many officers were themselves provincial in origin and thus had little hope of promotion to friendlier districts closer to the imperial core.

The Inca and his substantial retinue employed and received tribute from numerous artisans, mostly conquered provincials. Such specialists included architects, khipu-keepers, civil engineers, metalworkers, stonecutters, weavers, potters, wood-carvers, and many others. Unlike the Aztecs, the Incas did not tolerate free traders, instead choosing to manage the distribution of goods and services as a means of exercising state power. Partly as a result, chattel, or market-oriented, slavery appears not to have existed under the Incas, although some conquered young men and women spared from death or exile were absorbed into the labor force as personal servants. Most Inca subjects and tribute payers were peasants belonging to kin groups whose lives revolved around agriculture and rotational labor obligations. For them, the rigors of everyday life far outweighed the extra demands of Inca rule. Only in the case of recently conquered groups, or those caught in the midst of a regional rebellion or succession conflict, was this not true. Even then, subsistence remained the average Andean's most pressing concern; battlefields were abandoned at planting and harvest times.

Andean artisans living under Inca rule produced remarkable textiles, metalwork, and pottery, but the empire's most visible achievements were in the fields of architecture and civil engineering. The Incas' extensive road systems, irrigation works, and monumental temples were unmatched by any ancient American society. No one

Inca Road

Stretching nearly 10,000 miles across mountains, plains, deserts, and rain forests, the Inca Royal Road held one of the world's most rugged and extensive empires together. Using braided fiber bridges to span chasms and establishing inns and forts along the road, the Incas handily moved troops, supplies, and information—in the form of khipu records and messages—across vast distances. The Royal Road had the unintentional consequence of aiding penetration of the empire by Spanish conquistadors on horseback. (akg-images/Aurélia Frey.)

Material Achievements

else moved or carved such large stones or ruled such a vast stretch of terrain. Linking coast, highlands, and jungle, the Incas' roads covered nearly ten thousand miles. Draft workers and soldiers paved them with stones whenever possible, and many sections were hewn into near-vertical mountainsides by hand. Grass weavers spanned breathtaking gorges with hanging bridges strong enough to sustain trains of pack llamas for years at a time. These engineering marvels enabled the Incas to communicate and move troops and supplies across great distances with amazing speed, yet they also served the important religious function of facilitating pilgrimages and royal processions. Massive irrigation works and stone foundations, though highly practical, were similarly charged with religious power. Thus, the Inca infrastructure not only played an important practical role in imperial government, but it also expressed the Incas' belief in the connection between their own rule and the cosmic order.

The Incas appropriated and spread ancient Andean metalworking techniques, which were much older and thus far more developed than those of Mesoamerica. On the brink of a genuine Bronze Age by 1500, Inca metallurgy ranged from fine decorative work in specially prepared alloys to toolmaking for the masses. As in many parts of the early modern world, the forging of metals was as much a religious as an artistic exercise in the Andes, and metals themselves were regarded as semidivine. Gold was associated with the sun in Inca cosmology, and by extension with the Sapa Inca and his solar cult. Silver was associated with the moon and with several mother goddesses and Inca queens and princesses. Copper and bronze, considered less divine than gold and silver, were put to more practical uses.

Another ancient Andean tradition inherited by the Incas was weaving. Weaving in fact predates even ceramics in the Andes. Inca textiles, made mostly from native Peruvian cotton and alpaca fibers, were of extraordinary quality, and cloth became in essence the coin of the realm. Cooperative regional lords were rewarded by the Incas with substantial gifts of blankets and ponchos, which they could then redistribute among their subjects. Unlike some earlier coastal traditions, Inca design features favored geometric forms over representations of humans, animals, or deities. Fiber from the vicuña, a wild relative of the llama, was reserved for tunics and other garments worn only by the Sapa Inca. Softer than cashmere, it was the gold standard of Andean textile components. Some women became master weavers, but throughout most of the Inca Empire men wove fibers spun into thread by women, a gendered task division later reinforced by the Spanish.

With such an emphasis on textiles, it may come as no surprise that the Incas maintained a record-keeping system using knotted strings. Something like the Chinese abacus, or accounting device, in its most basic form, the **khipu** enabled bureaucrats and others to keep track of tributes, troop movements, ritual cycles, and other important matters. Like bronze metallurgy, the khipu predates the Inca Empire, but was most developed by Inca specialists. Although the extent of its capabilities as a means of data management remains a subject of intense debate, the khipu was sufficiently effective to remain in use for several centuries under Spanish rule, long after alphabetic writing was introduced.

Social Relations

Other ancient Andean traditions appropriated and spread by the Incas include reciprocity, the expectation of equal exchange and returned favors, complementary gender roles, and a tendency to view all social relations through the lens of kinship. Villagers, for example, depended on one another for aid in constructing homes, maintaining irrigation works, and tilling and harvesting fields. Whereas they chafed at service to the Inca ruler, they regarded rotational group work and communal care for disadvantaged neighbors not as burdens, but rather—after the work was done—as excuses for drinking parties and other festivities. Even in such a reciprocal environment, stresses and strains accumulated. In some villages, aggression was periodically vented during ritual fights between clan divisions.

Throughout the Andes, women occupied a distinct sphere from that of men, but not a subordinate one. For example, sources suggest that although the majority of Andeans living under Inca rule were patrilineal, or male-centered, in their succession preferences, power frequently landed in the hands of sisters and daughters of headmen. Literate Inca descendants described a world in which both sexes participated equally in complementary agricultural tasks, and also in contests against neighboring clans. Women exempted from rotational labor duties handled local exchanges of food and craft goods. Whether or not they were allowed to accumulate property as a result of these exchanges remains unknown.

Women's fertility was respected, but never equated with warfare, as in Aztec society. Interestingly, Andean childbirth was almost regarded as a nonevent, and rarely involved midwives. The Andean creator god, Wiracocha (weer-ah-COACH-ah), somewhat similar to the Aztecs' Tlaloc, had both male and female aspects. As in many traditional societies, Andean social hierarchy was described in terms of age and proximity of kin relation. "Mother" and "father," for example, were terms used to describe both gods and the most prominent earthly individuals (including one's parents). Next in line were numerous aunts, uncles, cousins, and so on down the family tree. Almost any respected elder was referred to as "uncle" or "aunt."

As in most early modern societies, parents treated Inca children much like miniature adults, and dressed them accordingly. Parents educated children by defining roles and duties early, using routine chores deemed appropriate to one's sex and status as the primary means of education. Girls and boys also participated in community and even state-level

khipu Knotted cotton or alpaca fiber strings used by the Incas and other Andeans to record tributes, troop numbers, and possibly narratives of events.

work projects. The expectation of all children was not to change society but to reproduce and maintain it through balanced relations with deities and neighbors. Contact with the Inca himself was an extremely remote possibility for most children living in the empire. A rare exception was capacocha sacrificial victims, such as the headman's daughter described at the opening of this chapter.

Just as maize was native to highland Mesoamerica and served as the base for urban development, the potato was the indigenous staple of the central Andes. A hearty, high-yield tuber with many varieties, the potato could be roasted, stewed, or naturally freeze-dried and stored for long periods. Control of preserved food surpluses was a hallmark of enduring imperial states, in large part because marching armies needed to eat. Maize could also be dried or toasted for storage and snacking, but among Andeans it was generally reserved for beer making. Along with maize, many lowland dwellers subsisted on manioc, peanuts, beans, and chili peppers.

Unique in the Americas, though common in much of Eurasia and Africa, Andean pastoralism played a critical role in Inca expansion. Andean domesticated animals included the llama, alpaca, and guinea pig. Llamas, in addition to carrying light loads, were sometimes eaten, and alpacas provided warm cloth fiber, much appreciated in the cold highlands. Slaughter of domestic animals, including fertilizer-producing guinea pigs, usually accompanied ritual occasions such as weddings or harvest festivals. Although like most early modern elites, the Inca and other nobles preferred to dine on freshly hunted deer, wild pig, and other meats. The average Andean diet was overwhelmingly vegetarian. Nevertheless, a common component of Inca trail food was *charqui* (hence "jerky"), bits of dried and salted llama flesh. Apparently for cultural rather than practical reasons, llamas and alpacas were never milked. Like many other peoples, Andeans restricted consumption of and even contact with certain animal fluids and body parts.

Khipu

The Incas did not invent the knotted-string record-keeping method known as khipu, but they used it extensively as they rapidly built their vast empire. Khipu masters braided and knotted cords of different colors and thicknesses in many combinations. Some khipus were kept as stored records and others sent as messages carried across the Andes by relay runners. (The Art Archive/Archaeological Museum Lima/Gianni Dagli Orti.)

Food and Subsistence

The high Inca heartland, though fertile, was prone to periodic droughts and frosts. The warmer coast was susceptible to catastrophic floods related to the so-called El Niño phenomenon, or periodic fluctuation in the eastern Pacific Ocean's surface temperature and resulting onshore moisture flow. Only by developing food storage techniques and exploiting numerous microenvironments were the Incas and their subjects able to weather such events. Added to these cyclical catastrophes were volcanic eruptions, earthquakes, mudslides, tsunamis, and plagues of locusts. Still, the overall record suggests that subsistence under the Incas, thanks to the "vertical archipelago," was much less precarious than under the Aztecs.

The Great Apparatus Breaks Down

In its simplest form Inca expansion derived from a blend of religious and secular impulses. As in Aztec Mexico, religious demands seem to have grown more and more urgent, possibly even destabilizing the empire by the time of the last Sapa Inca. As emperors died, their mummy cults required permanent and extravagant maintenance. In a context where the dead were not separate from the living, such obligations could not be shirked. The most eminent of mummies in effect tied up huge tracts of land. Logically, if vainly, successive emperors strove to make sure their mummy cults would be provided for in equal or better fashion. Each hoped his legacy might outshine that of his predecessor. Given the extraordinary precedent set by Pachacuti Inca, some scholars have argued that excessive mummy veneration effectively undermined the Inca Empire.

Despite this potentially unsustainable drive to conquer new territories, it was the Incas' notable organizational and diplomatic skills that held their enormous, geographically fractured empire together until the arrival of the Spanish in 1532. The Incas' ability to control the distribution of numerous commodities over great distances, to maintain communications and transport despite the absence of written texts and wheeled vehicles, to erect temples and centralize religious observation, and finally, to monopolize violence, all marked them as an imperial people.

As with the Aztecs, however, rapid growth by means of competitive violence sowed seeds of discontent. On the eve of the Spanish arrival both empires appear to have been on the verge of contraction rather than expansion, with rebellion at court and in the provinces the order of the day. The Incas had never done well against Amazonian and other lowland forest peoples, and some such enemies kept up chronic raiding activities. Highlanders such as the Cañaris of Ecuador and the Chachapoyas of northern Peru had cost the Incas dearly in their conquest, only just completed in 1525 after more than thirty years. Like the Tlaxcalans of Mexico, both of these recently conquered groups would ally with Spanish invaders in hopes of establishing their independence once and for all.

The Inca state was highly demanding of its subjects, and enemy frontiers abounded. Yet it seems the Incas' worst enemies were ultimately themselves. A nonviolent means of royal succession had never been established. This was good for the empire in that capable rather than simply hereditary rulers could emerge one after another, but bad in that the position of Sapa Inca was always up for grabs. In calmer times, defense against outside challengers would not have been much trouble, but the Spanish had the good fortune to arrive in the midst of a civil war between two rivals to the throne, Huascar and Atawallpa (also "Atahualpa"). By 1532 Atawallpa defeated his half-brother in a series of epic battles, only to fall prey to a small number of foreign interlopers.

COUNTERPOINT
The Peoples of North America's Eastern Woodlands 1450–1530

FOCUS

How did the Eastern Woodlanders' experience differ from life under the Aztecs and Incas?

By 1450 a great variety of native peoples, several million in all, inhabited North America's eastern woodlands. East of the Great Plains, dense forests provided raw materials for shelter, cooking, and transportation, as well as habitat for game. Trees also yielded nuts and other edible byproducts, and served as fertilizer for crops when burned. The great mound-building cultures of the Mississippi Basin had mostly faded by this time, their inhabitants having returned to less urban, more egalitarian ways of life. Villages headed by elected chiefs, not empires headed by divine kings, were the most common form of political organization (see Map 16.4).

Most of what we know about the diverse native inhabitants of eastern North America in early modern times derives from European documents from the contact period (1492–1750), plus archaeological studies. Although far less is known about them than about the Aztecs or Incas, the evidence suggests that Eastern Woodlands peoples faced significant changes in both their politics and everyday lives at the dawn of the early modern period, just before Europeans arrived to transform the region in other ways. Climate change may have been one important factor spurring conflict and consolidation.

Eastern Woodlands peoples were like the Aztecs in at least one sense. Most were maize farmers who engaged in seasonal warfare followed by captive sacrifice. According to archaeological evidence, both maize planting and warrior sacrifice spread into the region from Mesoamerica around the time of the Toltecs (800–1100 C.E.). The century prior to European contact appears to have been marked by rapid population growth, increased warfare, and political reorganization. Multisettlement ethnic alliances or leagues, such as the Iroquois Five Nations of upstate New York and the Powhatan Confederacy of Tidewater, Virginia, were relatively new to the landscape. Some confederacies were formed for

Population Growth and Political Organization

MAP 16.4

Native Peoples of North America, c. 1500

To the north of Mesoamerica, hundreds of native American groups, most of them organized as chiefdoms, flourished in a wide array of climate zones, from the coldest Arctic wilderness to the hottest subtropical deserts. Populations were highest where maize and other crops could be grown, as in the Mississippi Valley, Great Lakes, and eastern woodlands regions. Dense, sedentary populations also developed in the Pacific Northwest, where peoples such as the Kwakiutl lived almost entirely from gathering, hunting, and fishing. Nomadic hunters lived throughout the Great Plains, the Rocky Mountains, the Sierra Nevada, and the desert Southwest. Conflict between sedentary farmers and nomadic hunters was common, and some groups formed alliances to defend themselves against these and other attackers.

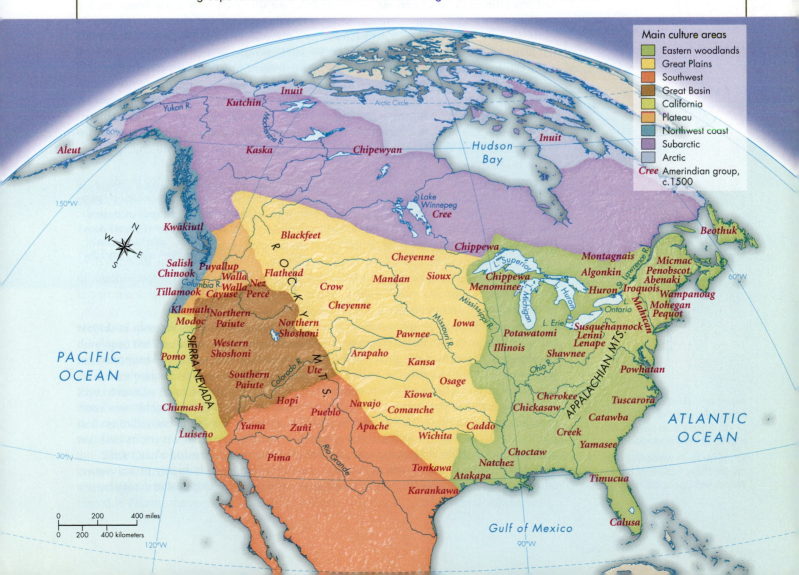

Huron Wampum Belt

For many Eastern Woodlands peoples such as the Huron, seashells like the New England quahog (a variety of clam) were sacred trade goods. Shell beads, generically called *wampum* after the arrival of Europeans, were woven into ceremonial belts whose geometrical designs and color schemes represented clans and sometimes treaties between larger groups. The linked-hands motif in this belt suggests a treaty or covenant. (National Museum of the American Indian, Smithsonian Institution. Catalog number: 1/2132. Photo by Katherine Fogden.)

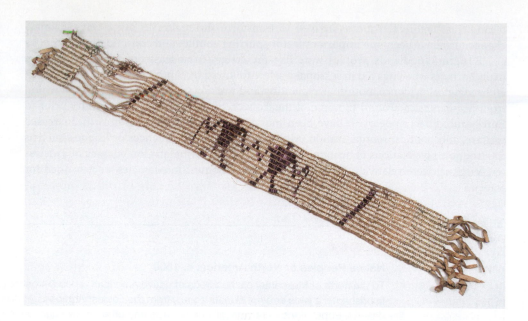

temporary defensive or offensive purposes, and others were primarily religious. Village populations sometimes exceeded two thousand inhabitants, and confederacies counted up to twenty thousand or more. As in the Andes, clan divisions were fairly common, but overall population densities were considerably lower.

Gathering-hunting groups, which made up a minority of the total Eastern Woodlands population, tended to occupy large but rocky, cold, or otherwise challenging landscapes. Notably, thanks to their varied diet, these nonsedentary peoples seem to have suffered fewer vitamin and mineral deficiencies than settled maize eaters. Even maize farmers, however, were generally taller than their European (or Mesoamerican) contemporaries. Throughout the eastern forests, including the vast Great Lakes region, metallurgy was limited to simple manipulation of native copper. Raw copper, found in abundance in northern Michigan, was regarded as a sacred substance and was associated with chiefly power. Beads made from polished seashells, or **wampum**, were similarly prized.

Nearly all Eastern Woodlands groups, including small gatherer-hunter bands, were headed by chiefs. These men were usually exceptional warriors or shamans elected by popular agreement. Chiefs retained power, however, only by redistributing goods at periodic ceremonies; generosity was the hallmark of leadership. Since surplus food, game, and war booty were far from predictable, chiefs could be unceremoniously deposed at any time. Few chiefdoms were hereditary. As in many societies, individual Eastern Woodlanders, particularly young men, yearned for independence even as circumstances forced them to cooperate and subordinate their wills to others. If the chief's generosity was a centripetal force, egalitarian desires formed a powerful centrifugal one.

Matrilineal Society

Some agricultural peoples, such as the Huron of central Ontario, Canada, had male chiefs or headmen but were organized matrilineally. This meant that society was built around clans of mothers, daughters, and sisters. Matrilineal clans occupied **longhouses**, or wooden multifamily residential buildings, typical of most Eastern Woodlands peoples. Elder women consulted with chiefs regularly, and all women played a part in urging men to war. Agriculture was regarded as a strictly female preserve among the Huron, closely linked to human fertility. Huron men were relegated to risky, perennial activities such as hunting, warfare, and tree felling. Their sphere of influence lay almost entirely outside the village. Men's exploits abroad, including adolescent vision quests, conferred status. Among all Eastern Woodlanders, public speech making, or rhetoric, was as highly prized among adult men as martial expertise. Only the most esteemed men participated in councils.

wampum Beads made of seashells; used in eastern North America as currency and to secure alliances.

longhouse A wooden communal dwelling typical of Eastern Woodlands peoples.

Children's lives were generally unenviable among North America's Eastern Woodlanders (keeping in mind that this was true of childhood throughout the early modern world). Thanks to a multitude of vermin and pathogens, generally poor nutrition, smoky residences, and manifold hazards of war and accident, relatively few children survived to adulthood. Partly for these reasons, Eastern Woodlands cultures discouraged severe discipline for children, instead allowing them much freedom.

Playtime ended early for surviving girls and boys, however, as each was schooled before puberty in the arts and responsibilities deemed appropriate for their sex. Girls learned to farm and cook, boys to hunt and make war. Soon after puberty young people began to "try out" mates until a suitable match was found. This preference for trial marriage over forced arrangements was found in the Andes and other parts of the Americas as well. Though this and the seemingly casual practice of divorce among Eastern Woodlanders were considered scandalous by early modern European standards, stable monogamy prevailed.

Warfare was endemic throughout the Eastern Woodlands in the summer season, when subsistence itself was less of a battle. In form, these wars resembled blood feuds, or vengeance cycles. According to European witnesses, wars among the Iroquois, Mahicans, and others were spawned by some long-forgotten crime, such as the rape or murder of a clan member. As such, they did not constitute struggles over land or other natural resources, which were relatively abundant, but rather male contests intended to prove courage and preserve honor.

Warfare closely resembled hunting in that successful warriors gained status for their ability to ambush and capture their equivalents from the opposite camp. These unlucky individuals were then brought to the captor's longhouse for what can only be described as an excruciating ordeal, nearly always followed by slaughter and ritual consumption. (Female and child captives, by contrast, were "adopted" as replacements for lost kin.) The religious significance of captive sacrifice among Eastern Woodlands peoples has been less clearly explained than that of the Aztecs and other Mesoamericans, but it seems to have been tied to subsistence anxieties.

Religious thought among Eastern Woodlands peoples varied, but there were commonalities. Beyond the realm of everyday life was a complex spirit world. Matrilineal societies such as the Huron traced their origins to a somewhat malevolent female spirit whose grandsons were responsible for various technical innovations and practices considered essential to civilized human life. The sky itself was often more important than the sun or moon in Eastern Woodlands mythologies, and climatic events were associated with enormous bird spirits, such as the thunderbird.

Like Andean peoples, many Eastern Woodlanders believed that material things such as boulders, islands, and personal charms contained life essences, or "souls." Traders and warriors, in particular, took time to please spirits and "recharge" protective amulets with offerings and incantations. Periodic feasts were also imbued with spiritual energy, but were unlike those of the Aztecs or Incas in that none was held on a specified date. As in many nonurban societies, religious life was an everyday affair, not an institutionalized one. Instead of priesthoods, liturgies, and temples, most Eastern Woodlands peoples relied on elders and shamans to maintain traditions and remind juniors of core beliefs.

Dreams and visions were carefully analyzed for clues to personal and group destinies. Dreams were also analyzed for evidence of witchcraft, or malevolent spell casting, within the group. Stingy or secretive individuals were sometimes suspected of this practice, often associated with jealousy, greed, and other socially unacceptable impulses. As in many semisedentary cultures worldwide, malicious witchcraft was blamed for virtually all sickness and death.

Unlike many other native American groups, most Eastern Woodlanders did not regard death as a positive transition. They believed that souls lived on indefinitely and migrated to a new home, usually a recognizable ethnic village located in the western distance. Even dogs' souls migrated, as did those of wild animals. The problem with this later

Children's Lives

Warfare

Religion

existence was that it was unsatisfying. Dead souls were said to haunt the living, complaining of hunger and other insatiable desires. The Huron sought to keep their dead ancestors together and send them off well through elaborate burial rituals, but it was understood that ultimately little could be done for them.

Conclusion

By the time Europeans entered the Caribbean Sea in 1492, the two continents and many islands that make up the Americas were home to over 60 million people. Throughout the Western Hemisphere, native American life was vibrant and complex, divided by language, customs, and sometimes geographical barriers, but also linked by religion, trade, and war. Cities, pilgrimage sites, mountain passes, and waterways served as crossroads for the exchange of goods and ideas, often between widely dispersed peoples. Another uniting factor was the underlying religious tradition of shamanism.

The many resources available in the highland tropics of Mesoamerica and the Andes Mountains promoted settled agriculture, urbanization, and eventually empire building. Drawing on the traditions of ancestors, imperial peoples such as the Aztecs and Incas built formidable capitals, road systems, and irrigation works. As the Inca capacocha and Aztec warrior sacrifices suggest, these empires were driven to expand at least as much by religious beliefs as by material desires. In part as a result of religious demands, both empires were in crisis by the first decades of the sixteenth century, when Europeans possessing steel-edged weapons, firearms, and other technological advantages first encountered them. Other native peoples, such as the Huron, Iroquois, and Powhatan of North America's eastern woodlands, built chiefdoms and confederacies rather than empires, and to some degree these looser structures would prove more resilient in the face of European invasion.

NOTES

1. For the archaeologist's own account of these discoveries, see Johan Reinhard, *The Ice Maiden: Inca Mummies, Mountain Gods, and Sacred Sites in the Andes* (Washington, DC: National Geographic, 2005).
2. Miguel León-Portilla, *Pre-Columbian Literatures of Mexico* (Norman: University of Oklahoma Press, 1969), 87.
3. Juan de Betanzos, *Narrative of the Incas*, c. 1557, trans. Roland Hamilton and Dana Buchanan (Austin: University of Texas Press, 1996), 92.

RESOURCES FOR RESEARCH

Many Native Americas

Native American history has long been interdisciplinary, combining archaeology, anthropology, history, linguistics, geography, and other disciplines. Here is a small sample of works on the last centuries before European arrival plus several venerable encyclopedias.

Conrad, Geoffrey, and Arthur Demarest. *Religion and Empire*. 1984.

Denevan, William, ed. *The Native Population of the Americas in 1492*, 2d ed. 1992.

National Museum of the American Indian, Washington, DC: http://www.nmai.si.edu/.

Steward, Julian, ed. *The Handbook of South American Indians*, 7 vols. 1946–1959.

Sturtevant, William E., ed. *The Handbook of North American Indians*, 20 vols. 1978–2008.

Trigger, Bruce, ed. *The Cambridge History of the Native Peoples of the Americas*, 3 vols. 1999.

Tributes of Blood: The Aztec Empire, 1325–1521

Scholarship on the Aztecs has exploded in recent years. The following small sample includes new works that synthesize the perspectives of history, anthropology, and comparative religions.

Carrasco, Davíd. *City of Sacrifice: The Aztec Empire and the Role of Violence in Civilization.* 1999.

Carrasco, Davíd, and Scott Sessions. *Daily Life of the Aztecs, People of the Sun and Earth,* 2d ed. 2008.

Clendinnen, Inga. *Aztecs, an Interpretation.* 1994.

For more on Mexico City's Templo Mayor, see: http://archaeology.asu.edu/tm/index2.htm.

Hassig, Ross. *Aztec Warfare: Imperial Expansion and Political Control,* 2d ed. 2006.

Townsend, Richard F. *The Aztecs,* rev. ed. 2000.

Tributes of Sweat: The Inca Empire, 1430–1532

As with the Aztecs, studies of the Incas have proliferated in recent years. Exciting work has taken place in many fields, including archaeology, linguistics, history, and anthropology.

D'Altroy, Terrence. *The Incas.* 2002.

McEwan, Gordon F. *The Incas: New Perspectives.* 2006.

On khipus, see also Prof. Urton's Web site: http://khipukamayuq .fas.harvard.edu.

Urton, Gary. *Signs of the Inka Khipu: Binary Coding in the Andean Knotted-String Records.* 2004.

Von Hagen, Adriana, and Craig Morris. *The Cities of the Ancient Andes.* 1998.

COUNTERPOINT: The Peoples of North America's Eastern Woodlands, 1450–1530

The history of North America's Eastern Woodlands peoples was pioneered by Canadian and U.S.-based anthropologists and historians. It has continued to grow and broaden in scope. Indigenous voices are best heard in James Axtell's documentary history.

The American Indian Studies Research Institute, University of Indiana, Bloomington. http://www.indiana.edu/%7Eaisri/ index.shtml.

Axtell, James. *Natives and Newcomers: The Cultural Origins of North America.* 2001.

Axtell, James, ed. *The Indian Peoples of Eastern North America: A Documentary History of the Sexes.* 1981.

Richter, Daniel. *The Ordeal of the Longhouse: The Peoples of the Iroquois League in the Era of European Colonization.* 1992.

Trigger, Bruce. *The Children of Aataentsic: A History of the Huron People to 1660,* 2d ed. 1987.

▶ **For additional primary sources from this period,** see *Sources of Crossroads and Cultures.*

▶ **For Web sites, images, and documents related to topics in this chapter,** see Make History at bedfordstmartins.com/smith.

The major global development in this chapter ▶ The diversity of societies and states in the Americas prior to European invasion.

IMPORTANT EVENTS

c. 900–1600	Late Woodland period of dispersed farming and hunting
c. 1100	Aztecs leave Aztlán
c. 1200	Incas move into Cuzco region
c. 1270	Aztecs settle in Valley of Mexico
c. 1320	Aztecs ally with Colhua
c. 1325	Tenochtitlán founded at Lake Texcoco's edge
c. 1437	Incas defeat Chankas
c. 1440–1471	Sapa Inca Pachacuti expands empire into Ecuador and Bolivia
1450–1451	Great famine in Valley of Mexico
1471–1493	Incas conquer northern Chile and Argentina
1487–1502	Aztecs dedicate Coatepec (Templo Mayor) and expand sacrificial wars
1493–1525	Incas conquer northern Peru and highland Ecuador
1502–1519	Reign of Moctezuma II, conquered by Spanish
1525–1532	Inca succession war, followed by arrival of the Spanish
c. 1570	Formation of Huron Confederacy north of Lake Ontario and of Iroquois League south of Lake Ontario
c. 1580	Formation of Powhatan Confederacy in eastern Virginia

KEY TERMS

autosacrifice (p. 525)   **tribute** (p. 526)
chinampa (p. 523)   **vertical archipelago**
khipu (p. 536)   (p. 530)
longhouse (p. 540)   **waka** (p. 532)
shamanism (p. 518)   **wampum** (p. 540)

CHAPTER OVERVIEW QUESTIONS

1. In what ways was cultural diversity in the Americas related to environmental diversity?

2. Why was it in Mesoamerica and the Andes that large empires emerged in around 1450?

3. What key ideas or practices extended beyond the limits of the great empires?

SECTION FOCUS QUESTIONS

1. What factors account for the diversity of native American cultures?

2. What core features characterized Aztec life and rule?

3. What core features characterized Inca life and rule?

4. How did the Eastern Woodlanders' experience differ from life under the Aztecs and Incas?

MAKING CONNECTIONS

1. Compare the Aztec and Inca empires with the Ming (see Chapter 15). What features did they share? What features set them apart?

2. How did Aztec and Inca sacrificial rituals differ, and why?

3. What were the main causes of warfare among native American peoples prior to the arrival of Europeans?

ADDITIONAL CREDITS

Text Credits

Chapter 1

Kate Wong. "Meet the Oldest Member of the Human Family," *Scientific American*, July 11, 2002. Reproduced with permission. Copyright © 2002 Scientific American, a division of Nature America, Inc. All rights reserved.

Chapter 2

H. L. J. Vanstiphout. Tale of Enmerkar from H. L. J. Vanstiphout, *Epics of Sumerian Kings: The Matter of Aratta*. Society of Biblical Literature, 2004: 85. Used by permission of the Society of Biblical Literature.

J. S. Cooper. *Sumerian and Akkadian Royal Inscriptions I*, translated by J. S. Cooper, 1986. Used by permission of the American Oriental Society, University of Michigan.

Martha T. Roth. Excerpts from the Code of Hammurabi from Martha T. Roth, *Law Collections from Mesopotamia and Asia Minor*. Society of Biblical Literature, 1997: 133–134. Used by permission of the Society of Biblical Literature.

E. Edel. Nefertari to Puduhepa from *Die agyptisch-hethitische Korrespondenz aus Boghazkoy*, by E. Edel. Nordrhein-Westfälische Akademie der Wissenschaften, 1994. Used by permission of the publisher.

Chapter 3

Burton Watson. *Records of the Grand Historian by Sima Qian: Han Dynasty II*, translated by Burton Watson. Copyright © 1993 Columbia University Press. Reprinted with permission of the publisher.

William Theodore de Bary and I. Bloom. *Sources of Chinese Tradition*, 2nd edition, edited by William Theodore de Bary and I. Bloom, translated by Burton Watson. Copyright © 1991 Columbia University Press. Reprinted by permission of the publisher.

Chapter 4

Jan Assmann. Reprinted by permission of the publisher from *Moses the Egyptian: The Memory of Egypt in Western Monotheism*, by Jan Assmann, pp. 175–177 (Cambridge, Mass.: Harvard University Press). Copyright © 1997 by the President and Fellows of Harvard College.

Chapter 5

Rex Warner. Thucydides, *History of the Peloponnesian War*, translated by Rex Warner, 1972. Reproduced by permission of Penguin Books Ltd.

S. G. Benardete. "The Persians," from *Complete Greek Tragedies: Aeschylus II*, translated by S. G. Benardete, Chicago University Press, 1991. © 1956, 1991 by The University of Chicago Press. Used by permission of Chicago University Press.

Elizabeth Wyckoff. *Antigone*, from *Sophocles I*, translated by Elizabeth Wyckoff. Copyright 1954 by The University of Chicago. All rights reserved. Used by permission of Chicago University Press.

M. L. West. "On Women" (21 lines of poetry) from *Greek Lyric Poetry*, translated by M. L. West (1994), p. 19. Used by permission of Oxford University Press.

Chapter 6

Aimslee T. Embree. *Sources of Indian Tradition*, Vol. I, 2nd edition, edited by Aimslee T. Embree. Copyright © 1988 Columbia University Press. Reprinted with permission of the publisher.

Leonard Nathan. *The Transport of Love*. Berkeley: University of California Press, 1976. Used by permission of Julia Nathan.

A. L. Basham. Translation from E. Zurcher, "The Yueh-chih and Kaniska in the Chinese Sources," *Papers on the Date of Kaniska*, ed. A. L. Basham. Leiden: Brill, 1968: 364–365. Used by permission of Brill.

Victor H. Mair. *The Columbia Anthology of Traditional Chinese Literature*, edited by Victor H. Mair. Copyright © 1994 Columbia University Press. Reprinted by permission of the publisher.

A. K. Ramanujan. Tamil poetry from *Poems of Love and War*, translated by A. K. Ramanujan. Copyright © 1985 Columbia University Press. Reprinted by permission of the publisher and by permission of Krishna Ramanujan.

Chapter 7

Jane Rowlandson. *Women and Society in Greek and Roman Egypt*, edited by Jane Rowlandson. Cambridge University Press, 1998. Reprinted with the permission of Cambridge University Press.

Chapter 8

J. C. Beaglehole. *The Endeavour Journal of Joseph Banks 1768–1771*, edited by J. C. Beaglehole, Halstead Press, Sydney, 1962. Vol. I, p. 368, and Vol. II, p. 37. Courtesy of State Library of New South Wales.

Martin West. Sappho poetry translated by Martin West, *The Times Literary Supplement*, June 24, 2005. Reprinted with permission.

Chapter 9

N. J. Dawood. Passages from the Qur'an from *The Koran: With Parallel Arabic Text*, translated with notes by N. J. Dawood (Penguin Books, 1990). Copyright © N. J. Dawood 1956, 1959, 1966, 1968, 1990. Reproduced by permission of Penguin Books Ltd.

A. S. Tritton. *The Caliphs and Their Non-Muslim Subjects*, by A. S. Tritton (1930): "The Pact of Umar." By permission of Oxford University Press.

Chapter 11

Allen J. Christenson. Popul Vuh, *The Sacred Book of the Maya*, translated by Allen Christenson. Copyright © 2003 by O Books. University of Oklahoma Press, 2007. Used by permission of the publisher.

Chapter 12

Patricia Buckley Ebrey. *Family and Property in Sung China*, by Patricia Buckley Ebrey. © 1984 Princeton University Press. Reprinted by permission of Princeton University Press.

Chapter 13

Ichisada Miyazaki. From *China's Examination Hell*, by Ichisada Miyazaki, translated by Conrad Schirokauer, 1st edition, 1976. Protected by copyright under terms of the International Copyright Union. Reprinted by arrangement with Shambhala Publications, Inc., Boston, Mass., www.shambhala.com.

Franz Rosenthal. Ibn Khaldun, *The Muqaddimah*, translated by Franz Rosenthal. © 2005 by Princeton University Press. Reprinted by permission of Princeton University Press.

Richard Bowring. From *The Diary of Lady Murasaki* by Lady Murasaki, translated by Richard Bowring (Penguin Books, 1996). Translation copyright © Richard Bowring, 1996. Used by permission of Penguin Group, UK.

Spot Map: Mesoamerican Scripts. Based on Andrew Robinson, *Lost Languages: The Enigma of the World's Undeciphered Scripts*. Copyright © 2002 McGraw-Hill Companies, Inc. Used by permission of the publisher.

Chapter 14

Francesco Gabrieli. *Arab Historians of the Crusades*, edited by Francesco Gabrieli. Copyright © 1957 by Giulio Einaudi Editore S.p.A., Turin. Translation © Routledge & Kegan Paul Limited, 1969. Reproduced by permission of Taylor & Francis Books UK.

Bruno Scott James. *Bernard of Clairvaux, Letters*, translated by Bruno Scott

James, Burns, Oates, 1953. Reproduced by kind permission of Continuum International Publishing Group.

Robert Bartlett. *The Making of Europe*, © 1993 Robert Bartlett. First published in Great Britain by Penguin Books Ltd. 1994 Princeton University Press paperback edition. Reprinted by permission of Princeton University Press.

Chapter 15

Richard A. Newhall. *The Chronicle of Jean de Venette*, edited by Richard A. Newhall, Columbia University Press, 1953. Used by permission of Columbia University Press.

Chapter 16

Miguel Leon-Portilla. *Pre-Columbian Literatures of Mexico*, by Miguel Leon-Portilla, translated from the Spanish by Grace Lobanov. Copyright © 1969 by The University of Oklahoma Press. Used by permission of the publisher.

Matthew Restall, Lisa Sousa, and Kevin Terraciano, editors. *Mesoamerican Voices: Native-Language Writings from Colonial Mexico, Oaxaca, Yucatan, and Guatemala*. Copyright © 2005 Matthew Restall, Lisa Sousa, and Kevin Terraciano. Reprinted with the permission of Cambridge University Press.

Frank Salomon and George L. Urioste. From *The Huarochirí Manuscript: A Testament of Ancient and Colonial Andean Religion*, translated and edited by Frank Salomon and George L. Urioste, Copyright © 1991. By permission of the University of Texas Press.

Art Credits

Opener to Part 1

Chapter 1: Bridgeman Art Library; Chapter 2: Science Source/ PhotoResearchers; Chapter 3: The State Hermitage Museum, St. Petersburg, Russia/Bridgeman Art Library; Chapter 4: Kenneth Garrett; Chapter 5: The Art Archive/Gianni Dagli Orti; Chapter 6: Fitzwilliam Museum, University of Cambridge, UK/Bridgeman Art Library; Chapter 7: Somerset County Museum, Taunton Castle, UK/Bridgeman Art Library; Chapter 8: Private Collection/Boltin Picture Library/Bridgeman Art Library

Opener to Part 2

Chapter 9: Erich Lessing/Art Resource, NY; Chapter 10: Arthur M. Sackler Museum, Harvard University Art Museums/Bequest of Grenville L. Winthrop/Bridgeman Art Library; Chapter 11: Giraudon/Bridgeman Art Library; Chapter 12: Bibliothèque Nationale, Paris, France/Bildarchiv Preussischer Kulturbesitz/Art Resource, NY; Chapter 13: ISESCO; Chapter 14: The Art Archive; Chapter 15: Candace Feit

Opener to Part 3

Chapter 16: The Art Archive/Museo del Templo Mayor Mexico/Gianni Dagli Orti; Chapter 17: The Art Archive/Science Academy Lisbon/Gianni Dagli Orti; Chapter 18: Image copyright © The Metropolitan Museum of Art/Art Resource, NY; Chapter 19: Marco Pavan/Grand Tour/Corbis; Chapter 20: Photo by Ketan Gajria; Chapter 21: Yoshio Tomii Photo Studio/Aflo FotoAgency/Photolibrary; Chapter 22: Acervo da Fundação Biblioteca Nacional, Rio de Janeiro, Brasil

INDEX

Luxury goods
  Celtic trade for, 166
  in China, 77
  Italian, 500
  Southwest Asia trade in, 59–60
  trade in, 388
Lu Yu (Tang scholar-official), 318–319(b)
Lydia, coins from, 129, 129(i)
Lysistrata (Aristophanes), 153

Macedonia, 156
  Alexander the Great from, 127
  Greece and, 150(m)
  under Philip II (359–336 B.C.E.),
    156(m)
Machu Picchu (Peru), 512(i)
Madrasas (Islamic colleges), 417–419
  Crusades and, 448
  Firdaws (Aleppo, Syria), 418(i)
Magadha, kingdom of, 178
Magi (priests), 130
Magistrates, in Rome, 209
Magnetic compass, 382
Magyars, Khazars and, 311
Mahabharata epic, 183, 427
Mahajanaka (Indian king), 326(i)
Maharajas (great kings), 171, 426
Mahavira, Vardhamana, 174
Mahayana (Greater Vehicle) Buddhism,
    175–176, 312, 312(i), 407
  Diamond Sutra of, 432(i)
  in Southeast Asia, 329
Maiolica (ceramic ware), 500
Maize. See Corn (maize)
Majapahit kingdom (Southeast Asia,
    1292–1528), 493, 496
Malaya, people of, 493
Malayan language, 257
Malay navigators, 330
Mali
  Islam in, 491
  in Mande epics, 401(b)
  trade and, 397, 492
Malik Ibrahim (Islamic preacher), 493
Malta, 120
Maluku. See Molucca Islands
Mamluk Sultanate (Egypt), 449, 461, 463, 475
  decline of, 480–482
  economy of, 480
  karimi merchants and, 390, 391
  Latin Christians and, 467
  ruling class of, 465–466
  ulama and, 418–419
Mammoth bones, dwelling from, 20(i)
al-Mamum (Abbasid caliph), 297
al-Ma'muniya, Arib (slave), 296
Manchuria, 308, 309
  invasions from, 441
  Koguryo confederation from, 317

Manda (African town), 393, 394
Mandate of Heaven (China), 96–97
Mande peoples, blacksmiths of,
    400–401(b), 400(i)
Mani (Parthian Empire), 232–233
Manichaean religion, in Iran, 232–233
Manors, 285
  lords and serfs on, 377
al-Mansur (Abbasid caliph), 295
Manual skills, human, 13
Manufacturing
  in China, 93, 495
  Italy and, 500
Manuscripts
  book production and, 411–412
  in China, 193
  illustrated, 411(i)
  Mongol, 464(i)
Maps, Aztec, 521(b), 521(i)
Mapungubwe (African state), 393–394
al-Maqrizi (Egyptian historian), 480
Marathon, Battle of (490 B.C.E.), 150
Marayoor, 198
Marduk (god), 123
Margiana region, 99
Marienburg Castle, Teutonic Knights
    and, 468(i)
Maritime trade, 308, 388, 442(m), 478
  in Americas, 517
  in Asia (1350–1450), 494–498
  in Baltic region, 454
  in China, 393
  Crusades and, 448
  European, 382
  in India, 327, 393
  Muslim Arabs in, 492–493
  Phoenician, 120
Market(s)
  in Africa, 278
  Aztec, 523
  Byzantine intervention in, 287(b)
  in China, 315–316
  production and, 383
Market economy, 383
Market exchange. See also Exchange
  payments in goods and services
    and, 398
Marquesas Islands, 363, 366–367
  Hawaii and, 399–400
Marriage, 291(b)
  in Aboriginal society, 34
  Aztec, 527
  Aztec-Colhua, 522
  Christian-Jew, 448
  in Eastern Woodlands society, 541
  in Greece, 157
  in India, 325
  Maya, 350
  Muslim-Hindu forbidden, 428

Roman, 209
  in sub-Saharan Africa, 245
Married women. See also Gender; Women
  as workers, 384
Martin (Saint)
  basilica at grave of, 280
  Clovis and, 284
Martyrdom, Christian, 223, 279
Mary (Saint), 276
  as Mother of God, 276, 277(b), 277(i)
  as virgin, 224
Masculinity. See also Gender and gender
    issues; Men
  in India, 325
Masters
  in guilds, 414
  Sufi, 420
  as teachers, 411, 413
Material culture, after Roman Empire, 287
Mathematics
  in India, 183
  in Mesopotamia, 55(i), 56
Matriarchy, 30
  Harappan society and, 82
Matrilineal clans, of Eastern Woodlands
    peoples, 540
Matrilineal descent, in Bantu society, 245
Matrilineal societies, 30
Maui, Hawaii, royal lineage in, 402
Mauryan Empire (India), 172(m), 174, 176,
    178–180, 179(m)
Mawangdui, China, 193
Maximian (archbishop of Ravenna),
    278(i)
Maximilian I (Holy Roman Empire),
    484(i)
Maya Empire, 517. See also Teotihuacán
  blood sacrifices by, 339, 345, 347, 349,
    349(i)
  calendar of, 249, 250, 349
  city-state network of, 347–350
  dynasties of, 341
  Feathered Serpent of, 344–345, 344(i)
  frescoes of, 252(b), 252(i)
  game of, 338(i)
  in Guatemala, 519
  Olmec elites and, 248–249
  people and society of, 249–251, 339–342,
    343(m)
  script of, 250, 435–436
  states of, 340(m)
  women in, 349
  writing of, 260
McNeill, William, on Black Death, 479
Mead (alcoholic beverage), 299
Mecca, 273(m), 289
Médard (bishop of Noyon), 271
Medea (Euripides), 152–153
Medes, 123

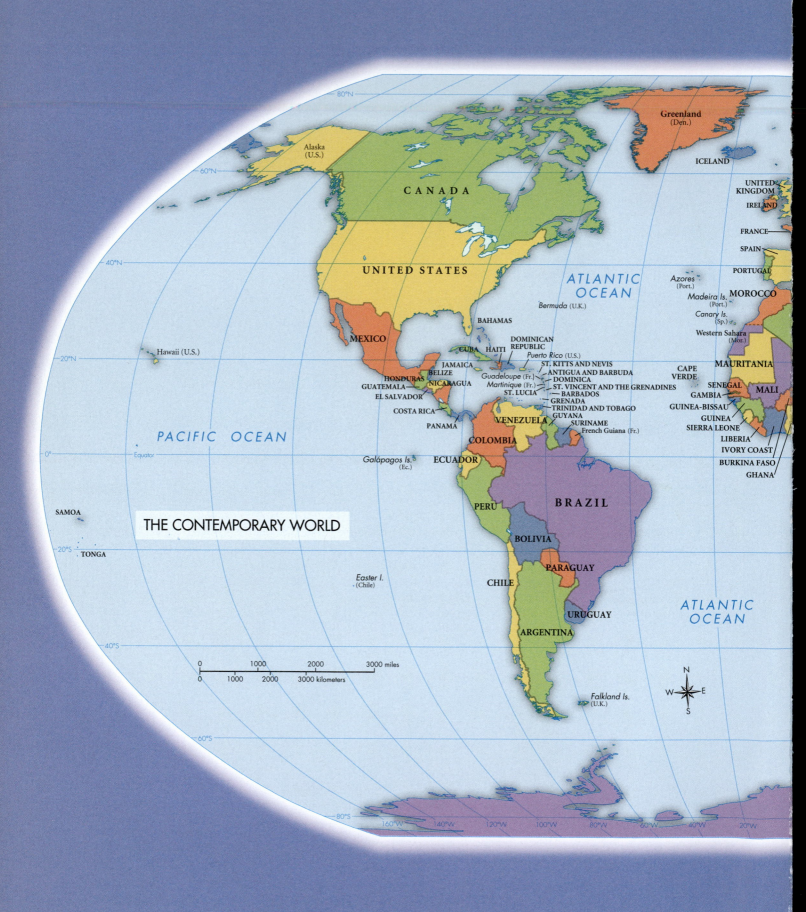

THE CONTEMPORARY WORLD

Greenland (Den.)

ICELAND

Alaska (U.S.)

CANADA

UNITED KINGDOM

IRELAND

FRANCE

SPAIN

PORTUGAL

ATLANTIC OCEAN

UNITED STATES

Azores (Port.)

Madeira Is. (Port.)

MOROCCO

Bermuda (U.K.)

Canary Is. (Sp.)

Western Sahara (Mor.)

BAHAMAS

MEXICO

CUBA

HAITI

DOMINICAN REPUBLIC

Puerto Rico (U.S.)

Hawaii (U.S.)

MAURITANIA

JAMAICA

ST. KITTS AND NEVIS

CAPE VERDE

BELIZE

Guadeloupe (Fr.)

ANTIGUA AND BARBUDA

DOMINICA

SENEGAL

MALI

HONDURAS

NICARAGUA

GUATEMALA

Martinique (Fr.)

ST. VINCENT AND THE GRENADINES

GAMBIA

EL SALVADOR

ST. LUCIA

BARBADOS

GUINEA-BISSAU

GRENADA

TRINIDAD AND TOBAGO

GUINEA

COSTA RICA

GUYANA

SIERRA LEONE

PANAMA

VENEZUELA

SURINAME

French Guiana (Fr.)

LIBERIA

IVORY COAST

COLOMBIA

BURKINA FASO

PACIFIC OCEAN

ECUADOR

Galápagos Is. (Ec.)

GHANA

PERU

BRAZIL

SAMOA

BOLIVIA

Easter I. (Chile)

TONGA

PARAGUAY

CHILE

URUGUAY

ARGENTINA

ATLANTIC OCEAN

0	1000	2000	3000 miles
0	1000	2000	3000 kilometers

Falkland Is. (U.K.)

N W E S

About the authors

BONNIE G. SMITH (Ph.D., University of Rochester) is Board of Governors Professor of History at Rutgers University. She has written numerous works in European and global history, including *Ladies of the Leisure Class*; *Changing Lives: Women in European History since 1700*; and *Imperialism*. She is editor of *Global Feminisms since 1945* and *Women's History in Global Perspective*; coeditor of the New Oxford World History series; and general editor of *The Oxford Encyclopedia of Women in World History*. Currently she is studying the globalization of European culture and society since the seventeenth century. **Bonnie treats the period 1750 to the present (Part 4) in *Crossroads and Cultures*.**

MARC VAN DE MIEROOP (Ph.D., Yale University) is Professor of History at Columbia University. His research focuses on the ancient history of the Near East from a long-term perspective and extends across traditionally established disciplinary boundaries. Among his many works are *The Ancient Mesopotamian City*; *Cuneiform Texts and the Writing of History*; *A History of the Ancient Near East*; *The Eastern Mediterranean in the Age of Ramesses II*; and *A History of Ancient Egypt*. **Marc covers the period from human origins to 500 C.E. (Part 1) in *Crossroads and Cultures*.**

RICHARD VON GLAHN (Ph.D., Yale University) is Professor of History at the University of California, Los Angeles. A specialist in Chinese economic history, Richard is the author of *The Country of Streams and Grottoes: Expansion, Settlement, and the Civilizing of the Sichuan Frontier in Song Times*; *Fountain of Fortune: Money and Monetary Policy in China, 1000–1700*; and *The Sinister Way: The Divine and the Demonic in Chinese Religious Culture*. He is also coeditor of *The Song-Yuan-Ming Transition in Chinese History* and *Global Connections and Monetary History, 1470–1800*. His current research focuses on monetary history on a global scale, from ancient times to the recent past. **Richard treats the period 500 to 1450 (Part 2) in *Crossroads and Cultures*.**

KRIS LANE (Ph.D., University of Minnesota) is the France V. Scholes Chair in Colonial Latin American History at Tulane University. Kris specializes in colonial Latin American history and the Atlantic world, and his great hope is to globalize the teaching and study of the early Americas. His publications include *Pillaging the Empire: Piracy in the Americas, 1500–1750*; *Quito 1599: City and Colony in Transition*; and *Colour of Paradise: The Emerald in the Age of Gunpowder Empires*. He also edited Bernardo de Vargas Machuca's *The Indian Militia and Description of the Indies* and *Defense and Discourse of the Western Conquest*. **Kris treats the period 1450 to 1750 (Part 3) in *Crossroads and Cultures*.**

About the cover image

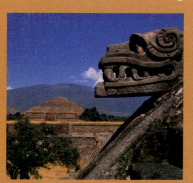

Teotihuacán, Mexico

Teotihuacán, located among the northern suburbs of Mexico City, was one of the Americas' first great urban centers. Just before its unexplained collapse around 700 C.E., the city was home to nearly 125,000 people, ranking it among the top-ten most populous cities in the world. Its rulers forged dynastic ties as far away as Guatemala, where the Classic Maya civilization was at its height, making Teotihuacán a humming, multiethnic crossroads.

RUSSIAN FEDERATION

KAZAKHSTAN

MONGOLIA

CHINA

N. KOREA
S. KOREA

JAPAN

PACIFIC OCEAN

NORWAY
SWEDEN
FINLAND
ESTONIA
LATVIA
LITHUANIA
NETH.
DEN.
BEL.
GERMANY
POLAND
BELARUS
LUX.
CZ.
SLK.
UKRAINE
AUS.
HUNG.
MOLDOVA
SWITZ.
ITALY
SLN.
SE.
ROMANIA
CR.
B.H.
BULGARIA
MO.
KO.
MAC.
GEORGIA
ALB.
GREECE
TURKEY
ARMENIA
AZERBAIJAN
UZBEKISTAN
KYRGYZSTAN
TURKMENISTAN
TAJIKISTAN
TUNISIA
MALTA
CYPRUS
SYRIA
LEBANON
IRAQ
ISRAEL
West Bank
Gaza Strip
JORDAN
KUWAIT
AFGHANISTAN
IRAN
PAKISTAN
NEPAL
BHUTAN
ALGERIA
LIBYA
EGYPT
SAUDI ARABIA
QATAR
UNITED ARAB
EMIRATES
BAHRAIN
OMAN
INDIA
BANGLADESH
MYANMAR
(BURMA)
NEPAL
VIETNAM
LAOS

NIGER
CHAD
SUDAN
YEMEN
ERITREA
DJIBOUTI
THAILAND
CAMBODIA

MALDIVES
SRI
LANKA
PHILIPPINES

Mariana Is.
(U.S.)
Guam
(U.S.)
MARSHALL
IS.

NIGERIA
BENIN
TOGO
CENTRAL
AFRICAN REP.
SOUTH
SUDAN
ETHIOPIA
SOMALIA
BRUNEI
PALAU
FEDERATED STATES
OF MICRONESIA

CAMEROON
EQ.
GUINEA
GABON
CONGO
DEM. REP. OF
THE CONGO
UGANDA
RWANDA
KENYA
BURUNDI
TANZANIA
SÃO
TOMÉ
& PRÍNCIPE
COMOROS
SEYCHELLES

MALAYSIA
SINGAPORE
INDONESIA
PAPUA
NEW
GUINEA
NAURU
KIRIBATI
TUVALU
SOLOMON
IS.

INDIAN OCEAN

TIMOR
LESTE

ANGOLA
ZAMBIA
MALAWI
NAMIBIA
ZIMBABWE
BOTSWANA
MOZAMBIQUE
SWAZILAND
SOUTH
AFRICA
LESOTHO
MADAGASCAR
MAURITIUS

Taiwan

VANUATU
FIJI

AUSTRALIA

New Caledonia
(Fr.)

NEW
ZEALAND

Tasmania
(Aust.)

ABBREVIATIONS

ALB.	ALBANIA
AUS.	AUSTRIA
BEL.	BELGIUM
B.H.	BOSNIA AND HERZEGOVINA
CR.	CROATIA
CZ.	CZECH REPUBLIC
DEN.	DENMARK
HUNG.	HUNGARY
KO.	KOSOVO
LUX.	LUXEMBOURG
MAC.	MACEDONIA
MO.	MONTENEGRO
NETH.	NETHERLANDS
SE.	SERBIA
SLK.	SLOVAKIA
SLN.	SLOVENIA
SWITZ.	SWITZERLAND

ANTARCTICA

20°E 40°E 60°E 80°E 100°E 120°E 140°E 160°E